SECOND CANADIAN EDITION

# PSYCHOLOGY

LESTER A. LEFTON | Tulane University

LINDA BRANNON | McNeese State University

MICHAEL C. BOYES | University of Calgary

NANCY A. OGDEN | Mount Royal College

PEARSON

and

Toronto

**National Library of Canada Cataloguing in Publication**

Psychology / Lester A. Lefton ... [et al.]. — 2nd Canadian ed.

Canadian ed. written by: Lester A. Lefton, Michael C. Boyes, and Nancy A. Ogden.
Includes bibliographical references and index.
ISBN 0-205-40380-8

1. Psychology—Textbooks. I. Lefton, Lester A., 1946– II. Lefton, Lester A., 1946– .
Psychology.

BF121.L43 2005        150        C2003-905392-X

Vice President, Editorial Director: Michael J. Young
Acquisitions Editor: Ky Pruesse
Executive Marketing Manager: Judith Allen
Supervising Developmental Editor: Suzanne Schaan
Editorial Coordinator: Söğüt Y. Güleç
Copy Editor: Susan Broadhurst
Proofreader: Susan McNish
Production Manager: Wendy Moran
Page Layout: Debbie Kumpf/Joan Wilson
Photo and Permissions Research: Sandy Cooke
Art Director: Mary Opper
Cover Image: Sandy Nicholson, Courtesy of Tatar Gallery, Toronto

The credits appear on pages 755–757. They should be considered an extension of the copyright page.

Statistics Canada information is used with the permission of the Minister of Industry, as Minister responsible for Statistics Canada. Information on the availability of the wide range of data from Statistics Canada can be obtained from Statistics Canada's Regional Offices, its World Wide Web site at http://www.statcan.ca, and its toll-free access number 1-800-263-1136.

1 2 3 4 5    09 08 07 06 05

Printed and bound in the USA.

For our children Michael Cryderman,
Daniel Cryderman, David Cryderman,
Danielle Boyes, Katie Boyes, and
Emily Boyes.

— M.C.B, N.A.O.

# Brief Contents

# Contents

# To the Student

Welcome to the Lefton learning experience! No matter who you are, this book will have meaning for you because it deals with everyday issues of human thought and behaviour. We believe very strongly in helping students retain all of the insights they can from a book; therefore, we have made a special effort to make psychology accessible, understandable, and interesting.

## Why This Book Was Written

The goal of this book is to help you appreciate the exciting field of psychology, to increase your knowledge, and to stimulate your interest and understanding of human behaviour and mental processes. The complexity of psychology makes the task hard but our passion for this discipline makes the task enjoyable. To share our enthusiasm and appreciation for psychology, we have chosen to focus on four themes that help explain and present psychology.

## Four Major Themes

The twentyfirst-century world is characterized by diversity and complexity and is increasingly interconnected. These factors strongly affect the field of psychology and contribute to making it the varied, complex, and challenging field that it is. We use the following themes to organize our presentation of the broad and rich discipline of psychology:

- the complex relationship between nature and nurture
- the changing impact and definition of diversity, which is of special interest within our multicultural Canadian society
- the importance of evolutionary and biological topics within the field of psychology
- the relevance of psychology in everyday life and the importance of critical thinking

## Be an Active Learner

The following important study tips will increase your effectiveness as a student and help reduce your stress level as you study:

- Become actively involved in the learning process: attend all of your classes, be an active listener, be open to new ideas, and think critically.
- Make new information meaningful by linking information that you are learning for the first time to your life experiences and knowledge.
- Be responsible for your own learning.

Many of the features of this text, outlined in the following pages, are designed to help you become an active learner.

# Pedagogical Features

Pedagogical features are integrated in *Psychology*, Second Canadian Edition, to stimulate your active involvement with and critical thinking about issues, as well as to help you learn more efficiently and effectively.

### BRAIN AND Behaviour

#### Art, Creativity, and Intelligence

People's intelligence, their creativity, and ultimately their humanity have a neurological basis. This is easy to forget because we think of such capacities as special and almost ethereal. Jacques Villeneuve's abilities in a race car, Vince Carter's grace on the basketball floor, or any number of talented writers, actors, and singers can transfix us with their abilities to bring us to a different place or time through their writings, acting, song, or dance.

What becomes intriguing, but difficult to resolve, is the relationship between these states or activities, which are hard to define and measure, and other states of being. Consider various mental illnesses. We know that people who have bipolar disorder (the proper term for what is often incorrectly called manic-depression) are often creative and exceptionally intelligent. Sometimes their long-lasting mood swings are accompanied by wild bursts of intelligence, exuberance, and creativity. Think historically for a moment. Mozart, Beethoven, Van Gogh, Edgar Allan Poe, and William Styron all were expansively creative and brilliant; they also suffered from ... They combined

mon theme here? Was it their heightened distractibility? Was their chronic unhappiness at the crux of their creativity? Kay Redfield Jamison (1993, 1996) thinks so; she makes the case that the artistic temperament and bipolar disorder in many cases are inextricably woven together.

The conclusion that Jamison leads to is the idea that physiologically underpinning both bipolar disorder and creative intelligence is one process, or at least one set of crossed connections. In reality there is little experimental evidence for this assertion, and critics argue that Jamison takes too narrow a view of mental disorders (Sass, 2001). But there is much anecdotal and correlational evidence. Enough data exist to make many psychologists and psychiatrists such as Jamison ask how we can study the brains of the exceptionally intelligent, the creative, and those who suffer from various psychological disorders to learn more about human thought, so as to maximize our human potential. Whether the two states of being—mental illness and creativity—are tied together is yet to be determined. Jamison asks probing questions, but the evidence that will firmly connect maladjustment with creativity is yet to be ascertained.

**BRAIN AND BEHAVIOUR.** The Brain and Behaviour feature reinforces one of the main themes of the text: the important role of biological and evolutionary topics within the rapidly changing field of psychology. These boxes introduce recent research and touch on topics such as the aging brain and Alzheimer's disease, social phobia, and neuroimaging and mental disorders.

### PSYCHOLOGY IN Action

#### Psychology in the Aftermath of Human Disaster

Following any major disaster, survivors and observers are left wondering why some survived when others did not. *Survivor guilt* is a term used to describe the feelings of some that emerge alive from a disaster that took the lives of others. Although irrational, these survivors blame themselves for surviving the fate of those who died. Survivors suffer from guilt and self-blame, which may result in either adaptive or maladaptive coping as individuals struggle to address feelings of powerlessness and loss (Garwood, 1996). Those with survivor guilt experience chronic and diffuse anger, anxiety, sleep disturbances, flashbacks, hypervigilance (constant alertness), and depression.

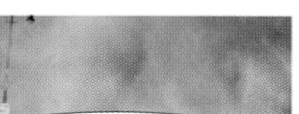

The Nazi attempt to annihilate the Jewish people, resulting in the murder of 6 million individuals, is one of the worst atrocities of all time. An ongoing research project by Peter Suedfeld and his colleagues (1997, 1998a, 1998b, 2000, 2003) at the University of British Columbia has been attempting to answer the many psychological questions that arise following human-produced disaster. The Holocaust has left us with many psychological questions that Suedfeld and many others (Dimsdale, 1974; Garwood, 1996; Krell & Sherman, 1997; Langer, 1991; McCann & Pearlman, 1990) have been attempting to answer.

Suedfeld, Fell, and Krell (1998a) suggest that the majority of survivors suffer no long-lasting distress and further cite evidence to demonstrate that the majority of Holocaust survivors, even young children released from death camps, go on to establish fairly normal lives in which they experience general contentment. Most survivors have a positive and powerful desire to bear witness to the events they were part of and to remember those who did not survive. Others, however, become unable to escape the past, paying penance through irrational and unending guilt.

**PSYCHOLOGY IN ACTION.** Featuring interesting topics, such as left-handedness, tickling, and seasonal affective disorder, the Psychology in Action boxes focus on how psychology can be applied to aspects of everyday life. The goal of these boxes is to show how psychologists build bridges between research and application, and to emphasize the theme that psychology is relevant to us all.

### POINT Counterpoint

#### Should Non-human Animals Be Used in Research?

**POINT:** The use of non-human animals is necessary for research to progress.

**COUNTERPOINT:** The use of non-human animals in research is ethically unacceptable.

Some people believe that animal research puts non-human animals through unfair and painful treatments, violating their basic rights and subjecting them to cruelty. They argue that animal researchers take it for granted that non-human animals are inferior to human beings and assert that this is a faulty assumption. Animal rights advocates also question whether the information scientists learn from animals is even relevant to human research because enormous variations exist between species in reaction to specific techniques, medicines, or manipulations. A further concern is how carefully federal guidelines on the treatment of animals in research are observed in laboratories and research facilities. Many religions, Buddhism included, assert that people cannot be hunters, fishers, trappers, or slaughterhouse workers; adherents are not allowed to kill animals, even when doing so will lead to discoveries that will pro-

complex distractions and variables that arise in studies involving humans. The use of animals also enables researchers to conduct studies that could not ethically be done with human beings. For example, it would be unethical to deprive human infants of visual stimulation to investigate the effects of visual restriction on their perceptual development. Furthermore, because most animals have shorter life spans than humans do, experimenters can control and observe an animal's entire life history, perform autopsies to obtain information, and study several generations within a short period of time. Research with animals has helped psychologists understand many aspects of behaviour, including eating, learning, perception, and motivation. In addition, for many diseases, such as multiple sclerosis, cancer, and Alzheimer's disease, animal research and experimentation have brought almost daily breakthroughs and raised legitimate hopes for

**POINT/COUNTERPOINT.** The new Point/Counterpoint feature focuses on controversial issues in psychology, such as the ethics involved in using animals for research, recovered memories, and whether homosexuality is biologically based or learned. Here we present current research results and discuss both sides of the issue.

## INTRODUCTION TO Research Basics

### Racism and Reactivity

Research has established that prejudice is typically a significant source of stress and negatively impacts quality of life. Testing a sample of residents of Prince George, British Columbia, researchers Alex Michalos of the University of Northern British Columbia and Bruno Zumbo of the University of British Columbia (2001) investigated the relationship between levels of ethnic or cultural diversity, social cohesion, and prejudice and quality of life.

**Design.** The study had a *quasi-experimental design* that constructed the independent variable, based on participants' self-reports, as Aboriginal, non-Aboriginal visible minority, or anything else. The researchers measured several dependent variables, including preference for one's own ethnic group, perception of the fairness of treatment of minorities, and general quality of life.

**Hypothesis.** Ethnic or cultural diversity, differences in social cohesion, and/or prejudice affect perceptions about quality of life.

contained items asking participants about their cultural or ethnic backgrounds, their cultural/ethnic relations, their preferences and experiences, and their satisfaction with particular domains of their lives (for example, job satisfaction, relationships). The questionnaire also contained two pages of demographic questions.

**Results.** On all significant comparisons, participants with Aboriginal backgrounds reported a generally lower quality of life than did those in either of the other two groups. The quality of life scores in the other two groups were almost identical. Members of the largest group tended to be the most prejudiced and the most optimistic, whereas people with Aboriginal backgrounds tended to be the least optimistic and the least prejudiced. People in the non-Aboriginal visible minority background tended to fall between the other two groups.

**Conclusions.** Differences in quality of life experienced by those in the Aboriginal group could not be attributed to differences in socio-economic background. Rather, these differences were largely attributable to differ...

**INTRODUCTION TO RESEARCH BASICS.** We believe that research is the foundation of psychology, and the second Canadian edition of *Psychology* reflects an increased emphasis on the important role of reasearch in the discipline. The Introduction to Research Basics boxes highlight the different research methods used in psychological research, and connect research methods with chapter-related content. These boxes, as a group, provide examples of methodological approaches.

### Be an ACTIVE LEARNER

**REVIEW**
> How common is sleep deprivation? What are its effects? pp. 137–138
> What brain structures regulate sleep and wakefulness? p. 140
> What is the most common sleep disorder? The most dangerous? pp. 140–141

**THINK CRITICALLY**
> How has sleep been affected by societal and tech-
...that began in the twentieth

**BE AN ACTIVE LEARNER.** According to learning theory, retention improves if you review and rethink what you have read. Throughout the text, short review sections called "Be an Active Learner" remind you to pause, answer questions, and think about what you have just learned. Some questions review material just read, others encourage critical thinking, and yet others ask you to apply what you have learned to real-world examples.

### PERIPHERAL [puh-RIF-er-al] NERVOUS SYSTEM

The part of the nervous system that carries information to and from the central nervous system through a network of spinal and

**KEY TERMS.** Key terms appear in boldface type in the text and are defined in the margin as well as in the end-of-book Glossary, with a pronunciation guide where appropriate. In addition, the key terms are listed with page references within each chapter's Summary and Review section, to provide you with an additional opportunity to review key concepts after you have finished the chapter.

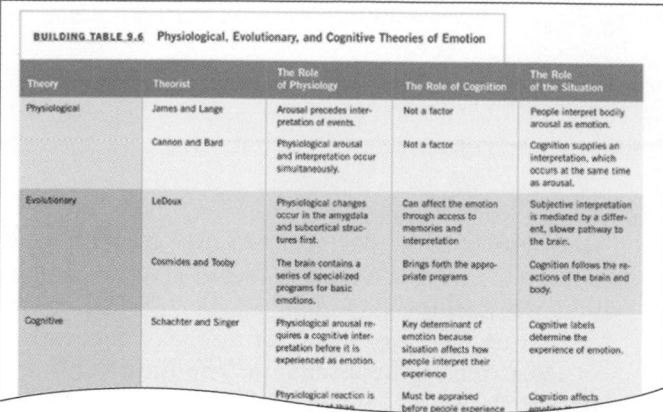

**BUILDING TABLES.** Presenting important theories and concepts in a way that shows the development of ideas is a major pedagogical element in this text. Widely applauded by many students and instructors, the Building Tables have remained a key feature of this second Canadian edition. As you are introduced to a new set of concepts, they are added to a Building Table for easy conceptual organization and review. These tables allow you to compare, contrast, and integrate concepts. They, too, are an excellent study and review aid.

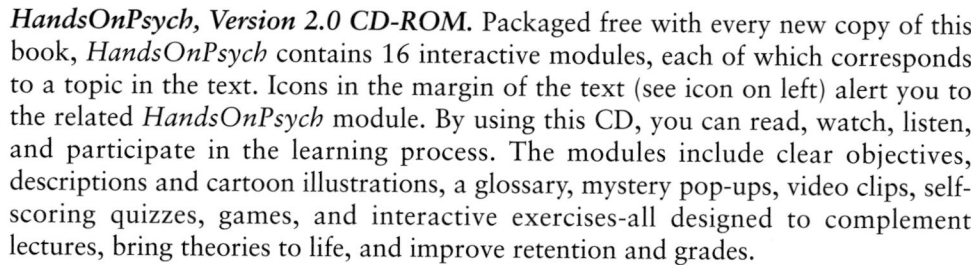

**CHAPTER SUMMARY AND REVIEW.** Every chapter ends with a carefully structured Summary and Review section. The summary is organized by section headings and includes page references to relevant portions of the text. The review is set up in a question-and-answer format and includes a list of key terms.

## Use the Supplements

You can further reinforce your learning by making use of the student supplements that are designed to enhance the Lefton learning experience.

**Development II**

*HandsOnPsych, Version 2.0 CD-ROM.* Packaged free with every new copy of this book, *HandsOnPsych* contains 16 interactive modules, each of which corresponds to a topic in the text. Icons in the margin of the text (see icon on left) alert you to the related *HandsOnPsych* module. By using this CD, you can read, watch, listen, and participate in the learning process. The modules include clear objectives, descriptions and cartoon illustrations, a glossary, mystery pop-ups, video clips, self-scoring quizzes, games, and interactive exercises-all designed to complement lectures, bring theories to life, and improve retention and grades.

*MyPsychLab. MyPsychLab* is a powerful interactive learning system that allows you to navigate a variety of exciting resources from the launching pad of an ebook version of *Psychology,* Second Canadian Edition. Pre- and post-tests allow you to assess your knowledge, and classic and contemporary experiments come to life through dynamic animations and simulations. Help with assignments and papers is provided by *Research NavigatorTM,* which offers an overview of the research process along with access to databases of reliable source material including the EBSCO Academic Journal and Abstract Database. Every new copy of this book comes with an access code that allows you to sign up free for *MyPsychLab.*

*Keeping Pace Plus.* *Keeping Pace Plus* is an active reading study guide. This carefully structured study guide helps you participate actively in learning about psychology. It contains book-specific exercises, learning objectives, review sections, and a language enrichment section for students who need help with vocabulary. With page-referenced reviews, *Keeping Pace Plus* guarantees a total learning experience for anyone who uses it.

**Companion Website (www.pearsoned.ca/lefton)** Visit the Lefton *Companion Website* for an online study guide. Graded practice tests help you review your knowledge of each chapter, and weblinks connect you to other sites for further research.

**Pearson Education Canada's Psych Supersite (www.pearsoned.ca/psychology)** Our supersite is your guide to exploring the fascinating and diverse world of psychology. On this site, you can find a variety of resources, including information on what psychology is about, help in gaining an understanding of the history of psychology, examples of the types of research done in the major fields of psychology, links to useful sites in the major areas of psychology, news links to current real-world issues in psychology, and summaries of cutting-edge research being conducted at Canadian universities.

# To the Instructor

Six strategic goals guided our work on *Psychology*, Second Canadian Edition. First and foremost, we wanted to remain current with new developments in psychology. For example, we have reworked a number of sections of the book in order to highlight new findings in the field of neuropsychology. We have also increased the coverage of evolutionary psychology and behavioural genetics. Second, we wanted to stress diversity and sensitivity to culture and gender; we were particularly interested in showing why psychologists take into account the impact of diversity on research. We want students to understand that, in order to make reasonable generalizations about human behaviour, psychologists have to consider the ways that ethnic, cultural, age, and gender differences affect behavioural outcomes in research as well as in real-world settings. Third, we wanted to show that research is a cornerstone of psychology; *Psychology*, Second Canadian Edition, reflects an emphasis on the role of research in psychology, highlighting important Canadian contributions. In emphasizing the importance of research, we especially wanted to focus on critical thinking as a key to good scientific thought and research-our fourth goal. Fifth, we wanted to focus on how applications grow from research and how psychologists build conceptual bridges between research and applications. Last, we wanted to be sure to sustain student interest and understanding. It can sometimes be difficult to blend four authorial voices, but to help accomplish this last goal, we have tried to harmonize four distinct voices into one highly personable, reader-friendly style.

## Content and Organization

CONTENT. *Psychology*, Second Canadian Edition, covers the core concepts of psychology in addition to emerging trends and topics. The chapters on the biological bases of behaviour, memory, and cognition have received particular attention to ensure that they reflect the most current thinking and research available. Moreover, the chapters on intelligence, development, psychological disorders, treatment, and social psychology were thoroughly scrutinized and revised. Current data and theories on neuropsychology, behavioural genetics, and evolutionary psychology are presented. The applied fields are similarly represented, with complete coverage of topics such as child development, gender differences, performance appraisal, and testing issues. The text covers high-interest topics including therapy, codependence, substance abuse, brain plasticity, and Alzheimer's disease. These topics are presented in an integrated manner, bringing science and application together and showing how they flow directly from traditional psychology. The content of the text reflects the current status of psychological science without being trendy or neglecting classic studies.

CANADIAN CONTENT. Canadian places and cultural icons, sports heroes and entertainers, demographics, census data, and laws are woven throughout the text to help students feel at home, and to give them a truer picture of the society in which they are studying psychology.

This text attempts to enhance that picture in two additional ways. First, significant Canadian research is highlighted where it is relevant and illustrates important psychological concepts. This alerts students to the fact that important psychological research has been done in the past and is being done now in this country, and it sets an encouraging example for those who want to go on to study psychology further.

Students will read about classic and contemporary Canadian research such as the sensory deprivation experiments at McGill in the 1950s, the work of Suedfeld and Coren at UBC on Restricted Environmental Stimulation, the pioneering work of Hebb on human memory and thinking, and Ames's work at Simon Fraser University on the adjustment of Romanian orphans adopted by Canadian parents. Second, this text reflects the ethnic diversity of Canadian society, which is obviously very different from that of American society and, in fact, unique in the world. Diversity topics covered include psychology that is uniquely Canadian, ethnic youth gangs in Manitoba and Toronto, self-perception in Canadians versus Japanese, Asian Canadians and mental health, and suicide in Aboriginal communities, to name just a few.

BRAIN AND BEHAVIOUR. *Psychology*, Second Canadian Edition, particularly emphasizes the relationship between biology and the environment. Psychologists now recognize that people are influenced by both genetics and the environment. We have integrated biology and neuropsychology throughout the text and have focused on high-interest topics in special sections called Brain and Behaviour. Topics include plasticity within the somatosensory areas of the brain, prosopagnosia, melatonin, the biological underpinnings of learning, and the neurochemistry of schizophrenia.

ORGANIZATION. We have consulted with instructors to try to determine the most logical and sought-after chapter sequence and internal chapter structure. You will notice that the social psychology chapter follows the chapter on personality; with its focus on the individual, this seemed to us the most logical placement. This decision was also a response to professors who preferred to see the growth of social psychology acknowledged by placing the chapter earlier in the text than is typical. Still, every chapter is written so that it can either stand alone or be read in alternative sequences relative to other chapters. Also, every chapter has been written with the aim of providing a structured approach, with a smooth, cohesive flow of information. The internal structure of each chapter attempts to match the way teachers present material.

## Supplements for Instructors

INSTRUCTOR'S RESOURCE CD-ROM. This CD-ROM brings together many of the instructor resources for this text, including the following components:

*Instructor's Resource Manual*, containing a wealth of classroom activities, demonstrations and handouts, and numerous additional teaching aids, such as learning objectives, annotated lecture outlines, lecture examples, and suggestions for using other supplements.

*Test Item File*, including over 3000 multiple-choice questions, many of which have been classroom-tested and validated. This test bank is offered in both Word and TestGen formats.

*Pearson TestGen*, providing the Test Item File within a testing software that enables instructors to view and edit the existing questions, add questions, generate tests, and print the tests in a variety of formats. Powerful search and sort functions make it easy to locate questions and arrange them in any order desired. TestGen also enables instructors to administer tests on a local area network, have the tests graded electronically, and have the results prepared in electronic or printed reports.

*PowerPoint Presentations*, covering the key concepts and figures in each chapter.

*Image Library*, offering digital versions of the text figures for instructor use in presentations or handouts.

Some of these resources can also be downloaded from Pearson Education Canada's Instructor Central website; this is a protected site for instructors only. An access code is required; apply online at **www.pearsoned.ca/instructor** or contact your local sales representative for details.

**HANDSONPSYCH FACULTY GUIDE.** The *HandsOnPsych, Version 2.0* CD-ROM is provided free with every new copy of this text. Icons in the margin of the text itself show you where each module fits with the content of the book. The *Faculty Guide* provides an overview of the CD to help you integrate the interactive modules into your course. For each module, the guide contains an annotated outline, activities, review questions and answers, and tests.

**MYPSYCHLAB.** *MyPsychLab* offers the timesaving convenience of a complete course management system (CourseCompass) with grade book, testing, and presentation options, plus an enhanced ebook version of the text (as described in the section on student supplements above).

**ONLINE LEARNING SOLUTIONS.** Pearson Education Canada supports instructors interested in using online course management systems. We provide text-related content in WebCT, Blackboard, and our own private label version of Blackboard called CourseCompass. To find out more about creating an online course using Pearson content in one of these platforms, contact your local Pearson Education Canada representative.

**ASSET.** For qualified adopters, Pearson Education is proud to introduce Instructor's ASSET, the Academic Support and Service for Educational Technologies. ASSET is the first integrated Canadian service program committed to meeting the customization, training, and support needs for your course. Our commitments are made in writing and in consultation with faculty. Your local Pearson Education sales representative can provide you with more details on this service program.

**INNOVATIVE SOLUTIONS TEAM.** Pearson's Innovative Solutions Team works with faculty and campus course designers to ensure that Pearson Technology products and online course materials are tailored to meet your specific needs. This highly qualified team is dedicated to helping schools take full advantage of a wide range of educational technology, by assisting in the integration of a variety of instructional materials and media formats.

## Acknowledgments for the Second Canadian Edition

You don't go off on your own to write a book like this. You actually work with an amazing array of talented and devoted people without whom there would be no book worth reading. We offer special thanks to our research assistant Kevin Wills for his facility with electronic resources and his ability to find us hard copies no matter how obscure, all with no notice whatsoever. We also wish to thank the staff of various agencies and organizations such as the Canadian Psychological Association, Statistics Canada and Health Canada, for providing us with the factual details for much of the Canadian content in the book. The folks at Pearson Education Canada impressed us yet again with their professionalism, competence and grace under fire as this project moved through the editorial and production processes. Especially deserving of our thanks are Ky Pruesse, Jessica Mosher, Suzanne Schaan, Söğüt Y. Güleç, Susan Broadhurst, and Susan McNish for their professionalism and attention to detail.

Finally, we owe our respectful thanks to those of our colleagues who reviewed our previous efforts prior to this second edition and to those who reviewed early versions of the current manuscript. Their collective thoughtfulness and careful suggestions were greatly appreciated. We would also like to particularly thank Ken Cramer of the University of Windsor, whose detailed, kind, yet constructively critical review of our early draft work moved the project significantly further than it might otherwise have gone. Additional reviewers included the following:

Anne Barnfield,
Brescia University College,
University of Western Ontario

Lisa Best,
University of New Brunswick

Wendy Bourque,
University of New Brunswick

Ross Broughton,
University of Winnipeg

Donald Gorassini,
King's College,
University of Western Ontario

Alain Morin,
Mount Royal College

James Parker,
Trent University

Timothy Parker,
Augustana University College

Glenda Prkachin,
University of
Northern British Columbia

Verna Raab,
Mount Royal College

Donald Sharpe,
University of Regina

The thoughtful reflections and feedback provided by these individuals provided us with much to think about and made this a better book. We are also indebted to the many reviewers who contributed to the U.S. eighth edition of *Psychology*, as new material from that edition has been incorporated into this one.

# Four Careers in Psychology

## LESTER A. LEFTON

I love teaching psychology. I hope my students here at Tulane University like the way I do it. My teaching technique and style began over three decades ago. My career in psychology began with a survey of sexual attitudes that I conducted in high school. I passed out questionnaires to the juniors and seniors, who were to respond anonymously. Then I spent days poring over, collating, and summarizing the data—which I, of course, found fascinating.

At Northeastern University in Boston, I majored in psychology and was particularly interested in clinical psychology. I took courses in traditional experimental psychology—learning, physiology, perception—but especially enjoyed abnormal psychology, child development, and personality. While in college, I worked in a treatment centre for emotionally disturbed children. The work was hard, emotionally gruelling, and stressful, and the pay wasn't particularly good—thus, the direct delivery of mental health services began to lose some of its appeal for me. Later, as a laboratory assistant, I collected and analyzed data for a psychologist doing research in vision. In contrast to my counselling experience, hunting for answers to scientific questions and collecting data were activities that held my interest.

My graduate studies at the University of Rochester included research in perception, and I studied visual information processing. In graduate school, my intellectual skills were sharpened and my interests were focused and refined. After earning my Ph.D., I became a faculty member at the University of South Carolina. My research in cognitive psychology involved studying perceptual phenomena such as eye movements. Now at Tulane University, I teach, do research, and write psychology textbooks. My goal is to share my excitement about psychology in the classroom, in my textbooks, and in professional journals.

Over time, my interests have changed, as I'm sure yours will. At first, I was interested in the delivery of mental health services to children. Later, I focused on applied research issues, such as eye movements among learning-disabled readers. But my primary focus remains in basic research issues. My evolving interests have spanned the three major areas in which psychologists work: applied research, human services, and experimental psychology—topics I present throughout the text.

I am married to a wonderful woman and have two daughters. I have applied in my family life much of what I have learned in my profession. My family hasn't been angry about it, although from time to time my "psychologizing" about issues can be annoying, I'm sure. I'm an avid bicyclist and computer hacker and occasional photographer. My life has generally revolved around my work and my family—not necessarily in that order. You'll probably gather that from many of the stories and examples I relate in this text.

I invite you to share in my excitement and my enthusiasm for psychology. Stay focused, read closely, and think critically. As you read, think about how the text relates to your own experiences—drawing personal connections to what you read will make it more meaningful. And please feel free to write me: *Lefton@tulane.edu*.

Good luck!

# LINDA BRANNON

My career in psychology began when I kept taking psychology courses as an undergraduate at the University of Texas at Austin. I was going to be a drama major, but I just couldn't stay away from the psychology courses because I was intrigued by how people understand the world in terms of language. Other areas of psychology, such as social psychology and child development, were almost equally exciting. Deciding which one to pursue was difficult, but I chose the program in human experimental psychology at the University of Texas at Austin.

During my years in graduate school, I was involved in researching language and cognitive processes. I spent many hours in the laboratory, collecting and analyzing data, and attempting to understand. The results of research studies fascinated me. I loved the data, and the printouts, and the patterns that the analyses revealed.

Toward the end of my doctoral studies, I got to teach a course in introductory psychology, and I also discovered that I loved teaching. When I finished my doctoral degree, I went to McNeese State University in Lake Charles, Louisiana. McNeese emphasizes teaching, and I taught a variety of courses, specializing in experimental psychology and biopsychology as well as continuing to teach introductory psychology.

In the early 1980s, I became interested in the developing field of health psychology. Along with Jess Feist, one of my colleagues in the department of psychology, I began to write a textbook for this new area. The result is *Health Psychology: An Introduction to Behavior and Health,* which is now in its fifth edition.

When I was a graduate student, a minority of students were women, but that situation changed, bringing changes to the entire field of psychology. It was exciting to be part of that transition and to watch women come into the discipline in large numbers. My research interest turned to gender issues, and an editor at Allyn and Bacon persuaded me that I should write a textbook on the topic. *Gender: Psychological Perspectives* is the result, and the course that I teach on the psychology of gender is one of my favourites.

I teach, do research in the area of gender, and write textbooks. In 1998, I was selected to be Distinguished Professor of the year at McNeese State University. I am married to a terrific guy, Barry Humphus, who has encouraged and helped me do things I did not think I could do, such as write three textbooks. I love movies (and movie trivia) and find wine both delicious and fascinating. I am an occasional hiker and reluctant jogger.

My students never stop teaching me, and I am grateful to them. Both Lester and I invite you to share our excitement and enthusiasm for psychology. If you want to tell me anything, contact me at *lbrannon@lightwire.net.*

# MICHAEL C. BOYES

Mike Boyes received his Ph.D. from the University of British Columbia in 1986. His research interests include cognitive and social development in children and adolescents as well as early intervention programs aimed at optimizing the development of at-risk children and families. He is on the faculty in the Psychology Department at the University of Calgary where he teaches introductory and child psychology.

# NANCY A. OGDEN

Nancy A. Ogden received her Ph.D. from the University of Calgary in 1994. Her research interests are primarily in cognitive, behavioural, and social development of children and adolescence as well as in research focusing on fostering the development of positive learning strategies among psychology students. She is on the faculty in the Behavioural Sciences Department at Mount Royal College in Calgary where she teaches introductory, lifespan, child, and adolescent psychology.

Nancy and Mike are married (to each other) and share a blended family consisting of six children along with three dogs and two cats.

## A Great Way to Learn and Instruct Online

The Pearson Education Canada Companion Website is easy to navigate and is organized to correspond to the chapters in this textbook. Whether you are a student in the classroom or a distance learner you will discover helpful resources for in-depth study and research that empower you in your quest for greater knowledge and maximize your potential for success in the course.

Companion Website

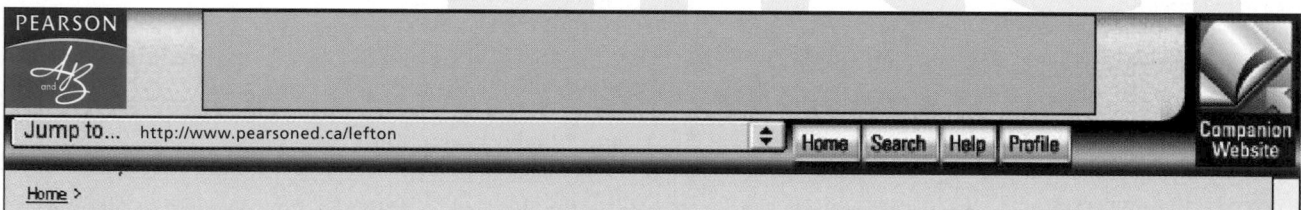

[**www.pearsoned.ca/lefton**]

Enter

---

**PEARSON**

Jump to... http://www.pearsoned.ca/lefton ⬍ | Home | Search | Help | Profile | Companion Website

Home >

### Companion Website

*Psychology*, Second Canadian Edition, by Lefton, Brannon, Boyes, and Ogden

PSYCHOLOGY

#### Student Resources

The modules in this section provide students with tools for learning course material. These modules include:

- Chapter Objectives
- Quizzes
- Essay Questions
- Psychology Links

In the quiz modules students can send answers to the grader and receive instant feedback on their progress through the Results Reporter. Coaching comments and references to the textbook may be available to ensure that students take advantage of all available resources to enhance their learning experience.

# MyPsychLab™

*to accompany Lefton, Brannon, Boyes, Ogden, Psychology, Second Canadian Edition*

This exciting new learning and teaching tool is designed to increase student success in the classroom *and* provide instructors with every resource needed to teach and administer an introductory psychology course!

**MyPsychLab** is an interactive and instructive multimedia resource that can be used as a supplement to a traditional lecture course, or to completely administer an online course. Its power lies in its design as an all-inclusive tool, combining an online version of the textbook plus multimedia, tutorials, audio, video, simulations, animations, and controlled assessments to completely engage students and reinforce learning.

Fully customizable, **MyPsychLab** meets the individual teaching and learning needs of *every* instructor and *every* student. It saves time, and it helps increase success in your course. What's more, it's EASY! Discover the benefits of using MyPsychLab for your psychology course today!

SIMULATE

WATCH

LISTEN

EXPLORE

PRE-TEST

PRACTICE

POST-TEST

EXAM

BIOGRAPHY

mypsych lab™
where learning comes to life!

# What Is Psychology?

Imagine this scene: A group of friends on a soccer team are meeting and trying to organize a joint holiday and tournament trip to a warmer part of the continent next fall. This is not always a respectful discussion, and some group members criticize and even insult others as they disagree about what they need to do next and how things should be arranged. Some team members form partnerships or alliances but sometimes lie or fail to keep their promises to their buddies. Too often members compete rather than cooperate, and many express their feelings in nasty and sometimes even violent ways. When violence occurs, it is usually perpetrated by a man. When someone cries, it is usually a woman. Indeed, the women and men often behave in ways considered stereotypical for their gender.

Is this an example of real life? Over the past few years, this type of scene has occurred again and again on the popular new type of television shows called reality TV. These programs place groups of people in unusual and often competitive situations, and viewers watch them interact. On *Real World, Survivor, Big Brother,* and *Temptation Island,* human behaviour is big entertainment. It can be intriguing to see how the players/actors/participants "use psychology" to influence others and gain advantage; their actions, words, and emotions can seem genuine and spontaneous.

Viewers find such shows compelling in part because they want to understand human behaviour and relationships. However, reality TV actually tells incredibly little about real people. For one thing, these shows' casts do not represent the range of humanity—cast members are usually chosen for their good looks, taut bodies, charisma, or energy. Events are scripted to maximize entertainment value, encouraging viewers to root for certain characters and dislike others. Also, the settings scarcely resemble reality—few people inhabit remote islands, live in multi-million-dollar homes, or compete every day for cash prizes. In fact, there may be a danger in taking reality TV seriously. The characters might be mistaken for models of "ideal people," though their behaviour and values rarely seem ideal as they often lie, taunt others, feign kindness, or try to win at any cost. Also, these programs often ridicule values that most people embrace; for example, *Temptation Island* shows no respect for faithfulness in a committed relationship.

Popular culture, including television, has created and nurtured some exaggerated ideas of what psychology is and what psychologists do. For example, one image of a research psychologist is a man in a white coat, working with rats in a lab. Though such experiments do in fact take place, today the researcher is almost as likely to be a woman, and the white coat is not necessary. During the 1940s and 1950s, white rats were the most common experimental subjects in research on learning, the most popular focus of research at the time. But this has changed—humans have replaced rats as the most common participants in psychology research, and learning is only one of many areas of study in psychology. Psychology is a much more varied field than the image implies.

Psychologists study and try to help people living their lives in the real world. Psychology helps us understand the nature of human interactions—how individuals grow up and grow independent, how people make their way in the world, form relationships with others, and lead fulfilling lives. It also addresses issues such as drug abuse and the abuse of women, children, and the elderly. We began and continue to study psychology because people fascinate us. You may be taking this course for the same reason.

Before we begin to explore psychology, it is important to carefully define and describe just what psychology is. Many students assume that psychology uses Freud's theories to provide therapy to clients reclining on couches. Although psychology does explore personality, maladjustment, and therapy, it encompasses far more. You will see that psychologists, whether practitioners or researchers, tend to be investigators who carefully and systematically attempt to discover the underpinnings of human behaviour and mental processes. Similarly, many students think of psychology as the science of the mind. It is that, of course, but—as this text emphasizes so strongly—it is also a biological science, and one that is increasingly interdisciplinary. Finally, some casual observers think of psychology as common sense; but the truth is that the hindsight of common sense, which explains past events so well, rarely allows people to make predictions about future behaviour and events—and this is a key goal of psychological inquiry. Students of psychology often think of themselves as psychological detectives, sifting through facts and theories in an orderly way, attempting to uncover the many causes of behaviour, so as ultimately to help individuals or organizations become everything they wish to be. Let's begin our exploration with a definition of the science that we find so exciting and that we believe will help you better understand the "real" reality outside of reality TV.

## What Is Psychology?

What exactly is psychology? It is as difficult for us to provide a definition of psychology that includes all of its elements as it would be for you to list all of the reasons why you might want to study it. We'll begin with a simple definition and gradually expand on it. Broadly defined, **psychology** is the science of behaviour and mental processes.

Let's look at the first part of this definition, because it is key to understanding what sets real psychology apart from the popular psychology of talk shows and tabloids. Psychology is a *science*. Because psychology is a science, psychologists use scientific principles, carefully defined methods, and precise procedures to present an organized body of knowledge and to draw inferences, or make predictions, about how people will behave in the future. Predicting behaviour is important, for it enables psychologists to help people anticipate their reactions to certain situations

PSYCHOLOGY
The science of behaviour and mental processes.

and learn how to express themselves in manageable and reasonable ways. For example, because excessive stress can cause anxiety, depression, and even heart attacks, psychologists use theories about stress to devise therapies to help people handle it more effectively.

Interestingly, there remain some, both inside and outside of university settings, who claim that psychology is not a science, who see human behaviour as either fixed or subject to little change, and who therefore do not believe that human behaviour is subject to scientific laws and principles. These divergent views exist cross-culturally as well; there is not the same degree of consensus about the usefulness of psychology around the world. Former Soviet bloc nations take a dim view of therapy, and as in some Asian cultures, people are expected to be self-reliant—accordingly, they are less likely to seek help from psychologists than are most mainstream Canadians.

Now for the second part of the definition: psychology as the science of *behaviour and mental processes*. Psychologists observe many aspects of human functioning—overt actions or behaviours, social relationships, mental processes, emotional responses, and physiological reactions. In cultures outside North America, especially former Soviet bloc nations, psychology also embraces paranormal phenomena such as telepathy and clairvoyance.

*Overt actions* are directly observable and measurable movements or the results of such movements. Walking, talking, playing, kissing, gestures, and expressions are examples of overt actions. Results or products of overt actions might be the papers you write, the piles of unsorted laundry in your bedroom, or the body you have kept in shape through regular exercise. *Social relationships* are the behaviours we engage in that define our interactions with other people. We make assumptions about the causes of other people's behaviours; we try to change their attitudes; we avoid them or engage them; we date, marry, and have children with them. *Mental processes*, which most of us consider the main grist for the psychological mill, include thoughts and ideas as well as more complex reasoning processes. *Emotional responses* basically are feelings such as anger, regret, lust, happiness, and depression. *Physiological reactions* are closely associated with emotional responses. They include an increased heart rate when you are excited, biochemical changes when light stimulates your eyes, and high blood pressure in response to stress. All of these are fair game for psychological scientists.

Psychology is considered a social and behavioural science because it deals with behaviour and mental processes. In recent years the Canadian Psychological Association has focused attention on the contributions of the behavioural and social sciences, which address many of our society's daunting challenges, and on the critical importance of psychology, which improves our country's health by eliminating child abuse and neglect and violence against women, and by increasing the safety and security of our communities. Psychology also contributes by helping educate our society to learn and think critically, training workers to be more efficient and productive, and sensitizing people to diversity—the broad range of customs and lifestyles we find within our borders and those we see in the world beyond. With these themes in mind, and because psychology is a science, it is crucial that we follow some key principles of science as we evaluate research and the applications of research. The application of these principles of science by psychologists over the years has led to the development of some detailed accounts of what we humans are like and why we act the way we do. Sometimes called "schools of psychological thought," these big ideas reflect particular ways of looking at humans and human nature that have been found to be useful at one time or another. We will run through some of these *big ideas* next in order to give you some things to think about when we go on after this next section to describe the scientific tools we use to critically review our past theories (we can be *very* critical of our own past work in psychology!) and to try to explain the human behaviour we see around us today.

# How Have Schools of Psychological Thought Developed?

If you think of psychology as a modern science you are not entirely wrong, and we will discuss some of the history of this modern psychology below, but if that was the extent of our discussion you might miss some of the important ideas about psychology and basic human nature offered by well-known early thinkers. We will point out a few of these before moving on to a discussion of the current issues and themes in psychology. (More detailed accounts of the early history of psychology can be found in the work of Canadian psychology historians Kurt Danziger [1990] and Raymond Fancher [1996], both of York University.)

It was none other than Socrates who suggested that an unexamined life is not worth living and that to live properly and well it is essential that we think clearly and rationally and that we realize the extent of our own ignorance. Know thyself is good advice that was offered initially by Socrates. From this early beginning we see in the writings of Plato, Aristotle, and others ongoing debate about the nature of human knowledge; the relationships among body, mind, and soul; and the possibility or processes of gaining knowledge and truth about the world and our place in it. These debates continue through the work of Descartes ("I think therefore I am") and his mind–body distinction, to the present. In the 1600s the work of a group of philosophers known as Empiricists (for example, John Locke and David Hume) began to insist that all our knowledge is linked to our experiences and acquired through our senses. Locke, in particular, argued that we arrive in the world as blank slates (*tabula rasa*) and are written upon by our experiences.

Psychology as a discipline and a science would not have been recognized as such 200 years ago. The psychological study of human behaviour has evolved over a relatively brief time span, beginning a little more than a century ago. Over that time, psychologists have subscribed to many different perspectives. Once fully developed and presented, these perspectives serve to orient researchers and provide them with a frame of reference through which to do new work. A specific perspective on the study of behaviour is called a *school of psychological thought*. This section discusses the development of schools of psychological thought. You will see that the study of behaviour and mental processes, despite its short life, has had a rich and varied history.

## THE EARLY TRADITIONS

### STRUCTURALISM—THE CONTENTS OF CONSCIOUSNESS.
Wilhelm Wundt (1832–1920) (pronounced *Voont*) developed the first widely accepted school of psychological thought. In Leipzig, Germany, in 1879, the former medical student and physiologist founded the first psychological laboratory; its focus was the study of mental life (Leahey, 1992). Before Wundt, the field of psychology simply did not exist; what are now considered psychological questions lay in the domains of philosophy, medicine, and theology. Wundt was a formal, humourless man, but his lectures were extremely popular and his dozens of graduate students were admiring followers. One of Wundt's major contributions was teaching his students to use the scientific method when asking psychological questions (Benjamin et al., 1992). Edward B. Titchener (1867–1927), an Englishman, helped popularize Wundt's ideas, along with his own, in the English-speaking world.

Wundt, Titchener, and others espoused structuralism. **Structuralism** was the school of psychological thought that considered the organized structure of immediate, conscious experience as the proper subject matter of psychology. Instead of looking at the broad range of behaviour and mental processes that psychologists consider today, structuralists tried to observe only the inner workings of the mind to find the elements of conscious experience.

STRUCTURALISM

The school of psychological thought that considered the organized structure of immediate, conscious experience to be the proper subject matter of psychology.

To discover these elements of conscious experience, Wundt and Titchener used the technique of **introspection**, or *self-examination*, the systematic description and analysis by a person of what he or she is thinking and feeling. In the process, they also conducted some of the first experiments in psychology. For example, they studied the speed of thought by observing reaction times for simple tasks.

By today's standards, of course, the structuralists focused too narrowly on individuals' conscious experiences. Understanding one person's conscious experience actually reveals little about another's. Thus, though they provided a starting point for psychological research, the structuralists' results allowed for few generalizations and the school made little progress in describing the nature of the mind.

**FUNCTIONALISM—HOW DOES THE MIND WORK?**   Before long, a new school developed, bringing with it a new, more active way of thinking about behaviour. Built on the basic concepts of structuralism, **functionalism** was the school of psychological thought that tried to discover not just the mind's structures but how and why the mind *functions* and is related to consciousness. It also sought to understand how people adapted to their environment.

This lively new school of thought, with Harvard University–trained physician and professor of anatomy William James (1842–1910) at its head, argued that knowing only the contents of consciousness (structuralism) was too limited. Unlike Wundt, James was charming, informal, outgoing, and vivacious; especially well liked by his students, James argued that a psychologist also had to know how the contents of consciousness functioned and worked together. Through such knowledge, the psychologist could understand how the mind (consciousness) guided behaviour. In 1890 James published *Principles of Psychology*, in which he described the mind as a dynamic set of continuously evolving elements. In this work he coined the phrase *stream of consciousness*, describing the mind as a river, always flowing, never remaining still.

James broadened the scope of structuralism by studying animals, by applying psychology in practical areas such as education, and by experimenting on overt behaviour rather than just mental processes. James's ideas influenced the life and writing of G. Stanley Hall (1844–1924), an American psychologist who was one of Wundt's early students. Hall, as Titchener was for structuralism, was an organizer and promoter of functionalist psychology.

Functionalists continued to use introspection as a technique; for them, psychology was still the study of consciousness. For many of the emerging schools of psychology, however, this scope was too limiting. The early schools of psychological thought were soon replaced by different conceptualizations: Gestalt psychology, psychoanalysis, behaviourism, and humanistic and cognitive approaches to psychology.

**GESTALT PSYCHOLOGY—EXAMINING WHOLES.**   In the early twentieth century, while some psychologists were feeling their way forward with structuralism and functionalism, others were developing very different approaches. One such approach was **Gestalt psychology** (*Gestalt* means "configuration")—the school of psychological thought that argued that it is necessary to study a person's total experience, not just parts of experience (the mind or behaviour). Gestalt psychologists such as Max Wertheimer (1880–1943) and Kurt Koffka (1886–1941) suggested that conscious experience is more than simply the sum of its individual parts, much as it is hard to fully understand how a car runs by studying all of its parts in detail. Arguing that each mind organizes the elements of experience into something unique, by adding structure and meaning to incoming stimuli, Gestalt psychologists analyzed the world in terms of perceptual frameworks. They proposed that people mould simple sensory elements into patterns through which they then interpret the world. By analyzing the whole experience—the patterns of a person's perceptions and thoughts—one could understand the mind and its workings.

INTROSPECTION

A person's description and analysis of what he or she is thinking and feeling; also known as *self-examination*.

FUNCTIONALISM

The school of psychological thought (an outgrowth of structuralism) that was concerned with how and why the conscious mind works; its main aim was to know how the contents of consciousness functioned and worked together.

GESTALT [gesh-TALT] PSYCHOLOGY

The school of psychological thought that argued that behaviour cannot be studied in parts but must be viewed as a whole; the focus was on the unity of perception and thinking.

▲ In the late 1800s and early 1900s Sigmund Freud published his famous works on emotional disorders and personality.

**PSYCHOANALYTIC**
[SYE-ko-an-uh-LIT-ick]
**APPROACH**

The school of psychological thought developed by Freud, which assumes that psychological maladjustment is a consequence of anxiety resulting from unresolved conflicts and forces of which a person may be unaware; includes the therapeutic technique known as *psychoanalysis*.

**BEHAVIOURISM**

The school of psychological thought that rejects the study of the contents of consciousness and focuses on describing and measuring only that which is observable directly or through assessment instruments.

Eventually Gestalt psychology became a major influence in many areas of psychology—for example, in therapy. A Gestalt-oriented therapist dealing with a "problem" family member might try to see how the "part" (the person perceived as the problem) could be better understood in the context of the "whole" (the family configuration). However, as broad as its influence was, Gestalt psychology seemed lacking in scientific rigour and somewhat mystical, and it never achieved as wide a following as did psychoanalysis.

**PSYCHOANALYSIS—PROBING THE UNCONSCIOUS.** One of the first researchers to develop a theory about emotional disturbance was Sigmund Freud (1856–1939). Freud grew up during a difficult time in the history of central Europe; he became a dark, brooding, complex, yet charismatic figure. Freud was a physician who was interested in helping people overcome anxiety; he worked in Vienna, Austria, focusing on the causes and treatment of emotional disturbances. Working from the premise that unconscious mental processes direct daily behaviour, he developed techniques to explore those unconscious processes; these techniques include free association and dream interpretation. He emphasized that childhood experiences shape and influence future adult behaviour and that sexual energy fuels day-to-day behaviour.

Freud created the **psychoanalytic approach**—the school of psychological thought that assumes that psychological maladjustment is a consequence of anxiety resulting from unresolved conflicts and forces of which a person generally is unaware. Its therapeutic technique is *psychoanalysis*. The psychoanalytic perspective has undergone many changes since Freud devised it. At times, in fact, it seems only loosely connected to Freud's basic ideas. When this approach was introduced in North America, most psychologists ignored it. But by the 1920s, when intellectual growth caused society to emerge from the repressed Victorian era, the influence of the psychoanalytic approach spread rapidly. Soon it was so influential and widely studied that it threatened to eclipse research-based laboratory psychology (Hornstein, 1992). Chapter 12 discusses Freud's theory of personality, and Chapter 16 discusses psychoanalysis as the therapeutic technique derived from his theory.

## PSYCHOLOGICAL SCHOOLS GROW BROADER

The early schools of psychology focused on the mind and how it functioned; for example, psychoanalysis examined how the unconscious operated and shaped later development. Yet it was not until the mid-1920s that the influences of learning were stressed, and it was not until the 1940s and 1950s that the roles of free will and self-expression were investigated. The 1970s saw the emergence of cognitive psychology, which stresses thinking processes; psychology in the 1980s and 1990s also has been heavily influenced by studies of the neurological and biological foundations of behaviour. Let's look at these more modern trends in the history of psychology.

**BEHAVIOURISM—OBSERVABLE BEHAVIOUR.** Despite their differences in focus, the structuralists, functionalists, Gestaltists, and psychoanalysts were all concerned with the functioning of the mind. They were all interested in private perceptions and conscious or unconscious activity. In the early twentieth century, however, North American psychology moved from studying the contents of the mind to studying overt behaviour. At the forefront of that movement was John B. Watson (1878–1958), the founder of behaviourism. **Behaviourism** is the school of psychological thought that rejects the study of the contents of consciousness and focuses instead on describing and measuring only behaviour—that which is observable directly through assessment instruments.

Watson was an upstart—clever, brash, and defiant. Trained as a functionalist, he argued forcefully that there was no reasonable, objective way to study the human mind, particularly through introspection. Watson, with great self-assurance, contended that behaviour, not the private contents of the mind, was the proper subject matter of psychology. According to Watson, psychologists should study only activities that can be objectively observed and measured; prediction and control should be the theoretical goals of psychology. This contention was a major break with previous psychological thought. Watson rejected the work of Wundt and most other early psychologists; he argued that psychologists should put the study of consciousness behind them.

After Watson, other researchers extended and developed behaviourism, so much so that in North America in the 1920s, behaviourism became the dominant and only acceptable view of psychology. Among those supporting the study of behaviourism, and certainly its most widely recognized proponent, was Harvard psychologist B. F. Skinner (1904–1990). In the 1940s Skinner attempted to explain the causes of behaviour by cataloguing and describing the relations among events in the environment (*stimuli*) and a person's or animal's reactions (*responses*). Skinner's behaviourism led the way for thousands of research studies on conditioning and human behaviour, a special focus on stimuli and responses, and the controlling of behaviour through learning principles.

Skinner is arguably the most influential psychologist ever trained in North America. Although he spent his research time studying animals, his writings focus on people. His theories about using principles of operant conditioning to design a utopian society brought him lasting fame. However, Skinner was more of an engineer, a behavioural technician, than he was a theorist. Determining the best time to get up in the morning, inventing a better hearing aid, designing a comfortable enclosed crib for his daughters—these were the kinds of tasks he found most rewarding. Skinner's thinking classified him as a behaviourist. He believed that we are what we do—that there is no "self," only a collection of possible behaviours. Skinner was also a determinist. In his view, our actions are more a result of past experiences than genetics. According to Skinner, our environment determines completely what we do. We control our actions about as much as a rock in an avalanche controls its resting place.

Behaviourists focus on how observable responses are learned, modified, or forgotten. They usually emphasize how current behaviour is acquired or modified rather than examine inherited characteristics or early childhood experiences. One of their fundamental assumptions is that disordered behaviour can be replaced with appropriate, worthwhile behaviour through traditional learning techniques (described in Chapter 5).

Early behaviourists took a relatively unbending view of the scope of psychology by refusing to study mental phenomena. Non-behaviourists of their time argued that not all behaviour can be explained by stimuli and responses alone. They focused instead on such topics as creativity, the origins of thought, and the expression of love. Today behaviourists are beginning to study a wider range of human behaviour, including mental phenomena such as decision making and maladjustment (Rachlin, 1995).

**HUMANISTIC PSYCHOLOGY—FREE WILL.** Another important perspective within modern psychology is **humanistic psychology**—the school of psychological thought that emphasizes the uniqueness of each human being's experience and the idea that human beings have free will to determine their destiny. Stressing individual free choice, the humanistic approach arose in the post–Second World War era. It was in part a response to disagreement with aspects of the psychoanalytic and behavioural views. Humanistic psychologists see people as inherently good and as striving to fulfil themselves; they believe that psychoanalytical theorists are wrong to say that people are fraught with inner conflict and that behaviourists are too narrowly focused on stimulus–response relations. Humanists focus on individual

▲ In 1913, John Watson advanced the behaviourist approach, the view that psychologists should only study that which can be observed.

▲ In the 1930s, B. F. Skinner laid the groundwork for his operant conditioning approach to psychology.

HUMANISTIC PSYCHOLOGY

The school of psychological thought that emphasizes the uniqueness of each human being and the idea that human beings have free will to determine their destiny.

SELF-ACTUALIZATION
The fundamental human need to strive to fulfil one's potential, thus a state of motivation, according to Maslow; from a humanist's view, a final level of psychological development in which a person attempts to minimize ill health, function fully, have a superior perception of reality, and feel a strong sense of self-acceptance.

COGNITIVE PSYCHOLOGY
The school of psychological thought that focuses on the mental processes and activities involved in perception, learning, memory, and thinking.

BIOLOGICAL PERSPECTIVE
The school of psychological thought that examines psychological issues based on how heredity and biological structures affect mental processes and behaviour and that focuses on how physical mechanisms affect emotions, feelings, thoughts, desires, and sensory experiences; also known as the *neuroscience perspective*.

uniqueness and decision-making ability; they assume that subjective experience contributes positively to establishing and maintaining a normal lifestyle.

Humanistic psychologists say that psychologists must examine human behaviour as individuals experience it. Proponents of the humanistic view, such as Abraham Maslow and Carl Rogers (both of whom we will study in Chapter 12), believe that human beings have the desire to achieve a state of **self-actualization**. Self-actualization is a final level of psychological development in which a person attempts to minimize ill health, function fully, have a superior perception of reality, and feel a strong sense of self-acceptance. Humanistic psychologists believe that people create their own perceptions of the world, choose their own experiences, and interpret reality in ways that lead toward self-actualization. Thus, for humanists, self-actualization is not only a final state but also an instinctual and motivational need. Researchers in this area examine the nature and roles of such concepts as hope, loneliness, happiness, despair, and self-actualization.

**COGNITIVE PSYCHOLOGY—THINKING AGAIN.**  In the 1960s and 1970s, many psychologists realized that behaviourism in its strict form had limitations, particularly its narrow focus on observable behaviour. As an outgrowth of behaviourism (and as a reaction to it), these psychologists developed **cognitive psychology**—the school of psychological thought that focuses on the mental processes and activities involved in perception, learning, memory, and thinking. In a short period, so many theories developed, and so many psychologists embraced them, that psychologists began to say that a cognitive revolution was taking place within the discipline. This perspective goes beyond behaviourism in considering the mental processes involved in behaviour—for example, how people solve problems and appraise threatening situations and how they acquire, code, store, and retrieve information. Though it is sometimes seen as anti-behaviourist, this perspective is not that. It simply views the strict behavioural approach as missing a key component—mental processes. Cognitive psychology encompasses theories on both symbolic thought processes and the physiological processes that underlie thought; for example, many cognitive theories are put forth to explain how the brain operates. Today cognitive psychology exerts a wide influence on psychological thinking.

The cognitive perspective asserts that human beings engage in behaviours, both worthwhile and maladjusted, because of ideas and thoughts. Cognitive psychologists may be clinicians working with maladjusted clients to help them achieve more realistic ideas about the world; the clients then use these changed thoughts to alter their behaviour and to adjust to the world more effectively. A cognitively oriented clinician might help a client realize that her distorted thoughts about her own importance were interfering with her ability to get along with co-workers, for example. Cognitive psychologists also may be researchers who study intelligence, memory, perception, and the mental processes underlying all thought.

Because cognitive psychology spans many psychological fields and research traditions, it is hard to identify a single person who could be called its leader. However, psychologists Albert Bandura, Albert Ellis, Aaron Beck, George Miller, Ulric Neisser, and Richard Lazarus have all taken a prominent role, and their work will be discussed in later chapters.

**BIOLOGICAL PERSPECTIVE—PREDISPOSITIONS.**  If you think that people are genetically predisposed to win, lose, be fat, be athletic, or be outgoing you might focus much of your research on the biological basis of behaviour. Indeed, researchers are increasingly turning to biology to explain behaviour. The **biological perspective**, also referred to as the *neuroscience perspective*, is the school of psychological thought that examines psychological issues based on how heredity and biological structures affect mental processes and behaviour and that focuses on how physical mechanisms affect emotions, feelings, thoughts, desires, and sensory experiences.

Researchers with a biological perspective might study genetic abnormalities, central nervous system problems, brain damage, or hormonal changes, for example. Today, exciting research is investigating whether a person's biological heritage leads to depression, learning disabilities, or homosexuality. Each day, groundbreaking research is occurring. Researchers Donald Hebb (memory), Michael Gazzaniga (perception), Noam Chomsky (language), Irving Gottesman (schizophrenia), and Robert Plomin (intelligence) are often cited as leaders of the biological perspective. You'll be hearing more about their work in the chapters to come.

The biological perspective is especially important in studies of sensation and perception, memory, and many types of maladjustment. It is pivotal in research on abnormal behaviour such as schizophrenia, which is linked in part to genetics, or on alcoholism, which in many cases has biological underpinnings. Because of the growing importance of the biological perspective, it has earned a prominent position in psychology—which you will see reflected in this text. We will revisit it many times, on many topics, in later chapters. In addition, most chapters will feature "Brain and Behaviour" boxes, which spotlight the latest breakthroughs in the study of brain–genetics–behaviour interaction.

**EVOLUTIONARY PSYCHOLOGY.** Is your sense of humour shaped by the same processes that shaped adaptive physical features such as our opposable thumb and erect posture? Did cave men and women laugh at life the way we do? Some psychologists think so; a distinctly psychobiological approach is **evolutionary psychology**—the psychological perspective that seeks to explain and predict behaviour by analyzing how specific behaviours, over the course of many generations, have led to adaptations that allow the species to survive. Evolutionary psychology assumes that behavioural tendencies that help organisms adapt, be fit, and survive will be passed on to successive generations through a greater likelihood of reproduction. Using ideas such as "survival of the fittest," these researchers argue that, in the same way that human beings have evolved physically, they have evolved in other areas that we might say are mental or psychological. Evolutionary psychology argues that significant portions of human behaviours and mental abilities are directly coded in the genome—they are innate. Language is but one example. Human beings may learn language from one another but they do so at about the same rate and the same age in a wide variety of cultures and languages. For this reason, psychologists think that language learning is a universal behaviour and ability that is encoded in the genome (Fischer, Lai, & Monaco, 2003). Other examples of common human behaviours in which evolutionary psychologists are especially interested are humour, emotions, parenting, and romantic love. In previous years, such behaviours have been called, among other things, "evolved cognitive structures," "special learning mechanisms," and "innate activities." Evolutionary psychologists assert that there is an evolved heredity in certain psychological traits; they argue that these traits were not always what they are today. For example, in the early stages of human evolution, language consisted merely of grunts, groans, and crude gestures. But through the course of generations, those who grunted good directions, warnings, and other communications were more likely to survive difficult circumstances. Those who survived taught their offspring, and over successive generations language developed and ultimately was encoded in the human genome.

It is not a new idea that the development of the brain is sensitive to experience. William James, the first American psychologist and the leader of functionalism, spoke of instincts at length in his classic book *Principles of Psychology*. James referred to instincts as specialized neural circuits that are common to every member of the species and are a product of that species' evolutionary history. Today, cognitive psychologists, evolutionary biologists, and neuroscientists are studying those neural circuits. They investigate how circuits are organized and specialized, and especially how they have evolved. Their approach assumes that the brain is a physical

EVOLUTIONARY PSYCHOLOGY
The psychological perspective that seeks to explain and predict behaviour by analyzing how specific behaviours, over the course of many generations, have led to adaptations that allow the species to survive; it assumes that behaviours that help organisms adapt, be fit, and survive will be passed on to successive generations through a greater chance of reproduction.

system whose operation is governed by a biochemical process, which can be organized and modified in a regular fashion, and that natural selection and a species' evolutionary history can determine how it currently operates. This means that the history of a species, over centuries, modifies the structure of the species' brain. Evolutionary psychologists argue (and most psychologists agree) that human behaviour and mental processes are *plastic*, or subject to change. The design of the brain and how it operates have been shaped by previous experiences, not only in an individual's lifetime, but also in the lifetime of the species. From an evolutionary perspective this constant change serves as an adaptive mechanism by which individuals, and their brains, are constantly evolving. So, our behaviour is affected not only by what goes on around us, but also by the experiences of our species.

**ECLECTICISM.** Psychologists now realize that there are complex relationships among the factors that affect both overt behaviour and mental processes. Therefore, most psychologists involved in applied psychology, especially in clinical and counselling psychology, are eclectic in their perspective. **Eclecticism** is a combination of theories, facts, or techniques. In clinical and counselling psychology, eclecticism means using a variety of approaches to evaluate data, theories, and therapies as appropriate for an individual client, rather than relying exclusively on the techniques of one school of psychology.

Eclecticism allows a researcher or practitioner to view a problem from several orientations. For example, consider depression, the disabling mood disorder that affects 10 to 20 percent of men and women in Canada at some time in their lives (Chapter 15 discusses depression at length). From a biological perspective, people become depressed because of changes in brain chemistry. From a behavioural point of view, people learn to be depressed and sad because of faulty reward systems in their environment. From a psychoanalytic perspective, people become depressed because their early childhood experiences caused them to form a negative outlook on life. From a humanistic perspective, people become depressed when they choose inaction because they have or had poor role models. From a cognitive perspective, depression is made worse by the interpretations (thoughts) an individual adopts about a situation. An eclectic practitioner recognizes the complex nature of depression and acknowledges each of the possible contributions; the practitioner evaluates the person, the depression, and the context in which it occurs.

ECLECTICISM
[ek-LECK-ti-sizm]

In psychology, a combination of theories, facts, or techniques; the practice of using whatever clinical and counselling techniques are appropriate for an individual client rather than relying exclusively on the techniques of one school of psychology.

# The Science of Psychology

## THREE PRINCIPLES OF SCIENTIFIC ENDEAVOUR

As a science, psychology is committed to objectivity, accuracy, and healthy scepticism about the study of behaviour and mental processes. These three basic principles are the very core of what makes psychology a science. These basic principles help psychologists constantly review our theories and our research and they can help you, too, be a critical thinker in your day-to-day life.

**OBJECTIVITY.** For psychologists, objectivity means evaluating research and theory on their merits, without preconceived ideas. For example, when scientists challenged the validity of lie detector tests, both believers and sceptics stepped up offering case studies, as well as anecdotal experiences, that supported or discounted their usefulness. Psychologists attempt to bring scientific objectivity to the research arena; they know that common sense approaches to phenomena often are anecdotal and can explain events that may have happened, but that such approaches can rarely predict behaviour or mental

*Be an*
**ACTIVE LEARNER**

**REVIEW**
> Why might thought be considered behaviour? p. 5
> Identify the key assumptions underlying each school of psychological thought. pp. 6–12
> Why was Watson's behaviourism such a departure from other schools of psychological thought? pp. 8–9

**THINK CRITICALLY**
> Think about the historical events occurring around the time that each school of psychological thought emerged. How might the historical era have helped give birth to each school of thought?
> John B. Watson ultimately went into the advertising business. How might he have applied behaviourist principles in that field?

**APPLY PSYCHOLOGY**
> Imagine a child pitching a fit in the grocery store because his parents refuse to buy him a highly sugared cereal. How might each of the schools of psychological thought explain the child's behaviour, and what sort of advice would a psychologist from each school likely offer the child's parents?

processes in the future. Remember, as scientists we want to describe *and* predict—common sense relies heavily on looking backward—having hindsight—but is not very objective or reliable in making predictions about behaviour.

**ACCURACY.** Psychologists are concerned with gathering data from the laboratory and the real world in precise ways—that is, with accuracy. For instance, to conclude from a small number of eyewitness accounts that large numbers of people have been abducted by aliens falls considerably short of scientific accuracy. Might there be other plausible explanations for why a number of people have told very similar accounts of small, ghostly figures levitating people to flying-saucer laboratories? Might those reporting such incidents suffer from similar psychological disorders? Rather than relying on limited samples and immediate impressions, psychologists base their thinking on detailed and thorough study that is as precise as possible.

**HEALTHY SCEPTICISM.** One needn't be a scientific researcher to realize that in science, and in life, we observe many amazing events and so a careful approach to reports of strange events and phenomena is necessary. Many people think twice when they hear stories about people charged with serious crimes claiming that voices or other personalities were responsible for the crimes with which they are charged. Appealing as it may be to believe accounts of alien abductions or criminal multiple personalities, psychologists maintain a healthy scepticism: a cautious view of data, hypotheses, and theories until results are repeated, verified, and established over time.

## THE SCIENTIFIC METHOD IN PSYCHOLOGY

Like other scientists, psychologists use the scientific method in developing theories that describe, explain, predict, and help change behaviour. The **scientific method** in psychology is the technique used to discover knowledge about human behaviour and mental processes; in experimentation, it involves *stating the problem, developing hypotheses, designing a study, collecting and analyzing data* (which often includes manipulating some part of the environment to better understand what conditions can lead to a behaviour or phenomenon), *replicating results,* and *drawing conclusions and reporting results* (see *Introduction to Research Basics*).

Let's break down the scientific method into its six basic steps, so that you can have an overview of how psychologists do their work. There will be more to say about the research process very shortly.

**STATING THE PROBLEM.** The question a psychologist asks must be stated in such a way that it can be answered; that is, it must be stated in a way that lends itself to investigation. For instance, if you ask the question "What is the mind?" little headway can be made even through rigorous techniques. But if you ask "To what extent is zinc effective in alleviating cold symptoms?" or "Does St. John's Wort work better than Prozac in treating depression?" the question can be tested with some degree of clarity.

**DEVELOPING HYPOTHESES.** In the next step of the scientific method, psychologists form educated guesses about how people are likely to react. Such a formulation is called a **hypothesis**—a tentative statement or idea expressing a relationship between two events or variables that are to be evaluated in a research study. A hypothesis might be that a specific diet—perhaps one low in refined sugar—is more effective than any other diet in controlling or reducing hyperactive behaviour in 10-year-old boys; further, the hypothesis might assert that such a diet will be 10 percent more effective than another diet or no special diet at all.

▲ Readers of tabloids need to assess the articles with a healthy degree of scepticism.

SCIENTIFIC METHOD
In psychology, the techniques used to discover knowledge about human behaviour and mental processes; in experimentation, the scientific method involves stating the problem, developing hypotheses, designing a study, collecting and analyzing data (which often includes manipulating some part of the environment to better understand what conditions can lead to a behaviour or phenomenon), replicating results, and drawing conclusions and reporting results.

HYPOTHESIS
A tentative statement or idea expressing a causal relationship between two events or variables that are to be evaluated in a research study.

## To Sleep, Perchance to Experiment

Let's walk through a research study and look at some of the key processes for experimental research discussed in this chapter. Imagine that you are a researcher interested in sleep, especially the effects of sleep deprivation. Psychologist Steve Joncas of the University of Montreal and his colleagues (Joncas et al., 2002) are such researchers; they are interested in the effects of sleep deprivation, specifically its effects on somnambulism (sleepwalking).

**Design.** The researchers chose to use a *quasi-experimental design* to investigate this question.

**Hypothesis.** Initially researchers form a *hypothesis,* a tentative statement or idea expressing a relationship between two or more variables. The hypothesis for this sleep deprivation study was that adult sleepwalking participants deprived of sleep for 38 hours would experience sleep fragmentation (disruptions in the normal patterns of sleep) resulting in increased episodes of sleepwalking.

**Variables.** The researchers asked participants to report to the Sleep Disorder Clinic in the Hôpital du Sacré-Coeur de Montréal three times. On each occasion researchers measured the participants' brain waves, eye movements, respiration, and other physiological variables. They also measured both the number and the complexity of movements made by the participants while sleeping (examples include sitting up in bed, playing with the bed sheets, trying to get out of bed).

**Participants.** The participants in the study were 20 men and women between the ages of 21 and 30.

**Control and Experimental Groups.** The sleep deprivation study compared two groups of participants. The experimental group consisted of 10 diagnosed sleepwalkers and the control group consisted of 10 age-matched participants who were not sleepwalkers (this means that for each sleepwalker in the study someone else of the same age was also included in the study).

**Procedure.** On the first night, participants were screened to ensure that they were free of any sleep disorders. On the second night, participants slept normally and each participant's sleep pattern was recorded as a baseline measure for comparison to the sleep deprivation night. The third night of measurement occurred after the patient had been awake for 38 consecutive hours. Presence or absence of a past history of sleepwalking was the *independent (manipulated) variable*. This is a *quasi-experiment* because participants cannot be randomly assigned to sleepwalking or non-sleepwalking groups. The *dependent variables* were the number and complexity of nocturnal (nighttime) behaviours observed, as well as the physiological variables.

**Results.** None of the control participants deprived of sleep for 38 hours showed any differences in the number or complexity of nocturnal behaviours from their baseline night. However, the sleepwalking group showed both greater numbers of nocturnal behaviours as well as increased complexity of nocturnal behaviours following sleep deprivation. By comparing the number and complexity of nocturnal behavioural measures (the dependent variable) of the experimental and control groups, the researchers determined that the independent variable (presence or absence of sleepwalking) was responsible for the difference in the dependent variable between the groups.

**Conclusions.** A study of this type allows researchers to suggest that sleep deprivation can be an effective means for inducing sleepwalking episodes in the laboratory and thus suggests that psychologists could use sleep deprivation to assist in diagnosing sleepwalking.

**Limitations and Problems.** Even successful studies have limitations. For example, this study on sleep deprivation used young adults as participants, and that choice in itself is a limitation. A *sample* is a group of participants who represent a larger group. In this case, the larger group is all young adults between ages 21 and 30. The extent to which this age group differs from the general population limits the ways in which researchers can generalize their results. What holds true for young adults may not be true for the older general population. Therefore, the sampling process represents a limitation for psychology research.

Good experiments allow researchers to draw conclusions about cause-and-effect relationships between independent and dependent variables. Though this basic plan is simple, arranging for two (or more) groups to be equal in all important ways except for the independent variable and choosing and measuring an appropriate dependent variable are not easy tasks. Before researchers can suggest that one situation causes another, they have to be sure that several specific conditions are met. A relationship between the variables is not sufficient to determine that one caused the other. *Correlational studies* demonstrate a relationship between two variables, but correlated variables may not be causally related. This caution is an important one. The *Introduction to*

*Research Basics* box in Chapter 2 describes correlational studies and emphasizes how these studies do not allow researchers to determine causation.

Bias can enter the research process at many points, and researchers must be careful in making design choices to minimize these biases. They pay close attention to how the data are collected and to whether the results of a study are repeatable in additional experiments. To make meaningful causal inferences, researchers must create situations in which they can limit the likelihood of obtaining a result that is simply a chance occurrence or caused by irrelevant factors. Only by using carefully formulated experiments can researchers make sound interpretations of results and cautiously extend them to other situations.

We will present some of the problems that plague research design and show how scientists solve these problems in *Introduction to Research Basics* boxes throughout this book. We have concentrated on the experimental method because researchers favour this method, but scientific research in psychology includes a variety of methods, each with advantages and limitations. Other methods of inquiry will be presented in the *Introduction to Research Basics* boxes, along with their strengths and limitations.

The research process is central to psychological inquiry, but it can also be applied to your own thinking. Indeed, thinking critically—not only about psychology research but about other issues—can make you a more effective student.

After stating the problem and developing a hypothesis, psychologists sometimes develop a theory from their current knowledge and past research. A **theory** is a collection of interrelated ideas and facts put forward to describe, explain, and predict behaviour and mental processes. For example, a theory that parental neglect, poverty, and a bad peer group contribute to delinquency might put together related facts about personality, gender differences, cultural differences, and the demographics of delinquency. Such a theory must organize data well and must create testable predictions to check the theory. Such testing usually occurs within the context of a well-designed research study.

**DESIGNING A STUDY.** Researchers next have to develop an approach to studying a problem, which will test a hypothesis or theory. They identify key variables, responses, and techniques that will help them understand the issue at hand. At the outset, the key elements of the study must be defined. The behaviours to be examined have to be carefully specified: How are they to be measured, with what instruments, how frequently, and by whom? In children who are identified as delinquents, some behaviours are fairly easily specified—for example, criminal behaviour. Other behaviours, such as anxiety and lack of self-esteem, which may be related to delinquency, are more difficult to define precisely—in delinquent children, or in anyone else for that matter.

**COLLECTING AND ANALYZING DATA.** After researchers have specified the key elements and chosen the participants for an experiment, they conduct the experiment, hoping it will yield interpretable, meaningful results. This requires carefully designed techniques for data collection so as not to bias the results in favour of one hypothesis or another. Data gathering techniques can include participant verbal reports, behaviour measures of things like reaction time, or physiological measures of blood characteristics, heart rate, or brain wave activity. The data also must be collected, organized, coded, and simplified in a way that allows for a reasonable set of conclusions to be drawn. For example if a researcher has 10 000 observations of 300 participants, something must be done to make sense of all this information. Statistical or mathematical techniques usually are called upon to help summarize and condense the data. For example, looking

THEORY

In psychology, a collection of interrelated ideas and facts put forward to describe, explain, and predict behaviour and mental processes.

▼ Certain physiological reactions, such as patterns of brain activity, must be measured with instruments to be observable.

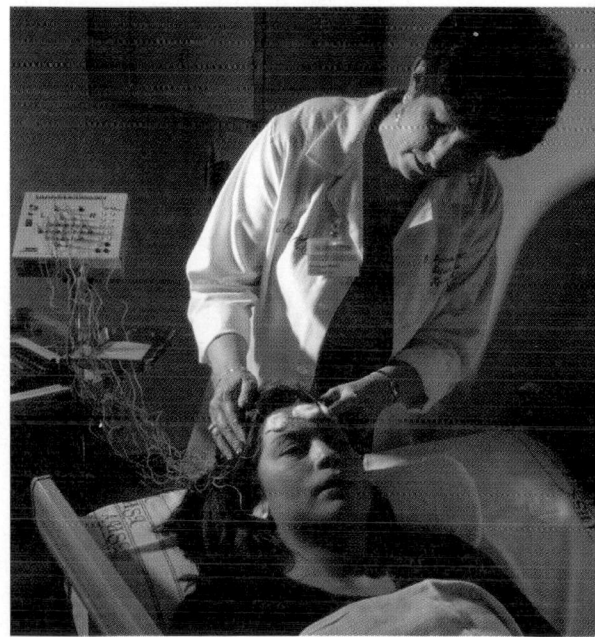

## Be an
## ACTIVE
## LEARNER

**REVIEW**
> Identify three key principles of scientific endeavour to which scientists must be committed. pp. 12–13
> Describe the steps followed when using the scientific method. pp. 13–16
> Why would successfully replicating a research study be so important to scientists? p. 16

**THINK CRITICALLY**
> You may have read that scientists have theorized that for women, estrogen replacement therapy may increase memory loss in Alzheimer's disease, a progressive degenerative disorder affecting memory. What questions would you ask, and what issues would you be concerned with, in attempting to test this hypothesis?

**APPLY PSYCHOLOGY**
> Watch several episodes of reality TV and make notes on how the participants "use psychology" on each other. Keep these notes and compare this portrayal of psychology to the information you learn as you read this book. How "real" is reality TV?

**HandsOnPsych**
Version 2.0

**Research Methods and Statistics**

EXPERIMENT

A procedure in which a researcher systematically manipulates and observes elements of a situation in order to answer a question and, usually, to test hypotheses and make inferences about cause and effect.

VARIABLE

A condition or characteristic of a situation or a person that is subject to change (that varies) within or across situations or individuals.

INDEPENDENT VARIABLE

The variable in a controlled experiment that the experimenter directly and purposely manipulates to see how the other variables under study will be affected.

DEPENDENT VARIABLE

The variable in a controlled experiment that is expected to change because of the manipulation of the independent variable.

at the average amount of time, over 10 or 20 trials, it takes a person in a driving simulator to apply the brakes when a hazard appears would provide a more accurate picture of this variable than just measuring it once with each person in the study.

**REPLICATING RESULTS.** Most researchers are aware of their own all-too-human tendency to *bias*, or subtly predetermine, the outcomes of their research so that they obtain precisely the results they expected. One way to control such bias is to *replicate*, or repeat the experiment, or to have another researcher try to reproduce the same results. If the results of a replicated experiment are the same, a researcher generally will say that the results are reliable and are likely to occur again given the same set of circumstances.

**DRAWING CONCLUSIONS AND REPORTING RESULTS.** When results are organized and statistics are calculated, researchers try to organize ideas and observations to make predictions about behaviour. They begin to draw conclusions about results and relate those conclusions to the data that they have collected. Ultimately, researchers report their results to the scientific community by publishing their study—they report their findings as well as their interpretations of what they think the results mean.

Now that we have a general overview of the research process, let's go into more detail, to examine how psychologists go about the process of scientific inquiry.

## The Research Process

If you ever have the opportunity to tour a psychologist's laboratory or to observe psychologists gathering research data in the field, you should do so. Even better, if you ever have the opportunity to assist a psychologist in research, take advantage of it. Although psychologists use most of the techniques other scientists use, they adapt these techniques to deal with the uncertainties of human behaviour. The typical research process in psychology is quite systematic and begins with a specific question—the "stating the problem" step of the scientific method. The process may take the form of an **experiment**—a procedure in which a researcher systematically manipulates and observes elements of a situation in order to answer a question and, usually, to establish causality. For example, if a researcher wants to determine the relationship between an animal's eating behaviour and its weight, the researcher could systematically vary (manipulate) how much the animal ate and then weigh (observe) the animal each day to infer that eating behaviour and weight are causally related. There are many other valid forms of research used in psychology, some of which will be discussed below.

### VARIABLES, HYPOTHESES, AND EXPERIMENTAL AND CONTROL GROUPS

**VARIABLES.** A **variable** is a condition or a characteristic of a situation or person that is subject to change (that varies) either within or across situations or individuals. Researchers manipulate some variables in order to measure how the changes in them affect other variables. There are two types of variables in any experiment: independent and dependent variables. The **independent variable** is the variable in a controlled experiment that the experimenter directly and purposely manipulates. The **dependent variable** is the variable that is expected to change as a result of manipulation of the independent variable. For example, a researcher might hypothesize that increases in temperature would adversely affect behaviour. The researcher therefore might raise the temperature in a room and measure whether a person's activity level is increased or decreased by the manipulation of the temperature.

Or imagine a simple reaction time experiment intended to determine the effects of sleep loss on behaviour. The participants in the study might be a large group of university students who normally sleep about seven hours a night. The independent (manipulated) variable might be the number of hours university students are allowed to sleep. The dependent variable could be the students' reaction times to a stimulus—for example, how quickly they push a button when a light is flashed.

HYPOTHESES.   As we saw earlier, a *hypothesis* is a tentative statement or idea expressing a relationship between two events or variables that are to be evaluated in a research study. The hypothesis of the sleep loss experiment might be that students deprived of sleep will react more slowly to a stimulus than will students allowed to sleep their regular seven hours. Suppose the participants sleep in the laboratory on four successive nights and are tested each morning on a reaction time task. The participants sleep seven hours on each of three nights but sleep only four hours on the fourth night. If the response times after the first three nights are constant and if all other factors are held equal, any observed differences in reaction times on the fourth test (following the night of four hours of sleep) can be attributed to the number of hours of sleep. That is, changes in the independent variable (numbers of hours of sleep) will produce changes in the dependent variable (reaction time). If the results show that students deprived of sleep respond on the reaction time task a half-second slower than they did after normal sleep, the researcher could feel justified in concluding that sleep deprivation acts to slow down reaction time. The researcher's hypothesis would have been supported by the experiment.

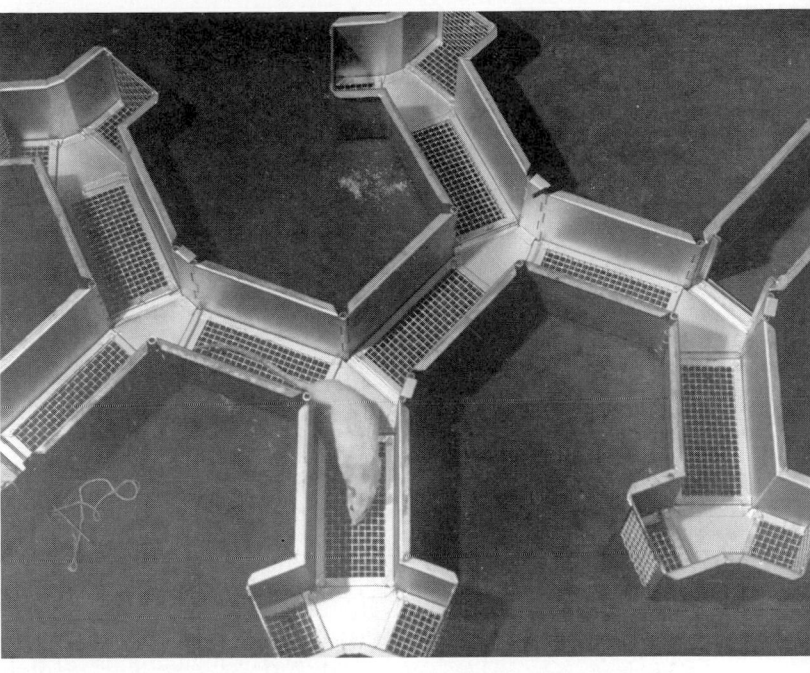

▲ During the 1940s and 1950s, white rats were the most common experimental subjects in research on learning.

EXPERIMENTAL AND CONTROL GROUPS.   Researchers must determine whether it is actually the changes in the manipulated variable, and not some unknown extraneous factor, that cause a change in the dependent variable. One way to do this is to set up at the start of the experiment at least two groups of participants who are identical in important ways. **Participants** are human individuals who take part in experiments and whose behaviour is observed for research data collection (previously referred to as *subjects*, this term was changed at the recommendation of the Canadian and American Psychological Associations to reflect the fact that people actively and voluntarily participate in experiments). Note that while we refer to human participants here, it is worth remembering that many of the studies we will talk about in the following chapters were conducted with animals rather than humans. The attributes that participants must have in common will depend on what the experimenter is testing. For example, because reflexes slow down as a person grows older, the researcher in the reaction time experiment would want to ensure that the two groups were composed of participants of the same or nearly the same age.

Once the participants are known to be similar on important attributes, they are assigned randomly to either the experimental or the control group. *Random assignment* means that the participants are assigned by lottery rather than on the basis of any particular characteristic, preference, or situation that might have even a remote possibility of influencing the outcome. The **experimental group** is the group of participants to whom a treatment is given. Some psychologists even refer to the

PARTICIPANT

A human individual who takes part in an experiment and whose behaviour is observed for research data collection; previously known as a *subject*.

EXPERIMENTAL GROUP

In an experiment, a group of participants to whom a treatment is given.

CONTROL GROUP

In an experiment, the comparison group—the group of participants tested on the dependent variable in the same way as the experimental group but for whom the treatment is not given.

experimental group as the *treatment group*. The **control group** is the comparison group—the group of participants tested on the dependent variable in the same way as the experimental group but for whom the treatment is not given. In the reaction time experiment, the students who sleep a full seven hours on all four nights are the control group. Those who are allowed to sleep only four hours on the last night are the experimental group. Their treatment was being deprived of sleep; of course, in other research studies, their treatment may be being allowed more sleep, a drug, or perhaps some special sleep techniques. By comparing the reaction times (the dependent variable) for the experimental and control groups, the researcher can determine whether the independent variable is responsible for any differences in the dependent variable between the groups.

If the researcher is confident that all of the participants responded with the same reaction time before the experiment—that is, that the two groups are truly comparable—then the researcher can conclude that sleep deprivation is the cause of the experimental group's decreased performance. Without comparable groups, the effect of the treatment variable is not clear, and few real conclusions can be drawn from the data.

Of course, extraneous, or irrelevant, variables can also make interpretation difficult. *Extraneous variables* are factors that affect the results of an experiment but that are not of interest to the experimenter. An example of an extraneous variable is a thunderstorm that occurs during an experiment in which anxiety is being measured through a physical response such as rises in skin conductivity. It would be difficult or impossible for the researchers to ascertain how much of the increased skin conductivity was due to manipulations they created and how much was due to anxiety about thunder. When extraneous variables occur during an experiment (or just before it), they may *confound results*—make data difficult to interpret.

## OPERATIONAL DEFINITIONS, SAMPLE SIZE, AND SIGNIFICANT DIFFERENCES

**OPERATIONAL DEFINITIONS.**   A key component of successful scientific research is that all terms used in describing the variables and the procedure must be given operational definitions. An **operational definition** is a definition of a variable in terms of a set of the methods or procedures used to measure or study that variable. When a researcher manipulates or observes real differences in an organism's state of hunger, the concept *hunger* must be defined in terms of the procedures necessary to produce hunger. For example, a researcher might be interested in the effects of hunger (the independent variable) on exploratory behaviour (the dependent variable) in mice. The researcher might deprive mice of food for 6, 10, 12, or 24 hours and then observe and record their exploratory behaviour. The researcher might operationally define hunger in terms of the number of hours of food deprivation and exploratory behaviour in terms of the number of times the mice walked farther than 60 centimetres down a path.

OPERATIONAL DEFINITION

Definition of a variable in terms of the set of methods or procedures used to measure or study that variable.

**SAMPLE SIZE.**   Another important factor in an experiment is the size and representativeness of the sample. A **sample** is a group of participants who are assumed to be representative of the population about which an inference is being made. A **population** is the entire group (large or small) of people you might be interested in studying. For example, a researcher studying Canadians' attitudes about mental illness would put together a sample of people that properly reflects the makeup of the Canadian population. If, however, the researcher was only interested in adolescent rural Canadian women's attitudes about mental illness, the population to be sampled could be all rural Canadian women under 19 years of age.

The number of participants in a sample is very important. If an effect is obtained consistently with a large enough number of participants, the researcher can reasonably rule out individual differences and chance as causes. The key

SAMPLE

A group of participants who are assumed to be representative of the population about which an inference is being made.

POPULATION

The entire group (large or small) of people you might be interested in studying.

assumption is that a large sample better represents the population to which the researcher wishes to generalize the results. Larger samples also tend to produce less variable results, making it easier to decide if the differences you observe in a sample are, in fact, reflective of real differences in the general population from which the sample was drawn.

**SIGNIFICANT DIFFERENCES.**   Researchers want to be sure that the differences they find are significant. For psychologists, a **significant difference** in an experiment is a difference that is statistically unlikely to have occurred because of chance alone and that is most likely due to the systematic manipulation of the independent variable. For example, when one therapy technique appears to be more effective than another, the researcher wants to be sure that the results with the first technique are significantly different from the results with the second and that the difference is large enough to be important in the outside world. The results are significantly different only if they are not likely due to chance, due to the use of only one or two participants, or due to a unique set of participants. Such conclusions can come only from experiments in which participants are randomly assigned to experimental and control groups, an independent variable is systematically manipulated, and attempts are made to control extraneous variables. If experimental results are not statistically significant, they are not considered to have established a finding or confirmed a hypothesis. You can read more about the important role that statistics play in psychological research in the Statistical Methods appendix at the end of this book.

## SUCCESSFUL EXPERIMENTS AVOID PITFALLS

Good experiments often involve several experimental groups, each tested under different conditions. Another study of the effects of sleep deprivation might involve a control group and five experimental groups. The participants in each of the experimental groups might be deprived of sleep for a different length of time (sleep deprivation operationally defined in terms of number of hours of sleep lost from the normal number of hours slept). In this way, the researcher could examine the effects of several different degrees of sleep deprivation on reaction time.

In a well-designed experiment, the experimenter also looks closely at the nature of the independent variable. Are there actual values for the independent variable above or below which results will differ markedly? For example, the researcher might find that a one-hour loss of sleep has no effect, that a two-hour deprivation produces only a modest effect, and that every additional hour of deprivation markedly slows reaction time. These results would show that reaction time is dependent on the amount of sleep deprivation. The use of several experimental groups yields better understanding of how the independent variable (sleep deprivation) affects the dependent variable (reaction time).

**EXPECTANCY EFFECTS.**   Frequently, things turn out just the way a researcher expects. Researchers are aware, however, that their *expectancies*, or expectations, about results may influence their findings, particularly where human behaviour is concerned. Knowing this, however, does not mean there will be no influence (Rosenthal, 2002). A researcher may unwittingly create a situation that leads to specific prophesied results—a **self-fulfilling prophecy**. For example, a teacher may develop expectations about a student's performance early in the year, then unconsciously set low (or high) standards for that student. Sensing those standards, the student will often confirm the teacher's expectations, even when the expectations may not reflect the student's potential ability. In these instances, the student's performance has fulfilled the teacher's prophecy, regardless of other factors. Sometimes researchers investigate expectancy effects directly when they study placebo effects. A **placebo** is a treatment that has no effect but is presented as possibly producing certain effects, for example, randomly substituting a child's hyperactivity medication with non-active copies of the real pills for some days and doing this in a way that anyone interacting with the child does not know which day is which. If the child's behaviour is reported to be as good on the placebo days as on the real drug days (one experimenter keeps track of which day is which, often in a sealed record) then it may be that the expectations of the child and those around him are exerting a powerful influence on his behaviour and that the effectiveness of the drug itself with that child should be reviewed.

To avoid the risk of self-fulfilling prophecies, researchers often use a **double-blind technique**—a research technique in which neither the experimenter nor the participants know who is in the control group or the experimental group. In this situation, someone who is not connected with the research project keeps track of which participants are assigned to which group. The double-blind technique minimizes the effect that a researcher's subtle cues might have on participants. (In a single-blind experiment, the researcher knows who is in the experimental group and who is in the control group, but the participants do not know who is assigned to which group or whether they are being presented with a manipulated variable.)

Researchers also try to minimize the demand characteristics of studies. **Demand characteristics** are the elements of a study situation that might direct how things happen or tip off a participant as to the purpose of the study and perhaps thereby elicit specific behaviour from the participant. Participants who even *think* they know the real purpose of a study may try to behave "appropriately" and in so doing may distort the results. Some techniques that minimize the impact of demand characteristics are the use of computers to decrease interaction with people (participants are less likely to want to act appropriately for a computer), of unobtrusive measures such as tape recording rather than note taking, and of deception (concealing the real purpose of the study; see the section on ethics beginning on page 27) until the end of the research section.

Even when a double-blind procedure is used and demand characteristics are minimized, participants often just behave differently when they are in a research study. This finding is known as the **Hawthorne effect,** after some early research studies at the Hawthorne industrial plant that showed that people behave differently (usually better) when they know they are being observed. This meant that any change in the plant (for example, to lighting levels) had a positive effect on productivity. Researchers therefore attempt to make participants feel comfortable and natural and to create experimental situations that minimize the effects of participation. They often do not collect data until after participants have adapted to the experimental situation and have become less distracted about being part of the research study.

## CORRELATION IS NOT NECESSARILY CAUSATION

Consider this statement: In general, the more education you have, the higher your yearly income will be. This is a true descriptive statement, but only up to a point. After a person receives a university or college degree, adding a professional degree is less likely to add significant additional income to the person's yearly take-home pay. It is not accurate to say that each unit of education causes income to rise; rather, education allows a person to open new doors and creates opportunities to earn more. At a certain point, another master's degree helps little in increasing opportunities. In short, more education does not directly cause more yearly income.

Designing an experiment to test this claim would not be ethical, for to conduct it you systematically would have to allow some people to study for advanced degrees and disallow others from doing so. Many things that are of interest to psychologists are of this nature. As a result, psychologists have devised other ways to study these more natural phenomena. While these other study designs require some care where causality questions are concerned, they can still provide a useful means for testing specifically stated hypotheses. Correlational studies are examples of informative research designs that can be used when strict experimentation is not possible.

**Research Methods and Statistics**

Two events are *correlated* when the increased presence (or absence) of a particular situation is regularly associated with a high (or low) presence of another situation, event, or situational feature. For example, a researcher who finds that children whose parents are divorced have more emotional problems and commit more crimes than children from intact families can state that there is a correlation. However, the researcher cannot directly conclude that parental divorce *causes* emotional problems or crime (see Figure 1.1). Events are considered causally related only when one event makes another event occur—when one event or situation is contingent on another. **Correlation coefficients** are statistical values that can be calculated between two scores to determine the nature and degree of relatedness between those variables. Correlation coefficients range from –1 through 0 to +1 with numbers closer to –1 or +1 reflecting stronger (closer) relationships (0 = no relationship) and the negative or positive sign indicating the direction of the relationship (for example, in a positive correlation both values increase together whereas in a negative correlation one value goes up and the other goes down). You can read more about the statistical procedures used to quantify correlations in the Statistical Methods appendix at the end of this book.

## THINKING CRITICALLY AND EVALUATING RESEARCH

Psychologists, like all scientists, are trained to think, to evaluate research critically, and to put their results into a meaningful framework. An important part of the investigative process is presenting your research publicly and to other psychologists through conferences, journals, and books. Psychology journals and many conferences use a *peer review* process (in which other psychologists read and critically evaluate the research study report) to evaluate research using the criteria outlined earlier and to decide whether to publish the study. Descriptions of this process can be found inside virtually any psychology journal (examples of which can be found in your university or college library). Psychologists follow a traditional approach to evaluating research. To benefit from this textbook, you might find it helpful to use the same critical thinking skills and framework in order to follow psychologists' logic, to understand their approach, and to evaluate their research.

*Critical thinking* consists of collecting and evaluating the evidence, sifting through the choices, assessing the outcomes, and deciding whether the conclusions make sense. When you think critically, you are being evaluative. You are not accepting glib generalizations; instead you are determining the relevance of facts and looking for biases and imbalances, as well as for objectivity and testable,

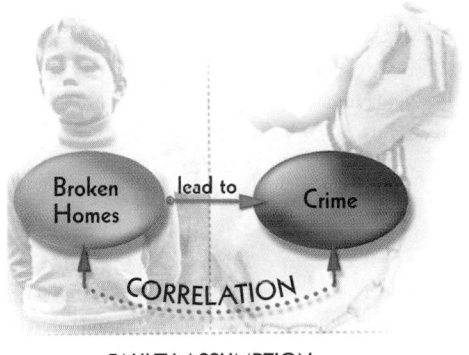

FAULTY ASSUMPTION

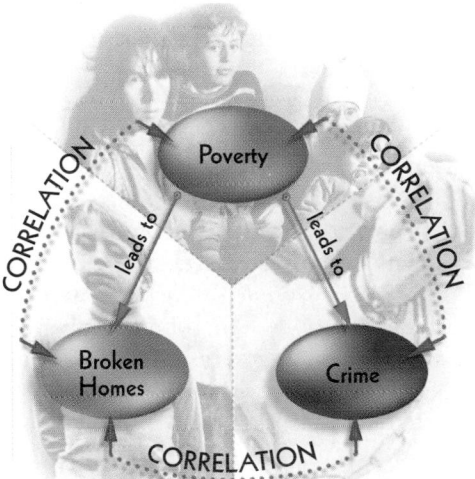

MORE LIKELY ASSUMPTION

**FIGURE 1.1**
**Correlation Is Not Necessarily Causation**

Although research shows that broken homes and crime are correlated, it does not show causation. Poverty, a third variable, may be the cause of both crime and broken homes.

repeatable results. A critical thinker identifies central issues and is careful not to draw cause-and-effect conclusions from correlations. A critical thinker also has to tolerate some uncertainty and be patient—all of the answers do not come at once.

When you think critically about research, you become a detective sorting through facts. You look objectively at the facts, question the hypotheses and conclusions, avoid oversimplification, and consider all of the arguments, objections, and counter-arguments. You evaluate all assumptions and assertively seek out conflicting points of view. You revise your opinions when the data and your conclusions call for it. Whenever you have to evaluate a research study in this text, the popular press, or a psychological publication, you will find it helpful to focus on five research criteria: purpose, methodology, participants, repeatability, and conclusions.

**PURPOSE.**   What is the purpose of this research? What is the researcher trying to test, demonstrate, or prove? Has the problem been clearly defined? Is the researcher qualified to conduct this research? Is the researcher biased?

**METHODOLOGY.**   Is the methodology appropriate and carefully executed? Is the method of investigation used (for example, a case study, survey, or experiment) the most appropriate one for the topic? Has the method been used properly? Is there a control group? Have variables been carefully (operationally) defined? Has the researcher followed ethical guidelines (a topic considered on p. 27)?

**PARTICIPANTS.**   Was the sample of participants properly chosen and carefully described? How was the sample selected? Does the sample accurately reflect the characteristics of the population of individuals about which the researcher would like to make generalizations? Will any generalizations be possible from this study?

**REPEATABILITY.**   Are the results repeatable? Has the researcher shown the same finding more than once? Have other investigators made similar findings? Are the results clear and unambiguous—that is, not open to criticism based on poor methodology? If other researchers cannot reproduce the results of a study using its own methodology, this seriously calls the results of the original study into question.

**CONCLUSIONS.**   How logical are the conclusions, implications, and applications suggested by the study? Does the researcher's data support them? Has the researcher gone beyond the data, drawing conclusions that might fit a predisposed view rather than conclusions that follow logically from the facts of the study? What implications do the data have for psychology as a science and a profession? What are the potential implications for you as an individual? Has the researcher considered alternative explanations?

Think again about the sleep deprivation experiment described earlier. Use the five criteria to evaluate this research. The participants were college students deprived of sleep and tested on a reaction time task.

*Was the purpose of the study clear?* The purpose was to assess the effect of sleep loss on reaction time.

*Was the methodology appropriate?* The method involved depriving participants of sleep after they had become used to sleeping in a controlled environment; participants were tested each morning. The task was operationally defined.

*Was the sample of participants properly chosen?* The participants were college students who were in good health. Reasonable generalizations from their reaction times to the reaction times of other similarly aged people might be possible.

*Are the results repeatable?* If the results were obtained with several groups of participants, and if the results were consistent within each of those groups, the repeatability of the results would seem assured.

*How logical are the conclusions?* Limited conclusions can be drawn from such a research study. There was only one age group—college students, a very convenient population for college and university researchers and a very good group with which to start research. There were no controls on other factors in the students' environment, such as workloads, school pressure, energy expenditures, and history of sleep loss. A simple conclusion about sleep deprivation could be drawn: In a controlled research study of college students, sleep deprivation tends to slow down reaction time. However, not much more could be said, and no generalizations could be applied to, say, children, older adults, or the chronically mentally ill. The results of the study do not contradict common sense, but they add little to our overall understanding of sleep deprivation.

A key to thinking critically about research is to be evaluative, to question all aspects of the study. Think about the advantages as well as the limitations of the research method used. You can also apply your critical thinking skills to nonacademic material. When a TV commercial tells you that 9 out of 10 doctors recommend Brand X, think critically about that claim. What kind of doctors, for what kind of ailment, for patients of what age, and for what extent of usage?

Look for research findings. Has there been any research done to support the claims being made? Was the research properly designed? For example, people often claim that their horoscopes seem to them to be accurate predictors of their daily experience. Have you read any research to support these claims? What about reports of psychic phenomena? Believing in the ability to read minds because others have told you they have experienced it is not thinking critically. Basically, the more carefully designed a study of psychic phenomena is the *less* likely it is to produce significant results supporting the existence of psychic phenomena or abilities. Look for and examine the data!

As you read this text, evaluate research findings. We will present the research to you in ways that allow you to critically evaluate it and to draw your own conclusions. From time to time in each chapter we will also ask you some *Be an Active Learner* questions called *Think Critically*. These questions will suggest new ideas and perspectives for you to consider as you evaluate the research studies presented. These are not the only places in the text where you should use your critical thinking skills, but they are specific instances in which you definitely can be evaluative.

## METHODS FOR GATHERING PSYCHOLOGICAL DATA

So far we have not specifically discussed how psychological researchers actually collect the data that are the central part of their studies. Direct measurement is useful but so are techniques that provide descriptive information about behaviour and that capture how well one variable predicts another. These techniques include *questionnaires, interviews, naturalistic observation,* and *case studies.* These techniques can be used outside of laboratory settings to study behaviour in natural environments.

**QUESTIONNAIRES.**   A **questionnaire**, or *survey*, is usually a printed form with questions that is given to a large group of people. Researchers use questionnaires to gather a large amount of information from many people in a short time. A questionnaire being used to learn the typical characteristics of psychology students might be distributed to students enrolled in an introductory psychology course. It might ask each student to list age, sex, height, weight, previous courses taken, grades in high school, graduating exam scores, number of brothers and sisters, and parents' financial status. There might also be questions regarding sexual activity, career goals, and personal preferences in TV shows, clothing styles, and music.

One aim of surveys is to discover relationships among variables. For example, a questionnaire designed to assess aggressiveness might ask respondents to list their sex, the number of fights they have had in the past, their feelings of anger, and the sports they enjoy. The researcher who is analyzing the results might use the data to determine whether men and women tend to differ in reporting aggressive behaviours.

The strength of the questionnaire is that it gathers a large amount of information in a short time. Its weaknesses are that it is impersonal, it gathers only the

QUESTIONNAIRE

A printed form with questions, usually given to a large group of people; used by researchers to gather a substantial amount of data in a short time; also known as a *survey*.

▲ Interviews allow researchers to gather responses from a large number of people in a short period of time.

**INTERVIEW**
A face-to-face meeting in which a series of standardized questions is used to gather detailed information.

**NATURALISTIC OBSERVATION**
Careful and objective observation of events from a distance, without observer intervention.

**CASE STUDY**
A method of interviewing participants to gain information about their backgrounds, including data on factors such as childhood, family, education, and social and sexual interactions.

information asked by the questions, it limits the participants' range of responses, it cannot prevent respondents from leaving some questions unanswered or from being untruthful in their responses, and it does not provide a structure from which cause-and-effect relationships can be inferred (although correlations may be found).

**INTERVIEWS.** An **interview** is typically a face-to-face meeting in which a researcher (interviewer) asks an individual a series of standardized questions. The interviewer usually tape-records or writes down the participant's responses. The advantage of an interview over a questionnaire is that it allows for a wider range of responses. An interviewer who notes an exaggerated response, for example, might decide to ask related questions and thus explore more fully an area that seems important to the participant. The interview technique is time consuming, however, and, as with questionnaires, no cause-and-effect relationships can be inferred.

**NATURALISTIC OBSERVATION.** A seemingly simple way to find out about behaviour is to observe it. As we've discussed, however, people who are told they are going to be observed tend to become self-conscious and alter their natural behaviour. Therefore, psychologists often use the technique of **naturalistic observation**—careful and objective observation of events from a distance, without observer intervention. The intent is to see how people or animals behave in their natural settings.

A psychologist conducting research on persuasion might pretend to be a browsing shopper at car lots, furniture stores, and appliance centres to discover how salespeople convince customers to buy expensive products. For example, the researcher might observe that one particularly successful car salesperson tends to show budget-minded customers the most expensive automobiles first, so that mid-priced models will seem more affordable by comparison. The researcher also might watch a salesperson through a one-way mirror similar to the kind used to detect thefts in supermarkets.

The strength of naturalistic observation is that the data collected are unaffected by the researcher's presence or by a laboratory setting. Naturalistic observers must take their data where and how they find them. They cannot manipulate the environment, because that might alter the behaviour they are observing. Because variables cannot be manipulated, data from naturalistic observation, like those from questionnaires and interviews, are descriptive and do not permit cause-and-effect conclusions.

A second major weakness is that the behaviour the psychologist may wish to examine is not always exhibited. For example, sometimes groups of people do not act persuasively or become aggressive; sometimes animals do not engage in mating behaviour. For these reasons, naturalistic observation is also very time consuming.

**CASE STUDIES.** The **case study** is a method of interviewing participants to gain information about their background, including data on factors such as childhood, family, education, and social and sexual interactions. The information in a case study describes in detail a specific person's responses to the world; the case study is often used to describe a potential method of treatment.

The strength of the case study is that the information it provides is extensive, for one individual. A weakness is that the information describes only one person's particular situation. Because the behaviour of one person may be like that of others or may be unique, researchers cannot generalize from one individual to an entire population. They must be cautious even when generalizing from a number of case studies.

See Table 1.1 for a summary of the major approaches to data collection.

**TABLE 1.1** Five Approaches to Research

| Approach | Strengths | Weaknesses |
|---|---|---|
| Experiment | Manipulation of variables to control outside influences; best method for identifying causal relationships. | Laboratory environment is artificial; limited generalizability of findings; manipulation of some variables is unethical or impractical. |
| Questionnaire | Effective means of measuring actions, attitudes, opinions, preferences, and intentions of large numbers of people. | Lack of explanatory power; validity of findings is limited by sample; reliability is difficult to determine; self-report may be inaccurate or biased. |
| Interview | Allows a wide range of responses; follow-up questions are possible. | Does not enable researchers to draw conclusions about causal relationships; time consuming. |
| Naturalistic observation | Behaviour is unaffected by a researcher's manipulations. | Little opportunity to control variables; time consuming. |
| Case study | Extensive evidence is gathered on a single person. | Lack of generalizability of findings; time consuming. |

## AVOIDING GENDER, ETHNICITY, AND CULTURAL BIAS

Some people argue that human beings are all pretty much the same. But in 1896 William James cleverly wrote, "There is very little difference between one person and another, but what little difference there is, is very important" (pp. 256–257). James's comment reminds us that to ensure good experiments we have to have a large sample of participants who accurately reflect the population. In addition, researchers also must be careful to avoid subtle biases that influence results, such as gender, ethnicity, and cultural bias. At any stage of the research endeavour, an experimenter can influence the results and their interpretation by making assumptions about people, their tendencies, and how they might be affected by the variable under study. Such assumptions often are affected by researchers' attitudes about whether to report findings such as gender or ethnicity differences among participants.

Although many behaviours seem universal, truly universal behaviours are those that occur in all human beings regardless of their culture. When research studies are used to draw conclusions and make generalizations about people, it is important to understand that enormous differences exist among both individuals and groups of people. The young and the old may behave differently under similar conditions; research done only on men may yield different results from research done only on women. People are not all alike and do not all behave in the same way, even when in the same situation. Thus, researchers have become especially sensitive to issues of human diversity.

To do effective research, draw meaningful conclusions, and make generalizations that may be wide ranging, researchers must recognize and test for elements of diversity, even within one country, such as Canada. A society includes individuals from many different cultures, ethnicities, religions, and so on. Each subgroup has developed its own style of living, which may vary considerably from that of the majority culture and may lead to marked ethnic-related differences in day-to-day behaviour and in mental health (Al-Issa, 1982). Psychologists say that a community, organization, or nation is culturally diverse if it has differences in race, ethnicity, language, nationality, age, and religion within it.

**ETHNICITY.**   *Ethnicity* refers to people's common traits, background, and allegiances, which are often cultural, religious, or language-based; ethnicity is learned from family, friends, and experiences. Families of English and French Canadians along with a broad range of other groups bring to the Canadian experience a wealth of different world views and different ways of raising children, based on their particular heritages. The makeup of the Canadian population is diverse. The 2001 census revealed that French is the first language of about 23 percent of Canadians, about 7 percent of the Canadian population are of Asian descent, and about 3 percent of the population are Aboriginal (Statistics Canada, 2003a).

**CULTURE.** Culture reflects a person's racial and ethnic background, religious and social values, artistic and musical tastes, and scholarly interests. Culture is the unwritten social and psychological dictionary that each of us has learned and through which we interpret ourselves and others (Landrine, Klonoff, & Brown-Collins, 1992). Various cultural vantage points shape behaviour, values, and even mental health. One such vantage point that must be considered is the difference between individualist and collectivist cultures. Individualist cultures (such as Canada's) stress personal rather than group goals, and individual freedom and autonomy are valued; collectivist cultures (such as many Asian cultures) stress group needs over individual ones, and a tightly knit social fabric and willingness to go along with the group are highly valued.

**CLASS.** Closely tied to culture is a person's class. Although the Canadian class structure is not as rigid as it was in the last century or as it is in some non-Western countries, and although class distinctions are somewhat fuzzy, Canadians do fall into several socio-economic classes. Among these classes are the economically poor, the disadvantaged, the educated, and the middle class. In different socio-economic classes (which include individuals of different races and cultures), people may view the world differently and behave differently primarily because of their socio-economic status. A research study that is not sensitive to such variables may confuse the causes of its results. For example, not considering socio-economic class as a key variable in a study of drug use may lead to conclusions that are not true or, at a minimum, are not generalizable to all socio-economic classes.

**GENDER.** Psychologists know that due to both biological and social reasons, women often react differently than men do in psychological situations. This makes it easy to see that the gender of the sample in a research study is crucial (Denmark, 1994). For example, research on morality shows that, in general, women may see moral situations differently than men do; research on brain functions shows differences in brain structure between men and women; research on communication styles, aggression, and love shows sharp differences between men and women. Further, more than half of the people treated by mental health practitioners are women—this may be because men with mental health problems are less likely to seek therapy. These differences must be examined closely if we are to properly understand them.

▼ Due to both nature and nurture, men and women respond differently in social situations.

**AGE OR DISABILITIES.** The exceptional and the elderly are two other groups that shape research results in distinctive ways. The exceptional include individuals diagnosed with mental retardation, learning disabilities, or physical disabilities. Assessing and assisting exceptional individuals often require a special sensitivity on the part of professionals. In addition, the elderly are a growing percentage of the general population. More than 3.9 million Canadians are age 65 or older (Statistics Canada, 2003b), and the aging of the baby boomers means that number will continue to rise until about 2016. Psychologists are involved in developing programs that focus on the special needs of the exceptional and the elderly for social support, physical and psychological therapy, and continuing education.

**DIVERSITY WITHIN VERSUS BETWEEN GROUPS.** The differing perspectives on day-to-day behaviour that special groups bring to the fabric of society have not always been appreciated, understood, or even recognized in psychological research or theory. For example, psychologists now take Freud to task for developing a personality theory that is seen as clearly gender biased. (We will be evaluating Freud's personality theory in Chapter 12). In Freud's day, however, gender bias was not a matter for concern. Further, minorities and special groups such as the exceptional and the elderly were rarely—if ever—included in psychological research studies intended to represent the general population. Today psychologists seek to study all types of people to make valid conclusions based on scientific evidence. They see cultural diversity as an opportunity for both researchers and practitioners; they also recognize that they must research, learn about, and theorize about this diversity to help individuals optimize their potential (Hall, 1997). It is crucial to realize, though, that *there are usually more differences within a group than between groups.* For example, visual-spatial abilities differ more greatly among women than they do between men and women.

Individual circumstances exist, and people's individual experiences make broad generalizations impossible. Individuals and special populations often act just as the majority population does, but occasionally do so with a slightly different twist or variation. Here is the key point to remember as you read this book: While people are very much alike and share many common, even universal, experiences and behaviours, every individual is unique; each person's behaviour reflects diverse life experiences.

## Ethics in Psychological Research

Researchers must pay special attention to ethical considerations when conducting research with either human beings or animals. **Ethics** in research comprises the rules concerning appropriate and humane conduct that investigators use to guide their research; these rules govern the treatment of animals (see *Point/Counterpoint*), the rights of human beings, and the responsibilities of investigators.

### HUMAN PARTICIPANTS

Although animal research is an important part of psychological research, psychologists more often work with human participants. In such research, psychologists investigate many of the same processes they study with animals, as well as design experiments specifically for human participants. A psychologist who wishes to test whether an enhanced environment makes organisms smarter may use both animals and human participants. First, the researcher may train one rat to run complicated mazes while leaving its littermate in a barren environment. Several months later, the researcher, in examining the two animals, may discover that the brain cells of the maze-running rat are larger and have more internal connections. Along the same lines, the psychologist may test whether a decline in IQ scores among nursing home residents can be halted or reversed by enriching their environment with classes and special activities.

The Canadian Psychological Association (2001) has strict ethical guidelines for research with human participants. As well, the three major granting agencies in Canada (Medical Research Council, Natural Science and Engineering Research Council, and the Social Sciences and Humanities Research Council) have created a tri-council policy document on research involving humans (MRC, NSERC, & SSHRC, 1998). Participants cannot be coerced to do things that are harmful to them, that could have other negative effects, or that would violate standards of decency. The investigator is responsible for ensuring the ethical treatment of the participants in a research study. In addition, any information gained in an experimental situation is considered strictly confidential. Before a study begins, human

ETHICS

Rules of proper and acceptable conduct that investigators use to guide psychological research; these rules concern the treatment of animals, the rights of human beings, and the responsibilities of investigators.

## Should Non-human Animals Be Used in Research?

**POINT:** The use of non-human animals is necessary for research to progress.

**COUNTERPOINT:** The use of non-human animals in research is ethically unacceptable.

Some people believe that animal research puts non-human animals through unfair and painful treatments, violating their basic rights and subjecting them to cruelty. They argue that animal researchers take it for granted that non-human animals are inferior to human beings and assert that this is a faulty assumption. Animal rights advocates also question whether the information scientists learn from animals is even relevant to human research because enormous variations exist between species in reaction to specific techniques, medicines, or manipulations. A further concern is how carefully federal guidelines on the treatment of animals in research are observed in laboratories and research facilities. Many religions, Buddhism included, assert that people cannot be hunters, fishers, trappers, or slaughterhouse workers; adherents are not allowed to kill animals, even when doing so will lead to discoveries that will prolong human life.

Advocates of animal research argue that using non-human animals in research studies allows experimenters to isolate simple aspects of behaviour and to eliminate the

complex distractions and variables that arise in studies involving humans. The use of animals also enables researchers to conduct studies that could not ethically be done with human beings. For example, it would be unethical to deprive human infants of visual stimulation to investigate the effects of visual restriction on their perceptual development. Furthermore, because most animals have shorter life spans than humans do, experimenters can control and observe an animal's entire life history, perform autopsies to obtain information, and study several generations within a short period of time. Research with animals has helped psychologists understand many aspects of behaviour, including eating, learning, perception, and motivation. In addition, for many diseases, such as multiple sclerosis, cancer, and Alzheimer's disease, animal research and experimentation have brought almost daily breakthroughs and raised legitimate hopes for cures (Mehlhorn, Holborn, & Schliebs, 2000). Most researchers are aware of and sensitive to the needs of animals (Plous, 1996); furthermore, the Canadian Psychological Association has strict ethical guidelines for the humane and sensitive care and treatment of animals used in research. As well, the agencies that manage research grants, such as the Natural Science and Engineering Research Council (NSERC) and the Medical Research Council (MRC), also demand strict adherence to codes of humane treatment (see also Canadian Council on Animal Care, 1989). Only 8 percent of psychological research is done on non-human animals, but certain areas of scientific research, such as biology and medicine, rely heavily on non-human animals. Researchers who use animals argue that there is no realistic, viable alternative for non-human animals in the research they do, and that this research enhances human welfare. Animal research results in treatments and cures of animal diseases, but humans benefit more than non-human animals do. At present, research with non-human animals continues throughout the scientific community, but the controversy over this practice also continues.

participants also must give the researcher their **informed consent**—agreement through a signed document that they understand the nature of their participation in the research and have been fully informed of the general nature of the research, its goals, and its methods. Participants are free to decline to participate or to withdraw at any time without penalty. At the end of the project, participants must be debriefed. A **debriefing** informs participants about the true nature of an experiment, including hypotheses, methods, and expected or potential results. The debriefing is done *after* the experiment so that the validity of the participants' responses is not affected by their knowledge of the experiment's purpose.

These ethical guidelines also apply to the interactions between clinical psychologists and their clients in therapy. Clients must be fully informed as to the nature of the therapy the psychologist is going to provide and must be assured that what they say to the psychologist will be kept in confidence. They also may need to be informed that psychologists in Canada do not have the same legal protection or "privilege" in their interactions with clients that is afforded to lawyers and priests. For example, if a client confesses a crime to a psychologist or states an intention to harm himself or herself or someone else, the psychologist is bound ethically both to take care that no harm comes to the client and to ensure that no harm comes to others. In such a case the psychologist may seek assistance if the threat of harm seems imminent or may work with the client to avoid causing harm or to confess to law enforcement officials if a crime has been committed. Clients must be informed of the researcher's strict requirement that all their responses be kept in confidence and that the participants' names will not appear in any report of the study. Finally, researchers must be very careful to avoid any recruitment techniques that might seem to be coercive. Asking for volunteers in your own classes if you are the researcher could be seen as making it harder for students to refuse to participate.

## DECEPTION IN PSYCHOLOGICAL RESEARCH

Sometimes what psychologists want to investigate cannot be studied without temporarily deceiving the research participants as to the true purpose of the study. A researcher might mislead a person into believing that she is causing another person pain in order to examine the conditions under which she might refuse to continue to harm another. Is this acceptable? The answer to this question is carefully considered by research ethics review committees set up to review research involving human participants. Consider John Darley and Bib Latané, social psychologists who do research on when people provide help to others in need. Many of their studies required that they arrange for someone to pretend to be injured or otherwise in need of assistance in order to see when others would offer to help. They used deception, but mainly to explore the nature of prosocial behaviour. Researchers must not use deception unless the study has important scientific, educational, or applied value, and when it is clear there is no alternative means to conduct the study. And even then, two key procedures must be followed: obtaining informed consent and providing debriefing.

Some psychologists believe that deception is unacceptable under *any* circumstances. They assert that it undermines the public's belief in the integrity of scientists and that its costs outweigh its potential benefits. Most psychologists do not conduct research in which there is deception; those who do are particularly careful to use rigorous informed consent procedures and extensive debriefing to minimize potentially harmful effects. Whenever deception must be used to achieve some legitimate scientific goal, psychologists go to extraordinary lengths to protect the well-being, rights, and dignity of the participants;

INFORMED CONSENT

The agreement of participants expressed through a signed document that indicates that they understand the nature of their participation in upcoming research and have been fully informed of the general nature of the research, its goals, and its methods.

DEBRIEFING

A procedure to inform participants about the true nature of an experiment after its completion.

*Be an*
**ACTIVE LEARNER**

**REVIEW**
> Distinguish between the independent variable and the dependent variable as well as the control group and the experimental group. pp. 16–18
> Identify two elements in the design of an experiment that are especially important to making generalizations about the results. pp. 18–19
> Why is it important for psychologists to consider the cultural context in which behaviour occurs? pp. 25–26

**THINK CRITICALLY**
> Imagine a research study testing the effects of a low dosage of a drug that helps relieve anxiety. The participants are a sample of 50 men who suffer from job-related stress. What are the limitations of such a study? Would you say that such a study is poorly designed, or that it has a flawed methodology?
> Why do you think sample size is so important in psychological research?
> As psychologists are increasingly considering themselves biomedical researchers, what kind of special training do you think they need in ethics?

**APPLY PSYCHOLOGY**
> The next time you are watching television make note of a couple of claims made about "what people are like." These claims could occur in an ad or in a show. Later, think about what sort of study you might design to test those claims to see if they are true.

anything less is considered a violation of CPA guidelines (Canadian Psychological Association, 2000).

You may be wondering what kinds of people actually do this work of psychology. Who are these people handing out questionnaires and depriving students of sleep? Next we'll examine who psychologists are and what they do on a day-to-day basis.

## Who Are These People We Call Psychologists?

Sometimes people mistakenly assume that all psychologists primarily assist those suffering from debilitating mental disorders, such as schizophrenia and severe depression; however, psychologists actually do a much broader range of things. Psychologists study nearly every aspect of life, not only to understand how people behave but to help them lead happier, healthier, more productive lives. Some psychologists practise psychology; others teach or do research. Most are involved in a combination of activities.

While some psychologists help people with problems, others help well-adjusted people by providing services such as career counselling and assistance with community projects. Some psychologists seek to provide people with interpersonal skills and knowledge about self-help techniques. And, as *Psychology in Action* reveals, some psychologists work with professional athletes and musicians to improve their public performances.

**PSYCHOLOGIST**

A professional who studies behaviour and uses behavioural principles in scientific research or applied settings.

**Psychologists,** then, are professionals who study behaviour and use behavioural principles in scientific research or applied settings. Most have an advanced degree, usually a Ph.D. Many psychologists also train for an additional year or two in a specialized area such as mental health, physiology, or child development.

Founded in 1939, the Canadian Psychological Association (CPA) is the largest professional organization for psychologists in Canada. Its purpose is to advance psychology as a science, a profession, and a means of promoting human welfare. The CPA disseminates research publications (for example, *Canadian Psychology*, *Canadian Journal of Experimental Psychology*, and *Canadian Journal of Behavioural Psychology*) that serve as a primary means for many psychologists to present their research to other professionals. In addition to belonging to the CPA many Canadian psychologists also belong to the American Psychological Association (APA) through a reciprocal arrangement that allows them to become members for a reduced fee if they are already members of the CPA.

The CPA is not the sole voice of psychology within Canada. Many specialty groups have emerged over the years. For example, organizations consisting mainly of developmental, behavioural, cognitive, or neuroscience psychologists have been formed. In 1990 the Canadian Society for Brain, Behaviour, and Cognitive Science (CSBBCS) was founded; it has a membership of about 600 psychologists with academic interests and focuses on scientific research rather than on practice or applied interests. Two of its goals are to preserve the scientific base of psychology and to promote public understanding of psychology as a science. In addition, psychological associations in each province and territory are responsible for overseeing the chartering (or certification) of practising psychologists.

**CLINICAL PSYCHOLOGIST**

A mental health practitioner who views behaviour and mental processes from a psychological perspective and who uses research-based knowledge to treat persons with serious emotional or behavioural problems or to do research into the causes of behaviour.

**PSYCHIATRIST**

A physician (medical doctor) specializing in the treatment of patients with emotional disorders.

People are often unsure about the differences among clinical psychologists, psychiatrists, and psychoanalysts. All are mental health practitioners who help people with serious emotional and behaviour problems, but each looks at behaviour differently. **Clinical psychologists** usually have a Ph.D. in psychology and view behaviour and emotions from a psychological perspective. In contrast, **psychiatrists** are physicians (medical doctors) who have chosen to specialize in the treatment of emotional disorders. Patients who see psychiatrists often have both physical and emotional problems. As physicians, psychiatrists can prescribe drugs and admit patients for hospitalization. In 1995 the APA voted to pursue the development of curricula that would prepare psychologists to prescribe drugs.

Clinical psychologists generally have more extensive training than psychiatrists do in research, assessment, and psychological treatment of emotional problems. Their non-medical perspective gives them different roles in hospital settings and encourages them to examine social and interpersonal variables more than psychiatrists do. Psychiatrists are physicians and use a medical approach, which often involves making assumptions about behaviour—for example, that abnormal behaviour is disease-like in nature—which many psychologists do not make. Clinical psychologists and psychiatrists often see a similar mix of clients and often work together as part of a mental health team. Most psychologists and psychiatrists support collaborative efforts.

**Psychoanalysts** are frequently psychiatrists (as physicians they are able to prescribe medications); they have training in the technique of psychoanalysis and use it to treat people with emotional problems. As we'll soon see, psychoanalysis was originated by Sigmund Freud and includes the study of unconscious motivation and dream analysis. In a strict Freudian psychoanalysis, a course of daily therapy sessions is required; the patient's treatment may last for several years. In the past, psychoanalysts had to be physicians. In 1988, however, Freudian psychoanalytic institutes began to accept non-physicians into their training programs, a practice begun earlier by Jungian institutes. Thus, all practitioners may treat similar clients, but therapists' individual training and assumptions may vary, and this may be reflected in their choice of treatment.

PSYCHOANALYST
A psychiatrist or, occasionally, non-medical practitioner who has studied the technique of psychoanalysis and uses it to treat people with emotional problems.

## Choosing Psychology as a Career

When we were first attracted to psychology as a career, it was because we had a desire to help others. We recognized that psychology is an optimistic profession—the truth is that psychologists unabashedly admit to this bias. Psychologists generally don't assume that our lives are fixed and instead believe that there is much we can do to make our lives more productive and enjoyable.

Many psychologists help others through the delivery of mental health services. However, many psychologists are intrigued by the analysis of data; they focus on research and the discovery of knowledge. These psychologists seek out careers as scientists, practitioners, or consultants because they enjoy the process of searching for and explaining the causes of human behaviour (see Figure 1.2).

Psychology attracts many students who like the idea of understanding human behaviour and helping others. The causes and implications of behaviour intrigue these students; they realize that psychology is part of the fabric of daily life. Psychology is one of the most popular undergraduate majors. Today's psychology students are increasingly female, ethnically diverse, and interested in many of its sub-specialties, such as health psychology, child psychology, or social psychology. And there is good news for students who go on to graduate school: Unemployment among psychologists is low. Most experts agree that employment opportunities will continue to be good; psychology is often cited as one of the top 10 growth areas for jobs. Furthermore, compensation for psychologists is good.

Training, of course, is the key to employment. A psychologist who (1) obtains a Ph.D. in clinical psychology, (2) writes a professional practice exam, and (3) completes an approved internship can become chartered by their provincial College of Psychologists and will have a wide variety of job opportunities available in both the private and the public

**FIGURE 1.2**
**What Psychologists Do**
(Based on data from the College of Psychologists of Ontario, May 31, 1999.)

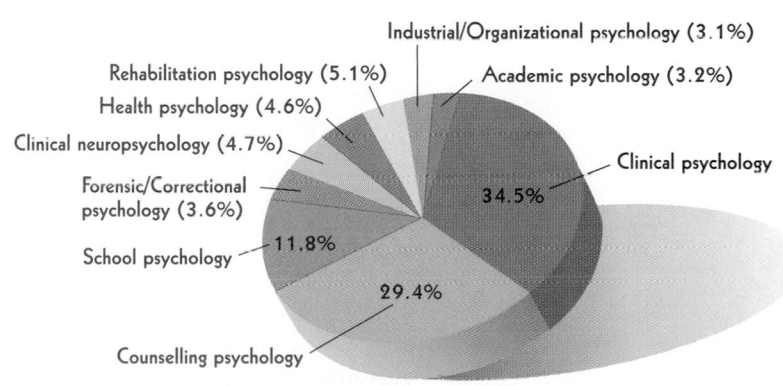

Industrial/Organizational psychology (3.1%)
Academic psychology (3.2%)
Rehabilitation psychology (5.1%)
Health psychology (4.6%)
Clinical neuropsychology (4.7%)
Clinical psychology 34.5%
Forensic/Correctional psychology (3.6%)
School psychology 11.8%
Counselling psychology 29.4%

## Using Psychological Knowledge to Improve Performance

You may be wondering what psychology can do for you as you go about your life. Psychology might appear to be just another academic subject, a set of theories and concepts to be learned in order to pass an exam and complete a course requirement. Not so. Psychology can be applied to everyday life in an endless variety of ways, as we'll see throughout this book. Let's look at just one example.

Did you take piano lessons as a child? Do you remember those dreaded days when you and your teacher's other students had to perform in recitals? You froze, staring at the keyboard. The teacher placed the sheet music in front of you, but you had no idea what the notes meant. Somehow you eventually managed to stumble through the performance, all the while saying to yourself, "But I know this piece! Why can't I play it?"

You or a friend of yours may have a similar problem when it comes to writing exams. Despite being well prepared you become so anxious during the exam that you have trouble recalling even the most basic facts correctly.

How can psychological knowledge help in such situations? These episodes stem from a phenomenon called performance anxiety, and they can be avoided, or at least alleviated, with a little knowledge of psychological processes. In fact, many top athletes are assisted by sport psychologists, who help them maintain their focus and avoid becoming too emotionally involved in their performances. The athlete can then concentrate on the specific actions necessary while still enjoying the experience of competing. The same principles can be applied to other types of performances, including piano recitals and public speaking.

People need to separate the judgmental part of the personality from the part that's performing. The best performances occur when the athlete or musician isn't actually thinking about the performance—not giving the body a lot of instructions, not telling it to correct mistakes, not evaluating the action in any way. Instead, good performances occur when the performer is in a state of effortless concentration. It's a matter of not trying too hard but simply focusing on the action itself. Musicians can achieve this type of concentration by focusing on each measure as it is being played, rather than saying to themselves, "I've got to be careful to hit all the sixteenth notes in that tough section coming up next."

Psychologists offer advice based on well-known psychological concepts that we will encounter throughout this book (see especially Chapter 17, which deals with applied psychology, including sport psychology). An understanding of the processes of learning and thinking (Chapters 5 and 7) can be helpful in developing ways to mute our judgmental side and allow our natural abilities to come through. Knowledge of the principles of motivation and emotion (Chapter 9) also can be helpful. And while writing exams is not as physically demanding as figure skating or high-jumping, the same issues of concentration and relaxation apply. If you are experiencing serious problems writing exams, especially when you are sure your preparations for them have gone well, you may find that assistance is available through your university or college's student counselling centre free of charge.

You use psychological principles all the time, and, in truth, all of human behaviour is part of psychology—the subject of this book. You will see that the many subfields of psychology that affect individual performance are related to one another. The way we as individuals can improve our individual performance—indeed, improve our lives—is by understanding basic psychological processes.

sectors. Individuals with a master's degree can function in a variety of settings, and even those with a bachelor's degree can play an important role in delivering psychological services. Salaries, responsibilities, and working conditions tend to be commensurate with level of training in the discipline. Psychologists with Ph.D.s are increasingly filling supervisory roles in the delivery of mental health services (Humphreys, 1996).

Many of the members of the CPA who work in the field of psychology deliver human services. Most of these psychologists work in clinics, community mental health centres, veterans' hospitals, general hospitals, and mental health hospitals. The others are private practitioners who maintain offices and work in schools, universities, business, and numerous other public and private settings.

Most psychologists employed by hospitals spend their time in the direct delivery of human services, including individual and group therapy. Business, government,

## We've Come a Long Way

"I couldn't get myself to react. I felt very still and very empty, the way the eye of a tornado must feel, moving dully along in the middle of the surrounding hullabaloo." Like many other well-known writers of the twentieth century, Sylvia Plath, author of those words from *The Bell Jar* (1971, p. 3), felt as though she had spent most of her life in a rarefied atmosphere, as if in a bell jar. Emotionally devastated, depressed, angry, agitated, and sometimes alcoholic, Plath, Zelda Fitzgerald, Robert Lowell, William Styron, and Tennessee Williams were labelled "despondent," "disturbed," or "melancholy." Those of them who were wealthy, and those who did not commit suicide, were sent to sanatoriums for rest and recuperation. In the early part of the twentieth century, the mentally ill were routinely locked up, kept in back rooms, or, at best, shunned by society. The causes of their problems were unknown, and treatments were haphazard and often downright dangerous. Thousands of them were told to take rest cures and breathe fresh, clean air. Experimental treatments consisted of cold-water baths, special diets, occupational therapy, and exercise. But for the vast majority of individuals, rest and fresh air was not a cure.

Schizophrenia and depression were the real problems these people faced—often made worse by alcoholism and other drug abuse. We will have much to say about schizophrenia, depression, and their causes and treatment in Chapters 15 and 16. For now, from a historical point of view, several key ideas are worth noting. First, disorders such as depression, in which a person becomes overwhelmingly sad and dejected and loses interest in most of life's activities, are now considered psychological disorders, not diseases of the blood or kidneys that call for rest and clean air. Second, depression and most other psychological disorders are now considered treatable. Third, and perhaps most important from a psychologist's point of view, we now know that specific brain mechanisms are responsible for many disorders such as depression, and that drugs can be part of the treatment.

One technique we use for diagnosis is brain imaging or brain scanning. Brain scans (discussed in Chapter 2) make the examination of the brain easier and more precise, thereby providing detailed information about its workings. For example, research shows that small brain lesions (areas of damaged tissue, often due to disease or injury) are common in the elderly and are a natural part of the aging process. But more importantly, researchers are establishing links among brain lesions, neurochemistry, and depression.

Unlike early twentieth-century practitioners, today's psychologists are combining old-school "talking therapy" with high-tech diagnostic tools and drug therapy. They've learned that people who suffer from depression sometimes have brain lesions but usually have changed levels of substances in the brain called neurotransmitters (we'll have more to say about them later). Whether neurotransmitters cause the depression or whether depression causes such changes in brain chemistry is not yet completely clear. Nevertheless, when people are seriously depressed, certain drug therapies can be effective in altering neurotransmission processes. When they are on drug therapies such as Prozac (Chapter 16), changes in people's thought processes can be tracked (Chapter 7). We can observe the brain in action through various imaging techniques (Chapter 2). And we can help people cope with the stressors in their life (Chapter 14) to better meet the demands of their environments. All of this has come about because we now better understand the links between brain and behaviour.

The connections between what we feel, think, and do and our biological inheritances are being explored intensively today. Is our eating behaviour, sexuality, or shyness biologically determined? Do we have a predisposition to aggressiveness? Is our genetic heritage our destiny? All these questions, and many more, are being addressed through studies of links between the brain and behaviour. It is easy to see the brain's control over other structures of the body—especially when people take psychoactive drugs (drugs that affect the nervous system and the brain itself). A person takes a drug, which affects the firing of neurons and the flow of neurotransmitters in the brain; these changes make the person feel different. The person responds to the feeling, and further brain changes take place. In other words, the brain affects behaviour, and behaviour in turn affects the brain. Such brain-behaviour connections can be found in other situations as well.

Throughout this book, we will attempt to show you some of these links through special features called *Brain and Behaviour*, which will highlight situations where the connections are especially notable or where research is making important breakthroughs. These connections related to depression are quite dramatic—drugs act on brain substances to help people who are depressed. In other areas of behaviour such connections may be important as well—drugs to help you sleep, adjust to time changes, or remember things better, for example. In still other areas, research on brain-behaviour connections is more tenuous. Changing people's attitudes about safe driving is less about brain-behaviour relations and more about laying out rules and providing motivation. So, we will try to focus on the unique brain-behaviour relationship where it is most appropriate to do so: where psychologists have done solid research on the key relationships.

We've come a long way since the time when people said that a disturbed person was suffering from "the vapours" or was the "black sheep of the family"—psychologists are now coming to understand the complex and important relationship between our brains and our behaviour.

and industry employ a small percentage of psychologists. Many psychologists are employed by universities, nearly half of them in psychology departments. University psychologists spend most of their time researching and teaching.

## PSYCHOLOGY THAT IS UNIQUELY CANADIAN

Psychology is a discipline that spans borders and continents. The research of Canadian psychologists contributes not just to Canadian psychological knowledge but to psychological knowledge in general. The work of Canadian psychologists will be highlighted, when and where appropriate, in this textbook. On the topic of diversity, however, there are a number of types of psychological research that, while they may not be done only in Canada, Canadian psychologists either are especially well prepared to address or in which the issue is somewhat unique to Canadian society.

Canada is constitutionally a bilingual country. Unlike in the United States, where English is the sole language of government and commerce, there are many regions in Canada where bilingualism is the norm. Canadian researchers are in the forefront of studies that examine bilingualism and second-language learning. Canadian elementary school immersion programs are considered models for how such programs should be set up and run. As well, Canadian researchers are actively involved in research on literacy for children and adults from homes where English or French is not the family's first language.

Canada has a federal policy of multiculturalism, which means that, unlike the American "melting pot" approach of integrating immigrants into mainstream culture, we in Canada are committed to a distinct approach that blends Canadian citizenship and ethnic heritage. A recent federal survey revealed that 95 percent of

▲ Canadians view their ethnic heritage as distinct from that of the United States.

Canadians are proud both of being Canadian and of their ethnic heritage. Psychologists are studying the effects that this general social policy has on the process of acculturation faced by new immigrants to Canada.

A large proportion of Canada is referred to as the North, even by Canadians. There are distinct challenges to living in the sometimes harsh conditions found in northern latitudes. In addition to cold and snow, there is a lack of sunlight in the winter months, which has implications for seasonal affective disorder, a form of depression linked to lack of sunlight. Social issues also have arisen, including the evaluation of decisions to relocate groups of Innu and Inuit living in the North. Canadian psychologists are learning much about the community/social conditions that have led to dramatic increases in the suicide rate among young members of those communities.

## APPLIED RESEARCH, HUMAN SERVICES, AND EXPERIMENTAL PSYCHOLOGY

Applied research, human services, and experimental psychology have much in common. Actually, human services is a subfield of applied research, but it comprises such a large proportion of psychologists that it generally is viewed as a separate field of psychology. All psychologists consider research and theory to be the cornerstones of their approach (Beutler et al., 1995). A human service provider also may do research, and a researcher who works in a university also may provide human services to the university or the community at large. For example, a human service psychologist may help an alcoholic patient by applying learning principles discovered in an experimental laboratory. Similarly, problems discovered by therapists challenge researchers to investigate causes in the laboratory. This cross-fertilization is stimulating. Let's look at each of these areas.

**APPLIED RESEARCH.** Applied psychologists do research and then use that research to solve practical problems. Many use psychological principles in business, government, and institutions such as hospitals.

*Engineering psychologists* (sometimes called *human factors psychologists*) use psychological principles to help people design machines for safe and efficient use (for example, an easy-to-use ATM machine). We will discuss this field in Chapter 17.

*Educational psychologists* focus on such topics as how learning occurs in the classroom, how intelligence affects performance, and the relationship between personality and learning. We also will discuss this field in Chapter 17.

*Forensic psychologists* deal with legal issues, often working in courts and correctional systems. They evaluate whether inmates are ready for parole, whether a rehabilitation program is achieving its goals, or whether an accused criminal has lied, deserves an "insanity defence," or is likely to give false testimony.

*Health psychologists* determine how lifestyle changes can improve health. They devise techniques for helping people avoid medical and psychological problems. We will discuss this field further in Chapter 14.

*Behavioural medicine psychologists* help people who suffer from chronic physical problems such as back pain and migraine headaches to learn to cope and develop techniques to manage pain.

*Sport psychologists* are in an emerging field that focuses on brain–behaviour interactions, the role of sports in healthful lifestyles, and the motivation and preparation of athletes. We will discuss this field in Chapter 17.

*Industrial/organizational psychologists* help employers evaluate employees; they also focus on personnel selection, employee motivation and training, work behaviour, incentives, and work appraisals. They apply psychological research and theory to organizational problems such as productivity, turnover, absenteeism, and management–labour relations. Working in human resources offices and in other departments at universities and businesses, they also evaluate organizational programs. Industrial/organizational psychologists are discussed in greater detail in Chapter 17.

**HUMAN SERVICES.** Many human service psychologists use behavioural principles to teach people to cope with life more effectively. They try to help people solve problems and promote well-being. Within the human service area are the subfields of clinical, counselling, community, and school psychology.

*Clinical psychologists* help clients with personal problems such as anger, shyness, and depression. They work either in private practice or at hospitals, mental institutions, or social service agencies. They administer psychological tests, interview potential clients, and use psychological methods to treat emotional problems. Many universities employ psychologists to help students and staff handle the pressures of academic life.

*Counselling psychologists*, like clinical psychologists, work with people who have personal problems. They also help people handle career planning; adjustment problems such as marriage, family, and parenting problems; and substance abuse. Counselling psychology began in the 1940s, and at first the problems presented by its clients were less serious than those presented by clients of clinical psychologists. However, since the 1980s, the problems of layoffs, spousal abuse, and violence have been addressed for treatment, and counselling psychologists increasingly have used psychotherapy and other therapies that previously were used exclusively by clinical psychologists. According to many practitioners and researchers, counselling and clinical psychology are converging (Fitzgerald & Osipow, 1986).

Counselling psychologists may work for public agencies such as mental health centres, hospitals, and universities. Many work in college or university counselling centres, where they help students adjust to the academic atmosphere and provide them with vocational and educational guidance. Like clinical psychologists, many counselling psychologists research the causes and treatment of maladjustment.

*Community psychologists* strengthen existing social support networks and stimulate the formation of new networks to meet a variety of challenges (L. R. Gonzales et al., 1983). Their goal is to help individuals and their neighbourhoods or communities to grow, develop, plan for the future, and prevent problems from developing. Community psychology emerged in response to the widespread desire for an action-oriented approach to individual and social adjustment, and one of its key elements is community involvement to effect social change. For example, community psychologists have been instrumental in organizing social support groups that help AIDS patients and their families handle the stress and loss of self-esteem produced by this catastrophic illness. Community psychologists work in mental health agencies, government, and private organizations. We will discuss this field in Chapter 17.

*School psychologists* help students, teachers, parents, and administrators to communicate effectively with one another and accomplish mutually agreed-upon goals. School psychology began in 1896 at the University of Pennsylvania in a clinic founded to study and treat children considered to be "morally or mentally defective." Early leaders such as G. Stanley Hall and Lightner Witmer were crucial in promoting psychological interventions and techniques in schools (Fagan, 1992). Today school psychologists administer and interpret tests, help teachers with classroom-related problems, and influence school policies and procedures (Bardon, 1983). They foster communication among parents, teachers, administrators, and other psychologists at schools. They also provide information to teachers and parents about students' progress and advise them on how to help students achieve more.

**EXPERIMENTAL PSYCHOLOGY.** Experimental psychologists try to identify and understand the basic elements of behaviour and mental processes. Theirs is an approach, not a specific field. That is, experimental psychology involves the use of a set of *techniques*; it is not defined simply by the topics it examines. For example, applied psychologists may be involved in experimental research. However, experimental psychologists focus on understanding basic research issues, whereas applied psychologists generally use experimental techniques to improve a specific situation, help a mental health practitioner, or work with an employer.

Experimental psychology covers many areas of interest, some of which overlap with fields outside psychology. Experimental psychologists may be interested, for example, in visual perception, in how people learn language or solve problems, or in how hormones influence behaviour. *Physiological psychologists* (sometimes called *neuropsychologists*) try to understand the relationship between the brain and behaviour (see *Brain and Behaviour*). They may examine drugs, hormones, and the effects of brain damage caused by strokes. We will discuss some of their explorations in Chapter 2. *Cognitive psychologists* focus on thought processes, especially on the relationships among learning, memory, and perception. They may, for example, examine how organisms process and interpret information on the basis of some internal representation in memory. We will discuss this field further in Chapter 7. *Developmental psychologists* focus on the emotional, physical, and intellectual changes that take place throughout people's lives. We will return to this field in Chapters 10 and 11. Personality psychologists examine the nature and structure of the dimensions along which people seem to view themselves and others. We will take a closer look at what they do in Chapter 12. *Social psychologists* study how other people affect an individual's behaviour and thoughts and how people interact with one another. For example, they may examine attitude formation, aggressive versus helping behaviour, or the formation of intimate relationships. We will discuss this field in Chapter 13.

*Be an*
**ACTIVE LEARNER**

REVIEW
> Identify the focuses of applied research, human services, and experimental psychology. pp. 34–36
> What makes experimental psychologists different from applied psychologists? p. 36

THINK CRITICALLY
> Which types of practitioners do you think would be best suited to work with William Sampson, who was released from a Saudi prison in the summer of 2003 after spending 31 months under a death sentence and having been tortured?
> If you were to seek help for marital conflict, what would be the key reason for choosing a psychologist rather than a psychiatrist?

APPLY PSYCHOLOGY
> The next time you read through the newspaper pick an article or two that raises issues about human interaction (why do people act like that?) and then think about the sorts of psychologists and the sorts of studies that might answer the questions raised.

# Summary and Review

## WHAT IS PSYCHOLOGY?

### What do psychologists study?

> *Psychology* is the science of behaviour and mental processes. Psychologists observe many aspects of human functioning—overt actions, social relationships, mental processes, emotional responses, and physiological reactions. Overt actions are directly observable and measurable movements or the results of such movements. Social relationships are the behaviours people engage in that define their interactions with other people. Mental processes include thoughts, ideas, and reasoning processes. Emotional responses include feelings such as anger, regret, and happiness. Physiological reactions include biochemical changes in the optic nerves when light stimulates your eyes and an increased heart rate when you are excited.   **pp. 4–5**

**KEY TERM**

psychology, p. 4

## HOW HAVE SCHOOLS OF PSYCHOLOGICAL THOUGHT DEVELOPED?

### Identify the key assumptions underlying each school of psychological thought.

> Psychology became a field of study in the mid-1800s. *Structuralism*, founded by Wundt, focused on the contents of consciousness through *introspection* and was the first true school of psychological thought. *Functionalism*, led by James and others, emphasized how and why the mind works. *Gestalt psychology*, in contrast to structuralism and functionalism, focused on perceptual frameworks and suggested that conscious experience is more than simply the sum of its individual parts. Arguing that each mind organizes the elements of experience into something unique, the early Gestalt psychologists studied perceptual phenomena. The *psychoanalytic approach* developed by Freud is the school of psychological thought that assumes that psychological maladjustment is a consequence of anxiety resulting from unresolved conflicts and forces of which a person may be unaware; its therapeutic technique is psychoanalysis.   **pp. 6–8**

> Watson, the founder of *behaviourism*, argued that the proper subject of psychological study was observable behaviour. Skinner took up the behaviourist banner through much of the twentieth century. *Humanistic psychology* arose in response to the psychoanalytic and behavioural views and stresses free will and *self-actualization*. *Cognitive psychology* focuses on perception, memory, learning, and thinking and asserts that human beings engage in both worthwhile and maladjusted behaviours because of ideas and thoughts. The *biological perspective* examines how heredity and biological structures affect mental processes and behaviour. *Evolutionary psychology* examines behaviour by analyzing how specific behaviours, over the course of many generations, have led to adaptations that allow the species to survive. *Eclecticism* acknowledges the complex relationships among factors affecting behavioural and mental processes and combines theories and techniques as appropriate to the situation.   **pp. 8–12**

**KEY TERMS**

structuralism, p. 6; introspection, p. 7; functionalism, p. 7; Gestalt psychology, p. 7; psychoanalytic approach, p. 8; behaviourism, p. 8; humanistic psychology, p. 9; self-actualization, p. 10; cognitive psychology, p. 10; biological perspective, p. 10; evolutionary psychology, p. 11; eclecticism, p. 12

## THE SCIENCE OF PSYCHOLOGY

### Describe the steps in the scientific method.

> The discipline of psychology is committed to objectivity, accuracy, and healthy scepticism. In their research, psychologists use the *scientific method* to organize their ideas and to develop theories that describe, explain, predict, and help manage behaviour. The scientific method's six basic steps are stating a problem clearly, developing a hypothesis, designing a study, collecting and analyzing data, replicating results, and drawing conclusions and reporting results.   **pp. 12–16**

**KEY TERMS**

scientific method, p. 13; hypothesis, p. 13; theory, p. 15

## THE RESEARCH PROCESS

### Describe an experiment and indicate its key components.

> An *experiment* is a procedure in which a researcher systematically strives to discover and describe the relationship between variables. Only controlled experiments allow for cause-and-effect statements. A *variable* is a characteristic of a situation or person that is subject to change (that varies) either within or across situations or individuals. The experimenter directly and purposely manipulates an *independent variable*. The *dependent variable* is expected to change because of manipulations of the independent variable.   **p. 16–17**

> A hypothesis is a tentative statement or idea expressing a relationship between two events or variables that are to be evaluated in a research study.   **p. 17**

> An *operational definition* is a definition of a variable in terms of a set of procedures used to measure or study that variable. A *sample* is a group of participants who are assumed to be representative of the *population* about which an inference is being made. A *significant difference*

means that there is a statistically determined likelihood that a behaviour has not occurred because of chance alone.   **pp. 18–19**

> Correlational studies make it possible for us to examine how (or if) one variable affects another. While informing us about the magnitude and direction of this relationship, correlational research does not permit us to make direct statements about causation.   **pp. 20–21**

### How do researchers ensure objectivity?

> To ensure objectivity, researchers attempt to minimize *self-fulfilling prophecies* by using carefully controlled situations—for example, the *double-blind technique*, in which neither researcher nor participant knows who is assigned to the *experimental* or *control group*. The double-blind technique helps minimize *demand characteristics*—the elements of a study situation that might clue a participant as to the purpose of the study and thereby might elicit specific behaviour from the participant. It also helps minimize the *Hawthorne effect*—the tendency of people, as shown in early research studies at the Hawthorne industrial plant, to behave differently (usually better) when they know they are being observed.   **pp. 19–20**

> Critical thinking involves collecting and evaluating evidence, sifting through choices, assessing outcomes, and deciding whether conclusions make sense. When evaluating research studies, critical thinkers focus on five research criteria: purpose, methodology, participants, repeatability, and conclusions.   **pp. 21–23**

### What are the various methods for gathering psychological data?

> *Questionnaires*, or surveys, are used by researchers to gather large amounts of information from many people in a short time. *Interviews* typically are face-to-face meetings in which researchers (interviewers) ask individuals series of standardized questions. In *naturalistic observation*, psychologists observe from a distance how people or animals behave in their natural settings. By contrast, *case study* methods involve interviewing participants to gain information concerning their background, including data on such things as childhood, family, education, and social and sexual interactions.   **pp. 23–25**

### How might we avoid gender, ethnicity, and cultural bias?

> In addition to individual variation we must be aware that ethnicity, culture, social class, gender, and age or disabilities can all shape behaviour and expectations. Psychologists must be aware of these potential influences when doing research.   **pp. 25–27**

#### KEY TERMS

experiment, p. 16; variable, p. 16; independent variable, p. 16; dependent variable, p. 16; participant, p. 17; experimental group, p. 17; control group, p. 18; operational definition, p. 18; sample, p. 18; population, p. 18; significant difference, p. 19; self-fulfilling prophecy, p. 19; placebo, p. 19; double-blind technique, p. 20; demand characteristics, p. 20; Hawthorne effect, p. 20; correlation coefficients, p. 21; questionnaire, p. 23; interview, p. 24; naturalistic observation, p. 24; case study, p. 24

## ETHICS IN PSYCHOLOGICAL RESEARCH
### Describe the ethical considerations in psychological research.

> *Ethics* in research comprises the rules of conduct that investigators use to guide their research; these rules concern the treatment of animals, the rights of human beings, and the responsibilities of investigators. The Canadian Psychological Association (CPA) has strict ethical guidelines for animal research. Human participants cannot be coerced to do things that are harmful to themselves, that would have other negative effects, or that would violate standards of decency. In addition, any information gained in an experimental situation is considered to be strictly confidential. Human participants must give *informed consent* to a researcher and must undergo *debriefing* following an experiment so that they understand the true nature of the research. In general, researchers must not use deception unless the study has highly important scientific, educational, or applied value.   **pp. 27–29**

#### KEY TERMS

ethics, p. 27; informed consent, p. 29; debriefing, p. 29

## WHO ARE THESE PEOPLE WE CALL PSYCHOLOGISTS?
### Distinguish the various types of psychology professionals.

> *Psychologists* are professionals who study behaviour and use behavioural principles in scientific research or in applied settings. Most psychologists have an advanced degree, usually a Ph.D. A *psychiatrist* is a medical doctor who has specialized in the treatment of emotional disorders. *Psychoanalysts* are usually psychiatrists; they have training in the specialized Freudian technique of psychoanalysis for treating people with emotional problems. **pp. 30–31**

#### KEY TERMS

psychologist, p. 30; clinical psychologist, p. 30; psychiatrist, p. 30; psychoanalyst, p. 31

## CHOOSING PSYCHOLOGY AS A CAREER
### In what fields are psychologists likely to be employed?

> A majority of psychologists work in human service fields such as clinical, counselling, and school psychology. Most others work in universities, business, and government doing research, teaching, and evaluation of programs. Psychology is attracting an increasing number of women.   **pp. 31–34**

**Identify the focuses of applied research, human services, and experimental psychology.**

> The three main fields of psychology are applied research, human services, and experimental psychology. All three consider research and theory to be the cornerstone of the psychological approach. Applied researchers use research to solve practical problems. Human service psychologists focus on helping individuals solve problems and on promoting their well-being. Experimental psychologists usually focus on teaching and research.　**pp. 34–36**

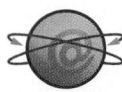 Take advantage of the multimedia resources available with this text! Follow the marginal icons to access the interactive modules on the *HandsOnPsych CD-ROM*; log on to *MyPsychLab* to explore the ebook, study aids, and other online resources; and visit the Companion Website at **www.pearsoned.ca/lefton** for additional exercises and links.

# The Brain
# and Behaviour

All the instructions for making a human being are packed within a surprisingly small number of genes—about 30 000. The genetic instructions for making a person take up less than two and a half centimetres of the two-metre-long strand of DNA that is packed inside nearly every cell in the human body. This information takes up merely 1 percent or so of the human genome. The genes can each produce one or, in some instances, several proteins—and the unique combinations of these proteins define individuals. How might we sort out those combinations? How might we begin to understand how diseases and traits that seem to run in families are coded in the genetic instructions? Where to start?

On February 16, 2001, human genome researchers provided us with a fantastic place to start dealing with these questions by publishing a map of the human genome—all the heritable traits carried in each cell of the human body. The sequencing and mapping of the human genome are considered the beginning of a new era in science. While we have not nearly explored all the genetic territory we now have an overall map to help us keep track of where we are as we search for the genetic forces that contribute to certain diseases and behaviours. But what effect does mapping the human genome have on psychology? What does understanding genetics have to do with understanding behaviour? Is it possible that at conception a switch, or hormonal trigger, is pulled that determines whether an individual will be outgoing, shy, musical, or happy? Are sexual urges determined before birth?

Your dreams, problem-solving abilities, friendships, and anxieties all have a biological basis. All behaviours and mental processes are in some way mediated by the neurons in our brains. While each of us may have a unique take on the world, with our own values and viewpoints, our ideas are coded, stored, processed, evaluated, and turned into mental processes or behaviours through the actions of the nervous system. In this chapter, we examine how the issues and findings from biology relate to human behaviour and mental processes. Beginning with the smallest of the biological building blocks of behaviour—genes and neurons—we will progress to the structure and functioning of the brain. We will focus on how biological processes affect behaviour; this focus is coming to dominate thinking in the field of psychology, and some insist that psychology is now rooted in brain science (Kolb, 1999). However, any simple interpretation that genes determine behaviour is incorrect (McGuffin, Riley, & Plomin, 2001); complex behaviours result from the interplay between environment and many genes (Plomin & Crabbe, 2000).

## Evolutionary Psychology, Behavioural Genetics, and Genes

When we say that genes influence behaviour, what do we mean? Does genetic makeup actually predetermine whether a person will be tall, depressed, or shy? Biologists first began to examine these questions, and many more, through the study of genetics, focusing on issues such as how blue eyes, black hair, extroversion, schizophrenia, diabetes, or high blood pressure were transmitted from one generation to the next. **Genetics** is the study of *heredity*, which is the biological transmission of traits and characteristics from parents to offspring. When parents transmit genes to their offspring does this mean that their children are inevitably predestined to demonstrate the traits or characteristics controlled by those genes? Absolutely not. Most genetic influences are not hard-wired; their effects are not inevitable. Although some genetic traits are determined at conception, combinations of many genes as well as environmental influences affect most characteristics and behaviours. Therefore, specific genes merely *influence* most complex human qualities.

### NATURE AND NURTURE

Psychologists recognize then that biology generally, and heredity specifically, plays a role in shaping human behaviour. There is a complex interplay between biology and experience, between inherited traits and encounters in the world. In general, it is simpler to determine relationships between biology and traits for chromosomal and single-gene disorders than for more complex traits. What role does biology play, if any, in these more complex behaviours? The controversy about the relative contributions of biology and environment toward complex behaviours has been traditionally referred to as the *nature versus nurture controversy*. However, it is currently accepted that both biology and environment contribute to developmental outcomes. **Nature** consists of a person's inherited characteristics determined by genetics; **nurture** refers to all non-genetic influences, that is, all prenatal, postnatal, biochemical, and social environmental events.

Decades ago, psychologists believed that characteristics of human behaviour were almost entirely the result of environmental influences. Some who consider nurture more important than nature suggest that people are not limited by their genetic heritage because learning, training, and hard work can stretch their potential. John B. Watson, a pioneer in the field of behaviourism (which we will examine further in Chapter 5) sang the praises of nurture:

> Give me a dozen healthy infants, well-formed, and my own specialized world to bring them up in and I'll guarantee to take any one at random and train him to become any type of specialist I might select—doctor, lawyer, artist, merchant-chief, and, yes, even beggar man and thief, regardless of his talents, penchants, tendencies, abilities, vocations, and race of his ancestors. I am exaggerating, of course, but so have the [proponents of the heredity position] . . . (1924, p. 104)

Virtually all contemporary psychologists, who acknowledge that both biology and experience contribute to behaviour, reject Watson's strong opinion of the importance of nurture. For example, a person with a special innate (inborn) talent will never develop proficiency unless provided with opportunities to express and develop his or her gift. For example, if Mozart had not had access to musical instruments, his talent would never have become apparent.

Thus, in human development nature and nurture work together as individuals select, modify, and create environments that correspond with their genetic predisposition. Contrary to traditional dogma, the genetic effects for many traits increases throughout childhood, rather than diminishing as previously claimed, yielding to environmental influence (McCartney, Harris, & Bernieri, 1990). How can it be that genetic influences become more important over time? One possible explanation is that a genetic predisposition leads people to choose, or even create, environments that foster the maintenance and further development of their genetically influenced abilities. For example, a quiet, introspective child in a family of animated outgoing siblings would end up being involved in many family activities that would not be his or her first choice. However, as the child approaches and enters adolescence he or she would have the freedom to choose activities more to his or her liking, thus expressing genetic predisposition.

As already mentioned, the nature versus nurture controversy is not a sensible distinction to maintain because behaviour exists only in the context of environmental influence. Most behaviour results from an interaction of genes and environment, each influencing the other. For example, Reiss and colleagues (2000) report that parents are more responsive to bright, inquisitive children, thus creating precisely the sort of environment that produces responsive, inquisitive behaviour in children. Importantly, genetic influences can also play a role in creating environments that cause stress (for example, aggression, hostility, etc.) and thereby threaten the physical and psychological well-being of the members of the family and the healthy development of children within the family.

Therefore, genetic traits provide the framework for behaviour. But within this biological framework, experiences ultimately shape what individuals feel, think, and do. To develop a better understanding of these two critical components of human behaviour it is necessary to acquire a basic understanding of each individual component. The remainder of this chapter will explore the biological approach to human development while the environmental approach will figure more prominently in other chapters of this book.

## THE EVOLUTIONARY APPROACH TO PSYCHOLOGY

The human genome did not emerge in its present form and remain unchanged over time. Rather, we know that human beings evolved, and through that selection process, our genes have their present configuration. If you accept that human behaviour is influenced by our genetic heritage, then understanding our evolutionary history is an important aspect of learning about our current behaviour. **Evolutionary psychology** is the psychological perspective that seeks to explain and predict behaviour by analyzing how the human brain developed over time and how evolutionary history affects the behaviour of humans today; it seeks to explain human behaviour by considering how behaviour is affected from the vantage point of evolutionary biology. Evolutionary psychologists argue that significant portions of human behaviours and mental abilities have endowed the human brain with specific selected abilities, such as the ability to learn, to acquire language, and to choose suitable mates.

**NATURAL SELECTION.** Evolutionary theory in biology assumes that natural selection is a key factor in changes that appear in different organisms over time. **Natural selection** is the principle that those characteristics and behaviours that help organisms adapt, be fit, and survive are the ones that will be passed on to successive generations because flexible, fit individuals have a greater chance of reproduction.

EVOLUTIONARY PSYCHOLOGY
The psychological perspective that seeks to explain and predict behaviour by analyzing how the human brain developed over time and how evolutionary history affects the behaviour of humans today; it seeks to explain human behaviour by considering how behaviour is affected from the vantage point of evolutionary biology.

NATURAL SELECTION
The principle that those characteristics and behaviours that help organisms adapt, be fit, and survive are the ones that will be passed on to successive generations because flexible, fit individuals have a greater chance of reproduction.

## Correlation Is Not Causation

Many people believe that genetic inheritance determines behaviour in much the same way it determines eye colour. However, scientists can draw conclusions about what causes a particular behaviour only based on evidence gained through experiments. Very few genetic studies, especially those conducted with human participants, are experimental. Instead, genetic researchers use a variety of methods that can be classified as *descriptive research,* which measures variables and attempts to develop an understanding of these variables and the relationships that may exist among them. In a research study conducted jointly with researchers from England, Wales, and Canada, Peter McGuffin and his colleagues (2003) conducted a descriptive study with pairs of twins to determine the relative contributions of heredity and environment to bipolar affective disorder (BPD), a serious disorder characterized by cycling states of mania (a mood state that includes rapid speech, inflated self-esteem, impulsiveness, decreased need for sleep, and euphoria) and depression (a sad and hopeless mood state).

**Design.** This study was a **correlational study**, a type of descriptive research design that establishes the degree of relationship between two variables. McGuffin and his colleagues wanted to establish the degree of relationship between diagnoses of mental disorders in pairs of twins. A correlation exists between two variables when an increase in the value of one variable is regularly accompanied by an increase or a decrease in the value of a second variable. Correlations are measured using the **correlation coefficient**, a number that expresses the degree and direction of a relationship between two variables. Correlation coefficients always range from –1 (a perfect negative correlation) to +1 (a perfect positive correlation). Any correlation coefficient greater or less than 0, regardless of its sign, indicates that the variables are somehow related. The closer the correlation coefficient is to 1, the stronger the relationship between the variables.

**Hypothesis.** BPD will show a stronger relationship in monozygotic (also called identical) twins than in dizygotic (also called fraternal) twins; that is, if one twin of a monozygotic pair exhibits symptoms of the disorder, the other will be likely to exhibit symptoms as well. In dizygotic twins, if one twin exhibits symptoms, the other should be no more likely to exhibit symptoms than other siblings do.

**Participants.** Participants were a total of 67 pairs of same-gender twins (30 monozygotic and 37 dizygotic) born in England between 1948 and 1992 with at least one twin diagnosed with BPD and 177 pairs of same-gender twins (68 monozygotic and 109 dizygotic) born in England between 1948 and 1985 with at least one twin diagnosed with unipolar disorder (depressive symptoms only).

**Procedure.** Researchers screened records from a twin register in London, England, to identify instances where one or both twins were given a hospital diagnosis of mania, depression, or both in order to determine the prevalence of unipolar depression or BPD.

**Results.** The prevalence of BPD was 3 percent for this population of twins in England. The correlation between diagnoses of BPD for monozygotic twins was .85, whereas the correlation for dizygotic twins was .41. Researchers concluded from their analyses that 85 percent of the variation in BPD is due to inherited factors. This estimate is higher than that of previous studies.

**Limitations.** Although the correlation between twin pairs was high, especially for monozygotic twins, the relationship of genetic inheritance and BPD is far from perfect. If BPD were genetically *determined,* 100 percent of monozygotic twins would be diagnosed with BPD whenever one member of the pair was. Although the strength of the correlation obtained in McGuffin's research definitely suggests that inherited factors are involved in the development of BPD, it is also clear that environmental factors contribute to it as well.

Correlations between behaviour and genetics are never sufficient to indicate that genes cause behaviour. That is, *correlated events are not necessarily causally related.* We say that we have a *correlation,* or that two events are *correlated,* when the increased presence (or absence) of a particular situation or condition is regularly associated with a high (or low) presence of another situation, or condition. McGuffin and his colleagues have data that suggest that BPD has strong genetic links. However, to definitively state that genes cause BPD, behavioural genetics researchers would have to gather data that would causally link specific genes to BPD. These links would have to produce information concerning how genes affect neurotransmitters, causing them to produce behavioural abnormalities, or to demonstrate how genes affect brain structure, producing the behaviours symptomatic of BPD. These specific links would be necessary to demonstrate that genes *cause* BPD. Research in the future may succeed in establishing these links, but this correlational research does not have the power to show such a causal relationship.

Using ideas such as survival of the fittest, these researchers argue that traits have evolved slowly over time, and this has led to humans with distinct physiological mechanisms that push them toward certain behaviours and away from others. When a trait or inherited characteristic has increased in a population, evolutionary researchers say that an **adaptation** has occurred—and that it occurred to help solve a problem of survival or reproduction. Evolutionary psychologists argue that certain psychological traits were not always what they are today; they assert that these traits are clear adaptations and represent evolved heredity. Evolution has created an instinct in human beings to protect their offspring from danger; there is a natural— evolutionary psychologists assert, genetically coded—tendency for parents to protect their young from danger (Geary, 2000). In doing so they ensure the survival of the species. Another example comes from the development of communication: In the early stages of human evolution, communication consisted merely of grunts. However, through the course of generations, those in difficult circumstances who grunted good commands, advice, and other ideas were more likely to survive. Those who lived taught their children, and over succeeding generations language developed and was ultimately encoded in the human genome. The timetables for evolutionary change vary, with characteristics like communication evolving over the last several hundred thousand years while other characteristics, like our visual systems, evolved much earlier, on the order of millions of years ago. Jealousy is reasoned to have an evolutionary base (Buss, 2000a); even self-esteem is hypothesized to have developed through evolutionary processes. Zimmerman (2000) maintains that our devotion to sports teams, the need to be right (rather than wrong), personal pride, and even arrogance are part of a sense of self-esteem determined through evolution.

**EVOLUTION AND DETERMINISM.**   Cognitive psychologists, evolutionary biologists, and neuroscientists together are studying the brain and its circuits to see how it is organized and specialized and especially how evolutionary history affects current thought processes. They all assume that the brain is a system whose function is governed by biological processes, whose evolutionary history influences how the brain currently operates. Evolutionary theory does not hold that behaviour is determined or controlled exclusively by innate mechanisms (Buss, 1999). All human behaviour occurs within some context, and the cultural environment of behaviour is a necessary component for an evolutionary explanation of behaviour because environment shapes physiological as well as psychological characteristics. Evolutionary psychologists are quick to point out that this approach does not constitute support for *behavioural determinism*, whereby evolutionary history determines behaviour in an inalterable way (Buss, 1999; Caporael, 2001).

To some, the study of human behavioural genetics carries the threat of racism and class elitism. This perception is due in part to conclusions drawn by American Arthur Jensen (1969) as well as Canadian Philip Rushton (1988) of the University of Western Ontario suggesting that differences in the average IQs of blacks and whites might be partly due to genetic factors. There has been little support for this extreme genetic interpretation of racial differences in intelligence, with many researchers demonstrating the importance of environmental influence on such complex characteristics as intelligence (Pinker, 2002).

Certainly at the level of the individual, culture and environment affect behaviour. Individuals are capable of change throughout their lives. Over time individuals develop new, different connections among brain cells that did not exist at birth. Furthermore, connections that existed at birth may disappear. Our brains are constantly being organized and reorganized, forming new and useful connections. We see evidence for such reorganization if a person has an accident or stroke and recovers the ability to speak, read, or walk—despite damage to the brain tissue that was the basis for that behaviour (Rossini & Pauri, 2000). Connections that are useful survive, grow, and mature; those that are not used are pruned away.

ADAPTATION

Occurs when a trait or inherited characteristic has increased in a population.

CORRELATIONAL STUDY

A type of descriptive research design that establishes the degree of relationship between two variables.

CORRELATION COEFFICIENT

A number that expresses the degree and direction of a relationship between two variables.

Evolution is a continuous process, adapting to new obstacles as they appear and then moving on to solve the next obstacle that comes along. The evolutionary approach argues that the design of the brain and its functioning are shaped by previous experiences—not only those in an individual's lifetime, but also those of the species. From an evolutionary perspective, this constant change serves as an adaptive mechanism that allows individuals, and their brains, to continue to evolve (Fernald & White, 2000). As Low (2000, p. 245) says, "Our evolved tendencies interact with today's novel environments." Psychologists strive to understand current behaviour, and evolutionary psychologists believe that studying the challenges faced in human prehistory offers a way to understand contemporary behaviour. Yet scientists such as Paul Ehrlich and Marc Feldman (2003) caution us to remember that we are not captives to our genes and that biology and evolution only make sense within the context of a culture.

**KEY QUESTIONS.** Evolutionary psychology is interesting because it addresses questions that psychology has often ignored in the past. It not only strives to understand mating and reproduction—behaviours closely associated with natural selection—but also how human beings have developed coping mechanisms, self-esteem, creativity, problem-solving abilities, and even a sense of awareness of ourselves. In some ways, evolutionary psychology is going beyond the question of how the mind works, asking how it got to work the way it does, why, and where it might go next.

Like most theories, evolutionary psychology has its proponents and critics. Proponents such as David Buss (1999, 2000a), Douglas Kenrick (2001), and Leda Cosmides and John Tooby (1999) assert that this new approach helps explain unanswered questions: issues of jealousy, aggression, and altruism. However, critics such as Bernardo Dubrovsky (2003) of McGill University and Stephen Jay Gould (1997, p. 60) maintain that evolutionary psychology goes too far in its explanations: "there are many evolutionary biologists who view everything that happens in evolution—every feature, every behavior—as directly evolved for adaptive benefit. And that just doesn't work." For most behaviours, adaptive explanations are incomplete or overly simplistic. For example, the presence of nurturing behaviour in women (often claimed to be an adaptive trait) could also be seen as due to ongoing cultural roles and expectations. Another type of criticism comes from Jerry Coyne (2000, p. 27), who points out the problems with taking an evolutionary approach to behaviour: "Unlike bones, behavior does not fossilize, and understanding its evolution often involves concocting stories that sound plausible but are hard to test."

Like all appealing theories, evolutionary psychology will go through refinements and changes in focus; if it is a good, workable theory that explains data and phenomena well, it will stand the test of time (Ketelaar & Ellis, 2000). For now, evolutionary psychology is opening a brave new world of questions just as behavioural geneticists are unlocking the keys to how genes express themselves.

## HUMAN BEHAVIOURAL GENETICS

Psychologists' efforts to explore the influences of nature and nurture have taken them into the field of behavioural genetics. Human **behavioural genetics** seeks to determine both genetic (nature) and environmental (nurture) contributions to individual variations in human behaviour. Behavioural genetics is distinct from evolutionary psychology in that it focuses on the role of genetic contributors to individual differences rather than on their role in accounting for shared species characteristics.

Differences among individuals are caused by environmental factors and/or by one or many genes. Accordingly, research in behavioural genetics is designed to explore the relative roles of genetic and environmental factors in creating differences in behavioural traits. Behavioural geneticists ask questions about whether human characteristics such as shyness, impulsiveness, or intelligence have a genetic,

BEHAVIOURAL GENETICS

Seeks to determine both genetic (nature) and environmental (nurture) contributions to individual variations in human behaviour.

**Development I**

## Identical Twins May Not Be So Identical

Psychologists and other scientists often study monozygotic twins when conducting research designed to determine which aspects of behaviour are influenced by genetic heritage and which aspects can be attributed to environmental influence. Monozygotic twins are the result of a single fertilized egg splitting at some point in time following conception. At the point of separation, which may occur soon after conception or later in the developmental process, each of these cell groups forms an individual, creating two genetically similar siblings. In Canada, multiple births (that is, births involving two or more babies) represent 2 percent of all births, with 4 sets of monozygotic twins occurring for every 1000 births.

Monozygotic twins are also commonly referred to as *identical twins* because they are assumed to share the same

genetic heritage. However, the adjective *identical* is deceptive because it leads to erroneous and confusing assumptions about the biology of monozygotic twins. Fiona Bamforth of the University of Alberta and her colleagues have demonstrated that monozygotic twins are *not* identical (Bamforth, Machin & Innes, 1996; Machin, 1996). There may in fact be significant *discordance* (differences in characteristics assumed to be genetic) between monozygotic twins on a variety of genetically determined traits, such as birth weight, genetic disease, and congenital anomalies (Gringras, 1999). There is a great deal of speculation about what causes these monozygotic differences. Theories that might account for monozygotic genetic dissimilarities include suggestions that perhaps biological events responsible for stimulating the separation caused these genetic differences in monozygotic twins or that during the split the allocation of cells to each twin is unequal (Machin, 1996). Researchers have also suggested that genes on the X chromosome may vary in their patterns of activation between each twin in the pair (St. Clair et al., 1998).

The finding that monozygotic twins have genetic differences has implications for scientific researchers. Concordance rates and heritability estimates obtained from twin studies need to be cautiously interpreted in light of these data. It is certain that genes play a causal role in development and that monozygotic versus dizygotic twin influences give us critical information about the relative contributions of heredity and environment (Turkheimer, 2000). Importantly, however, *every* individual is genetically unique and research findings will continue to be hampered by this inconvenient fact.

inherited basis. If they do, then to what extent is a given behaviour inherited or biological in origin, and to what extent is it learned or due to experience?

With the possible exception of identical twins (see *Brain and Behaviour*), every human being is genetically unique. Although each of us shares traits with our siblings and our parents, none of us is identical to them or to anyone else. One important explanation for this uniqueness is that a large number of genes influence each person's physical, cognitive, and emotional characteristics.

Researchers thus talk of the **heritability** of a trait or behaviour. Heritability can be determined for any trait. The concept of heritability refers to estimates of the proportion of variation in a trait in a population determined by heredity—with the remainder determined by environment. It is important to keep in mind that heritability is a descriptive statistic of a trait in a particular population, not of that trait in an individual. That is, how heritable a trait or characteristic is reflects estimates of how much variation in a *group* is due to genetic differences in that group (not in a specific person). Assume, for example, that the heritability of intelligence is about 65 percent. This means that researchers estimate that about 35 percent of

HERITABILITY

Refers to estimates of the proportion of variation in a trait in a population determined by heredity—with the remainder determined by environment.

intelligence is attributable to environmental factors. This does not mean that each individual inherits 65 percent of his or her intelligence. Many heritable characteristics—for example, depression, substance abuse, and height—exist and vary among individuals in a population.

Twins share the same uterine environment and experience similar patterns of nutrition and other prenatal influences. Dizygotic twins (fraternal twins) occur when two sperm fertilize two ova (eggs) and the resulting zygotes (fertilized eggs) implant in the uterus and develop alongside one another. The genes of these twins are not identical, so these twins are only as genetically similar as any sibling pair born in different years. Dizygotic twins can be of the same or different sexes. Monozygotic twins (also called identical twins) occur when one zygote splits into two virtually identical cells, which then develop independently into two genetically very similiar organisms, always of the same sex. Comparing monozygotic and dizygotic twins informs researchers about the influence of genes on a particular trait. In twin studies, researchers compare concordance rates or the degree to which a condition or trait is shared. Higher rates of concordance (the percentage of twins who share the disorder or trait) among monozygotic twins than dizygotic twins suggests a genetic influence on the disorder.

Several types of adoption studies have also been used to identify the relative contributions of genes and environment. To assess genetic influences, genetically alike individuals who live apart are studied. Such studies include biological parents and their adopted offspring, or twins separated early in life. To assess environmental influences, genetically unrelated individuals living together are compared. Such studies typically include adoptive parents and their adopted children or genetically unrelated children reared in the same family.

Recently, researchers have begun to search for pieces of DNA associated with particular behaviours or traits using family, twin, and adoption studies. Although this recent technique has been valuable in identifying potential locations for genes involved with atypical developmental conditions assumed to have strong genetic components, such as schizophrenia or bipolar disorder, it has been less helpful in identifying genetic influences associated with characteristics such as shyness or aggression that are more greatly influenced by environmental factors.

For complex traits and disorders, a carrier of a gene identified with a particular condition does not necessarily mean that the particular trait will inevitably develop. The presence of certain genetic factors can enhance or repress other genetic factors. Thus people are not simply "alcoholic" or "depressed" or "dyslexic"; rather, the potential to express those characteristics is genetically inherited but the combination of genes and experiences unique to each individual contributes to how much, if any, of a trait will be expressed.

## MAPPING THE GENOME

GENOME

The total DNA blueprint of heritable traits contained in every cell of the body.

GENETIC MAPPING

Dividing the chromosomes into smaller fragments that can be characterized and ordered (mapped) so that the fragments reflect their respective locations on specific chromosomes.

Biologists have mapped the human **genome**—the total DNA blueprint of heritable traits contained in every cell of the body. **Genetic mapping** involves dividing the chromosomes into smaller fragments that can be characterized, and ordering (mapping) the fragments to reflect their respective locations on specific chromosomes. DNA is a double-stranded molecule built of four simple building blocks, called bases, which are grouped together in long strings. Resembling a twisted ladder and referred to as a *double helix,* the steps of the spiral ladder comprise pairs of these bases. The human genome consists of more than 3 billion base pairs, and the sequence of these bases of strings constitutes the genetic code. There are about 30 000 to 40 000 human genes—genes are simply chemicals that direct the production of other chemicals. This information is converted into proteins, which act as enzymes and catalysts that turn various chemicals into still others, some of which affect behaviour. So, each unique DNA sequence in each person may produce enzymes that influence an individual to feel sad or behave erratically—and this varies from location to location, sequence to sequence, and person to person. Thus, each person's heredity and response are unique, despite each human being's similarity to others.

It is important to recognize that human beings all share a very similar gene pool. Contrary to popular belief, chromosomes among groups of people who are geographically distant, ethnically diverse, and considered to be of different races show little genetic variation—99.9 percent of DNA sequences found in the human genome are the same in all people (Venter et al., 2001). But that one-tenth of 1 percent makes for some interesting differences among us!

Researchers have identified the exact location or sites of genes contributing to muscular dystrophy, Huntington's disease, sickle cell anemia, some cancers, and learning problems such as dyslexia (Peltonen & McKusick, 2001). Behavioural traits such as temperament and intelligence and disorders such as Alzheimer's disease and schizophrenia also have genetic components. Some researchers even argue that the nature of family social interactions has a genetic basis, because elements of personality, maladjustment, and language acquisition may be genetically determined (O'Connor & Plomin, 2000; O'Connor et al., 2000).

In 2001, the focus of research shifted from demonstrating the existence of genetic influence to exploring its extent and significance. Of course, researchers in this area face the crucial question of what to do with the expanding knowledge of the human genome. When scientists understand the basic genetic and biological mechanisms plus their relationship to behaviour, they will be better able to predict situations in which maladjustment and behaviour disorders may occur. Yet this ability to predict will no doubt create some difficult ethical dilemmas: If a particular pattern of genes is found to be associated with aggressiveness, how should society respond? Would it be desirable or ethical to screen newborns to identify those at risk of developing schizophrenia? Could this information be used to justify terminating pregnancies? Medical ethicists and psychologists argue that genetic screening cannot and should not be used for such purposes. Ethical considerations and legislation to guard people's rights must be high on the agenda of genetic researchers. Those who carry on the ethical debate must consider that genetics only lays the framework for behaviour; because many events, life experiences, and cultural influences affect us, genetic influences must not be considered the sole determiner of behaviour. Genes may bias us to respond in a specific way—for example, to feel lonely—but genes do not determine what a person who feels lonely will do about it (McGuire & Clifford, 2000).

## THE BASICS OF GENETICS

Each human cell normally contains 23 pairs of chromosomes (46 chromosomes in all). **Chromosomes** are microscopic strands of deoxyribonucleic acid (DNA) found in the nucleus (centre) of every body cell (see Figure 2.1). Chromosomes carry self-replicating genetic information in their basic functional units, known as genes—thousands of which line up along each chromosome. **Genes** are the fundamental units of hereditary transmission, consisting of DNA. Genes provide templates that allow protein production—which doesn't sound very impressive except these functions control various aspects of a person's physical makeup, including eye colour, hair colour, and height—and they influence behaviour as well. Genetically determined characteristics are controlled by pairs of genes, located in parallel positions on chromosome pairs. Both of these corresponding genes influence the same trait, but they may carry different forms of the genetic code for that trait. Genes can either be dominant or recessive. Dominant genes are expressed whenever they are present. Recessive genes are expressed only if a

**CHROMOSOMES**

Microscopic strands of deoxyribonucleic acid (DNA) found in the nucleus (centre) of every body cell.

**GENES**

The fundamental units of hereditary transmission, consisting of DNA.

▼ The Y chromosome in these 23 pairs of human chromosomes means this person is male.

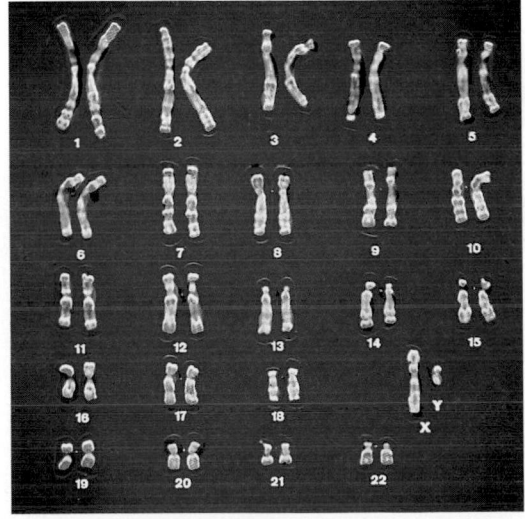

FIGURE 2.1

## Building Blocks of Genetics

Each of the trillions of cells in the human body has 23 pairs of chromosomes in its nucleus. Each chromosome is essentially a long, threadlike strand of DNA, a giant molecule consisting of two spiralling and cross-linked chains. Resembling a twisted ladder and referred to as a *double helix*, each DNA molecule carries thousands of genes—the basic building blocks of the genetic code—which direct the synthesis of all the body's proteins.

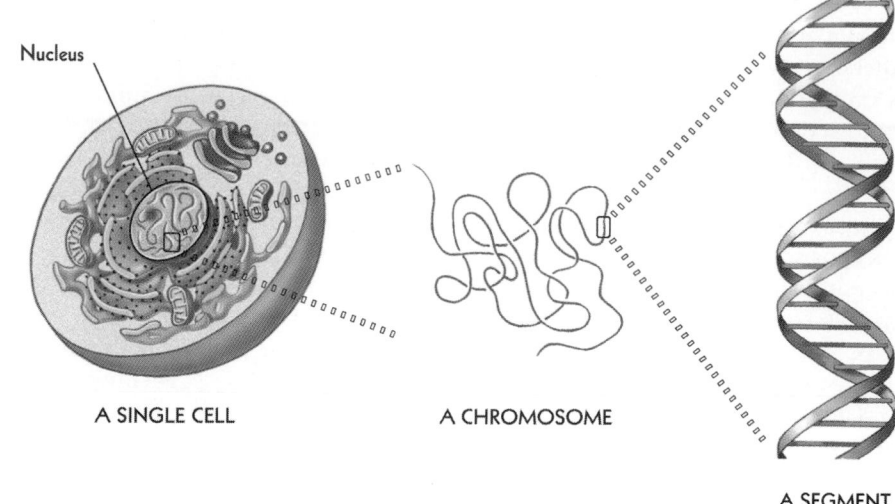

Nucleus

A SINGLE CELL     A CHROMOSOME

A SEGMENT OF DNA

second recessive gene for the trait is also inherited. For example, if an individual's two genes for eye colour carry the genetic codes for blue and brown, the individual will be brown-eyed, because the brown version of the gene is *dominant*. Only when both genes in the pair carry the genetic code for blue will the recessive gene exert its influence, resulting in a blue-eyed individual.

A **genotype** is a person's genetic makeup and is fixed at conception; however, a genotype may or may not appear in observable characteristics—**phenotypes**. Consider eye colour again; a mother and a father may both have brown eyes, but they may each also carry a recessive gene for blue eyes. Thus, their genotype includes a gene for blue eyes, but their phenotype is brown-eyed. We see many more brown-eyed than blue-eyed people because brown is dominant and is expressed in the phenotype when it is present in the genotype. The two brown-eyed parents may have offspring with brown eyes (very likely) or blue eyes (far less likely). Sometimes changes in genotypes occur in ways that are not expected, are not always evident in phenotype, and create unusual characteristics of body or behaviour—we call these unexpected changes in gene replications **mutations**. Mutations are principal sources of diversity in the human gene pool; some mutations cause desirable changes, but most do not.

Eye colour is a simple trait compared to traits such as intelligence or jealousy, and so you can see that analyzing the origin of traits can be complicated. In its simplest form it works like this: Each parent's sperm or ovum (egg) contains 23 chromosomes—half of the total of 46 contained in all other body cells. Of these 23 pairs of chromosomes, 22 carry the same types of genetic information in both men and women, and the twenty-third pair determines a person's sex. In women, the twenty-third pair contains two X chromosomes; in men, it contains one X and one Y chromosome. At the moment of conception, a sperm and an ovum, each containing 23 chromosomes, combine, and the chromosomes form 23 new pairs. There are 8 388 608 possible ways for the 23 pairs of chromosomes to form, with 70 368 744 000 000 possible combinations of genes. You can see that the chance of any two individuals being exactly alike is exceedingly slim.

---

*Be an*
## ACTIVE LEARNER

**REVIEW**
> What is the distinction between nature and nurture? p. 42
> Define natural selection. p. 43
> What is heritability? p. 47
> What fundamental assumption can researchers make about identical twins that causes them to be ideal participants in nature-versus-nurture studies? p. 48
> Distinguish between genotypes and phenotypes. p. 50

**THINK CRITICALLY**
> What potential environmental influences can alter people's inherited characteristics? Can such influences be limited? Should they be?
> Can you think of a behaviour that evolutionary approaches might better explain than traditional psychological approaches? Explain your answer.

**APPLY PSYCHOLOGY**
> Automobiles have not been part of human history long enough to produce an evolutionary adaptation to them, yet we are able to deal with automobiles. What evolved abilities help us deal with them? Give another example of how evolved abilities are used to master other challenges in modern society.
> The next time you see a pair of twins or, better yet, the next time you talk with someone about twins, think about what your expectations are regarding the twins. How similar do you expect them to look, or to act?
> The effort to map the genome and understand the biological characteristics associated with particular gene patterns has ethical implications. What if scientists find genes strongly associated with criminality, for example? What should be done with this knowledge?

Until now we have been discussing our current knowledge of the genetic blueprint for human growth. We now turn our attention to the building blocks of the actual structure of a human being as we begin to consider neurons and the human nervous system and brain.

## Communication in the Nervous System

Even the simplest tasks require smooth functioning of the communications system we call the nervous system. When there is a misfire, a glitch, in the communications process, people have trouble. For example, Shaywitz and colleagues (1998) showed that people with dyslexia, who have difficulty with reading and often reverse letters and words, don't use the usual pathways and regions of the brain that non-dyslexics do. While this has not yet led to a specific treatment approach, it does highlight the fact that the actions of the nervous system underlie all behaviour.

Walking, running, or driving a car requires a large number of coordinated movements, and that's without considering the need to pay attention to the surroundings and perhaps carry on a conversation at the same time. In some ways the nervous system acts like the conductor of a symphony orchestra, sending, receiving, processing, interpreting, and storing vital information. Many psychologists study how electrical and chemical signals in the brain represent and process such information. By studying how the nervous system's components work together and how they are integrated, psychologists learn a great deal about the nature and diversity of human behaviour.

The **nervous system** is made up of the structures and organs that allow all behaviour and mental processes to take place. The nervous system consists of two divisions—the *central nervous system* (the brain and spinal cord) and the *peripheral nervous system* (nerves connecting the central nervous system with the rest of the body). We'll examine these two divisions shortly. First, however, you need to understand how communication proceeds within the system as a whole. The nervous system is composed of billions of cells, many of which receive information from thousands of other cells (Nauta & Feirtag, 1986). The most elementary unit in the nervous system is the neuron, the building block of the entire system, which is where we will begin.

### THE NEURON

The basic unit of the nervous system is a single cell: the **neuron**, or *nerve cell*. There are billions of neurons throughout the body (as many as 100 billion in the brain alone), differing in shape, size, and function. Some neurons operate quickly, others relatively slowly. Some neurons are large; others are extremely small. Often neurons are grouped together in bundles; the bundles of neuron fibres are called *nerves* if they exist in the peripheral nervous system and *tracts* if they are in the central nervous system.

Not all of the neurons in your body are active at once. Nonetheless, they are always on alert, ready to convey information and signals to some part of the nervous system. Nerve pathways allow signals to flow (1) *to* the brain and spinal cord from the sense organs and muscles, and (2) *from* the brain and spinal cord to the sense organs and muscles, carrying messages for initiating new behaviour. Each type of neuron involved in this two-way neuronal firing has a name: **Afferent neurons** (from the Latin *ad*, "to," and *ferre*, "carry") send messages to the spinal cord and brain; **efferent neurons** (from the Latin *ex*, "out of," and *ferre*, "carry") send messages from the brain and spinal cord to other structures in the body (see Figure 2.2).

**TYPES OF NEURONS.**   There are three types of neurons: sensory neurons, motor neurons, and interneurons. *Sensory neurons* are afferent neurons that convey information from the body's sense organs to the brain and spinal cord. *Motor neurons*

FIGURE 2.2
**The Action of Afferent and Efferent Neurons**

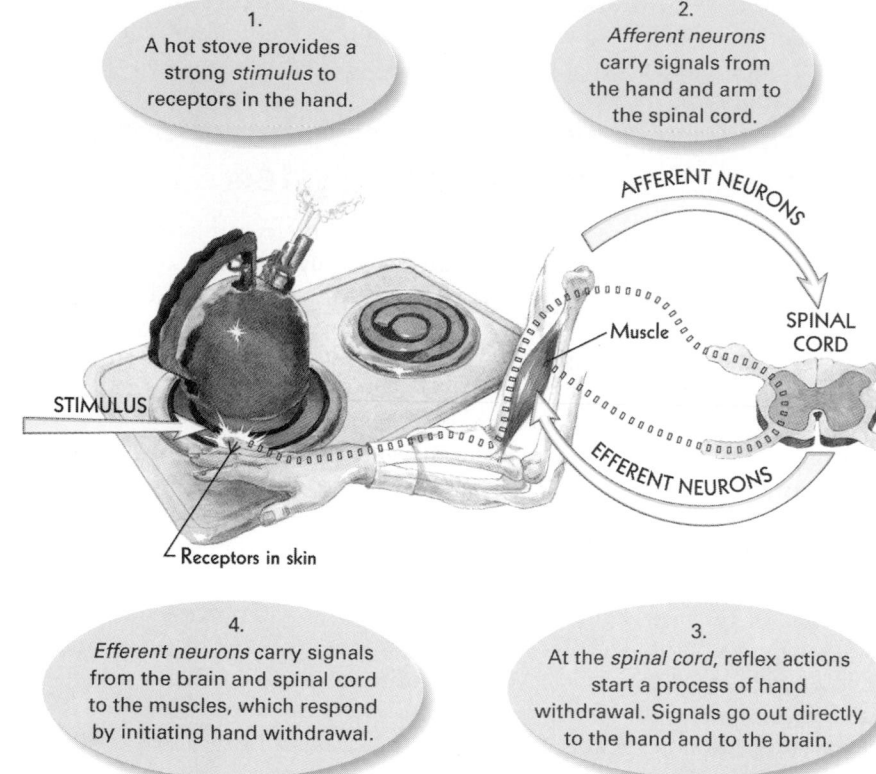

1.
A hot stove provides a strong *stimulus* to receptors in the hand.

2.
*Afferent neurons* carry signals from the hand and arm to the spinal cord.

AFFERENT NEURONS

SPINAL CORD

Muscle

STIMULUS

EFFERENT NEURONS

Receptors in skin

4.
*Efferent neurons* carry signals from the brain and spinal cord to the muscles, which respond by initiating hand withdrawal.

3.
At the *spinal cord*, reflex actions start a process of hand withdrawal. Signals go out directly to the hand and to the brain.

**HandsOnPsych**
Version 2.0

**Brain and Behaviour**

DENDRITES

Thin, bushy, widely branching fibres extending from the neuron cell body that receive signals from neighbouring neurons and carry them back to the cell body.

AXON

A thin, elongated process that leads from the neuron cell body and serves to transmit signals from the cell body through the axon terminal to adjacent neurons, muscles, or glands.

are efferent neurons that carry information from the brain and spinal cord to the muscles and glands. *Interneurons* connect neurons together and combine the activities of sensory and motor neurons. There are many more interneurons than sensory or motor neurons; the interneurons form a network that allows the other neurons to interact with one another. Neurons are surrounded by *glial cells*, which nourish the neurons and help hold them in place. Glial cells constitute about 90 percent of the cells in the brain and are also important in forming connections between neurons (Ullian et al., 2001). Glial cells are small—and 10 times more numerous than sensory neurons, motor neurons, or interneurons. They help insulate the brain from toxins, and they are the basis of the neurons' *myelin sheath*. The axons of many neurons, especially the longer ones, are *myelinated*, or covered with a thin white substance (the myelin sheath) that allows them to conduct signals faster than unmyelinated neurons.

**PARTS OF A NEURON.**  Typically, neurons are composed of four primary parts: dendrites, a cell body, an axon, and axon terminals (see Figure 2.3). **Dendrites** (from the Greek word for "tree," because of their branchlike appearance) are thin, bushy, widely branching fibres that become narrower as they spread away from the cell body. Dendrites are the principal signal reception sites for neurons; they receive signals from neighbouring neurons and carry them to the cell body (Kennedy, 2000). At the *cell body*, the signals are transformed and continue to travel along the **axon** to the *axon terminals* (the end points of each neuron). Like dendrites, axons have branches at their endings.

**NEURONAL SYNAPSES.**  For almost all neurons, the axon terminals (the button-like structures in the photo in Figure 2.4) of one neuron lie very close to receptor sites (dendrites, cell body, or axons) of other neurons. The microscopically small space between the axon terminals of one neuron and the receptor sites of another is

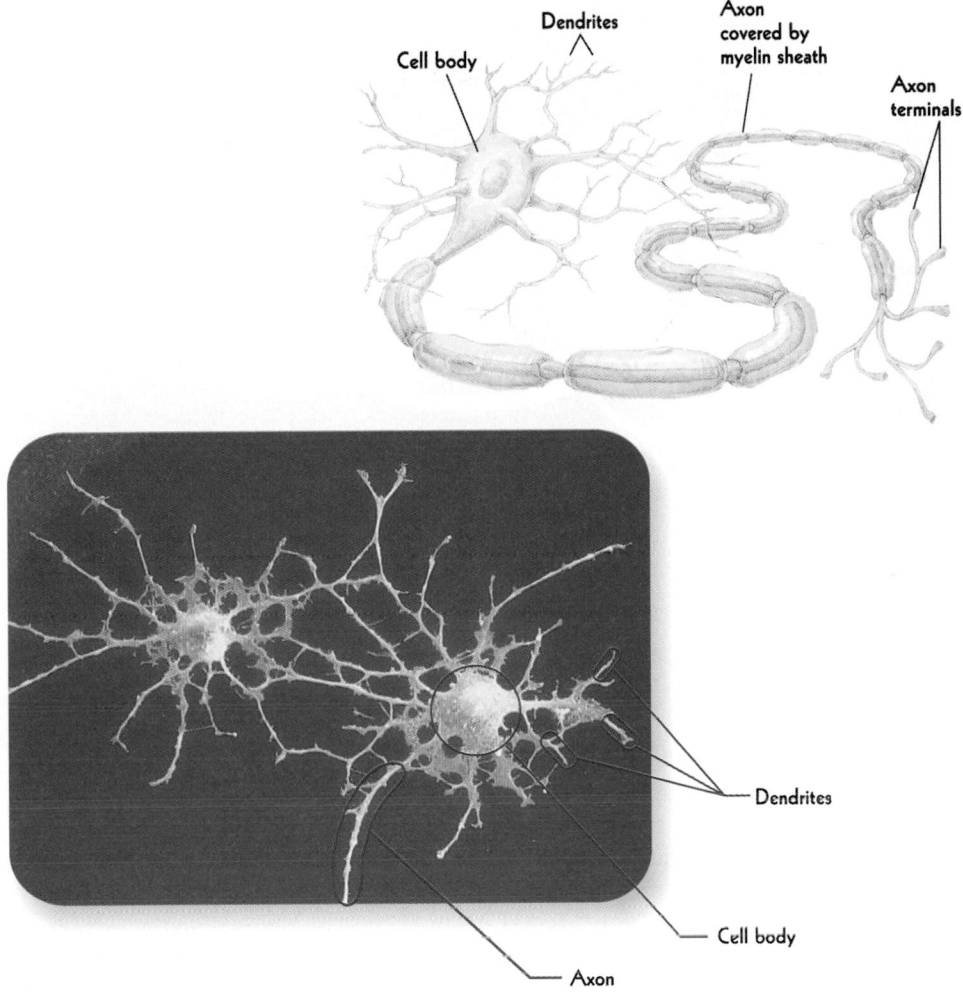

Cell body

Dendrites

Axon
covered by
myelin sheath

Axon
terminals

**FIGURE 2.3**
**The Basic Components
of a Neuron**

Neurons appear in many forms, but
all possess the basic structures
shown here: a cell body, an axon
(with myelin sheath and axon
terminals), and dendrites.

Dendrites

Cell body

Axon

called a **synapse** (see Figure 2.4). The signal from one neuron may travel across the synapse to another neuron. You can think of many neurons strung together in a long chain as a relay team sending signals, conveying information, or initiating some action in a cell, muscle, or gland. Neurons may receive information from as many as 1000 neighbouring neurons and may "synapse on" (transmit information to) as many as 1000 to 10 000 other neurons (Nauta & Fiertag, 1986).

**ELECTROCHEMICAL PROCESSES.** How do neurons communicate? What kind of signals do they transmit? Neuroscientists know that nerves are more complex than relay circuits and are affected by a wide array of electrical and chemical (*electrochemical*) variables. Two types of electrochemical processes take place. The first involves activity within a neuron; the second involves neurotransmitter substances (chemicals) that are released from the axons of one neuron and act on neighbouring neurons.

Understanding how information is transmitted within a neuron involves learning about how electrochemical impulses travel from the dendrites to the axon terminals. A widely accepted explanation of these electrochemical processes is that an extremely thin (less than 0.00001 millimetre thick) membrane surrounds every neuron, and there are channels, or "gates," in this permeable membrane through which electrically charged ions and small particles can pass. Normally the inside of the neuron is in a resting state in which it remains negatively charged, relative to the outside. This resting state is maintained by the cell membrane. The cell membrane is *polarized*; that is, the internal electrical state of the neuron (negatively charged) differs from its external state (positively charged).

SYNAPSE [SIN-apps]

The microscopically small space
between the axon terminals of one
neuron and the receptor sites of
another neuron.

**Brain and Behaviour**

## FIGURE 2.4
## The Synapse

The synapse is very small. Chemicals released by the axon terminals cross the synapse to stimulate the cell body or the dendrites of another neuron.

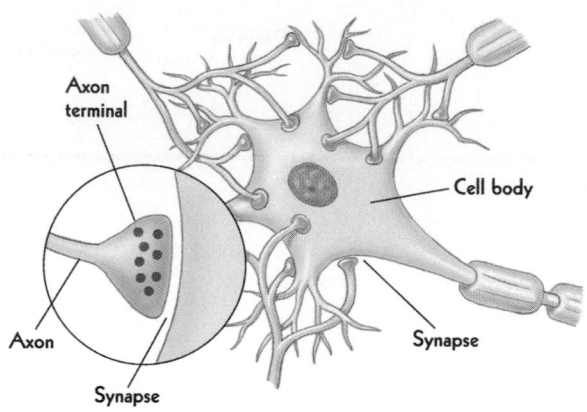

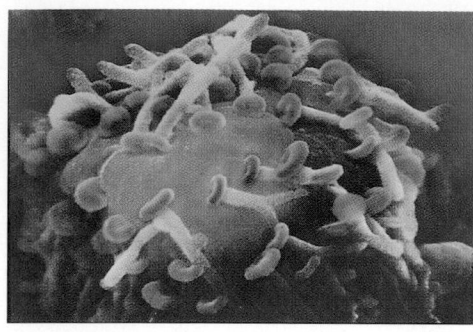

**ACTION POTENTIAL**

An electrical current sent down the axon of a neuron, initiated in an all-or-none fashion by a rapid reversal of the electrical balance of the cell membrane. Also known as a *spike discharge*.

**ACTION POTENTIALS.** When the neuron has been stimulated (its resting state has been disturbed), the cell membrane's permeability is altered, resulting in a reduced voltage difference (the inside of the cell is less negative), and the cell is said to be *depolarized*. If a sufficient amount of stimulation occurs, the axon reaches its threshold and the sodium "gates" of the cell membrane open, causing a rapid reversal of electrical polarity. Positively charged sodium ions rush into the axon. At this point an action potential has been generated (see Figure 2.5). The **action potential**, or *spike discharge*, is an electrical current that is sent down the axon of a neuron and initiated by a rapid reversal of the electrical balance of the cell membrane. Once the sodium ions reach a concentration that eliminates the negative potential inside the axon, the sodium gates close and a mechanism referred to as the *sodium-potassium pump* ejects sodium ions until the original resting potential is restored.

## FIGURE 2.5
## Generation of an Action Potential

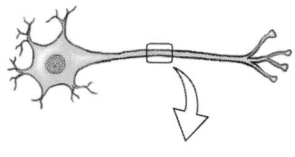

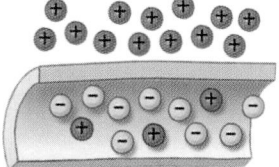

1. When the neuron is at rest, the inside is negatively charged relative to the outside.

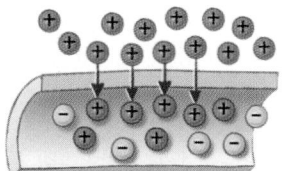

2. When the neuron is stimulated, positively charged particles enter. The action potential is initiated—the neuron is *depolarized*.

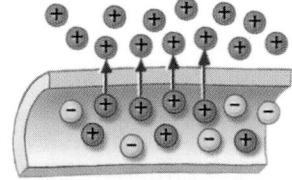

3. After a brief period, some positively charged particles are pushed outside the neuron, and the neuron moves back toward its polarized state.

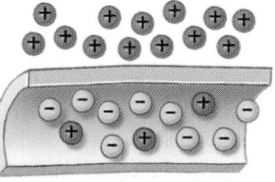

4. The neuron has finally returned to its initial polarized resting state.

A neuron does not necessarily fire or produce an action potential every time it is stimulated. If the level of polarization across the cell membrane has not been disturbed enough to generate an action potential—in other words, if the neuron has not reached its threshold (or the level of stimulation intensity that when exceeded causes a stimulus to be effective)—the cell will not fire. Neuron impulse is an **all-or-none** proposition—either the neuron fires or it doesn't. Action potentials are all the same size (Kandel, 2001)—that is, stronger stimuli do not produce stronger action potentials. However, neurons can convey information about the strength of a stimulus. They do this by varying the rate at which they fire action potentials. A stronger stimulus will cause a cell to fire a rapid volley of neural impulses. For example, a bright beam of light from a spotlight will cause some cells in the visual areas of the brain to fire over and over again very quickly, but a flicker of a candle may cause the same cells to fire much less often. Action potentials occur in 2 to 4 milliseconds; therefore, neurons normally cannot fire more than 500 times per second. After each firing a neuron needs time to recover; the time needed for recovery is called the **refractory period**. During the refractory period action potentials are much less likely to occur.

NEUROTRANSMITTERS.     When an action potential reaches the end of an axon, it triggers the release of **neurotransmitters**—chemicals that normally reside in the axon terminal within synaptic vesicles (small storage structures in the axon terminal) (Dunant & Israel, 1985). The neurotransmitters that are released into the synapse move across the synaptic space and bind to receptor sites on an adjacent cell, thereby transmitting the impulses to the next neuron (see Figure 2.6). We will examine the various types and effects of neurotransmitters shortly. When a neurotransmitter has affected the adjacent neuron, it has accomplished its main mission; the neurotransmitter is then either neutralized by an enzyme or taken back up by the neuron that released it in a process called *reuptake*. Sometimes neurotransmitters excite, or cause the receiving neurons to fire *more* easily (depolarization); sometimes they inhibit, or cause the receiving neurons to fire *less* easily (hyperpolarization). A change in the membrane potential of a neuron due to the release of neurotransmitters is called a *postsynaptic potential (PSP)*. *Excitatory PSPs* make it *easier* for the cell to fire; *inhibitory PSPs* make it *harder* for the cell to fire. Because thousands of neurons may synapse on a single cell, a single neuron can receive both excitatory and inhibitory PSPs at once (Abbott et al., 1997). The neuron then "sums" these inputs and only fires after reaching the threshold.

ALL-OR-NONE

Either at full strength or not at all; a principle by which neurons fire.

REFRACTORY PERIOD

The recovery period of a neuron after it fires, during which it cannot fire again; this period allows the neuron to re-establish electrical balance with its surroundings.

NEUROTRANSMITTER
[NYER-oh-TRANS-mitt-er]

Chemical substance that resides in the axon terminals and within synaptic vesicles and that, when released, moves across the synaptic space and binds to a receptor site on adjacent neurons.

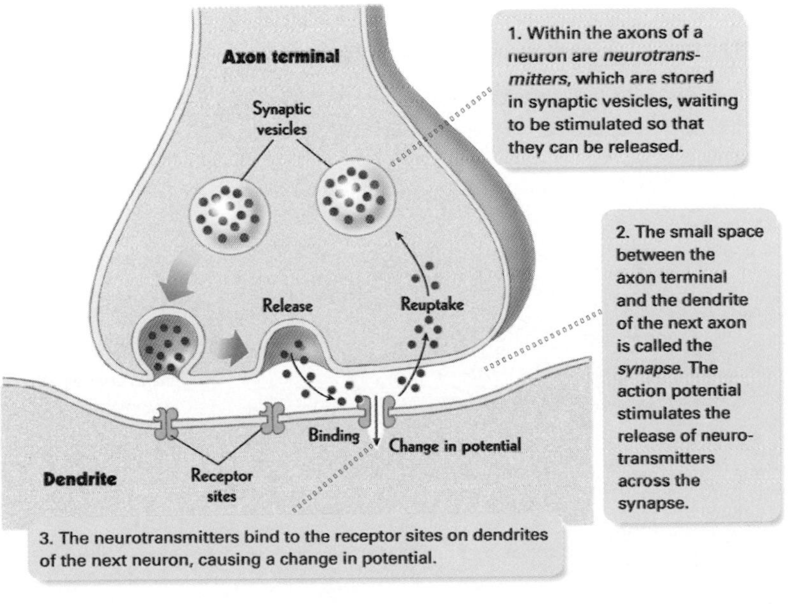

1. Within the axons of a neuron are *neurotransmitters*, which are stored in synaptic vesicles, waiting to be stimulated so that they can be released.

2. The small space between the axon terminal and the dendrite of the next axon is called the *synapse*. The action potential stimulates the release of neurotransmitters across the synapse.

3. The neurotransmitters bind to the receptor sites on dendrites of the next neuron, causing a change in potential.

FIGURE 2.6
Major Steps in Neuronal Transmission

## NEUROTRANSMITTERS AND BEHAVIOUR

There are a large number of neurotransmitters; at least 70 have been identified. One of them, gamma-aminobutyric acid (GABA), is involved in virtually every behaviour. Another important neurotransmitter, *serotonin*, is located throughout the brain, is especially important in sleep (McGinty & Szymusiak, 1988), and has been implicated in depression (Delgado et al., 1990). The most well known neurotransmitter, however, is *acetylcholine*, which is found in neurons throughout the brain and spinal cord. Acetylcholine is crucial to excitation of the skeletal muscles, the muscles that allow you to move. It is also important in such day-to-day functions as memory, learning, and sexual behaviour. The memory problems associated with Alzheimer's disease (discussed in Chapter 6) appear to be related to an inability to produce sufficient amounts of acetylcholine. Table 2.1 describes five key neurotransmitters and their effects.

**RESEARCH ON NEUROTRANSMITTERS.** Although scientists have known about the existence of neurotransmitters for a long time, only recently have they realized the significance of these substances in the study of human behaviour. For example, researchers have found that serotonin affects motivation and mood and that schizophrenia is associated with increased levels of activity in neural circuits that use certain neurotransmitters. Serotonin is implicated in the debilitating disorder of autism. In addition, researchers find that people with Parkinson's disease, whose symptoms include weakness and uncontrollable shaking, have low levels of the neurotransmitter dopamine. When clinicians give these people drugs that have the same effects as dopamine (such as L-dopa), many of their symptoms are alleviated temporarily. Although it is unlikely that one neurotransmitter alone can cause a disorder such as autism, schizophrenia, or Parkinson's disease, a single neurotransmitter may play an important role in the onset or maintenance of such an illness. Neuropeptides are chains of amino acids that act much like neurotransmitters, and are, for this reason, sometimes referred to as pseudotransmitters. The effects of endorphins, naturally produced neuropeptides perhaps most well known for inducing "runner's high," are mimicked by the actions of the narcotic morphine. Similar to the ways in which morphine affects hospitalized patients, endorphins inhibit certain synaptic transmissions—particularly those involving pain—and generally make people feel good (e.g., Miller et al., 1993). We will examine pain, endorphins, and pain management in more detail in Chapter 3.

### TABLE 2.1  Five Key Neurotransmitters

| Neurotransmitter | Location | Functions |
|---|---|---|
| Acetylcholine | Brain, spinal cord, autonomic nervous system, selected organs | Released at neuromuscular junctions. Also involved in memory. |
| Norepinephrine | Brain, spinal cord, selected organs | Regulates physical and psychological arousal. Also involved in learning, memory, and emotions. |
| Dopamine | Brain | Linked to muscle activity, emotional arousal, learning, and memory. |
| Serotonin | Brain, spinal cord | Linked to activity level, sleep, appetite, and emotion. |
| GABA | Brain, spinal cord | Involved in motor behaviour and level of arousal. |

At first, researchers thought that only one type of neurotransmitter existed in each neuron and that each neurotransmitter acted on only one type of receptor. Today researchers know that neurons often hold more than one type of neurotransmitter, and that these may act on more than one receptor, causing different effects. Some neurotransmitters (especially neuropeptides) are released into the bloodstream, so their effects may be far-reaching. Researchers now think of these neurotransmitters as neuromodulators. **Neuromodulators** are chemical substances that function to increase or decrease the sensitivity of widely distributed neurons to the specific effects of other neurotransmitters. A neuropeptide released into the bloodstream, for example, affects not only a single cell's immediate ion transfer but also whole classes, groups, or networks of cells, such as those within the limbic system, a brain structure known to be involved with emotional responses.

**PSYCHOPHARMACOLOGY.** The study of how drugs affect the body is called pharmacology, and *psychopharmacology* is the study of how drugs affect behaviour. Researchers study many types of drugs to learn the physiological mechanisms that underlie behavioural reactions. Psychopharmacological research may hold the key to treating drug addiction and other behaviour problems. Such research may uncover drugs that will effectively block the addictive properties of drugs such as cocaine and lead to more successful forms of treatment for addiction (Robinson & Berridge, 2000). Research has shown that many common drugs alter the amount of a neurotransmitter released at synapses; other drugs alter the way neurotransmitters operate; yet other drugs change the speed at which neurotransmitters are disabled after release. Thus, for example, a drug may change behaviour by changing the speed of neurotransmitter release, which increases the number of action potentials formed when the released neurotransmitter is excitatory or decreases the number of action potentials when the neurotransmitter is inhibitory.

Chemicals can also be used to mimic or facilitate the actions of neurotransmitters; such chemicals are called **agonists**. When an agonist is present, it is as if the neurotransmitter itself has been released. Other chemicals, called **antagonists**, oppose the actions of specific neurotransmitters. When an antagonist is present, receptor sites are blocked, and the neurotransmitter cannot have its usual effect. Schizophrenia, a disabling mental disorder, is often treated with antagonists. Neurons that normally respond to dopamine are blocked from doing so by being exposed to certain drugs that act as antagonists, and symptoms of schizophrenia are thereby diminished. (We will discuss dopamine and schizophrenia in more detail in Chapter 15.) Some drugs block the reabsorption, or reuptake, of neurotransmitters from their receptor sites. An example is the popular drug Prozac, part of a class of drugs known as selective serotonin-reuptake inhibitors (SSRIs). It exerts its effect by blocking the reuptake of serotonin, prolonging the ability of released serotonin to stimulate the postsynaptic cell. This drug has proved highly useful in the treatment of depression (Julien, 1995). The success of Prozac has been attributed to the relative lack of serious side-effects associated with its use. Moreover, Prozac has also been shown to be effective against other disorders, such as anxiety, the inability to experience pleasure, a fear of failure, and extreme sensitivity to criticism (Pinel, 2003).

When neurons fire, information is transferred from the sense organs to the brain and then from the brain to the muscular system and the glands. If psychologists knew precisely how this transfer occurred, they could more successfully predict and manage the behaviour of people with neurological damage, mood disorders, or epilepsy, for example. However, the firing of neurons and the release of neurotransmitters do not in themselves completely explain the biological bases of human behaviour. The firing of individual neurons presents a close-up look at the function of the nervous system, but a wider view of brain structure is necessary to understand the relationship between brain and behaviour. We turn next to that view of the brain and nervous system.

▲ Strenuous exercise and stress are experiences that release endorphins.

NEUROMODULATOR
Chemical substance that functions to increase or decrease the sensitivity of widely distributed neurons to the specific effects of neurotransmitters.

AGONIST [AG-oh-nist]
Chemical that mimics the actions of a neurotransmitter, usually by occupying receptor sites and facilitating neurochemical transfers.

ANTAGONIST
Chemical that opposes the actions of a neurotransmitter, usually by preventing the neurotransmitter from occupying a receptor site.

▼ Both the somatic and autonomic divisions of the peripheral nervous system are involved in swerving to avoid a crash.

PERIPHERAL [puh-RIF-er-al] NERVOUS SYSTEM

The part of the nervous system that carries information to and from the central nervous system through a network of spinal and cranial nerves.

SOMATIC [so-MAT-ick] NERVOUS SYSTEM

The part of the peripheral nervous system that carries information to skeletal muscles and thereby affects bodily movement; it controls voluntary, conscious sensory and motor functions.

# Organization of the Nervous System

It is a dark, wet evening; you are driving down a deserted road, listening to some 1980s oldies. Though you believe you have had enough sleep, you find your eyes getting heavy and eventually are startled when the right tires of your car hit the gravel on the shoulder of the road. Suddenly very alert, you ease off the gas and bring the car to a safe stop. You wait a bit for your breathing and heart rate to return to normal before driving on to look for a safe place to get some rest. On just such a second-by-second basis, the nervous system controls behaviour. It is therefore essential for psychologists to understand the organization and functions of the nervous system and its mutually dependent systems and divisions. The nervous system is made up of the peripheral nervous system and the central nervous system. The central nervous system consists of the brain and spinal cord; the peripheral nervous system connects the central nervous system to the rest of the body. Let's examine them both in detail.

## THE PERIPHERAL NERVOUS SYSTEM

The **peripheral nervous system** is the part of the nervous system that carries information to and from the spinal cord and the brain through spinal nerves attached to the spinal cord and by a system of 12 cranial nerves, which carry signals directly to and from the brain. The peripheral nervous system contains all of the neurons and nerves (groups of axons) that are not in the central nervous system; its nerves focus on the *periphery*, or outer parts, of the body. Its two major divisions are the somatic nervous system and the autonomic nervous system.

### THE SOMATIC NERVOUS SYSTEM.
The **somatic nervous system** is the part of the peripheral nervous system that both responds to the external senses of sight, hearing, touch, smell, and taste and acts on the outside world. Generally considered under the individual's voluntary control, the somatic nervous system is involved in perceptual processing (processing information gathered through one's senses) and in control of movement and striate muscles. Because it carries information from the sense organs to the brain and from the brain and spinal cord to the consciously controlled muscles, it consists of both sensory (afferent) and motor (efferent) neurons. The somatic system allows you to see an oncoming truck and to get out of its way.

### THE AUTONOMIC NERVOUS SYSTEM.
The **autonomic nervous system** is the part of the peripheral nervous system that controls the vital processes of the body, such as heart rate, digestion, blood pressure, and functioning of internal organs. In contrast to the somatic nervous system, it operates continuously and involuntarily (although the technique of biofeedback, discussed in Chapter 4, sometimes has proved to be effective in bringing a few of these processes under partial voluntary control). The system is called "autonomic" because many of its subsystems are self-regulating, focused on the use and conservation of energy resources. The autonomic nervous system is made up of two divisions: the sympathetic nervous system and the parasympathetic nervous system, which work together to control the activities of muscles and glands (see Figure 2.7).

The **sympathetic nervous system** is the part of the autonomic nervous system that responds to emergency situations. Its activities are easy to observe and measure. Activation results in a sharp increase in heart rate and blood pressure, slowing of digestion, dilation of the pupils, and general preparation for an

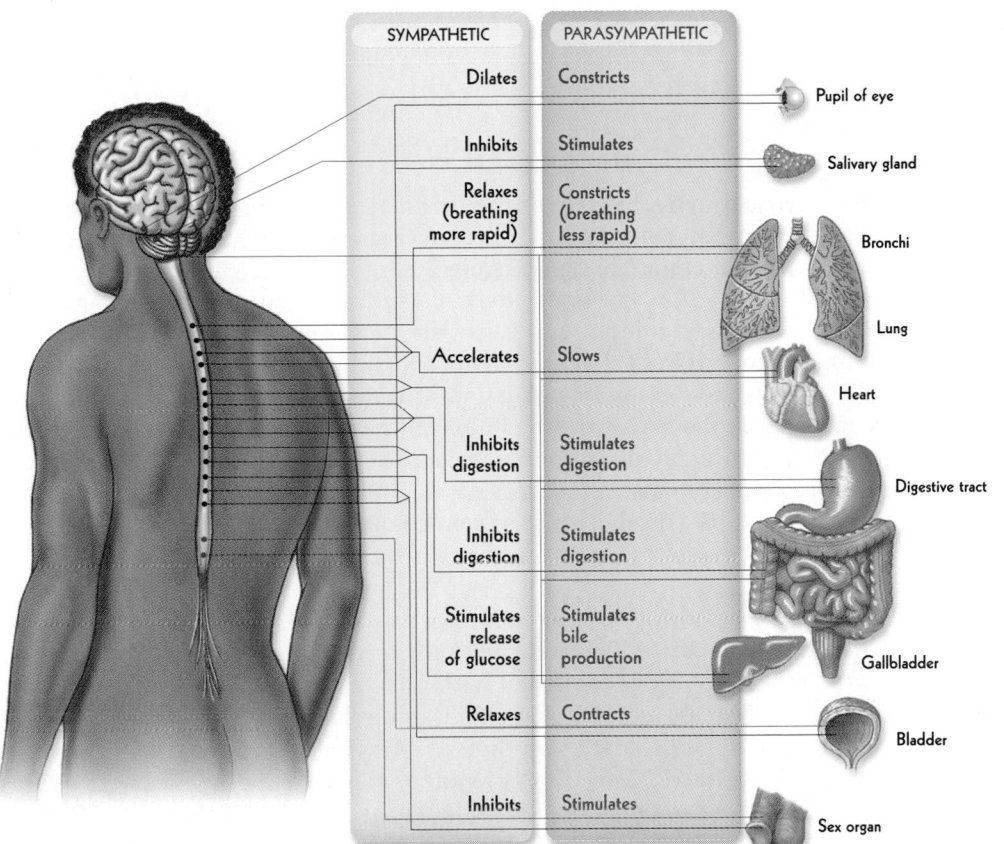

FIGURE 2.7

**The Two Divisions of the Autonomic Nervous System**

SYMPATHETIC | PARASYMPATHETIC

| Dilates | Constricts | Pupil of eye |
| Inhibits | Stimulates | Salivary gland |
| Relaxes (breathing more rapid) | Constricts (breathing less rapid) | Bronchi / Lung |
| Accelerates | Slows | Heart |
| Inhibits digestion | Stimulates digestion | Digestive tract |
| Inhibits digestion | Stimulates digestion | |
| Stimulates release of glucose | Stimulates bile production | Gallbladder |
| Relaxes | Contracts | Bladder |
| Inhibits | Stimulates | Sex organ |

emergency—sometimes called the *fight-or-flight response*. These changes usually are accompanied by an increased flow of epinephrine, or adrenalin, which is a substance released by the adrenal gland (to be discussed later in this chapter), and they are regulated by a set of neurons in the hypothalamus and brain stem (to be discussed shortly) (Jansen et al., 1995). Increased activity of the sympathetic nervous system is what makes your heart pound and your mouth go dry when your car drives off the road.

When the sympathetic nervous system is active and the organism is in a fight-or-flight position, the somatic nervous system also is activated. For example, when a large, snarling dog chases a cyclist, the cyclist's adrenal gland is stimulated by the sympathetic nervous system; the burst of energy produced by epinephrine (released by the adrenal gland) affects the somatic nervous system, making the cyclist's muscles respond strongly and rapidly. Thus, changes in the sympathetic nervous system can produce rapid changes in the organism's somatic nervous system; these changes usually are seen in emotional behaviour and in stress reactions (discussed in detail in Chapters 9 and 14). Even simple responses, such as blushing from embarrassment, are regulated by the sympathetic nervous system.

The **parasympathetic nervous system**, which is active most of the time, is the part of the autonomic nervous system that controls the normal operations of the body, such as digestion, blood pressure, and heart rate. In other words, it keeps the body running smoothly. This system calms everything down and moves the heartbeat back to normal after an emergency. Unlike the sympathetic system, the parasympathetic activity does not show sharp changes on a minute-by-minute basis.

It is important to note that in reality these two systems are not as independent as the previous discussion may suggest. Rather, the overall state of an organism depends on the *balance* between the sympathetic and parasympathetic systems. For example, an increase in heart rate can result from either an increase in

**AUTONOMIC [au-toe-NOM-ick] NERVOUS SYSTEM**

The part of the peripheral nervous system that controls the vital and automatic processes of the body, such as heart rate, digestion, blood pressure, and functioning of internal organs.

**SYMPATHETIC NERVOUS SYSTEM**

The part of the autonomic nervous system that becomes most active in response to emergency situations; it calls up bodily resources as needed for major energy expenditures.

**PARASYMPATHETIC [PAIR-uh-sim-puh-THET-ick] NERVOUS SYSTEM**

The part of the autonomic nervous system that controls the ongoing maintenance processes of the body, such as heart rate, digestion, and blood pressure.

sympathetic activity or a decrease in parasympathetic activity. Often, a strong parasympathetic system response occurs following a prolonged period of sympathetic system dominance.

## THE CENTRAL NERVOUS SYSTEM

The **central nervous system** is one of the two major parts of the nervous system. Consisting of the brain and the spinal cord, it serves as the main processing system for most information in the body (see Figure 2.8).

Although exactly how the brain functions remains a mystery that is far from being completely understood, neuroscientists do know that the brain operates through many mutually dependent systems and subsystems to affect and control behaviour. As you've seen in our discussion of neuronal activity, millions of brain cells are involved in the performance of even simple activities. When you walk, for example, the visual areas of the brain are active and your sight guides you, the brain's motor areas help make your legs move, and the cerebellum helps you keep your balance. It is the central nervous system communicating with the muscles and glands, under the control of the brain, that allows all of these things to happen so effortlessly.

The brain is the control centre, but it receives much of its information from the spinal cord, the main communication line to the rest of the body, and from the cranial nerves. The **spinal cord**, contained within the spinal column, receives signals from the sensory organs, muscles, and glands and relays these signals to the brain. Not all behaviours involve the brain directly. Among them are *spinal reflexes*—actions that are controlled almost solely by the spinal cord and a system of neurons that create a reflexive response. The knee jerk, elicited by a tap on the tendon below the kneecap, is one such spinal reflex. A sensory input (the tap) is linked to a motor response (the knee jerk) without first passing through the brain. Most signals eventually make their way up the spinal cord to the brain for further analysis, but the knee jerk response happens at the level of the spinal cord, before the brain has had time to register and act on the tap.

The spinal cord's importance cannot be overstated. When a person's spinal cord is severed, the information exchange between the brain and the muscles and glands below the point of damage is halted. Spinal reflexes still operate, and knee jerk responses are evident. However, individuals such as Rick Hansen or actor Christopher Reeve who suffer spinal cord damage lose voluntary control over

**FIGURE 2.8**
**The Basic Divisions of the Nervous System**

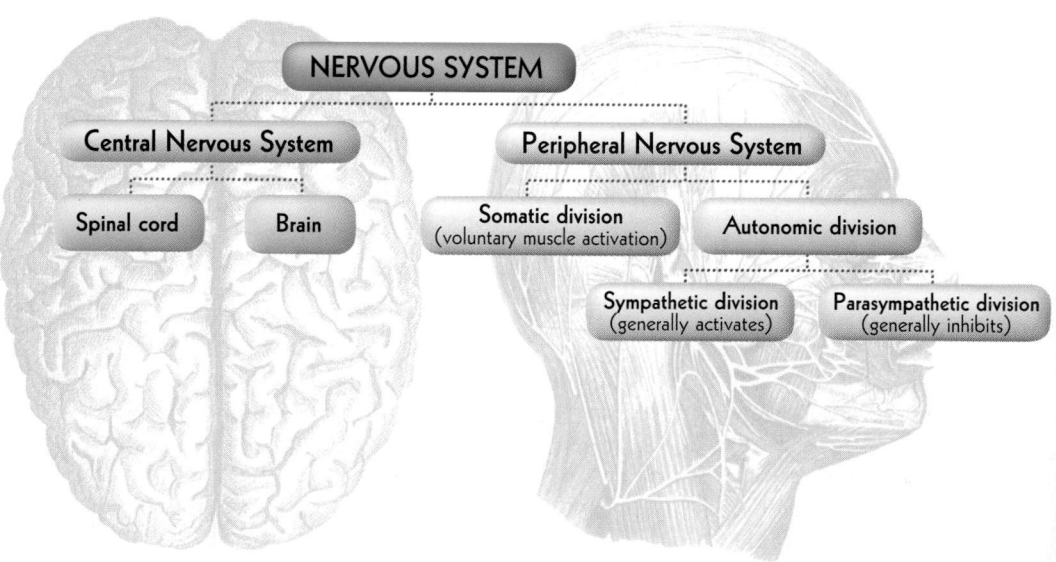

muscles in the parts of their bodies below the site of the injury. This shows that the spinal cord serves a key communication function between the brain and the rest of the body. Let's turn next to the brain itself.

# Organization of the Brain

A person's intelligence, personality traits, and ability to communicate through language reside in a small organ protected by the skull—the brain. The human brain is highly evolved, complex, and specialized. It is this specialization that allows humans—in contrast to other animals—to think about the past and the future and to communicate possibilities. Scientists have studied its structure, its functions, its interconnections, and what happens to it when it is damaged, yet they still have much to learn.

## FIVE PRINCIPLES GOVERNING BRAIN ORGANIZATION

The **brain** is the part of the central nervous system that regulates, monitors, processes, and guides other nervous system activity. Located in the skull, the human brain is an organ weighing about 1.4 kilograms composed of two large *cerebral hemispheres*, one on the right side and one on the left. More will be said later about what each hemisphere is responsible for. A large bundle of nerve fibres, the *corpus callosum*, connects the two hemispheres and permits the transfer of information between them. Besides being divided into right and left halves, the brain is often described as having three main divisions: the hindbrain, the midbrain, and the forebrain.

These specialized systems operate separately but often work together; in general, they follow five key operating principles (Amaral, 2000). *First,* each system involves several brain regions that carry out different types of information processing. *Second,* there are identifiable pathways, groups of neurons bundled together, that project from one area of the brain to the next. *Third,* each part of the brain projects to the next in an orderly fashion, creating what are called topographically organized regions that can be mapped spatially. *Fourth,* the brain is hierarchically organized; that is, it is organized in a logical sequence usually starting with simple cells, projecting to more complex areas of the brain, and ultimately winding up with the most complex processing taking place in the forebrain—and most of the major connections can be followed or mapped. *Last,* the brain systems are organized so that one side of the brain controls the other side of the body. Although we are not sure why, most brain structures are bilaterally symmetrical (the same on both sides) and cross over and control operations on the other side of the body. Many brain activities are localized in one specific area, but some are not. For example, most speech and language activity can be pinpointed to a specific area, usually on the left side of the brain (Damasio & Damasio, 2000). Other activities occur in both hemispheres, such as visual activity in the visual cortex of both sides of the brain as well as in subcortical structures.

## THE BRAIN'S MAIN DIVISIONS

Initially, the brain forms three divisions—hindbrain, midbrain, and forebrain—and we usually refer to brain organization this way (see Figures 2.9 and 2.10). As a general principle, the structures lower in the brain tend to be responsible for basic, reflexive functions, and those toward the top are involved in more complex and abstract mental functions.

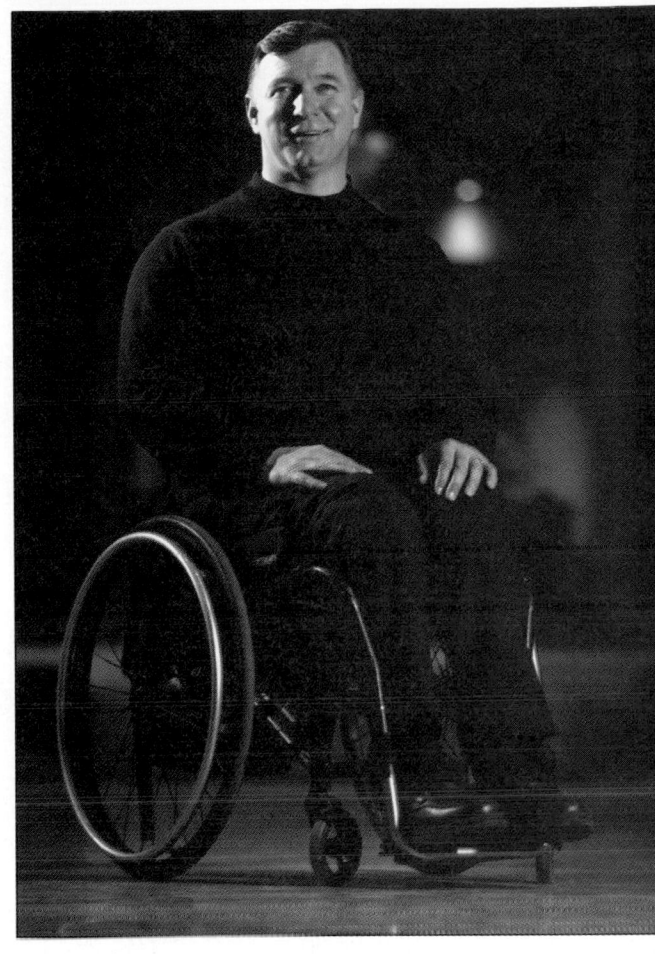

▲ For people such as Rick Hansen, spinal cord damage results in loss of voluntary control over muscles.

**BRAIN**

The part of the central nervous system that is located in the skull and that regulates, monitors, processes, and guides other nervous system activity.

**HandsOnPsych**
Version 2.0

**Brain and Behaviour**

FIGURE 2.9
**The Human Brain**

The human brain is divided into three major sections: the forebrain, the midbrain, and the hindbrain. Each of these is revealed in progressively more detail here.

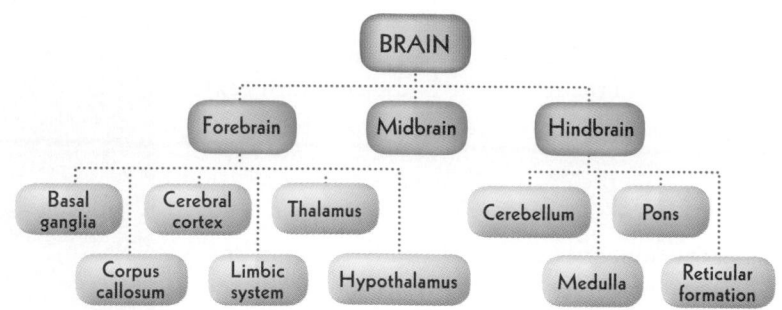

**FIGURE 2.10**

**Cross-Section of the Human Brain**

This cross-section illustrates the three major sections of the brain.

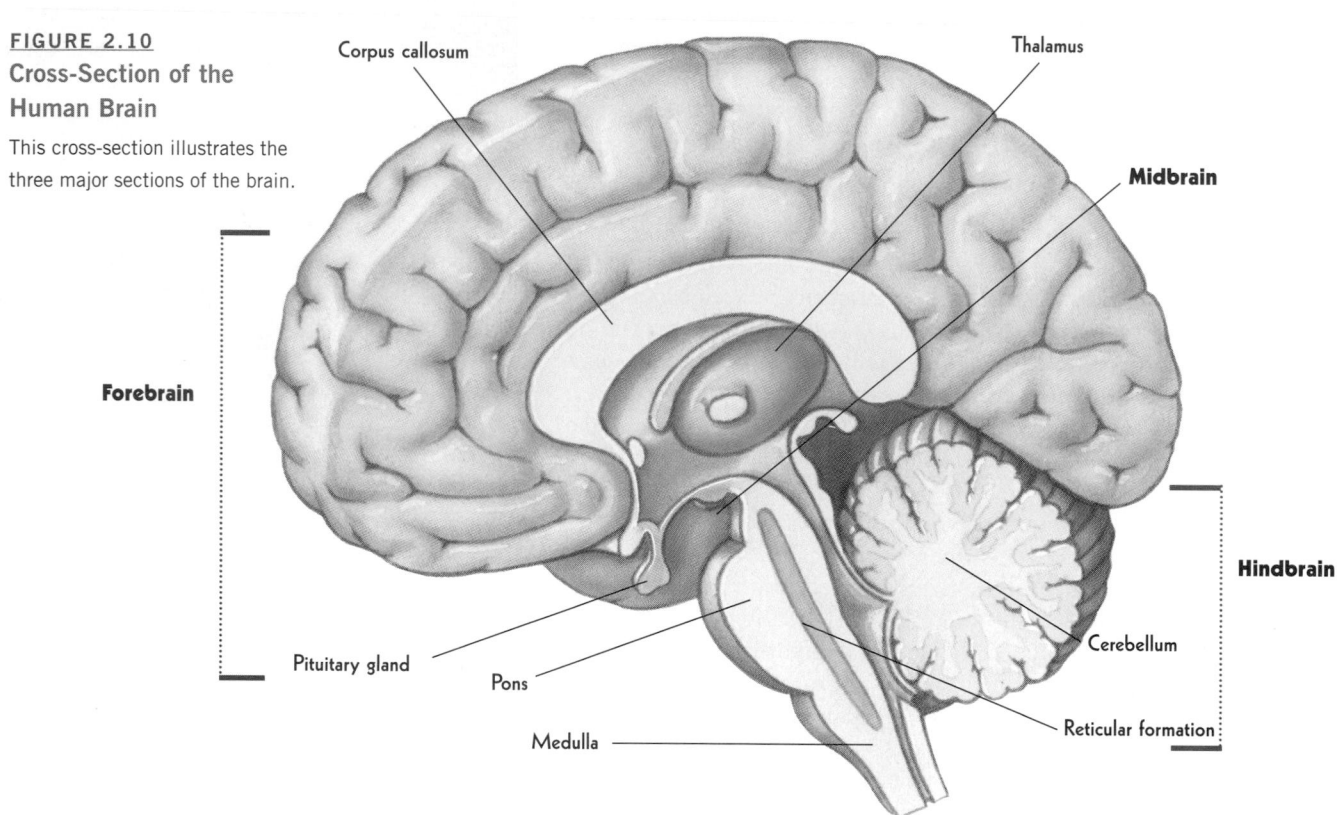

In examining the brain, we begin where the spinal cord and the brain meet. As we move higher up and toward the top of the brain, we find structures with more complicated but less essential functions. The cortex—the deeply fissured grey surface matter that covers the cerebral hemispheres—exhibits the highest complexity of functioning. The cortex is the location of thought processing—one of the most advanced abilities of humans.

## THE HINDBRAIN AND MIDBRAIN

Every time Mike Weir wins another golf tournament, it is a tribute to his cerebellum. If his cerebellum functioned even slightly less proficiently, he would be a duffer rather than a champion. The **hindbrain** consists of the medulla, the reticular formation, the pons, and the cerebellum (see Figure 2.11). The structures of the hindbrain receive afferent signals from other parts of the brain and from the spinal cord; they interpret the signals and either relay the information to more complex parts of the brain or immediately cause the body to act.

HINDBRAIN

The most primitive organizationally of the three functional divisions of the brain, consisting of the medulla, the reticular formation, the pons, and the cerebellum.

MEDULLA [meh-DUH-lah]

The most primitive and lowest portion of the hindbrain; controls basic bodily functions such as heartbeat and breathing.

**Structures of the brain**

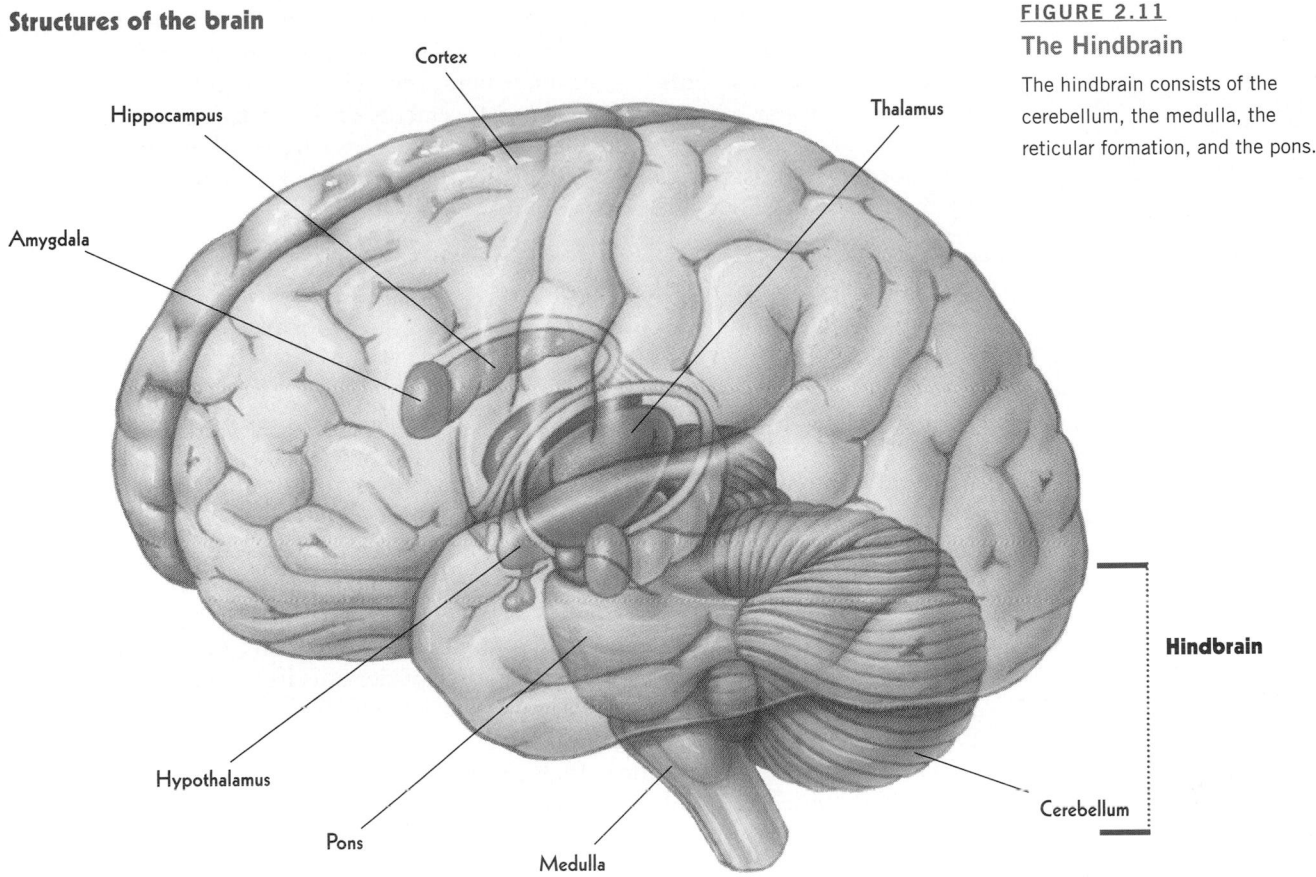

Cortex
Hippocampus
Amygdala
Thalamus
Hypothalamus
Pons
Medulla
Hindbrain
Cerebellum

FIGURE 2.11

**The Hindbrain**

The hindbrain consists of the cerebellum, the medulla, the reticular formation, and the pons.

The hindbrain includes the **medulla**, the dense package of nerves lying just above the spinal cord that controls heartbeat and breathing and through which many afferent and efferent signals pass. Within the medulla is a lattice like network of nerve cells, *the reticular formation*, which controls a person's state of arousal. Damage to it can result in coma and death, and its normal function controls waking and sleeping. The reticular formation extends into and through the pons and the midbrain, with projections toward the cortex.

The **pons** provides a link between the lower brain and the rest of the brain; like the medulla, the pons affects sleep and dreaming. The **cerebellum** (or "little brain"), a structure attached to the back surface of the brain stem, influences balance, coordination, and movement, including single joint actions such as the flexing of an elbow or knee. The cerebellum constitutes only 10 percent of the total volume of the brain but contains more than half of its neurons! The cerebellum allows you to walk in a straight line, type accurately on a keyboard, and coordinate the many movements involved in dancing—and if you're Mike Weir, hit a golf ball better than almost anyone ever has. The cerebellum may also be involved in some types of thinking and learning, although its functions in these areas are not yet clearly established (Thach, 1998).

The **midbrain**, the least understood area of the brain, is a very small structure in the human brain that consists of nuclei (collections of cell bodies) that receive afferent signals from other parts of the brain and from the spinal cord. Like the hindbrain, the midbrain interprets the signals and either relays the information to a more complex part of the brain or causes the body to act at once. The midbrain has two divisions (Pinel, 2003). One division includes the inferior and superior colliculi, which have auditory and visual functions, respectively. The second division contains

PONS

A structure of the hindbrain that provides a link between the medulla and the cerebellum and the rest of the brain; it affects sleep and dreaming.

CEREBELLUM
[seh-rah-BELL-um]

A large structure that is attached to the back surface of the brain stem and that influences balance, coordination, and movement.

MIDBRAIN

The second level of the three organizational structures of the brain; it receives afferent signals from other parts of the brain and from the spinal cord, interprets the signals, and either relays the information to a more complex part of the brain or causes the body to act at once; considered important in the regulation of movement.

FOREBRAIN

The largest, most complicated, and most advanced organizationally and functionally of the three divisions of the brain, with many interrelated parts: the thalamus and hypothalamus, the limbic system, the basal ganglia and corpus callosum, and the cortex.

THALAMUS

A large structure of the forebrain that acts primarily as a routing station to send information to other parts of the brain but probably also performs some interpretive functions; nearly all sensory information proceeds through the thalamus.

HYPOTHALAMUS

A relatively small structure of the forebrain, lying just below the thalamus, that acts through its connections with the rest of the forebrain and the midbrain and affects many complex behaviours, such as eating, drinking, and sexual activity.

the reticular formation, which extends from the hindbrain into the midbrain, as well as areas important for sensorimotor function and pain mediation. The midbrain also governs smoothness of movement, temperature regulation, and other reflexive movements (Stein et al., 2002). Movements of the eyeball in its socket, for example, are controlled by the *superior colliculus,* whereas other smooth body movements (such as swinging at a baseball or getting out of a chair) are controlled by the *substantia nigra* (a structure in the midbrain).

## THE FOREBRAIN

The **forebrain** is the most advanced brain structure organizationally and structurally; it is also the largest and most complicated of the brain structures because of its many interrelated parts: the thalamus and hypothalamus, the limbic system, the basal ganglia and corpus callosum, and the cortex (see Figure 2.12).

**THALAMUS AND HYPOTHALAMUS.**   The **thalamus** acts primarily as a relay station for sensory information. It integrates and analyzes this input and sends the information on to the primary sensory cortex. Therefore, all sensory information (except for olfaction) proceeds through the thalamus before being routed to other areas of the brain. The **hypothalamus,** which is relatively small (the size of a pea) and located just below the thalamus, has numerous connections with the rest of the forebrain and the midbrain and affects many species-specific behaviours, such as eating, drinking, and sexual arousal. It plays a crucial role in regulating the body's internal environment by maintaining homeostatic balance in such areas as blood sugar levels or body temperature. It also is involved in regulating the endocrine system. We will discuss the role of the hypothalamus in more detail in Chapter 9.

**LIMBIC SYSTEM.**   One of the most complex and least understood structures of the brain is the **limbic system** (see Figure 2.13). This system is located between the brain stem and the cerebral hemispheres and is an interconnected group of structures (including parts of the cortex, thalamus, and hypothalamus) involved in emotions, memory, motivation, and brain disorders such as epilepsy. Within the

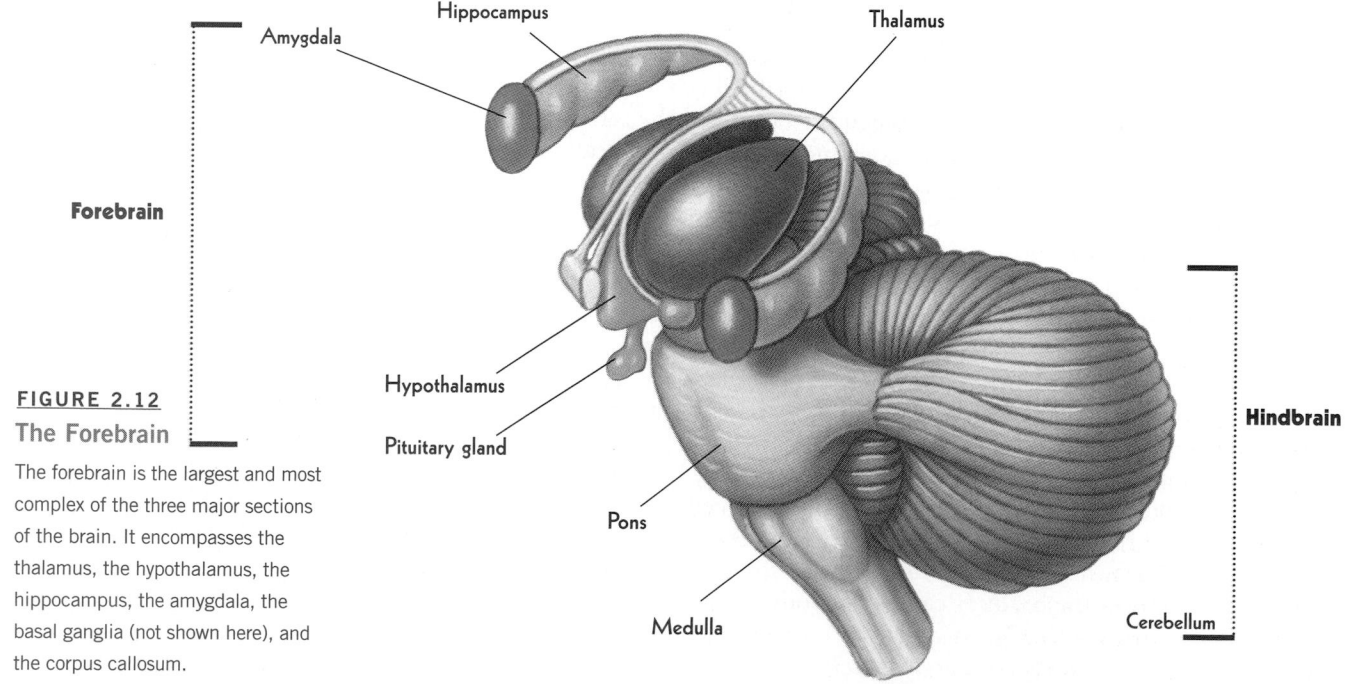

**FIGURE 2.12**
The Forebrain

The forebrain is the largest and most complex of the three major sections of the brain. It encompasses the thalamus, the hypothalamus, the hippocampus, the amygdala, the basal ganglia (not shown here), and the corpus callosum.

limbic system are the hippocampus and the amygdala. The *hippocampus* is located deep within the temporal lobe and is involved in new learning, in encoding and retrieving long-term memories, in navigating about the world, and in some emotional functions (Maguire et al., 1998).

The *amygdala*, a set of nuclei connected to the hippocampus, is also involved in emotional control and in the formation of emotional memories. Canadian researchers Brian Kolb and Ian Wishaw (1996) indicate that the amygdala is particularly important in directing attention to emotionally salient characteristics of behaviour. Stimulation of the amygdala in animals, for instance, produces attack responses. As another example, rabies leads to the deterioration and eventual destruction of the amygdala. That deterioration is associated with uncontrolled fits of violence. Surgical removal of the amygdala in human beings was once a radical way of treating people who were extremely violent, however, this technique is no longer considered an ethical treatment option. The amygdala is now considered also to play a significant role in learning of fear and other emotional responses (Bechara et al., 1995; Damasio, 1994). Stimulation of several areas of the limbic system in rats also produces what appear to be highly pleasurable sensations. Olds and Milner (1954) discovered that, when given small doses of electrical current in some of the limbic areas as a reward for pressing a bar, rats chose bar pressing over eating, even if they had been deprived of food for long periods. The researchers called the areas of the amygdala being stimulated in this experiment *pleasure centres*; researchers have recently investigated the link between addictive behaviours and stimulation of this brain region (Wise, 1996).

**THE BASAL GANGLIA AND CORPUS CALLOSUM.** The *basal ganglia* are a series of nuclei located deep in the forebrain to the left and right of the thalamus that link the thalamus and the cortex. They control movements and posture and are also associated with Parkinson's disease. Parts of the basal ganglia influence muscle tone and initiate commands to the cerebellum and to higher brain centres. Damage to this important neurological centre can have severe behavioural consequences. Parts of the basal ganglia are also involved in cognitive function. The *corpus callosum* is a thick band of 200 million or so nerve fibres that provide cross-hemisphere connections that convey information between the cerebral hemispheres; damage to it results in essentially two separate brains within one skull. We'll return to the corpus callosum shortly.

**CORTEX.** The brain has two major portions, referred to as the left and right cerebral hemispheres (we'll discuss brain specialization in more detail shortly). In terms of evolution, these two hemispheres are the youngest parts of our brains. The exterior covering of these hemispheres, called the **cortex**, is about two millimetres thick and consists of six thin layers of nerve cells. Most of the human cerebral cortex is called neocortex (new cortex) because it is a newer evolutionary adaptation than older brain areas in the midbrain and hindbrain. The cortex is *convoluted*, or furrowed. These **convolutions** (called gyri and fissures), folds in the tissue of the cerebral hemispheres and the overlying cortex, create more surface area within a small space. The overall surface area of the cortex is at least 0.13935 square metres but is collapsed and folded so that it can fit into the skull. A highly developed cortex is evident in human beings, but not all mammals show such specialization, and most other mammals' brains are less deeply fissured. The cortex plays a special role in behaviour because it is intimately involved in thought and reason.

**FIGURE 2.13**

**Principal Structures of the Limbic System**

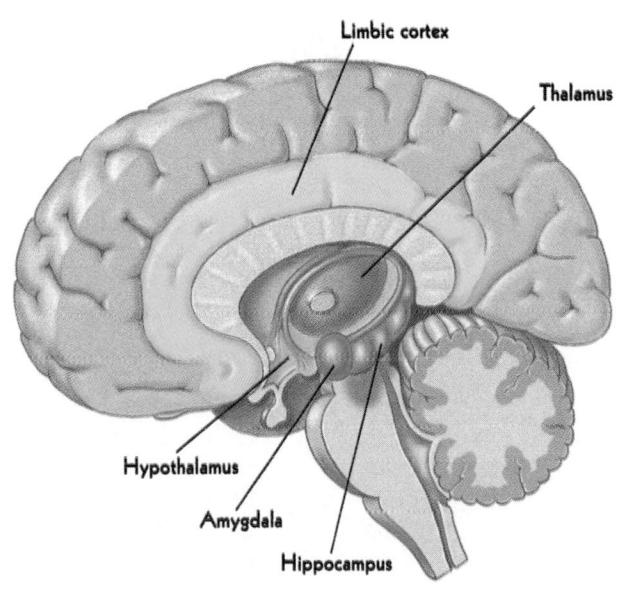

A traditional way to divide the cortex is to consider it to be a series of lobes, or areas, each with characteristic structures and functions. The most prominent structures are two deep fissures (very deep furrows, or folds)—the *lateral fissure* and the *central fissure*—that divide each hemisphere of the brain into four lobes. These easily recognizable fissures are like deep ravines that run among the convolutions, separating the various lobes; these deep cortical valleys are thought to be especially important in thought (Markowitsch & Tulving, 1994). Although for most tasks many disparate areas of the entire brain work in concert, each of the lobes of the brain is somewhat specialized in the functions it performs.

The *frontal lobe* is in front of the central fissure and is concerned with higher-order functions such as memory (Goldman-Rakic, 1998); monitoring, organizing, and directing thought processes; and planning and paying attention. A specialized speech and language production area, called Broca's area, is located in the left hemisphere of the frontal lobe. The famed Montreal neurosurgeon Wilder Penfield (Penfield & Boldrey, 1937; Penfield & Rasmussen, 1950), world renowned for his groundbreaking maps of the brain, discovered the role of a band of cortex in the frontal lobe, called the *primary motor cortex,* responsible for the control of body movements. Canadian researcher Donald Stuss of the University of Toronto and the Rotman Institute has studied the importance of the right frontal lobe in appreciating humour (Shammi & Stuss, 1999) and in self-awareness (Stuss, 1991). Damage to the frontal lobe can result in changes in personality, loss of the ability to plan, and impulsivity.

The *parietal lobe* is behind the central fissure and is involved in integrating visual input and monitoring the body's position in space. A specialized band of tissue in the parietal lobe, called the *somatosensory cortex,* registers information from the skin senses (such as touch, temperature, or pain). Ronald Melzack (1999) of McGill University has worked on a fascinating problem that may be related to the neurons in the parietal lobe. If someone loses a limb, through an accident or for medical reasons, they will often report that they can still "feel" the missing limb and particularly that they can feel pain in the limb that is no longer there. This *phantom limb* phenomenon is thought by Melzack and others to be due to a parietal lobe function that keeps track of our general "body sense." It is theorized that the model for one's whole body, including the missing limb, continues to exist there and relay information about the now-missing limb even after it is removed. Damage to the parietal lobe differs depending on whether the right or left lobe has been injured. Damage to the left lobe tends to produce *aphasias* (language disorders) or *agnosias* (inability to perceive objects) whereas damage to the right lobe causes the individual to neglect the left side of the body, for example, failing to dress or wash the affected side.

Below the lateral fissure and the parietal lobe is the *temporal lobe*. The left temporal lobe contains an important language comprehension area called Wernicke's area. Wernicke's area is connected to Broca's area so that the ability to understand and produce language is inexorably linked. The temporal lobe is also important for memory function and social understanding, and it contains the auditory cortex. Temporal damage causes memory loss as well as altered emotional responding.

The *occipital lobe* is located at the back of the head and processes visual input. The primary visual cortex receives sensory input directly from the eyes. The occipital lobe and the parietal lobe work in concert to control hand-eye coordination. Figure 2.14 summarizes each lobe and its primary functions.

It is important to recognize that the divisions of function based on anatomical location given above for the cerebral cortex are oversimplified. Many pathways conduct information through the brain and can function independently, in parallel, or in a hierarchical serial fashion (Zeki, 1993). Moreover, specific pathways may have separate functions. For example, Melvin Goodale and Keith Humphrey (2001) of the University of Western Ontario have conducted research that supports the view (see also Ungerleider and Mishkin, 1982; Courtney and Ungerleider, 1997) that the ventral and dorsal streams of the visual system have separate functions. The

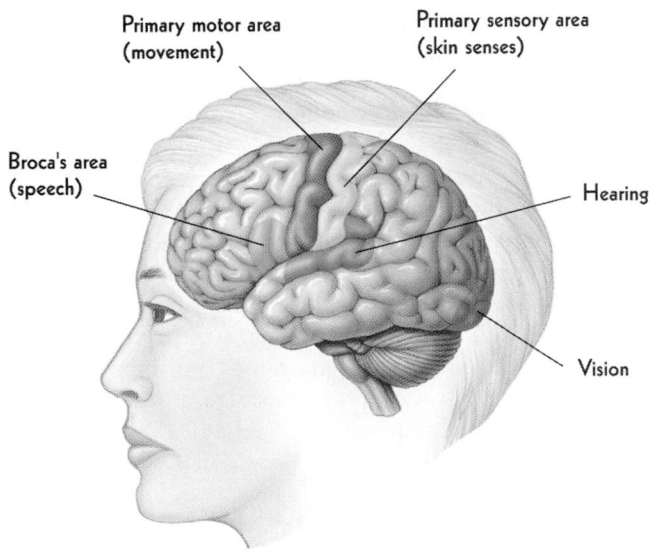

Primary motor area (movement)

Primary sensory area (skin senses)

Broca's area (speech)

Hearing

Vision

Specific areas of the brain control and influence both sensory and motor functions.

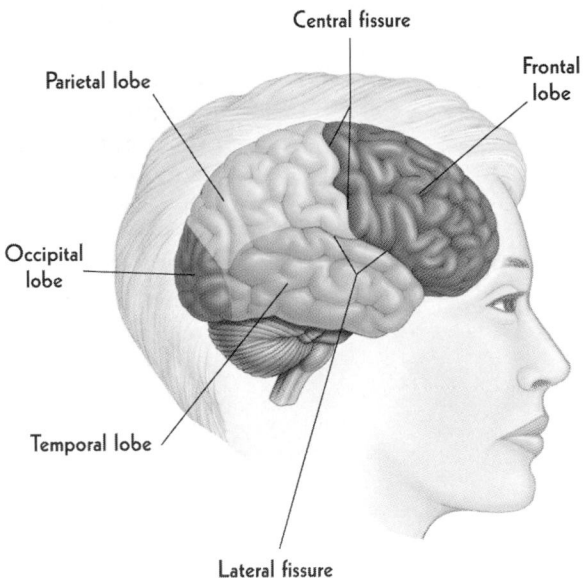

Central fissure

Parietal lobe

Frontal lobe

Occipital lobe

Temporal lobe

Lateral fissure

The *lateral fissure* divides the temporal lobe from the parietal lobe; the *central fissure* divides the frontal lobe from the parietal lobe.

|  | Location | Function |
|---|---|---|
| **Frontal lobe** | In front of the central fissure; contains the motor cortex and Broca's area | Memory Movement Speech and language production |
| **Parietal (paa-RYE-i-tal) lobe** | Behind frontal lobe | Sense of touch and body position |
| **Temporal lobe** | Below lateral fissure and parietal lobe | Speech, hearing, and some visual information processing |
| **Occipital (ok-SIP-i-tal) lobe** | Back of the brain, next to and behind parietal and temporal lobes | Visual sense |
| **Association cortex** | Areas between parietal, temporal, and occipital lobes | Believed to be responsible for complex behaviours that involve thinking and sensory processes |

ventral system is important for perceiving and identifying objects whereas the dorsal system is important for localizing objects. Goodale and Humphrey's work shows that these two systems likely evolved together and play complementary roles. Thus, although it is easier to recall functions for specific areas of the cortex, it is important to remember that this degree of specification is not completely accurate.

## The Brain at Work

In the eighteenth century, people called *phrenologists* measured the size of heads and examined bumps and prominent features such as a large protruding forehead; their reasoning was that prominent features might be associated with certain kinds of thoughts. Today scientists have come a long way from phrenology. They know that the brain plays a central role in controlling behaviour, and they are continually trying to understand it better, but now they use scientific techniques that go far beyond simple observation. Knowledge of the brain and its relationship to behaviour comes about in part through the study of *neuroanatomy*—the structures of the

**FIGURE 2.14**

**The Cortex and the Lobes of the Brain**

The cortex is the exterior covering of the cerebral hemispheres. It consists of four major lobes and the association cortex. The cortex plays a special role in behaviour because it is directly involved in thought.

nervous system. Some neuroanatomists do post-mortem (after death) studies of the brains of people who have died of tumours, brain diseases, and trauma (injury) to the brain. These researchers are attempting to correlate the type of brain damage or disruption with the loss of specific abilities, such as seeing, reading, and writing. Some brain damage occurs through accidents, strokes, and brain tumours; observing the behaviour and mental processes of individuals with known damage provides further information. Neuroanatomists who study behaviour often use *ablation* as a principal technique. In ablation, researchers remove or destroy a portion of an animal's brain and study the animal to determine which behaviours have been disrupted. Today, ablation studies are complemented by electrical recording techniques such as EEGs, MRIs, and CT and PET scans. Still other researchers study brain–behaviour relationships by watching animals or children as they interact with their environment and solve problems.

## MONITORING NEURONAL ACTIVITY

To fully understand neural function, researchers must study a living nervous system; dissection alone will not reveal a complete picture about how the brain works. Researchers have taken several approaches to this problem, including studying the function of a single neuron and using sophisticated technology to see the brain as it works.

One technique is *single unit recording*, in which researchers insert a thin wire, needle, or glass tube containing an electrolyte solution into or next to a single neuron to measure its electrical activity. Because neurons fire extremely rapidly, data are often fed into a computer, which averages the number of times the cell fires in one second or one minute. Scientists typically perform this type of recording technique on the neurons of rats, cats, or monkeys. For example, Brian Bland at the University of Calgary and his colleague Scott Oddie of Red Deer College have extensively mapped the functions of the hippocampus by recording the activities of individual hippocampal neurons under various conditions (Bland & Oddie, 2001; Bland, 2000).

There are widely scattered neural clusters that act together, in synchrony, and identifying all of them is a task of Herculean proportion. However, synchronized neural firing is very relevant to understanding movement and perception; synchronized output from widely spaced neurons may be at the heart of perception and thought, and of consciousness itself (Crick & Koch, 1998; Riehle et al., 1997; Rodriguez et al., 1999). For example, groups of neurons, called cell assemblies, probably represent objects in the visual system by firing synchronously and binding separate kinds of information such as motion, colour, and shape together (Engel et al., 1992). Such synchronized firing of diverse cells has allowed specialization to take place in different brain regions and yet combines neural output for higher-order thought.

Another technique, *electroencephalography*, measures electrical activity in the nervous systems of both animals and human beings. It produces a record of brain wave activity called an **electroencephalogram**, or **EEG** (*electro* means "electrical," *encephalon* means "brain," and *gram* means "record"). A small electrode placed on the scalp records the gross electrical activity of the brain by simultaneously measuring the output of thousands of cells beneath the skull to produce an EEG. EEGs, which generally are computer analyzed, are used for a variety of purposes, including the assessment of brain damage, epilepsy, tumours, and other abnormalities. When brain waves that are normally synchronized become erratic, this is usually evidence of an abnormality requiring further investigation and analysis.

In normal, healthy human beings, EEGs show a variety of characteristic brain wave patterns, depending on the person's level and kind

**ELECTROENCEPHALOGRAM (EEG)** [eel-ECK-tro-en-SEFF-uh-low-gram]
Record of electrical brain wave patterns obtained through electrodes placed on the scalp.

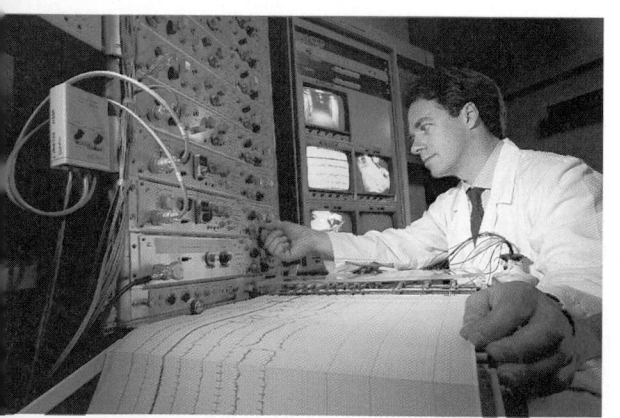
▼ Certain physiological reactions, such as patterns of brain activity, must be measured with instruments to be observable.

of mental activity. Researchers usually describe brain waves in terms of their *frequency* (the number of waves in a unit of time) and *amplitude* (the relative height or size of the waves). If people are awake, relaxed, have their eyes closed, and are not engaged in active thinking, their EEGs are predominantly composed of *alpha waves*, which occur at a moderate rate (frequency) of 8 to 12 cycles per second and are of moderate amplitude. When people are excited, their brain waves change dramatically from alpha waves to *beta waves*, which are of high frequency and low amplitude. At different times during sleep, people show varying patterns of high-frequency and low-frequency brain waves correlated with dreaming activity and restorative functions, both of which are discussed in Chapter 4.

Three revolutionary diagnostic techniques for measuring the activity of the nervous system have emerged in the last two decades: CT, PET, and MRI scanning. **CT (computerized tomography) scans** are computer-assisted X-ray images of the brain (or any area of the body) in three dimensions—essentially a computerized series of X-rays that show photographic slices of part of the brain or body. CT scans are particularly helpful in locating tumours or regions destroyed by strokes, accidents, or other brain abnormalities.

**PET (positron emission tomography)** tracks radioactive markers injected into the bloodstream to enable researchers to observe metabolic activity by recording glucose use taking place in the brain; the scans measure local variations in cerebral blood flow, which is correlated with neural activity. PET scans allow researchers to watch the actual functioning of the brain, to observe how the brain modifies itself as mental activity occurs, and to predict human behaviour from brain functioning. PET scans are relatively new to neuroscientists but research in this area is growing rapidly. For example, the PET scan technique allowed researchers to find a relationship between blood flow and cognitive activity (Koski & Petrides, 2001). Specific brain regions have been found to be associated with specific types of memory or thought processes (Anderson et al., 2000), and those areas showed more blood flow for particular tasks. For example, recall tasks showed greater blood flow compared to recognition tasks (Cabeza & Nyberg, 2000). The potential of PET scans has yet to be fully realized, but researchers are using them to study a wide range of psychological coding processes as well as psychological disorders such as schizophrenia (Andreasen, 1997). The biggest problem with PET scans is that, although they efficiently display cortical function, they lack spatial resolution (resolution is approximately 10 millimetres) and precise anatomical localization of the activated region.

**MRI (magnetic resonance imaging)** uses magnetic fields instead of X-rays to produce brain scans that have far greater clarity and resolution than CT scans. MRI can distinguish brain parts as small as one or two millimeters, providing highly detailed images of the brain's tissue and having the power to reveal many kinds of abnormalities. MRIs are not invasive—nothing needs to be injected—and no radiation is involved, making MRI scans preferred over PET scans in many situations.

A variation of MRI allows observation of the functioning of the brain. **Functional MRI (fMRI)** is an imaging technique that registers changes in the metabolism (energy consumption) of cells in various regions of the brain and thus allows observation of activity in the brain *as it takes place*. A person performs a particular task while the imaging is taking place. The area of the brain responsible for this task experiences an increase in metabolism that ultimately shows up on the fMRI image as a colour change. By having a person perform specific tasks, it is possible to locate the corresponding regions of brain activation (e.g., Reichle, Carpenter, & Just, 2000). Unlike PET, which requires a break between scans (to allow radioactive traces to leave the system), fMRI allows for alternating experimental conditions in the same individual—a distinct and important advantage. And the newest fMRI techniques are exploiting its ability to track changes in brain activity over time (Mitchell et al., 2000; Ng et al., 2000).

Typically, a researcher will image the brains of two or more participants under different experimental conditions and then compare the images and activity of the

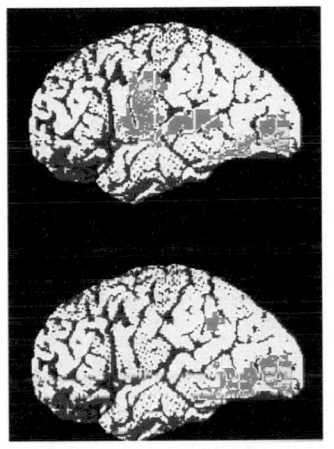

▲ PET scans reveal varying activity in different areas of the brain for reading aloud (top) versus reading silently (bottom).

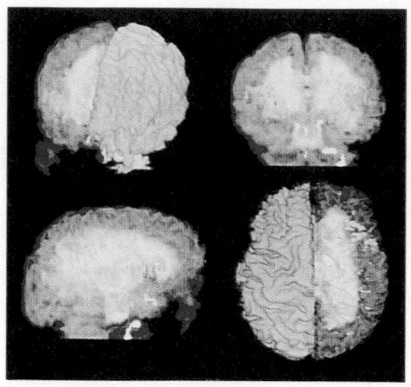

brains in the different conditions and between the two people (e.g., Dupont et al., 2000). Often the participants in one group are healthy individuals and those in a different group have some type of disorder; often the tasks are cognitive ones that require participants to read, imagine, or perhaps calculate. Research shows that specific brain sites are indeed affected by specific tasks. For example, one study that used the fMRI technique showed that individuals with the reading disability dyslexia use their brains differently than, and not as well or efficiently as, individuals without dyslexia (Shaywitz et al., 1998). These researchers asked participants, both normal readers and those with dyslexia, to do tasks such as naming letters and identifying words. Among participants with normal reading ability, the expected areas of the brain became active, notably the visual cortex, the angular gyrus, and the left temporal-parietal area (Wernicke's area). People with dyslexia showed little activity in these areas but activity in other places not typically associated with reading. The researchers asserted that the brain activation patterns provided a "neural signature" for the impairment—that is, a way of identifying and diagnosing it (Fullbright et al., 1997). This example demonstrates the promise of fMRI to investigate brain functioning that accompanies behaviour (Speck et al., 2000). Table 2.2 summarizes the four important imaging techniques we have just discussed.

Remember that imaging techniques such as PET and fMRI do not detect mental activity directly—rather, they measure changes in blood flow or metabolism that are related to energy consumption by brain cells. Nevertheless, these techniques, especially fMRI, are creating a revolution in neuroscience—allowing researchers not only to explore anatomy but also to learn how the brain operates (see Table 2.2). For example, researchers have been able to show that small brain lesions (small areas of damaged brain tissue, often due to disease or injury) are common in elderly people and are a natural part of aging. Further, researchers are establishing tentative links among brain lesions, illness, neurochemistry, and depression. Even newer techniques are being developed, including one that induces a lesion-like disruption of brain activity that allows researchers to investigate attention, discrimination, and

| TABLE 2.2 | Four Important Imaging Techniques |
|---|---|
| **Technique** | **Function and Application** |
| CT (computerized tomography) | Produces computer-enhanced, three-dimensional X-ray images of the brain (or any part of the body), essentially a series of X-rays showing photographic slices of the brain (or other part of the body) |
| PET (positron emission tomography) | Tracks radioactive markers that were injected into the bloodstream, enabling researchers to monitor marked variations in cerebral activity, which are correlated with mental processes |
| MRI (magnetic resonance imaging) | Uses magnetic fields instead of X-rays to produce highly detailed images of brain tissue that have far greater clarity and resolution than CT scans; can distinguish brain parts as small as one or two millimetres |
| fMRI (functional MRI) | Registers changes in the metabolism (energy consumption) of cells in various regions of the brain and thus allows observation of activity in the brain as it takes place |

plasticity. This non-invasive technique is called *transcranial magnetic stimulation (TMS)* (Harmer et al., 2001). TMS is the application of a brief magnetic pulse to the scalp to induce changes in the local electrical activity in the underlying surface of the brain.

Lawyers are now using various brain scans as part of the defence in some criminal trials. For example, an attorney may assert that PET scans show damage to the client's brain that traditional neurological tests could not have found. In one California case, a diagnosis of a mental disorder, confirmed through a PET scan, kept a man from going to the gas chamber.

One caution is necessary when considering all studies involving imaging techniques. Just because there is a correlation between two events—in these cases, brain activity and behaviour—does not mean one *causes* the other in a simple way. Research on brain activity such as that from PET and fMRI studies must be analyzed with caution because many parts of the brain become active simultaneously and neural circuits are widely interconnected. Understanding the causality in these complex patterns will not be simple.

## BRAIN SPECIALIZATION—THE LEFT AND RIGHT OF THINGS

Are there specific places in the brain that control specific behaviours and thoughts? Does one side of the brain have more control over certain behaviours (for example, hand preference—see *Psychology in Action*) than the other side does? Some science writers have concluded that brain hemisphere dominance may affect your choice of occupation, and even your world view. Let's explore the evidence.

### SPLITTING THE BRAIN.

Most of our body's organs are represented bilaterally (arms, legs, kidneys) and do the same thing. We know that human beings can lose one of their kidneys and function well. Our general symmetry may be misleading, however. Studies of brain structure show that different areas of the two-sided brain are responsible for different functions. Noted brain and consciousness expert Robert Ornstein (1997) likens the two sides of the brain to a tale of two cities in which complex operations exist in each hemisphere but are often as different as Montreal and Beijing!

Since the early 1970s, Nobel Prize winner Roger Sperry (1913–1994) and Michael Gazzaniga have been at the forefront of research in brain organization. Gazzaniga has concluded that the human brain has a modular organization—it is divided into discrete units that interact to produce mental activity (Gazzaniga, 2000). Importantly, more recent research suggests that the more experience an organism has with a particular event, situation, or concept, the more specialized the brain becomes (Jacobs, 1997).

Studies by Sperry (1985) and Gazzaniga (1983) show that in most human beings one cerebral hemisphere, usually the left, is specialized for the processing of speech and language; the other, usually the right, appears better able to handle spatial tasks and musical and artistic endeavours. Such hemispheric specialization within the brain frequently is referred to as right or left *brain dominance*. Some of the evidence for such hemispheric specialization comes from studies monitoring brain wave activity in normal participants exposed to different kinds of stimuli. For example, when normal participants are asked to look at or think about letters, or perhaps to rehearse a speech, some characteristic brain wave activity can be detected on the left side of the brain. When these participants are asked to perform creative tasks or are told to reorganize some spatial pattern, brain wave activity is apparent on the right side of the brain. Although studies of brain waves do not yield complete or thoroughly convincing knowledge of brain function or brain structure, evidence is mounting. For example, research using MRI scans supports a left–right distinction for pitch and music perception and indicates a difference between individuals who have perfect pitch and the rest of us (Schlaug et al., 1995). Similarly, an

## Left-handed in a Right-handed World

In his book *The Left-Hander Syndrome* (1992), Stanley Coren, a well-known psychologist at the University of British Columbia, meticulously details the many ways in which a small portion of our population is inconvenienced simply because they use their left hand for most major tasks. In fact, about 10 percent of the population is left-handed, depending on how you define it. Our handedness—left-handedness especially—affects our lives directly.

It appears that only a couple of different genes control whether you use principally your left hand or your right hand—what psychologists call "handedness" (Klar, 1996). One of the genes probably controls whether you are left- or right-hemisphere dominant; the other likely determines whether your brain dominance controls your handedness. Most left-handed people are right-brain dominant, and right-handed people are left-brain dominant. Because handedness is a genetically determined trait, in adoption studies we see a correlation of handedness with biological parents, and not with adoptive parents. Left-handedness is determined before birth, appears in all cultures, and has been observed for thousands of years. Unlike humans, while 54 percent of animals (cats, mice, and rats at least) have a dominant paw, they are virtually equally divided between whether the right paw or the left paw is dominant (Annet, 1985).

However, as with all things, handedness is not entirely genetically determined. There also is a strong environmental contribution; parents reinforce right-handed behaviour and our world is set up to accommodate those who are right-handed. School desks are made to support your right arm and hand for writing. Computer mice are organized and shaped for people who use their right hand. Safety levers on mechanical equipment are placed for right-handed people to grab. Sitting at a crowded table to eat dinner becomes an elbow-clashing ordeal for those who are left-handed. Until recently, left-handed people were discriminated against and parents and teachers were urged to encourage children to switch hands.

Although attitudes are shifting, left-handers continue to face discrimination. Despite recent changes such as specially designed (and more expensive) computer mice, which have reversible buttons for lefties, the world is still structured for the right-handed. As a consequence, left-handed people are more likely to have accidents (Graham & Cleveland, 1995). Perhaps because their accidents are more frequent and more severe, the left-handed suffer more pain from accidents (Coren & Previc, 1996), and even, according to Coren, die at a younger age (Halpern & Coren, 1991). Although this is a hotly disputed assertion (Harris, 1993), it is difficult to prove or disprove.

The research on left-handedness, especially on accidents and death rates, is controversial for a number of reasons, many of which reflect methodological problems. First, to do good research, we have to separate "strong right-handers" from "strong left-handers"—and this often has not been done. How does a researcher define people as left- or right-handed? By which hand they use for writing? Drawing? Throwing a ball? Depending on how one defines left-handedness, it turns out that some people are solely left-handed—they do everything with their left hand. Others are solely right-handed, and many people are ambidextrous (using both hands). For example, up to half of left-handed writers throw a ball with their right hand (McManus et al., 1999). Furthermore, research shows that most right-handed people (about 95 percent) process speech and language exclusively with the left hemispheres of their brains—they are clearly left-hemisphere dominant for many activities. However, only 50 percent of left-handed people process speech and language exclusively in the right hemispheres of their brains—they have a mixed dominance and are more likely to use both hemispheres to process language (Hiscock & Kinsbourne, 1987). Whether left-handed people are at increased risk for illness, accidents, and early death or merely for increased inconvenience has yet to be determined by science.

---

**SPLIT-BRAIN PATIENTS**

People whose corpus callosum, which normally connects the two cerebral hemispheres, has been surgically severed.

array of studies asserts a right-brain dominance for men in spatial tasks but a left-brain dominance for women in reading comprehension (Ornstein, 1997).

What happens to behaviour and mental processes when connections between the left and right sides of the brain are cut? Many important studies have involved **split-brain patients**—typically, these are people with uncontrollable, life-threatening epilepsy. Epilepsy is a neurological disorder in which the affected individual typically suffers recurrent seizures. Split-brain patients have undergone an operation to sever the *corpus callosum* (the band of fibres that connects the left and right hemispheres of the brain) to prevent seizures from spreading across the hemispheres. Special testing revealed that after the operation there was little or no perceptual or cognitive interaction between the hemispheres; the patients seemed to have two distinct, independent brains, each with its own abilities. Yet these patients appeared unaffected by this procedure and were able to live normal, productive lives. Studies of split-brain patients are invaluable to scientists seeking to understand how the brain works—in particular, how the left and right hemispheres function together (e.g., Blanc-Garin, Fauré, & Sabio, 1993). (See Figure 2.15.)

In a normal brain, each cerebral hemisphere is neurologically connected to the opposite side of the body; thus, the left hemisphere normally controls the right side of the body (Johnson, 1998). Split-brain patients are unable to use the speech and language capabilities located in the left hemisphere to describe activities carried out by the right hemisphere. In experimental conditions, when stimulus information is presented exclusively to their left hemispheres (by presenting it in the right visual field while participants stare straight ahead), they can identify the stimulus, describe it, and deal with it in essentially normal ways. However, when the same stimulus is presented to their right hemispheres, they can perform matching tasks (saying that two items are identical) but are unable to describe the stimulus verbally (a left-hemisphere task). Such artificial viewing situations must be generated in a laboratory. In day-to-day life, split-brain patients encounter stimuli that are presented to both hemispheres and so are able to perform normally.

Studies of split-brain patients have revealed that some brain functions are localized in one hemisphere and that many more abilities draw from a complex interconnection of structures (Metcalfe, Funnell, & Gazzaniga, 1995; Walsh, 1999). Lary Mosley of the University of Calgary is among a number of researchers who have contributed to the growing body of brain imaging research. Their research shows that many activities that were considered exclusively left-brain (such as listening to someone speaking) or right-brain functions (such as listening to music) actually involve both hemispheres (Doty, 1999; Waldie & Mosley, 2000). Philip Bryden, who worked at the University of Waterloo prior to his untimely death in 1996, developed a formal causal model of the Geschwind theory of cerebral lateralization (Geschwind &

## FIGURE 2.15
## The Effects of Severing the Corpus Callosum

Imagine that a man whose corpus callosum has been severed is staring directly before him at a screen on either side of which a researcher can flash words or pictures. The researcher flashes a picture of an apple on the right side of the screen. The man is able to name the image because it has been sent via his optic nerve only to his brain's left hemisphere—where verbal processing occurs. When the researcher flashes the word *spoon* on the left side of the screen, the man's optic nerve sends an image exclusively to his right hemisphere—which predominantly processes nonverbal stimuli. Now, because the right hemisphere is nonverbal, when the man is asked to name what he sees on the screen, he is unable to name the image as the word *spoon*. If he is asked to use his right hand, which is controlled by the left hemisphere, to pick out the object named on the screen (a spoon) from several objects, by touch alone, he will not be able to do so. However, if the man is asked to use his left hand to touch the object named on the screen, he can do so. The left hand is controlled by the right hemisphere, which is spatially adept and has been exposed to the word *spoon*.

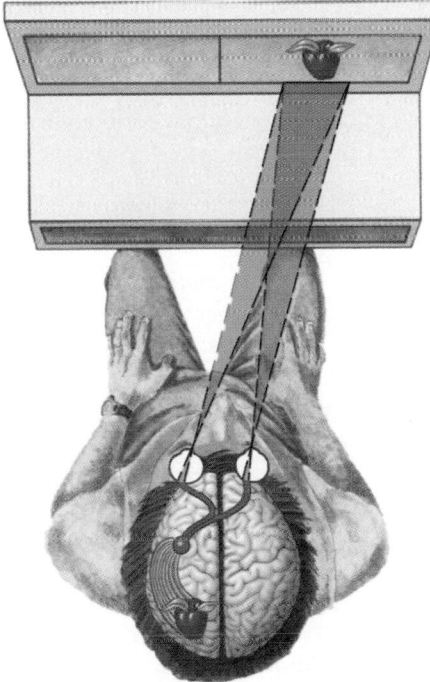

"I see an apple."

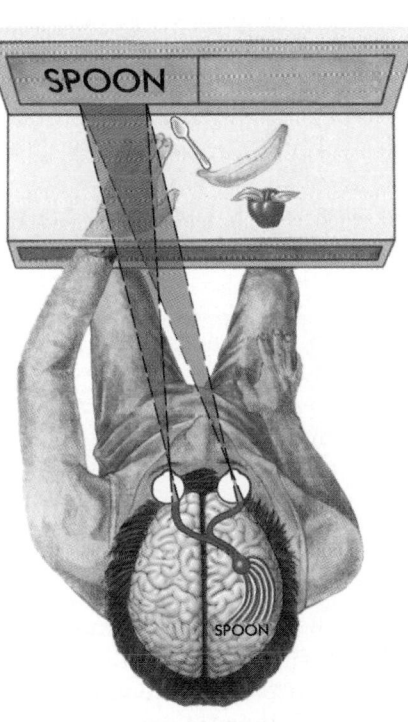

"I don't know what the image is."

Galaburda, 1985a, 1985b, 1985c) by focusing on handedness patterns and investigating cross-cultural differences (Ida & Bryden, 1996) as well as genetic explanations of hand preference (McManus et al., 1999; Bryden et al., 1997).

There is no doubt that human beings and other animals exhibit lateralization and specificity of functions. Unfortunately, the popular press and TV newscasters oversimplify the specificity of functions and, in some cases, overgeneralize their significance to account for school problems, marital problems, artistic abilities, and gender differences. One example in the popular misconception of hemispheric specialization is that the right hemisphere is "creative." This belief is an overgeneralization from the right hemisphere's abilities in spatial visualization and drawing. The right hemisphere *is* better at drawing, but not necessarily more creative than the left; it depends on the task. For example, the right hemisphere is not capable of creative writing, and both hemispheres must work together to produce poetry—the left hemisphere must find the words and the right hemisphere must construct the meter. Typically, the two hemispheres work together in everyday tasks; for example, the left side of the brain may recognize a stimulus, but the right side is necessary to put that recognition into context (Doty, 1999).

The full extent of hemispheric specialization is yet to be determined. Although it is recognized that the left side of the brain performs a recognition task and that the right side is necessary to put that recognition into context (Ornstein, 1997), most scientists and critical thinkers maintain a healthy scepticism about the existence of "two minds" in one.

**GENDER AND THE BRAIN.** People's misconceptions of brain hemispheric specialization have also led to theories on gender differences. Although there *are* studies indicating that men and woman have differences in their cerebral hemisphere functioning (see below), this research has led some people to the false conclusion that there are masculine and feminine sides of the brain. The left side is seen as logical and rational and thus masculine, and the right side is considered to be emotional and holistic and thus feminine. This theory is mistaken not only in its gender stereotyping but also in its overgeneralization of the findings on the brain's hemispheres.

Recent research does indicate that men's and women's brains may differ in their cerebral hemispheres. The best evidence shows that women are less lateralized than men (Springer & Deutsch, 1998). Men have their language functions more strongly lateralized in the left hemisphere and their spatial functions in the right, while women have both abilities distributed in both hemispheres. PET and fMRI imaging has confirmed these differences in studies where men and women have solved problems as their brain functions are scanned. For example, when asked to decide on rhyming words (a language-related task), men's brains became active in their left hemispheres and women's brains became active in both hemispheres (Shaywitz et al., 1995).

Do these studies indicate that women's and men's brains function differently? And if so, does one gender's brain function "better" than the other gender's? Recent research suggests that there is no clear answer to the first question—while some studies such as the rhyming study discussed above do show gender differences, the results are still considered inconclusive. For example, the differences demonstrated in the rhyming study reflected average differences between the brains of men and women, but not every individual in this study conformed to the pattern typical of his or her gender. That is, individuals varied in their patterns of brain activation—about 40 percent of the women showed an activation pattern typical of men. This point leads to an important caution to keep in mind—individual variation is much larger than the gender differences between men's and women's cerebral hemispheres. The second question is far easier to answer: These studies have not shown a performance difference in the tasks; rather, they have shown only a difference in brain activation patterns. Both men and women were able to perform the same tasks equally well.

## PLASTICITY AND CHANGE

Basic brain organization is established well before birth and does not change in any substantial way after birth; however, details of brain structure and functions, particularly in the cerebral cortex, are subject to continued growth and development. What happens in one cell affects what happens in neighbouring cells, so psychologists recognize that the brain is still *malleable* (changeable), especially during the formative years. This ability to change is often referred to as *plasticity* (see *Brain and Behaviour*). Within limits, the nervous system can be modified and fine-tuned by experience, which can be acquired over many years (Shatz, 1992), and the brain can be trained to relearn and simulate previous learning that may have been lost through an accident or some other brain trauma (Singer, 1995; Hinton, Plaut, & Shallice, 1993).

Experience with specific stimuli reinforces the development of neural structures (Kilgard & Merzenich, 1998). The developing brain can be likened to a highway system that expands with use. Less travelled roads are abandoned, but popular ones are broadened and new ones are added as needed. When neural structures are used, reused, and constantly updated, they become faster and more easily accessed (Moser et al., 1998; Zhang et al., 1997). Brain circuitry is constantly changing as a function of experience. Bryan Kolb and his colleagues at the University of Lethbridge are attempting to discover how factors such as stress, drugs, pre- and postnatal experiences, and many others influence brain organization and function. During early fetal and infant development, the neural links, connections, and interconnections are embellished (Crair, Gillespie, & Stryker, 1998) and if unused may begin to disappear (Colman, Nabekura, & Lichtman, 1997). Such elaboration and refinement is greater when organisms are placed in complex, super-enriched (for example, visually stimulating) environments (Chang, Isaacs, & Greenough, 1991). For example, one study showed that children with language-based learning impairments could be taught to use repetitive and adaptive training exercises to overcome their problems. The exercises are assumed to change neuronal structures and allow improvement in speech and language processing (Merzenich et al., 1996).

Can enhanced plasticity in fetal cells be used to treat damaged or diseased brains? For example, could we transplant brain tissue from a healthy individual to one who is ill? Researchers are focusing on this question in an effort to help patients with brain disorders such as Alzheimer's disease or Parkinson's disease. Neurotransplantation techniques in which either fetal cells or stem cells are transplanted to replace damaged structures have shown mixed results. The outcomes for Parkinson's patients who underwent bilateral transplantation of fetal substantia nigra cells (to reintroduce dopamine-releasing cells) have been mixed, with some patients experiencing modest improvements, others responding little if at all (Kopyov et al., 1996), and still others experiencing debilitating and uncontrollable writhing and chewing movements (Greene et al., 2000). So, can this type of intervention work? Maybe. With such ambiguous results and with the many ethical issues involved but such unlimited potential, this debate has only begun.

## Hormones and Glands

In 1978, Dan White fatally shot both San Francisco mayor George Moscone and city supervisor Harvey Milk. In court, White's attorney successfully argued that a diet of junk food had jumbled his client's brain and reduced his capacity for moral behaviour. White spent only three years in prison for committing the double homicide. Although

**Be an ACTIVE LEARNER**

**REVIEW**
> Describe the subdivisions of the autonomic nervous system. pp. 58–59
> Identify the differences between single unit recording and the EEG. pp. 68–69
> Why is the corpus callosum so essential to effective communication in the brain? pp. 65, 72–74

**THINK CRITICALLY**
> What do you think would happen to behaviour if the pons were damaged?
> What is the *potential* function of the convolutions of the cortex?
> If the brain is so malleable and sensitive to change, what—if anything—can individuals do to optimize their growth and potential?

**APPLY PSYCHOLOGY**
> Think about the scientific and ethical implications we would face if we could find a way to help brain cells regrow in damaged areas. How would your thinking about this possibility change if you knew that the most promising way to do this involves using cells grown from tissue collected from miscarried or aborted fetuses? This is an example of an increasingly large number of biomedical ethics issues we will have to face very soon.

## What If You Lost Just a Bit of Your Brain?

What would be the effect if someone lost a part of his or her brain? Even for the purposes of scientific research researchers cannot ethically "mess around with people's brains" in the literal sense. This question really asks how we might determine what parts of our brains do. Wilder Penfield, a professor of neurology and neurosurgery at McGill University from 1933 to 1954, was interested in this very question. While performing neurosurgery on live patients under local anesthetic he would electrically stimulate areas of the exposed brain with a *minute* charge. Medically, this assisted him in determining which areas of the brain were damaged. Interestingly, when patients underwent this procedure they would occasionally report that they had remembered something from long ago. Unfortunately, it was difficult to verify if what the patient reported was an actual memory of an actual event that had occurred years earlier. It also could have been a kind of waking dream caused by the electrical stimulation but *not* reflective of a real memory. So, if electrical stimulation doesn't yield reliable results, how might we study the functions of certain brain regions?

One method is to observe the effects of brain surgery performed for medically necessary reasons. For example, removing a substantial portion of the temporal lobe can stop uncontrollable, debilitating seizures in some patients. Claude Braun of the Cognitive Neuroscience Centre at the Université du Québec à Montréal, Jeanette McGlone of Dalhousie University and the Queen Elizabeth II Health Sciences Centre, and Natalie Philips of Concordia University have each studied the effects of temporal lobectomies on human patients. They were interested in how such radical surgery affected these patients, but were also committed to determining whether the benefits of temporal lobectomy are worth the costs in terms of effects on cognitive functioning.

Braun (Braun et al., 1994) compared the facial and emotional recognition performance of people with right or left temporal lobectomies as well as the performance of some right or left frontal lobectomized individuals. Findings indicated that the temporal lobectomized participants, on average, scored about 22 percent lower than the comparison group on facial and emotional recognition (both thought to be temporal lobe functions).

McGlone (McGlone & Wands, 1991) studied the effects of temporal lobectomies on people's memory. She compared the reports of memory functioning of some temporal lobectomized people with that of a number of people awaiting the procedure as well as a non-epileptic comparison group. The results suggested that both the lobectomized and the pre-surgery groups reported deficits in memory abilities. This suggests that memory loss may be attributed both to the epilepsy itself and to the removal of the affected brain lobe. However, a follow-up three years after the surgery indicated that the lobectomized individuals began to show improvements in memory while the memory functioning of those waiting for surgery continued to decline, suggesting that the epilepsy itself posed a greater risk to memory loss than did the surgery.

Phillips and McGlone (1995) tested 50 temporal lobectomized patients one year after surgery. They assessed the participants' general neurological functioning and directly assessed their memory abilities. They found that on the majority of measures (68 percent) there was no change in functioning, and that on the remaining measures people were as likely to improve as to do worse. This finding suggests that the benefits of such surgery seem to outweigh the costs.

In making sense of these studies it is important to bear in mind that they are all correlational studies, so their results *do not* allow us to say that memory and/or facial and emotional recognition resides in the temporal lobe. Researchers can only infer that the temporal lobe is involved in these functions.

Moreover, these results do not mean that psychosurgery will always be of benefit to the patient. Donald Struss, an expert on frontal lobes, led a study at the Rotman Research Institute (affiliated with the University of Toronto). The data from this study indicate that damage to the frontal lobes can significantly change personality, causing affected individuals to be less empathic and sympathetic, to make inappropriate judgments, and to lose the ability to appreciate humour. The data suggest that these effects are particularly noticeable when damage has occurred to the right frontal lobe. Damage to the left frontal lobe is associated with loss of language function. In fact, prefrontal lobotomies performed regularly in the late 1940s to treat mental illness (see Valenstein, 1986) were of little therapeutic benefit and were associated with a lack of moral understanding, an inability to plan, dulled emotional affect (unresponsive), epilepsy, and loss of bladder control. For this reason, in every case, the benefits of surgery must be scientifically weighed against the costs of the surgery.

the "Twinkie defence" is no longer a legal defence in California, White's lawyer capitalized on the fact that a person's body chemistry—even an imbalance in blood sugar levels—can have a dramatic impact on behaviour. It is true that body chemistry, hormones, and learned experiences can work together to influence a person. But does this render people unaccountable for their own actions, as Dan White's lawyer claimed?

Combinations of factors are usually the answer to many complex psychological questions, but research shows that some abilities and behaviours have a direct hormonal link—that is, hormones directly affect the behaviour. For example, in a paper presented at a scientific meeting in 1988, psychologist Doreen Kimura of the University of Western Ontario reported that when some women experience low estrogen levels during and immediately after menstruation, they excel at spatial tasks but perform less well on motor tasks. The differences are small and do not occur in all women. Work in this area is in its early stages, but it is interesting because of the links indicated between hormones and behaviour and because of the differences observed between men and women. The links are mediated by the endocrine glands and show the complexity of the relationship of behaviour, body structures, and hormones and other substances that flow through our bodies.

## ENDOCRINE GLANDS

Throughout each day, glands manufacture and secrete substances that affect many of our behaviours. Psychologists are particularly interested in the **endocrine glands**—ductless glands that secrete hormones directly into the bloodstream, rather than through a specific duct into a target organ. (See Figure 2.16 for the location of several endocrine glands.) **Hormones** are chemicals produced by the endocrine glands that regulate the activities of specific organs or cells; they travel through the bloodstream to target organs containing cells that respond specifically to particular hormones. Although researchers do not know the extent to which hormones control people's behaviour, there is no doubt that the glandular system is involved in regulating bodily activities. Each hormone affects behaviour and eventually other glands, which in turn affect other behaviours. A disorder in the thyroid, for example, affects not only the metabolic rate but also the pituitary gland, which in turn regulates many other glands. The glands, hormones, and target organs interact; the brain initiates the release of hormones, which affect the target organs, which in turn affect behaviour, which in turn affects the brain, and so on. *Point/Counterpoint* explores the question of whether gender differences are caused by hormones.

**ENDOCRINE [END-oh-krin] GLANDS**

Ductless glands that secrete hormones directly into the bloodstream, rather than through a specific duct into a target organ.

**HORMONES**

Chemicals produced by endocrine glands that regulate the activities of specific organs or cells.

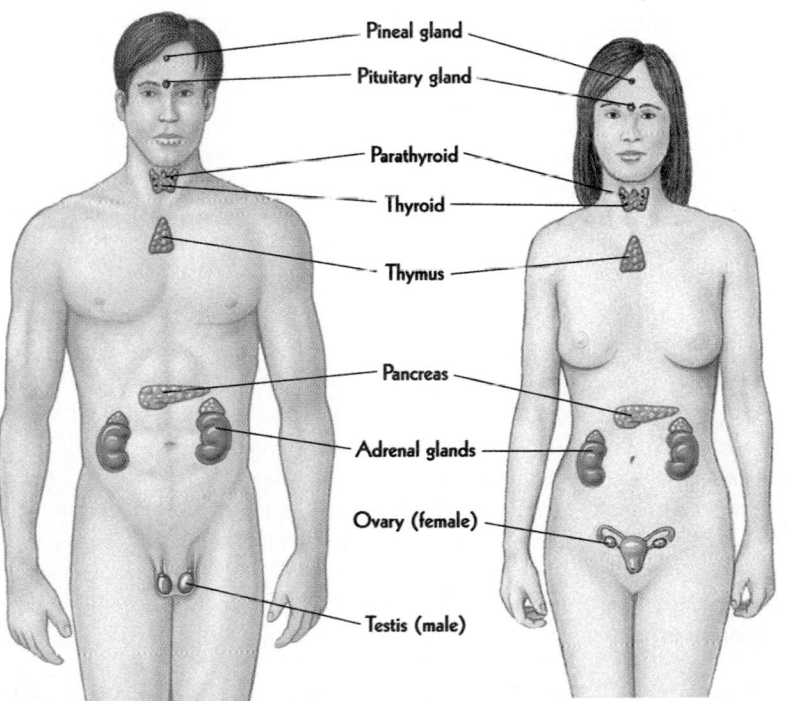

**FIGURE 2.16**

**The Endocrine Glands**

The endocrine glands are situated throughout the body. Though small in size, they exert enormous influences on behaviour.

Pineal gland
Pituitary gland
Parathyroid
Thyroid
Thymus
Pancreas
Adrenal glands
Ovary (female)
Testis (male)

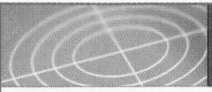 

POINT Counterpoint

## Do Gender Differences Lie in Our Brains or in Our Glands?

**POINT:** Men's and women's brains start out very similar and are then changed by the different hormones they are exposed to in ways that can produce structural brain differences.

**COUNTERPOINT:** As we change the social structures that limit our behavioural options we are seeing fewer and fewer differences between men and women. This means that many of the differences we observe have societal and not brain structure origins.

Some people believe that men and women are essentially the same; however, research does show some important biological and behavioural differences. In recent years, research on gender differences in brain organization has created a volatile debate.

Let's look at some facts. During fetal development, sex hormones are present in the fetus and help create sexual differentiation. Sex hormones also are thought to create permanent changes in brain development that become evident in later behaviour. Research shows that, on average, men do better than women on some spatial tasks—for example, the mental rotation of objects (Linn & Petersen, 1985). Men also do better, on average, in mathematical reasoning and in some motor tasks, such as guiding projectiles through space (Halpern, 1986).

By contrast, women do better than men on some perceptual tasks—for example, the rapid matching of items. Women have greater verbal fluency than men and outperform men in some arithmetic calculations (Hyde, Fennema, & Lamon, 1990). They also do better than men at reading emotions from photographs. For other tasks on which both sexes do equally well—for example, rhyming— men and women use different areas of the brain to perform the task (Shaywitz et al., 1995). Women tend to use both sides of the brain in cognitive tasks such as spelling, for example; men use primarily the left side of the brain. While women use both ears equally, men favour the right ear. Not all gender differences appear at all ages and at all phases of learning, however. Gender differences in problem solving, for example, tend to favour females in elementary school and males after puberty (Hyde, Fennema, & Lamon, 1990).

At birth, human brains are remarkably alike. Doreen Kimura (2000, 2002) of Simon Fraser University asserts that differing patterns of abilities probably reflect different hormonal influences after birth, which result in structural asymmetries. In males, androgens (male hormones) predominate; they may affect the size and function of brain structures such as the hypothalamus. For example, when newborn rats are administered large doses of androgens, their brains develop differently than when

they are administered large doses of estrogens (female hormones), and this difference alters their behavioural abilities permanently.

Of course, making the leap to human beings is difficult, because ethics preclude the manipulation of hormone levels of newborns. However, it is possible to make inferences from hormone levels and task performance in humans. Researchers have measured the abilities of human adults while simultaneously measuring their levels of the male hormone testosterone. Testosterone is present in all human beings, although men show significantly higher levels than women do. Valerie Shute measured these levels in men and women and found that women with high levels of testosterone performed better on spatial tasks than women with low levels; in men, the reverse was true. Shute's conclusion was that testosterone levels in men and women affect performance (Shute et al., 1983).

Are gender differences also influenced by the social environment—by the way in which individuals are raised? The answer to this question is certainly yes. Some gender differences may be biologically based, but Western culture emphasizes and encourages them. Psychologist Sandra Lipsitz Bem (1993) asserts that many traditionally held gender stereotypes are embedded in culture and in social institutions and perpetuate a society that values males more than females. For example, boys traditionally have been encouraged to participate in rough-and-tumble sports, while girls have been encouraged to take part in domestic activities. Men traditionally have been expected to be the providers—the wage earners and problem solvers—whereas women have been expected to be the nurturers—mothers and caregivers.

Today, however, more men and women in Western societies are sharing roles and responsibilities; in raising children, many parents are showing a greater understanding that boys and girls should have equal opportunities. The effects of changing societal values are becoming more evident in individual behaviour. In some Western cultures, differences between men and women that have long been apparent are diminishing; access to and enrolment in courses where problem solving is encouraged—for example, engineering or physics—are increasing among women. Unfortunately, many girls experience direct and indirect devaluing from peers, parents, and teachers (Reiss et al., 2000) and avoid advanced mathematics and science courses due to diminished self-esteem (Benbow & Arjmand, 1990). This in turn perpetuates stereotypes and in some cases causes discrimination. In Chapter 11, we'll discuss the fact that many differences between males and females in mathematical ability are exceedingly small and perhaps social in origin, and that the extent of those differences is shrinking each year.

Most important is the fact that *there are usually more differences within a gender than between genders*. For example, there are greater differences among individual women's spatial abilities than between women's and men's spatial abilities. This idea is especially important to consider when you are trying to determine the relevance of gender differences you may observe. It becomes impossible to generalize results to all people if the data are taken only from a small sample of women or men.

**SEXUAL BEHAVIOUR.** In newborn animals, hormones have an irreversible effect on sexual behaviour—they set specific behaviour patterns in motion by permanently affecting brain development. In human adults, sexual behaviour is to some extent under hormonal control. One study, for example, showed a significant correlation between married couples' hormone levels and frequency of intercourse (Persky, 1978). Hormones such as testosterone and estrogen, whose release is affected by the pituitary gland, the adrenal gland, the testes, and the ovaries, are certainly involved in sexual activity.

**PITUITARY GLAND.** The most important endocrine gland is the **pituitary gland,** which is often called the body's master gland because it regulates the actions of many other endocrine glands (see Figure 2.17). The pituitary gland is located at the base of the brain and is directly controlled by the hypothalamus. One of its major functions is the control of growth hormones.

PITUITARY
[pit-YOU-ih-tare-ee] GLAND
The body's master gland located at the base of the brain and closely linked to the hypothalamus; regulates the actions of other endocrine glands; major function is the control of growth hormones.

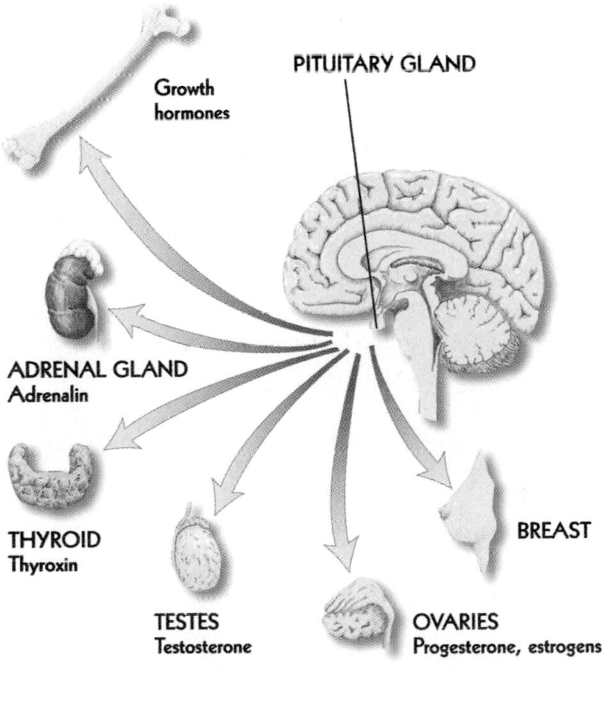

**FIGURE 2.17**
**The Pituitary Gland**

The pituitary gland is often called the body's master gland because it regulates many of the other endocrine glands. Located at the base of the brain, the pea-sized pituitary gland affects behaviour indirectly through control of other glands and directly through release of hormones—including growth hormones and sex hormones—into the bloodstream.

## Be an
# ACTIVE
# LEARNER

**REVIEW**

> What evidence has led researchers to conclude that hormonal differences in development affect behaviour in adulthood? pp. 75–77, 79–80

> Why are researchers justified in concluding that the pituitary gland is the master gland? pp. 79–80

**THINK CRITICALLY**

> What are the social implications of the conclusion researchers have reached about gender differences in intellectual and other abilities? Should men and women be expected to do things differently?

**APPLY PSYCHOLOGY**

> We suspect you can think of several behaviours that you identify as being *male* or *female* at a basic level. Make a short list of those behaviours (for example, aggressiveness, nurturing, etc.) and think about what you believe to be the bases of those behaviours (for example, biological or social). Now see if you can construct an alternative sociocultural explanation.

INSULIN

A hormone produced by the pancreas; facilitates the transport of sugar from the blood into body cells, where it is metabolized.

DIABETES MELLITUS

[mel-LIGHT-us]

A condition in which too little insulin is produced, causing sugar to be transported insufficiently out of the blood and into body cells.

HYPOGLYCEMIA

[hi-po-gly-SEE-me-uh]

A condition in which overproduction of insulin results in a very low blood sugar level.

The pea-sized pituitary gland is divided into two lobes, the anterior and the posterior. Secretions from the lobes produce direct changes in bodily functions, such as growth, and affect other glands. The *anterior lobe* produces a number of hormones—including those that stimulate the thyroid and adrenal glands, each of which controls specific behaviours; growth hormones (called somatotrophins), which control the body's development; and sex hormones (called gonadotrophins), which are involved in sexual behaviour. A person's psychological state influences the secretions from the anterior pituitary; for example, viewing sexually explicit films raises the level of gonadotrophins (LaFerla, Anderson, & Schalch, 1978). The *posterior lobe* of the pituitary gland stores and secretes two major hormones, antidiuretic hormone (ADH) and oxytocin. ADH is a vasopressin, acting on the kidneys to increase fluid absorption and decrease the amount of urine produced by the body as well as constricting blood vessels and hence raising blood pressure. Oxytocin stimulates uterine contractions in pregnant women and causes labour to begin. It also helps nursing mothers release milk.

**PANCREAS.** Another endocrine gland, the *pancreas*, is involved in regulating the body's sugar levels. Sugar in the blood determines a person's energy level. When blood sugar is high, people are energetic; when it is low, they feel weak and tired. Cells in the pancreas called the *islets of Langerhans* control the production of **insulin**—the pancreatic hormone that facilitates the transport of sugar into body cells, where it is metabolized. Two insulin-related problems are diabetes and hypoglycemia. **Diabetes mellitus** is a condition in which an insufficient amount of insulin is produced, causing sugar to be transported inefficiently out of the bloodstream into the cells and thus allowing too much sugar to accumulate in the blood. Some types of this condition can be treated through diet and weight loss, while other types require regular injections of insulin. If the pancreas errs in the opposite direction, the result is hypoglycemia. **Hypoglycemia** is a very low blood sugar level caused by the overproduction of insulin. Hypoglycemic patients have little energy. The condition usually can be controlled through diet, with careful monitoring of types of food eaten and daily calorie intake.

**ADRENAL GLANDS.** The *adrenal glands*, which are also involved in behaviour, are located just above the kidneys and are divided into two parts. The *adrenal medulla*, located deep within each adrenal gland, produces epinephrine (adrenalin), a substance that dramatically alters energy levels and affects a person's reactions to stress through stimulation of the sympathetic nervous system. Imagine that you are being chased through a dark alley. The release of epinephrine makes your heart pound and gives you a burst of energy to help you outdistance your pursuer. The *adrenal cortex*, the outer layer that covers each adrenal gland, secretes a hormone that is involved in growth and development as well as others that are involved in increasing blood sugar levels and boosting energy.

# Summary and Review

## EVOLUTIONARY PSYCHOLOGY, BEHAVIOURAL GENETICS, AND GENES

### What is the distinction between nature and nurture?

> Psychologists generally assert that human behaviour is influenced by both *nature* (heredity) and *nurture* (environment). Psychologists study the biological bases of behaviour to better understand how these two variables interact.   **pp. 42–43**

### What is evolutionary psychology, and why has it become so important?

> *Evolutionary psychology* is the psychological perspective that seeks to explain and predict behaviour by analyzing how the human brain developed over time, how it functions, and how input from the social environment affects human behaviour; it seeks to explain human behaviour by considering how behaviour is affected from the vantage point of evolutionary biology.   **p. 43**

> Evolutionary theory assumes that natural selection shapes physiology and behaviour—*natural selection* is the principle that among the range of behaviours those that help organisms adapt, be fit, and survive are the ones that will be passed on to successive generations because flexible, fit individuals have a greater chance of reproduction. When a trait or inherited characteristic increases in the population, *adaptation* has occurred.   **p. 43, 45**

> From an evolutionary perspective a person's current state of evolutionary development reflects traits and behaviours that have enabled survival in the world.   **p. 45**

### How is behavioural genetics distinct from evolutionary psychology?

> Behavioural genetics focuses on the role of specific genetic contributions to individual difference rather than on trying to account for characteristics shared by an entire species.   **p. 46**

> Identical twins share most of their genetic heritage; they come from one ovum and one sperm and are always the same sex. Fraternal twins are produced by two ova and two sperm and therefore can be both males, both females, or one male and one female. They share genetic characteristics to the same degree as other siblings do. Studying twins allows researchers to clarify the effects of nature and nurture on developmental processes.   **p. 48**

### What do we mean by heritability?

> When scientists say that a trait is *heritable,* especially when they attach a percentage to that heritability, they mean that a percentage of the variation (differences) among a group of people is attributable to heredity.   **p. 47**

### What is the human genome, and why is it important?

> The *genome* is the total DNA blueprint of heritable traits contained in every cell of the body. *Genetic mapping* involves dividing the chromosomes into smaller fragments that can be characterized, and ordering (mapping) the fragments to reflect their respective locations on specific chromosomes. Researchers have identified the exact location or sites of genes contributing to an array of traits; they argue that the nature of family social interactions has a genetic basis because elements of personality, maladjustment, and language acquisition may be genetically determined (at least in part).   **pp. 48–49**

### What is genetics, and why do psychologists study it?

> *Genetics* is the study of heredity—the biological transmission of traits and characteristics from parents to offspring. *Chromosomes* carry each person's inherited genetic makeup. Each chromosome contains thousands of *genes*, made up of DNA. Genes are the basic unit of heredity. The twenty-third pair of chromosomes determines the sex of a fetus.   **pp. 49–50**

> One's *genotype* is one's genetic makeup and is fixed at birth; but one's genotype may or may not be seen in observable characteristics. One's observable characteristics are one's *phenotype,* shaped by genotype and by the environment. Changes in gene replication produce *mutations,* which are the principal source of genetic diversity.   **p. 50**

#### KEY TERMS

genetics, p. 42; nature, p. 42; nurture, p. 42; evolutionary psychology, p. 43; natural selection, p. 43, adaptation, p. 45; correlational study, p. 45; correlation coefficient, p. 45; behavioural genetics, p. 46; heritability, p. 47; genome, p. 48; genetic mapping, p. 48; chromosomes, p. 49; genes, p. 49; genotype, p. 51; phenotypes, p. 51; mutations, p. 51

## COMMUNICATION IN THE NERVOUS SYSTEM

### Describe the full journey of a neural impulse from one neuron to another.

> The basic unit of the *nervous system* is the *neuron,* or nerve cell, made up of *dendrites,* a cell body, an *axon,* and axon terminals. The space between the axon terminals and another neuron is the *synapse.*   **pp. 51–53**

> The *action potential* is caused by the stimulation of the neuron. If there is enough stimulation at the cell body to exceed the threshold, a spike discharge occurs (with a rapid reversal of cell membrane polarity). The neuron fires on an *all-or-none* basis and has a *refractory period,* during which it cannot fire. The action potential

propagates down the axon and stimulates the release of *neurotransmitters* that reside in the axon terminal's synaptic vesicles. The neurotransmitters move across the synaptic gap and bind to receptor sites on the neighbouring cells, thereby conveying information to other neurons.   **pp. 54–55**

## What is the focus of psychopharmacology?

> Psychopharmacology is the study of how drugs affect behaviour. Research often focuses on *agonists* and *antagonists*. An agonist is a chemical that mimics or facilitates the actions of a neurotransmitter, usually by occupying receptor sites. An antagonist is a chemical that opposes the actions of a neurotransmitter, usually by preventing it from occupying receptor sites.   **pp. 57–58**

**KEY TERMS**

nervous system, p. 51; neuron, p. 51; afferent neurons, p. 51; efferent neurons, p. 51; dendrites, p. 52; axon, p. 52; synapse, p. 53; action potential, p. 54; all-or-none, p. 55; refractory period, p. 55; neurotransmitters, p. 55; neuromodulator, p. 57; agonist, p. 57; antagonist, p. 57

## ORGANIZATION OF THE NERVOUS SYSTEM
### Describe the subdivisions of the nervous system.

> The nervous system is composed of two subsystems: the central and peripheral nervous systems. The *central nervous system* consists of the brain and the *spinal cord*. The *peripheral nervous system* carries information to and from the spinal cord and brain through spinal and cranial nerves. The peripheral nervous system is further divided into the *somatic* and *autonomic nervous systems*. The autonomic nervous system is made up of two divisions: the *sympathetic* and *parasympathetic nervous systems*, each having different functions.   **pp. 58–61**

**KEY TERMS**

peripheral nervous system, p. 58; somatic nervous system, p. 58; autonomic nervous system, p. 59; sympathetic nervous system, p. 59; parasympathetic nervous system, p. 59; central nervous system, p. 60; spinal cord, p. 60

## ORGANIZATION OF THE BRAIN
### What are the major sections of the brain, and what are its structures?

> The *brain* is divided into three sections: the hindbrain, the midbrain, and the forebrain (which includes the cortex). The *hindbrain* consists of four main structures: the *medulla*, the reticular formation, the *pons*, and the *cerebellum*. The *midbrain* is made up of nuclei that receive afferent signals from other parts of the brain and from the spinal cord, interpret them, and either relay the information to other parts of the brain or cause the body to act at once. The *forebrain* is the largest and most complicated brain structure; it comprises the *thalamus* and the *hypothalamus*, the *limbic system*, the basal ganglia,

the corpus callosum, and the *cortex*. Two prominent structures of the cortex are the deep fissures—the lateral fissure and the central fissure—that divide the cortex's four lobes: frontal, parietal, temporal, and occipital.   **pp. 61–67**

**KEY TERMS**

brain, p. 61; hindbrain, p. 62; medulla, p. 62; pons, p. 63; cerebellum, p. 63; midbrain, p. 63; forebrain, p. 64; thalamus, p. 64; hypothalamus, p. 64; limbic system, p. 65; cortex, p. 65; convolutions, p. 65

## THE BRAIN AT WORK
### Describe several techniques for studying brain activity and functions.

> One technique for measuring the activity of the nervous system is single-unit recording, in which scientists record the activity of a single cell by placing an electrode within or next to the cell. Another technique uses graphical records of brain wave patterns, called *electroencephalograms (EEGs)*, to assess neurological disorders and the types of activities that occur during thought, sleep, and other behaviours.   **pp. 68–69**

> Three significant techniques for measuring the activity of the nervous system have been developed in the past two decades. *CT (computerized tomography) scans* are computer-enhanced X-ray images. *PET (positron emission tomography)* uses radioactive markers to allow researchers to capture an image showing which brain areas are most active during various mental processes. *MRI (magnetic resonance imaging)* uses magnetism rather than radiation and produces a higher resolution image than CT scans. *Functional MRI (fMRI)* is an imaging technique that allows researchers to observe brain activity as it takes place, while a participant performs a task.   **pp. 69–71**

### How does the function of the left and right hemisphere differ?

> Research shows that in most human beings one cerebral hemisphere—usually the left—is specialized for processing speech and language; the other—usually the right—appears better able to handle spatial, musical, and drawing tasks.   **pp. 71–72**

> Normal cerebral hemispheres are connected to each other by the corpus callosum. *Split-brain patients* have their cerebral hemispheres surgically disconnected and as a result they cannot internally access their left hemisphere language functions from their right hemisphere or their right hemisphere spatial capabilities from their left hemisphere.   **pp. 72–74**

### What does it mean to say that the brain is plastic?

> The brain is malleable, or able to change during development. Brain circuitry is modified by experience. This is particularly true for infants and children, but is also true for adults.   **p. 75**

> This plasticity means that the brain has the ability to recover, at least in part, from trauma. **p. 75**

**KEY TERMS**

electroencephalogram (EEG), p. 68; CT (computerized tomography) scans, p. 69; PET (positron emission tomography), p. 69; MRI (magnetic resonance imaging), p. 69; functional MRI (fMRI), p. 69; split-brain patients, p. 72

## HORMONES AND GLANDS

### How does the endocrine system affect behaviour?

> The *endocrine glands* are a group of ductless glands that affect behaviour by secreting *hormones* into the bloodstream. Each gland influences different aspects of behaviour, but all are regulated in one way or another by the *pituitary gland*. The pituitary gland is appropriately referred to as the master gland because of its central role in regulating hormones; another important gland is the pancreas, which is involved in regulating the body's sugar levels. **pp. 75–77, 79–80**

**KEY TERMS**

endocrine glands, p. 77; hormones, p. 77; pituitary gland, p. 79; insulin, p. 80; diabetes mellitus, p. 80; hypoglycemia, p. 80

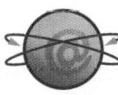 Take advantage of the multimedia resources available with this text! Follow the marginal icons to access the interactive modules on the *HandsOnPsych CD-ROM*; log on to *MyPsychLab* to explore the ebook, study aids, and other online resources; and visit the Companion Website at **www.pearsoned.ca/lefton** for additional exercises and links.

# 3 Sensation and Perception

You sit down at your desk to study psychology. You look over at the bookshelf, see this text, reach over and pick it up and place it on the desk. You look over your desktop until you see your highlighter pen and pick it up. Those acts of looking, seeing, recognizing, and retrieving seem so simple that they could only involve a single low-level mental process, right? Well, the reality of how we accomplish such simple things gets more and more interesting (and more and more complicated) the more we study it.

Consider a person who has been studied extensively by Mel Goodale of the University of Western Ontario (Goodale, 1996; Goodale et al., 1991). Referred to by her initials, D.F., this woman had suffered carbon monoxide poisoning that had damaged her visual system. When she was shown simple objects such as a pen or a letter opener on a table in front of her, she was unable to name them or even to describe them in any way. Yet, when asked by the researchers to pick up one of the objects, she did so smoothly, automatically adjusting her wrist, hand, and finger positions to grasp the object appropriately every time.

Consider also Dr. P, who was a patient of Oliver Sacks (1985), a neurologist. When handed a rose and asked if he knew what it was, Dr. P stated that it was a "convoluted red form with a linear attachment." He could not name it. When asked to smell the rose he looked confused and then gave it a sniff, at which point he smiled and said, "Beautiful. An early rose. What a heavenly smell." What both of these examples show us is that the processes of seeing and interpreting (of sensation and perception) are neither simple nor automatic. In the case of D.F., Goodale argues that two visual systems are at work: the ventral system, which works to help us catalogue what we see and compare new objects to existing object descriptions, and the dorsal system, which manages how we respond physically to objects. D.F.'s case clearly indicates that it is possible to damage one of these systems but leave the other intact. The case of Dr. P suggests that if there is damage to the ventral system it is possible to work around that damage using other sensory information input routes (that is, by smelling the rose instead of just looking at it). The existence of people such as D.F. and Dr. P help us piece together a detailed account of how we see and recognize things in the world.

# The Perceptual Experience

Whenever you are exposed to a stimulus in the environment—a word on a page or a breeze through your hair—the stimulus initiates an electrochemical change in the receptors in your body. That change in turn initiates the processes of sensation and perception. Psychologists study sensation and perception because what people sense and perceive determines how they understand and interpret the world. Such understanding depends on a combination of environmental stimulation, past experiences, and current interpretations. Although the relationship between perception and culture has not been extensively researched, it is clear that culture can affect perception—through socialization people learn what to believe, pay attention to, notice, and expect in the environment. For example, composers have long known that a person's experiences with music can make some melodies, especially non-Western ones, sound unfamiliar and dissonant.

**FIGURE 3.1**
**Bottom-up and Top-down Processing**

Bottom-up perceptual processing builds from an analysis of individual stimulus to perception. Top-down processing begins with a perception, then determines the exact "fit" with features that are discernable.

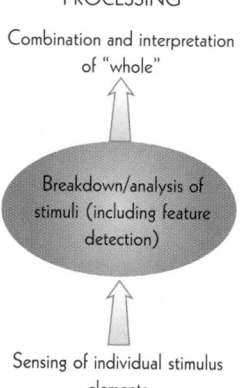

BOTTOM-UP
PROCESSING

Combination and interpretation of "whole"

Breakdown/analysis of stimuli (including feature detection)

Sensing of individual stimulus elements

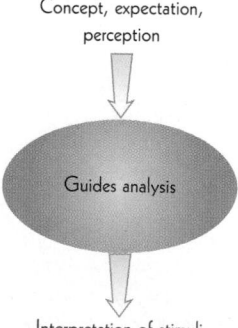

TOP-DOWN
PROCESSING

Concept, expectation, perception

Guides analysis

Interpretation of stimuli

## SENSATION AND PERCEPTION

Traditionally, psychologists have studied sensation and perception together as closely related—as we do in this chapter. **Sensation** is the process in which the sense organ receptor cells are stimulated and relay their initial information to higher brain centres for further processing. **Perception** is the process whereby an organism selects and interprets sensory input to give it meaning. Thus, sensation provides the stimuli for further perceptual processing. For example, when light striking the eyeball initiates electrochemical changes, you experience the sensation of light. However, your interpretation of the pattern of light and its resulting neural representation as a specific image are part of perception.

When researchers examine sensation and perception they usually adopt an approach that starts at the most fundamental level of sensation—where the stimulus meets the receptors—and work up to more complex perceptual tasks involving interpretation. This is often called *bottom-up processing* (see Figure 3.1). Bottom-up processing tends to be involuntary, almost automatic, and helps us discern and discriminate fast-changing information that occurs to our sense organs. Other researchers examine complex perceptual phenomena from more complex interpretations or memories—not surprisingly, called *top-down processing*. (See *Point/ Counterpoint*.) This type of processing focuses on aspects of the perceptual process such as selective attention and active decision making. For example, when we decide to search for a friend in a crowd, we establish a series of relevant criteria (tall, red-headed, wearing a blue shirt) through a series of decision rules based on our representation of our friend in memory. Top-down processing probably holds the key to our understanding not only of perception, but also of consciousness because perception and consciousness are more than reflexive discrimination processes; rather, both perception and consciousness require integration of current sensory experiences (bottom-up analysis) with past experiences and even cultural expectations (top-down analysis).

These two approaches, top down and bottom up, are both necessary and useful because sensation and perception involve whole sets of neurons and previous experiences, as well as stimulation from the environment that occurs at the sense organs. Because of this, perceptual psychologists generally think in terms of *perceptual systems*—the interacting sets of structures, functions, and operations by means of which people perceive the world around them. Sensory and perceptual processes rely so closely on each other that many researchers think of the two processes as being inseparable. So, sensation and perception together form an entire process through which an organism acquires sensory input, converts it into electrochemical energy, and interprets it so that it acquires organization, form, and meaning. It is through such processes that people explore the world and discover its rules. Such complex processes involve the nervous system in interaction with sensory receptors for vision, hearing, taste, smell, and/or touch.

# PSYCHOPHYSICS

Although perceptual systems are different, they share a common process. In each case, an environmental stimulus creates an initial stimulation of the sensory receptors. Receptor cells translate that form of energy into neuronal impulses, and the impulses are then sent to specific areas of the brain for further processing. Many psychologists who study such relationships use techniques from the area of **psychophysics**—focusing on the relationship between physical stimuli and people's conscious experience of those stimuli.

Psychophysical studies attempt to relate the physical dimension of stimuli to psychological experience. This often begins with studying sensory thresholds. We often speak of a *threshold* as a dividing line, the point at which things become different. In perception, a threshold is the value of a sensory event at the point at which things are perceived as being different. Early researchers, such as Ernst Weber and Gustav Fechner, sought to investigate *absolute thresholds*, the minimum levels of stimulation necessary to excite a perceptual system, such as vision. They asked, for example, what minimum intensity of light is necessary for a person to say, "I see it," or what minimum pressure is necessary to feel something against the skin. It turns out that a simple absolute threshold describing everyone's experiences is impossible to determine, because no two individuals see or feel at exactly the same minimum amount of intensity due to many variables. So, for a psychologist, the definition of **absolute threshold** is the minimum level of stimulation necessary to define the transition from what is undetectable to that which is detectable 50 percent of the time. In other words, the absolute threshold is an intensity that an observer can just barely detect (see Figure 3.2). For example, how loud does your CD player have to be for you to be just able to hear it? Another type of threshold is the *difference threshold*—the amount of change necessary for an observer to report 50 percent of the time that a level of stimulation (say, mass) has changed or is different from another value (that is, has gotten heavier or lighter). For example, if you were holding 100 cotton balls, how many more would someone have to add before the pile felt heavier to you?

Psychologists have devised a variety of methods for studying perceptual thresholds. In one—the *method of limits*—various values of a stimulus are presented in ascending or descending order. For example, a psychologist may present lights of very low intensity, then slightly higher intensity, and then higher still. A participant's task is to say when he or she finally sees the light—or, in the case of descending limits, no longer sees it. In another method—the *method of constant stimuli*—values of a signal are presented in random (not ascending or descending) order; the participant's task is to respond "yes" or "no," indicating that he or she has either detected a stimulus or not.

Both the method of limits and the method of constant stimuli have methodological weaknesses—they do not allow for key factors in the human observer. That is, human observers may be motivated to report stimuli they may really be unable to detect in order to appear competent and cooperative. In the last few decades, researchers studying thresholds have used the method of signal detection theory. **Signal detection theory** holds that an observer's perception is dependent not only on the intensity of a stimulus but on the observer's motivation; for example, when you are worried about a friend being late, you listen especially carefully for cars that may be coming down the street. Your perception also is dependent on the level of auditory stimulation that enables you to state, "Yes, that is enough for me to say that I detect the signal—the sound of a car." Your perception also is dependent on the *noise* (the unstructured, constant background activity) present; in our example, the noise of

**HandsOnPsych**
Version 2.0
**Sensation**

PSYCHOPHYSICS
[SYE-co-FIZ-icks]

The subfield that focuses on the relationship between physical stimuli and people's conscious experience of them.

ABSOLUTE THRESHOLD

The statistically determined minimum level of stimulation necessary to excite a perceptual system.

SIGNAL DETECTION THEORY

The theory that holds that an observer's perception is dependent on the intensity of a stimulus, on the observer's motivation, on the criteria he or she sets up, and on the "noise" present.

**FIGURE 3.2**
**Absolute Threshold**

When stimuli are detected less than 50 percent of the time, they are considered to be subliminal.

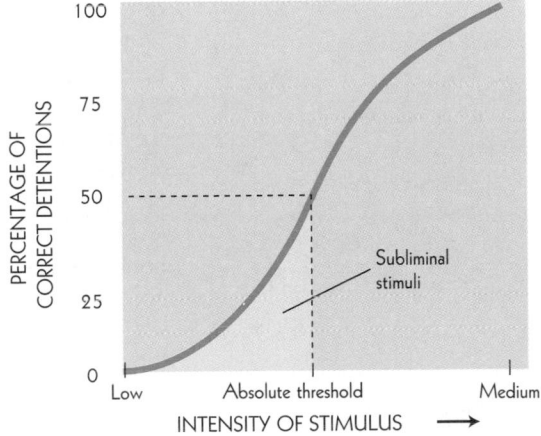

children playing in the street, birds chirping, or the television from the next apartment all make detecting the sound of your friend's automobile more difficult. Therefore, researchers manipulate signal intensity but also manipulate motivation levels (by offering varying rewards for detection), criteria (for example, by telling participants to be *very* sure before they respond, "Yes, I detect the signal"), and levels of noise. It turns out that all four of these variables affect a person's willingness to say, "Yes, I detect the signal." This important finding lends support to the idea that there is no single or absolute threshold—each individual's response will vary from one type of situation to the next.

## SUBLIMINAL PERCEPTION

**Subliminal perception** is perception below the threshold of awareness. Do subliminal self-help audiotapes do all that they claim? If a visual or auditory stimulus is presented so quickly or at such a low intensity or volume that you cannot consciously perceive it, can it affect your behaviour? Is it affecting your brain organization?

Modern studies of this type of perception began in the 1950s with tales of an innovative advertising ploy. The story was that a marketing executive had superimposed messages on a movie that said, among other things, "Buy popcorn." According to some enterprising advertising agents, movie theatres could induce audiences to buy more popcorn by flashing advertisements on the screen at speeds too fast to be consciously observed. Although psychological research has shown that there are no strong effects of this sort of advertising (Trappey, 1996), other research suggests that a large proportion of the public clearly believes that it works and that it is being used regularly by advertisers (Rogers & Smith, 1993).

Subliminal perception is possible. In fact, many cognitive scientists build theories around it (e.g., Draine & Greenwald, 1998; Kihlstrom, Barnhardt, & Tataryn, 1992). However, historically the concept of subliminal perception has been controversial. Many of the early studies in the 1960s lacked control groups and did not specify the variables being manipulated. Some did not adjust the presentation duration of the words they used to take individual differences into account. Other studies presented sexual words to see if they affected responses more than neutral or emotionally uncharged words did. Would the sexual words be emotionally arousing and lead participants to perceptually block out these stimuli? Initial results showed that participants did indeed show increased thresholds and had higher autonomic activity for these words, indicating arousal. Of course it is very likely that, even if detected, some participants were too embarrassed to repeat the noxious words to the experimenter (often a person of the opposite sex) and so denied having seen them.

To avoid some of these methodological problems, later experiments presented participants with both threatening and neutral words for very brief durations. Participants responded by repeating the words or by pressing a button as soon as they saw a word they had been told to look for. In these experiments, threatening words had to be presented for a longer time or at a greater intensity level than non-threatening words in order to be identified.

Evidence exists for subliminal effects in a variety of experimental settings from the work of Phil Merikle (2000) at the University of Waterloo and others (Monahan, Murphy, & Zajonc, 2000). The presentation of a threatening message—for example, an aggressive or sexual message—may raise the perceptual threshold above normal levels, making it harder for the participant to perceive subsequent subliminal words. Some researchers suggest that the unconscious mind or some other personality variable acts as a censor (Pratkanis, 2001; Silverman, 1983). Balay and Shevrin (1988) suggest that a higher processing stage beyond the sensory or perceptual stage affects the perceptual process. They maintain that subliminal perception can be explained in terms of non-perceptual variables such as motivation, previous experience, repetition, and unconscious or critical censoring processes that influence perceptual thresholds.

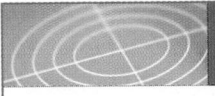

## Scotopic Sensitivity Syndrome: Fact or Fiction?

**POINT:** Subgroups of readers with reading disabilities demonstrate significant improvements in reading accuracy and comprehension when using coloured overlays (Irlen lenses).

**COUNTERPOINT:** The case for the use of Irlen lenses is not based on valid scientific research.

In 1983 Helen Irlen, an educational psychologist, identified a unique syndrome that she named "scotopic sensitivity syndrome (SSS)." Individuals diagnosed with this syndrome complained of sore, tired eyes, visual distortions, and glare during the reading process. While reading, they claimed to experience visual stress, perceptual distortions, and headaches. Irlen (1991) attributed SSS (also called Irlen Syndrome) to a visual-perceptual dysfunction caused by excessive sensitivity to particular wavelengths of light. She stressed then as now that this dysfunction is not an optical problem (that is, there is nothing wrong with the visual apparatus itself); rather she claims that for those diagnosed with SSS there is a defect within the nervous system that affects how visual information is encoded and decoded. This perceptual deficit, Irlen claims, prevents people from reading effectively or efficiently.

To combat the reading problems experienced by those diagnosed with SSS, Irlen advocates the use of precision tinted coloured overlays, coloured filters, coloured lenses in glasses or coloured computer monitors (collectively referred to as Irlen lenses). When text is presented using these coloured lenses or normal text is covered with a coloured overlay, supporters for Irlen lenses argue that visual information processing is enhanced leading to significant reading gains as well as improved comprehension and reading speed (Tyrrell, et al., 1995; Wilkins, et al., 2001).

Critics of the Irlen lenses claim that the case for the effectiveness of Irlen filters is unscientific and largely unsubstantiated. They correctly indicate that the term "scotopic" refers to processing within the rod system of the retina (a separate system from the colour processing cone system) and question this unsuitable name for the syndrome. Moreover, detractors claim that it is not only the treatment approach that is suspect but also question the validity of SSS as a legitimate medical syndrome. They argue that there are no established criteria for SSS and say that the identification of the syndrome relies on vague, non-specific symptoms. In fact they argue that the only way to definitively diagnose a person with SSS is to identify benefit derived from coloured lenses while reading. This circular diagnostic process is flawed, say critics. Furthermore, critics warn that readers using coloured overlays may be demonstrating a placebo effect. Placebo effects occur when a person believes that an intervention will help them and are therefore motivated to perform at a higher level than usual.

In sum, there is data to support both sides of this debate (Robinson & Foreman, 1999). It does appear that some children with reading disabilities experience reduced perceptual distortions and visual stress when using the coloured filters. However, this intervention does not eliminate the need for reading remediation to address underlying reading problems.

In some controlled situations, subliminal stimuli can influence perception, attitudes, and behaviour (Greenwald, Klinger, & Schuh, 1995; Krosnick et al., 1992; Underwood, 1994). In the real world, however, we are constantly faced with many competing sensory stimuli. Therefore, what grabs our attention depends on many variables, such as importance, prominence, and interest. Should we fear mind control by advertisers or other unsolicited outside stimuli? The answer is no, because such attempts are ineffective (Schredl et al., 1999; Trappey, 1996). Can backward speech in rock music be interpreted and understood? Again, the answer is no (Begg, Needham, & Bookbinder, 1993). Can listening to tapes while we are asleep help us learn Greek or Latin? Once more, the answer is no (Moore, 1995). In the end, subliminal perception, and any learning that results from it, is subtle at most (Channouf, 2000; Smith & Rogers, 1994) and greatly affected by such non-perceptual, non-biological variables as expectation, motivation, previous experience, personality, and other learned, culturally based behaviours (Miller, 2000; Pratkanis, 2001).

## SELECTIVE ATTENTION

Have you ever tried to study and listen to quiet music at the same time? You may have thought that the music barely reached your threshold of awareness, yet you

▲ The cocktail party phenomenon allows traders to discern the content of specific conversations amid the chaos around them.

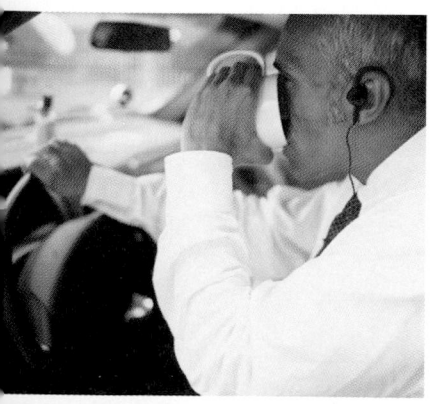

▼ People have limited ability to divide their attention between tasks—such as driving, drinking coffee, and talking on the phone.

may have found your attention wandering. Did certain melodies or words start to interrupt your studying? Research on attention shows that human beings constantly extract signals from the world around them. Although we receive many different messages at once, we can watch, listen, and attend to only a small number of stimuli at a time.

Because people can pay attention to only one or two things at a time, psychologists sometimes call the study of attention the study of *selective attention*. Early researchers in this area (Broadbent, 1958) described the *cocktail party phenomenon*, whereby a person can hear his or her name spoken across a crowded and noisy room. The person cannot discern the content of conversations across the room under such conditions, but does hear his or her name.

Perceptual psychologists are interested in the complex processes through which people extract information from the environment. These psychologists hope to answer the following question: To which stimuli do people choose to listen? They study the *allocation* of a person's attention. For example, measuring selective attention in the auditory senses can involve the use of selective-listening tasks in which participants wearing pairs of headphones simultaneously receive different messages in each ear. Their task often is to *shadow*, or repeat, a message heard in one ear. Typically, they report that they are able to listen to a speaker in *either* the left ear or the right ear and can provide information about the content and quality of that speaker's voice but are unable to attend to qualities of the stimuli in both ears at the same time.

There are several theories about how people attend selectively, two of which are the filter theory and the attenuation theory. The *filter theory* states that human beings possess a limited capacity to process information and that perceptual "filters" screen out extraneous information. The *attenuation theory* states that all information is analyzed but that intervening factors inhibit (attenuate) attention so that only selected information reaches the highest centres of processing. Hundreds of selective-listening studies have examined the claims of filter theory versus attenuation theory, and recent research favours attenuation theory (Cowan & Wood, 1997). Regardless of whether people filter or attenuate information, selective-attention studies show that human beings must select among available stimuli. It is impossible, for example, to attend to four lectures at once. A listener can extract information from only one speaker at a time. Admittedly, you can do more than one task at a time—for example, you can drive a car and listen to the radio—but you cannot use the same channel (such as vision) or concentrate equally on information from many channels for several tasks simultaneously. For example, you cannot sing along with the radio, study, and identify an odour at the same time.

Clearly, our sensory systems have limited capacities. People have limited ability to divide their attention between tasks and must allocate their perceptual resources for greatest efficiency. But what happens when the need to divide is not necessary? What occurs when there is a restricted environment?

## RESTRICTED ENVIRONMENTAL STIMULATION

Imagine utter loneliness . . . darkness . . . complete lack of light and sound. Imagine being in an isolation tank where you don't have to adapt to the light—because there is absolutely none. This was the case described in a compelling 1978 novel, a page-turner by Paddy Chayefsky entitled *Altered States,* and in its movie version starring William Hurt. It is a great story that raises provocative questions about human perceptual systems and consciousness—and the relationship between the two.

In 1956, at McGill University, neurophysiologist John Lilly enlisted modern technology to find out what would happen if the brain were deprived of all sensory input—he created a situation much like that described in Chayefsky's novel. Lilly constructed an isolation tank that excluded all light and sound and was filled with heavily salted water, which allows for easy floating. In this artificial sea, deprived of all external stimuli, Lilly experienced dreams, reveries, hallucinations, and other altered states.

Psychologists call such a situation one of restricted environmental stimulation. Some researchers argue that psychological benefits can be derived from sensory restriction (deprivation)—isolation from sights, sounds, smells, tastes, and feeling. The past president of the Canadian Psychological Association, Peter Suedfeld, has studied the effects of restricted environmental stimulation therapy (REST) for years at the University of British Columbia. Suedfeld and Coren (1989) have explained that early research participant reports of discomfort and hallucinations likely were due to poor participant selection (some people hallucinate without experiencing a REST situation) and to the stressful way in which those REST experiences were handled (participants were led to believe they might see things or feel discomfort, and so some participants obliged). Suedfeld and his colleagues have found that spending time in a REST chamber (either lying on a cot in the dark or floating in a bath of Epsom salts) can reduce anxiety (Sakata et al., 1995; Suedfeld, 1998), enhance sports performance (Suedfeld, Collier, & Hartnett, 1993; Suedfeld & Bruno, 1990), reduce the frequency of tension headaches (Wallbaum et al., 1991), help people modify habits such as smoking and overeating (Suedfeld, 1990), treat addictions (Borrie, 1991), and even improve the functioning of autistic children (Suedfeld & Schwartz, 1981).

There are a number of hypotheses about why REST has such a broad range of effects. These include simple relaxation or becoming "focused" as one might through meditation or concentration. Or it may be that the REST experience allows the non-dominant cerebral hemisphere to exert more influence than usual on functioning, as the screening function of the dominant hemisphere seems to be diminished in low stimulation conditions (Suedfeld et al., 1994). Once fully understood, the range of REST's effects very likely will tell us a great deal about our perceptual systems.

▲ An isolation tank removes all external stimuli and may alter an individual's mental state.

## INATTENTIONAL BLINDNESS

When you drive down a road, listen to a concert, or watch a favourite movie, you display an inability to detect unexpected objects; you show *inattentional blindness*. Research on this phenomenon shows that unless you pay attention, you can miss even the most conspicuous events around you (Scholl, 2000). For example, while people paid close attention to a visual scene with sports figures in it, a person in a gorilla suit appeared, pounded its chest, and then disappeared—and it went completely unnoticed (Most et al., 2001; Simons & Chabris, 1999).

Experimental research on attention shows that when you pay full attention to an object, scene, or event, other (unexpected) events go unnoticed (Simons, Franconeri, & Reimer, 2000). This means that an airline pilot, closely attending to hundreds of dials and switches, may completely miss an unanticipated plane approaching from the left. Similarly, if you are intently focused on a video game, you may not notice the arrival of a friend, roommate, or parent in your room. The more you pay attention to the main event, the less likely you will be to notice the unexpected one (Most et al., 2001). The more the unexpected event differs from what you are attending to or accustomed to, the more likely you will be to miss it (Lachter, Durgin, & Washington, 2000; Simons & Chabris, 1999).

Inattentional blindness is important because it reminds us that the brain can do only so much at one time—we can only encode so much. It prompts us to realize that "top-down" processes may tune an observer's attention to specific objects or events. It forces us to ask a question that remains unanswered for now. What

## Be an
# ACTIVE LEARNER

**REVIEW**
> Why have modern researchers viewed perception as a unitary rather than a two-step (sensation followed by perception) process? p. 86
> What evidence exists to show that, when a person receives more than one incoming message at the same time, the person can attend to only one? pp. 89–90

**THINK CRITICALLY**
> How does the culture prime, or pre-cue, individuals to focus their attention in important ways?
> What assumptions does a researcher make when depriving an organism of sensory experience and then measuring behaviour?

**APPLY PSYCHOLOGY**
> Think of two ways to restrict environmental stimulation to help people lead calmer, more relaxed lives.
> Think of three exercises to help athletes "reject" some inputs (screaming fans) while focusing on other inputs (catching a ball).

**LIGHT**

The portion of the electromagnetic spectrum visible to the eye.

information will get coded and what happens to the stimuli we do not register? These questions require us to look more closely at the visual system itself, our next topic.

# The Visual System

Imagine that you are in an unfamiliar house at night when the power goes out. You hear creaking sounds but have no idea where they are coming from. You stub your toe on the coffee table, then frantically grope along the walls until you reach the kitchen, where you fumble through the drawers in search of a flashlight. You quickly come to appreciate the sense of sight when you are suddenly without it.

Human beings derive more information through sight than through any other sense. By some estimates, the eyes contain 70 percent of the body's sense receptors. Visible **light** exists as a small band of energy contained within the electromagnetic spectrum, the entire spectrum of waves initiated by the movement of charged particles. The electromagnetic spectrum includes gamma rays, X-rays, ultraviolet rays, visible light, infrared rays, radar, broadcast bands, and AC currents (see Figure 3.3). Note that the light that is visible to the human eye is a very small portion of that spectrum. Light may come directly from a source or may be reflected from an object. The impact of light is complex and affects about 30 areas of the brain that are involved in sensation and perception. We begin our analysis of the visual system with a bottom-up analysis of the effect of light on the structure of the eye. Such an analysis will show that the visual system is exceedingly intricate. Although often likened to a camera, which records images, the visual system is interpretive, and a later top-down analysis will show that the camera analogy explains only part of the process.

## THE STRUCTURE OF THE EYE

Figure 3.4 shows the major structures of the human eye. Light first passes through the *cornea*—a small, transparent bulge covering both the *pupil* (the dark opening in the centre of the eye) and the pigmented (coloured) *iris*. Behind the pupil is the *lens*, which is about four millimetres thick. Together, the cornea, the pupil, the iris, and the lens focus images onto the retina. The *retina*, a layer of neurons that lines the back of the eye, captures images and sends them to the brain for processing, which ultimately will produce conscious visual experience. The iris regulates the amount of light entering the eye. Constriction of the iris makes the pupil smaller, letting in less light but creating a more sharply focused image on the retina. Dilation of the iris makes the pupil bigger and allows in more light, but the images produced will appear more blurred.

**FIGURE 3.3**

**The Electromagnetic Spectrum**

People can perceive only a small part of the total electromagnetic spectrum.

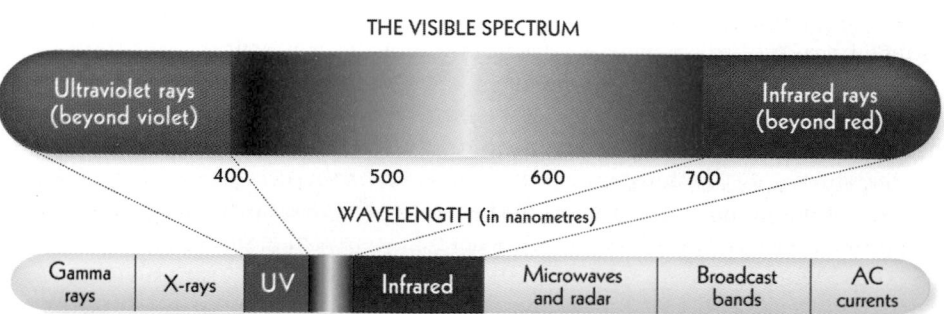

THE VISIBLE SPECTRUM

Ultraviolet rays (beyond violet)

Infrared rays (beyond red)

400    500    600    700

WAVELENGTH (in nanometres)

| Gamma rays | X-rays | UV | Infrared | Microwaves and radar | Broadcast bands | AC currents |

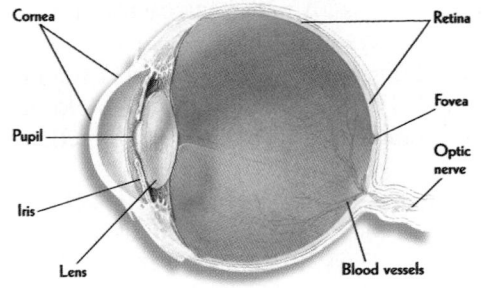

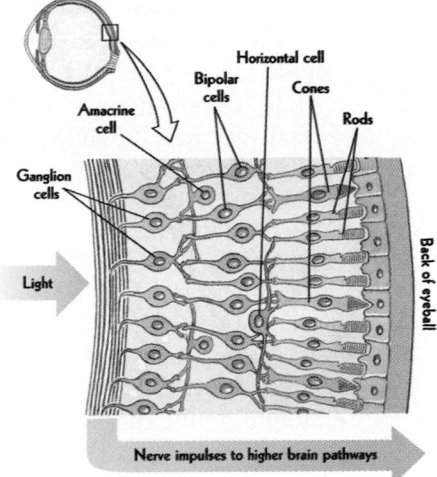

**FIGURE 3.4**
**The Main Structures**
**of the Eye**

The photoreceptors of the retina are connected to higher brain pathways through the optic nerve. Light filters through layers of retinal cells before hitting the receptors (rods and cones), located at the back of the eyeball and pointed away from the incoming light. The rods and cones pass an electrical impulse to the bipolar cells, which in turn relay the impulse back out to the ganglion cells. The axons of the ganglion cells form the fibres of the optic nerve.

To form a useful image, it is necessary for light from an object to be focused on the retina. The cornea and the lens both contribute to image formation. If either of these elements is too long or too short, a blurred image is formed. People with elongated eyeballs are **myopic**, or *nearsighted*; they are able to see things that are close to them but have trouble seeing objects at a distance, because the image falls in front of the retina. **Hyperopic**, or *farsighted*, people have shortened eyeballs. They have trouble seeing things up close because the image is focused behind the retina, but they are able to see objects at a distance.

The *retina* has a complex multi-layered organization consisting of a network of neurons. Of these, the most important are the **photoreceptors** (the light-sensitive cells). After light passes through several layers of other cells it strikes the photoreceptor layer, which consists of *rods* (large, rod-shaped receptors) and *cones* (small, cone-shaped receptors). Here light energy is transformed into electrical energy in a process called **transduction**. This electrical energy is transferred from the rods and cones to the *bipolar cells*.

**RODS AND CONES.** Each eye contains more than 120 million rods and 6 million cones. These millions of photoreceptors do not have individual pathways to the higher visual centres in the brain. Instead, through the process of *convergence*, electrochemical signals from many rods come together onto a single bipolar cell. At the same time, hundreds of cones synapse and converge onto other bipolar cells. From the bipolar cells, electrochemical energy is transferred to the *ganglion cell layer* of the retina. Dozens of bipolar cells synapse and converge onto each ganglion cell (there are about 1 million ganglion cells). The axons of the ganglion cells make up the *optic nerve*, which carries information that was initially received by the rods and cones to the brain. Still further coding takes place at the brain's **visual cortex**, or *striate cortex*. The visual cortex, the most important area of the brain's occipital lobe, further processes information from the *lateral geniculate nucleus* (one of the major visual projection areas in the visual system—see page 95).

The *duplicity theory of vision* (sometimes called the *duplexity theory*), which is now universally accepted, asserts that there are two separate receptor systems in the retina: the rods and the cones. It also states that rods and cones are structurally different and accomplish different tasks. Cones are for the most part tightly packed in the centre of the retina, at the *fovea*, and are used for day vision, colour vision, and fine visual discrimination. Rods (together with some cones) are found on the rest of the retina (the periphery) and are used predominantly for night vision (see Figure 3.5). The functioning of the cones is demonstrated in the visual acuity test

MYOPIC [my-OP-ick]

Able to see things that are close but having trouble seeing objects at a distance. Also known as *nearsighted.*

HYPEROPIC [HY-per-OP-ick]

Having trouble seeing things that are close but able to see objects at a distance. Also known as *farsighted.*

PHOTORECEPTORS

The light-sensitive cells in the retina: rods and cones.

TRANSDUCTION

The process by which a perceptual system analyzes stimuli and converts them into electrical impulses. Also known as *coding.*

VISUAL CORTEX

The most important area of the brain's occipital lobe, which receives information from the lateral geniculate nucleus. Also known as *striate cortex.*

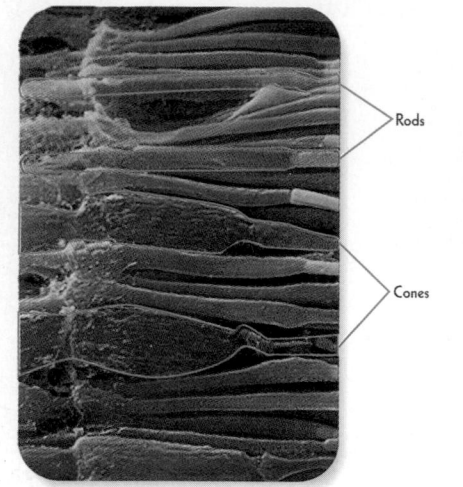

▲ Cones are packed tightly in the centre of the retina and used for day vision, while rods are found on the rest of the retina and are predominantly used for night vision.

DARK ADAPTATION

The increase in sensitivity to light that occurs when the illumination level changes from high to low, causing chemicals in the rods and cones to regenerate and return to their inactive state.

you take when you apply for a driver's licence. A *visual acuity* test measures the resolution capacity of the visual system—the ability to see fine details. Cones principally mediate this ability. You do best on such a test in a well-lit room (cones operate at high light levels) and when looking directly at the test items (again, more cones are in the centre of the retina than in any other place).

Your eyes are always in some state of light or dark adaptation. Rods and cones are sensitive to light, but they are less sensitive in a well-lit room than they are after having been in the dark. **Dark adaptation** is the increase in sensitivity to light that occurs when the illumination level changes from high to low. In dark adaptation, chemicals in the photoreceptors (rods and cones) regenerate and return to their original state, increasing the eyes' light sensitivity. If you go from a well-lit lobby into a dark theatre, for example, you experience a brief period of low light sensitivity, during which you are unable to distinguish empty seats. Your ability to discern objects and people in the theatre increases with each passing moment. Within 30 minutes, your eyes will have almost fully adapted to the dark and will be far more light sensitive. For this reason, after leaving a dark theatre and returning to the afternoon sunlight, you must squint or shade your eyes until they become adapted to the light.

Figure 3.6 shows a dark adaptation curve. The cones determine the first part of the curve; the second part is determined by the rods. The speed at which the photochemicals in these receptors regenerate determines the shape of the two parts of the curve. The cone-only portion of the curve was obtained by having a participant look at a small light that fell on only the fovea, which is all cones. The rod-only curve was obtained by testing a participant whose fovea contained only rods because of a genetic defect. The broken curve represents that which is obtained when a participant has normal vision. Typically, a participant is first shown bright light for two minutes. The light is then turned off, and the participant waits in a totally dark room for 15 seconds. Next, a very dim test spot of light is turned on for half a second, and the participant is asked if he or she sees it. Usually, the participant will report seeing the test spot only after several successive presentations, because dark adaptation

**FIGURE 3.5**

## The Distribution of Rods and Cones and the Blind Spot

The centre of the retina (the fovea) contains only cones. At about 18 degrees of visual angle (a measure of the size of images on the retina), there are no receptors at all. This is the place where the optic nerve leaves the eye, called the blind spot. Because the blind spot for each eye is on the nasal side of the eyeball, there is no loss of vision; the two blind spots do not overlap (Pirenne, 1967).

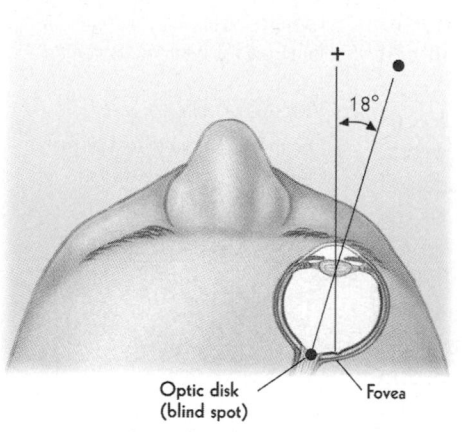

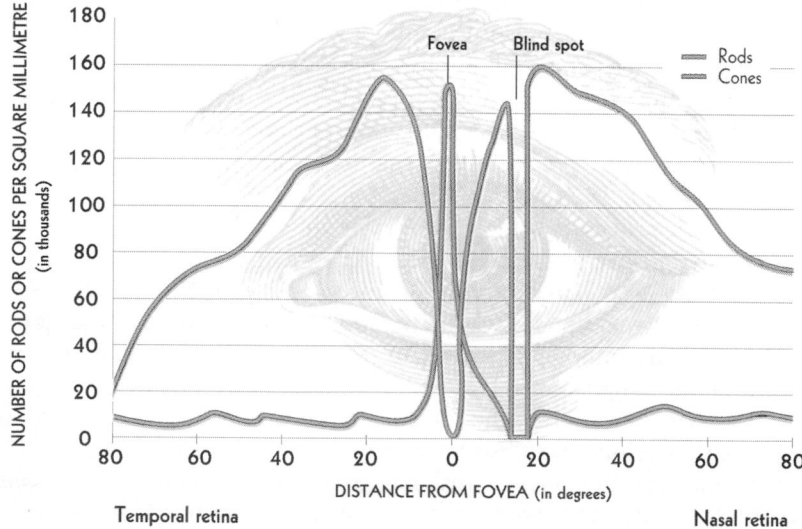

occurs gradually. This is why, when you are driving at night, you may have trouble seeing clearly for a brief time after a car drives toward you with its high beams on; the photochemicals in the rods take some time to regenerate.

**HIGHER PATHWAYS.**   As electrical impulses leave the retina through the optic nerve, they proceed to higher centres of the brain, including the lateral geniculate nucleus and the visual cortex (also called the striate cortex) (see Figure 3.7). These connections are quite specific. Knowledge about the way visual structures are connected to the brain aids not only psychologists but also physicians, who can determine, for example, whether a stroke victim with poor vision has a blood clot that is obstructing circulation in one hemisphere of the brain.

Each eye is connected to both sides of the brain, with half of its optic nerve fibres going to the left side of the brain and the other half connecting to the right side. The point at which the crossover of half the optic nerve fibres from each eye occurs is called the **optic chiasm** (see Figures 3.7 and 3.8). This crossover of impulses allows the brain to process two sets of signals from an image and helps human beings perceive form in three dimensions. Severing of the optic nerves at the optic chiasm results in tunnel vision—a condition in which peripheral vision is severely impaired and a person can see only items whose images fall on the central area of the eye, the fovea.

## THE ELECTROCHEMICAL BASIS OF PERCEPTION

You can probably find your way around your room in the dark; you know where light switches and doorknobs are. You can reach out and touch just about any object when you need it. Your memory for object locations and how to reach out is coded electrochemically, and scientists know which neurons are involved (Graziano, Hu, & Gross, 1997). In fact, vision and all other perceptual processes are electrochemical in nature. When receptors in the perceptual systems are stimulated, the information is coded and sent to the brain for interpretation and further analysis. Using this basic information about electrochemical stimulation, researchers are working on a visual prosthesis—a device to help the blind see—that bypasses the eyes and directly stimulates the visual cortex (Bak et al., 1990).

**RECEPTIVE FIELDS.**   Scientists in a wide range of related fields have carried out research on the organization of vision and

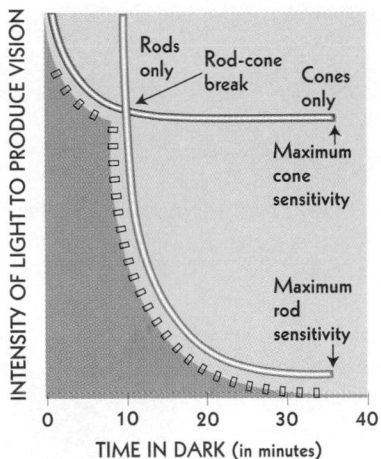

**FIGURE 3.6**

**A Dark Adaptation Curve**

The dashed line represents a typical overall dark adaptation curve. The two solid lines represent separate dark adaptation for rods and cones. Most dark adaptation occurs within 10 minutes. Rods, however, continue to adapt for another 20 minutes, reaching greater levels of sensitivity.

**FIGURE 3.7**

**The Major Components of the Visual System**

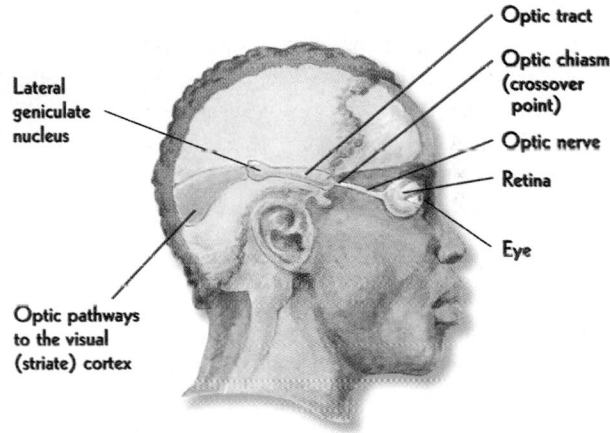

OPTIC CHIASM [KI-azm]
Point at which half of the optic nerve fibres from each eye cross over and connect to the other side of the brain.

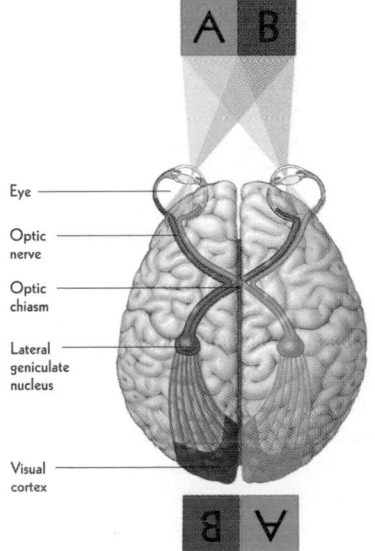

**FIGURE 3.8**

**A Visual Image Is Projected to Both Hemispheres of the Brain**

## Prosopagnosia—Do I Know You?

Wayne Gretzky, Michael J. Fox, Céline Dion, and Dan Ackroyd all have striking faces. So do Jean Chrétien and Prince Charles. Faces define and differentiate people. We all engage in the perceptual task of gazing at, discerning, analyzing, remembering, and recognizing faces. Even in the first weeks of life, newborns are able to distinguish faces from other objects, and they quickly develop the ability to recognize their principal caregiver's face (Fantz, 1961).

Research on brain structure shows that there is something special about face perception that distinguishes it from other kinds of perception. Some interesting evidence comes from studies of agnosia (Bauer & Demery, 2003). People with **agnosia** have normal, intact perceptual systems—for detecting colour, shape, and motion—and have no verbal, memory, or intellectual impairment, yet they are unable to recognize things they should be able to. Agnosia usually occurs because of injury to the brain from an accident, or perhaps because of a stroke. A patient with agnosia can see stimuli but cannot name them. When presented with an object—a cup or a candle, for example—an agnosic is not able to name it. Some visual agnosias are very specific—for example, colour agnosia, movement agnosia, and object agnosia.

Ruth M. had a special type of agnosia that prevented her from recognizing people by their facial characteristics. She could identify objects, scenes, and places, but if presented with the face of a friend, she went blank. This kind of agnosia is called *prosopagnosia*—the inability to recognize faces. When such patients are shown a picture of a spouse, mother, friend, or even themselves, they cannot name the person in the photo. They know that an image is a face, but they cannot tell one face from another. Research shows that such patients often have other perceptual problems as well, but that their ability to recognize faces is exceptionally impaired (Farah, Levinson, & Klein, 1995).

Is it possible that there are special regions of the brain responsible for prosopagnosia? Are there "face detectors"? Several lines of evidence support this notion. First, research shows that certain brain cells are activated by facial stimuli and not by other stimuli (Renault et al., 1989). Some individual cells (around the temporal lobes) respond best to faces, sometimes even to faces in a particular orientation, such as frontal or profile views. Unfortunately, the appealing idea of "one-face, one-neuron" is somewhat flawed, because it would not be adaptive to rely solely on one neuron to recognize important and

familiar people in our lives (neurons die all the time!). We know that people are particularly skilled at recognizing faces, but when faces are distorted, turned upside down, or otherwise taken out of normal perspective, face recognition is far more difficult (Farah et al., 1998; McNeil & Warrington, 1993), though still possible. The photo in this box shows a sculpture of Prince Charles. Despite the comical exaggeration of his features, you can still tell who he is.

Daniel Saumier, Martin Arguin, and Maryse Lassonde (2001) of Université de Montréal were interested in whether face recognition required that each discrete part of the face first be perceived individually. Their findings suggest that people do indeed integrate individual facial features (for example, noses or eyes) into a more global (or holistic) perception that allows identification of unique individuals. Although people with prosopagnosia are able to identify specific features, they are incapable of forming an entire perception from distinct facial characteristics and are therefore impaired in their ability to recognize others. In the end, this leads some researchers to believe that face perception depends on a specialized, neurophysiologically distinct processing system.

Remember that patients with agnosia have lesions or damage to a specific area of the brain, so the conclusion that specific brain areas are responsible for perceptual abilities is logical. However, face perception cannot occur through analysis of perception of specific features. We know that single features in isolation, or even incomplete combinations of them, do not allow for any meaningful level of facial recognition (Saumier, Arguin, & Lassonde, 2001; Farah, O'Reilly, & Vecera, 1993). The whole—the face—seems to be more than the sum of its parts. So, prosopagnosics may suffer from such deficits because the visual system is interactive—when one part is not operating well, or is damaged, other parts are also affected (Tovee & Cohen-Tovee, 1993). Our ability to recognize faces depends on an ability to recognize components—eyes, ears, teeth, and so on—but it also depends on many systems from both sides of the brain acting together (Wacholtz, 1996; Rapcsak et al., 1994). These findings lead to the conclusion that our visual system is made up of interacting and interdependent parts that create a whole visual experience. So, although some tasks require very specific object recognition, other tasks, such as face perception, may require a more holistic, interactive analysis that depends on both hemispheres of the brain (Rumiati & Humphreys, 1997) and on the whole brain acting in concert (Farah, 1990).

electrical coding for a long time. For example, Von Senden (1932) reported case histories of people who were born with cataracts (which cloud vision) and had them removed in adulthood. These individuals, seeing clearly for the first time as adults, experienced several deficiencies. For example, they were unable to recognize simple forms presented in an unfamiliar colour or context. Some time later, Hirsch and Spinelli (1971) conducted a series of experiments in which they controlled the visual experiences of newborn kittens. The kittens wore goggles that let them perceive either vertical lines or horizontal lines. When the goggles were later removed, kittens raised with only horizontal experiences bumped into vertical chair legs but could leap into a horizontal chair seat; kittens raised with only vertical experiences had problems with horizontal surfaces. Such studies indicate that although most of the connections in the visual system are present in newborns, the proper functioning of the system depends on the organism's experiences, the task given, and even the other senses (Creem & Proffitt, 2001; Macaluso, Frith, & Driver, 2000).

Current knowledge about how the brain processes electrochemical signals comes from studies of single cells and of receptive fields and associated pathways. **Receptive fields** are the areas of the retina that, when stimulated, produce a change in the firing of cells in the visual system. For example, specific cells in the retina will fire, or become active, if a vertical line is presented to a viewer but not if a horizontal line is presented. Many perceptual psychologists refer to these stimulated visual system cells as *feature detectors*. Hubel and Wiesel (1962; 2000) found receptive fields that are sensitive to features of a stimulus line, such as its position, length, movement, colour, and intensity (see Figure 3.9). Hubel and Wiesel characterized the feature detectors as simple, complex, or hypercomplex cells. *Simple cells* respond to the shape and size of lights that stimulate the receptive field. *Complex cells* respond most vigorously to the movement of light in one direction (e.g., Taylor et al., 2000). *Hypercomplex cells* are the most specific; they respond only to a line of the correct length and orientation that moves in the proper direction (e.g., Anderson et al., 2000; Blakemore & Campbell, 2000). From Hubel and Wiesel's point of view, electrical coding becomes increasingly complex as information proceeds through the visual system (Anderson et al., 2000; Sonnenborg, Anderssen, & Arendt-Nielsen, 2000). The work of Hubel and Wiesel earned them a Nobel

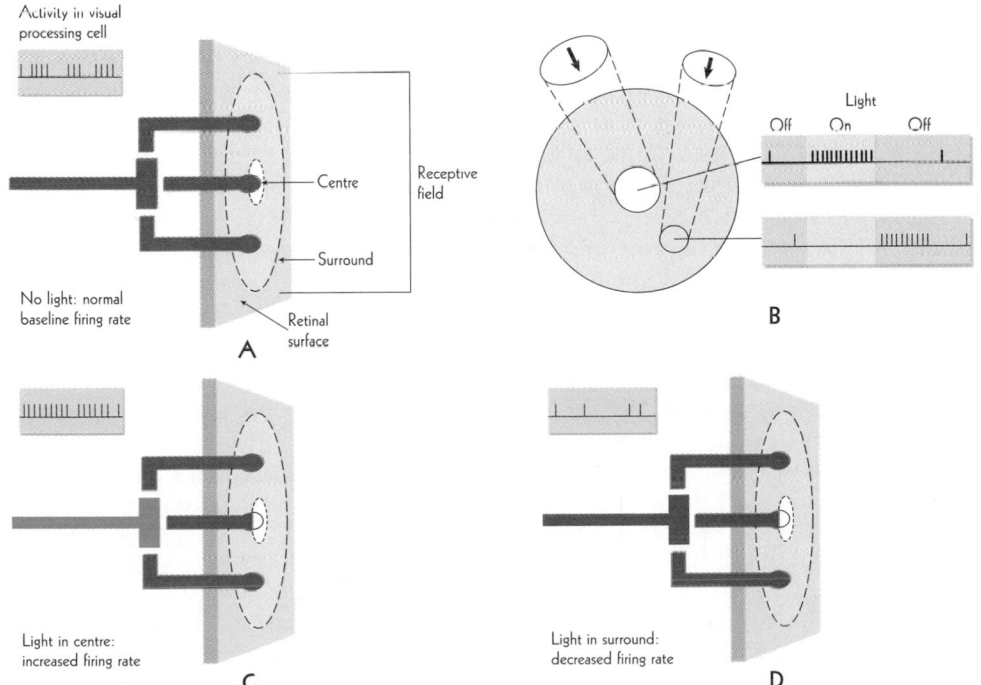

**FIGURE 3.9**
**Receptive Fields**

Hubel and Wiesel (1962) found that cells fire when stimulated in the centre of their receptive field but do not fire when stimulated outside the centre area. (A) Receptive fields in the retina are often circular with a centre-surround arrangement. Light striking the centre of the field produces the opposite result of light striking the surround. (B) Here, light in the centre produces increased firing in the visual cell (C) and light in the surround produces decreased firing. (D)

Prize in 1981 and has been supported and extended by other noted researchers (see Livingstone & Tsao, 1999).

Scientists now know that receptive fields also help link visual perception of space to body movements—as when Jackie Chan judges just the right time to leap from a helicopter to a floating barge, or when you see a ball and then slide to catch it (Graziano & Gross, 1994). Receptive fields are associated not only with every area of the visual cortex but also with some nonvisual areas (Polonsky et al., 2000); for example, receptive fields stimulate cells in the parietal cortex, which is adjacent to the visual cortex and is associated with the control of movement (Corbetta & Vereijken, 1999). Receptive fields not only help you recognize vertical and horizontal lines and balls flying through the air, but they also seem to be critically involved in the recognition of faces and other common objects (Allison et al., 1994). Receptive fields may be linked together in complex ways (B. B. Lee, 1999), and probably not by direct, strong connections between individual cells—the perceptual system is just too complicated and flexible (Crick & Koch, 1998; Heeger, 1999).

**WHAT AND WHERE.**  Remember that the task of perception is difficult; a face, a building, a flower may all be seen from different angles and distances, and these can change from moment to moment. Herein lies a central, key problem for perception researchers: How does the brain perceive constancy though sensory input—views of the world—is constantly changing? Data about an image are probably kept in a storage location for a brief time while other data are being collected, and then these are integrated (e.g., Tenenbaum, de Silva, & Langford, 2000). Parts of these data are based on information about what and where. We know that the visual system processes an object's form and colour (*what* it is) separately from its spatial location (*where* it is). A person can know where something is but not know what it is. Mecklinger (2000) found distinctions in memory stores, and "what" information affects our ability to make "where" discriminations (Carlson-Radvansky, Covey, & Lattanzi, 1999). Furthermore, some neurons seem to be tuned to detect either "what" information *or* "where" information; other cells seem to respond to both what and where an object is. Kilgard and Merzenich (1998) have found high degrees of "what" and "where" specificity for cells in the prefrontal cortex and suggest that they may hold the key to understanding how we get around, by linking objects (what) to places (where), as when we follow directions according to landmarks such as "the Tim Hortons at the corner of 2nd and Main" (Rybak et al., 1998).

Researchers' study of electrochemical changes in the visual system shows that the brain simultaneously processes many components of an image—what it is, where it is, when it is perceived, colours, movement, and so on (Deco & Schürmann, 2000). Such simultaneous processing of information taking place in multiple locations of the brain is referred to as *parallel processing,* in contrast to *serial processing,* which occurs in a step-by-step, linear fashion. Parallel processing allows for fast recognition of complexities in the world; it also explains why brain-damaged individuals can recognize some elements of a scene and not others. It helps explain why people with reading disabilities can be smart and astute, able to play the piano and draw, but unable to make sounds correspond to letters. The representation and interpretation of the world happen in multiple brain locations, and some of those locations may not be operating well or efficiently, or even be primarily visual (Frey & Hinton, 1999; Kreiman, Koch, & Fried, 2000).

**GENDER DIFFERENCES—AN EVOLUTIONARY PERSPECTIVE.**  Boys and girls are more alike than different on most visual tasks. However, when it comes to spatial abilities—tasks that require the perception of a relationship of parts to a whole—boys have an edge in mental rotation of three-dimensional objects and perhaps in map reading, puzzles, and mazes (McBurney et al., 1997). When it comes to remembering where something is, women excel. Early researchers thought that the differences might have emerged because men were exposed to and trained in map reading and other tasks—a strong environmental point of view. Evolutionary researchers have asserted that as human beings evolved, men predominately hunted while women foraged—human beings were hunter-gatherers. Over time and through the process of natural selection, these hunter-gatherer activities fostered spatial (hunting) skills in men and spatial remembering (gathering) skills in women (Silverman et al., 2000).

If evolutionary theory is correct, it has some implications for everyday life. For example, women and men tend to use different strategies to find their way in the world. Men's strategies rely more on geography and directions, whereas women use landmarks in navigation (Schmitz, 1999). Men's use of geography and directions may be related to their proficiency in spatial orientation. Some researchers have related people's ability to find their way to spatial ability. Much of this research focuses on gender differences. The results from some studies show that men are more confident and learn to find their way around an unfamiliar place faster than women do (Schmitz, 1999; Silverman et al., 2000), but other researchers find that, despite the difference in strategies, women and men do equally well in navigating the world (Malinowski, 2001). Thus, the support for gender differences based on evolutionary theory is not clear.

▲ Women and men tend to use different strategies to find their way in the world. Men's strategy relies more on geography and directions, whereas women's navigation uses landmarks.

## EYE MOVEMENTS

Your eyes are constantly in motion. They search for familiar faces in a crowded classroom, scan the headlines on a page in a newspaper, or follow a baseball hit high into right field for a home run. You notice when someone else is eyeing something over your shoulder and when someone is fixating on a spot on top of your head (is there a spider there?). Research on eye movements reveals what people are looking at, how long they look at it, and perhaps where they will look next. It also helps psychologists understand the visual link with auditory processing and sentence production (Griffin & Bock, 2000) and some visual problems, such as reading disabilities. Zangwill and Blakemore (1972) studied the eye movements of a man who had difficulty reading. They found that he was moving his eyes from right to left across the page, rather than in the usual left to right direction. Eye movements also depend on the context in which they are measured. The eye movements of a reader are different from those of someone keyboarding text, even when both are examining the same material. The keyboarder is processing the text merely in order to transcribe it, not to absorb its meaning, as the reader is doing (Inhoff, Starr, & Shindler, 2000). Thus, when researchers study eye movements, they work from the bottom up and from the top down, from the physiology and nature of the actual movements to the functions they perform (Schiller, 1998).

**Saccades** are the most common type of eye movement—in fact, your eyes make at least 100 000 saccades per day. These are rapid voluntary movements of the eyes when you are reading, driving, or looking for an object. The eye can make only four or five saccades in a second. Each movement of the eye takes only about 20 to 50 milliseconds, but there is a delay of about 200 to 250 milliseconds before the next movement can be made. During this delay, the eye fixates on some part of the visual field. People use eye *fixations* to form representations of the visual world, probably by integrating successive glances into memory. This integration requires that observers move their eyes, pay attention to key elements of a visual scene, and exert careful, systematic control over eye movements (Rayner, Reichle, & Pollatsek, 2000) (see Figure 3.10).

SACCADES [sack-ADZ]
Rapid voluntary movements of the eyes.

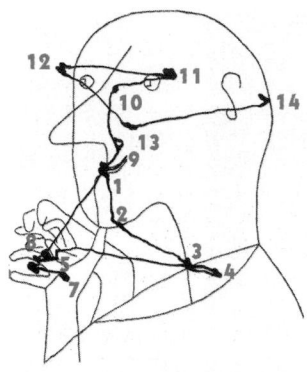

**FIGURE 3.10**

**Patterns of Eye Movement**

Eye movements made by a person viewing a drawing adapted from Paul Klee's *Old Man Figuring*. The numbers show the order of the visual fixations. Lines between the numbers represent saccades, which occupied about 10 percent of the viewing time. The remainder of the time was spent fixating.

HUE

The psychological property of light referred to as colour, determined by the wavelengths of reflected light.

BRIGHTNESS

The lightness or darkness of reflected light, determined in large part by the light's intensity.

**FIGURE 3.11**

**Spectral Sensitivity Curve**

The average observer's sensitivity to visible light during daylight reaches a peak at 555 nanometres. Thus, the normal human eye is more sensitive to yellow wavelengths than to red or blue. The curve in the graph is called a *spectral sensitivity curve*.

Eye movements have been used to determine the *perceptual span*—the size of the region a person sees when fixating visually; for example, the perceptual span is the number of letters you see when you fixate on a specific point on this page. Research shows that people use information gathered by both central vision (at the fovea) and peripheral vision (at noncentral regions of the eye) to determine the location of their next eye movements; this information ultimately affects the size of the perceptual span (Machado & Rafal, 2000; Rayner, 1998). Like so many other psychological phenomena, the size and nature of the perceptual span depend on the situation and personal variables; that is, the size of the perceptual span increases and decreases according to variables such as interest, motivation, and the presence of observers. People also tend to direct their gaze to a point just to the left of centre of words when they are reading. This site (left of centre) may help them make inferences about the rest of the word and even where they will look next (Inhoff, Starr, & Shindler, 2000).

## COLOUR VISION

Think of all the different shades of blue (navy blue, sky blue, baby blue, royal blue, turquoise, aqua). If you have normal vision, you have no trouble discriminating among a wide range of colours. Colour depends on the wavelengths of the visible light that stimulates the photoreceptors. It has three psychological dimensions: hue, brightness, and saturation. These dimensions correspond to three physical properties of light: wavelength, intensity, and purity.

When people speak of the colour of an object, they are referring to its **hue**—whether the light reflected from the object looks red, blue, orange, or some other colour. *Hue* is a psychological term, because objects themselves do not possess colour. Rather, a person's perception of colour is determined by how the eyes and brain interpret reflected wavelengths. In the visible spectrum, a different hue is associated with each range of wavelengths. Light with a wavelength of 400 to 450 nanometres looks blue; light with a wavelength of 700 nanometres looks red.

The second psychological dimension of colour is **brightness**—how light or dark the hue of an object appears. Brightness is affected by three variables: (1) the greater the intensity of reflected light, the brighter the object; (2) the longer the wavelength of reflected light, the less bright the object; (3) the nearer the wavelengths are to the range of 500 to 600 nanometres, the more sensitive the photoreceptors (see Figure 3.11). This is why school buses are often painted yellow—it makes them more visible to motorists, because yellow falls at about 580 nanometres and is therefore easily detected.

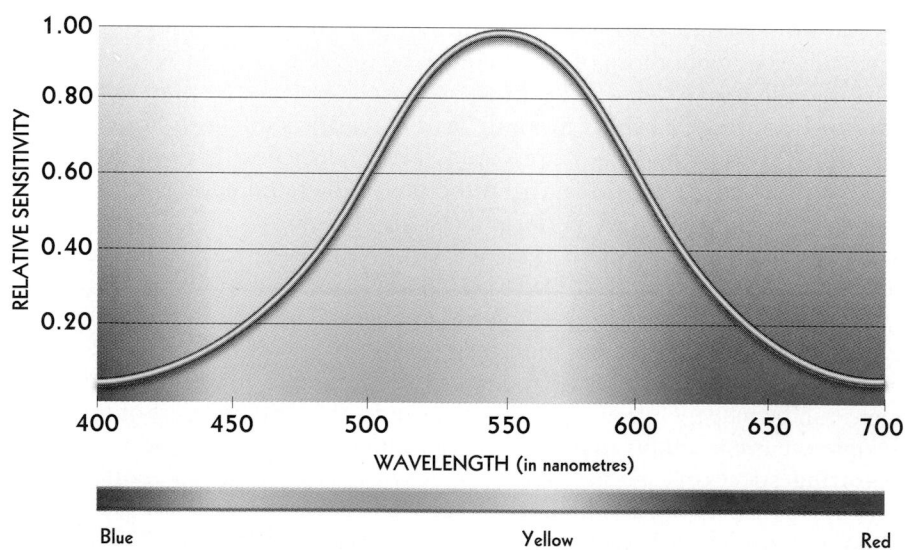

The third psychological dimension of colour is **saturation**, or *purity*—the depth and richness of the hue, determined by the homogeneity of the wavelengths contained in the reflected light. Few objects reflect light that is totally pure. Usually objects reflect a mixture of wavelengths. Pure, saturated light has a narrow band of wavelengths and, thus, a narrow range of perceived colour. A saturated red light with no blue, yellow, or white in it, for example, appears as a very intense red. Unsaturated colours are produced by a wider band of wavelengths. Unsaturated red light can appear to be light pink, dark red, or rusty brown, because its wider range of wavelengths makes it less pure (see Figure 3.12).

THEORIES OF COLOUR VISION.    How does the brain code and process colour? Two nineteenth-century scientists, Thomas Young and Hermann von Helmholtz, working independently, proposed that different types of cones provide the basis for colour coding in the visual system. *Colour coding* is the ability to discriminate among colours on the basis of differences in wavelength. According to the **trichromatic theory**, or the *Young-Helmholtz theory*, mixing three basic colours—red, green, and blue—can make all colours. (*Trichromatic* means "three colours"—*tri* meaning "three" and *chroma* meaning "colour.") All cone cells in the retina are assumed to respond to all wavelengths of light; but there are three types of cones that are especially likely to respond to red, green, or blue wavelengths (see Figure 3.13). The combined neural output of the red-sensitive, green-sensitive, and blue-sensitive cones provides the information that enables a person to distinguish colour. If the neural output from one type of cone is sufficiently greater than that from the others, that type of colour receptor will have a stronger influence on a person's perception of colour. Because each person's neurons are unique, it is likely that each of us sees colour somewhat differently.

Unfortunately, the trichromatic theory does not account for some specific visual phenomena. For example, it does not explain why some colours look more vivid when placed next to other colours (colour contrast). It does not explain why people asked to name the basic colours nearly always name more than three. Further, the trichromatic theory does not do a good job of explaining aspects of **colour blindness**—the inability to perceive different hues (described below). For example, many people with colour blindness cannot successfully discriminate colours in two areas of the visual spectrum. In 1887, to solve some of the problems left unsolved by the

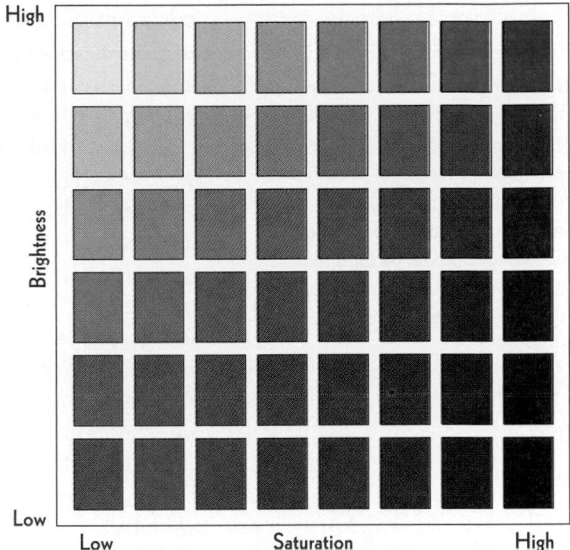

**FIGURE 3.12**

**Hue, Brightness, and Saturation**

These colours have the same dominant wavelength (hue) but different saturation and brightness.

SATURATION

The depth and richness of a hue determined by the homogeneity of the wavelengths contained in the reflected light; also known as *purity*.

TRICHROMATIC
[try-kroe-MAT-ick] THEORY

Visual theory, stated by Young and Helmholtz, that all colours can be made by mixing the three basic colours: red, green, and blue; also known as the *Young-Helmholtz theory*.

COLOUR BLINDNESS

The inability to perceive different hues.

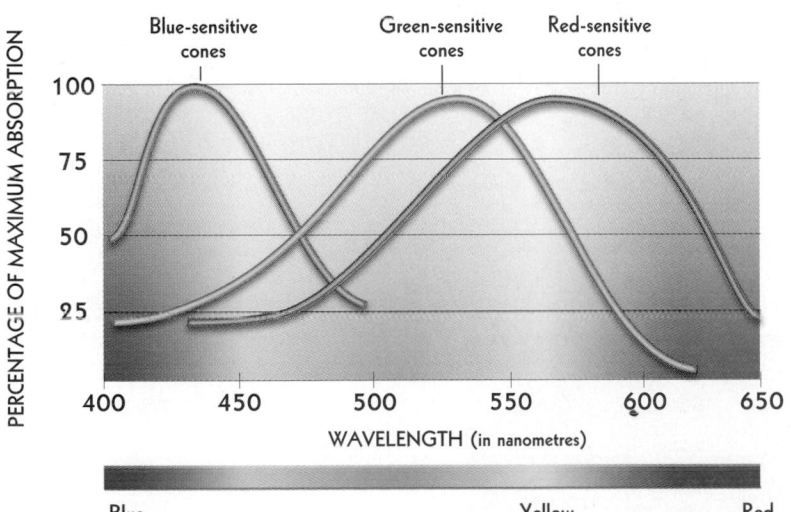

**FIGURE 3.13**

**Three Types of Cones**

Each of the three types of cones in the eye has peak sensitivity in a different area of the visible spectrum. Thus, certain cells are more responsive to some wavelengths than to others (Marks, Dobell, & MacNichol, 1964).

trichromatic theory, Ewald Herring proposed another theory of colour vision—the **opponent-process theory**. According to this theory, at the level of the retinal ganglion cell, sensory input from three cone types is translated into an opponent colour system with red opposing green, blue opposing yellow, and white (intense light) opposing black (no light). Three pairs of mechanisms respond to light intensity and wavelength in opposite ways. Each member of the pair responds antagonistically to the other; that is, excitation of one inhibits the other. Thus, red and green are mutually exclusive; an object may appear green or it may appear red but it cannot be red and green at the same time. Nor can an object appear blue and yellow simultaneously (see Figure 3.14). Colour opponent processing also explains visual afterimages. If you look at a green object for about a minute and then transfer your gaze to an empty space, you will experience a red afterimage (see Figure 3.15). According to opponent processing, the neural mechanisms for green become fatigued and the receptors respond with an "unfatigued" red response.

Thus, if a red light is shone on the retina, a red-green cell will increase its rate of firing. A green light would cause the cell to decrease firing. The red- and green-sensitive cones in the retina relay the sensory input they receive to the red-green opponent process. The same is true for the blue cones. The yellow opponent process cannot receive input from a yellow cone since there isn't one, so it receives simultaneous input from the red- and green-sensitive cones. Both the trichromatic theory and the opponent-process theory have received support from research (e.g., Hurvich & Jameson, 1974). Physiological studies of the retina do show three classes of cones. Thus, the trichromatic theory seems to describe accurately the coding at the

**FIGURE 3.14**

**The Role of Opponent Processing in Colour Vision**

Retinal cone cells convey information to opponent-process cells higher in the brain. These opponent-process cells in turn signal the colour-processing cells in the cortex with precise information about the colours present by sending information about whether they are excited or inhibited based on the information they received from the cone cells.

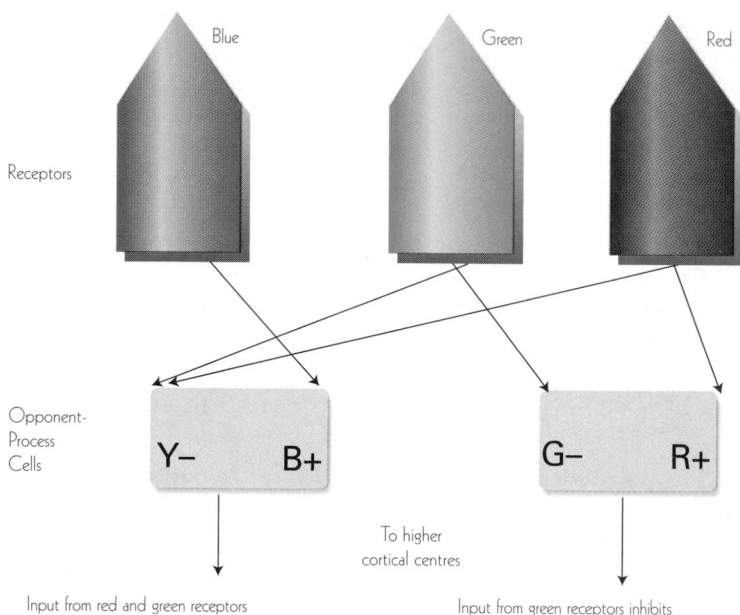

**FIGURE 3.15**

**Demonstration of a Negative Afterimage**

Stare at the dot in the middle of the flag image for one minute. Then shift your gaze to the blank space. You should experience a negative afterimage (a red and white Canadian flag).

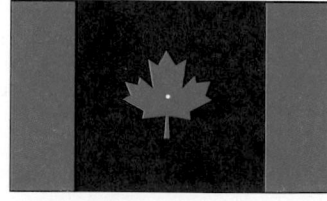

retina (Marks, Dobell, & MacNichol, 1964). Support for the opponent-process theory comes from microelectrode studies of the lateral geniculate nucleus in monkeys. Cells in this nucleus respond differently to various wavelengths. When the eye is stimulated with light of a wavelength between 400 and 500 nanometres, some cells in the lateral geniculate nucleus decrease their rate of firing. If the eye is stimulated with light of a longer wavelength, their firing rate increases (DeValois & Jacobs, 1968). This change is predicted by the opponent-process theory. Exactly how colour information is transferred from the retina to the lateral geniculate nucleus remains to be discovered (Engel, 1999).

**COLOUR BLINDNESS.** In 1794, John Dalton, formulator of the atomic theory of matter, believed he had figured out why he couldn't distinguish his red stockings from his green ones. He reasoned that something blue in his eyeball absorbed red light and prevented him from seeing red. Although Dalton was the first to try to describe colour blindness scientifically, he was not the first—or the last—person to suffer from it.

Most human beings have normal colour vision and can distinguish among about 100 different hues; they are considered trichromats. **Trichromats** are people who can perceive all three primary colours and thus can distinguish any hue. A very few people (less than 1 percent) do not see any colour. These people, known as **monochromats**, are totally colour-blind and cannot discriminate among wavelengths, often because they lack cones in their retinas (Boynton, 1988). The lack of the specific colour-absorbing pigment or chemical in the cones makes accurate colour discriminations impossible. Fortunately, most people with colour vision deficiencies (about 8 percent of men and 1 percent of women) are only partially colour-blind (Nathans, 1989). **Dichromats** are people who can distinguish only two of the three basic colours; they have difficulty distinguishing between either red and green or blue and yellow. About 2 percent of men cannot discriminate between reds and greens (Wyszecki & Stiles, 1967). What does the world look like to a person who is a dichromat? Such a person sees all the colours in a range of the electromagnetic spectrum as similar.

The full role of genetics in colour blindness is not clear, but this perceptual problem is transmitted genetically from mothers to their male offspring. The fact that more men than women are colour-blind is due to the way this genetic information is coded and passed on to each generation. Colour blindness results from inherited alterations in the genes that are responsible for cone pigments; these genes are located on the X chromosome. Since girls have two X chromosomes and boys have only one, a girl will be colour-deficient only if she inherits the defective gene from both parents. Boys who inherit an X chromosome with a defective gene will have deficient colour vision.

**TRICHROMATS**

People who can perceive all three primary colours and thus can distinguish any hue.

**MONOCHROMATS**

People who are totally colour-blind and cannot discriminate among wavelengths, often because they lack cones in their retinas.

**DICHROMATS**

People who can distinguish only two of the three basic colours; they have difficulty distinguishing between either red and green or blue and yellow.

**Be an ACTIVE LEARNER**

**REVIEW**
> What does it mean to be myopic? p. 93
> What are three important differences between rods and cones? pp. 93–94
> Describe the process of dark adaptation. pp. 94–95

**THINK CRITICALLY**
> Why do you think boys and girls might vary on some visual tasks?

**APPLY PSYCHOLOGY**
> Design an invention—a pair of glasses—that might help a partially colour-blind person see colour better.
> How might you design a better pair of everyday corrective lenses? What might ensure better vision?

# Visual Perception

As we said at the beginning of this chapter, perceptual experiences use sensory input but also involve past events in addition to current stimulation. Integrating previous experiences with new events makes perceptual encounters more meaningful. For example, it is only with experience that children learn that an object stays the same size and shape when it is moved away from their immediate location. In this section, we will look at a range of visual perceptual phenomena that rely heavily on the integration of past and current experiences.

### PERCEPTION OF FORM: CONSTANCY

Perceptual constancy is the maintenance of a stable perception in the presence of continual, substantial variation in physical stimulation. For example, you recognize

**HandsOnPsych**
Version 2.0

**Perception**

# INTRODUCTION TO Research Basics

## Have You Ever Smelled a Colour?

Occasionally a phenomenon that is mildly mystifying presents itself to a psychologist. Such topics are often difficult, but not impossible, to assess experimentally—consider synesthesia.

Synesthesia is a bizarre phenomenon in which sensory images or qualities of one modality, such as vision, are transferred to another modality, such as taste or hearing (Marks, 2000; Ramachandran, 2000). To a synesthetic person, a sip of lemonade may take on a green colour as well as a sour-sweet flavour, or a soprano's aria may take on visual form that changes in shape, size, and colour. In synesthesia, therefore, a stimulus produces two kinds of responses at the same time: the principal sensory experience that is normally associated with the stimulus and a second experience in another modality (Armel & Ramachandran, 1999). In synesthesia we hear shapes, see colours as sound, and may perceive a shirt as noisy (Martino & Marks, 2001).

The incidence of synesthesia is estimated to be approximately 1 in 25 000 individuals. There is probably a genetic component; it runs in families, and 15 percent of people with synesthesia have an immediate family history of other neurological abnormalities, including dyslexia, autism, and attention-deficit disorder. Typically, the synesthetic individual is female, left-handed, and of normal intelligence (Grossenbacher & Lovelace, 2001).

Canadian synesthesia researcher Phil Merikle of the Synaesthesia Research Centre at the University of Waterloo and his colleagues (Dixon et al., 2000) have investigated the phenomenon by looking at a specific form of synesthesia called *coloured number synesthesia*.

**Design.** A *case study design* was chosen for this study. This procedure involves carefully studying the behaviour and responses of a single individual with synesthesia. Conditions such as synesthesia are so distinct and so rare that while it is often not possible to put a large research sample together, even the examination of the behaviours and responses of a single individual with the condition can be very instructive.

**Hypothesis.** Merikle and his colleagues hypothesized that people with synesthesia would be influenced by the perceptual qualities of visual displays prompted by their synesthesia as well as by primary sensory properties.

**Participants.** One individual, an adult woman diagnosed with coloured letter synesthesia, served as participant.

**Procedure.** The participant completed a series of perceptual tests. In one, the participant was shown a series of black letters and asked to report on her experiences. In another, she was asked to think of a letter without the letter actually being presented.

**Results.** The results were compelling. The participant with synesthesia reported specific colours related to individual letters. More interestingly, she reported the same colours when asked to think about the letters but not look at them.

**Conclusions.** Merikle and his colleagues assert that the phenomenon of synesthesia is a real perceptual process. Furthermore, they argue that these specific cross-modal perceptions are wired at a fairly "high" level in the perceptual system, as they can be evoked by conceptual reflection alone. This wiring is unusual, but the researchers suggest that it is more common among artists and poets than others. Their results suggest that synesthesia is a real phenomenon, one that can and should be investigated and that probably has a unique physiological basis. This subject needs further investigation.

**Limitations.** A main limitation with case studies concerns their generalizability. Basically, the behaviours of a single participant may not generalize (or be the same as) the behaviours of other people in similar circumstances. Case studies are still very valuable as they provide us with rich detailed information about conditions that may be rare but that may also give us very valuable hints about how the human perceptual system is wired (and how it may become wired to provide different, unique experiences).

your dog whether you are viewing it from the side, the front, or the back. You recognize it in low light, whether it is close or far away. Despite variations in size, shape, and luminance you recognize your pet. This ability to perceive enduring qualities in the face of enormous change is impressive. Thus the perceptual constancy task cannot simply rely on sensory stimuli. We must evaluate and interpret the sensory input, relying on our memories of and our experiences with stable objects and a reasonably permanent world.

**SIZE CONSTANCY.**    People generally can judge the size of an object, even if the size of its image on the retina changes. For example, you can estimate the height of a six-foot-tall man who is standing 15 metres away and who casts a small image on the retina; you can also estimate his height from only two metres away, when he casts a much larger image on the retina. **Size constancy** is the ability of the perceptual system to recognize that an object remains constant in size regardless of its distance from the observer or the size of its image on the retina.

Three variables determine a person's ability to maintain size constancy: (1) experience with the true size of objects, (2) the distance between the object and the person, and (3) the presence of surrounding objects. As an object is moved farther away, the size of its image on the retina decreases and its perceived distance increases (see Figure 3.16). These two processes always work together. Moreover, as an object is moved away, its size relative to the objects around it does not change. This is why knowing the size of surrounding objects helps people determine the moved object's distance as well as its actual size.

Researchers have studied how experience helps people establish and maintain size constancy. Bower (1966) trained 50- to 60-day-old infants to look toward a specific object by reinforcing their direction of gaze (the reinforcement was an adult saying "peekaboo"). He then placed other objects of different sizes at various distances from the infants so that the sizes of their retinal images varied. Finally, he arranged the objects so that the small ones were close to the infants and the large ones were farther away, causing the sizes of retinal images to be the same. In all of these situations, the infants showed size constancy. They turned their heads only toward the original reinforced object, not toward the other objects that produced images of the same size on the retina. It is clear that infants attain size constancy by the age of six months and probably as early as four months (Luger, Bower, & Wishart, 1983; McKenzie, Tootell, & Day, 1980).

**SHAPE CONSTANCY.**    Another important aspect of form perception is **shape constancy**—the ability to recognize a shape despite changes in the angle or position

SIZE CONSTANCY

The ability of the perceptual system to recognize that an object remains constant in size regardless of its distance from the observer or the size of its image on the retina.

SHAPE CONSTANCY

The ability to recognize a shape despite changes in the orientation or angle from which it is viewed.

**FIGURE 3.16**
**Perceptual Constancies**

*Size constancy* is the perceptual system's ability to recognize that an object remains the same size regardless of its distance from an observer or the size of its image on the retina. *Shape constancy* is the perceptual system's ability to recognize a shape despite changes in the angle or position from which it is viewed.

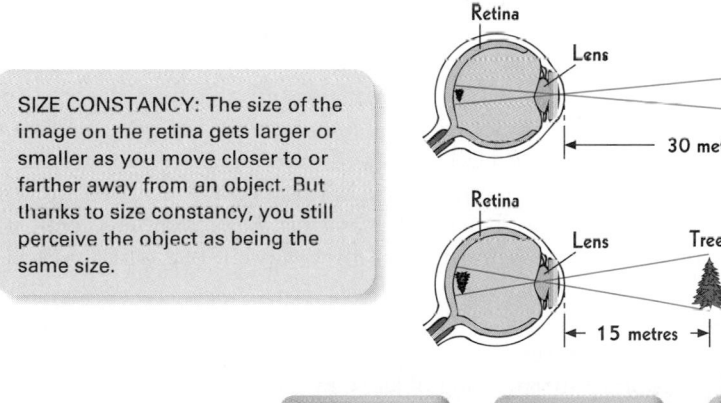

SIZE CONSTANCY: The size of the image on the retina gets larger or smaller as you move closer to or farther away from an object. But thanks to size constancy, you still perceive the object as being the same size.

SHAPE CONSTANCY: A door is a door is a door . . . whether it is open, shut, or viewed at an angle.

▲ Zen landscape artists use the principles of depth perception to create seemingly expansive, rugged gardens out of small plots of land.

**HandsOnPsych**
Version 2.0

**Perception**

MONOCULAR
[mah-NAHK-you-ler]
DEPTH CUES

Depth cues that do not depend on the use of both eyes.

from which it is viewed (see Figure 3.16). For example, even though you usually see trees standing perpendicular to the ground, you can recognize a tree when it has been chopped down and is lying in a horizontal position. Similarly, an ice cream cone looks triangular when you view it from the side; yet you perceive it as an ice cream cone even when you view it from above, where it appears more circular than triangular.

## DEPTH PERCEPTION

For centuries, Zen landscape artists have used the principles of perception to create seemingly expansive, rugged gardens out of tiny plots of land. Although a Zen landscape artist can fool the eye, you judge the distance of objects every day when you drive a car, catch a ball, or take a picture. You estimate your distance from an object and the distance between one object and another. These cues are operative and evident even in infants (Sen, Yonas, & Knill, 2001). Closely associated with these two tasks is the ability to see in three dimensions—that is, in terms of height, width, and depth. Both monocular (one-eyed) and binocular (two-eyed) cues are used in depth perception. Binocular cues predominate at close distances, and monocular cues are used for distant scenes and two-dimensional fields of view, such as paintings. Because the visual system is still plastic (modifiable) early in life, where and how depth information is coded depends on an infant's experiences. Research shows, for example, that binocular depth information is coded at different places if there is a deprivation of depth experience (Trachtenberg, Trepel, & Stryker, 2000).

**MONOCULAR DEPTH CUES.** Depth cues that do not depend on the use of both eyes are **monocular depth cues** (see Figure 3.17). There are dynamic and static monocular depth cues. Two important dynamic monocular depth cues relate to the effects of motion on perception. The first cue, *motion parallax*, occurs when a moving observer stares at a fixed point. The objects behind that point appear to move in the same direction as the observer; the objects in front of the point appear to move in the opposite direction. For example, if you stare at a fence while riding in a moving car, the trees behind the fence rails seem to move in the same direction as the car (forward) and the bushes in front of the rails seem to move in the opposite direction (backward). Motion parallax also affects the speed at which objects appear to move. Objects at a greater distance from the moving observer appear to move more slowly than objects that are closer. The second monocular depth cue derived from movement is the *kinetic depth effect*. Objects that look flat when they are stationary appear to be three-dimensional when set in motion. For example, a bent paperclip lying in a stationary position appears two dimensional, but when picked up and rotated it appears three-dimensional.

Static monocular depth cues are often seen in photographs and paintings. For example, larger or taller objects usually are perceived to be closer than smaller ones, particularly in relation to surrounding objects. In addition, *linear perspective* affects perception; this cue is based on the principle that distant objects appear to be closer together than nearer objects. For example, a painter shows distance by making parallel lines converge as they recede. Another monocular cue for depth is *interposition*. When one object blocks part of another, the first appears to be closer. Another monocular cue is *texture*; surfaces that have little texture or detail seem to be in the distance. Artists often use the additional cues of *highlighting* and *shadowing*. Highlighted (light) objects appear close; shadowed (dark) objects appear to be farther away. In addition, the perceptual system picks up other information from shadowing, including the curvature of surfaces (Cavanagh & Leclerc, 1989). Still another monocular depth cue is *atmospheric perspective*, which relates to light wavelengths themselves. Distant mountains often look blue, for example, because

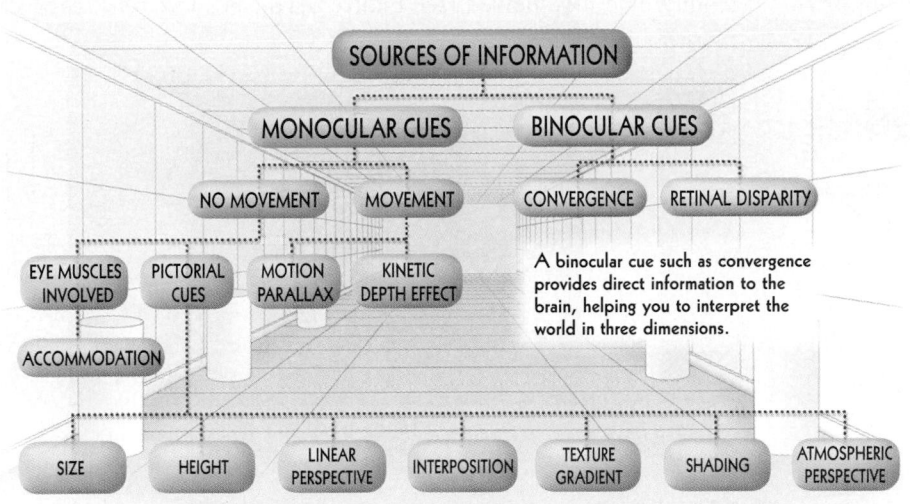

SOURCES OF INFORMATION

MONOCULAR CUES   BINOCULAR CUES

NO MOVEMENT   MOVEMENT   CONVERGENCE   RETINAL DISPARITY

EYE MUSCLES INVOLVED   PICTORIAL CUES   MOTION PARALLAX   KINETIC DEPTH EFFECT

A binocular cue such as convergence provides direct information to the brain, helping you to interpret the world in three dimensions.

ACCOMMODATION

SIZE   HEIGHT   LINEAR PERSPECTIVE   INTERPOSITION   TEXTURE GRADIENT   SHADING   ATMOSPHERIC PERSPECTIVE

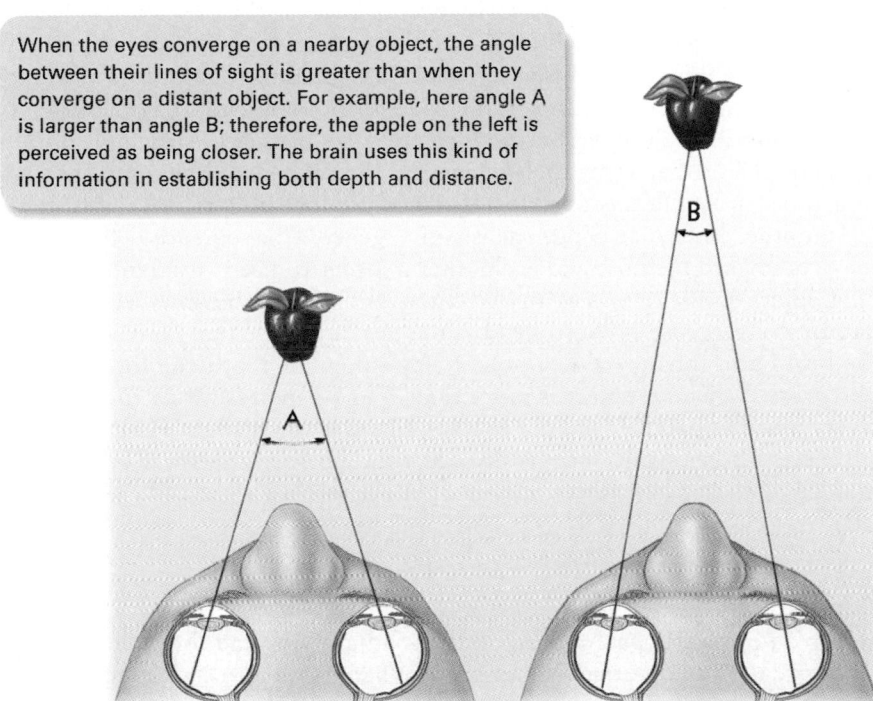

When the eyes converge on a nearby object, the angle between their lines of sight is greater than when they converge on a distant object. For example, here angle A is larger than angle B; therefore, the apple on the left is perceived as being closer. The brain uses this kind of information in establishing both depth and distance.

B

A

long (red) wavelengths are more easily scattered as they pass through the air, allowing more short (blue) wavelengths to reach our eyes. Leonardo da Vinci used this phenomenon in his paintings; he even developed an equation for how much blue pigment should be mixed with the natural colour of an object so the object would appear as far away as he wished. Michelangelo's angels seem to float off the ceiling of the Sistine Chapel because he used colour so effectively to portray depth.

If a person looks from one object to another object at a different distance, the lenses of the eye will accommodate—that is, change shape to adapt to the depth of focus. This monocular cue is available from each eye separately. **Accommodation** is the change in the shape of the lens that enables the observer to keep an object in focus on the retina when the object is moved or when the choice of objects changes. Muscles attached to the lens control this change, which provides information about the shape of the lens to the higher processing systems in the brain.

ACCOMMODATION
The change in the shape of the lens of the eye to keep an object in focus on the retina when the object is moved closer to or farther away from the observer.

▲ Mountains in the distance often look blue because of the monocular depth cue atmospheric perspective. Similarly, Michelangelo's figures seem to float off the ceiling of the Sistine Chapel because he used colour so effectively to portray depth.

**BINOCULAR DEPTH CUES**

Any visual cues for depth perception that require the use of both eyes.

**RETINAL DISPARITY**

The slight difference between the visual images projected on the two retinas.

**CONVERGENCE**

The movement of the eyes toward each other in order to keep visual input at corresponding points on the retinas as an object moves closer to the observer.

**ILLUSION**

A perception of a physical stimulus that differs from measurable reality and normal expectations about its appearance.

**BINOCULAR DEPTH CUES.**    Most people, even infants, also use **binocular depth cues**—cues that require the use of both eyes. One important binocular depth cue is **retinal disparity**, which is the slight difference between the visual images projected on the two retinas. Retinal disparity occurs because the eyes are physically five to seven centimetres apart, which causes them to see objects from slightly different angles. To see how retinal disparity works, hold a finger up in front of some distant object. Examine the object first with one eye and then with the other eye. Your finger will appear in different positions relative to the object. The closer objects are to the eyes, the farther apart their images on the retinas will be—and the greater the retinal disparity. Objects at a great distance produce little retinal disparity.

Another binocular depth cue is convergence. **Convergence** is the movement of the eyes toward the nose and each other in order to keep visual input at corresponding points on the retinas as an object moves closer to the observer. Like accommodation, convergence is controlled by muscles in the eye that convey information to the brain and thus provide a potent physiological depth cue for stimuli close to observers. When an object is more than 7 to 10 metres away, the eyes are aimed pretty much in parallel, and the effect of this cue diminishes. When we wish to look at objects farther away, our eyes diverge, rotating outward toward the temples, each moving in an opposite direction (the right eye moving right and the left eye moving left).

## ILLUSIONS

Have you ever seen water ahead on the road, only to find that it has disappeared a moment later as you drive by that spot? When the normal visual process and depth cues seem to break down, you experience an optical illusion. An **illusion** is a perception of a physical stimulus that differs from measurable reality and the commonly expected appearance; many consider it to be a misperception of stimulation.

A common illusion is the *Müller–Lyer illusion*, in which two equal-length lines with arrows attached to their ends appear to be of different lengths. A similar illusion is the *Ponzo illusion* (sometimes called the railroad illusion), in which two horizontal lines of the same length, bracketed by slanted lines, appear to be of different lengths. (See Figure 3.18 for examples of these two illusions and three others. Figure 3.19 presents another perceptual phenomenon.) One natural illusion is the moon illusion. Although the actual size of the moon and the size of its image on the retina do not change, the moon appears about 30 percent larger when it is near the horizon than when it is overhead. The *moon illusion* is quite striking. In just a few minutes, the size of the moon appears to change from quite large to quite small. The moon illusion is even seen in photographs and paintings (Coren & Aks, 1990; Suzuki, 1998).

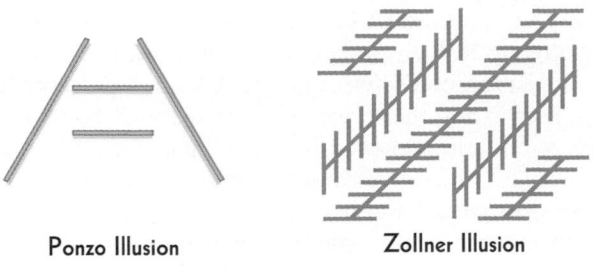

Ponzo Illusion

Zollner Illusion

**FIGURE 3.18**

**Five Well-Known Illusions**

In the Müller-Lyer and Ponzo illusions, lines of equal length appear to differ in length. The photos with the Müller-Lyer illusion show how the arrows can represent a "near corner" and a "far corner." In the Zollner illusion, the short lines make the longer ones seem not parallel, even though they are. In the Wundt illusion, the centre horizontal lines are parallel, even though they appear bent. In the Poggendorf illusion, the line disappears behind a solid and reappears in a position that seems wrong.

Müller-Lyer
Illusion

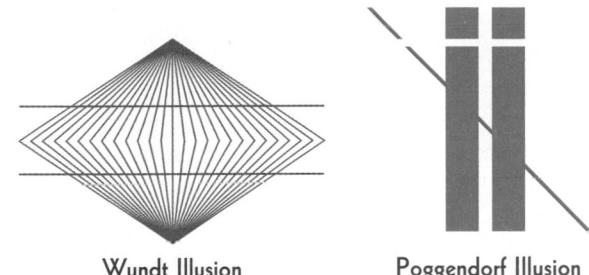

Wundt Illusion

Poggendorf Illusion

How do visual illusions work? No completely satisfactory explanations have been found. Recent theories account for them in terms of the backgrounds against which the objects are seen.

These explanations are based on the observer's previous experiences and well-developed perceptual constancies. For example, the moon illusion is explained by the fact that, when seen overhead, the moon has a featureless background, whereas at the horizon objects are close to it. Objects in the landscape provide cues about distance that change the observer's perception of the size of the moon (Baird, Wagner, & Fuld, 1990; Restle, 1970). To see how the moon illusion depends on landscape cues, try this: When the moon is at the horizon, bend over and look at it from between your legs. Since that position screens out some of the horizon cues, the magnitude of the illusion will be reduced.

The Ponzo illusion is similarly accounted for by the linear perspective provided by the slanted background lines. The Müller–Lyer illusion occurs because of the angle and shape of the arrows attached to the ends of the lines. Lines angled inward are often interpreted as far corners—those that are most distant from the observer. Lines angled outward are commonly interpreted as near corners—those that are closest to the observer. Therefore, lines with far-corner angles attached to them appear longer because their length is judged in a context of distance.

These are not the only ways of explaining illusions. Some researchers assert that people see the moon as having different sizes on the horizon and overhead because they judge it as they judge other moving objects that pass through space. Because the moon does not move closer to them, they assume it is moving away. Objects that move away get smaller; hence the illusion of a change in the size of the moon (Reed, 1984). This explanation focuses on constancies but also takes into account movement, space, and the atmosphere.

## GESTALT LAWS OF ORGANIZATION

Gestalt psychologists suggest that conscious experience is more than the sum of its parts. They argue that the mind organizes the elements of experience to form something unique; they thus view the world in

**FIGURE 3.19**

**Impossible Figures**

Many types of drawings trick the perceiver because they portray *impossible figures*. The longer you stare at this drawing by M. C. Escher, the more visually confusing you'll find the arrangement of its components.

terms of perceptual frameworks. Analyzed as a whole experience, the patterns of a person's perceptions make sense. The first Gestalt psychologists—including Max Wertheimer, Kurt Koffka, and Wolfgang Köhler—greatly influenced early theories of form perception. These psychologists assumed (wrongly) that human perceptual processes *solely* reflect brain organization and that they could learn about the workings of the brain by studying perception. Researchers now know, of course, that the relationship between brain structure and function is much more complex—perception is a process that not only represents stimuli but also reflects past experiences.

The early Gestaltists focused their perceptual studies on the ways in which people experience form and organization. These early researchers believed that people organize each complex visual field into a coherent whole rather than seeing individual, unrelated elements. That is, they believed that people see groups of elements, not fragmented parts. According to this idea, called the **law of Prägnanz**, items or stimuli that *can* be grouped together and seen as a whole, or a form, *will* be seen that way; people see the simplest shape consistent with available information. So, for example, people tend to see the series of 16 dots in the lower left portion of Figure 3.20 as a square. Not only did the Gestaltists see the world through the lenses of grouping and form but they also felt that retinal stimulation was directly reflected in physiological processing.

The law of Prägnanz was based on principles of organization for the perception of figures, especially contours, which help define figure–ground relationships. Gestalt psychologists focused on the nature of *figure–ground relationships*, contending that people perceive *figures* (the main objects of sensory attention—the

**LAW OF PRÄGNANZ**
[PREG-nants]

The Gestalt principle that when items or stimuli *can* be grouped together and seen as a whole, they *will* be.

**FIGURE 3.20**
**Gestalt Laws**

Gestalt principles are the organizing elements humans use to group perceptual fragments into the coherent wholes by which they perceive the world.

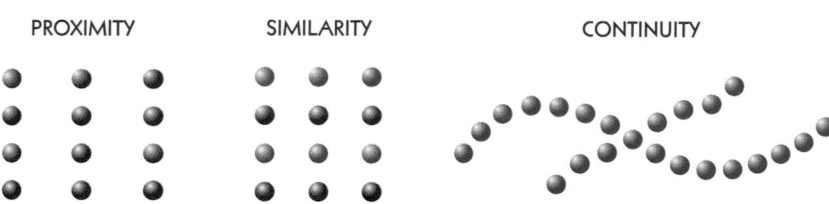

PROXIMITY  SIMILARITY  CONTINUITY

According to the Gestalt law of proximity, the circles on the left appear to be arranged in vertical columns because items that are close together tend to be perceived as a unit. According to the law of similarity, the red and blue circles in the middle appear to be arranged in horizontal rows because similar items tend to be perceived in groups. According to the law of continuity, an observer can predict where the next item should occur in the arrangement on the right because the grouping of items projects lines into space.

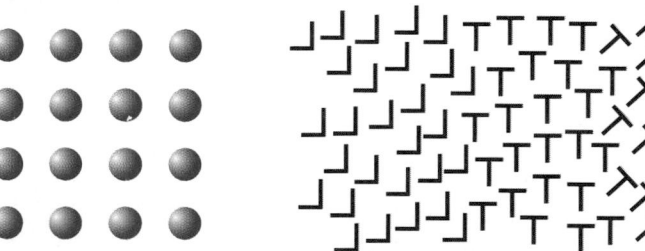

The law of Prägnanz: Items or stimuli that *can* be grouped together as a whole *will* be. These 16 dots are typically perceived as a square.

In a study asking people to divide these objects into two groups, Beck (1966) found that participants generally placed the boundary between upright and tilted *Ts* rather than between the backward *Ls* and the upright *Ts* because the latter appear more similar. Beck argued that this result supports the law of Prägnanz.

foregrounds) as distinct from the *grounds* (the backgrounds) on which they are presented (see Figure 3.21). Gestalt psychologists developed the following series of laws, the first three of which are illustrated in the upper part of Figure 3.20, for predicting which areas of an ambiguous pattern would be seen as the figure (foreground) and which would be seen as the ground (background):

- *Law of proximity*—elements close to one another in space or time will be perceived as groups.
- *Law of similarity*—similar items will be perceived as groups.
- *Law of continuity*—a string of items will indicate where the next item in the string will be found.
- *Common fate principle*—items that move or change together will be perceived as a whole.
- *Law of closure*—parts of a figure that are not presented will be filled in by the perceptual system.

Beck (1966) conducted a well-known study that examined Gestalt principles (see the lower right portion of Figure 3.20). However, Beck's work showed that Gestalt principles are vague: They apply whether participants choose orientation or shape to break up the figure, but they do not explain why orientation predominated in Beck's study. Gestalt laws are not always obeyed, nor are they always consistent with current knowledge of brain organization. For example, when a figure is made up of other figures people are not always consistent in what they choose to pay attention to, the larger figure or the embedded smaller ones (Rock & Palmer, 1990). Furthermore, our "what" and "where" processing cells are located in various locations throughout the brain—processing is not merely bottom up but also top down. Nevertheless, these early investigations continue to influence perceptual psychologists as springboards that have some elements of truth.

# Hearing

You may have heard the oft-repeated idea that blind people can hear better than sighted individuals; at least with some tasks, it turns out to be true (Bavelier et al., 2000; Rosenbluth, Grossman, & Kaitz, 2000). Hearing is taken for granted by most of us, but the ability and task of a listener is exceedingly complex. Consider music. Listening closely to a Beethoven symphony is delightful and intriguing, but it is difficult because so much is going on at once. With more than 20 instruments playing, the listener must process many sounds, rhythms, and intensities simultaneously. Like seeing, hearing is a complex process that involves converting physical stimuli into a psychological experience. For example, suppose that a tuning fork is struck or a stereo system booms out a bass note. In both cases, sound waves are being created and air is being moved. The movement of the air and the accompanying changes in air pressure (physical stimuli) cause your eardrum to move back and forth rapidly. The movement of the eardrum triggers a series of *electromechanical* and *electrochemical* changes that you ultimately experience as sound.

## SOUND

When a tuning fork, the reed of a clarinet, or a person's vocal cords are set in motion, the resulting vibrations cause sound waves. You can place your hand in front of a stereo speaker and feel the displacement of the sound waves when the volume rises. **Sound** is the psychological experience that occurs when changes in air pressure are transduced to nerve impulses at the receptive organ for hearing. The

**FIGURE 3.21**
**The Figure–Ground Relationship**

Gestalt psychologists studied the figure–ground relationship. In this drawing, figure and ground can be reversed. You can see either two faces against a white background or a goblet against a dark background.

**Be an ACTIVE LEARNER**

**REVIEW**
> What are the key variables that allow a person to maintain size constancy? p. 105
> Explain how monocular and binocular depth cues help people see depth. pp. 106–108
> How do perceptual psychologists account for the moon illusion? pp. 108–109

**THINK CRITICALLY**
> What do Gestalt researchers mean when they say that the whole is greater than the sum of its parts?
> How do you think culture exerts its influence on your perceptual systems?

**APPLY PSYCHOLOGY**
> If you were to design a robot, and the robot had "what" and "where" detectors, what other types of visual sensors might you add to it? Why?
> Could a computer be trained to distinguish between real phenomena and human illusions? What would a developer have to do to teach a computer to experience an illusion?

**SOUND**

The psychological experience that occurs when changes in air pressure take place at the receptive organ for hearing; the resulting tones, or sounds, vary in frequency and amplitude.

FIGURE 3.22

## The Frequency and Amplitude of Sound Waves

A person's psychological experience of sound depends on the frequency and amplitude of sound waves.

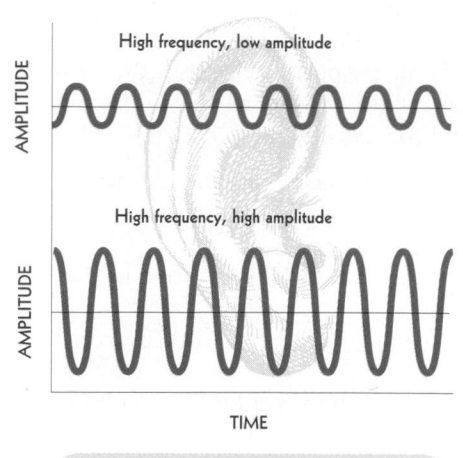

High frequency, low amplitude

AMPLITUDE

High frequency, high amplitude

AMPLITUDE

TIME

**High-frequency sound waves** have a large number of complete cycles per second and a high pitch; they can be of low amplitude (soft sound) or high amplitude (loud sound).

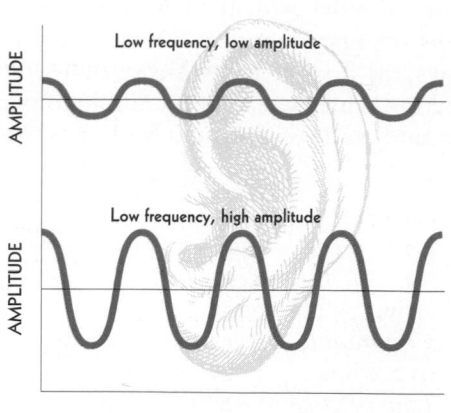

Low frequency, low amplitude

AMPLITUDE

Low frequency, high amplitude

AMPLITUDE

TIME

**Low-frequency sound waves** have a small number of complete cycles per second and a low pitch; they can be of low amplitude (soft sound) or high amplitude (loud sound).

### FREQUENCY

In sound waves, a measure of the number of times a complete change in air pressure occurs per unit of time; expressed in hertz (Hz), or cycles per second.

### PITCH

The psychological experience that corresponds with the frequency of an auditory stimulus. Also known as *tone*.

### AMPLITUDE

The total energy of a sound wave, which determines the loudness of a sound. Also known as *intensity*.

**FIGURE 3.23**

## Psychological Responses to Various Sound Intensities

High-amplitude sound waves, such as those generated by a rock band, have greater energy than low-amplitude waves and a greater impact on the sensitive structure of the ears.

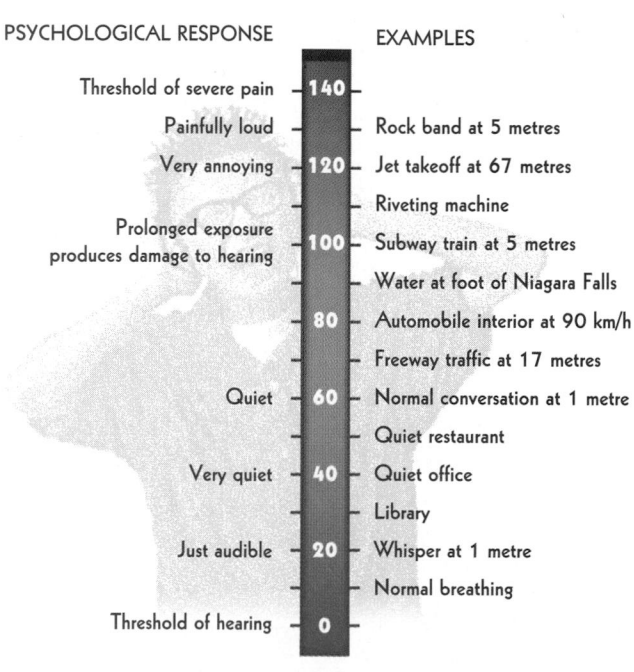

| PSYCHOLOGICAL RESPONSE | | EXAMPLES |
|---|---|---|
| Threshold of severe pain | 140 | |
| Painfully loud | | Rock band at 5 metres |
| Very annoying | 120 | Jet takeoff at 67 metres |
| | | Riveting machine |
| Prolonged exposure produces damage to hearing | 100 | Subway train at 5 metres |
| | | Water at foot of Niagara Falls |
| | 80 | Automobile interior at 90 km/h |
| | | Freeway traffic at 17 metres |
| Quiet | 60 | Normal conversation at 1 metre |
| | | Quiet restaurant |
| Very quiet | 40 | Quiet office |
| | | Library |
| Just audible | 20 | Whisper at 1 metre |
| | | Normal breathing |
| Threshold of hearing | 0 | |

DECIBEL SCALE

resulting tones, or sounds, vary in frequency and amplitude. Sound is often thought of in terms of two psychological aspects, pitch and loudness, which are associated with the two physical attributes of frequency and amplitude.

As shown in Figure 3.22, **frequency** is the number of times a complete change in air pressure occurs during a given unit of time. Within one second, for example, there may be 50 complete changes (50 cycles per second) or 10 000 complete changes (10 000 cycles per second). Frequency is usually measured in hertz (Hz); one Hz equals one cycle per second. Frequency determines the pitch, or *tone*, of a sound; **pitch** is the psychological experience that corresponds with the frequency of an auditory stimulus. High-pitched tones usually have high frequencies. When a piano hammer strikes a short string on the right-hand end of a piano, the string vibrates at a high frequency and sounds high in pitch; when a long string (at the left-hand end) is struck, it vibrates less frequently and sounds low in pitch.

**Amplitude**, or *intensity*, is the total energy of a sound wave, and determines the loudness of a sound. High-amplitude sound waves have more energy than low-amplitude waves; they apply greater force to the ear. Amplitude is measured in *decibels*. Every increase of 20 decibels corresponds to a tenfold increase in intensity. (Decibels are measured on a logarithmic scale, which means that increases are exponential, not linear; thus, increases in sound intensity measured in decibels are quite steep.) As Figure 3.23 shows, normal conversation has an amplitude of about 60 decibels, and sounds at about 120 decibels are painfully loud.

Amplitude and frequency are not correlated. A low-frequency sound can be very loud or very soft; that is, it can have either high or low amplitude. Middle C on a piano, for example, can be loud or soft. The frequency (pitch) of the sound stays the same—it is still middle C—

only its amplitude (loudness) varies. The psychological perception of loudness depends on other factors, such as background noise and whether the person is paying attention to the sound. Another psychological dimension, *timbre*, is the complexity of a sound—the different mixture of amplitudes and frequencies that make up the sound. For example, a piano or guitar produces many harmonics and so has greater timbre than a flute, which produces clear, pure tones. People's perceptions of all of these qualities depend on the physical structure of their ears.

## THE STRUCTURE OF THE EAR

The receptive organ for *audition*, or hearing, is the ear: It translates physical stimuli (sound waves) first into mechanical motion and then into electrical impulses the brain can interpret. The ear has three major parts: the outer ear, the middle ear, and the inner ear. The tissue on the outside of the head (the *pinna*) is part of the outer ear. The eardrum (*tympanic membrane*) is the boundary between the outer and middle ear. When sound waves enter the ear, they produce changes in the pressure of the air on the eardrum. The eardrum responds to these changes by vibrating.

The middle ear is quite small. Within it, tiny bones (*ossicles*) known as the *hammer*, *anvil*, and *stirrup* help convert the large forces striking the eardrum into a small, concentrated force. Two small muscles are attached to the ossicles; these muscles serve a protective function and contract reflexively in response to intense sounds. They help protect the delicate mechanisms of the inner ear from the damaging effects of a loud noise that could overstimulate them (Borg & Counter, 1989).

Ultimately, the middle ear bones stimulate the *basilar membrane*, which runs down the middle of the *cochlea*, a spiral tube in the inner ear. Figure 3.24 shows the major structures of the middle and inner ear, and Figure 3.25 shows the basilar membrane. In the cochlea, which is shaped like a snail's shell and comprises three chambers, sound waves of different frequencies stimulate different areas of the basilar membrane. These areas, in turn, stimulate hair cells, which bring about the initial electrical coding of sound waves. These hair cells are remarkably sensitive. Hudspeth (1983), for example, found that hair cells respond when they are displaced as little as 100 picometres (trillionths of a metre).

Electrical impulses make their way through the brain's auditory nervous system in much the same way as visual information proceeds through the visual nervous system. The electrochemical neuronal impulses proceed through the auditory nerve to the midbrain and finally to the auditory cortex. Studies of single cells in the auditory areas of the brain show that some cells are more responsive to certain frequencies than to others. Katsuki (1961) found cells that are maximally sensitive to certain narrow frequency ranges; if a frequency is outside their range, these cells might not fire at all. This finding is analogous to the findings reported by Hubel and Wiesel, who discovered receptive visual fields in which proper stimulation brought about dramatic changes in the firing of a cell. Research supports a highly organized columnar organization in the auditory system, much like that of the visual system (DeCharms, Blake & Merzenich, 1998).

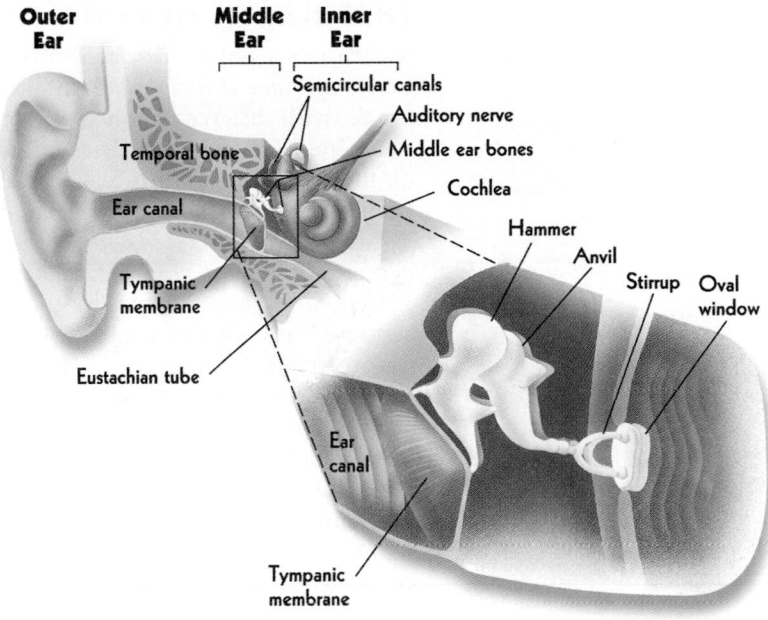

**FIGURE 3.24**
**The Major Structures of the Ear**

**FIGURE 3.25**
**The Basilar Membrane**

In this view, the cochlea has been unwound and cut open to reveal the basilar membrane, which is covered with thousands of hair cells. Pressure variations in the fluid that fills the cochlea cause oscillations to travel in waves along the basilar membrane, stimulating the hair cells

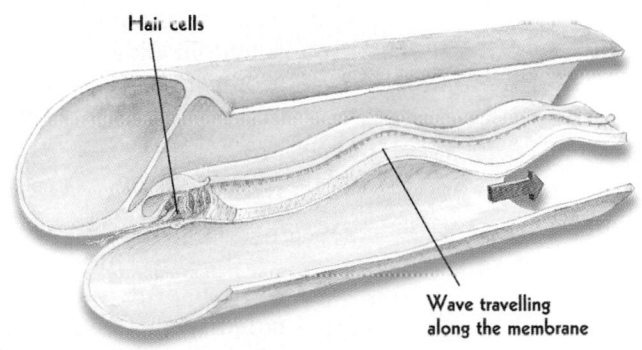

## THEORIES OF HEARING

Most theories of hearing fall into two major classes: place theories and frequency theories. *Place theories* claim that the analysis of sound occurs in the basilar membrane, with different frequencies and intensities affecting different parts (places) of the membrane. These theories assert that each sound wave causes a travelling wave on the basilar membrane, which in turn causes changes in the hair cells on the membrane. These changes then trigger specific information about pitch.

In contrast, *frequency theories* maintain that the analysis of pitch and intensity occurs at higher centres (levels) of processing, perhaps in the auditory area of the cortex, and that the basilar membrane merely transfers information to those centres. These theories suggest that the entire basilar membrane is stimulated and that its overall rate of responding is transferred to the auditory nerve and beyond, where analysis takes place.

Like theories that attempt to explain colour vision, both place theories and frequency theories present theoretical problems. And neither type of theory explains all of the data about pitch and loudness. For example, hair cells do not act independently (as place theories suggest) but instead act together (as frequency theories suggest). Further, the rate at which hair cells fire is not fast enough to keep up with sound waves (typically having frequencies of 1000 to 10 000 cycles per second), as frequency theories suggest.

To get around these difficulties, modern researchers have developed theories of auditory information processing that attempt to explain pitch in terms of both specific action in parts of the basilar membrane and complex frequency analyses at higher levels. Theories that seem at odds with one another can work together to explain pitch and loudness when the best parts of them are combined. (Does this remind you of the debate over the trichromatic and opponent-process theories of colour vision we discussed earlier?)

## SOUND LOCALIZATION

How do you know where to turn when you hear a baby crying? Although not as direction-sensitive as many animals, human beings have amazingly efficient sound localization (direction-determining) abilities. Researchers have learned much about such abilities by presenting sound through headsets, with one sound presented to one ear and another sound presented to the other ear. Such experiments have revealed that there are two key concepts in sound localization: interaural time differences and interaural intensity differences. Because you have two ears, a sound made to the left of your head will arrive at the left ear before the right ear. Thus, you have an *interaural time difference*. In addition, the sound will reach the two ears at different intensities. A sound made at your left will be slightly more intense to the left ear than to the right ear; thus, there is an *interaural intensity difference*. These two pieces of information are analyzed in the brain at nuclei that are especially sensitive to time and intensity differences between the ears.

Some potential ambiguities exist in sound localization, however. What happens when the sound source is just in front of you, and thus is equidistant from your two ears? It turns out that head and body movements help resolve the source of a sound. You rotate your head or move your body when you are unsure of the source of a sound. In addition, the external ear (pinna) has ridges and folds that bounce sounds around a bit. This creates slight delays that help you localize sounds. Finally, sight and past experiences with sounds aid in the task of localizing sounds in space.

## HEARING IMPAIRMENTS

Sixteen percent of adults and more than one-third of people over age 60 have a hearing loss. In total, about 4 out of 100 Canadians have a hearing impairment (National Advisory Council on Aging, 1997). Older individuals are often discriminated against because of their hearing problem, with younger people assuming a lack of intellect rather than a lack of hearing. The causes of the impairments are numerous and include both environmental and genetic factors, and they lead to varying degrees of conduction deafness, sensorineural deafness, or a combination of the two (Vahava et al., 1998).

**Conduction deafness** is deafness resulting from interference with the transmission of sound to the neural mechanism of the inner ear. The interference may be caused by something temporary, such as a head cold or a buildup of wax in the outer ear canal. Or it may be caused by something far more serious, such as hardening of the tympanic membrane, destruction of the tiny bones within the ear, or diseases that create pressure in the middle ear. If the affected person can get help with transmission of the sound past the point of the conduction problem, hearing can be improved.

**Sensorineural deafness** is deafness resulting from damage to the cochlea, the auditory nerve, or higher auditory processing centres. The most common cause of this type of deafness is ongoing exposure to very high-intensity sound, such as that of rock bands or jet planes. Listening to even moderately loud music for longer than 15 minutes a day can cause permanent deafness.

An audiometer, which presents sounds of different frequencies through a headphone, measures hearing loss; results are presented as an *audiogram*, which is a graph showing hearing sensitivity at selected frequencies. The audiogram of the person being tested is compared with that of a person with no known hearing loss. A simpler way to assess and diagnose hearing impairment is to test a person's recognition of spoken words. In a typical test of this sort, a person listens to a tape recording of speech sounds that are standardized in terms of loudness and pitch. Performance is based on the number of words the participant can repeat correctly at various intensity levels. Non-medical personnel, who then refer individuals who may have hearing problems to a physician, often administer this type of test.

You can easily see that hearing and vision have many similarities in their perceptual mechanisms. In both perceptual systems, physical energy is transduced into electrochemical energy. Coding takes place at several locations in the brain, and people can have impairments in either visual or auditory abilities. Nevertheless, the auditory system, like the visual system, is plastic and can be trained and retrained after an accident or other trauma, especially when the person is young (Klinke et al., 1999).

## Taste and Smell

Try the following experiment. Cut a fresh onion in half and inhale its odour while holding a piece of raw potato in your mouth. Now chew the potato. Does the potato taste like an onion? This experiment demonstrates that taste and smell are closely linked. Food contains substances that act as stimuli for both taste and smell.

There is one taste most people have a special fondness for: sweetness. Babies prefer sweet foods, as do great-grandmothers. But researchers know that a sweet tooth involves a craving for more than the taste of sugar. People with a sweet tooth crave candy, cake, ice cream, and sometimes liquor. Their bodies learn that sweetness is associated with many foods that are high in carbohydrates and fat. Carbohydrates act almost as sedatives. So your cravings for some substances—your desire to taste or smell or eat or drink them—are affected by a number of variables, including the composition of the food, its smells, what it ultimately does to you, and your previous experiences with it.

### TASTE

Try to think back to some memorable taste experiences you had recently or remember having had as a child. How about the first time

CONDUCTION DEAFNESS
Deafness resulting from interference with the transmission of sound to the neural mechanism of the inner ear.

SENSORINEURAL
[sen-so-ree-NEW-ruhl]
DEAFNESS
Deafness resulting from damage to the cochlea, the auditory nerve, or higher auditory processing centres.

Be an
**ACTIVE LEARNER**

**REVIEW**
> What is the difference between pitch and frequency? pp. 111–112
> How does a person locate a sound in space? p. 114
> Distinguish between conduction deafness and sensorineural deafness. p. 115

**THINK CRITICALLY**
> Why do scientists consider sound a psychological experience rather than a physical one?
> Why might an inner ear infection cause light-headedness?

**APPLY PSYCHOLOGY**
> What is the potential impact of an inner ear infection?
> Can you design a device that might be developed so as to create the most natural hearing possible for the deaf?

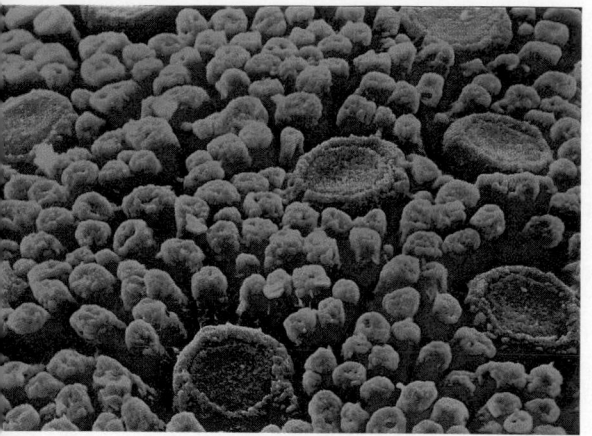

▲ Each taste bud consists of 5 to 150 taste cells. These cells last only about 10 to 14 days and are constantly being renewed.

you remember eating Brussels sprouts (if you have ever tried them). How about your first cup of coffee? Can you remember ever being very surprised by the taste of something? Perhaps biting into a lemon wedge while thinking it was an orange? Taste sensations are very powerful.

Taste is so complex that it is usually studied from the bottom up. Taste is a chemical sense; food placed in the mouth is partially dissolved in saliva and stimulates the *taste buds*, the primary receptors for taste stimuli (see Figure 3.26). When substances contact the taste buds, you experience taste. The taste buds are found on small bumps on the tongue—papillae. Each hill-like papilla is separated from the next by a trench-like moat; on the walls of this moat are the taste buds, which can be seen only under a microscope. Each taste bud (human beings have about 10 000 of them) consists of 5 to 150 *taste cells*. These cells last for only 10 to 14 days and are constantly renewed.

Although psychologists do not know exactly how many tastes there are, most agree that there are four basic ones: sweet, sour, salty, and bitter. Most foods contain more than one primary taste; Hawaiian pizza, for example, offers a complicated taste stimulus and also stimulates the sense of smell. All taste cells are sensitive to all taste stimuli, but some cells are more sensitive to some stimuli than to others. (In this regard, they are much like the cones in the retina, which are sensitive to all wavelengths but are especially sensitive to a specific range of wavelengths.) By isolating stimuli that initiate only one taste sensation, psychologists have found that some regions of the tongue seem to be more sensitive to particular taste stimuli than others. The tip of the tongue, for example, is more sensitive to sweet tastes than the back of the tongue, and the sides of the tongue are especially sensitive to sour tastes (see Figure 3.26).

Some people are more sensitive to taste than others, and this seems to be genetically determined. In fact, there are vast differences in sensitivity among people. Some individuals are considered non-tasters, most are considered medium tasters,

**FIGURE 3.26**

**Taste Buds Are Found on the Surface of the Tongue**

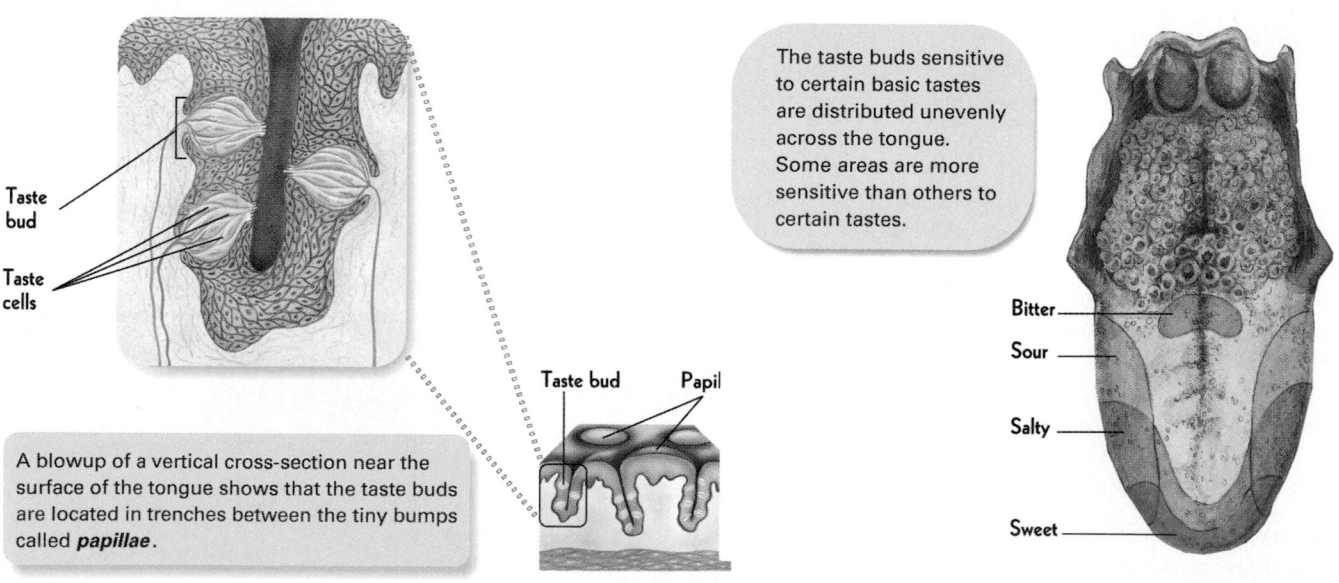

Taste bud

Taste cells

A blowup of a vertical cross-section near the surface of the tongue shows that the taste buds are located in trenches between the tiny bumps called *papillae*.

Taste bud    Papil

The taste buds sensitive to certain basic tastes are distributed unevenly across the tongue. Some areas are more sensitive than others to certain tastes.

Bitter
Sour
Salty
Sweet

and some are considered super tasters. Well-known taste researcher Linda Bartoshuk and her colleagues (1996, 2000) found that non-tasters had as few as 11 buds per square centimetre on the tip of the tongue, whereas super tasters had as many as 1100 taste buds per square centimetre. Super tasters taste sweet foods as too sweet, bitter foods as too bitter, and so forth, while non-tasters cannot distinguish among basic tastes and require additional samples of food to discern flavour. Interesting, and not yet explained, is the finding that women are more likely to be super tasters (Bartoshuk, Duffy, & Miller, 1994).

The taste of a particular food depends not only on its chemical makeup and the number of taste buds a person has, but on past experiences with that or similar foods, how much saliva is mixed into food, and how long the food is chewed. Food that is chewed well has a strong taste. However, food that rests on the tongue for a long time loses its ability to stimulate. This phenomenon is called *sensory adaptation,* or the temporary change in responsiveness of a receptor, often due to repeated high levels of stimulation. A food that loses its texture by being mashed up, blended, or mixed with other foods has less taste and is less appealing to most adults. Thus, a taste experience, much like other perceptual experiences, depends not only on a sensory event but also on past experiences and other sensory and perceptual variables (Friedrich & Laurent, 2001).

## SMELL

Try eating potatoes and onions while holding your nose and you will quickly discover that they taste alike, as do carrots and apples. Smell is such an important sense that those who lose it feel disabled. Like the sense of taste, **olfaction**—the sense of smell—is a chemical sense. That is, the stimulus for smell is a chemical in the air. The olfactory system in human beings is remarkably sensitive: Humans can distinguish approximately 10 000 different scents and can recognize a smell from as few as 40 or 50 molecules of the chemical. For the sensation of smell to occur, chemicals must move toward the receptor cells located on the walls of the nasal passage. This happens when you breathe the chemicals in through your nostrils or take them in through the back of your throat when you chew and swallow food. When a chemical substance in the air moves past the receptor cells, it is partially absorbed in the mucus that covers the cells, thereby initiating the process of smell.

For human beings to perceive smell, information must be sent to the brain (Scott et al., 2001; Vroon, 1997). At the top of the nasal cavity is the *olfactory epithelium* (see Figure 3.27), a layer of cells that contains the olfactory receptor cells—the nerve fibres that process odours and transmit information about smell to the olfactory bulbs (the enlargements at the end of the olfactory nerve) and on to higher centres of the brain. There can be as many as 30 million olfactory receptor cells in each nostril, which is what makes the olfactory system so sensitive and the electrochemical coding so complex (Laurent, 1999; Scott et al., 2001; Wilson, 2000). This fact is dramatically illustrated by perfume manufacturing, which is a complex process. Perfume makers may combine hundreds of scents to make one new perfume; dozens of perfumes actually have the same basic scent and vary only slightly. The manufacturer's task is to generate a perfume that has a distinctive top note—the first impact of a smell. If the substance that creates a smell is not chemically pure, a middle note and an endnote will follow the top note. The middle note follows after the top note fades away and the endnote remains long after the top and middle notes have disappeared.

Theories of smell involve both the stimulus for smell and the structure of the receptor system. Some theories posit a few basic smells; others suggest many—including fragrant, putrid, fruity, resinous, spicy, and burnt. Psychologists have not agreed on a single classification system for smells, nor do they completely understand how odours affect the receptor cells. Research into the coding of smell is being done, and physiological psychologists make headway each year; for example,

OLFACTION [ole-FAK-shun]
The sense of smell.

**HandsOnPsych**
Version 2.0

**Sensation**

FIGURE 3.27
The Olfactory System

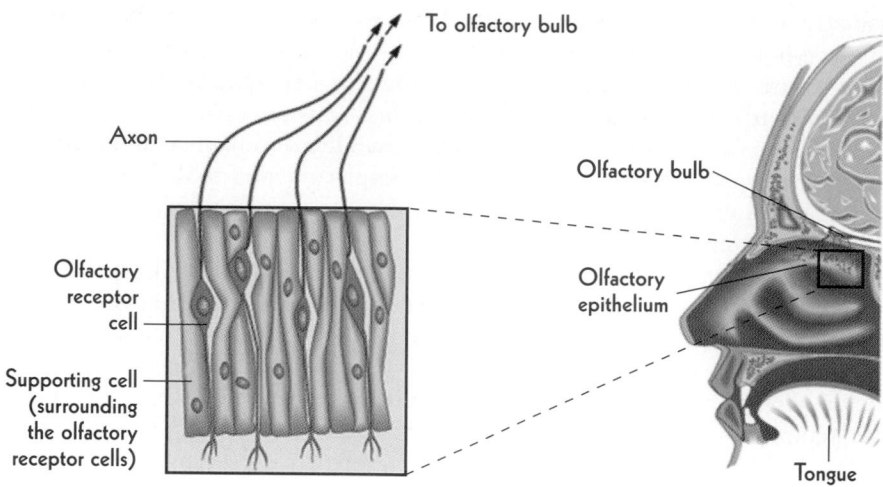

we know that memory for odours is long-lasting and that odours can evoke other memories—of past events, childhood, and especially emotional times in our lives (Herz & Engen, 1996; Engen & Engen, 1997). Another area in which important progress has been made is the question of whether and how odours affect human behaviour. We consider this issue next.

## SMELL AND COMMUNICATION

Animals secrete *pheromones* (pronounced FER-uh-moans)—scented chemical substances that are detected by other animals. Pheromones act as a means of communication. In fact, scents released by one animal even may influence the physiology of another animal.

Pheromones are widely recognized as initiators of sexual activity among animals. For example, female silkworms release a pheromone that can attract male silkworms from miles away. Similarly, when female hamsters are sexually receptive, they emit a highly odorous substance that attracts males (Montgomery-St. Laurent, Fullenkamp, & Fischer, 1988); mice are similarly equipped (Coppola & O'Connell, 1988) and rats and elephants behave similarly (Fornai & Orzi, 2001; Rasmusen & Krishnamurthy, 2000).

Many animals emit pheromones to elicit specific behavioural reactions; others, notably dogs, use scents in their feces and urine to maintain territories and identify one another. Beavers attempt to keep strangers out of their territory by depositing foul-smelling substances emitted by sacs near the anus. Reindeer have scent glands between their toes that leave a trail for the rest of the herd. Communication through pheromones is found throughout the animal world. But do human beings share this ability?

Although people have always believed that a kind of "chemistry" exists between close friends, few really believed that one person's secretions might alter another person's behaviour. It was generally thought that human beings did not communicate through smell. However, groundbreaking research in the 1970s began to change psychologists' thinking about smell and communication. McClintock (1971) found that the menstrual periods of women living in a college dormitory who were either roommates or close friends became roughly *synchronous*. That is, after the women lived together for several months, their menstrual cycles began and ended at about the same time. In more recent experimental research, McClintock and her colleagues (Jacob & McClintok, 2000; McClintock, 1996) found that women emit an array of chemical signals that affect synchronicity and behaviour. No one has actually discovered human pheromones.

The effects of pheromones in animals are profound, but the role of pheromones in human beings remains relatively controversial because of its implications. Nevertheless, perfume makers have been sent into a frenzy of activity trying to make a perfume with pheromone-like capabilities. Is it reasonable for them to assert that perfumes, like pheromones, can attract members of the opposite sex? Probably not. Pheromones probably are not as powerful in human beings as they are in animals, because so many other environmental stimuli affect human behaviour, attitudes, and interpersonal relations.

## The Skin Senses

Your skin, an organ of your body, contains a wide range of receptors for relaying information about the *skin senses*—touch, pain, and temperature (warmth and cold). In each case a stimulus is converted into neural energy, and then the brain interprets that neural energy as a psychological experience. Skin receptors ultimately send information to the somatosensory cortex of the brain.

### TOUCH

The skin is more than just a binding that holds your body together. It acts as the housing for your *sense of touch*—your tactile system. The skin of an adult human being measures roughly two square metres and comprises three layers: the epidermis, the dermis, and the hypodermis. The top layer, the *epidermis* (*epi* means "outer," among other things), consists primarily of dead cells and varies in thickness. On the face it is thin; on the elbows and the heels of the feet it is quite thick. The epidermis is constantly regenerating; in fact, every 28 days or so, all of its cells are replaced. The layer underneath the epidermis—the *dermis* (from *derma*, or "skin")—contains live cells as well as a supply of nerve endings, blood, hair cells, and oil-producing (sebaceous) glands. The dermis and epidermis are resilient, flexible, and quite thick. They protect the body against quick changes in temperature and pressure, and the epidermis in particular guards against pain from small scratches, cuts, and bumps. The deepest layer—the *hypodermis* (*hypo* means "under")—is a thick, insulating cushion.

The specialized receptors for each of the skin senses   touch, pain, and temperature—vary in shape, size, number, and distribution. For example, the body has many more cold receptors than heat receptors; it has more pain receptors behind the knee than on the top of the nose. In the most sensitive areas of the hand, there are as many as 1300 receptors per square centimetre.

The skin sense receptors appear to interact with one another; sometimes one sensation seems to combine with or change to another. Thus, increasing pressure can become pain. Similarly, an itch seems to result from a low-level irritation of nerve endings in the skin; however, a tickle can be caused by the same stimulus and produce a reflex-like response (see *Psychology in Action*). Further, people are far more sensitive to pressure in some parts of their bodies than in other parts (compare your fingers to your thigh); the more sensitive areas, such as the neck and the back of the knees, have more receptors than do the less sensitive areas. Complicating matters further, women have greater sensitivity to some pain stimuli than do men and are better able to discriminate painful stimuli (Berkley, 1997).

Many of your determinations of how something feels are relative. When you say a stimulus is cold, you mean it is cold compared to normal skin temperature. When you say an object is warm, you mean it feels warmer than normal skin temperature. When you feel a child's head with the back of your hand and say the child has a fever, you are comparing normal skin temperature to a sick child's elevated skin temperature (and you wouldn't make such a determination immediately after being outside in −10-degree Celsius weather).

## A Ticklish Subject

All of us have been tickled at some point in our lives. Some of us are especially ticklish. We smile, laugh, squirm, and sometimes howl when tickled. But why?

Nineteenth-century speculations suggested that people laugh and are ticklish because of a "pleasant state of mind." But today researchers are showing that tickling and its results are in part physical and in large part psychological. People respond to a light touch on the sole of the foot or on the spine, but if they anticipate the touch, if they are with a friend or relative, or if there is an element of surprise, the response is much stronger. That may be why people can't tickle themselves—there is no element of surprise, and tickling requires a social interaction and a tension that can occur only between two or more people (Claxon, 1975). Another possible explanation is that when you tickle yourself you have up-front access to the internal motor commands that initiate the tickle, thus removing all the uncertainty and surprise that makes tickles work (Blakemore et al., 2000). A

third possible explanation is that being ticklish in areas that are vulnerable during arm-to-arm combat motivates us to protect those areas (Harris, 1999) and suggests that tickle play is a form a self-defence training.

Think back to your childhood. When your mom or dad said, "I'm going . . . to . . . *tickle* you!" and started to wiggle his or her fingers, you would likely squirm and giggle even before you were touched. Upon the actual tickle, you may have convulsed in laughter. Those who laugh easily at humour are more likely to respond to tickling (Harris & Christenfeld, 1997). Also, a physiological response to tickling is more likely when with others, particularly friends (Christenfeld et al., 1997), and if one feels comfortable with one's body and is disposed to perceive pleasurable stimuli (Ruggieri et al., 1983).

When researchers used "tickle machines" to lightly stimulate the soles of the feet, the effects of tickling were far more likely to occur when preceded by something else that was funny or when in the presence of another person. Although a tickle response may be a reflexive one, it is highly enhanced by social interactions (Christenfeld et al., 1997). Think of it as top-down *and* bottom-up processing; we laugh because it's a reflex (bottom up) and because of the situation in which we find ourselves (top down). You might chuckle at a joke when a friend tells it, but you're more likely to laugh at the same joke if a comedian tells it. And if the joke is embedded within a long string of other funny jokes, your response would be more intense.

Our response to humour and our ability to be tickled seem to be somewhat related. Both tickling and humour are universal traits found in human beings and in some primates. They are traits that occur at an early age, and specific pathways can be identified—elements of an evolved response. Indeed, the responses to both humour and tickling serve an evolutionary purpose—those of us with a humorous outlook on life may live longer (Weisfeld, 1993).

## PAIN

Everyone has experienced an acute painful episode at one time or another: headache, childbirth, dental pain, arthritic pain, or perhaps a kidney stone or stomach flare-up. For most people pain comes and goes, and they are thankful or relieved when it is over. Pain is a perceptual experience with particular negative qualities (Fernandez & Turk, 1992). Pain is the most common symptom found in medical settings; nevertheless, it is adaptive and necessary. In rare cases, children have been born without the ability to feel pain, which places them in constant danger. Their encounters with caustic substances, violent collisions, and deep cuts elicit no painful cautions to avoid such experiences. Further, they do not recognize serious conditions that would send most of us to the doctor for attention—for example, broken bones, deep burns, or the sharp pains that signal appendicitis.

Studying pain is difficult, because pain can be elicited in so many ways. For example, stomach pains can be due to hunger or the flu, toothaches due to a cavity or an abscess, and headaches due to stress or eye strain. Myriad kinds of pain exist, including sunburn, pain from terminal cancer, labour pains, low back pain, frostbite, and even pain in a "phantom limb" lost as a result of trauma or surgery. Psychologists use several kinds of stimuli to study pain, including chemicals, extreme heat and cold, and electrical stimulation.

Most researchers believe that the receptors for pain are small, free nerve endings located throughout the body that are sensitive to intense potentially harmful stimulation—and there are various types, each more sensitive to certain types of stimulation than another. Some areas of the body are more sensitive to pain than others. For example, the sole of the foot and the ball of the thumb are less sensitive than the back of the knee and the neck. Also, though an individual's pain threshold remains fairly constant, different individuals possess different sensitivities to pain. Some people have a low threshold for pain; they will report a comparatively low-level stimulus as being painful. Others have fairly high pain thresholds. When you experience pain, you know where it hurts, how much it hurts, and the quality of the pain (sharp, burning, localized); your body responds with autonomic nervous system activity—increased heart rate, blood pressure, sweating, and so forth. You then, in turn, respond: You also know whether you are frightened, anxious, or annoyed.

The perception of pain is physical and psychological; much depends on a person's attitudes, previous experiences, and culture (Keefe & France, 1999). For example, athletes often report not feeling the pain of an injury until after competition has ended. Athletes, such as Canadian rower Silken Laumann, can sometimes overcome amazing amounts of pain to triumph in their sports. Laumann's leg was shattered in a boating accident while training and yet, despite five operations in ten days, she was rowing again in three weeks and rowed to the Olympic bronze medal just eight weeks after the accident. Some cultures are more stoical about pain and teach individuals to endure individual suffering; in Western cultures, there is a widespread illusion that pain and suffering are ennobling (Berkowitz, 1993). Also, boys and girls within Western cultures often are taught to respond differently to pain (Wall, 2000).

What allows pain suppression? How does the body process, interpret, and stop pain? Neuromatrix theory may offer an answer.

**NEUROMATRIX THEORY.** One explanation of how the body processes pain is the *neuromatrix theory* developed by Ronald Melzack (1999) of McGill University and originally called the Melzack-Wall gate control theory (Melzack & Wall, 1965). The theory takes into account the sizes, level of development, and interplay of cells that initiate pain sensations; it also considers inhibitory cells that can diminish pain sensations. The theory contends that the brain possesses a neural network, the body–self neuromatrix (BSN), that integrates inputs to produce an output pattern that we experience as pain. The BSN comprises a widely distributed neural network and is determined by genetic and sensory influences. Melzack refers to this neuromatrix pattern as a neurosignature. The neurosignature output of the neuromatrix—patterns of nerve impulses of varying temporal and spatial dimensions—is produced by neural programs genetically built into the neuromatrix.

Multiple inputs act on the neuromatrix programs, including (1) sensory inputs; (2) visual and other sensory inputs that influence the interpretation of the situation; (3) emotional inputs from other areas of the brain; (4) neural self-modulation; and (5) the activity of the body's stress-regulation systems.

If the theory is correct (and the research is still being done), the brain has been prewired to realize that its body is going to have a right arm. Even if the right arm is amputated, the brain is still prewired to believe that the arm is there. If the brain believes that limb is there, it might tell the limb to move by stimulating key neural pathways in the neuromatrix. Since the limb is not there, and the brain receives no sensory feedback, it will increase the strength of its stimulation, thus causing what we call phantom pain (Schultz & Melzack, 1999).

**ENDORPHINS.** There have been some exciting breakthroughs in research on pain receptors and the nature of pain. Consider, for example, the study of endorphins. **Endorphins** (from *endogenous*, meaning "naturally occurring," and *morphine*, an opiate painkiller usually derived from opium) are painkillers that are produced naturally in the brain and pituitary gland. There are many kinds of endorphins, and they help regulate several bodily functions, including the control of blood pressure and body temperature (Bloom, 1981; Koob, Wall, & Bloom, 1989). Endorphins also can produce euphoria and a sense of well-being in the way that morphine does, but to an even greater extent. Stress, anticipated pain, and engaging in athletic activities bring about an increased endorphin level. During and after running, runners often report experiencing a "runner's high," a sensation many believe is related to their increased endorphin level.

Endorphins bind themselves to receptor sites in the brain and spinal cord, thereby preventing pain signals from going to higher levels of the nervous system. Naturally produced endorphins include some that increase tolerance to pain and others that actually reduce pain. *Enkephalin*, for example, is an innate brain endorphin that blocks pain signals (Blum et al., 2000, Samoriski & Gross, 2000). Another naturally produced painkiller, nocistatin, is being tested on a variety of painful conditions and may be able to be synthetically produced (Okuda-Ashitaka et al., 1998). Physicians prescribe synthetic endorphins or endorphin-like substances, such as morphine, to block pain when traditional medications are ineffective.

**ACUPUNCTURE.** Many people who suffer chronic, unrelieved pain have sought help from acupuncture (Olausson & Sagvik, 2000). Initially developed in China thousands of years ago, *acupuncture* is a technique in which long, slender needles are inserted into the body at specific locations to relieve particular kinds of pain. Controlled studies of acupuncture have yielded varying results (Pan et al., 2000). Acupuncture seems to help when needles are placed near the site of pain; this is in contrast to the traditional Chinese view that the key sites are located along life-force meridians found on acupuncture charts (Wall, 2000). It is possible that the needles stimulate endorphins that may help block the pain (Murray, 1995) or alter serotonin levels (Nash, 1996; Fishbain, 2000) and alleviate pain or other problems (Bernstein, 2000). For some people, acupuncture may be a reasonable option and an effective treatment (Baischer, 1995). The National Institutes of Health in the United States concluded that acupuncture may be effective for some kinds of pain—migraines, arthritis, and post-operative pain from dental surgery—but that more research is needed because controlled research studies on the results of acupuncture are still inconclusive.

**PAIN MANAGEMENT.** Usually the pain resulting from a headache, toothache, or small cut is temporary and can be alleviated with a simple pain medication such as aspirin. For millions of people, however, aspirin is not enough. For those who suffer from constant pain caused by back injury, arthritis, or cancer, drug treatment either is not effective or is dangerous because of the high dosages required; in addition, each type of pain may require a different treatment. Sometimes painkillers are not prescribed because of fear of addiction—a fear that is often exaggerated by caring, well-meaning family and friends (Melzack, 1990).

New technologies are emerging to help people manage pain. Leaders in pain research reason that something must happen at the site of an injury to trigger endorphin production. What if a drug could stop the whole pain perception process at the actual place where an injury occurs? Researchers are studying the receptor

**ENDORPHINS** [en-DOR-finz]
Painkillers produced naturally in the brain and pituitary gland.

sites in skin tissue and observing how chemicals bind to them. They hope to find compounds that will stop the entire pain perception process, even before endorphin production starts. The compounds they discover may not be total pain relievers; however, in combination with other pain medications, such as aspirin, they may be effective.

Practitioners who deal with pain recognize that it can have both physical and psychological sources. Although pain initially may arise from physical complaints, it sometimes continues even after the physical cause abates because it provides other benefits to the sufferer (Gatchel & Turk, 1999) such as enforced inactivity or increased social support. As well, the work of Michael Sullivan and colleagues (1995) at Dalhousie University clearly indicates that psychological factors play a central role in the nature and level of pain that individuals experience. People who score high on Sullivan's pain catastrophizing scale report experiencing more pain and more negative thoughts during ice-water immersion than do low scorers. Treatment focuses on helping people cope with pain regardless of its origins and increasing a patient's knowledge and skills to control pain (Hardy, 1995).

Hypnosis has been used to treat pain. Patients may be instructed to focus on other aspects of their lives and may be told that after the hypnotic session their pain will be more bearable. Although some suggest that two-thirds of patients who are considered highly susceptible to suggestion can experience some relief of pain through hypnosis, the National Institutes of Health concluded that a more accurate estimate was 15 to 20 percent.

Anxiety and worry can make pain worse. People who suffer from migraine headaches, for example, often make their condition worse by becoming fearful when they feel a headache coming on. Researchers find that biofeedback training, which teaches people how to relax and cope more effectively, can help those who suffer from chronic pain and migraine headaches—again, results are mixed. Another treatment, closely related to biofeedback, is cognitive coping. A poor or hopeless attitude can make pain worse. Cognitive coping strategies teach patients to have a better attitude about their pain. Patients learn to talk to themselves in positive ways, to divert attention to pleasant images, and to take an active role in managing their pain and transcending the experience.

**Be an ACTIVE LEARNER**

**REVIEW**
> Why are taste and smell called chemical senses? pp. 116–118
> What is the evidence that animal behaviour is directly affected by pheromones? p. 118
> What are the most and least sensitive parts of the body? p. 119
> Why is the study of pain so complicated? p. 121

**THINK CRITICALLY**
> Some individuals are born without a sense of smell. What effect would this have on their sense of taste, and why?
> Why do you think the study of endorphins might have relevance to your life?

**APPLY PSYCHOLOGY**
> What can people do to help alleviate seemingly uncontrollable pain through traditional means?
> What could you do to enhance your sense of smell?

## Kinesthesis and the Vestibular Sense

If you are a dancer or an athlete, you rely mightily on your body to provide you with information about hand, arm, and leg movements. You try to keep your balance, be graceful, and move about with coordinated skill. Two sensory systems allow for skilled, accurate, and smooth movement—the often ignored, but vitally important, kinesthetic and vestibular systems.

**Kinesthesis** is the awareness aroused by movements of the muscles, tendons, and joints. It is what allows you to touch your finger to your nose with your eyes closed, leap over hurdles during a track-and-field event, and dance without stepping on your partner's feet. The study of kinesthesis provides information about bodily movements. The movements of muscles around your eye, for example, help you know how far away objects are. Kinesthesia and your other internal sensations (such as an upset stomach) are *proprioceptive cues* (kinesthesia is sometimes called *proprioception*)—sensory cues coming from within your body and providing information about bodily movements and internal sensations.

The **vestibular sense** is the sense of bodily orientation and postural adjustment. It helps you keep your balance and sense of equilibrium. The structures essential to these functions are in the ear. Vestibular sacs and semicircular canals, which are linked indirectly with the body wall of the cochlea, provide information about the

**KINESTHESIS**
[kin-iss-THEE-sis]
The awareness aroused by movements of the muscles, tendons, and joints.

**VESTIBULAR**
[ves-TIB-you-ler] SENSE
The sense of bodily orientation and postural adjustment.

▲ Riding a roller coaster usually affects your vestibular sense—the sense of bodily orientation and postural adjustment.

**HandsOnPsych**
Version 2.0

**Perception**

orientations of the head and body (Parker, 1980). The vestibular sense allows you to walk on a balance beam without falling off, to know which way is up after diving into the water, and to sense that you are turning a corner when riding in a car, even when your eyes are closed.

Rapid movements of the head bring about changes in the semicircular canals. These changes induce eye movements to help compensate for head changes and changes in bodily orientation. They also may be accompanied by physical sensations ranging from pleasant dizziness to unbearable motion sickness. Studies of the vestibular sense help scientists understand what happens to people during space travel and under conditions of weightlessness.

## Extrasensory Perception

Vision, hearing, taste, smell, touch, and even pain are all part of the normal sensory experience of human beings. Some people, however, claim there are other perceptual experiences that many human beings do not recognize as such. People have been fascinated by *extrasensory perception (ESP)* for hundreds of years. The British Society for the Study of Psychic Phenomena has investigated reports of ESP since the nineteenth century. ESP includes telepathy, clairvoyance, precognition, and psychokinesis. *Telepathy* is the transfer of thought from one person to another. *Clairvoyance* is the ability to recognize objects or events, such as the contents of a message in a sealed envelope, that are not present to normal sensory receptors. *Precognition* is unexplained knowledge about future events, such as knowing when the phone is about to ring. *Psychokinesis* is the ability to move objects by using only one's mental powers.

Thinking about ESP is a good place to practise your critical thinking skills. Wanting or wishing that ESP were real does not mean you shouldn't carefully scientifically evaluate ESP claims. When we do this we routinely find that experimental support for the existence of ESP is weak, and the more carefully controlled our ESP experiments are the less likely it is that we see effects. Moreover, ESP phenomena such as "reading people's minds" or bending spoons through mental power cannot be verified by experimental manipulations in the way that other perceptual events can be. None of these criticisms means that ESP does not exist. However, psychologists see so much trickery and falsification of data and so many design errors in experiments on this subject that they remain sceptical. Much of the debate turns on the related questions of whether the studies done on ESP used appropriate controls and whether they used appropriate or comparable statistical analytic procedures (Bem & Honorton, 1994; Milton & Wiseman, 1999).

# Summary and Review

**How does the study of the psychological aspects of perception help explain individuals' attending to and attaching meaning to stimuli?**

> *Sensation* is the process in which the sense organs' receptor cells are stimulated and relay initial information to higher brain centres for further processing.  **p. 86**

> *Perception* is the process through which people attach meaning to sensory stimuli by means of complex processing mechanisms. Each perceptual system operates in a similar way; although all are different, they share common processes.  **p. 86**

> *Psychophysics* is the study of the relationship between physical stimuli and people's conscious experience of them. Psychophysical techniques allow researchers to study and approximate the *absolute threshold*—the statistically determined minimum level of stimulation necessary to excite a perceptual system.  **p. 87**

> If a visual or auditory stimulus is presented so quickly or at such a low level that a person cannot consciously perceive it, psychologists say that it is presented subliminally. Research on *subliminal perception* is controversial, and many researchers maintain that it can be explained in terms of non-perceptual variables such as motivation, previous experience, and unconscious or critical censoring processes.  **p. 88**

> The cocktail party phenomenon, which allows a person to hear his or her name spoken across a crowded and noisy room, is a basic finding of selective attention studies, which show that people have a limited capacity to pay attention to stimuli.  **p. 90**

> Studies of sensory deprivation and especially of sensory restriction have shown that profound relaxation can occur in an environment of extreme sensory restriction. **pp. 90–91**

**KEY TERMS**

sensation, p. 86; perception, p. 86; psychophysics, p. 87; absolute threshold, p. 87; signal detection theory, p. 87; subliminal perception, p. 88

## THE VISUAL SYSTEM

**Describe the structures of the visual system.**

> The main structures of the eye are the cornea, pupil, iris, lens, and retina. The retina is made up of 10 layers, of which the most important are the *photoreceptors,* the bipolar cells, and the ganglion cells. The axons of the ganglion cells make up the optic nerve.  **pp. 92–93**

**What is the duplicity theory of vision?**

> The duplicity theory of vision states that rods and cones are structurally unique and are used to accomplish different tasks. That is, the two types of receptors have special functions and operate differently: Cones are specialized for colour, day vision, and fine acuity, and rods are specialized for low light levels but contribute little to colour vision or acuity.  **pp. 93–94**

**What do receptive fields tell researchers about the perceptual process?**

> *Receptive fields* are areas on the retina that, when stimulated, produce changes in the firing of cells in the visual system. Cells at the lateral geniculate nucleus and the visual cortex are called feature detectors, and some of them are highly specialized—for example, for detecting motion or colour.  **pp. 97–98**

**What are the trichromatic and opponent-process theories of colour vision?**

> The three psychological dimensions of colour are *hue, brightness,* and *saturation.* They correspond to the three physical characteristics of light: wavelength, intensity, and purity. Young and Helmholtz's *trichromatic theory* of colour vision states that all colours can be made by mixing three basic colours and that the retina has three types of cones. Herring's *opponent-process theory* states that colour is coded by a series of receptors that respond either strongly or weakly to different wavelengths of light.  **pp. 100–103**

> *Colour blindness* is the inability to perceive different hues; many people with colour blindness cannot successfully discriminate colours in two areas of the visual spectrum.  **p. 103**

**KEY TERMS**

light, p. 92; myopic, p. 93; hyperopic, p. 93; photoreceptors, p. 93; transduction, p. 93; visual cortex, p. 93; dark adaptation, p. 94; optic chiasm, p. 95; agnosia, p. 97; receptive fields, p. 97; saccades, p. 99; hue, p. 100; brightness, p. 100; saturation, p. 101; trichromatic theory, p. 101; colour blindness, p. 101; opponent-process theory, p. 102; trichromats, p. 103; monochromats, p. 103; dichromats, p. 103

## VISUAL PERCEPTION

**What are size constancy and shape constancy?**

> *Size constancy* is the ability of the perceptual system to recognize that an object remains constant in size regardless of its distance from the viewer or the size of the retinal image. *Shape constancy* is the ability of the visual perceptual system to recognize a shape despite changes in its orientation or the angle from which it is viewed. **pp. 105–106**

**What kinds of depth cues help people see depth?**

> The *monocular depth cues* include motion parallax, the kinetic depth effect, linear perspective, interposition, texture, highlighting and shadowing, atmospheric perspective, and *accommodation*. The two primary *binocular depth cues* are *retinal disparity* and *convergence*. **pp. 106–108**

**What is an illusion?**

> An *illusion* is a perception of a physical stimulus that differs from measurable reality or from what is commonly expected. **pp. 108–109**

**What did the Gestalt psychologists contribute to scientists' understanding of perception?**

> According to a Gestalt idea called the *law of Prägnanz*, stimuli that *can* be grouped together and seen as a whole, or a form, *will* be seen that way. Using the law of Prägnanz as an organizing idea, Gestalt psychologists developed principles of organization for the perception of figures, especially figure–ground relationships. **pp. 109–111**

**KEY TERMS**

size constancy, p. 105; shape constancy, p. 105; monocular depth cues, p. 106; accommodation, p. 107; binocular depth cues, p. 108; retinal disparity, p. 108; convergence, p. 108; illusion, p. 108; law of Prägnanz, p. 110

## HEARING

**What are the key characteristics of sound?**

> *Sound* refers to the psychological experience of changes in pressure in a liquid or gaseous medium—usually air. The *frequency* and *amplitude* of a sound wave determine in large part how a listener will experience a sound. **pp. 111–113**

**Describe the anatomy of the ear and how sound is processed.**

> The ear has three main parts: the outer ear, the middle ear, and the inner ear. The eardrum (tympanic membrane) is the boundary between the outer ear and the middle ear. Tiny bones (ossicles) in the middle ear stimulate the basilar membrane in the cochlea, a tube in the inner ear. Place theories of hearing claim that the analysis of sound occurs in the inner ear; frequency theories claim that the analysis of pitch and intensity takes place at higher centres of processing. **pp. 113–114**

> Because you have two ears, you can locate the source of sound. A sound produced to the left of the head will arrive at the left ear before the right. This creates an interaural time difference. In addition, a sound produced to the left will be slightly more intense at the left ear than the right; thus, there is an interaural intensity difference. **p. 114**

**Distinguish between conduction deafness and sensorineural deafness.**

> *Conduction deafness* results from interference in the delivery of sound to the neural mechanism of the inner ear. *Sensorineural deafness* results from damage to the cochlea, the auditory nerve, or higher auditory processing centres. **p. 115**

**KEY TERMS**

sound, p. 111; frequency, p. 112; pitch, p. 112; amplitude, p. 112; conduction deafness, p. 115; sensorineural deafness, p. 115

## TASTE AND SMELL

**Describe the anatomy of the tongue and explain how it allows for taste differences.**

> The tongue contains thousands of bumps, or papillae, each of which is separated from the next by a moat. The taste buds are located on the walls of these moats. Each taste bud consists of many taste cells. All taste cells are sensitive to all taste stimuli, but certain cells are more sensitive to some stimuli than to others. **pp. 116–117**

**Why are taste and smell called chemical senses?**

> For taste or smell to occur, chemicals must come into contact with the receptor cells. For the sense of smell, the receptors are located on the walls of the nasal passage. When a chemical substance in the air moves past these receptor cells, it is partially absorbed into the mucus that covers the cells, thereby initiating the process of smell. The olfactory epithelium contains the olfactory receptor cells—the nerve fibres that process odours and enable an individual to perceive smell. **pp. 116–118**

**KEY TERM**

olfaction, p. 117

## THE SKIN SENSES

**Describe the anatomy of the skin.**

> The skin is made up of three layers. The top layer is the epidermis. The layer underneath the epidermis is the dermis. The deepest layer, the hypodermis, is a thick insulating cushion. The skin sense receptors appear to interact with one another; sometimes one sensation seems to combine with or change to another. **p. 119**

**What theory of pain is most prominent now?**

> A widely accepted explanation of how pain sensations are processed is that the brain possesses a neural network, the body–self neuromatrix (BSN), that integrates inputs to produce the output pattern of pain. The BSN comprises a widely distributed neural network; Melzack refers to this neuromatrix pattern as a neurosignature. The neurosignature output of the neuromatrix is produced by neural programs genetically built into the neuromatrix. **pp. 121–122**

**What are the body's naturally produced painkillers?**

> *Endorphins* are painkillers that are produced naturally in the brain and pituitary gland. They help regulate several bodily functions, including blood pressure and body temperature. Stress, anticipated pain, and athletic activities bring about an increased level of endorphins. **p. 122**

**KEY TERM**

endorphins, p. 122

## KINESTHESIS AND THE VESTIBULAR SENSE

**What sense involves the orientation of the entire body?**

> *Kinesthesis* is the awareness that is aroused by movements of the muscles, tendons, and joints. One kinesthetic sense is the *vestibular sense*—the sense of bodily orientation and postural adjustment—which helps you keep your balance and sense of equilibrium.    **pp. 123–124**

**KEY TERMS**

kinesthesis, p. 123; vestibular sense, p. 123

## EXTRASENSORY PERCEPTION

**Is there a "sixth sense"—ESP?**

> ESP includes telepathy, clairvoyance, precognition, and psychokinesis. Experimental support for the existence of ESP is generally weak. Psychologists remain sceptical about ESP because they see so much trickery and falsification of data, as well as experimental design errors. **p. 124**

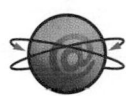 Take advantage of the multimedia resources available with this text! Follow the marginal icons to access the interactive modules on the *HandsOnPsych* CD-ROM; log on to *MyPsychLab* to explore the ebook, study aids, and other online resources; and visit the Companion Website at **www.pearsoned.ca/lefton** for additional exercises and links.

CHAPTER

# 4 Consciousness

Many people have proclaimed that they are "dead tired," but very few actually die from lack of sleep. Members of one Italian family, however, are among those who do. This family has a genetic defect that produces a failure to be able to sleep. The affected individuals usually develop symptoms in their fifties. They feel exhausted but cannot sleep; they sweat profusely; their pupils become constricted; they lose weight. As the disease progresses, they become confused and begin to hallucinate. Sometimes they fall into a very light sleep, but this sleep neither refreshes them nor prevents their continuing degeneration. After several months, they fall into a coma and die (Max, 2001).

The history of this disorder goes back to the 1700s and has affected dozens of members of this family. In 1986, the disorder was named fatal familial insomnia (FFI), and the genetics of the disorder was established. Many puzzles remain. Not all family members who have the gene develop the disorder; some develop it earlier than middle age. Even more puzzling is the brain deterioration that underlies the disorder. In the brains of those who have died from FFI, the thalamus is filled with small holes, though the thalamus is seen mostly as a relay station for sensory information; it is not one of the brain structures believed to be important for sleep.

This mysterious sleep disorder is only one of the many puzzles of sleep. Most people do not die when they fail to sleep, mostly because the urge to sleep is so strong that they eventually are overtaken by it. Almost everyone has the opposite problem of those with FFI—we all sleep, even when we want to stay awake. This situation highlights the most important puzzle: the reason for sleep. Why is it necessary for us to spend time unconscious? What about sleep is so important that we must sleep or die? This question remains unanswered, but researchers have discovered the answers to other important questions about sleep and other states of consciousness.

# Consciousness

In both the Disney and classical versions, Pinocchio is seeking to be more human, to experience feelings and emotions the way human beings do. He is trying to be sentient, to have subjective feelings and awareness of them. To a great extent, Pinocchio is trying to develop a human consciousness.

Part of Pinocchio's problem is that consciousness is difficult to describe, let alone program. Psychologists are acutely aware of this issue. The study of consciousness has waxed and waned as a valid pursuit in psychology. Early psychologists, such as Wilhelm Wundt, studied little else but the content of consciousness; later psychologists, such as William James, studied how consciousness operates. But in the 1920s, behaviourists such as John B. Watson argued that consciousness should be eliminated as a subject of psychological study—because it is not a physical structure that can be examined, probed, or diagrammed. As the behavioural approach came to dominate North American psychology, the study of consciousness and thought was all but forgotten. In the 1960s and 1970s, when the information processing model and computers were being developed, however, cognitive psychology emerged as a subdiscipline in its own right, investigating thought, perception, memory, and how all of these are interwoven. Consciousness again became a viable topic. The tide had clearly turned; today, consciousness—like other areas of cognitive psychology—is a topic of strong scientific and popular interest.

## DEFINING CONSCIOUSNESS

Almost all psychologists agree that a person who is conscious is aware of the environment; for example, you are conscious when you listen to a lecture (at least some of the time!). However, consciousness also refers to inner awareness—knowledge of your own thoughts, feelings, and memories (sentience); of your own mental shopping list for the afternoon, your anger at a rude driver, and the scent of lilac that reminds you of your fourth-grade teacher.

When early psychologists studied the mind and its contents, they were studying consciousness. Wundt and his students in the late 1880s had research participants report the contents of their consciousness while sitting still, while working, and while falling asleep. At the turn of the century, Sigmund Freud moved to change the study of consciousness quite dramatically. According to Freud, people have different levels of consciousness—conscious thoughts of which they are aware and unconscious thoughts in the form of needs, wishes, and desires of which they are unaware. He further argued that much of what shapes our actions exists at a level of consciousness to which we do not have access.

The early psychologists came out of a dualistic model, one that saw the mind and body as separate—various dualistic conceptions saw different levels of interaction between the two. *Dualism* has a long and rich tradition that dates back to Descartes, who asserted that the mind and body were completely separate things. Dualism has crept into our language; we say, "These athletes are prepared in both mind and body," suggesting that the mind and body are separate entities having no relationship to one another. However, today, almost all psychologists reject dualistic ideas. The mind does not exist independent of the body; researchers today acknowledge that our mental life has a physiological basis rooted in the brain—this approach is referred to as *materialism*. Not only is materialism the dominant approach, but today's psychologists also take a less black-and-white view of the distinction between "conscious" and "unconscious." They assert that people are more aware of certain mental processes and less aware of others. For example, when you drive along a very familiar route, you suddenly may realize that you drove five kilometres of highway seemingly unaware of what you passed. You know the route so well that you drove automatically, or with less awareness. Cognitive psychologists generally do not speak about the unconscious but instead refer to controlled (deliberate or aware) versus automatic (less aware) processes.

Most psychologists—including the early structuralists, Freud, and today's cognitive researchers—have acknowledged that people experience different *levels* of consciousness. They agree that consciousness can be seen as a process or a continuum—ranging from the sort of alert attention required to read this textbook to dreaming, hypnosis, or drug-induced states. Following this view of consciousness, a person who does not pay attention or who is not alert is not as "conscious" as one who is vigilant and alert. The idea of a continuum of awareness guides many researchers who believe that consciousness is made up of several *levels* of awareness, from alertness to total unresponsiveness. Researchers who favour this view suggest, for example, that a person who is drinking heavily enters, temporarily, a lower (deeper) *level* in the range of conscious levels—that of intoxication. A person who is in a state of consciousness that is dramatically different from ordinary levels of awareness and responsiveness is in an *altered state of consciousness*. A person who is asleep has pretty much "turned off" both his or her body and consciousness (Hobson, 1999).

Not only do researchers acknowledge levels of consciousness, but they also know that some people are better able to think about their own thinking—a process called *metacognition*. Researchers examine metacognition by asking individuals to think about their problem-solving abilities or their perceptual strategies. They ask them to make assessments about their own level of consciousness and their use of information (Flavell & Wellman, 1977; Gleitman, 1985). Researchers ask individuals to monitor their level of alertness and their mood, through the day and over a longer period. You probably know what time of day you are most alert and when you are likely to be sleepy, and you may have noticed that while some of your friends share this pattern with you others do not. Understanding the rhythm to your consciousness is one of many metacognitive skills.

What is the function of consciousness? Clearly, our consciousness allows us to monitor our bodily and mental states. It also allows us, to a certain extent, to control our bodily and mental states. When we feel too anxious, we breathe more deeply. When we are falling asleep we sit up, yawn (to gather extra oxygen), and perhaps blink. Our consciousness allows us to monitor and control our daily lives; the extent to which we can do this depends on how aware we are, whether we are at a low level of consciousness—such as asleep—or whether in some special situation such as hypnotized, meditating, or drugged. Before we go too far with these ideas, though, let's agree to define **consciousness** as the general state of being aware of and responsive to events within ourselves and in the environment.

CONSCIOUSNESS
The general state of being aware of and responsive to events in the environment, including one's own mental processes.

## THEORIES OF CONSCIOUSNESS

As in other areas of psychology, theory guides research. Several researchers have proposed biologically based theories of consciousness in which understanding the evolution of the human brain is key to understanding consciousness. Jaynes (1976) believes that consciousness originates in differences in the function and physiology of the two hemispheres of the brain (and that in the ancient past, some people who heard God speaking to them actually were listening to the other side of their brain). In a similar way, Robert Ornstein (1977), using physiology and brain structure, suggests that there are two modes of consciousness, each controlled by its own side of the brain. These are the active-verbal-rational mode (called the *active mode*) and the receptive-spatial-intuitive-holistic mode (called the *receptive mode*). Ornstein believes that evolution has made the active mode automatic; this is the "default," or normal, mode of operation for human beings. Human beings limit their awareness automatically to shut out experiences, events, and stimuli that do not relate directly to their ability to survive. When people need to gain perspective and judgment about what they are doing, however, they can expand their normal awareness by using the receptive mode. According to Ornstein, techniques such as meditation, biofeedback, hypnosis, and even the use of certain drugs can help people learn to use the receptive mode, as their primitive ancestors did, to balance the active mode.

Ornstein and his collaborator, David Galin, support many of their ideas with laboratory data showing that the brain is divided and specialized in significant ways. They point out that the left-dominated and right-dominated modes of consciousness operate in a complementary and alternating fashion, one working while the other is inhibited (Galin, 1974; Ornstein, 1976). In Ornstein's (1977) model, intellectual activities take place in the active, or left-dominated, mode; intuitive activities take place in the receptive, or right-dominated, mode. The integration of these two modes underlies the highest human accomplishments. However, since the structure of the brain does not necessarily explain its function, support for this idea is still weak.

Among the newest explanations of consciousness are those from Daniel Dennett (1991, 1996) and Richard Restak (1994). In his book *Consciousness Explained*, Dennett asserts that human beings possess many sources of information, which together create a conscious experience. He argues that the brain creates multiple drafts (copies) of experiences, which are constantly being reanalyzed. According to Dennett, the brain develops a sense of consciousness as well as a sense of self (which is made up of multiple copies of past experiences) through this constant updating and reanalysis of experience. Further, Dennett argues that language may be essential to these updating and reanalysis processes and thus essential to consciousness (creating an interesting question about the location of consciousness in the split-brain patients described in Chapter 2). The theory is as yet untested, is not widely accepted, and has been criticized (Mangan, 1993); however, it takes a new path in bringing together perceptual, physiological, and historical information in one individual to explain consciousness. Such ideas are supported by the arguments of neurologist Restak, who asserts in his book *The Modular Brain* that it is the brain's various modules, sections, or parts that control behaviour. Consciousness is not centrally organized but rather resides in these modules; if you lose a module through a car crash or a sporting accident, you will lose certain, but not all, key abilities. Adolphs and Damasio (1995) also follow this line of reasoning and suggest that the modules are hierarchically organized; Calvin (1996) asserts that these modules are at work generating, synthesizing, and creating throughout our lives, when we are awake, asleep, at work, and at play. Calvin argues that it is this activity—which does not always work well—that creates interesting thought patterns and in many cases creative, ingenious thoughts.

Consciousness is an important issue in evolutionary psychology. Evolutionary theorists such as Leda Cosmides and John Tooby (1997) and Steven Pinker (1997) take the materialist position, maintaining that the mind is what the brain does—nothing more. In addition, evolutionary psychologists explain consciousness as an adaptation that gave humans a survival advantage. According to this view, the mind is a set of systems for computation, designed by natural selection to solve the kinds of problems our ancestors faced in their foraging way of life. Pinker argues that the "problem" of consciousness can be broken into three issues: sentience, access, and self-knowledge. *Sentience* refers to subjective experience and awareness—feelings. *Access* refers to the ability to report on the content and product of rational thought—to take deliberate, reasoned actions based on memory, rational ideas, and past experiences. *Self-knowledge* refers to the ability of individuals to recognize that their experiences are uniquely their own and to be aware that they are experiencing as they are doing it. Sentience is difficult to assess, but access and self-knowledge are cognitive activities that can be analyzed from a variety of vantage points, including the physiological, such as through fMRI scans and even biofeedback. From Pinker's view, such an analysis is crucial, because it is the only way for scientists to understand the true nature of consciousness. Pinker argues that the mind is a neural computer, fitted by natural selection with systems for reasoning.

Evolutionary psychologists see consciousness as only part of what the mind does; much of the mind's function is guided by brain functions that are outside awareness (Cosmides & Tooby, 1997). Complex neural circuits underlie functions such as vision that seem simple and automatic. These processes are arranged so that we are not aware of some and do have conscious awareness of others. Thus, evolutionary psychologists see a variety of levels of consciousness, all of which can be traced to neural circuitry that has been selected for during evolution. The result is our current multi-level consciousness.

The problem of consciousness is a classic one in philosophy, and some philosophers do not believe that neuroscience and evolutionary theory are on the right track to solve the puzzle of consciousness. David Chalmers (1996) is one of the philosophers who believe that neuroscience will not be the answer to the origins of consciousness. He contends that the problems neuroscience will solve are the "easy problems," whereas the existence of consciousness is the "hard problem." Chalmers considers consciousness to be a problem of another order, separate from issues of physiology, but he does not believe that this problem is unsolvable. He accepts that a solution is possible, but believes that the current research in neuroscience will not provide it.

Thus, the larger issues are difficult to frame, and the answers are far from complete. To work toward a more complete overall understanding of consciousness, researchers often focus on particular states of consciousness. So, in the remainder of this chapter, we will look at many of those states. Some of them are desirable and normal; others alter human behaviour in less desirable ways. We begin with a very familiar state of consciousness—sleep.

**Be an ACTIVE LEARNER**

**REVIEW**
> What is the dualist position? p. 130
> What are the key characteristics of consciousness? pp. 130–131
> Compare the view that consciousness comes from the working of the brain to Descartes's view. pp. 130–133

**THINK CRITICALLY**
> Why might neuroscience researchers and philosophers have different views of consciousness?
> What functions of consciousness are important from an evolutionary point of view?

**APPLY PSYCHOLOGY**
> What are the advantages of having consciousness?
> Over the next week, list the things you do on "automatic pilot," then analyze the things these situations have in common. Where do they occur? Are you alone or with others? What types of activities cause you to go into this altered state of consciousness?

# Sleep

The Italian family whose members die because they cannot sleep is very unusual. Most people—indeed, most creatures—sleep. Some animals are awake during daylight and sleep at night, whereas other have the opposite cycle, but cycles of sleep and waking are the rule. Research on sleep is just one part of the larger puzzle of human awareness, human consciousness, and altered states of being. It is a very important part, however, given our increasing tendency to live in a constantly sleep-deprived state (Coren, 1996).

### THE SLEEP–WAKEFULNESS CYCLE: CIRCADIAN RHYTHMS

In the far north in summer it is impossible to tell night from day. There is no darkness, activity can continue outdoors 24 hours a day, and you can even get a tee-time at midnight. People never seem to sleep; it is as if there *is* no day or night. But people do sleep; they give in to their bodily urge to rejuvenate themselves. Their bodies tell them they are tired even if there is no clock on the wall to give them a reminder. Humans are not at the mercy of light and darkness to control their activities, but seem instead to have an internal biological clock ticking to control the sleep–wakefulness cycle. This clock seems to run in about a 24-hour cycle; thus, the term *circadian* was born—from the Latin *circa diem* ("around a day"). **Circadian rhythms** are internally generated patterns of body functions, including hormonal signals, sleep, blood pressure, and temperature regulation, that have an approximate 24-hour cycle and occur even in the absence of normal cues about whether it is day or night.

Human beings are sensitive to light, which helps keep their biological clocks in sync (Boivin et al., 1996). However, when time cues (clocks, windows, temperature changes as the sun goes down) are removed from the environment for a long time,

▲ Light is an important cue for regulating circadian rhythms.

**CIRCADIAN** [sir-KAY-dee-an] **RHYTHMS**

Internally generated patterns of body functions, including hormonal signals, sleep, blood pressure, and temperature regulation, that have an approximate 24-hour cycle and occur even when normal day and night cues are removed.

Jet lag is a problem with circadian rhythms, which may create safety problems for pilots.

an interesting thing happens—circadian rhythms run a bit slowly. When human beings are placed in artificially lit environments and are allowed to sleep, eat, and read whenever they want to, they sleep a constant amount of time, but on each "day" they go to sleep a bit later (Lavie, 2001). This is because the full sleep–wakefulness cycle runs about 24.5 to 25.5 hours. Body temperature and other bodily functions tend to follow a similar circadian rhythm.

Because there are daylight, clocks, and arbitrary schedules, however, circadian rhythms alone do not control sleep and wakefulness. You can see the impact of circadian rhythms when your routine is thrown off by having to work through the night, then sleep, then rise, and so forth—your body's clock may not match your work clock. This disruption becomes especially apparent if you are an airline pilot, a surgeon, or a firefighter—one of the many people who work at night (Czeisler et al., 1990). When you put in long hours that stretch through the night and into the dawn, and when these hours are not regular, you become less attentive, think less clearly, and even may fall asleep from time to time. As well, you may have difficulty allowing your body to adjust to your work schedule because on your days off you naturally want to socialize with your friends and family and they are awake when you normally would be asleep (Coren, 1996). Thus, employers, workers, and consumers need to be aware of the potential decreased efficiency of night workers who vary their schedules, especially airline pilots, police officers, and medical interns. Research shows that circadian rhythms can be reset by shining lights on people's bodies, even while they are asleep (Campbell & Murphy, 1998, Lavie, 2001)—this is an important finding for those, such as frequent air travellers, who are perpetually readjusting their internal clock.

Consider the air traveller's common problem—jet lag. If you travel from, say, Toronto to London, England, the trip will take about seven hours. If you leave at 9 p.m., you will arrive in London seven hours later, at 4 a.m.—at least as far as your body is concerned. It seems very late at night. However, local London time is 9 a.m. You are exhausted. You finally go to bed and sleep, but your body still has to adjust. You experience exhaustion and disorientation, a set of feelings referred to as *jet lag*. You may want to sleep during the day and stay up at night. If you are experiencing jet lag or if you work long, irregular shifts, your work performance may not be at its peak. Psychologists have learned this through studying sleep, the sleep–wakefulness cycle, and sleep deprivation.

## SLEEP: A RESTORATIVE PROCESS

SLEEP

Non-waking state of consciousness characterized by general unresponsiveness to the environment and general physical immobility.

Sleep is a natural state of consciousness experienced by everyone. **Sleep** is a non-waking state of consciousness characterized by general unresponsiveness to the environment and general physical immobility. Some psychologists think that sleep allows the body to recover from the day's expenditure of energy; they see it as a restorative process. Others perceive sleep as a holdover from a type of hibernation. They believe that an organism conserves energy during sleep, when its expenditure would be inefficient (night is not a good time for some animals to catch or produce food). Still others see sleep as a time when the brain itself recovers from exhaustion and overload; they believe that sleep has little effect on basic physiological processes in the rest of the body. Horne (1988) asserts that sleep can be divided into two major types: core and optional. *Core sleep* repairs the effects of waking wear and tear on cerebral functions; it is thus restorative. *Optional sleep* fills the time from the end of core sleep until waking. These views of sleep—as physical restoration, hibernation, brain restoration, and core repair—guide researchers' investigations into sleep patterns.

How much sleep do people really need? Most people require about eight hours a day, but some can function with only four or five hours, while others need as many as nine or ten. Young teenagers tend to need more sleep than college students, and elderly people tend to sleep less than young people do. Most young adults (65 percent) sleep between 6.5 and 8.5 hours a night, and about 95 percent sleep between 5.5 and 9.5 hours (Horne, 1988). Do you think people who are active and energetic require more sleep than those who are less active? Surprisingly, this is not always the case. Bedridden hospital patients, for example, sleep about the same amount of time as people who are on their feet all day. Although the amount of sleep a person needs is determined genetically, heavy exercise, on any particular day, seems to increase a person's need for sleep (Youngstedt, O'Connor, & Dishman, 1997).

## SLEEP CYCLES AND STAGES: REM AND NREM SLEEP

The sleep–wakefulness cycle is repetitive, determined in part by circadian rhythms and in part by work schedules and a host of other events. When early sleep researchers such as Nathaniel Kleitman and William Dement studied the sleep–wakefulness cycle, they found stages within sleep that could be characterized through **electroencephalograms (EEGs)**—records of electrical brain patterns—and by eye movements that occur during sleep. Researchers working in sleep laboratories study the EEG patterns that occur in the brain during sleep by attaching electrodes to a participant's scalp and forehead and monitoring the person's brain waves throughout the night. Research in this area has become broader with the development and use by people such as Broughton at the Institute for Medical Engineering at the University of Ottawa of portable devices that now allow the recording of brain waves throughout the day as well (Broughton, 1991).

Recordings of the brain waves of sleeping participants have revealed that during an eight-hour period, people typically progress through five full cycles of sleep (see Figure 4.1). A full sleep cycle lasts approximately 90 minutes. We characterize the first four stages within a cycle as **non-rapid eye movement (NREM) sleep**. The other, very different, stage is **rapid eye movement (REM) sleep**—a stage of sleep characterized by high-frequency, low-voltage brain wave activity, rapid and systematic eye movements, and many vivid dreams. When people first fall asleep, they are in stage one; their sleep is light, and they can be awakened easily. Within the next 30 to 40 minutes, they pass through stages two, three, and four. Stage four is very deep sleep;

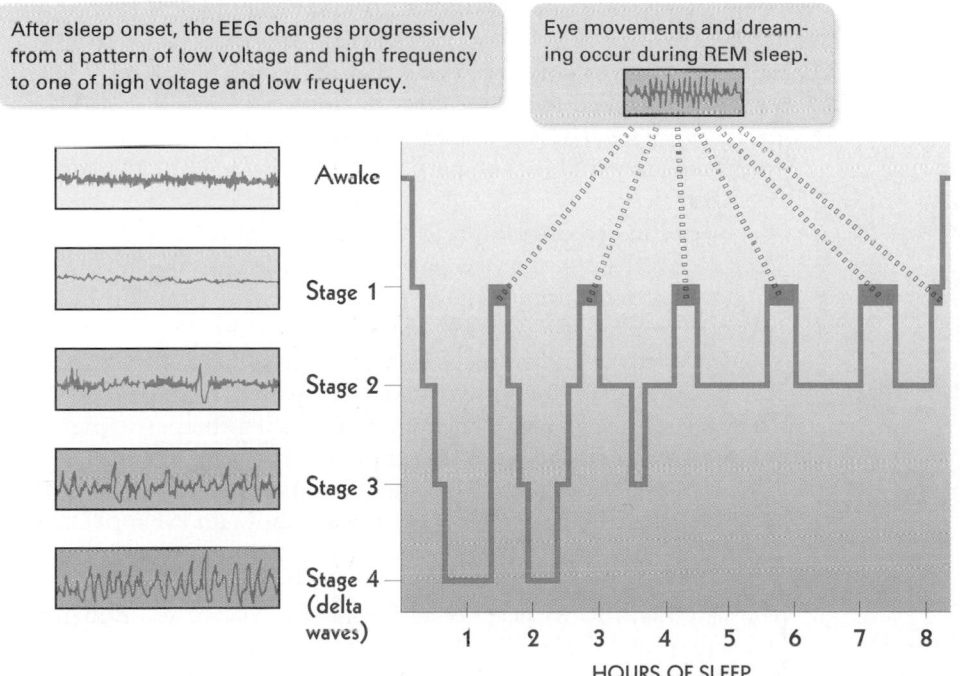

After sleep onset, the EEG changes progressively from a pattern of low voltage and high frequency to one of high voltage and low frequency.

Eye movements and dreaming occur during REM sleep.

Awake
Stage 1
Stage 2
Stage 3
Stage 4 (delta waves)

HOURS OF SLEEP

**FIGURE 4.1**
**EEG Activity during Sleep**

EEGs show distinctive and characteristic patterns during the wakeful state, REM sleep, and each of the four NREM sleep stages. Most people complete about five sleep cycles per night.

CONSCIOUSNESS

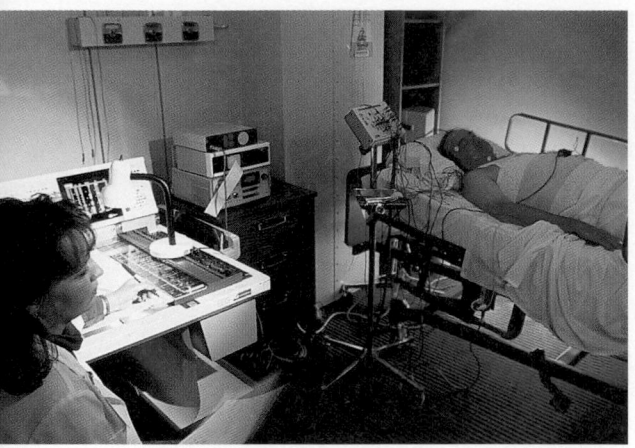

▲ Researchers in sleep laboratories study the EEG patterns of sleeping participants.

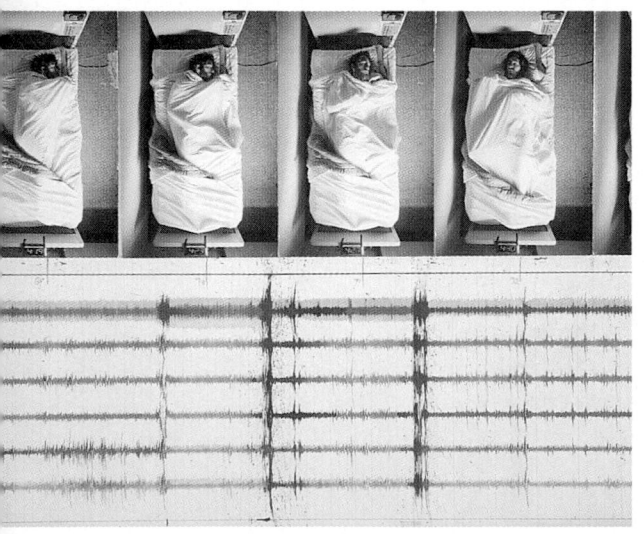

▼ During REM sleep, breathing and heart rate increase, eye movements become rapid, and EEG waves are of high frequency and low amplitude.

when participants leave that stage, they pass again through stage three and then two (both are described in the following paragraph) on their way to REM sleep.

The descent into stage four sleep may take 40 minutes or longer; then a curious event occurs. People move back through stages three, two, and sometimes stage one and then nearly awaken when they go into REM sleep for about 10 minutes. Breathing and heart rate increase, eye movements become rapid, imagery becomes vivid, and other physiological excitement occurs. Also, the longer people sleep (and the more sleep cycles they go through), the more REM sleep they experience (Agnew & Webb, 1973; Barbato et al., 1994). Figure 4.1 shows the distinctive brain wave patterns of wakefulness, the four stages of NREM sleep, and REM sleep in a normal adult. The waking pattern exhibits a fast, regular rhythm. In stage one, sleep is light; the brain waves are of low amplitude (height) but are relatively fast, with mixed frequencies. Sleepers in stage one can be awakened easily. Stage two sleep shows low-amplitude, non-rhythmic activity combined with special patterns called sleep spindles and K complexes. A *sleep spindle* is a rhythmic burst of brain waves that waxes and wanes for one or two seconds. A *K complex* is a higher-amplitude burst of activity seen in the last third of stage two. Sleep spindles and K complexes appear only during NREM sleep. Sleepers in stage two are in deeper sleep than those in stage one but still can be easily awakened. Stage three sleep is a transitional stage between stages two and four, with slower but higher-amplitude activity than during stage two. Stage four sleep, the deepest sleep stage, has even higher-amplitude brain wave traces, called *delta waves*. During this stage, people breathe deeply and have a slowed heart rate and lowered blood pressure. Stage four sleep has two well-documented behavioural characteristics. First, people are difficult to awaken. People awakened from stage four sleep often appear confused and disturbed and take several seconds to rouse themselves fully. Second, people in this stage of sleep generally do not dream as much as they do in REM sleep. Early research on sleep and dreaming suggested that dreams were a sole function of REM sleep, but we now know that dreams during NREM sleep occur and have many of the same characteristics of REM sleep dreams (Foulkes, 1996).

Research participants who are awakened, especially during REM sleep, can report in great detail the imagery and mental activity they have been experiencing. Because REM sleep is considered necessary for normal physiological functioning and behaviour, it might be expected to be a deep sleep; however, it is an active sleep, during which the brain wave activity resembles that of an aware person. For this reason, REM sleep is often called *paradoxical sleep* (Jouvet, 1999). In REM sleep, participants seem agitated; their eyes move and their heart rate and breathing are variable. Yet, participants are difficult to awaken during REM sleep.

In an EEG recorded during a transition from NREM stage two sleep to REM sleep, the first part of the tracing would show a clear K complex, indicating stage two sleep; the last part would show waves characteristic of REM sleep. Researchers can identify the stage in which an individual is sleeping by watching an EEG recording. If delta waves are present, the participant is in stage four sleep. To confirm this, an experimenter may awaken the participant and ask whether he or she was dreaming.

Sleep cycles develop before birth, and they continue to change into adulthood. Initially, sleeping fetuses show no eye movements. Later, they show eye, facial, and bodily movements. Newborns spend a little less than half of their sleep time in REM sleep. From age 1 to 10, the ratio of REM sleep to stage four sleep decreases dramatically (see Figure 4.2). The elderly experience greater fragmentation of sleep patterns than do younger adults.

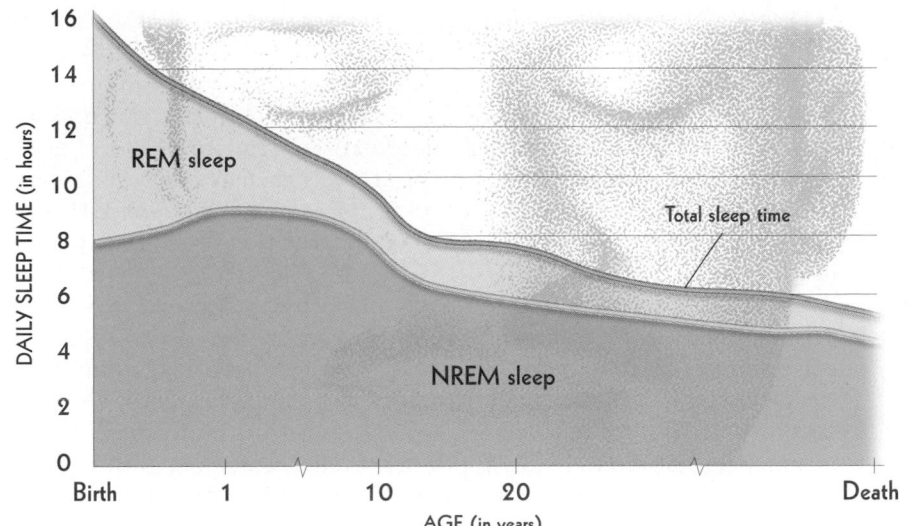

FIGURE 4.2

**Changes in Sleep Patterns over a Lifetime**

Children spend more time in REM sleep than adults do; the proportion of time spent in REM sleep decreases every year. NREM sleep accounts for nearly half of a newborn's sleep time. In adulthood, 80 to 85 percent of sleep is NREM.

Although REM sleep is an active sleep at all ages, PET scan research shows that not all areas of the brain are equally active. Braun and his colleagues (1998) found that the primary visual cortex is nearly shut down during REM sleep, but that other key visual areas are highly active. This lack of integration of key visual areas may account for some of the confused nature of dreams and their bizarre content. Without interpretation from important visual areas it is like looking at a map without key exits, roads, and directional arrows marked on it. We'll have more to say about this finding in a bit.

## SLEEP DEPRIVATION: DOING WITHOUT REM

In January 1964, at age 17, Randy Gardner made history by setting a world's record by staying awake for more than 260 hours—just short of 11 days. He enlisted two friends to help keep him awake, and he took no stimulants, not even coffee. After two days, sleep researcher William Dement began supervising Gardner's progress, much to the relief of his parents. Although Gardner did not suffer any serious physical symptoms, there were marked psychological effects. On day 2, he had trouble focusing his eyes. On day 3, he experienced mood changes. On day 4, he was irritable and uncooperative; he also began to hallucinate. By day 6, Gardner had some memory lapses and difficulty speaking. By day 9, his thoughts and speech were sometimes incoherent. On day 10, blurred vision became more of a problem, and he was regularly forgetting things. Mornings were his most difficult time. Despite these behavioural changes, Gardner never became violent or behaved in a socially deviant manner.

One of the most interesting aspects of Gardner's adventure is what happened to his sleep after his deprivation. Dement followed up by monitoring and observing Gardner for several days to see how well he recovered, what happened to his sleep patterns, and whether he made up for the sleep he had lost. Dement found that for the three nights following his deprivation, Gardner slept an extra 6.5 hours; on the fourth night, he slept an extra 2.5 hours (Gulevich, Dement, & Johnson, 1966; Johnson, Slye, & Dement, 1965). Therefore, Gardner did not make up all the sleep he lost in his 11 days of sleep deprivation.

Gardner's experience was unusual in terms of the length of his sleep deprivation, but going without sleep is a part of many people's lives. According to Stanley Coren of the University of British Columbia and data collected by Statistics Canada

**Be an ACTIVE LEARNER**

**REVIEW**
> What are circadian rhythms and what affects them? pp. 133–134
> Describe three different theories of the functions of sleep. p. 122
> Differentiate between REM and NREM sleep, and characterize the various sleep stages. p. 134
> What functions are served by the stages of sleep? pp. 135–137

**THINK CRITICALLY**
> See if you can think of some ways to make some connections between what we see on a PET scan while people are asleep and their subjective experiences while they are asleep. Do these methodological problems have any implications for what we can know in this area?

**APPLY PSYCHOLOGY**
> Describe your own sleep–wakefulness cycle for a day, keeping in mind that sleep specialists have a name for "morning people" (*larks*) and "night people" (*owls*). Are you a lark or an owl?

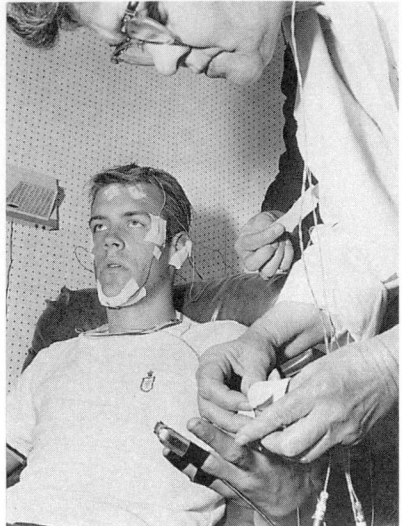

▼ Researchers studied Randy Gardner as he experienced 260 hours of sleep deprivation.

(Coren, 1996; Williams, 2001), 50 to 60 percent of adults in Canada get less than the recommended amount of sleep; many say that sleepiness interferes with activities in their lives, including work performance. People miss sleep in order to work, but they also neglect sleep in order to have fun, such as partying and watching TV. What are the effects of sleep deprivation? How much harm does going without sleep cause, especially at typical levels such as a few hours per night? If Randy Gardner's experience is typical, missing a few hours of sleep doesn't cause many problems, but many hours of deprivation produce major problems in functioning.

Some of the results from research on sleep deprivation are not at all surprising, but other results point to how drastically sleep deprivation can affect performance. The obvious result is that the longer people go without sleep, the sleepier they get and the worse their performance becomes (Devoto et al., 1999). One night of total sleep deprivation affects motor performance and memory (Forest & Godbout, 2000). But even a few hours of missed sleep can affect performance. A study that made this point in a dramatic way compared driving performance for people who were deprived of various amounts of sleep compared to those who had drunk various amounts of alcohol (Arnedt et al., 2001). The results showed that even low levels of alcohol impair driving ability, and sleep deprivation is comparable to drinking in its effects on driving. Indeed, driving skills worsen after staying awake only three hours longer than usual.

Do these results about sleep deprivation and driving explain the underlying reason for many traffic accidents? Research with long-haul truckers suggests that sleep deprivation is a serious safety problem. A team of researchers (Mitler et al., 1997) undertook a study of long-haul truck drivers to assess this safety issue. The researchers reasoned that such truckers, whose livelihood depends on delivering goods in a timely fashion, would sleep less than they needed to and that their sleep patterns would be altered in ways that would impair their driving skills. To do this study, these researchers had to conduct around-the-clock physiological monitoring while the truckers were on the job, which is an interesting contrast to typical laboratory sleep research. The participants were driving 10 to 13 hours per day, and performance on the various measures was repeatedly tested over a 5-day period on more than 200 trips totalling 328 000 kilometres.

The truckers averaged just over 5 hours of sleep per 24-hour period, which is about 2 hours less than what they reported as their ideal amount of sleep. The monitoring revealed that sleepiness was a substantial problem. For 7 percent of the time while they were actually driving, drivers exhibited signs of being in the first stage of sleep. In addition, 56 percent of the participants had at least one six-minute period of drowsiness. The most likely times for such drowsy episodes were late at night and early in the morning, or between 11 p.m. and 5 a.m.

Truckers are not the only people who neglect sleep and engage in activities that can be dangerous. Airline and ship pilots, health-care workers, police, and those who monitor nuclear facilities can endanger the lives of others by their sleepiness. But millions of people endanger their own and others' lives by driving while drowsy; 60 percent of young adults admit that they have done so, and 17 percent say they have dozed off while driving (Harvey, 2000).

Pioneering sleep researcher William Dement (1999) argues that the modern world experiences massive sleep deprivation and that we suffer because of our sleepiness. He describes this problem as *sleep debt*. Think of your sleep needs as a cheque book, with the total amount of sleep having to be in balance at the end of a week. After sleep deprivation, you owe your body sleep time. If you don't pay up, you pay the price in terms of sleepiness, trouble with concentration and attentiveness, poor mood, and lack of judgment, which may put you in danger.

What about complete sleep deprivation? What happens when people do not sleep at all? We know relatively little about this topic, for obvious reasons of ethics. Researchers cannot completely deprive people of sleep to see what happens, but we do know what happens to rats and to those with fatal familial insomnia: They die. Rats completely deprived of sleep die after two to three weeks of complete sleep deprivation (Rechtschaffen, 1998). Some of the symptoms in sleep-deprived rats are similar to those experienced by the Italian family with FFI—they show signs of terrible exhaustion, they lose the ability to regulate body temperature, and they lose weight. Sleep is obviously important, but what does it do?

## WHY DO WE SLEEP?

Researchers have established what happens during sleep but not why we sleep. Several theories attempt this task, but none is completely satisfactory (Rechtschaffen, 1998). The most obvious approach is to say that we sleep because we are tired—sleep provides some type of restorative function. If so, researchers have not identified what sleep restores. And fatigue does not relate directly to the need for sleep. Bedridden hospital patients, for example, sleep about the same amount of time as people who are on their feet all day. Heavy exercise seems to increase the need for sleep on any particular day, but these variations are not large (Youngstedt, O'Connor, & Dishman, 1997). And people can be exhausted and yet unable to sleep; an extreme example is the members of the Italian family afflicted with FFI.

The evolutionary approach is not very successful in explaining sleep. The adaptive advantage of spending hours per day unconscious is difficult to explain. The argument that forced unconsciousness keeps creatures out of danger can be countered with the point that being unconscious increases vulnerability. In addition, while we are asleep, we are not able to do other things that would increase our survival advantage, such as gather food, care for children, or have sex (Rechtschaffen, 1998). Therefore, considering the evolutionary cost of sleep *raises,* rather than answers, questions about why we sleep.

Another theory emphasizes sleep as part of circadian rhythms and emphasizes the brain mechanisms underlying the regulation of sleep and waking (Lavie, 2001). The circadian theory of sleep takes a broad approach, examining the cross-species differences and similarities in amount of sleep and sleep stages. This theory explains the mechanisms of sleep better than the underlying reasons of why sleep seems necessary.

Some theories of sleep concentrate on the stages of sleep, especially on REM sleep. One theory within this group holds that REM activity is important to memory formation, but two opposing camps disagree over what involvement REM has in memory. One version proposes that REM sleep is necessary to eliminate unnecessary and mistaken neural connections formed during waking (Crick & Mitchison, 1983), whereas another version hypothesizes that REM activity is important to memory formation (Stickgold et al., 2000). Related to this second theory is the view advanced by Carlyle Smith of Trent University and others (Maquet, Smith, & Stickgold, 2003) that brain plasticity, or the capacity for physical brain changes, is facilitated by sleep. For example, one study showed that cats given an opportunity to sleep for six hours after an environmental challenge showed more brain changes than did cats that continued to experience the challenge over the six-hour period. Yet another theory holds that REM plays an essential role in neural maturation, pointing to the finding that infants and babies spend more time in REM sleep than adults and older people do (Dement, 1999). This theory of sleep shows promise but leaves a great deal about sleep and its other stages unexplained.

No single theory has yet explained why we sleep, and perhaps none ever will. Perhaps one theory alone would be inadequate for this task anyway. Sleep serves multiple functions, and thus several theories may be necessary to explain those various functions (Rechtschaffen, 1998).

## IS THERE A SLEEP SWITCH?

If you find yourself in a theatre that's a little too hot, watching a film that's a bit boring, after a night in which you didn't have quite enough sleep, you might start to doze off. Is there a physiological structure that regulates and initiates sleep? Researchers are now suggesting that there may be certain cells deep within the brain that are "turned on" in such situations, while other brain cells are "shut off." Like cells in the visual system, which are activated when exposed to certain stimuli, these specialized brain cells may be selectively active.

Sherin and colleagues (1996) found that when rats were in various stages of sleep, cells in their brains seemed to turn on or off depending on the stage. The specific area of the brain in which these cells are located is the front region of the hypothalamus, called the *ventrolateral preoptic area* (VLPO). When rats were deprived of sleep for 9 to 12 hours, researchers found a certain protein present throughout most of the brain but not in the VLPO; in contrast, when rats were not deprived of sleep, the protein was found in the VLPO but not in the rest of the brain. According to these researchers, this very small area of the brain may constitute a subpopulation of sleep-controlling cells, whose actions determine the organism's state of consciousness. Further research has confirmed the importance of the VLPO in promoting sleep and has added information about how this area might work (Gallopin et al., 2000). The neurons in the VLPO produce GABA, an inhibitory neurotransmitter (see Table 2.1, p. 56). In addition, cells in the VLPO have connections to other locations in the brain and may be related to not only the control of sleep but also wakefulness.

Researchers have known for years that a collection of neurons in the *suprachiasmic nucleus* (SCN) (an area just above where the optic nerves meet and cross) is essential to the regulation of circadian rhythms. Dement (1999) argues that the biological clock actually promotes waking, which he calls clock-dependent alerting. The function of this internal clock helps us wake at two times during the 24-hour day: once in the early morning and again in the evening. Its effect is weak during the afternoon. Dement says that these effects explain why we are drowsy in the afternoon, feeling as if we just can't make it until bedtime, but start to feel more alert as the evening progresses. The longer we stay awake, the sleepier we get, so the effects of alerting are overtaken by sleepiness, so we sleep. Connections between the VLPO and the SCN are likely to be part of this regulation, but research must establish this connection and identify the neurotransmitters that allow it to occur.

## SLEEP DISORDERS

Do you snore so loudly that you keep others awake; fall asleep at inappropriate times, such as while driving a car; have trouble falling asleep; or sleepwalk? You may have a sleep disorder. People who fall asleep suddenly and unexpectedly have a disorder known as *narcolepsy*. This disorder affects about 1 in 2000 people and can cause them to have a very restricted life—they never know when they will have an attack. Narcolepsy has a genetic component (Takahashi, 1999), and an effective drug treatment has recently been developed (Dement, 1999).

Another sleep disorder, *sleep apnea*, causes airflow to stop for at least 15 seconds, so the person ceases breathing and wakens briefly. People with this disorder often have as many as 100 apnea episodes in a night; during the day, they are exceedingly sleepy and sometimes have memory losses. Because of their interrupted sleep, people with severe apnea may have work-related accidents and severe headaches, and they may fall asleep during the day. Drug therapy and some minor surgical techniques to create better airflow have been used to treat those with sleep apnea—and also may relieve the loud snoring that accompanies the disorder. Monitoring equipment for prolonged breathing pauses also has been used to wake the sleeper (Sheridan, 1985). Sleep apnea affects about 40 in 1000 individuals, but males are more likely than females to suffer from it (Ingbar & Gee, 1985). Sleep apnea also has been proposed as a possible explanation for sudden infant death syndrome (SIDS), in which infants die suddenly during sleep for no obvious reason. Alcohol and other central nervous system depressant drugs often contribute to sleep apnea in adults.

**Insomnia**, a prolonged inability to sleep, is a very common sleep disorder, often caused by anxiety or depression; 1 in 10 people report suffering from it at some time in their lives. Sleep disturbances and insomnia are especially common among older adults (Prinz et al., 1990). Insomniacs tend to be listless and tired during the day and may use sleeping pills or other drugs to induce sleep at night. Ironically, researchers have found that these drugs do not induce natural sleep; instead, they reduce the proportion of REM sleep (Webb & Agnew, 1975). (Recall that the body's normal response to sleep deprivation is to *increase* REM sleep.) Researchers such as Dement have found that lack of REM sleep may alter normal behaviour; accordingly, people with chronic insomnia should not regularly use drugs that force sleep. Various researchers have proposed behavioural methods that do not rely on drugs to help solve the problem; among these are relaxation training, thought restructuring, and self-hypnosis (e.g., Morin et al., 1994). Vitiello (1989) asserts that diet affects sleep by affecting sympathetic nervous system activity, which may stimulate people in the middle of the night. Research on diet and insomnia is still in its early stages. However, since diet affects mood and sleepiness, this idea does have experimental support. Another promising option for insomniacs is discussed in *Brain and Behaviour*.

*Night terrors*, another sleep disorder, consist of panic attacks that occur within an hour after a person falls asleep. Sitting up abruptly in a state of sheer panic, a person with a night terror may scream, breathe quickly, and be in a total state of fright. Night terrors are especially common in young children between the ages of three and eight. They usually disappear as a child grows older and do not seem to be a symptom of any psychological disorder. The cause of night terrors is not fully established, but they may be due to electrochemical processes overloading during NREM sleep.

In *sleepwalking*, a disorder that tends to run in families, an individual appears both asleep and awake at the same time. Sleepwalking is common among children. A sleepwalking child may reach out to a parent for a hug, navigate a darkened room, avoid a piece of furniture, walk into the street, or seem to be trying to accomplish a task—yet still be asleep. More boys sleepwalk than girls, and children who sleepwalk tend to outgrow it as they mature. Brain activity of sleepwalkers, when recorded with an EEG, shows stage four sleep. Research shows that different parts of a sleepwalker's brain display different levels of activity: more primitive motor portions of the brain are active; higher-level cognitive portions are deeply asleep. Contrary to popular belief, there is no danger in waking a sleepwalker. More likely, you may not be able to wake the sleepwalking individual because he or she is so deeply asleep (Dement, 1999). In very rare cases people can do dangerous things while sleep walking. Have a look at the strange case of Kenneth Parks in *Psychology in Action*.

Sleep disorders probably have several origins and will require the development of a research methodology, a theory, and a set of treatment plans that reflect the complexity of the problem. To date, no single approach has been found to be universally successful.

# Dreams

Why do some people rarely remember their dreams while others can recall theirs in vivid detail? Do dreams contain hidden meanings and mysterious symbols to be deciphered? Sometimes lifelike, sometimes surreal, and sometimes incoherent, dreams may replay a person's life history or venture into the unknown. Dreams have long occupied an important place in psychology, but only since the 1950s have they

INSOMNIA

A prolonged inability to sleep.

**Consciousness**

**Be an ACTIVE LEARNER**

**REVIEW**
> How common is sleep deprivation? What are its effects? pp. 137–138
> What brain structures regulate sleep and wakefulness? p. 140
> What is the most common sleep disorder? The most dangerous? pp. 140–141

**THINK CRITICALLY**
> How has sleep been affected by societal and technological changes that began in the twentieth century?
> What does the research on sleep deprivation reveal about the reasons for sleep?
> How can the evolutionary view explain sleep disorders?

**APPLY PSYCHOLOGY**
> Calculate your current sleep debt, and make a schedule that would allow you to pay back this debt. How difficult would it be for you to carry out this schedule?
> You probably know someone who experiences sleepwalking. Devise a plan to prevent this person from harming himself or herself.

## Melatonin—A Drug That Induces Sweet Dreams?

If you were a drug researcher seeking a new drug that could make you a billionaire, you might be looking for a drug that has the effect of melatonin. Melatonin induces a sweet and easy sleep without side effects, even among people with insomnia.

Melatonin is a natural nightcap; it is a hormone normally released by the pea-sized pineal gland at the base of the brain. Melatonin is involved in keeping the biological clock in sync, among other things (Middleton, Arendt, & Stone, 1997). Melatonin levels in a person's bloodstream vary when the amount of light in the person's environment changes (Mishima et al., 1994) and when circadian rhythms are disturbed (Dollinset et al., 1993; Haermae et al., 1994). However, research shows that melatonin given in small doses to human beings induces sleep and eases jet lag—quickly and easily,

even in midday. Richard Wurtman of the Massachusetts Institute of Technology has reported that, given in very small doses, the hormone is a sleep inducer without sleeping pill side effects such as feeling hung over and losing REM sleep (Dollins et al., 1993). Melatonin has proved especially effective in the treatment of sleep disorders (Jan, Espezel, & Appleton, 1994) and is widely used for jet lag (Brown, 1994). Melatonin has been claimed to positively affect sex drive, life span, heart disease, and even cancer outcomes—these claims have been exaggerated, however, and little evidence exists to support these beneficial effects.

Researchers are not sure how melatonin works. It may fool the body into thinking that it is night. It may act on other brain centres. It may affect other natural sleep-inducing hormones. What researchers do know is that people who take melatonin in small doses have less trouble sleeping. Currently it is available as a nutritional supplement, not yet as a prescription drug.

Should you take melatonin? Lots of people do. But, as a critical thinker, you have to be wary of unproven drugs. Clinical trials with double-blind procedures have yet to be conducted. Dosage levels are untested and people use dosages ranging from as little as one-tenth of a milligram to 200 milligrams. Some people, about 10 percent, report negative side effects including nightmares, headaches, and lowered sex drives. Researchers do not know how the hormone affects old people compared with younger ones. Do men and women respond differently? (There is reason to believe that they do.) Does the drug have any long-term side effects? The potential of melatonin is enormous: It may help people who suffer from sleep disorders; it may aid those who work irregular shifts, including physicians, nurses, and airline pilots. Melatonin may revolutionize how and when people sleep—but the operative word is *may*. The outcome must await carefully controlled, scientific double-blind research on human beings.

come under close scientific scrutiny. Dream research is difficult to conduct; in addition, because the data from dream research are always memories of past events, they are sometimes difficult to quantify and verify (Koulack, 1991) and this is especially true with youngsters who have difficulty reporting dreams from their own perspective (Foulkes & Kerr, 1994).

**DREAM**

A state of consciousness that occurs during sleep and is usually accompanied by vivid visual, tactile, or auditory imagery.

### WHAT IS A DREAM?

A **dream** is a state of consciousness that occurs during sleep and is usually accompanied by vivid visual imagery, although the imagery also may be tactile or auditory. During a dream there is an increase in heart rate, the appearance of rapid eye movements, a characteristic brain wave pattern, and a lack of bodily movements.

## Homicidal Somnambulism: The Strange Case of Kenneth Parks

On May 23, 1987, at 1:30 a.m., Kenneth Parks, a married Toronto man with a mother-in-law and father-in-law whom he liked and cared for deeply, arose from the couch on which he had fallen asleep, put on his shoes, and drove 37 kilometres to the home of his in-laws. There he assaulted his father-in-law, leaving the man unconscious on the floor, and stabbed his mother-in-law to death. He then drove to the local police station and, in a confused state, told them he thought he had killed someone, not even noticing that his hands were very seriously cut.

In court, Parks' defence attorney successfully argued that Parks was in fact sleepwalking at the time of the murder and that, as such, he lacked the coherent state of mind necessary to be held accountable for his actions. A team of researchers led by Roger Broughton of the University of Ottawa conducted a thorough assessment of Parks and in an article for the journal *Sleep* (Broughton et al., 1994) pointed to a number of features of the case that led to the court's acceptance of the sleepwalking defence. It is important to note that Broughton's assessment did not prove scientifically that Parks was wholly unaware of his actions—it only provided the court with what it saw as reasonable reasons to doubt that Parks was aware of his actions.

Parks had a history of sleepwalking, talking in his sleep, and night terrors as a child. In the year prior to the incident described above, Parks had developed a serious gambling problem and had embezzled money from the company he worked for to cover his debts. In worrying about his situation up to and after being fired for stealing and having to reveal the extent of the problem to his wife, Parks did not sleep much or well, averaging four to six hours a night. After his daughter's birth, even those few hours of sleep were often interrupted. In the week leading up to May 23, Parks had joined Gamblers Anonymous and had made a commitment to tell his grandmother and his in-laws about his problem. He hardly slept at all the night before the fateful evening and had played rugby for several hours that afternoon, coming home completely exhausted. All of these factors have been shown in the past to increase the likelihood that one who is prone to sleepwalking will, in fact, walk in their sleep.

Following his arrest, Parks' brain wave patterns were assessed while sleeping and through several forced awakenings. The patterns observed were consistent with those of other sleepwalkers and unrelated to those seen in people with mental illness, on drugs, or suffering from organic brain damage. This evidence along with the fact that Parks cared deeply for his in-laws and expressed genuine grief at what had occurred led experts to recommend to the court that Parks had killed his mother-in-law "during noninsane automatism as part of a presumed episode of somnambulism." Parks was acquitted and left the courtroom a free man.

Although dreams occur more often in REM sleep, they also occur during NREM sleep; during NREM sleep, they tend to be less visual and less bizarre (Casagrande et al., 1996). Dreams during REM sleep are intensely visual, may be action-oriented, and are more likely to be emotional than are NREM dreams. NREM dreams, such as those that occur at the beginning of sleep (Vogel, 1991), are more "thoughtlike" (Foulkes, 1985).

Most people dream four or five times per night, and their dreams last from a few seconds to several minutes. The first dream in a typical night occurs 90 minutes after a person has fallen asleep and lasts for 10 minutes. You dream more in the second part of the night than at the beginning of it (Casagrande et al., 1996). With about 4 dreams per night and 365 days per year, a person dreams more than 100 000 dreams in a lifetime. However, people remember only a few of their dreams. Usually, they recall a dream because they woke in the middle of it or because it had powerful emotional content or imagery.

## CONTENT OF DREAMS

Sometimes the content of a dream is related to day-to-day events, to a desire a person wishes to fulfil, or to reliving an unpleasant experience. Sometimes the same dream or a sequence of related dreams is experienced over and over again. Dreams are mostly visual, and they occur mostly in colour. Most dreams are commonplace, focusing on events related to people with whom the person comes into contact frequently—family, friends, or co-workers. Common dream themes include sex, aggressive incidents, and misfortunes. Sounds and other sensations from the environment that do not awaken a sleeper are often incorporated into a dream. For example, when a researcher sprayed water on the hands of sleepers, 42 percent (of those who did not awaken) later reported dreaming about swimming pools, baths, or rain (Dement & Wolpert, 1958).

A six-year-old described a dream in which she was being chased by a monster. In the dream she realized that she was dreaming, and turned and made friends with the monster. Like this child, people sometimes report that they are aware of dreaming while the dream is going on; this type of dream is a lucid dream. Most people have had a **lucid dream** at one time or another, particularly as children. When people have experienced a lucid dream, they often report that they were inside and outside of the dream at the same time. For some people this is upsetting, and they may wake themselves from the dream.

LUCID [LOO-sid] DREAM
A dream in which the person is aware of dreaming while it is happening.

## DREAM THEORIES

Some psychologists assume that dreams express desires and thoughts that may be unacceptable to the conscious mind. Many therapists who interpret and analyze dreams assume that dreams represent some element of a person that is seeking expression; this view—widely held—suggests that dreams put emotions into a context and that dreaming allows the expression of emotions in a safe place (Hartmann, 1995, 1996). Some psychologists see much symbolism in dreams and assert that the content of a dream hides the dream's true meaning. Other psychologists find dreams meaningless. The suggested meaning of a dream depends on the psychologist's orientation. Two theorists who made much of the meaning of dreams are Freud and Jung; both wrote extensively on the meaning of dreams, yet there is little or no scientific support for their theories and much evidence to the contrary (Blagrove, 1996) (see Table 4.1). Others see dreams as a biological phenomenon with little meaning, and cite the fact that dreams are often disconnected and incoherent as evidence of this fact.

MANIFEST CONTENT
The overt story line, characters, and setting of a dream—the obvious, clearly discernible events of the dream.

**PSYCHODYNAMIC VIEWS.** Sigmund Freud described dreams as "the royal road to the unconscious." For Freud, a dream expressed desires, wishes, and unfulfilled needs that exist in the unconscious. In his book *The Interpretation of Dreams* (1953), Freud spoke about the manifest and latent content of dreams. The **manifest content** of a dream consists of its overt story line, characters, and setting—the

---

**TABLE 4.1  Theories of Dreaming**

| Theory | Explanation |
|---|---|
| Psychodynamic theory | Psychodynamic theorists such as Freud view dreams as expressions of desires, wishes, and unfulfilled needs that exist in the unconscious. |
| Jungian theory | Jungian theorists see dreams not only as expressions of needs and desires, but as reflections of a collective unconscious shared by everyone within a particular cultural group. |
| Physiological model | Physiological models of dreaming view dreams as combinations of neural signals that are randomly generated and see analysis of dreams as a futile effort to make sense out of random events. |

obvious, clearly discernible events of the dream. The **latent content** of a dream is its deeper meaning, usually involving symbolism, hidden content, and repressed or obscured ideas and wishes—often involving sex or other uncomfortable, anxiety-provoking issues. We will see in Chapters 12 and 16 that Freud used dreams extensively in his theory of personality and in his treatment approach. Freudian psychoanalysts use dream analysis as a therapeutic tool in the treatment of emotional disturbance. Many contemporary therapists use patients' dreams to understand current problems and may see the dreams themselves only as a starting point. It is important to note that despite its possible use as a clinical tool, there is little research support for Freud's view of dreams. Try to figure out how we could test any of his claims.

Carl G. Jung (1875–1961) studied Freudian approaches to therapy and personality analysis, and he, too, considered the dream a crucial way to understand human nature. However, Jung took it for granted that a dream was nature's way of allowing humans access to their own unconscious. He believed that an individual's dreams express his or her deepest feelings in an uncensored form; they were a dreamer's attempt to make sense of life's tasks, compensate for unconscious urges, and predict the future (McLynn, 1997). Jung asserted that dreams give visual expression to instincts and that all humans share in the **collective unconscious**, a storehouse of primitive ideas and images inherited from one's ancestors. These inherited ideas and images, whose representations emerge in dreams, are termed *archetypes,* and are emotionally charged and rich in meaning and symbolism. One especially important archetype is the *mandala,* a mystical symbol, often with a circular pattern, that in Jung's view represents a person's inner striving for unity. Dream analysis is also important in Jungian therapy, with a focus on understanding and accepting one's humanity. We will consider this approach in more detail in our study of personality in Chapter 12.

Today psychoanalytic dream theories still see dreams as keys to the unconscious, but they also suggest that dreams integrate past experiences with current ones to produce a structure of ideas and feelings that are organized and help restore psychological balance. Thus theorists like Fosshage (1997) assert that a dream speaks to us by telling stories of our ongoing psychological transformation. As appealing as these ideas are to some psychologists, there are scant data to suggest that such notions are correct (Blagrove, 1996).

LATENT CONTENT
The deeper meaning of a dream, usually involving symbolism, hidden content, and repressed or obscured ideas and wishes.

COLLECTIVE UNCONSCIOUS
In Jung's dream theory, a storehouse of primitive ideas and images in the unconscious that is inherited from one's ancestors; these inherited ideas and images, called *archetypes*, are emotionally charged and rich in meaning and symbolism.

▲ Jung believed that the *mandala* represented a person's inner striving for unity.

**COGNITIVE VIEWS.** Many contemporary researchers believe that dreams are connected to reality, have meaning, and even have a "grammar" of their own, without having a hidden, deep, latent content. These cognitive researchers—for example, Foulkes (1985, 1996)—suggest that dreams express current wishes, desires, and issues with which a person is dealing. Dieters dream of food, those quitting smoking do dream of cigars, and individuals who are depressed dream of bleak futures (e.g., Hajek & Belcher, 1991). As illustrated in *Introduction to Research Basics*, this connection between dreams and reality is not limited to human beings. Similarly, young lovers dream about the future, and the elderly dream about the past. Not only do we dream about current situations, but our culture and language affect dream content; for example, bilinguals' dream content is related to the language that dominated their waking hours before sleep (Foulkes et al., 1993). Thus, Foulkes (1990) argues that the creation of a dream depends on active, integrative intelligence and that by studying the content of dreams we can study not only development, intelligence, and language, but also how cognitive processes develop.

**BIOLOGICAL VIEWS.** We know that dreaming is solely neither a right-hemisphere nor left-hemisphere function—both hemispheres are required (McCormick et al.,

# INTRODUCTION to Research Basics

## Caught in a Maze

Have you ever had a dream about being caught in a giant maze, trying to find your way out? If you have, maybe some of the corridors in the maze ended in dead ends, and you weren't sure where you were going. If so, you aren't alone—rats have similar dreams, at least the ones in the Massachusetts Institute of Technology laboratory of Kenway Louie and Matthew Wilson (2001). These two researchers conducted a descriptive study in which they compared the pattern of neural activity during maze learning with the pattern during REM sleep. They wanted to determine whether the two types of patterns were similar enough to conclude that the rats were dreaming of their daytime maze-running activities.

**Hypothesis.** Neural activity in the hippocampus, a brain structure involved in memory formation, will be similar during REM sleep and during maze running.

**Design.** The design was a descriptive study using correlation. **Descriptive studies** are a type of research method that allows researchers to measure variables so that they can develop a description of a situation or phenomenon. Louie and Wilson wanted to know the degree of relationship between the firing patterns of neurons in the hippocampus during maze running and during REM sleep. This method allowed them to make some inferences about dream content in non-human animals, a topic that has been difficult to study because rats cannot report their dreams. However, rats do have the same five sleep stages that humans experience, including REM sleep.

**Procedure.** Louie and Wilson measured the pattern of activation in the rats' hippocampus (see Chapter 2, p. 65) and then compared that pattern to the activation in the hippocampus during REM sleep. These researchers placed four rats in a circular maze and made recordings from neurons in their brains during this activity. Then they made neural recordings of more than 40 REM periods in the rats that had run the maze.

**Results.** Some REM periods showed brain activity that was not at all similar to the pattern during maze running, but about half of the REM periods showed a very similar pattern of activity in the hippocampus. The researchers measured the similarity by using a correlation statistic (see Chapter 2 for a more detailed explanation of this technique) to determine the degree of association between neural activity during maze running and during REM sleep. They found patterns that seem to be so similar that they could be considered neural "signatures" of this specific activity.

**Conclusions.** These researchers believe that the rats are replaying their maze experiences during their dreams. The replay was the same length as the experience of traversing the maze, and the researchers could match the patterns of activity closely. Not only does this research tell us that rats dream but that both rat and human dreams may serve to consolidate memory. One version of the biological theory of dreaming holds that REM sleep is important for memory formation, and this research strengthens that claim.

---

**DESCRIPTIVE STUDIES**

A type of research method that allows researchers to measure variables so that they can develop a description of a situation or phenomenon.

1997). However, both sides of the brain may not be operative simultaneously or even work in congruence. Is it possible that this lack of coordination means that dreams have no underlying meaning and are just random, fleeting images? Two researchers from Harvard Medical School, Allan Hobson and Robert McCarley (1977), believe that dreams (and for that matter all consciousness) have a physiological basis but represent little more than incoherent, haphazard, transient images. They argue that during periods of REM sleep, the parts of the brain responsible for long-term memory, vision, audition, and perhaps even emotion are spontaneously *activated* (stimulated) from cells in the hindbrain, especially the pons. The cortex tries to *synthesize*, or make sense of, the messages it receives from these parts of the brain. Because this activity is not organized by any external stimuli, the resulting dream is often fragmented and incoherent (Hobson, 1989, 1994). Activation–synthesis theory is supported by researchers who assert that the brain (especially the cortex) basically does its daily "housecleaning" during sleep, scanning previous memories, refreshing old storage mechanisms, and maintaining active memory. Other researchers, however, point out that dreamlike activity occurs even when cells in the pons are not active. In this view, the dream is a random collection of images and means little or nothing of importance. Braun and colleagues' (1998) research lends support to the idea of disconnects in brain activity; not all parts of the brain are activated during sleep. This lack of integration of brain activity thus may account for the random nature of images and dream content.

## Controlling Consciousness: Biofeedback, Hypnosis, and Meditation

Can you learn to control your own consciousness? Can you manipulate your mental states to achieve certain bodily reactions? Research and anecdotal data suggest that you can. People have long been taught to relax and breathe in special ways so as not to experience pain—for example, during childbirth. Marathons have been won through intense mental concentration that allowed contestants to endure particularly difficult physical circumstances. Laboratory research also shows that people can bring some otherwise autonomic bodily states (see Chapter 2), such as blood pressure, under conscious control through a technique called biofeedback.

**Be an ACTIVE LEARNER**

**REVIEW**
> How do dreams in REM and NREM states differ? p. 143
> Jung and Freud both believe that the content of a dream is meaningful. In what ways do their views differ? pp. 144–145
> How do researchers know when people dream? p. 142

**THINK CRITICALLY**
> What, if anything, would probably happen to you if you cut short your normal sleep time by two hours a night for a period of several months?
> If someone like Freud told you what one of your dreams meant, how would you argue with him if you did not think the interpretation made sense?

**APPLY PSYCHOLOGY**
> Keep a notepad at your bedside, and record several nights' dreams immediately on awakening. (You otherwise may forget them by the time you have breakfast.) Which theory of dreaming seems to explain your dreams best?

### BIOFEEDBACK

Imagine a special clinic where people could be taught to treat themselves for headaches, high blood pressure, and stress-related illnesses, even for nearsightedness. By learning to influence consciously what are normally involuntary physiological reactions, patients might be able to help themselves. Such a psychological–medical clinic may exist in the future if biofeedback proves to be the healing tool some researchers predict it will be.

Physicians and psychologists once assumed that most biological functions, especially those involving the autonomic nervous system, could not be controlled voluntarily except through drugs or surgery. Since the 1960s, however, studies have explored the extent to which participants can learn to control these functions through biofeedback. **Biofeedback** is a general technique by which individuals can monitor and learn to control the involuntary activity of some of the body's organs and functions. A well-known psychologist, Neal E. Miller, was one of the first researchers to train rats to control certain glandular responses. Miller (1969) suggested that the same techniques could be used to help human beings manage their bodies and behaviour. Since then, studies have shown that people can indeed manipulate their bodies. We do not normally control processes such as blood flow, and in truth we may not have any conscious awareness of where blood actually flows. However, in theory, biofeedback gives us that awareness and allows us to directly modify brain systems that control it. The appropriate brain changes are reinforced by the feedback. A relaxed person viewing his or her own brain waves on a monitor, for example, can increase the frequency of those waves by becoming more alert and by paying attention. Similarly, a participant whose heart rate is displayed on a monitor can see the rate decrease as he or she relaxes, thereby learning about the physiological states that allow the body to work easily and efficiently. The person can learn which behaviours relax the heart and lower blood pressure and, in time, can learn to control heart rate and blood pressure by reproducing behaviours associated with reduced heart rate, sometimes without actually being sure how he or she is doing it.

Some researchers contend that biofeedback training is not effective (Drennen & Holden, 1984); others point out that the same effects can be obtained without real feedback (Plotkin, 1980). Some are sceptical about the long-term effectiveness of biofeedback. Still others claim to have used

**BIOFEEDBACK**

A technique by which individuals can monitor and learn to control the involuntary activity of some of the body's organs and functions.

▼ Biofeedback uses electronic equipment to measure physical responses, such as muscle tension or EEG activity, which allows the person to learn to control those responses.

biofeedback successfully to treat people with stress-related symptoms, hyperactivity, stuttering, depression, nearsightedness, and learning disabilities. For example, Dietvorst (1978) successfully used biofeedback to help heart attack patients reduce their anxiety and fear of future attacks. He trained participants to decrease their level of arousal, and thus their level of anxiety, by monitoring one measure of their autonomic activity—hand temperature.

Many laboratory studies have demonstrated biofeedback's effectiveness in helping people manage a wide range of physiological problems; however, only carefully controlled research will answer persistent questions about its usefulness. For example, under what conditions, with what kinds of problems, and with what types of individuals is biofeedback effective (Middaugh, 1990)? Methodological issues such as those described in Chapter 1 (expectancy effects or attempts to please a researcher, for example) make this a challenging research area.

## HYPNOSIS

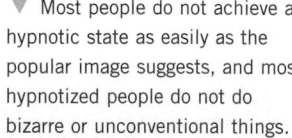

HYPNOSIS

An altered state of consciousness brought about by procedures that may induce a trance.

"You are falling asleep. Your eyelids are becoming heavy. The weight on your eyes is becoming greater and greater. Your muscles are relaxing. You are feeling sleepier and sleepier. You are feeling very relaxed." These instructions are typical of those used in *hypnotic induction*—the process used to hypnotize people. **Hypnosis** is an altered state of consciousness brought about by procedures that may induce a trance. A common public view of hypnosis is that hypnotized individuals are in a trancelike state of consciousness and give up control over much of their behaviour. They are aware of their surroundings and are conscious, but their level of awareness and responses to others are altered. A person's ability to be hypnotized or willingness to follow unconventional instructions given by the hypnotist, such as to make funny noises, is called *hypnotic susceptibility*, or *suggestibility*. Most people can be hypnotized to some extent (Hilgard, 1965). Children between the ages of 7 and 14 are the most susceptible; those who daydream also are particularly susceptible (Hoyt et al., 1989). Crawford (1994) argues that highly hypnotizable people have stronger attention-focusing abilities than those who are not suggestible.

**EFFECTS OF HYPNOSIS.** People who have been hypnotized report that they know they have been hypnotized and are aware of their surroundings. Some report being in a special, almost mystical state; most report a sense of time distortion (Bowers, 1979). One reported time distortion effect of hypnosis is *age regression*—the ability to recount details about an experience that took place many years earlier or to feel and act like a child. Because few studies that report age regression during hypnosis have been controlled for accuracy of recall, the authenticity of age regression has been questioned (Nash, 1987). The age at which such recall is said to occur is important, because it is difficult to remember events before age three (Perner & Ruffman, 1995). It is possible that individuals are only reporting what they believe may have happened at an earlier age.

▼ Most people do not achieve a hypnotic state as easily as the popular image suggests, and most hypnotized people do not do bizarre or unconventional things.

*Heightened memory* is another purported effect of hypnosis. Evidence indicates that hypnosis helps participants recall information (e.g., McConkey & Kinoshita, 1988). However, techniques that do not involve hypnosis may work just as well for this purpose. In fact, in a contradictory study by Putnam (1979), hypnotized and non-hypnotized participants were asked to recall events they had seen earlier on videotape. Hypnotized participants made more errors when answering leading questions than did non-hypnotized participants. Putnam suggests that hypnotized participants not only make more errors (misrecollection) but mistakenly believe that their memories are accurate (Sheehan & Tilden, 1983). These results have led researchers to question the use of hypnosis in courtroom settings; in fact, some states do not allow the testimony of hypnotized persons as evidence (Sanders & Simmons, 1983; Smith, 1983).

Hypnosis is also used for pain reduction. In a case reported by Siegel (1979), hypnosis successfully reduced lower-leg pain in a woman who had undergone an above-the-knee amputation. (The phenomenon of pain in a part of the body that no longer exists is called *phantom pain*; it occurs in some amputees.) Hypnosis also has been used to reduce pain from heat, pressure, and childbirth (Chaves & Dworkin, 1997; Miller & Bowers, 1993). Few studies of pain management, however, are conducted with adequate experimental rigour. Critics of hypnosis note that most patients show signs of pain even when hypnotized. Also, in many cases analgesic drugs (pain relievers) are used along with hypnotism. Some researchers challenge the ability of hypnosis to reduce pain, reasoning that relaxation and a patient's positive attitude and lowered anxiety account for reported reductions in pain.

Hypnosis continues to be widely used as an aid in psychotherapy. Most clients report that, if nothing else, it is a pleasant experience. Therapists assert that in some cases it can (1) help focus a client's energy on a specific topic, (2) aid memory, or (3) help a child cope with the after-effects of child abuse. Many therapists use hypnosis to help patients relax, enhance their memory, reduce stress and anxiety, lose weight, or stop smoking (Ballen, 1997; Kinnunen & Zamansky, 1996; Kirsch et al., 1995). Some psychologists assert that hypnosis can help athletes concentrate (Morgan, 1992) and help obese patients lose weight (Johnson, 1997). Research into the process and effects of hypnosis continues, with an emphasis on defining critical variables in hypnosis itself and in the participants who are most and least easily hypnotized (e.g., Nilsson, 1990) and on ascertaining potential negative effects (e.g., Lynn et al., 1997; Sapp, 1996).

## MEDITATION

Meditation has become an important daily routine for one of our colleagues. Previously, searing migraines, stomach pains, and high blood pressure had afflicted her during stressful periods. Despite prescription drugs and frequent visits to the doctor, she had found little relief. Then, at a stress management clinic, she discovered how to ease her tensions through meditation. Now, instead of taking a pill when she feels a migraine coming on, she meditates.

**Meditation** is a state of consciousness induced by a variety of techniques and characterized by concentration, restriction of incoming stimuli, and deep relaxation to produce a sense of detachment. For centuries meditation has been used to alter consciousness and help relieve health problems. Those who practise it use a variety of positions—sitting, lying, or reclining—and report that it can reduce anxiety, tension headaches, backaches, asthma, and the need for sleep. It also can increase self-awareness and feelings of inner peace (West, 1980, 1982). Meditation is not relaxation, but relaxation is a by-product of meditation.

Practitioners distinguish between two major types of meditation: *mindful* and *concentrative*. Each type uses different techniques to induce an altered state of awareness. Both direct the focus of attention away from the outside world through intense concentration. One begins *mindful meditation* by trying to empty the mind and just be still. As random and intrusive thoughts arise, one notices them (becomes mindful of their content) without reacting to them, judging them good or bad, or dwelling on them. They eventually become mere wisps of thought that pass through consciousness while the person meditating remains serene. Eventually, one becomes aware that how they react to their thoughts is the problem (it causes suffering) and that such reactions are not necessary in order to have thoughts. In *concentrative meditation*, on the other hand, one concentrates on a visual image or a mantra (repetition of a phrase), and when the mind wanders to a random thought, one brings the mind back to the image

MEDITATION
A state of consciousness induced by a variety of techniques and characterized by concentration, restriction of incoming stimuli, and deep relaxation to produce a sense of detachment.

▼ Meditation involves concentration and deep relaxation.

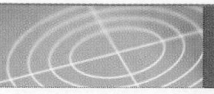

## Is Hypnosis an Altered State of Consciousness?

**POINT:** Hypnosis is an altered state of consciousness characterized by suggestibility, relaxation, and concentration.

**COUNTERPOINT:** Hypnosis involves no alteration of consciousness.

Some authorities, including Ernest Hilgard (1965) and Josephine Hilgard (Hilgard, Hilgard & Barber, 1994), define hypnosis as an altered state of consciousness during which a person's consciousness is divided or dissociated. They argue that in a hypnotized state, people are more highly suggestible, and they can therefore control physiological processes they cannot control during normal waking, such as pain perception. In addition, the participants in the Hilgards' studies showed changes in brain activation in an area of the cerebral cortex associated with attention. They argue that this distinct pattern of brain activity is further evidence that people who are hypnotized experience an altered state of consciousness.

Joseph Barber (1991) and Nicolas Spanos (1991), a researcher at Carlton University until his death several years ago, contend that the concepts of hypnosis and the hypnotic trance are meaningless and misleading. According to them, the behaviour of hypnotized participants is no different than the behaviour of participants willing to think about and imagine themes suggested to them. If participants' attitudes toward a situation lead them to expect certain effects, those effects are more likely to occur. These researchers' approach is a social-cognitive one and is sometimes called a *cognitive–behavioural view* because it stresses the role of social processes in changing people's thoughts and behaviour during hypnosis (Lynn, 1992; Barber, Spanos, & Chaves, 1974). Barber's and Spanos's studies show that participants who undergo hypnotic induction and participants given task-motivating instructions (such as to concentrate deeply, fix their attention, or breathe deeply) perform similarly. Typically, more than half of the participants in experimental groups showed responsiveness to task suggestions, in contrast to 16 percent in control groups that were given no special instructions. From the results, the researchers concluded that task-motivating instructions are almost as effective as hypnotic induction in increasing participants' responsiveness. Those who accept this view believe that hypnosis is more like *playing the role* of a

hypnotized person than attaining an altered state of consciousness.

A third definition for hypnosis proposes that it is a state of focused attention that allows people to relax and learn to control bodily functions (Olness, 1993). This definition concentrates on the characteristics associated with and the benefits that can be derived from hypnosis. So, in the end, we have three views of hypnosis.

These views are incompatible, and all argue that they have research support, though at times it is not always clear which view a study best supports. The definition of hypnosis as an altered state of consciousness received support from a study in which researchers used PET brain-imaging technology to study people during hypnosis (Rainville et al., 1999). This study compared people during relaxation, hypnosis, and hypnosis with suggestions about suppressing pain. While hypnotized, people's brains showed a complex pattern of changes, including increased activation of the frontal lobes and chronic headaches, especially migraine headaches (Compas et al., 1998). Many of its benefits are related to relaxation, and other consciousness-controlling techniques are often as effective as biofeedback.

Barber's studies have received support from other research. Salzberg and DePiano (1980), for example, found that hypnosis did not facilitate performance any more than task-motivating instructions did. In fact, they argued that for cognitive tasks, task-motivating instructions are more effective than hypnosis. However, the evidence showing that effects similar to those from hypnosis can be achieved in many and various ways (e.g., Bryant & McConkey, 1989) does not mean that psychologists must discard the concept or use of hypnosis. It simply means they should reconsider traditional assumptions and stop thinking about hypnosis as either existing or not existing. The ultimate view of hypnosis is unlikely to be strictly state or social-cognitive, but instead will consider motivation, intention, expectancy, memory, and automated responses (Kirsch & Lynn, 1998b).

or mantra without noticing the content of the thought. In this case, the image or mantra is the important thing. This form of meditation is closely tied with religions such as Tibetan Buddhism and Hinduism, but it also has been commercially exploited and because of this has acquired a bad reputation in some circles.

One concentrative approach, *Zen*, is especially popular among those interested in healing and nutritional approaches to health. People using Zen techniques highlight the experience of enlightenment and the possibility of attaining it in this life. Zen techniques urge people to concentrate on their breathing and count their breaths. The immediate aim is to focus attention on a specific visual stimulus; the ultimate aim is to achieve a spiritual state of being.

Supporters of meditation claim that it is a unique state, capable of causing profound physiological and psychological changes. They argue that mindful meditation produces a different mode of cognitive processing by training people to maintain awareness of ongoing events and increasing attention. However, a study comparing the physiological responses of meditating participants with those of hypnotized participants found their responses to be nearly identical (Holmes, 1984). Experimental studies also show that individuals trained simply to relax and concentrate have been able to achieve bodily states similar to those who meditate (Fenwick et al., 1977).

Although most theories that explain the nature and effects of meditation rely on concepts that are not scientifically measurable or observable, some controlled studies have been done. The data from these studies have shown that those who meditate can alter their physiological responses, including oxygen consumption, brain wave activity, and sleep patterns (Pagano et al., 1976). Such evidence encourages some scientists to continue to investigate meditation for relieving tension, anxiety, and arousal.

**Be an ACTIVE LEARNER**

**REVIEW**
> What happens during biofeedback that allows people to gain control of autonomic processes? p. 147
> Which characteristics of hypnosis are undisputed? Which are controversial? pp. 148–149
> What do the different types of meditation have in common? pp. 149–151

**THINK CRITICALLY**
> Evaluate who would be the better hypnotic subject—an elderly person or a child.
> How would you go about demonstrating that hypnosis and meditation are different states of consciousness?

**APPLY PSYCHOLOGY**
> If you wanted to try biofeedback, hypnosis, or meditation to help control stress, which would be the easiest to do? Which would be the most economical approach?
> Your roommate smokes and would like to quit. He asks you if you would recommend hypnosis as a therapy for quitting. What is your advice?

## Altering Consciousness with Drugs

In each of the past few years, Canadian physicians have written millions of prescriptions for drugs. At least 4 percent of the Canadian population is currently taking tranquilizers. At least 20 percent of adult Canadians use some kind of consciousness-altering drug that changes both brain activity and daily behaviour. We use drugs to help us wake up in the morning, to get us through daily stresses, and to help us sleep. Drugs may be legal or illegal; they may be used responsibly or abused with tragic consequences. A **drug** is any chemical substance that alters normal biological processes. Many widely used drugs are both psychoactive and addictive. A **psychoactive drug** is one that alters behaviour, thoughts, or emotions by altering biochemical reactions in the nervous system, thereby affecting consciousness. An **addictive drug** is one that causes a compulsive physiological need and that, when withheld, produces withdrawal symptoms. Addictive drugs also usually produce tolerance.

In studying drug (or substance) use and abuse, we have to consider the drug itself, its properties, and the context of its use. For example, not all people respond in the same way to the same drug, and one person may respond differently on different occasions. Two important questions we need to ask are the following: Does the drug produce dependence? Are there adverse reactions to the drug for the user or adverse consequences for other people or society (Newcomb & Bentler, 1989)? There is no single explanation for substance use and abuse. Societal factors, individual family situations, medical problems, and genetic heritage are all potentially part of a person's reasons for using or abusing drugs. The use versus abuse issue is an especially problematic one for young people, who have to sort out the conflicting messages that society delivers. Newcomb and Bentler (1989) argue, "Adolescents are quite adept at spotting hypocrisy and may have difficulty understanding a policy of 'saying no to drugs' when suggested by a society that clearly says 'yes' to the smorgasbord of drugs that are legal as well as the range of illicit drugs that are widely available and used" (p. 242).

**DRUG**
Any chemical substance that alters normal biological processes.

**PSYCHOACTIVE [SYE-koh-AK-tiv] DRUG**
A drug that alters behaviour, thoughts, or emotions by altering biochemical reactions in the nervous system, thereby affecting consciousness.

**ADDICTIVE DRUG**
A drug that causes a compulsive physiological need and that, when withheld, produces withdrawal symptoms.

**Consciousness**

## WHAT IS SUBSTANCE ABUSE?

A **substance abuser** is a person who overuses and relies on drugs to deal with stress and anxiety. Most substance abusers turn to alcohol, tobacco, and other readily available drugs such as cocaine and marijuana, but substance abuse is not confined to these drugs. A growing number of people are abusing legal drugs such as tranquilizers and diet pills, as well as illegal drugs such as amphetamines and heroin. A person is a substance abuser if all three of the following statements apply:

- The person has used the abusive substance for at least a month.
- The use has caused legal difficulties or social or vocational problems.
- There is recurrent use in hazardous situations such as driving a car.

Substance abuse can lead to psychological dependence, pathological use, or both. **Psychological dependence** is a compelling desire to use a drug, along with an inability to inhibit that desire. *Pathological use* involves out-of-control episodes of use, such as alcohol binges. Most drugs produce a physiological reaction when they are no longer administered; in general, this reaction is evidence of physical dependence. Without the drug, a dependent person suffers from withdrawal symptoms. **Withdrawal symptoms** are the physiological reactions that occur when an addictive drug is no longer administered to an addict. These reactions may include headaches, nausea, and an intense craving for the absent drug. In addition, addictive drugs usually produce **tolerance**—progressive insensitivity to repeated use of a specific drug in the same dosage and at the same frequency of use. Tolerance forces an addict to use increasing amounts of the drug or to use the drug at an increased frequency to achieve the same effect. For example, alcoholics must consume larger and larger amounts of alcohol to become drunk. Most addictive drugs produce both dependence and tolerance. Shepard Siegel (Weise-Kelly & Siegel, 2001; Siegel et al., 2000) of McMaster University has demonstrated that tolerance is only partly due to physiological factors and that addicts become conditioned to the effects of their drugs when taken in familiar settings, requiring more drugs for a comparable high.

Psychoactive drugs change behaviour by altering a person's physiology and normal state of consciousness. Some drugs increase alertness and performance; others promote relaxation and relieve high levels of arousal and tension. Some produce physical and psychological dependence. All psychoactive drugs alter a person's thoughts and moods; they are all considered to be consciousness-altering drugs.

## WHY DO PEOPLE ABUSE DRUGS?

Some people are likely to develop a substance abuse problem for physiological and genetic reasons; others may have emotional problems caused by stress, poverty, boredom, loneliness, or anxiety. People may turn to drugs to relax, be sociable, forget their worries, feel confident, or lose weight. Parental drug use, peer drug use, poor self-esteem, stressful life changes, divorce, and social isolation have all been implicated.

In any culture, determining the causes of drug abuse is complicated by the definition of addiction. Addictive drugs are generally defined by saying that they are habit-forming (reinforcing) or that they produce a physiological dependence—for example, dependence on alcohol or barbiturates. These two processes are not independent, however; physiological processes may lead to addictive reinforcement patterns. Many drugs that affect the brain differently all share the property of being addictive—alcohol and cocaine are two examples. To help develop drug policies, researchers today are attempting to develop models that account for psychological variables such as cravings, physiological variables such as changes in brain structures and firing patterns, and social variables such as family support and therapy.

Substance abusers rarely have identical abuse patterns. Some people use only one drug—for example, alcohol. Others are *polydrug abusers*, taking several drugs; a heroin addict, for example, might also take amphetamines. When amphetamines are difficult to obtain, the person might switch to barbiturates. Some researchers assert that many people are addiction-prone (Sutker & Allain, 1988). Others note that addicts are often ambivalent about whether they want to give up their drug (Bradley, 1990). Still other researchers note that later addictive behaviour can be predicted from anti-social childhood behaviour (Nathan, 1988; Shedler & Block, 1990).

Let's take a closer look at some of the most commonly used drugs and their consciousness-altering properties. We begin with alcohol, the source of one of the most complicated and widespread drug problems in our society.

## ALCOHOL

Alcohol consumption in Canada has been declining over the past decade. According to the Canadian Centre on Substance Abuse (McKenzie, 1997), about 72 percent of urban Canadian adults report having used alcohol at some time; just over 9 percent of those who drink report having problems related to alcohol and just under half a million Canadians are classified as alcoholics. The highest proportion of people reporting problems with alcohol are in the 15- to 24-year-old range.

Alcohol is the most widely used sedative–hypnotic. A **sedative–hypnotic** is any of a class of drugs that relax and calm people and, in higher doses, induce sleep. Because alcohol is readily available, relatively inexpensive, and socially accepted, addiction to this drug is easy to establish and maintain. In fact, most Canadians consider some alcohol consumption appropriate in a variety of situations; they often consume alcoholic beverages before, during, and after dinner, at weddings and funerals, at religious ceremonies, and during sporting events.

**EFFECTS OF ALCOHOL.** Alcohol is a depressant that decreases inhibitions and thus increases some behaviours that are normally under tight control. For example, it may diminish people's social inhibitions and make them less likely to restrain their aggressive impulses (Steele & Josephs, 1990). The physiological effects of alcohol vary, depending on the amount of alcohol in the bloodstream and the gender and weight of the user (see Figure 4.3). After equal amounts of alcohol consumption, women have higher blood alcohol levels than men do, even allowing for differences in body weight; this occurs because men's bodies typically have a higher percentage

**SEDATIVE–HYPNOTIC**
A drug that relaxes and calms people and, in higher doses, induces sleep.

▼ Alcohol meets the definition of a psychoactive drug because it alters thought and behaviour, and produces both tolerance and dependence.

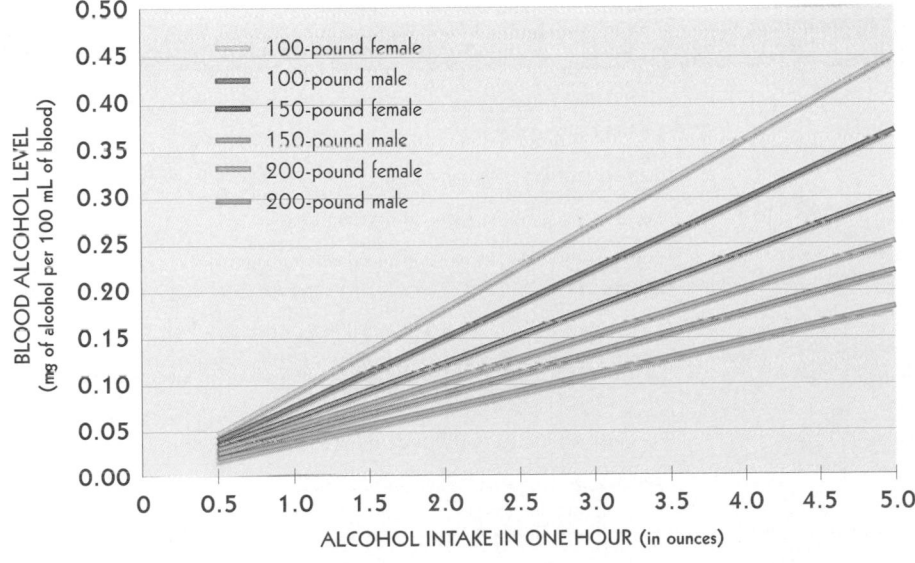

**FIGURE 4.3**
**Relationship between Alcohol Consumption and Blood Alcohol Level, by Gender and Weight**

Note that one ounce of alcohol is equivalent to two glasses of wine, two cans of beer, or one mixed drink.

Legend:
- 100-pound female
- 100-pound male
- 150-pound female
- 150-pound male
- 200-pound female
- 200-pound male

Y-axis: BLOOD ALCOHOL LEVEL (mg of alcohol per 100 mL of blood)
X-axis: ALCOHOL INTAKE IN ONE HOUR (in ounces)

of fluid than do women's. With less blood and other fluids in which to dilute the alcohol, women may end up with higher blood alcohol concentrations after fewer drinks than men (Frezza et al., 1990; York & Welte, 1994).

With increasing amounts of alcohol in the bloodstream, people typically exhibit progressively slowed behaviour; often they exhibit severe motor disturbances, such as staggering. A blood alcohol level greater than 0.08 percent (0.08 milligrams of alcohol per 100 millilitres of blood) usually indicates that the person has consumed too much alcohol to function responsibly. In all provinces, legal intoxication is a 0.08 percent (or higher) blood alcohol level; police officers may arrest drivers who are found to have at least this level of blood alcohol. Table 4.2 shows the behaviours associated with various blood alcohol levels.

The nervous system becomes less sensitive to, or accommodates to, alcohol with increased usage. After months or years of drinking, drug tolerance develops, and a person has to consume ever-increasing amounts of alcohol to achieve the same effect. Thus, when not in an alcoholic state, a heavy drinker develops anxiety, cravings, and other withdrawal symptoms (Levin, 1990).

**PROBLEM DRINKERS VERSUS ALCOHOLICS.** *Alcohol-related problems* are medical, social, or psychological problems associated with alcohol use. A person who shows an alcohol-related problem such as missing work occasionally because of hangovers, spending a paycheque to buy drinks for friends, or losing a driver's licence because of drunk driving is abusing alcohol. Alcohol-related problems caused by chronic (repeated) alcohol abuse may include liver deterioration, memory loss, and significant mood swings (Nace, 1987). A person with alcohol-related problems, a problem drinker, who also has a physiological and psychological need to consume alcohol and to experience its effects is an **alcoholic**. All alcoholics are problem drinkers, but not all problem drinkers are alcoholics. Without alcohol, alcoholics develop physiological withdrawal symptoms. In addition, they often develop tolerance; a single drink or even a few will not affect them.

Are some people more likely than others to become alcoholics? The answer is yes, according to researchers who study the biological aspects of alcoholism. Researchers assert that genetics, blood and brain chemistry, and specific brain structures predispose

ALCOHOLIC

A problem drinker who also has both a physiological and a psychological need to consume alcohol and to experience its effects.

| TABLE 4.2 Behavioural Effects Associated with Various Blood Alcohol Levels | |
|---|---|
| **Blood Alcohol Level\*** | **Behavioural Effects** |
| 0.05 | Lowered alertness, impaired judgment, release of inhibitions, feelings of well-being or sociability |
| 0.10 | Slowed reaction time and impaired motor function, less caution |
| 0.15 | Large, consistent increases in reaction time |
| 0.20 | Marked depression in sensory and motor capability, decidedly intoxicated behaviour |
| 0.25 | Severe motor disturbance and impairment of sensory perceptions |
| 0.30 | In a stupor but still conscious—no comprehension of events in the environment |
| 0.35 | Surgical anesthesia; lethal dose for about 1 percent of adults |
| 0.40 | Lethal dose for about 50 percent of adults |

\*In milligrams of alcohol per 100 millilitres of blood

some people to alcoholism. Children of alcoholics are more likely to become alcoholics, even if they are raised by non-alcoholic adoptive parents. The correlations suggest that certain individuals' physiology predisposes them to alcoholism.

An important study of the inheritance factor and the vulnerability of women to alcoholism shows similar results. According to Kenneth Kendler and his colleagues (1994), the transmission of vulnerability to alcoholism from parents to their daughters is due to genetic factors. This study showed that genetic vulnerability was transmitted equally from fathers and mothers to their daughters. It may be that a parent's alcohol use affects a woman's ova or a man's sperm (Cicero, 1994). That inheritance is involved in alcoholism for both men and women is clear; how inheritance interacts with the environment, parental influence (Chassin et al., 1993), and especially thought processes (Goldman et al., 1991) is the question researchers must answer next (Hawkins, Catalano, & Miller, 1992).

**SOCIAL AND MEDICAL PROBLEMS.** Although alcoholism is seen as a social disease because of its devastating social consequences, it is also a medical problem. Biomedical researchers study the effects of alcohol on the brain, as well as anything about the brains and basic genetics of alcoholics that may predispose them to alcoholism (Tarter & Vanyukov, 1994). Researchers know that chronic excessive drinking is associated with loss of brain tissue, liver malfunctions, and impaired cognitive and motor abilities (e.g., Ellis & Oscar-Berman, 1989).

**TREATMENT PROGRAMS.** For some alcoholics, psychological and medical treatment is successful. The most widely known program is Alcoholics Anonymous, which helps individuals abstain from alcohol by providing a therapeutic and emotionally nurturing environment. Treatment programs make abstinence their goal. The fundamental assumptions, based on the difficulty alcoholics have controlling their drinking, are that an alcoholic is an alcoholic forever and that alcoholism should be considered an incurable disease (McCrady, 1994).

Some practitioners, on the other hand, believe that limited, non-problem drinking should be the goal of treatment programs (Vaillant & Milofsky, 1982). This view assumes that alcohol abuse is a learned behaviour that therefore can be unlearned. Those who prefer controlled use with the goal of minimizing the harmful effects of alcohol consumption (Fromme et al., 1994; Marlatt et al., 1993) claim that alcohol abuse is merely a symptom of a larger underlying problem, such as poor self-esteem or family instability (Sobell & Sobell, 1982). Researchers such as Marlatt claim that a controlled drinking model is preferable to abstinence-only or "zero tolerance" approaches because it supports any behaviour change that reduces the harm of problems due to alcohol. However, most researchers believe that controlled drinking is not a reliable answer for most alcoholics, although it may be a reasonable alternative for young heavy drinkers who are not yet alcoholics (Nathan & Skinstad, 1987; Rosenberg, 1993).

Family therapy is generally considered an important part of treatment for alcoholism, because the alcohol problem of one family member becomes a problem for the entire family. A multimodal treatment approach (one involving many modes of treatment) is often the best plan; the objective is to combine individual or group therapy with participation in Alcoholics Anonymous or some other self-help group (Levin, 1990). Few systematic, carefully controlled studies of alcoholism and procedures for its treatment exist. Some researchers are investigating the use of behavioural therapies and drugs to control alcohol intake—including drugs such as naltrexone, which has been used to treat heroin addiction but shows positive effects for alcoholism (Kranzler & Anton, 1994). Others are studying the effectiveness of treatment in detoxification centres and halfway houses. Still others are trying to determine who is at risk (who is likely to become an alcoholic), in the hope that early intervention can prevent alcoholism (e.g., Hawkins, Catalano, & Miller, 1992). Table 4.3 presents some of the warning signs that alcoholism is developing.

**TABLE 4.3** Warning Signs of Alcoholism

You drink more than you used to and tend to gulp your drinks.

You try to have a few extra drinks before or after drinking with others.

You have begun to drink alone.

You are noticeably drunk on important occasions.

You drink the "morning after" to overcome the effects of previous drinking.

You drink to relieve feelings of boredom, depression, anxiety, or inadequacy.

You have begun to drink at certain times, to get through difficult situations, or when you have problems.

You have weekend drinking bouts and Monday hangovers.

You are beginning to lose control of your drinking; you drink more than you planned and get drunk when you do not want to.

You promise to drink less but do not.

You often regret what you have said or done while drinking.

You are beginning to feel guilty about your drinking.

You are sensitive when others mention your drinking.

You have begun to deny your drinking or lie about it.

You have memory blackouts or pass out while drinking.

Your drinking is affecting your relationships with friends and relatives.

You have lost time at work or school because of drinking.

You are beginning to stay away from people who do not drink.

## OTHER SEDATIVE–HYPNOTICS

Like alcohol, most barbiturates and tranquilizers are considered to be in the sedative–hypnotic class of drugs (sometimes they are referred to as depressants). They relax or calm people, and when taken in higher doses they often induce sleep. *Barbiturates* decrease the excitability of neurons throughout the nervous system. They calm the individual by depressing the central nervous system. The use of barbiturates as sedatives, however, has diminished; they largely have been replaced by another class of drugs—tranquilizers.

*Tranquilizers* are a group of drugs (technically benzodiazepines) that sedate and calm people. With a somewhat lower potential for abuse, they are sometimes called *minor tranquilizers*. Valium and Xanax are two of the most widely used tranquilizers prescribed by physicians for relief of mild stress. Such drugs have been widely abused by all segments of society because of their availability.

## OPIATES: HEROIN

Perhaps among the oldest drugs known to human beings are derivatives of the drug morphine, which is a component of the opium produced naturally by some poppy plants. In general, drugs that have such a derivation are referred to as opiates. **Opiates** are a class of drugs with pain-relieving and sedative properties that are addictive and produce tolerance. Heroin is an opiate that dulls the senses, relieves pain, tranquilizes, and induces euphoria. Like many other addictive drugs, heroin is considered biologically reinforcing.

OPIATE

A drug with pain-relieving and sedative properties that is addictive and produces tolerance.

Opiates have been used for everything from relieving children's crying to reducing pain from headaches, surgery, childbirth, and menstruation. Today, most opiates are illegal, but heroin and other opiates (such as morphine, which is illegal when not prescribed by a physician) are readily available from drug dealers. The high cost of these illegal drugs leads many addicts to engage in crime to support their habits.

Heroin can be smoked, swallowed, or, more typically, injected into a vein, sometimes as often as four times a day. A recent and especially dangerous trend, because of the likelihood of overdose, is for the user to snort heroin through the nose.

Heroin addicts tend to be young, poor, and undereducated. Most become addicts as a result of peer pressure. Estimates of the number of heroin addicts range dramatically, but the most reliable is about 1 percent of the Canadian population. Heroin addicts often use other drugs in combination with heroin; among these are alcohol, barbiturates, amphetamines, and cocaine (the last two drugs will be described in a later section). This polydrug use makes it difficult to classify heroin users as addicts of one drug or another. Moreover, even when classification is possible, treatment is complicated by the medical, psychological, and social problems associated with using many drugs at once.

The major physiological effect of heroin is impaired functioning of the respiratory system. Other effects are some detrimental changes in the heart, arteries, and veins, as well as constipation and loss of appetite. Contrary to popular beliefs, few heroin addicts actually die of overdoses from injections. A lethal dose of the drug would be much larger than that injected even by heavy users. More often than not, heroin addicts die from snorting lethal doses of pure heroin, from taking a mixture of drugs (such as heroin and alcohol), or from disease—especially AIDS, contracted from non-sterile needles and other paraphernalia used to inject the substance into the bloodstream. Some lawmakers advocate community programs to distribute sterile needles to drug users to prevent the spread of AIDS. However, as you might expect, such programs are extremely controversial.

The only major successful treatment program for heroin addiction is methadone maintenance. Like heroin, methadone is an addictive drug and must be consumed daily to avoid withdrawal symptoms. Unlike heroin, however, methadone does not produce euphoria or tolerance in the user, and daily dosages do not need to be increased. Because methadone blocks the effects of heroin, a normal injection of heroin has no effect on individuals who are on methadone maintenance. Moreover, because methadone is legal, many users are able to hold jobs to support themselves and stay out of jail. Research suggests that methadone treatment combined with psychotherapy and behaviour modification techniques to reduce illicit drug use may be far more effective than methadone treatment by itself (Stitzer, 1988). Unfortunately, most methadone treatment programs simply prescribe methadone. Thus, they have been criticized as being unethical because they make money by perpetuating addictive behaviour.

## PSYCHOSTIMULANTS: AMPHETAMINES AND COCAINE

Amphetamines and cocaine are considered psychostimulants and are highly addictive. A **psychostimulant** is any drug that increases alertness, reduces fatigue, and elevates mood when taken in low to moderate doses. *Amphetamines* are a group of chemical compounds that act on the central nervous system to increase excitability, depress appetite, and increase alertness and talkativeness. They also increase blood pressure and heart rate. After long-term use of an amphetamine, a person has cravings for the drug and experiences exhaustion, lethargy, and depression without it.

MDMA (methylenedioxymethamphetamine), or Ecstasy, is a synthetic psychoactive drug with properties related to both amphetamines and hallucinogens. In the brain it acts on the serotonin system and also seems to have some effect on the dopamine system (though more notably over prolonged use). Ecstasy produces feel-

PSYCHOSTIMULANT

A drug that in low to moderate doses increases alertness, reduces fatigue, and elevates mood.

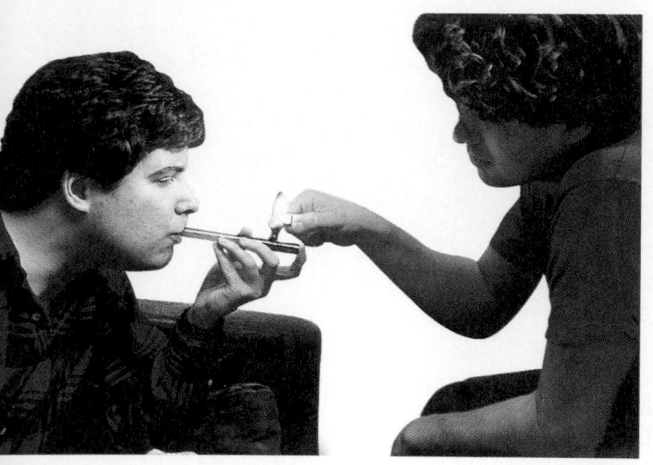

▲ Crack is a smokable form of cocaine and meets the definition of a stimulant because it increases alertness and also acts as an anesthetic.

ings of happiness and giddiness, reduces inhibitions, and seems to "rev" people up, all of which account for its popularity at raves (late-night, all-night dance parties). It has a number of potentially serious side effects, including confusion, depression, anxiety, and paranoia, often weeks after use, as well as heart rate and blood pressure increases. It may deplete the brain's supplies of serotonin and reduce effective dopamine production as well.

Cocaine is a central nervous system stimulant and an anesthetic. It acts on neurotransmitters such as norepinephrine (noradrenalin) and especially dopamine (it blocks the reuptake of dopamine so that once dopamine is released it stays longer in the synaptic cleft). It also stimulates sympathetic activity in the peripheral nervous system, causing dilation of the pupils; increases in heart rate, blood pressure, and blood sugar; and decreased appetite. The drug produces euphoria—a light-headed feeling, a sense of alertness, increased energy, sexual arousal, and sometimes a sense of infallibility—but this euphoria is short-lived.

Cocaine can be snorted, smoked, or injected. Snorting is the most popular method. Once inhaled, the drug is absorbed into the tiny blood vessels that line the nose. Within five minutes, the user starts to feel its effects; the peak effect occurs in 15 minutes and may last for 20 to 30 minutes. The processed, smokable form of cocaine, *crack* (so called because of the crackling sound that often occurs when the mixture is heated), delivers an unusually large dose and induces euphoria in a matter of seconds. While this method of use seems to bring about the fastest effect, it turns out to be the most addictive. Cocaine also can be injected, since it is soluble in water. However, because of concerns about contracting AIDS through infected needles, intravenous injections are less common than they used to be.

Cocaine is not as widely used in Canada as it is in the United States. About 7 percent of American high-school students have used cocaine at least once, while only 1.3 percent of Canadian high-school students report having tried the drug. (Table 4.4 summarizes the effects of cocaine and other commonly abused drugs.) What is the appeal of cocaine? First, cocaine acts as a powerful reward and is highly addictive. In laboratory studies, for example, animals will work incessantly, even to the point of exhaustion, to obtain it. Further, cocaine produces both tolerance and potent urges and cravings. A cocaine high is pleasurable but also brief; users wish to repeat the sensation almost immediately. When the cocaine wears off, its effects give way to unpleasant feelings (known as crashing). These feelings can be alleviated only through more cocaine use (Washton, 1989).

What are some of the problems of cocaine use? At a minimum, the drug is extremely addictive and produces irritability and eating and sleeping disturbances. It also seems to precipitate other disturbances, such as panic attacks. Further, cocaine can produce serious mental disorders, including paranoia, agitation, and suicidal behaviour. Overdosing causes physical problems such as heart attacks, hemorrhages, and heat stroke. Complications associated with cocaine administration include nose sores, lung damage, infection at injection sites, and AIDS. Even those who stop using cocaine often experience medical problems later as a result of damage done to their bodies during the time they were abusing the drug. Using cocaine during pregnancy may result in premature birth, malformations of the fetus, and spontaneous abortions. Lastly, the effects of cocaine are enhanced by its combination with alcohol, but the consequences of this mixture are severe; when people mix cocaine with alcohol they significantly increase the risk of sudden death.

Because a drug treatment for cocaine addiction has not been developed, psychological therapy is the sole option. Treatment usually includes education, family involvement, group and individual therapy, a focus on abstinence, and long-term follow-up; it is time-intensive and expensive (Hall, Havassy, & Wasserman, 1991).

**TABLE 4.4** Commonly Abused Drugs

| Type of Drug | Examples of Drug | Effects of Drug | Tolerance? | Physiological Dependence? |
|---|---|---|---|---|
| Sedative–hypnotics | Alcohol | Reduces tension | yes | yes |
| | Barbiturates (e.g., Seconal) | Reduce tension; induce sleep | yes | yes |
| | Tranquilizers (e.g., Valium) | Alleviate tension; induce relaxation | yes | yes |
| Opiates | Opium<br>Morphine<br>Heroin | Alleviate pain and tension; induce a high | yes | yes |
| Psychostimulants | Amphetamines | Increase excitability, alertness, and talkativeness; decrease appetite | yes | yes |
| | MDMA (Ecstasy) | Lowers social inhibitions, promotes physical activity (dancing) | yes | yes |
| | Cocaine | Increases alertness, decreases fatigue, stimulates sexual arousal | yes | yes |
| Psychedelics | LSD | Changes perception | no | no |
| | Ecstasy | Produces sense of well being and connection to others | no | possibly |
| | Marijuana | Changes mood and perception | no | no |

Note: Even though a drug may not produce physiological dependence, it may produce a psychosocial need that compels repeated use.

## PSYCHEDELIC DRUGS

A consciousness-altering drug that affects moods, thoughts, memory, judgment, and perception and that is usually self-administered for the purpose of producing these results is called a **psychedelic**. Psychedelic drugs are sometimes called *hallucinogens*; regardless of their names, they have as their principal action creating mind-altering and vivid imagery. The term *psychedelic* means mind-expanding. The impact of psychedelics varies widely with each individual, and a range of drugs from LSD to Ecstasy fall within this category. Lysergic acid diethylamide (LSD), commonly referred to as "acid," is sold as tablets, capsules, and occasionally in liquid form. With increases in respiration, sweating, and a dry mouth also come rapid mood swings and visual imagery; perception of time and distance changes, and perceptual imagery changes and sometimes frightens users. Although not considered an addictive drug, many LSD users have reported flashbacks—recurring experiences of being high without having taken the drug.

**MARIJUANA** Perhaps the most widely used psychedelic drug is marijuana, the dried leaves and flowering tops of the *cannabis sativa* plant, whose active ingredient is *tetrahydrocannabinol* (THC).

Marijuana can be ingested (eaten), but in Canada, where recent court decisions have essentially decriminalized simple possession, it is most commonly smoked, a process in which 20 to 80 percent of the THC is lost. Smoked as a cigarette (called a joint or a nail), in a pipe, or as a cigar (blunts), marijuana alters consciousness, alleviates depression, or merely acts as a distraction. Most users report a sense of elation and well being; others assert that the drug induces wild flights of fancy. Some users report other, adverse reactions, such as sleeplessness, bad dreams, paranoia, and nausea. There is likely a genetic basis for a person's reaction to the drug; people react differently to it and some individuals are far more susceptible. Marijuana's

**PSYCHEDELIC**

A consciousness-altering drug that affects moods, thoughts, memory, judgment, and perception and that is usually self-administered for the purpose of producing these results.

Be an
## ACTIVE
## LEARNER

**REVIEW**
> How can researchers test the hypothesis that alcoholism may have genetic components? pp. 154–155
> What are the principal risks of cocaine use? p. 158

**THINK CRITICALLY**
> To what extent is it true that one can be "born" an alcoholic?
> What do you think is the best way to treat alcoholism? Why? Would you treat cocaine addiction with the same procedures? Why?

**APPLY PSYCHOLOGY**
> Think about people you know or have known and about how they use alcohol or other substances. If you were a psychologist evaluating them for substance abuse, what would you look for?

effects are felt about one minute after smoking, begin to diminish within an hour, and disappear almost completely after three to five hours—although traces of THC can be detected in the body for weeks. Individuals under the influence of marijuana demonstrate impaired performance on simple intellectual and psychomotor tasks. They become less task-oriented and have slower reaction times. Marijuana also interferes with attention and memory. Little is known about how marijuana affects fetal development and reproductive abilities, and about its long-term effects on those who use it from early adolescence until middle age. Marijuana has been widely used only since the late 1960s; it will take a couple of generations before researchers know all of its long-term effects. However, recent research suggests that long-term use can produce lasting brain changes—including problems with attention, memory, and learning—similar to those caused by other major drugs that are abused (Solowij, 1998).

Although researchers agree that marijuana is not physiologically addictive, many argue that it produces psychological dependence. People use and become dependent on marijuana for a variety of reasons. One reason is that it is more easily available than substances such as barbiturates and cocaine. Another reason is the relief from tension that marijuana users experience. Further, most people wrongly believe the drug has few, if any, long-lasting side effects.

Despite considerable social acceptance of marijuana use in Canada, its sale and possession are still against the law. About 25 percent of high-school students report having tried it. For the most part, laws against the sale and possession of marijuana have been ineffective, and the drug is widely available across the country in both urban and rural areas. Some experts consider legalization of marijuana to be a good idea, although few legislators take the idea seriously.

# Summary and Review

## CONSCIOUSNESS

### What are the key characteristics of a definition of consciousness?

> *Consciousness* is a general state of being aware of and responsive to events in the environment, including one's own mental processes. It can range from alert attention to dreaming, hypnosis, or drug-induced states. An altered state of consciousness is a pattern of functioning that is dramatically different from that of ordinary awareness and responsiveness. **pp. 130–131**

**KEY TERM**

consciousness, p. 131

## SLEEP

### Describe the cycles of sleep and wakefulness.

> A biological clock that ticks within each person controls the sleep–wakefulness cycle; *circadian rhythms* are the internally generated bodily rhythms. When time cues such as daylight and the clock on the wall are removed from the environment, circadian rhythms run a bit slowly. **pp. 133–134**

> Recordings of the brain waves of sleeping participants have revealed distinct cycles of sleep. Each cycle has four stages of *non-rapid eye movement (NREM) sleep* and one stage of *rapid eye movement (REM) sleep*. During REM sleep, rapid and systematic eye movements occur. A full sleep cycle lasts about 90 minutes, so five complete sleep cycles occur in an average night's sleep. People deprived of REM sleep tend to catch up on REM sleep on subsequent nights. **pp. 134–138**

### What happens when someone suffers from a sleep disorder?

> Snoring loudly, sleepwalking, and falling asleep at inappropriate times may be signs of a sleep disorder. People who fall asleep suddenly and unexpectedly have a sleep

disorder known as narcolepsy. Narcolepsy is probably a symptom of an autonomic nervous system disturbance and lowered arousal but also may reflect neurochemical problems. Another sleep disorder, *insomnia*, is a prolonged inability to sleep, which is often caused by anxiety or depression.　**pp. 140–141**

### KEY TERMS

circadian rhythms, p. 133; sleep, p. 134; electroencephalogram (EEG), p. 135; non-rapid eye movement (NREM) sleep, p. 135; rapid eye movement (REM) sleep, p. 135; insomnia, p. 141

## DREAMS

### What evidence supports the assertion that people dream in the middle of the night rather than solely at the end of the evening?

> A *dream* is a state of consciousness that occurs largely during REM sleep and is usually accompanied by vivid visual imagery, although the imagery also may be tactile or auditory. REM sleep occurs four or five times a night, so most people dream four or five times a night. The first dream of a typical night occurs 90 minutes after a person has fallen asleep and lasts for approximately 10 minutes. **pp. 142–143**

### How have key theorists explained dreaming?

> For Freud, a dream expressed desires, wishes, and unfulfilled needs that exist in the unconscious—dreams were "the royal road to the unconscious." Freud referred to the *manifest content* of a dream (its overt story line, characters, and settings) and the *latent content* of a dream (its deeper meaning, usually involving symbolism, hidden content, and repressed or obscured ideas and wishes). **pp. 144–145**

> Jung asserted that each person shares in the *collective unconscious*, a storehouse of primitive ideas and images in people's unconscious that are inherited from their ancestors. **p. 145**

> Hobson and McCarley believe that dreams have a physiological basis and that, during periods of REM sleep, the parts of the brain responsible for long-term memory, vision, audition, and perhaps even emotion are spontaneously activated (stimulated) from cells in the hindbrain, especially the pons. The cortex attempts to synthesize, or make sense of, the messages. **pp. 145–146**

### KEY TERMS

dream, p. 142; lucid dream, p. 144; manifest content, p. 144; latent content, p. 145; collective unconscious, p. 145; descriptive studies, p. 146

## CONTROLLING CONSCIOUSNESS: BIOFEEDBACK, HYPNOSIS, AND MEDITATION

### Differentiate three key means of controlling consciousness.

> *Biofeedback* is the general technique by which individuals can monitor and learn to control the involuntary activity of some bodily organs and functions. Laboratory studies have demonstrated biofeedback's effectiveness in helping people manage a wide range of physiological problems such as headaches and high blood pressure, but only carefully controlled research will answer persistent questions about its usefulness. **pp. 147–148**

> *Hypnosis* is an altered state of consciousness brought about by procedures that may induce a trance. Hypnosis can produce special effects such as age regression, heightened memory, and pain reduction. **pp. 148–149**

> Physical states produced by *meditation* resemble those achieved by individuals trained to relax and concentrate. The two major types of meditation are mindful and concentrative; both induce an altered state of awareness. People using mindful meditation focus on trying to empty the mind and be still. Concentrative meditation focuses on a visual image or a mantra; when the mind wanders to random thoughts, the person meditating brings attention back to the image or mantra without noticing the content of the thoughts. **pp. 149–151**

### KEY TERMS

biofeedback, p. 147; hypnosis, p. 148; meditation, p. 149

## ALTERING CONSCIOUSNESS WITH DRUGS

### What are the different broad categories of drugs?

> A *drug* is any chemical substance that alters normal biological processes. A *psychoactive drug* is a drug that alters behaviour, thoughts, or emotions by altering biochemical reactions in the nervous system, thereby affecting consciousness. An *addictive drug* is a drug that causes a compulsive physiological need and that, when withheld, produces withdrawal symptoms. **p. 151**

### What are the defining characteristics of a substance abuser?

> *Substance abusers* have used drugs for at least one month, have experienced legal, personal, social, or vocational problems due to drug use, and have used a drug in hazardous situations. Most researchers agree that no single explanation can account for drug use and abuse. **pp. 152–153**

### How does alcohol affect behaviour, and who is an alcoholic?

> Alcohol affects behaviour in proportion to its level in the bloodstream and the gender and weight of the user. A person with a blood alcohol level of 0.08 percent or more is generally considered intoxicated; if driving, the person can be arrested. **pp. 153–154**

> An *alcoholic* is a person who has alcohol-related problems and who also has a physiological and psychological need to consume alcoholic products and experience their effects. Without alcohol, alcoholics develop physiological *withdrawal symptoms*. In addition, they often develop *tolerance*, whereby a single drink or even a few drinks will not affect them. All alcoholics are problem drinkers, but not all problem drinkers are alcoholics. **p. 154**

**Describe the risks and effects of different classes of drugs.**

> Barbiturates and tranquilizers are in the class of drugs called *sedative–hypnotics*. They relax and calm individuals and, when taken in higher doses, can induce sleep. Barbiturates are considered to produce a deeper relaxation than tranquilizers. Tranquilizers are widely overused because of their availability.  **p. 156**

> Heroin is one of the class of drugs called *opiates*. It has become a social problem in part because it is illegal; thus, addicts commit crimes to get money to obtain the drug. Heroin addiction has been treated successfully with methadone, which blocks heroin's effects. Methadone programs are criticized, however, because of their lack of treatment to help addicts become totally drug-free.  **pp. 156–157**

> In general, a *psychostimulant* is any drug that increases alertness, reduces fatigue, and elevates mood when taken in low to moderate doses. Amphetamines, Ecstasy (MDMA), and cocaine are psychostimulants. Cocaine is more widely abused in the United States than in Canada; cocaine addiction is difficult to treat and has numerous medical complications.  **p. 157**

> *Psychedelics* such as marijuana are consciousness-altering drugs that affect moods, thoughts, memory, judgment, and perception and that are usually self-administered for the purposes of producing these results. **pp. 159–160**

**KEY TERMS**

drug, p. 151; psychoactive drug, p. 151; addictive drug, p. 151; substance abuser, p. 152; psychological dependence, p. 152; withdrawal symptoms, p. 152; tolerance, p. 152; sedative–hypnotic, p. 153; alcoholic, p. 154; opiate, p. 156; psychostimulant, p. 157; psychedelic, p. 159

---

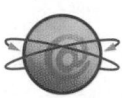

Take advantage of the multimedia resources available with this text! Follow the marginal icons to access the interactive modules on the *HandsOnPsych CD-ROM*; log on to *MyPsychLab* to explore the ebook, study aids, and other online resources; and visit the Companion Website at **www.pearsoned.ca/lefton** for additional exercises and links.

Animals can be trained to do extraordinary things. Dolphins and whales can be taught to do high jumps on command in front of crowds. Bears can be taught to ride bicycles and mice can be taught to climb ladders, raise flags, and salute. Animals are taught these complex behaviours in a step-by-step learning process in which each small step is rewarded until the final goal is attained. Techniques similar to these training methods have been used for thousands of years to teach dogs to herd sheep, horses to accept riders, and donkeys to pull farm equipment.

However, recently scientists have developed techniques that will allow distant animals to be guided by remote control by microstimulating key areas of their brains (Talwar et al., 2002). In this research stimulating electrodes were implanted into particular brain areas of the frontal and parietal lobes of rats. Specifically, an electrical stimulus was generated that presented a "virtual touch" to both the right and the left whisker representations in the somatosensory cortex of each rat in order to guide the rat. Each time the rat responded in the desired way, it was rewarded with stimulation to a "pleasure centre" in the brain. In this way, virtual cues and rewards were used to guide rats through complex environments and over terrains that they would normally avoid. For example, rats were guided through pipes, across ledges, and elevated surfaces and could be instructed to climb and jump. Use of such learning techniques, which eliminate the need for delivery of rewards by more traditional means, may eventually result in the use of "guided animals" as navigators in search and rescue efforts in areas of urban destruction following natural disaster or for landmine detection. A remote human in a way similar to that used with "intelligent" robots could guide the animals through these potentially treacherous environments.

Learning is at the core of psychology. We have learned, for example, that a long day at the beach may result in a painful sunburn and that we should approach a strange dog with caution. We also have learned sophisticated, complicated processes, such as how to drive a car or how to appreciate music ranging from Bach to Blue Rodeo. Some people also learn socially deviant behaviours, such as stealing and drug abuse. Whatever the associations are, our ability to learn about the past and to think about and modify our future behaviour is part of what distinguishes human beings from other organisms: We learn and can think about and reflect on that learning.

In general, learning is the process by which people acquire new knowledge. Psychologists define **learning** as a relatively permanent change in an organism that occurs as a result of experiences in the environment and that is often *observed in overt behaviour*. This last point means that, because the internal processes of learning cannot be *seen*, psychologists study the *results* of learning. To do so, they may examine such overt behaviour as solving an algebra problem or throwing a ball. They also may measure physiological changes, such as brain wave activity, heart rate, and temperature. Psychologists' definition of learning has three other important parts: (1) experience in the environment, (2) change in the organism, and (3) permanence.

Behaviour is always being modified; new experiences affect learning, and what is learned may be forgotten. Along with the external environment, an organism's internal motivation, abilities, and physiological state influence its ability to learn. For example, if you are tired, learning the material in this chapter will be particularly difficult. Also, practice and repeated experiences ensure that you will remember and easily exhibit newly acquired learning, information, and skills. Furthermore, when learning has occurred, physiological changes—for example, in synapse organization or levels of dopamine—have occurred as well, so that after you learn, you're no longer the same.

The factors that affect learning are often studied in animal behaviour, because the genetic heritage of animals is easy to control and manipulate and because all details of an animal's history and environmental experiences can be known. Although some psychologists claim that different processes underlie animal and human learning, most believe—and experiments show—that the basic processes are similar. Differences become apparent and important, however, when complex behaviours are being evaluated and in experiments that require the use of language.

As you read this chapter, ask yourself whether you favour specific study spots, have special fears associated with specific places, or have learned to associate and anticipate exciting, fearful, or special events in your world. Chances are that you will begin to see in yourself a whole range of learned associations that shape your daily interactions. You will see how your conditioning and the resulting associations illustrate the three basic learning processes that are the subject of this chapter: classical conditioning, operant conditioning, and cognitive learning.

## Pavlovian, or Classical, Conditioning Theory

You may have noticed that you have developed an association between your favourite study location and success in exams. It involves a small self-deception on your part, but one that gives you some stress relief in preparation for examinations. To a real extent, you have become conditioned.

In a general sense, psychologists use the term *conditioning* to mean learning. But **conditioning** is actually a systematic procedure through which associations and responses to specific stimuli are learned. It is one of the simplest forms of learning. For example, consider this situation. You go to a fellow classmate's home for the first time and are surprised to find that you spend much of the time you are there

LEARNING
A relatively permanent change in an organism that occurs as a result of experiences in the environment.

CONDITIONING
A systematic procedure through which associations and responses to specific stimuli are learned.

thinking fondly about your grandmother. It isn't until later that you realize you were thinking of your grandmother because your classmate's house smelled of freshly baked bread. Your grandmother loves to bake for you and always has fresh bread as a special treat when you go to visit her. Thus, you have been *conditioned* to associate the odour of freshly baked bread with your grandmother. In the terminology used by psychologists, the odour of bread is the *stimulus*, and the fond thought of your grandmother is the *response*.

Conditioned behaviours and reflexive behaviours are different. When psychologists first studied conditioning, they found automatic (reflexive) relationships between specific stimuli and responses. Each time a certain stimulus occurs, the same reflexive response, or behaviour, follows. For example, the presence of food in the mouth leads to salivation; a tap on the knee leads to a knee jerk; a bright light in the eye leads to contraction of the pupil and an eye blink. A **reflex** is an involuntary, automatic behaviour in response to a stimulus; it occurs without prior learning and usually shows little variability from instance to instance. Conditioned behaviours, in contrast, are learned. Many people have learned the response of fear to the stimulus of sitting in a dentist's chair, since they associate the chair with drilling and pain. A chair by itself (a neutral stimulus) does not elicit fear, but a chair associated with pain becomes a stimulus that can elicit fear. This is an example of *conditioning*.

Conditioned behaviours may occur so automatically that they appear to be reflexive. Like reflexes, conditioned behaviours are involuntary; unlike reflexes, they are learned. In classical conditioning (to be defined shortly), previously neutral stimuli such as chairs, lights, and buzzers become associated with specific events and lead to responses such as fear, eye blinks, and nervousness. This type of learning, then, involves stimuli of biological significance.

In 1927, Ivan Pavlov (1849–1936), a Russian physiologist, summarized a now famous series of experiments in which he uncovered a basic principle of learning—conditioning. His research began quite accidentally while studying saliva and gastric secretions in the digestive processes of dogs. He knew that it is normal for dogs to salivate when they eat—salivation is a reflexive behaviour that aids digestion—but he noticed that the dogs were salivating *before* they tasted their food. Pavlov reasoned that this might be happening because the dogs had learned to associate the trainers, who brought them food, with the food itself. Anxious to know more about this basic form of learning, Pavlov abandoned his research on gastric processes and redirected his efforts into teaching dogs to salivate to a new stimulus, such as a bell.

## TERMS AND PROCEDURES

The terminology and procedures associated with Pavlov's experiments are precise and can be confusing; however, the basic ideas are actually quite straightforward. Let's explore them systematically. What Pavlov described was **classical conditioning**, or *Pavlovian conditioning*, in which a neutral stimulus is paired with a stimulus that elicits a reflexive response. For example, the process might occur as follows: A researcher first would identify a stimulus that elicits a reflexive response; for instance, an electric shock elicits a flinching or withdrawal response in an animal (or human). The researcher then would pair this reflexive stimulus and response (shock–flinching) with a neutral stimulus (a light). The researcher might turn on the light as the animal is shocked—this would represent one pairing. This would be repeated a number of times, after which turning the light on without shocking the animal produces a flinching response. The animal has learned something about the light and the shock; that is, it has made an association between the light and the shock.

REFLEX
An involuntary, automatic behaviour that occurs in response to a stimulus without prior learning and usually shows little variability from instance to instance.

▲ When your eye is exposed to intense light, it responds by reflex: Your pupil contracts and your eye blinks.

CLASSICAL CONDITIONING
A conditioning process in which an originally neutral stimulus, by repeated pairing with a stimulus that normally elicits a response, comes to elicit a similar or identical response. Also known as *Pavlovian conditioning*.

HandsOnPsych
Version 2.0

**Learning**

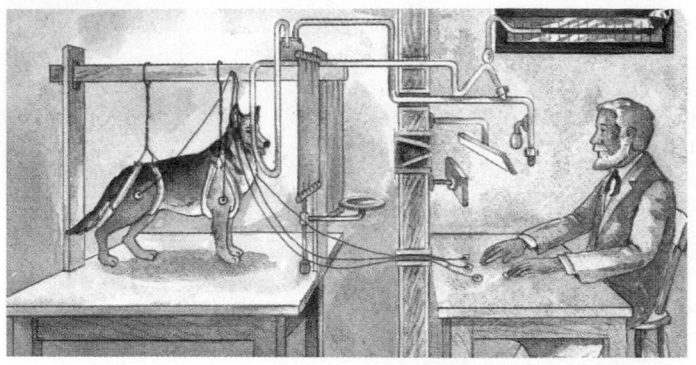

**FIGURE 5.1**
Pavlov's Experimental
Setup

UNCONDITIONED STIMULUS
A stimulus that normally produces
a measurable involuntary response.

UNCONDITIONED RESPONSE
An unlearned or involuntary
response to an unconditioned
stimulus.

CONDITIONED STIMULUS
A neutral stimulus that, through
repeated association with an
unconditioned stimulus, begins to
elicit a conditioned response.

CONDITIONED RESPONSE
A response elicited by a
conditioned stimulus.

Pavlov called the stimulus that normally produces a response (for example, food) an **unconditioned stimulus**; as its name implies, it elicits relevant activities from the outset, that is, unconditionally. He called the response to this stimulus (for example, salivating) an **unconditioned response**. The unconditioned response occurs involuntarily, without learning, in response to the unconditioned stimulus.

In a series of experiments, Pavlov taught dogs to salivate in response to a bell. First, he surgically altered the location of each dog's salivary gland to make the secretions of saliva accessible. He then attached tubes to the relocated salivary glands to measure precisely the amount of saliva produced by the food—the unconditioned stimulus. Then he introduced a bell—the new stimulus (see Figure 5.1). He called the bell a neutral stimulus, because the sound of a bell is not necessarily related to salivation and generally elicits only a response of orientation or attention. To demonstrate this prior to training, Pavlov measured the amount of saliva the dogs produced when a bell was rung by itself; the amount was negligible. He then began the conditioning process by ringing the bell and immediately placing food in the dogs' mouths. After he did this several times, the dogs salivated in response to the sound of the bell alone. Pavlov reasoned that the dogs had associated the sound of the bell with the presentation of food. He called the bell, which elicited salivation as a result of learning, a conditioned stimulus. A **conditioned stimulus** is a neutral stimulus that, through repeated association with an unconditioned stimulus, becomes capable of eliciting a conditioned response. As its name implies, a conditioned stimulus becomes capable of eliciting a response because of (conditional upon) its pairing with the unconditioned stimulus. He called the salivation—the learned response to the sound of the bell—a **conditioned response** (the response elicited by a conditioned stimulus). From his experiments Pavlov discovered that the conditioned stimulus (the bell) brought about a similar but somewhat weaker response than the unconditioned stimulus (the food). Pavlov originally called the conditioned response a "conditional" response because it was conditional upon events in the environment—it was dependent on them. Errors in the translation of his writings brought about the term used most often today: conditioned response. The process of Pavlovian conditioning is outlined in Figure 5.2.

The key characteristic of classical conditioning is the use of an originally neutral stimulus (here, a bell) to elicit a response (here, salivation) through repeated pairing of the neutral stimulus and an unconditioned stimulus that elicits the response naturally (here, food). The conditioned response is acquired gradually. On the first few trials of such pairings, conditioning is unlikely to occur. With additional trials, there is a greater likelihood that the neutral stimulus will yield a conditioned response. Psychologists generally refer to this process as an *acquisition process* and say that an organism has acquired a response. Figure 5.3 shows a typical acquisition curve.

Classical conditioning occurs regularly in the everyday world. When you enter a dentist's office, your heart rate may increase and you may begin to exhibit nervous behaviours because of learned associations you have developed. When classical conditioning occurs, behaviour changes.

## CLASSICAL CONDITIONING IN HUMANS

After Pavlov's success with conditioning in dogs, psychologists were interested in determining whether conditioning also occurs in human beings. In 1931, for example, Marquis showed classical conditioning in infants. Marquis knew that when an object touched an infant's lips, the infant immediately started sucking, because the object was usually the nipple of a breast or bottle, from which the infant got milk. The nipple, an unconditioned stimulus, elicited sucking, an unconditioned response.

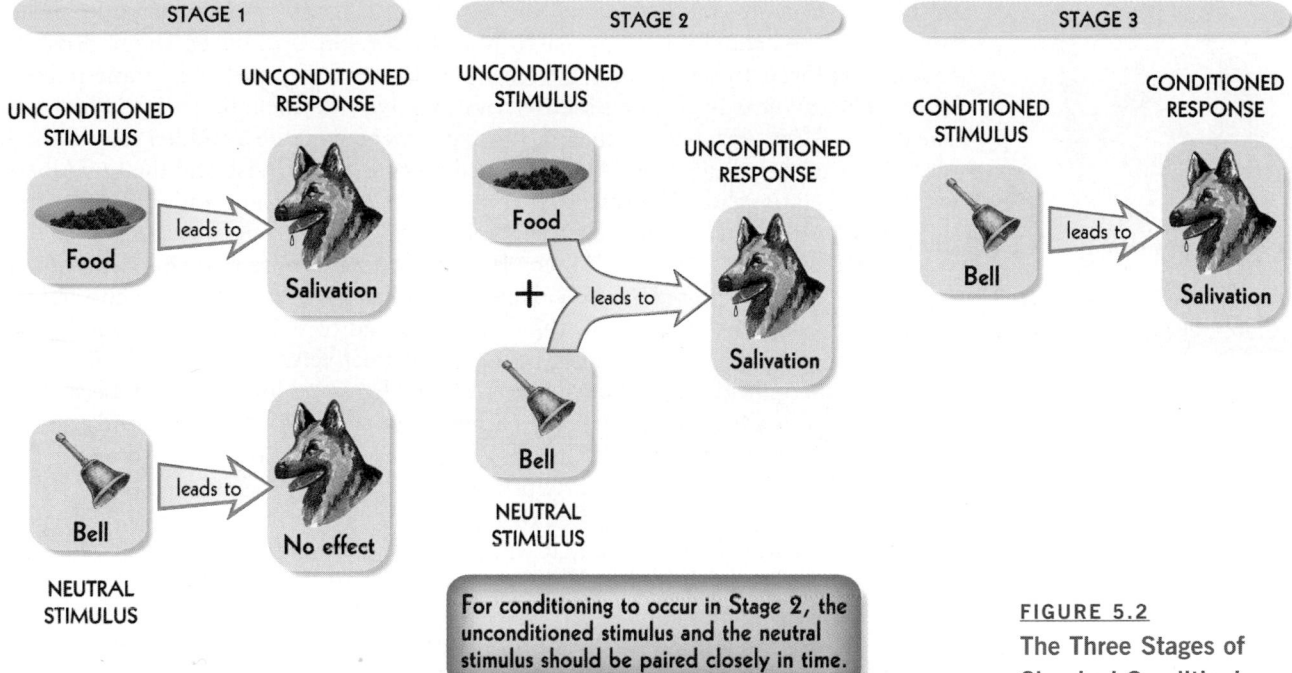

FIGURE 5.2
The Three Stages of
Classical Conditioning

For conditioning to occur in Stage 2, the unconditioned stimulus and the neutral stimulus should be paired closely in time.

After repeated pairings of a sound or light with a nipple, infants were conditioned to suck when only the sound or light was presented.

Sucking is one of many reflexive behaviours in human beings; thus it is only one of many responses that can be conditioned. A puff of air delivered to the eye, for example, produces the unconditioned response of an eye blink. When a light or buzzer is paired with puffs of air to the eye, it eventually will elicit the eye blink by itself. This effect can be produced in many animals, as well as in human adults and infants (Solomon et al., 1998).

The complex equation that allows for learning is not automatic, and depends on an array of events, including an organism's past experiences with the conditioned and unconditioned stimulus. This is especially true with complex conditioned responses. Both pleasant and unpleasant emotional responses can be classically conditioned. Consider the following: If a child who is playing with a favourite toy is repeatedly frightened by a sudden loud noise, the child may be conditioned to be

FIGURE 5.3
A Typical Acquisition Curve

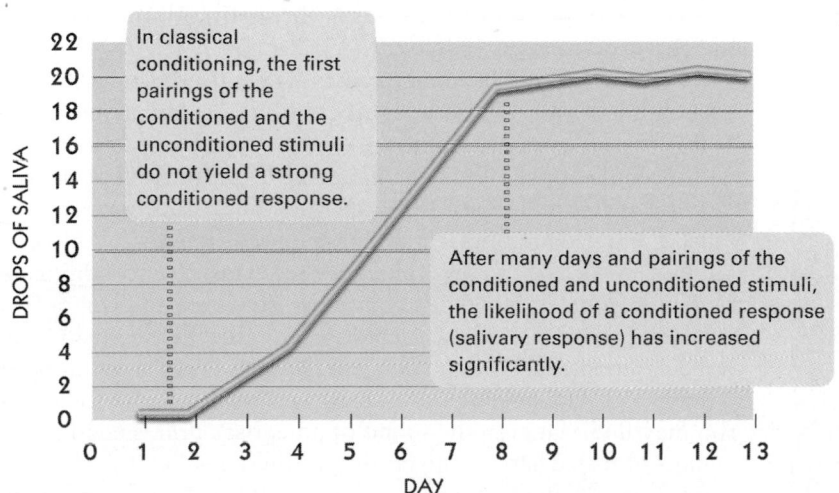

In classical conditioning, the first pairings of the conditioned and the unconditioned stimuli do not yield a strong conditioned response.

After many days and pairings of the conditioned and unconditioned stimuli, the likelihood of a conditioned response (salivary response) has increased significantly.

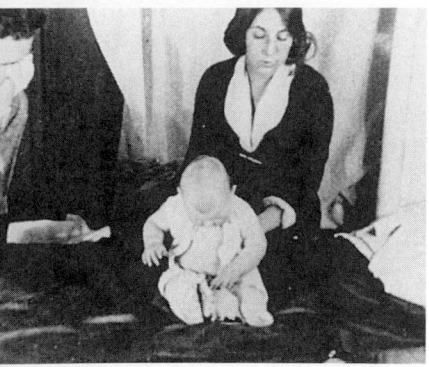

In their now famous experiment, Watson and Rayner gave baby Albert a white rat to play with. However, after Watson and Rayner repeatedly paired the rat (conditioned stimulus) with a loud noise (unconditioned stimulus), Albert learned to associate the two and grew afraid of the rat.

afraid each time he or she sees the toy. In a famous 1920 experiment, one of the founders of the behaviourist approach, John B. Watson, and his colleague Rosalie Raynor explored this type of relationship with an 11-month-old infant named Albert. The infant was given a series of toys to play with, including a live white rat. One day, as Albert reached for the rat, the experimenters made a sudden ear-splitting noise that frightened the child. After repeated pairing of the noise and the rat, Albert learned the relationship. The rat served as a conditioned stimulus and the loud noise as the unconditioned stimulus; on each subsequent presentation, the rat evoked a conditioned response of fear in Albert. It is important to note that this experiment would now be considered unethical under the current Canadian Psychological Association guidelines because of the distress caused to Albert and the possibility that the fear, once created, might not be removed effectively.

Classical conditioning can be observed simply by watching television, because it is widely used in advertising. Many ads attempt to lead us to associate food, coffee, and perfume, for example, with salivatory responses, relaxation, and sexual appeal. Beer commercials apply conditioning principles by featuring beautiful people enjoying their favourite beer while also enjoying a warm, sunny beach or socializing in a cozy ski chalet. Advertisers hope that when viewers associate the can of beer (a neutral stimulus) with an unconditioned stimulus that naturally elicits a positive emotional response (the pleasant scene), the beer will similarly elicit a positive response. In other words, they hope to condition people to feel good whenever they think about this beer. The powerful role of classical conditioning in advertising has been supported by experimental studies with adults in the laboratory (Stuart, Shimp, & Engle, 1987).

## HIGHER-ORDER CONDITIONING

After a neutral stimulus becomes a conditioned stimulus, it elicits the conditioned response whenever it is presented. Moreover, another phenomenon that may occur is **higher-order conditioning**—the process by which a neutral stimulus takes on conditioned properties through pairing with another conditioned stimulus. Suppose a light is paired with mild electric shocks to a dog. On seeing the light, the dog exhibits fear; the light has thus become a conditioned stimulus that elicits a set of fear responses. If a bell is now paired with or presented just before the light, the new stimulus (the bell) can also take on properties of the conditioned stimulus (the light). After repeated pairings, the dog will learn to associate the two events (the light and the bell), and either event by itself will elicit a fear response. When a third stimulus—say, an experimenter in a white lab coat—is introduced, the dog may learn to associate the experimenter with the bell or light. After enough trials, the dog may have conditioned fear responses to each of the three stimuli: the light, the bell, and the experimenter (Pavlov, 1927; Rescorla, 1977). Thus, higher-order conditioning permits increasingly remote associations, which can result in a complex network of conditioned stimuli and responses. At least two factors determine the extent of higher-order conditioning: (1) the similarity between the higher-order stimulus and the original conditioned stimulus, and (2) the frequency and consistency with which the two conditioned stimuli are paired (Rescorla, 1978).

In daily life and in every culture we see evidence of conditioning. The oil light in your car blinks on, your pulse quickens, and you pull over to the side of the road. If you became violently ill with the flu after eating a particular food, you may find that you have developed a conditioned taste aversion; you cannot even look at that food again without feeling a bit ill. You may find that even the sound of a dentist's drill is enough to cause feelings of fear. There is universality to these responses—they occur in Japan, Uganda, and Venezuela as well as in Canada. In fact, conditioned

HIGHER-ORDER CONDITIONING
A process by which a neutral stimulus takes on conditioned properties through pairing with a conditioned stimulus.

**Be an**
**ACTIVE**
**LEARNER**

**REVIEW**
> Identify the fundamental difference between a reflex and a conditioned behaviour. p. 167
> Distinguish between a conditioned and an unconditioned response. pp. 167–168

**THINK CRITICALLY**
> Provide an example of how classical conditioning and higher-order conditioning occur in your life.
> What sorts of things might be done using classical conditioning that could be viewed as ethically problematic?

**APPLY PSYCHOLOGY**
> Can you think of a situation in which you might want to facilitate higher-order conditioning? How might you increase the likelihood of this kind of learning taking place?
> Think over the past few days and see how many examples of classical conditioning you can find in your own experiences.

taste aversions are among the most powerful conditioned phenomena ever demonstrated. You can see that successful pairing of conditioned and unconditioned stimuli— that is, successful classical conditioning— involves many key variables.

# Key Variables in Classical Conditioning

Classical conditioning is not as simple a process as Pavlov might have thought. As we suggested earlier, such learning is not automatic and depends on a matrix of events, including an organism's past experiences with the conditioned and unconditioned stimulus as well as some key stimulus variables. For example, how bright must the oil light signal in your car be? How loud does the buzzer have to be? How long does the bell have to ring? How sinister must a movie's scary music be? How many times must someone experience pain in a dentist's chair, and how strong does that pain have to be? As with other psychological phenomena, situational variables affect when, if, and under what conditions classical conditioning will occur. Cultural variables are also important; while the principles of conditioning are the same in every culture, what constitutes a fear-producing stimulus will vary from culture to culture.

Some of the most important variables in classical conditioning are the strength, timing, and frequency of the unconditioned stimulus. When these variables are optimal, conditioning occurs easily.

## STRENGTH, TIMING, AND FREQUENCY

**STRENGTH OF THE UNCONDITIONED STIMULUS.**   A puff of air delivered to the eye will easily elicit an unconditioned response, but only if the puff of air (the unconditioned stimulus) is sufficiently strong. Research shows that when the unconditioned stimulus is strong and elicits a quick and regular reflexive (unconditioned) response, conditioning of the neutral stimulus is likely to occur. On the other hand, when the unconditioned stimulus is weak, it is unlikely to elicit an unconditioned response, and conditioning of the neutral stimulus is unlikely to occur. Thus, pairing a neutral stimulus with a weak unconditioned stimulus will not lead reliably to conditioning.

**TIMING OF THE UNCONDITIONED STIMULUS.**   For conditioning to occur, an unconditioned stimulus usually must be paired with a conditioned stimulus close enough in time for the two to become associated; that is, they must be temporally contiguous. For optimal conditioning, the conditioned stimulus should occur at least half a second (and in many cases substantially longer) before the unconditioned stimulus and overlap with it, particularly for reflexes such as the eye blink. (In Pavlov's experiment, conditioning would not have occurred if the bell and the food had been presented an hour apart.) The two stimuli may be presented together or may be separated by a brief interval. Some types of conditioning can occur with fairly long delays, but the optimal time between the onset of the two stimuli (often cited as half a second) varies from one study to another and depends on many things, including the type of conditioned response sought (e.g., Schwarz-Stevens & Cunninghan, 1993; Cunningham et al., 1999).

**FREQUENCY OF PAIRINGS.**   Occasional or rare pairings of a neutral stimulus with an unconditioned stimulus at close intervals usually do not result in conditioning (with the exception of food–illness pairings); generally speaking, frequent pairings and pairings that establish a relationship between the unconditioned and the conditioned stimulus are necessary. If, for example, food and the sound of a bell are paired on every trial, a dog is conditioned more quickly than if the stimuli are paired on every other trial. The frequency of the natural occurrence of the unconditioned stimulus is also important. If the unconditioned stimulus does not occur frequently but is always associated with the conditioned stimulus, more rapid conditioning is likely, because one stimulus predicts the other (Rescorla,

1988). Once the conditioned response has reached its maximum strength, additional pairings of the stimuli do not increase the likelihood of a conditioned response. There are exceptions to this general rule, though, and specific one-time pairings can produce learning.

## PREDICTABILITY

A key factor determining whether conditioning will occur is the predictability of the association of the unconditioned and conditioned stimuli. Closeness in time and regular frequency of pairings promote conditioning, but these are not enough. Predictability—being able to anticipate future events—facilitates, and turns out to be a central factor in, conditioning (Rescorla, 1988).

Pavlov thought that classical conditioning was based on *contiguity* (a close connection between the unconditioned stimulus and the conditioned stimulus). Research now shows, however, that if the unconditioned stimulus (such as the food) can be predicted by the conditioned stimulus (such as the bell), then conditioning is rapidly achieved. Conditioning is achieved not because of the number of times the two events have occurred but rather because of the reliability with which the conditioned stimulus predicts the unconditioned stimulus. Pavlov's dogs learned that bells were good predictors of food; the conditioned stimulus (bells) reliably predicted the unconditioned stimulus (food), so conditioning was quickly achieved.

In Rescorla's (1988) view, what is learned in conditioning is the predictability of events—bells predicting food, light predicting puffs of air to the eye, dentist chairs predicting pain. That there is some sort of relationship between the conditioned and unconditioned stimulus is important. Predictability is one of the key elements in classical conditioning, but without other contextual cues it usually is not enough (Papini & Bitterman, 1990). Many researchers consider predictability to be a cognitive concept; in fact, animals and human beings make predictions about the future based on past events in an array of circumstances (Siegel & Allan, 1996; Seigel et al., 2000). As we will see in the next two chapters (on memory and cognition), such thought is based on simple learning but become even more complex. You'll also see how the predictability and relationship of events become consequential in phenomena such as extinction and spontaneous recovery, considered next.

## EXTINCTION AND SPONTANEOUS RECOVERY

Some conditioned responses last for a long time, some for less time. Much depends on whether the conditioned response still predicts the unconditioned one. Consider the following: What would have happened to Pavlov's dogs if he had rung the bell each day but never followed the bell with food? What would happen if you went to the dentist every day for two months, but the dentist only brushed your teeth with pleasant-tasting toothpaste and never drilled, or the drilling that occurred was never accompanied by any discomfort?

If a researcher continues Pavlov's experiment by presenting the conditioned stimulus (bell) but no unconditioned stimulus (food), the likelihood of a conditioned response decreases with every trial; it undergoes extinction. In classical conditioning, **extinction** is the process through which *not* presenting the unconditioned stimulus gradually reduces the probability (and often the strength) of a conditioned response. Imagine a study in which a puff of air is associated with a buzzer that consistently elicits the conditioned eye-blink response. If the unconditioned stimulus (the puff of air) is no longer delivered in association with the buzzer, the likelihood that the buzzer will continue to elicit the eye-blink response decreases over time (see Figure 5.4). When presentation of the buzzer alone no longer elicits the conditioned response, psychologists say that the response has been *extinguished* (Rescorla, 2001a, 2001b).

EXTINCTION
[egg-STINK-shun]

In classical conditioning, the process through which not presenting the unconditioned stimulus gradually reduces the probability of a conditioned response.

However, an extinguished conditioned response may not be gone forever. It can recur, especially after a rest period, in a phenomenon called **spontaneous recovery**. If the dog whose salivation response has been extinguished is placed in the experimental situation again after a rest period of 20 minutes, its salivary response to the bell will recur briefly (although less strongly than before). This behaviour shows that the effects of extinction are not permanent and that the learned association is not totally forgotten (see Figure 5.5).

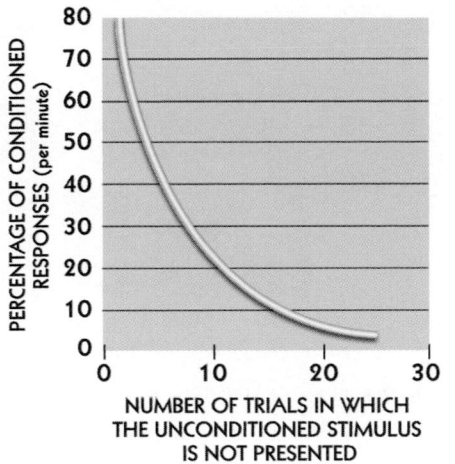

FIGURE 5.4
**A Typical Extinction Curve**

Numerous experiments have demonstrated that the percentage of times an organism displays a conditioned response decreases over a number of trials in which the unconditioned stimulus is not presented. When presentation of the conditioned stimulus alone no longer elicits the conditioned response, the response has been extinguished.

## STIMULUS GENERALIZATION AND STIMULUS DISCRIMINATION

Imagine that a three-year-old child pulls a cat's tail and receives a painful scratch in return. It will not be surprising if the child develops a fear of that cat; but the child actually may develop a fear of all cats, and even of dogs and other four-legged animals. Adults may respond in the same way to similar stimuli—a phenomenon that psychologists call stimulus generalization.

SPONTANEOUS RECOVERY
Recurrence of an extinguished conditioned response following a rest period.

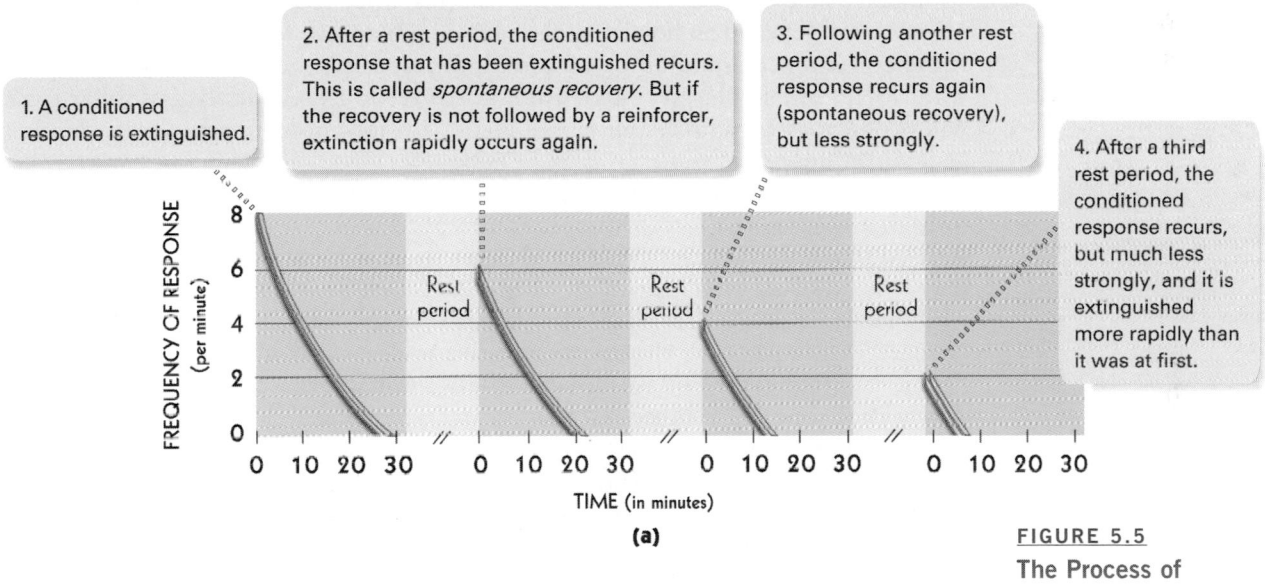

1. A conditioned response is extinguished.

2. After a rest period, the conditioned response that has been extinguished recurs. This is called *spontaneous recovery*. But if the recovery is not followed by a reinforcer, extinction rapidly occurs again.

3. Following another rest period, the conditioned response recurs again (spontaneous recovery), but less strongly.

4. After a third rest period, the conditioned response recurs, but much less strongly, and it is extinguished more rapidly than it was at first.

(a)

FIGURE 5.5
**The Process of Spontaneous Recovery**

The graph in part (b) shows some of Pavlov's actual data from an experiment published in 1927. Pavlov brought about extinction in a series of six trials by omitting the presentation of the unconditioned stimulus; but after a 20-minute rest period, spontaneous recovery occurred.

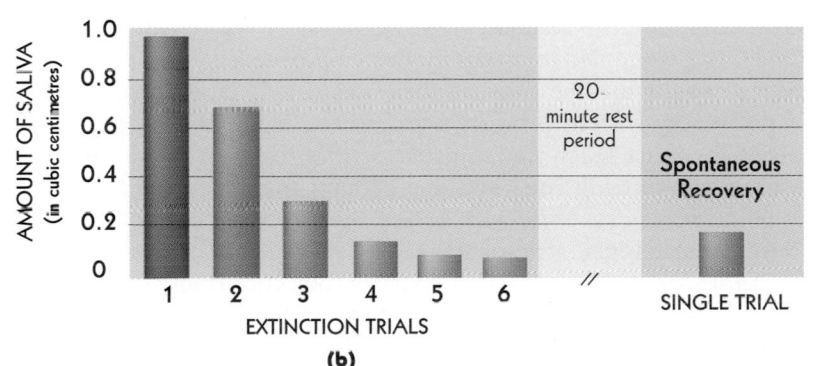

20-minute rest period

Spontaneous Recovery

SINGLE TRIAL

EXTINCTION TRIALS

(b)

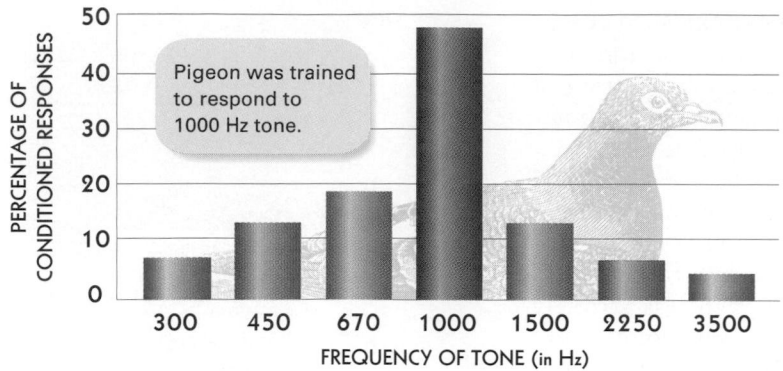

FIGURE 5.6

**Stimulus Generalization**

Stimulus generalization occurs when an organism (an animal or a human being) exhibits a conditioned response to a stimulus that is similar but not identical to the original conditioned stimulus. In this experiment, a pigeon was trained to respond to a tone of 1000 Hz by pecking a key. Later, the pigeon was presented with tones of different frequencies so that the experimenter could determine whether it would respond to those dissimilar frequencies. Results showed that the percentage of responses decreased as the tone's frequency became increasingly different from the training frequency. (Based on Jenkins & Harrison, 1960.)

STIMULUS GENERALIZATION

Occurrence of a conditioned response with a stimulus that is similar but not identical to the original conditioned stimulus.

STIMULUS DISCRIMINATION

Process by which an organism learns to respond only to a specific reinforced stimulus and not to other irrelevant stimuli.

**Stimulus generalization** occurs when an organism develops a conditioned response to a stimulus that is similar but not identical to the original conditioned stimulus. The extent to which an organism responds to a stimulus similar to the original one depends on how alike the two stimuli are. If, for example, a loud tone is the conditioned stimulus for an eye-blink response, then tones that are somewhat lower but similar also may produce the response. A totally dissimilar tone will produce little or no response. See Figure 5.6 for another example of stimulus generalization.

**Stimulus discrimination** is the process by which an organism learns to respond only to a specific reinforced stimulus and not to other irrelevant stimuli. Pavlov showed that animals that have learned to differentiate between pairs of stimuli display frustration or even aggression when discrimination is made difficult or impossible. He trained a dog to discriminate between a circle and an ellipse and then changed the shape of the ellipse on successive trials to look more and more like the circle. Eventually, the dog was unable to discriminate between the shapes; it randomly chose one or the other and also became aggressive.

Human beings exhibit similar disorganization in behaviour when placed in work or home situations in which they feel compelled to make a response but don't know how to respond correctly. In such occasions, where one must make a response choice but where choosing a response becomes difficult or impossible, behaviour can become repetitive or limited in scope; people may choose either not to respond to the stimulus or to respond always in the same way (Lundin, 1961; Maier & Klee, 1941). For example, an assembly line employee asked to remove flawed products from a rapidly moving conveyer belt may simply let all products pass or may elect to pull every fiftieth product off the belt, if the flaws are not obvious. Often, therapists must teach maladjusted people to learn to be more flexible in their responses to difficult situations and perhaps to acknowledge when a task is beyond their abilities. *Psychology in Action* discusses techniques that therapists use to address maladaptive, irrational fears.

Table 5.1 (on page 176) summarizes four important concepts in classical conditioning: extinction, spontaneous recovery, stimulus generalization, and stimulus discrimination.

## Getting Rid of Phobias

Have you ever heard of the following terms?

- Claustrophobia—fear of enclosed spaces
- Technophobia—fear of technology
- Sciophobia—fear of shadows
- Decidophobia—fear of making decisions
- Nyctophobia—fear of night
- Electrophobia—fear of electricity
- Topophobia—fear of performing (stage fright)
- Tropophobia—fear of moving or making changes
- Peladophobia —fear of bald-headed people
- Pogonophobia—fear of beards

We all have fears, but most of them are manageable. Fear becomes a phobia when we lose control over our ability to control fear of a particular situation or object. Formally, we define a *phobia* as an anxiety disorder involving excessive irrational fear of, and consequent avoidance of, specific objects or situations. People with a phobic disorder exhibit avoidance and escape behaviours, show increased heart rate and irregular breathing patterns, and report thoughts of disaster and severe embarrassment. Many psychologists agree that phobias are established (learned) and maintained by the release a person receives from escaping or avoiding the feared circumstances.

Millions of people suffer from phobias. However, the out look for them has improved greatly. In fact, people with simple phobias can often find relief in a matter of weeks. Psychologists use a variety of techniques usually linked to their viewpoint about the cause of the disorder. It turns out that many of these techniques share a common feature: They all require that patients meet the source of their discomfort head-on and then *learn* a new response. The therapy is usually (but not always) behavioural and the key word here is *learn.*

One behavioural technique, systematic desensitization, requires the client to learn formal, deep-muscle relaxation. It is up to the client to create a list of fear-provoking stimuli. The client is then asked to imagine the least fear-provoking scene from the list. At the same time, he or she is asked to relax. By remaining comfortable while at the same time imagining the feared situation, the client may weaken the association between the situation and feelings of anxiety. Once the client has become thoroughly comfortable imagining the least threatening situation, he or she moves up the list and conquers each level of fear in turn.

Of course, exposure to such situations gradually lets the client get used to the fear-provoking stimulus—that is, the client ultimately learns that there is no real danger. Gradually, slowly, the anxiety is extinguished. Some therapists believe that the more quickly such exposure takes place, the more quickly the phobia will be eliminated. There is some evidence that treatment is most effective when systematic desensitization of thoughts is used along with real life, or "in vivo," exposure. Programs incorporating in vivo exposure techniques have become widely used in the treatment of simple phobias. There is a catch, however—often, clients with phobias have trouble getting better because they avoid the object or situation that elicits the anxiety, and even the therapy that deals with the phobia.

Behaviour therapy techniques to help clients confront and overcome their fears use principles of learning. For example, in cognitive-behaviour therapy, clients with phobias are trained to become aware of their own negative thought statements, such as, "I'll die if I go there" or "I can't do it." They learn to replace such thoughts with positive coping statements such as "Of course, I can do it." (We will have more to say about cognitive behaviour therapy in Chapter 16.) In general, phobia treatment programs that are based on learning principles are widely available and effective.

Of course, not every form of treatment is appropriate for every patient or client. Some phobia programs offer psychotherapy, behaviour therapy, and medications. Sometimes a combination of these treatments is necessary. Because phobias are so widespread, you likely know someone who suffers from one. Effective treatment is available. Encourage the person to seek help.

## CLASSICAL CONDITIONING IN DAILY LIFE

Whether you have noticed it or not, it is very likely that you respond to various types of music with conditioned responses over and over again. Hear a particular kind of music while watching a suspense or horror film and you practically look over your own shoulder. Hear the theme song from the latest romantic film and you may get teary-eyed. During your lifetime, you've been conditioned not only to music, but also to the sight of good-looking cars and to the thought of walking

**TABLE 5.1** Four Important Concepts in Classical Conditioning

| Property | Definition | Example |
|---|---|---|
| Extinction | The process of reducing the probability of a conditioned response by presenting the conditioned stimulus alone. | A dog is conditioned by the presentation of food to salivate in response to a tone. When the tone is presented without the food, the dog ceases to salivate in response to the tone. |
| Spontaneous recovery | The recurrence of an extinguished conditioned response following presentation of the conditioned stimulus. | A dog's conditioned salivary response to a tone has been extinguished. After a rest period, the dog again salivates in response to the tone, though less than before. |
| Stimulus generalization | The occurrence of a conditioned response to stimuli that are similar but not identical to the original conditioned stimulus. | A dog conditioned to salivate in response to a high-pitched tone also salivates in response to a somewhat lower-pitched tone. |
| Stimulus discrimination | The process by which an organism learns to respond only to a specific reinforced stimulus. | A dog is conditioned to salivate only in response to high-pitched tones, not to low-pitched tones. |

along a beach with someone you love. All of us become conditioned to respond in one way or another, and much of that conditioning is Pavlovian classical conditioning. Let us examine some important examples that have helped us understand ourselves as well as conditioning.

THE GARCIA EFFECT. Imagine the following scenario: A six-year-old sits down with her parents after her friends have left her birthday party and eats a ham sandwich with lettuce. She decides that since she is now almost "grown up" she will have mustard on her sandwich, just like her parents. Two hours later, she becomes ill—fever, vomiting, chills, and swollen glands. It was the flu that actually made her ill, but as far as she is concerned, the mustard made her sick. As an adult she still refuses to eat mustard.

This association of mustard and nausea is an example of a conditioned taste aversion. In a famous experiment, John Garcia gave animals specific foods or liquids to eat or drink and then induced nausea (usually by injecting them with a drug or by exposing the animals to radiation). He found that after only one pairing of a food or drink (the conditioned stimulus) with the drug or radiation (the unconditioned stimulus), the animals avoided the food or drink that preceded the nausea (see, e.g., Garcia & Koelling, 1971; Linberg et al., 1982).

Two aspects of Garcia's work startled the research community. First, he showed that a conditioned taste aversion could be obtained even if the nausea was induced several hours after the food or drink had been consumed. This contradicted the previously held assumption that the time interval between the unconditioned stimulus and the conditioned stimulus had to be short, especially if conditioning was to occur quickly. Recent research confirms Garcia's finding (Schafe, Sollars, & Bernstein, 1995; De La Casa & Lubow, 2000). Garcia also showed that not all stimuli could become associated. He tried to pair bells and lights with nausea to produce a taste aversion in rats, but he was unable to do so—learning depended on the relevance, or appropriateness, of the stimuli to one another. This led him to conclude that "strong aversions to the smell or taste of food can develop even when illness is delayed for hours after consumption [but] avoidance reactions do not develop for visual, auditory, or tactile stimuli associated with food" (Garcia & Koelling, 1971, p. 461). Such appropriateness of stimuli may be due to whether they "belong" together in nature; bells and nausea have little to do with one another, but smells and nausea are far more likely to be related in the world and so a smell might quickly become a conditioned stimulus (Hollis, 1997). In the end, Garcia disproved two accepted principles of learning.

Conditioned taste aversion, sometimes called the *Garcia effect,* has survival value and practical application. In one trial or instance, animals learn to avoid foods that make them sick by associating the smells of poisonous foods with the foods themselves. This clearly has survival value; that is, animals that do not develop rapid aversions to foods that make them sick likely do not survive. Animals that do have this ability survive to reproduce and thus produce offspring that also likely have the rapid aversion ability. Conditioned taste aversion is unaffected by intervening events during the delay between the taste and the illness (Holder et al., 1989). Anyone who has suffered from food poisoning or who has had the misfortune to develop a nasty flu after eating a (formerly!) favourite food can attest to the lasting memory of the food or meal that caused it.

Conditioned taste aversion also has practical uses. Coyotes and wolves often attack sheep and lambs. Garcia laced lamb meat with a substance that causes a short-term illness and put the food on the outskirts of sheep ranchers' fenced-in areas. Coyotes that ate the lamb meat became sick and developed an aversion to lamb. After this experience, they approached the sheep as if ready to attack, but nearly always backed off (see, e.g., Garcia et al., 1976). By using conditioned taste aversion, Garcia deterred coyotes from eating sheep.

What all this seems to suggest is that we may be biologically prepared to learn some responses more easily than others. Think about the sorts of things about which people develop phobic fears. These include snakes, heights, open spaces, and water, to name a few. What all these things share is the very real potential, in some natural circumstances, to represent serious threats—that is, in some situations being wary of those sorts of things has survival value. On the other hand, people rarely develop phobic fears about chairs, trees, or stoves—all things that do not tend to threaten our safety. Therefore, it may be that we are *biologically prepared,* as a result of evolutionary influences, to develop some fears and not others (Mineka, 1992).

**LEARNING AND CHEMOTHERAPY.** Cancer patients often undergo chemotherapy; an unfortunate side effect of this therapy is vomiting and nausea. The patients often lose their appetite and lose weight during treatment. Is it possible that they lose weight because of a conditioned taste aversion? According to researchers (Bernstein, 1991; Montgomery et al., 1998; Montgomery & Bovbjerg, 1997), some cancer patients become conditioned to avoid food. They check into a hospital, have a meal, are given chemotherapy, become sick, and thereafter avoid the food that preceded the therapy. Schafe and Bernstein (1996) conducted research with children and adults who were going to receive chemotherapy. Their research showed that patients given food before therapy, especially foods rich in protein such as eggs and cheese, developed specific aversions to those foods; control groups who were not given those foods before their therapy did not develop aversions to them. Gary Challis and Hank Stam (1992), working at the University of Calgary, identified several factors that seem to predict who will be most influenced by this effect. Depression and anxiety appear unrelated to the effect, while self-absorption and a focus on one's physical functioning predict a stronger reaction.

Patients develop food aversions even when they know it is the chemotherapy that induces the nausea. Bernstein (1988, 1991) suggested an intervention based on learning theory: Patients were given a "scapegoat" food, such as coconut or root beer LifeSavers, just before chemotherapy, so that any conditioned aversion that developed would be to a nutritionally unimportant food rather than to a nutritious food.

**CONDITIONING OF THE IMMUNE SYSTEM.** Think of a person's fear of the dentist's chair; chairs, dentists, hygienists, and even the smells associated with the dentist's office can lead to fear responses. Classical conditioning explains a wide range

▲ Conditioned taste aversion, or the Garcia effect, has been used successfully to deter coyotes from attacking sheep.

of human behaviour, including some physical responses to the world, such as heart rate acceleration and changes in blood pressure.

Substances such as pollen, dust, animal dander, and mould initiate an allergic reaction in many people. Cat fur, for example, may elicit an allergic reaction, such as an inability to breathe, in persons with asthma. Asthma attacks, like other behaviours, can be conditioned to occur. For example, if Lindsay's asthmatic friend has *always* found cat fur in Lindsay's house (a regular pairing), classical conditioning theory predicts that even if all of the cat hair is removed, the friend still may have an allergic reaction upon entering Lindsay's house. (A conditioned stimulus, the house, predicts an unconditioned response, the allergic reaction.) Researchers have shown that people with severe allergies can have an allergic reaction from merely seeing a cat (or entering Lindsay's house, even long after the cat's demise), even if there is no cat fur present.

Even the body's immune system can be conditioned (Ader & Cohen, 1993). Normally, the body releases antibodies to fight disease when toxic substances appear in the blood. In a striking series of studies, animals were classically conditioned in a way that altered their immune responses (Ader, 1997, 2000; Ader & Cohen, 1985, 1993). The experimenters paired a sweet-tasting solution with a drug that produced illness and, as a side effect, also suppressed the immune response. The animals quickly learned to avoid the sweet-tasting substance that seemed to predict illness. When later presented with the sweet-tasting substance alone, the animals showed a reduction in immune system antibodies. The experimenters had classically conditioned an immune system response that was previously thought not to be under nervous system control (Hiramoto et al., 1997).

**CONDITIONING IN ADDICTS.** Research also shows that drug users become well conditioned (see *Brain and Behaviour*). When heroin addicts inject heroin, their bodies produce compensatory responses to protect them from an overdose; this is a natural response. Shepard Siegel (1984; Seigel & MacCrae, 1984) of McMaster University argues that some of these responses become classically conditioned; that is, they become associated as conditioned responses to the environmental setting in which the addict is injecting the drug. If the addict always injects the drug in the same room, the room itself may serve to initiate compensatory responses, without the heroin ever actually being administered. When a user injects the drug in a new and different location, such compensatory responses are not created—as a result, too much of the drug may be administered, leading to an overdose. A comprehensive theory of drug use, abuse, tolerance, and withdrawal will need to incorporate environmental cues and bodily reactions that are Pavlovian in origin—addicts' bodies react not only to effects of the drug but also in an anticipatory way to the sight of needles, drugs, and locations (Siegel & Allan, 1996).

Building Table 5.1 summarizes some of the key elements of classical conditioning. Although classical conditioning explains a wide range of phenomena, not all behaviours are the result of such associations. Many complex behaviours result from another

| BUILDING TABLE 5.1 | Types of Learning: Classical Conditioning | | |
|---|---|---|---|
| **Type of Learning** | **Procedure** | **Result** | **Example** |
| Classical Conditioning | A neutral stimulus (such as a bell) is paired with an unconditioned stimulus (such as food). | The neutral stimulus becomes a conditioned stimulus— it elicits the conditioned response. | A bell elicits a response in a dog. |

## Conditioning in Drug Addicts

Drug abuse cannot be blamed on any one event, person, family, or set of circumstances; drug seeking will not be accounted for by one approach (Drummond, 2001). We know that drug dependence is a physiological phenomenon. Initially, most illegal and abused drugs produce a feeling that the user finds positive, followed upon withdrawal by an unpleasant effect—this happens because the brain "demands" more of the drug to feel good or go back to "normal." This cycle of pleasure and need leads to repeated use and may result in addiction—users learn to use drugs to satisfy the physiological needs created by the drug (O'Brien et al., 1998). They learn to place confidence in their drug of choice—like alcohol—rather than in work, family, or other areas of life (O'Brien et al., 1998). After extensive and repeated use, alcoholics and other drug abusers resent people and events that do not fit in with their drug use.

In addition, and making matters worse, we also know that drug users become conditioned. For example, when addicts inject heroin, their bodies produce an anti-opiate substance to protect them from an overdose; this is a natural response. Siegel (1999) argues that if the addict always injects the drug in the same room, the place itself may serve to initiate an anti-opiate response, without any use of the drug. That is, the location of heroin use can serve as a conditioned stimulus for the anti-opiate response. When the user injects the drug in a different location, the well-developed anti-opiate response does not occur—the body is not doing something that it has become accustomed to. As a consequence, the user may inject too much of the drug, leading to an overdose. The stimulus for the increased use may have been merely the location of the drug consumption (Baptista et al., 1998).

A comprehensive theory of drug use, abuse, tolerance, and withdrawal will have to incorporate the neurobiology of addiction (Koob, 2000) and environmental cues (Carter & Tiffany, 1999) and bodily reactions that are Pavlovian in origin. Addicts' bodies react not only to effects of the drug but also in an anticipatory way to the sight of needles, drugs, and locations (Losa, 1999; Siegel & Allen, 1996).

---

form of learning—operant conditioning—which focuses on behaviour and its consequences. Operant conditioning is discussed next.

## Operant Conditioning

Bells, whistles, lights, and salivation may occur in the world, and associations may be formed, but in all of these situations the organism, the learner, has little control over the events. A light is presented before food is delivered, and an association is formed. But what happens when a child accidentally breaks a valued clock or a teacher pats a child on the head after class? Do consequences result from such events? Is anything learned? Many psychologists believe that the consequences of behaviour have powerful effects that change the course of subsequent behaviour. Unlike classical conditioning, this view sees the organism as operating on and within the environment, and as a result the organism receives and observes rewards or punishments. Let's explore this distinction further because it helps explain the how and why of what we do.

*Be an*
**ACTIVE LEARNER**

**REVIEW**
> How do the variables of strength, timing, and frequency affect learning? pp. 171–172
> What happens to the conditioned response if a researcher presents the conditioned stimulus but no unconditioned stimulus? p. 172

**THINK CRITICALLY**
> What led Garcia to conclude that taste aversion can occur in one trial or one instance? What other examples of learning could occur in one trial or one instance?

**APPLY PSYCHOLOGY**
> Drug abuse is seen by many as a psychological and physical problem. Psychologically, what are some conditioned responses that might lead to drug overdoses among addicts?

### PIONEERS: B. F. SKINNER AND E. L. THORNDIKE

In the 1930s, B. F. Skinner (1904–1990) challenged and began to change the way psychologists think about conditioning and learning. In fact, Skinner questioned whether the passive Pavlovian (classical) conditioning that focused on reflexive, automatic responses should be studied at all. Skinner maintained that organisms operate on the environment, with every action followed by a specific event, or consequence. He focused only on an organism's observable behaviour—thought

**HandsOnPsych**
Version 2.0

**Learning**

processes, consciousness, brain–behaviour relationships, and the mind were not considered the proper subject matter of psychology. Skinner's early work was in the tradition of such strict behaviourists as John Watson advocating a strict focus upon stimuli and responses in a completely measurable manner, although Skinner ultimately modified some of his own most extreme positions. His 1938 book, *The Behavior of Organisms*, continues to have an impact on studies of conditioning.

According to Skinner, many behaviours are acquired and maintained through operant conditioning, not through Pavlov's classical conditioning. Skinner used the term *operant conditioning* because the organism *operates* on the environment, with every action followed by a specific event, or consequence. **Operant conditioning**, or *instrumental conditioning*, is conditioning in which an increase or decrease in the likelihood that a behaviour will recur (will be repeated) is affected by the delivery of a rewarding or punishing event as a consequence of the behaviour. The conditioned behaviour is usually voluntary, not reflex-like as in classical conditioning. Another key difference between classical conditioning and operant conditioning is that the reward or punishment *follows*, rather than coexists with, the behaviour.

Consider what happens when a boss rewards and encourages her overworked employees by giving them unexpected cash bonuses. If the bonuses improve morale and induce the employees to work harder, the employer's conditioning efforts have been successful. In turn, the employees could condition the boss's behaviour by rewarding her generosity with further increases in productivity, thereby encouraging her to continue giving bonuses. In the laboratory, researchers have studied similar sequences of behaviours followed by rewards. One of the most famous of these experiments was conducted by the American psychologist E. L. Thorndike (1874–1949), who pioneered the study of operant conditioning during the 1890s and first reported his work in 1898. Thorndike placed hungry cats in boxes and put food outside the boxes. The cats could escape from the boxes and get food by hitting a lever that opened a door in each box. The cats quickly performed the behaviour Thorndike was trying to condition (hitting the lever), because doing so (at first by accident and then deliberately) gave them access to food. Because the response (hitting the lever) was important (instrumental) in obtaining the reward, Thorndike used the term *instrumental conditioning* to describe the process and called the behaviours *instrumental behaviours*.

Although Skinner spoke of operant conditioning and Thorndike spoke of instrumental conditioning, the two terms are often used interchangeably. What is important is that both Skinner and Thorndike acknowledged that first the behaviour is *emitted* (displayed), and then a consequence (for example, a reward) follows. This is unlike classical (Pavlovian) conditioning, in which first there is a change in the environment (for example, bells and food are paired) and then the conditioned behaviour (usually a reflexive response) is *elicited* (see Figure 5.7).

In operant conditioning, such as in Thorndike's experiment with cats, an organism emits a behaviour and then a consequence follows. The type of consequence that follows the behaviour is a crucial component of the conditioning, because it determines whether the behaviour is likely to be repeated. Principally, the consequence can be a reinforcer or a punisher. As in classical conditioning, a reward acts as a *reinforcer*, increasing the likelihood that the behaviour targeted for conditioning will recur; in Thorndike's experiment, food was the reinforcer for hitting the lever. A *punisher*, on the other hand, decreases the likelihood that the targeted behaviour will recur. If an electric shock is delivered to a cat's paws each time the cat touches a lever, the cat quickly learns not to touch the lever. Parents use reinforcers and punishers when they link the behaviour of their teenagers to the use of the family car. A teenager on a date is more likely to return home at an appropriate hour if doing so will ensure use of the car again. (We will discuss punishment and its consequences in more detail later in this chapter.)

OPERANT [OP-er-ant] CONDITIONING

Conditioning in which the probability that an organism will emit a response is increased or decreased by the subsequent delivery of a reinforcer or punisher. Also known as *instrumental conditioning*.

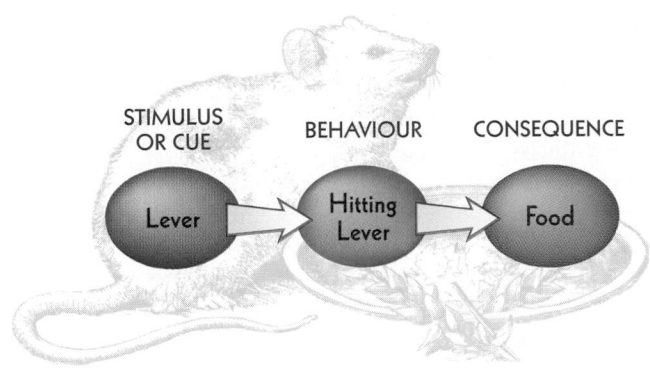

FIGURE 5.7

**The Process of Operant Conditioning**

Operant conditioning is different from classical conditioning in that the behaviour to be conditioned (such as hitting a lever) is reinforced *after* it occurs.

## THE SKINNER BOX AND SHAPING

Much of the research on operant conditioning has used the apparatus that most psychologists call a Skinner box—even though Skinner never approved of the idea of naming it after him. A **Skinner box** is a box that contains a mechanism for delivering a consequence whenever the animal in the box makes a readily identifiable response that the experimenter has decided to reinforce or punish. In experiments that involve rewards, the delivery mechanism is often a small lever or bar in the side of the box; whenever the animal presses it, the pressing behaviour may be rewarded. Punishment often takes the form of electric shocks delivered through a grid on the floor of the box. Early in Skinner's career, he believed so strongly in creating controlled environments that he devised a controlled living space for his daughter—it became known as the "baby box." The baby box held temperature, light, and humidity at comfortable levels. It also allowed Skinner to "control" the environment and help shape his daughter's behaviour. This personal decision on Skinner's part was quite controversial; although his daughter grew up to be quite normal, ethical questions were raised about manipulating children in this way. However, most of Skinner's work was done with animals—pigeons and rats.

In a traditional operant conditioning experiment, a rat that has been deprived of food for a short time is placed in a Skinner box. The rat moves around the box, often seeking to escape; eventually it stumbles on the lever and presses it. Immediately following that action, the experimenter delivers a pellet of food into a cup. The rat moves about some more and happens to press the lever again; another pellet of food is delivered. After a few trials, the rat learns that pressing the lever brings food. A hungry rat will learn to press the lever many times in rapid succession to obtain food. Today, psychologists use computerized devices to quantify behaviour such as bar pressing and to track the progress an organism makes in learning a response.

Teaching an organism a complex response takes many trials because most organisms need to be taught in small steps, through *shaping*. **Shaping** is the process of reinforcing behaviour that approximates (comes close to) a desired behaviour. To teach a hungry rat to press a bar in a Skinner box, for example, a researcher begins by giving the rat a pellet of food each time it enters the side of the box on which the bar is located. Once this behaviour is established, the rat receives food only when it touches the wall where the bar is located. It then receives food only when it approaches the bar—and so on, until it receives food only when it actually presses the bar. At each stage the reinforced behaviour (entering the half of the box nearest the

**SKINNER BOX**

Named by others for its developer, B. F. Skinner, a box that contains a responding mechanism (usually a lever) capable of delivering a consequence, often a reinforcer, to an organism.

**SHAPING**

A gradual training of an organism to give the proper responses through selective reinforcement of behaviours as they approach the desired response.

▼ The "baby box" allowed Skinner to shape his daughter's behaviour in certain ways.

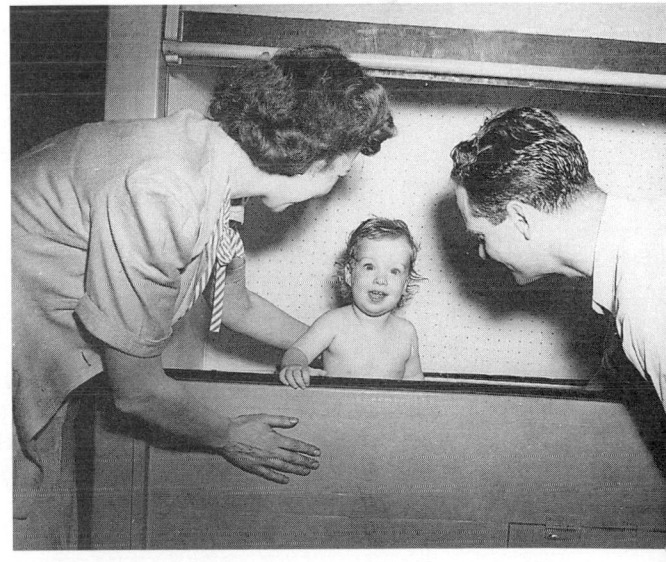

▲ Pet owners can use shaping to teach animals to obey. Each time this dog makes a closer approximation to the owner's goal of having it sit, the owner rewards it with a treat.

bar, touching the wall that houses the bar, and so on) more closely approximates the desired behaviour (pressing the bar). The sequence of stages used to elicit increasingly closer approximations of a desired behaviour is sometimes called the *method of successive approximations*, which means the same thing as *shaping*.

Shaping is effective for teaching animals new behaviours; for example, shaping is used to train a dog to sit on command. The trainer generally does this by pairing a dog treat with a push on the dog's rear while verbally commanding, "Sit!" With a treat as a reinforcer following the sitting, the dog begins to sit with less and less pressure applied to its rear; eventually, it sits on command. Shaping is also helpful in teaching people new behaviours. For example, were you taught how to play baseball? If so, first you probably were taught how to hold the bat correctly, then how to swing it, then how to make contact with the ball, and finally how to get a base hit.

Teaching new behaviours by means of operant conditioning is time consuming and often must be done in several stages, especially if the behaviours are complex. For example, a father who wants his son to make his bed neatly will at first reinforce *all* of the child's attempts at bed-making, even if the results are sloppy. Over successive weeks, the father will reinforce only the better attempts, until finally he reinforces only neat bed-making. Patience is important, because it is essential to reinforce all steps toward the desired behaviour, no matter how small (Fischer & Gochros, 1975). Shaping embodies a central tenet of behaviourism—*reinforced behaviours recur*. Skinner is the individual most responsible for advancing that notion; psychologists attribute to him the idea that various consequences can redirect the natural flow of behaviour. Among the most important of these consequences is reinforcement.

## REINFORCEMENT: A CONSEQUENCE THAT STRENGTHENS A RESPONSE

To really understand operant conditioning, you need to study the basic principles of reinforcement. To psychologists, a **reinforcer** is any event that increases the probability of a recurrence of the response that preceded it. Thus, a behaviour followed by a desirable event is likely to recur. Examples of reinforcement abound in daily life: A person works hard in a factory and is rewarded with high pay; a student studies long hours for an examination and is rewarded with a top grade; sales agents call on hundreds of clients and sell many of their products; young children behave appropriately and receive affection and praise from their parents. The specific behaviours of working hard, studying a great deal, calling on clients, and behaving well for parents are established because of reinforcement. Such behaviours can be taught by means of either or both of two kinds of reinforcers: positive and negative.

**POSITIVE REINFORCEMENT.** Most people have used positive reinforcement at one time or another. **Positive reinforcement** is the presentation of a rewarding or pleasant stimulus after a particular response, to increase the likelihood that the response will recur. When you teach your dog tricks, you reward it with a biscuit or a pat on the head. When a child raises her hand in school, her teacher praises her for waiting her turn; the praise is a reinforcer. The dog and the child continue the behaviours because they have been rewarded with something that is important or desired; their behaviours have been positively reinforced.

Some reinforcers are more powerful than others, and a reinforcer that rewards one person may not have reinforcing value for another. A smile from an approving parent may be a powerful reinforcer for a two-year-old; high grades may be the most effective reinforcer for a student; money may be effective for one adult, while position or status is effective for another.

**NEGATIVE REINFORCEMENT.** Whereas positive reinforcement increases the probability of a response through delivery of a reward, **negative reinforcement** increases the probability of a response through removal of an *aversive* (unpleasant or noxious) stimulus. *Negative reinforcement is still reinforcement*, because it strengthens or increases the likelihood of a response; its reinforcing properties are associated with its removal. For example, suppose a rat is placed in a maze with an electrified grid that delivers a shock every 50 seconds, and the rat can escape the shock by turning to the left in the maze. The behaviour to be conditioned is turning to the left in the maze; the reinforcement is termination of the painful stimulus. In this case, negative reinforcement—termination of the painful stimulus—increases the probability of the response (going left) because that is the way to escape the unpleasant stimulus. As another example, consider the last time you took a remedy for a headache. The headache's disappearance will negatively reinforce your remedy-taking behaviour. That is, next time you have a headache you will *repeat* the remedy-taking behaviour.

There are two types of negative reinforcement. In *escape conditioning*, an animal receives a shock just strong enough to cause it to thrash around until it bumps against a bar, thereby stopping the shock. In just a few trials, the animal learns to press the bar to escape being shocked, to bring the unpleasant situation to an end. In *avoidance conditioning*, the same apparatus is used, but a buzzer or some other cue precedes the shock by a few seconds. In this case, the animal learns that when it is presented with a stimulus or cue such as a buzzer, it should press the bar to prevent the shock from occurring—to avoid it. Avoidance conditioning generally involves escape conditioning as well. First the animal learns how to escape the shock by pressing the bar. Then it learns how to avoid the shock by pressing the bar when it hears the buzzer that signals the oncoming shock or it learns to push the bar or to leave the area (if possible) as soon as it is put in the apparatus.

In avoidance conditioning, the organism learns to respond in such a way that the noxious stimulus is never delivered. For example, to avoid receiving a bad grade on an English quiz, a student may study before an examination or not take an English course at all. And when an adult develops an irrational fear of airplanes, the person may avoid airplane travel. If the person can get to where he or she needs to go by some other means, the person may never unlearn the fear of planes. Thus, avoidance conditioning can explain adaptive behaviours such as studying before an exam, and it can also explain why some people maintain irrational fears.

Most children master both escape and avoidance conditioning at an early age; appropriate signals from a disapproving parent often result in an emitted avoidance response so punishment will not follow. Similarly, just knowing the possible effects of an automobile accident will make most cautious adults wear seatbelts. Both positive and negative reinforcements *increase* the likelihood that an organism will repeat a behaviour. If the reinforcement is strong enough, is delivered often enough, and is important enough to the organism, it can help maintain behaviours for long periods.

**THE NATURE OF REINFORCERS.** The precise nature of reinforcers is a murky issue. Early researchers recognized that events that satisfy biological needs are powerful reinforcers. Later researchers added events that decrease a person's various needs—for example, conversation that relieves boredom, sounds that relieve sensory deprivation, and money that relieves housing congestion. Then, in the 1960s, researchers acknowledged that an array of events can be reinforcers. *Probable behaviours*—behaviours likely to happen, including biological behaviours such as eating and social behaviours such as playing tennis, writing letters, or talking—can reinforce less probable or unlikely behaviours such as cleaning closets, studying calculus, or pressing levers. Researchers call this idea the *Premack principle*, after David Premack, whose influential writings and research fostered it (Premack, 1962, 1965). Parents employ the Premack principle when they tell their children that they can go outside to play *after* they clean up their room.

The Premack principle and its refinements focus on the problem of determining what is a good reinforcer. Therapists and learning theorists know, for example, that something that acts as a reinforcer for one person may not do so for another, and something that acts as a reinforcer on one day may not do so for the same person on the next day. Therefore, psychologists are very careful about determining what events in a client's life—or a rodent's environment—act as reinforcers. If someone were to offer you a reinforcer for some extraordinary activity on your part, what would be the most effective reinforcer? Do reinforcers change with a person's age and experiences, or do they depend on how often the person has been reinforced? Today, researchers are trying to find out ahead of time what reinforcers will work in practical settings such as the home and the workplace (Farmer-Dougan, 1998; Timberlake & Farmer-Dougan, 1991).

A reinforcer that is known to be successful may work only in specific situations. The delivery of food pellets to a hungry rat that has just pressed a lever increases the likelihood that the rat will press the lever again. However, this reinforcer works only if the rat is hungry; for a rat that has just eaten, food pellets are not reinforcing. Psychologists studying learning and conditioning create the conditions for reinforcement by depriving animals of food or water before an experiment. In doing so, they motivate the animals and allow the delivery of food to take on reinforcing properties. In most experiments, the organism is motivated in some way. Chapter 9 discusses the role of an organism's needs, desires, and physiological state in determining what can be used as a reinforcer.

A **primary reinforcer** is a reinforcer that has survival value for the organism (for example, food, water, or the termination of pain); its value does not have to be learned. Food can be a primary reinforcer for a hungry rat, water for a thirsty one. A **secondary reinforcer** is a neutral stimulus (such as money or grades) that initially has no intrinsic value for the organism but that when linked with a primary reinforcer can become rewarding. Many human pleasures are secondary reinforcers that have acquired value—for example, leather coats that keep people no warmer than cloth ones and sports cars that take people around town no faster than four-door sedans. The secondary reinforcer acquires value because it predicts the primary reinforcer (that is, an association has been made between the secondary and primary reinforcers).

**SUPERSTITIOUS BEHAVIOURS.** Because reinforcement plays a key role in our learning of new behaviours, parents and educators intentionally try to reinforce children and students on a regular basis. But what happens when a person or animal is *accidentally* rewarded for a behaviour—when a reward has nothing to do with the behaviour that immediately preceded it? Under this condition, people and animals may develop **superstitious behaviour**—behaviour learned through coincidental association with reinforcement. Superstitious behaviour often represents an attempt to gain some control over a situation that may be unpredictable. For example, a hockey player may try to extend his scoring streak by always wearing the same "lucky" socks or engaging in small repetitive rituals (Bleak & Frederick, 1998). A student may study at the same place in the library because she earned an A after studying there for the last exam. Many superstitious behaviours—including fear responses to the number 13, black cats, and walking under ladders—are centuries old and have strong cultural associations. Individual superstitious behaviours generally arise from a purely random event that occurred immediately after the behaviour.

Animals have been observed learning superstitious behaviours in a Skinner box. For example, on trials in which a pigeon learns the bar-pressing response, the bird may turn its head to the right before pressing the bar and receiving reinforcement. Although the reinforcement is actually contingent only on pressing the bar, to the pigeon it may seem that both the head turning and the bar pressing are necessary (Skinner, 1948). Therefore, the pigeon will continue to turn its head before pressing the bar.

PRIMARY REINFORCER

A reinforcer (such as food, water, or the termination of pain) that has survival value for an organism; thus, its value does not have to be learned.

SECONDARY REINFORCER

A neutral stimulus that has no intrinsic value for an organism initially but that can become rewarding when linked with a primary reinforcer.

SUPERSTITIOUS BEHAVIOUR

Behaviour learned through coincidental association with reinforcement.

**ELECTRICAL BRAIN STIMULATION.**   Until the 1950s, researchers assumed that reinforcers were effective because they satisfied some need or drive, such as hunger, in an organism. Then James Olds (1955, 1969) found an apparent exception to this assumption. He discovered that rats find electrical stimulation of specific areas of the brain to be rewarding in itself.

Olds implanted electrodes in the hypothalamus of rats and attached the electrodes to a stimulator that provided a small voltage. The stimulator was activated only when the rats pressed a lever in a Skinner box. Olds found that the rats pressed the lever thousands of times in order to continue the self-stimulation. In one study, they pressed it at a rate of 1920 times per hour (Olds & Milner, 1954). Rats even crossed an electrified grid to obtain this reward. Animals who were rewarded with brain stimulation performed better in a maze, running faster with fewer errors. And hungry rats often chose self-stimulation over food.

Stimulation of specific areas of the brain initiates different drives and activities. In some cases, it reinforces behaviours such as bar pressing; in others, it increases eating, drinking, or sexual behaviour. Psychologists are still not sure how electrical stimulation reinforces a behaviour such as lever pressing, but they do know that certain neurotransmitters play an important role. For example, Peter Milner of McGill University found that when levels of specific neurotransmitters, such as dopamine, are increased after bar pressing, a rat is far more likely to continue bar pressing (Milner, 1991; White & Milner, 1992). The area of the brain stimulated (initially thought to be the medial forebrain bundle but now recognized to include large parts of the limbic system), the state of the organism, its particular physiological needs, and the levels of various brain neurotransmitters are all important. A hungry rat, for example, will self-stimulate faster than a rat that is not hungry. In addition, a hungry rat generally will choose electrical brain stimulation over food, but will not starve to death by always making this choice.

## PUNISHMENT: A CONSEQUENCE THAT WEAKENS A RESPONSE

You already know that the consequences of an action—whether reward or punishment—affect behaviour. Clearly, rewards can establish new behaviours and maintain them for long periods. How effective is punishment in manipulating behaviour? **Punishment** is the process of presenting an undesirable or noxious stimulus, or removing a desirable stimulus, to decrease the probability that a particular preceding response will recur. Punishment, unlike reinforcement, aims to *decrease* the probability of a particular response. There are two forms of punishment, generally described as positive and negative punishment. In this instance the word *positive* refers to the nature of the contingency. A positive punishment occurs when a noxious stimulus follows an undesired behaviour. For example, when a dog growls at visitors, its owner reprimands it. When children write on the walls with crayons, their parents scold them or make them scrub the walls clean. In both cases, people indicate displeasure by the delivery of an action in an effort to suppress (decrease) an undesirable behaviour. *Introduction to Research Basics* illustrates how positive punishment (also referred to as aversive conditioning) can be therapeutically useful.

Researchers use the same approach—a form of punishment, **positive punishment**—to decrease the probability that a behaviour will recur. They deliver a noxious or unpleasant stimulus, such as a mild electric shock, when an organism displays an undesirable behaviour. If an animal is punished for a specific behaviour, the probability that it will continue to perform that behaviour decreases.

Another form of punishment, **negative punishment**, involves removal of a pleasant stimulus. For example, if teenagers stay out past their curfew, they may lose privileges (be grounded) for a week. If children misbehave, they may be forbidden to watch television. One effective negative punishment is the time out, in which a person is removed from an environment containing positive events or reinforcers. For example, a child who hits and kicks may be put in a corner where there are no toys, television, or people.

PUNISHMENT

The process of presenting an undesirable or noxious stimulus, or removing a desirable stimulus, to decrease the probability that a particular preceding response will recur.

POSITIVE PUNISHMENT

A form of punishment in which an unpleasant stimulus is added in an effort to decrease an undesirable behaviour.

NEGATIVE PUNISHMENT

A form of punishment in which a pleasant stimulus is taken away in an effort to decrease an undesirable behaviour.

## Positive Punishment: Olfactory Aversion as a Treatment for Deviant Sexual Behaviour

Learning theory provides a possible means for assisting individuals who exhibit deviant sexual tendencies such as pedophilia (a desire for sexual activity with children) or sexual sadism (taking pleasure in others' physical pain). Richard Laws (2001), who runs a private practice out of Victoria, British Columbia, has conducted research into the effectiveness of using olfactory (smell) aversion conditioning as a technique to reduce deviant sexual behaviours.

**Design.** The design Laws uses is called the *multiple baseline case study procedure* in which an individual is presented with a noxious smell in the presence of deviant sexual images or thoughts. The procedure is repeated with or without the noxious odour at regular intervals over the next few weeks. A device called a penile plethysmograph (PPG) that measures degree of erectile response was used to measure the degree of sexual response to deviant and non-deviant sexual images.

**Hypothesis.** The pairing of a noxious odour (an aversive or punishing stimulus) with the presentation of deviant sexual images or thoughts will reduce or eliminate the magnitude of the individual's sexual arousal to those images or thoughts.

**Participants.** As these studies arise out of clinical practice, they are conducted one participant or client at a time. In this case, the study or intervention focused on one individual who had been convicted of pedophilia.

**Procedure.** The individual's sexual response to deviant sexual images was first measured using the PPG. During the training phase, as the individual viewed deviant sexual images he was also required to break open ammonia capsules (smelling salts) and inhale deeply while viewing the material (a *very* noxious experience). He was not required to inhale ammonia while viewing non-deviant sexual images. This procedure was repeated over three sessions. Sexual responsiveness to deviant material was then measured with the PPG weekly for 14 weeks.

**Results.** The individual's sexual responsiveness to deviant images dropped dramatically over the first six weeks and stabilized at a very low level. The individual's responsiveness to non-deviant sexual images increased consistently during this period and remained high through the 14 weeks of the study.

**Conclusions.** Laws suggests that this olfactory aversion procedure can provide a means for assisting individuals in managing their deviant sexual tendencies. An advantage of this technique is that the individuals can administer it themselves and so can run their own follow-up or behavioural maintenance program.

**Limitations.** The main limitation of this study is that it is focused only on a single individual. Therefore, it is up to clinical psychologists using this technique to monitor its effectiveness with their individual clients.

---

Thus, punishment can involve either adding a noxious event, such as a scolding (positive punishment), or subtracting a positive event, such as TV watching (negative punishment). In both cases, the aim is to decrease the likelihood of a behaviour. (See Figure 5.8 for a summary of the effects of adding or subtracting a reinforcer or punisher.)

**THE NATURE OF PUNISHERS.** Figure 5.9 on page 188 illustrates the difference between negative reinforcement and punishment. Remember that reinforcement always increases the behaviour it is associated with and punishment always decreases the behaviour it is associated with.

Just as reinforcers are used for reinforcement, *punishers* are used for punishment. They can be primary or secondary. A **primary punisher** is a stimulus that is naturally painful to an organism; two examples are an electric shock to an animal or a piercing high-pitched sound. A **secondary punisher** is a neutral stimulus that takes on punishing qualities; examples are a verbal no, a shake of the head, or indifference. Secondary punishers can be effective means of controlling behaviour, especially when used in combination with reinforcers for desired behaviour. However, as with reinforcement, what is punishing for one person or in one culture may not have the same properties for another person or in another culture. For example, a

PRIMARY PUNISHER

Any stimulus or event that is naturally painful or aversive to an organism.

SECONDARY PUNISHER

A neutral stimulus with no intrinsic negative effect on an organism that acquires punishment value through repeated pairing with a primary punisher.

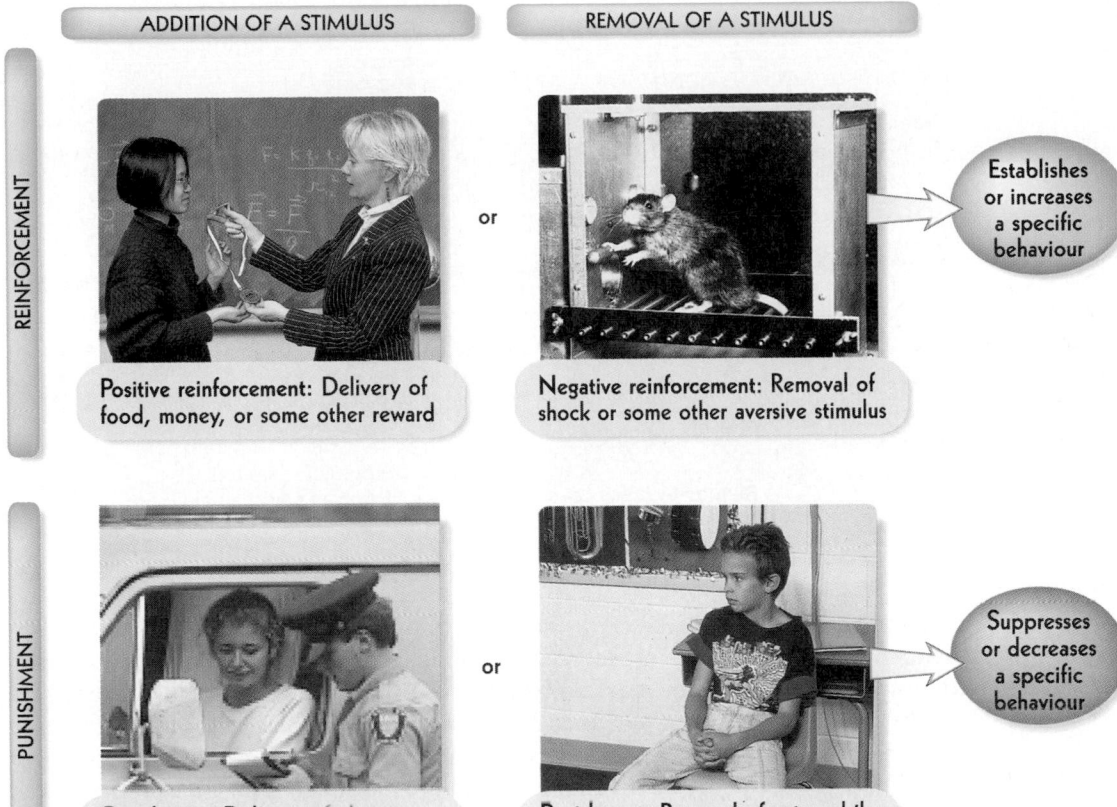

| ADDITION OF A STIMULUS | REMOVAL OF A STIMULUS | |
|---|---|---|
| **REINFORCEMENT** Positive reinforcement: Delivery of food, money, or some other reward | or Negative reinforcement: Removal of shock or some other aversive stimulus | Establishes or increases a specific behaviour |
| **PUNISHMENT** Punishment: Delivery of electric shock, a slap on the hand, or some other aversive stimulus | or Punishment: Removal of automobile, television, or some other pleasant stimulus | Suppresses or decreases a specific behaviour |

FIGURE 5.8
Effects of Reinforcement and Punishment

frown of disapproval from a teacher in Japan, where obedience to authority is culturally expected, would probably be more punishing to a Japanese student than would a similar experience for a Canadian student.

PUNISHMENT PLUS REINFORCEMENT. Psychologists have long known that punishment by itself is not an effective way to control or eliminate behaviour. Punishment can suppress simple behaviour patterns, but once the punishment ceases, animals and human beings often return to their previous behaviour. Generally, punishment is most effective if it is immediate, if positive alternative behaviours are available, if it quickly follows the behaviour it is intended to reduce, and if it is accompanied by feedback that specifies the relationship between the bad behaviour and the punishment (Schwartz & Robbins, 1995). Therefore, those who study children in classrooms urge the combination of punishment for anti-social behaviour and reinforcement for prosocial behaviour. A combination of private reprimands for disruptive behaviour and public praise for good behaviour is often the most effective method for controlling behaviour.

LIMITATIONS OF PUNISHMENT. A serious limitation of punishment as a behaviour-shaping device is that it suppresses only existing behaviours. It cannot be used to establish new, desired behaviours. Punishment also has serious social consequences (Azrin & Holtz, 1966). If parents use excessive punishment to control a child's behaviour, for example, the child may try to escape from the home so that

FIGURE 5.9

## Comparison of Negative Reinforcement and Punishment

Punishment involves the presentation of an aversive stimulus to *decrease* the likelihood of a behaviour recurring. Negative reinforcement increases a behaviour by removing an aversive stimulus. Thus, punishment and negative reinforcement have opposite effects on behaviour.

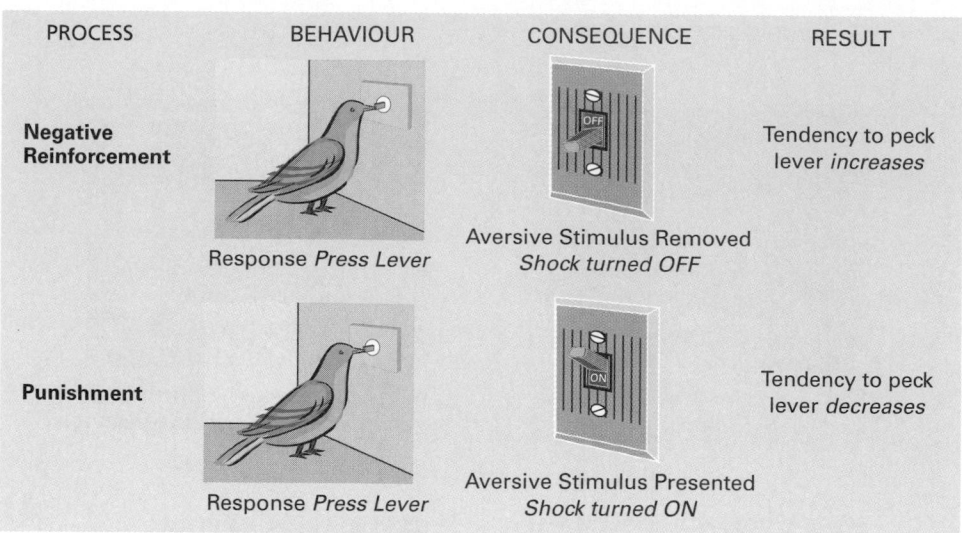

PROCESS     BEHAVIOUR     CONSEQUENCE     RESULT

**Negative Reinforcement**

Response *Press Lever*

Aversive Stimulus Removed
*Shock turned OFF*

Tendency to peck lever *increases*

**Punishment**

Response *Press Lever*

Aversive Stimulus Presented
*Shock turned ON*

Tendency to peck lever *decreases*

**LEARNED HELPLESSNESS**
The behaviour of giving up or not responding, exhibited by people or animals exposed to negative consequences or punishment over which they have no control.

**Be an ACTIVE LEARNER**

**REVIEW**
> How could a child's undesirable behaviour (hitting the family cat, for example) be shaped to a desired behaviour? pp. 181–182
> What types of reinforcers are most likely to ensure that a behaviour will be repeated? pp. 182–184
> What are some examples showing that probable behaviours can reinforce less probable or unlikely behaviours (the Premack principle)? pp. 183–184
> Distinguish between primary reinforcers and secondary reinforcers. p. 184

**THINK CRITICALLY**
> What are the fundamental differences between positive reinforcement, negative reinforcement, and punishment? Give an example of each.

**APPLY PSYCHOLOGY**
> Your neighbour tells you, "Punishment just doesn't work with my kids any more. I keep escalating the punishments, and they keep acting worse and worse! I don't know what to do!" What do you think is going on here, and what would you advise your neighbour to do?

punishment cannot be delivered. Further, children who receive physical punishments often demonstrate increased levels of aggression when they are away from the punisher. Punishment may control a child's behaviour while the parents are nearby, but it also may serve to alienate the child from the parents. In fact, the issue of spanking or corporal punishment is currently under debate at the highest level in Canada. The Ontario Court of Appeal has upheld a law that gives parents and teachers the right to use corporal punishment to correct children's behaviour. The Supreme Court of Canada is currently considering a request to appeal that decision and outlaw spanking and other forms of corporal punishment.

Research also shows that children imitate aggression. Joan Grusec of the University of Toronto found that parents who punish children physically are likely to have children who are physically aggressive (Grusec, Goodnow, & Kuczynski, 2000). A child may strike out at the person who administers punishment in an attempt to eliminate the source of punishment, sometimes inflicting serious injury. Punishment also can bring about generalized aggression. For example, if two rats in a Skinner box both receive painful shocks, they will strike out at each other. Similarly, punished individuals are often hostile and aggressive toward other members of their group. This is especially true for prison inmates, whose hostility is well recognized, and for class bullies, who are often the children most strictly disciplined by their parents or teachers. Skinner (1988) believed that punishment in schools is unnecessary and harmful; he advocated non-punitive techniques, which might involve developing strong bonds between students and teachers and reinforcing school activities at home (Comer & Woodruf, 1998; Comer, 1988). In general, procedures that lead to a perception of control on the part of an individual are much more likely to extinguish undesired behaviour, even when the disciplining agent (often Mom or Dad) is not around.

Further, if punishment is delivered inconsistently or without reference to the organism's behaviour or culture (Rudy & Grusec, 2001), it may lead to **learned helplessness**, the reaction of a person or animal that feels powerless to control the punishment and so stops making any response at all (LoLordo & Taylor, 2001; Maier, Peterson, & Schwartz, 2000; Shatz, 2000; Springer, 2000). For example, if a parent responds with open hostility and constant criticism toward a child, the child will eventually stop trying to please the parent and may perhaps stop trying to please any adult. The child needs to see a connection between his or her behaviour and the consequences of that behaviour. When that connection does not exist, the child stops trying. He or she has *learned* to be helpless.

# Key Variables in Operant Conditioning

As with classical conditioning, many variables affect operant conditioning. Most important are the strength, timing, and frequency of consequences (either reinforcement or punishment).

## STRENGTH, TIMING, AND FREQUENCY OF CONSEQUENCES

**STRENGTH OF CONSEQUENCES.** Studies comparing productivity with varying amounts of reinforcement show that the greater the reward, the harder, longer, and faster a person will work to complete a task (see Figure 5.10). For example, if you were a gardener, the more money you received for mowing lawns, the more lawns you would want to mow. Similarly, the stronger the punishment, the more quickly and longer the behaviour can be suppressed. If you knew you would get a $500 ticket for speeding instead of just paying a small fine, you would be less likely to speed.

The strength of a consequence can be measured in terms of either time or degree. For example, the length of time a child stays in a time-out room without positive reinforcements can affect how soon and for how long an unacceptable behaviour will be suppressed. Thus, a two-minute stay might not be as effective as a ten-minute stay. Likewise, a half-hearted "Oh no, sweetie" is not as effective as a firm "Don't do that again."

Punishment, whatever its form, is best delivered in moderation; too much may be as ineffective as too little. If too much punishment is delivered, it may cause strong anxiety, decrease the likelihood of an appropriate response, or even elicit behaviour that is contrary to the goals of the punishment.

**TIMING OF CONSEQUENCES.** Just as the interval between presenting the conditioned stimulus and the unconditioned stimulus is important in classical conditioning, the interval between a desired behaviour and the delivery of the consequence (reward or punishment) is important in operant conditioning. Generally, the shorter the interval, the greater the likelihood that the behaviour will be learned (see Figure 5.10).

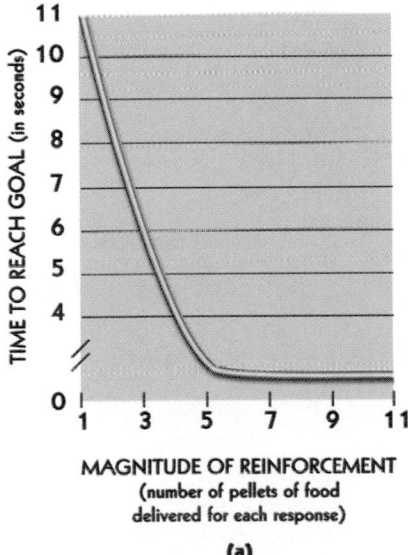

(a)

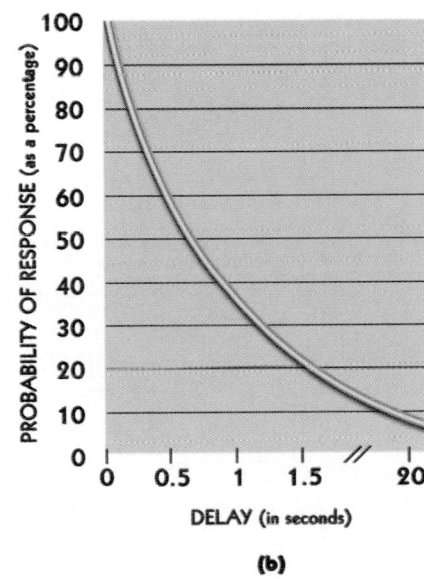

(b)

**FIGURE 5.10**

**The Magnitude and Delay of Reinforcement**

(a) As the amount of a reinforcer (its strength or magnitude) increases, the time it takes an organism to reach a goal usually decreases. (b) As a delay is placed between a response and reinforcement, the probability that a behaviour will recur decreases. Short delays (or no delays) between a response and reinforcement increase the chances that a behaviour will recur.

**FREQUENCY OF CONSEQUENCES.** How often do people need to be reinforced? Is a paycheque once a month sufficient? Will people work better if they receive reinforcement regularly or if they receive it at unpredictable times? Up to this point, our discussion has generally assumed that a consequence follows each response. What if people are reinforced only some of the time, not continually? When a researcher varies the frequency with which an organism is to be reinforced, the researcher is said to manipulate the *schedule of reinforcement*—the pattern of presentation of the reinforcer over time. The simplest and easiest reinforcement pattern is **continuous reinforcement**—reinforcement for every occurrence of the targeted behaviour. Continuous reinforcement results in faster learning but this learning is easily extinguished (unlearned). Furthermore, most researchers, or parents, do not reinforce a behaviour every time it occurs; rather, they reinforce occasionally or intermittently, a pattern known as **partial reinforcement**. What determines the timetable for reinforcement? Partial reinforcement is generally based on either intervals of time or on frequency of responses. Some schedules establish behaviours quickly; however, quickly established behaviours are more quickly extinguished than are behaviours that are slower to be established. (We'll discuss extinction in operant conditioning later in this section.) Researchers have devised four basic schedules of partial reinforcement; two are *interval schedules* (which deal with time periods between reinforced responses), and two are *ratio schedules* (which deal with work output).

Interval schedules can be either fixed or variable. Imagine that a rat in a Skinner box is being trained to press a bar in order to obtain food. If the experiment is on a **fixed-interval schedule**, the reward will follow the first required response that occurs after a specified interval of time since the previous reinforced response. That is, the rat will be given a reinforcer if it presses the bar at least once after a specified time interval, regardless of whether the rat works a great deal or just a little. As Figure 5.11 shows, a fixed-interval schedule produces a scalloped graph line. Just after reinforcement (shown by the tick marks in the figure), both animals and human beings typically respond slowly; just before the reinforcer is due, there is an increase in performance.

**CONTINUOUS REINFORCEMENT**
Reinforcement for every occurrence of the targeted behaviour.

**PARTIAL REINFORCEMENT**
Reinforcement that is occasional or intermittent.

**FIXED-INTERVAL SCHEDULE**
A reinforcement schedule in which a reinforcer (reward) is delivered after a specified interval of time, provided that the required response occurs at least once after the interval.

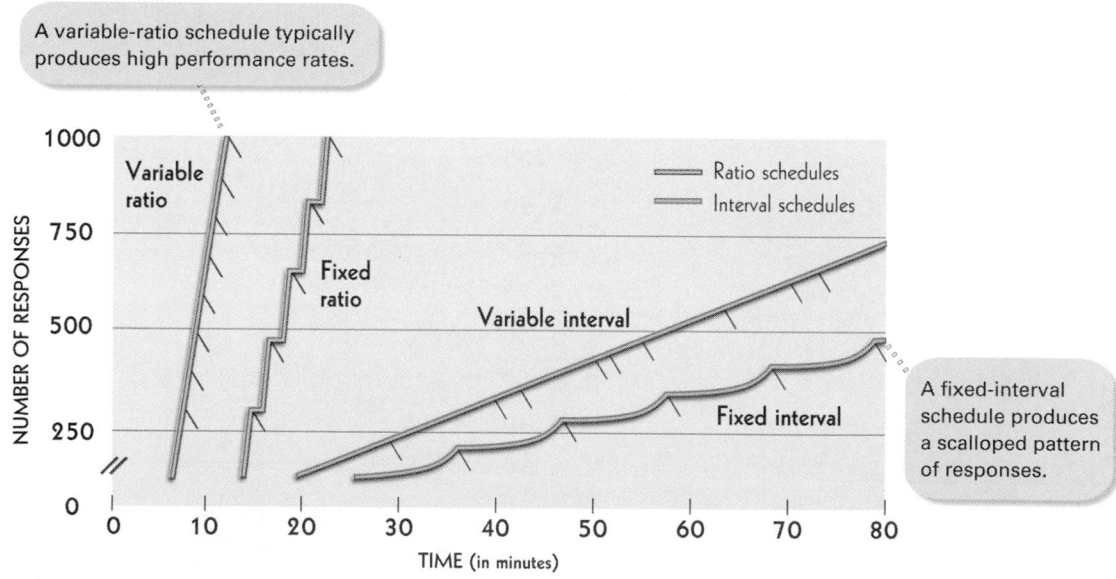

**FIGURE 5.11**

**The Four Basic Types of Reinforcement Schedules**

Each tick mark indicates presentation of a reinforcer. Steep slopes represent high work rates. In general, the rate of response is higher under ratio schedules than under interval schedules.

Under a **variable-interval schedule**, the reinforcer is delivered after predetermined but varying amounts of time, as long as an appropriate response is made at least once after each interval following the previous reinforced response. The organism may be reinforced if it makes a response after 40 seconds, after 60 seconds, and then after 25 seconds. For example, if grades are posted at unpredictable intervals during a semester, you probably will check the bulletin board at a fairly regular rate. Rats reinforced on a variable-interval schedule work at a slow, regular rate, without showing the scalloped effect of those on a fixed-interval schedule. The work rate is relatively slow, because the delivery of the reinforcer is tied to time intervals rather than to output.

Ratio schedules, which also can be either fixed or variable, deal with output instead of time. In a **fixed-ratio schedule**, the subject is reinforced for a specified number of responses (amount of work). For example, a rat in a Skinner box might be reinforced after every tenth bar press. In this case, the rat will work at a fast, regular rate until it is reinforced, pause, and then begin to work at a fast, regular rate again. It has learned that hard work brings regular delivery of a reinforcer, but that reinforcers do not occur one after the next, so it has learned that it can pause following reinforcement. Figure 5.11 shows that the work rate of a rat on a fixed-ratio schedule is much higher than that of a rat on an interval schedule. In the same way, a teenager who is paid for each lawn mowed (that is, for the amount of work completed) probably will mow more lawns than a teenager who is paid by the hour.

Variable-ratio schedules can achieve very high rates of response. In contrast to a fixed-ratio schedule, a **variable-ratio schedule** reinforces the subject for a predetermined but variable number of responses (amount of work). Thus, a rat learns that hard work produces a reinforcer, but it cannot predict when the reinforcer will be delivered. Therefore, the rat's best bet is to work at a regular, high rate, thereby generating the highest available rate of response. Sales agents for insurance companies know that the more prospects they approach, the more insurance they will sell. They may not know who will buy, but they do know that a greater number of selling opportunities ultimately will result in more sales. Similarly, gamblers pour quarters into slot machines because although they do not know when they will be reinforced with a jackpot they do know that the slot machine is programmed to pay off at some point. Table 5.2 summarizes the four schedules of reinforcement.

An efficient way to teach a response is to have an organism learn the response on a fixed ratio schedule, then introduce a variable-ratio schedule. For example, a rat initially can be reinforced on every trial so that it will learn the proper response quickly. It then can be reinforced after every other trial, then after every fifth trial, and then after a variable number of trials. Once the rat has learned the desired response, very high response rates can be obtained even with infrequent reinforce-

**VARIABLE-INTERVAL SCHEDULE**

A reinforcement schedule in which a reinforcer (reward) is delivered after predetermined but varying intervals of time, provided that the required response occurs at least once after each interval.

**FIXED-RATIO SCHEDULE**

A reinforcement schedule in which a reinforcer (reward) is delivered after a specified number of responses has occurred.

**VARIABLE-RATIO SCHEDULE**

A reinforcement schedule in which a reinforcer (reward) is delivered after a predetermined but variable number of responses has occurred.

**TABLE 5.2** Types of Reinforcement Schedules

| Schedule | Description | Effect |
|---|---|---|
| Fixed interval | Reinforcement is given for the first response after a fixed time. | Response rate drops right after reinforcement but then increases near the end of the interval. |
| Variable interval | Reinforcement is given for the first response after a predetermined but variable interval of time. | Response rate is slow and regular. |
| Fixed ratio | Reinforcement is given after a fixed number of responses. | Response rate is fast and regular. |
| Variable ratio | Reinforcement is given after a predetermined and variable number of responses. | Response rate is regular and high. |

ment. When an experimenter implements a *variable*-ratio or a *variable*-interval schedule, the frequency for each ratio or the length of each interval is predetermined, though it will not appear so to the subject. These schedules can be combined easily for maximum effect, depending on the targeted behaviour (e.g., Worsdell et al., 2000; Zarcone et al., 1999).

**USING SCHEDULES OF CONSEQUENCES.** The study of reinforcement has many practical implications. Psychologists use the principles of reinforcement to study such frequently asked questions as these: How can I change my little brother's rotten attitude? How can I get more work out of my employees? How do I learn to say no? How do I get my dog to stop biting my ankles? To get your brother to shape up, you can shape his behaviour. Each time he acts in a way you like, however slight, reward him with praise or affection. When he acts poorly, withhold attention or rewards and ignore him. Continue this pattern for a few weeks; as he becomes more pleasant, show him more attention. Remember, reinforced behaviours tend to recur.

Most workers are paid a fixed amount each week. They are on a fixed-interval schedule—regardless of their output, they get their paycheque. One way to increase productivity is to place workers on a fixed-ratio schedule. A worker who is paid by the piece, by the report, by the page, or by the widget is going to produce more pieces, reports, pages, or widgets than one who is paid by the hour and whose productivity therefore does not make a difference. Automobile salespeople, who are known for their persistence, work on a commission basis; their pay is linked to their ability to close a sale. Research in both the laboratory and the business world shows that when pay is linked to output, people generally work harder.

## STIMULUS GENERALIZATION AND STIMULUS DISCRIMINATION

*Stimulus generalization* and *stimulus discrimination* occur in operant conditioning much as they do in classical conditioning. The difference is that in operant conditioning the reinforcement is delivered only after the organism correctly discriminates between the stimuli. For example, suppose an animal in a laboratory is shown either a vertical or a horizontal line and is given two keys to press—one if the line is vertical, the other if the line is horizontal. The animal gets rewards for correct responses. The animal usually will make errors at first, but after repeated presentations of the vertical and horizontal lines, with reinforcements given only for correct responses, discrimination will occur. Stimulus discrimination also can be established with colours, tones, and more complex stimuli.

The processes of stimulus generalization and discrimination are evident daily. Children often make mistakes by overgeneralizing. For example, a child who knows that cats have four legs and a tail may call all four-legged animals with a tail "cat." With experience and with help, guidance, and reinforcement from his or her parents, the child will learn to discriminate between dogs and cats, using body size, shape, fur, and sounds as criteria.

## EXTINCTION AND SPONTANEOUS RECOVERY

In operant conditioning, if a reinforcer or punisher is no longer delivered—that is, if a consequence does not follow an instrumentally conditioned behaviour—the behaviour either will not be well established or, if it is already established, will undergo extinction (see Figure 5.12). **Extinction**, in operant conditioning, is the process by which the probability of an organism's emitting a conditioned response is reduced when reinforcement no longer follows the response. Suppose, for example, that a pigeon is trained to peck a key whenever it hears a high-pitched tone.

Pecking in response to a high-pitched tone brings reinforcement, but pecking in response to a low-pitched tone does not. If the reinforcement process ceases entirely, the pigeon eventually will stop working. If the pigeon has been on a variable-ratio

**EXTINCTION**

In operant conditioning, the process by which the probability of an organism's emitting a conditioned response is reduced when reinforcement no longer follows the response.

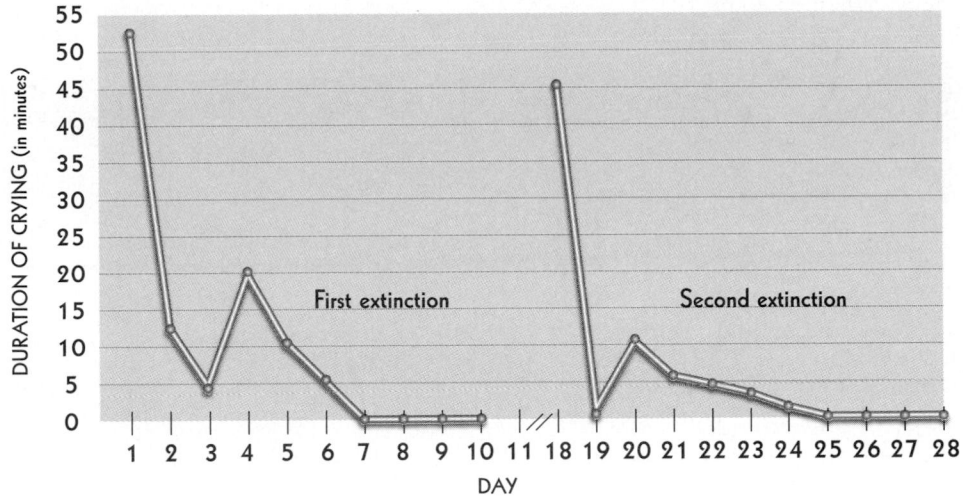

FIGURE 5.12
The Process of Extinction
When an organism's behaviour is
no longer reinforced, the
likelihood that the organism will
continue to respond decreases;
psychologists say that the
behaviour has undergone
*extinction*. Extinction is seen
with both animals and human
beings. One study (Mindell,
1999) found that a child was
throwing tantrums at bedtime to
get attention. The parents were
instructed to pay no attention to
the tantrums. After several days,
the number of minutes the child
cried decreased to zero. A week
later, an aunt put the child to
bed; when the child made a fuss
(spontaneous recovery), the aunt
reinforced the child with
attention. The parents then had
to initiate a second extinction
process.

schedule and thus expects to work for long periods before reinforcement occurs, it probably will work for a very long time before stopping. If it is on a fixed-interval schedule and thus expects reinforcement within a short time, it will stop pecking after just a few trials in which it is not reinforced.

One way to measure the extent of conditioning is to measure how resistant a response is to extinction. *Resistance to extinction* is a measure of how long it takes, or how many trials are necessary, to achieve extinction. Consider a pigeon that is trained to peck when it hears a high-pitched tone and that is rewarded each time it pecks correctly. The pigeon is tested for 30 minutes a day for 60 days. On the sixty-first day it is not reinforced for its correct behaviour. For the first few minutes, the pigeon continues to work normally. But soon its work rate decreases, and by the end of the 30-minute session, it is not pecking at all. When the pigeon is presented with a tone the next day, it again responds with pecking but receives no reinforcement. Within a short time, the pecking behaviour is extinguished. Certainly parents know that when they stop reinforcing a child's misbehaviour with a lot of attention (even if that attention consists of scolding), the misbehaviour often decreases. Note that the decrease in response is not always immediately apparent, however. When a reinforcer is withheld, organisms sometimes work harder—showing an initial increase in performance. In such cases, the curve depicting the extinction process shows a small initial increase in performance, followed by a decrease (Allen, Turner, & Everett, 1970).

As in classical conditioning, *spontaneous recovery* also occurs in operant conditioning. If an organism's conditioned work behaviour has undergone extinction and the organism is given a rest period and then retested, the organism will show spontaneous recovery of the behaviour. If the organism is put through this sequence several times, its overall work rate in each session will decrease. After one rest period, the organism's work rate will almost equal what it was when the conditioned response was reinforced. However, after a dozen or so rest periods (with no reinforcements), the organism may make only one or two responses; the level of spontaneous recovery will have decreased markedly. Eventually, the behaviour will disappear completely.

People also show spontaneous recovery. When you answer a question in class, reinforcement usually follows: The instructor praises you for your knowledge. However, if the instructor stops reinforcing correct answers or does not call on you when you raise your hand, you will probably stop responding (your behaviour will be extinguished). After a vacation, you may start raising your hand again (spontaneous recovery), but you will quickly stop if your behaviour again is not reinforced. Instructors learn early in their careers that if they want to have lively classes, they

**TABLE 5.3** Four Important Concepts in Operant Conditioning

| Property | Definition | Example |
|---|---|---|
| Extinction | The process of reducing the probability of a conditioned response by withholding the reinforcer after the response. | A rat trained to press a bar stops pressing when it is no longer reinforced. |
| Spontaneous recovery | The recurrence of an extinguished conditioned response following a rest period. | A rat's continued bar-pressing behaviour has undergone extinction; after a rest period, the rat again presses the bar. |
| Stimulus generalization | The process by which an organism learns to respond to stimuli that are similar but not identical to the original conditioned stimulus. | A cat presses a bar when presented with either an ellipse or a circle. |
| Stimulus discrimination | The process by which an organism learns to respond only to a specific reinforced stimulus. | A pigeon presses a key only in response to red lights, not to blue or green ones. |

need to reinforce not just correct answers but also attempts at correct answers. In doing so, they help shape their students' behaviour.

Table 5.3 summarizes four important concepts in operant conditioning: extinction, spontaneous recovery, stimulus generalization, and stimulus discrimination.

## OPERANT CONDITIONING IN DAILY LIFE

Our world is full of reinforcers and punishers. We can work for rewards such as money. We can volunteer our time for such worthy causes as the Red Cross, shelters for battered women, and AIDS research. Of course, sometimes people feel that there are more punishers in the world than need be. Government taxes our income; the cost of living keeps rising; drunk drivers penalize all of us. But by and large, most of us feel in control of our reinforcers and punishers. We know that many of our rewards and punishments are indeed contingent on our behaviours. Each of us, to various extents, experiences operant conditioning in daily life.

INTRINSICALLY MOTIVATED BEHAVIOUR. Psychologists have shown that reinforcement is effective in establishing and maintaining behaviour. However, some behaviours are intrinsically rewarding—they are pleasurable in themselves. People are likely to repeat *intrinsically motivated behaviours* for their own sake; for example, they may work on craft projects for the feeling of satisfaction these activities bring. People are likely to perform *extrinsically motivated behaviour,* such as working for a paycheque, for the sake of the external reinforcement alone. Interestingly, if reinforcement is offered for intrinsically motivated behaviour, performance actually may decrease. Imagine, for example, that a man does charity work because it makes him feel good. Paying the man could cause him to lose interest in the work, because it no longer would offer the intrinsic reward of selfless behaviour. A student pianist may lose her desire to practise when her teacher enters her in a competition; practice sessions become ordeals, and the student may wish to stop playing altogether. For every person and for every culture, rewards are individualistic and determined by a host of learning experiences. Chapter 9 considers this issue at greater length, especially the topic of potential hidden costs of rewards.

BEHAVIOURAL SELF-REGULATION. *Behavioural regulation theorists* assume that people and animals make choices and that they will choose, if possible, activities that seem optimal to them. Rats, for

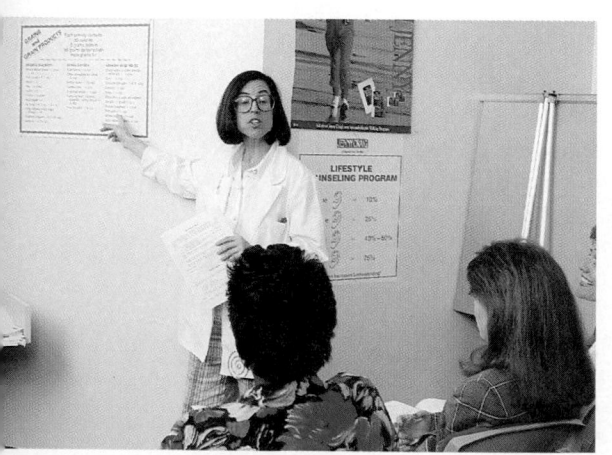

▼ Weight Watchers, an organization that emphasizes behavioural self-regulation, helps its members control their weight by encouraging them to analyze and amend their own eating habits.

example, spend their time eating, drinking, and running on a wheel—activities they find pleasurable. An experiment by Bernstein and Ebbesen (1978) showed that human beings readjust their activities in a systematic manner. The researchers paid participants to live in an isolated room 24 hours a day, 7 days a week, for several weeks. The room had all the usual amenities of a home—bed, tables, shower, books, cooking utensils, and so forth. The experimenters observed the participants through a one-way mirror and recorded their baseline activity—the frequency of participants' specific behaviours when no restrictions were placed on them. The researchers found, for example, that one participant spent nearly twice as much time knitting as studying. The experimenters used the participant's baseline to determine the reinforcing activity—in this case, knitting.

The experimenters then imposed a contingency. In the case of the participant who liked to knit, for example, they insisted that she study for a specific amount of time before she could knit. If she studied only as much as she did before, she would be able to knit for much less time. As a consequence, the subject altered her behaviour so that she could knit more. She began to study for longer periods of time—eventually more than doubling the time she spent studying.

Behavioural self-regulation has other practical applications. It is effective within classrooms (Winsler et al., 2000) and in other social situations where it can modulate disruptive behaviour (Cavalier, Ferretti, & Hodges, 1997). Members of the diet program Weight Watchers may be told to keep track of when and what they eat, when they have the urge to eat, and what feelings or events precede those urges. The aim is to help people think clearly, regulate themselves, and thus manage their lives better. This decision process and the focus on thinking are clearly seen in studies of cognitive learning, considered shortly.

Building Table 5.2 summarizes key points of comparison between classical and operant conditioning.

**Be an ACTIVE LEARNER**

**REVIEW**
> Why are variable reinforcement schedules more effective than other reward schedules? pp. 191–192
> What happens in extinction? How can researchers measure extinction? pp. 192–193

**THINK CRITICALLY**
> Would you agree or disagree with the view that all intrinsically motivated behaviours must at some point have been reinforced? Why?
> When doing human and animal research on learning, researchers often record baseline activity. Why is such evidence important?

**APPLY PSYCHOLOGY**
> Physiologically, are there ways in which a person might facilitate learning and consolidation? Explain your answer.

# The Biology That Underpins Learning

This chapter is about learning and experiences in the environment that shape behaviour, yet it is impossible to consider learning without recognizing the complex interplay of a person's biological heritage with that person's day-to-day experiences, the role of evolution, and how learning is coded.

| BUILDING TABLE 5.2 | Types of Learning: Classical Conditioning and Operant Conditioning | | |
|---|---|---|---|
| **Type of Learning** | **Procedure** | **Result** | **Example** |
| Classical Conditioning | A neutral stimulus (such as a bell) is paired with an unconditioned stimulus (such as food). | The neutral stimulus becomes a conditioned stimulus—it elicits the conditioned response. | A bell elicits a response in a dog. |
| Operant Conditioning | A behaviour is followed by a consequence—either reinforcement or punishment. | The behaviour increases or decreases in frequency. | A rat will press a bar 120 times per hour to achieve a reward or to avoid punishment. |

## ARE EVOLUTIONARY THEORY AND LEARNING THEORY INCOMPATIBLE?

At first blush it might seem that evolutionary theory, with its emphasis on evolved psychological mechanisms, focuses on built-in behaviour patterns that have taken root in organisms over successive generations and have become part of the genome (see Chapters 1 and 2). Evolutionary theory is largely biological in focus and may seem to exclude consideration of the central concern of learning theory—changes that occur in an organism due to experiences in life. (Remember that we define *learning* as a relatively permanent change in an organism that occurs *as a result of experiences in the environment*.) Yet learning theory and evolutionary theory are more compatible than they might appear.

Evolutionary theory does not rule out learning, and evolution does not strictly determine behaviour—in fact, genes and the genome do not code for any specific behaviour (Petrinovich, 1997). Indeed, humans and other animals must be capable of learning or they would not be very adaptive. Genetically determined tendencies are modified by the environment, and so evolutionary theory recognizes differences in societies and distinct, even unique, learning patterns in different cultures. Nevertheless, all human beings exhibit some characteristics everywhere in the world—for example, all human beings smile. That human beings learn and adapt is a key evolved psychological mechanism. This mechanism helps human beings survive and allows us to look toward the future, evaluate the past, and not feel hopelessly locked into a determined, rule-bound set of behaviours.

Evolutionary theory asserts that evolution is continuously setting the framework for human learning, and throughout life individuals adapt to their surroundings; some do so better than others. In the long run, those that adapt and learn the best will survive and reproduce. Thus, learning and evolutionary theory are more compatible than many think.

## LEARNING AND THE NERVOUS SYSTEM

Whenever learning occurs, there is a relatively permanent change in behaviour; this change is reflected in the nervous system. Donald O. Hebb (1904–1985), a Canadian psychologist who worked at McGill University, was one of the first to suggest that, with each learning situation, the structure of the brain changes. He argued that certain groups of neurons act together, and that their synaptic transmissions and general neural activity form a recurring pattern. He referred to such a group of coordinated neurons as a *reverberating circuit*. The more the circuit that represents a concept or experience is stimulated, the better that concept or experience will be remembered and the more the structure of the brain is altered.

Remember that learning is a process that occurs because of unique interactions among hundreds of thousands of neurons in the brain. Using this fact, Hebb (1949) suggested that stimulation of particular groups of neurons causes them to form specific patterns of neural activity. The evolution of a temporary neural circuit into a more permanent circuit is known as *consolidation*. According to Hebb, consolidation serves as the basis of learning and memory. If Hebb is correct, then when people first sense a new stimulus, only temporary changes in neurons take place; but repetition of the stimulus causes consolidation, and the temporary circuit becomes a permanent one.

Many psychologists today believe that the consolidation process provides the key to understanding learning—that individual differences in ability to learn (or remember) may be due to differing abilities to consolidate neural circuits (Gabriel & Talk, 2001; Nadel & Bohbot, 2001; Vianna et al., 2001). Confirmation of this notion comes from studies using electroconvulsive shock therapy (discussed in Chapter 15) to disrupt consolidation, which results in impaired learning and memory in both human beings and animals. Further support comes from studies showing that recent (less consolidated) memories are more susceptible to loss through amnesia than are older (more consolidated) memories (Craik, 2001; Parkin, 2001; Winocur, McDonald, & Moscovitch, 2001).

The consolidation process may even play a role in the brain's physiological development. Researchers have compared the brains of animals raised in enriched environments, where toys and other objects are available for the animals to play with and learn from, with the brains of animals raised in deprived environments. The brains of animals raised in rich environments have more elaborate networks of nerve cells, with more dendrites and more synapses with other neurons (Greenough et al., 1999). This means that stimulating a neuron over and over again may cause it to branch out and become more easily accessible to additional synaptic connections. These findings may indicate that when key neurons are stimulated, the events that cause the stimulation may be better remembered and more easily accessed—this may be part of the reason why practice makes perfect (McGaugh, 2002; O'Mara, Commins, & Anderson, 2000). Although there has been less work done with human beings in this area, Jacobs and his colleagues (1993) found that people with more education have more dendritic elaboration; and Scheibel's research team (1990) found that parts of the body that are used more (fingers versus the wall of the chest) have more elaborate dendritic organization in the brain.

**Be an ACTIVE LEARNER**

**REVIEW**
> Does evolutionary theory rule out learning as a process? p. 196
> What is a Hebbian reverberating circuit? p. 196

**THINK CRITICALLY**
> How might the consolidation process make learning possible?
> Why is synaptic plasticity in learning so important?

**APPLY PSYCHOLOGY**
> The effort to map the human genome may have key findings for learning theory. What could be done with this new knowledge? In what ways might we rethink how we go about teaching school children based on such knowledge?

# Cognitive Learning

"Enough!" shouted Patrick after four gruelling hours of trying to write a program on his personal computer. Bugs were rampant in his program, all resulting from the same basic problem; however, he didn't know what the problem was. After dozens of trial-and-error manipulations, Patrick turned off the computer and went to study for his history exam. Then, while staring at a page in the text, he saw a difficult phrase that was set off by commas; he thought about it and suddenly realized his programming mistake. He mistakenly had put commas in his program's if–then statements. It was correct English, but incorrect computer syntax.

**Learning**

Patrick solved his problem by thinking. His learning was not a matter of simple conditioning of a simple response with a simple reinforcer, or trial and error. Learning researchers have actively focused on learning that involves reinforcement. Is a reinforcer always necessary for learning? Can a person learn new behaviours just by thinking or using imagination? These questions are problematic for traditional learning researchers—but not for cognitive psychologists or learning researchers with a cognitive emphasis.

Some of the most famous psychologists of the early part of this century examined learning when reinforcement was not evident and behaviour was not shown. Their early studies focused on insight and latent learning. Recent research has focused on generative learning and observational learning. Still other cognitive research has focused on problem solving, creativity, and concept formation (which will be discussed in Chapter 7). All of this work indicates that there are many different aspects to what is learned and how learning takes place, as the discussion in *Point/Counterpoint* clearly shows.

## INSIGHT

When you discover relationships between a series of events, you may say that you have had an *insight*. Insights usually are not taught to people but rather are discovered after a series of events has occurred. Like Patrick's discovery of the extra commas in his computer program, many types of learning involve both sustained thought and insight.

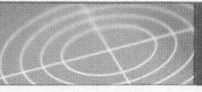

## POINT Counterpoint

### Do Men and Women Learn Differently?

**POINT:** There is no evidence that men and women learn differently.

**COUNTERPOINT:** Men and women have different cognitive styles, which lead them to learn differently.

Although many people believe that men and women think in very different ways, psychologists have been able to find little evidence that learning varies by gender. Psychologists have found small differences in abilities—girls and women have advantages on some verbal tasks, and men and boys have advantages on some spatial tasks (Halpern, 1997). These differences in abilities can be manifested as differences in interests, such as course choices, college majors, and careers, but abilities are not the same as the process of learning.

Psychologists have been assessing cognitive learning styles for decades; in doing so, they have found that males

and females are taught to learn differently. Boys and girls are taught different behaviour on the playground, at home, and in the classroom—and these behaviours influence the way they learn. In general, boys are taught to win, whereas girls are encouraged to enjoy the game and the process of playing and are taught to get along, communicate, and cooperate (Kohn, 1993). As a consequence, girls and

women tend to feel more comfortable in cooperative learning situations, whereas boys and men tend to prefer a classroom hierarchy with a leader who is in charge. Some research has supported these gender differences (Galotti et al., 1999; Knight, Elfenbein, & Martin, 1997), but other research (Severiens & Ten-Dam, 1997) suggests that gender role rather than gender is the factor related to these preferences. The notion that men's and women's learning styles differ led to the creation of same-sex classes, with the argument that each sex needs to use its own style for most effective learning. At some university campuses, women are taking classes called "Women in Business," as well as traditional literature and math classes in which the students are all women.

Some educators argue that female students work better in groups, in cooperative efforts that stimulate connections among their ideas and emphasize critical thinking (Gillies & Ashman, 1996). Critical thinking, which focuses on integrating ideas rather than memorizing information, is at the core of such efforts. Same-sex settings appear to be better for women when it comes to problem solving (Inzlicht & Ben-Zeev, 2000). Research on the role of learning styles confirms some differences between men and women—although there are still more differences among women and among men than between men and women. Gender differences in learning styles tend to be small, to be focused on a narrow range of abilities, and to emerge primarily when special types of processing are encouraged by test developers, teachers, or employers (Meyers-Levy & Maheswaran, 1991). Men's and women's preferences for different learning styles do not mean that each is incapable of either; in fact, men and women are almost identical in their ability to learn (Galotti et al., 1999).

Discovering the sources of insight was the goal of researchers working with animals during the First World War. Wolfgang Köhler, a Gestalt researcher, showed that chimps developed insights into methods of retrieving food that was beyond their reach. The chimps discovered they could pile boxes on top of one another to reach food or could attach poles together, making a long stick, to grab bananas. They were never reinforced for the specific behaviours that led to their recovering the food;

rather, they learned how to get the food through insight, by putting their behaviours together in novel ways. Once a chimp learns how to pile boxes, or once Patrick realizes his programming error, the insight is not forgotten. The insight occurs through thought, without direct reinforcement, but does depend on appropriate prior experience. Once it occurs, no further instruction, investigation, or training is necessary. The role of insight is often overlooked in studies of learning; however, it is an essential element in problem solving, a topic discussed in Chapter 7.

## LATENT LEARNING

After a person has an insight, learns a task, or solves a problem, the new learning is not necessarily evident. Researchers in the 1920s placed hungry rats in mazes and recorded how many trials it took the rats to reach a "goal"—the spot where food was hidden. It took many days and many trials, but the hungry rats learned the mazes well. Other hungry rats were put into the mazes but were not reinforced with food on reaching the same goal; instead, they merely were removed from the maze. A third group of hungry rats, like the second group, was not reinforced; however, after 10 days, these rats were given food on reaching the goal. Surprisingly, in one day, the rats in the third group were reaching the goal with few errors. During the first 10 days of maze running, they must have been learning something but not showing it. After being given a reward, they had a reason to reach the goal quickly.

Researchers such as E. C. Tolman (1886–1959) argued that this was an example of **latent learning**—learning that is not demonstrated when it occurs. Tolman showed that when a rat is given a reason (such as food) to show learning, the behaviour will become evident. In other words, a rat—or a person—without motivation may not show learning, even if it exists. Tolman's idea of latent learning was especially significant because the definition of learning at the time was strictly behavioural. Observable behaviour was an essential part of the definition. His early work laid the foundation for later studies of latent learning (e.g., Prados, Chamizo, & Mackintosh, 1999) and of generative learning and cognitive maps, and learning to learn. We consider each in turn.

**LATENT LEARNING**
Learning that occurs in the absence of any direct reinforcement and that is not necessarily demonstrated in any observable behaviour, though it has the potential to be exhibited.

## LEARNING TO LEARN AND COOPERATIVE LEARNING ARE KEY FACILITATORS

Most students in their final year of university or college believe they are much better students than they were when they began their post-secondary education. What makes the difference? How do students learn to learn better? Today, educators and cognitive researchers are focusing on *how* information is learned, as opposed to *what* is learned.

Human beings learn how to learn; they learn special strategies for special topics, and they devise general rules that depend on their goals. When you go fishing, you not only catch fish, but also learn something about the sport of fishing. The techniques for learning how to fish are different from those for learning foreign languages and from those needed to learn mathematics. Researchers (Lin, McKeachie, & Kim, 2001; McKeachie, 2003) have argued that lack of effective learning strategies is a major cause of low achievement by university and college students. They suggest that students can benefit from using certain general cognitive techniques:

- *Elaboration*—translating concepts into one's own language and actively trying to relate new ideas to old ones.
- *Attention*—focusing one's concentrative abilities and staying on task.
- *Organization*—developing skills that allow one to perform the tasks of learning and concept formation in an orderly manner.
- *Scheduling*—developing routine times for studying (which turns out to be a key element of both organization and managing anxiety).

- *Managing anxiety*—learning to focus anxiety on getting a task done, rather than becoming paralyzed with fear.
- *Expecting success*—developing an expectation of success rather than failure.
- *Note taking*—acquiring the skills necessary to take notes that will be a worthwhile learning tool.
- *Learning in groups*—developing good cooperative learning styles that make the most of interactions with other students.

Making students aware of the processes used in learning and remembering is key. This awareness (thinking about thinking and learning about learning) is called *metacognition*. When students think about their own learning, they do better; when they act strategically to modify their strategies, they learn more (Wynn-Dancy & Gillam, 1997) and are able to do better across a curriculum (Perkins & Grotzer, 1997). After people learn *how* to learn, the differences become obvious; indeed, some researchers think of creativity as a metacognitive process involving thinking about one's own thoughts (Pesut, 1990). Individuals can learn to reason, learn, and make better choices across a variety of domains (Larrick, Morgan, & Nisbett, 1990).

One way to create a better learning environment is to have students cooperate with each other, rather than compete against one another. Research shows that cooperative interactions among students—not just between students and teachers or between students and books—play a significant role in real learning (Kohn, 1993).

In fact, studies show that forming teams of students in which no one gets credit until everyone understands the material is a more effective learning approach than competitive or individualized learning. Whether the students are preschoolers or college age, whether they are studying English or physics, they have more fun, enjoy the subject matter more, and learn more when they work together (Karabenick & Collins, 1997). Students' achievements and attitudes are both improved through cooperative learning (Leikin & Zaslavsky, 1997; Whicker, Bol, & Nunnery, 1997).

**Learning**

▼ Research shows that—no matter their age—many students learn more and have more fun when collaborating in a group, rather than learning individually.

### THE THEORY OF OBSERVATIONAL LEARNING

A truly comprehensive learning theory of behaviour must be able to explain how people learn behaviours that are not taught through reinforcement. For example, everyone knows that smoking cigarettes is unhealthy. Smokers regularly try to stop smoking, and most people find their first smoking experience unpleasant. Nonetheless, adolescents light up anyway. They inhale the smoke, cough for several minutes, and feel nauseated. It is a punishing experience for them, but they try it again. Over time, they master the technique of inhaling and, in their view, look "cool" with a cigarette dangling from their fingers. That's the key to the whole situation: Adolescents observe other people with cigarettes, think they look cool, want to look cool themselves, and therefore imitate the smoking behaviour.

Such situations present a problem for traditional learning theorists, whose theories give a central role to the concept of reinforcement. There is little reinforcement in establishing smoking behaviour; instead, there is punishment (coughing and nausea). Nonetheless, the behaviour recurs. To explain this type of learning, Alberta-born, University of British Columbia–educated, Stanford University psychologist Albert Bandura has contended that the principles of classical and operant conditioning are just two of the ways in which people learn.

During the past 30 years, Bandura's ideas, expressed through observational learning theory, or *social learning theory*, have expanded the range of behaviours that can be explained by learning theory (Woodward, 1982). **Observational learning theory** suggests that organisms learn new responses by observing the behaviour of a model and then imitating it. Observational learning theory focuses on the role of thought in establishing and maintaining behaviour. Bandura and his colleagues conducted important research to confirm their idea that people can learn by observing and then imitating the behaviour of others (Bandura, 1969, 1977b; Bandura, Ross, & Ross, 1963). In their early studies, conducted at the University of Waterloo, they showed a group of children some films with aggressive content, in which an adult punched an inflated doll; they showed another group of children some films that had neither aggressive nor passive content. They then compared the play behaviour of both groups and found that the children who had viewed aggressive films tended to play aggressively afterward, whereas the other children showed no change in behaviour (Bandura, Ross, & Ross, 1963; Bandura & Walters, 1963). Bandura's research and many subsequent studies have shown that observing aggression creates aggression in children, although children do not imitate aggressive behaviour when they also see the aggressive model being punished for the actions (Goldstein, 2001).

Building Table 5.3 compares observational learning with the other two major types of learning discussed in this chapter: classical conditioning and operant conditioning.

Everyday experience also shows that people imitate the behaviour of others, especially those whom they hold in high esteem. Parents regularly say to children, "Now watch me..." or "Yes, that's the right way to do it." They provide a seemingly endless string of situations in which children can watch and copy their behaviour and then be reinforced for imitation (Masia & Chase, 1997). Children emulate their parents by putting their seatbelts on while riding in a car. Young girls become interested in gymnastics or skating after watching Olympic competitions. Unfortunately, not all observational learning is positive. Alcohol and other drug use often begins when children and teenagers imitate people they admire.

Laboratory studies of observational learning show that people can learn new behaviours merely by observing them, *without being reinforced*. For example, people who stutter can decrease their stuttering by watching others do the same (Martin & Haroldson, 1977). Children who fear animals can learn to be less fearful by watching other children interact with animals (Bandura & Menlove, 1968). Even cats learn by observing. John and colleagues (1968) found that cats can learn

OBSERVATIONAL LEARNING THEORY

A theory that suggests that organisms learn new responses by observing the behaviour of a model and then imitating it. Also known as *social learning theory*.

BUILDING TABLE 5.3    Types of Learning: Classical Conditioning, Operant Conditioning, and Observational Learning

| Type of Learning | Procedure | Result | Example |
|---|---|---|---|
| Classical Conditioning | A neutral stimulus (such as a bell) is paired with an unconditioned stimulus (such as food). | The neutral stimulus becomes a conditioned stimulus—it elicits the conditioned response. | A bell elicits a response in a dog. |
| Operant Conditioning | A behaviour is followed by a consequence—either reinforcement or punishment. | The behaviour increases or decreases in frequency. | A rat will press a bar 120 times per hour to achieve a reward or to avoid punishment. |
| Observational Learning | An observer attends to a model to learn a behaviour. | The observer learns a sequence of behaviours and becomes able to perform them at will. | After watching TV violence, children are more likely to show aggressive behaviour. |

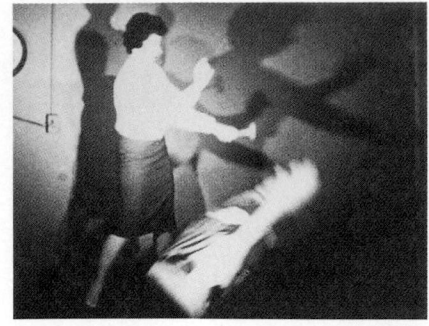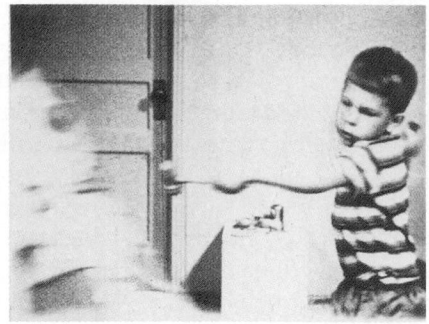

▲ After watching an adult take aggressive action against a Bobo doll, children imitated the aggressive behaviour.

to avoid receiving a shock through a grid floor by watching other cats successfully avoid the shocks by performing a task.

Moreover, if a person observes an action that is not reinforced, but rather is punished, the person will *not* imitate that action—at least not right away. Recall that latent learning may occur without behavioural evidence (see page 199). Children who observe aggression that is punished do not behave aggressively immediately; nevertheless, they may learn aggressive responses that will become evident in the future. Learning may take place through observation, but performance of specific learning may depend on a specific setting and a person's expectations about the effect of exhibiting the learned behaviour.

**KEY VARIABLES IN OBSERVATIONAL LEARNING.** Whether a person learns about an event or a behaviour depends on the extent to which he or she is involved in it. A child who has a direct experience with smoking, for example, is far more likely to remember and copy the behaviour than a child who merely hears about smoking or one who watches a film depicting it. Direct experience will always be a far more potent way for a person to remember and learn (Murachver et al., 1996). In real-world learning situations—classrooms, playgrounds, and homes—children and adults learn best when they are engaged in learning and observing. They are reinforced in some cases, observe and imitate in other cases, and sometimes change the way they are learning in midstream. Greeno (1998) maintains that all learning is active, takes place within a context, constantly changes, and depends on the active participation, consciously or unconsciously, of the learner.

Given that people can learn through many sources, we know that the effectiveness and likelihood of learning is affected by some key elements. One is the *type and power of the model* employed. Nurturing, warm, and caring models, for example, are more likely to be imitated than indifferent, angry ones; authoritative parents are more likely to be imitated than passive ones. In a classroom, children are more likely to participate with and imitate peers whom they see as powerful and dominant.

Another element is the *learner's personality and degree of independence*. Dependent children are more likely to learn from and imitate models than are independent children. Generally, the less self-confidence a person has, the more likely the person is to imitate a model, given that they undervalue their own opinions and behaviour.

A third factor is the *situation*. People are more likely to imitate others when there is uncertainty about correct behaviour. A teenager going on a first date, for example, takes cues about appropriate dress from peers and imitates their behaviour. A person who has never before been exposed to death but who loses someone close may not know what to say or how to express his or her feelings. Watching other people express their grief provides a model for behaviour. However, not everyone learns well, and there is wide variation in how people learn.

**Be an ACTIVE LEARNER**

**REVIEW**
> What evidence is there that students who are taught how to learn make gains in many areas, including grades and motivation? pp. 199–200
> What fundamental assumptions do observational learning theorists make about reinforcement in the learning process? pp. 200–202

**THINK CRITICALLY**
> Who are the best types of models for a behaviour that is to be learned through observational learning?

**APPLY PSYCHOLOGY**
> Given what you now know about observational learning, what advice would you give to parents about allowing their children to watch violent television programs or films?

# Summary and Review

## PAVLOVIAN, OR CLASSICAL, CONDITIONING THEORY

**Identify the fundamental difference between learning and reflexes.**

> *Learning* is a relatively permanent and stable change in an organism that occurs as a result of experiences in the environment. In contrast, *reflexes* occur involuntarily, quickly, and without prior learning.   **p. 166**

**Describe how classical conditioning works.**

> *Classical conditioning* involves the pairing of a neutral stimulus (for example, a bell) with an *unconditioned stimulus* (for example, food) so that the *unconditioned response* (for example, salivation) becomes a *conditioned response*. In *higher-order conditioning*, a second neutral stimulus takes on reinforcing properties by being associated with the *conditioned stimulus*. For classical conditioning to occur, the unconditioned stimulus and the conditioned stimulus usually must be presented in rapid sequence, and the conditioned stimulus must predict the occurrence of the unconditioned stimulus. **pp. 166–171**

**KEY TERMS**

learning, p. 166; conditioning, p. 166; reflex, p. 167; classical conditioning, p. 167; unconditioned stimulus, p. 168; unconditioned response, p. 168; conditioned stimulus, p. 168; conditioned response, p. 168; higher-order conditioning, p. 170

## KEY VARIABLES IN CLASSICAL CONDITIONING

**What are the most important variables in classical conditioning?**

> The most important variables in classical conditioning are the strength, timing, and frequency of the unconditioned stimulus.   **p. 171**

**How may conditioned responses vary depending on the situation?**

> *Extinction* is the process of reducing the likelihood of a conditioned response by withholding (not pairing) the unconditioned and conditioned stimulus. *Spontaneous recovery* is the recurrence of an extinguished conditioned response following a rest period, showing that previously learned associations are not totally forgotten. **pp. 172–173**
> *Stimulus generalization* is the occurrence of a conditioned response to stimuli similar to, but not the same as, the training stimulus. In contrast, *stimulus discrimination* is the process by which an organism learns to re-spond only to a specific reinforced stimulus and not to other irrelevant stimuli.   **p. 174**

**What are the key findings in studies of conditioned taste aversion?**

> In conditioned taste aversion, or the Garcia effect, it takes only one pairing of a food or drink (the conditioned stimulus) with a nausea-inducing substance (the unconditioned stimulus) to make organisms avoid the food or drink that preceded the nausea. Taste aversion can be learned even if the nausea is induced several hours after the food or drink has been consumed; this is important because learning theorists previously had assumed that closeness in time between the two events was essential.   **pp. 176–177**

**KEY TERMS**

extinction, p. 172; spontaneous recovery, p. 173; stimulus generalization, p. 174; stimulus discrimination, p. 174

## OPERANT CONDITIONING

**What takes place in operant conditioning?**

> *Operant conditioning* is conditioning in which an increase or decrease in the likelihood that a behaviour will recur is determined by whether the behaviour is followed by a consequence of reward or punishment. The process often occurs through shaping; *shaping* is reinforcing behaviour that approximates a desired behaviour. A key component of operant conditioning is reinforcement. **pp. 179–182**

**How do reinforcement and punishment work?**

> A *reinforcer* is any event that increases the probability that the response that preceded it will recur. *Positive reinforcement* increases the probability that a desired response will occur by introducing a rewarding or pleasant stimulus. *Negative reinforcement* increases the probability that a desired behaviour will occur by removing an aversive stimulus.   **pp. 182–183**
> *Primary reinforcers* have survival value for the organism; their value does not have to be learned. *Secondary reinforcers* are neutral stimuli that have no intrinsic value for the organism initially but that become rewards when they are paired with a primary reinforcer. **p. 184**
> Punishment, unlike reinforcement, decreases the probability of a particular response. *Punishment* is the process of presenting an undesirable or noxious stimulus, or removing a positive, desirable stimulus, to decrease the probability that a particular preceding response will recur.   **p. 185**

## KEY VARIABLES IN OPERANT CONDITIONING

### What are the most important variables affecting operant conditioning?

> The most important variables affecting operant conditioning are the strength, timing, and frequency of consequences. Strong consequences delivered quickly yield high work rates. However, consequences do not have to be continuous. Studies of schedules of consequences, especially of reinforcement, have shown that consequences can be intermittent. *Fixed-interval* and *variable-interval schedules* provide reinforcement after fixed or variable time periods. *Fixed-ratio* and *variable-ratio schedules* provide reinforcement after fixed or variable amounts of work. Variable-ratio schedules produce the highest work rates, while fixed-interval schedules induce the lowest work rates.   **pp. 189–192**

### Distinguish between extrinsic and intrinsic motivation.

> Psychologists have shown that reinforcement (extrinsic motivation) is effective in establishing and maintaining behaviour. However, some behaviours are intrinsically motivated; they are performed because they are pleasurable in themselves. Behavioural regulation theorists assume that organisms make choices and that, if possible, they will engage in the activities that seem optimal to them. If they are prevented from performing a desired activity, they will readjust their activities.   **pp. 194–195**

## THE BIOLOGY THAT UNDERPINS LEARNING

### Are learning theory and evolution incompatible?

> Evolutionary theory does not mean, nor demand, genetic determinism. Genetically determined tendencies are modified by learning and so evolutionary theory recognizes differences in societies and distinct, even unique, learning patterns.   **p. 196**

### What is a reverberating circuit?

> Hebb argued that certain groups of neurons act together, and their synaptic transmissions form a recurring pattern—he referred to such a group of coordinated neurons as a reverberating circuit. The evolution of a temporary neural circuit into a more permanent circuit is known as consolidation.   **pp. 196–197**

## COGNITIVE LEARNING

### What is the focus of cognitive learning psychologists?

> Cognitive learning psychologists focus on thinking processes and on thought that helps process, establish, and maintain learning. Some of the early studies focused on insight and latent learning. When you discover relationships between a series of events, psychologists say that you have had an insight. *Latent learning* is learning that occurs in the absence of any direct reinforcement and that is not necessarily demonstrated in any observable behaviour, though it has occurred and has the potential of being exhibited.   **pp. 197–199**

### What fundamental assumptions do observational learning theorists make about the learning process?

> *Observational learning theory* (also called social learning theory) suggests that organisms learn new responses by observing the behaviour of a model and then imitating it. Observational learning theory has expanded the range of behaviours that can be explained by learning theorists and focuses on the role of thought in establishing and maintaining behaviour.   **pp. 200–202**
> Some key variables in observational learning are the type and power of the model, the learner's personality and degree of independence, and the situations in which people find themselves.   **p. 202**

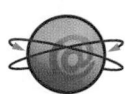

Take advantage of the multimedia resources available with this text! Follow the marginal icons to access the interactive modules on the *HandsOnPsych* CD-ROM; log on to *MyPsychLab* to explore the ebook, study aids, and other online resources; and visit the Companion Website at **www.pearsoned.ca/lefton** for additional exercises and links.

CHAPTER

# 6  Memory

With the exception of those times when you are struggling to re-call an important study or theory to answer an exam question, you may not think much about the central role that memory plays in how you experience, organize, and live your life. However, your memory gets you through the day by keeping track of your ap-pointments, your belongings, and even your identity. If you have any doubts about the importance of memory, consider a few case studies of people with memory problems.

Is it possible to have too much memory? What if you re-membered absolutely everything you saw or heard? Perhaps writ-ing exams might be easier, but there could be a real downside, too. "S," a patient studied by Luria and written about in his book *The Mind of the Mnemonist* (1968), was unable to forget. Even days, months, or years after hearing them, S could remember very long lists of words, letters, or numbers, and could state cor-rectly what he had been wearing and where he had been sitting when he first heard the lists. He could not, however, distinguish between trivial and significant information (Turkington, 1996). Everything he heard or read created vivid images in his mind that helped him recall simple information but, for example, made reading books virtually impossible. The first part of a sentence would create one image but the end of the same sentence would suggest another image; this would cause him to start reading the sentence again or risk missing the meaning of the sentence en-tirely. Finally overwhelmed, S spent the final years of his life in a mental hospital. It could be said that he had too much memory.

What about the opposite case, when memory falls short of what it should be? Imagine what life would be like if you were similar to "H. M." In an attempt to control severe seizures asso-ciated with extreme epilepsy, surgeons removed the hippocam-pus and several related structures from each side of H. M.'s brain. As a result, H. M. suffers from severe memory problems (Milner, Corkin, & Teuber, 1968; Corkin, 1984). He cannot add new information to his long-term memory. That is, he remembers clearly all that he knew before the surgery but he is unable to store any new memories. This leaves him with a sense that the world is moving on without him. He describes his condition as being "dead but alive." He can experience new events but cannot remember them. As a consequence his identity, his life, and his world effectively have stopped in time, and yet even that fact is only vaguely available to him.

The central role of memory to identity and functioning also is abundantly clear in the case of people suffering from Alzheimer's disease. Alzheimer's attacks the brain mechanisms that store memories; as the disease progresses patients gradually lose more and more of their memories, and consequently more and more of their identities. The particular tragedy of this disorder is that its onset is usually so gradual that patients can clearly notice and track its early progress and effects.

Memory is the means by which we store not only our experiences but our reactions to those experiences. We keep track of who we are through our storehouse of memories. So, with the importance of memory clearly in mind, let us look at how memory has been studied by psychologists.

**MEMORY**

The ability to remember past events, images, ideas, or previously learned information or skills; the storage system that allows for retention and retrieval of previously learned information.

Psychologists have long recognized that recalling well-learned facts sometimes can be difficult. Even though something has been *learned*, it may not always be *remembered*. You might easily remember the words to "O Canada," for example, but forget the name of someone you were introduced to last weekend at a friend's house. From Chapter 5, recall that learning is a *relatively* permanent change in an organism that occurs as a result of experience; this change is often, but not always, seen in overt behaviour. **Memory** is the ability to remember past events, images, ideas, or previously learned information or skills; it is also the storage system that allows a person to retain and retrieve previously learned information. Memory allows you to store information and to retrieve it. You may learn something, but this knowledge does you little good without the aid of memory and your ability to reconstruct the past.

## Memory: The Brain as Information Processor

Some people tell you that they have a good memory; others tell you that their memory is failing them; still others—often politicians who are being questioned—tell you that they just can't remember. Memory is not a thing you can weigh; it is not found in one small corner of the brain, with some people having more and others having less of it. Rather, memory is an ability and a process, and it is studied from many different perspectives. Traditionally, psychologists have examined memory solely from a psychological/behavioural perspective, focusing on issues such as what is remembered and what affects memory. Early memory studies at the turn of the twentieth century focused on how quickly people learned lists of nonsense words and how long they remembered them or how quickly they forgot them. Early physiological psychologists likened the brain to a huge map with certain areas that code vision, others that code auditory events, and still others that code, analyze, and store memory. Their goal was to discover the spatial layout of the brain and to see how the brain operated. Studies in the post–Second World War era became more practical, focusing on variables such as how the organization of material might affect retention and forgetting. Today, research is focusing on how people code information and use memory aids, imagery, and other learning cues to retrieve information from memory. Researchers also are examining the neuroscience of memory and studying the variables and conditions that determine what is remembered and what is forgotten.

In this age of computers and information technology it is not surprising that researchers have likened the brain to a computer—an information processor—and this has guided their thinking about memory. In the 1960s and 1970s, when the

**Memory**

▼ Researchers have compared the brain to computers—both are information processing systems.

Information Age was still young, researchers began to recognize the brain's complex interconnections and processing abilities. Today, researchers know that the brain is far more complex than ever before thought. The truth is that human brains, of course, are not computers; nor do they work exactly as computers do. They make mistakes, and they are influenced by biological, environmental, and interpersonal events. Nevertheless, enough similarities exist between human brains and computers for psychologists to discuss learning and memory in terms of information processing.

Psychologists use the term *information processing* to refer to organizing, interpreting, and responding to incoming information in the environment in a meaningful way. The information processing approach typically describes and analyzes a sequence of steps or stages for key memory processes. This approach assumes that the stages and processes are separate, though related, and that each can be analyzed by scientific methods. Although psychologists once considered memory a step-by-step, linear process, today they recognize that many of these steps take place simultaneously, *in parallel*.

In virtually every approach to understanding memory that has been offered, rejected, or modified, researchers seem to agree that three key processes exist. The names of these processes derive from information technologies and will sound familiar to you if you know how computers work. The first process is *encoding*; in the second, data or information is placed in some type of *storage*, either temporarily or permanently; in the third, information is made available through a *retrieval* process. We will use this three-process approach to guide our discussion of memory. You will see that memory involves all three of these processes and that multiple activities take place in multiple memory stores—so that you may be retrieving some information while encoding other information. Memory does not always function linearly, with one step preceding another and not being used again.

# Encoding

If you travel to a foreign country you may find that you are able to manage reasonably well speaking only your own language. With help, you probably will be able to order food and make travel arrangements. However, your experience will be much better if you learn to speak the foreign language. To do this you have to be able to understand the language, and to respond in a meaningful way; this requires encoding.

In Chapter 3, we defined *coding* as the process whereby the perceptual system analyzes stimuli and converts them into electrical impulses. In the same way, the term *encoding* means getting information into the system to be processed, converting it into a usable form. The conversion of an experience into electrochemical energy, coding, is the first step of encoding and establishing a memory. In the language of memory, **encoding** is the organizing of information so that the nervous system can process it, much as a computer programmer writes code that the computer can understand. The sensory information can be of any type: visual, auditory, olfactory, and so on.

The role of *attention* is important for encoding (Brown & Craik, 2000). In general, *attention* refers to the process of directing mental effort to some features of the environment and not to others. People can focus their attention on one idea, one event, one person, or one memory task, or they can shift their attention among several tasks or events. Divided attention during encoding interferes with the process, and people who are forced to divide their attention during encoding tend to perform more poorly during retrieval; they experience a type of memory failure we can describe as encoding failure. Such failures are very common because many stimuli compete for a person's attention.

Researchers also want to know about processes that occur once information enters memory, for example, how a person recalls information so as to make

**ENCODING**

The organizing of information so that the nervous system can process it.

LEVELS-OF-PROCESSING APPROACH

A memory theory that suggests that the brain processes and encodes information in different ways, to different extents, and at different levels, depending on how shallow or how deep the degree of analysis.

inferences. Even the monitoring of one's own awareness and memory, a process called *metacognition*, has become a focus of research. We encode various kinds of information in a range of ways and to different extents. The type and extent of encoding affect what we remember.

## LEVELS OF PROCESSING

Does the human brain encode and process some information at a deeper, more complex level than it does other information? Do thinking processes depend on the depth of analysis? Research conducted at the University of Toronto by Fergus Craik and Robert Lockhart (1972) suggested that people encode and process stimuli in different ways, to different extents, and at different levels. Craik and Lockhart called their theory a **levels-of-processing approach**. They claimed that we process information in one of two ways: We process information in a *shallow*, or superficial way, coding words by repeating them or making a sensory judgment about them (for example, one might be in italics and another might be in bold). Alternatively, we can use a more effortful, or *deep processing*, route (for example, determining whether two words rhyme, such as *sister* and *mister*). We can increase the depth of processing by examining words for shared meaning (for example, *sister* and *sibling*) or by putting words together in a sentence (for example, *My favourite sibling is my sister Joyce.*) and so on. You can see how this works by examining the example in Figure 6.1. Follow either the first or second set of instructions depending on the first letter of your last name (as described in the instructions) then spend one minute examining the words as instructed. Wait three minutes. Without looking at the list look at the number of words you can recall.

If you followed the first set of instructions to examine these words while looking for the letters with curves versus straight lines, you will have focused on the shape of the letters, and you will have analyzed them in these more shallow, sensory terms. If you followed the instructions to try to understand what property the words had in common, you would have done a more effortful type of analysis, which relates to the meaning and properties of the words. The second type of instructions made you encode, analyze, and store the words at a deeper level. If you analyzed in depth, you probably remembered most of the words on the list. However, if you used a more shallow approach, you likely did not remember more than a few words on the list. According to this view of encoding, how information is processed determines how it will be stored for later retrieval.

Cognitive psychologists began to equate the level of processing with the degree or depth of analysis involved. When the level of processing becomes more complex, they theorized, the code goes deeper into memory. Thus, the memory for the lines and angles of the letters may be fleeting and short-lived, the memory for the words themselves may last longer, and the memory for the meaning of the words may last longest. You can demonstrate a second effect of this last type of processing for yourself later in this chapter (p. 234).

Encoding is not a discrete step that happens all at once, before memory stores information. Rather, some levels of encoding happen quickly and easily, whereas other levels take longer and continue for some time. You may continue to encode information while other data are being stored. According to Craik and Lockhart, encoding in various memory levels involves different operations, and memory features are stored in different ways and for different durations.

The levels-of-processing approach generated an enormous amount of research. It explained why some information, such as your family history, is retained for long periods, and other information, such as the dry cleaner's phone number, is quickly forgotten. It also showed that when people are asked to encode information in only one way, they do not encode it in other ways. Thus, when people are not asked to encode words for meaning, but simply to memorize or quickly repeat them (for example, to remember a list of items to buy at the supermarket), they can recall very few of them later.

However, some researchers did not fully accept the levels-of-processing approach, which dealt primarily with establishing memory. These researchers suggested that recall differences originate from how memories are elaborated on or made distinctive. For example, the link between encoding and the later process of retrieval is explained by the **encoding specificity principle**, which asserts that the effectiveness of a specific retrieval cue depends on how well it matches up with the originally encoded information. The more sharply your retrieval cues are defined and the more closely they are paired with memory stores, the better your recall will be and the less likely you will be to experience retrieval failures. For example, students usually recognize their professors on campus but sometimes fail to recognize them if they happen to meet them in the grocery store. In such cases students are experiencing a retrieval error because their professors are not in a context that matches the type of encoding the student has already done.

Deriving from the encoding specificity principle is the idea of **transfer-appropriate processing**, which occurs when the initial processing of information is similar to the process of retrieval. When there is a close relationship between encoding and retrieval in terms of the modality of information (whether it is visual, auditory, or in some other form) and the processing required, retrieval is enhanced. Researchers have given participants instructions to encode words either for sound or for meaning; if a participant codes for sound but is then asked to recall meaning, recall is far less extensive than if they are asked to encode for sound and to recall sound (Franks et al., 2000; Morris, Bransford, & Franks, 1977; Rajaram, Srinivas, & Roediger, 1998).

The levels-of-processing research and its subsequent refinements and extensions shape the way cognitive researchers think about memory. These researchers argue that the way information is encoded relates to how it is stored, processed, and later recalled. They are aware that encoding processes are flexible; they are affected by both the cues provided and the demands of the retrieval tasks. The processes of encoding are also affected by preconceived biases people have; humans tend to notice and encode information that confirms beliefs they already hold—a tendency

> *Take Home Tip*
> ## FOR THE ACTIVE LEARNER
> When you study for a test, you should study in the same way you will be tested. If a test will be in essay format, study by writing essays rather than by underlining text. If a test will consist of geometry problem sets, study by doing problem sets rather than studying proofs or principles.

called *confirmation bias* (Jonas et al., 2001). This tendency to "see what you expect to see" is a powerful force in allowing people to retain inaccurate beliefs.

## NEUROSCIENCE AND ENCODING

Memories are retained in electrochemical form in the brain. Researchers are exploring the neurobiological bases of memory: How does the brain store memories? Where are memories stored? Are memory traces localized or distributed? Researchers using positron emission tomography (PET) techniques (described in Chapter 2) are studying the location, extent, and timing of processing in the brain as it occurs. We will explore the neuroscience approach to memory in more detail later in this chapter.

As shown in Figure 6.2, the frontal lobes constitute about one-third of the brain; the prefrontal lobes with their overlying cortex are the large areas on the left

ENCODING SPECIFICITY PRINCIPLE

The notion that the effectiveness of a specific retrieval cue depends on how well it matches up with the originally encoded information.

TRANSFER-APPROPRIATE PROCESSING

Initial processing of information that is similar in modality or type to the processing necessary in the retrieval task.

**FIGURE 6.1**
**For the Active Learner: Levels of Processing**

*If your last name begins with one of the letters A through K:* Examine the following list of words, counting the number of letters with only curves (such as C and S) versus the number of letters with only straight lines (such as K and N). Do not count letters with a combination of curved and straight lines (such as B and R).

*If your last name begins with one of the letters L through Z:* Examine the following list of words, analyzing their meaning and trying to determine any possible relationships among them.

FINGERPRINTS
INVESTIGATION
SUSPECT
NEWSPAPER
MIDNIGHT
ATTORNEY
NEPHEW
MOTIVE
ARREST
INHERITANCE
KITCHEN

## Be an ACTIVE LEARNER

**REVIEW**

> What are the key assumptions of the information processing approach to memory? pp. 208–209

> What is the underlying assumption of the levels-of-processing approach? pp. 210–211

**THINK CRITICALLY**

> Much of the research on encoding as a factor in retrieval has been done on memory for verbal information. How might encoding as a factor in retrieval apply to memory for skills and motor performance?

**APPLY PSYCHOLOGY**

> What changes would you have to make in your study strategies to allow the encoding specificity principle to improve your studying?

and right at the very front of the brain, behind the forehead. The drive to understand the roles of specific brain areas began years ago, but only recently have researchers identified specific memory functions of the prefrontal cortex. Canadian Endel Tulving and his colleagues at the Rotman Research Institute showed that the left prefrontal cortex is used more in *encoding* of new information into memory, whereas the right prefrontal cortex is involved more in memory *retrieval* (Nyberg, Cabeza, & Tulving, 1996; Tulving et al., 1994). Research using PET and fMRI imaging shows that when participants engage in various tasks, left and right brain scans are quite different—that is, there is different blood flow in different portions of the prefrontal cortex (Courtney et al., 1998; Craik et al., 1999).

Researchers have long known that the temporal lobes of the cerebral cortex are related to memory (Squire & Kandel, 1999), and brain imaging studies have furnished more specific knowledge of how the temporal lobes interact with other brain structures. An fMRI study demonstrated that the posterior (back) part of the medial (middle) temporal lobes are activated during the encoding process, but a different part of the temporal lobes becomes active during retrieval (Gabrieli et al., 1997). This research provides neurological confirmation that encoding and retrieval are different processes with different underlying brain centres.

Researchers have also examined the pattern of brain activation during encoding by using PET imaging and have found that encoding activated the medial temporal lobe (Anderson et al., 2000). In addition, the left prefrontal cortex became active, but this activation was not the same for all participants—older adults showed some different brain activation, which may be related to their decreased encoding ability and memory problems.

## Storage

Suppose a friend of yours goes to school in Europe for a year and stores all of his possessions in your spare closet. He stacks box upon box in your closet and labels each one. He numbers the boxes and develops a master list that he posts on the closet door. You are informed that if he needs anything he will have a copy of the master list, and you will be able to access his books, tapes, and clothes very easily. Your friend has developed an elaborate storage system.

**FIGURE 6.2**

**Areas of the Brain Involved in Encoding**

The prefrontal cortex and the temporal lobes are involved in the process of encoding.

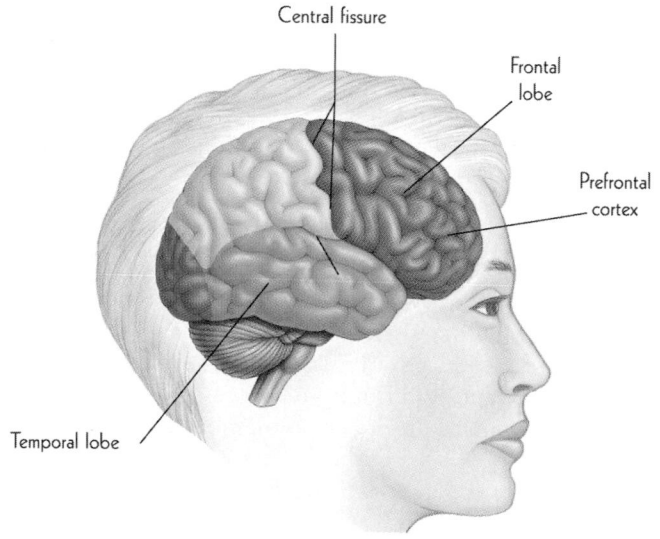

Central fissure

Frontal lobe

Prefrontal cortex

Temporal lobe

**Storage** is the process of maintaining or keeping information readily available; it also refers to the locations where information is held, which researchers call *memory stores*. The duration of storage may be a few seconds or many years, but if people have access to information they no longer sense, then memory is involved. For example, if you look up a telephone number, go to the telephone, and dial the number while no longer looking at it, then memory is involved, even if only for seconds.

Researchers have conceptualized a three-stage model for memory storage: (1) sensory memory, (2) short-term storage, and (3) long-term memory. *Sensory memory* is a very brief storage based on the sensory systems. When you hear a song, see a photograph, or touch a piece of silk, sensory memory starts. This very brief storage allows for attention and coding processes to begin. Information from sensory memory may pass into *short-term storage*, which is limited both in how long information can stay and how much information can fit. This storage is similar to a computer's random access memory (RAM), holding information for processing. Another similarity between your memory and your computer's RAM is fragility—information in short-term storage is easily lost, just as it is when the electricity goes off unexpectedly in your computer. Similarly, if you look up a telephone number but do not dial it immediately, you quickly lose that information. In a computer, information is stored for longer periods of time on the hard disk or on a floppy disk. In the brain, information is stored in *long-term memory*, from which a person can recall, retrieve, and reconstruct previous experiences.

## SENSORY MEMORY

As George Sperling demonstrated in the early 1960s, **sensory memory,** or the *sensory register*, performs initial encoding and provides brief storage of stimuli. The brief image of a stimulus appears the way lightning does on a dark evening: The lightning flashes and you retain a brief visual image of it. In his experiments, Sperling (1960) briefly presented research participants with a visual display consisting of three rows of letters, which they saw for only a fraction of a second. He asked the participants to recite the letters, and they typically responded by reciting three or four letters from the first row. This limit for their performance suggests that they record only three or four items in their sensory register. However, when he cued them (with a tone that varied for each row), Sperling found that participants were able to recall three out of four letters from any of the rows. This result suggests that the sensory register records a complete picture. When Sperling delayed the cue signalling which row to report, recall decreased, which suggests that sensory memory fades very rapidly (see Figure 6.3).

From Sperling's studies and others that followed, researchers concluded that we have a brief (250 milliseconds, or 0.25 second), rapidly fading sensory visual memory. Although some researchers have challenged the existence and physiological basis of sensory memory (Sakitt & Long, 1979), most researchers still see it as the first stage of encoding (Healy & McNamara, 1996).

Sensory memory captures a visual, auditory, or chemical stimulus (such as an odour) into a form the brain can interpret. Consider the visual system. Initial coding usually contains information in the form of a picture. Sensory memory establishes the visual stimulus in an electrical or neural

STORAGE

The process of maintaining or keeping information available; it also refers to the locations of memory, which researchers call "memory stores."

SENSORY MEMORY

The mechanism that performs initial encoding and brief storage of stimuli. Also known as the *sensory register*.

▼ When lightning flashes, you retain a brief visual image of it in sensory memory.

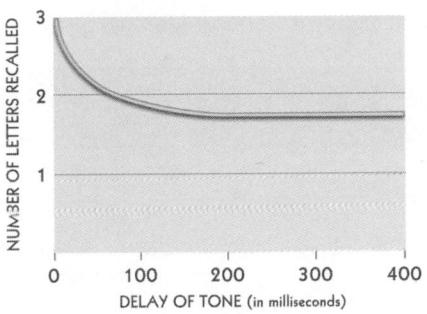

A display like this was presented briefly. Then a tone of varying pitch told the participant which row of four letters to report.

X B D F
M P Z G
L C N H

**FIGURE 6.3**

**Sperling's Discovery of a Visual Sensory Memory**

The graph plots participants' accuracy in reporting a specified row of letters. At best, participants recalled about three out of the four letters in a row. As the tone was delayed, the accuracy of recall decreased. However, note that there were no further decreases in accuracy when the tone was delayed more than 200 milliseconds. *(Based on data from Sperling, 1960, p. 11.)*

NUMBER OF LETTERS RECALLED

3

2

1

0    100    200    300    400

DELAY OF TONE (in milliseconds)

form and stores it for 0.25 second with little interpretation, in an almost photographic manner. This visual sensory memory is sometimes called an *icon*, and the storage mechanism is called *iconic storage*. For the auditory system, the storage mechanism is called *echoic storage*; it stores an auditory representation for about three seconds.

Sensory memory is temporary and extremely fragile. Once information is established there, it must be transferred elsewhere for additional encoding and storage or it will be lost. For example, when you locate a phone number you need in a rapidly scrolling computer display, it is established in visual sensory memory (iconic storage). However, unless you quickly transfer the phone number to short-term working memory by writing it down, repeating it over and over to yourself, or elaborating on it by associating it with something else in your memory, you will forget it. Building Table 6.1 summarizes the key processes in sensory memory.

## SHORT-TERM WORKING MEMORY

Once captured in sensory memory, stimuli either fade or are transferred to a second stage—short-term storage. Initially, researchers spoke of *short-term memory*, to emphasize its brief duration. After extensive research, however, the nature of short-term storage became clearer, and researchers began to recognize its active nature, giving it the term *working memory*. Both terms apply to the brief, fragile storage that occurs between sensory memory and long-term memory, but people who use the term *short-term memory* have a slightly different conceptualization of that storage from those who use the term *working memory* (Baddeley, 2000; Kail & Hall, 2001). We use the term *short-term storage* as a general term to refer to this type of brief memory; we use the terms *short-term memory* and *working memory* to refer to research on those specific topics.

**EARLY RESEARCH ON SHORT-TERM MEMORY.** Thousands of studies were done on the components and characteristics of storage in short-term memory. Early research focused on its duration, its capacity, and its relationship to rehearsal.

Researchers had been studying memory and retrieval for decades, but it was not until 1959 that Lloyd and Margaret Peterson presented experimental evidence for the existence of short-term memory. In a laboratory study, the Petersons asked participants to recall a three-consonant sequence, such as *xbd*, after varying intervals. During the interval participants were required to count backward by threes to prevent them from repeating (rehearsing) the consonant sequence. Figure 6.4 presents their results. As the interval between presentation and recall increased, accuracy of recall decreased until it fell to levels that could have been due to chance. The Petersons' experiment, like many others that followed, showed that information contained in short-term memory is available for less than 20 to 30 seconds at most. After that, the information must be transferred to long-term memory or it will be lost.

**Memory**

**FIGURE 6.4**
**Results of Peterson and Peterson's Classic Experiment**

Peterson and Peterson (1959) found that when they delayed the report of three-letter syllables by having subjects count backward, accuracy of recall decreased over the first 18 seconds.

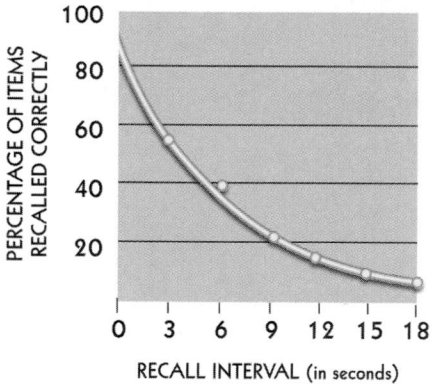

| BUILDING TABLE 6.1 | Key Processes in Sensory Memory | | | | |
|---|---|---|---|---|---|
| Stage | Encoding | Storage | Retrieval | Duration | Forgetting |
| Sensory Memory | Visual or auditory (iconic or echoic storage). | Brief, fragile, and temporary. | Information is extracted from stimulus presentation and transferred to short-term memory. | Visual: 250 milliseconds; auditory: about 3 seconds. | Rapid decay of information; interference is possible if a new stimulus is presented. |

In 1956, George Miller argued that human beings can retain about seven (plus or minus two) items in short-term memory. The number of items a person can produce from short-term memory is the **memory span**. However, what constitutes an "item" is not consistent. For example, a person can recall about five letters, about five words, and about five sentences. Therefore, people can group information in ways that expand short-term memory capacity. The groupings are called **chunks**—manageable and meaningful units of information organized in a familiar way for easy encoding, storage, and retrieval. Short-term memory will hold one or two chunks. Many people remember their social insurance number in three chunks and their telephone number in two chunks. Chunks can be organized on the basis of meaning, past events, associations, perception, rhythm, or some arbitrary strategy devised by a learner to help encode large amounts of data (Brown & Craik, 2000). Research has confirmed the widespread occurrence of chunking and the use of seven plus or minus two units of information per chunk (Baddeley, 1994). Determining what constitutes a chunk is sometimes difficult, though, because what is perceptually or cognitively grouped together by one individual may be grouped differently by other individuals.

Researchers agree that a key operation—rehearsal—is especially important in memory. Rehearsal usually involves more than simply repeating information to prevent it from fading. **Rehearsal** is the process of verbalizing, thinking about, or otherwise acting on or transforming information in order to keep it active in memory. Psychologists distinguish two important types of rehearsal: maintenance and elaborative. **Maintenance rehearsal** is the repetition of information with little or no interpretation. This shallow form of rehearsal involves the physical stimulus, not its underlying meaning. It generally occurs just after initial encoding has taken place—for example, when you repeat a phone number just long enough to dial it. **Elaborative rehearsal** involves repetition plus analysis, in which the stimulus may be associated with other events and further processed; elaboration links a stimulus to other information. When a shopper attempts to remember the things he needs to purchase to make dinner, he may organize them in a meaningful pattern, such as the order of the aisles in the supermarket. Elaborative rehearsal, when information is made personally meaningful, is especially important in the encoding processes. This type of rehearsal allows information to be transferred into longer-term memory. Maintenance rehearsal alone usually is not sufficient for information to be permanently stored. In general, information held in short-term memory is either transferred to long-term memory or lost.

## FOR THE ACTIVE LEARNER

The chunking memory technique works well with numbers, letters, and words, as you have read. However, it can also be effective in remembering ideas, which you can also group together. For example, if you were studying for a test on this chapter, you could "chunk together" a list of factors that increase recall, to help you remember them on test day. Another chunk might be factors that contribute to forgetting.

Maintenance rehearsal is adequate to keep information active in memory, but elaborative rehearsal allows information to be transferred to long-term memory.

MEMORY SPAN

The limited number of items a person can reproduce from usually one or two chunks.

CHUNKS

Manageable and meaningful units of information that can be easily encoded, stored, and retrieved

REHEARSAL

The process of verbalizing, thinking about, or otherwise acting on or transforming information in order to keep it active in memory.

MAINTENANCE REHEARSAL

The repetition of information with little or no interpretation.

ELABORATIVE REHEARSAL

Involves repetition and analysis, in which the stimulus may be associated with (linked to) other information and further processed.

**THE EMERGENCE OF WORKING MEMORY.** Until the 1970s, psychologists used the term *short-term memory* to refer to memory that lasts for less than a minute. In the 1970s researchers Alan Baddely and Graham Hitch (1974, 1994) began to

**215**

**WORKING MEMORY**

The storage mechanism that temporarily holds current or recently attended-to information for immediate or short-term use and that is composed of several subsystems: a component to encode and rehearse auditory information, a visual–spatial "scratch pad," and a central processing mechanism, or executive, that balances and controls information flow.

**LONG-TERM MEMORY**

The storage mechanism that keeps a relatively permanent record of information.

**Memory**

reconceptualize short-term memory as a more complex type of brief storage they called *working memory*. Their model contains several substructures operating simultaneously to maintain information while it is being processed. Earlier, psychologists often concentrated on single memory tasks, trying to understand each of the components in encoding, storage, and retrieval. However, the concept of working memory goes beyond individual stages to describe the active integration of both conscious processes (such as repetition) and unconscious processes. This model of memory emphasizes how human memory meets the demands of real-life conscious mental activities such as listening to the radio, reading, or mentally calculating the sum of 74 and 782.

**Working memory** is the storage mechanism that temporarily holds current or recent information for immediate or short-term use. In working memory, information is not simply stored; it is further encoded, and then maintained for about 20 to 30 seconds while active processing takes place. A person may decide that a specific piece of information is important; if the information is complicated or lengthy, the person will need to rehearse it actively to keep it in working memory. As we saw earlier, *rehearsal* is the process of repeatedly verbalizing, thinking about, or otherwise acting on or transforming information in order to keep it in memory.

The addition of new information also may *interfere* with the recall of other information in working memory. Baddeley and Hitch (1974) demonstrated the limited capabilities of several components, or subsystems, of working memory by having participants recall digits while doing some other type of reasoning task. If one subsystem is given a demanding task, the performance of the others will suffer. One subsystem in working memory encodes, rehearses, and holds auditory information such as a person's name or phone number. Another subsystem is a visual–spatial scratch pad or blackboard, which stores visual and spatial information, such as the appearance and location of objects, for a brief time and then is erased to allow new information to be stored. A third subsystem is a central processing mechanism, something like an executive, that balances the information flow and allows people to solve problems and make decisions. This executive controls the processing flow and adjusts it when necessary. Research shows that the type of information being processed by working memory affects the accuracy of the processing (Kruley, Sciama, & Glenberg, 1994).

Figure 6.5 illustrates the now widely accepted view of short-term memory as working memory. Building Table 6.2 summarizes the key processes in the first two stages of memory.

## LONG-TERM MEMORY

Information such as names, faces, dates, places, smells, and events—both important and trivial—can be found in a relatively permanent form in **long-term memory**. The duration of information in long-term memory is indefinite; much of it lasts a lifetime. The capacity for long-term memory is seemingly infinite; the more information a person acquires, the easier it is to acquire further information. Using the library analogy again, we can say that long-term memory includes all of the books in the library's collection. However, as in a library, information can be lost ("misshelved") or unavailable for some other reason.

A wide variety of information is stored in long-term memory—for example, the words to "O Canada," the meaning of the word *sanguine*, how to operate a CD player, the place where your psychology class meets, and what you did to celebrate your high-school graduation. Different types of information seem to be stored and called on in different ways. On this basis, psychologists have made a number of distinctions among the types of memory.

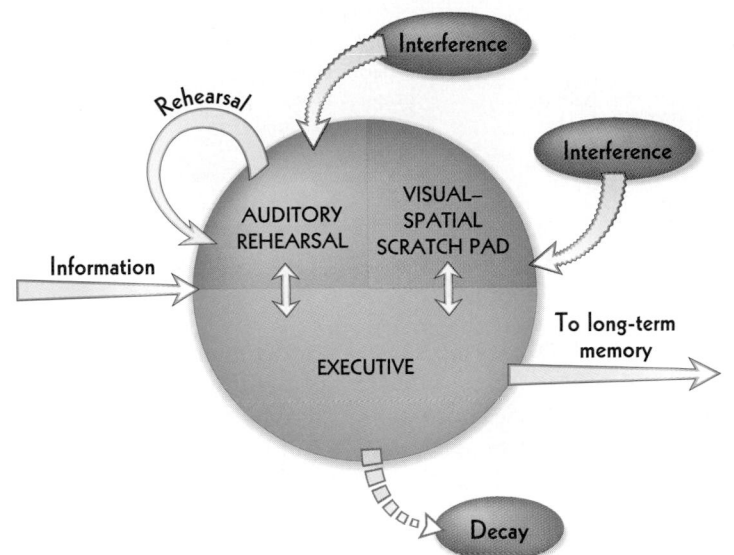

FIGURE 6.5
**Short-term Working
Memory**

In short-term working memory,
active processing occurs.
Information is assumed to be held
in a visual–spatial scratch pad and
transferred back to an executive, or
central processing mechanism.
Meanwhile, auditory information is
in a rehearsal loop.

**PROCEDURAL AND DECLARATIVE MEMORY.** **Procedural memory** is memory for skills, including the perceptual, motor, and cognitive skills required to complete complex tasks (see Figure 6.6). Driving a car, in-line skating, or cooking a meal involves a series of steps that include perceptual, motor, and cognitive skills—and thus procedural memory. Acquiring such skills is usually time-consuming and difficult at first; but once the skills are learned, they are relatively permanent and automatic. **Declarative memory** is memory for specific information, such as who Ralph Klein is (the premier of Alberta), which member of the group REM left the band (drummer Bill Berry), and the meaning of the word *sanguine* (hopeful and confident). Declarative memories may be established quickly, but the information is more likely to be forgotten over time than is the information in procedural memory. Not all declarative memories are the same, and some researchers subdivide declarative memory into episodic and semantic memory.

PROCEDURAL MEMORY
Memory for skills, including the perceptual, motor, and cognitive skills required to complete complex tasks.

DECLARATIVE MEMORY
Memory for specific information.

**BUILDING TABLE 6.2    Key Processes in the First Two Stages of Memory**

| Stage | Encoding | Storage | Retrieval | Duration | Forgetting |
|---|---|---|---|---|---|
| Sensory Memory | Visual or auditory (iconic or echoic storage). | Brief, fragile, and temporary. | Information is extracted from stimulus presentation and transferred to short-term memory. | Visual: 250 milliseconds; auditory: about 3 seconds. | Rapid decay of information; interference is possible if a new stimulus is presented. |
| Short-term Working Memory | Visual and auditory. | Repetitive rehearsal maintains information in storage, perhaps on a visual–auditory "scratch pad" where further encoding can take place. | Maintenance and elaborative rehearsal can keep information available for retrieval; retrieval is enhanced through elaboration and further encoding. | No more than 30 seconds, probably less than 20 seconds; depends on specific task and stimuli. | Interference and decay affect memory; new stimulation causes rapid loss of information unless it is especially important. |

FIGURE 6.6
Procedural and Declarative
Long-term Memory

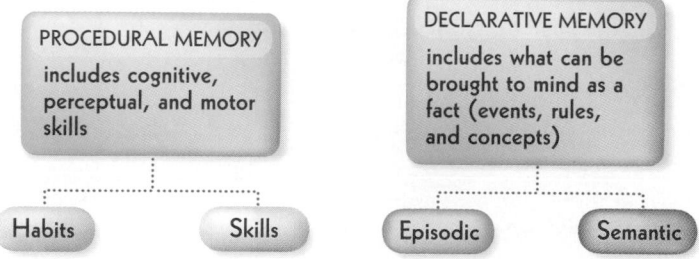

EPISODIC [ep-ih-SAW-dick]
MEMORY

Memory of specific personal events
and situations (episodes), tagged
with information about time.

SEMANTIC MEMORY

Memory of ideas, rules, words, and
general concepts about the world.

EXPLICIT MEMORY

Conscious memory that a person is
aware of, such as a memory of a
word in a list or an event that
occurred in the past.

IMPLICIT MEMORY

Memory a person is not aware of
possessing; considered an almost
unconscious process, implicit
memory occurs almost
automatically.

**EPISODIC AND SEMANTIC MEMORY.** **Episodic memory** is memory of specific personal events and situations (episodes), tagged with information about time. An episodic memory includes where, when, and how you obtained the information, plus chronological dating or tagging, so you know the sequence of events within your episodic memory. Examples include having breakfast this morning, the movie you saw last night, and what you did on holiday two summers ago. Episodic memory is often highly detailed: You may recall not only the plot of the movie you saw last night and who starred in it, but also the temperature of the theatre, the smell of the popcorn, what you were wearing, who accompanied you, and many other details of the experience.

Episodic memory about ourselves—our own personal story—can be termed *autobiographical memory*. In some sense, we *are* our autobiographical memories; we need these memories to construct a personal view of self (Fivush, 2001). People's autobiographical memories can last for many years (Neisser & Libby, 2000); when autobiographical memory is lost, people lose some of their personal sense of self. This type of long-term memory storage is durable and fairly easy to access if a helpful retrieval cue, such as a smell associated with the event, is available. These memories are also subject to a variety of distortions (which we will consider in a later section). A defining characteristic of autobiographical memories is their organization by temporal markers, such as what happened the summer after you graduated from high school (Shum, 1998).

**Semantic memory** is memory for ideas, rules, words, and general concepts about the world. It is your personal, generalized knowledge, based on a set of concepts about the world, about previous events, experiences, and learned information. It is not time-specific; it refers to knowledge that may have been gathered over days or weeks, and it continues to be modified and expanded over a lifetime. Your knowledge of what a typical horse looks like comes from semantic memory; knowledge of your last encounter with a horse is episodic memory. Semantic memory develops earlier in childhood than does episodic memory (Tulving, 1993; Wheeler, 2000).

▼ Procedural memory includes
motor skills such as skating.

**EXPLICIT AND IMPLICIT MEMORY.** **Explicit memory** is conscious memory that a person is aware of, such as a memory of a word in a list or an event that occurred in the past; most of the memory tasks we have been looking at require explicit recall of information. Both semantic and episodic memory are explicit, consisting of voluntary, active memory store. When you tap semantic memory, you are accessing explicit memory. In contrast, **implicit memory** is memory a person is not aware that he or she possesses; considered an almost unconscious process, implicit memory is accessed almost automatically and unintentionally.

For example, you may remember things that you are supposed to remember (explicit memories), but you are also likely to recall things you did not deliberately attempt to learn—the colour of a book you are studying or the name of the book's publisher, the size of a piece of cake you were served, or perhaps the make of a computer in the office of a professor you have visited (implicit memories). Implicit memory occurs without conscious awareness; it demonstrates that people can learn without intentional effort (Boronat & Logan, 1997), and that what they learn explicitly and how they are asked to recall it may affect their implicit memories (Nelson, McKinney, & Gee, 1998). Lending physiological support to the explicit/implicit distinction is the finding that these memory stores seem to be found in different locations in the brain (Fleischman et al., 1997).

The distinction between explicit and implicit memory adds another dimension to researchers' understanding of long-term memory, suggesting that memory storage is varied and complex. These distinctions also suggest that these different types of memory may have differing representations in the brain and that the functioning of one system is independent of others. (*Brain and Behaviour* discusses the impact of Alzheimer's disease on various memory systems.)

**PRACTICE.** Obviously, practice is a factor in storage, but research indicates that the *timing* of practice is an important factor. Data indicate that distributing the total number of practice hours over a number of sessions is more effective than practising for the same amount of time in a single block. Researchers have learned that the effectiveness of distributed practice depends on many variables, including the method, order, and speed of presentation. Distributed practice is especially effective for perceptual motor skills, where eye–hand coordination is important.

## NEUROSCIENCE AND STORAGE

Using both PET and fMRI, researchers can now identify the neural machinery that underlies brain functions, and some of the most exciting research involves studies of the neural activity and brain locations associated with working memory. The visual–spatial scratch pad of working memory is embodied physically in the brain. When Smith and colleagues (1995) had participants engage in either a spatial memory task or an object memory task, the spatial task activated only right-hemisphere prefrontal regions, whereas the object task activated primarily left-hemisphere regions. In later research, Smith (1997) found different working memory subsystems for spatial, object, and verbal information. Further, other researchers (Gabrieli et al., 1997; Jonides et al., 1997) showed that as a working memory task grew more difficult, participants' brain scans became more active, especially in the prefrontal cortex. This and other results (Nyberg & Cabeza, 2000) suggest that the prefrontal cortex may be the place where this coordinating, or executive, function of working memory is carried out.

One patient with brain damage has been very important in focusing attention on the brain mechanisms underlying the transition of information from short-term storage to long-term memory. Well-known Canadian psychologist Brenda Milner (1966) of McGill University reported the case of H. M. (already mentioned at the beginning of the chapter), a man whose brain was damaged as a result of surgery to control his epilepsy. His short-term storage was intact, but he was unable to form new long-term declarative memories. As long as H. M. was able to rehearse information and keep it in short-term storage, his recall performance was normal. However, as soon as he could no longer rehearse, his recall became poor. That is, his ability to shift information from short-term to long-term storage was impaired. (His procedural memory was not so severely affected, and he was able to learn new skills.) Milner's account of this case provides support for a neurological distinction between short-term

▲ Some time after you look at this photo, try to recall details about what is in it. You will probably discover that you remember things you noticed consciously (explicit memory), but you may also find that you recall information that you didn't consciously observe (implicit memory).

*Take Home Tip*
**FOR THE ACTIVE LEARNER**
When you study, distribute your practice and rehearsal over time. For optimum learning, you should study each subject for a relatively short period every day or every other day, instead of trying to cram all of your studying into one long session, right before a test. Distributing your study time instead of cramming will increase the amount of material you can learn and remember *without* increasing your total study time.

and long-term memory and focused researchers' attention on the role of the *hippocampus*, a brain structure in the temporal lobes. Subsequent research has shown that this brain structure is an important component in memory formation, especially the transfer of information from short-term to long-term storage (Zola & Squire, 2000).

The process of changing a temporary memory to a permanent one is called **consolidation**, and this concept plays an important role in one of the leading theories of neuroscience and storage. Canadian psychologist Donald Hebb (1904–1985) presented one of the major physiological theories of memory. Hebb (1949)

**CONSOLIDATION**
[kon-SOL-ih-DAY-shun]

The process of changing a short-term memory to a long-term one.

## BRAIN AND Behaviour

### The Aging Brain and Alzheimer's Disease

Will your memory decline as you get older? Is memory loss an inevitable consequence of aging? As people age, they often lose some memory abilities but not others. The largest problems come from storage of long-term episodic memories, but sensory memory and implicit memory tasks show little decline in healthy older people (Balota, Dolan, & Duchek, 2000). However, several diseases can devastate memory, and Alzheimer's disease is the most disastrous and, unfortunately, the most common.

Alzheimer's disease is a degenerative disease of the brain, and its diagnosis can only be confirmed after death, during an autopsy. An examination of neurons in the brain, especially in the medial temporal and frontal lobes, will show a pattern of neurofibrillary tangles (tangled bundles of neurons) as well as

a buildup of plaque (tissue that interferes with the functioning of neurons). The underlying cause of Alzheimer's disease is unknown, but one rare version is linked to a defective gene, and all versions may have some genetic involvement.

Problems with memory are the most prominent feature of Alzheimer's disease and the most common complaint among Alzheimer's patients (Hodges, 2000). The symptoms of early Alzheimer's disease include problems with forming new memories. This pattern is not surprising, considering the damage that is occurring to the medial temporal lobes and the hippocampus. People with more advanced Alzheimer's are unable to retrieve large areas of personal memory. They lose their past more completely than people with other types of memory loss.

The progress of Alzheimer's disease affects other parts of the brain, damaging other memory systems. Working memory is less affected than other memory systems, but intact working memory helps keep people functioning in the present, not the past. Alzheimer's patients typically have impairments in semantic memory, which means they forget items of general knowledge. This type of memory loss is more devastating than personal memory loss because it means that these individuals may forget important information they need to get along in the world, such as what keys are and what belongs in a kitchen. In addition, Alzheimer's disease can produce deficits in procedural memory, so patients may not only forget what a fork is but also how to eat. Other types of memory loss rarely affect procedural memory.

People with advanced Alzheimer's disease are unable to care for themselves and need constant attention. The population of Canada and many other industrialized countries is aging, and age is the leading risk factor for Alzheimer's disease. Few people younger than 65 are affected, but as many as 50 percent of those over age 85 are (Evans et al., 1989). Thus, this devastating disease may affect as many as 6 million people in North America by 2040.

suggested that when groups of neurons are stimulated, they form patterns of neural activity. When specific groups of neurons fire frequently, this activity establishes regular neural circuits through the process of consolidation. According to Hebb, this process must occur for short-term memory to become long-term memory. When key neurons and neurotransmitters are repeatedly stimulated by various events, those events may be better remembered and more easily accessed—this may be part of the reason that practised behaviours are so easily recalled (Kandel & Abel, 1995).

If a neuron is stimulated, the biochemical processes involved make it more likely to respond again later; this increase in responsiveness is referred to as *long-term potentiation*, a phenomenon that is especially evident in areas of the brain such as the hippocampus. In addition, clear evidence exists that specific protein synthesis occurs just after learning and that long-term memory depends on this synthesis (Squire & Kandel, 1999). Psychologists now generally accept the idea that the structure of synapses changes after learning, and especially after repeated learning experiences. As Hebb said, "Some memories are both instantaneously established and permanent. To account for the permanence, some structural change seems necessary" (1949, p. 62).

If the changes in the physical brain that form the basis for memory occur at the level of the synapse, then no one brain structure should be specifically associated with long-term memory. Researchers worked for years trying to find a structure in the cerebral cortex that formed the specific brain basis for memory. They failed. Although complete agreement has not been reached, many authorities now accept that memory is distributed throughout the brain rather than localized in one spot. As we have seen, structures in the medial temporal lobe, including the hippocampus, are critically important in forming long-term storage, but the temporal lobes are not the site of long-term memory (Markowitsch, 2000). Therefore, the picture of long-term memory in the brain is extremely complex. Memories are distributed over the cerebral cortex and even in lower brain structures, and their encoding and retrieval activate pathways that include the prefrontal cortex and the medial temporal lobes.

*Be an*
**ACTIVE LEARNER**

**REVIEW**
> What evidence shows that sensory memory is temporary and fragile? pp. 213–214
> How does the idea of working memory expand the initial concept of short-term memory? pp. 215–216
> What structures are important for memory storage in the brain? pp. 219–220

**THINK CRITICALLY**
> In terms of memory systems, why does reading a book about tennis not help your tennis game?
> Do you think it makes evolutionary or adaptive sense to have memory representations all over the brain? Or would it be better if memory were located in a specific place? Explain your reasoning.

**APPLY PSYCHOLOGY**
> Analyze how you typically study for tests, and compare your strategy to the recommendations from the research on storage in long-term memory. Then list some ways in which you could become a more effective learner.

# Retrieval

**Retrieval** is the process by which stored information is recovered from memory. Recalling your social insurance number, remembering the details of an assignment, and listing the names of all seven dwarfs from the fairy tale Snow White are retrieval tasks. A person may encode information quickly, deal with the information in working memory, and enter the information into long-term memory. But once information is coded and stored, the person must be able to retrieve the information and use it in a meaningful way. It turns out that the ability to retrieve information depends on how retention is measured and how the information is encoded and stored.

Some contemporary researchers assert that every memory is retained and available but that some memories are less accessible than others. Think once again of the library analogy: All of the books in the library are there, but some cannot be found (perhaps because they are misshelved), making retrieval difficult or impossible. When retrieval of information is blocked, that information is effectively forgotten.

**RETRIEVAL**

The process by which stored information is recovered from memory.

## MEASURES OF RETENTION

As teachers, we hope our students will be able to recall key ideas, recognize important concepts, reconstruct elements of our lectures, and be able to visualize key graphs and other images. We hope students will associate the facts in meaningful, personally relevant ways. But first, they have to be able to learn and access the information. Recall, recognition, reconstruction, and pictorial memory are all measures of *retention*. The most widely investigated measures of retention have been recall and recognition. *Recall* is remembering the details of a situation or idea and placing them together in a meaningful framework (usually without any cues or aids). Asking someone to name the make of the vehicle Princess Diana was riding in at the time of the fatal collision is a test of recall. *Recognition* is remembering whether one has seen a stimulus before—whether the stimulus is familiar. Asking someone whether the same vehicle was a Mercedes is a test of recognition. *Reconstruction* is the procedure of restoring a disrupted sequence of events (for example, a series of events in a person's history) to its original order. This is often aided by *pictorial memory*.

**RECALL.** In recall tasks, participants are asked to remember previously presented information. (Essay exams require you to recall information.) In experiments, the information usually comprises strings (or lists) of digits or letters. A typical study might ask participants to remember 10 nonsense syllables, which are presented one at a time on a screen every half-second. The participants then would have to repeat the list at the end of the five-second presentation period.

Three widely used recall tasks are free recall, serial recall, and paired associate tasks. In *free recall tasks*, participants can recall items in any order, much as you might recall the items on a grocery list. *Serial recall tasks* are more difficult; the items must be recalled in the order in which they were presented, as you would recall a telephone number. In *paired associate tasks*, participants are given a cue to help them recall the second half of a pair of items. In the learning phase of a study, the experimenter might pair the words *tree* and *shoe*. In the testing phase, participants would be presented with the word *tree* and would have to respond with the correct answer, *shoe*. People are amazingly good at such tasks; we recall groups of words, events, animals, and so forth together, which of course lends credence to the idea that information is contained in *semantic networks*, loosely related organization based on meaning.

**RECOGNITION.** In a multiple-choice test, you are asked to recognize relevant information. Psychologists have found that recognition tasks can help them measure subtle differences in memory ability better than recall tasks can. That's because, although a person may be unable to recall the associated details contained in a previously studied fact, he or she may recognize the fact. Asked to name the capital of Prince Edward Island, you would probably have a better chance of answering correctly if you were given four options: Halifax, Charlottetown, Sherbrooke, or Regina.

**RELEARNING.** *Relearning* focuses on the effects of repeated attempts to learn or better learn the information already partially in memory. The German philosopher, Hermann Ebbinghaus (see also p. 230), was the first person to investigate memory scientifically and systematically and was interested in how quickly people forget. He studied this question by measuring how long it took him to memorize a list of nonsense syllables, and after various delays, measuring how long it took him to relearn the same list. The shorter the delay between the first memory task and the second, the less time he had to spend relearning the list. He referred to this faster learning time on the second occasion as "savings." And, once the information was in memory and could be recalled after a significant period of time even without rehearsal, such memories appeared to be relatively permanent, that is, they could not be forgotten. This pattern of forgetting, rapid initial loss of memories followed by more gradual loss, is common to many kinds of tasks.

## RETRIEVAL SUCCESS AND FAILURE

Research on retrieval focuses on how people encode information and on the cues that help them recall it. If you are given a cue for retrieval that relates to some aspect of the originally stored information, retrieval is easier, faster, and more accurate. For example, if you were asked to recall the name of Jim Black, it would be easier if he had a bushy black beard than if he were a redhead. When a retrieval cue is present, retrieval is easier; this evidence supports the encoding specificity principle.

Recall that the value or effectiveness of a specific retrieval cue depends on how well it matches up with information in the original encoded memory. (This evidence supports the *encoding specificity principle*. This principle predicts that people who encode information under one set of circumstances should find it easier to retrieve that information under the same circumstances. The more clearly and sharply your memory cues are defined and paired, the better your recall will be and the less likely you will be to experience retrieval failures. To increase your access to information stored in memory, you should match the retrieval situation to the original learning situation as much as possible.(For a view on how long information can be accessible, see *Introduction to Research Basics*.) The encoding specificity principle is apparent in studies of state-dependent learning and retrieval.

**STATE-DEPENDENT LEARNING AND RETRIEVAL.** Psychologist Gordon Bower (1981) used the following story to describe a phenomenon known as state-dependent learning:

> When I was a kid I saw the movie *City Lights* in which Charlie Chaplin plays the little tramp. In one very funny sequence, Charlie saves a drunk from leaping to his death. The drunk turns out to be a millionaire who befriends Charlie, and the two spend the evening together drinking and carousing. The next day, when sober, the millionaire does not recognize Charlie and even snubs him. Later the millionaire gets drunk again, and when he spots Charlie treats him as his long lost companion. So the two of them spend another evening together carousing and drinking and then stagger back to the millionaire's mansion to sleep. In the morning, of course, the sober millionaire again does not recognize Charlie, treats him as an intruder, and has the butler kick him out by the seat of his pants. The scene ends with the little tramp telling the camera his opinion of high society and the evils of drunkenness. (p. 129)

The millionaire remembers Charlie only when he is intoxicated, the same state in which he originally met him. Psychologists find that information learned while a person is in a particular physiological state is recalled most accurately when the person is again in that physiological state. This phenomenon, known as **state-dependent learning**, includes state-dependent retrieval. This dependence of retrieval on learning state is associated with states involving drugs, time of day (Holloway, 1977), mental illness (Weingartner, 1977), and traumatic experiences (Perry, 1999).

In a typical study of state-dependent learning, Weingartner and colleagues (1976) had four groups of participants learn lists of high- and low-imagery words. To induce intoxication, all participants except those in the control group drank vodka and fruit juice. The control group learned and recalled while sober, a second group learned and recalled while intoxicated, a third group learned while sober and recalled while intoxicated, and a fourth group learned while intoxicated and recalled while sober. The results showed that participants recalled the lists best when they were in the same state in which they had learned the lists. (This is not to say that memory is better when you are drunk! All else being equal, recall is better in sober individuals.)

Several theories attempt to explain state-dependent learning. A widely accepted explanation focuses on how altered or drugged states affect the storage process.

▼ The millionaire character in Charlie Chaplin's movie *City Lights* remembers Charlie only when he is intoxicated, which is known as state-dependent learning.

STATE-DEPENDENT LEARNING
The tendency to recall information learned in a particular physiological state most accurately when one is again in that physiological state.

## Testing Very Long-term Memory

Most memory research takes place in a laboratory, with participants who learn a selection of material and then have their memory tested. The testing for memory typically occurs within minutes. Sometimes, researchers test after hours or days have elapsed, but studies of longer retention are rare because keeping track of participants is such a problem. Harry Bahrick solved that problem by finding material that many people had already learned at the same time in their lives and testing their memory for that material years later. He has used this approach in a number of studies, including memory for photos in high school yearbooks and memory for courses taken in high school and college (Bahrick, 2000). This approach has allowed Bahrick to study memory in real-life contexts, over time spans as long as 50 years.

**Design.** Bahrick's (1984) approach is not experimental. His research method is a type of descriptive study called an **ex post facto study**, a type of design that contrasts groups of people who differ on some variable of interest to the researcher. He did not manipulate the information presented to participants as typical memory researchers do when they vary the type of material (nouns or numbers) or amount of information (10 or 20 words) participants must memorize. Instead, he chose participants who already had the experiences of interest, such as studying a foreign language, and he tested them. This approach may look like an experiment because the participants are tested in a lab, but it has important differences. By choosing participants who already differ, researchers such as Bahrick do not manipulate an independent variable but instead choose participants with the appropriate level of the variable they have selected. This variable is called a *subject variable* because it describes characteristics of the subjects (participants) in the study. Because the researchers do not manipulate an independent variable, they have no possibility of exerting control over other variables, so they are restricted from making conclusions about cause-and-effect relationships. However, this approach can tell about differences among people with varying characteristics, which was Bahrick's goal.

**Hypothesis.** Bahrick hypothesized that people who had completed more Spanish courses would have better retention of Spanish, even many years later. That is, he hypothesized that practice would be a factor in very long-term memory. In addition, he hypothesized that the amount of time that elapsed would show a relationship to memory.

**Participants.** Bahrick found 733 volunteers who agreed to complete a Spanish reading, vocabulary, and grammar examination and to furnish background information about their coursework and grades (along with permission to verify this information). These participants had taken at least one Spanish course during high school or college. This instruction took place between 2 months and 50 years prior to testing.

**Procedure.** Bahrick grouped participants according to the time that had passed since their last Spanish instruction. He also assessed how much Spanish instruction each person had received, creating a procedure to make coursework equivalent to university or college semesters and placing participants in 10 different categories of instruction. These 10 categories were the levels of his subject variable, amount of Spanish instruction. Bahrick determined that most of the participants did not practise Spanish after they finished the courses, so rehearsal was not a factor in his study.

**Results.** Bahrick found that both elapsed time and amount of Spanish instruction were important factors in memory. He found that, regardless of the age of the participants or how long ago they had studied Spanish, the greatest memory loss occurs within three to six years after completing the last Spanish course. Retention then remains constant for several decades, but declines again after about 30 years.

The number of courses completed was also an important factor in memory. The best predictor of memory for Spanish was the number of Spanish courses completed.

**Conclusions.** Even without rehearsal or great personal relevance, some information in semantic long-term memory persists for 25 years or longer. Original training is the best predictor of retention in long-term memory. So practice, indeed, does seem to make memory permanent—for at least 30 years.

---

**EX POST FACTO STUDY**

A type of research design that contrasts groups of people who differ on some variable of interest to the researcher.

According to this view, part of learning involves the encoding of stimuli in specific ways at the time of learning (encoding specificity principle); to access the stored information, a person must evoke the same context in which the encoding occurred (Schramke & Bauer, 1997). When you study for an examination with music in the background but are tested in quiet conditions, your recall may not be as good. The reasons for retrieval failures are not completely clear, but studies of mood and its impact on memory and of state-dependent learning may hold the key (Izquierdo & Medina, 1997; Eich, 1995). Studying after exercise, when in a good mood, or when well rested is likely to lead to better recall.

## FLASHBULB MEMORY

Where were you when you heard about the terrorist attacks on the World Trade Center and the Pentagon? How did you hear about these events? What were you doing? What were your first thoughts? Do you remember those details more vividly than you remember what you had for lunch two days ago? These terrorist attacks made an indelible impression on most North Americans as well as on many people around the world. Are these public, dramatic events the basis of a special kind of memory?

Your memories of seeing or hearing about the terrorist attacks on the United States on September 11, 2001, may be the type of major event that is referred to as *flashbulb memory*. Such events are dramatic, and memory of them tends to be vivid.

Brown and Kulik (1977) were the first to research this type of memory. They argued that there is a special type of memory for events that have a critical level of emotional impact and what they called *consequentiality*. Most people immediately understand the concept of flashbulb memory and can identify personal examples of it. The attack on the World Trade Center is one example, but the Columbine shootings and the death of Princess Diana are also dramatic, public events that many people put into the category of flashbulb memory. The types of events that are likely to be flashbulb memories vary among countries. For example, people living in the United Kingdom are more likely to have such a memory for the resignation of Prime Minister Margaret Thatcher than are residents of North America (Conway et al., 1994). Thus, more Canadians and Europeans than Americans have flashbulb memories of the death of Princess Diana, but this event is the type of public, emotionally charged event that prompts the formation of these memories. The concept of flashbulb memories has not only generated a great deal of research but also has prompted debate over its validity.

The concept of flashbulb memory holds that people will have complete, detailed, and accurate memories from such events. Brown and Kulik argued that a special memory mechanism creates flashbulb memories, which explains their special characteristics. Other psychologists argue that the processes of encoding and retrieval can account for flashbulb memories, just as for other memories (Schooler & Eich, 2000); the emotional component of these memories makes them more distinctive (affecting encoding) and more often rehearsed (affecting retrieval).

Another point of argument involves the accuracy of flashbulb memories. Brown and Kulik argued that the special mechanism for creating these memories should make them very accurate—just like the photograph made by the flashbulb. Researchers approached the topic by focusing on some public event that generated emotion; they collected people's memories of various events (earthquakes, assassinations, and the space shuttle *Challenger* explosion) and compared the detail and accuracy to those of other memories. Results indicate that flashbulb memories are far from perfectly accurate, and they change over time, but people still retain the feeling of vividness for these memories (Koriat, Goldsmith, & Pansky, 2000). Thus, flashbulb memories are probably created by the same mechanisms that form other memories. They are certainly vivid, but other emotionally charged personal memories share the same level of detail and persistence.

▼ Millions of people have a flashbulb memory for this emotionally charged event.

Men's memory tends to be better for hardware than for groceries.

## GENDER AND MEMORY

Although many people believe that the differences between women and men extend to every type of behaviour, research shows very few differences in memory. For example, no gender differences appeared in a study involving recalling pictures and words (Ionescu, 2000). Women were slightly better than men at recalling the names and faces of their high-school classmates after as many as 50 years, but Bahrick's (2000) analysis of that difference held that women were better at learning the information, not at recall. This gender difference in attention and learning is probably the basis of any differences in memory—men and women attend to different types of information. Differential attention leads to encoding differences and thus to retrieval differences.

The factors that prompt gender differences in attention conform to gender stereotypes. For example, one study asked women and men to memorize a shopping list and the directions of how to get to a particular place (Hermann, Crawford, & Holdsworth, 1992). The results showed the expected stereotypical differences: Women performed slightly better on the shopping list and men on the directions. However, the study showed that memory could be manipulated along stereotypical lines. Of the participants who received information that the shopping list related to groceries, women did better, but for participants who were told that the list pertained to hardware, men's memory for the items was better. Therefore, memory efficiency can be manipulated not only by attention but also by how well the memory task matches gender-stereotypical information.

## EXTRAORDINARY MEMORY

Nearly perfect recall is rare. But is it possible for an average person to develop a remarkable memory? We saw that the memory span for most adults is limited to around seven items, plus or minus two items. Research shows, however, that with practice and the use of special chunking strategies, memory span can be increased greatly. In two different studies, participants' memory spans were increased to 79 digits (Ericsson, Chase, & Faloon, 1980) and 106 digits (Staszewski, 1987). The participants in these experiments developed strategies for effective encoding and efficient retrieval of meaningful chunks of information; the process was effortful and deliberate.

Attempting to increase digit span is a time-consuming process. In the two studies just discussed, 20 months were needed in the first case and 5 years were needed in the second—and the results did not carry over to other study materials. However, exceptional memory skills can be seen in other research domains. For example, Staszewski (1988) presented research on "lightning mental calculators"—individuals who can solve complex arithmetic problems (such as 54 917 × 63) with remarkable speed and accuracy. The key to such achievement is steady practice, efficient use of memory, and extensive knowledge of numerical relationships. A person cannot train to be a lightning mental calculator without extensive daily and weekly practice. Nor can a person learn to calculate calendar date problems (for example, the day of the week on which July 27, 1946, fell) without extensive practice and considerable knowledge of day, date, and calendar rules (Howe & Smith, 1988). Individuals can learn to overcome working memory limitations, but it requires supervised, prolonged practice that is maintained at high daily levels (Ericsson, Krampe, & Tesch-Römer, 1993). In rare cases people can do astounding things. There was a person once who could listen to a single reading of Dante's *Divine Comedy* in Italian and then repeat lines afterwards even though he could not speak

PRIMACY EFFECT

The more accurate recall of items presented first in a series.

RECENCY EFFECT

The more accurate recall of items presented last in a series.

IMAGERY

The creation or recreation of a mental picture of a sensory or perceptual experience.

a word of Italian. As well, extraordinary musical or athletic skills that take years to perfect provide evidence that procedural memory benefits from intensive supervised practice (Ericsson & Charness, 1994).

## WHAT FACILITATES RETRIEVAL?

Study the list of words in Figure 6.7 for 45 seconds, trying to memorize them in the order in which they appear. After 45 seconds, cover the list and write down as many of the words as you can, in the order that they appeared.

Long-term memory studies have brought forth some interesting findings about retrieval and have generated hundreds of other studies focusing on factors that can facilitate or inhibit accurate recall. Two of these factors are primacy and recency effects and imagery. You use both every day.

**PRIMACY AND RECENCY EFFECTS.** In a typical memory experiment, a participant may be asked to study 30 or 40 words, with a word presented every 2 seconds. A few seconds or minutes later, the person is asked to recall the words so that the researcher can determine whether the information was transferred from short-term to long-term memory. Such experiments typically show an overall recall rate of 20 percent. However, recall is higher for words at the beginning of a list than for those in the middle, a phenomenon termed the **primacy effect**. This effect occurs because no information related to the task at hand is already stored in short-term memory; at the moment a new task is assigned, a person's attention to new stimuli is at its peak. In addition, words at the beginning of a series get to be rehearsed more often, allowing them to be transferred to long-term memory. Thus, the primacy effect is associated with long-term memory processes. However, recall is *even higher* for words at the end of a list—a phenomenon termed the **recency effect**. This effect occurs because these more recently presented items are still being held in short-term memory, where they can still be actively rehearsed, and are not being subjected to any interference from newer information prior to being encoded into long-term memory. The recency effect is thus thought to be related to short-term memory. Figure 6.8 shows the recall rate for words in various positions in a list. It is called a *serial position curve* and presents the accuracy or speed of recall as a function of item position in a list or series of presented items.

In politics, campaign managers attempt to capitalize on the primacy and recency effects through their candidates' speeches. For example, they urge their candidates to speak both very early in the campaign and very late, just before people vote. If several candidates are to speak back-to-back, campaign managers will try to schedule their candidates either first or last. Primacy effects suggest that attention is at its peak at the beginning of the speeches; recency effects suggest that speaking last will be effective because other speakers won't interfere with the transfer of information from short-term to long-term memory. Of course, if days and weeks pass, new information will interfere, and primacy effects will be greater than recency effects.

**IMAGERY.** People use perceptual imagery every day as a long-term memory retrieval aid. In imagery, people create, recreate, or conjure up a mental picture of a sensory or perceptual experience to be remembered. People constantly invoke images to recall things they did, said, read, or saw. People's imagery systems can be activated by visual, auditory, or olfactory stimuli or by other images (Tracy & Barker, 1994). Even a lack of sensory stimulation can produce vivid imagery. Imagery helps you answer questions such as these: Which is darker green, a pea or a Christmas tree? Which is bigger, a tennis ball or a baseball? Does the person you met last night have brown eyes or blue eyes?

**FIGURE 6.7**
**For the Active Learner: Memory Retrieval Activity**

*Study this list of words for 45 seconds, especially focusing on their order. After 45 seconds, cover the list and write down as many of the words as you can, in the order that they appeared. Then return to the text to find out what your performance on this task says about your memory.*

horse
cabin
water
field
model
apple
heart
scene
constitutional
earth
bugle
night
voice
ocean
child
movie
grape

**FIGURE 6.8**
**A Serial Position Curve**

The probability of recalling an item is plotted as a function of its serial position on a list of items. Generally, the first several items are fairly likely to be recalled (the primacy effect), and the last several are recalled very well (the recency effect).

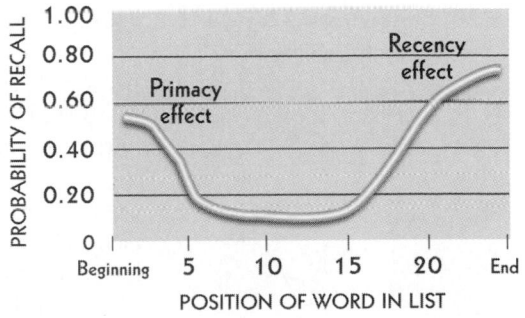

One technique that researchers use to measure imagery is to ask participants to imagine objects of various sizes—for example, an animal such as a rabbit next to either an elephant or a fly. In a 1975 study by Stephen Kosslyn of Harvard University, participants reported that when they imagined a fly, plenty of room remained in their mental image for a rabbit. However, when they imagined an elephant, it took up most of the available space. One particularly interesting result was that the participants required more time and found it harder to see a rabbit's nose when the rabbit was next to an elephant than when it was next to a fly, because the nose appeared to be extremely small in the first instance (see Figure 6.9).

Although they are mental, not physical, phenomena, images have "edges" like those on a photograph—points beyond which visual information ceases to be represented (Kosslyn, 1987). These and other properties of mental images have been useful in a wide variety of studies designed to measure the nature and speed of thought (see, for example, Figure 6.10).

**FIGURE 6.9**

**Kosslyn's Imagery Studies**

(Based on Kosslyn, 1975, after Solso, 1979.)

Kosslyn had subjects imagine elephants, flies, and rabbits. An imagined rabbit appeared small in size next to an elephant.

Next to a fly, however, an imagined rabbit appeared large in size.

**FIGURE 6.10**

**The Speed of Thought**

The speed of thought can be assessed through studies of mental rotation. Shepard and Metzler (1988) asked participants to see as quickly as possible whether visual stimuli were in fact the same stimuli, but rotated, or were different stimuli.

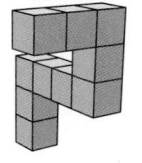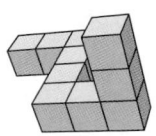

Imagery is an important perceptual memory aid. In fact, a growing body of evidence suggests that it is a means of preserving perceptual information that might otherwise decay. According to Allan Paivio (1971) of the University of Western Ontario, a person told to remember two words may form an image combining those words. Someone told to remember the words *house* and *hamburger*, for example, might have an easier time remembering those words by forming an image of a house made of hamburgers or of a hamburger on top of a house. When the person is later presented with the word *house*, the word *hamburger* will come to mind. Paivio suggests that words paired in this way become conceptually linked, with the crucial factor being the image.

How images facilitate recall and recognition is not yet fully understood, but one possibility is that an image could add another code to semantic memory. Thus, with two codes, semantic and imaginal, a person has two ways to access previously learned information. Some researchers argue that imagery, verbal encoding mechanisms, and semantic memory operate together to encode and to aid in retrieval (Marschark et al., 1987).

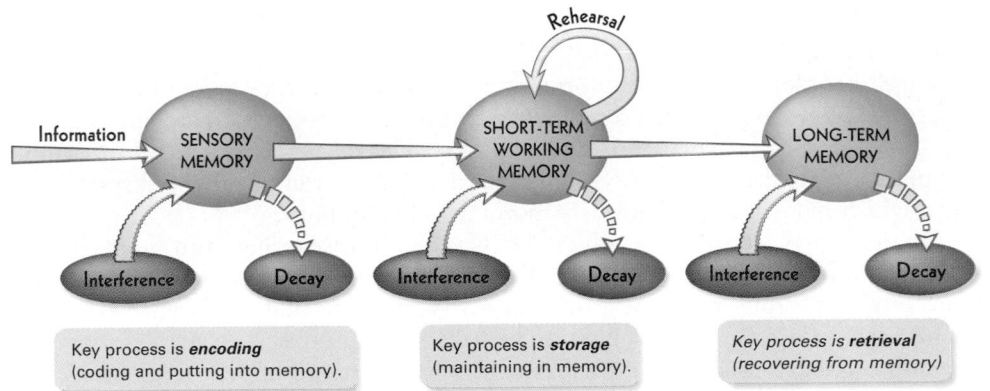

Figure 6.11 presents an overall view of the processes of encoding, storage, and retrieval at various stages of memory.

---

*Be an*
## ACTIVE LEARNER

**REVIEW**
> What techniques have researchers used to assess memory retrieval? pp. 221–223
> What evidence do some researchers cite when arguing that flashbulb memories do not result from a unique type of memory process? p. 225
> How do primacy and recency effects influence memory retrieval? p. 227

**THINK CRITICALLY**
> Is flashbulb memory more explicit or implicit? Explain.
> What makes unusual imagery better than ordinary images as memory aids?

**APPLY PSYCHOLOGY**
> Can you see any differences in memory for the women and men in your family? Do stereotypical gender differences apply? Give examples.
> Provide three examples of how imagery can assist retrieval, drawing these examples from the classes you are taking now.

---

*Take Home Tip*
## FOR THE ACTIVE LEARNER

Some people are good at creating images, but for those of us who are not, a rhyme can help: *one is a bun, two is a shoe, three is a tree, four is a door, five is a hive, six is sticks, seven is heaven, eight is a gate, nine is a vine, and ten is a hen.* Now you can use your memory of this rhyme to learn other material by creating an image that attaches the new material to the items in the rhyme. Make the image unusual so that it will be memorable, and picture the image. If the order of the items is important, you must stick to the order in the rhyme, but otherwise you can rearrange the list to maximize the outrageous imagery. For example, if you have to remember to get milk, peanut butter, apples, and mouthwash at the store, create images that pair each item with one on the list. For the association between milk and bun, imagine opening a package of buns and pouring milk into the package so that they are wet, soggy, and disgusting; picture that image. Then think about polishing your shoes with peanut butter, spreading it evenly over the shoes. Create an image for each item. To recall the items, all you have to do is think, "One is a bun," and your image of milk-soaked buns should prompt your memory. "Two is a shoe" should prompt you to retrieve....

---

# Forgetting: When Memory Fails

Quick! Name your first-grade teacher. Recite your social insurance number. Give your best friend's middle name. Where you went on your last holiday. In general, your memory serves you amazingly well. Nevertheless, at times you may have trouble recalling the name of someone you know well, where you read an interesting article, or the phone number of a close friend. And have you ever started an exam only to have your mind suddenly go blank? In some ways, forgetting is the opposite, or flip side, of memory—it's the inability to recall, reconstruct, or, in general, remember.

There are many causes of forgetting, including not rehearsing information well enough, not making good elaborative associations (links), or not using learned information for a long time. Forgetting also occurs because of interference from other learned information, because information is unpleasant, or because of physiological problems. Moreover, forgetting occurs with both short-term and long-term memory.

▲ Hermann Ebbinghaus was the first researcher to investigate memory scientifically.

## EARLY STUDIES

**EBBINGHAUS AND FORGETTING.** Hermann Ebbinghaus (1850–1909) studied how well people retain stored information. Ebbinghaus earnestly believed that the contents of consciousness could be studied by scientific principles. He tried to quantify how quickly participants could learn, relearn, and forget information. Ebbinghaus was the first person to investigate memory scientifically and systematically, which made his technique as important as his findings.

In his early studies, in which he was both researcher and participant, Ebbinghaus assigned himself the task of learning lists of letters in order of presentation. First, he strung together groups of three letters to make nonsense syllables such as *nak, dib, mip,* and *daf* because he believed that nonsense syllables carry no previous associations to contaminate the measurement of learning. Next, he recorded how many times he had to present lists of these nonsense syllables to himself before he could remember them perfectly. Ebbinghaus found that when the lists were short, his learning was nearly perfect after one or two trials. When they contained more than seven items, however, he had to present them over and over to achieve accurate recall.

Later, Ebbinghaus did learning experiments with other participants, using the technique of *relearning.* He had them learn lists of syllables and then, after varying amounts of time, measured how quickly the participants relearned the original list, which he called the *saving method,* because what was initially learned was not totally forgotten. Ebbinghaus's research showed that forgetting occurs very rapidly. Recall falls from perfect performance to less than 50 percent correct within 20 minutes. After the first several hours, forgetting levels off to a very slow decrease, indicating that most forgetting occurs quickly. (See Figure 6.12, which shows Ebbinghaus's "forgetting curve.")

**BARTLETT AND FORGETTING.** In 1932, English psychologist Sir Frederick Bartlett reported that when college students tried to recall stories they had just read, they changed them in several interesting ways: They shortened and simplified details, a process Bartlett called *levelling;* they focused on or emphasized certain details, a process he called *sharpening;* and they altered facts to make the stories fit their own views of the world, a process he called *assimilation.* In other words, the students constructed memories that distorted the events.

Contemporary explanations of this distortion have centred on the reconstructive nature of the memory process—memory retrieval is more like a reconstruction than a replay. This reconstructive process occurs partly because people develop a **schema**—a conceptual framework that organizes information and allows a person

*SCHEMA* [SKEEM-uh]

A conceptual framework that organizes information and allows a person to make sense of the world.

**FIGURE 6.12**
**Ebbinghaus's Forgetting Curve**

Ebbinghaus found that most forgetting occurs during the first nine hours after learning.

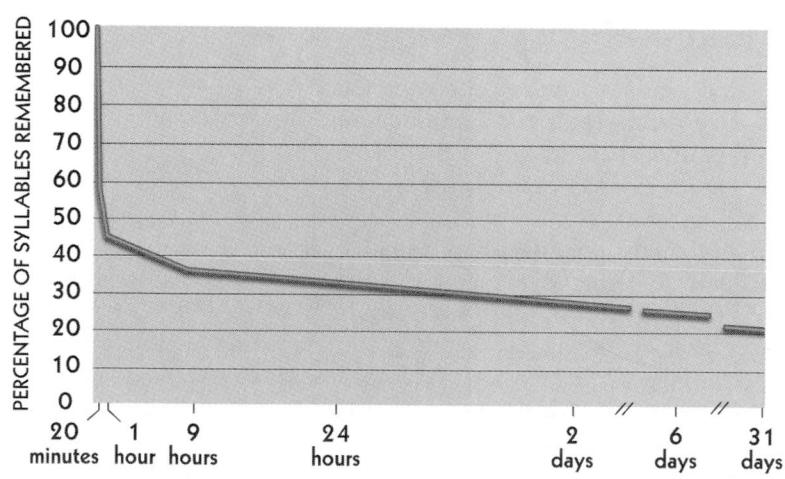

ELAPSED TIME BETWEEN LEARNING OF SYLLABLES AND MEMORY TEST

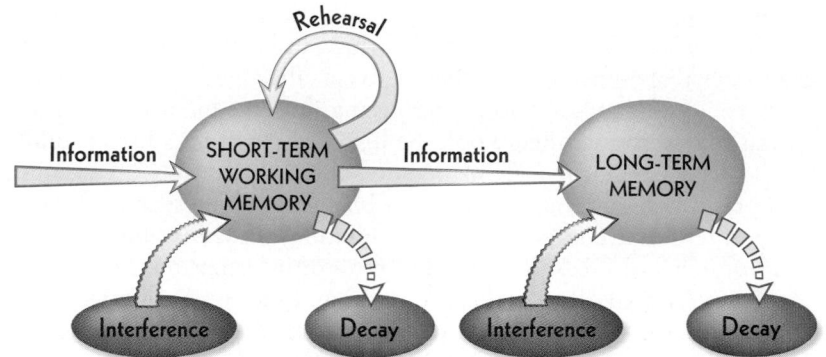

**FIGURE 6.13**

**Decay and Interference in Short-term Working Memory and Long-term Memory**

The transfer of information from short-term working memory to long-term memory is crucial for accurate recall at a later time. Note that decay and interference affect both stages of memory.

to make sense of the world. Because people cannot remember *all* the details of an event or situation, they keep key facts and lose minor details. Schemas group together key pieces of information. In general, people try to fit an entire memory into some framework that will be available for later recall. Distortion is important in forgetting, but so is the type of decay that Ebbinghaus researched.

## KEY CAUSES OF FORGETTING

Daniel Schacter (2001) wrote about the types of problems that can plague memory, referring to them as "sins of memory." Schacter's memory sins include factors that affect the reasons that people fail to retrieve information when they need it and the processes that make memory inaccurate. Two processes, decay and interference, account for several "memory sins" and can affect both short-term storage and long-term memory (see Figure 6.13).

**DECAY OF INFORMATION.** **Decay** is the loss of information from memory as a result of disuse and the passage of time. In decay theory, unimportant events fade from memory, and details become lost, confused, or fuzzy if not recalled every once in a while. Another way to look at decay theory is this: Memory exists in the brain in a physiological form known as a *memory trace*. With the passage of time and a lack of active use, the trace disintegrates, fades, and is lost.

Decay theory was popular for many years but is not widely accepted today. Many early studies did not consider several important variables that affect memory processes, such as the rate and mode of stimulus presentation. Although decay is a small part of the final explanation of forgetting, it is probably less important than other factors, such as interference.

**INTERFERENCE IN MEMORY.** **Interference** is the suppression of one bit of information by another received either earlier or later or the confusion of two pieces of information. In interference theory, the limited capacity of short-term memory makes it susceptible to interference from, or confusion among, other learned items. That is, when competing information is stored in short-term memory, the crowding that results affects a person's memory for particular items. For example, if someone looks up a telephone number and is then given another number to remember, the second number probably will interfere with the ability to remember the first one. Moreover, interference in memory is more likely to occur when a person is presented with a great deal of new information. (In this text, you are being provided with a great deal of new information. Organizing your studying into coherent chunks will help you avoid confusing the information you are trying to enter into long-term memory.)

**DECAY**

Loss of information from memory as a result of disuse and the passage of time.

**INTERFERENCE**

The suppression of one bit of information by another received either earlier or later or the confusion of two pieces of information.

| *Take Home Tip*<br>**FOR THE ACTIVE LEARNER** | This text is providing you with a great deal of new information. Interference will be a problem, but you can prevent interference by organizing your studying. |
|---|---|

For example, pay attention to the headings and subheadings within chapters. Attending to the outline of chapters or sections can help you understand the organization of the material, which can minimize the impact of interference.

Research on interference theory shows that the extent and nature of a person's experiences both before and after learning are important. For example, someone given a list of nonsense syllables may recall 75 percent of the items correctly. However, if that person had earlier been given 20 similar lists to learn, the number of items correctly recalled would be lower; the previous lists would interfere with recall of the current list. If the person subsequently were given additional lists to learn, recall would be even lower. Psychologists call these interference effects proactive and retroactive interference (or inhibition). **Proactive interference**, or *proactive inhibition*, is a decrease in accurate recall of information due to interference from previously learned or presented information. **Retroactive interference**, or *retroactive inhibition*, is a decrease in accurate recall resulting from the subsequent presentation of different information. (See Figure 6.14 for an illustration of both types of interference.) Proactive and retroactive interference help explain recall failures in long-term memory.

Here is an illustration of proactive and retroactive interference: Suppose that you attend a series of speeches, each of which is five minutes long. According to psychological research on proactive and retroactive interference, you will be most likely to remember the first and last speeches. There will be no proactive interference with the first speech and no retroactive interference with the last speech. Your memory of the middle speeches, however, will suffer from both proactive and retroactive interference. This effect is closely related to primacy and recency effects discussed earlier.

**INTERFERENCE IN ATTENTION.** According to Schacter (2001), interference in attention is responsible for one of the most annoying types of memory failure—absentmindedness. This problem plagues almost everyone, even people who have excellent memories, because this type of interference prevents information from getting into long-term memory.

Absentmindedness is encoding failure. You really can't remember where you put your keys because that information is not there to retrieve. This problem is common because the competition for attention leads us to ignore some stimuli at critical points in the flow of information through the memory system, and we do not remember where we put our keys, book, really important paper, glasses, wallet, and so forth.

When people try to attend to more than one thing at a time, their attention is divided, which is another form of interference in attention. Divided attention

▲ Listening to a series of speeches, you will be most likely to recall the first and last ones.

**FIGURE 6.14**
**Proactive and Retroactive Interference**

In memory, proactive and retroactive interference occur when information interferes with (inhibits recall of) other information.

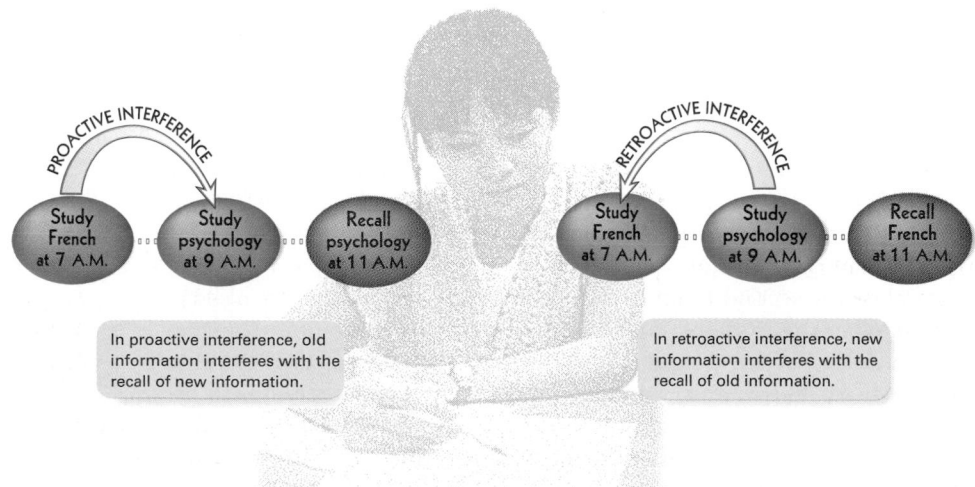

PROACTIVE INTERFERENCE

Study French at 7 A.M. → Study psychology at 9 A.M. → Recall psychology at 11 A.M.

In proactive interference, old information interferes with the recall of new information.

RETROACTIVE INTERFERENCE

Study French at 7 A.M. → Study psychology at 9 A.M. → Recall French at 11 A.M.

In retroactive interference, new information interferes with the recall of old information.

presents a problem for both encoding and retrieval processes, but these effects are not equal: Distraction during encoding is a much bigger problem than during retrieval (Brown & Craik, 2000).

For many years, interference in attention was used to explain what is called the *Stroop effect* (Stroop, 1935). The Stroop test is a procedure in which people are presented with the names of colours, printed in ink that is not the same as the colour named. Figure 6.15 illustrates the Stroop effect. When people read column A, naming the word, most people find it difficult to attend to the word and ignore the colour of ink (the Stroop effect). Their performance is slower and has more errors than for column B, when the words are in standard black ink, or in column C, when the words are printed in the same colour ink as the name of the word. The colour of the ink produces interference. This explanation has been popular—but attention, rather than interference, is now considered more important in explaining the Stroop effect (MacLeod, 1991).

## SPECIAL TYPES OF FORGETFULNESS

Psychologists have learned that there are special kinds of forgetting that are not so easily explained by mere decay or simple interference. You have probably heard about these kinds of forgetting in the popular press, but psychologists have given them special attention in studies of eyewitness testimony and of motivated forgetting.

**EYEWITNESS TESTIMONY.** You've seen it on television dozens of times. A witness is asked to look through a book of mug shots in the hopes that he can identify a perpetrator. A mug shot is identified; the witness identifies the perpetrator. If the witness is then shown a lineup of six individuals, he is now more likely to identify the perpetrator than if he wasn't shown the mug shots. When a witness looks through a book of mug shots it actually biases him to choose the perpetrator from the lineup. The witness is more confident that he is identifying the correct perpetrator during the lineup, although the mug shot is actually what is being remembered.

If someone witnesses an accident or a crime, can that person accurately report the facts of the situation to the police or the courts? The answer is yes and no. The police and the courts generally have accepted *eyewitness testimony* as some of the best evidence that can be presented. Eyewitnesses are people who saw the crime, have no bias or grudge, and swear to tell (and recall) the truth. But do they?

If memory is a reconstructive process, as many psychologists contend, it is not a literal reproduction of the past (Schacter, 1996). In fact, research shows that eyewitnesses often forget; they recall events incorrectly, make mistakes, and sometimes identify the wrong people as being involved in the events (Bekerian & Bowers, 1983; Loftus, 1979). When people make such incorrect identifications, they are often confident in their judgments (Wells, Luus, & Windschitl, 1994). Nevertheless, eyewitnesses of the same event often report seeing different things.

To complicate the matter, eyewitnesses often enhance their memories over time (recall Bartlett's theory of assimilation). Harvard law professor Alan Dershowitz (1986) asserts that the memories of witnesses—particularly those with a stake in the eventual outcome—tend to get better with the passing of time. Dershowitz calls this process *memory enhancement* and argues that it occurs when people fit their hazy memories into a coherent theory and pattern of other results. Ironically, the more detailed a witness is (even about irrelevant details), the more credible that witness is assumed to be, even if he or she is recalling things inaccurately (Bell & Loftus, 1989).

Much of these observations also apply to "ear witnesses," people who are asked to identify a voice they have heard before. Daniel Yarmey (2001) of the University of Guelph has studied this issue extensively. Generally, he finds that witnesses do a poorer job of identifying people from voice alone, but that the identification rate improves as the length of the voice sample increases.

*Take Home Tip*
## FOR THE ACTIVE LEARNER

If you have a choice about when to make a speech or when to be interviewed, go first or last if you want to be remembered.

**FIGURE 6.15**

**For the Active Learner: Stroop Effect**

Read the words in each column as fast as you can.

| A | B | C |
| --- | --- | --- |
| red | blue | green |
| green | red | yellow |
| blue | green | blue |
| yellow | yellow | red |
| blue | red | blue |
| red | blue | green |
| yellow | yellow | red |
| green | red | blue |
| blue | blue | green |
| red | green | yellow |
| green | yellow | red |
| blue | red | yellow |
| yellow | blue | green |
| green | yellow | blue |

▲ Elizabeth Loftus, a memory researcher, has served as an expert witness in more than 200 trials.

**MOTIVATED FORGETTING.** Freud (1933) was the first to suggest formally the idea of *motivated forgetting*—that frightening, traumatic events might be forgotten simply because people want or need to forget them. He stated that such memory loss occurs through *repression*—the burying of traumatic events in the unconscious, where they remain but are inaccessible. The controversy surrounding the concept of repressed memories gained public attention when the topic of sexual abuse of children began to gain widespread publicity (see *Point/Counterpoint*).

Most researchers agree that motivated forgetting probably is a real phenomenon, but it is not the type of phenomenon that can be investigated experimentally in a laboratory. It would obviously be unethical to attempt to traumatize participants. Many clinical psychologists have experience in dealing with people who have lived through traumatic events, both in childhood and later in life. However, most researchers are reluctant to rely solely on subjective clinical evidence (Pope, 2000). Thus, the phenomenon of motivated forgetting due to repression is accepted, but many psychologists are critical of its use regarding recovered memories of childhood abuse without more empirical evidence.

To further complicate this complex area, repression is not necessary for the creation of false memories, nor are such memories unique to traumatic experiences. In Figure 6.1, we asked you to examine a group of words to illustrate levels of processing, but your memory for this list can also illustrate another memory phenomenon. Without looking at the list again, identify which of the following words were on that list—*sweet, needle, arrest, homicide*. If you followed the set of instructions to analyze the meaning and relationship among the words, you will probably say that *sweet* and *needle* were not on the list, which is correct. You are also likely to say that the other two words appeared on the list. That is not correct; only one of those words—*arrest*—was part of the list. People tend to identify the other two words as part of that list because *homicide* has a conceptual relationship with the other 12 words on that list (Roediger & McDermott, 1995). If you misidentified this word, you have experienced a false memory. It wasn't related to a personal trauma, and your forgetting wasn't motivated in any way, but it demonstrates how everyone is subject to the memory processes that can lead to false memories.

Why are our memories so vulnerable to interference, distortion, and error? The adaptive benefits of memory are obvious, so the evolutionary benefit of memory is clear. However, some of that benefit is negated by memory problems, which seem difficult to reconcile in an evolutionary framework. Perhaps the problems of memory are not so serious (Anderson & Schooler, 2000). The same processes that produce memory problems may have advantages, or alternatively, these errors are not so damaging as to hamper reproductive success. For example, most of the information that we cannot recall is not critically important, at least in a life-threatening way, and we seem to be able to retrieve the information that is important at any given time. We forget information such as the function of the suprachiasmic nucleus all too often during a test, but we do not forget that walking into traffic is dangerous. Indeed, even people with profound types of memory loss rarely lose memory to the extent that they endanger themselves.

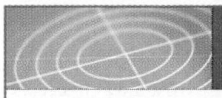 

## Are Recovered Memories Real?

**POINT:** The process of repression leads to motivated forgetting, and these memories represent traumatic events in people's past.

**COUNTERPOINT:** Recovered memories are usually false memories that occur through suggestion rather than recall.

The concept of motivated forgetting is critical to the controversy over recovered memories. If motivated forgetting can occur, then these repressed memories can resurface and the memories can be recovered. This process is exactly what some people claim has happened: As adults, people can recover the memories of childhood abuse. The debate over recovered memories has become intense and divisive, at times pitting clinical psychologists against researchers.

Memory researchers typically draw from laboratory studies that demonstrate everyday memory processes as well as errors and distortions in retrieval. Based on this type of research, some memory researchers have asserted that victims of sexual abuse could not forget their childhood events for long durations (Garry & Loftus, 1994; Pendergrast, 1997) and that there is nothing special about a traumatic memory (Shobe & Kihlstrom, 1997).

Clinicians and researchers have accused each other of acting improperly. The clinicians who have worked with patients claim that the laboratory research cannot be generalized to patients because laboratory research is restricted from presenting traumatic events and studying the memory consequences (Pope, 2000). Generalizing laboratory research to traumatized patients is not valid. Researchers have accused misguided therapists of helping people "recover" events that never occurred.

Three key questions need to be addressed: First, can someone forget horrible experiences and remember them years later? Second, is there a potential physiological basis for such recall? And third, is memory fallible? Clinical psychologists are concerned with the first issue; physiologists, the second; and memory researchers, the third.

The third question is the easiest to answer. Yes, memory is fallible in a number of ways, including remembering events that never took place. People can be led on and can attribute information to the wrong source; people can fail to retrieve information that is in their long-term memory.

In answer to the second question, there may be perceptual and physiological explanations for these memory errors (Payne et al., 1997; Schacter, 1997). Even more interesting, true memories may produce different patterns of brain activity than do false memories (Cabeza et al., 2001; Fabiani, Stadler, & Wessels, 2000).

The first question is the most difficult to answer, and researchers and clinicians have furnished different answers. Let's look at the areas of agreement. Without any question, many women and men have been sexually abused as children, and this abuse can be a factor in psychological problems, both during childhood and continuing into adulthood (Knapp & VandeCreek, 2000). No facet of the recovered memory controversy should minimize or discount the reality of the problem of sexual abuse during childhood.

Many abused children do not talk about the situation. Failing to tell someone is not the same as failing to remember. Many people tell therapists about sexual abuse because their therapist may be the first person who has asked or the first person who is trusted. Thus, allegations of sexual abuse during childhood may first appear years later, but this situation is not part of the recovered memory controversy. These memories were not recovered because they were never lost; they simply were not disclosed.

Most victims of sexual abuse remember the experience, but all do not. Some of those who remember are patients in therapy. These cases are at the centre of the recovered memory debate. According to a review of surveys of therapists, patients with recovered memories of abuse are rare, but they exist (Knapp & VandeCreek, 2000). Also, a question by the therapist concerning sexual abuse during childhood is not a sufficient suggestion to create a false memory. Suggestive techniques, especially those involving hypnosis, are ways to create false memories.

# NEUROSCIENCE OF FORGETTING: STUDIES OF AMNESIA

Much of the early work on the neuroscience of memory began with the study of patients in hospitals who for one reason or another had developed amnesia, often as the result of an accident. Television soap operas frequently portray people with amnesia, but in fact the condition is relatively rare. **Amnesia** is the inability to remember information, usually because of physiological trauma (such as a blow to the head). Typically, amnesia involves loss of memory for all events within a specific period.

There are two basic kinds of amnesia: retrograde and anterograde. **Retrograde amnesia** is the inability to remember events and experiences that preceded a traumatizing event. The loss of memory can cover the period just before the event, as in the minutes leading up to an accident, or a period of several years before it. Recovery tends to be gradual, with earlier events remembered before more recent ones. **Anterograde amnesia** is the inability to remember events and experiences that occur *after* an injury or brain damage. People suffering from anterograde amnesia are stuck in the lives they lived before being injured; new events are often completely forgotten. For example, if the onset of the amnesia occurred in 1996, the person may be able to remember clearly the events of 1995, or earlier, but may have a difficult time recalling what he or she did only half an hour ago. The person may meet someone for the hundredth time and think he or she is being introduced to a perfect stranger, yet may learn a new motor skill. People with anterograde amnesia are better at forming new procedural memories than declarative memories (Squire & Kandel, 1999) and long-term memories.

Most people who develop amnesia do so because of head injury; others develop symptoms because of Korsakoff's syndrome, an affliction resulting from drinking too much, eating too little, vitamin deficiencies, and brain damage. Diseases, especially viral ones, can cause amnesia as well. These types of causes for amnesia may seem completely unrelated, but research shows that head injury, Korsakoff's syndrome, and viral disease affect a group of loosely related neural circuits that link the temporal lobes, hippocampus, and frontal lobes. In studying patients with brain damage or those who have undergone surgery for major epileptic attacks, researchers have found that the hippocampus (see pages 64–65) may play a critical role in the transfer of new information to long-term memory. Milner showed that if certain regions of the brain are damaged or removed, people can remember old information but not new information (Milner, 1966; Milner, Corkin, & Teuber, 1968). The ability to remember remote events seems to depend on brain mechanisms that are separate and distinct from those required for new learning of recent events (Shimamura & Squire, 1986). These studies do not conclusively confirm the existence of separate places or processes in the brain for different types of memory, but they are suggestive. Moreover, research on learning and memory of emotional responses by Kim and Fanselow (1992) supports the idea that memory is not a single process or one encoded in a single place (Shen & McNaughton, 1996; Shallice et al., 1994). MRI studies indicate that men and women who have undergone traumas show changes in the size of various areas of the brain, especially the hippocampus. All of this research supports an important point: Memories may be coded in one or many places, and they may be affected by a range of physical events, past experiences, and current ones—thus, memory is as much a process as it is an event or a thing.

Building Table 6.3 summarizes key processes in the three stages of memory and forgetting.

AMNESIA [am-NEE-zhuh]

Inability to remember information (typically all events within a specific period), usually due to physiological trauma.

RETROGRADE [RET-ro-grade] AMNESIA

Loss of memory for events and experiences that occurred in a period preceding the amnesia-causing event.

ANTEROGRADE AMNESIA

Loss of memory for events and experiences that occurred after the amnesia-causing event.

**Be an ACTIVE LEARNER**

**REVIEW**

> What are the differences between Ebbinghaus's and Bartlett's approaches to forgetting? pp. 230–231
> Describe the differences between proactive and retroactive interference. p. 232
> Distinguish retrograde from anterograde amnesia. p. 236

**THINK CRITICALLY**

> At what point in the investigation of a crime is it most critical to the witness to correctly identify a perpetrator? Why?
> What types of evidence would you need in order to accept as valid the recovered memories of alien abductions? Would this evidence differ from that needed to validate recovered memories of childhood sexual abuse? If so, are the differing standards reasonable and objective?

**APPLY PSYCHOLOGY**

> What type of study and testing environment will minimize interference in encoding and retrieving memory, and how can you build such an environment?

| Stage | Encoding | Storage | Retrieval | Duration | Forgetting |
|---|---|---|---|---|---|
| Sensory Memory | Visual or auditory (iconic or echoic storage). | Brief, fragile, and temporary. | Information is extracted from stimulus presentation and transferred to short-term memory. | Visual: 250 milli-seconds; auditory: about 3 seconds. | Rapid decay of information; interference is possible if a new stimulus is presented. |
| Short-term Working Memory | Visual and auditory. | Repetitive rehearsal maintains informa-tion in storage, per-haps on a visual–auditory "scratch pad" where further encoding can take place. | Maintenance and elaborative rehearsal can keep information available for re-trieval; retrieval is enhanced through elaboration and further encoding. | No more than 30 seconds, probably less than 20 sec-onds; depends on specific task and stimuli. | Interference and decay affect memory; new stimulation causes rapid loss of information unless it is especially important. |
| Long-term Memory | Salient or important information processed by short-term working memory is transferred into long-term memory through elaborative rehearsal. | Storage is organized on logical and se-mantic lines for rapid recall; organization of information by categories, events, and other structures aids retrieval. | Retrieval is aided by cues and careful or-ganization; errors in retrieval can be intro-duced; long-term memory is fallible. | Indefinite; many events will be recalled in great detail for a lifetime. | Both decay and interference contribute to retrieval failure. |

# Summary and Review

## MEMORY: THE BRAIN AS INFORMATION PROCESSOR

### Define memory.

> *Memory* is the ability to remember past events or previously learned information or skills; it is also the storage system that allows retention and retrieval of information.   **pp. 208–209**

### What is the information processing approach to memory?

> The information processing approach assumes that each stage of learning and memory is separate, though related, and can be analyzed by scientific methods.   **pp. 208–209**

**KEY TERM**

memory, p. 208

## ENCODING

### What is encoding?

> *Encoding* is the organizing of information so that the nervous system can process it; it is the process of getting stimuli into a form usable by the nervous system.   **p. 209**

### What are the underlying assumptions of the levels-of-processing approach?

> The *levels-of-processing approach* holds that a person can process a stimulus in different ways, to different ex-tents, and at different levels. When the level of process-ing becomes more complex, the theory asserts, the coding occurs at a deeper level of memory.   **p. 210**

> The *encoding specificity principle* asserts that the effec-tiveness of a specific retrieval cue depends on how well it matches up with the originally encoded information. The more clearly and sharply retrieval cues are defined, the better recall will be.   **p. 211**

### What is the neurological basis of encoding?

> PET and fMRI brain imaging techniques indicate that the prefrontal cortex and areas in the medial temporal lobes are involved in encoding, but different areas are important for retrieval.   **pp. 211–212**

**KEY TERMS**

encoding, p. 209; levels-of-processing approach, p. 210; encoding specificity principle, p. 211; transfer-appropriate processing, p. 211

## STORAGE

### Describe the role of sensory memory.

> *Storage* refers to the process of maintaining information as well as the locations where information is held. **p. 213**

> *Sensory memory* is the mechanism that performs initial encoding and brief storage of sensory information. Once information is established in sensory memory, it must be transferred elsewhere for additional encoding or it will be lost. **pp. 213–214**

### Describe short-term working memory.

> Short-term working memory was initially conceptualized as short-term memory, which maintains a limited amount of information (7 plus or minus 2 items) for about 20 to 30 seconds. *Working memory* is a more recent conceptualization that is seen as consisting of three subsystems: an auditory loop to encode and rehearse auditory information; a visual–spatial "scratch pad," and a central processing mechanism, or executive, that balances the information flow. **p. 214**

### What is rehearsal?

> The limited number of items that can be reproduced easily after presentation is called the *memory span*. The immediate memory span usually contains one or two *chunks*—manageable and meaningful units of information. **p. 215**

> *Rehearsal* is the process of repeatedly verbalizing, thinking about, or otherwise acting on or transforming information in order to remember it. *Maintenance rehearsal* is the repetitive review of information with little or no interpretation; this shallow form of rehearsal involves the physical stimulus, not its underlying meaning. *Elaborative rehearsal* involves repetition in which the stimulus may be associated with other events and further processed; this type of rehearsal is usually necessary to transfer information to long-term memory. **p. 215**

### What is long-term memory, and what are the different types of long-term storage?

> *Long-term memory* is the storage mechanism that keeps a relatively permanent record of information. It is divided into procedural memory and declarative memory. *Procedural memory* is memory for the perceptual, motor, and cognitive skills necessary to complete complex tasks; *declarative memory* is memory for specific facts, which can be subdivided into episodic and semantic memory. **pp. 216–217**

> *Episodic memory* is a personal memory for specific events and situations, including time sequence. *Semantic memory* is memory of generalized knowledge of the world, including ideas, rules, and general concepts based on experiences and learned knowledge. **p. 218**

> *Explicit memory* is conscious memory that a person is aware of, such as memory of a word in a list or an event that occurred in the past; generally speaking, most recall tasks require participants to recall explicit information.

Explicit memory is a voluntary, active memory store. In contrast, *implicit memory* is memory a person is not aware of possessing; considered an almost unconscious process, implicit memory occurs unintentionally and almost automatically. **pp. 218–219**

### What is the neurological basis of memory storage?

> Structures in the prefrontal cortex and the medial temporal lobes are important for working memory, and the hippocampus, a structure in the medial temporal lobes, is critical in transferring memories from short-term to long-term storage. *Consolidation* is the term that describes this transformation. The repeated stimulation of neurons may produce changes in the synapses of neurons and long-term potentiation, which may be the underlying neurological basis for memory. **pp. 219–221**

**KEY TERMS**

storage, p. 213; sensory memory, p. 213; memory span, p. 215; chunks, p. 215; rehearsal, p. 215; maintenance rehearsal, p. 215; elaborative rehearsal, p. 215; working memory, p. 216; long-term memory, p. 216; procedural memory, p. 217; declarative memory, p. 217; episodic memory, p. 218; semantic memory, p. 218; explicit memory, p. 218; implicit memory, p. 218; consolidation, p. 220

## RETRIEVAL

### What are recall, recognition, and relearning?

> *Retrieval* is the process by which stored information is recovered from memory. Recall, recognition, and relearning can be used to assess retrieval success. Recall is reproducing the details of a situation or idea and placing them together in a meaningful framework (usually without any cues or aids). Recognition is remembering whether one has seen a stimulus before—whether the stimulus is familiar. After information has been learned, relearning can determine how long it takes to reacquire the information. **pp. 221–222**

### How does a person's physiological or emotional state affect retrieval?

> Physiological and emotional states affect retrieval. *State-dependent learning* is the tendency to recall information learned in a particular physiological or emotional state most accurately when one is again in that state. **pp. 223–225**

> Flashbulb memories are vivid memories associated with a state of emotional arousal. **p. 225**

### Does gender relate to memory?

> Gender is not a very important factor in memory, but gender stereotypes have an impact on attention, which can affect memory. **p. 226**

### What distinguishes the primacy effect from the recency effect?

> The *primacy effect* is the more accurate recall of items presented first in a series; the *recency effect* is the more accurate recall of items presented last. **p. 227**

## What is imagery?

> *Imagery* is the cognitive process of creating a mental picture of a sensory event. People's imagery systems can be activated by visual, auditory, or olfactory stimuli. **p. 227**

### KEY TERMS

retrieval, p. 221; state-dependent learning, p. 223; ex post facto study; p. 224; primacy effect, p. 226; recency effect, p. 226; imagery, pp. 226–227

## FORGETTING: WHEN MEMORY FAILS

### How and why is information lost from memory?

> Memory distortions occur in part because people develop a schema, a way to organize information, that fails to include all details of a situation. **pp. 229–231**

> *Decay* is the loss of information from memory as a result of disuse and the passage of time. According to interference theory, the limited capacity of short-term working memory makes it susceptible to *interference. Proactive interference* is a decrease in accurate recall as a result of the effects of previously learned or presented information. *Retroactive interference* is a decrease in accurate recall as a result of the subsequent presentation of different information. **pp. 231–232**

## What do eyewitness testimony and recovered memories reveal about the memory process?

> Both types of memory processes show that memory is subject to errors, including distortion and suggestibility. These errors indicate that memory is more of a reconstruction than a replay. Everyone is subject to these memory problems, but memory is an adaptive process that has many more advantages than disadvantages. **pp. 233–234**

### Distinguish retrograde from anterograde amnesia.

> *Amnesia* is the inability to remember information, usually because of some physiological trauma (such as a blow to the head). *Retrograde amnesia* is the inability to remember events that preceded a traumatizing event; *anterograde amnesia* is the inability to remember events that occur after such an event. **p. 236**

### KEY TERMS

schema, p. 230; decay, p. 231; interference, p. 231; proactive interference, p. 232; retroactive interference, p. 232; amnesia, p. 236; retrograde amnesia, p. 236; anterograde amnesia, p. 236

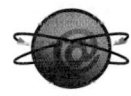 Take advantage of the multimedia resources available with this text! Follow the marginal icons to access the interactive modules on the *HandsOnPsych* CD-ROM; log on to *MyPsychLab* to explore the ebook, study aids, and other online resources; and visit the Companion Website at **www.pearsoned.ca/lefton** for additional exercises and links.

# 7 Cognition: Thought and Language

Larry Barnett was more or less typical of men his age. At age 52, his kids were finishing college, he was at his peak earning potential, he didn't smoke, he drank only occasionally, and he didn't exercise very much. In fact, his wife called him a "weekend warrior," suggesting that he expended energy only on the weekends. That day seemed like any other day—driving in congested traffic to get to a stressful office. However, unlike any other day, an event was taking place within Larry's body, one that would change the course of his life forever. Larry suffered a stroke behind the wheel of his well-padded Volvo. He lost consciousness, slammed into the car in front of him, spun around, and wound up on the side of the highway. Other cars were damaged, but no lives were lost. Larry lay in the hospital for three weeks in a semi-coma. Six weeks after the incident Larry awoke and began to do better.

But, some pieces of Larry's intellectual life had been disconnected. Larry seemed aware of the world around him and was able to process what people were saying. Yet he had trouble speaking. He seemed to know things but was unable to articulate what he knew. If shown a picture of a cat and asked to identify it, he would indicate that he knew what it was. In fact, if asked questions about cats—for example, if they had four legs, if they purred, if they had long tails—he knew the correct answers. However, if asked to name the animal, he couldn't. Larry Barnett was suffering brain damage due to his stroke.

Parts of his brain that connected the sections involved in speech, language, and thought were damaged. After a stroke, if a patient is lucky, some areas of the brain may recover, some may have to be retrained, and some take over for other portions. A long road lay ahead for Larry. Neuroscientists understand what happens when a stroke occurs and that the common, day-to-day behaviours that we all take for granted are intricately interwoven and easily damaged. Speech, language, and thinking are separate yet interconnected processes, all of which rely on the brain.

Every day, each of us faces and tries to sort out problems both small and large. Researchers attempt to learn how we do this, to better understand thought and help people maximize their potential. Researchers try to break down thought and language into their constituent parts, analyzing each step separately. Some biologists and even many neuroscientists assert that psychologically complex phenomena such as speech and language must be analyzed according to the laws of evolution, molecular biology, and physics (Wilson, 1998). But the truth is—and most social scientists agree on this point—that human behaviour, especially thought and language, is far too complex, original, and spontaneous to be explained simply in terms of molecules, genes, and DNA. Human behaviour is so complex and varied that no single field of study or theoretical approach can explain it.

In searching for a comprehensive theory of psychology—one that accounts for individual differences—research has recognized that thought and language are separate, but closely related, aspects of human behaviour. Thought allows human beings to reflect on and assess the past and to develop new ideas and technology. Language provides human beings with a unique vehicle for expressing thoughts about the past, present, and future. This chapter therefore covers both cognition (thought) and language, the symbolic system people use to communicate their thoughts verbally. Let's take the next step toward understanding human behaviour.

## Cognitive Psychology: An Overview

How are a tiger and a domestic cat similar? Who is the governor general of Canada? How is an omelette made? Answering each of these questions requires a different mental procedure. To answer the first question, you likely drew mental images of both felines and then compared the images. In answering the second question, you simply may have known the right name because of news stories. To answer the third question, you likely mentally walked through the procedure of preparing an omelette and described each step. The thinking you used to answer all of these questions required knowledge, language, and images.

**Cognitive psychology** is the study of the overlapping fields of perception, learning, memory, and thought; it is the study of how people attend to, acquire, transform, store, and retrieve knowledge (and increasingly, *cognitive neuroscience* studies how these processes are accomplished within the brain). In a real sense, cognitive psychology is the overall study of thought; we have been discussing it for the past three chapters, and it will help us understand other fields such as intelligence (Chapter 8). In this chapter, however, we will focus on two core topics of cognitive psychology: thought and language. The word *cognition* derives from the Latin *cognoscere*, "to know." Cognitive psychologists are interested primarily in mental processes that influence the acquisition and use of knowledge as well as the ability to *reason*, the process by which people generate logical and coherent ideas, evaluate situations, and reach conclusions. Cognitive researchers assume that mental processes exist, that people are active processors, and that cognitive processes can be studied primarily using techniques that measure time to respond and the accuracy of responses (Ashcraft, 1989).

The history of cognitive psychology began in the late nineteenth century. In the 1920s, behaviourism—with its focus on directly observable behaviour—became the mainstream psychology, and there was little reference to internal cognitive processes. Discussion and research of such "mentalistic" phenomena as imagery were avoided, because these phenomena were deemed fleeting and incapable of being observed and measured. In the 1940s, psychology changed in profound ways. During the Second World War rudimentary computers that could store instructions in their memory were being built. In the late 1950s and early 1960s, the flow charts and concepts such as encoding, storage, and retrieval used to construct, program, and run computers were used to begin to construct models of how human "computers" or minds processed information. Research into the nature of human thinking had begun in earnest.

The intellectual world wasn't concerned solely with computers, though. Jean Piaget (whom we will discuss in later chapters) argued that children think *differently* than adults. George Miller (1956) speculated on exactly how humans code information. Noam Chomsky (1957) suggested that language acquisition is a "wired-in" process. Donald Broadbent (1958) wrote on the nature of attention and thought. Ulric Neisser (1967) published an important book called *Cognitive Psychology*. Also in 1967, Posner and Mitchell published one of the first true experimental studies of cognitive processes. In 1972, Fergus Craik (Craik & Lockhart, 1972) of the University of Toronto proposed a new model for understanding memory processes, and Endel Tulving (1972) of the Rottman Institute advanced memory research by studying components of memory retrieval. The next wave of theorists in cognitive studies came from psychology, biology, linguistics, computer science, and philosophy (especially logic).

It is sometimes hard to pinpoint exactly what cognitive psychology is. This chapter demonstrates the breadth of cognitive psychology and its growth since its origins in the 1950s. We begin with the study of concept formation, which is crucial for all cognition.

## Concept Formation: The Process of Forming Mental Groups

Each day, people solve problems, make decisions, and behave logically, often following steps that are complicated but orderly. Many researchers conceive of reasoning itself as an orderly process that takes place in discrete steps, one set of ideas leading to another (Rips, 1990). To perform this process, people need to be able to form, manipulate, transform, and interrelate concepts. **Concepts** are the mental categories people use to classify events and objects according to common properties. Many objects with four wheels, a driver's seat, and a steering wheel are automobiles; "automobiles" is a concept. More abstract is the concept of "justice," which has to do with legality and fairness. "Animal," "computer," and "lecturer" are all examples of concepts that have various *exemplars*, or specific instances, so there are many kinds of animals, for example, dogs, giraffes, and whales. The study of *concept formation* is the examination of the way people organize and classify events and objects, usually in order to solve problems.

Concepts make events in the world more meaningful by helping people organize their thinking. People develop progressively more complex concepts throughout life. Early on, infants learn the difference between "parent" and "stranger." Within a year, they can discriminate among objects, colours, and people and comprehend such simple concepts as "animal" and "flower." By age two they can verbalize these differences.

Much of what young children are taught involves *classification*—the process of organizing things into categories—because this is a key to organizing and understanding this complex world (see Figure 7.1). Think back to your early school years and to TV shows such as *Sesame Street*. You were taught to classify colours; different animals (and their sounds); shapes such as triangles, circles, and squares; and the letters in the alphabet. The process of developing concepts through the process of classification is lifelong. It involves separating dissimilar events and finding commonalties (Ariely, 2001). But what is the best way to study the processes by which children and adults classify and organize information? As a type of thinking, concept formation is relatively easy to study in controlled laboratory situations. Psychologists design laboratory studies in which the participants form concepts through a range of tasks. For example, suppose you were asked to make judgments in response to questions such as this: Is a bicycle a toy or a vehicle? The experimenter would

CONCEPT

A mental category used to classify an event or object according to a common property.

**FIGURE 7.1**

**Classification Tasks Require Choosing among Alternatives That Share Properties**

In a typical classification task for children, the objective is to circle the picture that is most like the sample.

SAMPLE

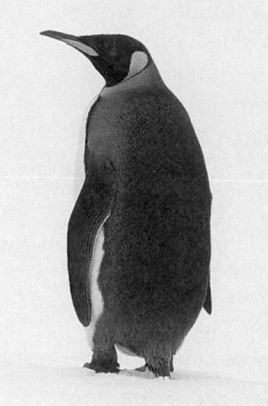

▲ Although quite distinct, this blue jay and this penguin share common characterisitics.

PROTOTYPE

An abstraction of a pattern, object, or idea stored in memory, against which similar patterns are evaluated to see how closely they resemble each other; it is the best example of a class of items.

**Be an ACTIVE LEARNER**

**REVIEW**
> What is the fundamental difference between a positive and a negative instance in concept formation? p. 244
> How do we use prototypes in forming concepts? p. 244

**THINK CRITICALLY**
> Cognitive psychology is expansive in scope. How is this a strength of the field? How is it a weakness?

**APPLY PSYCHOLOGY**
> If you were designing a course to help people develop concept formation skills, what exercises might you include?

time your response and also ask you to express your thought processes out loud. Even more complicated concept formation tasks can be devised in which subtleties between categories are hard to discern—for example, you could be asked to distinguish between a street, a drive, and a boulevard.

A key requirement in laboratory situations studying concept formation is that participants understand and be able to form rules—statements of how features are related. For example, if all objects that have four sides and are red are exemplars of a target concept, participants can learn that any time they see a red rectangle or square, they should press a button. Here is a common task used in laboratory investigations of concept formation: An experimenter presents you with a stimulus and tells you that something about the objects to come makes them similar. You are asked to identify this characteristic, this rule. Each time the researcher presents a stimulus, you ask whether it has the property (characteristic) being targeted; the experimenter answers yes or no. Suppose the first stimulus is a picture of a large bird. The experimenter tells you that it is a *positive instance* (a stimulus that is an example of the concept under study). You now know that the concept may be largeness or being a bird. The second stimulus is a small red bird; the experimenter says that this, too, is a positive instance. You now know that size is not important. The third stimulus is a large blue bird; it, too, is a positive instance. Although the property could be "things that fly" or "animals," you surmise that the relevant property is being a bird. When, on the fourth trial, the stimulus is a small blue toy car and the experimenter says it is a *negative instance* (a stimulus that is not an example of the concept), you might say with conviction that being a bird is the concept.

Laboratory studies allow for examination of how concepts are formed and organized. However, concepts in the real world are not always so clear-cut. For example, you know that professors and high-school instructors are teachers, but do priests and ministers qualify as teachers? Do scout troop leaders qualify? Is the prime minister of Canada a teacher? Each of these individuals acts as a teacher—at least, from time to time. The same problem exists with concepts such as "family." One concept of a family consists of two parents and 2.4 kids. But what of single-parent families, blended families, adoptive families, communal families, extended families? Many researchers define a family as any group of people who care about each other in significant ways. You can see that concepts are often fuzzy.

Eleanor Rosch has asserted that when people are presented with *fuzzy concepts*, they tend to define them in terms of *prototypes*, or best examples, of a class of items (Rosch, 1973, 1978). A **prototype** is an abstraction of a pattern, object, or idea stored in memory, against which similar patterns are evaluated to see how closely they resemble each other; it is the best example of a class of items. A high-school English teacher may be a prototype of a teacher; ministers, hiking instructors, and psychologists are also examples, but not "best" examples. Some concepts make for easily defined prototypes; others are hard to define. When you think about the concept of "furniture," you recognize that chairs, sofas, and tables are good examples—but telephones, pianos, and mirrors are all furniture as well; this is a fuzzy concept. The concept of "computer modem" is much less fuzzy: There may be a few shapes and sizes, but nearly all computer modems do the same thing, in pretty much the same way—they allow for digital computer signals to be reconfigured and sent along analog telephone communication lines. Of course, many variables affect how easily concepts are defined, including properties of the concept as well as an individual's unique experiences with that concept. It is these experiences that help people build strategies and solve problems.

# Problem Solving: Confronting Situations That Require Solutions

You are generally unaware of your cognitive processes; you don't usually think about thinking. And yet you are thinking all the time—sorting through choices, deciding where to go, what to do, and when to do it. When you think, you engage in a wide variety of activities, from daydreaming to planning your next few steps on a mountain path.

How do you manage to study for your psychology exam when you have an English paper due tomorrow? How can you arrange your minuscule closet so all of your clothes and other belongings will fit in it? Your car gets a flat tire on the Trans-Canada Highway; what should you do? These are all problems to be solved. In important ways, your approaches to these dilemmas represent some of the highest levels of cognitive functioning. Human beings are wonderful at **problem solving**, at confronting situations that require going beyond the available information (insight) or that require information gaps to be filled in. Because you can form concepts and group things together in logical ways, you are able to organize your thoughts and attack a problem to be solved. Psychologists (e.g., Knoblich & Ohlsson, 1999) believe that the process of problem solving has four stages, summarized in Figure 7.2.

Huge differences exist in people's problem-solving abilities; but psychologists can help people become more effective problem solvers. When people, and machines for that matter, solve problems they tend to use two basic approaches: algorithms and heuristics. An **algorithm** is a procedure for solving a problem by using a set of rules to implement particular steps over and over again until the problem is solved. *An algorithm, if performed correctly, guarantees a correct solution.* Many mathematics problems (for example, finding a square root) make use of algorithms.

Algorithms also are used in a wide variety of real-life problems, from increasing the yield of a recipe (say, by doubling each ingredient) to writing a computer program (even a relatively simple program requires several algorithms). To implement an algorithm, you follow the rules regarding which task to implement at which point in the procedure. For example, an algorithm for doubling a recipe might be: "Find the list of ingredients. For each ingredient, find the measured amount of the ingredient, multiply that amount by two, and use the product as the new amount for the ingredient. Repeat this procedure until there are no more ingredients listed in the recipe." It's monotonous, but it works. However, because algorithms are sets of rules and procedures that *must* be followed, the necessary time and effort may make them impractical for some uses. Chess-playing computer programs like the University of Alberta's "Deep Blue" (Schaeffer & Plaat, 1997) use algorithms to calculate which of all possible chess moves is best at a given moment. Human problem solvers, such as chess master Gary Kasparov, use rules of thumb so that they do not have to follow rigid sets of rules to solve problems. These rules of thumb are integral to heuristic problem-solving strategies.

**PROBLEM SOLVING**

The behaviour of individuals when confronted with a situation or task that requires insight or determination of some unknown elements.

**ALGORITHM**
[AL-go-rith-um]

A simple, precise, and exhaustive problem-solving procedure that follows a set of rules to implement a step-by-step analysis, as in working out a math problem

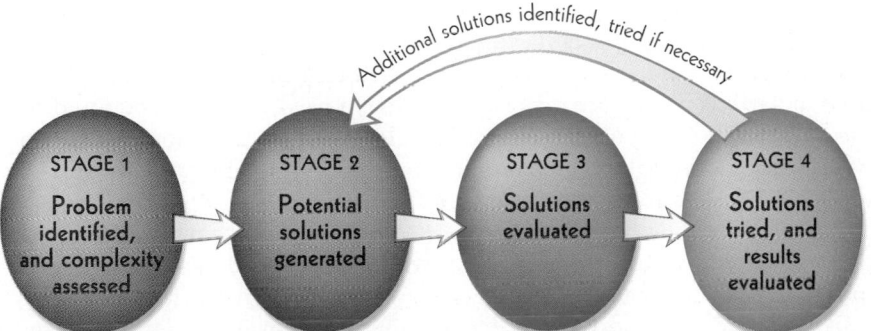

**FIGURE 7.2**

**Stages in Problem Solving**

Problem solving can be conceived of as a four-stage process.

Heuristics are sets of strategies that act as flexible guidelines—not strict rules and procedures—for discovery-oriented problem solving. *A heuristic may quickly lead you to a correct solution, but it does not guarantee one.* Heuristic procedures reflect the processes used by the human brain, and involve making rough estimates, guesses, and subjective evaluations that might be called hunches, or intuitions (Bowers et al., 1990; Rumelhart, 1997). For example, the coach of a hockey team might evaluate the team's first-period performance and intuit that different plays might better its chances against that opponent.

Most heuristic approaches focus on the goal that is to be achieved. In one approach called **subgoal analysis**, a problem is taken apart or broken down into several smaller steps, each of which has a subgoal. For example, the writing of an essay could be broken into subgoals such as formulating the problem, doing library research, and drafting an outline. In **means–ends analysis**, the person compares the current situation or position with the desired end (the goal) to determine the most efficient *means* for getting from one to the other—for example, a person might recognize that getting out of debt first means cutting up credit cards. The objective is to reduce the number of steps needed to reach the goal. A **backward search** involves working backward from the goal, or endpoint, to the current position, both to analyze the problem and to reduce the steps needed to get to the goal. Some problems are most easily solved by starting at the objective and working backward toward the opening or beginning position. People often solve puzzles using this approach, because there are usually a smaller number of choices at the end than at the beginning of a puzzle. This strategy reduces the near infinite number of options available from the opening of the puzzle.

Table 7.1 summarizes the major advantages and disadvantages of algorithms and heuristics.

## BARRIERS TO PROBLEM SOLVING

Although people's problem-solving abilities are usually quite good, they may be subject to certain limitations. Researchers study these hindrances to gain a better understanding of the processes of problem solving.

**FUNCTIONAL FIXEDNESS: COGNITION WITH CONSTRAINTS.** Young children often become distressed if an object is being used for something other than its intended purpose. For example, if an adult uses a pencil to stir coffee, the child is upset by the inappropriate use of the drawing tool. In this example, the child is exhibiting a basic characteristic of most people: functional fixedness. **Functional fixedness** is the inability to see that an object can have a function other than its stated or usual one. When people are functionally fixed, they have limited their choices and conceptual framework; they see too few meanings or responses to an object or idea. In many ways this constitutes a breakdown in problem solving.

Studies of functional fixedness show that often the name or the meaning given to an object or tool limits its function (German & Defeyter, 2001). In a typical study, a participant is presented with a task and provided with tools that can be used in various ways. One laboratory problem used to show functional fixedness is the two-string problem (see Figure 7.3). In this task, a person is put in a room in which there are two strings hanging from the ceiling and some objects lying on a table. The task is to tie the two strings together, but it is impossible to reach one string while holding the other. The only solution is to tie a weight (such as a magnet or a pair of pliers) to one string, set it swinging back and forth, take hold of the second string, and wait until the first string swings within reach. This task is difficult because people's previous experiences with objects such as pliers may prevent them from considering using them as potential tools in an unusual situation.

▲ Coaches use heuristics when relating the moves they believe are most likely to succeed, based on past experience. A coach might ask, "What move has usually enhanced our strategic position in the game?"

**HEURISTICS**
[hyoo-RISS-ticks]

Sets of strategies that act as guidelines, not strict rules and procedures, for discovery-oriented problem solving.

**SUBGOAL ANALYSIS**

A heuristic procedure in which a task is broken down into smaller, more manageable steps, each of which has a subgoal.

**MEANS–ENDS ANALYSIS**

A heuristic procedure in which the problem solver tries to move closer to a solution by comparing the current situation with the desired goal and determining the most efficient way to get from one to the other.

**BACKWARD SEARCH**

A heuristic procedure in which a problem solver works backward from the goal or endpoint to the current position, both to analyze the problem and to reduce the steps needed to get from the current position to the goal.

**FUNCTIONAL FIXEDNESS**

The inability to see that an object can have a function other than its stated or usual one.

**TABLE 7.1  Algorithms and Heuristics: Two Approaches to Problem Solving**

| Approach | Procedure | Advantages | Disadvantages | Example |
|---|---|---|---|---|
| Algorithm | Exhaustive, systematic consideration of all possible solutions; a set of rules. | Solution is guaranteed. | Can be very inefficient, effortful, time-consuming. | You have forgotten your friend's phone number so you call every John Smith in the phone book until you find him. |
| Heuristics | Strategies; rules of thumb that have worked in the past. | Efficient; saves effort and time. | Solution is not guaranteed. | Person attempting to repair a car uses past experience to rule out possible problems. |
| • Subgoal Analysis | Breaks task into smaller units. | — | — | Getting a summer job involves several means for achieving the goal: You must create a resumé, contact references, look for work opportunities you are qualified for, etc. |
| • Means–Ends Analysis | Final goal is identified and the most efficient means for reaching it is established. | — | — | Reflecting on your need to get in shape most efficiently involves increasing your activity level as well as monitoring food intake. |
| • Backwards Search | Similar to means–ends except it involves working from the goal backward toward the start rather than the other way around. | — | — | You might determine how a clock functions by taking one apart, starting with one that works. |

**MENTAL SET.** Psychologists have found that most individuals are flexible in their approaches to solving problems. In other words, they do not use preconceived, or "set," solutions but often think about objects, people, and situations in new ways. A rigid approach would not allow an astronaut to make a device for filtering air out of duct tape and other spare parts (remember the scene from the film *Apollo 13*?). These solutions require limber thought processes (Wiley, 1998).

However, sometimes people develop a rigid strategy, or approach, to certain types of problems. Creative thinking requires that people break out of their *mental set*—their limited ways of thinking about possibilities. Having a mental set is the opposite of being creative. It limits innovation and prevents a person from solving new and complex problems (McKelvie, 1984; Holland, 1975). In an increasingly complex and changing world, such limitations can be problematic. Here's a problem that is difficult because it requires you to overcome a mental set. In Figure 7.4, draw no more than four lines that will run through all nine dots—without lifting your pen from the paper. The answer is provided in Figure 7.5 on page 250.

**FIGURE 7.3**

**The Two-String Problem**

In the two-string problem, the person must set one string in motion in order to tie the strings together. This solution illustrates that sometimes in order to solve problems people need to overcome functional fixedness and use tools in new ways.

FIGURE 7.4

For the Active Learner:
The Nine-Dot Problem

Because people tend to group things in familiar ways, it is hard for them to overcome their psychological set to connect the nine dots as instructed.

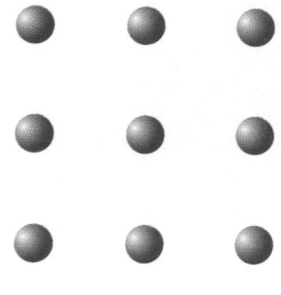

Try to connect all nine dots with no more than four lines, without lifting your pen from the paper.

CREATIVITY

A feature of thought and problem solving that includes the tendency to generate or recognize ideas considered to be high quality, original, novel, and appropriate.

CONVERGENT THINKING

In problem solving, the process of narrowing down choices and alternatives to arrive at a suitable answer.

DIVERGENT THINKING

In problem solving, widening the range of possibilities and expanding the options for solutions.

BRAINSTORMING

A problem-solving technique that involves considering all possible solutions without making initial evaluative judgments.

*Psychology in Action* offers suggestions for overcoming barriers to problem solving and improving your critical thinking skills.

## CREATIVE PROBLEM SOLVING

A number of Canadian cities have had problems in the past with young people hanging around subways or other transit stations and creating disturbances or intimidating transit users. In Calgary, the problem was creatively addressed relatively inexpensively, without installing expensive video surveillance systems or hiring more security. Instead, classical music was played through the existing address system; most of the young people moved on and the problems ceased.

**Creativity** is a feature of thought and problem solving that includes the tendency to generate or recognize high-quality ideas that are original, novel, and appropriate (Sternberg, 2001b). An *original response* is a response not copied from or imitative of another response; that is, the respondent originated the idea. A *novel response* is a response that is new or that has no precedent. Unless an original and novel solution is also appropriate, however, psychologists do not call it creative. An *appropriate response* is a response that is reasonable in terms of the situation. Building your home out of soap bubbles may be an original and novel idea, but it is clearly not appropriate. Two key issues in studies of creativity are how people break mental sets and become more creative in their thinking and who is likely to be creative (Mumford et al., 2001; Sternberg, 2000a). You don't have to be an Einstein or a Picasso to be creative, as the Calgary transit solution demonstrated. To ensure that a creative solution is appropriate, effective problem solvers form a hypothesis and then test it to evaluate potential solutions. Creativity is simply a different way of thinking.

According to well-known creativity researcher Mihalay Csikszentmihalyi (pronounced CHICK-sent–me-high-ee, 1996, 2001), creative individuals are those who have changed the surrounding culture in some way that involves original thinking. Csikszentmihalyi asserts that creativity is the process of redefining or transforming a domain (either a professional field or an area of interest such as gardening, music, or painting) to create a new domain. However, he also acknowledges—indeed, stresses—the idea that individuals work and create within culture; creativity is culturally dependent—in Western cultures creativity is often measured as a work product, but in Eastern traditions creativity is often seen as a process of finding inner truth (Lubart, 1999).

When people sort through alternatives to try to solve a problem, they attempt to focus their thinking, discarding inappropriate solutions until a single appropriate option remains. To do so, they *converge* on an answer (or use convergent thinking skills). **Convergent thinking** is narrowing down choices and alternatives to arrive at a suitable answer. **Divergent thinking**, in contrast, is widening the range of possibilities and expanding the options for solutions; this lessens the likelihood of functional fixedness or mental set. Guilford (1967) defined creative thinking as divergent thinking. According to other psychologists, any solution to a problem that can be worked out only with time and practice is not a creative solution. To foster creativity, people need to rethink their whole approach to a task (Greeno, 1989). Successful entrepreneurs know this to be the case (McClelland, 1998), and those who develop new technologies, products, and services are often well rewarded for their creativity.

Another way to stimulate creative problem solving is a technique called brainstorming. In **brainstorming**, people try to generate as many possible solutions as they can without making any initial judgments about the validity of those solutions. This procedure can be used to illuminate alternative solutions to problems as diverse as how a city can dispose of its waste and how a topic for a group project can be selected. The rationale behind brainstorming is that people will produce more high-quality ideas if they do not have to evaluate the suggestions immediately.

## Be a Critical Thinker

Every day, you have to make judgments, classify ideas, and follow logic—that is, engage in reasoning—to solve problems. Being able to think critically will improve your reasoning and thus your problem-solving skills. Besides the guidelines presented in Chapter 1 (pp. 21–23), several other tips can make you a better critical thinker:

- *Don't fixate on availability.* Things that come to mind quickly are not necessarily the best solutions to problems. Don't choose the first answer just because it's there.
- *Don't generalize too quickly.* Just because most elements in a group follow a pattern does not mean all elements in the group will follow the pattern. For example, just because the florist removed the thorns from most of the red roses you bought for Valentine's Day does not mean he didn't miss one.

- *Don't settle for an easy solution.* People often settle for a solution that works, even though other solutions may work even better. Look at all the alternatives.
- *Don't choose a solution just because it fits pre-existing ideas.* People often accept ideas too quickly when they conform to previously held views. This is a serious mistake for researchers, who need to be open to new ideas, a state of mind that often requires conscious effort.
- *Don't fail to consider any possible solution.* If you do not evaluate *all* of the available alternatives, you are likely to miss the correct, or most logical, answer.
- *Don't be emotional.* Sometimes people become emotionally tied to a specific idea, premise, or conviction. When this happens, the likelihood of being able to critically evaluate the evidence drops sharply. Critical thinkers are cool and evaluative, not headstrong and emotional.

---

Brainstorming attempts to release the potential of the participants: to free them from potential functional fixedness, increase the diversity of ideas, and promote creativity.

**THE INVESTMENT THEORY OF CREATIVITY.** Robert Sternberg has developed a novel approach to studying creativity. He argues that we bring six interactive resources to a problem: intelligence, thinking styles, knowledge, personality, motivation, and environment. People sometimes use their creativity to develop a solution that others have ignored or dismissed. They can later "sell" their creative idea. This notion of working on undervalued problem solutions and marketing them later is why Sternberg calls his approach an *investment theory of creativity* (Sternberg & Lubart, 1993, 1996, 1999). Sternberg argues that if people emphasize their interactive resources such as thinking style and motivation, they can be more creative; he contrasts this approach with traditional ideas of creativity that often define truly creative people as those with exceptionally high levels of certain personality attributes. From Sternberg's point of view, anyone who brings all six interactive resources to bear on a problem can be creative (Sternberg, 2001a).

# Reasoning and Decision Making: Generating Ideas and Reaching Conclusions

Deciding whether to take a run at lunchtime, have a sandwich and soft drink, or study for an upcoming quiz may be a regular decision for you. Each option has benefits and costs; because you make this decision day in and day out, the process usually occurs quickly. But how do you make such decisions? When cognitive psychologists study

**Be an ACTIVE LEARNER**

**REVIEW**
- What are the important differences between heuristics and algorithms? pp. 245–246
- Identify and describe three research-proven ways of improving problem-solving abilities. pp. 248–249
- Characterize the investment theory of creativity. p. 249

**THINK CRITICALLY**
- What mental habits might you develop to break through functional fixedness when you need to solve a problem?
- What kinds of situations cause people to become irrational when they try to solve a problem?

**APPLY PSYCHOLOGY**
- In school settings, people solve theoretical problems and answer questions that might be divorced from reality (such as how to solve the problem of worldwide poverty in one year). How does this approach facilitate problem solving? Or does it? Explain your answer.

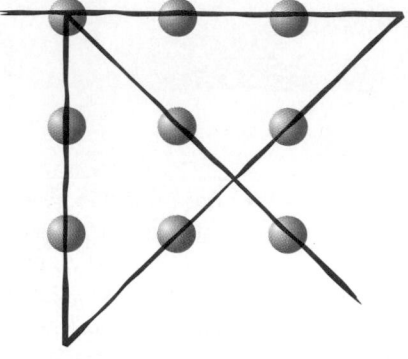

**FIGURE 7.5**

For the Active Learner:
The Nine-Dot Solution

Here is a creative solution to the nine-dot problem presented in Figure 7.4. Note that you have to think beyond your psychological set and not see the nine dots as forming a square.

REASONING

The purposeful process by which people generate logical and coherent ideas, evaluate situations, and reach conclusions.

LOGIC

The system or principles of reasoning used to reach valid conclusions or inferences.

DECISION MAKING

Assessing and choosing among alternatives.

*thinking* they generally attempt to study the systematic day-to-day processes of reasoning and decision making (Galotti, 1989). **Reasoning** is the purposeful process by which people generate logical and coherent ideas, evaluate situations, and reach conclusions. The system or principles of reasoning used to reach valid conclusions or inferences is called **logic.** You can think about reasoning and logic as proceeding in an ordered way or as comprising a process in which ideas and beliefs are continuously updated in a loose, unstructured way (Rips, 1990)—both approaches are valid, and both types of reasoning occur.

**Decision making** means assessing and choosing among alternatives. You make decisions that involve the probability of some event (how likely is it that my friends will want to go on this trip with me?) and others that involve expected value (how important is *this* trip, rather than some other one?). Your decisions vary from the trivial to the complex: what to eat for breakfast, which courses to take, what career to pursue. The trivial decisions are usually made quickly, without much effort or conscious thought. The complex ones require conscious, deliberate, effortful consideration.

Some students have trouble with the distinction between problem solving and decision making. Think of it like this: Both focus on making a good rational solution, but problem solving involves the self-generation of options followed by choosing the best one; decision making often involves narrowing options presented to you.

Psychologists have devised numerous approaches for looking at decision-making processes. We examine estimating probabilities used in situations in which the answer or decision is uncertain.

## UNCERTAINTY: ESTIMATING PROBABILITIES

How do people decide what to wear, where to go, or how to answer a question on a test? How do they decide when something is bigger, longer, or more difficult? Many decisions are based on formal logic, some are based on carefully tested hypotheses, and some are based on educated guesses. Making an *educated guess* implies knowing something from past experience. When you see rain clouds, for example, you guess—but cannot be 100 percent certain—that it will rain. The likelihood of rain is expressed as a percentage—that is, as a probability.

Psychological factors, especially previous events, affect how people estimate probabilities of events. Consider a study conducted by Nobel Laureate Daniel Kahneman, while working at the University of British Columbia, and his colleague Amos Tversky (Tversky & Kahneman, 1973) in which participants were asked to judge whether a list of names contained more men than women. Participants were given the names of 40 famous people—20 men and 20 women, with a probability of 50 percent of each gender. In one case, the participants read a list in which the men were more famous than the women; in another, the participants read a list in which the women were more famous than the men. After reading their respective lists, the participants were asked if their list contained more men or women. The participants who read the list with more famous men said there were more men on the list; those who read the list with more famous women said there were more women on the list. The critical variable affecting the results was the participants' familiarity with the names of the famous people. In other words, the fact that the people of one gender were more famous affected the participants' perceptions and their estimates of probability. (See Figure 7.6 for an example of this phenonmenon.)

People make probability estimates of all types of behaviours and events. In election years, they estimate the likelihood of a Liberal victory. On the basis of past experience, they estimate the probability of staying on a study schedule, an exercise regime, or a diet. They can judge whether a particular event increases or decreases the probability of another event. When several factors are involved, their compounding and mitigating effects alter the probability of the outcome. For example, the probability that there will be rain when there are thunderclouds, high winds, and low barometric pressure is much higher than the probability of rain when it is merely cloudy.

Study participants asked to make probability judgments about the real world, particularly about fairly rare events such as airplane crashes, are less likely to make accurate judgments than people given laboratory problems (Chase, 2000). The farther in the future the event to be predicted is, the more ambiguity exists for the predictor; also, people are likely to be affected by past behaviour and therefore make mistakes about the future (Payne, Bettman, & Johnson, 1992). Also, according to Norman Brown (1997) at the University of Alberta, people judge the frequency of target events by trying to recall as many similar events as possible and then counting their recollections. For example, a person might estimate the probability of contracting the West Nile virus as high based on the number of news reports they have heard or read about the virus (when in fact the probability of contracting the disease is very small). This strategy, of course, is significantly influenced by how the questions are asked and the contexts in which they are posed. People make mistakes and errors in judgment and may act irrationally. They may ignore key pieces of data and thus make bad (or irrational) decisions that are not based on probability. For this reason, a person afraid of contracting the West Nile virus might use dangerous chemicals in their home and yard to reduce their (unfounded) perception of risk. Sometimes, people's world views colour their probability decision making. For example, having strong religious or political views can influence a person's strategies and decision estimates.

Finally, people are not machines or computers; their past experiences, personalities, and cultural backgrounds can influence their thought processes, sometimes in unpredictable ways. However, cognitive psychologists have suggested ways for

| | | |
|---|---|---|
| Mike Myers | Emily Smith | Marion Lancaster |
| Martin Short | Tracy Conners | Jim Carrey |
| Michael J. Fox | Dave Thomas | Tracy Roberts |
| Matthew Perry | John Candy | Cindy Cox |
| Joan Brown | Michelle Jones | Patty Johnson |
| Susan Richards | Brenda Williams | Eugene Levy |
| Tom Green | Graham Greene | Kathryn Moore |
| Roberta Lynch | Dan Aykroyd | Jason Priestley |
| Beverly Matthews | Howie Mandel | |

The answer may surprise you. There are an equal number of male and female names. However since the men listed are all famous Canadian actors and comedians, it is easier to recall their names, leading to an overestimation of the number of male names.

**FIGURE 7.6**
**For the Active Learner: The Availability Heuristic**

Read the names and answer the following question. *Without counting,* are there more men's names or women's names in this list? What is your impression?

▲ Diverse world views affect how people in the East and the West solve problems.

individuals to become the most efficient learners and thinkers they can be, and researchers have found that people can be taught to weigh costs and benefits more accurately and to be less influenced by their frames of reference (Bayster & Ford, 2000; Blount & Larrick, 2000). Research by Kevin Dunbar (1994) at McGill University, for example, indicates that the stated goals of a sample research project (finding evidence that supports a hypothesis) strongly affect whether the researcher can look past expectations and react appropriately to negative research findings. One way to break out of traditional frames of reference is to use analogies. When researchers examined how students could best learn scientific concepts, they found that analogies were especially useful. Analogies involve using past experiences with similar situations to find a solution to a current problem. For example, you may enjoy success when fishing a new river by recalling that on other rivers you have fished you had good luck when casting into slower-moving, deeper areas. Details are reported back well through traditional learning of text, but analogies—especially creative ones—provide conceptual bridges that facilitate learning, memory, and concept development (Donnelly & McDaniel, 1993).

## BARRIERS TO GOOD DECISION MAKING

In the same way that people's problem solving can be hampered by mental sets, their decision making can be hindered by a range of stumbling blocks. By studying and learning about those limitations we can hope to overcome some of them.

**GAMBLER'S FALLACY.**   If you know about probability, you know that people have misconceptions about the probabilities of events. A common fallacy is the *gambler's fallacy*—the belief that the chances of an event occurring increase if the event has not occurred recently or that things can be done to increase the odds of winning. This fallacy has resulted in millions of people leaving thousands of dollars in casinos. In reality, every time you flip a coin the chance of getting "heads" is 1 in 2, or 50 percent—regardless of what happened on the last flip.

**BELIEF IN SMALL NUMBERS.**   Limiting the number of observations we make also contributes to poor decision making. When we choose to draw conclusions from a small sample of individuals or observations—a *belief in small numbers*—results are likely to be far more variable and not representative of a larger sample. Even a single compelling story example can influence us. People are willing to infer conclusions from a small sample—say, 10 neighbours—and assume that such a sample is representative of an entire town, province, or country.

**AVAILABILITY HEURISTIC.**   Although it is generally known that air travel is quite safe—safer than walking through the parking lot of a nearby shopping mall—many people are still afraid to fly. People with such fears overestimate the probability of events in their lives and are likely to make poor decisions when they follow those beliefs. Such exaggeration is probably due to the wide media attention given to infrequent catastrophic events; accordingly, such information is more "available" than other information and therefore it is easy to think of examples of these events. Psychologists refer to this phenomenon as the *availability heuristic*—the tendency to judge the probability of an event by how easy it is to think of examples of it. The number of fatalities due to plane crashes, tornadoes, and icebergs is overestimated by most people.

**OVERCONFIDENCE.**   When people develop ideas about the world they often become overconfident and overestimate the accuracy of their judgments and knowledge. Such *overconfidence* is a major stumbling block to good decision making. Imagine the surprise of a student who is rejected from the only law school she applied to because she was sure—absolutely convinced—that she would be accepted. Individuals become so committed to their ideas and beliefs that they are more often confident than correct; when challenged they often become more rigid and fixed in their beliefs.

**CONFIRMATION BIAS.** Perhaps the greatest challenge to making good decisions is that people tend to cling to beliefs despite contradictory evidence; psychologists call this phenomenon the *confirmation bias*. People tend to discount information that does not fit with their pre-existing views. For example, older drivers may believe that all young drivers are reckless despite numerous examples of responsible young drivers on the road. The older driver only makes note of examples of careless driving by young people. People rarely dwell on missed opportunities to make money from investments; rather, they seek to confirm their good judgment by telling how they have made money (or did not lose any) through the investments they did make. Such a narrow, single-minded focus certainly can lead to poor reasoning and decision making. As you will see when we study social psychology in Chapter 13, the confirmation bias leads to stereotypes and prejudices that are often ill-informed and wrong.

## CULTURE AND REASONING

Problem solving, reasoning, and decision making seem like straightforward thought processes. Everybody recognizes difficult situations, complexities, and even barriers to good decision making and problem solving. However, people also believe that, in the end, all people go about reasoning in the same way. This just isn't so.

It turns out, for example, that the intellectual traditions of the East and the West are quite different, and so are the reasoning and decision-making tendencies of their peoples (Peng & Nisbett, 1999). For example, when given contradictory statements to reason through, people from China prefer compromise solutions; European Canadians prefer noncompromising ones. Chinese traditions hold that reality is a process, does not stand still, and is in constant flux. Chinese tradition recognizes contradictions in life and that such contradictions must be embraced. It further argues that all things are in one way or another connected. Western intellectual traditions use reasoning that is analytical and logical; reality is considered to be objective, fixed, and identifiable; reality is precise and constant; and many things are isolated and independent of one another.

Such different world views affect how people in the East and the West solve problems; they think about problems differently (Peng & Nisbett, 1999). Therefore, when the conclusions of business leaders, politicians, and soldiers of the East puzzle Westerners, it should not be surprising. We have much more to learn about cognition by studying such cultural variation. One potentially illuminating research method will be to study multicultural individuals. What is a person's reasoning like when she is raised in one culture but then moves to another? How much time must be spent in the new culture before she realizes a new mode of thinking? Is it even possible for people to switch modes of thinking? Tomasello (2000) asserts that culture is learned at very young ages. However, Hong and colleagues (2000) have found that people are able to switch modes of thought, especially about a recently evaluated thought. There is much more work to be done concerning multicultural individuals, who constitute a growing segment of the world's population.

## EVOLUTION AND REASONING

How do evolutionary theorists and researchers account for reasoning? First and foremost, remember that evolutionary psychologists assume that people have specific abilities because those skills have helped them be fit, survive, and reproduce.

The world is a complex place, filled with information and many decisions to make. Evolutionary psychologists believe that humans have built-in mechanisms to help them sift through the information and make decisions, concentrating on the decisions that are most relevant for survival and reproduction. Most psychologists believe that cognition is shaped by general mechanisms, cognitive processes, and ways of handling information that apply to a variety of situations. Evolutionary psychologists argue that human brains have specific "programs," specialized ways of handling certain information, that shape our cognition and reasoning (Cosmides & Tooby, 1997). Thus, some of our reasoning is determined by the type of information processing our brains are set up to do. This type of cognition and reasoning is easier than other types. For example, "If a person eats cookies, then the person must wash dishes first." This situation also involves "if–then" logic, but it is framed as a benefit that occurs only when the person performs the required task. If people eat cookies and have not washed dishes first, then they have violated the rule—they have cheated. Cosmides and Tooby argue that people have evolved "cheater detectors" that allow them to detect this type of social contract violation. This specialized mechanism allows people to be good at this type of logic problem. Evolutionary psychologists argue that cognitive psychology has focused on problems that are difficult for humans rather than studying the types of reasoning that the human brain is programmed to do. Therefore, evolutionary psychologists claim that cognitive psychology has ignored some of the most important problems.

# Artificial Intelligence

As the 1990s unfolded and people gave thought to the approaching new millennium, much was written about the role of computers in society. There is no question that computers have transformed what we do and how we do it. Today's computers are small, fast, and powerful; in some ways, they reflect the values of our society—power, speed, and disposability after four years or so. By simulating specific models of the human brain, computers help psychologists understand human thought processes. Specifically, computers help shape theoretical development (as in hypotheses about information processing and perception), assist researchers in investigating how people solve problems, and enable psychologists to test models of certain aspects of behaviour, such as memory. They also assist human beings in performing many real-life chores. When computer programs implement or produce some type of human activities, they are said to involve *artificial intelligence (AI)*.

## THE COMPUTER AS INFORMATION PROCESSOR

The information processing approach to perception, memory, and problem solving is a direct outgrowth of computer simulations. Flow charts showing how information from sensory memory reaches short-term working memory and long-term memory rely implicitly on a computer analogy. Those who study memory extend the computer analogy further by referring to hypothetical storage areas in the brain as "buffers" and biological information processing mechanisms as "central processors." The information processing approach is widely used, although it has come under attack because it tends to reduce memory to small mechanistic elements (Bruner, 1990).

The most widely investigated aspect of computer simulation and artificial intelligence is problem solving. Playing chess was one of the first human activities that researchers tried to duplicate with computers, and ever since then human beings like Gary Kasparov have been challenging the computers for dominance—with some modest successes and some notable failures! Jonathan Schaeffer (1997) of the computer science department at the University of Alberta has taken game modelling to new heights by designing a program called Chinook that plays checkers so well that it is now, in fact, the world champion, having beaten several top-ranked players in tournament play. If you think your checkers skills are pretty good, try them out against Chinook at **www.cs.ualberta.ca/~chinook/**. Good luck!

▲ Jonathan Schaeffer's Chinook program is now the checkers world champion.

Computers can solve complicated problems involving large amounts of memory. The most sophisticated programs incorporate aspects of human memory and decision making and have been used to solve a wide array of problems, including issues of computer chip design and human resource management (Lawler & Elliot, 1996).

Although computers can be programmed to process information in similar ways to human beings and can process certain complex information infinitely more quickly, they lack human ingenuity and imagination (see *Point/Counterpoint*). In addition, computers do not have a referential context in which to interpret situations. Further, they cannot evaluate their own ideas or improve their own problem-solving abilities by developing heuristics.

## NEURAL NETWORKS

As we have seen, the comparison of the brain to a computer is a compelling one. Interesting research has focused on the brain's ability to represent information in a number of locations simultaneously. Take a moment to imagine a computer. You may conjure up an image of an IBM or a Macintosh, a laptop or a mainframe terminal. You also may start thinking about programming code, computer screens, even your favourite gaming console. Your images of specific computers or representations of what the computers can do are stored and coded at different places in the brain. No one suggests that you have a "computer corner" where all information about computers is stored. Since various pieces of information are stored in different portions of the brain, their electrical energy must be combined at some point, in some way, for you to use the word *computer*, understand it, and visualize it what it stands for.

The brain has specific processing areas. However, these areas are located throughout the brain, and thus a "convergence" zone, or centre, is necessary to mediate and organize the information, according to Antonio Damasio (Adolphs & Damasio, 2000; Damasio, 2000; Parvizi & Damasio, 2001). Signals from widely separated clusters of neuronal activity come together in convergence zones to evoke words. That convergence zones are located away from specific pieces of information helps explain why some stroke victims and patients with various brain lesions (injuries) can tell you some things about a given topic—say, pianos—but not everything they once knew. For example, a stroke victim may be able to look at a picture of a piano and tell you that it has keys and a pedal but be unable to name it. According to Damasio's view, a key convergence zone has been damaged.

The idea of convergence zones has led to the development of models of where and how the brain operates to represent the world, develop concepts, solve problems, and process day-to-day tasks such as reading and listening (Posner & Pavese, 1998). It also helps explain why people who have had damage to the visual cortex can sometimes have knowledge of things that they do not acknowledge seeing. This residual vision—sometimes referred to as *blindsight*—is attributed to secondary, less important visual pathways. Place (2000) and Jackson (2000) reported cases of individuals who demonstrated blindsight. A patient who has incurred localized brain damage is periodically able to discriminate visual information of which they claim to have no visual awareness (claiming to be merely "guessing"). Such multi-stage models of knowledge of the world—with multiple sources of input—suggest convergence zones and multiple levels and layers of processing.

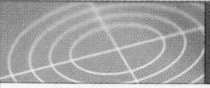

## Do Computers Think the Way Human Beings Do?

**POINT:** Computers have problem-solving and decision-making abilities; these abilities correspond to human thinking.

**COUNTERPOINT:** A computer's ability to store information and answer questions does not constitute thought, and those who state that a computer thinks exaggerate its abilities.

The computer has transformed the workplace and the home. Its miniaturization has led to small phones, smart phones, and wireless miniature phones. We have palm devices, robots, and the Internet, which has transformed commerce. But does the computer think, or does it merely process preprogrammed ideas and thoughts that human beings put into it?

Clearly computers know how to solve problems; they also have decision-making abilities. Computers can be given mathematical, economic, social, and weather models and make highly accurate predictions. In fact, when predicting the weather, a computer acts in much the same way human beings do. The computer can take multiple variables into account, factor in subtle potential changes, and be as good as the CBC meteorologist. The truth is that computers can be programmed with both general and specific rules. They can relate symbols and build organized structures. A computer's capabilities are far ranging, it does not get tired, it can hold huge amounts of information—theoretically, unlimited amounts—and it will work at blinding speeds, 24 hours per day. Computers have already been shown to have reasoning properties in common with the thought processes of human beings. Although a computer's processing methods are often clear-cut and repetitive, this is not necessarily a basis for denying computers thinking status.

However, computers are not human beings, and they operate differently. They do not use strategies that can be considered perceptual in nature. Their approach tends to be step by step rather than intuitive. Once committed to a strategy—usually an algorithm—a computer cannot change its mind. In fact, it has no mind and thus cannot use multiple strategies. People, unlike computers, can interpret language (and the world) not because they run the right computer code but because they are organisms with a biological structure capable of producing action, purpose, learning, perception, insight, and other planned experiences. Computers do not reflect or think about themselves and their purpose for being. You cannot find a computer that can tease, dream, or fall head over silicon in love.

In the end, the real question is this: Can a computer think like a human being? The answer is not entirely clear. Computers are not human, they do not intuit, they do not have imagination, they are not endowed with a spirit that makes them soar when they hear music or become depressed at the demise of another computer; however, they compute like crazy, they have nearly infinite memory, and they are able to solve problems, anticipate events, and increasingly behave more and more like human beings.

In recent years, mathematicians, physiologists, and psychologists have joined forces to develop specific models of how neural structures represent complicated information (e.g., Crosson, 2000). Their work is often based on the concept of *parallel distributed processing (PDP)*, which suggests that many operations take place simultaneously and at many locations within the brain. Most desktop computers can perform only one operation at a time—admittedly very quickly, but still only one at a time. In contrast, the largest of modern computers can operate hundreds or even thousands of processors at once. Today's supercomputers are made up of many powerful computers that operate simultaneously (in parallel) to solve problems. PDP models assert that the brain can process many events, store them simultaneously, and compare them to past events (Grossberg, 1995).

To study parallel distributed processing, researchers have devised artificial neural networks. These networks typically are composed of interconnected "units" that serve as model neurons. Each unit, or artificial neuron, receives signals of varying and modifiable weight, to represent signals that would be received by a real dendrite. Activity generated by the unit is transmitted as a single out-going signal to other neural units. Both input and output to units can be varied electronically, as can interconnections among units. Layers of units can be connected to other layers, and the output of one layer may be the input to another.

A neural network can be a physical entity, but researchers usually prefer to use computers to create complex, fast, electronic neural networks that simulate specific activities. For example, some electronic neural networks have sophisticated pattern recognition abilities and can be taught to recognize handwritten letters and other simple patterns. A network can be presented with a stimulus, say, the letter A. In addition, a network can learn to recognize a range of forms that look like the letter A. In this case, the network is said to have learned a *prototype*. Prototypes may constitute the network's basis of form and letter perception.

An interesting aspect of networks is what happens when one portion of a network is destroyed. The network does not crash, but it makes mistakes, much as the brain would. When portions of the brain are ablated (surgically destroyed or removed) or injured in an accident, the person is still able to complete some tasks. For example, one patient lost the ability to perceive motion, seeing the world as a series of still photos. This made crossing the road very hazardous, as she would glance up and see a stationary image of a car and assume it was safe to cross when in fact the car was bearing down on her.

Neural networks, like the brain, learn and remember. A neural network learns by noticing changes in the weights or values associated with various connections. Sophisticated networks learn quickly and easily, and modify themselves based on experience. The connections between various units within the network are changed because of experience in a way that reflects Hebb's theory: Those units that are frequently activated will become more pronounced, will have a lower threshold of activation, and will be more easily accessed in the future (Posner, DiGirolamo, & Frenandez-Duque, 1997). This access is part of the retrieval process; easy access means easy retrieval, and both are dependent on clear, unambiguous learning.

That neural networks operate efficiently is clear; but they're fallible. Although they can learn speech and handwriting, chess and checkers strategies, and spatial layouts, they are subject to error (see Nass et al., 1995). Furthermore, they do not have the creativity and personality that human beings possess. They lack a sense of humour and the ingenuity that perseverance, motivation, and intelligence bring to a task. Neural networks help us understand human cognition, but they will not take its place.

## Language

Linguists have a name for the study of how the social context of a sentence affects its meaning: *pragmatics*. A **language** is a system of symbols, usually words, that convey meaning; in addition to the symbols, a language also has rules for combining symbols to generate an infinite number of messages (usually sentences). Therefore, language is symbolic, it is a structured system, it is used to represent meaning, and it is generative, allowing an infinite number of sentences to be created. We will examine these key elements in a moment. But for now, think about how amazing it is that we have such complex language structure, and that we are able to process it so effortlessly, despite its complexity. Languages evolve and grow; they reflect a person's culture; they allow individuals to share ideas and values almost effortlessly. Thus language is a social tool. Language takes place in a context, and the same words can have different meanings depending on who says them

**HandsOnPsych**
Version 2.0

**Language, Intelligence, and Problem Solving**

LANGUAGE

A system of symbols, usually words, that convey meaning; in addition, it also has rules for combining symbols to generate an infinite number of messages.

▲ Walk down any street that is under construction, and you may see the warning sign "Men Working"—even though you are likely to see women as part of the construction crew.

and when, whether they are said with a smile, with a grunt, or in a song (Trimble, 2000). Language is often also expressed with gestures. Language is also clearly rule governed—the rules we use are called grammar (more on it later). Importantly, language is a generative system—knowledge of a language's rules allows a user to generate or create an infinite number of meaningful ideas and sentences.

## LANGUAGE AND GENDER STEREOTYPES

In churches, synagogues, and mosques around the country, people are trying out, and getting used to, gender-neutral language. In some liturgies, God is no longer referred to as "father," and "forefathers" are called "ancestors." Research shows that such changes affect listeners' responses to liturgy and sermons (Greene & Rubin, 1991). In general, the English language has evolved in such a way that its words define many roles as male, except for roles that traditionally have been played by women (nurses, teachers) and considered softer and weaker—and less powerful (Lakoff, 2000).

Language with a sexist bias expresses stereotypes and expectations about men and women. For example, men are often described using active, positive words (for example, *successful, strong, independent,* and *courageous*). Women have traditionally been described with words implying passiveness (such as *gentle, loving,* or *patient*), or even with negative terms (*the weaker sex, timid, frail*). When language indicative of strength or courage is applied to a woman, it is often in the context of incongruity—for example, "She thinks like a man."

Lakoff (2000) asserts that people still see the world through a male frame of reference and that this is assumed to be the preferred value system. Research supports the idea that men and women are perceived and treated differently and that they speak differently. Frable (1989) concluded that if people believe in gender-specific abilities, they are likely to apply that belief to their decision making. Frable found that people with strong gender-typed ideas were especially likely to pay attention to the gender of job applicants and then to devalue the interview performance of the women.

Gender differences in language use are usually context-dependent; researchers know that men's and women's language is different and English does appear to have more female-valued terms (Sankis, Corbitt, & Widiger, 1999), but they also know that the differences must be considered within a larger context of ethnicity, class, age, and gender—not to mention social norms and personality (Pennebaker & King, 1999; Wodak & Benke, 1997).

Although gender stereotypes continue to exist, some women and men accept the value of *androgyny,* the state of possessing characteristics traditionally considered masculine as well as those considered feminine. People are becoming more accepting of individuals whose behaviour is gender-flexible—for example, men who cook and women who repair cars. Even more important, people are becoming more sensitive to how language shapes their concept of the world and their problem-solving abilities. Research shows that people can adapt their language style depending on whom they talk to; that is, they "gender" their language depending on whether the listener is a man or a woman (Thomson, Murachaver, & Green, 2001).

## THOUGHT, CULTURE, AND LANGUAGE

In the 1950s researchers discovered that Inuit languages had many more nouns to refer to snow than English does. From this finding, anthropologist and linguist

Benjamin Whorf reasoned that the Inuit languages shaped Inuits' thinking about snow—that is, verbal and language abilities must affect thought directly. In Whorf's view, the structure of the language that people speak directly determines their thoughts and perceptions (Whorf, 1956).

Even though human beings are sensitive to odours, they have an impoverished language structure to describe them. Research shows that although odours are easily detected, naming such odours can be difficult. Such names are often based on personal experiences and sometimes are coded in terms of a personal biographical event (for example, Granddad's pipe tobacco, Mother's perfume, Aunt Maria's attic) (Richardson & Zucco, 1989). Linguistic processes play a limited role in the processing of smell; the language of odours is determined by factors other than simply perceptions of odours. *Language may influence thought but language does not determine thought* (Lillo-Martin, 1997).

▲ Culture has an important influence on both language and thought.

Certainly thought and language interact. Culture has a great influence on both language and thought. Fairly rigid linguistic customs reflect hundreds of years of history; for example, in the French language, there are formal and informal means of address. The word *you* for friends is *tu*; in more formal settings, one uses *vous*. Japan has even greater culturally determined distinctions in formality of language; who a person is in the workplace—boss, manager, supervisor, worker—affects how he or she is addressed and whether he or she will be shown deference. (In Chapter 17, we will consider workplace psychology in more detail.) Language is thus an expression of ethnic, geographic, cultural, and religious tendencies (Williamson, 1991).

Many people are bilingual, speaking at least two languages. Although bilingualism promotes cognitive flexibility, research shows that when bilingual people are asked to respond to a question, take a personality test, or otherwise interact in the world, they do so in a culturally bound way—depending on the language in which they respond. When responding to a personality inventory written in Chinese, native speakers of Chinese are likely to reflect Chinese values; when they respond to an English version of the same personality test, their responses are more likely to reflect Western values (Dinges & Hull, 1993; Dinges, Atlis, & Vincent, 1997; Dinges & Cherry, 1995).

As Matsumoto (2000) asserts, language and culture are intertwined; culture affects language, *and* it affects a person's attitudes and world view. Studies of culture suggest that language does not determine thought, but rather subtly influences it.

## LINGUISTICS

**Linguistics** is the study of language, including speech sounds, meaning, and grammar. **Psycholinguistics** is the study of how language is acquired, perceived, understood, and produced. Among other things, psycholinguists seek to discover how children learn the complicated rules necessary to speak correctly.

For most of us language is conveyed through spoken words and then, later, writing. However, other means of communication exist. For example, many deaf individuals communicate through American Sign Language (ASL). ASL is visual rather than auditory and is composed of precise hand shapes and movements; interpreters are required to translate spoken English into ASL. It is the native language of many deaf men and women, as well as some hearing children born into deaf families. Like spoken English or French, ASL is capable of communicating subtle, complex, and abstract ideas. Research shows that ASL is complex and expressive. It has its own distinct grammatical structure that is not a form of English; in fact, ASL shares more with spoken Japanese than it does with English. The rules and grammar of ASL must be mastered in the same way as the grammar of any other language (Siple, 1997).

**LINGUISTICS**
[ling-GWIS-ticks]
The study of language structure and language change, including speech sounds, meaning, and grammar.

**PSYCHOLINGUISTICS**
The study of how language is acquired, perceived, understood, and produced.

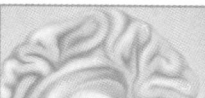 Children are astonishingly adept at understanding the basic rules of spoken language.

Children are astonishingly adept at understanding and using the basic rules of spoken language. Even children only 18 months old, who have vocabularies of perhaps 50 words, understand the world around them; psychologists say that their *receptive vocabulary* is greater than their *productive vocabulary*—but that eventually changes. A three-year-old, noticing that many nouns can be turned into verbs by the addition of a suffix, may say, "It sunned today," indicating that she understands the rule. By the time most English-speaking people reach adulthood, they recognize about 40 000 words.

The miracle of language acquisition in children has long fascinated linguists and psycholinguists. Psychological studies since the early 1970s show that children first acquire the simple aspects of language and then learn progressively more complex elements and capabilities. Studies have also revealed *linguistic structures*—the rules and regularities that exist in, and make it possible to learn, a language. We will examine three major areas of psycholinguistic study: *phonology*, the study of the sounds of language; *semantics*, the study of the meanings of words and sentences; and *syntax*, the study of the relationships among words and how they combine to form sentences. In each of these areas, researchers have tried to identify the universal characteristics that exist in all languages, not just English.

## BRAIN AND Behaviour

### Is Anything about Thought Hard-wired?

Is the brain hard-wired for some cognitive activities? Researchers have conducted EEG studies to see if there are observable differences in the brain waves, brain structures, or neuroanatomical details of young and old people and of individuals while they perform new and well-learned tasks.

Research using brain-imaging techniques and language studies provides some suggestions about brain development and structure. PET and fMRI scans, which trace the distribution and timing of activity in the brain while a person is involved in a cognitive task, show that specific brain areas do seem to be activated while people are performing certain functions (Simpson et al., 2000). The occipital lobe becomes more involved in visual activities, the temporal lobe in more cognitive functions, and the left superior temporal gyrus in auditory language comprehension (e.g., Yancey & Phelps, 2001). Such scan studies thus lend credence to the traditional view that there is correspondence between brain structure and function.

Research is constantly challenging traditional findings, however. Language functions have traditionally been thought to be based solely in the left hemisphere for right-handed people (about 90 percent of the population). An area on the left side of the brain, called the sylvian fissure, has been thought to be responsible for the expression and comprehension of spoken and written language—closely associated activities.

But left–right asymmetries disappeared as children grew older and developed more sophisticated language ability (Eliot, 1999). Furthermore, Baynes and colleagues (1998) found that writing functions may be located in the right side of the brain. Baynes found that for a patient who had undergone a surgical split-brain procedure (see Chapter 2, p. 72), in which the left and right sides of the brain are disconnected, the abilities to read and speak were left-brain activities but writing was a right-brain activity. This new finding—that spoken and written language may be controlled by independent hemispheres—has yet to be substantiated, but it raises new questions about brain function (Langdon & Warrington, 2000). Some researchers think that the brain may consist of many more modules, or parts, than previously thought, and that these parts may operate both independently and together to create language. So, is the brain hard-wired for some cognitive activities? Perhaps. We saw in Chapter 2 that the brain is plastic, malleable, and sensitive to experience and that it changes over time in a developmental sequence (Epstein, 2001). The brain may have specific structures and functions that are hard-wired, but their proper operation requires sophisticated control and coordination that may depend on experience and even on the context and culture in which people mature (Zhou, 2001). Perhaps it is this coordination that allows each of us to develop unique and potentially creative thought processes.

# LANGUAGE STRUCTURE

The key components of language are its sounds, how its sounds acquire meaning, and its overall organization. Let's consider these elements, known more formally as phonology, semantics, and syntax.

**PHONOLOGY.**   The crying, spitting, and burping noises that infants first make are caused by air passing through the vocal apparatus. By about six weeks, infants begin to make speech such as cooing sounds. During their first 12 months, babies' vocalizations become more varied and frequent. Eventually a baby can combine sounds into pronounceable units. As psychologists have studied people's speech patterns, they have helped define a field—phonology. **Phonology** is the study of the patterns and distribution of speech sounds in a language and the tacit rules for their pronunciation.

The basic units of sound that compose the words in a language are called **phonemes**. One hundred phonemes exist over all of the world's languages, and babies use all of them for a short period of time when first babbling. In English, phonemes are the sounds of single letters, such as *b, p, f,* and *v,* and of combinations of letters, such as *th* in "these." All of the sounds in the English language are expressed in 45 phonemes; of those, just 9 make up nearly half of all words. **Categorical speech perception** refers to the ability to discriminate sounds that belong to the same phonemic class. Janet Werker and Richard Tees (1999, 2002) at the University of British Columbia have clearly demonstrated that infants can make more distinctions among phonemes than adults can. Unlike mature speakers of their native language, young infants are able to distinguish the differences between speech sounds that do not actually exist in their native language; they have universal *phonetic sensitivity.* However, in the second half of their first year, as infants focus on the phonemic distinctions that are important in their native language, they begin to lose the ability to respond to sounds outside of their usual language environment. That is, they tune in the sounds contained in the language they will learn to speak and tune out the sounds that are not relevant.

Words consist of **morphemes**, the basic units of meaning in a language. A morpheme consists of one or more phonemes combined into a meaningful unit. The morpheme *do,* for example, consists of two phonemes, *d* and *o.* Adding prefixes and suffixes to morphemes can form other words. Adding *un-* or *-ing* to the morpheme *do,* for example, results in *undo* or *doing. Morphology* is the study of word meaning.

No matter what language people speak, one of their first meaningful utterances is the sound *da.* It is coincidental that *da* is a word in English. Other frequently heard early words of English-speaking children are *bye-bye, mama,* and *baby.* In any language, the first words often refer to a specific person or object, especially food, toys, or animals. At about one year of age, children make the first sounds that can be classified as communicative speech. Initially they utter only one word, but soon they are saying as many as four or five words. Once they have mastered 100 or so words, there is a rapid increase in the size of their vocabulary. Interestingly, there is considerable variation in when this "vocabulary spurt" takes place; some children exhibit it far earlier than others (Dromi, 1997). In the second year, a child's vocabulary may increase to more than 200 words, and by the end of the third year, to nearly 900 words. Figure 7.7 shows vocabulary growth through age nine.

**SEMANTICS.**   At first, babies do not fully understand what their parents' utterances mean. As more words take on meaning, however, the growing child develops semantic capability. **Semantics** is the analysis of the meaning of language, but especially of individual words, the relationships among words, and the significance of words within particular contexts.

**PHONOLOGY**

The study of the patterns and distribution of speech sounds in a language and the tacit rules for their pronunciation.

**PHONEME [FOE-neem]**

A basic unit of sound in a language.

**CATEGORICAL SPEECH PERCEPTION**

The ability to discriminate sounds that belong to the same phonemic class.

**MORPHEME [MORE-feem]**

A basic unit of meaning in a language.

**SEMANTICS [se-MAN-ticks]**

The analysis of the meaning of language, especially of individual words.

FIGURE 7.7

## Vocabulary Changes in Childhood

The average size of children's vocabulary increases rapidly from age 18 months until age 6, when children are fully functional—with a vocabulary of more than 2500 words.

(Adapted from Moskowitz, 1978 on work done by Smith.)

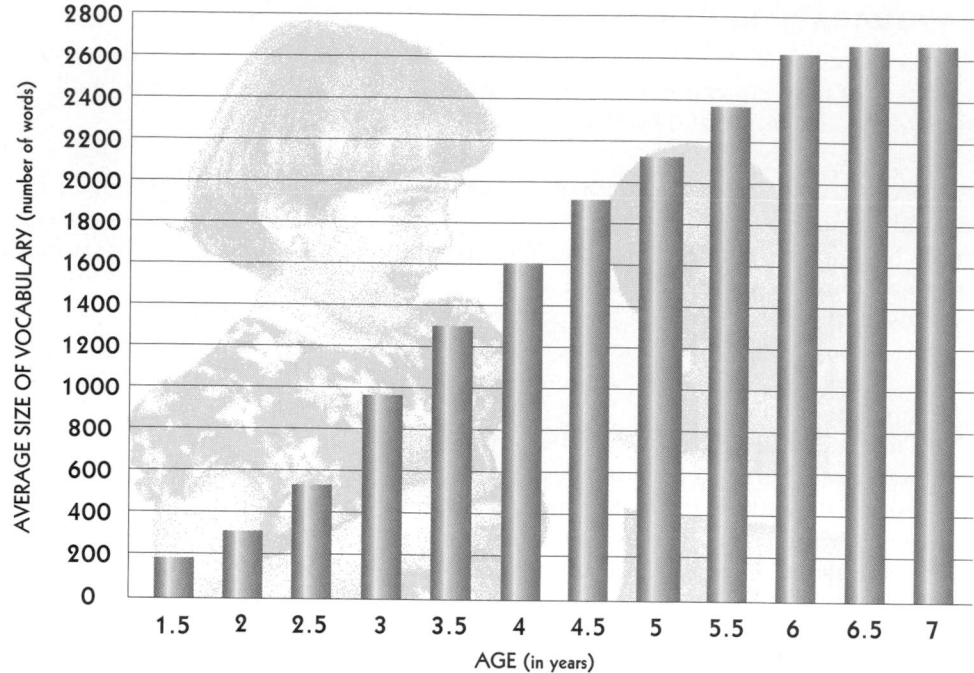

Consider how a four-year-old child might misconstrue what her father says to her mother: "I've had a terrible day. First, the morning traffic made me a nervous wreck. Then, I got into an argument with my boss, who became so furious he almost fired me." The child might think her father got into a car accident and was nearly set on fire. In trying to understand what is being said, a child is faced with understanding not only the meanings of single words but also the relationships of those words to other words. As everyone who has attempted to learn a new language knows, the meaning of a sentence is not always the same as the meanings of the individual words added together. Although children acquire words daily, the words they acquire mean different things, depending on their context. Of course, even adults use only a small set of words over and over again; most other words are used rarely. People who learn a new language usually concentrate on the most widely used words. Teachers of French or Spanish rarely attempt to have students learn the words for *aura* or *modality*. The focus tends to be on basic, utilitarian vocabulary and syntax.

SYNTAX.    Young children use single words to represent whole sentences or ideas; they say, "Milk" or "Blankie." We understand that they mean that they want more milk, or that they want their blanket. Linguists call such one-word utterances *holophrases*. Eventually, children begin to combine words into short sentences, such as "Mama, look" or "Bye-bye, Daddy." This slightly expanded, but still reduced, speech in which unimportant words are left out is referred to as *telegraphic speech* or *telegraphese*. This type of speech is only observed in children who are learning languages in which word order conveys meaning, such as French or English. Over a period of time children must learn to convey meaning using appropriate grammatical structures. **Syntax** is the way that words and groups of words combine to form phrases, clauses, and sentences. Syntactic capability enables children to convey more meaning. For example, children acquire a powerful new way of making their demands known when they learn to combine the words *I want* or *give me* with appropriate nouns. Suddenly, they can ask for cookies, toys, or Mommy without any of them being within pointing range. The rewards that such linguistic behaviour brings children are powerful incentives for them to learn more language. Children begin to use sentences at different ages; but once they begin, they tend to develop at similar rates (Brown, 1970).

SYNTAX [SIN-tacks]

The way that words and groups of words combine to form phrases, clauses, and sentences.

The rate at which language skill develops largely depends on the nature of the language being learned. For example, English grammar relies heavily on word order and less on adding suffixes to words (morphology). Inuktitut, spoken by Inuit in Canada's North, relies more heavily on morphology than on word order to convey meaning. As a result, telegraphic speech is not seen among Inuit toddlers. As well, the Turkish language relies on inflections to communicate meaning, whereas Serbo-Croatian uses word order (similar to English and French) as well as inflection. Because word order systems are more complex, those languages are acquired more slowly than systems based partly or completely on inflection.

Early studies of children's short sentences suggested that descriptions of the positions and types of words used could characterize early speech, but later analyses showed these descriptions to be inadequate. Later investigations suggested that young children possess an innate grammar and that they use grammatical relationships in much the same ways that adults do (McNeill, 1970). That is, they have an understanding of the rules for word order that goes beyond the small sentences they can produce. **Grammar** is the linguistic description of how a language functions, especially in terms of the rules and patterns used for generating appropriate and comprehensible sentences.

Table 7.2 summarizes some of the linguistic milestones in a child's life.

## THE BIOLOGICAL AND EVOLUTIONARY BASIS OF LANGUAGE

In 1957, linguist Noam Chomsky began the development of an idea that has found wide support. He suggested that one of the defining characteristics of human beings—language—is innate. He put forward the idea that human beings have an inborn, biologically based, universal grammar that allows them to master the language of their caregivers easily. This universal grammar, he asserted, is an innate word–sound–sentence generational mechanism capable of forming meaningful sentences. You can think of this universal grammar as a set of built-in "super-rules" that are instinctive, unconscious, and innate.

Evidence for the biological readiness of human beings to learn a language comes from physiological brain studies showing that infants—even very young ones—begin to respond physiologically to the language to which they are first

▲ Inuit toddlers do not use telegraphic speech because word order is not critical to conveying meaning in the Inuktitut language.

GRAMMAR

The linguistic description of how a language functions, especially the rules and patterns used for generating appropriate and comprehensible sentences.

| TABLE 7.2 | Early Linguistic Milestones |
|---|---|
| **Age** | **Language Activity** |
| 12 weeks | Smiles when talked to; makes cooing sounds spontaneously |
| 16 weeks | Turns head in response to human voices |
| 20 weeks | Makes vowel and consonant sounds while cooing |
| 6 months | Changes from cooing to babbling |
| 12 months | Imitates sounds; understands some words |
| 18 months | Uses 3 to 50 words (some babies use very few words at this age—as few as 3—while others use as many as 100); understands basic speech |
| 24 months | Uses between 50 and 250 words; uses 2-word phrases |
| 30 months | Uses new words daily; has good comprehension of speech; vocabulary of about 500 words |
| 36 months | Has vocabulary of more than 850 words; makes grammatical mistakes, but their number decreases significantly with each passing week |

**Be an ACTIVE LEARNER**

**REVIEW**

> Does the structure of spoken language determine people's thoughts and perception? Explain your answer. pp. 258–259

> Distinguish between a phoneme and a morpheme. p. 261

**THINK CRITICALLY**

> Do you think that learning two languages as a child facilitates cognitive development? Why or why not?

> Why do you think that American Sign Language shares more with spoken Japanese (or any other language, for that matter) than it does with English?

> If there is one universal grammar, do you think that people around the world make the same grammatical mistakes? Why or why not?

**APPLY PSYCHOLOGY**

> If a person is going to learn a second language, where is the best place to do it, and when? Why?

exposed (Werker & Vouloumanos, 1999). This means that the infant brain must be prewired, plastic, and ready to adapt to the sounds and meanings of speakers (Bates & Roe, 1999).

Evidence also exists from studies of congenitally deaf infants and children who have never been taught a sign language. For example, Goldin-Meadow and Mylander (1998) found that deaf children in the United States and in the Republic of China (Taipei) evoked spontaneous signing—despite the fact that parents tried to communicate through lip reading and speech. Not only did they spontaneously emit signs, but also they did so in a consistent, grammatically coherent pattern that shared commonalities. Their gestures were in gesture sentences rather than single signs, and the sentences did not conform to the grammars of English or Mandarin. This is more evidence for an innate (signing) grammar (Goldin-Meadow, 2000).

Chomsky (1999) and Pinker (1994, 1997, 1999) argue that there is but one grand-grammar, innate and thus biologically based in the human genome, that underpins the specific grammars of English, Swahili, or Hebrew. From a strictly evolutionary point of view, the reasons human beings have language—and animals do not—is a part of the process of natural selection. Language has enormous adaptive value, and those adaptations that help the species survive and prosper will lead to their further development. Pinker (1999) points out that from an evolutionary viewpoint we learn language (be it Spanish or Farsi), but we have an instinctive tendency to speak, babble, and acquire knowledge and words.

## Language Acquisition

That human beings acquire language is one of our uniquely defining characteristics. It is a major achievement in the life of a child (for more on this, see *Introduction to Research Basics*), continues to define us as adults, and separates us from other species (Bickerton, 1998). All of our historic and cultural achievements, let alone advances in science and technology, depend on the use of language. Language development is an individual achievement that occurs within a sociocultural context (Clark, 1996). Since language is a unique human gift, a special ability, was there an evolutionary turn of events that set humans apart in this respect (MacWhinney, 1998)? If language were solely an evolutionary unfolding, the story would be simple, but research shows that language and thought are sensitive to both genetic inheritance (nature) and experience (nurture). As in other areas of human behaviour, the debate continues about the relative contribution of each factor. If language is based on the evolutionary development of biological structures, two things should be true: (1) Many aspects of language ability should be evident early in life. (2) All children, regardless of their culture or language, should develop syntax and grammar (an understanding of language patterns) in a similar way. If environmental factors account for language acquisition, the role of learning should predominate.

### LEARNING THEORIES

The learning approach to language acquisition is quite simple. We speak and understand language because specific language structures (that is, grammatical categories) are reinforced and repeated. Babies attend in a focused way, listening intently and repeating the sounds they hear, especially those they have heard before (Johnson & Jusczyk, 2001). Infants are attentive listeners and parents modify their speech so that it is short, direct, repetitive, and intentionally exaggerated (Kuhl et al., 1997).

A behaviourist might describe the following scenario. As a baby produces sounds, parents often repeat the baby's words in proper English so that the baby can hear its words spoken correctly. Parents also reinforce the baby by responding

## Acquiring a First Language

In the early 1960s, the process of acquiring a first language was not well understood. Roger Brown (1973) and a group of researchers at Harvard University conducted a classic study that changed the understanding of language development and how researchers approach this problem.

**Hypothesis.** Children develop language in a sequence of stages that is similar for all children.

**Design.** Brown and his group conducted a naturalistic observation of language development. **Naturalistic observation** is a descriptive research method in which researchers study behaviour in its natural context. This method involves no manipulation of variables; indeed, researchers typically do not interact with participants and may attempt to "make themselves invisible" so that their presence will not affect the participants' behaviour.

**Participants.** Participants were three children, one that was 18 months old and two who were 27 months old when the study began. Two were girls, and one was a boy. The children's parents varied in educational level from high school through graduate school education.

**Procedure.** Brown and his research team obtained the parents' permission and cooperation to go into the children's homes and make audio recordings of at least 30 minutes of speech per week for each child. The recordings included not only the children's speech but also people who were interacting with each child at the time, including mothers, fathers, and other visitors in the home. At least one member of Brown's research team was present to take notes about the situation in which the vocalizations occurred. These weekly recordings continued for a year for one of the children and for four years for two of them.

**Results.** The researchers analyzed the progress that the children made in constructing sentences. They found that all three children developed language through a similar series of stages, but age was not a good predictor of this sequence. In fact, the youngest child made the most rapid progress, and her sentence complexity at age 18 months was comparable to that of the other two children at age 27 months.

**Conclusions.** Children go through a similar process of developing a first language, but they acquire language at different rates. Therefore, age is not a good way to divide children when considering language development; four-year-olds may differ a great deal in their development. This finding of similarity is consistent with the belief that there is an underlying, universal basis for language acquisition.

---

in some way to the baby's utterance. The baby might say, "Daddy, baby, wasue." In response, the parent may say, "You want Daddy to give you water?" The baby smiles, is given a drink, and the process continues until eventually, over days and weeks, the baby learns the "proper" words and word order. Thus, learning approaches use traditional learning (operant conditioning) theories and more modern (social/observational learning) theories to explain the acquisition of language.

## BIOLOGICAL THEORIES

Learning theories emphasize the role of environmental influences, or nurture, in language acquisition. But learning theories cannot account for the fact that people have the ability to generate an almost infinite number of correctly formed sentences in their native language. This means that people can comprehend sentences they have never heard and generate sentences they have never before produced. Because this ability cannot be acquired solely through imitation or instruction, many researchers (e.g., Miller, 1965) assert that human beings are biologically equipped with an innate, unique capacity to acquire and develop language. Such nativist positions assume that a hypothetical structure, a *language acquisition device* or LAD (Chomsky, 1957), exists to process and facilitate the learning of language.

NATURALISTIC OBSERVATION
A descriptive research method in which researchers study behaviour in its natural context.

Although Miller and Chomsky do not exclude experience as a factor in shaping children's language, they claim that human nature itself, through a LAD, allows children to pay attention to language in their environment and ultimately to use it. Nonetheless, even the strongest proponents of the nature (biological) argument do not contend that a specific language is inborn. Rather, they agree that a predisposition toward language exists and that human beings are born with a "preprinted" blueprint for language. As a child matures, the blueprint provides the framework through which the child learns a language and its rules (e.g., Marcus et al., 1999). Three major sources of evidence support the biological side of the nature–nurture debate: (1) studies of brain structure, lateralization, and convergence zones, (2) studies of learning readiness, and (3) studies of language acquisition in children and chimpanzees.

**BRAIN STRUCTURE, LATERALIZATION, AND CONVERGENCE ZONES.** As early as 1800, researchers knew that the brain of a human being was specialized for different functions. At that time, researchers began mapping the brain and discovered that if certain areas were damaged (usually through accidents), the injured person suffered from severe disorders in language abilities. Later work, some of it conducted by Norman Geschwind (1972), led to the idea of *lateralization*—the localization of a particular brain function primarily in one hemisphere. As Chapter 2 showed, considerable evidence suggests that the left and right hemispheres of the brain (normally connected by the corpus callosum) have some distinctly different functions.

Some researchers argue that the brain has unique processing abilities in each hemisphere. For example, for most people, important language functions are predominantly, but not exclusively, left-hemisphere functions (Corina, 1999). However, the available evidence for hemispheric specialization is not clear-cut. Although each hemisphere seems to play a dominant role in some functions, it interacts with the other hemisphere in the performance of other functions (Baynes et al., 1998).

Antonio Damasio asserts that the brain has many specific language-processing areas, some of which are lateralized (Damasio & Damasio, 1992). Information about a single thing or event may be stored in multiple locations throughout the brain. However, data connect through a convergence zone, or centre, that mediates and organizes all of the relevant information. Thus, signals from physically distant clusters of neuronal activity come together in convergence zones to elicit words, generate sentences, and fully process language.

**LEARNING READINESS.** Researcher Eric Lenneberg (1967) claimed that human beings are born with a grammatical capacity and a readiness to produce language. He theorized that language simply develops as people interact with their environment. One important aspect of this theory is that a child's capacity to learn language depends on the maturation of specific neurological structures. Lack of maturity of certain brain structures limits infants' ability to speak in the first months of life. However, the structural maturation that has occurred by about 18 to 24 months permits children to acquire grammar. Lenneberg's view derives in part from observations that most children learn the rules of grammar at a very early age. Lenneberg believed that the brain continues to develop from birth until about age 13, with the greatest developmental leap taking place around age 2. During this period, children develop grammar and learn the rules of language. After age 13, there is little room for improvement or change in their neurological structure. Lenneberg supported this argument with the observation that brain-damaged children can relearn some speech and language, whereas brain-damaged adolescents or adults who lose language and speech are unable to completely regain the lost ability. Lenneberg's view is persuasive, but some of his original claims have been seriously criticized, particularly his idea of the role of a critical time period in language development (e.g., Tchernichovski et al., 2001).

## LANGUAGE STUDIES WITH CHIMPANZEES

We have long known that animals communicate with one another. Whales use clicks and squeals, and monkeys make various sounds to signal one another, especially when predators appear. But do animals communicate with one another through language? If they do, is that language the same as, similar to, or totally different from the language of human beings? Most importantly, what can human beings learn from animals about the inborn aspects of language?

Some researchers claim that not only human beings but also other organisms—perhaps surprisingly, parrots—may have some rather sophisticated language acquisition skills. Irene Pepperberg (Pepperberg, 1994; Pepperberg, Brese, & Harris, 1991), for example, has conducted an extensive series of studies on a number of parrots, including Alex, who she bought in 1977. Alex can name 50 objects, name colours, and count to 8. He can classify objects by both number and colour and shows evidence of understanding the concepts of *same* and *different*. As well, there is evidence that he may practise speech in private in ways similar to that of young human language learners. The suggestion that parrots may have complex language ability is controversial, but even more hotly debated is the question of whether chimpanzees are born with a grammatical capacity and readiness for language.

The biological approach to language suggests that human beings are "prewired"—born with a capacity for language. Experience is the key that unlocks this existing capacity and allows its development. The arguments for and against the biological approach to language acquisition use studies showing that chimpanzees naturally develop some language abilities. Playful and curious, chimps share many physical and mental abilities with human beings. Their brains have a similar organization, and some language-like functions may even be lateralized in chimpanzees (Gannon et al., 1998). This is an especially important and interesting finding because psychologists generally have believed that only human beings exhibited brain asymmetries related to lateralization of language functions. Researchers are not sure what this lateralization means, but hope that it will provide some insight into chimp language abilities. What it does *not* mean is that chimps have human language—structure does not necessarily imply its function.

Chimps are especially useful to study because researchers can control and shape the environment in which chimps learn language, something they cannot do in studies involving human beings. For these reasons, chimpanzees have been the species of choice for psychologists studying language in animals.

However, all attempts to teach animals to talk have failed. Until recently, this failure led most psycholinguists to conclude that only human beings have the capacity to acquire language.

**WASHOE.** From age one, the chimpanzee Washoe was raised like a human child by Allen and Beatrice Gardner (1969). Rather than being taught to speak words, Washoe was taught American Sign Language, making signs that stood for words as well as simple concepts and commands (for example, *more, come, give me, flower, tickle,* and *open*). Washoe learned a large number of signs that refer to specific objects or events. She was able to generalize these signs and to combine them in meaningful order to make sentences. There is no proof, however, that she used a systematic grammar to generate novel kinds of sentences.

**SARAH.** The chimp Sarah was raised in a cage, with more limited contact with human beings than Washoe had. Psychologist David Premack (1971) used magnetized and coloured plastic icons to teach Sarah words and sentences (see Figure 7.8). Sarah gradually developed a small but impressive vocabulary. She learned to make

▲ Many researchers studied language differences between the chimpanzee and the human and eventually concluded that chimps just do not use language the way humans do.

**FIGURE 7.8**

**Icons Used by Sarah in Premack's Study**

Sarah learned to construct sentences using pieces of magnetized plastic that varied in colour and shape. (Premack, 1971)

Give     Take

Apple     Banana

Sarah     Mary

compound sentences, to answer simple questions, and to substitute words in a sentence construction. There is no evidence, however, that she could generate a new sentence, such as "Where are the apples?"

**LANA.** The chimp Lana learned to interact with a computer at the Yerkes Primate Research Center at Emory University. Researchers Rumbaugh, Gill, and Von Glaserfeld (1973) gave Lana six months of computer-controlled language training. Lana learned to press a series of keys imprinted with geometric symbols. Each symbol represented a word in an artificial language the researchers called Yerkish. The computer varied the location of each Yerkish word and the colour and brightness of the keys. Through conditioning, Lana learned to demonstrate some of the rudiments of language acquisition. Lana did not show that she could manipulate grammatical relations in meaningful and regular ways.

The studies of chimps just described show that their language usage is similar to that of very young children: it is concrete, specific, and limited. However, chimps do not show the ability to generate an unlimited number of grammatically correct sentences, an ability that human beings begin to acquire at a fairly young age.

**KANZI.** A Bonobo ape, Kanzi, was born at the Yerkes Field Station and subsequently brought, with his mother Matata, to Emory University at six months of age. Although exposed to his mother's lexigram training sessions, Kanzi himself was never taught the lexigrams. However, when he was 2.5 years of age he began to correctly use the 10 lexigrams on his mother's keyboard. He also knew the English words that corresponded to the appropriate lexigrams. He was the first non-human primate to demonstrate an ability to connect specific spoken words to symbols. Today Kanzi can produce more than 200 words and understands 500 words. Importantly, Kanzi also understands syntactically complex novel sentences, demonstrating a clear understanding of grammatical rules.

**NIM.** Columbia University psychologist Herbert Terrace reports significant differences between chimp language and the language of young children. Terrace taught his chimp, Nim Chimpski (a play on the name of the famous linguist Noam Chomsky), to communicate using manual signs. Terrace found that Nim's signed communications did not increase in length, as young children's sentences do. Nim acquired many words, but only 12 percent of Nim's utterances were spontaneous; the remaining 88 percent were responses to her teacher. Terrace points out that a significantly greater percentage of children's utterances are spontaneous. Terrace also found no evidence of grammatical competence in either his own data or that of other researchers.

**CHIMP LANGUAGE?** Unlike young children, who spontaneously learn to name and to point at objects (often called *referential naming*), chimps do not spontaneously develop such communication skills. Terrace (1985) agrees that the ability to name is a basic part of human consciousness. He argues that, as part of socialization, children learn to refer to various inner states: feelings, thoughts, and emotions. Chimps can be taught some naming skills, but the procedure is long and tedious. Children, on the other hand, develop these skills easily and spontaneously at a young age. Accordingly, researchers generally assert that chimps do not interpret the symbols they use in the same way that children do. These researchers question the comparability of human and chimp language.

In the end, chimps do not culturally transmit sign language from ape to ape to ape. Chimps do not have sophisticated referential naming. Chimps do not have the ability to be generative—to form new words, sentences, and ideas. So chimps do not use language the way human beings do. The answers to researchers' questions about language acquisition are far from complete, but the quest is exciting and is being extended to other species, including dolphins (Kuczaj, 1998; Schusterman & Gisiner, 1996).

## AND WHAT ABOUT DOLPHINS?

It is widely known that dolphins communicate with one another through squeaks and groans. It is also well accepted that dolphins learn quickly and well. But do they have language? Not in a human sense. They have no vocal cords to modulate their speech, and they do not gesture. Nevertheless dolphins do communicate with one another. They repeat signals from other dolphins; Vincent Janik (2000) showed that wild bottlenose dolphins listened, learned the whistles of other dolphins, and repeated those signals. This ability is an early part of language.

Researchers Miller and Bain (2000) presented evidence that whales not only communicate with one another, but do so with flair. They found that whales repeat sounds, like dolphins, but do so with inflections, almost like a tone of voice among human beings. Miller and Bain found that whales, their offspring, and even a third generation of whales possess some calls or sounds that are distinct to their families. Do dolphins or whales have language? The answer is no. Do they have communicative abilities? The answer is surely yes.

## SOCIAL INTERACTION THEORIES: A LITTLE BIT OF EACH

The development of language is a wonderful example of how debates in psychology emerge, grow, and help us understand human behaviour. Early learning theorists took a rigid view of the role of reinforcement in language development. Later, biological researchers assumed that the physical underpinning of language was just too strong to deny the role of physiology in language. But neither view by itself is correct. Children are born with a predisposition to language—there is no doubt about that. And nearly everybody will agree that children are reinforced for their language behaviour. But all language takes place within a social setting that changes daily with different caretakers and with the moods and needs of both child and caregivers. So language is in part innate and in part reinforced—rigid, unbending views of innate grammars, reinforced behaviours, and polarized approaches are probably too limited in their conception of language acquisition (Seidenberg, 1997).

Like so many other behaviours, we must consider the context in which language occurs. At feeding time, babies are far more likely to express their needs vocally because they are hungry. During play times, babies are far more likely to be self-centred, making utterances that do not necessarily have communicative functions. Parents often articulate words, sentences, and emotional expressions in a teaching mode when talking to babies. For example, we know that infants acquire phonetic properties of their native language in the early months of life by listening to adults speak (a social/observational approach).

A key to understanding language acquisition is to consider not only the structure of language, but also its function and the context in which it is learned, expressed, and practised. For human beings, who are very much social organisms, that expression takes place within groups of people where communication serves a vital function as a way for children to get attention and make their needs known. So, while a child may be "prewired" for language and reinforced for using language correctly, language nearly always takes place in an interactive social setting.

*Be an*
**ACTIVE LEARNER**

**REVIEW**
> What is the crucial assumption of biological approaches to language acquisition? p. 265
> Why are studies of lateralization important to studies of language? p. 266
> What important differences between chimp language and the language of human children did Terrace's work point out? p. 268

**THINK CRITICALLY**
> The two learning approaches to language acquisition—conditioning and social/observational learning—differ with respect to what key underlying principle?
> What is the implication of the finding that chimps do not culturally transmit sign language from ape to ape to ape?

**APPLY PSYCHOLOGY**
> Since the critical period for language development seems to end with adolescence, should the school curriculum be more language-based during the elementary-school years?

# Summary and Review

## COGNITIVE PSYCHOLOGY: AN OVERVIEW

**What is the focus of cognitive psychology?**

> *Cognitive psychology* is the study of the overlapping fields of perception, learning, memory, and thought. Cognitive psychology focuses on how people attend to, acquire, transform, store, and retrieve knowledge. Cognitive psychologists study thinking; they assume that mental processes exist, are systematic, and can be studied scientifically.   **pp. 242–243**

**KEY TERM**

cognitive psychology, p. 242

## CONCEPT FORMATION: THE PROCESS OF FORMING MENTAL GROUPS

**What is involved in the process of concept formation?**

> *Concepts* are the mental categories used to classify events or objects according to common properties or features. Concept formation involves classifying and organizing events or objects by grouping them with or isolating them from others on the basis of a shared characteristic. In laboratory studies of concept formation, participants are presented with stimuli that are either positive or negative instances of a concept. They are asked to identify the concept.   **pp. 243–244**

> A *prototype* is an abstraction, an idealized pattern of an object or idea that is stored in memory and used to decide whether similar objects or ideas are members of the same class of items.   **p. 244**

**KEY TERMS**

concept, p. 243; prototype, p. 244

## PROBLEM SOLVING: CONFRONTING SITUATIONS THAT REQUIRE SOLUTIONS

**What are the fundamental differences between algorithms and heuristics?**

> *Algorithms* are problem-solving procedures that implement a particular series of steps repeatedly. *Heuristics* are sets of strategies that act as guidelines, not strict rules, for problem solving.   **pp. 245–246**

> In *subgoal analysis*, a problem is broken down into several smaller steps, each of which has a subgoal. In *means–ends analysis*, the current situation or position is compared with the desired end to determine the most efficient means for getting from one to the other.   **p. 246**

**What are some barriers to effective problem solving?**

> *Functional fixedness* is the inability to see that an object can have a function other than its stated or usual one. Functional fixedness has been shown to be detrimental to problem solving.   **pp. 246–247**

> *Creativity* is the ability to develop responses that are original, novel, and appropriate. According to Guilford, creative thinking is divergent thinking. *Divergent thinking* is the process of widening the range of possible solutions. In contrast, *convergent thinking* is the process by which the number of possible options is reduced until one option remains as the answer. To solve problems creatively, some people use the technique of *brainstorming*.   **pp. 248–249**

**KEY TERMS**

problem solving, p. 245; algorithm, p. 245; heuristics, p. 246; subgoal analysis, p. 246; means–ends analysis, p. 246; backward search, p. 246; functional fixedness, p. 246; creativity, p. 248; convergent thinking, p. 248; divergent thinking, p. 248; brainstorming, p. 248

## REASONING AND DECISION MAKING: GENERATING IDEAS AND REACHING CONCLUSIONS

**Differentiate between reasoning and decision making.**

> *Reasoning* is the purposeful process by which a person generates logical and coherent ideas, evaluates situations, and reaches conclusions. The system or principles of reasoning used to reach valid conclusions or make inferences is called *logic*. *Decision making* is the assessment of alternatives; people make decisions that sometimes involve the probability of occurrence of an event or the expected value of the outcome.   **p. 249–250**

**What is a psychological approach to studying decision making?**

> Psychological factors, especially previous events, affect how people estimate probabilities of behaviours and events. Sometimes a person may ignore key pieces of data and thus make bad (or irrational) decisions not based on probability; also, a person's world view may affect decision making.   **pp. 250–252**

**What is the effect of culture on reasoning?**

> The intellectual traditions of the East and the West are quite different, and so are the reasoning and decision-making tendencies of their peoples—different world views affect how people in the East and West solve problems.   **p. 253**

**How do evolutionary theorists and researchers account for reasoning?**

> Evolutionary psychologists assert that reasoning is a direct consequence of evolution and adaptations to a complex, even dangerous world—reasoning is an adaptation.   **pp. 253–254**

## ARTIFICIAL INTELLIGENCE

### What is artificial intelligence?

> Computer programs that mimic some type of human cognitive activities are said to use artificial intelligence (AI). A computer analogy of perception and reasoning has been the model for most studies of AI; this work is often based on the concept of parallel distributed processing (PDP), which suggests that many operations take place simultaneously and at many brain locations. **pp. 254–256**

### Describe how neural networks work.

> Electronic neural networks simulate specific cognitive activities, including recognizing patterns, recognizing handwriting, planning computer moves, and recognizing spatial layouts. Neural networks learn and remember by noting changes in the weights or values associated with various connections between their units. Those units that are frequently activated become more pronounced, have lower thresholds of activation, and can be more easily accessed. **pp. 255–257**

## LANGUAGE

### How are language, thought, and culture interrelated, and what are the key elements of language?

> Research shows that language structure alone is unlikely to account for the way people think because culture also influences language and thought. **pp. 257–258**

> The English language has evolved in such a way that its words define many roles as male; many people still see the world through a male frame of reference and assume that this is the preferred value system. Although gender stereotypes continue, some women and men are becoming more androgynous. **p. 258**

> *Linguistics* is the study of language, including speech sounds, meaning, and grammar. *Psycholinguistics* is the study of how people acquire, perceive, understand, and produce language. *Phonemes* are the basic units of

sounds in a language; *morphemes* are the basic units of meaning. *Semantics* is the study of the meaning of language components. *Syntax* is how words and groups of words are related and how words are arranged into phrases and sentences. *Grammar* is the linguistic description of a language, in terms of its rules and patterns for generating comprehensible sentences. **pp. 259–260**

## LANGUAGE ACQUISITION

### How do theorists explain language acquisition?

> Learning plays an important part in language acquisition. However, people have the ability to generate an unlimited number of correctly formed sentences in their native language. This ability cannot be acquired solely through imitation or instruction, which suggests the existence of an innate language ability. **pp. 264–266**

> Damasio asserts that the brain has specific language-processing areas, some of which are lateralized. Information about any thing or event may be stored in multiple locations throughout the brain. However, the locations are connected through convergence zones, or centres that mediate and organize the information. **p. 266**

> Studies of language ability in chimpanzees have produced some impressive results, although few psychologists are completely convinced that the ways in which chimps use language parallels human use of language. The criticisms, however, do not diminish the chimps' language abilities or accomplishments. **pp. 267–268**

> A key to understanding language acquisition is to consider not only the structure of language, but also its function and the context in which it is learned, expressed, and practised. Communication serves a vital function and nearly always takes place in an interactive, social setting. **p. 269**

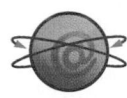

Take advantage of the multimedia resources available with this text! Follow the marginal icons to access the interactive modules on the *HandsOnPsych* CD-ROM; log on to *MyPsychLab* to explore the ebook, study aids, and other online resources; and visit the Companion Website at **www.pearsoned.ca/lefton** for additional exercises and links.

# 8 Intelligence

Two parents are meeting with their son's schoolteacher and the resource teacher for the school to discuss their son's current school experiences. The resource teacher says, "We think it would be helpful in our planning for your child if we had the psychologist administer the Wechsler Intelligence Scale for Children." Two questions likely come quickly to mind for the parents: "Why does my child need testing at all?" and "Why an intelligence test?" It could be that the son has shown clear signs of giftedness in school and the teachers are going to recommend that he be referred to a Gifted and Talented Education (GATE) program. Applications to such GATE programs must be accompanied by an official (done by a psychologist) WISC assessment indicating that the child's IQ score is at least 130, putting him in the top 2 percent of the population. It could be that the child is not doing as well in school as the teachers think he should be based on their general impression of his intellectual abilities. In this case the psychologist might find an overall score on the WISC that is in the average to above-average range but, in addition, one of several distinctive patterns among the subscale scores suggesting a high degree of variability across the basic ability areas. Alternatively, there may be one or two areas where the child scores noticeably lower than on other subtests — perhaps on the arithmetic subtest, on subtests requiring quick processing speed, or on subtests reflecting basic reading or comprehension skills. Any of these patterns might lead the psychologist to recommend additional assessments in order to investigate the possibility that the child has a learning disability related to language processing, math skills, or attentional focus. Once identified, there are many ways that children with learning disabilities can be helped to enjoy academic success.

Some individuals do so poorly on tests such as the WISC that their overall level of intelligence can seem immeasurable. It may be, however, that there are islands of full-blown brilliance among an overall ability profile that is very low. For example, Neil Charness and his colleagues at the University of Waterloo (Charness, Clifton, & MacDonald, 1988) assessed an individual whose general level of intellectual functioning was very low and impossible to measure on the WISC, yet the individual had phenomenal musical skill, being able to reproduce note for note on piano, organ, or harmonica any melody he had ever heard. Laurent Mottron and Sylvie Belleville (1998) at the University of Montreal assessed a 34-year-old individual who functioned at about a 6-year-old level, yet could draw architectural-quality pictures of objects, photos, and imagined scenes.

A test of intelligence figured in all these assessments but a question that is not answered here is, "What is intelligence?" Is it a single capacity that some people (such as the gifted child discussed above) seem to have a lot of? Is it a small number of abilities usually evenly distributed but open to patterns that lead to the need, as with learning disabled children, to develop special strategies for instruction and studying to optimize success? Or is it a great many things such that individuals with what has been called savant syndrome can have islands of profoundly superior ability in the midst of a general profile that is very much below the population average? It is to this complicated question that we turn in this chapter.

## What Is Intelligence?

Human beings are capable of artistic greatness, such as Michelangelo's frescos in the Vatican or Yo Yo Ma's virtuoso cello performances. Humans can achieve enormously difficult tasks such as building the pyramids with relatively primitive tools; we exhibit great compassion for others, as did Gandhi and Mother Teresa; and we are capable of communicating effectively with each other to bring about peace. We are an intelligent species that can think about our past, predict our future, and use our abilities for good as well as for evil; our capabilities and achievements are immense. But how can we quantify these achievements? Should we? From a historical perspective, it is not clear how one can even begin to compare Michelangelo's frescos to the achievements of Mother Teresa. But how do we compare individual achievement at a given point in time? How do we predict future outcomes?

From a scientist's point of view, the important task becomes quantifying intelligence so as to make accurate measurements and predictions about human behaviour. And so the intelligence test was designed, or as most of us know it, the IQ test. Everyone has heard of IQ tests, but do they actually measure intelligence? Can any test measure it? Further, what causes us to be so intellectually different from one another?

What is intelligence? For some psychologists, intelligence is all mental abilities; for others, it is the basic general factor necessary for all mental activity; for still others, it is a group of specific abilities. However, all agree that intelligence is a concept, a hypothetical structure, not an identifiable thing.

Early psychologists sought to separate normal children from mentally retarded children, and developed tests to do so. Later researchers developed elaborate theories of the "factors" that make up intelligence. Along the way, they developed complicated testing procedures. From the beginning, researchers have sought to know the source of intelligence. Is it inherited from our parents through genetics or acquired from our learning and environment? The history of psychology has been punctuated with thousands of research papers on intelligence and its nature. Part of the problem is defining what intelligence is and is not. Part is determining whether intelligence has one or many components. And again, part is determining what causes intelligent behaviour—nature or nurture.

Recognizing these complexities, we can still formulate a working definition of intelligence: **Intelligence** is the overall capacity of the individual to act purposefully, to think rationally, and to deal effectively with the environment. It is a person's ability to learn and understand. By this definition, intelligence is expressed behaviourally. It is shown in the ways people act and in their abilities to learn new things and to use previously learned knowledge. Most importantly, intelligence has to do with people's ability to adapt to the social and cultural environment. Intelligence is thus not a thing but a process, a product, and a capacity, which is affected by a person's day-to-day experiences in the environment. One's intelligence is *not* his or her IQ, which is merely a score derived from a test.

▲ Is the musical genious of Yo Yo Ma evidence of a high general intelligence or of a specific musical gift?

**INTELLIGENCE**

The overall capacity of the individual to act purposefully, to think rationally, and to deal effectively with the environment.

# THEORIES OF INTELLIGENCE—ONE ABILITY OR MANY?

Clearly, all people do not act intelligently all of the time. The realization of individual differences in behaviour has been a problem for psychology from its beginnings. Psychologists want to study individual behaviour and how it varies over time and in different circumstances, but they also want to make generalizations about human behaviour.

A key issue has been, and continues to be, whether there is one intelligence or many. Is intelligence a singular property, or does it consist of many, more or less independent components? Today, the most influential views on this issue are Wechsler's theory, factor theories, Jensen's two-level theory, Vygotsky's view, Gardner's theory of multiple intelligences, and Sternberg's triarchic theory.

**WECHSLER'S THEORY.** David Wechsler viewed intelligence from the perspective of a tester. As one of the developers of a widely used and respected intelligence test (which we will examine later), Wechsler knew that such tests are made up of many subparts, each measuring a fairly narrow aspect of a person's functioning and resourcefulness. He argued that intelligence tests involving spatial relations and verbal comprehension reveal little about someone's overall capacity to deal with the world. In Wechsler's view, psychologists need to remember that intelligence is more than simply mathematical or problem-solving ability; it is the broader ability to deal with the world.

**FACTOR THEORIES.** Factor theories of intelligence use a correlation technique known as *factor analysis* to explore what makes up intelligence. **Factor analysis** is a statistical procedure designed to discover the independent elements (factors) in any set of data. With regard to intelligence testing, factor analysis attempts to find a cluster of items that measure a common ability. Results of tests of verbal comprehension, spelling, and reading speed, for example, usually correlate highly, suggesting that some underlying attribute of verbal abilities (a factor) determines a person's score on those three tests.

In the early 1900s, Charles E. Spearman (1863–1945) used factor analysis to show that intelligence consists of two parts: a general factor affecting all tasks, which he termed the *g* factor, and specific factors associated with particular tasks. According to Spearman, some amounts of both the general factor and the appropriate specific factor(s) were necessary for the successful performance of any task. This view of intelligence is known as the *two-factor theory of intelligence*. Experts assert that a general factor underlies the diverse cognitive abilities (Brody, 1997), and there is physiological evidence for it (Duncan et al., 2000).

Louis L. Thurstone (1887–1955) further developed Spearman's work by postulating a general factor analogous to Spearman's, as well as seven other basic factors, each representing a unique mental ability: verbal comprehension, word fluency, number facility, spatial visualization, associative memory, perceptual speed, and reasoning. Known as the *factor theory of intelligence*, Thurstone's theory included a computational scheme for sorting out these seven factors. The factor theory is not universally accepted. Many assert that there is a general factor of intelligence and that it cannot be separated into distinct parts that account for specific abilities; rather, the same overall factor accounts for success in both academic work and other pursuits (Kranzler, 1997).

**JENSEN'S TWO-LEVEL THEORY.** Arthur Jensen (1969, 1970, 1987) suggests that intellectual functioning consists of associative abilities and cognitive abilities. *Associative abilities* enable people to connect stimuli and events; they involve little reasoning or transformation. Items testing associative abilities might, for example, ask someone to repeat from memory a seven-digit number sequence and to identify geometric shapes or classify them into categories. *Cognitive abilities*, on the other hand, involve reasoning and problem solving. What is novel is Jensen's claim that associative and cognitive abilities are inherited, which adds fuel to the nature–nurture controversy about intelligence (which we'll consider later in this chapter).

FACTOR ANALYSIS
Statistical procedure designed to discover the independent elements (factors) in any set of data.

**VYGOTSKY'S VIEW.** Lev Vygotsky (1896–1934) was a Russian psychologist who saw intellectual development as occurring in a social context that includes communication, with the self and with others. Intelligence is not one task, but many, which are interwoven. Children, for example, engage in private speech to plan their own actions and behaviour; when they use such speech, they do better at various intellectual tasks. Vygotsky suggested that private speech helps a child understand his or her world. For Vygotsky (1962), even the earliest speech is essentially social and useful and a key part of intelligence; in fact, he asserted that social speech comes first, followed by egocentric (self-centred) speech, then inner speech.

Vygotsky held that when children are presented with tasks that are beyond their current abilities, they need the help of society to accomplish them. The child eventually incorporates new skills into his or her repertoire of behaviours and thus shows intelligence. Since children solve practical tasks with the help of their own inner speech, psychologists have to watch how and when that speech develops. Vygotsky ultimately believed that psychologists must examine not only the result of intellectual growth, but also the process of getting there. Since many tasks are involved, intelligence is not so much a product as a process; this argument is supported by a number of contemporary thinkers who assert the existence of multiple intelligences.

**GARDNER'S MULTIPLE INTELLIGENCES.** Howard Gardner (1983/1993, 1995; Gardner & Hatch, 1989) has proposed that there are multiple types of intelligences and that traditional intelligence tests do not measure them. Gardner argues that human competencies, of which there are many, do not all lend themselves to measurement on a standard test. He maintains that people have multiple intelligences—"an intelligence" being an ability to solve a problem or create a product within a specific cultural setting. Gardner's eight types of intelligences are summarized in Table 8.1.

▲ Vygotsky held that when children develop problem-solving skills, language, and thought in general, it is done in a cultural and social context.

### TABLE 8.1  Gardner's Multiple Intelligences

| Type of Intelligence | Exemplar | Core Components |
|---|---|---|
| Linguistic | Poet<br>Journalist | Sensitivity to the sounds, rhythms, and meanings of words; sensitivity to the different functions of language |
| Logical–mathematical | Scientist<br>Mathematician | Sensitivity to and capacity to discern logical or numerical patterns; ability to handle long chains of reasoning |
| Musical | Composer<br>Violinist | Ability to produce and appreciate rhythm, pitch, and timbre; appreciation of the forms of musical expressiveness |
| Spatial | Navigator<br>Sculptor | Capacity to perceive the visual–spatial world accurately and to perform transformations on initial perceptions |
| Bodily–kinesthetic | Dancer<br>Athlete | Ability to control bodily movements and to handle objects skilfully |
| Naturalist | Botanist<br>Chef | Ability to make fine discriminations among the flora and fauna of the natural world or the patterns and designs of human artifacts |
| Interpersonal | Therapist<br>Salesperson | Capacity to discern and respond appropriately to the moods, temperaments, motivations, and desires of other people |
| Intrapersonal | Person with detailed, accurate, self-knowledge | Access to one's own feelings and the ability to discriminate among them and draw on them to guide behaviour; knowledge of one's own strengths, weaknesses, desires, and intelligence (Gardner & Hatch, 1989) |

Gardner's view has been praised for its recognition of the cultural context of intelligence, its consideration of multiple human competencies, and the framework it offers in which to analyze intelligence in school and other applied settings. The criticisms of his multiple intelligences approach focus on terminology—for example, are talents one type of intelligence? Some critics assert that Gardner's "intelligences" are all highly correlated with one another, essentially measuring the same thing. Others claim that the intelligences seem to resemble lists of learning and personality styles, not competencies or intelligence. The scientific jury is still out, but Gardner's work on multiple intelligences has certainly influenced other theorists, including Sternberg.

**STERNBERG'S TRIARCHIC THEORY.**   Robert J. Sternberg maintains that traditional tests used by universities and colleges to make admissions decisions—including the SAT, LSAT, GRE, and even IQ tests—measure only limited aspects of behaviour and do not predict future success very well (Sternberg, Grigorenko, & Bundy, 2001; Sternberg & Williams, 1997). He feels that psychologists keep using the same populations and the same tasks in the same contexts and keep drawing the same results—often wrong and not generalizable to all peoples (Sternberg & Grigorenko, 2000b).

Sternberg (1997a) asserts that a solid theory of intelligence must focus on *successful intelligence*, or the ability to adapt to, shape, and select environments to accomplish one's goals and those of society. Sternberg believes that psychologists should investigate not how much intelligence people have, but how they use it; this makes his theory highly applicable cross-culturally. Sternberg (1985, 1997a; Sternberg et al., 2001) has proposed a *triarchic theory* in which intelligence has three dimensions: analytic, practical, and creative (see Figure 8.1).

The *analytic dimension* of intelligence involves an individual's ability to use intelligence for problem solving in specific situations where there is one right answer. This part of the triarchic theory focuses on how people shape their environments so that their competencies can be used to best advantage. In Western societies, analytical intelligence is measured on tests and valued in classrooms. For

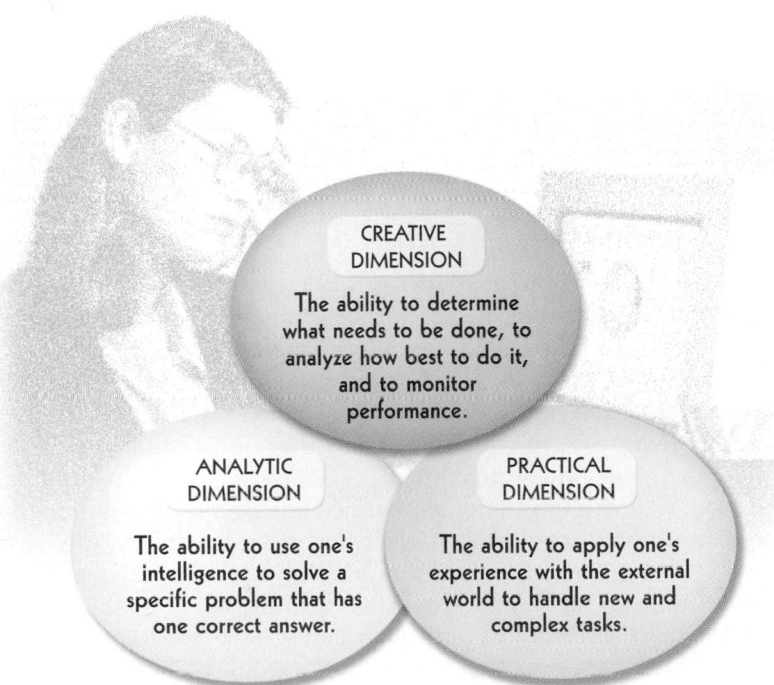

**FIGURE 8.1**
Sternberg's Triarchic Theory of Intelligence

CREATIVE DIMENSION
The ability to determine what needs to be done, to analyze how best to do it, and to monitor performance.

ANALYTIC DIMENSION
The ability to use one's intelligence to solve a specific problem that has one correct answer.

PRACTICAL DIMENSION
The ability to apply one's experience with the external world to handle new and complex tasks.

example, a person might organize a situation in a meaningful way, perhaps by grouping similar items together. However, the analytic dimension does not refer to any mental operations required to carry out problem solving, and thus it is likely to be culture-free. It may be used by an African herdsman weaving leaves to build walls for a dwelling, a machinist cleaning a well-used lathe, or a student solving a problem in long division.

The *practical dimension* has to do with a person's application of his or her experience with the external world and with everyday tasks. According to this part of Sternberg's theory, a test measures intelligence if it assesses a person's ability both to handle novel tasks and to master tasks so that they can be performed in an automatic manner. An example of such mastery through experience is memorizing verb forms in a foreign language or troubleshooting malfunctioning electronic equipment. Initially, such tasks are usually difficult and tedious, but practice makes them nearly automatic (Sternberg & Grigorenko, 2000a).

The *creative dimension* of Sternberg's triarchic intelligence is the glue that holds the other two dimensions together. It describes the mental mechanisms underlying what are commonly considered intelligent behaviours. Creative intelligence includes a person's ability to determine which tasks need to be done, to determine the order in which subtasks should be undertaken, to analyze their subparts, to decide which information should be processed, and to monitor performance. This is the aspect of intelligence necessary to write a love poem or a computer program. Tasks involving analogies, vocabulary, and syllogisms can be used to measure the elements of creative intelligence.

Few behaviours engage all three dimensions of intelligence, so Sternberg asserts that various tasks measure intelligence to a different extent. Thus, from Sternberg's point of view, new batteries of tests are needed to fully analyze the three basic dimensions of intelligent behaviour. Good predictors of a person's academic achievement will take into account knowledge of the world—practical intelligence or common sense—in addition to verbal comprehension and mathematical reasoning (Sternberg, 2000b). Too often, children do poorly in school and in life despite having obvious intellectual skills. These individuals often do not know how to allocate their time or how to work effectively with other people. Such skills need to be taught, because some students do not develop them on their own. As Ceci (2000) asserts, schools foster the learning of specific skills, not necessarily general problem-solving abilities. In addition, schools often promote specific ways of thinking about problems, but researchers and tests need to value alternative modes of thought and creativity. For example, tests—especially IQ tests—should begin to probe for wise responses (Sternberg, 1998). The issue of the multiplicity of intelligence becomes even more complex when emotions enter the equation, as we'll see next.

## EMOTIONS—A DIFFERENT KIND OF INTELLIGENCE?

Being highly intelligent is no guarantee of success in life. It is true that doing well in school is important in getting ahead, but there is more to success in business, and in life, than superior cognitive ability. You probably know individuals who are quite bright intellectually, but who have little common sense, few leadership skills, or very little motivation. In 1995, Daniel Goleman published a book entitled *Emotional Intelligence*, in which he claims that one's emotional life can matter much more than one's intellectual life.

Goleman argues that traditionally defined intelligence stands alongside and separate from emotional intelligence. According to Goleman, emotional intelligence seems to be the key to getting ahead in life. Emotional intelligence includes self-awareness, impulse control, persistence, self-motivation, the ability to recognize emotions in others, and social agility. Goleman gives credit to psychologists such as Gardner and Sternberg who stress the multiplicity of intelligence, but he feels that they don't go far enough.

**HandsOnPsych**
Version 2.0

**Language, Intelligence, and Problem Solving**

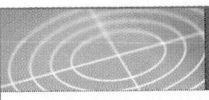
## Is the Idea of Multiple Intelligences Flawed?

**POINT:** Intelligence must be considered from multiple vantage points, with many competencies making up intelligence.

**COUNTERPOINT:** Theories of multiple intelligences, such as Howard Gardner's, involve circular reasoning and are misleading.

All people are unique in the way they go about life; while human beings share a common genome, how they express their heredity is affected by a myriad of variables—prenatal nutrition, playground encounters, and parental exchanges large and small. So it is not surprising that as adults people express their intelligence, and their humanity for that matter, in many ways. Howard Gardner (1998) maintains that people have multiple intelligences—"an intelligence" being an ability to solve a problem or create a product within a specific cultural setting. Gardner ultimately describes eight types of intelligence. Similarly, Sternberg (2000b) boils his "intelligences" down—in his case to three types. Both Gardner's and Sternberg's approaches have had an enormous impact on educators' thinking.

However, having intuitive appeal and being widely popular doesn't make the multiple intelligences theories right—or so say critics such as Perry Klein (1997), who argue that theories of multiple intelligences do not tell us anything new, that these intelligences are not independent of one another, that the intelligences are so closely related that they cannot really be distinguished from one another, and that telling people that they are high or low in one

form of intelligence or another may discourage initiative and do more harm than good.

Gardner and Sternberg argue that we have to keep in mind that people can excel in many ways and that facility on the dance floor is quite different than computer fluency or verbal fluency. They argue that the different kinds of intelligences must be recognized and fostered in the classroom. Klein counters that these "intelligences" are nothing more than special abilities and that labelling them as intelligences does little or nothing to help us understand human intelligence.

The multiple intelligences approach is seen by many as a deeper analysis, a more subtle, nuanced explanation of this thing we call intelligence; yet the unitary approach that argues that there is one general factor called Intelligence has been around for decades and has withstood many assaults on its validity. Time—and a great deal of research—will tell. We can't wait to see what the research will say in the next decade. If you would like to get a general sense of your own intelligence profile, visit the Canada Career Consortium Web site for an online scored measure: **www.careerccc.org/products/cp_99_e/ section1/quiz.cfm**

Cognitive ability and emotional intelligence are not mutually exclusive. Highly intelligent people can be bright and productive, but they also can be cold, unresponsive, and detached (low emotional intelligence). Alternatively, a bright, productive person can be outgoing, cheerful, poised, sympathetic, and caring (high emotional intelligence). Goleman's assertion is that, all other things being equal, those with high emotional intelligence will nearly always do better than those with low emotional intelligence. Of course, people who are bright do not have only low or high emotional intelligence. Like other types of intelligence, emotional intelligence is displayed in a wide range of degrees.

Goleman proposes that people who develop a high emotional intelligence can better manage the difficulties of life, such as inappropriate aggression, eating disorders, depression, or alcoholism. He argues that people can be taught to recognize emotions and understand relationships, to develop better frustration tolerance and anger management, to focus better on the task at hand and pay attention (thus becoming less impulsive), and to take another person's perspective. Goleman's point has been emphasized by researchers who assert that only when people can accurately perceive, appraise, and express their emotions, can they better harness their intellectual lives. Mayer, Salovey, and Caruso (2000) argue that when people use

**Be an**
## ACTIVE LEARNER

**REVIEW**
> What is the central and most important part of a definition of intelligence? pp. 274–275
> What did theoreticians mean by a *g* factor? p. 275

**THINK CRITICALLY**
> What might be the implications for researchers of Vygotsky's claim that scientists must examine the process of intelligence, not just its products?
> Is love an emotionally intelligent feeling? Can a person's feelings and thoughts be separated from his or her intelligence? If so, how?
> What are some key competencies that you think should be in an intelligence test?
> Identify ways that people can keep emotions from determining thoughts.

**APPLY PSYCHOLOGY**
> What do you think the goal of intelligence testing should be?
> Identify some elements that you would put in a test of emotional intelligence.

their emotions to facilitate thought they can help regulate emotions and thus facilitate growth. Mayer, Salovey, and Caruso try to separate the effects of emotion and intelligence, and assert that each affects the other; they contend that a definition such as Goleman's focuses too much on the motivational properties of emotional states and too little on the feelings of emotions.

Psychologists have to ask some critical questions: To what extent are cognitive ability and emotions independent? Are they affected by the same environmental variables? Can emotional intelligence be fostered, boosted, or enhanced? (We will see in Chapter 10 that programs such as Better Beginnings, Better Futures have successfully enhanced academic skills. Might the same be done for emotional intelligence?) How do we measure Goleman's criteria for emotional intelligence? Psychologists know a great deal about both intelligence and emotion, but there is little research evidence to support this new concept of emotional intelligence, despite its intuitive appeal (Davies, Stankov, & Roberts, 1998). Until solid, systematic research is done, it remains an interesting working hypothesis, an imaginative idea that deserves investigation. It very likely will be tested in longitudinal studies over the next decade or two.

# The Process of Test Development

You may have been administered one or more intelligence tests during your school years. These tests may have determined your educational track from elementary school onward. However, psychologists are among the first to admit that intelligence tests have shortcomings, and researchers continue to revise these tests to correct their inadequacies and ensure that they have practical benefits and applications in educational, occupational, and clinical settings (Daniel, 1997).

Intelligence tests have had a long history. In the late nineteenth century, Sir Francis Galton developed what he considered to be an objective measure of intelligence. He assessed mental ability by measuring sensory processes, reasoning that elementary sensations form the foundations for thought. He measured reaction time and response to colour among other things. Not surprisingly, since his measures were actually unrelated to thought, his test was not effective in measuring intelligence. Galton's efforts did, however, serve to pique interest in measuring mental ability. Thus he set the stage for Alfred Binet. Binet (1857–1911), a French psychologist, began to study mental behaviour and ability. He later employed Theodore Simon (1873–1961), a 26-year-old physician; their friendship and collaboration became famous. In 1904, Binet was commissioned to identify procedures for educating children in Paris who were in need of special education. Binet was chosen for the task because he had been lobbying for action to help schools (French schools had only recently been made public, and mentally retarded children were doing poorly and dropping out). As Stagner (1988) suggests, this may have been the first government-sponsored psychological research.

Binet coined the phrase *mental age*, meaning the age level at which a child is functioning cognitively, regardless of chronological age. Binet and Simon developed everyday tasks, such as counting, naming, and using objects, to determine mental age. The scale they developed is often considered the first useful and practical test of intelligence. A century later, psychologists are still following some of their recommendations about how tests should be constructed and administered. In fact, one of the most influential intelligence tests in use today—the Stanford–Binet test—is a direct descendant of Binet and Simon's early tests.

▼ Binet and Simon are best known as the founders of the psychological testing movement. In 1904, Binet (shown here) attempted to devise procedures for identifying and educating Parisian children with mental retardation.

## DEVELOPING A TEST

Imagine that you are a seven-year-old child taking an intelligence test, and you come to the following question: "Which one of the following tells you the temperature?" Below the question are pictures of the sun, a radio, a thermometer, and a pair of mittens. Is the thermometer the only correct answer? Suppose there are no thermometers in your home, but you often hear the temperature being given on radio weather reports. Or imagine that you "estimate" the temperature each morning by standing outside to feel the sun's strength, or that you know it's cold outside when your parents tell you to wear mittens. According to your experiences, any one of the answers to the question might be appropriate.

**WHAT DOES A TEST MEASURE?**   Your predisposition to respond to this hypothetical test question based on your experience—your social and cultural biases—illustrates the complexity of intelligence test development. In general, a *test* is a standardized device for examining a person's responses to specific stimuli, usually questions or problems. Because there are many potential pitfalls in creating a test, psychologists follow an elaborate set of guidelines and procedures to make certain that their questions are properly constructed. First, a psychologist must decide what the test will measure. For example, will it measure musical ability or knowledge of geography, mathematics, or psychology? Second, the psychologist needs to construct and evaluate items for the test that will give examiners a reasonable expectation that success on the test means something. Third, the test must be standardized.

**HandsOnPsych**
Version 2.0

**Personality and Health**

**STANDARDIZATION.**   **Standardization** is the process of developing uniform procedures for administering and scoring a test and for establishing norms. **Norms** are the scores and corresponding percentile ranks of a large and representative sample of individuals from the population for which the test was designed. Norms are used to compare an individual's test performance with those of the general population. A **representative sample** is a sample of individuals who match the population with whom they are to be compared on key variables such as socio-economic status and age. Thus, a test designed for all Canadian university and college students might be given to 2000 students, including an equal number of males and females, 16 to 20 years old, who graduated from large and small high schools, from different areas of Canada, and who represent different ethnic groups and socio-economic levels.

Standardization ensures that there is a basis for comparing future test results with those of a standard reference group. After a test is designed and administered to a representative sample, the test developers examine the results to establish norm scores for different segments of the test population. Knowing how people in the representative sample have done allows psychologists and educators to interpret future individual test results properly. The scores of those in the representative sample serve as a reference point for comparing individual scores.

STANDARDIZATION

The process of developing uniform procedures for administering and scoring a test and for establishing norms.

NORMS

The scores and corresponding percentile ranks of a large and representative sample of individuals from the population for which a test was designed.

REPRESENTATIVE SAMPLE

A sample of individuals who match the population with whom they are to be compared on key variables such as socio-economic status and age.

**NORMAL CURVE.**   Test developers generally plot the scores of the representative sample on a graph that shows how frequently each score occurs. On most tests some people score very well, some score very poorly, and most score somewhere in the middle. When test scores are distributed in that way, psychologists say they are *normally distributed*, or fall on a normal curve. A **normal curve** is a bell-shaped graphic representation of data arranged to show what percentage of the population obtains a particular score. As Figure 8.2 illustrates, most people fall in the middle range, with a few at each extreme. An individual's test score can then be used to estimate his or her rank in the general population by noting where it falls on the normal distribution. (The Appendix discusses the normal distribution in detail.) As Figure 8.2 illustrates, 68 percent of cases fall within one standard deviation of the mean. For most IQ tests the mean is set at 100 and the standard deviation is set at 15. This means that 68 percent of the population has IQ scores ranging from 85 to 115.

NORMAL CURVE

A bell-shaped graphic representation of data arranged to show what percentage of the population falls under each part of the curve.

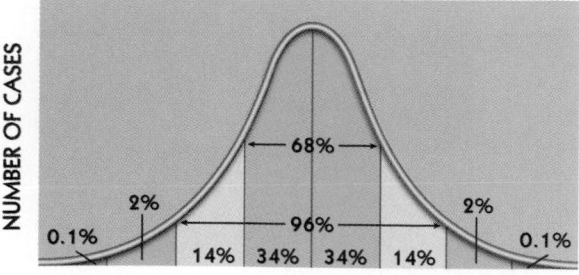

**FIGURE 8.2**

**A Normal Distribution**

The bell-shaped curve shows a standard normal distribution. As in normal distributions of height, weight, and even intelligence, very few people are represented at the extremes.

RAW SCORE

A test score that has not been transformed or converted in any way.

STANDARD SCORE

A score that expresses an individual's position relative to those of others based on the mean score and how scores are distributed around it.

PERCENTILE SCORE

A score indicating what percentage of the test population obtained a lower score.

Higher and lower IQ scores are obtained by fewer people in the population as scores become increasingly extreme. It is important to note that frequency distributions can take many forms. However, intelligence scores tend to be normally distributed based on the deviation of the persons' score from the norms of others the same age.

**SCORES.** The simplest score on a test is the **raw score**—the number of correct answers unconverted or transformed in any way. The raw score, however, is seldom a true indicator of a person's ability. For many tests, particularly intelligence tests, raw scores need to be adjusted to take into account a person's age, gender, and grade level; that is, to ensure that they are being compared to an appropriate comparison group. Such scores commonly are expressed in terms of a **standard score**—a score that expresses an individual's position relative to those of others based on the mean score and how scores are distributed around it. If, for example, a 100-item intelligence test is administered to students in grades 3 and 11, test developers expect those in grade 11 to answer more items correctly than those in grade 3. To adjust for these differences in age, scoring procedures provide for each student's score to be compared to the score typically achieved by other students at the same grade level. Thus, if those in grade 11 typically answer 70 questions correctly, a student in grade 11 who answers 90 questions correctly will have done better than most other students at that grade level. Similarly, if those in grade 3 usually answer 25 questions correctly, a student in grade 3 who answers 15 questions correctly will not have performed as well as other students at that grade level. A standard score is generally a **percentile score**—a score indicating what percentage of the test population obtained a lower score. If, for example, someone's percentile score is 84, then 84 percent of the people taking the test obtained a lower score than that person did.

**INTELLIGENCE QUOTIENTS.** Binet and Simon's test to determine mental age clearly qualifies as an intelligence test—even though it was a relatively crude one. In the early 1900s, intelligence was measured by a simple formula. To obtain an intelligence quotient (IQ), a psychologist divided a person's mental abilities, or mental age, by the person's chronological age and multiplied the result by 100. (See Table 8.2 for examples.) Mental ages of children were estimated from the number of correct answers on a series of test items; the higher the number, the higher the mental age.

A problem with the traditional formula—mental age divided by chronological age, then multiplied by 100—is that young children are far more variable in their answers than are older children or adults; it is as if their intelligence is less stable, less repeatable, and more subject to change. This variability makes predictions and comparisons difficult. To simplify measures of IQ, psychologists and testers began

| TABLE 8.2 | Traditional Calculation of Intelligence Quotient for Three People | | |
|---|---|---|---|
| | **Person 1** | **Person 2** | **Person 3** |
| Mental Age (MA) | 6 years | 15 years | 15 years |
| Chronological Age (CA) | 6 years | 18 years | 12 years |
| MA ÷ CA | 6 ÷ 6 = 1 | 15 ÷ 18 = 0.83 | 15 ÷ 12 = 1.25 |
| (MA ÷ CA) x 100 | 1 × 100 = 100 | 0.83 × 100 = 83 | 1.25 × 100 = 125 |
| IQ | 100 | 83 | 125 |

using **deviation IQ**—a standard IQ test score for which the mean and variability remain constant at all ages. According to deviation IQs, a child of 9 and an adolescent of 16, each with an IQ of 116, have the same position relative to others who have taken the same IQ test. Both are above the eighty-fourth percentile; that is, both scored better than 84 percent of all others their age who took the same IQ test.

Perhaps the most important goal in the development of IQ tests is ensuring that tests are both reliable and valid. If a student obtains different scores on two versions of the same test, which score is correct? Furthermore, does the test measure what it is supposed to measure and only that?

## RELIABILITY

*Reliability* refers to the consistency of test scores. **Reliability** is a test's ability to yield very similar scores for the same individual over repeated testing. (When a researcher says that test scores have consistency, the researcher is assuming that the person taking the test is in the same emotional and physiological state each time the test is administered.) If a test's results are not consistent over several testing sessions or for two comparable groups of people, useful comparisons are impossible. A test is rarely perfectly reliable; the question is, "Is it *generally* consistent and does it yield similar results over multiple testings?"

There are several ways to determine whether a test is reliable. The simplest method, termed *test–retest*, is to administer the same test to the same person on two or more occasions. If, for example, the person achieves a score of 87 one day and 110 another, the test is probably not reliable (see Table 8.3). Of course, the person might have remembered some of the test items from one occasion to the next. To avoid that problem, testers use the *alternative-form method*, which involves giving two different versions of the same test. If the two versions test the same characteristic, differing only in the test items used, both should yield the same result. Another way to test reliability is to use the *split-half method*, which involves dividing a test into two parts; on a reliable test, the scores from the two halves should yield similar, if not identical, results.

Even the most reliable test will not yield identical results each time it is taken; however, a good test will have a relatively small standard error of measurement. The *standard error of measurement* is the number of points by which a score varies because of imperfect reliability. Consider an IQ test that has a standard error of measurement of three, for example. If someone scores 115 on that test, the test developer can state with a high degree of confidence that the individual's real score is between 112 and 118—3 points above or below the obtained score.

## VALIDITY

If a psychology exam included questions such as "What is the square root of 647?" and "Who wrote *The Grapes of Wrath*?" it would not be a valid measure of your

---

TABLE 8.3  **Test–Retest Reliability**

*Test–retest reliability* indicates whether people who are given the same or a similar test on repeated occasions achieve similar scores each time.

| | Test with High Reliability | | Test with Low Reliability | |
|---|---|---|---|---|
| | **First Testing** | **Second Testing** | **First Testing** | **Second Testing** |
| **Person 1** | 92 | 90 | 92 | 74 |
| **Person 2** | 87 | 89 | 87 | 96 |
| **Person 3** | 78 | 77 | 78 | 51 |

VALIDITY

The ability of a test to measure only what it is supposed to measure and to predict only what it is supposed to predict.

knowledge of psychology. That is, it would not be measuring what it is supposed to measure. To be useful, a test must have not only reliability but also **validity**—the ability to measure only what it is supposed to measure and to predict only what it is supposed to predict.

**TYPES OF VALIDITY.**   *Content validity* is a test's ability to measure the knowledge or behaviour it is intended to measure and is based on a detailed examination of the contents of the test items. A test designed to measure musical aptitude should not include items that assess mechanical aptitude or personality characteristics.

In addition to content validity, a test should have *predictive validity*—the ability to predict a person's future achievements with at least some degree of accuracy. Critics of intelligence tests like to point out, however, that test scores are not always accurate predictors of people's performance, that the correlation between IQ test scores and school grades is only about 0.6 at best (1.0 represents perfect correlation). Tests cannot take into account high levels of motivation or creative abilities. Nevertheless, many law schools use the Law School Admission Test (LSAT) scores of applicants to decide who should be accepted for admission—thus assuming that the scores accurately predict ability to succeed in law school.

Two additional types of validity are *face validity*, the extent to which a person can judge a test's appropriateness by reading or examining the test items, and *construct validity*, the extent to which a test actually captures or measures the hypothetical quality or particular trait it is supposed to measure, such as intelligence, anxiety, or musical ability.

**A CRITIQUE OF INTELLIGENCE TEST VALIDITY.**   There are six basic criticisms of the validity of intelligence tests and testing. The first is that there is no way to measure intelligence because no clear, agreed-upon definition of intelligence exists. The defence to this argument is that, although different IQ tests seem to measure different abilities, the major tests have face validity.

The second criticism is that, because IQ test items usually consist of *learned information*, they reflect the quality of a child's schooling rather than the child's actual intelligence. The response to this challenge is that most vocabulary items on IQ tests are learned in the general environment, not in school; moreover, the ability to learn vocabulary terms and facts seems to depend on the general ability to reason verbally. Further, scores on other measures of ability seem independent of schooling and correlate highly with traditional test scores (Richardson, 2000).

The third criticism is that the administration of intelligence tests in *school settings* may adversely affect IQ and other test scores, not only because tests are often administered inexpertly but also because of the halo effect (e.g., Crowl & MacGinitie, 1974; Darley & Gross, 2000). The **halo effect** is the tendency for one particular or outstanding characteristic of an individual (or a group) to influence the evaluation of other characteristics. A test administrator can develop a positive or negative feeling about a person, a class, or a group of students that may influence the administration of tests or the interpretation of test scores (Nathan & Tippins, 1990). People who defend testing against this charge acknowledge that incorrectly administered tests are likely to result in inaccurate test scores, but they claim that this effect is less powerful than opponents think it is, especially among properly trained test administrators.

Two other criticisms of testing are less directly related to the issue of validity. One criticism is that some people are *test-wise*. These individuals make better use of their time than others, guess the tester's intentions, and find clues in the test. Practice in taking tests improves these people's performance. The usual defences are that the items on IQ tests are unfamiliar even to experienced test takers and that the effects of previous practice are seldom or never evident on IQ tests. Another criticism is that individuals' scores often depend on their *motivation to succeed* rather than on actual intelligence. Claude Steele has argued that whenever members

HALO EFFECT

The tendency for one particular or outstanding characteristic of an individual (or a group) to influence the evaluation of other characteristics.

of ethnic or other minorities concentrate explicitly on a scholastic task, they worry about confirming negative stereotypes of their group (Steele, 1999; Steele & Aronson, 2000). This extra burden may drag down their performance, through what Steele calls *stereotype threat*—people fear being reduced to a stereotype and then do worse because of their fear. Stereotype threat probably occurs in part because of subtle instructional differences and in part because of situational pressure that may undermine a test taker's self-confidence. Unless members of minority groups are resilient to such threats their performance is likely to suffer (Steele, 1999).

Lastly, success in Canada—economic, social, and political—is heavily influenced by one's academic achievement and the ensuing opportunities that emerge from completing university or college. In making educational placement decisions on the basis of IQ test scores, it is argued that our society creates the correlation between academic success, schooling, and IQ test scores. The defence, again, is that IQ test scores correlate with other measures of intelligence that seem to be independent of schooling.

Critics of IQ tests are concerned about the interpretation of scores. It is important to remember that intelligence tests generally are made up of different subtests or subscales, each of which yields a score. There also may be a general score for the entire test. All of these scores require knowledgeable interpretation; that is, test scores must be given a context that is meaningful to the person who receives the information (Daniel, 2000). Without such a context, a score is little more than a number. The interpretation of test scores is the key to understanding IQs; without such interpretation, a single IQ score can be biased, inaccurate, or misleading.

# Four Important Intelligence Tests

What is the best intelligence test? What does it measure? Can you study for an intelligence test and get a higher score? As in other areas of science, theory leads to application; many theorists applied their ideas to the development of intelligence tests. The four tests we examine here—the Stanford–Binet Intelligence Scale, the Wechsler scales, the Kaufman Assessment Battery for Children, and Woodcock–Johnson–III— are all widely used. They were developed by well-known and respected researchers, and they predict performance well. Their results all correlate well with one another, and research shows that they are reliable and valid. We'll begin by examining the first real IQ test, the Stanford–Binet Intelligence Scale.

## STANFORD–BINET INTELLIGENCE SCALE

Most people associate the beginning of intelligence testing with Alfred Binet and Theodore Simon. As noted earlier, Binet collaborated with Simon to develop the Binet–Simon Scale in 1905. The original test actually was 30 short tests arranged in order of difficulty and consisting of such tasks as distinguishing food from non-food and pointing to objects and naming them. The Binet–Simon Scale was heavily biased toward verbal questions and was not well standardized.

From 1912 to 1916, Lewis M. Terman revised the scale and developed an intelligence test now known as the Stanford–Binet Intelligence Scale. (*Stanford* refers to Stanford University, where the test was further developed.) In the Stanford–Binet, a child's mental age (intellectual ability) is divided by that child's chronological age and multiplied by 100 to yield an intelligence quotient (IQ). For decades psychologists have used the original and revised versions of the Stanford–Binet scale. This test traditionally has been a good predictor of academic performance, and many of its subtests correlate highly with one another.

A newer version of the Stanford–Binet Intelligence Scale, published in 1986, contains items designed to avoid favouring men or women or stressing ethnic stereotypes. It is composed of four major subscales and tests individuals ages 2 through 23, yielding one overall IQ score. The test administration time varies, because the number of subtests given is determined by age. All examinees first are given a vocabulary test; along with their age, this test determines the level at which all other tests begin. There are 15 possible subtests, which vary greatly in content. Some require verbal reasoning, others require quantitative reasoning, and still others require abstract visual reasoning. In addition, there are tests of short-term memory.

Each of the subtests consists of a series of levels, with two items at each level. The tester begins by using entry-level items and continues until a higher level on each subscale is established (until the test taker fails a prescribed number of items). (See Figure 8.3 for a description of the new Stanford–Binet Intelligence Scale.)

Raw scores, determined by the number of items passed, are converted to a standard score for each age group. The new Stanford–Binet scale is a powerful test; one of its great strengths is that it can be used over a wide range of ages and abilities. Nonetheless, like all tests, it has limitations. One of these limitations is that examinees are not given the same battery of subtests at different ages; this makes comparisons across age groups difficult (Sattler, 1992). However, the new Stanford–Binet scale correlates well with the previous version, as well as with the Wechsler scales and the Kaufman Assessment Battery for Children (which are examined next).

## WECHSLER SCALES

David Wechsler (1896–1981), a Romanian immigrant who earned a Ph.D. in psychology from Columbia University, was influenced by Charles Spearman and Karl Pearson, two English statisticians with whom he studied. In 1932, Wechsler was appointed chief psychologist at Bellevue Hospital in New York City. Wechsler recognized that the Stanford–Binet Intelligence Scale was inadequate for testing the IQs of adults. He also maintained that some of the Stanford–Binet items lacked validity. In 1939, Wechsler developed the Wechsler–Bellevue Intelligence Scale to test adults. In 1955, the Wechsler Adult Intelligence Scale (WAIS) was published; it eliminated some technical difficulties of the Wechsler–Bellevue scale. The latest revision of the test is the WAIS–III. Figure 8.4 shows some examples from the WAIS.

**FIGURE 8.3**

**The Modern Stanford–Binet Intelligence Scale**

The most recent version of the Stanford–Binet Intelligence Scale measures intelligence with a composite score made up of four scores on broad types of mental activity: verbal reasoning, quantitative reasoning, abstract visual reasoning, and short-term working memory. Each of the scores is obtained through a series of subtests that measure specific mental abilities.

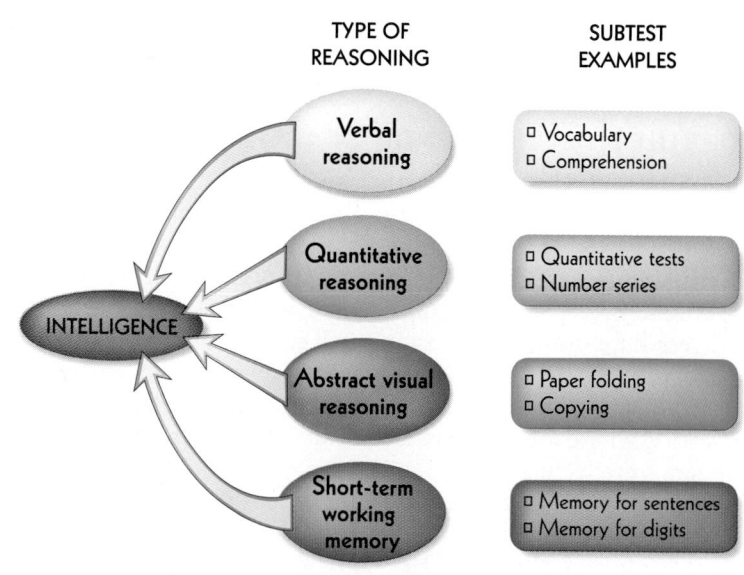

TYPE OF REASONING

SUBTEST EXAMPLES

Verbal reasoning
- Vocabulary
- Comprehension

Quantitative reasoning
- Quantitative tests
- Number series

INTELLIGENCE

Abstract visual reasoning
- Paper folding
- Copying

Short-term working memory
- Memory for sentences
- Memory for digits

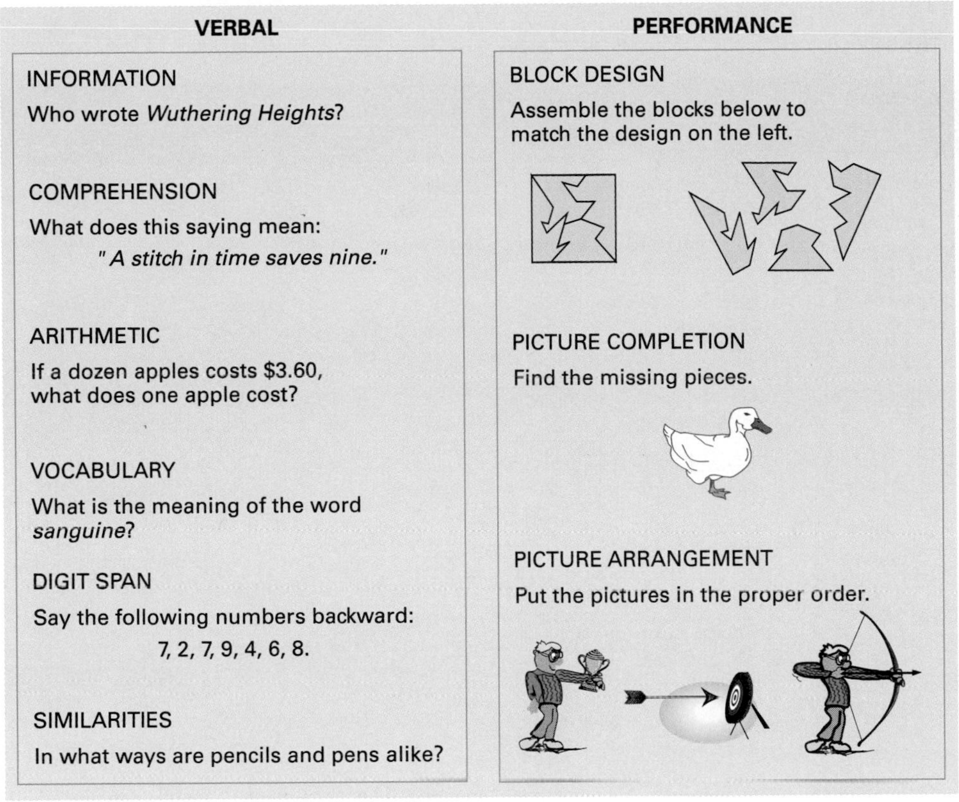

FIGURE 8.4

Items from the WAIS-III Verbal and Performance Subtests

**VERBAL**

INFORMATION

Who wrote *Wuthering Heights*?

COMPREHENSION

What does this saying mean:
"*A stitch in time saves nine.*"

ARITHMETIC

If a dozen apples costs $3.60, what does one apple cost?

VOCABULARY

What is the meaning of the word *sanguine*?

DIGIT SPAN

Say the following numbers backward:
7, 2, 7, 9, 4, 6, 8.

SIMILARITIES

In what ways are pencils and pens alike?

**PERFORMANCE**

BLOCK DESIGN

Assemble the blocks below to match the design on the left.

PICTURE COMPLETION

Find the missing pieces.

PICTURE ARRANGEMENT

Put the pictures in the proper order.

Wechsler also developed the Wechsler Intelligence Scale for Children (WISC), which covers children ages 6 through 16. It was revised in 1974, becoming the WISC–R; the 1991 revision is the WISC–III. Table 8.4 shows some of the typical subtests included in the WISC–R. In 1967, the Wechsler Preschool and Primary Scale of Intelligence (WPPSI) was developed for children ages 4 through 6.5; it was revised in 1989, becoming the WPPSI–R.

The Wechsler scales group test items by content. For example, all of the information questions are presented together, and all of the arithmetic problems are presented together. The score on each subtest is calculated and converted to a standard (or scaled) score, adjusted for the test taker's age. The scaled scores allow for a comparison of scores across age levels. Thus, an 8-year-old's scaled score of 7 is comparable to an 11-year-old's scaled score of 7. An overall IQ score is reported as well as subscale scores. Thousands of studies have been conducted to assess the reliability and validity of the Wechsler scales.

## KAUFMAN ASSESSMENT BATTERY FOR CHILDREN

Psychologists Alan and Nadeen Kaufman contend that their Kaufman Assessment Battery for Children (K–ABC) uses tasks that tap the experience of all people, regardless of background. A memory task in the K–ABC, for example, might ask a child to look at a picture of a face and then pick it out from pictures of other faces a few moments later. The K–ABC examines the intelligence of participants ages 3 to 18 and was revised in 2001.

The K–ABC was designed especially for assessment of school problems. School psychologists, the primary users of the K–ABC, act as evaluators and consultants to families and schools, helping them to set and achieve appropriate educational goals. The K–ABC consists of four global scales. Three measure mental processing abilities (sequential processing, simultaneous processing, and a composite of the two); the

**TABLE 8.4** Typical Subtests of the WISC–III

| Verbal Test | | Performance Test | |
| --- | --- | --- | --- |
| Subtest | Type of Task | Subtest | Type of Task |
| Information | When questioned, recall a general fact that has been acquired in a formal or informal school setting | Picture completion | Point out the part of an incomplete picture that is missing |
| Similarities | Use another concept in describing how two ideas are alike | Picture arrangement | Put a series of pictures that tell a story in the right sequence |
| Arithmetic | Solve a word problem without pencil and paper | Block design | Use real blocks to reproduce a picture of a block design |
| Digit span | Recall an orally presented string of digits | Object assembly | Put the pieces of a jigsaw-like puzzle together to form a complete object |
| Vocabulary | Define a vocabulary word | Coding | Given a key that matches numbers to geometric shapes, fill in a form with the shapes that go with the listed numbers |
| Comprehension | Answer a question requiring practical judgment and common sense | | |

fourth assesses achievement. A sequential task requires that stimuli be manipulated in sequential order. For example, a child might be asked to repeat a series of digits in the order in which the examiner presented them. A simultaneous-processing task involves organizing and integrating many stimuli at the same time. Here, a child might be asked to recall the placement of objects on a page that was presented only briefly.

The K–ABC assesses how well and in what way a child solves problems on each task, minimizing the role of language and of acquired facts and skills. A separate part of the test, the achievement scale, involves demonstrating such skills as reading comprehension, letter and word identification, and computation. These tasks resemble those typically found on other IQ tests in that they are heavily influenced by language experience and verbal ability. The Kaufmans believe that the sequential- and simultaneous-processing scales measure abilities synonymous with intelligence—that is, the ability to process information and the ability to solve problems (Kaufman, 1983).

### THE WOODCOCK–JOHNSON–III

There are thousands of tests and hundreds of intelligence tests. The Stanford–Binet, Wechsler, and K–ABC are widely used, but many practitioners have used the Woodcock–Johnson for many years. The Woodcock–Johnson–III is a test for measuring general intellectual ability, specific cognitive abilities, scholastic aptitude, oral language, and academic achievement. It consists of several subparts, and is one of the most comprehensive test batteries available. Recently revised, this widely used test is given to children in kindergarten through adults in graduate school. Its strengths are that it measures and evaluates domain-specific skills with related cognitive abilities as well as traditional ability/achievement discrepancies; it is a useful diagnostic tool and can be used across the life span.

## The Environmental and Biological Partnership

The political, cultural, and scientific issues involved in the debate about what intelligence is and what intelligence tests actually measure are complicated. Ethnic and

## Seeing What You Expect to See

Scores on IQ tests are important, especially in the school setting. Children's scores influence educational and career decisions. Test administrators are supposed to be fair and objective in giving and interpreting the tests, but other opportunities for bias are possible in how test scores are used. Possibilities for bias arise through the **self-fulfilling prophecy**, the creation of a situation that unintentionally allows personal expectancies to influence participants. This effect is also called the *experiment expectancy effect*, and Robert Rosenthal and Lenore Jacobson (1966) investigated how this effect applies in classroom situations involving intelligence and intelligence testing.

**Design.** This study was an **experimental design** in which the researchers manipulated the information that they furnished to teachers about their students' IQs in order to produce different expectancies about students' abilities. The difference in expectation was the *independent variable*, and the *dependent variable* was students' scores on an IQ test. (See Chapter 1 for more details on experimental designs.)

**Hypothesis.** Rosenthal and Jacobson hypothesized that teachers' expectancies would influence students' performance—that is, the information about IQ would produce a self-fulfilling prophecy.

**Participants.** Participants were 18 teachers (16 women and 2 men) who taught grades 1 through 6 in an elementary school.

**Method.** Rosenthal and Jacobson conducted their study in an elementary school that had administered an IQ test to all students in grades one through six. This situation allowed the researchers to manipulate the information that teachers received about their students' scores on the IQ test. They told the teachers that some students' scores were in the top 20 percent, indicating that these students would "bloom" within the next year and show big gains in their learning ability. This group was the experimental group. Rosenthal and Jacobson said that students whose scores were low would continue to make progress, but they would not experience a spurt in intellectual growth. This group was the control (comparison) group. These stories were both untrue, but the false feedback allowed the researchers to create differential expectancies in the teachers by manipulating the information received. In fact, Rosenthal and Jacobson randomly assigned which students were "bloomers" and which were not.

**Results.** Examining students' scores on the IQ test at the end of the academic year, Rosenthal and Jacobson found that teacher expectancies made a significant difference for student performance. The students who were supposed to intellectually "bloom" did so, showing significantly higher IQ scores than the comparison students who were not expected to make dramatic gains. The effect was much stronger for grades one and two than for grades three through six.

**Conclusions.** Self-fulfilling prophecy applies to teachers in classroom situations. The effect can be powerful, accounting for gains in IQ of up to 30 points. This effect probably occurs through the ways that teachers communicate with and encourage students; teachers give more attention and encouragement to those students for whom they have high expectations. The results highlight one of the ways that information about IQ can be used to perpetuate discrimination. This study has many implications for teachers, counsellors, and supervisors whose expectations can affect the behaviour of students, clients, and workers.

other minority groups have joined some psychologists and educators both from mainstream culture and from ethnic and minority groups in challenging the usefulness of IQ tests. In *Introduction to Research Basics* we examine how the results from IQ testing can be misused. Underlying public concern and scientific debate is the fundamental issue of how much of intelligence is due to heredity and how much is due to a person's upbringing and culture. Further, if culture is a major factor, are tests biased?

## ARE IQ TESTS CULTURALLY BIASED?

A major argument against IQ testing is that the tests are culturally biased and thus effectively discriminate against individuals who are not typical of the test makers' environments, which are usually white, middle class, and suburban. A test item or

**SELF-FULFILLING PROPHECY**

The creation of a situation that unintentionally allows personal expectancies to influence participants.

**EXPERIMENTAL DESIGN**

A design in which researchers manipulate an independent variable and measure a dependent variable to determine a cause-and-effect relationship.

subscale is considered culturally biased when, with all other factors held constant, its content is more difficult for members of one group than for those of other groups. Because experiments have shown some tests to be culturally biased, many educators and parents have urged a ban on intelligence tests in all public schools. Groups of individuals who are not exposed to the same education and experiences as the middle-class group for whom the tests were designed are bound to perform less well and, as a consequence, may not be provided appropriate educational experiences. To understand how a test can be culturally biased, imagine that the child of an immigrant is given the multiple-choice temperature problem posed earlier. If the child is unfamiliar with thermometers and radios, he might choose the sun as the best answer. However, if the test designer has deemed "thermometer" to be the correct answer, the child's answer would be considered wrong. Table 8.5 lists some questions that might bias an intelligence test. Each test represents a very different set of skills and knowledge. It is conceivable that a person might do well on one test but not on the other, depending on his or her experiences.

Clearly, those who interpret IQ test scores must be particularly sensitive to any potential biases in the tests. Nonetheless, although researchers find differences among the IQ scores of various racial, ethnic, and cultural groups, they have found no consistent and conclusive evidence of bias in the tests themselves. Differences between siblings are usually as great as differences between ethnic groups; there is as great a variability between individuals as between groups. It is simply not the case that tests such as the WISC–R involve systematic discrimination on the basis of ethnicity. It is possible that any bias that appears to exist in an IQ test actually arises from how the results are used (a point to be examined shortly).

IQ tests cannot predict or explain all types of intellectual behaviour. They are derived from a small sample of a restricted range of cognitive activities. Intelligence can be demonstrated in many ways; an IQ test provides little information about someone's ability to be flexible in new situations or to function in mature and responsible ways. Intelligence tests do reflect many aspects of people's environments—how much individuals are encouraged to express themselves verbally, how much time they spend reading, and the extent to which parents have urged them to engage in academic pursuits (e.g., Barrett & Depinet, 1991).

Since the early 1970s, the public, educators, and psychologists have scrutinized the weaknesses of IQ tests and have attempted to eliminate cultural bias in testing by creating better tests and establishing better norms for comparison. The tests have attempted to control the influences of different cultural backgrounds (Helms,

| TABLE 8.5 | Tests Can Be Constructed to Have a Bias |
| --- | --- |
| **Test A** | **Test B** |
| 1. What are the colours in the Canadian flag? | 1. Of what is butter made? |
| 2. Who is the prime minister of Canada? | 2. Name a vegetable that grows above ground. |
| 3. What is the longest river in Canada? | 3. Why does seasoned wood burn more easily than green wood? |
| 4. How can banks afford to pay interest on the money you deposit? | 4. About how often do we have a full moon? |
| 5. What is the freezing point of water? | 5. Who was the prime minister of Canada during the Second World War? |
| 6. What is a referendum in government? | 6. How can you locate the pole star? |

1992). In isolation, IQ scores mean little. Information about an individual's home environment, personality, socio-economic status, and special abilities is crucial to understanding intellectual functioning.

Cross-cultural differences in IQ scores, SAT scores, and other measures of achievement are narrowing. In addition—and especially important—differences among individuals within a group are often greater than differences between groups.

## CULTURAL DIMENSIONS OF INTELLIGENCE

Differences in IQ scores, LSAT scores, and other measures of achievement or ability are narrowing for various ethnic groups within North America (Fan, Chen, & Matsumoto, 1997; Williams & Ceci, 1997). This narrowing may be due to a variety of factors, including more equal opportunities under the law, intervention programs for at-risk children, and more equal academic preparation for ethnic minority students. As ethnic minority students' enrolment in advanced mathematics courses rises, these students' scores on achievement tests also increase. Historical and cultural background has a significant effect on people's patterns of mental ability and achievement (Geary, 1996) and the instrument used to test any child must be culturally relevant (Greenfield, 1997). Furthermore, differences among individuals within a group are often greater than differences between groups, a situation that minimizes the importance of between-group differences and highlights the importance of considering the individual rather than the ethnic group (Zuckerman, 1990).

One conclusion is strikingly clear: *Rather than measuring innate intellectual capacity, IQ tests measure the degree to which people adapt to the culture in which they live*. In many cultures, to be intelligent is to be socially adept. In Western society, because social aptitude is linked with schooling, the more schooling you have, the higher your IQ score is likely to be (Ceci & Williams, 1997). All individuals have special capabilities (not necessarily intellectual ones), and how those capabilities are regarded depends on the social environment. Being a genius in traditional African cultures may include being a good storyteller; in Canada, it may mean being astute and assertive (Eysenck, 1995). In Canada, however, the concept of genius is too often associated solely with high academic achievement. Concern about the implications of this limited conception of intelligence is one reason why some educators are placing less emphasis on IQ scores.

Researchers now assert that the typical intelligence test is too limited because it does not take into consideration the many forms of intelligent behaviour that occur outside the testing situation but within the diverse culture of Canada (Sternberg, 2000b). Real-life problem situations might be used to supplement the usual psychological tests—intelligence must be evaluated on many levels, including the environment in which a person lives and works. Yet, in spite of all the limitations of IQ scores, research continues to show that they are the best overall predictor of school performance (Kuncel, Hezlett, & Ones, 2001). This situation should be no surprise—Binet and Simon developed the first IQ test for the Paris school system.

## ENVIRONMENTAL AND GENETIC IMPACT

If you came from a well-bred, upper-class family and had access to schooling and appropriate family connections, you would likely be smart. Or so thought Sir Francis Galton in the nineteenth century. Galton was among the first to speculate that genetics was a factor in intelligence, arguing that intelligence—a measurable trait or ability—is passed from generation to generation. Today, psychologists recognize that both the genetic heritage established before birth (nature) and a person's life experiences (nurture) play an important role in intelligence.

▲ Cross-cultural differences in IQ scores, SAT scores, and other measures of achievement are narrowing. In addition—and especially important—differences among individuals within a group are often greater than differences between groups.

**HERITABILITY.** Few would debate the idea that the environment, and especially schooling, has a potent effect on performance of intellectual tasks (Ceci & Williams, 1997). Certainly, persistent poverty clearly has detrimental effects on children (McLoyd, 1998); still, Ramey, Ramey, and Lanzi (2001) assert that children from impoverished homes can achieve more on standardized tests if cognitive training begins early in life and continues for an extended period. However, efforts to unravel the fixed genetic component from the environmental impact have required some sophisticated research and statistical techniques. The main goal of such studies has been to determine various traits' **heritability**, the genetically determined proportion of a trait's variation among individuals in a population. Recall from Chapter 2 that heritability estimates are based on kinship studies and estimate to what degree genetics contributes to a given characteristic. The heritability of some traits is fairly obvious; for example, height is a highly heritable trait. Children who have two tall parents have a strong likelihood of being tall—the heritability of height is high, and thus scientists say that heredity is a key factor in determining height. When scientists say that a trait is heritable, especially when they attach a percentage to that heritability—for example, 50 percent—they mean that 50 percent of the variation (differences) among a *group* of people is attributable to heredity. Note that this is *not* the same as saying that 50 percent of a *specific person's* intelligence, height, or any other variable is determined by heredity. One last caution: Although heritability is a biological phenomenon, even highly heritable traits such as height can be modified by the environment. Deprive the child of tall parents of a nutritious diet during the growth years and the child will be less likely to be tall. So even highly heritable traits are modifiable by the environment.

Estimates of the heritability of intelligence have varied widely, as have research techniques that attempt to measure it. To establish how much of intelligence is heritable, several researchers have studied adopted children, who are raised apart from their biological parents (e.g., Finkel et al., 2000; McGue & Bouchard, 2000). Researchers compare an adopted person's intelligence test scores and other measures of cognitive ability with those of biological parents, adoptive parents, biological siblings, and adoptive siblings. The goal is to see if scores later in life more greatly resemble those of biological relatives or adoptive relatives. A French adoption study showed a 14-point increase in IQ scores for children from impoverished homes after they were adopted into families in a higher socio-economic class (Schiff et al., 1982). This study demonstrated that the environment in the adoptive home had a strong effect on intellectual abilities. Other data, however, strongly suggest that the biological mother's IQ score has a more important effect than the adoptive home environment on an adopted child's IQ score. In fact, as time passes, the correlation between the IQ of an adopted child and those of the adoptive parents decreases, and the correlation with the IQ of the child's biological parents increases (Plomin & DeFries, 1999; Plomin et al., 1997; Stoolmiller, 1999). Eysenck (1998) explains this finding by asserting that when an adopted child is young, his or her environment is determined solely by the adopted parents, leading to a correlation between their IQs. However, as the child grows older and makes more life choices, he or she becomes less subject to restrictive parental environmental influences. His or her biological predispositions become more evident, and the result is a greater correlation between the child's IQ and the biological parents' IQ.

One type of adoptive study compares the intellectual abilities of adopted identical twins who were separated at birth; because the twins share the same genetic heritage, any differences in IQ scores *must* be the result of environmental influences. Figure 8.5 summarizes the correlation between the IQ scores of related and unrelated children and parents in different studies. If genetics were the sole determinant of IQ scores, the correlation for identical twins would be 1.0 whether they were reared together or apart. However, identical twins, whether raised together or apart, do not have identical IQ scores—although their scores are similar. In general, researchers

HERITABILITY

The genetically determined proportion of a trait's variation among individuals in a population.

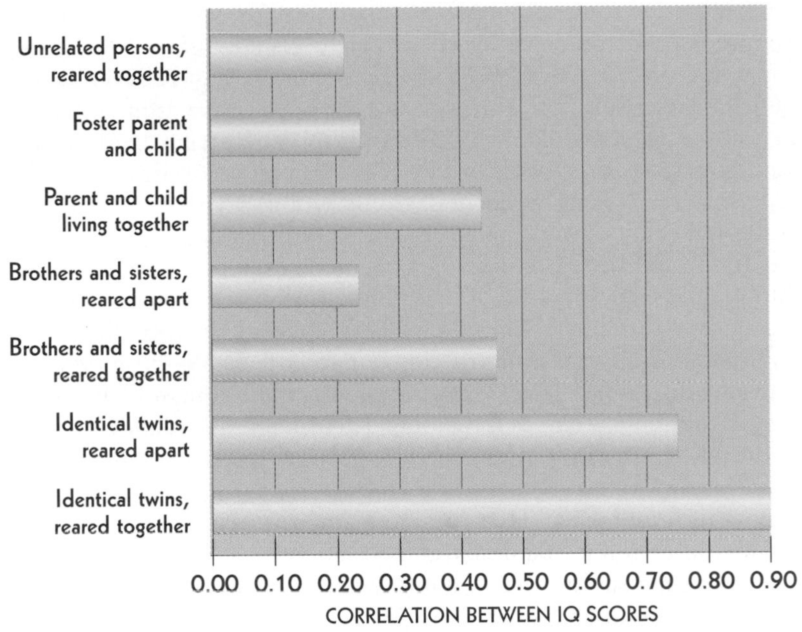
Unrelated persons, reared together
Foster parent and child
Parent and child living together
Brothers and sisters, reared apart
Brothers and sisters, reared together
Identical twins, reared apart
Identical twins, reared together
0.00 0.10 0.20 0.30 0.40 0.50 0.60 0.70 0.80 0.90
CORRELATION BETWEEN IQ SCORES

**FIGURE 8.5**
**Correlations Between IQ Scores of Persons of Varying Relationships**
The closer the biological relationship of two individuals, the more similar their IQ scores—strong support for a genetic component to intelligence.
(Based on data from Bouchard & McGue, 1981, and Erlenmeyer-Kimling & Jarvik, 1963.)

conclude that about 50 percent of the similarities in IQ test scores of identical twins can be accounted for by genetics. Interestingly, most of the data about IQ scores and the role of genetics come from studies of identical twins and their performance early in life; only recently have data emerged from studies of older identical twins, who have lived full lives and had a wide range of experiences (Finkel et al., 1998; McClearn et al., 1997). These data confirm the idea that about half of the similarity in scores of identical twins—even into old age—can be accounted for by genetics (Petrill et al., 1998).

These strong findings supporting genetic influence do not mean that the role of environment is insignificant. In fact, an effect commonly referred to as the "Flynn effect" strongly supports the role of environment. Flynn (1999) gathered data to suggest that IQ scores are, on average, 20 points higher today than they were in the 1930s. Since the gene pool could not have altered in 70 years, this finding has to be attributed to environmental influence. The nature of that influence is unknown. Researchers have hypothesized that the media and video games have had a positive effect on cognitive and visuospatial skills; others argue that better nutrition, smaller families, and a better-educated population may account for this finding. Whatever the cause, the effect is clear and cannot be explained by genetic influence.

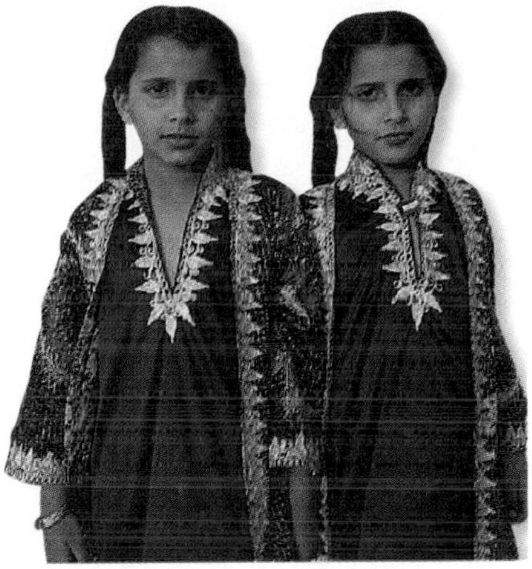

▲ One type of adoptive study compares the intellectual abilities of adopted identical twins who were separated at birth; because such twins share the same genetic heritage, any differences in IQ must be the result of environmental influences.

## EVOLUTION AND INTELLIGENCE

It is important to remember that a fundamental assumption of evolutionary psychology is that human behaviour can be explained in terms of striving to fulfil some evolutionary goal. Intelligent human behaviour can be seen as an adaptation (see p. 43) whose purpose is to increase the chances for reproduction. From an evolutionary perspective then, intelligence develops because smart human beings were able to avoid predators, developed the use of tools, and planted crops that provided nutrition; ultimately, over the course of generations, smarter people predominated. In this way, over hundreds of generations, the elements of complex intellectual functioning are acquired.

Not all scientists agree with this view of evolution and natural selection. Scientists such as Stephen Jay Gould (1997) assert that the evolutionary perspective has failed to appreciate other principles of evolutionary change such as accidental

genetic changes due to catastrophic events that might wipe out a city or country. Furthermore, Gould contends, by identifying a genetic origin for intelligence, the evolutionary perspective would have us believe that human behaviours are far more absolute than they really are. The evolutionary perspective argues that most of our intelligence has been crafted over thousands of generations by natural selection, whereas theorists such as Gould believe that human attributes as basic as human intelligence may, in fact, be accidental. Gould would say that human intelligence is just not the end result of predictable evolutionary progress.

John Tooby and Leda Cosmides (1997), among the foremost intellectual leaders of evolutionary psychology, argue that Gould misrepresented evolutionary theory and that he overstated its assumptions. They contend that intelligence and other adaptations do not determine our destiny but are affected by both random and purposeful events in people's lives. Has evolution helped human beings develop their intelligence? Certainly it has. Is it the only determinant? Certainly not.

In the end, volumes of arguments from evolutionary theorists as well as data from child-rearing studies attempt to demonstrate the genetic and environmental components of intelligence. However, to frame the argument as a debate with a winner and a loser is a mistake; nature and nurture work together in partnership. The idea that a genetically influenced behaviour or characteristic cannot be changed is a myth. Genes do not fix behaviour; instead, they establish a range of possible reactions. The concept of a reaction range suggests that genetics establishes the upper boundaries for intelligence and environment determines where in that range a given individual will score. Individuals in impoverished environments will score at the low end of their range whereas individuals in enriched environments will score at the high end of their range (Ceci & Williams, 1997). Thus, the study of nature and nurture together is essential to an understanding of intelligence.

## THE BELL CURVE

Publication in 1994 of *The Bell Curve*, by Richard J. Herrnstein and Charles Murray, stirred up a whirlpool of controversy. Among its controversial positions, the book makes the argument that IQ is largely genetically determined; that U.S. minority groups, especially African Americans, are trapped in an IQ-lowering environment from which they are unlikely to emerge; and that any attempts to reverse this situation are doomed to failure. Let's take a look at the authors' claims and see if critical thinking supports them.

*The Bell Curve* asserts that the United States is ruled by a cognitive elite whose members are selected by IQ tests, SAT scores, and admission to prestigious colleges. This elite is said to occupy the top of the socio-economic ladder, while the rest of society is assigned to inferior and subordinate status—and, Herrnstein and Murray claim, the situation is likely to stay that way. Herrnstein and Murray suggest that unless something is done to alter the present trends, the United States will be permanently split between a ruling cognitive elite and an ever-increasing and powerless underclass made up primarily of low-IQ blacks, whites, Latinos, and immigrants. Yet Herrnstein and Murray consider it futile to attempt to raise the poor, the disadvantaged, and the cognitively impaired above the limits of their own genetics.

Not surprisingly, others hold the opposite point of view. For example, Myerson and his colleagues (1998) argue that people are most likely to take tests of academic ability at the point in life when ability differences are most pronounced; blacks gain more from university and college educations than do whites, and if students were given IQ tests as they finished university or college, the gap between scores would be much smaller. Flynn (1999) convincingly shows that average IQs of groups of individuals can change over time and that ethnic- or race-based arguments about genetically rooted differences just do not follow from the data. Hout (2002) presents additional evidence that social factors—for example, schools, the family, and labour markets—are the main determinants of social inequality. Crane (1996; Phillips et al., 1998) and

Hall (2001) assert that there is simply no evidence that the race gap in cognitive test scores is caused by genetically determined differences. They argue that, in contrast, there is a good deal of evidence that supports an environmental explanation.

It is crucial to remember that the concept of race is fraught with issues; Fish (2002) cautions that the human species does not have "races" in the biological sense, although cultures have a variety of folk concepts of "race." Although any debate about race, ethnicity, IQ, and genetics is inherently controversial, Herrnstein and Murray present data in a way that makes careful critical analysis especially difficult. For example, they omit much historical data, fail to separate the effects of nature and nurture in some early childhood data, present limited new data, and make a series of questionable claims and assumptions (Horn, 2002). In addition, heritability is a concept that deals with groups of people, and their recommendations about education focus on individuals—a classic flaw in scientific thinking. Among their weak assumptions are that IQ represents a general quality, that IQ largely or solely reflects genetics, that IQ is fixed and immutable, and that there is a cause-and-effect relationship between low IQ and problematic social behaviours. Average differences between groups more likely reflect the environment than genetics—remember again, differences within groups are usually greater than differences between groups. Psychologists, however, recognize the multidimensional nature of intelligence, the modifiability of intelligence, and the fact that IQ is neither the only predictor of performance on a job or in life nor always a very good one.

## THE STABILITY OF INTELLIGENCE TEST SCORES

Many Canadians have taken an intelligence test at some time. Was the test you took in grade two a good predictor of your academic ability when you were in high school? Does an IQ score remain stable over a long period of time? Early examinations of IQ score stability showed that the IQ scores of infants did not correlate well with their IQ scores when they were school age (Bayley, 1969). Researchers quickly realized that it is not possible to measure the same capabilities in infants and in older children and adults. Further, correlations of the IQ scores of school-age children and adults show that such scores can change, sometimes substantially. Yet some research indicates that to a certain extent infant IQ can predict school-age IQ (DiLalla et al., 1990; Rose & Feldman, 1995). Note that the items included on tests vary quite substantially over the years; first-graders are asked quite different questions than are tenth-graders. What remains stable is a person's score in relation to those of his or her peers of the same age.

What about the IQ scores of adults? Do IQ scores remain stable throughout adulthood? In general, psychologists have shown that intelligence and achievement test scores at first increase with age, then level off in adulthood, only to decline in late adulthood. The results of a 40-year study of IQ showed that, in general, the intellectual functioning of men increased a bit around age 40 and then gradually declined to its earlier level when the men were in their fifties (Schwartzman et al., 1987). In other words, despite the passage of years, cognitive performance remained relatively stable. The effect of aging on IQ scores is difficult to assess because some aspects of the scores decrease more with age than others. For example, scores on numerical portions of IQ tests tend to show a more significant decrease with advancing age than do scores on verbal portions. In addition, not everyone shows age-related IQ declines; people who continue their education throughout their lives show relatively small decreases.

There is now ample evidence that IQ scores remain relatively stable once test subjects reach adulthood. However, the scores of infants and children are so prone to change that they are not reliable predictors of later IQ scores. Of course, a child who achieves a high score on an IQ test at age 9 is likely to do well or perhaps even better at age 10. The data show enough fluctuation, though, especially at younger ages, to make predictions uncertain.

## The Abecedarian Intervention

In this section, we saw that *The Bell Curve* argued that there is no way out for the poor and disadvantaged; no matter how many early educational programs are introduced, children will be held back by cognitive disabilities created by their genetics. However, research that began in 1972 shows evidence to the contrary (Ramey & Campbell, 1984, 1992; Ramey, Ramey, & Lanzi, 2001). The Abecedarian Project was a carefully controlled study in which 57 infants from low-income families were randomly assigned to receive early intervention in a high-quality child-care setting and 54 infants were placed in a no-treatment control group. All of the infants were considered at risk for delayed and poor intellectual development because of issues of poverty, for example. The children who received care had full-time, high-quality educational intervention from infancy through age five; each child had an individualized scheme of educational activities that usually consisted of "games" built into the child's day. The activities focused on social, emotional, and cognitive areas of development but gave special emphasis to language activities. Progress was monitored over time, with follow-up studies conducted at ages 12, 15, and 21.

The results showed that children who participated in the program had higher cognitive test scores from the toddler years to age 21. Academic achievement in both reading and math was higher. Not only that, but those treated completed more years of education and were more likely to attend a university or college. Enhanced language development appears to have been especially influential in raising cognitive test scores.

In the end, young adults who received *early* educational intervention had significantly higher mental test scores from toddlerhood through age 21 than did untreated participants. The truth is that large gains in IQ test scores can be obtained with intensive early intervention programs, especially when the program is sustained for long periods of time (Ramey & Sackett, 2000; Ramey et al., 2000). Instead of poor children lagging behind even in the early school years, the Abecedarian Project shows that early intervention works and works well. Ed Zigler's Project Head Start (see p. 361) would take no issue with these findings, and students who do service learning activities in early intervention provide first-hand testimony. Similar early intervention programs are running across Canada under names such as Head Start and Healthy Families, Early Intervention, and Home Visitation. The federal government, with provincial support, has in recent years provided additional funding for these sorts of early intervention programs through the Early Child Development Initiative.

▲ Students today are learning critical-thinking skills, which helps them obtain higher IQ scores.

## ARE THERE GENDER DIFFERENCES IN INTELLIGENCE?

Many psychologists believe there are gender differences in verbal ability, with girls surpassing boys in most verbal tasks during the early school years. However, most differences have been found to be due to the expectations of parents and teachers. For example, parents and teachers have long encouraged boys to engage in spatial, mechanical tasks. Two interesting trends have been observed in Canada in recent decades, though. First, many parents have been encouraging both girls and boys to acquire math, verbal, and spatial skills; that is, they have endeavoured to avoid gender stereotyping. Second, the observed cognitive differences between boys and girls have been diminishing each year (American Association of University Women Educational Foundation, 1998).

In fact, the old consensus about gender differences is at least exaggerated, if not simply wrong (Halpern, 1997). Janet Shibley Hyde has investigated and explored the results of thousands of studies on sex differences in a variety of domains—self-esteem, mathematics, stress, and cognitive ability. These studies had tested more than 1 million individuals (Hyde, 1996; Jaffee & Hyde, 2000; Plant et al., 2000). Although Hyde and Linn (1988) found a gender difference in verbal ability in favour of women, it was exceedingly small. They further argued that more refined tests and theories of intelligence are needed to examine any gender differences that may exist. The differences found today exist only in certain special populations; for example, among the very brightest mathematics students, boys continue to outscore girls, although the boys' scores vary more than girls' scores (Hedges & Nowell, 1995). Boys are motivated to achieve more and strive harder at math, in part because more of them have career aspirations that involve mathematical skills. As a consequence of these aspirations, boys tend to take more math courses and more advanced ones—this puts them still further ahead on standardized tests. It is important to remember that the small gender differences (and ethnic differences) that do exist are based on group averages and say nothing about individual abilities (Halpern, 1997; Suzuki & Valencia, 1997). In general, differences between the test scores of males and those of females are disappearing, and this trend has been observed in many cultures (Geary, 1998).

## Exceptional Individuals

Canadian society is oriented toward looking for, testing, and educating special or exceptional children. As early as during the first few weeks of grade one, most children take some kind of reading readiness test; by the end of grade four, students usually are classified and labelled according to their projected development, again largely on the basis of tests. Educators often use the term *exceptional* to refer to people who are gifted as well as to those who suffer from learning disabilities, physical impairments, and mental retardation.

### GIFTEDNESS

Gifted individuals represent one end of the continuum of intelligence and talent. Exceptional ability is not limited to cognitive skills, however. Most six-year-olds enrolled in a ballet class probably will show average ability, but ballet teachers report that an occasional child will exhibit a natural ability for dance. In the same way, many children and adults learn to play the piano, but only a few excel at it. And over a wide range of behaviours, some people excel in a particular area but are only average in other areas (Winner, 2000).

As discussed further in *Brain and Behaviour*, the phenomenon of gifted children has been established and the basis of giftedness researched for some time. Some gifted children, such as Mozart, display their genius musically. Others display it in science, creative writing, dance, etc. There is no universally accepted definition of *giftedness* (just as there is no universally agreed-on definition of *intelligence*). Gifted children may have superior cognitive, leadership, or performing arts abilities. Moreover, many require special schooling that goes beyond the ordinary classroom; their instruction needs to be individualized (Detterman & Thompson, 1997). Without it, these children may not realize their full potential. In truth, all children need individualized instruction because most students—especially the gifted—are underchallenged (Winner, 1997). There is no federally mandated program for gifted students in Canada. Each school board or district may have a special program for the gifted; however, some school systems have none, and others allocate special instruction only in brief periods or to small groups and still do not challenge the extraordinarily gifted. Some systems provide special schools for children with superior cognitive abilities, performing arts talents, or science aptitude. The special needs of gifted students (and of those with mental retardation—considered next) should not be addressed for only one day a week, only in grades one through six, or with traditional teaching techniques.

*Be an*
**ACTIVE LEARNER**

REVIEW
> What are the chief differences between the Kaufman Assessment Battery for Children (K–ABC) and the Stanford–Binet, Wechsler, and Woodcock–Johnson–III scales? pp. 287–288
> If IQ tests do not examine innate ability, what do they measure? p. 291
> What is the main goal of heritability studies? p. 292
> Gould believes that human attributes such as basic human intelligence may, in fact, be accidental rather than a result of natural selection. How might this occur? pp. 293–294

THINK CRITICALLY
> What conclusions about nature versus nurture can be drawn from data on correlations between IQ scores and child-rearing environments for both related and unrelated children?
> What is a possible explanation for an over-representation of ethnically diverse students in special education classes?

APPLY PSYCHOLOGY
> If you had to design a series of selection procedures for a university or college or a program for gifted students, what procedures would you choose?
> If you were designing an early intervention project, what features would you consider absolutely essential to having an impact on intelligence?

## Art, Creativity, and Intelligence

People's intelligence, their creativity, and ultimately their humanity have a neurological basis. This is easy to forget because we think of such capacities as special and almost ethereal. Jacques Villeneuve's abilities in a race car, Vince Carter's grace on the basketball floor, or any number of talented writers, actors, and singers can transfix us with their abilities to bring us to a different place or time through their writings, acting, song, or dance.

What becomes intriguing, but difficult to resolve, is the relationship between these states or activities, which are hard to define and measure, and other states of being. Consider various mental illnesses. We know that people who have bipolar disorder (the proper term for what is often incorrectly called manic-depression) are often creative and exceptionally intelligent. Sometimes their long-lasting mood swings are accompanied by wild bursts of intelligence, exuberance, and creativity. Think historically for a moment. Mozart, Beethoven, Van Gogh, Edgar Allan Poe, and William Styron all were expansively creative and brilliant; they also suffered from depression and perhaps bipolar disorder. They combined new ideas, were creative, and were unhappy. Is there a common theme here? Was it their heightened distractibility? Was their chronic unhappiness at the crux of their creativity? Kay Redfield Jamison (1993, 1996) thinks so; she makes the case that the artistic temperament and bipolar disorder in many cases are inextricably woven together.

The conclusion that Jamison leads to is the idea that physiologically underpinning both bipolar disorder and creative intelligence is one process, or at least one set of crossed connections. In reality there is little experimental evidence for this assertion, and critics argue that Jamison takes too narrow a view of mental disorders (Sass, 2001). But there is much anecdotal and correlational evidence. Enough data exist to make many psychologists and psychiatrists such as Jamison ask how we can study the brains of the exceptionally intelligent, the creative, and those who suffer from various psychological disorders to learn more about human thought, so as to maximize our human potential. Whether the two states of being—mental illness and creativity—are tied together is yet to be determined. Jamison asks probing questions, but the evidence that will firmly connect maladjustment with creativity is yet to be ascertained.

## MENTAL RETARDATION

The term *mental retardation* covers a wide range of behaviours, from slow learning to severe mental and physical impairment. Many people with mental retardation are able to cope well. Most learn to walk and to feed and dress themselves; many learn to read and are able to work. In 1992, the American Association on Mental Retardation adopted a new formal definition of mental retardation:

**MENTAL RETARDATION**

Below-average intellectual functioning, as measured on an IQ test, accompanied by substantial limitations in functioning that originate before age 18.

**Mental retardation** refers to substantial limitations in present functioning. It is characterized by significantly subaverage intellectual functioning, existing concurrently with related limitations in two or more of the following applicable adaptive skill areas: communication, self-care, home living, social skills, community use, self-direction, health and safety, functional academics, leisure, and work. Mental retardation manifests before age 18.

This definition requires that practitioners consider (1) cultural and linguistic diversity, (2) how adaptive skills interact with a person's community setting, (3) the fact that specific skills often exist with limitations, and (4) the likelihood that life functioning generally will improve with age.

There are a variety of causes for mental retardation—from deprived environments (especially for those with mild retardation) to genetic abnormalities, infectious diseases, and physical trauma (including trauma caused by drugs taken by the mother during pregnancy). There are two broad ways to classify mental retardation. The first focuses on biological versus environmental causes; the second, more prevalent, approach focuses on levels of retardation as reflected in behaviour.

**LEVELS OF RETARDATION.** A diagnosis of mental retardation involves three criteria: a lower-than-normal (below 70) IQ score as measured on a standardized test, such as the WISC–III or the WAIS–III; difficulty adapting to the environment; and the presence of such problems before age 18. There are four basic levels of mental retardation, each corresponding to a different range of scores on a standardized IQ test (see Table 8.6 and Figure 8.6): mild, moderate, severe, and profound.

Mild Retardation. Approximately 90 percent of those classified as mentally retarded have mild mental retardation (Wechsler IQ score of 55 to 69). Through special programs, they are able to acquire academic and occupational skills, but they generally need extra supervision of their work (e.g., Allington, 1981). As adults, people with mild mental retardation function intellectually at about the level of 10-year-olds. Thus, with some help from family and friends, most people with mild mental retardation can cope successfully with their environment.

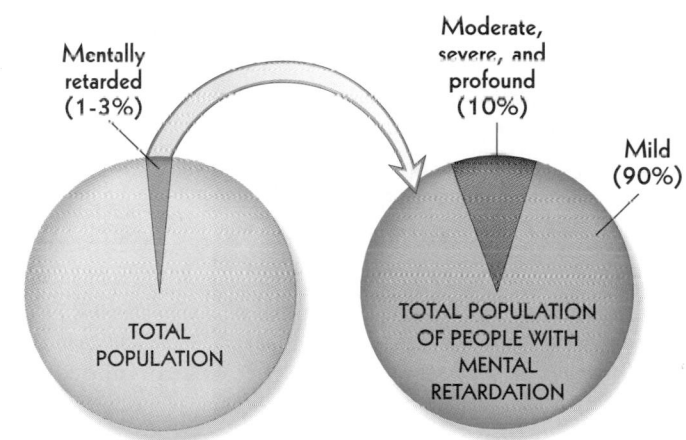

▲ Individuals with mental retardation often have functional limitations; however, many participate and succeed in many activities, including sports.

Moderate Retardation. People with moderate mental retardation (Wechsler IQ score of 40 to 54) account for approximately 6 percent of those classified as mentally retarded. Most live in institutions or as dependants of their families. Those who are not institutionalized need special classes; some can hold simple jobs, although few are employed. People with moderate mental retardation are able to speak, write, and interact with friends, but their motor coordination, posture, and social skills are clumsy. Their intellectual level is equivalent to that of five- to six-year-olds.

Severe Retardation. Only about 3 percent of the people with mental retardation are severely retarded (Wechsler IQ score of 25 to 39). People with severe mental retardation show great motor, speech, and intellectual impairment and are almost totally dependent on others to take care of their basic needs. Severe retardation often results from birth disorders or traumatic injury to the brain.

**FIGURE 8.6**
**Mental Retardation in the Population**

Profound Retardation. Only 1 percent of the people with mental retardation are classified as profoundly retarded (Wechsler IQ score below 25). These people are unable to master even simple tasks and require total supervision and constant care. Their motor and intellectual development is minimal, and many are physically underdeveloped. Physical deformities and other congenital defects (such as deafness, blindness, and seizures) often accompany profound mental retardation.

Mentally retarded (1-3%)

Moderate, severe, and profound (10%)

Mild (90%)

TOTAL POPULATION

TOTAL POPULATION OF PEOPLE WITH MENTAL RETARDATION

| TABLE 8.6 | Mental Retardation as Measured on the Wechsler Scales | |
|---|---|---|
| **Classification** | **Wechsler IQ Score** | **Percentage of the Mentally Retarded** |
| Mild | 55–69 | 90 |
| Moderate | 40–54 | 6 |
| Severe | 25–39 | 3 |
| Profound | Below 25 | 1 |

**EDUCATING AND EMPLOYING THOSE WITH MENTAL RETARDATION.** Until recently, thousands of children were given a substandard education after doing poorly on an intelligence test. Labelled as slow learners or perhaps even as mentally retarded, these children received neither special education nor special attention. The situation is somewhat better today. In the United States, federal legislation Public Law (102-119, Individuals with Disabilities Education Act—IDEA) guarantees a free, appropriate education to children with disabilities. In Canada, there is no such legislation, but nonetheless our educational systems are significantly more inclusive of children with special needs than they used to be.

Mainstreaming—the integration of all children with special needs into regular classroom settings, whenever appropriate, with the support of special education services—has been tried to varying degrees within our educational systems. In mainstreaming, children are assigned to a regular class for at least half of their school day. They spend the rest of the day in special education classrooms or vocational training situations. Although research studies have produced conflicting data on the effectiveness of mainstreaming, psychologists and educators generally support it (Zigler & Hodapp, 1991).

Real progress has been made with mainstreaming, but problems remain in many school settings. Too often children are mainstreamed not into the academic (classroom) aspects of school, but only into its social aspects (athletics, lunch). This is done to avoid stigmatization, but one consequence is a lack of delivery of adequate special academic services to children who require them (Zigler & Hodapp, 1991). Because of such problems, some schools now keep students with special education needs in regular classrooms and bring support to them rather than bringing the children to supportive services—an approach called *inclusion*. Not without its critics, inclusion focuses on the needs of individual children in new ways; research on its success is still a decade away.

Mainstreamed children can become good workers. Companies are realizing that if people with mild mental retardation are placed in the right job, are properly trained, and are effectively motivated, they can be counted on to be good workers. As a result, many companies now hire workers with mental retardation who were once thought to be unemployable.

There are some drawbacks to hiring such workers. One is that training them often requires extra patience. Even a relatively simple task may have to be broken down into 30 or 40 individual steps. As well, workers with mental retardation sometimes need help to remain focused on their job. Nonetheless, there are many great success stories. Those workers who have been through training programs do exceptionally well. Workers with mental retardation are likely to stay in jobs that others tire of. In addition, they may be more dependable, motivated, and industrious than other workers.

MAINSTREAMING

The integration of all children with special needs into regular classroom settings, whenever appropriate, with the support of special education services.

**Be an ACTIVE LEARNER**

**REVIEW**
> Define *mental retardation.* p. 298
> What is mainstreaming? p. 300

**THINK CRITICALLY**
> A diagnosis of mental retardation involves a lower-than-normal IQ score. What does this imply about IQ tests as predictors of behaviour?
> If gifted children often develop more quickly than others, how do you distinguish early developers from the gifted?

**APPLY PSYCHOLOGY**
> What might a practitioner do to diagnose mental retardation differently?
> Identify five individuals whom you consider gifted and explain why they are gifted.

# Summary and Review

## WHAT IS INTELLIGENCE?

**Identify the key features of a definition of intelligence.**

> *Intelligence* is the overall capacity of an individual to act purposefully, to think rationally, and to deal effectively with the environment.   **pp. 274–275**

**Describe several different approaches to intelligence.**

> Wechsler examined the components of intelligence and argued that intelligence tests made up of subparts involving spatial relations and verbal comprehension reveal little about someone's overall capacity to deal with the world.   **p. 275**

> A *factor analysis* approach to evaluating intelligence uses correlational techniques to determine which tasks are involved in intellectual ability. In factor analysis, the assumption is that tasks with high correlations test similar aspects of intellectual functioning.   **p. 275**

> Vygotsky argued that the most significant moment in the course of intellectual development occurs when speech and practical activity, two previously completely independent lines of development, converge. Thus, researchers need to study the processes of intelligence in a social context, not just the products of intelligence.   **p. 276**

> Gardner maintains that people have multiple intelligences (at least eight). An intelligence is an ability to solve a problem or create a product within a specific cultural setting. He argues that not all human intelligences, or competencies, lend themselves to measurement by a test, and he criticizes IQ tests because they place so much emphasis on linguistic and logical–mathematical skills.   **pp. 276–277**

> Sternberg takes an information processing view of intelligence. Like Gardner's view that intelligence has many parts, Sternberg's triarchic theory divides intelligence into three dimensions: analytic, practical, and creative. Sternberg's theory focuses on adaptation to the world.   **pp. 277–278**

**KEY TERMS**

intelligence, p. 274; factor analysis, p. 275

## THE PROCESS OF TEST DEVELOPMENT

**Why were Binet and Simon significant in the development of intelligence tests?**

> Binet coined the phrase *mental age*, meaning the age level at which a person is functioning cognitively, regardless of chronological age. He and Simon applied everyday tasks, such as counting, naming, and using objects, to determining mental age. The scale they developed can be considered the first useful and practical test of intelligence.   **p. 280**

**What criteria must be addressed in order to develop a fair and accurate intelligence test?**

> *Standardization* is the process of developing uniform procedures for administering and scoring a test. This includes developing *norms*—the scores and corresponding percentile ranks of a large and representative sample of test takers from the population for which the test was designed. A *representative sample* is a sample of individuals who match the population with whom they are to be compared, with regard to key variables such as socio-economic status and age.   **p. 281**

> A *normal curve* is a bell-shaped graphic representation of data, showing what percentage of the population falls under each part of the curve. The simplest score on a test is the *raw score*—the number of correct answers unconverted or transformed in any way. Scores are commonly expressed in terms of a *standard score*—a score that expresses an individual's position relative to those of others and based on the mean and how scores are distributed around it. A standard score is generally a *percentile score*—a score indicating what percentage of the test population would obtain a lower score. A *deviation IQ* is a standard IQ test score whose mean and standard deviation remain constant for all ages.   **pp. 281–283**

> There are several types of *reliability*. A test is considered reliable if it yields a very similar score for the same individual over repeated testings. All tests are unreliable to some degree. The standard error of measurement is the number of points by which a score varies because of the imperfect reliability of a test. A test's *validity* is its ability to measure what it is supposed to measure; if a test does not have validity, no inferences can be drawn from test results.   **pp. 283–284**

> There are several basic criticisms of—and defences of—the validity of intelligence tests and testing. The first is that there is no agreed-on definition of intelligence. The second is that intelligence tests measure learned information rather than intelligence. The third is that school settings may adversely affect IQ test results. Another criticism of testing is that some people may be test-wise, which improves performance. A fifth criticism is that IQ test scores may depend on people's motivation to succeed. Finally, some claim that society helps create the correlation between academic success and IQ test scores.   **pp. 284–285**

> Critics of IQ tests are concerned about the interpretation of scores. Intelligence tests are generally made up of different subtests or subscales, each yielding a score; there may also be one general score for the entire test. All of these scores require knowledgeable interpretation; that is, test scores must be given a context that is meaningful to the person who receives the information—without such context, a test score is little more than a number.   **p. 285**

## FOUR IMPORTANT INTELLIGENCE TESTS

**Describe the Stanford–Binet Intelligence Scale, the Wechsler scales, the Kaufman Assessment Battery for Children (K–ABC), and the Woodcock–Johnson–III.**

> The Stanford–Binet Intelligence Scale consists of four major subscales and one overall IQ test score. It has been a good predictor of academic performance, and many of its tests correlate highly with one another; its newer items minimize gender and racial characteristics. **pp. 285–286**

> The Wechsler scales group test items by content. The score on each subtest is converted to a standard (or scaled) score, adjusted for the subject's age. The test yields verbal, performance, and overall IQ scores.   **pp. 286–287**

> The K–ABC consists of four global scales. Three measure mental processing abilities—sequential and simultaneous processing, and a composite of the two; the fourth assesses achievement.   **pp. 287–288**

> The Woodcock–Johnson–III measures general intellectual ability, specific cognitive abilities, scholastic aptitude, oral language, and academic achievement.   **p. 288**

## THE ENVIRONMENTAL AND BIOLOGICAL PARTNERSHIP

**What is the effect of cultural variables and gender on intelligence test scores?**

> Although researchers find differences among the IQ test scores of various ethnic groups, they find little or no consistent and conclusive evidence of bias in the tests themselves. The evidence of many studies of a variety of intelligence tests used with ethnic minority groups indicates that intelligence tests are not culturally biased. However, IQ test scores in isolation mean little. Intelligence can be demonstrated in many ways, including through mature and responsible behaviour.   **pp. 289–291**

> Cross-cultural differences are evident in IQ test scores; for this reason, many psychologists (1) de-emphasize overall test scores, (2) focus on interpretation of test results, (3) remember that IQ test scores do not measure innate ability, and (4) focus on intellectual functioning in the context of real-life situations.   **p. 291**

> Proponents of the environmental (nurture) view of intelligence believe that intelligence tests do not adequately measure a person's adaptation to a constantly changing environment. Many researchers claim that the question of nature versus nurture will never be resolved because factors such as family structure, family size, and other environmental variables are important and impossible to measure accurately. The *heritability* of a trait is the genetically determined proportion of a trait's variation within a population of individuals. Heredity (nature) does not fix a person's intelligence; it sets a framework within which intelligence is shaped by the environment. **pp. 291–293**

> The extent of gender differences in verbal and mathematical abilities has been exaggerated; gender differences in verbal ability are so small that they can be ignored. **pp. 296–297**

## EXCEPTIONAL INDIVIDUALS

**Describe the ends of the continuum of intelligence— giftedness and mental retardation—and their implications for educational settings.**

> Giftedness means having superior cognitive, leadership, or performing arts abilities. Gifted children represent one end of a continuum of cognitive and other abilities. Such individuals need special schooling to meet their needs.   **p. 297**

> *Mental retardation* is below-average intellectual functioning, together with substantial limitations in adaptive behaviour, originating before age 8. Retardation can affect communication, self-care, home living, social skills, self-direction, health and safety, leisure activities, and work. There are four basic levels of mental retardation; each corresponds to a specific range of scores on a standardized intelligence test. The behaviours associated with mental retardation vary from slow learning to an inability to care for oneself because of impaired physical, motor, and intellectual development.   **pp. 298–300**

> *Mainstreaming* is the integration of all children with special needs into regular classroom settings wherever appropriate, with the support of special services. The purpose of mainstreaming is to help normalize the life experiences of children with special needs; unfortunately, mainstreaming is most often done with regard to the social aspects of school rather than academic ones.   **p. 300**

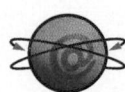

Take advantage of the multimedia resources available with this text! Follow the marginal icons to access the interactive modules on the *HandsOnPsych CD-ROM*; log on to *MyPsychLab* to explore the ebook, study aids, and other online resources; and visit the Companion Website at **www.pearsoned.ca/lefton** for additional exercises and links.

# Motivation and Emotion

Terry Fox, Steve Fonyo, and Rick Hansen are three amazing Canadians who can be said to have gone the distance in many more ways than one. Each undertook a marathon of personal challenge and hardship for something he believed in and showed Canada and the world the extent to which humans can motivate themselves to achieve.

Terry Fox embarked on a cross-country run for cancer research in April 1980. Terry had lost most of one leg to cancer but trained hard and undertook to run across Canada to raise money for cancer research. After a slow start, in terms of public awareness, Terry's determination and characteristic hopping run soon captured the attention and imaginations of Canadians. By the time he was forced to stop his run in Thunder Bay due to a recurrence of cancer, Terry had achieved an amazing feat. Though he died a year later without being able to resume his run, Terry came to embody, for Canadians, grit, determination, and personal motivation.

At 18 years of age, Steve Fonyo followed in Terry's footsteps. Also having lost a leg to cancer, Steve began a cross-country run on March 31, 1984, intending to complete what Terry Fox had begun. More than a year and 7924 kilometres later, he arrived in Victoria on May 29, 1985, completing his marathon. He raised more than $30 million. Throughout his run, Steve showed the same motivated determination that had carried Terry through his marathon. Steve followed up his accomplishment with a similar run in Britain. Following that, he retired from marathons but then appeared to lose direction. He was young when he completed his first run and seemed unsure how to develop his identity after his early accomplishments. He considered suicide, turned to cocaine use, and eventually faced a number of serious criminal charges, including assault with a weapon, fraud, theft, and firearms offences. Steve has since worked through this difficult period and rediscovered some of his earlier motivational drive. He has completed training as a helicopter pilot and mechanic.

Rick Hansen faced a different challenge. A friend of Terry Fox, Rick lost the use of his legs at 15 years of age as a result of a truck crash. Rick showed heroic determination as he excelled in wheelchair sports and was the first disabled athlete to earn a physical education degree at the University of British Columbia. In 1985, Rick took on his greatest challenge. The Man in Motion World Tour had Rick wheeling through 34 countries and covering more than 40 000 kilometers to raise money and awareness of disabilities and spinal cord research. The tour raised more than $26 million and the Hansen Foundation that was created with the money has since raised more than $148 million for spinal cord injury causes, including research, awareness, and rehabilitation.

Understanding what allows individuals such as Terry Fox, Steve Fonyo, and Rick Hansen to drive themselves to such heights of accomplishment requires an understanding of the basics of human motivation. If we can better understand their accomplishments, perhaps we can find ways to help ourselves get through our days more effectively.

## Theories of Motivation

Researchers have always sought to discover what drives people to take various actions—from simple, seemingly instinctual ones such as eating to complex ones such as learning to juggle. The word *motivation* derives from the Latin *movere*, meaning "to move," and refers to the forces that energize. **Motivation** is any condition, although usually an internal one, that can be inferred to initiate, activate, or maintain an organism's goal-directed behaviour.

Let's examine the four basic parts of this definition of motivation. First, motivation reflects an *internal condition* that cannot be directly observed. Regardless of whether the motivation develops from simple physiological needs or from complex psychological desires, such as the desire to help others, to obtain approval, or to earn a higher income, the source for motivation is internal. Second, motivation is *inferred to be* the link between a person's internal conditions and external behaviours; an observer can infer its presence from its behavioural effects. Third, motivation *initiates, activates, and maintains behaviour*. If a person wants to make a good grade in a college class, that motivation will require the person to maintain class attendance, study regularly, and develop good test-taking behaviours. Finally, motivation generates *goal-directed behaviour*. Goals vary widely across individuals and situations. Some goals are concrete and immediate—for example, to eat, to remove a painful stimulus, or to win a diving match. Other goals are more abstract and long term.

The study of motivation can be considered the study of what people choose to do, why they choose to do it, and how much energy they spend doing it (Edwards, 1999). Many theories of motivation have been developed to explain human behaviour, and these theories fall into five broad categories, each of which has generated research activity: evolutionary theories, drive theory, arousal theory, cognitive theories, and humanistic theory. Let's examine each of these categories in turn and then look at some basic types of motivation, before turning to how emotions and motivation are intertwined.

### EVOLUTIONARY THEORIES

In the early days of psychology, theorists such as Konrad Lorenz spoke of *instincts*, referring to fixed behavioural patterns that occur throughout a species and appear without learning or practice. What these researchers studied were often elaborate stereotyped behaviour patterns associated with hunting and mating. Researchers quickly realized that the study of such rigid behaviour patterns—whether of geese or wolves—had limited relevance to human beings. However, their early theorizing did give way to a more contemporary, *evolutionary perspective* that asserts that

**MOTIVATION**

Any condition, although usually an internal one, that can be inferred to initiate, activate, or maintain an organism's goal-directed behaviour.

**Emotion and Motivation**

natural selection, the process of selective reproduction of the fittest organisms, would explain certain basic human behaviours. Animals, and human beings for that matter, who are motivated to engage in behaviours that make it more likely they will succeed, stay alive, and reproduce are more likely to be represented in the population. Ultimately, only the fittest organisms contribute to the gene pool.

Evolutionary psychology has brought back the concept of instinct, claiming that the behaviour of humans and other animals is motivated by many instincts. Rather than hypothesizing that humans are less controlled by instinct than other animals, evolutionary psychologists believe that humans have *more* instincts. These instincts give humans a variety of built-in, complex programs that automatically deploy behaviours that were adaptive in our evolutionary history. However, many of these built-in behaviour sequences occur automatically and thus without conscious thought or decision making. These programs endow humans with natural competencies, and their automatic activation makes such responses rapid. This view of many automatic behaviours is contrary to the view of much of psychology, but Leda Cosmides and John Tooby (1997) claim that the rest of psychology is "instinct blind" because other psychological orientations cannot see how prominent and important instincts are.

According to David Buss (1995), Steven Pinker (1997), and McMaster University's Denys deCatanzaro (1999), motivation and emotion are inseparable. Motivation pushes people toward a number of behaviours, possibly simultaneously, but emotion sets priorities about what to do at any particular time. A person may be motivated to eat, even moving toward food, but a threatening noise in the next room will change that motivated behaviour to another very quickly.

Evolutionary psychologists examine motivations in the framework of understanding how they help organisms survive and reproduce. According to the evolutionary view, things that produce pleasure or pain will be motivating because these feelings relate to survival. Thus, eating, drinking, pain avoidance, temperature regulation, and reproductive behaviours are all of interest to evolutionary psychologists, who assume that these behaviours have built-in bases.

## DRIVE THEORY

Some of the most influential and best-researched motivation theories are forms of drive theory. **Drive theory** is an explanation of behaviour that assumes that an organism is motivated to act because of a need to attain, re-establish, balance, or maintain some goal. Stimuli such as hunger and pain create, energize, and initiate such behaviour. A person who is hungry will be driven to seek food.

A **drive** is an internal aroused condition that directs an organism to satisfy some physiological need. Drive theory focuses on **need**—a state of physiological imbalance usually accompanied by arousal. (We will explore arousal in greater depth in the next section.) Physiological needs are said to be *mechanistic*, because the organism has no choice but to be pushed, pulled, and energized by them, almost like a machine. An organism motivated by a need is said to be in a *drive state*. The ultimate goal is to attain **homeostasis**—maintainance of a constant state of inner stability or balance. The processes by which organisms seek to re-establish homeostasis are a key part of drive theory. For example, a thirsty animal will seek out water to re-establish its body fluid level (psychologists refer to this normally maintained level as a steady state). In motivation theory, the goal that satisfies a need is an *incentive*. Incentives can be positive and lure us, like food or a sexually attractive person, or they can repel us and cause us to avoid a painful situation or someone we dislike. Behaviours such as eating and drinking, which reduce a biological need (and re-establish homeostasis), are reinforced when their incentives are attained; such behaviours are therefore especially likely to recur. Behaviours such as juggling, which does not reduce a biological need, are less likely to recur. (See Figure 9.1 for an overview and examples of drive theory.)

DRIVE THEORY

An explanation of behaviour that assumes that an organism is motivated to act because of a need to attain, re-establish, balance, or maintain some goal that helps with the survival of the organism or the species.

DRIVE

An internal aroused condition that directs an organism to satisfy physiological needs.

NEED

A state of physiological imbalance usually accompanied by arousal.

HOMEOSTASIS

A tendency to attempt to maintain a constant state of inner stability or balance.

FIGURE 9.1

An Overview of Drive
Theory

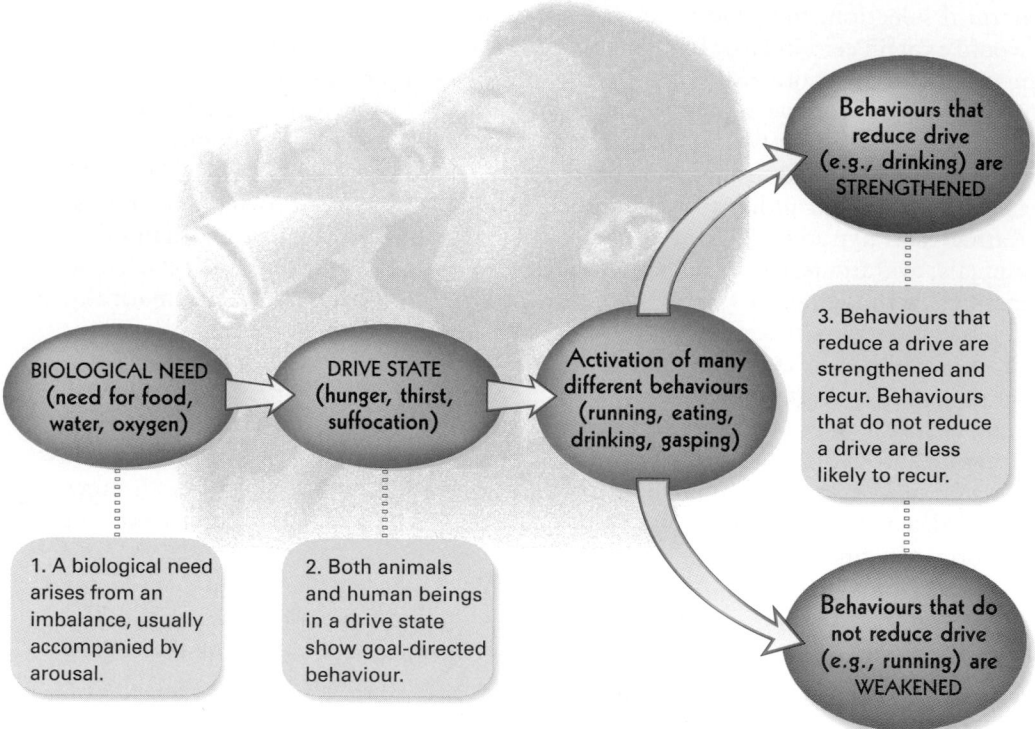

BIOLOGICAL NEED
(need for food,
water, oxygen)

DRIVE STATE
(hunger, thirst,
suffocation)

Activation of many
different behaviours
(running, eating,
drinking, gasping)

Behaviours that
reduce drive
(e.g., drinking) are
STRENGTHENED

Behaviours that do
not reduce drive
(e.g., running) are
WEAKENED

1. A biological need
arises from an
imbalance, usually
accompanied by
arousal.

2. Both animals
and human beings
in a drive state
show goal-directed
behaviour.

3. Behaviours that
reduce a drive are
strengthened and
recur. Behaviours
that do not reduce
a drive are less
likely to recur.

Physiologically based behaviors such as eating and drinking offer clear examples of motivation according to the drive reduction point of view. In the 1950s, drive reduction theorist Clark Hull asserted that the actions of reinforcers in developing stimulus–response associations were in part determined by the motivational drive state of the organism. In his elaborate, and mechanistic, theory of motivation and learning, Hull argued that only hungry organisms find food a good reinforcer and are thus motivated to engage in tasks that lead to food. Organisms are also motivated to avoid pain, and escaping from situations with negative consequences can be strong motivation. The possibility that a person can experience drives both toward and away from certain goals can result in conflict.

## AROUSAL THEORY

According to drive theory, arousal is a component of all motivational systems. **Arousal** is generally thought of as physical activation, including the central nervous system, the autonomic nervous system, and the muscles and glands. The evolution of drive theory into arousal theory was prompted by findings that deprivation or conflict is not necessary for motivated behaviour; an animal does not have to be need-deprived to seek a goal. For example, if you have ever had a hamster or gerbil as a pet, you noticed that it had a strong motivation to explore its environment and to run, climb, and play in the tunnels, wheels, and chambers of its home cage. These behaviours were not all oriented toward seeking food or water—it looks very much as if the animals are playing. The motivation to seek novel stimulation applies to humans as well as hamsters—amusement parks allow us to play in tunnels, wheels, and chambers. Some motivational theorists have concentrated on this finding and suggest that organisms seek to maintain optimal levels of arousal by actively varying their exposure to sensory stimuli.

Unlike hunger and thirst, lack of sensory stimulation does not result in a physiological imbalance; yet both human beings and animals seem motivated to seek such stimulation. When deprived of a normal amount of visual, auditory, or tactile stimulation, some people become irritable and consider their situation or

AROUSAL

Activation of the central nervous system, the autonomic nervous system, and the muscles and glands; according to some motivational theorists, organisms seek to maintain optimal levels of arousal by actively varying their exposure to arousing stimuli.

environment to be intolerable ("I'm so bored"). This motivation is not unique to humans: Kittens like to explore their environment; young monkeys investigate mechanical devices and play with puzzles.

*Arousal theory* attempts to bridge the gap by explaining the link between a behaviour and a state of arousal. R. M. Yerkes and J. D. Dodson first scientifically explored the link between performance and arousal in 1908. They described a relationship involving arousal and performance that ultimately was called the *Yerkes–Dodson principle*. This law suggests that arousal and level of task difficulty are related: On easy tasks, moderate to high levels of arousal produce maximum performance; on difficult tasks, low levels of arousal yield better performance. Think of athletics: In a 100-metre sprint, a fairly high level of arousal may facilitate performance, but in a more complex triathlon, where strategy is necessary, too much arousal may yield poor decision making, for example, by going all-out too soon in a multi-hour event. Contemporary researchers have refined the Yerkes–Dodson law by suggesting that when a person's level of arousal and anxiety is either too high or too low, performance will be poor, especially on complex tasks. The inverted U-shaped curve in Figure 9.2 illustrates this relationship between level of arousal and level of performance.

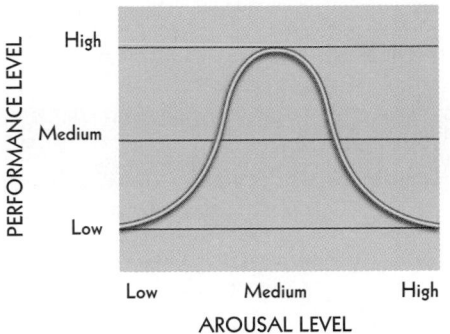

**FIGURE 9.2**

**Performance and Arousal**

Performance is at its peak when arousal is at moderate levels; too much or too little arousal results in low performance levels.

Thus, people who do not care about what they are doing have little anxiety but also have little arousal, and therefore usually perform poorly in both work and play. If arousal increases to the point of high anxiety, performance also suffers. Think of an activity that you practise often, and in which you occasionally either compete or perform publicly. For example, you may be a diver, an actor, or a member of a debating team. Chances are you performed most poorly when you were not interested in practising or when you were exceedingly nervous about your performance, such as during an important competition. Conversely, you probably did your best when you were eager to practise or when you were moderately excited by the competition. This phenomenon explains why some hockey players perform exceptionally well at the beginning of the season, when pressure is only moderately high, and then commit numerous errors when pressure mounts—for instance, in the final games of the Stanley Cup. It also explains why the same tasks at different points in our lives seem to bring far more interest, pressure, and concern. High-school students are far more concerned about final exams than are fifth-graders or university graduates. Even among high-school students, events are interpreted differently; pressure surrounding final exams varies depending on how important they are to a student and how prepared that student is for them.

Canadian researcher Donald Hebb (1904–1985) suggested that behaviours vary from disorganized to effective, depending on a person's level of arousal. He demonstrated that human functioning is most efficient when people are at an optimal level of arousal (Hebb, 1955). It is important to realize that the stimulus itself—for example, final exams, the Grey Cup, or a date on Saturday night—does not produce arousal; it is a person's internal response to these events that determines how he or she behaves. Hebb's theory shifted researchers' focus from stimuli, drives, and needs to the idea that arousal energizes behaviour but does not direct it. The development of optimal-arousal theories helped psychologists explain the variation in people's responses to situations in terms of a state of internal arousal rather than solely in terms of responses to stimuli. This shift in emphasis marked a subtle but important transition from a strictly mechanistic drive reduction theory toward learning, expectancy, and more cognitive theories. (See Building Table 9.1 for a comparison of drive and arousal theories.)

| Theory | Theorist | Principally Explains | Key Idea | View of Behaviour |
|---|---|---|---|---|
| Drive | Hull | Learning through stimulus–response associations and drive reduction | *Homeostasis*—the organism seeks physiological balance. | Largely mechanistic |
|  | Nisbett | Obesity |  |  |
| Arousal | Hebb | Optimal arousal | Performance depends on level of arousal. | The efficiency of behaviour is determined by the level of physiological arousal. |

## COGNITIVE THEORIES

**COGNITIVE THEORIES**
In the study of motivation, an explanation of behaviour that asserts that people actively and regularly determine their own goals and the means of achieving them through thought.

**EXPECTANCY THEORIES**
Explanations of behaviour that focus on people's expectations about reaching a goal and their need for achievement as energizing factors.

**MOTIVE**
A specific (usually internal) condition, usually involving some form of arousal, that directs an organism's behaviour toward a goal.

**SOCIAL NEED**
An aroused condition that directs people to behave in ways that allow them to feel good about themselves and others and to establish and maintain relationships.

In the study of motivation, **cognitive theories** focus on goals that people actively determine and how they achieve them. For these theorists, thought is an initiator and determinant of behaviour. For some cognitive theorists, expectation about reaching a goal is a key factor in motivation.

**EXPECTANCY THEORIES.**   Explanations of behaviour that focus on people's expectations about reaching a goal and their need for achievement can be described as **expectancy theories**. Such theories connect thought and motivation. A key element of these theories, as expressed by achievement researcher David McClelland (1961), among others, is that people's thoughts, their expectations, guide their behaviours. A **motive** is a specific (usually internal) condition, typically involving some form of arousal, that directs an organism's behaviour toward a goal. Unlike a drive, which always has a physiological origin, a motive does not necessarily have a physiological basis. The motives and needs people develop are not initiated because of some physiological imbalance. Rather, people learn through their interactions in the environment to have needs for mastery, affiliation, and competition. These needs are based on their expectations about the future and about how their efforts will lead to various rewarding outcomes.

Expectations are based on experience that occurs in a social context, and some expectancies originate in social needs. A **social need** is an aroused condition that directs people to behave in ways that allow them to feel good about themselves and others and to establish and maintain relationships. The needs for achievement and affiliation are determined by many factors, including socio-economic status and ethnicity. For example, Asian Canadian families often stress school achievement even more strongly than families from other ethnic groups, so Asian Canadian children fulfil both needs for achievement and acceptance by their families by doing well in school. The need to feel good about oneself often leads to specific behaviours that the individual hopes will be evaluated positively by others (Geen, 1991). We will explore this topic in more detail when we discuss achievement later in this chapter and when we consider social psychology in Chapter 13. (See Building Table 9.2 for a comparison of expectancy theories and drive and arousal theories.)

In the study of motivation, cognitive theory is an explanation of behaviour that asserts that people are actively and regularly involved in determining their own goals and the means of achieving them. Like expectancy theory, cognitive theory focuses on thought as an initiator and determinant of behaviour. However, more than expectancy theory does, cognitive theory emphasizes the role of conscious decision making in all areas of life. For example, you are actively involved in

| Theory | Theorist | Principally Explains | Key Idea | View of Behaviour |
|--------|----------|----------------------|----------|-------------------|
| Drive | Hull | Learning through stimulus–response associations and drive reduction | *Homeostasis*—the organism seeks physiological balance. | Largely mechanistic |
|  | Nisbett | Obesity |  |  |
| Arousal | Hebb | Optimal arousal | Performance depends on level of arousal. | The efficiency of behaviour is determined by the level of physiological arousal. |
| Expectancy | McClelland | Achievement motivation | Humans learn the need to achieve. | Partly cognitive, partly mechanistic—achievement is a learned behaviour. |

deciding how much time you will spend studying for a psychology exam, how hard you will work to become an accomplished pianist, or how much commitment you will give to a new diet or exercise routine.

As early as 1949, Donald Hebb anticipated how cognitive theory would influence psychology to move away from mechanistic views of motivation and behaviour by suggesting that it is unsatisfactory to equate motivation with biological need. Other factors, such as arousal and attention, are also important determinants of motivation. Contemporary researchers consider, and many emphasize, the role of active decision making and the human capacity for abstract thought. These cognitive theorists assume that individuals set goals and decide how to achieve them.

**INTRINSIC AND EXTRINSIC MOTIVATION.**   A child may love playing video games, doing puzzles, or colouring in colouring books, yet need to be coaxed or ordered to practise the piano or do homework. Why do some activities seem like fun and others seem like work? Are there things psychologists can do to make activities fun? What are the critical variables?

In general, psychologists find that some activities are intrinsically fun—people like to do them for their own reward. Others, however, are not nearly as much fun; people need to be motivated to perform them, either with reinforcers or with threats of punishment. Psychologists talk about *intrinsic* and *extrinsic* motivation—whether things are done for fun or for rewards. **Extrinsic motivation** is supplied in the form of rewards that come from the external environment. Praise, a high grade, and money given for a particular behaviour are extrinsic rewards. Such rewards can strengthen existing behaviours, provide people with information about their performance, and increase feelings of self-worth and competence. In contrast, behaviours engaged in for no apparent reward except the pleasure and satisfaction of the activity itself arise from **intrinsic motivation**. Edward Deci (1975) suggests that people engage in such behaviours for two reasons: to obtain cognitive stimulation and to gain a sense of accomplishment, competence, and mastery over the environment. Individuals vary widely with respect to the need for cognitive stimulation; each person's experiences and genetic makeup affect the strength of this need (Cacioppo et al., 1996).

**EXTRINSIC MOTIVATION**
[ecks-TRINZ-ick]
Motivation supplied by rewards that come from the external environment.

**INTRINSIC MOTIVATION**
[in-TRINZ-ick]
Motivation that leads to behaviours engaged in for no apparent reward except the pleasure and satisfaction of the activity itself.

▼ People are motivated to engage in some activities that offer intrinsic motivation.

OVERJUSTIFICATION EFFECT

The decrease in likelihood that an intrinsically motivated task, after having been extrinsically rewarded, will be performed when the reward is no longer given.

In studies focusing on intrinsic motivation, Deci compared two groups of university-age participants engaged in puzzle solving. One group received no external rewards, while the other group did receive rewards. Deci found that participants who initially were given rewards generally spent less time solving puzzles when rewards were no longer given. Those who were never rewarded, on the other hand, spent the same amount of time solving puzzles on all trials (Deci, 1972). Robert Vallerand and his colleagues at the Université du Québec à Montréal have shown clearly that intrinsic motivation is a key to academic success in a college or university setting (Vallerand & Bissonnette, 1992). They found that students who persisted to the end of a compulsory course rather than drop out were much more likely to be intrinsically motivated academically. This effect is known as the **overjustification effect**, the decrease in likelihood that an intrinsically motivated task, after having been extrinsically rewarded, will be performed when the reward is no longer given.

Research on the overjustification effect has been extensive and controversial. Research by Judy Cameron and W. David Pierce (2002) at the University of Alberta focusing on the basic finding that extrinsic rewards can have detrimental effects suggests that these detrimental effects occur only under restricted situations. In fact, Cameron and Pierce assert that when goals are attainable, extrinsic rewards have negligible effects on intrinsic motivation, but that some people report liking the task better after verbal extrinsic rewards. More recent research criticized these advocates, saying that rewards have drawbacks in a number of situations, not only in laboratories but also in classrooms and workplace settings; children are more strongly affected than adults (Deci et al., 1999). When a task is interesting, tangible rewards can decrease the intrinsic motivation for that task.

Keep in mind that the overjustification effect is limited. Verbal reinforcement does not have the same effect as tangible reward; verbal reinforcement can act as positive feedback, which increases intrinsic motivation. When rewards increase feelings of mastery and control, they can be effective in boosting intrinsic motivation (Cialdini et al., 1998). In addition, the overjustification effect applies only to inherently *interesting* tasks—activities that people would do even without reward. The value of reward as a factor in performance of uninteresting tasks is not part of this controversy. Reward is a way to get both children and adults to work at a task they find inherently uninteresting or dull. However, reward becomes the motivation, and people do not have the opportunity to develop internal self-regulation for those rewarded behaviours. When parents offer their child money for making good grades, they may be focusing on the goal of good grades too much to realize that their child needs to develop a sense of accomplishment by mastering the school subjects. The money can become the motivation, which may decrease the child's motivation to learn.

## HUMANISTIC THEORY

HUMANISTIC THEORY

An explanation of behaviour that emphasizes the entirety of life rather than individual components of behaviour; focuses on human dignity, individual choice, and self-worth.

SELF-ACTUALIZATION

In humanistic theory, the final level of psychological development in which individuals strive to realize their uniquely human potential—to achieve everything they are capable of achieving, including minimizing ill health, attaining a superior perception of reality, and feeling a strong sense of self-acceptance.

**Humanistic theory** is an explanation of behaviour that emphasizes the entirety of life rather than individual components of behaviour. It focuses on human dignity, individual choice, and self-worth. Humanistic psychologists believe that individuals' behaviour must be viewed within the framework of the individuals' environment and values.

As we saw in Chapter 1, one of the founders and leaders of the humanistic approach was Abraham Maslow (1908–1970), who assumed that people are essentially good—that they possess an innate inclination to develop their potential and to seek beauty, truth, and harmony. Maslow believed that people are born open and trusting and can experience the world in healthy ways. In his words, people are naturally motivated toward self-actualization. **Self-actualization** is the final level of psychological development in which individuals strive to realize their uniquely human potential—to achieve everything they are capable of achieving. This includes attempts to minimize ill health, to attain a superior perception of reality, and to feel a strong sense of self-acceptance.

Maslow's influential theory conceives of motives as forming a hierarchy, which can be represented as a pyramid, with fundamental physiological needs at the base and the needs for love, achievement, understanding, and self-actualization near the top (see Figure 9.3). According to Maslow, as lower-level needs are satisfied, people strive for the next higher level; the pyramid culminates in self-actualization. Although Maslow's theory provides an interesting way to organize aspects of motivation and behaviour, its global nature makes experimental verification difficult. Moreover, his levels of motivation seem closely tied to middle-class Western cultural experiences; Western cultures are highly individualistic compared to Eastern cultures, which are more collectivist. So Maslow's theory may not be valid for all cultures or socio-economic strata.

Building Table 9.3 adds Deci's cognitive theory and Maslow's humanistic theory to the comparative summary of motivation theories.

**Be an ACTIVE LEARNER**

**REVIEW**
> What are the necessary components of a homeostatic system? pp. 307–308
> What is the difference between the concepts of drive and motive? p. 310
> How do cognitive theories of motivation differ from arousal theory? pp. 309–310

**THINK CRITICALLY**
> How comprehensive is the concept of homeostasis; that is, to how many different motivations can this concept apply? What are the problems with this broad application?
> Why are humanistic theories difficult to test experimentally?

**APPLY PSYCHOLOGY**
> Can you think of an example from your life of the overjustification effect—when receiving a reward for a behaviour decreased your motivation?
> At what level on Maslow's hierarchy are you motivated?

## FIGURE 9.3

**Maslow's Hierarchy of Needs**

Physiological needs are at the base of the pyramid. Successively higher levels represent needs that are increasingly learned social ones.

(Pyramid from top to bottom: SELF-ACTUALIZATION NEEDS, AESTHETIC NEEDS, COGNITIVE NEEDS, ESTEEM NEEDS, BELONGINGNESS NEEDS, SAFETY NEEDS, PHYSIOLOGICAL NEEDS)

**BUILDING TABLE 9.3**  Drive, Arousal, Expectancy, Cognitive, and Humanistic Theories of Motivation

| Theory | Theorist | Principally Explains | Key Idea | View of Behaviour |
|---|---|---|---|---|
| Drive | Hull | Learning through stimulus–response associations and drive reduction | *Homeostasis*—the organism seeks physiological balance. | Largely mechanistic |
| | Nisbett | Obesity | | |
| Arousal | Hebb | Optimal arousal | Performance depends on level of arousal. | The efficiency of behaviour is determined by the level of physiological arousal. |
| Expectancy | McClelland | Achievement motivation | Humans learn the need to achieve. | Partly cognitive, partly mechanistic—achievement is a learned behaviour. |
| Cognitive | Deci | Intrinsic motivation | Intrinsic motivation is self-rewarding because it makes people feel competent. | Cognitive—motivation is inborn, but extrinsic rewards often decrease it. |
| Humanistic | Maslow | Learned needs for fulfilment and feelings of self-actualization | Self-actualization | Cognitive—humans seek to attain self-actualization after they have fulfilled basic needs for food and security. |

# Hunger: A Physiologically Based Need

Now that you understand the theoretical work that has been done on motivation, let's look at a few very basic *types* of motivation. All of us have been hungry, felt sexually aroused, and experienced such learned motives as those for achievement. These three motivators—food, sex, and achievement—illustrate how motivation leads to both basic biological behaviours and some complex and culturally determined ones. It is to those types of motivation that we turn next, beginning with perhaps the most basic, drive-based motivation—hunger. You will see that in motivation, as in other areas of psychology, there is a complex interplay of biology and learning with one or the other predominating at different times.

## THE PHYSIOLOGICAL DETERMINANTS OF HUNGER

The basis of eating and hunger may seem very clear—we need energy to fuel our bodies, and eating furnishes this fuel. When depleted of energy, our bodies send out signals that prompt us to seek food and consume it. The first part is correct: We need energy in the form of calories to fuel our bodies, and we get that energy as well as other nutrients from food. However, the explanation of hunger as energy depletion and eating as the automatic response to low fuel levels is too simple to be correct. In addition, this biologically based motivation has learned and cultural influences.

Food intake is only one factor in the weight maintenance equation. To maintain weight, the energy expenditures must equal the energy intake. Those expenditures include physical activity and basal metabolism, and maintenance of basic cellular and body functions. Physiological explanations of hunger have focused on the concept of *homeostasis*, which we encountered earlier in this chapter (p. 307). Applied to weight maintenance, homeostasis is a balance of energy intake and output that results in a stable weight. When you eat as many calories as you burn, your weight remains the same.

Many people maintain a relatively stable weight over many years, which led researchers to look for a homeostatic mechanism for weight control. Weight stability is consistent with the concept of a *set point* for weight—a predetermined weight that the body maintains. Such a system requires a mechanism to set the weight and some way to signal when body weight gets out of line with the set point. Richard Nisbett (1972) proposed that fat cells are the basis of the body's set point. Fat cells vary with both genetic and environmental factors; the number of fat cells an infant has can increase during the first several years of life. Have you noticed the similarity in body shape among family members? This similarity is a result of the inheritance of fat cell distribution on the body, creating similar body shapes. Recent research has supported the possibility that body fat provides a basis for weight regulation. The other component for a homeostatic weight control system is a signalling system that notes nutritional excess or deficit and sends signals that prompt the increase or decrease of food intake. Researchers have considered several possibilities. One hypothesis involved the level of glucose that circulates in the blood, and another hypothesis concentrated on fat metabolism. Digestion and metabolism produce both glucose and fats that circulate through the blood and thus could be part of the signalling system that prompts eating. However, blood levels of neither glucose nor fat fall low enough to initiate eating or rise rapidly enough after a meal to terminate eating (Woods et al., 2000). Therefore, some of the obvious possibilities for a homeostatic mechanism to regulate eating are not the key factors.

Two hormones appear to be important in maintaining a weight balance. These two hormones are *insulin*, which is produced by the pancreas and allows glucose to be taken into body cells and used, and *leptin*, which is produced by fat cells. The discovery that fat cells produce a hormone prompted a rush to research the effects of this hormone and resulted in a better understanding of weight regulation. Both of these hormones furnish signals to the brain, which contains receptors for these hormones. The complex chain of events in the brain has not yet been established, but the hypothalamus (see Chapter 2, p. 64) is important in receiving the signals that insulin and leptin send and in forming connections with other brain structures involved in the control process. It's really difficult to develop a picture of how these factors function because they happen on a cellular level in your brain and body. You know about feeling hungry or full, but you generally don't know how your hormone levels change in relation to food metabolism.

Researchers have known for years that the hypothalamus is involved in eating because surgery to this brain structure alters eating behaviour; surgery that damages the ventromedial hypothalamus produces extreme overeating, and surgery that damages the lateral hypothalamus produces a drastic decrease in eating (see Figure 9.4). The actions of insulin and leptin on the neural pathways in the brain produce a complex cascade of events that appear to signal hunger and satiation.

People (and other animals) do not begin eating a meal because their blood glucose or fat levels have fallen to low levels. Instead, eating begins *before* bodies actually need food (Woods et al., 2000). This arrangement prevents energy levels from falling too low, which seems like an excellent adaptation. Animals that protect themselves against starvation are much more likely to survive and reproduce than those that were on the verge of starvation before they felt the urge to eat. This conceptualization of eating brings up a question: If energy deficit is not the reason why people start eating, what is?

## LEARNING TO BE HUNGRY: ENVIRONMENTAL AND CULTURAL INFLUENCE

The physiological mechanisms that underlie eating are not the whole story of hunger and eating. People do not eat because they are energy deficient; they eat *before* they are. However, we *feel* hungry, and that feeling prompts us to seek food. Research shows that learning and experience are important in feeling hungry. Stimuli in the environment associated with food can be the signal to eat (Sclafani, 1997). One of those powerful stimuli is time of day. Most of us feel hungry at specified times. You have probably missed a meal and had the experience of feeling very hungry for an hour or so, but then your hunger diminished. This experience shows how eating at regular times leads to hunger at those times. Both rats and humans are susceptible to training to eat on a schedule.

We also learn what to eat, and the enormous cultural variations in desirable and forbidden foods reflect the strength of this experience. Almost every substance that has nutritional value is eaten by the people of some culture in some part of the world (Rozin, 1999). Refried beans and tortillas are foods that most Canadians know, but until fast-food restaurants began marketing breakfast burritos, most non-Latino Canadians did not consider them to be appealing breakfast foods. Fried grasshoppers—or other insects—are not considered desirable foods by most university and college students in Canada, but in some cultures insects are a favourite. Margaret Visser, Canadian author and frequent contributor to the old Morningside program on the CBC, points out that Canadian favourites are not accepted worldwide; an extensive advertising campaign attempted to market corn flakes to Spanish children, but this effort was not very successful because in general the Spanish do not pour milk over any

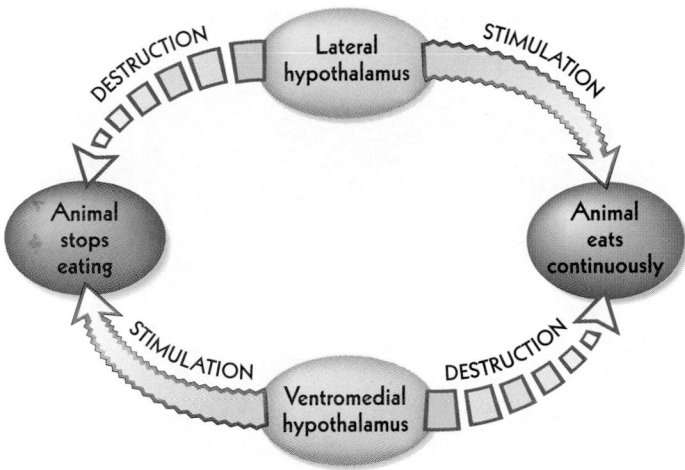

**FIGURE 9.4**
**The Effects of the Hypothalamus on Eating Behaviour**

The stimulation or destruction (ablation) of a rat's hypothalamus alters the rat's eating behaviour; the location of the hypothalamic stimulation or destruction—ventromedial or lateral—affects the results.

▼ Shown here are a normal rat (right) and a rat with a ventromedial hypothalamic lesion (left).

Fried grasshoppers are considered repulsive by many Canadians, but people in some cultures find insects delectable.

foods before eating them. Indeed, milk is not a staple in the Spanish diet as it is in Canada, so the marketing campaign was pitted against a cultural tradition that made corn flakes a hard sell in Spain (Visser, 1999).

Cultural experiences are not the only learned factor in food preferences; individuals also develop food likes and dislikes. Those preferences are guided by some innate preferences and some family, peer, and advertising influences. Examining the foods that were available in human prehistory, those with sweet or salty tastes were usually safe and nutritious, whereas bitter foods often contained poisonous toxins, which has led to an inborn preference for sweet and salty foods and a tendency to avoid bitter foods (Rozin, 1999). Another component of taste preference is sensitivity to various tastes, and some taste sensitivities have a genetic component (Tepper, 1998). For example, vegetables in the broccoli and cabbage family contain a chemical to which people have varying genetic sensitivities that may relate to their preferences for this taste. So, if you dislike broccoli, it may be in your genes. Early family experiences, peer pressure, and advertising also play a role in individual food choices, creating a wide range of variation in liked and disliked foods (Nestle et al., 1998).

Sometimes hunger is not even a factor in eating; people eat for pleasure, and pleasure is an important factor in eating. When tasty food is available, people eat, even if they are not hungry. Almost everyone has had the experience of yielding to the temptation of a luscious dessert after eating a large meal. Despite being full (perhaps uncomfortably so) from the meal, a person finds the dessert just too good to resist. We would not be as tempted to eat more of the same food that we had just consumed, but a different food can prompt additional eating. This situation suggests that variety is a factor in eating, and research and personal experience support this view (Sokolov, 1999). A variety of tasty food can produce overeating in both rats and humans, and variety is a key factor in the pleasure of eating. Even your favourite food—turkey with dressing, pepperoni pizza, a ripe peach, chocolate—would eventually become unappealing if it were the only thing you could eat.

## EATING AND OBESITY

Despite widespread signs of health consciousness (low-fat foods, health clubs, strong sales of sports gear), it seems there is an ever-growing tendency for Canadians to be ever growing. Twenty-five to thirty-five percent of Canadians are obese (Health Canada, 1999)—a rate almost twice as high as it was two decades ago. No one tries to be obese—indeed, most people want to be slim. Is it the ever-increasing variety of junk food, time spent watching television, not enough exercise? What is the underlying reason for obesity? Both physiological and psychological explanations have been offered to account for it.

**HandsOnPsych**
Version 2.0

**Personality and Health**

EVOLUTIONARY AND PHYSIOLOGICAL EXPLANATIONS OF OBESITY.   One type of explanation for obesity comes from an examination of evolutionary history. For humans and other animals, food scarcity and potential starvation were serious threats. A good fat supply was one way to diminish that threat, so animals with a tendency to develop fat stores had a survival advantage. This interpretation suggests that humans and other animals have a tendency to get fat when food is readily available. That hypothesis is confirmed by obesity rates in industrialized countries. In Canada and many other countries, the food supply is steady and plentiful, and these countries have a much higher obesity rate than poorer countries. Yet the evolutionary explanation of obesity leaves some unanswered questions. For example, why are most people, even in circumstances with lots of food, able to maintain a stable weight? Why is there such variation among people, with some individuals getting fat and others staying slim?

One possibility for individual variation comes from an inherited tendency to store fat, which varies among people. Some researchers insist that obesity has a genetic basis and that behavioural and biological patterns for the distribution of body fat are inherited (Bar-Or et al., 1998; Comuzzie & Allison, 1998). If you have an overweight parent, your likelihood of being overweight as an adult increases dramatically, even if your weight was normal as a youngster. The possibility of a genetic predisposition for obesity is based partly on the observation that fat runs in families, but additional evidence is necessary because eating habits also run in families. The other piece of evidence for the genetics of obesity comes from research on rats and mice. During the 1990s, researchers discovered a genetic mutation in mice and another in rats that affected the hormone leptin, a hormone that forms a brain-level signalling system related to eating. Mice that do not produce leptin and rats that have faulty brain receptors for this hormone are obese, leading researchers to hypothesize that some genetically determined problem with leptin may be involved in human obesity (Woods et al., 2000; Carlson, 2001; Oberbauer et al., 2001).

Further, some studies suggest that people can inherit both a tendency to overeat and a slow (or low) metabolism. A slow metabolism has a lower basal metabolic rate, which uses available energy (calories) from food efficiently and stores unused calories as fat. This type of metabolism is an advantage in protecting against starvation but tends to result in obesity when people with a low metabolism eat what would otherwise be a normal diet. For example, the Pima Indians of Arizona are prone to obesity; 80 to 90 percent of the tribe's young adults are dangerously overweight. According to Ravussin and his colleagues (Norman et al., 1998; Ravussin et al., 1988; Tataranni et al., 1997), who have studied these Native Americans extensively, the Pima have unusually low metabolic rates. During any 24-hour period, the typical Pima (who is as active as the average European American) burns about 80 calories less than an average European American. Ravussin's view is that the Pima, whose ancestors spent generations in a desert environment where they went through periods of famine, developed a metabolism that adapted to this on-again, off-again pattern of food availability. However, in the twentieth century the Pima abandoned their traditional low-fat diet and began to eat like other Americans. Their metabolisms, which had developed a disposition to be "thrifty" and store fat, became a liability as the proportion of fat in their diet increased.

▲ Hunger is not always a factor in eating; people eat for pleasure.

PSYCHOLOGICAL EXPLANATIONS OF OBESITY. Even people with low metabolic rates are not destined to be obese. They can balance their food intake to their metabolic rate or increase their energy output by exercising. Nor are people with a normal metabolic rate guaranteed lifelong thinness. All of us are bombarded with food-oriented messages that have little to do with nutritional needs. Advertisements proclaim that merriment can be found at a restaurant or a supermarket. Parents coax good behaviour from their children by promising them desserts or snacks. Thus, eating acquires a significance that far exceeds its role in satisfying physiological needs: It serves as a centre for social interaction, a means to reward good behaviour, and a way to fend off unhappy thoughts and reduce stress (Greeno & Wing, 1994). Eating has many meanings beyond nutrition. In addition to promoting excessive food intake, the Canadian environment both encourages physical activity and offers multiple opportunities to avoid it.

▼ Some groups are prone to obesity, with more than 80 percent being overweight.

▲ Despite her obvious emaciation, this woman most likely feels that her weight is "just right" or that she needs to "lose a few more pounds."

The problem is that the human body has developed effective mechanisms for gaining weight and weak ones for shedding pounds that are no longer needed (Hill & Peters, 1998). Researchers through the past five decades have identified four key factors that contribute to overeating. First, food is readily available—from drive-through windows and vending machines, restaurants and street vendors, at home, at work, and everywhere in between. Second, portion sizes are growing ever bigger—fast-food restaurants have supersize meals. Third, the average person's diet is higher in fat than ever before—fat provides nearly twice the calories per gram as protein or carbohydrates. Fourth, most children and adults do not engage in regular, sustained physical activity. Put all of this together—low physical activity, eating too much, too often, of the wrong things—and the result is an overweight population that has trouble losing weight.

To make the situation even worse, being thin has become increasingly desirable, especially for women. So dieting has become a way of life for many Canadians who hope to be thin. The majority of normal-weight dieters are women who want to attain the very thin body that has become the ideal in modern Western society. This ideal has led to chronic dieting and other eating disorders, which are more common among women than men. In recent years, an increasing number of men have been developing eating disorders (Lakkis, Ricciardelli, & Williams, 1999). See Chapter 11 for more on this topic.

The quest for thinness is most often unsuccessful; most dieters gain back the weight they lose. People who are obese are not often successful in losing enough weight to enter the normal weight range. If they do, they too are likely to gain it back. The same factors that make obesity increasingly likely push the newly thin toward weight gain. This evidence supports the notion of a set point for weight, to which people return when they lose. However, increasing obesity is evidence against set points as the only factor in weight maintenance: If people gain weight, they should also return to the set point. The increasing number of obese Canadians is evidence for psychological and social factors in weight gain.

Obviously, there is no simple answer to this nature-versus-nurture question with respect to obesity. Research from the 1990s, especially the discovery of the hormone leptin, has led to a renewed excitement about the possibilities of understanding how the brain experiences hunger and the ways in which these brain signals initiate eating and the feeling of being satiated (Woods et al., 2000). This research has led to the view that obesity is a chronic health problem that requires treatment (Mokdad et al., 2000). The active research in the molecular biology of eating and its behavioural implications may lead to the development of effective treatments for obesity in the near future.

## Sexual Behaviour: Physiology Plus Thought

When it was first reported that Prince Charles had had a long-standing affair with friend and confidant Camilla Parker-Bowles, the London tabloids had a field day. American President Bill Clinton's affairs have had a similar effect in the United States. People's preoccupation with the sex lives of national figures indicates that they are fascinated with and often define themselves in terms of their sexuality—a type of motivation that, unlike physiologically based hunger, is not necessary to sustain life. So we immediately see an important difference between sexual behaviour and activities such as food seeking. The sexual behaviour of lower organisms is controlled largely by their physiological and hormonal systems. In contrast, in human beings the sex drive is to a great extent under psychological control.

*Be an*
**ACTIVE LEARNER**

**REVIEW**
> What brain structures and hormones are related to hunger and eating? pp. 314–315
> What cultural and psychological factors influence eating? pp. 315–316

**THINK CRITICALLY**
> How does obesity fit with the concept of set point? Why should some people have a set point that is set at obesity?
> Why might the one-food diet described in the next point be an effective (if not pleasant) weight reduction strategy?

**APPLY PSYCHOLOGY**
> Choose a favourite food and make it your personal diet. Eat only this one food for every meal and every snack. Keep a diary of your eating and your feelings about the experience. How long did it take for you to become tired of this favourite food? Do you think you could lose weight on this diet?

This means that not only physiology, especially sex hormones, but ideas, past behaviour, emotions, expectations, and goals all influence the sexual behaviour of human beings. The relative contributions of these factors vary. For some people, sights, sounds, and smells are sexual initiators, triggers for sexually motivated behaviour. For others, thoughts, feelings, and fantasy either initiate or in many cases satisfy sexual impulses. Men and women respond differently, the old respond differently than the young, the religious background of individuals affects their sexual behaviour, and the culture in which a person is raised has profound influences. Western ideas about sexuality differ significantly from Eastern approaches, and even within Western cultures there exists great diversity. For example, Europeans are more open and expressive sexually than are Canadians. And the British find sexual indiscretions among politicians more outrageous and titillating than do Canadians, who find ethical scandals less entertaining. Keeping in mind this cultural diversity, let us first look at some of the initiators of sexual behaviour and then at the sexual behaviours in which human beings engage.

## WHAT INITIATES THE SEX DRIVE?

Hardly a day goes by that you are not bombarded with sexually suggestive advertisements. Perfume ads abound in magazines; attractive, and often half-clad, models sell cars. Youthful, sexually desirable men and women sell sports equipment; even toothpaste is sold by alluring women and men. Advertisers use learning principles to pair attractive people and situations with their products in the hope that their products will assume an arousing glamour—and to hint that if you use their product, you may become as alluring as their models. The advertisers are seeking to initiate an activity—that is, buying activity—by activating the sexual drive. They know, of course, that people's thoughts, rather than their hormones, direct buying behaviour. But hormones do play a vital role in sexual behaviour.

SEX HORMONES.   Sex hormones are important for sexual behaviour in humans, beginning before birth. Both males and females produce both androgens (the "male" hormones) and estrogens (the "female" hormones), but in different proportions. In males, the testes are the principal producers of androgens. In females, the ovaries are the principal producers of estrogens. During prenatal development, the presence of testosterone prompts the development of the male reproductive system; its absence allows development of the female system. The release of androgens and estrogens initiates the onset of the secondary sex characteristics in developing teenagers (see Chapter 11, p. 383). The presence of these hormones is important for the development of sexual desire, and their regulation is essential for the development and maintenance of fertility. Women's levels of sex hormones vary according to their menstrual cycles and then decrease at menopause, whereas men's levels of sex hormones do not vary as much or in a cyclic fashion. However, men's levels of testosterone also decline as they age. For humans, hormone levels are involved in but not directly responsible for sexual behaviour.

In the animal kingdom, the relationship between sex hormones and sexual behaviour is clear. Female rats, for example, are sexually responsive only when they are fertile, and both sexual receptivity and fertility are regulated by a complex series of hormones released into the bloodstream (when they are "in heat"). If the testes of male rats are removed, the animals show a marked decrease in sexual interest and performance. Most sexual responses in non-human animals do not occur without hormonal activation. Human beings, on the other hand, can choose whether to respond sexually at any given time. In human beings, the removal of hormone-generating organs has a much less drastic effect on sexual interest and behaviour.

SIGHTS, SOUNDS, SMELLS, AND FANTASY.   In animals, a female may show her sexual receptivity by releasing pheromones; this acts as a trigger for sexual activity. Other times, a suggestive movement may signal receptivity and will trigger sexual behaviour in another animal. Thought plays an enormous role in human sexuality; people's thoughts, fantasies, and emotions initiate and activate sexual desire and behaviour. PET studies have recently located specific areas of the brain that are activated when people are experiencing sexual arousal (Stoléru et al., 1999).

## HUMAN SEXUAL BEHAVIOUR

While Western culture is saturated with sexually suggestive advertisements and sexually explicit movies, it also shows considerable reluctance to examine and talk about sexual behaviour scientifically. Efforts to examine sexuality in a systematic way are often viewed with scepticism.

STUDYING SEXUALITY.   Despite this reluctance to look at sex objectively, various researchers have studied sex, mostly by conducting surveys. One of the first and most famous was conducted by a biologist, Alfred Kinsey, and his colleagues. For years, the Kinsey surveys were the main source of information about sexual attitudes and behaviour, but contemporary researchers such as Morton Hunt (1974), Masters, Johnson, and Kolodny (1994), and Edward Laumann and his colleagues (1994; Michael et al., 1998) have conducted more recent and more representative sex surveys. Comparisons of the results from these surveys allow conclusions to be drawn about how sexual behaviour has changed over the past 50 years.

When Kinsey and his colleagues conducted their sex surveys, the results showed differences between women's and men's sexual behaviour. Later surveys have revealed a decrease in those differences; the percentage of women and men who engage in masturbation, premarital sex, and extramarital sex are now more similar than in the 1950s. Men and women are more likely today than in the 1950s to have intercourse before marriage, and there has been a slow and steady decrease in the age of first intercourse for both boys and girls (see also Feldman et al., 1997; Wadsworth et al., 1995). Today, people express their sexuality more often and more openly—and seek to understand their own feelings and behaviours.

In general, reports about sexual practices show that individuals engage in sexual behaviours more when they are younger than when they are older. For example, the frequency of intercourse decreases from the early twenties to the fifties or sixties (Call, Sprecher, & Schwartz, 1995). Similarly, the duration of any specific sexual activity decreases with increasing age. Older people are less happy with their sex lives, and many older women have no sexual partners (Laumann et al., 1994). For all ages, sexuality occurs within a context, and the most common context is a relationship. Laumann and his colleagues (1994) found that most individuals have sex with someone they know and live with (usually a spouse) and that people who are sexually active think about and desire sex more than do individuals who are not sexually active. Further, when people do engage in an extramarital affair, it is usually not a casual encounter but a relationship with one person they know (Wadsworth et al., 1995).

According to an annual international survey (Durex, 2002), Canadian adults have sex about 150 times per year, ranking fourth among 22 countries. The picture of sexuality in Canada is not completely happy, and Canadian sexuality has negative aspects. Compared with other industrialized countries, individuals in Canada begin sexual activity at younger ages, and although pregnancy rates have fallen among Canadian adolescents, the pregnancy rate is substantially higher than in other developed countries (Singh & Darroch, 2000). Other negative factors include a high incidence of sexually transmitted diseases, the continuing spread of AIDS, and the continuation of risky sexual behaviours, such as not using condoms (Downey & Landry, 1997). The rates of *sexual dysfunction*—the term for sexual problems—are high: 43 percent for women and 31 percent for men. Young women and older men are more likely to suffer from sexual dysfunction, including inability to experience orgasm, low sexual desire, problems attaining an erection in men, and painful intercourse in women. These problems have both health-related and psychological components (Laumann, Paik, & Rosen, 1999). Unfortunately, embarrassment prevents many people from seeking treatment. Despite these problems, most people report their sex lives as being satisfactory (Laumann et al., 1994).

SEXUAL ORIENTATION.    One's sexual orientation is the direction of one's sexual interest. A person with a *heterosexual orientation* has a romantic and erotic attraction and preference for members of the other sex; a person with a *homosexual orientation* has a romantic and erotic attraction to and preference for members of the same sex. A *bisexual orientation* is a romantic and erotic attraction to members of both sexes. Kinsey introduced the idea of a continuum of sexual behaviours ranging from exclusively homosexual behaviours through some homosexual behaviours, to mostly heterosexual behaviours, to exclusively heterosexual behaviours. Kinsey also recognized that a same-sex sexual experience does not make a person homosexual. In addition, a person may have a homosexual or bisexual orientation without ever having had a sexual experience with someone of the same sex. It is thus an overgeneralization to define a person's sexual orientation based solely on a single, or even on multiple, sexual encounters (Haslam, 1997).

The Kinsey survey of male sexual behaviour reported that 37 percent of men had had at least one same-sex sexual experience and that 10 percent of men were primarily homosexual in orientation. Other surveys reported lower rates, and most sex researchers consider the Kinsey statistics to be overestimates. The Laumann study (1994) found that 2.8 percent of men and 1.4 percent of women identified themselves as primarily homosexual, and other studies confirm these lower figures (Cameron & Cameron, 1998; Sell, Wells, & Wypij, 1995). However, as further discussed in *Introduction to Research Basics* on page 322, a study done by Chris Bagely (Bagely & Tremblay, 1988) at the University of Calgary indicates that these estimates can be significantly affected by how the questions about sexual orientation are asked, and his results suggest that the true figure for homosexuality in urban populations may actually be closer to 10 to 15 percent. Regardless of the percentages, people who are not heterosexual experience discrimination and censure. Perhaps more than people in other cultures, Canadians as well as Americans still have great difficulty with homosexuality as an acceptable sexual orientation. For example, having gays in the military causes intense debate, and an important part of this debate is the basis of homosexuality (see *Point/Counterpoint* on page 323).

## Achievement: A Social Need

Personality psychologists such as Henry Murray assert that key events and situations in people's environment determine behaviour. Murray used the word *press* for the way these environmental situations may motivate a person (Murray, 1938). The environment may *press* an individual to excel at sports, be a loving caretaker to a grandparent, or achieve great wealth. The *press* of poverty may produce a social need for financial security; it therefore may cause a person to work hard, train, and become educated to achieve wealth.

The most notable theories for measuring the results of press are expectancy theories that focus specifically on the **need for achievement**—a social need that directs people to strive constantly for excellence and success. According to such achievement theories, people engage in behaviours that satisfy their desires for success, mastery, and fulfilment. Tasks not oriented toward these goals are not motivating and either are not undertaken or are performed without energy or commitment. There may be even more negative effects when people feel that making an effort is useless.

> **Be an ACTIVE LEARNER**
>
> **REVIEW**
> > What changes in sexual behaviour have occurred over the past 50 years in Canada? p. 320
> > Summarize the evidence supporting each side of the debate about the determination of sexual orientation. pp. 321, 323
>
> **THINK CRITICALLY**
> > Do you think the federal government should study sexual behaviour? Why or why not?
> > Many people argue that homosexual orientation is a matter of choice, but heterosexual orientation is innate. How can both positions be true?
>
> **APPLY PSYCHOLOGY**
> > When you read the statistics on different sexual behaviours presented by sex researchers, which ones surprised you? Which ones did not? What is the basis for your reactions?

NEED FOR ACHIEVEMENT

A social need that directs people to strive constantly for excellence and success.

## Sex Surveys

The most common approach to studying sexuality has been to survey or interview people about their sexual behaviour. A **survey** is one of the descriptive methods of research; it requires construction of a set of questions to administer to a group of participants. Analysis of the responses enables researchers to better understand their research topic. This method has a built-in limitation: people do not always tell the truth when asked about their behaviour. All survey researchers must deal with the challenge of obtaining truthful answers from their research participants.

Despite this limitation, several groups of researchers have surveyed people about their sexual behaviour. To be accurate, surveys must include a **representative sample**, a sample that reflects the composition of the population from which it is drawn. However, normal random sampling methods often incorrectly sample homosexual and lesbian groups. This occurs for a number of reasons. First, many homosexual and lesbian groups live in dense communities within large cities but are underrepresented in other areas. Thus, depending on whether the sampling occurred in Vancouver or in Brandon, these populations might be quite differently represented. Second, there can be problems in definition (for example, if, as an adolescent, you had one sexual experience with a person of the same sex, would you consider yourself to be homosexual or lesbian, bisexual, or heterosexual?). Third, information about sexuality is considered by many to be private; individuals are therefore reluctant to disclose details about their sexuality to strangers. Moreover, because homosexuals and lesbians are stigmatized, many individuals may be afraid to disclose. For these reasons, and others, Christopher Bagely and Pierre Tremblay (1998) conducted a survey in Calgary to assess the effects of child sexual abuse on the mental health of young adult males. Due to the unusually stringent stratified sampling method they used, they were able to accurately assess the prevalence of homosexuality within their sample.

**Design.** The relevant part of the study for this discussion was a survey that included an extensive list of questions about sexual activity and orientation, which participants answered using a computerized response format.

**Participants.** Participants were 750 adult males between ages 18 and 27 living in Calgary. All participants were paid for their time. Participants were selected to be representative of the adult population. Males were tested outside of Calgary's city centre, where gay and bisexual males are most concentrated.

**Procedure.** Teams of trained interviewers conducted face-to-face interviews asking participants about childhood events and adjustment issues. Respondents were then asked to complete an anonymous computer questionnaire. The researchers were very careful to explain that participants' responses to the computer questionnaire would be entirely anonymous; that is, no one would be able to link participants' names with their responses. This was done to decrease the effects of participant concerns related to the issues discussed above.

**Results.** Unlike many samples reporting a 1 to 3 percent estimate for the prevalence of homosexuality, data from this study suggest that 13 percent of young adult males in middle- to lower-class socio-economic groups in Calgary identified themselves as homosexual or bisexual. Most reported that they were currently homosexually active.

**Conclusions.** This survey included a representative sample of male adults in one Canadian city, using a confidential response method. These data vary significantly from some other survey data and, as a result, suggest that errors exist in demographic work relying on telephone and face-to-face interviews. In fact, these data support the 1 in 10 estimate commonly believed by those in the gay community.

**Limitation.** Like all survey research, the main limitation of this survey is its reliance on self-reports. Because our society is homophobic and homo-punitive, disclosure under even these circumstances may be open to question.

SURVEY

One of the descriptive methods of research; it requires construction of a set of questions to administer to a group of participants.

REPRESENTATIVE SAMPLE

A sample that reflects the composition of the population from which it is drawn.

One of the leaders in early studies of achievement motivation was David C. McClelland, whose early research focused on the idea that people have strong social motives for achievement (McClelland, 1958). McClelland showed that achievement motivation is learned in an individual's home environment during childhood. Adults with a high need for achievement had parents who stressed excellence and who provided physical affection and emotional rewards for high achievement. These individuals also generally walked early, talked early, and had a high need for achievement even in elementary school (e.g., Teevan & McGhee, 1972). A high need for achievement is most pronounced in first-born children, perhaps because

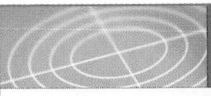

## POINT Counterpoint

### Is Sexual Orientation Determined by Biological Factors?

**POINT:** Sexual orientation is determined by nature; innate, biological factors produce homosexuality.

**COUNTERPOINT:** Sexual orientation is determined by nurture; social experiences determine homosexuality.

The causes of homosexuality have been debated for decades, and the argument has developed into a classic nature-versus-nurture one. Those on the nature side of the debate assert that biological factors determine sexual orientation, and most see genetics as the determining factor. They cite data showing that homosexual men and women knew when they were young children that they were "different." Studies have pointed to genes, prenatal events, and brain structures as possible biological contributors to homosexual orientation. Many studies have confirmed the family association of homosexuality; studies of twins and adopted children confirm that sexual orientation runs in families (Pillard & Bailey, 1998). Gay men tend to come from extended families that have included other gay men. Further, Dean Hamer and his colleagues (Hamer et al., 1993; LeVay & Hamer, 1994) reported that they found unique DNA markers on the X chromosomes of gay men—that is, a "gay gene"—but other researchers (Rice et al., 1999) failed to confirm this finding. Thus, the possible location, or even the existence, of the gene remains uncertain, but the search is still in progress. Another possibility for a physiological basis for sexual orientation lies within the brain. Research found differences between gay and heterosexual men in a specific area within the hypothalamus (LeVay, 1991; Swaab & Hofman, 1995). More recent research has not yet replicated these differences.

On the nurture side of the debate, Daryl Bem (1996, 2000) has developed a theory that explains the development of sexual orientation through the interaction of innate personality traits and experience. Bem suggests that children develop feelings of familiarity for those with whom they associate, making the unfamiliar exotic and exciting. He argues that during preadolescence, the exotic becomes erotic through association with heightened autonomic activity, leading to sexual attraction. Most children associate with same-sex peers and develop feelings of familiarity for them, thus never developing erotic feelings for individuals of the same sex. However, Bem argues that since some adolescents associate primarily with other-sex peers, this makes those of the same sex the exotic ones; he asserts that these individuals are likely to develop homosexual orientation. Bem (2000) cited evidence from surveys of gay men and lesbian women that shows a strong preference for other-sex peers that, he argues, supports his theory. However, many researchers contend that Bem's interpretation of these survey results is incorrect and that the role of experience remains unknown (Krisel, 2001).

As with many aspects of nature-versus-nurture debate, however, the most important questions have to do with how we, as a society, decide to handle the issue. Both nature and nuture arguments have been used in the past to persecute people who "can't" or "won't" change. In Canada, we have recently entered another level of debate with the Supreme Court striking down laws that do not permit gay couples to marry. This is a social matter, not a scientific matter, and it remains to be seem whether we, as Canadians, use this as an opportunity to broaden our view of ourselves or decide to draw more lines within our society.

parents typically have more time to give them direction and praise. It is also especially evident in cultures—for example, in many Asian cultures—that stress achievement-related activities and foster a fear of academic failure in children (Eaton & Dembo, 1997). However, factors related to achievement in Asian cultures

The Thematic Apperception Test (TAT) is used to measure achievement motivation.

vary from those in Western cultures. One difference is independence, which is positively related to achievement in Western cultures but not in Asian cultures, which are more collectivist than individualist. Interdependence is highly valued in Asia, and need for achievement and need for affiliation are positively related there (Ang & Chang, 1999). In Western cultures, factors emphasizing the individual are more strongly related to achievement needs, including a willingness to leave family and country. The need for achievement was found to be positively related to willingness to immigrate for students in Albania, the Czech Republic, and Slovenia (Boneva et al., 1998). Not surprisingly, these achievement-oriented students had lower affiliation needs than those less willing to leave their countries. Therefore, need for achievement occurs in Asian and European cultures, but the other characteristics that relate to this need vary among these cultures.

Achievement motives often are measured in terms of scores derived from an analysis of the thought content of imaginative stories. Early studies of people's need for achievement used the *Thematic Apperception Test (TAT)*. In this test, people are shown scenes with no captions and vague themes, which are thus open to interpretation. The test takers are instructed not to think in terms of right or wrong answers but to answer four basic questions for each scene:

1. What is happening?
2. What has led up to this situation?
3. What is being thought?
4. What will happen next?

Using a complex scoring system, researchers analyze participants' descriptions of each scene. They have found that persons with a high need for achievement tell stories that stress success, getting ahead, and competition (Spangler, 1992).

With tests such as the TAT, a researcher can quickly discern which individuals have a high need for achievement and which have a low need. For example, Lowell (1952) found that when he asked participants to rearrange scrambled letters (such as *wtse*) to construct a meaningful word (*west*), subjects with a low need for achievement improved only slightly at the task over successive testing periods. In contrast, participants who scored high in the need for achievement showed greater ongoing improvement over several periods of testing (see Figure 9.5). The researchers reasoned that, when presented with a complex task, persons with a high need for achievement find new and better ways of performing the task as they practise it, whereas those with a low need for achievement try no new methods. People with a high need for achievement constantly strive toward excellence and better performance; they have developed a belief in their self-efficacy and in the importance of effort in determining performance (Carr, Borkowski, & Maxwell, 1991; McClelland, 1961).

Those people with high need for achievement also tend to be high in **self-efficacy**, the belief that they can successfully engage in and execute a specific behaviour. The relationship between self-efficacy and achievement motivation was demonstrated in a study of children's occupational aspirations (Bandura et al., 2001). This study measured self-efficacy for both academics and occupations in girls and boys around age 12.

**SELF-EFFICACY**

A person's belief that he or she can successfully engage in and execute a specific behaviour.

**FIGURE 9.5**

**Performance on a Scrambled-Letter Task**

The graph shows performance on a scrambled-letter task for successive two-minute periods. Performance is affected by a person's overall approach to achievement-related tasks. Participants with a low need for achievement improved overall; however, those with a high need for achievement improved even more. (Based on data from Lowell, 1952.)

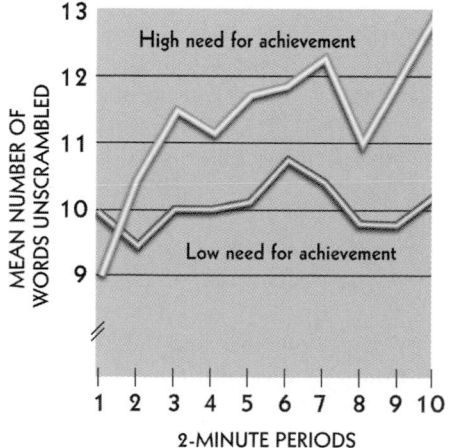

These researchers found that parents convey achievement-related messages to their children, and these messages influence children's occupational aspirations, mediated through feelings of academic self-efficacy. Children with higher academic self-efficacy were more likely to choose occupations that require higher achievement, regardless of the type of occupation. For example, children with high academic self-efficacy for scientific careers were more likely to choose the occupational activities of scientists rather than scientific assistants.

The study of self-efficacy and career development also considered the factor of gender and the differences between career achievement for women and men, relating those differences to self-efficacy beliefs (Bandura et al., 2001). The results showed no overall gender difference in self-efficacy for occupations, but boys were attracted to careers in the military and technology and girls to occupations involving social services and caregiving—traditional gender differences. This continuing pattern prevents men and women from considering some types of achievement, and those who do not consider possibilities do not pursue them. Self-efficacy is not the only factor that influences achievement motivation, but the expectations of parents, teachers, and peers influence a person's belief in his or her ability to be successful in various activities, which makes self-efficacy an important concept in the need for achievement.

**Be an ACTIVE LEARNER**

**REVIEW**
> Define *need for achievement*, and explain how psychologists measure it. pp. 321–324
> What is self-efficacy, and how does it relate to the need for achievement? pp. 324–325

**THINK CRITICALLY**
> Do you think that second- and third-born children have needs that are different from or greater than those of first-born children? What might those needs be?
> What cultural components shape women and men to have different achievement needs?

**APPLY PSYCHOLOGY**
> As a parent, what would you do to build achievement needs in your child?

# Emotion

In July 2003, after working determinedly for several years, large groups of people from three locations gathered in Prague to get some good news and some bad news. Representing Canada were Jean Chrétien, Wayne Gretzky, and many others. Pyeongchang, South Korea, and Salzburg, Austria, were also well represented. After two votes the Canadian contingent were jubilant, for they had been awarded the 2010 Olympic Winter Games in Vancouver/Whistler. Representatives of the other venue hopefuls were heartbroken, especially the Austrian contingent, which had only garnered 15 votes in the first round despite considering themselves to be in a neck-and-neck race with Canada.

That motivation and emotion are interconnected should come as no surprise. Grief causes people to engage in acts of kindness. Anger can cause you to hurl an object across a room or to lash out at a friend. Happiness can make you smile all day long or stop to help a motorist with a flat tire. Fear can electrify you and make your legs pump faster as you sprint down a dark, shadowy alley. Although emotions, including love, joy, and fear, can motivate behaviour, these emotional states and categories remain difficult to define (Panksepp, 2000).

▼ The Olympic Bid Committee celebrates the awarding of the 2010 Olympic Games to Vancouver, British Columbia.

## WHAT IS EMOTION?

The word *emotion* refers to a wide range of subjective states, such as love, fear, sadness, and excitement. We all have emotions, talk about them, and agree on what represents them; but this agreement is not scientific. The psychological investigation of emotion has led to a more precise definition. Most psychologists acknowledge that emotion consists of three elements: feelings, physiological responses, and behaviours. An **emotion** is a subjective response (feeling), usually accompanied by a physiological change, which is often interpreted by an individual and then readies the individual for some action that is associated with a change in behaviour. These elements often fit together, but they are separable. For example, a person may feel angry but not give any outward signs of this feeling.

**EMOTION**

A subjective response (feeling), usually accompanied by a physiological change, which is often interpreted by an individual and then readies the individual for some action that is associated with a change in behaviour.

While watching the World Trade Center attacks on September 11, 2001, people displayed a variety of emotions.

**HandsOnPsych**
Version 2.0

**Emotion and Motivation**

## PHYSIOLOGICAL THEORIES OF EMOTION

Researchers who take a physiological orientation feel that happiness, rage, and even romantic love are physiologically based. They argue that the wide range of emotions that human beings experience and express is in large part controlled by neurons located in an area deep within the brain, the limbic system. The *limbic system* is composed of cells in the hypothalamus, the amygdala, and other cortical and sub-cortical areas. Studies of these crucial areas began in the 1920s, when Bard (1934) found that the removal of portions of the cortex of cats produced sharp emotional reactions to simple stimuli such as a touch or a puff of air. The cats would hiss, claw, bite, arch their backs, and growl—but their reactions did not seem directed at any specific person or target. Bard referred to this behaviour as *sham rage*, a behaviour sequence that showed the signs of rage but without appropriate motivation. Later researchers stimulated portions of the brain with electrical current and found that many brain centres were involved in the experiencing of emotions—they deduced that the cortex was integrating information. Two major biological approaches to the study of emotion dominated psychology for decades: the James–Lange theory and the Cannon–Bard theory. Both are concerned with the physiology of emotions and with whether physiological change or emotional feelings occur first. More recent theories have questioned whether the limbic system is the foundation of emotion, focusing on specific brain structures. Another recent approach goes back to the beginning—the evolutionary theory of emotion.

**THE JAMES–LANGE THEORY.** According to a theory proposed by both William James (1842–1910) and Carl Lange (1834–1900) (who are given joint credit because their approaches were so similar), people experience physiological changes and *then* interpret them as emotional states. People do not cry because they feel sad; they feel sad because they cry. People do not run because they are afraid; they feel afraid after they run. In other words, the James–Lange theory says that people do not experience an emotion until after their bodies become aroused and begin to respond with physiological changes; feedback from the body produces feelings or emotions (James, 1884; Lange, 1922). For this approach, in its most simplified form, *feeling* is the essence of emotion. Thus, James (1890, p. 1006) wrote, "Every one of the bodily changes, whatsoever it be, is felt, acutely or obscurely, the moment it occurs."

A modern physiological approach suggests that facial movements, by their action, can create emotions. Called the *facial feedback hypothesis*, this approach suggests that sensations from the face provide cues or signals to the brain that act as feedback to help a person determine an emotional response. In some ways, this approach derives from the James–Lange theory. According to this theory, a facial movement such as a smile or an eye movement may release the appropriate emotion-linked neurotransmitters (Ekman, 1993; Izard, 1990; Neumann & Strack, 2000). Other research suggests that facial expression is not alone in shifting emotions; body posture (Flack, Laird, & Cavallaro, 1999) and tone of voice may also play a role (Siegman & Boyle, 1993). In this version of the theory, the facial feedback hypothesis is also called the *peripheral feedback hypothesis*.

**THE CANNON–BARD THEORY.** Some physiologists, notably Walter Cannon (1871–1945), were critical of the James–Lange theory. Cannon and colleague Philip Bard argued that the physiological changes associated with many emotional states are identical. They reasoned as follows: If increases in blood pressure and heart rate accompany feelings of both anger and joy, how can people determine their emotional state simply from their physiological state? Cannon spoke of undifferentiated arousal—the physiological response underlying the fight-and-flight response (the body's response to emergency situations that includes activating resources needed for energy to fight or flee) is the same.

Cannon argued that when a person is emotional, two areas of the brain—the thalamus and the cerebral cortex—are stimulated simultaneously (he did not know the whole story about the limbic system). Stimulation of the cortex produces the emotional component of the experience; stimulation of the thalamus produces physiological changes in the sympathetic nervous system. According to Cannon (1927), emotional feelings *accompany* physiological changes; they neither produce nor result from such changes. Building Table 9.4 presents a contrast of these two physiological approaches to emotion.

When Cannon and Bard were formulating their theory, they knew relatively little about how the brain operates. For example, physiological changes in the brain do not happen exactly simultaneously. Further, people report that they often have an experience and then have physiological and emotional reactions to it. Neither the James–Lange nor the Cannon–Bard approach considered how a person's thoughts about a situation might alter physiological reactions and emotional responses. However, the James–Lange and Cannon–Bard approaches provided a conceptual bridge to newer approaches. One of those approaches concentrates on the role of a brain structure called the amygdala (see *Brain and Behaviour*), and the other approach considers the evolutionary value of emotions.

**EVOLUTIONARY THEORY.** Evolutionary psychologists see complex behaviour as a series of specialized subprograms that are called into action by specific situations (Cosmides & Tooby, 2000). Emotions have a prominent role in evolutionary psychology, furnishing the coordination and ordering of many different specialized programs. Repeated situations in human evolutionary history organized these programs around emotions, so that when specific situations arise, emotions occur, and along with them the behaviours governed by these programs. In this view, emotional responses are hard-wired into the brain's circuits, and subjective feelings follow them. Fear responses—such as freezing up at the sight of a natural predator—occur automatically without thought and have adaptive advantages that caused these behavioural sequences to become part of evolutionary biology. LeDoux's (1996; LeDoux & Phelps, 2000) view of fear (see *Brain and Behaviour*) is very much an evolutionary one; evolution has prepared humans (and other animals) to respond in certain basic emotional ways to some stimuli. Through the process of natural selection, the human brain has evolved the ability to be very sensitive to fear-inducing situations and to respond rapidly to avoid such situations (see Building Table 9.5). Indeed, the situations that elicit such an alert do not have to produce fear—any new or unusual stimulus should provoke a response orienting the animal to this new element. The new element could be trouble or, alternatively, it could be food (Cacioppo & Gardner, 1999).

---

**BUILDING TABLE 9.4** Physiological Theories of Emotion

| Theory | Theorist | The Role of Physiology | The Role of Cognition | The Role of the Situation |
|---|---|---|---|---|
| Physiological | James and Lange | Arousal precedes interpretation of events. | Not a factor | People interpret bodily arousal as emotion. |
| | Cannon and Bard | Physiological arousal and interpretation occur simultaneously. | Not a factor | Cognition supplies an interpretation, which occurs at the same time as arousal. |

## Experiencing and Recognizing Fear

Joseph LeDoux (1995, 1996; LeDoux & Phelps, 2000) has investigated the physiological bases of emotions, concentrating on the emotion of fear. His research has centred on one brain structure—the amygdala and its connections. In his popular book The Emotional Brain, LeDoux asserts that a person's feelings and subjective experiences are initiated through a trail to the amygdala.

For LeDoux, emotional experiences are determined by stimulation of two routes. The first route is a fast system that makes use of subcortical structures, including the amygdala, and results in the ability to react quickly. These reactions include arousal in various other brain structures and automatic responses in the body—release of hormones, sweating, and facial changes. The other route involves the cerebral cortex as well as the amygdala. This route allows an evaluation of the situation and the inclusion of thoughts and past experiences in the assessment of the situation and decisions about what steps to take. For example, an unexpected touch is often enough to produce a quick fear reaction, but the experience of fear will be different if the touch occurs in your home by a friend versus in a dimly lit corridor by a stranger. In the end, LeDoux (1996)

asserts that there seem to be two routes for fear, one subcortical and one cortical, but both involving the amygdala.

The amygdala is also important for forming memories related to fear, probably through its connections to the neighbouring hippocampus (LeDoux & Phelps, 2000). Studies using brain imaging techniques show that the amygdala is active when people see photos of fearful faces. Humans with damage to the amygdala show altered perceptions of fear (Davidson, Jackson, & Kalin, 2000); they have difficulty identifying a photograph as expressing fear (but can recognize other emotions). One patient with damage to the amygdala has problems in recognizing but not in showing fear (Anderson & Phelps, 2000). This problem is not restricted to facial expressions; people with damage to the amygdala also have problems in recognizing vocal signs of fear.

People with psychological problems related to fear also show increased activity in the amygdala (Davidson, Jackson, & Kalin, 2000). Brain imaging studies of people with anxiety disorders and phobias (unreasonable fears) show that these individuals' amygdalas react more strongly to their feared situations than the amygdalas of comparison participants.

Fear of heights, snakes, or insects has an evolutionary basis; encountering any of these situations can be dangerous, and built-in responses to these stimuli can be adaptive. Of course, the modern world is drastically different from that of our ancestors, and such fears today may be unreasonable phobias—tall buildings are

BUILDING TABLE 9.5   **Physiological and Evolutionary Theories of Emotion**

| Theory | Theorist | The Role of Physiology | The Role of Cognition | The Role of the Situation |
|---|---|---|---|---|
| Physiological | James and Lange | Arousal precedes interpretation of events. | Not a factor | People interpret bodily arousal as emotion. |
| | Cannon and Bard | Physiological arousal and interpretation occur simultaneously. | Not a factor | Cognition supplies an interpretation, which occurs at the same time as arousal. |
| Evolutionary | LeDoux | Physiological changes occur in the amygdala and subcortical structures first. | Can affect the emotion through access to memories and interpretation | Subjective interpretation is mediated by a different, slower pathway to the brain. |
| | Cosmides and Tooby | The brain contains a series of specialized programs for basic emotions. | Brings forth the appropriate programs | Cognition follows the reactions of the brain and body. |

typically safe, and people see snakes more often in zoos or as pets than in the street. Thus, some of our programs from prehistory are not nearly as adaptive in the modern world as they were in the past. Indeed, this discrepancy may be one source of discontent with modern life (Buss, 2000b). Our evolutionary history has prepared us to perceive fear and to be competitive, and enacting these tendencies can produce major problems. Evolutionary psychology also explains that humans have the capacity to experience a range of positive emotions (Buss, 2000b). Humans lived in groups during prehistory, and their history of living in small groups and forming close, mating relationships gives humans the evolutionary predisposition to form close personal relationships and to derive great satisfaction from them. That is, evolutionary psychology sees love and friendship as part of our evolved history. Indeed, these close relationships should be the basis for many people's most satisfying experiences, and studies of happiness confirm this view (Myers, 2000).

Evolutionary psychologists have been interested in identifying "basic" emotions and determining whether these emotions are evident among all humans, and even all primates. Facial expressions have provided a means to this goal. Facial expressions are easily observed and interpreted by others. Paul Ekman and his colleagues (1992; Keltner & Ekman, 2000) conducted cross-cultural studies of the perception of emotion, finding a great deal of consistency among cultures in people's ability to interpret facial expressions. In addition, people are extremely good at detecting changes in facial expressions (Edwards, 1998; Farah et al., 1998). However, the claims for universality of facial expressions are the target of criticism (Russell, 1994); also, facial expressions do not always reflect people's feelings. People can "put on a happy face" to mask sadness. Further, some cultural variations exist in both the interpretation of expressions and the situations that elicit them (Keltner & Ekman, 2000). For example, laughter is common at funerals in some cultures but very unusual in others, and individuals from Southeast Asia show a wider variety of facial expressions to reflect embarrassment than do people in Western cultures. For a demonstration that emotions are both easy and difficult to read, see Figure 9.6.

## COGNITIVE THEORIES OF EMOTION

Fear, sadness, rage, and excitement all have readily recognizable emotional and physiological manifestations, but these emotions also are accompanied by thoughts and feelings. And what about more complex emotions? Consider, for example,

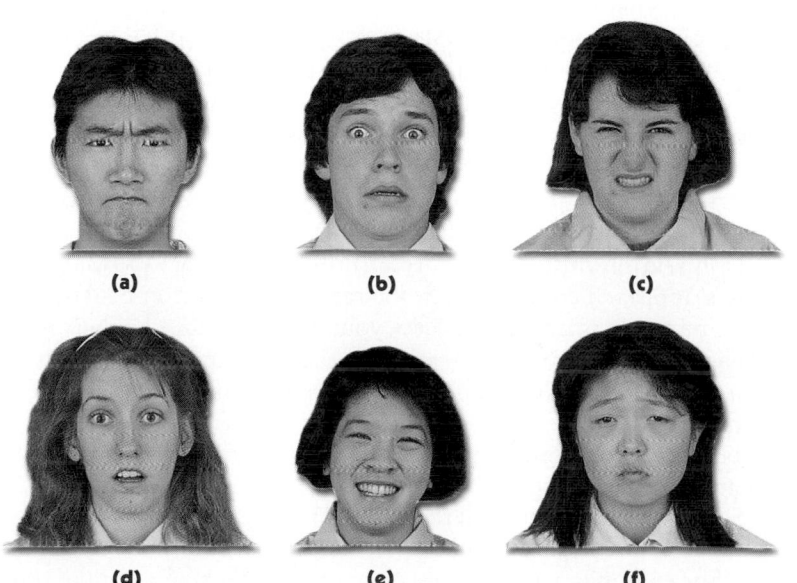

(a)   (b)   (c)

(d)   (e)   (f)

**FIGURE 9.6**

**For the Active Learner: Recognizing and Naming Emotions**

Look carefully at the six photographs. Which of the following six emotions is portrayed in each photo?

1. Happiness
2. Sadness
3. Fear
4. Anger
5. Surprise
6. Disgust

Answers: (a) 4; (b) 3; (c) 6; (d) 5; (e) 1; (f) 2

pride, embarrassment, or guilt. All of these require a far more subtle and complex analysis—one that focuses on thought (Lewis, 1995). Cognitive theories of emotion focus on mental interpretation as well as physiology.

**THE SCHACHTER–SINGER APPROACH.** The Schachter–Singer view of emotion is a cognitive approach that focuses on emotional activation and incorporates elements of both the James–Lange and the Cannon–Bard theories. Stanley Schachter and Jerome Singer observed that people do indeed interpret their emotions, but not solely from bodily changes. They argued that people interpret physical sensations within a specific context. They knew that bodily states, including chemically induced states brought on by alcohol or other drugs, changed moods. However, a person (as well as observers of the person) cannot interpret what emotional behaviour means unless they know something about the situation in which the behaviour occurs. If a man cries at a funeral, observers suspect he is sad; if he cries at his daughter's wedding, they suspect he is joyful. Thus, according to the Schachter–Singer view, an emotion is created by cognitive factors as a person tries to account for a state of perceived activation (Lang, 1994). You may have experienced the sensation of being somewhat edgy and irritated and been unable to account for it. Then you recall that except for five cups of coffee you haven't had anything to eat or drink all day. You attribute your emotional reaction to the caffeine in your system and probably go get something to eat.

To demonstrate their contention, Schachter and Singer (1962) manipulated participants' level of physiological arousal plus the emotional climate of their surroundings by injecting volunteers with epinephrine (adrenalin), a powerful stimulant that increases physiological arousal in areas such as heart rate and blood pressure, often creating sensations of butterflies in the stomach. These participants were compared to a group who received saline injections, which have no physiological effects. To see if they could affect how participants interpreted their aroused state, Schachter and Singer manipulated the emotional settings in which the volunteers received the injection. The researchers hired confederates, undergraduate students trained to act either happy or angry. The hired confederates pretended that they were volunteers in the drug study, but they were actually behaving according to a script; their emotional behaviour was strictly an act. The "happy" confederates had a great time in the experiment; they shot wads of paper into a wastebasket and flew paper airplanes around the room. The "angry" ones complained about the questionnaire they had to fill out and voiced their dissatisfaction with the experiment.

Schachter and Singer found that both of their manipulations were successful. All of the experimental participants who received epinephrine injections showed increased physiological arousal when compared to the participants who received saline. Those who interacted with the happy stooges reported that the drug made them feel good; those who interacted with the angry ones reported feeling anger. Schachter and Singer reasoned that when people have no label for the cause of their physiological arousal (especially when arousal levels are low), they will label their feelings in terms of the experiences available to them—in this case, thoughts stimulated by their interactions with the confederates.

Don Dutton of the University of British Columbia showed how Schachter and Singer's approach could work in the real world (Dutton & Aron, 1974). He had a female research assistant interview young men standing either in the middle of the Capilano Suspension Bridge that spans the spillway of the dam holding Vacouver's water supply or in the middle of a much lower, more stable bridge. The natural adrenalin rush of the suspension bridge led to much higher ratings when the participants interviewed there were asked how much they thought the research assistant was attracted to them.

Schachter and Singer had the kernel of an important idea: Arousal does intensify emotions. However, it does not work alone. People don't live in an experiential vacuum. For example, when people first smoke marijuana or take other psychoactive drugs, they tend to approach the experience with definite expectations. If told the drug produces feelings of hunger, new users report feeling hungry; if told the drug is a downer, new users often interpret their bodily sensations as depressed. In Schachter and Singer's view, people experience internal arousal, become aware of the arousal, seek an explanation for it, identify an external cue, and then label the arousal. In an important way, arousal provides the fuel—the energy—for the physiological reaction, but the labelling determines the feeling.

These findings have been the target of criticism of several types, including both relying too much and too little on physiological arousal to explain emotion. That is, some critics believe that thoughts alone are sufficient to produce emotion (Reisenzein, 1983). And the physiological theorists argue that brain arousal or excitation of the autonomic nervous system is the controlling factor in the experience of emotion.

**THE LAZARUS APPROACH.**   Richard Lazarus (1991) formulated a theory of emotion that also relies heavily on cognition. Like Schachter and Singer, Lazarus considered both physiology and cognition important in emotion, and he also believes that the situation is critical in people's experience of emotion. Lazarus argues that cognition affects emotion through people's appraisal of the situation and its impact on them. **Appraisal** is the evaluation of the significance of a situation or event for a person's well-being. Thus, people's evaluation of a situation in personal terms is important for emotion. Lazarus's cognitive theory of emotion is controversial, but his insistence on the importance of thoughts and personal appraisal in the experience of emotion fits well with the varieties of emotional experience that occur. Building Table 9.6 allows you to contrast the key elements of physiological, evolutionary, and cognitive theories of emotion.

APPRAISAL

The evaluation of the significance of a situation or event as it relates to a person's well-being.

**BUILDING TABLE 9.6**   Physiological, Evolutionary, and Cognitive Theories of Emotion

| Theory | Theorist | The Role of Physiology | The Role of Cognition | The Role of the Situation |
|--------|----------|------------------------|-----------------------|---------------------------|
| Physiological | James and Lange | Arousal precedes interpretation of events. | Not a factor | People interpret bodily arousal as emotion. |
| | Cannon and Bard | Physiological arousal and interpretation occur simultaneously. | Not a factor | Cognition supplies an interpretation, which occurs at the same time as arousal. |
| Evolutionary | LeDoux | Physiological changes occur in the amygdala and subcortical structures first. | Can affect the emotion through access to memories and interpretation | Subjective interpretation is mediated by a different, slower pathway to the brain. |
| | Cosmides and Tooby | The brain contains a series of specialized programs for basic emotions. | Brings forth the appropriate programs | Cognition follows the reactions of the brain and body. |
| Cognitive | Schachter and Singer | Physiological arousal requires a cognitive interpretation before it is experienced as emotion. | Key determinant of emotion because situation affects how people interpret their experience | Cognitive labels determine the experience of emotion. |
| | Lazarus | Physiological reaction is less important than cognition. | Must be appraised before people experience emotion | Cognition affects emotion through appraisal of the situation. |

## VARIETIES OF EMOTIONAL EXPERIENCE

Over the years, researchers have tried to identify the "basic" emotional expressions of feeling. One noted researcher (Izard, 1997) isolated 10 such basic emotions (joy, interest, surprise, sadness, anger, disgust, contempt, fear, shame, and guilt). But such cataloguing is difficult because of the enormous variations in emotional expression. Research can be seen as finding basic emotions in the kinds of emotions people experience, but other factors vary, including intensity, quality, and situation. Emotional responses are also moulded by strong cultural expectations. Fear, for example, can be praised or punished, depending on the culture, and children may learn to hide some emotions. One person's sense of joy may differ from another's, and the ways of expressing joy differ from individual to individual and from culture to culture.

The experience of emotion is private and personal, but the expression of emotion is observable behaviour. Thus, people may experience similar emotions but behave differently. *Display rules* are the rules that govern the display of emotion, and these rules vary according to age, culture, and gender, creating wide differences in emotional expression. For example, in Canada we consider temper tantrums to be unacceptable behaviour, but these displays are more expected and accepted for 3-year-olds than for 30-year-olds.

**CULTURE AND EMOTION.** Most emotions are expressed in most cultures, indicating some type of commonality across cultures. However, the expressions vary in degree and especially in the circumstances under which they occur, indicating some variation. Thus, emotions show both consistency and variation among cultures. Questions about cultural variation in emotion are important to those theorists who argue that emotions are universal and biologically based. Research indicates that even for "basic" emotions such as disgust, fear, and happiness, some cultural and individual variation exists (Keltner & Ekman, 2000; Scherer, 1997; Scherer, Walbott, & Summerfield, 1986). Individuals from different cultures vary in how they interpret the underlying meaning of facial expressions and how intensely people judge the underlying emotion. In addition, different cultures allow the display of very different emotions in very similar situations. For example, Japanese children are taught to smile when an elder scolds or corrects them (they should be grateful for this useful information). Children in Canada are not taught to frown and pout, but they learn that these responses are expected and accepted when they are scolded.

Culture is not specific to national boundaries, and culture can vary within a country, for example, between different ethnic groups living in the same country. Culture can also be shared across countries, and one survey (Scherer, 1997) found that the greatest differences among cultures came from people's evaluations of the situations and events that provoke emotion. This survey revealed differences among geopolitical regions but similarities within these regions. For example, people in Latin America had opinions about morality, fairness, and justice that varied from those of people in Africa, and both differed from those in Western Europe. These differences in judgments of such events might produce substantial differences in the emotions and reactions that people experience.

One of the most frequently assessed variables in cross-cultural research is the distinction between individualist and collectivist cultures. Individualist cultures stress the individual, whereas collectivist cultures stress how the individual fits within a group and within the entire society. People living within these different cultures show some variations in emotionality (Mesquita, 2001). Contrasting people from collectivist cultures in Surinam and Turkey with those from the individualist culture of Holland showed that people from

▼ Canadian children frequently respond by pouting when they are scolded.

collectivist cultures were more likely than those from the individualist culture to see emotion as reflecting reality rather than their own individual experience. In addition, the collectivist cultures tended to foster the attitude that emotion resides in the interaction between people rather than within the person.

Emotions are also differently valued by collectivist and individualist cultures. In a study of people in 61 countries (Suh et al., 1998), the relationship between positive emotions and life satisfaction was stronger in individualist than in collectivist cultures. In collectivist cultures, life satisfaction was more closely related to achieving the culture's norm for happiness. This result suggests that people in individualist cultures use their own emotions as the standard to judge their happiness, whereas people in collectivist cultures use social standards to make that judgment. People in individualist cultures are not necessarily more satisfied with life or happier than those in collectivist cultures, but the life situations and feelings that relate to happiness vary for these two cultural patterns (Diener, 2000). For example, self-esteem and self-respect are more strongly related to happiness in individualistic than in collectivist cultures. One factor that does not vary with happiness is gender (Myers, 2000), but women and men show other differences in emotion.

GENDER AND EMOTION.    In this society, it is widely believed that women are more emotional than men, but that assumption requires that people concentrate on some emotions and overlook others. People are thinking of sympathy, fear, and sadness when they associate women with emotion, but they are overlooking anger when they consider men unemotional (Plant et al., 2000). These beliefs about men and women are widely accepted. However, research shows that the degree to which these stereotypes reflect reality may be due to the power of the stereotypes to shape that reality. People who do not conform to generally held beliefs might be punished through social rejection, and people who do conform are rewarded for such behaviour. People have a tendency to notice and recall examples that conform to their stereotypes and to ignore and forget examples that do not. This tendency helps shape and perpetuate these gender stereotypes of emotionality. In addition, people interpret situations that are not clear in stereotypical terms. All of these tendencies perpetuate gender stereotypes of emotion and limit both men's and women's full expression of their emotionality.

Consider, for example, the gender stereotype that men experience more anger than women. This stereotype is largely inaccurate because it focuses on the behavioural expression of anger through aggression but ignores the experience of anger and anger expressed in other ways. Research on the experience of anger indicates that few gender differences exist in feelings of anger (Larson & Pleck, 1999). Considering other expressions of anger, women often verbalize more intense anger and for longer periods of time than do men— especially women who are in close heterosexual relationships. Men in a similar situation more frequently "stonewall" by inhibiting facial expressions and minimizing listening behaviours as well as eye contact (Gottman, 1998). Yet the physiological reactions of men and women in these situations are much more similar than their behaviours indicate. Even in less personally involving situations, such as viewing an emotion-arousing movie, the physiological reactions of women and men are similar (Kring & Gordon, 1998). Thus, the experience and feelings of anger are probably very similar for men and women.

Even when their experience of emotion is similar, men and women differ in their expression of emotions (Kring & Gordon, 1998). A great deal of this difference is due to display rules. Gender stereotypes of emotionality hold that women are more emotional, giving them the freedom to express a wider variety of

▼ Men and women differ in the ways in which they express emotion.

emotions than men can. However, women are restricted in their expression of anger, so even though they feel anger as frequently and as intensely as men, they display their anger verbally or indirectly rather than in direct, physical confrontations. Men are similarly restricted in their expressions of sadness, fear, affection, and most emotions except anger. Women and men learn to conform to the display rules deemed appropriate to their gender, and this learning suggests that people can learn to control their emotions. But if one component of emotion comes from brain and nervous system arousal, how can emotions be controlled?

CAN WE CONTROL EMOTIONS? Whether we can control our emotions depends on which of the three components of emotion we mean—physiology, feelings, or behaviours. If we are concentrating on the physiological component of emotion, then control is quite difficult. The changes that occur in brain structures and the resulting activity of the peripheral nervous system and changes to hormone levels happen automatically and largely outside the level of conscious thought. Controlling these physiological reactions is possible but difficult (see Chapter 4 and the discussion on biofeedback, p. 147). A controversial example of the difficulty of controlling emotional reactions is the use of those physiological responses to detect emotionality with polygraphs (see *Psychology in Action*).

Changing feelings and behaviour holds more promise in the management of emotion. If cognitions are an important component of emotional experience, then changes in how people think about a situation should produce alterations in the emotions. Indeed, the notion that cognitions can change emotions is the basis for one type of psychotherapy, rational–emotive therapy (see Chapter 16, p. 596). When people learn to think about their problems and situations in different ways, they can change their feelings about their lives. This process is not easy, but it is possible. An easier approach involves changing the situations that provoke emotions, preventing the unwanted emotions from occurring (Gross, 1999). People can elect to avoid certain situations, modify some component of the situation, or attend to some other aspect of the situation. For example, if you had to work with someone whom you found annoying, you might try to avoid the person, change the way you interact, or attend to some positive aspect of the person's behaviour. Any of these strategies could be successful in managing your emotions.

Of the three components of emotion, changing the behaviours associated with emotion is the easiest. We can "put on a happy face," "turn the other cheek," or use our "poker face" rather than expressing our true feelings. We also have the option of behaving in some way that is different from our first impulse. When we are angry with someone, our first impulse may be to lash out, either verbally or physically, but people have been taught since childhood to control these behaviours. Some people have more trouble with this type of control than others.

*Be an*
**ACTIVE LEARNER**

**REVIEW**
> Identify the fundamental ideas that distinguish the James–Lange view from the Cannon–Bard view of emotion. pp. 326–327
> How does the evolutionary view differ from other physiological theories of emotion? pp. 327–329
> What finding from Schachter and Singer's study prompted them to give cognitions such a prominent role in emotion? p. 330
> What findings from cross-cultural and gender research argue against universal experience of certain emotions? pp. 331–334

**THINK CRITICALLY**
> Do you think using lie detectors should be permitted in the public or private sector? Why or why not?
> How do domestic violence issues relate to gender differences in emotional expressiveness?

**APPLY PSYCHOLOGY**
> Design a program to help people control anger, targeting the components of physiology, feelings, and behaviour.

## Lie Detectors and Emotion

Would you take a job if one of the conditions for employment was taking a polygraph examination whenever the employer asked? How would you feel if you were actually asked to take such an examination? How nervous would you be? Would you feel guilty, even if you hadn't done anything wrong? Many employees are put into this position because some employers attempt to guard against employee dishonesty by administering "lie detector" tests. (Employees in Ontario and New Brunswick may not be asked or required to take lie detector tests except by police in an actual criminal investigation.) The accuracy of this type of testing is the subject of intense debate. The basis for the procedure is our nervous system response to emotional situations. Many physiological changes associated with emotion are caused by an increase in activity in the sympathetic branch of the autonomic nervous system. When the sympathetic nervous system is activated, many different responses take place almost simultaneously. For example, arousal of the sympathetic nervous system slows or halts digestion, increases blood pressure and heart rate, deepens breathing, dilates the pupils, decreases salivation, and tenses the muscles. Recognition that the autonomic nervous system provides direct, observable, measurable responses that can be quantified in a systematic manner led to the development of the *polygraph device*, commonly called the *lie detector*.

A polygraph test involves recording many physiological responses that indicate changes in the activity of the sympathetic branch of a person's autonomic nervous system. Most autonomic nervous system activity is involuntary, and lying is usually associated with an increase in autonomic activity. A trained polygraph operator compares a person's physiological responses while answering a series of relatively neutral questions to the person's responses while answering questions about the issue being explored. During neutral questioning (such as requesting the person's name or address), autonomic nervous system activity remains at what is considered the baseline level. During critical questioning (such as asking whether the person used a knife as a holdup weapon or took money from the cash register), however, a person with something to hide usually shows a dramatic increase in autonomic nervous system activity.

Polygraphs do not measure lying and are far from perfect in allowing operators to conclude who is telling the truth and who is not. Critics argue that even well-trained operators do not use polygraphs as standardized tests but as interrogation devices (Frater, 2000). In addition, critics claim that polygraphs are little better than flipping a coin in deciding about truth telling, with nearly 50 percent of innocent responders showing as "guilty"(Phillipps, 1999). However, the results may not be random, but worse—some people

show little or no change in autonomic activity when they lie (Honts, 1994). Such people seem to able to lie without becoming emotionally aroused and thus can systematically "beat the machine." Equally important is the finding that some people who tell the truth may register changes in autonomic nervous system activity because of anxiety. If you believe you would be so nervous being hooked up to the machine that your testing would not be valid, you may be correct. Lie detectors are subject to significant errors in both directions. Because of this uncertainty, the Supreme Court of Canada has outlawed the use of lie detector evidence in court.

In less formal settings there a few things you can do to detect deception or lies. According to DePaulo and colleagues (2003), liars are less forthcoming than truth tellers, and tell less compelling stories. Liars' stories contain fewer ordinary imperfections or unusual contents. Judee Burgoon and colleagues (1995) tell us that deceptive communications are less complete, less direct, involve more hesitation, and are less personalized. They also tell us, unfortunately, that liars with better social skills are far more likely to be believed, so practice seems to pay off here too.

Paul Ekman (2003; Ekman, O'Sullivan, & Cavallaro, 1999) studied the ability of a 30-year police veteran, James Newberry, to tell liars from truth tellers and found that what Newberry was good at was detecting those faint or fleeting expressions in a suspect's face that seemed inconsistent with what he was saying or with other clues. Ekman called them "microexpressions." Ekman now trains police officers to look for these microexpressions when questioning suspects. So, while we do not have a lie detecting technique that is yet reliable enough for use in court, we can, by paying attention, perhaps do a bit better when playing cards or buying used cars—that is, when we have to evaluate others' claims at "face" value.

# Summary and Review

**Distinguish between a motivation and a need.**

> A *motivation* is any internal condition that can be inferred to initiate, activate, or maintain an organism's goal-directed behaviour. Motivation is inferred from behaviour and is caused by needs, drives, or desires. A *need* is a state of physiological imbalance that is usually accompanied by arousal.   **pp. 306–307**

**Differentiate among the various theories of motivation.**

> Evolutionary psychologists believe that humans are motivated by many instincts, innate behaviour sequences. These motivations are the result of evolutionary history and have produced people motivated by forces that relate to survival and reproduction.   **pp. 306–307**

> *Drive theory* is an explanation of behaviour that assumes that an organism is motivated to act because of a need to attain, re-establish, or maintain some goal. A *drive* is an internal arousal condition related to a need. A drive explanation of behaviour is said to be mechanistic, viewing the organism as being pushed and pulled, almost like a machine. The goal of many drives is *homeostasis*, the maintenance of a constant state of inner stability or balance.   **pp. 307–308**

> According to *arousal theory*, individuals seek an optimal level of stimulation. The Yerkes–Dodson law asserts that behaviour varies from disorganized to effective to optimal, depending on the person's level of *arousal*. Contemporary researchers have extended the idea by suggesting that when a person's level of arousal and anxiety is too high or too low, performance will be poor, especially on complex tasks. Performance peaks when arousal is at a moderate level.   **pp. 308–309**

> *Cognitive theories* are explanations of behaviour that emphasize the role of thoughts and active decision making regarding life goals and the means of achieving them. *Expectancy theories* are cognitive theories of motivation that focus on people's expectations about reaching a goal and their need for achievement. A *motive* is typically an internal condition that directs an organism's behaviour toward a goal, but a motive is not based on physiology. Needs are also learned, and a *social need* directs people to behave in ways that establish and maintain relationships.   **pp. 310–311**

> *Intrinsic motivation* gives rise to behaviours a person performs to obtain cognitive stimulation and a sense of competence and accomplishment. *Extrinsic motivation* is supplied by rewards that come from the external environment. The *overjustification effect* is the decrease in likelihood that an intrinsically motivated task will be performed once it has been extrinsically rewarded and then the reward is no longer given.   **pp. 311–312**

> *Humanistic theory* emphasizes that people are drawn toward *self-actualization*, fulfilling their full human potential. Theorists such as Maslow describe how motivation can be arranged in a hierarchy, ranging from physiological need to self-actualization. This theory focuses on human dignity, individual choice, and self-worth, but such concepts are difficult to verify experimentally.   **pp. 312–313**

**KEY TERMS**

motivation, p. 306; drive theory, p. 307; drive, p. 307; need, p. 307; homeostasis, p. 307; arousal, p. 308; cognitive theories, p. 310; expectancy theories, p. 310; motive, p. 310; social need, p. 310; extrinsic motivation, p. 311; intrinsic motivation, p. 311; overjustification effect, p. 312; humanistic theory, p. 312; self-actualization, p. 312

## HUNGER: A PHYSIOLOGICALLY BASED NEED

**What causes hunger?**

> People do not eat because their energy levels are low; they eat before energy deficits occur. The hormones insulin and leptin provide signals to the brain, including the hypothalamus, where a complex series of events signal hunger and satiation.   **pp. 314–315**

> Learning is also important for hunger and eating. The initiation of eating is affected by habit and learning, and food preferences are strongly influenced by cultural and individual factors.   **pp. 315–316**

**Why are people obese?**

> There is no clear, convincing answer to the question of whether nature or nurture is a more important determinant of obesity. Genetics plays a role, but a person's history with food and current weight also influence the likelihood of recurrence or development of obesity.   **pp. 316–318**

## SEXUAL BEHAVIOUR: PHYSIOLOGY PLUS THOUGHT

**What are the roles of hormones and thought in human sexual behaviour?**

> Sexual behaviour in human beings is in part under hormonal control, and the hormones are different in men and women. In men, the androgens produced by the testes predominate, and in women, estrogens produced by the ovaries do. These sex hormones control prenatal development of the reproductive systems and prompt the development of sexual behaviour and fertility during puberty.   **p. 319**

> Thought plays an enormous role in the sexual behaviour of human beings; thoughts, fantasies, and images can initiate and activate sexual desire and activity. pp. 319–320

**How have sex lives changed over the past 50 years?**

> The Laumann study, the most recent and comprehensive study of sexual behaviour, has shown that the sex lives of most Canadians are predictable and not as active as many assume, but most people are satisfied with their sex lives. In contrast with the Kinsey reports, the Laumann study showed that men and women are more likely today than they were 50 years ago to have had intercourse before marriage and that there has been a slow and steady decrease in the age of first intercourse. Men think about sex more than women do, and married men and women have more sex than do unmarried people. p. 320

> A person with a heterosexual orientation has an erotic attraction and preference for members of the other sex; a person with a homosexual orientation has an erotic attraction and preference for members of the same sex. According to the Laumann study, only 2.8 percent of men and 1.4 percent of women identify themselves as exclusively homosexual in orientation. These figures are substantially lower than Kinsey reported in the 1950s. p. 321

**KEY TERMS**

survey, p. 322; representative sample, p. 322

## ACHIEVEMENT: A SOCIAL NEED

**How does expectancy theory explain the need for achievement?**

> *Need for achievement* is a social need that directs a person to strive constantly for excellence and success. According to expectancy theories, people engage in behaviours that satisfy their desires for success, mastery, and fulfilment. Tests such as the TAT have been used to measure need for achievement. Achievement values vary among and within cultures, and personal *self-efficacy* is related to the need for achievement. pp. 321–325

**KEY TERMS**

need for achievement, p. 321; self-efficacy, p. 324

## EMOTION

**What is an emotion, and what are the components of emotion?**

> An *emotion* is a subjective response (a feeling), usually accompanied by a physiological change, which is interpreted in a particular way by the individual and often leads to a change in behaviour. Thus, the three components of an emotion are feelings, physiological responses, and behaviour. These components usually function together but are separable. p. 325

**Identify the fundamental ideas that distinguish various theories of emotion.**

> Physiological theories of emotion include the James–Lange theory, the Cannon–Bard theory, and evolutionary theory. The James–Lange theory states that people experience physiological changes and then interpret those changes as emotions. The Cannon–Bard theory states that when people experience emotions, two areas of the brain are stimulated simultaneously, one creating an emotional response and the other creating physiological changes. Evolutionary theory, including LeDoux's view of the emotional brain, views emotion as preparing people to adapt to situations and to increase their survival and reproductive advantages. Facial expressions have been used as a way to assess universal emotional experience, which the evolutionary theory hypothesizes. pp. 326–330

> According to cognitive theories of emotion, for example, the Schachter–Singer approach and Lazarus's approach, thoughts and an appraisal of the situation are an important, even a determining component of emotion. pp. 330–331

**What factors relate to varieties of emotional experience?**

> Culture and display rules affect the expression of emotion. pp. 331–333

> Gender may not produce differences in the feelings or physiological reactions involved in emotion, but women and men are governed by different display rules that lead to different behavioural expression of emotion. pp. 333–334

**KEY TERMS**

emotion, p. 325; appraisal, p. 331

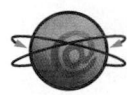

Take advantage of the multimedia resources available with this text! Follow the marginal icons to access the interactive modules on the *HandsOnPsych* CD-ROM; log on to *MyPsychLab* to explore the ebook, study aids, and other online resources; and visit the Companion Website at **www.pearsoned.ca/lefton** for additional exercises and links.

# 10 Child Development

Do four-year-olds think about the world the same way that we as adults do? If you are not sure, try this experiment first used as part of a study by Janet Astington (Astington & Gopnick, 1988) of the University of Toronto. Buy a box of Smarties, empty the box, and replace the Smarties with golf pencils. Show the box to a four-year-old and, after giving it a shake, ask her what is inside. Most four-year-olds will smile in anticipation and say, "Smarties!" Now open the box carefully and reveal the pencils, at which point the child will likely respond, "Ohhh ... pencils?" Put the pencils back into the box and ask the four-year-old what she thought was in the box when you first showed it to her. She will most likely say, "Pencils!" Ask her to predict what a friend of hers would say if he was asked what was in the box and she will predict "Pencils." It is as if the four-year-old has a one-track mind in which new information (such as that Smarties boxes now contain pencils) replaces old information, which is then lost. Children stop making errors like this by five years of age. Trying to understand how and why children think differently about the world and how they respond to the social and emotional situations they encounter in their day-to-day lives makes up much of what developmental psychologists do. It is to this fascinating area of psychological study that we now turn.

Part of the goal of this chapter will be to focus on normal developmental processes in children—physical, cognitive, moral, emotional, and social development. We will also see how people's genetic makeup interacts with their environments to produce unique individuals. Our examination will help explain how parents can affect their children's development so profoundly. The next chapter will look at adolescence, adulthood, and aging—showing that development is a process that lasts a lifetime.

**Development I**

# Key Issues, Theories, and Research Designs

**Developmental psychology** is the study of the lifelong, age-related processes of change in the physical, cognitive, emotional, and social domains of functioning; such changes are rooted in biological mechanisms that are genetically controlled (for example, maturational processes involved in the growth of the nervous system) as well as in social interactions. Psychologists study all of these changes—biological, maturational, and social—to find out how people grow, develop, and transform from young children to mature, functioning adults and to learn what causes those changes. Developmental psychologists recognize that development involves gains and losses over time as people respond in positive and negative ways to life's experiences. They also recognize that development must be viewed from multiple perspectives and within a historical context. Today's developmental researchers acknowledge that the interaction of genetics and the environment is a complex issue (Smith & Thelen, 1993) and that there is considerable diversity in developmental growth (Baltes, 1987). In their study of development, psychologists have focused on a few key issues, theories, and research methods to unravel the causes of behaviour. The goal is always the same: to describe, explain, predict, and potentially help manage human development.

## KEY ISSUES

There are a number of key issues in the study of development that help researchers form their questions and construct their theories. Three of the most important are nature versus nurture, stability versus change, and continuity versus discontinuity.

**NATURE AND NURTURE.** One way to look at individual development is to consider to what extent the developing person's abilities, interests, and personality are determined by evolutionary or biological influences, by *nature*, or by environmental influences, by *nurture*. The nature-versus-nurture issue has been raised before, in Chapters 2 and 9. Attempting to separate biological from environmental causes of behaviour is a complex matter and one of the classic theoretical issues in this area of psychology; the answer to any specific question about human behaviour usually involves the interaction of both nature and nurture. For this reason, many theorists now view the nature versus nurture debate as over. Virtually all behaviour can be attributed to complex interactions between nature *and* nurture. To separate the roles played by genetics and the environment, researchers have studied identical twins (who share the same genetic makeup) who have been reared apart (in different environments). In doing so, they have found extraordinary similarities between such siblings beyond the obvious genetic traits such as height, hair colour, or allergies (Lykken, McGue, Tellegen, & Bouchard, 1992). In one study, Lykken and his colleagues found an identical twin who was an accomplished storyteller with a collection of amusing anecdotes. Later, his twin brother was asked if he knew any funny stories. "Why, sure," he responded, very like his brother, and leaning back with a practiced air he continued, "I'll tell you a story." Other twins shared interests in dogs, smoked the same cigarettes, or were both politically conservative. One pair of twins shared a phobia for water at the beach; both would enter the water backward, and then only up to their knees. In the Lykken study there were two firefighters, two gunsmiths, and two people who obsessively counted things; all of these pairs were identical twins. Lykken and his colleagues argued that genetics plays an especially important role in human development. However, many psychologists believe that although genetics plays a crucial role in development, a child's environment has an equal, if not more important, impact. They argue that children's experiences in and outside the home can expand or hinder the developmental possibilities provided by genetics. Similarly, many parents think they can enhance their children's environment and optimize the likelihood of their living stimulating, well-reasoned, satisfying lives.

**STABILITY VERSUS CHANGE.**　Do individuals stay pretty much the same throughout their lives—cognitively, emotionally, and socially—or do they change, adapt, emerge from, and be affected profoundly by events in their environment? The issue of stability versus change is a recurring theme in developmental psychology. It is closely associated with nature and nurture, because when researchers assume stability they often assume that stable traits—for example, shyness—are inherited and genetically determined. Those who favour an environmental view are more likely to believe that people change over the course of a lifetime because of unique life events—for example, the loss of a sibling in a car accident or exposure to chicken pox, which later may be implicated in the development of multiple sclerosis.

**CONTINUITY VERSUS DISCONTINUITY.**　A third debate focuses on development as continuous or discontinuous. A *continuous view* sees development as a process of gradual growth and change with skills and knowledge added one bit at a time, with one skill building on another. Development also can be viewed as *discontinuous*, with growth, maturation, and understanding of the world occurring at various stages with changes appearing abruptly—almost suddenly. For example, a 12-month-old does not seem to recognize herself in a mirror, but in a few short months she will show that she does recognize herself by touching her nose in curiosity if a blob of red rouge has secretly been placed on it.

▲ Monozygotic twins raised apart often demonstrate extraordinary similarities.

## KEY THEORIES

Most developmental psychologists also have a point of view about development—a theoretical orientation. They develop orderly, coherent ideas that describe, explain, and hopefully predict behaviour from a particular theoretic perspective. Developmental theories give shape and order to sets of data about physical, cognitive, and social development. Some developmental theories today reach back to early psychological leaders for ideas; other developmental theories have modernized earlier ideas; still others are breaking new ground, looking at development and maturation from unique vantage points. These theories reflect the history of psychology and the diversity of the discipline.

**PSYCHOANALYTIC.**　One of the earliest modern theories of development was Freud's. As you will see when we study personality in Chapter 12, Freud believed that early childhood experiences, especially those before the age of six, shape a person's biologically determined urges—leading, for example, to the development of a conscience. Interestingly, Freud never studied children; his theories developed out of studies of disordered adults. We'll have much more to say about Freud later. Erik Erikson, who we will discuss in more detail in the next chapter, took Freud's view and modified it, making it more focused on normal personality development, more focused on development across the life span, and more focused on social and cultural influences on development, rather than focused on sexual and aggressive impulses.

**BEHAVIOURISM.**　In sharp contrast to the psychoanalytic tradition, which emphasizes the unconscious and the role of early childhood experiences, behaviourists focused on observable, quantifiable behaviours. Clark Hull focused on drive reduction theories, which consider how people are motivated by biological needs. B. F. Skinner focused on the antecedents of behaviour and the reinforcers following behaviour. Behaviourists have claimed that a child's development can proceed in any number of directions depending entirely on his or her particular reinforcement history. Today many behaviourists also consider cognitive aspects of behaviour and how thought influences behaviour.

**COGNITIVE THEORY.**    The development of thought has been studied closely by a number of researchers. The key theorist in this area, Jean Piaget, argued that development occurs in an orderly, biologically determined manner, but also emphasized that development involves a process of adaptation to the world in which a child adjusts to its ever-changing demands. Piaget developed an exceedingly influential theory of cognitive development (Flavell, 1996). A second cognitive theory, *the information processing perspective,* views human beings as problem solvers who attempt to make sense of the world. These theorists attempt to look more closely at basic processes such as attention, memory, and problem solving and offer an alternative way of describing and explaining why young children think differently than older children. Most information processing approaches see people as active decision makers responding to environmental demands; these approaches attempt to explain how hard-wired brain systems work by enabling people to learn from and build on their experiences.

**ECOLOGICAL SYSTEMS THEORY.**    A distinctly different approach that has had a wide impact is *ecological systems theory.* Described by a number of researchers, with Urie Bronfenbrenner at its forefront, this approach argues that children develop within a system of complex human relationships and that those relationships exist in a series of overlapping and non-overlapping immediate environments such as families and neighbourhoods and larger environments such as communities, provinces, and countries. Children grow within families, within larger family relationships, within neighbourhoods and workplaces, and within a country and culture that stresses certain values. This approach emphasizes the role of culture and social relationships in the small world of individuals and in larger society. You will see that Bronfenbrenner shares this theoretic perspective with others. For example, Lev Vygotsky, who stressed that dialogue between children and members of society fuels child development, promoted a sociocultural perspective more than 70 years ago. His work, along with Bronfenbrenner's, reminds us that we have to look at behaviour in the social context in which it occurs because we do not live in a social vacuum.

## KEY RESEARCH DESIGNS

Good researchers know that the method they use to study a problem often influences the results. To interpret what the results might mean, a researcher must, at a minimum, take into account the particular research design used. In developmental research, two widely used designs for describing developmental changes are the cross-sectional and the longitudinal designs. In the *cross-sectional research design*, a psychologist will compare many different individuals of different ages at the same time to determine how they differ on some important dimension. In the *longitudinal research design*, a psychologist studies the same group of people repeatedly over time to examine changes that have occurred over a long period of time.

Each design has its advantages and disadvantages. For example, the cross-sectional design suffers from the fact that the participants' backgrounds (parents, family income, and nutrition) differ. Moreover, if differences between age groups are observed, it is difficult to determine whether such differences are due to development or to pre-existing differences. The various age groups being examined may have had different life experiences—for example, one generation may have received substantially less education than the next and that factor will affect results when measuring IQ.

Lastly, with cross-sectional design, individual differences are impossible to assess because participants generally are tested only once whereas in a longitudinal design the same person is tested repeatedly. This allows comparisons to be made from one testing time to the next for the same person as well as comparisons to be made between the person and other participants.

However, the longitudinal design also has problems. It requires repeated access over time to the same people, but some participants may move, withdraw from the study, or even die. Also, after repeated testing on the same task (even though the tests may be months or years apart), participants may improve because of practice (that is, experience with taking the test may improve performance). If testing occurs over a long period of time, the tests themselves may become obsolete. Longitudinal research sometimes takes years to complete; this can cost a lot of money. Also, if the welfare of children could be affected (for example, by a study that examines which approach to teaching children how to read works best), it may be desirable to implement the study's results as quickly as possible rather than waiting for 5-, 10-, or 20-year outcome data. Another disadvantage to this design is that important changes may occur in the environment and/or in the social worlds of the participants, making it difficult to discern whether observed changes should be attributed to development or to environmental change. For example, if a group of children in Bosnia was tested for stability of personality, it would be difficult to conclude that their particular traits were due to development and not influenced by the extreme circumstances of their lives. See Figure 10.1 for a comparison of the cross-sectional and longitudinal research designs.

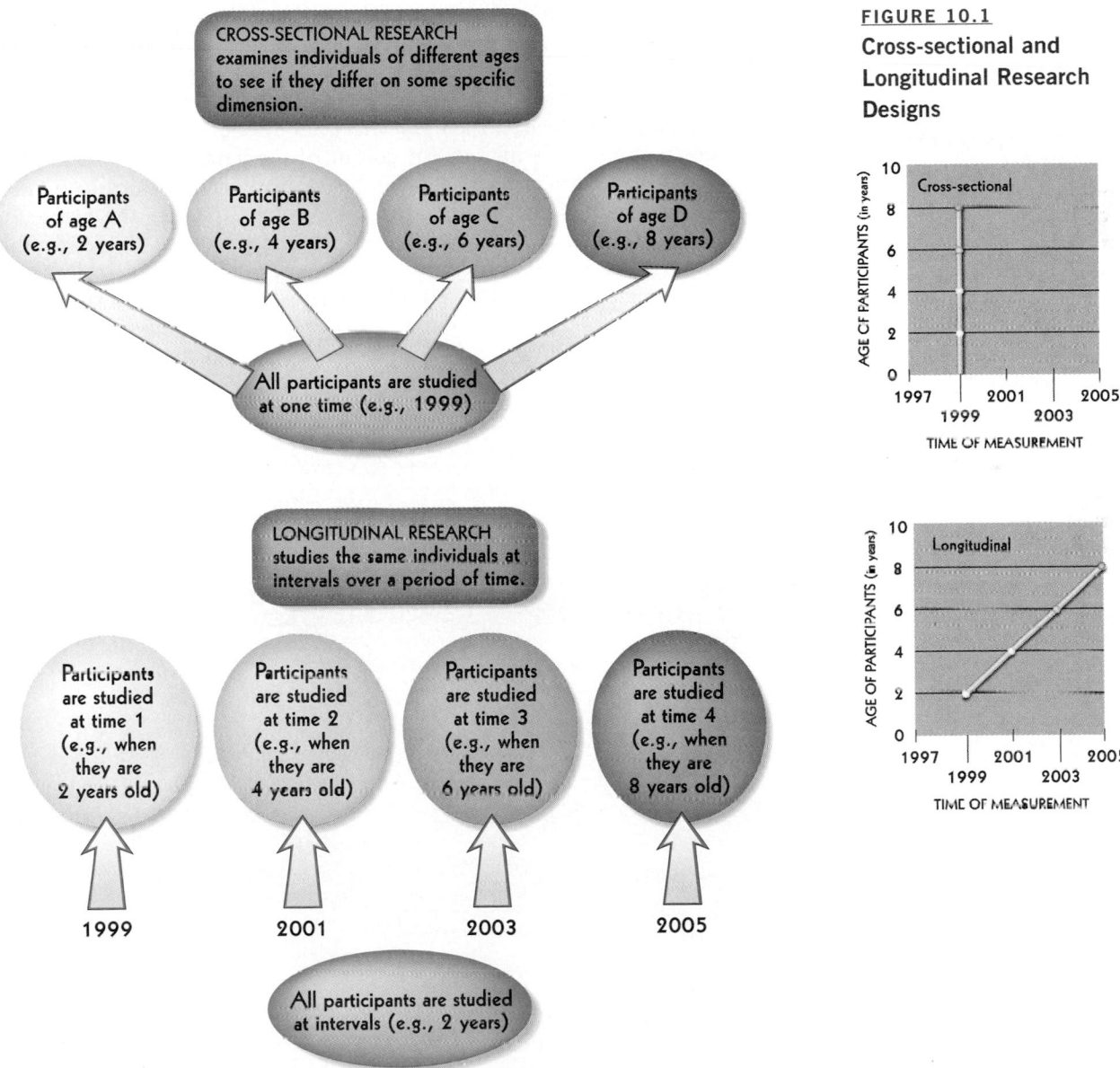

**FIGURE 10.1**

**Cross-sectional and Longitudinal Research Designs**

**Development II**

# Physical Development: The First 10 Months

Understanding how and why adolescents or adults turn out the way they do can't be done by simply examining a mere slice of their lives and saying that "this caused that"; human behaviour is sufficiently complex and affected by so many subtle influences that developmental change has multiple sources. Those sources begin with our basic constitution, our biology—our bodies. Our development begins long before birth. Developmental events before birth are referred to as *prenatal* development; in the month after birth, they are *neonatal* development. Both terms derive from the Latin word *natus*, meaning "born."

## PRENATAL DEVELOPMENT

The lifelong journey of human development begins with conception. Conception occurs when an ovum and a sperm join in a woman's fallopian tube to form a **zygote**—a fertilized egg. During the next seven to nine days, the zygote floats down the fallopian tube to implant itself in the blood-lined wall of the uterus. From the time implantation is complete (about the second week following conception) until the eighth week after conception, the organism is called an **embryo**. Then, from the eighth week until birth, the organism is called a **fetus**. On average, maturation and development of the fetus takes 266 days, or about 38 weeks. Table 10.1 summarizes the prenatal (before birth) and postnatal (after birth) periods of development.

Although the prenatal environment—especially the mother's diet (Sigman, 1995)—can have an influence, the basic characteristics of an individual are established at conception; these include the colour of the hair, skin, and eyes; the sex (gender); the likelihood that the person will be tall or short, fat or lean; and perhaps basic intellectual abilities and personality traits. Within 10 hours, the zygote divides into four cells, forming a *blastocyst*. During the first week, a cluster of about a dozen cells drifts from the fallopian tube to the uterus. There, the cells begin the process of *differentiation*: Organs and other parts of the body begin to form. Some cells form the *umbilical cord*—a group of blood vessels and tissues that connect the zygote to the placenta. The **placenta** is a mass of tissue in the uterus that acts as the life-support system for the fetus by supplying oxygen, food, and antibodies and by eliminating wastes—all by way of the mother's bloodstream.

ZYGOTE [ZEYE-goat]
A fertilized egg.

EMBRYO [EM-bree-o]
The prenatal organism from implantation to the eighth week following conception.

FETUS [FEET-us]
The prenatal organism from the eighth week following conception until birth.

PLACENTA [pluh-SENT-uh]
A mass of tissue in the uterus that acts as the life-support system for the fetus by supplying oxygen, food, and antibodies and by eliminating wastes—all by way of the mother's bloodstream.

| TABLE 10.1 | Life Stages and Approximate Ages in Human Development | |
| --- | --- | --- |
| **Period** | **Life Stage** | **Approximate Age** |
| **Prenatal period** | Zygote | Conception to day 7 to 9 |
| | Embryo | To week 8 |
| | Fetus | Week 8 to birth |
| **Postnatal period** | Neonate | Birth to 1 month |
| | Infancy | 1 to 18 months |
| | Toddlerhood | 18 months to 3 years |
| | Early childhood | 3 to 6 years |
| | Middle childhood | 6 to 13 years |
| | Adolescence | 13 to 20 years |
| | Young adulthood | 20 to 40 years |
| | Middle adulthood | 40 to 65 years |
| | Late adulthood | 65 plus |

TABLE 10.2    Major Developments during the Prenatal Period

| | Age | Size | Characteristics |
|---|---|---|---|
| **First trimester**<br>**1–12 weeks** | 7–9 days | 150 cells | Zygote attaches to uterine lining. |
| | 2 weeks | Several thousand cells | Placental circulation established. |
| | 3 weeks | 1/10 inch | Heart and blood vessels begin to develop. Basics of brain and central nervous system form. |
| | 4 weeks | 1/4 inch | Kidneys and digestive tract begin to form. Rudiments of ears, nose, and eyes are present. |
| | 6 weeks | 1/2 inch | Arms and legs develop. Jaws form around mouth. |
| | 8 weeks | 1 inch, 1/30 ounce | Bones begin to develop in limbs. Sex organs begin to form. |
| | 12 weeks | 3 inches, 1 ounce | Gender can be distinguished. Kidneys are functioning, and liver is manufacturing red blood cells. Fetal movements can be detected by a physician. |
| **Second trimester**<br>**13–24 weeks** | 16 weeks | 6½ inches, 4 ounces | Heartbeat can be detected by a physician. Bones begin to calcify. |
| | 20 weeks | 10 inches, 8 ounces | Mother feels fetal movements. |
| | 24 weeks | 12 inches, 1½ pounds | Vernix (white waxy substance) protects the body. Eyes open; eyebrows and eyelashes form; skin is wrinkled. Respiratory system is barely mature enough to support life. |
| **Third trimester**<br>**25–38 weeks** | 28 weeks | 15 inches, 2½ pounds | Fetus is fully developed but needs to gain in size, strength, and maturity of systems. |
| | 32 weeks | 17 inches, 4 pounds | A layer of fat forms beneath the skin to regulate body temperature. |
| | 36 weeks | 19 inches, 6 pounds | Fetus settles into position for birth. |
| | 38 weeks | 21 inches, 8 pounds | Fetus arrives at full term—266 days from conception. |

11 weeks

4 weeks

20 weeks

Table 10.2 summarizes the major physical developments during the prenatal period.

## HARMFUL ENVIRONMENTAL EFFECTS

People have long assumed that the behaviour of a pregnant woman affects prenatal development. Medieval European doctors advised pregnant women that uplifting thoughts would help their babies develop into good, happy people, while fright, despondency, and negative emotions might disrupt the pregnancies and possibly influence the infants to become sad or mean-spirited. Research with animals shows that stress during pregnancy has effects on the emotional development of offspring, as indicated when the offspring are later tested as adults (Pfister & Muir, 1992).

## Critical Periods

An experienced researcher in the area of early intervention, Jack Shonkoff, argues that early experiences that affect brain development lay the foundations for intelligence, emotional health, and moral development. However, he also argues that the focus on a period from birth to age three is too narrow: "The neurological window of opportunity does not slam shut at age 3 or 5 . . . the disproportionate focus on 'zero to three' begins too late and ends too soon" (Shonkoff, 2000).

There are established critical periods for brain development but it would appear that other developmental issues are also time-sensitive. For example, attachments to other people—especially caregivers, usually moms and dads—form at an early point in life, typically assumed as critical development prior to the age of three, although the window for forming attachments is probably wider than traditionally believed (Thompson, 2001; Thompson & Nelson, 2001). However, in the area of cognitive development, missed opportunities in the first three years may be missed opportunities indeed (Ramey & Sackett, 2000). In general, researchers assert that specific learning is not what is essential in the first three or four years—rather, stimulation prepares children for future learning, laying down important foundational pathways in the brain. But must specific tasks, skills, or knowledge be learned at a specific age—a critical period—or remain unlearned? A critical period is a time in the development of an organism when it is especially sensitive to

certain environmental influences; outside of that period the same influences will have far less effect.

Newport and her colleagues studied second-language learning and found that this learning is harder later in life (Johnson et al., 1996). Young children acquire a second language with greater ease and fewer mistakes than adults do. Furthermore, the neural systems underlying learning a second language show differences depending on the age of learning. For children under the age of four, brain responses tend to be isolated in the left hemisphere—where you would expect them to be. For children over age four, however, there is much more right-hemisphere activity. Of course, language is not a single system; it involves sounds, words, meaning, and grammar, and emerges at different times. Brain organization is structured, ready for language at a young age—a critical period—and later learning deviates from this inherent pattern, both in physiology and in efficiency (Neville & Bavelier, 2000; Weber-Fox & Neville, 1999).

The brain continues to develop throughout life, but it is especially plastic during childhood. Children before puberty have the most plastic brains, and so it is not surprising that second-language acquisition grows more difficult after that period (Gao, Levine, & Huttenlocher, 2000; Huttenlocher, 1998, 1999). People continue to grow and develop throughout life, but brain development and chemistry are most sensitive and most plastic and easily changed in the younger developmental years.

---

**CRITICAL PERIOD**

A time in the development of an organism when it is especially sensitive to certain environmental influences; outside of that period the same influences will have far less effect.

**TERATOGEN** [ter-AT-oh-jen]

A substance that can produce developmental malformations (birth defects) during the prenatal period.

While a fetus is not affected by the mother's condition to the extent suggested by medieval doctors, the environment and life-support systems provided by the mother do influence the embryo and fetus from conception until birth. Environmental factors such as diet, infection, radiation, and drugs affect both the mother *and* the baby. The child is especially affected during *critical periods*, during which there is rapid development and special sensitivity to environmental stimuli. During the first two years of life, the brain is especially sensitive; neuronal connections are undergoing many changes. Although the basic architecture of the brain is in place before birth, how individual connections of neurons are made is subject to considerable influence or damage. The issue of critical periods is discussed further in *Brain and Behaviour*.

Substances that can produce developmental malformations (birth defects) during the prenatal period are known as **teratogens**. Birth defects are the leading cause of death of infants in their first year of life in North America. Probably the most widely known teratogen is alcohol. If the mother drinks alcoholic beverages in early and middle pregnancy, the baby is more likely to be born prematurely, to have a lower birth weight, and to suffer from mental retardation or attention deficit disorder (Streissguth, Barr, & Martin, 1983). Extreme effects are associated with a syndrome called *fetal alcohol syndrome (FAS)*. Children with FAS often have smaller brains, heart defects, and distinctive facial abnormalities and are mentally retarded. In many cases other defects are also present. Although these effects are typically observed in the offspring of alcoholic mothers, the mother does not have to be an alcoholic, or even a heavy drinker, to cause these effects. One study showed that drinking more than three ounces of 100-proof liquor per day during pregnancy was significantly related to a deficit in four-year-olds' intelligence test scores and poor attention span (Streissguth et al., 1989). Any deficits that occur usually are related to both the amount of alcohol consumed and when it was consumed during the pregnancy. It is estimated that about 350 children with FAS are born each year in Canada (Health Canada, 2002).

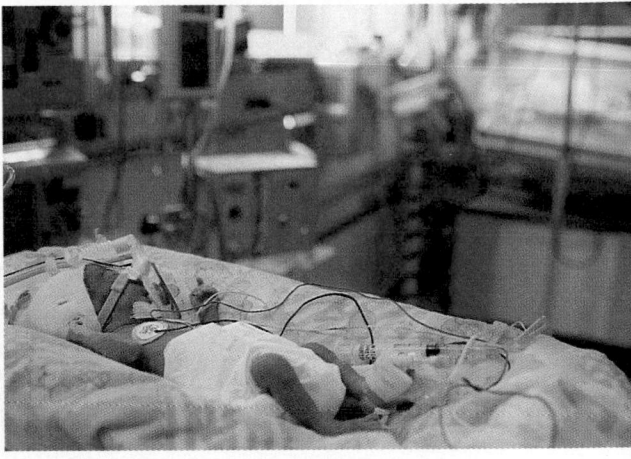

▲ Mothers who abuse drugs and alcohol have babies of low birth weight who are also often born prematurely.

Studies also show that many drugs can affect prenatal development. High doses of aspirin, for example, may cause fetal bleeding, although the evidence is controversial (Werler, Mitchell, & Shapiro, 1989). Cigarette smoking constricts the oxygen supply. Babies born to mothers who smoke cigarettes tend to be of lower birth weight, may be at increased risk for cleft palate and childhood cancers, and are more likely to die in infancy. Certain drugs, including tranquilizers, can be teratogenic, producing potentially irreversible malformations of the head, face, and limbs as well as neurological disorders (Kopp & Kaler, 1989; Lester & Dreher, 1989). Tragically, in recent years, hundreds of thousands of infants have been born addicted to various illegal drugs. Infants born to mothers who smoked crack during pregnancy suffer from low birth weight and central nervous system damage (Kaye, Elkind, Goldberg, & Tytun, 1989). Users of cocaine during pregnancy give birth to babies at increased risk for sudden infant death as well as a number of behavioural and physical problems (Klonoff-Cohen & Lam-Kruglick, 2002; Fares, McCulloch, & Raju, 1997; Ostrea, Ostrea, & Simpson, 1997). The influence of drugs can be especially severe during the embryonic stage of development—a critical period—when the mother may not realize she is pregnant.

## NEWBORNS COME WELL-EQUIPPED

Newborns grow rapidly and they are not nearly as helpless as many people believe. At birth infants can hear, see, smell, and respond to the environment in adaptive ways; in other words, they have good sensory systems. They also are directly affected by experience. To help infants develop in optimal ways, psychologists try to find out how experience affects their perceptual development. In doing so, psychologists need to discover how infants think, what they perceive, and how they react to the world. Researchers therefore have devised ingenious ways of "asking" newborns questions about their perceptual world, such as: What are a child's inborn abilities and reflexes? When do inborn abilities become evident? How does the environment affect inborn abilities?

**GROWTH.** An infant who weighs 7.5 pounds at birth may weigh as much as 20 or 25 pounds by 12 months. At 18 months, the infant is usually walking and beginning to talk. For psychologists, infancy continues until the time when the child begins to represent the world abstractly (for example, through language). Thus, *infancy* is the period from 1 to 18 months (the infant is referred to as a neonate in the first month); *childhood* is the period from 18 months to about age 13—when *adolescence* begins.

The rapid growth that occurs in the early weeks and months after birth is quite extraordinary and mirrors embryonic development in important ways. A newborn's head is about one-fourth of its body length; a two-year-old's head is only one-fifth of its body length. This pattern of growth is called the *cephalocaudal trend* (from the Greek word *kephalé*, "head," and the Latin word *cauda*, "tail"). Another growth pattern—the *proximodistal trend*—has growth moving from the centre (proximal part) of the body outward (to the more "distant" extremities). That is, the head and

FIGURE 10.2
**The Cephalocaudal
Trend of Growth**

Body proportions change
dramatically from fetal stages of
development until adulthood.
(From Berk, 1994.)

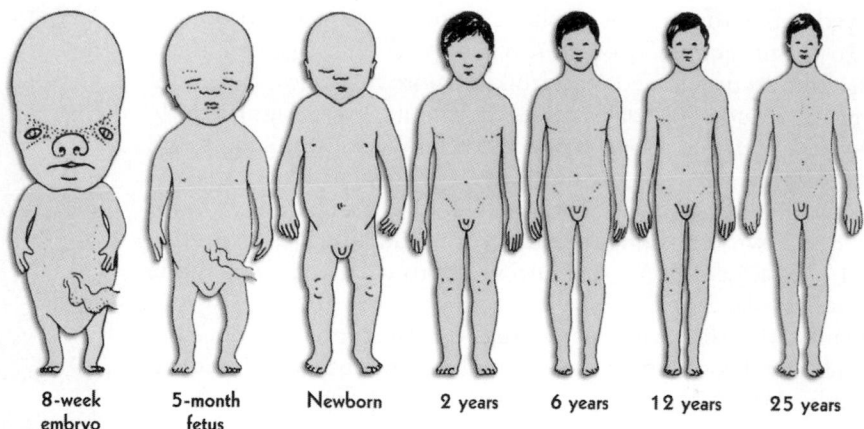

8-week embryo    5-month fetus    Newborn    2 years    6 years    12 years    25 years

torso grow before the arms, legs, hands, and feet do. Thus, a newborn's head is about the same circumference as the torso, and an infant's arms and legs are quite short, relatively speaking—but this changes very quickly (see Figure 10.2).

During the period of infancy and childhood, the child grows physically from a being that requires constant care, attention, and assistance to a nearly full-sized, independent person. This process of growth and maturation begins at birth. At the end of the first year and the beginning of the second year of life, children can walk, climb, and manipulate their environments—skills that often lead parents to use safety devices that block stairways, lock cabinets, and prevent medicine bottles from being opened. There is significant variability in the age at which a child begins to walk or climb. Some babies develop early; others are slow to develop these physical abilities. However, the age at which these specific behaviours occur seems unrelated to any other major developmental abilities, except in cases of severe delay.

Figure 10.3 shows the major achievements in motor development in the first two years.

**NEWBORNS' REFLEXES.** Touch the palm of a newborn baby and you'll probably find one of your fingers held in the surprisingly firm grip of a tiny fist. The baby is exhibiting a reflexive reaction. Babies are born with innate *primary reflexes*—unlearned responses to stimuli. Some, such as the *grasping reflex*, no doubt helped

FIGURE 10.3

**Development of Motor
Skills in the First Two
Years**

Infants typically develop motor
skills in the sequence shown here.
Normal, healthy infants may reach
any of these milestones earlier or
later than these average ages.

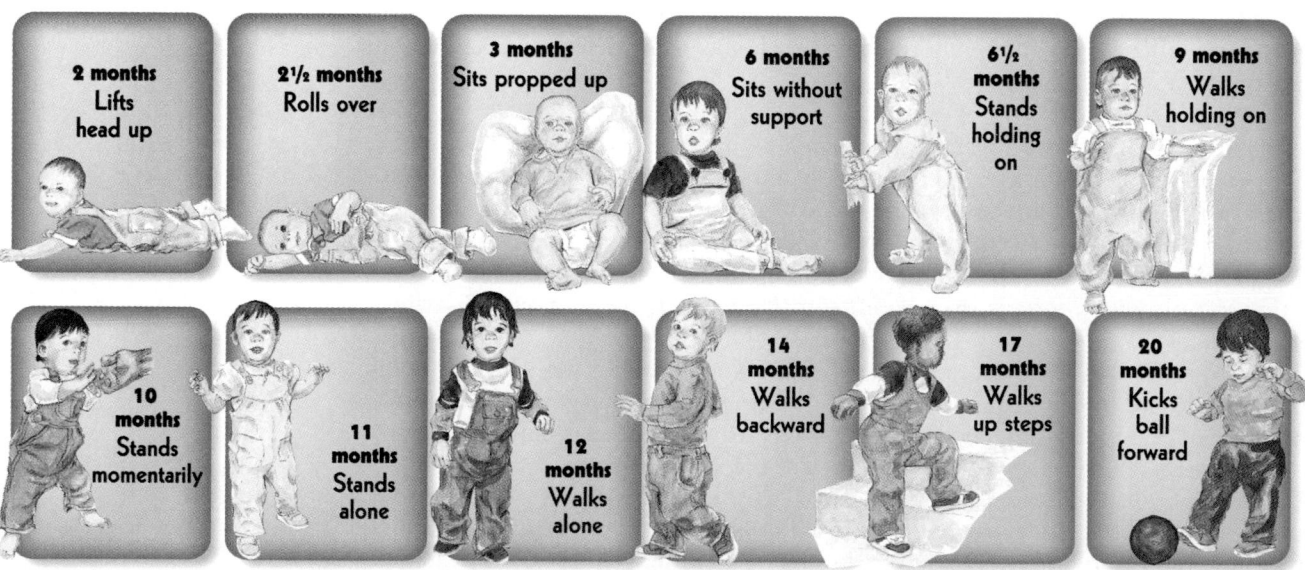

2 months — Lifts head up
2½ months — Rolls over
3 months — Sits propped up
6 months — Sits without support
6½ months — Stands holding on
9 months — Walks holding on
10 months — Stands momentarily
11 months — Stands alone
12 months — Walks alone
14 months — Walks backward
17 months — Walks up steps
20 months — Kicks ball forward

ensure survival in humanity's primate ancestors. Most of these reflexes disappear over the course of the first year of life. Physicians use the presence or absence of primary reflexes to assess neurological damage at birth and to evaluate an infant's rate of development. Table 10.3 summarizes the primary reflexes and their duration. One primary reflex exhibited by infants is the **Babinski reflex**—a projection of the toes outward and up in response to a touch to the sole of the foot. Another is the **Moro reflex**—an outstretching of the arms and legs and crying in response to a loud noise or a sudden, unexpected change in the environment. Newborns also exhibit the **rooting reflex**—the turning of the head toward a mild stimulus (such as a breast or hand) that touches their lips or cheek. They show the **sucking reflex** in response to a finger placed in their mouth and the **grasping reflex** in response to an object touching the palms of their hands—infants vigorously grasp objects touching their palm or fingers.

At first, an infant's abilities and reflexes are innate (biologically determined by the human genetic code). Gradually, learned responses, such as reaching for desired objects or grasping a cup, replace reflex reactions. The baby's experiences in the environment become more important in determining development. These complex interactions between nature and nurture follow a developmental time course that continues throughout life.

**INFANT PERCEPTION: FANTZ'S VIEWING BOX.**   An avalanche of research on infant perception shows that newborns have surprisingly well-developed perceptual systems. Robert Fantz (1961) did some of the earliest work on infant perception. He designed a viewing box in which he placed an infant; he then had a hidden observer or camera record the infant's responses to stimuli (see Figure 10.4).

**BABINSKI REFLEX**

A reflex in which a newborn projects its toes outward and up when the soles of its feet are touched.

**MORO REFLEX**

A reflex in which a newborn stretches out its arms and legs and cries in response to a loud noise or a sudden, unexpected change in the environment.

**ROOTING REFLEX**

A reflex in which a newborn turns its head toward a mild stimulus that touches its lips or cheek.

**SUCKING REFLEX**

A reflex in which a newborn makes sucking motions when presented with a stimulus to the lips, such as a nipple.

**GRASPING REFLEX**

A reflex in which a newborn vigorously grasps any object touching its palm or fingers or placed in its hand.

---

TABLE 10.3   Newborns' Reflexes

| Reflex | Initiated By | Response | Duration |
|---|---|---|---|
| Eye blink | Flashing a light in the infant's eyes | Closing both eyes | Continues throughout life |
| Babinski | Gently stroking the sole of the infant's foot | Flexing the big toe; fanning out the other toes | Usually disappears near the end of the first year |
| Withdrawal | Pricking the sole of the infant's foot | Flexing of the leg | Present during the first 10 days; present but less intense later |
| Plantar | Pressing a finger against the ball of the infant's foot | Curling all the toes under | Disappears between 8 and 12 months |
| Moro | Making a sudden loud sound | Extending the arms and legs; then bringing arms toward each other in convulsive manner; crying | Begins to decline in third month; gone by fifth month |
| Rooting | Stroking the infant's cheek lightly with a finger or a nipple | Turning the head toward the finger, opening the mouth, and trying to suck | Disappears at approximately three to four months |
| Sucking | Placing a finger in the infant's mouth | Sucking rhythmically | Often less intense and less regular during the first three to four days of life but continues for several months |

FIGURE 10.4
**Results of Fantz's Study**

Using a viewing box to observe
newborns' eye movements, Fantz
(1961) recorded the total time
infants spent looking at various
patterns. He found that they looked
at faces or patterned material
much more often than they looked
at plain fields.

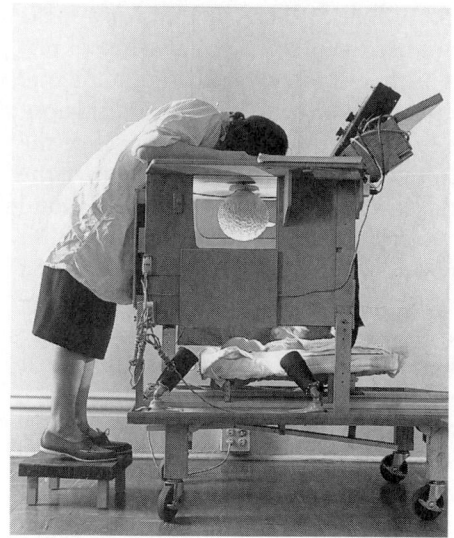

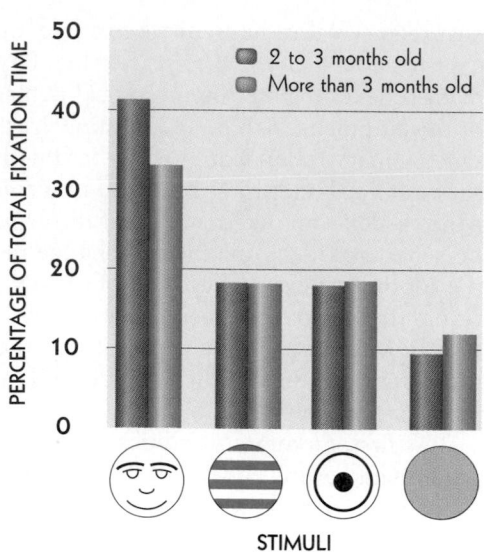

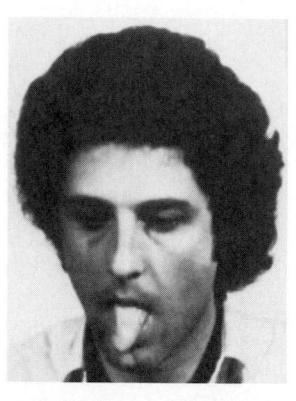

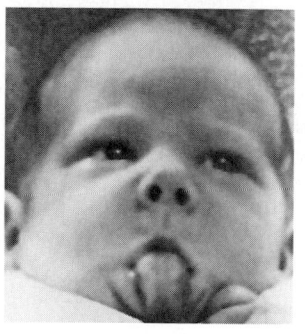

▲ Many researchers claim that
even very young infants are able to
imitate particular adult facial
expressions.

The exciting part of Fantz's work was not that he asked interesting questions but that he was able to get "answers" from the infants. By showing infants various pictures of faces and patterns and recording their eye movements, he discovered the infants' visual preferences. He recorded how long and how often the infants looked at each picture and calculated the total time they spent viewing each type of picture. Because they spent more time looking at pictures of faces than at pictures of random squiggles, Fantz concluded not only that they could see different patterns but also that they preferred faces.

Other researchers confirm that human and non-human infants prefer complex visual fields over simple ones, curved patterns over straight or angular ones, and human faces over random patterns or faces with mixed-up features (Walton & Bower, 1993; Wilson & Goldman-Rakic, 1994). Even in the first few months of life, babies can discriminate among facial features and prefer attractive faces to less attractive ones (Langlois et al., 1990, 1991). Newborns look at pictures of their parents more than at pictures of strangers (de Haan & Nelson, 1997). Babies as young as three months can discern a caregiver's shift of attention by observing their eyes and then shift their own attention to the same object or event (Hood, Willen, & Driver, 1998). Also, as the photos show, babies sometimes respond to caregivers by imitating their facial expressions (pursed lips, stuck-out tongues). Research in this area with very young infants is controversial, and not all researchers are able to find consistent imitation in young infants (Abravanel & deYong, 1997; Meltzoff, 1996).

By seven months, infants know happy faces and sounds and can discriminate among them. According to Arlene Walker-Andrews (1997), they recognize emotional expressions. Using a procedure similar to Fantz's, Walker-Andrews (1986) observed five- and seven-month-old infants who saw films of people with angry or happy facial expressions making angry or happy sounds. (The lower third of each face was covered so that the infants could not match the sounds to the lips.) Walker-Andrews showed that seven-month-old infants could tell when the sound and facial expression did not match, but five-month-olds could not. This research suggests a timetable by which infants develop the ability to discriminate among facial expressions.

Infant perception is quite good; it follows a maturational timetable, but there are discontinuities in perceptual development. At first, babies attend to the most prominent features in the world; as time passes, they attend to, recognize, and respond to the world based on their recognition of people and situations—they begin to make more cognitive-based perceptual decisions (Bhatt, 1997; Bronson, 1997).

**THE VISUAL CLIFF.** Gibson and Walk conducted a classic developmental research study in 1961. They devised the *visual cliff method* to determine the extent of infants' depth perception. In this method the researcher places an infant who can crawl on a glass surface, half of which is covered with a checkerboard pattern. The same pattern is placed several feet below the transparent half of the glass surface. Infants can crawl easily from the patterned area onto the transparent area. Infants who lack depth perception should be willing to crawl onto the transparent side as often as onto the patterned side. Conversely, infants who have depth perception should refuse to crawl onto the transparent side, even when encouraged to do so by their mothers. Walk and Gibson found that nine-month-olds avoided the transparent surface, thus proving that they have depth perception.

In sum, newborns enter the world with the ability to experience, respond to, and learn from the environment. In general the sensory systems of newborns are well formed but still developing; their development is very much shaped by experience, which ultimately alters brain connections permanently (Leon, 1992). Newborns are thus genetically equipped and ready to learn, perceive, and experience the world; their brains develop, neurons interconnect, and the complexity of neuronal development continues. Recall from Chapter 3 that, although most of the connections of a newborn's visual system are present at birth, the proper functioning of the system is sensitive to and depends on experience (Wong et al., 1995) and the tasks given to the individual (Jacobs & Kosslyn, 1994). Without proper and varied perceptual experiences, less than optimal brain development occurs. Babies' development proceeds in a certain order and according to a rough timetable of developmental events during infancy and early childhood. These events are the topics considered next.

▼ Walk and Gibson designed the visual cliff method to test the extent of infants' depth perception.

**Be an ACTIVE LEARNER**

**REVIEW**
> What are the fundamental differences between the psychoanalytic and the cognitive views of development? pp. 341–342
> What is the evidence that the embryonic stage is crucial for fetal development? pp. 346–347

**THINK CRITICALLY**
> What ancient survival value might each of the primary reflexes have had?
> What survival function might infants' preferences for human faces have?

**APPLY PSYCHOLOGY**
> Using the basic concepts you now have regarding infant perception, how might you advise a toy manufacturer to design toys that would stimulate an infant's developing brain?

## The Development of Thought: Cognitive Development

Why do some automobiles have childproof locks and windows? Why do parents use gates to guard stairs and gadgets to keep kitchen cabinets closed? Why are young children's toys made so that small parts cannot come off? The answer: Children are inquisitive and much more intelligent than many people give them credit for. Even three-month-olds can learn the order of a list of items, and when given age-appropriate prompts can remember that information a day later (Gulya et al., 1998).

The physical development of infants is visible and dramatic; parents of infants will tell you that their babies seem to grow and change every day. The cognitive changes that occur in young children are less visible but no less dramatic. Children are continually developing, both physically and cognitively; they focus their attention on coping with an ever-expanding world and, as they mature, can determine causes of events. Much of this developing ability is cognitively based (Miller & Aloise, 1989). Figure 10.5 shows some of the many cognitive activities of the first 12 months. Without question, the leading figure of the twentieth century in studying and theorizing about children's and adults' cognitive development was Jean Piaget; his work laid the foundation for our current understanding of the development of thought.

**HandsOnPsych**
Version 2.0

**Development II**

### JEAN PIAGET'S INSIGHTS

Swiss psychologist Jean Piaget (1896–1980) came to believe that the fundamental development of all thought and reasoning or cognitive abilities takes place during

**1 week**

- See patterns, light, and dark
- Are sensitive to the location of a sound
- Distinguish volume and pitch
- Prefer high voices
- Will grasp an object if they touch it accidentally
- Stop sucking to look at a person momentarily

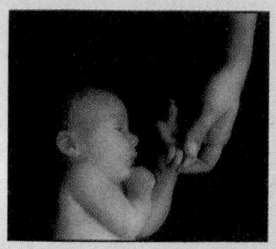

**1 month**

- Become excited at the sight of a person or a toy
- Look at objects only if in their line of vision
- Prefer patterns to plain fields
- Coordinate eyes sideways, up, and down
- Follow a toy from the side to the center of the body

**2 months**

- Prefer people to objects
- Stare at human faces; become quiet at the sound of a human voice
- Are startled at sounds and make a facial response
- Perceive depth
- Coordinate eye movements
- Reach out voluntarily instead of grasping reflexively
- Discriminate among voices, people, tastes, and objects

**3 months**

- Follow moving objects
- Glance from one object to another
- Distinguish near objects from distant objects
- Search with eyes for the source of a sound
- Become aware of self through exploration
- Show basic signs of memory

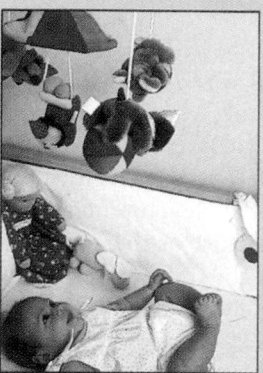

**4 to 7 months**

- See the world in color and with near-adult vision
- Pull dangling objects toward them
- Follow dangling or moving objects
- Turn to follow sound and vanishing objects
- Visually search out fast-moving or fallen objects
- Begin to anticipate a whole object when shown only part of it
- Deliberately imitate sounds and movements
- Recall a short series of actions
- Look briefly for a toy that disappears

**8 to 12 months**

- Put small objects into containers and pull them out of containers
- Search behind a screen for an object after they see it hidden there
- Hold and manipulate one object while looking at another object
- Recognize dimensions of objects

**FIGURE 10.5**

**Infants' Perceptual and Cognitive Milestones**

(After Clarke-Stewart, Friedman, & Koch, 1985, p. 191.)

the first two years of life; Piaget devised ingenious procedures for examining the mysteries of cognitive development of young children; he looked at what children did well, what mistakes they made, and generally at how they figured out the world. Piaget's theory focuses on *how* people think instead of on *what* they think, making it applicable to people in all societies and cultures. Although psychologists initially were sceptical of Piaget's ideas, and some criticisms persist, many researchers have shown that his assumptions are generally correct and can be applied cross-culturally.

There are also dissenters (notably Russian psychologist Lev Vygotsky, whose theories we will consider later), who stress the primary role that culture plays in shaping thought processes (Rogoff & Morelli, 1989). Piaget had a strong child emphasis, asserting that cognitive development grows out of the interaction between biological changes that take place within a child and a child's experience in using the mind to try to understand the world. What Piaget did best was focus on the details of a child's cognitive life; he observed them in minute detail and noticed discontinuities in children's limitations and abilities at various ages. It was from these observations that he developed his theory. Piaget's explanations of cognitive development follow the child's movement from a self-absorbed infant to an independent, thinking adolescent. He believed that this development is due to fundamental changes in how the child's thinking is organized.

KEY CONCEPTS.    Piaget believed that developmental changes in cognition occur as children try to make sense of their experiences. He called organized ways of interacting with the environment and experiencing the world **schemes**; schemes are mental structures or basic ways of knowing or making sense out of experience, that can also include actions (such as looking, reaching, and grasping). Initially, infants and toddlers develop schemes for motor behaviours, such as realizing that reaching out and touching an object will move it. Schemes develop because a child realizes that a particular action is associated with a particular outcome. Those results then, in turn, may affect the child's future behaviour and development; for example, the child learns that the amount of force he or she uses will determine how far the object will move. This entire process of constructing schemes through actions on and in the environment is called *adaptation*. As adaptation continues, a child organizes his or her schemes into more complex mental representations, linking one scheme with another. Ultimately, schemes develop about play, make-believe, and the permanence of objects, among other things. For a child to develop schemes, and for mental structures to grow more complex, two key processes must occur: assimilation and accommodation.

Both children and adults use the processes of assimilation and accommodation to deal with new information and experiences. **Assimilation** is the process by which a person absorbs new ideas and experiences and incorporates them into existing schemes. **Accommodation** is the process of modifying previously developed schemes to adapt them to new experiences. A child who learns to grasp a ball demonstrates assimilation by later grasping other round objects in a manner similar to the one used to grasp the ball. This assimilated behaviour then serves as a foundation for accommodation. The child can learn new and more complex behaviours for grasping forks, crayons, and sticks by modifying the earlier response—for example, by widening or narrowing the grasp. The two processes alternate in a never-ending cycle of cognitive growth throughout the four stages of development that Piaget described. The stages and processes involved are part of an active construction of reality and the world—babies and young children piece together their own constructions of the world, rather than directly absorb what adults teach them. Importantly, Piaget viewed children as active in their own cognitive development and therefore not simply as passive recipients of knowledge and information.

Four *stages* of cognitive development are central to Piaget's theory. Piaget believed that just as standing must precede walking, each stage of cognitive development must precede the next. For example, a preschooler does not understand the logical relationship between height and width. Therefore, even if a parent carefully measures a soft drink equally into two different-sized glasses, the preschooler feels cheated if the level of the soft drink in his shorter, wider glass is lower than that in his older brother's taller, narrower glass. The older brother understands that differences in height can compensate for differences in width and is therefore unsympathetic to the preschooler's "illogical" demand for more soda pop. Piaget's stages are

**SCHEME**

In Piaget's view, a specific mental structure; an organized way of interacting with the environment and experiencing it.

**ASSIMILATION**

According to Piaget, the process by which a person absorbs new ideas and experiences and incorporates them into existing schemes.

**ACCOMMODATION**

According to Piaget, the process of modifying previously developed schemes to adapt them to new experiences.

associated with approximate ages. The exact age for each stage varies with the individual, but children in all cultures go through the same stages in the same order. The four developmental stages he proposed are the sensorimotor stage, the preoperational stage, the concrete operational stage, and the formal operational stage.

**THE SENSORIMOTOR STAGE.**    Piaget considered the **sensorimotor stage**, which extends from birth to about age two, to be of critical importance, because the foundation for all cognitive development is established during this period. Consider the enormous changes that take place during the first two years of life. At birth an infant is a totally dependent, reflexive organism. Within weeks, infants learn some simple behaviours. They ingenuously smile at their caregivers; they attend to objects in their visual range, such as mobiles hanging overhead; they appear captured by human voices; they anticipate events in the environment, for example, by arching their backs in anticipation of being picked up. At two to three months, infants develop some motor coordination skills (Thelen, 1994; Thelan & Corbetta, 2002), a memory for past events, and an ability to predict future visual events (Gulya et al., 1998; Diedrich et al., 2001). According to Piaget, this early acquisition of memory is a crucial foundation for further cognitive development.

By the age of six to eight months, infants seek new and more interesting kinds of stimulation. They can sit up and crawl. No longer willing just to watch what goes on around them, they begin to actively manipulate their environment, attempting what Piaget called "making interesting sights last." They may throw a toy or their food onto the floor from their high chair over and over again so that they can watch the adults around them run about and react. Infants at this stage exhibit some fairly sophisticated cognitive abilities. For example, Karen Wynn (2002; Wynn, Bloom, & Chiang, 2002) suggests that infants at this age have some very basic numerical reasoning abilities that lay the foundation for further arithmetic reasoning development. At about eight months, infants can form simple intentions, and they attempt to overcome obstacles in order to reach goals. They can now crawl to the other side of a room to where the cat is lying or follow a parent into the next room.

From about eight months on, babies develop *object permanence*—the ability to realize that objects continue to exist even when they are out of sight. Prior to the development of object permanence, when an object moves out of a baby's range of sight, the baby acts as if it no longer exists. After object permanence develops, the baby can call up a mental representation or image of the vanished object and begin to develop search strategies to locate it. Infants can now begin to search in simple ways for objects that are no longer in sight because they remember that they exist. Although the exact age at which object permanence becomes evident has not yet been established, Renée Baillargeon (Hespos & Baillargeon, 2001) has shown the existence of object permanence for some tasks in four-month-olds—earlier than Piaget believed possible. Researchers assert that infants have knowledge of the physical world and that they have a specialized learning ability that guides their acquisition of such knowledge, with various aspects of object permanence evolving gradually throughout the sensorimotor stage (Meltzoff & Moore, 2001; Spelke et al., 1992; Spelke & von Hofsten, 2001). In the second half of the sensorimotor stage (from about 12 to 24 months), children begin to walk, talk, and deliberately act on their environment. Object permanence is more fully developed; the child can now follow a ball that rolls away and can search for his or her mother after she has left the room. Children also begin to use language to represent the world, an ability that allows them to create a symbol (word/idea) for an object. By age two, a child can talk about dolly, doggy, cookies, going bye-bye, and other people, objects, and events. No longer an uncoordinated, reflexive organism, the child has become a thinking, walking, talking human being.

Simultaneously, children may become manipulative and difficult to deal with. Parents often describe this stage as the terrible twos; it is characterized by the child's regular usage of the word *no!* The child's behaviour may vacillate between charming and noncompliant. This vacillation and the emergence of annoying new habits, such as being difficult to dress and bathe, are signs of normal development, marking the beginning of the stage of preoperational thought.

**THE PREOPERATIONAL STAGE.**     In the **preoperational stage**, which lasts from about age two to age six or seven, children begin to use their newfound ability to represent the world symbolically. By age two, a child can talk about Grandma, Daddy, doggy, cookies, Big Bird, going bye-bye, and other people, objects, and events. They can now engage in games of pretend (using a broom for a horse), they can defer imitation (sitting in a toy box imitating a bus driver from a trip with Grandpa two week ago), and they can use language. They are not restricted to the immediate present. No longer an uncoordinated, reflex-oriented organism, the child has become a thinking, walking, talking human being. The abilities to represent and to use symbols mark the beginning of the preoperational stage. Nonetheless, children continue to think about specifics and cannot deal with thoughts that are not easily represented visually. This can lead to faulty thinking, an example of which is outlined in *Introduction to Research Basics*.

▲ Children in the preoperational stage of development are able to engage in pretend play.

A key element of the preoperational stage—which affects a child's cognitive and emotional behaviour—is egocentrism. **Egocentrism** is the inability to perceive a situation or event except in relation to oneself. As discussed in the chapter opening, if a child has seen a toy hidden or a present wrapped, he will not be able to separate this "privileged" information (which he now knows) from what others know, and will expect others to know where to look for the hidden toy or the contents of what is in the wrapped package. For example, because of cognitive immaturity, a young child talking on the phone will answer questions by nodding her head in silence. The child still cannot put herself in the caller's (or anyone else's) position. Egocentrism also leads children at this stage to interpret the world entirely from their own perspective.

Piaget used a related term, **centration**, to refer to the consistent tendency for preoperational children to become *centred* or exclusively focused on one salient feature or dimension of the situations they encounter. As in the conservation problem shown in Figure 10.6, preoperational children centre upon the height of a liquid in a taller, thinner glass and decide that it has more liquid in it than a shorter, wider glass.

Piaget also claimed that preoperational children engage in **animistic thinking**, in which they attribute intentions or animate qualities to some objects or events. For example, they might say that the sun rises because it *wants to* or they may believe that their dreams happen in their rooms around them when they are asleep. This may explain why they sometimes believe that there are monsters in their closets or under their beds. If they have just dreamt about them and have just woken up, how far could such a being have gotten?

Piaget further held that children's understanding of space and their construction of alternative visual perspectives is limited during the preoperational stage. Recent evidence, however, suggests that Piaget may have underestimated the visual perspective abilities of children by using tasks that were too complex. For example, Piaget asked children about what a doll would see when it was placed on the other side of a detailed model of three mountains. He claimed that children either were confused about what the doll would see or attributed their own view to the doll. When much simpler displays are used (for example, three Disney character dolls arranged in a simple circle) children as young as three years of age show a rudimentary grasp of what someone seated opposite them would see and how it would differ from what they themselves see. Research now shows that even 3-year-olds can solve certain visual and spatial perspective problems previously thought to be solely in the domain of 7- to 10-year-olds (Newcombe & Huttenlocher, 2000).

**PREOPERATIONAL STAGE**
Piaget's second stage of cognitive development (lasting from about age two to age six or seven), during which initial symbolic thought is developed.

**EGOCENTRISM**
[ee-go-SENT-rism]
The inability to perceive a situation or event except in relation to oneself.

**CENTRATION** [sent-RAY-shun]
The tendency to focus on or reason with only the single most salient feature of a task or situation.

**ANIMISTIC THINKING**
The attribution of intentions or animate qualities to some objects or events

## INTRODUCTION TO Research Basics

### Understanding the Danger

According to Piaget's theory of cognitive development, children have cognitive limitations during the preoperational stage. These limitations prevent children from having a full understanding of many concepts, and Lockman and Summers (1999) believed that these cognitive limitations would influence children's understanding of poison and its dangers.

**Design.** Lockman and Summers designed a **cross-sectional study**, a type of research design that compares individuals of different ages to determine how they differ on a particular important dimension. Cross-sectional studies are one way to study age-related differences (see p. 343 for more on this method and another way to research age-related differences).

**Hypothesis.** Lockman and Summers hypothesized that younger children would have a less complete understanding of the concept of poison than do older children.

**Participants.** Of the 426 children who participated, 189 were four years old and 237 were seven years old. None of these children had experienced any type of education about poison.

**Procedure.** The researchers asked the children two questions about poison: They asked for the definition of poison and whether or not there was any poison in the children's homes.

**Results.** The four-year-olds and seven-year-olds showed different understandings of the concept of poison. This difference was not large in terms of the definition—76.4 percent of four-year-olds and 96.4 percent of seven-year-olds were able to define or give an example of poison. However, 86.8 percent of the younger children said that they did not know whether any poison existed in their homes or believed that none was present; only 8 percent of the older children shared this opinion.

**Conclusions.** Although young children may learn the definition of poison and be able to say that poison is dangerous, their cognitive limitations prevent them from fully realizing the immediacy of the dangers they face. Both parents and poison prevention educators need to understand children's cognitive capabilities to protect children more effectively.

---

**CROSS-SECTIONAL STUDY**

A type of research design that compares individuals of different ages to determine how they differ on a particular important dimension.

**CONCRETE OPERATIONAL STAGE**

Piaget's third stage of cognitive development (lasting from approximately age 6 or 7 to age 11 or 12), during which the child develops the ability to understand constant factors in the environment, rules, and higher-order symbolism.

**CONSERVATION**

The ability to recognize that perceptual changes (such as the "shape" of a liquid put in a different container) may not indicate that an underlying quality has changed (for example, the liquid still has the same weight, substance, and volume).

**THE CONCRETE OPERATIONAL STAGE.** The **concrete operational stage** is Piaget's third stage of cognitive development, lasting from approximately age 6 or 7 to age 11 or 12; during this stage, a child develops the ability to understand the basic logic of such things as the constant factors in the environment, rules, and higher-order symbolic systems such as arithmetic and geography. Children in this stage can look at a situation from more than one viewpoint. They have gained sufficient mental maturity to be able to *decentre* or to distinguish between appearance and reality and to think ahead one or two moves in checkers or other games. During this stage, children discover constancy in the world; they learn rules and understand the reasons for them. For example, a child learns not to build a sandcastle right at the water's edge, because the rising tide will inevitably destroy it. Cognitive and perceptual abilities continue to develop as children mature and, slowly and in different ways, begin to grasp ever more difficult concepts.

The hallmark of this stage is an understanding of **conservation**—the ability to recognize that objects can be transformed in some way, visually or physically, yet still be the same in number, weight, substance, or volume. This concept has been the subject of considerable research. In a typical conservation task, a child is shown three beakers or glasses. Two are short and squat and contain the same amount of liquid (water or juice); the other is tall, narrow, and empty (see Figure 10.6). While the child watches, the experimenter pours the liquid from one short, squat glass into the tall, narrow one and asks the child, "Which glass has more juice?" A preoperational child, who does not understand the principle of conservation will claim that the taller glass contains more, because the water is "more taller." A child who is able to conserve liquid quantity will recognize that the same amount of liquid is in both the tall and the short glasses.

FIGURE 10.6
**Development of
Conservation**

Conservation is the ability to
recognize that an object that has
been transformed is still the same
object, regardless of any changes it
has undergone.

1. A child examines two glasses of juice and sees that they are the same.

2. A researcher pours the contents of one glass into a taller and narrower glass.

3. The child is asked to choose the glass that has "more" in it. Children who have not yet developed the ability to conserve choose the taller glass and often declare, "It has more in it; it's bigger."

A child who has mastered one type of conservation (for example, conservation of liquid quantity) often cannot immediately transfer that knowledge to other conservation tasks. For example, the child may not understand that two stacked weights weigh the same as the two weights placed side by side. A child who masters the concept of conservation realizes that specific facts are true because they follow logically, not simply because they are observed. Thus, the child infers that the tall glass *must* contain the same amount of liquid as the short glass because no liquid was added or taken away when the contents of the short glass were poured into the tall one. Other examples of their new logical abilities include knowing that if A > B and B > C then A > C, not being confused by that fact that their fathers are also their grandfathers' sons, or knowing that they can mentally reverse actions. Thus, if you know how to get to a new school, you will also know how to get home again.

**THE FORMAL OPERATIONAL STAGE.**     The **formal operational stage** is Piaget's fourth and final stage of cognitive development (beginning at about age 12), during which the individual can think hypothetically, can consider all future possibilities, and is capable of deductive logic. Unlike children in the concrete operational stage, whose thoughts are still tied to immediate situations, adolescents can engage in abstract thought. They do this by forming hypotheses that allow them to think of different ways to represent situations, organizing them into all possible relationships and outcomes. The cognitive world of adolescents is full of informal theories of logic and ideas about themselves and life; they now can undertake scientific experiments where they form and test hypotheses.

By age 12, about the beginning of adolescence, the egocentrism of the sensorimotor and preoperational stages has for the most part disappeared, but another form of egocentrism has developed. According to Inhelder and Piaget (1958), "The adolescent goes through a phase in which he [or she] attributes an unlimited power to his [or her] own thoughts so that the dream of a glorious future or of transforming the world through ideas (even if this idealism takes a materialistic form) seems to be not only fantasy, but also an effective action which in itself modifies the empirical world" (pp. 345–346). The egocentrism and naive hopes of adolescents

FORMAL OPERATIONAL STAGE
Piaget's fourth and final stage of
cognitive development (beginning
at about age 12), during which the
individual can think hypothetically,
can consider all future possibilities, and is capable of deductive
logic.

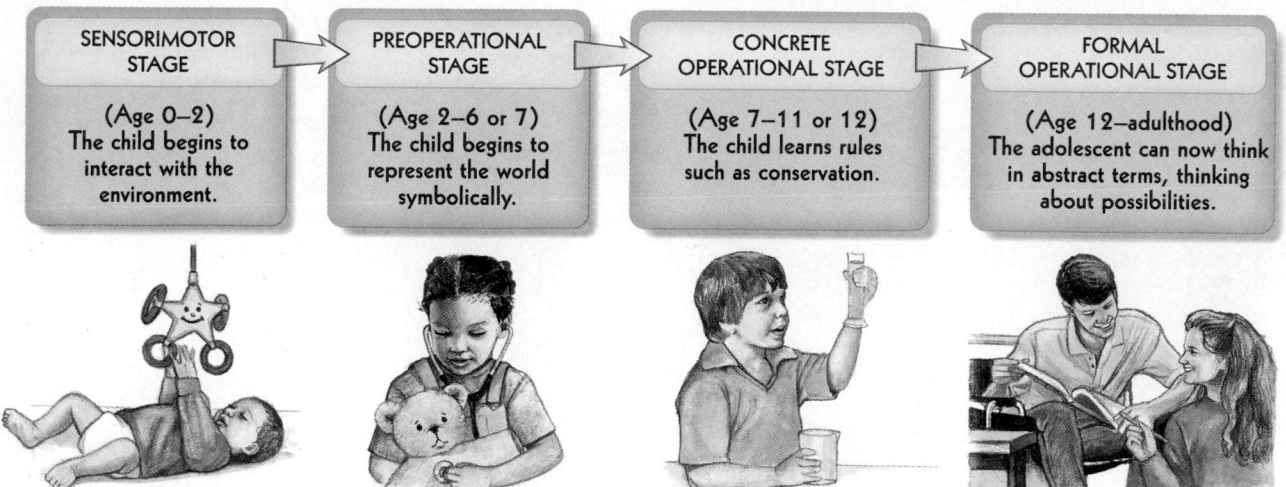

| SENSORIMOTOR STAGE | PREOPERATIONAL STAGE | CONCRETE OPERATIONAL STAGE | FORMAL OPERATIONAL STAGE |
|---|---|---|---|
| (Age 0–2) The child begins to interact with the environment. | (Age 2–6 or 7) The child begins to represent the world symbolically. | (Age 7–11 or 12) The child learns rules such as conservation. | (Age 12–adulthood) The adolescent can now think in abstract terms, thinking about possibilities. |

FIGURE 10.7
Piaget's Stages of Cognitive Development

eventually decrease as they face and deal with the challenges of life. Piaget's stages of cognitive development are summarized in Figure 10.7.

**PUTTING PIAGET IN PERSPECTIVE.** Parents, educators, and psychologists can enhance children's cognitive development by understanding how cognitive abilities develop. For example, Piaget recognized that parental love and parent–child interactions are always important to a child's development, but he asserted that they are *essential* in the first two years of life. For a child to develop object permanence, to learn how to make interesting sights last, and to develop the rudiments of numerical reasoning, it is necessary for caregivers to provide abundant physical and cognitive stimuli, especially stimuli that move and change colour, shape, and form. Research confirms that children and animals given sensory stimulation from birth through the early months develop more quickly both cognitively and socially than those who are not given such stimulation. Parents and educators who agree with Piaget have devoted their efforts to ensuring that the first years of life are ones in which stimulation is great, curiosity is encouraged, and exploration is maximized. A key to an enriched environment is that children be given the freedom to manipulate objects and see them from multiple vantage points; expensive toys are not necessary—variety is the key. Psychologists advising governments about early intervention programs such as Better Beginnings, Better Futures in Ontario agree that an enriched preschool environment could help children from disadvantaged backgrounds.

Although Piaget's ideas have had enormous influence on developmental psychology, some researchers have problems with his approach on three fronts. He may have underestimated children's cognitive development, he miscalculated the ages of stage transitions, and he placed too great an emphasis on the individual and de-emphasized the social world. Furthermore, Baillargeon (1998) has argued that infants are born with specialized learning mechanisms that allow for the acquisition of knowledge about the physical world. Other researchers agree, pointing out strong genetic effects on cognitive abilities early in development (Price et al., 2000; Rowe, Jacobson, & Van den Oord, 1999).

**INFORMATION PROCESSING THEORY.** After a great deal of interest in the implications of Piaget's big ideas for our understanding of child development, North American researchers shifted their attention toward the development of a theory of children's thinking that better fits our models of adult cognition. What was wanted was a theory that talked about how we process specific information as we solve problems and about how experience and practice help us think in more sophisticated ways but only in relation to the material we have practised. Out of this, *information processing theory* was born. This theory examines how children focus their attention, encode information, store it in memory and retrieve it later, and monitor these ongoing activities (metacognition). It does not assume that development proceeds in general universal stages but rather that children become more sophisticated by building specific knowledge bases. Chi (Chi & Koeske, 1983; Chi & Hutchinson, 1989) has studied how the memories and information processing strategies of experts in a particular knowledge area are far more mature than those of novices who do not know the area well, and indeed more mature than the experts' memories and strategies in areas outside of their expertise. Some children, for example, become experts in dinosaurs, able to stroll through the Royal Tyrrell Museum in Alberta and identify and provide the Latin name of every dinosaur skeleton displayed there. Their expertise, however, is limited to dinosaurs.

## VYGOTSKY'S SOCIOCULTURAL THEORY: AN ALTERNATIVE TO PIAGET

Piaget saw the child as an organism that is self-motivated to abstract reality from the world. The child, he held, is a busy constructor of reality, making interesting sights last, inventing games, and learning abstract rules. However, Lev Vygotsky (1896–1934) saw the child not as alone in this task but as part of a social world filled with communication with the self and others. For Vygotsky, children are constantly trying to extract meaning from the social world and mastering higher-order concepts, and are aided in this by the ways in which their experiences are structured by parents, teachers, siblings, peers, and others (Bruner, 1997). At first, children's mental life expresses itself in interaction with other people. Later, children engage in *private speech* (speech out loud, but to themselves) to plan and guide their own actions and behaviour; when they use such speech, they do better in various tasks (Bivens & Berk, 1990; Winsler, Carleton, & Barry, 2000). It is important to note that Piaget believed that private speech was egocentric, did not involve perspective taking, and therefore had no communicative intent or more general purpose. Vygotsky suggests just the opposite; private speech is essential in that it is self-directive and thus helps a child understand his or her world and that of other people. Think of the last time you engaged in a complex task—for example, putting something together or playing a video game—and admit that you may have been talking to yourself a bit at the time. For Vygotsky (1962), even the earliest speech is essentially social and useful; in fact, he asserts that social speech comes first, followed by private speech, then inner speech (fully internalized speech). Vygotsky wrote that "the most significant moment in the course of intellectual development . . . occurs . . . when speech and practical activity, two previously completely independent lines of development, converge" (Vygotsky, 1978, p. 24).

▼ Vygotsky's work focused on the importance of verbal interchange.

To a great extent, Vygotsky focused much of his writing on trying to understand what he called *culturally patterned dialogue*. Vygotsky emphasized extracting meaning from the world, especially through verbal (social) interchanges, and he particularly tried to examine the culture, situation, and context through which meaning is extracted. Vygotsky's approach can be considered *sociocultural* (Bruner, 1997), as it focuses on the social and cultural roots of human knowledge and development.

Vygotsky was especially concerned with how other people provide information about culture to children. From a Vygotsky perspective, skills and knowledge are culture bound (Meadows, 1998). He held that when children are presented with tasks that are just outside of their current abilities, they need the help of culture and society—usually parents—to accomplish them. Vygotsky referred to the *zone of proximal development* as the difference between what children can do on their own and what they can accomplish with the aid of a parent, teacher, sibling, or peer (or a large purple dinosaur, for that matter). When more skilled individuals help a child, the child can try out new skills and eventually incorporates those new skills and ideas into his or her repertoire of behaviour. The child can engage in an interactive process that can also be referred to as *scaffolding*, where one person sets a structure for another that enables that person to succeed at a task he or she could not accomplish alone. As a child learns, the adult gradually removes the scaffolding and makes the task slightly harder or more complicated so that the child learns the next rules of engagement. This interactive, collaborative process leads to developmental advancement for the child (Meadows, 1998; Stringer, 1998).

## THEORY OF MIND

Piaget investigated how and when children develop intellectual abilities; Vygotsky extended the study of children's intellectual development by considering its social context. Recently, developmental theorists have been focusing on how and when children acquire theories about causation, including the causes of human behaviour.

Adults use their knowledge of the world to construct informal and formal theories to explain behaviour, both other people's and their own. Adults are aware of their theories of human behaviour and can articulate them: They say that people do what they do because of internal mental states, such as desires and beliefs. Joe climbed up on the kitchen counter because he "wanted" cookies; Jill looked for her glasses in the study because she "thought" she left them on her desk. Thus, adults possess and apply a **theory of mind**—an understanding of mental states such as feelings, desires, beliefs, and intentions and of the causal role they play in human behaviour.

When do children first develop a theory of mind? Research indicates that children have little awareness of their own and other people's mental processes until about age three, but it does develop at about this point (Wellman, Phillips, & Rodriguez, 2000). A typical research study in this area focuses on a situation such as this: A child and two adults are in a room, with some object such as a ball in a box. One adult leaves the room, and the other moves the object, into a basket, for example. The child is then asked where the person who left the room will expect the object to be when he or she returns. A child who has developed a theory of mind will correctly predict that the person will look for the object where it last was (in the box), because the person will believe that it should still be there, not knowing it was moved. A younger child, who has not yet developed a theory of mind, will say that the person coming back into the room will look for the object in its new location (in the basket). Before the age of two or three, children are not able to set aside their own knowledge of the situation and realize that the person who left the room does not know that the object was moved. Developmental researchers say that these children don't yet have a theory of mind.

The concept of theory of mind has stimulated many lines of research, including studies of infant and child attention, infant desires, and the role of brain development in cognitive maturation. However, according to some researchers acquisition of a theory of mind is not an automatic developmental process. Astington (1999) asserts that children do not acquire such an understanding on their own; rather, through participation in social activities, they come to share their culture's way of seeing and talking about people's relations to one another and to the world. How and when children develop a theory of mind is partly determined by their interactions with others, especially family—a key variable in the development of intelligence (Cutting & Dunn, 1999). But it develops in all cultures, although not necessarily at the same pace (Tardif & Wellman, 2000). Thus, the notion that social relationships play a crucial role in cognitive development—which, as we saw earlier, was first introduced by Vygotsky—continues to influence developmental theory and research. As the next section shows, the psychologists who advised the federal government to begin Project Head Start in the 1960s, and who continue to advise on many ongoing programs, agreed that an enriched social environment can help children develop cognitively.

## THOUGHT IN A SOCIAL CONTEXT

Does growing up in an enriched environment facilitate learning and discovery? Can identifying children who are at risk for suboptimal development early on and providing support to their families improve the odds that the children will develop and do well when they reach school? Today there are many programs that seek to provide the support to families and the enrichment to children necessary to help maximize children's developmental outcomes. In a way, it all began in the United States with Project Head Start, which was initiated in the 1960s in an effort to break the poverty cycle by raising the social and educational competency of economically disadvantaged preschool children. Today, Head Start programs enrol more than 800 000 children a year in North America, most of them from the neediest families (Schnur, Brooks-Gunn, & Shipman, 1992). Health Canada is currently involved in funding a number of Head Start programs across the country.

In Head Start, children attend a school with a low teacher–student ratio and are provided with nutritional and medical services. Children receive focused, individual attention; efforts are made to build their self-confidence and self-esteem. The emphasis is on basic skills that may lead to more complex learning strategies, and preschoolers experience the joy of learning. Parent involvement is central; parents work on school boards and in the classroom and also receive related social services such as family counselling. Long-term follow-up studies have consistently shown that Head Start works and that children who have gone through Head Start are more likely to finish school and go on to post-secondary education and less likely to become involved in the criminal justice system. This has also been found to be true for a number of other early intervention programs, some beginning with prenatal contact with prospective parents and/or providing home visitation support in an effort to help new parents adjust to roles and connect with family resources in their communities. Ramey and colleagues (1999) outline several important findings: Interventions need to begin early in development and continue for a long period of time; intensive programs (more hours per week) are better than nonintensive ones; direct intervention (rather than intervention through parental training) works best; programs that use multiple routes to enhance development are especially effective; individual differences must be emphasized, and so it is essential to find the right fit between children and programs; and environmental support at home and in the community is necessary for lasting and effective early intervention.

In 2001, the federal government, through the Department of Human Resources Development Canada, committed $2.2 billion in support of early childhood development. The money is to be administered by the provinces. Ontario, for example, has formed an Early Years Plan to ensure that the early childhood development money is deployed effectively. In most provinces and territories the money is going to support a range of early childhood programs including early intervention, home visitation, Head Start, child care, and family resource centres. If you are interested, see if you can find out how the early childhood development initiative money is being spent in your province and community.

**Be an ACTIVE LEARNER**

**REVIEW**
> What is the difference between assimilation and accommodation? p. 353
> From Piaget's point of view, why are the first two years a critical time for cognitive development? p. 358
> How is Vygotsky's approach different from Piaget's? pp. 359–360

**THINK CRITICALLY**
> Assuming that Piaget did in fact overestimate the extent of egocentrism in young children, what might be another explanation for apparently egocentric behaviour in a child?
> What are the implications of Vygotsky's view that the most significant moment in intellectual development occurs when speech and practical activity converge?
> Describe how you might use scaffolding to teach a child a game.

**APPLY PSYCHOLOGY**
> If you have access to a preschool child, try out the conservation task. Make it a sort of game, but ask the child questions while running through the procedure and try to understand how he or she sees the liquid and its transformation from one glass to another.

# Moral Reasoning

Few children make it to adolescence without squabbling with their siblings. The adult in charge usually tells them to stop fighting with their sister or brother and announces that such behaviour is "unacceptable." As children grow, they develop the capacity to assess for themselves what is right and wrong. From childhood on, individuals develop **morality**—a system of learned attitudes about social practices, institutions, and individual behaviour that allows a person to evaluate situations and behaviour as being right or wrong, good or bad.

Children learn from their parents the behaviours, attitudes, and values considered appropriate and correct in their family and culture. Morality is also nurtured by teachers, by religious and community leaders, and by friends. Research by Larry Walker at the University of British Columbia and others indicates that morality is especially nurtured by daily interactions with caregivers in dialogues and conversations large and small (Laible & Thompson, 2000; Walker, Hennig, & Krettenauer, 2000). As children mature, they acquire attitudes that accommodate an increasingly complex view of reality. Your moral views when you were a 10-year-old probably differ from your views today.

## PIAGET AND KOHLBERG

Piaget examined children's ability to analyze questions of morality and found the results to be consistent with his ideas about cognitive development. Piaget's theory of moral development was based on descriptions of how children responded to specific kinds of questions about moral situations and the ages at which they gave different answers. Young children's ideas about morality are based on what others (their parents) tell them is right or wrong (called *heteronomous*, meaning directed by someone else); young children expect that immediate consequences will follow any transgression. When playing a game, a young child pays only passing attention to the rules and tends to focus on outcome, that is, on who wins and who loses. Older children, on the other hand, recognize that rules are established to regulate social interaction. Older children have developed a sense of *moral autonomy* (meaning self-directed morality), which allows them to recognize that situational factors affect perceptions and that if they play by the rules all involved should recognize that the game proceeded "fairly" despite who wins (Piaget, 1932).

According to Piaget, as children develop cognitively, their moral judgments move away from inflexibility and toward relativity (to context). When young children are questioned about lying, for example, they respond that it is always bad under any circumstances—a person should never lie. Between the ages of 5 and 12, however, children recognize that lying may be permissible in special circumstances—for example, when you lie to a bully so that he will not hurt your friend or when you lie to avoid hurting someone else's feelings.

The research of Harvard psychologist Lawrence Kohlberg (1927–1987) grew out of Piaget's work both on moral development and on general cognitive development. Kohlberg believed that moral development in general proceeds through three levels, each of which is divided into two stages (though he eventually dropped the sixth stage, as he could not find a significant number of people who used it consistently). The central concept in Kohlberg's theory is *justice*, the idea that morality ultimately comes down to a principled balance of individual rights and responsibilities. In his studies of moral reasoning, Kohlberg presented moral dilemmas to people of various ages and asked them to describe what the stories meant to them and how they felt about them (Kohlberg, 1969). Kohlberg believed that the ways people reasoned about their response was more important than the content of what they actually said. Table 10.4 shows how Kohlberg's theory of moral development and Piaget's theories of moral and cognitive development compare.

MORALITY

A system of learned attitudes about social practices, institutions, and individual behaviour that allows a person to evaluate situations and behaviour as being right or wrong, good or bad.

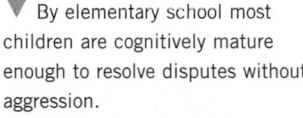
▼ By elementary school most children are cognitively mature enough to resolve disputes without aggression.

**TABLE 10.4** A Comparison of Piaget's Cognitive and Moral Theories and Kohlberg's Theory on Moral Development

| Piaget | | Kohlberg |
| --- | --- | --- |
| **Cognitive** | **Moral** | **Moral** |
| Sensorimotor and pre-operational (birth to 6 or 7 years) | Heteronomous morality | *Level 1—Preconventional morality*<br><br>Stage 1: Obedience and punishment orientation<br><br>Stage 2: Naively egoistic orientation |
| Concrete operational (7 to 11 or 12 years) | Autonomous morality | *Level 2—Conventional morality*<br><br>Stage 3: Good-child orientation<br><br>Stage 4: Authority-and–social order maintaining orientation |
| Formal operations (12 years and beyond) | | *Level 3—Postconventional morality*<br><br>Stage 5: Contractual–legalistic orientation<br><br>Stage 6: Conscience or principle orientation |

**THREE LEVELS OF MORALITY.** In one of Kohlberg's stories, Heinz, a poor man, considers stealing a drug for his wife, who will die without it. Presented with the story of Heinz, people at level 1, *preconventional morality*, either condemn Heinz's behaviour or justify it based on what he gets out of it (for example, prison time or a wife that lives). People at level 2, *conventional morality*, have internalized society's rules and say that Heinz broke the law by stealing and should go to jail or that the marital contract obliges him to do all he can to save his wife. Only people who have reached level 3, *postconventional morality*, can see that although Heinz's action was illegal, it may be justified on the principled grounds that the right to life takes precedence over rights to property (see Figure 10.8).

As individuals move toward level 3, *postconventional morality*, they become more able to move beyond fixed rules and laws and focus on principles. The principles at

**FIGURE 10.8**

**Development of Morality over Time**

In Kohlberg's theory of morality, a distinct progression of moral development emerges over a child's life. Children do not often achieve the highest, or postconventional, levels of moral reasoning.

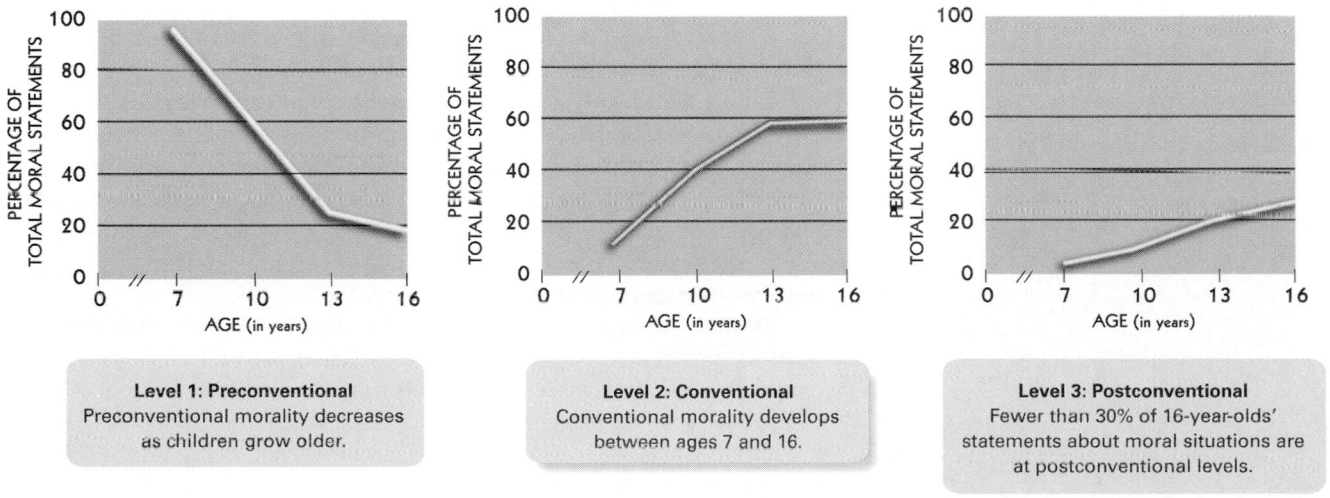

**Level 1: Preconventional**
Preconventional morality decreases as children grow older.

**Level 2: Conventional**
Conventional morality develops between ages 7 and 16.

**Level 3: Postconventional**
Fewer than 30% of 16-year-olds' statements about moral situations are at postconventional levels.

issue here are the sort found in documents such as the Canadian Charter of Rights and Freedoms. In level 3 morality, people make judgments on the basis of their perception of the needs of society, with the goal of maintaining community welfare and order. Only a minority reaches level 3. In advanced stages of level 3, people make judgments on the basis of personally constructed moral principles, rather than societal teachings.

Being capable of the highest level of moral reasoning does not guarantee that people will always operate at that level. Research conducted at the University of British Columbia by Brian de Vries and Lawrence Walker (1986) indicates that when thinking about issues such as capital punishment, about one-quarter of participants used reasoning that was a full stage lower than their highest possible stage. Much research is being done to determine what influences people's moral reasoning. Lawrence Walker (Walker & Pitts, 1998) has shown that, in addition to cognitive developmental advancement, the more advanced stages can also include aspects of virtue and religiosity, suggesting that there are a number of influential factors in moral development.

## GENDER DIFFERENCES? GILLIGAN'S WORK

Criticisms of Kohlberg's pioneering research came from Carol Gilligan (1982, 1994, 1997), who found that people look at more than justice when they analyze moral conflicts. Though Kohlberg and his colleagues generally had not reported differences between males and females, Gilligan did. She found that females are more concerned with caring, relationships, and connections with other people—she hypothesized a feminine orientation to moral issues. As younger children, girls are socialized toward a morality of caring, whereas boys are socialized toward a morality of justice. Drawing on work by Nancy Chodorow (1978), Gilligan asserts that the difference between boys and girls is established by gender socialization and by the child's relationship with the mother. Where children spend more time with their mothers or other female caregivers during their preschool years, Gilligan argues that boys, who have identified with their fathers as being male, work at being essentially different from the female adults who are caring for them. This establishes autonomy, assertiveness, and self-interest as central developmental goals. By identifying with their female caregivers, girls do not have to sever the close social ties that developed between them during the dependency of infancy and develop a sense of self based on those and other connections and relationships.

Gilligan asserts that the transition to adolescence is a crucial time, during which girls may develop their own voice—a voice based on caring and connection that too often is muted and suppressed (Gilligan, 1997). Gilligan shows that boys respond to Kohlberg's Heinz dilemma by indicating that sometimes people must act on their own to do the right thing. Girls, in contrast, are more likely to look for ways to discuss differences and seek compromise. Gilligan argued that this caring perspective might cause girls to score lower than boys on Kohlberg's Moral Judgment Interview. Further, she argues that the development of caring follows a time line, with caring initially felt only toward oneself, later felt toward others, and ultimately (in some people) a more mature stage of caring for truth. Gilligan's work has been influential with respect to psychologists' evaluations of morality, yet there is concern that her approach perpetuates gender stereotyping—women as nurturing, men as logical.

Despite widespread acceptance of Gilligan's view that Kohlberg's work is biased against women, there exists surprisingly little research examining just how these two models might function in normal development (Fisher & Bredemeier, 2000; Miller & Bersoff, 1999). There are data to suggest that the verbal responses given to the moral dilemmas are only moderately associated with actual behavioural responses in real life (Carpendale, 2000).

Be an
**ACTIVE LEARNER**

**REVIEW**
> Summarize the differences that characterize Kohlberg's pre-conventional, conventional, and postconventional levels of morality. pp. 363–364
> What is Gilligan's main criticism of Kohlberg's work? p. 364

**THINK CRITICALLY**
> If research on morality were done with a wide range of populations, what differences might emerge—for example, among French Canadian, Asian Canadian, and European Canadian groups?
> If morality is nurtured by teachers and by religious and community leaders, what might happen to children when one of those individuals is found to have betrayed his or her moral authority?

**APPLY PSYCHOLOGY**
> What can you as an individual do to foster a higher level of moral reasoning among your peers?

# Emotional Development

Anne Frank, the young Jewish girl who was hidden for a time from the Nazis during the Second World War, was eloquently thankful in the diary that survived her to the people who helped hide her and her family. She wrote extensively about all of her feelings—her hopes and fears, as well as her gratitude toward the people who were making sacrifices and putting their own lives at risk to help her family. Her attachment to her family and her emotional ties to those around her were evident. We do not grow and develop in isolation. We form connections to and interact with many others. Social and emotional developmental experience is essential for healthy development.

## ATTACHMENT: THE EARLIEST EMOTIONS

**Attachment** is the formal term psychologists use to describe the strong emotional tie that a person feels toward significant others. Attachment theory plays an important role in the emotional development of children. People's ability to express emotion and form attachments develops from birth through adulthood. Attachment behaviours develop in the early weeks and months of life and are evident during adolescence and adulthood, when people form close loving bonds with others. Most researchers consider these behaviours to be innate, even though they unfold slowly over the first year of life and are reinforced by caregivers. Emotional expressions—including attachment behaviours—not only appear in all cultures (see Chapter 9) but are found in deaf and blind people and in people without limbs, who have limited touch experiences (Izard & Saxton, 1988). Attachment, emotional expressions, and the bonds that form among people have been studied in depth. Heavily influenced by classic early work with rhesus monkeys done by Harry Harlow, this research was extended in the 1970s by later work on bonding.

**CLASSIC WORK: ATTACHMENT IN RHESUS MONKEYS.** To find out how people develop attachment behaviours, Harry Harlow (1905–1981), a psychologist at the University of Wisconsin, focused on the development of attachment in rhesus monkeys. In a classic experiment, Harlow placed infant monkeys in cages along with two wire-covered shapes resembling adult monkeys. One figure was covered with terry cloth; the other was left bare. Both figures could be fitted with bottles to provide milk. In some cases, the wire figure had the bottle of milk; in other cases, the terry-cloth figure had the bottle. Harlow found that the infant monkeys clung to the terry-cloth figures whether or not they provided milk. As well, they rushed to the terry-cloth figure whenever they were frightened or anxious, a clear sign of attachment. Harlow concluded that the wire figure, even with a bottle of milk, could not provide the comfort that the terry-cloth figure could provide (Harlow & Zimmerman, 1958).

However, Harlow also found that none of the monkeys grew up to be totally normal. They were more aggressive and fearful than monkeys raised normally. They also were unable to engage in normal sexual relations. Some of the infants raised with artificial mothers exhibited self-destructive behaviours (Harlow, 1962). Importantly, Harlow was able to demonstrate in another series of experiments that these anti-social behaviours could be modified or eliminated if the baby monkeys were allowed to engage in regular play periods with younger peers.

**BONDING.** In the 1970s and 1980s, it was widely, though incorrectly, believed that parents bond to their infants soon after delivery. **Bonding** is a special process of emotional attachment that may occur between parents and babies in the minutes and hours immediately after birth. It is neither a reflex nor a learned behaviour.

**Development II**

ATTACHMENT

The strong emotional tie that a person develops toward significant others.

▼ Baby rhesus monkeys preferred the terry-cloth mother whether "she" fed the baby or not.

BONDING

A special process of emotional attachment that may occur between parents and babies in the minutes and hours immediately after birth.

Pediatricians Marshall Klaus and John Kennell (1983) argued that a mother is in a state of heightened sensitivity to her child immediately after delivery and that she begins to form a unique, specific attachment to the child at that time. However, research has not supported claims for bonding. Eyer (1992) asserts that there is no evidence to support the existence of bonding and that, for humans at least, it is a fictional concept.

ATTACHMENT IN INFANTS.    John Bowlby (1907–1990) studied the close attachment between mothers and their newborns. Bowlby (1977) argued that an infant's emotional tie with its caregiver is innate and evolves as a set of behavioural responses that promote survival. Bowlby asserted that an infant's very early interactions with its parents are crucial to normal development. In support of this view, research now shows that mothers recognize their newborns by smell, touch, and sound (Kaitz et al., 1992), and that newborn infants similarly recognize their mothers (Leon, 1992). Many psychologists consider the establishment of a close and warm parent–child relationship to be one of the major developmental milestones of the first year of life. This attachment is considered to be a key developmental event that helps an infant develop basic feelings about trust and security.

By the age of seven or eight months, after achieving object permanence, attachment to the mother may become so strong that her departure from the room causes a fear response, especially to strangers; this response is known as *separation anxiety* and reflects insecurity on the part of the infant. When infants fear that their principal caregiver, usually the mother, may not be consistently available, they become clingy and object to her disappearing (Ainsworth, 1979; Bowlby, 1988; Cassidy & Berlin, 1994). Infants also may demonstrate a heightened fear of strangers at this time. In attempting to analyze attachment to parents, influential research conducted in Canada by Mary Ainsworth used a procedure called the *strange situation technique*, in which babies from 12 to 24 months of age are observed with parents, removed briefly from them, and then reunited. Research with this technique shows that most babies (about 60 percent) are secure; they are distressed by a parent leaving but are easily comforted. Other babies (about 20 percent) are neither distressed by separations nor comforted by reunions—these babies are categorized as *avoidant* and are considered to have an insecure attachment. Still other babies (about 15 percent) are *resistant*; these babies seek closeness to the parent but when separated are angry and then show mixed feelings of both anger and proximity seeking when they are reunited (Ainsworth, Blehar, Waters, & Wall, 1978). Lastly, some babies (about 5 percent) are characterized as *disoriented*; they show confused, contradictory attachment behaviours and may act angry, sad, or ambivalent at any time (Main & Soloman, 1990). Although attachment theory has been criticized for being largely based on behaviours observed during stressful situations that are somewhat artificial (Field, 1996), it is nevertheless a good predictor of later developmental outcomes (Ainsworth, 1989; Brennan & Shaver, 1996). Moreover, there are cross-cultural differences in attachment and in how children respond to stressful situations (Cole, 1999).

Researchers find that time spent with babies allows secure attachments (Scher & Mayseless, 2000); secure babies have mothers who are affectionate and appropriately responsive (Isabella, Belsky, & von Eye, 1989). According to some researchers, this mother–child relationship facilitates both current behaviours and later cognitive and emotional development (Call, 1999; Cassidy & Berlin, 1994; Hewlett et al., 1998). Not all researchers agree, and cross-cultural work shows significant variations (e.g., Tronick, Morelli, & Ivey, 1992), but studies indicate that the quality and nature of the mutual closeness formed between the young child and the mother can make a difference (Hewlett et

▲ Some children become obviously distressed when placed in a novel (new) situation.

al., 1998). Children who have not formed warm, close attachments early in life lack a sense of security and become anxious and overly dependent. As six-year-olds, they are perceived as more aggressive and less competent than their more secure counterparts (Cohn, 1990). Those who have close attachments require less discipline and are less easily distracted (Lewis & Feiring, 1989). There is evidence that early attachment relationships are predictive of other relationships as the child gets older. Ratings of older children's relationships with their mothers, for example, are positively correlated with ratings of infant attachment. Similarly, ratings of attachments with early teachers tend to predict the perceptions of later teachers. Such data led Howes, Hamilton, and Philipsen (1998) to conclude that early attachments exist in a wide variety of domains and affect later development. An important study of Canadian families conducted by Sarah Landy and Kwok Kwan Tam (1998) found that positive parenting practices acted as a protective factor for children living in at-risk environments. If a child's family had at least four risk factors (such as a single-parent home, a dysfunctional or low-income family), parenting could make the difference between positive and negative outcomes.

Once established, early attachment is fairly stable. Babies are fairly resilient (Kier & Lewis, 1997) and brief separations from parents, as in child-care centres, do not adversely affect attachment. Mary Ainsworth (1979) asserts that early attachment affects the child's later friendships, relations with relatives, and enduring adult relationships; other research confirms that people's relationships as adults are related to the attachment styles they had as children (Brennan & Shaver, 1995; Clark & Shaver, 1998). Adoptive parents can form the same type of secure, close attachment to the child as biological parents. A caretaking atmosphere that is warm, consistent, and governed by the infant's needs is the key to forming a secure attachment. Both adoptive and biological parents can provide such an atmosphere, and both adoptive and biological children can form strong secure attachments to their parents (Singer et al., 1985). In recent years, large numbers of children have been adopted from orphanages in countries such as Romania. Their early experiences were far less than optimal, but following adoption by Canadian parents their circumstances improved greatly. The studies featured in *Psychology in Action* provide some insight into the effects of early experiences and changes in parenting on attachment behaviour.

**WHAT ABOUT CHILD CARE?**   According to earlier traditions, mothers were expected to provide child care. However, the trend toward mothers being employed outside the home necessitates other arrangements. Child-care situations are becoming increasingly diverse as parents seek alternative arrangements for their children, but child-care centres provide care for about 30 percent of preschool children whose mothers are employed outside the home.

Maternal employment and day care have become the topic of many heated arguments and a great deal of guilt on the part of mothers. Does the research suggest negative consequences for leaving children in the care of someone other than a parent? This question is difficult to answer because many variables influence the placement of a child into day care, including the family's economic resources (some families hire nannies rather than put children into day care), the child's age, the security of the child's attachment to parents, and the stability of the child-care arrangement. Some research has suggested negative effects of current child-care practices (Kim, 1997), but the majority of studies find minimal effects. Broberg and his colleagues (1997) assert that being in day care did not place children at any disadvantage. Other research found virtually no difference in personality or attachment between children cared for at home and children who had received day care (Erel, Oberman, & Yirmiya, 2000; NICHD Early Child Care Research Network, 1997).

A comprehensive, multi-year study by Harvey (1999) assessed the cognitive, academic, behavioural, and emotional development of more than 6000 children

## Adopted Romanian Orphans in Canada

Following the fall of the Berlin Wall and the beginning of massive social restructuring in Eastern Europe, Canadians became dramatically aware of the plight of the youngest citizens of these changing countries. Perhaps most poignant were the conditions of infants and young children living in orphanages in Romania. With birth control unavailable and abortion illegal, many parents had children they could not care for and who were thus turned over to the state (Marcovitch et al., 1994). These children were living in developmentally hazardous conditions, often with infant–caregiver ratios of between 10 and 20 to 1. They had no toys or consistent stimulation, and feedings largely were conducted by propping up a bottle or having the infants hold their own bottles. Children would spend 20 to 24 hours a day in their cribs. As Elinor Ames (1990) of Simon Fraser University observed, their living conditions amounted to severe deprivation; possibly, this represented the most extreme form of systematic deprivation ever documented. The potential negative effects of such deprivation have been studied by Bruce Perry (2002), former medical director for provincial programs in children's mental health for the Alberta Mental Health Board. Perry has examined the long-term cognitive, behavioural, emotional, social, and physiological effects of neglect and trauma in children, describing how childhood experiences—including neglect and traumatic stress—change the biology of the brain and thereby the health of the child.

The public response to descriptions and pictures of these infants was significant and rapidly led to a large number of Canadians trying to adopt Romanian children and remove them from the conditions that were threatening their short-term welfare and long-term development. Between January 1990 and April 1991, 1013 Romanian children were issued visas to come to Canada for adoption (Ames & Carter, 1992). Past research had clearly indicated that children who spent their early years in similar conditions were at increased risk for less-than-optimal developmental outcomes, even if they were eventually placed in stable family environments. What would the Canadian experience of the Romanian orphans be like? How would they fare developmentally relative to Canadian children? Would the amount of time they spent in the orphanages be related to a level of developmental delay? Would early problems diminish with time spent with Canadian adoptive families?

Follow-up studies of these children and their experiences with their Canadian adoptive families have been conducted independently by Elinor Ames and her colleagues and by Sharon Marcovitch of the Child Development Clinic at Toronto's Hospital for Sick Children. The results obtained so far have been very instructive about the effects of the early orphanage experiences, but also reasonably positive about the longer-term developmental outcomes for these children.

A key variable seems to be the amount of time the children spent in an orphanage before adoption. Generally, those adopted before six months of age (Marcovitch et al., 1994; Ames & Chisholm, 2001) and those who spent little or no time in an orphanage prior to adoption had few developmental delays upon arrival in Canada, and their adoptive parents reported fewer problems related to their care (Fischer, Ames, Chisholm, & Savoie, 1997). Children who spent more time in orphanages arrived in Canada with more medical problems and eating problems (often eating all they were offered until their parents decided they had had enough). As well, they were more likely to have sleeping problems, the most common being a tendency to lie in bed in the morning without signalling that they had awakened. They were more likely to engage in rocking behaviour, most commonly when they were tired or alone. They were more likely to have problems with siblings and peers, the most common being a tendency to withdraw from or not engage in social interaction. Overall, children who spent more time in an orphanage exhibited a range of developmental delays when compared to non-orphaned preschool children (Fischer, Ames, Chisholm, & Savoie, 1997; Marcovitch et al., 1994) and their adoptive parents showed more signs of stress (Mainemer, Gilman, & Ames, 1998).

As bleak as this may sound, the final results of these investigations are actually positive. First, it is worth noting that the vast majority of these problems were present when the children first arrived in Canada. Except with regard to medical problems, the adoptive parents coped with the children effectively on their own, and with few exceptions all reported significant improvement in all problem areas through the preschool years. While researchers will have to wait until the children enter school to get a clear picture of where they stand developmentally relative to their Canadian peers, it appears that things are headed in the right direction.

As a final note, some of the researchers in this area (Fischer, Ames, Chisholm, & Savoie, 1997) have speculated as to whether it is appropriate to characterize the pattern of problems presented by these children as reflecting developmental abnormality. They point out that a similar pattern of problem behaviour in a non-orphanage-reared child very likely would raise serious concerns about the developmental course that child was following. However, consideration of the conditions within Romanian orphanages may suggest an alternative hypothesis. Could it be that the "problem" behaviours of these children actually reflect adaptations, on their part, to a very unusual environment? For example, there would be no point in indicating they were awake if no one was going to interact with them, no reason to learn to attend to satiety cues (which indicate a person is full) when they were constantly underfed, and no reason to expect them to be able to interact with siblings and peers if they have had no experience with the sort of energetic interactions we routinely see in children. The hope is that, with the new opportunities they now have as a result of being adopted into Canadian families, these children will learn to adapt to their new, more positive environments and get back on track developmentally. There is encouraging evidence that they are doing just that.

whose parents were both employed outside the home. The study tracked 12 600 mothers and their children, interviewing them each year starting in 1979, and it concluded that there were no permanent negative effects. The large sample size and the longitudinal nature of the study make it an important piece of evidence that parental employment and child care do not have significant negative effects—if the care is of high quality. Sandra Scarr (1998, p. 95) concludes: "Widely varying qualities of child care have been shown to have only small effects on children's current development and no demonstrated long-term impact, except on disadvantaged children, whose homes put them at developmental risk."

**EVOLUTIONARY PERSPECTIVES.** In a very real sense, one of the seminal figures in attachment theory, John Bowlby, was an evolutionary psychologist. Bowlby argued that the infant's attachment with the caregiver *evolves* because it *promotes survival*. Children who have strong attachments with their parents are more likely to grow up to be confident adults, form attachments to other people, reproduce, and pass on their genes to another generation. Of course, like so many adaptations that people make, a person's environment affects how his or her biological endowment plays out. Poverty, malnutrition, war, famine, and disease can all influence childhood attachment—thus, evolutionary psychologists assert that attachment is an evolved adaptation that facilitates a reproductive strategy (see Belsky, 1999).

## TEMPERAMENT

**Temperament** refers to early-emerging and long-lasting individual differences in disposition and in the intensity and especially the quality of a person's emotional reactions. Some psychologists believe that each person is born with a specific type of temperament: easygoing, wilful, outgoing, or shy, to name a few. Newborns, infants, and children, like the adults they will eventually grow to be, are all different from one another. Generalizations from one child to all children are impossible, and even generalizations from a sample of children to all children must be made cautiously. So many variables can affect a child's growth and development that researchers have painstakingly tried to determine which variables are critical and which are less important. Thomas and Chess (1977), in their pioneering work in the New York Longitudinal Study, in which a sample of children were studied from birth into adulthood, point out that temperament is not fixed and unchangeable.

Nevertheless, along with many other researchers, they argue that temperament refers to a complex set of processes—not a single thing—and that temperament refers to the way in which behaviour is expressed, independent of the content of behaviour or the motivation for behaviour. Temperament is biologically based, moderately stable across time and over situations, but not necessarily invariant across time or situations. Further, the expression of temperament can be influenced by biological, developmental, and contextual factors. With these cautions in mind, let's look at some studies of temperament.

TEMPERAMENT
Early-emerging and long-lasting individual differences in the intensity and especially the quality of a person's emotional reactions.

▲ Are children with aggressive or difficult temperaments more likely to use and abuse drugs in their teenage and adult years? Researchers say yes.

Data from the New York Longitudinal Study show that children tend to fall into four broad categories: easy (40 percent), difficult (10 percent), slow to warm up (15 percent), and unique (35 percent). *Easy* children are happy-go-lucky and adapt easily to new situations. This type of child would react to the first day of kindergarten with interest and excitement. *Difficult* children resist environmental change and often react poorly. This type of child would react to the first day of kindergarten with fear and intense anxiety, perhaps throwing a tantrum and refusing to enter the room. *Slow-to-warm-up* children respond slowly, have low-intensity responses, and often are negative. This type of child would react to the first day of kindergarten with anxiety, clinging to the parent. Many children are *unique* and show a variety of emotional reactions.

Many researchers contend that some specific initial temperamental characteristics may be biologically based. For example, Jerome Kagan and his colleagues found that two- and three-year-olds who were *extremely* inhibited—that is, cautious and shy—tended to remain that way for four more years. They also found physiological evidence that these children may be more responsive (by showing an increase in autonomic nervous system activity, for example) to change and unfamiliarity (Kagan, 1997; Woodward et al., 2000). During the earliest months of life, some infants smile or reach out to a new face and readily accept being held or cuddled. Others are more inhibited. Still others exhibit extreme reticence, even distress, in the presence of strangers. Such xenophobic infants (those who fear strangers) may turn out to be inhibited, meek, and wavering as adults (Caspi & Roberts, 2001). Researchers know, however, that infant behaviours are not necessarily stable over time and may not be evident in later behavioural styles (except in very extreme cases—intense shyness or diffidence, for example). Further, what parents observe (social wariness with unfamiliar people) is different from the shyness that teachers observe (concern about social evaluation by peers), and so shyness—social inhibition and anxiety—varies in different situations (Eisenberg et al., 1998). The fit between the temperament of an infant and the caregiver is critical. Some caregivers can do well with a calm infant but are inundated by an irritable one. Sometimes an interaction style familiar to a caregiver from caring for other children may not suit. The shared irritation can impair good socialization.

Biological factors play a key role in shyness (McEwen, 1999). Studies of identical twins on a range of emotional dimensions, especially temperament, also show support for a strong genetic component (DiLalla & Jones, 2000; Stroganova et al., 2000; Warren, Schmitz, & Emde, 1999). Even maternal actions, such as time spent in daylight during pregnancy, may have an effect; Gortmaker and colleagues (1997) found that short exposure to daylight during pregnancy was associated with a higher likelihood of shy behaviour in offspring. Further evidence for a biological predisposition comes from studies of basic physiological responsivity—infants' heart rates in response to a distracting stimulus are known to predict temperament (Huffman et al., 1998). However, shyness is influenced by culture; in one cross-cultural study, researchers found that shyness among native Chinese students helps them gain acceptance from teachers; the opposite tends to be true for students in Western countries (Chen, 2000). Western culture also has a controversial relationship with drug treatment for many disorders (see *Point/ Counterpoint*).

In addition, shyness and other aspects of temperament can be changed; human behaviour is the product of deliberative thought processes as well as biological forces. Imagine a child who is shy or diffident and not easy to coax into social situations. Researchers today suggest that such a disposition will affect parent–child interactions and parental discipline practices, and, ultimately, the child's socialization. As Greenspan (1997) argues, the qualities we often value more than any others—empathy, creativity, honour, the ability to love and trust—stem from relationships,

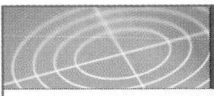

## Is Ritalin Use a Good Thing?

**POINT:** Ritalin is a useful drug that helps manage children with various disorders and helps them learn.

**COUNTERPOINT:** Ritalin is an overprescribed, powerful drug that has unwanted side effects.

Doctors prescribe it, parents pass it out to children, and school nurses supervise the administration of it because all believe the pill will calm children and stop their disruptive behaviour. Best known by the brand name Ritalin, methylphenidate (METH-el-FEN-i-date) was introduced in 1956 and is a stimulant in the same class as amphetamines. Experts agree that it affects the midbrain, the part of the brain that controls impulses.

Advocates of Ritalin assert that the drug is a blessing and that it has helped those with attention deficit/hyperactivity disorder (ADHD) concentrate. People diagnosed with ADHD are unable to sit still, plan ahead, finish tasks, or be fully aware of what's going on around them. To their family, classmates, or co-workers, they seem to exist in a cyclone of disorganized or harried activity. One of the most common mental disorders among children, it affects 3 to 5 percent of all children. Two to three times more boys than girls are affected and, on average, at least one child in every classroom needs help for the disorder (Health Canada, 1999).

Ritalin allows the patient to focus better on the task at hand (Jerome & Segal, 2001). Besides its use in treating the symptoms of ADHD, Ritalin is also prescribed for mild to moderate depression and in some cases of emotional withdrawal among elderly people. Initially Ritalin was used for children who were so restless that they were unreachable and unteachable. The National Institutes of Health (1998) support "the efficacy of stimulants and psychosocial treatments for ADHD and the superiority of stimulants relative to psychosocial treatments." The benefits of Ritalin are so strong that advocates say withholding the pills is a form of neglect. Those who claim diet, exercise, or other treatments work just as well are kidding themselves, say believers. A typical parental comment is the following:

> His homework took 3 hours—even with me helping him—to do because his mind was in the sky. He was a genius at video games, but not at homework. He was also at the point of being held back in school. He shed tears because he could not control himself; he hated the way he acted. I was always getting complaints about his spontaneous outbursts. And then he took Ritalin—and everything changed.

However, the situation is not all rosy. Critics say that doctors who work with teachers to keep boisterous children in line misdiagnose students. As awareness of ADHD has grown, the characterization of the disorder now encompasses a much broader range of behaviours—an increasing number of children seem to have conditions that meet the definition of ADHD.

Ritalin production has increased by more than 700 percent since 1990. Since then disorders for which Ritalin is prescribed have jumped an average of 21 percent per year. Researchers claim a disturbing reliance upon the drug to solve problems that have other solutions (McCubbin & Cohen, 1999).

Ritalin is a stimulant drug similar to cocaine, morphine, and methamphetamine—thus, there is potential for abuse or dependence. Ritalin is widely misused by drug addicts, and a large number of suicides and emergency room admissions are associated with it (Young, Longstaffe, & Tenenbein, 1999). Health Canada cautions that stimulant treatments may not "normalize" the entire range of behaviour problems, and children under treatment may still manifest a higher level of some behaviour problems than normal children. It also notes that there are no long-term studies testing stimulants or psychosocial treatments lasting for several years (Health Canada, 1999; also Snider, Frankenberger, & Aspenson, 2000).

Of course, an ADHD diagnosis can and often does lead to medication, special education facilities, and parental support groups. Today, children and teenagers with ADHD may be placed in a special classroom and get additional time on tests. Are the ADHD diagnosis and the Ritalin treatment being used for the wrong reasons by overzealous parents and well-meaning physicians (Pozzi, 2000)?

Is Ritalin effective? Yes, it is. Can it help children and teenagers with ADHD? Yes, it can. Are mistakes made in diagnosing ADHD? Of course. Is there overdiagnosis? Yes. Overdiagnosis usually occurs when a doctor is inexperienced, untrained, pressured, or predisposed to "find" ADHD. We need careful, controlled research into the impact and long-term effects of Ritalin—and those studies are still a few years away. We also need physician, teacher, and parent education into ADHD and the use of Ritalin.

**Be an**

## ACTIVE LEARNER

**REVIEW**
> How do psychologists know that children experience attachment? pp. 365–367
> Cite evidence that some traits, such as shyness, are inborn. p. 370

**THINK CRITICALLY**
> Describe some ways in which physical and emotional development might interact.
> What are the implications for later emotional development of cross-cultural differences in responsiveness toward infants?

**APPLY PSYCHOLOGY**
> As a parent, what critical variables might you consider if your child is prescribed Ritalin by a physician?

**HandsOnPsych**
Version 2.0

**Development II**

not genes, and from how, over time, caregivers relate to their children. Indeed, researchers assert that a child's conscience emerges because of these interactions and the growth of self-understanding (Stilwell, Galvin, & Kopta, 2000). Clearly, a child's temperament affects his or her interactions with parents in important ways and may determine in part how the parents treat the child—there is a reciprocal and mutually reinforcing influence. Parents recognize that they affect their child's temperament and personality—and they are right (Hesse & Main, 2000). They assume that their child-rearing practices strongly influence development and that a child who might be categorized as difficult by Thomas and Chess (1977) may, if treated with patience, become easy as an adolescent. But researchers also know that children with aggressive or difficult temperaments are more likely to use and abuse drugs in their teenage and adult years. Researchers are identifying temperament risk factors and behaviours that predict drug abuse (Chassin et al., 2001).

## Social Development

Any bookstore has shelves lined with how-to books on child rearing, written by physicians, parents, psychologists, and others. The variety of approaches and the number of experts show that ideas about child rearing are complicated and constantly changing. As society changes, so do beliefs and practices related to children's social development and ideas about how children form a sense of identity and self. As children move cognitively from being egocentric to a point of perceiving themselves as different from the rest of the world, they also develop the ability to think about social relationships. As we will see, children develop socially in not one but many environments.

The family is the first social environment. Regardless of culture, parents respond positively to what they judge to be good behaviours in children and negatively to bad ones. Although cultural differences exist (there is extensive scheduling of daytime childhood behaviours in France and noninterference and acceptance by Swedish parents, for example), parents worldwide respond to their children in similar ways (McDermott, 2001). Although parents exert a powerful influence on children, theirs is not the sole influence. Some such as Harris (1998) assert that a child has many environments, especially his or her play groups, that exert profound effects on social development.

### EARLY SOCIAL DEVELOPMENT AND CHILD REARING

Social development begins soon after birth, with the development of an attachment between parents and their newborn. The nature of a child's early interactions with parents is a crucial part of personality development. Infants have a great need to be hugged, cuddled, nurtured, and made to feel good. Eventually, the most important job for parents is teaching their children how to become independent and how to interact with others.

**THE ROLE OF FATHERS.** Typical patterns of how mothers and fathers interact with their children are changing. During the past three decades, women have entered the workforce in unprecedented numbers and, in so doing, have changed the structure and fabric of family life. Few fathers stay home to provide child care, but women, who traditionally did spend more time at home, are spending less time with their young children due to women's careers. Are fathers spending more of their time caring for children? Do fathers engage in basic caregiving activities, play, or both?

A father's involvement is important; his affection is important—and the research asserts that it is as important as love from mothers (Rohner, 1998; Silverstein & Auerbach, 1999). Today's fathers are more interested in their newborns and may be involved in their upbringing from the first moments of life, as evidenced by the fact that many more fathers are present in the delivery room when their children are born than was true in previous generations. In general, fathers are affectionate and responsive caregivers; they are concerned with their children's welfare (Fagan, 1997). Still, some men view parenting as a voluntary activity and themselves as helpers or assistants to their partners, whom they consider to be the primary caregivers. Fathers sometimes assert that they spend limited time with their children, but that this time is "quality" time.

Research on the quality and quantity of interactions between fathers and their children showed that some fathers spent significant time with their children, but most spent very little (Black, Dubowitz, & Starr, 1999). Some spent quality time (time devoted to active involvement with a child, as opposed to merely being present in the room with the child); others did not. Seventy-two percent had daily contact. Play turns out to be a prominent feature of the time men spent with their infants; in fact, the men were twice as likely to be involved in play as in basic caregiving activities (Hoosain & Roopnarine, 1994).

The quality of the time a father spends with his children is affected by the mother's attitudes (Beitel & Parke, 1998). For example, if mothers are highly supportive of a father's involvement, father involvement may be high or low, depending on the father, his work schedule, and his predispositions. However, if a mother opposes or does not support father involvement, the father will not be involved regardless of his individual disposition. Other factors also enter the picture, such as work schedules—a father's involvement has as much to do with each parent's work schedule as anything else (Averett, Gennetian, & Peters, 2000).

Although fathering is clearly good for children, it is also good for men—it enhances their self-esteem and feelings of competence. Children do not benefit merely from the presence of a father—fathers have to take part in family life.

**THE FIRST TWO YEARS.** In the first year of life, social interactions among children are limited; infants are largely egocentric and are basically unable to recognize any needs other than their own. By about the second half of the first year, children exhibit strong attachments to parents and other caregivers, along with fear of strangers.

As early as nine months, infants show that they like to play games by indicating their unhappiness when an adult stops playing with them (Ross & Lollis, 1987). They play by themselves, but as they grow older, especially after two years of age, they engage in more social play with other children (Howes & Tonyan, 1999).

By the end of their second year, children have begun to understand that they are separate from their parents—they are developing a sense of self. They begin to learn to interact with other people. They may play alongside other children, but they prefer to play with an adult rather than with another two-year-old—gradually, however, they begin to socialize with their peers (Howes & Tonyan, 1999).

**SHARING.** The noted pediatrician Benjamin Spock once said that the only two things children will share willingly are communicable diseases and their mother's age. Actually, from age two until they begin school, children vacillate between quiet conformity and happy sharing, on the one hand, and stubborn negative demands and egocentric behaviour, on the other. Because sharing is a socially desirable behaviour, learning to share becomes a top priority when children enter a day-care centre, nursery school, or kindergarten.

▼ Sharing is more likely after entry into kindergarten, which helps lead to a breakdown of egocentrism.

Although young children know that people experience mental states (Dad or Mom is in a bad mood, for example) (Wellman, Phillips, & Rodriguez, 2000), very young children still do not understand the concept of sharing—particularly the idea that if you share with another child, the other child is more likely to share with you. In a laboratory study of sharing, researchers observed pairs of children separated by a gate. Initially, one child was given toys and the other wasn't; then the situation was reversed. The researchers found that none of the children shared spontaneously; however, 65 percent shared a toy when their mothers asked them to. Moreover, a child who was deprived of a toy after having shared one often approached the child who now had the toy. One child even said, "I gave you a toy. Why don't you give me one?" Children do not initiate sharing at a young age; but once they share, they seem to exhibit knowledge about reciprocal arrangements. Of course, sharing is more likely among children who are friends because they have had more frequent social interaction and make more attempts at conflict resolution (Newcomb, Bukowski, & Bagwell, 1999). Sharing is also more likely after entry into kindergarten, which helps lead to a breakdown of egocentrism.

## GENDER ROLES

There is a distinction between sex and gender; the division focuses on biological traits dealing with reproductive capacity (sex) and behavioural and mental processes that are constructed and reinforced by society (gender). Everyone acknowledges that women differ from men—but women *and* men are powerful, resourceful, sensitive, intuitive, and analytical. Yet they exhibit those abilities in different circumstances (Hales, 1999). To an important extent, the study of gender differences is an investigation of when, how, and why those abilities are revealed.

A generation ago, many parents tended to tenaciously encourage "masculine" traits such as athletic prowess in their sons and "feminine" traits such as popularity in their daughters. Parents accepted, promoted, and vigorously reinforced gender-based social environments. Today, many parents de-emphasize gender-based interests in their children, seeking to reduce or eliminate society's tendency to stereotype people on the basis of sex.

When young people are given equal schooling, measures of academic performance for boys and girls tend to be equal. Socially, both men and women value intelligence and a sense of humour in the other sex. But men and women differ in their biological makeup, and their experiences are not the same. Researchers must place gender differences within meaningful contexts in order to analyze them. This means looking at how parents treat children as a function of their biological sex, how schools and religious institutions establish and reinforce gender-specific behaviours, and how society views the influence of gender in the daily life of children and young adults (Hannover, 2000; Tiedemann, 2000). We must also remember that children are active learners and take part in learning about gender and gendered behaviours (Martin, 1999).

▼ Boys tend to prefer to play with other boys in groups engaged in physical activities.

Modern medical technology has allowed parents to know the sex of their child during prenatal development, which allows them to begin treating the child differently on the basis of its sex before it is born; and so, from the beginning, girls and boys have different life experiences. As Collins suggests, parental influences on child development are neither unambiguous nor insubstantial (Collins et al., 2000). We see their impact from the beginning—for example, relatively few people have gender-neutral names such as Pat, Terry, Chris, or Lee (Van Fleet & Atwater, 1997). Moms and dads agonize over picking just the right name, one that will send the right signals and be gender-appropriate. Some psychologists assert that the way in which parents talk to and treat boys and girls creates special problems. For example, Pollack (1998) argues that parents have such strong expectations about how boys should behave—independent, strong, and tough—that the pressure of these expectations puts them at risk for various psychological problems. In addition, many parents put similar, but different, pressure on girls—to be independent, strong, and feminine. Children today sometimes get mixed messages, and they certainly have high expectations placed on them, far more than when children were expected to be "seen but not heard" (Maccoby, 1998).

## ERIK ERIKSON AND THE SEARCH FOR SELF

Developing an awareness of the self as different from others is an important step in early childhood social development. Self-perception begins when the child recognizes that he or she is separate from other people, particularly the mother; the self becomes more differentiated as a child develops an appreciation of his or her own inner mental world. Ideally, as children develop a concept of themselves, they develop self-esteem and significant attachments to others. Such cognitive, and then social, changes do not take place in isolation. They are influenced by the nature of a child's early attachments, by the cultural world surrounding the child, by the family's and society's child-rearing practices, and by how the child is taught to think about the causes of events in the world (Waters, Weinfield, & Hamilton, 2000). The construction of an identity—a self—occurs slowly and gradually and is affected by myriad variables.

Perhaps no one studied the challenges of social development and self-understanding more closely than the psychoanalyst Erik H. Erikson (1902–1994). With sharp insight, a linguistic flair, and a logical, coherent approach to analyzing human behaviour, Erikson, who studied with Freud in Austria, developed a theory of *psychosocial stages of development;* each of his stages contributes to the development of a unique self and helps define how a person develops a role, attitudes, and skills as a member of society. According to Erikson, a series of basic psychological conflicts determines the course of development. His theory is noted for its integration of individual disposition and environment with historical forces in the shaping of the self. Erikson's theory describes a continuum of stages, each involving a dilemma and a crisis, through which all individuals must pass. Each stage can have either a positive or a negative outcome. New dilemmas emerge as a person grows older and faces new responsibilities, tasks, and social relationships. A person may experience a dilemma as an opportunity and face it positively or may view the dilemma as a catastrophe and fail to cope with it effectively.

Table 10.5 lists the first four psychosocial stages in Erikson's theory, with their age ranges and the important events associated with them. These four stages cover birth through age 12. (We will look at Erikson's later stages, covering adolescence and adulthood, in Chapter 11.)

Stage 1 (birth to 12 to 18 months) involves the development of *basic trust versus basic mistrust.* During their first months, according to Erikson, infants make distinctions about the world and decide whether it is a comfortable, loving place in which they can feel basic trust. At this stage, they develop beliefs about people's essential trustworthiness. If their needs are adequately met, they learn that the world is a predictable and safe place. Infants whose needs are not met learn to distrust the world.

During stage 2 (18 months to 3 years), toddlers must resolve the crisis of *autonomy versus shame and doubt.* Success in toilet training and other tasks involving control leads to a sense of autonomy and more mature behaviour. Difficulties dealing with control during this stage result in fears and a sense of shame and doubt.

Stage 3 of Erikson's theory (3 to 6 years) is that of *initiative versus guilt,* when children begin to exercise their own inventiveness, drive, and enthusiasm. During this stage, they either gain a sense of independence and good feelings about themselves or develop a sense of guilt, lack of acceptance, and negative feelings about themselves. If children learn to dress themselves, clean their rooms and accomplish other similar tasks, and develop friendships with other children, they can feel a sense of mastery; alternatively, they can be dependent or regretful.

## TABLE 10.5  Erikson's First Four Stages of Psychosocial Development

| Stage | Approximate Age | Important Event | Description |
|---|---|---|---|
| 1. Basic trust versus basic mistrust | Birth to 12 to 18 months | Feeding | The infant must form a loving, trusting relationship with the caregiver or develop a sense of mistrust. |
| 2. Autonomy versus shame/doubt | 18 months to 3 years | Toilet training | The child's energies are directed toward the development of physical skills, including walking and controlling the sphincter. The child learns control but may develop shame and doubt if not handled well. |
| 3. Initiative versus guilt | 3 to 6 years | Independence | The child continues to become more assertive and to take more initiative but may be chastised for being too forceful, which can lead to guilt feelings. |
| 4. Industry versus inferiority | 6 to 12 years | School | The child must deal with demands to learn new skills or risk a sense of inferiority, failure, and incompetence. |

*Be an*
## ACTIVE LEARNER

**REVIEW**
> Identify two important variables that affect the quality of child care. pp. 367, 369
> What is a gender stereotype? p. 374

**THINK CRITICALLY**
> Why do you think that gender differences are minimized when children are observed individually?
> What does Erikson's theory have in common with Piaget's theory?

**APPLY PSYCHOLOGY**
> Should employers provide daycare for their employees' children? If yes, what might be the implications for workers and employers? If no, why not?

During stage 4 (6 to 12 years), children must resolve the issue of *industry versus inferiority*. Children either develop feelings of competence and confidence in their abilities or experience inferiority, failure, and feelings of incompetence.

Erikson's theory asserts that children must go through each stage, resolving its crisis as best they can. Many factors have a bearing on the successful navigation of these stages. Of course, children grow older whether or not they are ready for the next stage. A person of any age may still have unresolved conflicts, opportunities, and dilemmas from previous stages. These can cause anxiety and discomfort and make resolution of advanced stages more difficult. Because adolescence is such a crucial stage for the formation of a firm identity, the environment surrounding an adolescent becomes especially important. We will turn to this topic in the next chapter.

# Summary and Review

## KEY ISSUES, THEORIES, AND RESEARCH DESIGNS

### What is developmental psychology?

> *Developmental psychology* is the study of the lifelong, often age-related, processes of change in the physical, cognitive, emotional, moral, and social domains of functioning; these changes are rooted in genetically controlled biological mechanisms as well as in social interactions.  **p. 340**

### What are some issues in the study of human development?

> A key issue in development involves considering the extent to which a person's abilities, interests, and personality are determined by biological or genetic influences (by nature) or by environmental influences (by nurture). The issue of stability versus change is closely associated with that of nature versus nurture. Many researchers assume that stable traits are inherited and genetically determined, whereas those favouring an environmental view are more likely to believe that people change with life's events. A continuous view sees development as a process of gradual growth and change, but development can also be viewed as discontinuous, with growth, maturation, and understanding of the world occurring at various key periods and change appearing abruptly.  **pp. 340–341**

### What are the primary theories drawn from in the study of human development?

> Psychoanalytic theory argues that the role of the unconscious as well as the role of early experience is crucial in the development of the personality. Freud focused on disordered adults and from his observations developed a theory about development. Erikson modified Freud's theory by focusing primarily on the role of normative social development. Behaviourist theories focus on observable behaviours and argue that the development of the personality largely depended on the reinforcements and punishments experienced by individuals. Cognitive theories focus on the role of thought in development. Piaget focused on the interaction between the child and the environment whereas information processing theorists focus on the ability of individuals to solve problems. Ecological systems theories view development as occurring within a number of overlapping, interrelated social environments.  **pp. 341–342**

### What are the key methods of studying development?

> With a cross-sectional research design, researchers compare people of different ages to determine if they differ on some important dimension. With a longitudinal design, researchers study a group of people, usually of the same age, over a period of time to determine whether changes have occurred.  **pp. 342–343**

**KEY TERM**

developmental psychology, p. 340

## PHYSICAL DEVELOPMENT: THE FIRST 10 MONTHS

### Distinguish between an embryo and a fetus.

> Conception occurs when an ovum and a sperm join in a woman's fallopian tube to form a *zygote*—a fertilized egg.  **p. 344**

> The *placenta* is a mass of tissue that is attached to the wall of the uterus and acts as the life-support system for the fetus.  **p. 344**

> From the time implantation is complete (about the second week following conception) until the eighth week after conception, the prenatal organism is called an *embryo;* from that point until birth, it is called a *fetus.*  **p. 344**

> In the first months of life, an embryo is especially sensitive to teratogens. A *teratogen* is a substance that can produce developmental malformations; common teratogens include alcohol and other drugs.  **pp. 346–347**

### How is a newborn equipped to deal with the world?

> A newborn comes prepared with a set of primary reflexes, among them the *Babinski reflex*, the *Moro reflex*, the *rooting reflex*, the *sucking reflex*, and the *grasping reflex*. Newborns also have surprisingly well-developed perceptual systems.  **pp. 348–351**

**KEY TERMS**

zygote, p. 344; embryo, p. 344; fetus, p. 344; placenta, p. 344; critical period, p. 346; teratogen, p. 346; Babinski reflex, p. 349; Moro reflex, p. 349; rooting reflex, p. 349; sucking reflex, p. 349; grasping reflex, p. 349

## THE DEVELOPMENT OF THOUGHT: COGNITIVE DEVELOPMENT

### What is the difference between Piaget's concepts of assimilation and accommodation?

> Piaget's theory focuses on *how* people think, instead of on *what* they think. His theory includes the concept of the *scheme,* a mental structure that helps a child make sense of experience. Piaget identified two processes that enable the individual to gain new knowledge: assimilation and accommodation. *Assimilation* is the process of incorporating new information into existing understanding. *Accommodation* is the process of modifying one's

existing thought processes and framework of knowledge in response to new information.    pp. 352–354

### Describe Piaget's stages of cognitive development.

> Piaget believed that cognitive development occurs in four stages, each of which must be completed before the next stage begins. In the *sensorimotor stage,* covering roughly the first two years of life, the child develops some motor coordination skills and a memory for past events; the rudiments of intelligence are established.    pp. 353–354

> The *preoperational stage* lasts from about age two to age six or seven, when the child begins to represent the world symbolically. *Egocentrism,* the inability to perceive a situation or event except in relation to oneself, flourishes in this stage. At the end of the preoperational stage, children begin the process of decentration, gradually moving away from self-centredness.    p. 355

> *Conservation* is the ability to recognize that objects can be transformed in some way, visually or physically, yet still be the same in number, weight, substance, or volume.    pp. 356–357

> The *concrete operational stage* lasts from approximately age 6 or 7 to age 11 or 12; the child develops the ability to understand constant factors in the environment, rules, and higher-order symbolic systems.    pp. 356–357

> The *formal operational stage* begins at about age 12, when the individual can think hypothetically, consider future possibilities, and use deductive logic.    pp. 357–358

### How is Vygotsky's approach different from Piaget's?

> Vygotsky saw the child as part of an active social world in which communication with others and self-speech (private speech) help the child understand his or her world and that of other people. Vygotsky held that when children are presented with tasks that are outside of their current abilities, they need the help of society to accomplish them.    pp. 359–360

**KEY TERMS**

scheme, p. 353; assimilation, p. 353; accommodation, p. 353; sensorimotor stage, p. 354; preoperational stage, p. 355; egocentrism, p. 355; centration, p. 355; animistic thinking, p. 355; cross-sectional study, p. 356; concrete operational stage, p. 356; conservation, p. 356; formal operational stage, p. 357; theory of mind, p. 360

## MORAL REASONING
### How do Piaget's and Kohlberg's views of the development of morality differ?

> *Morality* is a system of learned attitudes about social practices, institutions, and individual behaviour that people use to evaluate situations and behaviour as right or wrong, good or bad. Piaget and Kohlberg studied moral reasoning, focusing on how people make moral judgments about hypothetical situations. Their theories differ in that Piaget thought of the stages of moral development as discrete, whereas Kohlberg viewed them as

overlapping. Kohlberg proposed that children's interactions with parents and friends might influence their conceptions of morality.    pp. 362–364

### What was Gilligan's main criticism of Kohlberg's work?

> Whereas Kohlberg showed that young children base their decisions about right and wrong on the likelihood of avoiding punishment and obtaining rewards, Gilligan found that children also focused on caring, relationships, and connections with other people. Most important, Gilligan found some differences between boys and girls. As young children, girls gravitate toward a morality of caring, while boys tend toward a morality of justice.    p. 364

**KEY TERM**

morality, p. 362

## EMOTIONAL DEVELOPMENT
### What is attachment, and why is it important?

> *Attachment* is the strong emotional tie that a person feels toward special other persons in his or her life.    p. 365

> *Bonding* is a special process of emotional attachment theorized to occur between parent and child in the minutes and hours immediately after birth; bonding is a controversial idea that is widely accepted but has little research support.    pp. 365–366

> Bowlby was one of the first to study the close attachment between mothers and their babies and to show that babies separated from their mothers exhibit characteristic responses he identified as secure, avoidant, resistant, and disoriented. Once established, early attachment is fairly permanent. Verbal exchanges between child and caregiver help establish ties, teach language, inform infants about the world, and socialize them.    pp. 366–367

### How permanent is temperament?

> *Temperament* refers to early-emerging and long-lasting individual differences in disposition and in the intensity and especially the quality of emotional reactions. Temperament is not fixed and unchangeable, although many researchers contend that some specific initial temperamental characteristics may be biologically based.    pp. 369–372

**KEY TERMS**

attachment, p. 365; bonding, p.369; temperament, p. 369

## SOCIAL DEVELOPMENT
### When do children begin to develop a sense of self?

> By the end of their second year, children have begun to understand that they are separate from their parents—they are developing a sense of self. Very young children do not understand the concept of sharing—particularly the idea that sharing with another child makes the other child more likely to share too.    pp. 373–374

**What are gender stereotypes?**

> A *gender stereotype* is an expectation of specific behaviour patterns based on a person's gender. Parents reinforce children selectively based on their gender to some extent, especially at young ages, but gender differences in behaviour are small and are apparent only in certain situations, such as on the playground and in groups. **pp. 374–375**

**Describe Erikson's stage theory of psychosocial development.**

> Erikson described psychosocial development throughout life as a series of stages during which people resolve various psychosocial issues. His theory suggests that at each stage a successful or unsuccessful resolution of a dilemma determines personality and social interactions. The first four stages are basic trust versus basic mistrust, autonomy versus shame and doubt, initiative versus guilt, and industry versus inferiority. **pp. 375–376**

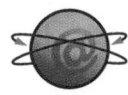

Take advantage of the multimedia resources available with this text! Follow the marginal icons to access the interactive modules on the *HandsOnPsych* CD-ROM; log on to *MyPsychLab* to explore the ebook, study aids, and other online resources; and visit the Companion Website at **www.pearsoned.ca/lefton** for additional exercises and links.

CHAPTER

# 11 Adolescence and Adulthood

One way or another, you have your parents for life. Parent–child relationships are not just a topic of preschool development. In fact, over the course of their lives, most people experience a very broad and changing range of relationships with their parents and, eventually, with their own children as well. You begin in a completely dependent relationship with your parents, relying on them for all of life's necessities. Through childhood and especially in adolescence, you increasingly work both to gain an independent sense of identity from your parents through friendships and academic endeavours and figure out what sort of connection you will maintain with your parents as you move into adulthood. Struggles over independence usually peak at about 14 years of age. From that point there is often a process of working out a different kind of relationship where your parents are not so much in charge as they are working with you to decide how you will live together for the next 10 years or so. You are never completely independent, however. Two hundred years ago, adults could expect that by the time they were 37 both of their parents would be dead. Today we can expect that one or both of our parents will be alive until we are in our late fifties. Should you go on and establish a work career and then start a family of your own, these days you will likely find that just when you are dealing with these sorts of issues with your own adolescent children you will also, as part of what is sometimes referred to as the *sandwich generation*, have to begin to come to terms with the fact that your parents may need some support and assistance as they deal with issues of retirement and aging. So, while we prize independence within Canadian culture we also constantly rework and maintain social relationships with many people. Those relationships, especially in the case of our parents, last a lifetime. It is to the many changing tasks and relationship changes that we face through adolescence and adulthood that we now turn our attention.

This chapter discusses some of the developmental changes that occur during adolescence and adulthood and traces the psychological processes underlying these changes. You'll see that a person's *chronological age* (actual age in years) is sometimes different from his or her *functional age* (the way the person actually performs in life). For example, some adolescents act "beyond their years," older and wiser than is expected of their peers. Among older adults—especially those over 65—some function in ways that seem more like what one would expect of people in their forties and fifties (Neugarten, 1968).

# Adolescence: Bridging the Gap

In Western culture, the transition from childhood to adulthood brings dramatic cognitive, social, and emotional changes. Generally, this transition occurs between the ages of 12 and 20, a period known as *adolescence,* which bridges childhood and adulthood but is like neither of those states. **Adolescence** is the period extending from the onset of puberty to early adulthood. **Puberty** is the time when the reproductive system matures; it begins with an increase in the production of sex hormones, which signals the end of childhood. Although adolescents are in many ways like adults—they are nearly mature physically and mentally, and their moral development is fairly advanced—their emotional development may be far from complete, and generally they have not yet become self-sufficient economically. Their stages of development—cognitive, physical, and emotional—have just not caught up with one another.

## VIEWING ADOLESCENCE IN MULTIPLE CONTEXTS

Adolescence is often referred to as a time of storm and stress brought on largely by raging hormones—and for some adolescents this is the case. It is a popular stereotype that adolescents are in a state of conflict resulting in part from a lack of congruity among the various aspects of their development—physical, cognitive, social, and emotional. There is some truth to this image. Most adolescents have normal conflicts, such as with parents, and some have atypical problems, such as poverty or parental alcoholism; what may compound these problems is that adolescents' coping mechanisms, or ways of dealing with such stressors, may not yet have evolved sufficiently. Consider alcohol abuse. Most adolescents know that underage drinking is illegal and that drinking is potentially deadly when combined with driving. Yet most do not stand up to peer pressure and make a conscious decision not to drink—especially those youths who are at high risk because of poverty, absent parents, or alcoholism in the home (Dishion, McCord, & Poulin, 1999; Taubman-ben Ari, 2000).

▼ Cultural context affects the process of development and the problems adolescents encounter.

Storm and stress do not give the whole picture of adolescence, however. Most adolescents go through this period of multiple changes without significant psychological difficulty (Arnett, 1999; Larson, 2000). Although spurts of hormones do affect adolescents' reactions, nonbiological factors seem to be especially important in moderating the effects of hormones on adolescents' moods (Archibald, 2000). Adolescence may be a challenging life period, just as adulthood is, but relatively few adolescents have serious difficulties (Roeser, Eccles, & Sameroff, 2000), and most psychologists agree that adolescence is not typically marked by great psychological turmoil. This does not mean that adolescence is conflict-free or that parent–child relationships do not change during this period; what it does mean is that adolescence does not *have* to be a stressful time (Galambos & Tilton-Weaver, 2000; Sagrestano et al., 1999). Most adolescents experience healthy emotional and social development during these years, and the frequency and intensity of conflicts decrease as adolescents grow older (Collins & Laursen, 2000). Thus, the current consensus among psychologists is that adolescence is not ordinarily a time of great psychological turmoil (Powers, Hauser, & Kilner, 1989) and that adolescents experience no greater incidence of psychological disturbances than the rest of the population (Hauser & Bowlds, 1990).

While it is almost a cliché for a teenager in Canada to feel that "no one understands me" (almost 20 percent of 12- to 19-year-old Canadians have low self-esteem; Statistics Canada, 2001), it is difficult to imagine a teenager growing up in the jungles of New Guinea expressing the same sentiment; her focus during the teen years is not on self-expression but on learning specific skills. Thus, the problems of adolescence must be considered in a cultural context. Even when adolescents grow up in the same country, they experience life's joys and disappointments in different ways. Some teenagers come from disadvantaged economic groups, perhaps from inner city ghettos or a poverty-stricken First Nations reserve. Some grow up in luxury, perhaps in a wealthy suburb of Montreal. Others are exposed to racial prejudice, alcohol and other drug abuse, violence, nonsupportive families, or other stressors that lead them to feel a lack of control over their lives (Kilpatrick et al., 2000). In the end, the culture in which a teenager grows and matures affects his or her view of the world, daily attitudes, and specific behaviours.

## PHYSICAL DEVELOPMENT IN ADOLESCENCE

The words *adolescence* and *puberty* are often used interchangeably, but in fact they mean different things. Puberty is the period during which the reproductive system matures. The age when puberty begins varies widely; some girls begin to mature physically as early as age 8, and some boys at 9 or 10 (Wilson, 1992). The average age at which individuals reach sexual maturity—the first menstruation (called menarche) for a girl, the first ejaculation for a boy—is 13, plus or minus a year or two (on average, girls enter puberty a year or two before boys). Just before the onset of sexual maturity, boys and girls experience significant *growth spurts*, gaining as much as 12 centimetres in height in a single year.

By the end of the first or second year of the growth spurt, changes have occurred in body proportions, fat distribution, bones and muscles, and physical strength and agility. In addition, the hormonal system has begun to trigger the development of secondary sex characteristics. **Secondary sex characteristics** are the genetically determined physical features that differentiate the sexes but are not directly involved with reproduction. These characteristics help distinguish men from women—for example, beards and chest hair in males, breasts in females. (Primary sex characteristics are the external genitalia and their associated internal structures, all of which are present at birth.) Boys experience an increase in body mass and a deepening of the voice, as well as the growth of pubic, underarm, and facial hair. Girls experience an increase in the size of the breasts, a widening of the hips, and the growth of underarm and pubic hair. Puberty ends with the maturation of the reproductive organs, at which time boys produce sperm and girls begin to menstruate. The order and sequence of these physical changes are predictable, but, as noted earlier, the age at which puberty begins and the secondary sex characteristics emerge varies widely from person to person. Over the past 30 years, many girls have been reaching puberty at younger and younger ages, and this has put increasing pressure on them to choose situations and activities that go together with their physical growth—regardless of their emotional development at that age.

**Development II**

SECONDARY SEX CHARACTERISTICS

The genetically determined physical features that differentiate the sexes but are not directly involved with reproduction.

▼ Just before the onset of sexual maturity, boys and girls experience significant growth spurts, with girls maturing earlier.

▲ Following puberty, on average boys tend to be taller than girls.

**HandsOnPsych**
Version 2.0

**Development II**

Puberty has received a good deal of research attention. For example, researchers have found that generally as boys pass through puberty, they feel more positive about their bodies, whereas girls are more likely to have negative feelings about their bodies. Puberty itself does not create psychological difficulty. However, adolescence means beginning to emerge as an adult, socially and sexually, and this requires significant adjustment. New forces affect the self-image of adolescents, and although these forces create new stresses, most adolescents perceive their new status as desirable. Physical maturation has implications for social development, because young people often gravitate to and choose environments and activities that complement their genetic tendencies (Collins et al., 2000). While they will eventually attain independence, we know that some adolescents often make bad decisions, take risks, and are vulnerable to abuse of alcohol and other drugs (Spear, 2000).

Researchers find that in junior high school, early-maturing adolescents enjoy several advantages, including increased confidence, superior athletic prowess, greater sexual appeal, and higher expectations from teachers and parents (Prokopcakova, 1998). However, some physically early-maturing adolescents seem to be at a disadvantage, in part because peers often treat them as outsiders (Archibald, 2000; Ge, Conger, & Elder, 1996). But such differences in adolescence seem to have few long-term negative consequences; in fact, the stresses of being an early or late maturer may help teenagers become adept at coping. Many who were at a disadvantage during their school years become self-assured adults. So many factors go into the making of a self-assured adult that psychologists are really not sure how significant the impact of early or late maturation is. During the teen years, the brain continues to consolidate circuits and hard-wire various abilities—physical ones such as catching baseballs, mental ones such as doing algebra problems, and artistic ones such as playing piano. It is important to remember that the brain is still maturing during the adolescent years, making new connections and interconnections. In young adulthood the brain is still organizing, pruning neural cells that are inoperative and no longer useful, and reorganizing often used, important circuits (Casey, Giedd, & Thomas, 2000).

## COGNITIVE DEVELOPMENT IN ADOLESCENCE

As children mature physically, they also develop cognitively in rather complex ways. Piaget and Vygotsky showed (see Chapter 10) that children's cognitive development has both biological and social components. But cognitive development does not stop in adolescence. Because most adolescents are now in the formal operational stage, they can think about the world abstractly, develop hypotheses, and learn new cognitive strategies (Marini & Case, 1994). Teenagers gain an expanding vocabulary, seek out creative solutions, and can fully use higher mental functions. Problem solving often becomes a focus for adolescent thought. Implications for this expanded cognitive ability are discussed in *Point/Counterpoint*. In spite of this newly acquired capacity for abstract thinking and the more mature cognitive abilities that accompany this thinking, for a brief time many adolescents become egocentric, idealistic, and critical of others—which may make decisions about everyday issues difficult for them.

Developing new cognitive abilities—moving into Piaget's formal operations—is quite liberating for adolescents. Teenagers begin to understand the world and its subtleties and can think about the world abstractly. This newfound ability is not always easy, as adolescents sometimes become argumentative and difficult. According to Inhelder and Piaget (1958, pp. 345–346): "The adolescent goes through a phase in which he attributes an unlimited power to his own thoughts so that the dream of a glorious future or of transforming the world through ideas (even

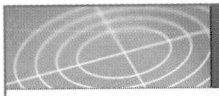
## Should Adolescents Be Allowed to Make Life-and-Death Decisions?

**POINT:** Adolescents are cognitively mature and can and should make their own medical decisions.

**COUNTERPOINT:** Adolescents may be mature but do not have the context of life experience to make life-and-death decisions.

Bethany Hughes died of leukemia in September 2002. Through the course of her treatment she received 38 transfusions despite the fact that her religious beliefs as a Jehovah's Witness led her to refuse the course of treatment that would require transfusions. She fought the court ruling that made her a ward of the province of Alberta and was supported in her fight by doctors at the Alberta Children's Hospital in Edmonton who argued that, as a mature minor, Bethany should have the right to refuse particular treatments. The court ruled that she was being influenced by her religion and was therefore not in a position to make a rational decision regarding her treatment.

This situation and ones similar to it occur in hospitals every day when adolescents and adults cope with chronic conditions such as leukemia and cystic fibrosis. There often comes a point at which many patients conclude that death is preferable to suffering and difficult treatment procedures that often offer little hope, or that alternative treatments are preferable. Adults make these decisions for themselves, usually in consultation with family and friends. But if you are a teenager, your views and wishes may be completely ignored. Parents have power over medical decision making. But should they? Are adolescents capable of making informed decisions about their lives and health? There are sharp divisions of opinion on this matter.

On one hand, research shows that adolescents in general are capable of making health decisions and providing informed consent. The argument is that adolescents above age 12 or 13 have the cognitive capacities to make knowledgeable decisions because they are cognitively mature. Most provinces also allow teenagers who are on their own to consent to medical treatment provided that the attending physicians are convinced that the teenager is capable of making rational decisions. Adolescents argue, and most parents agree, that they are capable of informed, intelligent decision making. Yet adolescents are not always given the ability to refuse various treatments—especially when the decision involves potential loss of life.

There is another side to this issue—adolescents take risks, often ill-informed risks. As a result, we have laws that suggest that minors under the age of 17 are incapable of understanding, deliberating, and making important health-care decisions. Thus, there is a focus on whether decisions about treatment are made knowingly, intelligently, and voluntarily. It's often been argued that adolescents, and many adults for that matter, don't meet these three criteria. Those who oppose adolescents making these decisions argue that there are scant research data to prove that adolescents are emotionally or cognitively mature enough to make life-and-death decisions. For example, do teenagers see all of the options that adults see? Are teenagers fully aware of the consequences of their decisions? Do teenagers value what adults value, and are they looking at multiple options concurrently? Are teenagers careful decision makers (Fischhoff, Downs, & de Bruin, 1998)?

We know that adolescents make risky decisions and favour their own experience and anecdotal evidence over systematic factual information (Haveman et al., 1997). As a consequence, society draws a line at age 17 or 19 and says that if you're younger than this age, you can't make the decision. Those who argue against adolescent decision making say that children need a protected period during which they can develop self-control, maturity, and the ability to make difficult decisions. They argue that children have limited world experience and that intellect should not be the only criterion. They further argue that if adolescents can make health-care decisions, why can they not make decisions about when they will drive, when they will come home, and when they shall vote?

In the end, mature children should not be ignored in the decision-making process. Physicians who treat minors have an ethical duty to promote the autonomy of minor patients by involving them in the medical decision-making process to a degree commensurate with their abilities. Parents should include their children and adolescents in the process, both to get their active support and to teach them how to make such decisions. The fact is, most parents do both, and it's generally only in fairly extreme circumstances that parents overrule adolescents. For now, the law limits adolescent decision making. Just before she died, Bethany made it clear that she wanted the fight for teenagers to have the right to make their own medical decisions to continue. It does.

▲ Adolescents often believe the world is focused around their individual lives—as if they are always "on stage."

if this idealism takes a materialistic form) seems to be not only fantasy, but also an effective action which in itself modifies the empirical world." Part of the problem is that teenagers become wrapped up in themselves and their own thoughts—they become quite egocentric. This transitional period, and its attendant *adolescent egocentrism*, leads to two cognitive distortions that were first documented by David Elkind (1967). The first is called the **imaginary audience**—the feeling adolescents have that they are "on stage," that there is an imaginary audience always watching them and the belief that this audience is as concerned about the adolescent's thoughts and behaviours as he or she is. "Everyone will notice," thinks a teenager, referring to his or her first pimple, or whatever else. The adolescent egocentrically believes the world is watching and therefore will do whatever is necessary to avoid embarrassment—usually by behaving like all of his or her friends or by seeking solitude (Vartanian, 2000).

Not only do adolescents believe that they are on stage, but they also develop an inflated sense of their own importance. This cognitive distortion is called the **personal fable**—the belief that their own ideas are special and unique, that other people cannot understand them, and that they are invulnerable so that risky behaviours, such as unsafe sex, that might harm other people will not harm them (Elkind & Bowen, 1979). The personal fable can lead to tragedy such as with the individual who thinks that he or she would never crash the car and can drive after drinking.

The imaginary audience and the personal fable are not a return to childhood egocentrism so much as side effects of cognitive growth and the ability to think about thinking. Adolescent egocentrism may be a bridging mechanism that allows adolescents to take on new roles, break away from parents, and integrate new views of the self (Lapsley, 1993). Whatever its origins, it starts to disappear by late adolescence (Vartanian & Powlishta, 1996).

Cognitive differences between boys and girls and between male and female adolescents are minimal. Gender differences in verbal and mathematical abilities are exceedingly small (Park, Bauer, & Sullivan, 1998). The cognitive differences found in recent research studies exist only in certain special populations—for example, among the very brightest mathematics students, where boys continue to outscore girls at least at the high-school level. However, boys' scores are especially variable (Hedges & Nowell, 1995). This does not mean that no differences are apparent; on certain tests, males as a group outperform females in mathematics (Park, Bauer, & Sullivan, 1998). What it does mean is that when certain socio-economic and cultural variables are controlled, gender differences are small and unimportant and refer only to overall group differences, not to any one individual's likelihood of accomplishment.

**IMAGINARY AUDIENCE**

A cognitive distortion experienced by adolescents, in which they see themselves as "on stage," with an imaginary audience always watching them.

**PERSONAL FABLE**

A cognitive distortion experienced by adolescents, in which they believe they are so special and unique that other people cannot understand them and risky behaviours will not harm them.

**Development II**

## EMOTIONAL AND SOCIAL DEVELOPMENT IN ADOLESCENCE

Early childhood social interactions as well as advances in cognitive development profoundly affect adolescent social adjustment. When children make poor adjustments early on, the likelihood of making good adolescent adjustments, social and otherwise, decreases. When Cairns and Cairns (1994, 2000) tracked 695 young people growing up over a 14-year period, they noticed that the youngsters' early patterns of social adjustment became predominant as the years went by. These researchers argue that the trajectories of social development do not change much; troubled boys and girls stay troubled (see *Psychology in Action*), and happy and well-adjusted children are more likely to stay well adjusted. But regardless of their previous adjustment, the egocentrism of the *imaginary audience* that they think exists and the *personal fable* that they invent complicates their emotional and social adjustment.

## If There Are Young People, Are There Gangs?

In his song "Northern Frontier" on his CD *xray sierra*, Tom Cochrane sings about the deaths of Joseph Beeper Spence and Jeff Giles in Winnipeg, both of whom were innocent bystanders killed by members of the "deuce" and "i.p." (Indian Posse) gangs because they were in the wrong place at the wrong time. According to information presented at a national forum on youth gangs convened by the federal Solicitor General's office and the Ministry of Justice, there is increasing discussion among police about possible links between gangs and organized crime, especially in areas such as drug trafficking, as well as concern about the perception that the level of gang-related violence is increasing (National Crime Prevention Centre, 1999). Do we have a problem with youth gangs in Canada? Are gangs an inevitable part of life? Are all adolescent gangs organized in the same ways and to the same extent? Before you jump to what may seem like obvious conclusions, think for a minute about how your answers may be influenced by the portrayals of youth gang activity in the American media (for example, movies such as *Dangerous Minds* and *American History X*, and especially television). Think about whether the assumption that full-blown gang activity is an inevitable part of adolescents' lives is a valid one, or whether it is just that—an assumption.

There is youth gang activity in Canada, but gangs do not exist in every high school. This is emphasized by students like Janice Crave from Courtney, British Columbia, who wrote of her concern about the assumption she noticed in an American questionnaire on gangs that there are gangs wherever there are young people (Crave, 1998). Gangs are mainly an urban phenomenon. While specific acts of violence are difficult to connect to gang activity (because police charge individuals, not groups), the amount and level of violent offences by young people in Canada is on the increase (Mathews, 1993). A number of police forces across

the country, including those in Vancouver, Calgary, Winnipeg, and Toronto, operate gang crime units. There is an increasing problem with gangs of middle-class youth in Toronto, native gangs in Winnipeg, and Asian gangs in Vancouver, Calgary, and Toronto. What are Canadian youth gangs like and what sorts of forces draw young people into (or steer them away from) involvement in gang activities?

First, according to Nick Bala of Queen's University, it is important to realize that the nature and extent of gang activity in Canada is in no way as serious as that found in the United States (Bala et al., 1994). Though the nature and extent of the violent images regularly presented to us via American media may be contributing to the increase in violence among Canadian youth, it is also contributing to an overestimation of the extent and seriousness of youth gang activities in Canada (Federation of Canadian Municipalities, 1994).

Second, despite the tendency of some older citizens to view groups of three or more young people as a gang, there is uncertainty as to just how to define a gang. Gangs definitely should be distinguished from peer groups, which are a central part of normal adolescent development. Researchers identify a continuum of youth crime organization ranging from a group to a gang. A group is a collection of friends that is loosely organized, has no clear leadership structure, has only spontaneous involvement in violence (if at all), and has little or no involvement in crime for profit (Mathews, 1993). Groups are likely to spend their time hanging out in malls and around convenience stores and street corners, and would describe themselves as friends. In the middle of this continuum are groups that gather mainly to engage in crime (for example, house break-ins), then go their separate ways when the crimes are completed. At the other end of this continuum are criminal youth gangs, which are highly organized, have a clear leadership hierarchy, are systematically violent, and are involved in crime for profit as a major activity (Mathews, 1993). These gangs have initiation rituals, recognizable clothing, and "turf" (or territory) that they protect. They are more likely to use violence systematically and to have a noticeable effect on their communities. They also may be linked to adult gangs. To quote a young gang member, "A group is a group of friends. A gang is a group of trouble" (Mathews, 1993).

To understand Canadian groups/gangs and the young people involved in them requires that you consider the developmental stage of adolescence and the diverse context in which Canadian young people are growing and living. Adolescence is a time when young people begin to stand on their own both cognitively and socially, and their peer groups

provide them with support for their emerging identities. A standard theory holds that gangs provide a level of support and access to social power, status, and resources such as money for young people growing up in severely economically challenged areas (Haskell, 1961). The actual role that the social context plays in the formation of youth groups in Canada partially fits this model but varies significantly by region.

In Winnipeg, for example, youth groups fall closer to the gang end of the continuum and a large proportion of their members are Aboriginal. Both poverty and a lack of strong social organization and future prospects contribute to the formation of these gangs (Smith, 1996). In southern Ontario, a lot of gang-related activity involves middle-class youth who appear to be involved for thrills rather than for monetary payoff. In Toronto, groups/gangs are quite diverse; some are ethnically based and others have mixed membership (Mathews, 1990). In British Columbia (and to a lesser extent in Toronto), the focus is on Asian gangs consisting of members drawn together either by their immigrant status (and thus their common language and, for many, lack of easy

access to money and status) or by the drug trade (Nyhuus, 1998).

The question of what to do about youth gangs is a difficult one. The Summit on Youth Crime concluded that to be effective any approach must simultaneously consider prevention and suppression of gang activity as well as intervention to reduce involvement and promote the reintegration of gang members into society. Certainly work can be done to help communities become better informed about the actual extent of the problem. In the case of youth groups, interventions at the community level that find or create other, more positive activities and facilities for young people can help. Specific social problems can be addressed in other areas; for example, committing necessary resources to English as a second language (ESL) training to speed assimilation may be of value. Finally, recognizing the difficult social problems faced by Aboriginal youth is a necessary step in addressing the problem in areas such as Winnipeg. Most of these approaches focus on providing support for more positive adolescent development—something that must occur if this problem is to diminish.

Adolescents develop a self-image based on beliefs about themselves that are both cognitively and emotionally based; but significant others (parents and peers) also generate expectations and beliefs about adolescents, and these beliefs also have an impact (Cairns & Cairns, 1994, 2000). Thus an adolescent's personality and sense of self-esteem are affected by childhood experiences, events such as the timing of puberty and how peers and parents react to that timing, and stage of cognitive development. Self-esteem is also affected by ethnic identity, religion, and involvement in community service (Youniss, McClellan, & Yates, 1999).

Parents and teachers can help troubled children and both early- and late-maturing adolescents develop a stronger sense of self-esteem. For example, research shows that involvement in athletics can be a buffer against the initially negative feelings about body image that can sometimes arise during this period. For both girls and boys, increased time spent playing sports is associated with higher satisfaction with body image and higher self-ratings on strength and attractiveness. Physical activity is associated with higher achievement, weight reduction, improved muscle tone, and stress reduction, all of which foster a positive self-image (Kirshnit, Richards, & Ham, 1988).

There are sharp individual differences in the development of adolescent self-esteem. In contrast to middle or later adolescence, early adolescence is associated with lower self-esteem and with feelings of insecurity, inadequacy, and shyness. Widespread publicity has claimed that this problem affects girls more than it does boys, but research shows that gender differences in self-esteem are small and that in some countries and ethnic groups, no gender difference exists (Kling et al., 1999). Adolescent girls face many barriers to achievement, but very low self-esteem is not a big problem for most.

Two important sources of influence on self-esteem and personality are parents and peers. Adolescents are responsive to parental influence (Otto, 2000; Resnick et al., 1997). Psychologists and parents disagree about the relative importance of peers versus parents (Harris, 1998), but most studies indicate that adolescents' attitudes fall somewhere between those of their parents and those of their peers (Bukowski, Sippola, & Hoza, 1999; Paikoff et al., 1997). As Chapter 10 pointed out, the influence of peer groups is especially formidable—especially in the middle years of adolescence. *Peer groups* are people who identify with and compare themselves to one another. They often consist of people of the same age, gender, and ethnicity, although adolescents may change their peer group memberships and may belong to more than one group. As adolescents spend more time away from parents and home, they experience increasing pressure to conform to their peer groups' values regarding society, government, religion, and even music. According to research by William Bukowski, Lorrie Sippola, and Betsy Hoza (1999) of Concordia University in Montreal, the desire for conformity especially affects same-sex peer relations (Bukowski, Sippola, & Newcomb, 2000). Peers constantly pressure one another to conform to behavioural standards, including standards for dress, social interaction, and even forms of rebellion, such as shoplifting and drug-taking. Most important, peers influence the adolescent's developing self-concept. And adolescents are vulnerable; those who are unpopular can be victimized, which only further erodes self-esteem and creates withdrawal and a range of problems (Hodges et al., 1999).

Parents and their child-rearing style undoubtedly affect an adolescent's self-esteem and self-confidence (Neumark-Sztainer et al., 2000). Are they democratic and open, nurturing, and at the same time firm, or are they heavy-handed and dictatorial, or perhaps more interested in being their child's friend and thus too permissive? Both parents and peers set standards by which the adolescent judges his or her own behaviour. These three sources of influence (parents, peers, and self-interpretation) can establish self-esteem and self-confidence and allow an individual to attain good social and emotional adjustment. Some of that social adjustment is gender-based, as we'll discover next.

## WHO AM I? THE SEARCH FOR GENDER IDENTITY

Gender matters. In fact, gender matters a great deal in both childhood and adulthood (Maccoby, 1998, 2000). Being a man or a woman in the Western world carries with it certain burdens. Men and women have different expectations for themselves and for members of the opposite sex and those expectations create gender inequality. The attitudes and values of white males still dominate our society (Rhode, 1997). Women still experience serious disparities in employment, pay, status, and access to leadership roles. This is a societal problem that stems from society's definition and value of gender roles.

We saw in Chapter 10 that gender differences are differences between males and females in behaviour or mental processes. Extensive research has revealed few significant biologically determined behavioural differences between the sexes (Geary, 1998). Although girls often reach developmental milestones earlier than boys do, this difference usually disappears by late adolescence (Cohn, 1991). On the other hand, experience and learning—the way a person is raised and taught—have a profound impact on behaviours.

GENDER IDENTITY.　As noted earlier, a key feature of adolescence is that it is a period of transition and change. Adolescents must develop their own identity, a sense of themselves as independent, mature individuals. One important aspect of identity is **gender identity**—a person's sense of being male or female. Children develop some sense of gender identity by age three. By age four or five, children realize that their gender identity is permanent; that is, they know that they will always be the sex they are, but children as old as six or seven can be confused about the constancy of gender. Some children in early elementary school believe that changing their hair, clothing, or behaviour will alter their sex.

GENDER IDENTITY
A person's sense of being male or female.

Consider the experience that adolescents have when their bodies change in appearance very rapidly, sometimes in unpredictable ways. During the transition to adulthood, adolescents often try out various types of behaviours, including those relating to male–female relationships and dating. Some adolescents become extreme in their orientation toward maleness or femaleness. Boys, especially in groups, may become overtly aggressive; girls may act submissively and be especially concerned with their looks. This exaggeration of traditional male or female behaviours, called *gender intensification,* is often short-lived, and it may be related to the increased self-esteem that boys feel during adolescence and the decreased self-esteem that girls experience (Aube et al., 2000; Kremen & Block, 1998).

Many psychologists believe that while children and adolescents are developing their gender identity, they attempt to bring their behaviour and thoughts into conformity with generally accepted gender-specific roles. **Gender schema theory** asserts that children and adolescents use sex as an organizing theme to classify and interpret their perceptions about the world and themselves (Bem, 1985; Maccoby, 2000). (A *schema* is a conceptual framework that organizes information and makes sense of the world. See Figure 11.1 for a description of gender schema theory.) Young children decide on appropriate and inappropriate gender behaviours by processing a wide array of social information, including sibling models (see *Introduction to Research Basics*). They develop shorthand concepts of what boys and girls are like; then they try to behave in ways that are consistent with those concepts (Levy, 1999). Thus, they show preferences for sex-related toys, activities, and vocations. In fact, children's and, later, adolescents' self-esteem and feelings of worth are often tied to their gender-based perceptions about themselves, many of which are determined by identification with the same-gender parent or by what they see as society's view of gender roles (Hudak, 1993).

**GENDER SCHEMA THEORY**

The theory that children and adolescents use gender as an organizing theme to classify and interpret their perceptions about the world and themselves.

**FIGURE 11.1**

**Gender Schema Theory**

According to gender schema theory, children and adolescents use gender as an organizing theme for classifying and interpreting their perceptions about the world.

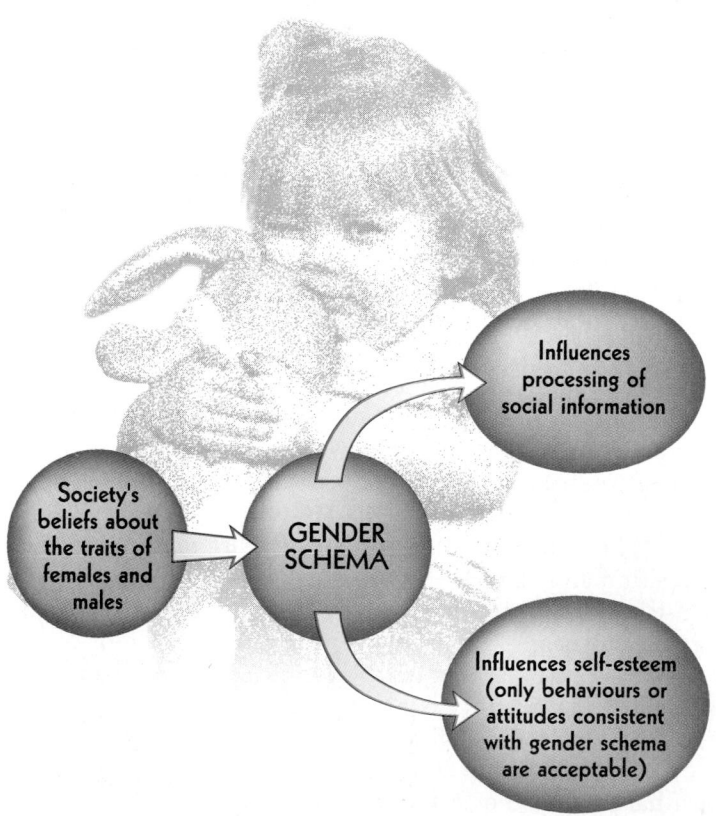

Society's beliefs about the traits of females and males

GENDER SCHEMA

Influences processing of social information

Influences self-esteem (only behaviours or attitudes consistent with gender schema are acceptable)

# Sibling Influences During Early Adolescence

Brothers and sisters are obviously important for children as they grow and develop, but psychologists have not devoted a great deal of research to the influence of siblings. Recently, two groups of researchers have studied the influence of siblings during early adolescence; one group used a longitudinal study and the other conducted a cross-sectional study. These two methods use different approaches to studying age-related changes in developmental psychology (see page 343 in Chapter 10).

**Study 1.** Susan McHale and her colleagues (McHale et al., 2001) explored the impact of the sex of the sibling and siblings' gender-role orientations as influences on gender-related behaviours during middle childhood and early adolescence.

**Design.** This was a **longitudinal study**, a research method that examines a specific group of individuals at different ages to discover changes that occur over time. This method falls within descriptive research techniques because the researchers do not manipulate variables; instead, they measure existing variables. Longitudinal studies are difficult to conduct; repeated measurements require locating a suitable selection of participants and following them over time. Though these studies are expensive and difficult, they give researchers helpful information about developmental trends.

**Hypothesis.** Older siblings' gender-role attitudes and behaviours will influence their younger siblings to adopt similar attitudes and behaviours.

**Participants.** Participants were 198 first-born and second-born siblings and their parents. With the exception of two adopted Asian children, all were white and members of the working class or middle class, and they resided in rural areas, towns, and small cities.

**Procedure.** The research involved three years of data collection; by the third year of the study, the second-borns were approximately the same age that the first-borns had been in year one. The researchers conducted home interviews with mothers, fathers, and the children; in addition, participants filled out a daily diary of activities. McHale and her colleagues assessed parents' and children's gender-role attitudes as well as their sex-typed personality qualities and interest in sex-typed leisure activities to determine the patterns of influence.

**Results.** In general, first-born siblings' behaviours in year one predicted second-born children's behaviours in year three. That is, there seemed to be a modelling effect for the second-born children. Among first-borns, parental influence was more evident, and first-borns changed in ways that made them different from (rather than similar to) their siblings. In addition, the gender of the sibling made a difference; for example, girls with younger brothers reported less traditional attitudes than those with younger sisters. Also, boys with less traditional mothers became less traditional over time.

**Conclusions.** Research using interviews and questionnaires—even longitudinal research that reveals developmental patterns—cannot provide conclusions concerning causality (what causes a behaviour). However, the results from McHale and her colleagues suggest that sibling influences operate in ways that make children from the same family both similar (in the case of younger siblings) and more different (older siblings). Families are complex interactive systems that include influences from parents and siblings. Each child experiences a unique pattern of interactions. Many of us can appreciate this idea as we look at our brothers and sisters and wonder why they are so different from us. This study demonstrated some ways in which these differences may develop.

**Study 2.** AmyKay Cole and Kathryn Kerns (2001) also studied the influence of siblings during early adolescence. Cole and Kerns focused on a comparison of three different ages and examined sibling interactions, with special attention to the gender composition of sibling pairs.

**Design.** Cole and Kerns used a cross-sectional rather than a longitudinal approach. A **cross-sectional study** is a type of research design that compares individuals of different ages to determine how they differ. Researchers who want to contrast behaviour at different ages often use this approach because it produces results more quickly than the longitudinal approach does. Cole and Kerns used this cross-sectional design to study intimacy, companionship, and conflict in preadolescent children and their siblings.

**Hypothesis.** Cole and Kerns hypothesized that the older participants and participants in same-gender pairs would have more intimate relationships and less conflict with their siblings than younger participants and those in mixed-gender pairs.

**Participants.** Participants were 60 students in grade four, 44 students in grade six, and 66 students in grade eight. All had at least one sibling.

**Procedure.** Participants filled out questionnaires that assessed the quality of their relationship with their siblings and the activities they and their siblings did together.

**Results.** Cole and Kerns found significant age differences for interactions with siblings, but not exactly as they had predicted. As predicted, intimacy was highest for eighth-graders, but lower for sixth-graders than for fourth-graders. Gender composition of sibling pairs also produced differences, especially between pairs of brothers and pairs of sisters. Brother pairs were lowest in intimacy and in conflict resolution; sibling pairs that included a girl showed higher intimacy levels.

**Conclusions.** Younger children have relationships with less intimacy than older children, and girls show more intimacy than boys. For siblings and friendships, boys engage in companionship-type activities and conflict. That is, the patterns of interactions between siblings during early adolescence showed similarities to the developmental patterns and gender differences seen in friendships. Cole and Kerns noted that the cross-sectional design of their study is one of its limitations, and in order to understand the developmental pattern of sibling interactions, a longitudinal study would be necessary.

---

**LONGITUDINAL STUDY**

A research method that examines a specific group of individuals at different ages to discover changes that occur over time.

**CROSS-SECTIONAL STUDY**

A type of research design that compares individuals of different ages to determine how they differ.

**ANDROGYNOUS**

Having both stereotypically male and stereotypically female characteristics.

## ANDROGYNY

Developing a gender identity in adolescence has always been part of the transition to adulthood. Today, this task is more complicated. In earlier decades of this century, most educated Canadian women were expected to pursue marriage and homemaking, which were considered to be full-time jobs. Today, women's plans often include a career outside the home, which may be interrupted for child rearing; men's plans often include active involvement with raising their children. In recent years, many women and men have developed new attitudes about sex roles—attitudes that encourage all people to cultivate both traditionally masculine and traditionally feminine traits. They have adopted behaviours that are **androgynous**—that represent a blend of stereotypically male and stereotypically female characteristics. Androgynous men and women may fix cars, pursue careers, do housework, and help care for children; they can be both assertive and emotionally sensitive. More than ever before, men today disparage violent toughness as part of the masculine role (Fischer & Good, 1998). Several studies have found that people who rate high in androgynous characteristics tend to feel more fulfilled and more competent when dealing with social and personal issues (Bem, 1993; Stake, 1997). Androgynous behaviours are being seen worldwide with specific cultural adaptations because some societies are more polarized than others about certain gendered behaviours (Sugihara & Katsurada, 2000).

## REAL MEN AND WOMEN

In the 1990s there was—and continues to be today—a growing awareness of the ways in which boys, girls, and teenagers are raised. Best-selling books such as *Reviving Ophelia* (1994) by Mary Pipher; *Raising Cain* (1999) by Dan Kindlon, Michael Thompson, and Teresa Barker; and *Real Boys* (1998) by William Pollack have argued that we have given girls and boys mixed messages that ask them to be all things to all people—strong, sensitive, and competent as well as docile, independent, and vulnerable. We are asking them to develop the abilities all at the same time, but often expressing only some of them—the ones we consider to be gender appropriate (Faludi, 1999). This creates confusion.

Boys are urged to mask their emotional vulnerability as early as possible. The code for boys, and then men, is to cut themselves off from feelings that society teaches are unacceptable and wear a mask of cheerfulness and resiliency—ultimately the goal is to be master of their universe. Pollack (1998) calls it the "boy code" and argues that it puts boys, teens, and men into emotional straitjackets.

Girls, teens, and women are similarly tied, but with a different set of knots. Feminism is still considered a pejorative term to some people; women work for lower wages and face corporate glass ceilings. And we still live in a society that is *gendered*—that is, jobs, roles, and responsibilities have male or female connotations (nurses are women, firefighters are men, for example). Pipher (1994) notes that the protected era that we once called adolescence has grown shorter, and the suffering that girls experience has grown stronger and is evident daily in eating disorders and depression. As explored further in *Brain and Behaviour*, adolescent girls today are at greater risk for psychological disorders than ever before, are pressured to excel and be tough—be as good as the boys—and at the same time convey a waiflike image of feminine sexuality. The problem is that waiflike, sexual, strong, independent, and competent all don't usually go together—and certainly not for all girls, teenagers, and women.

"By century's end," Faludi (1999, p. 451) writes, "the dictates of a consumer and media culture had trapped both men and women in a world in which top billing mattered more than building, in which representation trumped production, in which appearances were what counted." In Faludi's view, it's no longer enough just to be a traditional man who works hard, raises a family, and leads a good life. Today men, like women, have developed a hunger for stardom, for the role of the "leading" man. The dilemma men face, Faludi argues, is not so different from the forces straitjacketing women: The culture has taken from them much of their depth and relegated them to the status of ornaments.

In the end, men and women are being held to a near impossible standard of manhood or womanhood. The challenge for parents, educators, and psychologists is to allow children and teenagers to blossom fully, to emerge as adults unhindered by destructive emotional straitjackets of exaggerated gender stereotyping. Boys and girls, men and women all need to be able to be strong, independent, happy, sad, lonely, and unhappy.

## WHO ARE MY FRIENDS?

When you like someone who likes you, there is a good chance you call yourselves friends. Although some people have many friends and others have few, most people, at one time or another, find someone with whom they share values, ideas, and thoughts. At its simplest, a friendship is a close emotional tie between two peers (Kerns, 1998). Most teenagers report having between three and five good friends. As much as 29 percent of adolescents' waking hours are spent with friends; among adults, for a whole range of reasons, the time spent interacting with friends drops to 7 percent. If you had many friends as a child, you are more likely to have many as an adult, even if you don't spend a great deal of time with each one of them.

According to Hartup and Stevens (1997), there are some important developmental consequences of having or not having friends. Children and adolescents who have friends tend to be more socially competent than those who do not. Having friends provides someone to confide in, to be afraid with, and to grow with, and childhood friendships set the stage for intimacy as adults. Elementary school children tend to form same-gender friendships; cross-gender friendships are rare. Adolescent friendships can contribute to sharing and intimacy, although occasionally they can also be filled with conflict over social or political issues, drugs, gangs, and sexual behaviour. When friendships fall apart, a child's self-confidence is undermined (Keefe & Berndt, 1996).

Among adults, friendships between women differ from those between men; and both differ from a friendship between a man and a woman. In Western cultures, expectations for specific gender-based behaviours often control male–female interactions in friendship. Women talk more about family, personal matters, and doubts and fears than men do; men talk more about sports and work than do women. Women in general find friendships more satisfying than men do (Bleske & Buss,

## The Prevalence of Eating Disorders

Calista Flockhart, star of the TV show *Ally McBeal,* has been the subject of considerable speculation because of her extreme thinness. Flockhart claims she is just thin, but many critics and psychologists assert that she has an eating disorder. This issue grabbed the public's attention because nearly 1 in 150 girls has the eating disorder anorexia nervosa. Flockhart's weight and her eating behaviour are between her and her doctor, but it raises questions about role models for women and teenagers who always feel too fat compared to television stars. In some cases, this comparison leads teenagers to eating disorders.

Eating disorders are psychological disorders characterized by gross disturbances in eating behaviour and in the way individuals respond to food. Two important eating disorders are *anorexia nervosa* and *bulimia nervosa.* These disorders are very much culture-bound, Western diseases, but may have a physiological basis. Eating disorders affect about 3 percent of women in such societies at some time during their lives. In a recent study of nearly 2000 teenaged girls in Ontario (Jones et al., 2001) it was found that more than 27 percent of them showed disordered eating attitudes and behaviours.

**Anorexia nervosa**, which affects as many as 40 out of every 10 000 young women in Canada, is an eating disorder characterized by an obstinate and wilful refusal to eat. Individuals with the disorder, usually adolescent girls from

middle-class families, have a distorted body image. They perceive themselves as fat if they have any flesh on their bones or deviate from their idealized body image (Rieger et al., 2001). They intensely fear being fat and relentlessly pursue thinness. The anorexic person's refusal to eat eventually brings on emaciation and malnutrition (which may bring about a further distortion of body image). Victims may sustain permanent damage to their heart muscle tissue, sometimes dying as a result.

Many therapists believe that anorexia nervosa has strictly psychological origins. They cite poor mother–daughter relationships, excessively protective parents, other negative family interactions, and efforts to escape self-awareness as the main causes, as well as prejudice against the obese. Others are exploring possible physiological contributions to the disorder (Monteleone et al., 2001; Walsh & Devlin, 1998), including the many changes taking place at puberty that might influence its emergence. Some psychologists believe that people with eating disorders may lack a hormone that is thought to induce a feeling of fullness after a meal. John Pinel (2003) of the University of British Columbia suggests that the causes of anorexia nervosa are a complex interaction of psychological and physiological origin. People, primarily young women, respond to cultural pressure to be thin. Some become controlled, rigid, and obsessive and stop eating. At this point, well-meaning individuals try to force the anorexic to eat a meal, causing her to feel ill. In this way food becomes a stimulus. Over time, food loses its positive incentive value and the anorexic associates eating with feelings of illness.

Individuals with anorexia nervosa need a structured setting, and therapists often hospitalize them to help them regain weight. To ensure that the setting is reinforcing, hospital staff members are always present at meals. Individual and family therapy is provided. Patients are encouraged to eat and are rewarded for consuming specified quantities of food. Recently, Ahmed Boachie and his colleagues (Boachie, Goldfield, & Spettique, 2003) at the Children's Hospital of Eastern Ontario in Ottawa have reported success when adding an anti-psychotic drug (Olanzapine) into the treatment plan, mainly in cases where individuals are struggling to see themselves as needing to eat to survive. The drugs seem to help the anorexics stop "listening" to their self-destructive self-perceptions. Generally, psychotherapy is also necessary to help people with anorexia attain a healthy self-image. Even with treatment, however, as many as 50 percent of patients suffer relapses within a year.

**Bulimia nervosa** is an eating disorder characterized by repeated episodes of binge eating followed by purging. It tends to occur in women of normal weight with no history of anorexia nervosa. The binge eating (which the person recognizes as being abnormal) is accompanied by a fear of not being able to stop. Individuals who engage in binge eating become fearful of gaining weight; they become preoccupied with how others see them (Striegel-Moore & Cachelin, 1999). Therefore, they often purge themselves of unwanted calories, mostly through vomiting and the use of laxatives and diuretics. Other methods include compulsive exercising and use of weight-reduction drugs. The medical complications of bulimia are serious. They include cardiovascular and gastrointestinal problems, menstrual irregularities, blood and hormone dysfunctions, muscular and skeletal problems, and sharp swings in mood and personality.

Men and women are affected by eating disorders in similar ways (Olivardia et al., 1995), but the ratio of female to male bulimics is 10 to 1. Researchers theorize that women believe, more readily than men, that fat is ugly and thin is beautiful. Women of higher socio-economic classes are at greater risk of becoming bulimic, as are professionals whose weight is directly related to career achievement, such as dancers, athletes, and models. Whether dieting plays a role in

bulimia is unclear because many bulimics don't regularly engage in dieting (Lowe, Gleaves, & Murphy-Eberenz, 1998). Women with bulimia have lower self-esteem than women who eat normally, and they may have experienced some kind of clinical depression in the past. Alcohol dependency and a family history of bulimia are sometimes reported (Kozyk, Touyz, & Beumont, 1998). Some bulimics may become so wrapped up in food-related behaviours that they avoid contact with other people.

Bulimia may have a biological basis, taking the form of an imbalance of neurotransmitters, yet most researchers have focused on psychological explanations. Some people with bulimia may eat as a means of managing their mood, regulating tension, and escaping from self-awareness (Ball & Lee, 2000). After binges, however, they feel guilty. To lessen their guilt and avoid the potential consequence of eating (gaining weight), they purge themselves. Researchers believe the purges reduce post-binge guilt feelings. The problems of bulimia may not disappear completely when treated; one study found that after not being considered bulimic for an entire decade, women who had once been so diagnosed were much thinner than others in their communities (Sullivan et al., 1998).

2000); nevertheless, men experience and seek intimacy and support in friendships (Botschner, 1996).

Many researchers report that intimacy and shared values are the key variables that define a friendship. Ideally, close friends participate as equals, enjoy each other's company, have mutual trust, provide mutual assistance, accept each other as they are, respect each other's judgment, feel free to be themselves with each other, understand each other in fundamental ways, and are intimate and share confidences (Bender, 1999).

From a developmental point of view, friends are an important resource from childhood through old age, both cognitively and emotionally (Hartup & Stevens, 1997). But not all friendships are alike, and the meaning of a friendship is often buried below the surface conversation of shopping, school, or jobs.

**FRIENDS, THEN LOVERS: EVOLUTIONARY APPROACHES.** We may seek friends who share interests; we may also be shaped heavily by popular culture. But evolutionary psychologists assert that our current behaviour—including our self-esteem—is shaped through the process of natural selection and a series of adaptations that are ultimately coded in the genome. For example, those whom we seek out as mates and have children with are, at least in part, under evolutionary control—or so say evolutionary psychologists. They assert that those whom we are sexually drawn to are an evolved adaptation. From their view, men seek out as many women as they can to mate with, especially women who are fertile—men are polygamous (Hinsz, Matz, & Patience, 2001). Women have evolved to seek out a man who can provide status, wealth, and security for them and their offspring; accordingly, they will be far more selective about whom they mate with, tending to be monogamous. Thus, our genetic code, at its present state of evolution, makes men far more sexually promiscuous than women. The key from an evolutionary perspective is that this occurs due to natural selection.

ANOREXIA NERVOSA
An eating disorder characterized by an obstinate and wilful refusal to eat, a distorted body image, and an intense fear of being fat.

BULIMIA NERVOSA
An eating disorder characterized by repeated episodes of binge eating followed by purging.

▲ Most Canadian adolescents view sexual intimacy as an important and normal part of growing up.

Critics of evolutionary approaches are quick to point out that evolutionary psychology is nondevelopmental in its nature—it does not track changes in individuals over time, nor does it explain how evolution may express itself differently in different environments (think city living versus agrarian societies). In addition, our environment has grown more complex than it has ever been before, and evolution may be able to exert only so much of an influence; this is reflected in the sexual behaviour of adolescents.

## SEXUAL BEHAVIOUR DURING ADOLESCENCE

Sex. It fascinates and it captivates. It is biological and it is cultural. It happens a lot for some and very little for others. It is important to recognize and appreciate the fact that girls and women and boys and men tend to view sex and sexual behaviour somewhat differently. For example, you will get many different answers if you ask:

- What constitutes sex?
- Is oral sex, sex?
- How many sexual partners do you want to have in a lifetime?
- How often do you have sex?

Roy Baumeister and Dianne Tice (2001) point out that men tend to estimate and women tend to count; the former leads to high numbers of partners and encounters, the latter leads to low numbers. Any careful reading of the facts shows discrepancies and so data about human sexual behaviours—especially frequency data—must be viewed with careful analysis and critical thinking.

What changes in adolescent sexual behaviour have occurred? Canadian adolescents view sexual intimacy as an important and normal part of growing up; premarital heterosexual activity has become increasingly common among adolescents. Adolescents are having sexual experiences at younger ages than in previous decades, in part because knowledge and use of contraception are becoming more widespread, thus reducing the fear of pregnancy and diseases such as AIDS. Today, adolescents consider sexual behaviour normal in an intimate relationship (Graber, Britto, & Brooks-Gunn, 1999). Fifty-five percent of male teenagers have intercourse by age 18, and the same percentage of white female adolescents do so by age 19 (Gates & Sonenstein, 2000). Among African Americans, 60 percent of boys have intercourse by age 16, and 60 percent of girls do so by age 18. There are great individual differences with regard to age at first intercourse and the subsequent frequency of intercourse. It is not uncommon for a teenager to have first intercourse at age 14 or 15 and then not have sexual relations again for a year or two (Coley & Chase-Lansdale, 1998; Laumann & Mahay, 2002).

## Adulthood: Years of Stability and Change

Canadian adults today often have vastly different life experiences than did adults of the 1950s, whose lives tended to follow more predictable and prescribed timetables. In the 1950s, many people married when they were in their late teens or early twenties and had children soon after. Wives frequently stayed at home to raise the children, while husbands went to work to support the family. Today's adults tend to marry later, and some don't marry at all. Many people are postponing or rejecting parenting. While some women choose to stay at home to raise children, many are concentrating on careers. Many grown children are returning home after college, and divorce is

### Be an ACTIVE LEARNER

**REVIEW**
> How do the imaginary audience and the personal fable affect adolescent behaviours? p. 386
> What is gender-schema theory? p. 390
> Are today's teenagers being held to a near impossible standard of manhood or womanhood? How? pp. 392–393

**THINK CRITICALLY**
> Why do you think that teenagers have arguments with parents? Are such arguments necessary? Are they productive?
> How do you think an increase in androgyny might affect adolescent friendships? How might it change the nature of courting or of marriage?

**APPLY PSYCHOLOGY**
> As an adult who has gone through adolescence, is your personality pretty much the same, or have you gone through major changes? Explain your answer.
> Who do you think was more influential in your life, parents or peers? Were peers more influential in some areas than others?

common. The 1950s stereotype of a well-ordered, simple family structure has changed sharply in a relatively short period of time.

Psychologists are now focusing on development across cultures and throughout the life span. They are recognizing that a person encounters new challenges in every stage of life. Researchers study adult development by looking at the factors that contribute to stability or change, to a sense of accomplishment or feelings of despair, and to physical well-being or diminished functioning. To illustrate this, think about the decades after retirement, which can be a time of stability and feelings of completion and well-being, or a difficult, unhappy time full of physical and emotional troubles. Researchers today also are examining the differences between men and women, with emphasis on the unique experiences of women. Minorities are being studied, and theories are recognizing and focusing on cultural diversity.

Psychologists also are recognizing that a person's career, not just the person's family or life stage, is a defining characteristic of adulthood. Adults spend an enormous amount of time and energy on their careers. Until recently, this aspect of adult development was relatively ignored by psychologists. However, in general, as people age from adolescence to adulthood, and ultimately to old age, they become psychologically healthier (Carstensen & Charles, 1998; Jones & Meredith, 2000). Building Table 11.1 summarizes the major changes in important functional domains during young, early, and middle adulthood.

## PHYSICAL CHANGES

One hundred years ago only about half of all Canadians who reached age 20 lived beyond age 65. Today most people live well into their seventies, but despite this longevity we know little about the middle to late adult years. Psychologists study childhood physical development extensively, but in comparison pay little attention to adult physical development. Although physical development in adulthood is slower, less dramatic, and sometimes less visible than in childhood and adolescence, it does occur.

**HandsOnPsych**
Version 2.0

**Development II**

| BUILDING TABLE 11.1 | Major Changes in Important Domains of Adult Functioning | | | | |
| --- | --- | --- | --- | --- | --- |
| Age | Physical Change | Cognitive Change | Work Roles | Personal Development | Major Tasks |
| Young Adulthood, 18–25 | Peak functioning in most physical skills; optimal time for child-bearing | Cognitive skills high on most measures | Choice of career, which may involve several job changes | Conformity; task of establishing intimacy | Separate from family; form partnership; begin family; find job; create individual life pattern |
| Early Adulthood, 25–40 | Good physical functioning in most areas; health habits during this time establish later risks | Peak period of cognitive skill on most measures | Rising work satisfaction; major emphasis on career or work success; most career progress steps made | Task of passing on skills, knowledge, love (generativity) | Rear family; establish personal work pattern and strive for success |
| Middle Adulthood, 40–65 | Beginning signs of physical decline in some areas (strength, elasticity of tissues, height, cardiovascular function) | Some signs of loss of cognitive skill on timed, unexercised skills | Career reaches plateau, but higher work satisfaction | Increase in self-confidence, openness | Launch family; redefine life goals; redefine self outside of family and work roles; care for aging parents |

**FITNESS CHANGES.**   Most of the adult years are years of health and fitness; the leading cause of death, for example, for people ages 25 to 44 is an unintentional injury—for example, from a motor vehicle crash. Psychologists often speak of fitness as involving both a psychological and a physical sense of well-being. Physically, human beings are at their peak of agility, speed, and strength between ages 18 and 30. From age 30 to 40 there is some loss of agility and speed. Between ages 40 and 60, much greater losses occur (Merrill & Verbrugge, 1999). In general, strength, muscle tone, and overall fitness deteriorate gradually from age 30 on. People become more susceptible to disease. Respiratory, circulatory, and blood pressure problems are more apparent; lung capacity and physical strength are significantly reduced. Decrease in bone mass and strength occur, especially in women after menopause; the resulting condition is called *osteoporosis*. Immune system responsivity and the ability to fight disease diminish significantly among older adults.

**SENSORY CHANGES.**   In early adulthood, most sensory abilities remain fairly stable. But between ages 40 and 50 adults must contend with almost inevitable sensory losses that become more pronounced as they age. Vision, hearing, taste, and smell require increasingly higher levels of stimulation to respond at the same levels as younger people's senses do. Older people, for example, usually are unable to make fine visual discriminations without the aid of glasses, have limited capacity for dark adaptation, and often have some degree of hearing loss, especially in the high-frequency ranges. Reaction time slows and visual acuity decreases; the risks of glaucoma, cataracts, and retinal detachment increase. For example, Don Kline (Kline et al., 1992) at the University of Calgary has found that sensory changes can affect driving behaviour; elderly drivers have difficulty judging their own speed and making out instrument panel displays. By age 65, many people can no longer hear very high-frequency sounds, and some are unable to hear ordinary speech. Hearing loss is greater for men than for women.

**SEXUAL CHANGES.**   In adults of both sexes, advancing years bring changes in sexual behaviour and desire as well as physical changes related to sexuality. For example, in the child-rearing years, women's and men's sexual desires are sometimes moderated by the stresses of raising a family and juggling a work schedule. However, sexual activity remains a vital part of the lives of middle-aged adults. Although many people continue to experience sexual enjoyment to a similar or greater extent than in their younger years, there may be differences in their physical reactions. Men may need more time to achieve erection and women experience a thinning of the vaginal walls that may make intercourse painful. For women, midlife hormonal changes lead to the cessation of ovulation and menstruation at about 50 years of age, a process known as *menopause*. Menopause generally is not seen as a crisis for most but as a transition after which women no longer have to deal with pregnancy issues; for some, however, it is perceived as a crisis signalling the beginning of old age and a lack of youthful femininity. At about the same age, men's testosterone levels decrease, their ejaculations are weaker and briefer, and their desire for sexual intercourse typically decreases from previous levels (Rowland et al., 1993). Nevertheless, as Gerald Brock (Brock, McIntire, & Macchia, 2003) from the University of Western Ontario reported recently, older people continue to engage in sexual activities and find them enjoyable, and a significant percentage continue to find their sexual activities more satisfying than when they were younger.

**THEORIES OF AGING.**   Psychologists and physicians have been examining the behavioural and physiological changes that accompany aging only since the early 1970s. Three basic types of theories—based on heredity, external factors, and physiology—have been developed

▼ Visual loss afflicts a large number of older adults.

to explain aging. Although each emphasizes a different cause for aging, it is most likely that aging results from a combination of all three.

Genes determine much of a person's physical makeup; thus, it is probable that *heredity*, to some extent, determines how a person ages and how long he or she will live. Much supporting evidence exists for this genetic argument. For example, long-lived parents tend to have long-lived offspring. However, researchers still do not know *how* heredity exerts its influence over the aging process, simply that there are multiple mechanisms of aging, some of which are hereditary (Jazwinski, 1996). One promising area of study has been apoptosis, the process by which cells kill themselves. Normal human cells have a limited capacity to proliferate, which is most likely mediated by telomeres. *Telomeres* are end segments of DNA responsible for aging of the cell (Bodnar et al., 1998). After a certain finite number of cell divisions, time on the biological clock runs out; the cells "age" and stop dividing. The research shows that human cells grow older each time they divide because their telomeres shorten; in a way they are "chewed up" just a bit with each successive cell division. If a chromosome does not have telomeres of the proper length, the cell will not divide. This finding is still somewhat controversial but holds promise for an explanation of aging.

*External*, or *lifestyle*, *factors* also affect how long a person will live. For example, people who reside on farms live longer than those who reside in cities; normal-weight people live longer than overweight people; and people who do not smoke cigarettes, who are not constantly tense or hostile, who wear seatbelts, and who are not exposed to disease or radiation live longer than others. Because data on external factors are often obtained from correlational studies, cause-and-effect statements cannot be based on them; it is reasonable to assume, however, that external factors such as disease, smoking, and obesity affect a person's life span.

Several theories use *physiological explanations* to account for aging. Because a person's physiological processes depend on both hereditary and environmental factors, these theories rely on both concepts. The *wear-and-tear theory* of aging claims that the human organism simply wears out from overuse, like a machine (Hayflick, 1996); this idea has intuitive appeal but little research support. What little research does support this information focuses on how the body uses its energy stores and indicates that the more active a life a person lives, the less efficient may be the body's use of energy and the faster the aging process (Levine & Stadtman, 1992). A related theory, the *homeostatic theory*, suggests that the body's ability to adjust to stress and other variations in internal conditions decreases with age. For example, as the ability to maintain a constant body temperature decreases, cellular and tissue damage occur and aging results. Similarly, when the body can no longer control the use of sugar through the output of insulin, signs of aging appear. It is important to note, however, that aging may be the *cause* of deviations from homeostasis, rather than the result.

It is also important to distinguish between primary and secondary aging. *Primary aging* is the normal, inevitable change that occurs among human beings and is irreversible, progressive, and universal. Such aging happens despite good health; a consequence of such aging is that a person is more vulnerable to society's fast-paced and sometimes stressful lifestyles. *Secondary aging* is aging due to extrinsic factors such as disease, environmental pollution, or smoking. Lack of good nutrition is a secondary aging factor that can be a cause of poor health among lower-income elderly Canadians.

## THE SEARCH FOR IDENTITY: ADULT STAGE THEORIES

Some theorists think of life as a journey along a road from birth to death. This metaphor is encapsulated in Erik Erikson's stage theory, in which people move through a series of stages and must resolve a different dilemma in each stage in order to develop a healthy identity.

ERIK ERIKSON—REVISITED.　　An important aspect of Erikson's stage theory is that it encompasses the entire life span. At each stage, people attempt to solve a particular dilemma and they move toward greater maturity as they pass from stage to stage. In Chapter 10 we addressed stages 1 to 4, which focused on childhood. Let's now consider the stages that begin with adolescence.

Erikson's stage 5, *identity versus role confusion*, marks the end of childhood and the beginning of adolescence. According to Erikson, the growth and turmoil of adolescence creates an "identity crisis." The major task for adolescents is to resolve that crisis successfully by forming an *identity*: a sense of who they are, where they are going, and their place in the world. Adolescents have to form an identity that is multifaceted and includes vocational choices, religious beliefs, gender roles, sexual beliefs, and ethnic customs. The task is daunting, and this is one reason why adolescence is such a key stage of development. In Erikson's view, the failure to form an identity leaves the adolescent confused about adult roles and unable to cope with the demands of adulthood, including the development of mature relationships with members of the opposite sex (Erikson, 1963, 1968). James Marcia (2002) of Simon Fraser University has worked extensively in this area and extended much of what Erikson had to say about this stage, including that identity issues can carry forward well into adulthood. The special problems of adolescence—which occasionally include rebellion, suicidal feelings, and drug problems—also must be dealt with at this stage.

Stage 6 (young adulthood) involves *intimacy versus isolation*. Young adults begin to select other people with whom they can form intimate, caring relationships. They learn to relate on an emotionally deep basis with members of the opposite sex and commit to a lasting relationship. Failure to resolve the dilemma of intimacy results in feelings of isolation.

In stage 7 (middle adulthood), *generativity versus stagnation*, people become more aware of their mortality and develop a concern for future generations. They now hope to convey to the next generation, particularly to their children, information, love, and warmth. They do so through acts of caring (Bradley & Marcia, 1998). As adults, they hope to guide the following generations; otherwise they will stagnate (remain self-absorbed), feeling that they have done nothing for the next generation.

▼ In Erickson's "intimacy versus isolation" stage, young adults begin to relate emotionally to others and commit to a lasting relationship.

In stage 8 (late adulthood), *ego integrity versus despair*, people decide whether their existence is meaningful, happy, and cohesive, or wasteful and unproductive. Many individuals never fully complete stage 8, and some do so with regrets and a feeling that life is too short. Those who do master and complete this stage feel fulfilled, with a sense that they understand, at least partly, what life is about.

Table 11.1 summarizes stages 5 to 8 of Erikson's theory.

LEVINSON'S LIFE STRUCTURES.　　Another noted theorist, Daniel Levinson, has devised a different stage theory of adult development. He agrees that people go through stages and that they share similar experiences at key points in their lives. Like Erikson, Levinson also agrees that studying those shared experiences allows psychologists to help people better manage their lives. Unlike Erikson, however, Levinson does not see life as a journey toward some specific goal or objective leading to maturity. Rather, he believes that a theory of development should lay out the eras during which individuals master various developmental tasks. In his words (Levinson, 1980, p. 289): "We change in different ways, according to different timetables. Yet, I

## TABLE 11.1    Erikson's Last Four Stages of Psychosocial Development

| Stage | Approximate Age | Important Event | Description |
|---|---|---|---|
| 5. Identity versus role confusion | Adolescence | Peer relationships | The teenager must achieve a sense of identity that encompasses occupation, gender roles, sexual behaviour, and religion. |
| 6. Intimacy versus isolation | Young adulthood | Love relationships | The young adult must develop intimate relationships or suffer feelings of isolation. |
| 7. Generativity versus stagnation | Middle adulthood | Parenting and work | Each adult must find some way to contribute to and support the next generation. |
| 8. Ego integrity versus despair | Late adulthood | Reflection on and acceptance of one's life | Ideally, the person arrives at a sense of acceptance of oneself as one is and a sense of fulfilment. |

believe that everyone lives through the same developmental periods in adulthood . . . though people go through them in their own ways."

Levinson (1978) suggests that, as people grow older, they adapt to the demands and tasks of life. He describes four basic eras in the adult life cycle—adolescence, early adulthood, middle adulthood, and late adulthood—each with distinctive qualities and different life problems, tasks, and situations. Each era also brings with it different *life structures*—unique patterns of behaviour and ways of interacting with the world. These are the "themes" of one's life at a given time, as reflected in two or three major areas of chosen commitment. Levinson's theory highlights periods of questioning and doubt alternating with periods of stability. He said that the midlife crisis is one of those major questioning periods.

During *adolescence* (ages 11 to 17), young people enter the adult world but are still immature and vulnerable. During *early adulthood* (ages 18 to 45), they make their first major life choices regarding family, occupation, and style of living. Throughout this period, adults move toward greater independence and senior positions in the community. They raise their children, strive to advance their careers, and launch their offspring into the adult world. Early adulthood is an era of striving for, gaining, and accepting responsibility. By the end of this era, at about age 45, most people are no longer caring for young children but increasingly may be involved in assisting aging parents.

The midlife crisis occurs at the end of early adulthood. In fact, Levinson calls particular attention to it, asserting that most adults experience a crisis in their early forties. During this era, people often realize that their lives are half over—that if they are to change their lives, they must do so now. Of those who are dissatisfied with the life they have made, some resign themselves to their original course; others decide to change, grow, and strive to achieve new goals.

*Middle adulthood* spans the years from 46 to 65. Adults now learn to live with the decisions they made during early adulthood. Career and family usually are established. People experience either a sense of satisfaction, self-worth, and accomplishment or a sense that much of their life has been wasted. It is often during this period that people reach their peak in creativity and achievement (Simonton, 1988).

People approaching their sixties begin to prepare for late adulthood, making whatever major career and family decisions are necessary before retirement. People in their early sixties generally learn to assess their lives not in terms of money or day-to-day successes but according to whether life has been meaningful, happy, and cohesive. At this time, people typically try to optimize their life, because they know that at least two-thirds of it has passed and they wish to make the most of their remaining years. Depending on how well people come to accept themselves at this stage, the next decade may be one of great fulfilment or of great despair.

Levinson's fourth and final era, *late adulthood*, covers the years from age 65 on. During retirement, many people relax and enjoy life. Children, grandchildren, and even great-grandchildren can become the focus of an older person's life.

Levinson's stage theory is a bit more rigid about its timetable than is Erikson's, and it focuses on developmental tasks, or themes. Levinson's theory is an alternative to Erikson's, but difficult to evaluate experimentally.

**GENDER DIFFERENCES IN ADULT STAGES.**   Levinson developed his theory by studying 40 men in detail over several years. His subjects were interviewed weekly for several months and again after two years. Spouses were interviewed, and extensive biographical data were collected. Levinson's theory has achieved wide acclaim, but it has also been challenged. A major shortcoming of his research is that it was based on information gathered from a small sample of middle-class men between the ages of 35 and 45.

Levinson eventually developed a theory of female development. Women apparently follow life stages similar to those for men. As children, women are taught different values, goals, and approaches toward life, which often are reflected later in their choice of vocations, hobbies, and intellectual pursuits. Historically, women have pursued different career paths than men. More recently, women are increasingly entering areas previously dominated by men. For example, women now comprise nearly half of all law school students. However, this does not mean that all female lawyers choose to follow the traditional path from associate to partner that is generally chosen by males. In *The Seasons of a Woman's Life* (1996), Levinson points out the complexities of women's lives based on his interviews with a small sample of women. According to Levinson, women must deal with contradictory roles and responsibilities, which makes tracking of their life stages and transitions a complex task.

The developmental course of women, and especially of women's transitions, is similar to that of men; but some women tend to experience transitions and life events at later ages and in more irregular sequences (Smart & Peterson, 1994). In addition, women experience events such as midlife transitions differently than men. While some men approach a midlife crisis at age 40 as a last chance to hold on to their youth, many women see it as a time to reassess, refocus, and revitalize their creative energies (Apter, 1995; Levinson, 1996). At 50, many women become suddenly aware of their aging due to physical changes in their body—especially declining fertility—and this creates a different type of transition (Jarrett & Lethbridge, 1994; Pearlmann, 1993).

Women still face discrimination in the workplace, and society continues to be ambivalent in its expectations for women. Women still have the primary responsibility for child care; in the aftermath of a divorce, the woman often gets physical custody of the children. Women often must juggle multiple roles (Williams et al., 1991). The assumption of solo child-care responsibility after divorce has sharp economic consequences that alter the lifestyle, mental health, and course of life stages for many women (McBride, 1990). Further, the issues in women's transitions are often different from those in men's; women tend to focus more on intimacy and relationships than do men (Caffarella & Olson, 1993). Thus, obvious life stage differences exist for men and women—whether they are upper, middle, or lower class—but even greater differences exist *within* groups of demographically similar men or women. Even popular accounts of life span development such as Gail Sheehy's *New Passages* (1995) and *Men's Passages* (1998) recognize the enormous individual differences that exist in people's ability to alter, customize, and create their life courses.

## COGNITIVE CHANGES IN ADULTHOOD

Changes in intellectual functioning that occur with age are pretty small. Up to the age of 65, there is little decline in learning or memory; motivation, interest, and

**HandsOnPsych**
Version 2.0
**Development II**

recent educational experience (or lack of it) are more important than age with regard to a person's ability to master complex knowledge (Willis & Schaie, 1999). Although many people believe that declines in intellectual functioning are drastic and universal, they are not. Researchers do agree that certain cognitive abilities, especially in mathematics and memory functions, begin to deteriorate in many people after age 60.

Although most research indicates that cognitive abilities and memory functions typically decrease with advancing age (Anstey et al., 2001), many of the changes are of little importance for day-to-day functioning (Meinz & Salthouse, 1997; Salthouse, 1999; Schaie, 2000). For example, overall vocabulary decreases only slightly. Moreover, some of the changes observed in laboratory tasks (for example, reaction-time tasks) are small and can be forestalled or reversed through cognitive interventions. Yet there is no doubt that the brain encodes information differently in the young than in the old. See Table 11.2 for a summary of age-related changes in intellectual skills through adulthood.

Researchers generally acknowledge that some age-related decrements do occur, especially after age 65 (e.g., Hambrick, Salthouse, & Meinz, 1999; Salthouse, 2000; Sharit & Czajia, 1999); however, such effects are often less apparent in cognitively active individuals. Many researchers, including David Hultsch at the University of Victoria, suggest a "use it and you are less likely to lose it" approach (Hultsch et al., 1999; Kliegl et al., 2001). Research by Morris Moscovitch at the University of Toronto also supports this view, indicating that some of the effects of aging on memory may be due to effects on frontal lobe function and that ongoing mental activity may slow these effects (Dawson, Winocur, & Moscovitch, 1999; Moscovitch & Winocur, 1995). Most Canadians are aging well (Johnson, 1995) and with appropriate health care and social support systems, older individuals can do just fine, especially in everyday situations (Baltes, 1993).

## PERSONALITY DEVELOPMENT

A basic tenet of most personality theories is that, regardless of day-to-day variations, an individual's personality remains stable over time. That is, despite deviations from normal patterns of development, the way a person copes with life tends to remain fairly consistent throughout her or his lifetime. But personality may

| TABLE 11.2 Summary of Age-Related Changes in Intellectual Skills | | |
|---|---|---|
| **Ages 20–40** | **Ages 40–65** | **Age 65 and Older** |
| Peak intellectual ability between about 20 and 35 | Maintenance of skill on measures of verbal intelligence; some decline of skill on measures of performance intelligence; decline usually not functionally significant until age 60 or older | Some loss of verbal intelligence; most noticeable in adults with poorer health, lower levels of activity, and less education |
| Optimal performance on memory tasks | Little change in performance on memory tasks, except perhaps some slowing later in this period | Slowing of retrieval processes and other memory processes; less skilful use of coding strategies for new memories |
| Peak performance on laboratory tests of problem solving | Peak performance on real-life problem-solving tasks and many verbal abilities | Decline in problem-solving performance on both laboratory and real-life tests |

Source: Adapted from Bee (1987).

**Be an**
**ACTIVE LEARNER**

**REVIEW**
> What are the major sensory, physical, cognitive, and social changes that occur during adulthood? pp. 397–399
> In each of Erikson's eight stages, people face dilemmas. What are the consequences of a poor outcome at any one stage? pp. 400–401
> Why do some women experience transitions and life events at later ages and in less orderly sequences than men do? p. 402

**THINK CRITICALLY**
> What might be the implications of the finding that women follow a different developmental progression than do men?
> With so many people divorcing, what interventions might psychologists implement on a societal level to help decrease the divorce rate?
> Of how much importance are chance encounters in life? Why?

**APPLY PSYCHOLOGY**
> Write a brief set of hints to help parents better communicate with their teenage children; keep in mind that parents themselves are developing.
> What can individuals do as adults to help prepare themselves for retirement years? Make a list of at least five specific things that people in middle adulthood (ages 45 to 60) can do to prepare for growing older.

also be sensitive to the unique experiences of the individual, especially during the adult years. The adult years are filled with great personal challenges and opportunities and therefore require people to be innovative, flexible, and adaptive. Positive changes during adulthood—the development of a sense of generativity, the fulfilment of yearnings for love and respect—usually depend on some degree of success during earlier life stages. Adults who continue to have an especially narrow outlook are less likely to experience personality growth in later life.

It is important to remember that despite evidence that old age takes a toll, there are many remarkable examples of intellectual achievement by people 70 years of age or older. Golda Meir, for example, became prime minister of Israel at age 70. Chief Dan George's prominent film career began in his seventies. Arthur Rubinstein, the Polish-born concert pianist, gave one of his greatest recitals at age 81. Older individuals have a certain wisdom that comes with the experience of having lived a long life.

## Late Adulthood: Growing Older, Growing Wiser

No human being has lived past 122 years of age. Most of us will not achieve such longevity, but as we grow older, we age experientially as well as physically; that is, we gather experiences and expand our worlds. Nevertheless, in Western society, growing older is not always easy, especially because of the negative stereotypes associated with the aging process. Today, however, people are healthier than ever before, are approaching later years with vigour, and look forward to second and sometimes third careers. In general, being over age 65 brings with it new developmental tasks—retirement, coping with health issues, and maintaining a long-term standard of living.

How older people view themselves depends in part on how society treats them. Many Asian, First Nations, and African cultures greatly respect the elderly for their wisdom and maturity; in such societies, grey hair is a mark of distinction, not an embarrassment. In contrast, Western cultures tend to be youth-oriented and people spend a fortune on everything from hair dyes to facelifts to make themselves look younger. However, because the average age of North Americans is climbing, how the elderly are perceived by others and how they perceive themselves may be changing.

Approximately 12.7 percent of the Canadian population—or nearly 4 million Canadians—are 65 years of age or older. According to Statistics Canada (2002), the proportion of elderly people is expected to increase to 18 percent of the total population by the year 2021, when the number of Canadians over 65 will exceed 6.6 million. Figure 11.2 illustrates how Canada's population has been growing older over the past few decades. At present, the average life expectancy at birth in Canada is about 78 years, and the oldest of the old—those over 85—are the most rapidly growing elderly age group. Life expectancy is different for men and women, however. Women live about six years longer than men, on average.

For many people, the years after age 60 are filled with new activities and excitement. Both men and women enjoy doing things that they may not have been able to do before because of family commitments. Canadian seniors receive 60 percent of their income from private pensions, investments, and earnings and 40 percent from government pensions and benefits. The median income of Canadian families headed by a senior was about $33 000 (Health Canada, 1998). Most seniors maintain close friendships and stay in touch with family members. Some, however, experience loneliness and isolation because many of their friends and relatives have died or they have lost touch with their families. In Canada, there are now as many people over the age of 65 as there are under the age of 8.

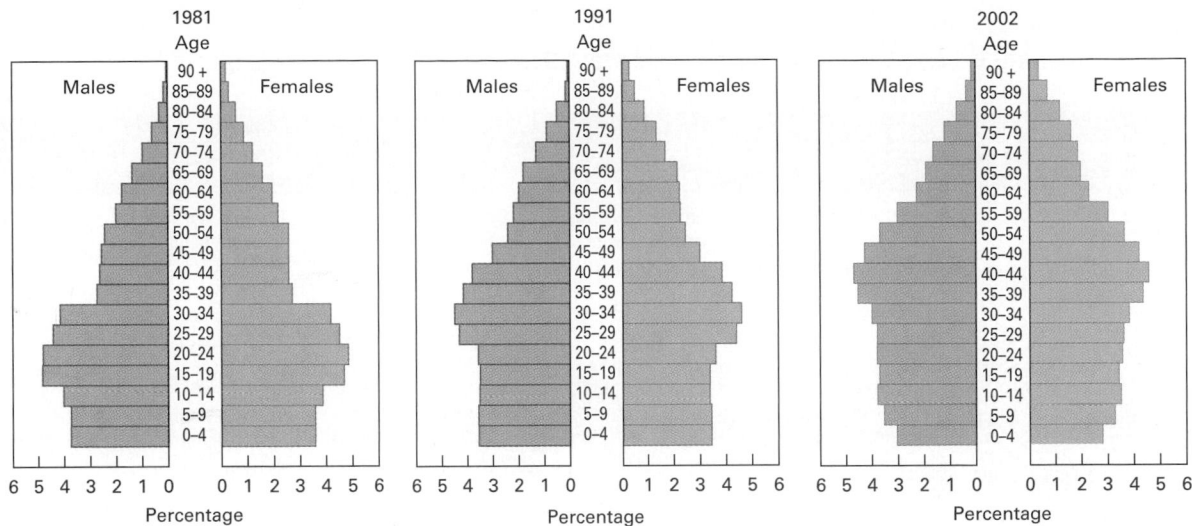

| 1981 | 1991 | 2002 |

MYTHS, REALITIES, AND STEREOTYPES

There is a widely held myth that older people are less intelligent than younger people, less able to care for themselves, inflexible, and sickly. The reality is that many elderly people are as competent and capable as they were in earlier adulthood. They work, play golf, run marathons, socialize, and stay politically aware and active. Most older adults maintain a good sex life (Bretschneider & McCoy, 1988) and positive mental health. Of course, some people will conduct life's activities in a frail, disorganized manner, even when young; others, although chronologically old, are youthful and vigorous and happy (Carstensen & Charles, 1998; Jones & Meredith, 2000). How engaged older adults become in life is a key factor; willingness to persevere, cope, and stay involved seems central to a happy set of elderly years (Nair, 2000). Building Table 11.2 summarizes important changes in adult functioning through late adulthood.

AGEISM.    Stereotypes about the elderly have given rise to **ageism**—prejudice against the elderly and the discrimination that follows from it. Ageism is prevalent in the job market, in which older people are not given the same opportunities as their younger co-workers, and in housing and health care. Ageism is exceptionally prevalent in the media—on television and in newspapers, cartoons, and magazines—and in everyday language (Schaie, 1993). Schmidt and Boland (1986) examined everyday language to learn how people perceive older adults. They found interesting differences. For example, *elder statesman* implies that a person is experienced, wise, or perhaps conservative. However, *old statesman* might suggest that a person is past his prime, tired, or useless. The term *old people* may allude to positive elements in older adults—for example, being the perfect grandparent—or to negative qualities such as grouchiness or mental deficiencies. What does *old* mean?

Older people who are perceived as representing negative stereotypes are more likely to suffer discrimination than those who appear to represent more positive stereotypes. This means that an older person who appears healthy, bright, and alert is more likely to be treated with the same respect shown to younger people. By contrast, an older adult who appears less capable may not be given the same respect or treatment. In Chapter 13, we'll see that first impressions have a potent effect on people's behaviour. This seems to be particularly true for older people. An older person's physical appearance may evoke

**FIGURE 11.2**
**A Nation Growing Older**

Note that, in 1981, the baby boom shows up in the 15 to 29 years age category; by 2002, the baby boom is in the 35 to 49 years age category.

Adapted from data in Statistics Canada (2002 and 2003).

AGEISM

Prejudice against the elderly and the discrimination that follows from it.

▼ For many individuals, the years after age 60 are filled with new activities and interests.

## BUILDING TABLE 11.2    Major Changes in Important Domains of Adult Functioning

| Age | Physical Change | Cognitive Change | Work Roles | Personal Development | Major Tasks |
|---|---|---|---|---|---|
| Young Adulthood, 18–25 | Peak functioning in most physical skills; optimal time for child-bearing | Cognitive skills high on most measures | Choice of career, which may involve several job changes | Conformity; task of establishing intimacy | Separate from family; form partnership; begin family; find job; create individual life pattern |
| Early Adulthood, 25–40 | Good physical functioning in most areas; health habits during this time establish later risks | Peak period of cognitive skill on most measures | Rising work satisfaction; major emphasis on career or work success; most career progress steps made | Task of passing on skills, knowledge, love (generativity) | Rear family; establish personal work pattern and strive for success |
| Middle Adulthood, 40–65 | Beginning signs of physical decline in some areas (strength, elasticity of tissues, height, cardiovascular function) | Some signs of loss of cognitive skill on timed, unexercised skills | Career reaches plateau, but higher work satisfaction | Increase in self-confidence, openness | Launch family; redefine life goals; redefine self outside of family and work roles; care for aging parents |
| Late Adulthood, 65–75+ | Significant physical decline on most measures | Small declines for virtually all adults on some skills | Retirement | Integration of ideas and experiences, perhaps self-actualization; task of ego integrity | Cope with retirement; cope with declining health; redefine life goals and sense of self |

ageism on sight, whereas a younger person may not be judged until more data are obtained. In any case, ageism can be reduced if people recognize the diversity that exists among aging populations.

## HEALTH IN LATE ADULTHOOD

Many people lead not only happy but also healthy lives well into late adulthood. Of course, as people age various aches, pains, and a certain slowing of responses occur. While some older people have serious problems with arthritis, hypertension, and some orthopedic problems, many lead active, relatively healthy lifestyles. Nevertheless there are problems for some older individuals. One of those problems is dementia.

You might assume that aging is inevitably accompanied by *senility,* a term once used to describe cognitive changes that occur in older people. Today, psychologists know that cognitive deficits are caused by brain disorders, sometimes termed *dementias,* that occur only in *some* older people. **Dementias** are long-standing impairments of mental functioning and global cognitive abilities in otherwise alert individuals, causing a memory loss and related symptoms. Only a small proportion of people ages 60 to 65 suffer from dementias. The percentage begins to increase after 65 years of age to 2.4 percent of people between 65 and 74 years, 11.1 percent of people ages 75 to 84, and 34.5 percent of those age 85 and older (Canadian Study of Health and Aging Working Group, 1994).

DEMENTIA

A long-standing impairment of mental functioning and global cognitive abilities in otherwise alert individuals, causing memory loss and related symptoms.

More than 70 conditions cause dementias. Among them are arteriosclerosis (hardening of the arteries), Parkinson's disease, Huntington's disease, syphilis, and multiple sclerosis. Moreover, the failing immune systems of AIDS patients can cause brain infections, which in turn can lead to dementia. Memory loss often first occurs for recent events and later occurs for past events. Additional symptoms include loss of language skills, reduced capacity for abstract thinking, personality changes, and loss of a sense of time and place. Severe and disabling dementias affect about 316 500 Canadians. With the increasing number of elderly citizens, these statistics are on the rise.

Some conditions that cause dementia can be treated, and that treatment often halts (but does not necessarily reverse) the dementia. Such *reversible dementias*, which can be caused by malnutrition, alcoholism, or toxins (poisons), usually affect younger people. *Irreversible dementias* are most commonly of two types: multiple infarct dementia and Alzheimer's disease. *Multiple infarct dementia* usually is caused by two or more small strokes (ruptures of small blood vessels in the brain); it results in a slow degeneration of the brain.

**Alzheimer's disease** is a chronic and progressive disorder of the brain and the most common cause of degenerative dementia in Canada. Named after Dr. Alois Alzheimer, a German physician who first studied its symptoms, it could well be the most widespread neurological disorder of all time (see Figure 11.3). At autopsy, threadlike tangles of protein (called neurofibrillary tangles) and clumps of protein and degenerating neurons (called amyloid plaques) are identified in the patient's brain.

People of all kinds can be victims of Alzheimer's disease, and all confront an unkind fate. In addition to memory loss, language deterioration, poor visual/spatial skills, and indifferent attitudes characterize this disease. It accounts for about 50 percent of the cases of progressive memory loss in aging individuals. (Vascular dementia and other similar disease processes account for 10 to 20 percent, and depression for about 1 to 5 percent. The other causes are metabolic, infectious, traumatic, inflammatory, and mass lesion disorders.)

As the population grows older, the number of cases of Alzheimer's disease increases. Currently, there are 160 000 diagnosed Alzheimer's patients in Canada (Health Canada, 2001) and nearly 20 million worldwide; in addition, there are an untold number of undiagnosed cases. Because Alzheimer's is a degenerative disease, its progression cannot be stopped; it is irreversible and ultimately ends in death. To date, there is no fully effective method of prevention, treatment, or cure.

Scientific findings about possible causes of the disease come from a wide variety of sources, and it is generally argued that there are multiple routes to the disease. Not only do researchers not know the exact causes of Alzheimer's disease, but no

**ALZHEIMER'S [ALTZ-hy-merz] DISEASE**
A chronic and progressive disorder of the brain that is the most common cause of degenerative dementia.

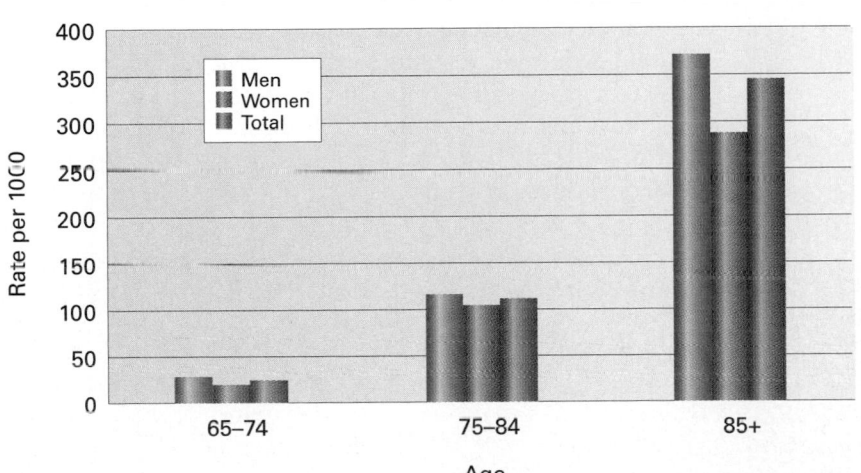

**FIGURE 11.3**

**Incidence of Dementia, by Age, Caused by Alzheimer's Disease or Strokes, Canada 1991–92**

Source: *Canadian Study of Health and Aging*, Health Canada, June 30, 2003, reproduced with the permission of the Minister of Public Works and Government Services Canada, 2004.

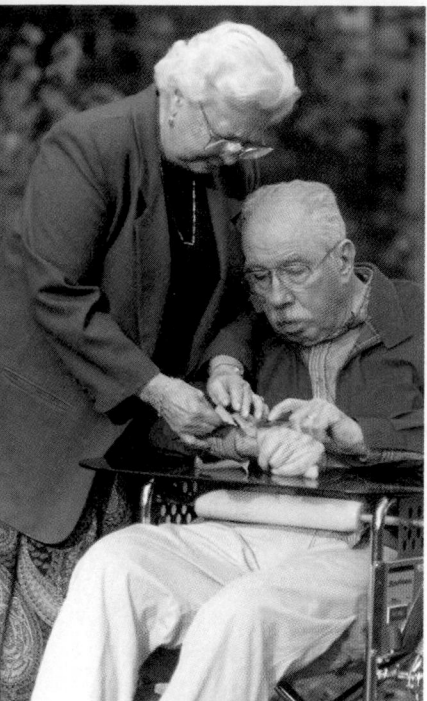

▲ To date, there is no effective method of prevention, cure, or treatment for Alzheimer's disease.

THANATOLOGY

The study of the psychological and medical aspects of death and dying.

**Be an**
### ACTIVE LEARNER

**REVIEW**
> Describe ageism and its impact on older individuals. pp. 405–406
> What is dementia? p. 406
> What are the effects of Alzheimer's disease? p. 407

**THINK CRITICALLY**
> How might the cognitive changes associated with aging influence the health and well-being of older adults?
> Why do you think people are living to older and older ages? What are new challenges that very old people face that old people of previous generations did not have to deal with?
> What special emotional problems might need to be addressed when a terminally ill person enters a hospice program?

**APPLY PSYCHOLOGY**
> Write a paragraph that describes the oldest person you know. Does the person's health and behaviour fit the stereotypes that most people have about older people?
> How would you define successful aging? Make a list of at least five criteria for successful aging.

one has developed an effective treatment. Research is showing that there may be specific genes on specific chromosomes that cause nearly all of the cases of early-onset familial Alzheimer's; such research may lead to an understanding of the biochemical causes of the disease (Sherrington et al., 1995). The discovery of these genes may lead to diagnostic tests that can be offered to individuals who are at risk because of family history.

## DEATH: THE END OF THE LIFE SPAN

People's overall health deteriorates as they age. For men, the probability of dying doubles in each decade after midlife. In some people, blood pressure rises, cardiac output decreases, and the likelihood of stroke increases, often as a result of cardiovascular disease, which also affects intellectual functioning by decreasing blood flow to the brain (Riegal & Bennett, 2000). Some individuals experience *terminal drop*—a rapid decline in intellectual functioning in the year before death. Some researchers attribute this change to cardiovascular disease, claiming that decreased blood flow (and resulting decrease in oxygen) to the brain causes declining mental ability and, ultimately, failing health. However, although there is evidence for the terminal drop, no satisfactory method exists for predicting death on the basis of poor performance on intelligence or neuropsychological tests (Petersen et al., 2001).

If you are young, perhaps an adolescent, you are more likely than older people to die from automobile accidents or AIDS. But the majority of the population dies at an older age and so the leading causes of death in Canada are heart disease, cancer, strokes, and accidents; in fact, 7 out of 10 older Canadians die from heart disease, cancer, or stroke. The number of Canadians who succumb to heart disease has decreased because of improved health, reduced smoking, and positive lifestyle changes among Canadians. Strokes take their toll every year by cutting off the blood supply to the brain; strokes are significantly less common among men and women who do not smoke, who manage their high blood pressure, and who exercise regularly. But cancer continues to increase; despite good cure rates, half of all cancers are found in men and women over the age of 65. A healthy lifestyle decreases the likelihood of disease, and research shows that older adults can achieve the fitness levels of younger adults (Danner & Edwards, 1992) and show increased self-esteem (Tiggemann & Williamson, 2000).

Everyone recognizes that death is inevitable, but in the twentieth century few people actually witnessed death (Aiken, 1985). Before the twentieth century, most people died in bed at home, where other people were likely to be with them. Today, nearly 80 percent of Canadians die in hospitals and nursing homes. **Thanatology**, the study of the psychological and medical aspects of death and dying, has become an interdisciplinary specialty. Researchers and theorists in several areas—including theology, law, history, psychology, sociology, and medicine—have come together to better understand death and dying. For psychologists, dealing with the process of dying is especially complicated because people do not like to talk or think about death. Nevertheless, considerable progress has been made toward understanding the psychology of dying.

# Summary and Review

## ADOLESCENCE: BRIDGING THE GAP

### Distinguish between puberty and adolescence.

> *Puberty* is the period during which the reproductive system matures; it signals the end of childhood. There is considerable variation among individuals as to its time of onset. *Adolescence* is the period extending from the end of childhood (often defined as the onset of puberty) to early adulthood.   **p. 382**

### What are the major changes experienced by adolescents?

> *Secondary sex characteristics* are the genetically determined physical features that differentiate the sexes but are not directly involved with reproduction. Examples are bodily hair patterns, pitch of voice, and muscle development.   **p. 383**

> Changes in intellectual abilities, body proportions, and sexual urges (together with changing relationships with parents and peers) create enormous challenges for adolescents. For some, the changes are problematic emotionally. Adolescents also develop cognitive distortions, especially the *imaginary audience* and the *personal fable*, in which they see themselves as "on stage" all the time and so special and unique that other people cannot understand them. The challenges of adolescence, however, must be considered in a cultural context, because most of the research on adolescence has been conducted with white, middle-class teenagers—who are clearly not representative of all adolescents.   **pp. 384, 386**

### Describe some factors that influence cognitive and social development in adolescence, especially with respect to gender similarities and differences.

> Cognitive differences between male and female adolescents are minimal, but social differences are significant. Adolescents develop a self-image based on a set of beliefs about themselves; other people also generate expectations and beliefs about adolescents, and these beliefs affect them. The influence on adolescents of peer groups, people who identify with and compare themselves to one another, is formidable.   **pp. 388–389**

> *Gender identity* is a person's sense of being male or female. Parents are the first and most important forces acting to shape gender identity; they influence a child from birth. Peers and schools are other important sources of influence. *Gender schema theory* asserts that children and adolescents use gender as an organizing theme to classify and interpret their perceptions about the world and themselves.   **pp. 389–390**

> Most people adopt gender role stereotypes—beliefs about which gender-based behaviours are appropriate and acceptable for each gender; such beliefs are strongly regulated and reinforced by society. But *androgyny*, in which some stereotypically male and some stereotypically female characteristics are apparent in one individual, is more common today than in the past.   **p. 392**

> Eating disorders are psychological disorders marked by gross disturbances in eating behaviour and in responses to food. *Anorexia nervosa* is an eating disorder characterized by the obstinate and wilful refusal to eat, a distorted body image, and an intense fear of being fat. *Bulimia nervosa* involves repeated episodes of binge eating accompanied by fear of not being able to stop eating. Bulimics often purge themselves of unwanted calories by vomiting and using laxatives and diuretics.   **pp. 394–395**

### What is friendship?

> Friendship is a close emotional tie between peers. Close friends ideally interact as equals, enjoy each other's company, have mutual trust, provide mutual assistance, accept each other as they are, respect each other's judgment, feel free to be themselves with each other, understand each other, and share confidences. High-school students typically report having three to five good friends. Adolescents spend as much as 29 percent of their waking hours with friends. Among adults in Western cultures, expectations for specific gender-based behaviours often control male–female interactions in friendship.   **pp. 393, 395**

### How have adolescent sexual behaviour and attitudes changed in recent years?

> More so than previous generations, today's adolescents view sexual intimacy as a normal part of growing up. Premarital heterosexual activity has become more common among adolescents, especially 13- to 17-year-olds. More relaxed attitudes concerning adolescent sexual behaviour have brought about increased awareness among adolescents about contraception and pregnancy. Yet teen pregnancy is still widely prevalent; thus, increased awareness does not imply that the problem is being solved.   **p. 396**

#### KEY TERMS

adolescence, p. 382; puberty, p. 382; secondary sex characteristics, p. 383, imaginary audience, p. 386; personal fable, p. 386; gender identity, p. 389; gender schema theory, p. 390; longitudinal study, p. 392; cross-sectional study, p. 392; androgynous, p. 392; anorexia nervosa, p. 395; bulimia nervosa, p. 395

## ADULTHOOD: YEARS OF STABILITY AND CHANGE

### Describe the effects of aging.

> Physical development and aging continue throughout adulthood. In general, strength, muscle tone, and overall

fitness deteriorate from age 30 on. There are also sensory changes, including slower reaction time after age 65. Sexual behaviour and desire typically change, and physical changes related to sexuality occur in adults of both sexes.  **pp. 397–398**

> Primary aging is the normal, inevitable change that occurs with age and is irreversible, progressive, and universal. Secondary aging is aging that is due to extrinsic factors such as disease, environmental pollution, and smoking.  **p. 399**

> Most research indicates that cognitive abilities decrease somewhat with advancing age, but many of the late-life changes are of little importance for day-to-day functioning and affect only some people.  **pp. 402–403**

### Describe Erikson's last four stages of psychosocial development.

> Erikson's stage 5, identity versus role confusion, marks the end of childhood and the beginning of adolescence; adolescents must decide who they are and what they want to do in life. Stage 6 (young adulthood) is characterized by intimacy versus isolation; young adults begin to select other people with whom they can form intimate, caring relationships. In stage 7 (middle adulthood), generativity versus stagnation, people become more aware of their mortality and develop a particular concern for future generations. Finally, in stage 8 (late adulthood), ego integrity versus despair, people decide whether their existence is meaningful, happy, and cohesive or wasteful and unproductive.  **pp. 400–401**

### Describe Levinson's theory of adult development.

> According to Levinson's stage theory of adulthood, all adults live through the same developmental periods, though people go through them in their own ways. His theory of adult development (which was generated from data on men) describes four basic eras: adolescence, early adulthood, middle adulthood, and late adulthood. Each has distinctive qualities and different life problems, tasks, and situations.  **pp. 400–402**

### Do women's life stages parallel men's?

> Women do not necessarily follow the same life stages as men. Women tend to experience transitions and life events at later ages and in less orderly sequences than those reported by Levinson.  **p. 402**

## LATE ADULTHOOD: GROWING OLDER, GROWING WISER

### Who are the aged, and how is life different in late adulthood?

> In general, being over age 65 classifies a person as being aged. Approximately 12.7 percent of the Canadian population—more than 3.6 million Canadians—are 65 years of age or older.  **p. 404**

> *Ageism* is discrimination on the basis of age, often resulting in the denial of rights and services to the elderly.  **p. 405**

> Brain disorders called *dementias* involve losses of cognitive or mental functioning. Reversible dementias, which may be caused by malnutrition, alcoholism, or toxins (poisons), usually affect younger people. Irreversible dementias are of two types: multiple infarct dementia and Alzheimer's disease.  **pp. 406–407**

> Currently, there are about 160 000 diagnosed Alzheimer's patients in Canada. *Alzheimer's disease* is a degenerative disorder whose progression cannot be stopped; it is irreversible and ultimately ends in death. Individuals who suffer from Alzheimer's disease slowly lose their memory. Within months, or sometimes years, they lose speech and language functions. Eventually, they lose all bodily and mental control.  **pp. 407–408**

### KEY TERMS

ageism, p. 405; dementia, p. 406; Alzheimer's disease, p. 407; thanatology, p. 408

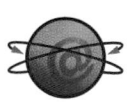

Take advantage of the multimedia resources available with this text! Follow the marginal icons to access the interactive modules on the *HandsOnPsych* CD-ROM; log on to *MyPsychLab* to explore the ebook, study aids, and other online resources; and visit the Companion Website at **www.pearsoned.ca/lefton** for additional exercises and links.

# 12 Personality and Its Assessment

Harry Potter's first encounter with Severus Snape, the potions master at Hogwarts School of Witchcraft and Wizardry, left Harry with the impression that the potions master was an unpleasant man who disliked him. After the second meeting, Harry believed that *hated* would be a more accurate description of Snape's feelings, and Harry formed some negative opinions of Snape's personality, too. Subsequent encounters led Harry (and other students) to consider Snape suspicious, malicious, and vengeful. Snape seemed to enjoy belittling Harry and finding opportunities to make trouble for Harry and his friends. Thus far in her best-selling Harry Potter series, J. K. Rowling highlights the evil in Snape, presenting his character, much as a child might see him, as one-dimensional and wholly predictable. Many of us are reading the new books in the series to see if this view of Snape's personality continues to make sense.

Such an emphasis on one dimension of a personality is consistent with the personality theory of Gordon Allport, who said that some people have a *cardinal trait* that is so dominant that a person's entire personality revolves around that one trait. According to Allport, most people do not have a cardinal trait, but those who do have one have personalities that are unmistakable. Harry Potter fans associate Snape with malice.

What do real people have in common with such characters? What is necessary to understand the personalities of real people, and are those personalities subject to the extremes that appear in Severus Snape? In Snape's case, what past experiences could have shaped his personality? We will explore some of these questions as we turn to a definition of personality and an examination of theories and assessment of human personality. For the complete story on Snape, we will have to keep reading the Harry Potter series.

# What Is Personality?

**HandsOnPsych**
Version 2.0

**Personality and Health**

Although personality psychologists may disagree on the meaning of the word *personality,* most agree that the term originated from the Latin *persona,* that is, the theatrical mask worn by Roman actors in Greek dramas. Despite the original meaning of the word, psychologists now speak of personality as something more than simply the role people play. **Personality** is a pattern of relatively permanent traits, dispositions, or characteristics that give some consistency to people's behaviour. More specifically, personality includes traits or dispositions that lead you to behave at least somewhat consistently in different environmental situations. However, the definition of personality must also allow for some inconsistency of behaviour. For example, you may behave quite aggressively in one situation but rather submissively in another, depending on the presence of other people, the behaviour of those people, and your own mood and motivation.

The traits, dispositions, or characteristics that make up your personality may be unique to you, common to your particular social group, or shared with all other people. Thus, you are identical to no other person, similar to others in your cultural group, and akin to all other people in some ways.

What causes people to have certain personality dimensions? Personality theorists differ in their answer to this question. Some, such as Freud, focus on unconscious conflicts that originated during childhood; others, such as Skinner, see human personality as largely learned from the environment. Yet others, such as Allport, emphasize the *pattern* of personal traits that characterize people; still others, such as Cattell and Eysenck, look for genetic influences that motivate behaviour and shape personality. Another group of theorists, such as Rogers and Maslow, see humans as moving toward fulfilment or self-actualization. Finally, some personality theorists, such as Bandura, emphasize a variety of cognitive factors that influence personality development and functioning.

Like all theories, personality theories should generate research as well as organize, explain, and predict data. These data help psychologists answer questions such as these:

- Does nature or nurture play a greater role in personality development?
- Do unconscious processes direct behaviour?
- What accounts for the development of stable behaviour patterns in humans?
- Does a person's behaviour depend on the situation?
- Do people behave consistently throughout their lives?

# Psychodynamic Theories

We begin our discussion of personality theories by examining psychodynamic theories—an approach to personality that focuses on how unconscious processes direct day-to-day behaviour. The most famous and perhaps the most widely disputed of these approaches is the psychoanalytic theory of Sigmund Freud. We follow Freud's theory with a discussion of two other psychodynamic theories, namely, the individual psychology of Alfred Adler and the analytical psychology of Carl Jung.

## THE PSYCHOANALYTIC THEORY OF SIGMUND FREUD

Sigmund Freud (1856–1939) was an Austrian physician whose influence on psychology was so great that some of his basic concepts are now taken for granted. Such terms as *ego, oral fixation, death wish, anal retentive, Freudian slip, unconscious motivation,* and *Oedipus complex* are part of everyday language. However, when Freud introduced his ideas, he was seen as strange and radical. Freud's exploration of the unconscious and his suggestion that children have sexual experiences were, to say the least, revolutionary.

Freud developed his theory by treating people with mental problems. Freud used hypnosis and, later, a process known as *free association* to treat people with physical and emotional problems. (We will discuss free association in Chapter 16.) Most of his patients were from the middle and upper classes of Austrian society. Many were married women of wealth and position who, because they lived in a repressive society, had limited opportunities for the release of anxiety and tension. Freud noticed that many of them needed to discuss their problems and often felt better after having done so. From his therapeutic work with these patients, Freud began to formulate a theory of behaviour that centred on early childhood experiences and fantasies. Originally, Freud believed that the neurotic symptoms of his adult patients sprang from their experiences of being sexually seduced by an older person, often a parent. However, he soon abandoned this seduction theory and replaced it with the *Oedipus complex*, a concept that places responsibility for childhood sexual experiences on fantasies of the child rather than the behaviour of the parents. Over time, Freud developed an elaborate theory of personality and an accompanying approach to therapy called *psychoanalysis*.

Psychoanalytic theory rests on several key assumptions:

1. Human experience takes place on three *levels of consciousness*—conscious, preconscious, and unconscious, with the unconscious dominating the other two.
2. Human functioning is influenced by three basic *structures of the mind*—id, ego, and superego.
3. The foundation of personality is shaped mostly by *early childhood experiences*.
4. Parental punishment of a child's *sexual and aggressive* behaviours results in repression of at least part of these experiences and leads to psychological conflict.
5. Unconscious psychological conflict creates anxiety, and all people learn to protect themselves against anxiety by adopting a variety of *defence mechanisms*.

**LEVELS OF MENTAL LIFE.** Freud assumed that mental life can take place on three levels: conscious, preconscious, and unconscious. **Consciousness** occupies a relatively minor place in psychoanalytic theory. It simply refers to those experiences that we are aware of at any given time. It is the only level of mental life directly available to us. The **preconscious** is that level of the mind that contains those experiences that are not currently conscious but may become so with varying degrees of difficulty. You can probably become aware of your social insurance number very easily, but you may have much difficulty recalling some date in history that you learned four years ago. Both the social insurance number and the history date are in your preconscious, but one is easily recalled whereas the other is quite difficult or perhaps impossible to remember.

The **unconscious** contains experiences that, by definition, are beyond the realm of awareness. They are not like the history date, which is simply forgotten; they must remain unconscious to prevent us from experiencing too much anxiety. However, unconscious urges can become preconscious, or even conscious, by adopting a disguise that prevents us from recognizing their true nature. For example, thoughts about harming a despised rival may be too anxiety provoking, so we disguise these thoughts by behaving in an overly friendly manner toward that person. This facade may slip, and we may say or do something that reflects our true feelings of hostility. These *Freudian slips* reveal our true but unconscious thoughts.

**THE STRUCTURE OF THE MIND.** According to Freud's theory, the primary structural elements of the mind and personality are three mental forces (not physical structures of the brain) that reside, fully or partially, in the unconscious: the id, the ego, and the superego. Each force accounts for a different aspect of functioning (see Table 12.1).

The **id** is the source of a person's instinctual energy, which, according to Freud (1933), is either sexual or aggressive. The id works mainly by the *pleasure principle*; that is, it tries to maximize immediate gratification through the satisfaction of raw

CONSCIOUSNESS

Freud's level of mental life that consists of those experiences that we are aware of at any given time.

PRECONSCIOUS

Freud's level of the mind that contains those experiences that are not currently conscious but may become so with varying degrees of difficulty.

UNCONSCIOUS

Freud's level of mental life that consists of mental activities beyond people's normal awareness.

ID

In Freud's theory, the source of a person's instinctual energy, which works mainly on the pleasure principle.

## TABLE 12.1 Comparison of Freud's Three Systems of Personality

| | Nature | Level | Principle | Purpose | Aim |
|---|---|---|---|---|---|
| **Id** | Represents biological aspect | Unconscious | Pleasure | Seek pleasure and avoid pain | Immediate gratification |
| **Ego** | Represents psychological aspect | Conscious, preconscious, and unconscious | Reality | Adapt to reality while controlling the id and superego | Safety, compromise, and delayed gratification |
| **Superego** | Represents societal and parental aspect | Conscious, pre-conscious, and unconscious | Moralistic and idealistic | Represent right and wrong | Perfection |

**EGO**

In Freud's theory, the part of personality that seeks to satisfy instinctual needs in accordance with reality.

**SUPEREGO** [sue-pur-EE-go]

In Freud's theory, the moral aspect of mental functioning, comprising the ego ideal (what a person would ideally like to be) and the conscience and taught by parents and society.

impulses. Residing deep within the unconscious, the demanding, irrational, and selfish id seeks pleasure—without regard for reality or morality.

While the id seeks to maximize pleasure and obtain immediate gratification, the **ego** (which grows out of the id) is the part of the personality that seeks to satisfy the individual's instinctual needs in accordance with reality; that is, it works by the *reality principle*. Whereas the id strives to achieve immediate gratification, the ego attempts to check the power of the id and delay gratification. The ego acts as a manager, adjusting cognitive and perceptual processes to balance the person's functioning, control the id, and keep the person in touch with reality. For example, a four-year-old boy who is in a grocery store sees candy; his id says, "Take the candy." However, his ego may recognize that he is likely to be caught and punished. His decision to leave the candy alone is *not* based on morality but on reality. Reality says, "If I take the candy, I will be caught and punished."

As children grow older, their **superego** develops and provides them with both an *ego ideal* and a *conscience*. A developed superego would provide a somewhat older child in the grocery store two additional reasons for not taking the candy. First, stealing candy is not consistent with the ego ideal, and second, the child's conscience does not permit stealing. The child's id may say, "Take the candy. It tastes good," and the ego may say, "I won't get caught. No one is looking," but the ego ideal says, "I'm not a person who steals candy" and the conscience says, "I would feel guilty if I took something that did not belong to me." The ego and superego thus attempt to moderate the demands of the id and direct it toward appropriate ways of behaving.

The superego in Freud's theory has something in common with the id—neither is in touch with reality. In other ways, however, they are direct opposites. The id seeks instant pleasure without regard for what is wise or possible, while the superego tells a person not to do anything merely because it would be immediately pleasurable. (See Figure 12.1 for an illustration of Freud's levels of consciousness and structure of the mind.)

**DEVELOPMENT OF PERSONALITY.** Freud strongly believed that if people looked at their past, they could gain insight into their current behaviour. This belief led him to create an elaborate psychosexual stage theory of personality development. Freud believed that the core aspects of personality are established early, remain relatively stable throughout life, and are changed only with great difficulty. He argued that all people pass through five critical stages of personality development: oral, anal, phallic, latency, and genital (see Table 12.2). At each of these stages, Freud (1933) asserted, people experience conflicts and issues associated with *erogenous zones*—areas of the body that give rise to erotic or sexual sensations when they are stimulated.

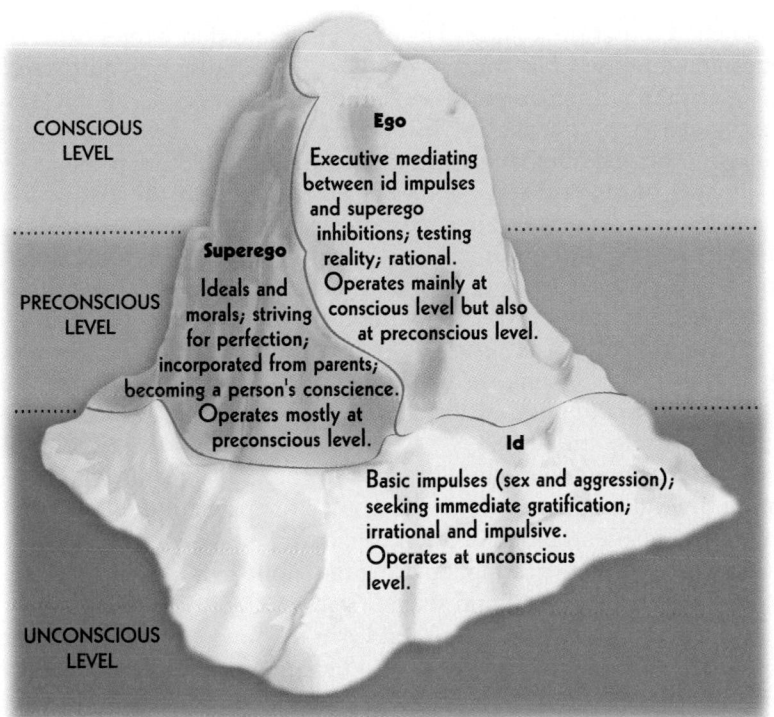

FIGURE 12.1
**Freud's View of Mental Forces**

Freud viewed consciousness as having three levels: the conscious, the preconscious, and the unconscious. Freud theorized that just as the greater part of an iceberg is hidden beneath the surface of the sea, most of the contents of the mind are below the level of conscious awareness. The *ego* is mainly a conscious and preconscious mental force. The *superego* operates mostly as a preconscious mental force. The *id* operates solely at an unconscious level.

| | | | |
|---|---|---|---|
| **TABLE 12.2** | **Freud's Five Psychosexual Stages of Personality Development** | | |

| Stage | Erogenous Zone | Conflicts/ Experiences | Adult Traits (Especially Fixations) Associated with Problems at a Stage |
|---|---|---|---|
| Oral (birth to 2 years) | Mouth | Infant achieves gratification through oral activities, such as feeding, thumb sucking, cooing. | Optimism, gullibility, passivity, hostility, substance abuse |
| Anal (2 to 3 years) | Anus | The child learns to respond to some parental demands (such as for bladder and bowel control). | Excessive cleanliness, orderliness, messiness, rebelliousness |
| Phallic (4 to 7 years) | Genitals | The child learns to realize the differences between males and females and experiences the Oedipus complex. | Flirtatiousness, vanity, promiscuity, chastity, disorder in gender identity |
| Latency (7 years to puberty) | None | The child continues developing but sexual urges are relatively quiet. | Not specified |
| Genital (puberty onward) | Genitals | The growing adolescent shakes off old dependencies and learns to deal maturely with the other sex. | Not specified |

▼ Toilet training often presents a conflict between parents and the child.

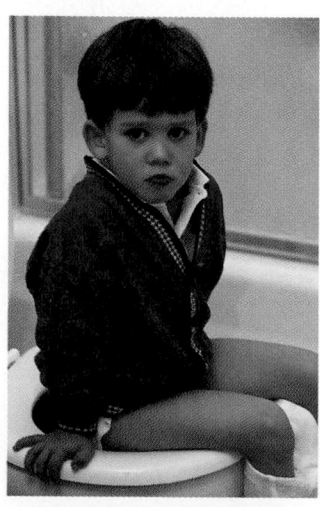

Freud believed that these stages began at birth and that babies experienced sexual feelings and impulses. His concept of infantile sexuality was quite controversial when he first began writing about the sexual life of young children. However, Freud had an expanded view of sexuality. To him, sexual pleasure was not limited to the genital areas of the body but included the mouth, anus, and other erogenous zones.

The concept of the **oral stage** is based on the fact that the instincts of infants (from birth to about age two) are focused on the mouth as the primary pleasure centre. Infants receive oral gratification through feeding, thumb sucking, and cooing during the early months of life, when their basic feelings about the world are being established. Relying heavily on symbolism, Freud contended that adults who consider the world to be a bitter place (referring to the mouth and taste senses) probably had difficulty during the oral stage of development and may have traits associated with passivity and hostility. Their problems tend to focus on their need for nurturing, warmth, and love.

Adults who continue to remain attached to the oral stage or who revert to this stage during times of intense anxiety will display the traits of an "oral" personality. They may take pleasure in biting objects (or making biting comments); smoking cigarettes, cigars, or pipes; overeating; or using the mouth for sexual pleasure.

The **anal stage** is Freud's second stage of personality development, from age two to about age three, during which children learn to control the immediate gratification they obtain through defecation and to become responsive to the demands of society. At about age two or three, children learn to respond to some of their parents' and society's demands. One parental demand is that children control their bodily functions of urination and defecation and become toilet trained. Most two- and three-year-olds experience pleasure in moving their bowels. This stage therefore establishes the basis for conflict between the id and the ego—between the desire for immediate gratification of physical urges and the demand for controlled behaviour. Freud claimed that during the anal stage, children may develop certain lasting personality characteristics related to control. Children who are able to rebel against the parents' demands for cleanliness and control may develop the anal-expulsion personality and become exceedingly sloppy, messy, and rebellious. On the other hand, children who do not successfully rebel against parents' attempts to toilet train them may acquire an anal-retentive personality pattern characterized by compulsive needs for orderliness, miserliness, and stubbornness. Thus, adults who had difficulty in the anal stage tend to have problems that focus on orderliness (or lack of it) and also might be compulsive in many behaviours.

The **phallic stage** is Freud's third stage of personality development, from about age four through seven, during which children obtain gratification primarily from the genitals. At about age four or five, children become aware of their genitals and the pleasure that comes from them. During the phallic stage, children pass through what Freud termed the **Oedipus complex**. According to Freud, this complex is a group (or complex) of unconscious wishes to have sexual intercourse with one parent and to kill or "remove" the other parent. Freud derived the term *Oedipus complex* from the story of Oedipus as told by the Greek playwright Sophocles. Oedipus unknowingly killed his father and married his mother.

The male Oedipus complex usually involves feelings of rivalry toward the father and sexual love for the mother. The boy develops feelings of hostility toward his father and believes that his attraction to his mother makes his father jealous. This rivalry produces *castration anxiety*, the fear that his father will remove the boy's penis as a punishment. This castration anxiety resolves the Oedipus complex. Freud argued that the Oedipus complex follows a slightly different course for girls than it does for boys. The female Oedipus complex typically involves hostile feelings for the mother and sexual love for the father. Freud held that when a girl realizes that she has no penis, she develops what he called *penis envy* and the desire to acquire a penis. Freud suggested that the girl could symbolically acquire a penis by forming a relationship with her father. A young girl might ask her father to marry her so that they can raise a family together. Thus, the actions of children during the Oedipus complex produce uneasiness within the family and cause anxiety for the children.

For both genders, the Oedipus complex is resolved through identification with the parent of the same sex and the acquisition of a developing superego, one based on the child's perception of the same-sex parent's morals and ideals. When the Oedipus complex is properly resolved, children will accept the authority of the same-sex parent and surrender the sexual nature of their love for the other-sex parent. In this way, a young boy begins to model his behaviour after that of his father and a young girl adopts her mother as a role model. For both boys and girls, the critical component in resolving the Oedipus complex is the development of identification with the parent of the same sex. Adult traits associated with problems at this stage usually involve sexuality and may include vanity, promiscuity, or excessive worry about chastity.

Whether the Oedipus complex explains behaviour is controversial and widely debated, especially because many people find the idea insulting to women. There is no doubt about Freud's view of women; he saw them as morally weaker and inferior to men. Most researchers now believe that Freud's notion of penis envy was imaginative but unconvincing, overdrawn, and lacking credibility (Breger, 2000; Webster, 1995). Is it a good explanation of the dynamics of four- and five-year-olds and their parents? Again, most researchers think not.

The **latency stage** follows the phallic stage and lasts from about age seven until puberty. During this period, children develop physically but sexual urges are inactive (latent). Much of children's energy is channelled into social or intellectual activities. Some psychoanalysts believe that this stage has nearly disappeared from the development of Canadian children because of their rapid physical and social maturation into adolescence.

Freud's last stage of personality development, the **genital stage**, begins at the onset of puberty and continues through adolescence into adulthood. When individuals reach this stage, sexuality re-emerges, along with the fears and repressed feelings of earlier stages. Repressed sexual feelings toward one's parents may also resurface at puberty. Over the course of the genital stage, the adolescent shakes off dependence on parents and learns to deal with members of the other sex in socially and sexually mature ways. Members of the other sex, who were ignored during the latency stage, are now seen as attractive. Many unresolved conflicts and repressed urges affect behaviour during this stage. Ideally, if people have passed successfully through previous stages of development, they will develop heterosexual relationships. If not, they may continue to have unresolved conflicts within their unconscious throughout their adult life.

As children proceed from one developmental stage to the next, they adjust their views of the world. Successfully passing through a stage requires resolution of that stage's principal conflict. Freud likened the process to military troops moving from battle to battle—a failure to successfully resolve one conflict weakens an army at its next.

**SEX AND AGGRESSION: THE TWO GREAT DRIVES.** Freud also theorized that people are energized to act the way they do because of two basic instinctual drives: the drive toward *life*, which is expressed through sex and sexual energy, and the drive toward *death*, which is expressed through aggression. These instincts are buried deep within the unconscious, and their expression is not always socially acceptable. Freud wrote little about aggression until late in his life; he focused mainly on energy from the sexual instinct, which he termed the **libido**—the instinctual (and sexual) life force that, working on the pleasure principle and seeking immediate gratification, energizes the id.

When people exhibit socially unacceptable behaviours or have feelings they consider to be socially unacceptable, especially sexual feelings, they often experience self-punishment, guilt, and anxiety—all forms of inner conflict. Freud's theory thus describes a conflict between a person's instinctual (often unconscious) need for

LATENCY [LAY-ten-see] STAGE
Freud's fourth stage of personality development, from about age seven until puberty, during which sexual urges are inactive.

GENITAL [JEN-it-ul] STAGE
Freud's last stage of personality development, from the onset of puberty through adulthood, during which the sexual conflicts of childhood resurface (at puberty) and are often resolved (during adolescence).

LIBIDO [lih-BEE-doe]
In Freud's theory, the instinctual (and sexual) life force that, working on the pleasure principle and seeking immediate gratification, energizes the id.

gratification and society's demand that each individual be socialized. In other words, it paints a picture of human beings caught in a conflict between basic sexual and aggressive desires and socialization. Personality functions as a delicate balancing act, with sexual and aggressive desires weighed against the demands of society, and the person attempting to satisfy both.

**DEFENCE MECHANISMS.** To defend itself against the anxiety brought about by sexual and aggressive drives, the ego adopts one or more **defence mechanisms**. Freud made several key assumptions about defence mechanisms:

1. They are normal and universal reactions.
2. When carried to extremes, they may lead to compulsive, unhealthy behaviours.
3. They operate on an unconscious level.
4. They protect the ego against anxiety.
5. They are helpful to the individual and generally harmless to society.
6. They all have some elements of repression.

Thus, **repression**, or the forcing of unwanted anxiety-laden experiences into the unconscious, is the basic Freudian defence mechanism.

What types of experiences are most likely to be repressed? Freud believed that childhood experiences involving sex and aggression are often unacceptable to the parents and eventually are denied or repressed by the child. For example, the Oedipal feelings of sexual attraction toward one parent and aggression toward the other are not acceptable to most parents in Western countries. After parents suppress their child's sexual and aggressive behaviours by either punishing or withholding reward for these behaviours, the child begins to develop anxiety about certain sexual and aggressive impulses and therefore forces them into the unconscious.

In addition to repression, Freud identified several other defence mechanisms:

- **Rationalization** is a defence mechanism by which people reinterpret undesirable feelings or behaviours in terms that make them seem acceptable. For example, a shoplifter may rationalize that no one will miss the things she steals or that she needs the things more than other people do. A student may cheat, asserting to himself that failing the course would hurt his parents far too much for them to bear.

- **Fixation** is a defence mechanism by which a person develops an excessive attachment to another person or object that was appropriate only at an earlier stage of development. For example, with an oral fixation, a person continues to receive pleasure from talking, biting, drinking, eating, smoking, and other oral functions. Examples of anal fixation would be anal-retentive people who hold on to their money or opinions in the same manner that they originally held on to their feces.

- **Regressions** are related to fixations, except they take place after a person has progressed through the various stages of development. During periods of extreme anxiety, a person may regress or move backward to an earlier state, typically the oral stage. For example, university or college students during final exams may increase their talking, eating, or smoking as a means of handling anxiety.

- **Projection** is a defence mechanism by which people attribute their own undesirable traits to others. A friend who inexplicably asks, "Are you mad at me?" may actually be mad at you but afraid to admit it to himself; instead, he sees *your* behaviour as angry. Similarly, a person with deep aggressive tendencies may see other people as acting in an excessively hostile way.

- **Reaction formation** is a defence mechanism by which people behave in a way opposite to what their true but anxiety-provoking feelings would dictate. A

**DEFENCE MECHANISM**

An unconscious way of reducing anxiety by distorting perceptions of reality.

**REPRESSION**

A defence mechanism by which anxiety-provoking thoughts and feelings are forced to the unconscious.

**RATIONALIZATION**

A defence mechanism by which people reinterpret undesirable feelings or behaviours in terms that make them appear acceptable.

**FIXATION**

An excessive attachment to some person or object that was appropriate only at an earlier stage of development.

**REGRESSION**

A return to a prior stage after a person has progressed through the various stages of development; caused by anxiety.

**PROJECTION**

A defence mechanism by which people attribute their own undesirable traits to others.

**REACTION FORMATION**

A defence mechanism by which people behave in a way opposite to what their true but anxiety-provoking feelings would dictate.

classic example of reaction formation is the behaviour of a person who has strong sexual urges but who becomes extremely chaste. Similarly, a person with strong but unconscious hostile feelings for her boss may behave in an overly friendly manner to him or her. Reaction formations can be detected by other people because they produce behaviour that is exaggerated or overly dramatic.

- **Displacement** is a defence mechanism by which people divert sexual or aggressive feelings for one person onto another person. For example, a woman who is mistreated by her employer may repress her hostility for her boss but take out her anger on her husband, children, pets, or even a stuffed animal. Displacement differs from reaction formation in that the behaviours are not exaggerated or overdone.

- **Denial** is a defence mechanism by which people refuse to accept reality or recognize the true source of their anxiety. For example, someone with strong sexual urges may deny any interest in sex rather than deal with those urges. Or, a person with drinking or drug problems may deny that these behaviours are causing problems.

- **Sublimation** differs from other defence mechanisms in that it can be helpful to society; other defence mechanisms help the person but do little or nothing to enhance society. With sublimations, people redirect socially unacceptable impulses toward acceptable goals. Thus, a man who has sexual desire for someone he knows is off limits (perhaps a cousin) may channel that desire into working 14-hour days for his church. Similarly, a student who wants to drop out of school may throw himself into artistic endeavours or athletics.

**FREUD TODAY.**   When Freud's psychosexual theory of development was first proposed, around 1900, it received a great deal of unfavourable attention. It was considered outrageous to suggest that young children had sexual feelings, especially toward their parents. Opinion changed, and Freud's theory became popular. If you watch how young children respond to and identify with their parents, you will see that there are elements of truth in Freud's conception of how personality development proceeds. Little girls do tend to idolize their fathers, and little boys often become strongly attached to their mothers. Also, it is widely accepted that individuals use projection and other defence mechanisms (Newman, Duff, & Baumeister, 1997).

Despite these observations, Freud's theory has been sharply criticized. Some psychologists object to Freud's basic conception of human nature—his emphasis on sexual urges toward parents and his idea that human behaviour is so biologically determined. Others reject his predictions about psychosexual stages and fixations. Still others assert that his theory does not account for changing situations and differing cultures. His case histories are seen by many today as "clinical romances" and intellectually contrived (Webster, 1995). At a minimum, his ideas are controversial, and many psychologists do not regard them as valid (Schatzman, 1992). *Point/Counterpoint* summarizes the continuing controversy over Freud within psychology.

## ADLER AND INDIVIDUAL PSYCHOLOGY

Although Alfred Adler (1870–1937) was one of the original members of Freud's Vienna Psychoanalytic Society, his differences with Freud led him to resign and to formulate an alternative personality theory. His theory, now called *individual psychology*, is quite different from Freud's in almost all aspects. Adler chose the term *individual* to suggest that personality is indivisible and must not be divided into various levels of consciousness or different regions of the mind.

In Adler's individual psychology, each concept relates to all others, making division of personality terms somewhat arbitrary. Nevertheless, we discuss the

**DISPLACEMENT**
A defence mechanism by which people divert sexual or aggressive feelings for one person onto another person.

**DENIAL**
A defence mechanism by which people refuse to accept reality or recognize the true source of their anxiety.

**SUBLIMATION**
[sub-li-MAY-shun]
A defence mechanism by which people redirect socially unacceptable impulses toward acceptable goals.

▼ Alfred Adler broke with Freud and went on to argue that individuals are motivated by their need for superiority or success.

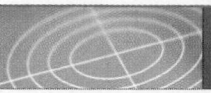
## Is Freud Still Relevant to Psychology?

**POINT:** Freud's theory is outdated and unscientific, making it irrelevant to contemporary psychology.

**COUNTERPOINT:** Freud has left an important legacy to contemporary culture and scientific psychology.

Freud's detractors have levelled many criticisms at him and his theory. These criticisms have ranged from the sexism of his theory to the difficulties of subjecting it to empirical testing. During the first half of the twentieth century, Freud went from obscurity to controversy to widespread acceptance. During the last half of the twentieth century, psychology moved in different directions, and the Freudian view was no longer prominent. Freud's theory depicts women in very derogatory ways, and the growing number of women in psychology was a factor in his theory's diminishing popularity.

Another type of criticism comes from problems in scientific testability. That is, critics cite Freud's use of poorly defined terms, his failure to distinguish between his observations and the inferences he made from them, and his reliance on the unconscious to explain any possible behaviour. Good scientific theories make specific predictions about behaviour, such as that people with fixations at the oral stage will prefer to drink beer from bottles rather than glasses. Freud's theory explains *any* possible behaviour, not just the ones that occur.

Thus, the theory's comprehensiveness is actually a drawback. Other psychologists argue that psychology moved beyond Freud, leaving unscientific personality theories behind and developing better alternatives. Summarizing the view of many psychologists, Frederick Crews (1996, p. 63) said, "[T]here is literally nothing to be said, scientifically or therapeutically, to the advantage of the entire Freudian system or any of its component dogmas."

Other psychologists argue that Freud has exerted a greater influence on psychology and Western culture than

has any other personality theorist. Proponents such as Drew Westen (1998, p. 333) explain that "Freud, like Elvis, has been dead for a number of years but continues to be cited with regularity." Westen criticizes Freud's critics, claiming that psychoanalytic thought has evolved into a theory that contributes to contemporary scientific knowledge. Westen argues that psychoanalytic thought is consistent with the beliefs of a wide variety of psychology researchers. These shared assumptions include the existence of the unconscious and its influence on behaviour, the importance of early childhood in personality formation, and the appropriate emphasis on sexuality and aggression. Westen claims that the belief in the unconscious is part of the renewed interest in consciousness among neuroscientists. In addition, Westen argues that support for the existence of the unconscious comes from experimental evidence for unconscious emotional processing. Westen also discusses the research on personality development, saying that most research highlights the importance of childhood for adult personality formation and functioning. In addition, a great deal of research indicates that childhood abuse and neglect produce psychological damage that persists into adulthood. Although personality development consists of more than controlling sexuality and aggression, these two tasks are important in forming socially responsible adults. Thus, contemporary psychoanalytic theorists argue that this theoretical view is far from dead; it has contributed to mainstream psychology research as well as Western thought and popular culture.

following concepts separately: striving for superiority or success, unity of personality, social interest, creative power, family constellations, and early recollections.

**STRIVING FOR SUPERIORITY OR SUCCESS.** According to Adler, people are motivated, or energized, by natural feelings of inferiority, which lead them to strive for superiority or success. We all begin life with small and fragile bodies. At the same time, we possess an innate striving force that combines with our inferior bodies to create *feelings* of inferiority. The criterion of successful striving is a matter of how we handle these inevitable feelings of inferiority. By the time we are three or four years old, we have adopted a *style of life* that may either lead us toward unhealthy striving for personal gain (superiority) or toward completion and psychological health (success). Thus, feelings of inferiority are not necessarily detrimental to personal development; they may lead to either a self-centred style of life or a desire to improve the human condition. Although we all strive as a *compensation* for feelings of incompleteness, many people *overcompensate* and strive in a fixed and rigid manner.

Adler recognized that people seek to express their need for superiority in different areas of life. Some seek to be superior artists; others seek to be superior parents or corporate executives. Thus, each person develops a unique style of life, in which attitudes and behaviours express a specific life *goal* or an ideal approach to achieving superiority.

**UNITY OF PERSONALITY.** Adler believed in the essential unity of personality. All of our thoughts, feelings, and actions serve a single purpose, one that is consistent with the *final goal* we set at about age four or five years. One person may set a final goal as achieving an overdependent relationship with his mother. As a child, he feels frightened when his mother is out of sight and fusses when his mother spends time with other children. As an adult, he looks for a woman to take care of him and allow him to continue his goal of having a dependent relationship with a mother figure.

According to Adler, inconsistent behaviour does not exist; a close look at another person's final goal reveals the unity of seemingly inconsistent behaviours. For example, our overly dependent boy might alternate between submissive and aggressive behaviours toward his mother. With both behaviours, he is attempting to solidify his dependency on his mother.

**SOCIAL INTEREST.** The pinnacle of Adlerian theory is the notion of **social interest,** or a feeling of oneness with all humanity. Adler (1927) regarded social interest as the "sole criterion" of human values, or the primary gauge for judging the worth of people's actions. The potential for social interest is acquired during the early parent–child relationship. Everyone who has survived infancy has received at least minimum care from an adult who has demonstrated some measure of social interest. However, children who are neglected will develop little social interest. These children strive for personal gain and grow up to believe that people cannot be trusted, living in "enemy territory" and feeling overly suspicious of people. They may get along with others on a superficial level, but their deficit of social interest leads them to believe that people cannot be trusted.

Adler believed that the effects of the early parent–child relationship may have a lasting influence on later development. By the time children are five or six years old, Adler said, their experiences with social interest (or lack of social interest) are sufficiently powerful to blur the effects of heredity. People with high levels of social interest are generally motivated by normal feelings of incompleteness, whereas those with low levels of social interest develop exaggerated feelings of inferiority and attempt to compensate for their incompleteness by setting personal goals and striving for personal superiority.

**CREATIVE POWER.** Adler acknowledged that heredity and environment furnish the building material of personality, but he insisted that each of us is our own architect, freely deciding how we wish to use the building materials. Adler called this ability to shape our own personality the *creative power.* Our creative power permits us to freely choose our final goal and to select our manner of striving toward that goal, generally placing us in control of our lives. Thus, we are much more than an interaction of heredity and environment; we are creative beings who not only react to our environment but also act on it and cause it to react to us. We can create either a healthy style of life or an unhealthy one; the choice is ours.

**SOCIAL INTEREST**
In Adler's theory, a feeling of oneness with all humanity.

**FAMILY CONSTELLATIONS.** Adler believed that psychologists could learn about people's personality from an understanding of their *family constellation*. Family constellation is not the same as birth order. Birth order is simply one's rank among siblings, whereas family constellation considers the gender and health of siblings as well as the age difference between siblings. Adler and others have observed some typical traits of four family positions: only child, first-born, second-born, and last-born (see Table 12.3). A first-born child, for example, is likely to have a different relationship with people than a second-born child does and is thus likely to develop a different style of life. Only children may be socially mature but may demand to be the centre of attention. First-borns are pushed by parents toward success, leadership, and independence and so tend to have a high need for achievement. Their early experiences make it likely that they will choose careers reflecting that need for achievement, such as corporate executive or politician. Second-born children, on the other hand, are usually more relaxed about achievement. If they feel competitive with an older sibling (as Adler did toward his older brother Sigmund), however, they may develop a strong need for achievement that will drive them toward public success. Youngest children are often pampered and allow older siblings to take care of them.

**EARLY RECOLLECTIONS.** Adlerian therapists are much more likely to use *early recollections* rather than birth order to reveal a person's style of life. With this technique, they simply ask the people to describe the earliest experience they can remember. The objective validity of the memory is of no importance; the crucial factor is people's interpretation of the event.

Although Adler believed that early recollections yield clues for understanding people's current style of life, he did not believe that the early event is the cause for present style of life. Rather, people reconstruct their early experiences to make them consistent with some theme that runs through their life. To illustrate this point, Adler (1964, p. 123) reported the case of one of his patients, a young man who was about to be married but who deeply and inexplicably distrusted women, including his fiancée. When asked his earliest recollection, the young man recalled that he was "going with my mother and little brother to market. Suddenly it began to rain and my mother took me in her arms, and then, remembering that I was the older, she put me down and took up my younger brother." This seemingly insignificant memory related to the man's current distrust of women. Having first gained the favourite position with his mother, he quickly lost it to his younger brother. Although women may initially love him, they cannot be trusted to continue their love. In the Adlerian interpretation, the man's present style of life continues to shape the way he perceives his early experiences.

---

### TABLE 12.3 Some of Adler's Hypotheses about Birth Order

| Birth Order | Hypothesis |
| --- | --- |
| Only child | The centre of attention, dominant; often spoiled because of parental timidity and anxiety |
| First-born | Driven to success; independent; high need for achievement; high levels of anxiety; protective toward others |
| Second-born | Actively struggling to surpass others; often competitive (especially with older sibling) |
| Last-born | The most pampered (the smallest and weakest); dependent on others; may excel by being different |

# JUNG AND ANALYTICAL PSYCHOLOGY

The second important theorist to break from Freud's psychoanalytic theory was Carl Gustav Jung (1875–1961), a Swiss psychiatrist. Jung, a brilliant thinker, had an intense personal relationship with Freud but ultimately left the Freudian group over several key issues. Compared to Freud, Jung placed relatively little emphasis on sex. He saw people's behaviour as less rigidly fixed and determined than Freud described. Jung also emphasized the search for meaning in life and focused on religiosity. By 1911, he and Freud were exchanging angry letters; in 1913, when Jung publicly declared his disagreements with Freud, the two severed their relationship—Freud was intolerant of followers who deviated too much from his positions.

Like Freud's *psychoanalytic approach*, Jung's *analytical psychology* emphasized unconscious processes as determinants of behaviour. Jung believed that people are ultimately motivated to attain self-realization or perfection and that our journey toward self-realization is exceedingly difficult, including many obstacles and several tests of courage.

Like Freud, Jung believed in an unconscious. However, his version of the unconscious was somewhat different from Freud's in that he added a collective unconscious. The **collective unconscious** is a shared storehouse of primitive ideas and images that reside in the unconscious and are inherited from one's ancestors. Called **archetypes**, these inherited ideas and images are emotionally charged and rich in meaning and symbolism. The archetypes of the collective unconscious emerge in art, in religion, and especially in dreams.

One important archetype is the *shadow*, or the dark side of our personality. The shadow represents those personal experiences we find distasteful and attempt to hide from ourselves and others. For example, we may enjoy reading about serial killers and other criminals because it allows us to deny parts of ourselves and to project our shadow onto other people. On our quest for self-realization, our first test of courage is to recognize our shadow, that is, to come to grips with the darkness and ugliness within ourselves. The second test of courage for men is to recognize their anima, or feminine side of their personality, and for women to make peace with their animus, or masculine side of their personality. Many men, and especially young men, have difficulty coming to grips with their feminine side. Often, they behave in ultramasculine ways to convince themselves and others that they are totally masculine.

Two other archetypes are the *great mother* and the *wise old man*. The great mother is the archetype of nourishment and destruction. Just as "Mother Nature" and our own mother can either nourish us or destroy us, the great mother archetype includes these two qualities. In fairy tales and legends, the great mother may appear as a fairy godmother, a witch, or Mother Earth. The wise old man is the archetype of wisdom, but this wisdom is often shallow, with no substance. The wizard in *The Wizard of Oz* is a good example—he seemed to be quite wise, but his wisdom, at best, was merely common sense. The wise old man is seen in dreams and legends as a father, grandfather, philosopher, doctor, priest, or rabbi.

The most important archetype is the *self*, the archetype of completion and wholeness. The self encompasses all other archetypes as well as the opposing sides of personality, such as extroversion and introversion, masculinity and femininity, conscious and unconscious, light and dark forces, and so on. Our final test of courage on the road to completeness is to realize the self—to bring all opposing forces of personality together. As an archetype, the self is symbolized by a person's ideas of perfection, completion, and wholeness, but its ultimate symbol is the mandala. The *mandala* is a mystical symbol, generally circular in form, that in Jung's view represents a person's inward striving for unity. Jung pointed out that many religions have mandala-like symbols; indeed, Hinduism and Buddhism use such symbols as aids to meditation.

▼ Carl Jung broke with Freud and formulated an alternative theory of personality.

COLLECTIVE UNCONSCIOUS
In Jung's theory, a shared storehouse of primitive ideas and images that reside in the unconscious and are inherited from one's ancestors.

ARCHETYPES [AR-ki-types]
In Jung's theory, the emotionally charged ideas and images that are rich in meaning and symbolism and exist within the collective unconscious.

▼ The *mandala* is a mystical symbol that holds significance in many religions.

# Be an
## ACTIVE LEARNER

**REVIEW**

> How do the id, ego, and super-ego develop through the psychosexual stages? pp. 416–419

> In Freud's view, why is the unconscious so important in personality development? pp. 415–417

> Summarize the common function of all of Freud's defence mechanisms. In what ways do they differ? p. 420

> What elements of Freud's theory did Adler and Jung object to? pp. 421, 425

**THINK CRITICALLY**

> Freud initially believed that seduction by a parent was an important cause of mental disorders, but he abandoned this theory and accepted the Oedipus complex in its place. Considering current statistics on child abuse, was Freud correct in his decision?

> What societal forces can shape a personality theorist's point of view?

**APPLY PSYCHOLOGY**

> Rent any of the Star Wars movies (*Star Wars* itself provides the best examples), and analyze the characters based on Jung's archetypes.

> Jung's ideas are widely known but not widely accepted by mainstream psychologists. Although their impact on psychodynamic theory is important, Jung's ideas never achieved prominence in leading psychological thought because they are so difficult to verify. Some theorists even view them as mere poetic speculation; others see them as attractive but untestable hypotheses.

# Skinner and Behavioural Analysis

We often speculate about what goes on "inside" the minds of our favourite movie stars, athletes, or other famous figures; we try to guess what their personal and professional lives might be like and infer things about their personalities. B. F. Skinner would have argued that such an exercise is a waste of time—you cannot see inside people's minds. Skinner (1904–1990), a leader of behaviourism, applied the principles of learning to all facets of behaviour, including personality. Behaviourists argue that speculating about private, unobservable behaviour is fruitless. They further assert that inner drives, psychic urges, and levels of consciousness are concepts that are impossible to define.

## THE POWER OF LEARNING

Behaviourists look at personality very differently than do any of the theorists described so far. They generally do not look within the psyche; they look only at overt behaviour. Behavioural approaches are often viewed as a reaction to the conceptual vagueness of traditional psychodynamic personality theories. Behavioural personality theorists assert that personality develops as people learn from their environments. The key word here is *learn*. According to behaviourists, personality characteristics are not fixed traits; instead, they are learned and subject to change. Thus, for behaviourists, personality is the sum of a person's learned tendencies.

How do people learn? The concept of *operant conditioning* is critical in a behavioural analysis of personality. The principles of operant conditioning come from experiments with non-human animals, mostly rats and pigeons, but these laboratory experiences can be generalized to humans. People (and other animals) learn mostly as a result of their experiences with reinforcement. As we saw in Chapter 5, *reinforcement* is any condition within the environment that strengthens a behaviour. Both positive reinforcement and negative reinforcement are synonymous with reward. More technically, a *positive reinforcer* is any positively valued condition that, when added to a situation, increases the probability that a given behaviour will occur. A child who receives a cookie for cleaning her room is being positively reinforced. A *negative reinforcer*, on the other hand, is any aversive stimulus that, when removed from a situation, increases the probability that a given behaviour will occur. If you take an aspirin when you have a headache and your headache goes away, you have been negatively reinforced and you are more likely to use this same technique in the future. Negative reinforcement must not be confused with punishment, which does not strengthen behaviour; punishment weakens behaviour. There are also two types of punishment: (1) adding an aversive stimulus to a situation and (2) taking away a positive valued stimulus. An example of the first type would be embarrassing a person telling a sexist joke by walking away before the story is finished. An example of the second type of punishment might be finding that your car has been stolen because you neglected to lock it.

How can you tell the difference between reinforcement and punishment? Behaviourists are very empirical, relying on observation. If any given behaviour increases in frequency, we know that it has been reinforced. For example, if a teacher scolds a child for misbehaving in class, and the child's rowdy behaviour increases, we know the admonishment is a reward for that child, not a punishment. The teacher may have meant to punish, but that was not the result. If a 12-year-old boy hides when his overly affectionate aunt comes for a visit, we know that the aunt's affectionate behaviours serve as a punishment for the boy, not as reinforcement.

## ACQUIRING A PERSONALITY

Theorists who take the behavioural analysis point of view believe that, in addition to the individual's experiences with reinforcement, personality is acquired through natural selection and cultural evolution (Skinner, 1987). As a species, our behaviours are partially shaped by the contingencies of survival. Throughout human history, those behaviours that were helpful to the species tended to survive, whereas those that were merely beneficial to an individual tended not to survive. For example, natural selection has favoured people who formed cooperative communities to protect themselves from outside forces. Today, cooperation remains an important human behaviour.

The evolution of cultures is also responsible for at least some human behaviour. Perhaps the two strongest contributors to modern life are the development of symbolic language and the continuing evolution of technology. Thus, your facility with language contributes at least some measure to your personality. Similarly, your experiences with important inventions, especially since the Industrial Revolution, have greatly shaped your life, making you a much different person than your ancestors of a thousand years ago.

Skinner and others who take the behavioural analysis view reject many of the concepts that other personality theorists use. Skinner emphasized learning, and personal learning history was the foundation of his approach to personality. Through experiences, people form stable tendencies to behave in similar ways over time. These tendencies, not underlying dimensions of personality, are the basis for behaviour. This approach is a sharp contrast with the psychodynamic view, as Building Table 12.1 shows.

# Trait and Type Theories: Stable Behavioural Dispositions

Ancient philosophers and medieval physicians believed that the proportions of various fluids (called *humours*) in the body determine a person's temperament and personality. Cheerful, healthy people, for example, were said to have a *sanguine* (hopeful and self-confident) personality because blood was their primary humour; those who had a preponderance of yellow bile were considered hot-tempered.

Cheerful and hot-tempered could be considered as traits. A **trait** is any readily identifiable stable quality that characterizes how an individual differs from other

TRAIT

Any readily identifiable stable quality that characterizes how an individual differs from other individuals.

---

| BUILDING TABLE 12.1 | Psychodynamic and Behavioural Approaches to Personality |

| Approach | Major Proponent | Core of Personality | Development | Structure of Personality | Cause of Problems |
|---|---|---|---|---|---|
| Psychodynamic | Sigmund Freud | Maximizes gratification while minimizing punishment or guilt; instinctual unconscious urges direct behaviour | Five stages: oral, anal, phallic, latency, genital | Id, ego, superego | Imbalances between the id, ego, and superego, resulting in fixations |
| Behavioural | B. F. Skinner | Patterns of behaviours learned through experience with the environment | Process of learning new responses | Responses | Faulty or inappropriate behaviours learned through experience with the environment |

## Are Personality Traits Stable?

Most personality theorists conceptualize personality as stable over time and resistant to change, but relatively few studies have measured the stability of personality. It is difficult to study the stability of personality on a day-to-day basis or to see how stable personality is over a course of years. The main reason for this lack is the difficulty of performing the required research. The method required is a longitudinal study, which is a research approach that follows a group of people over time to determine change or stability in behaviour. The process of making multiple measurements over a span of time makes this method difficult and expensive. Such studies have been done.

**Design.** Kirk Brown and Debbie Moskowitz (1998) at McGill University in Montreal examined the stability of personality dimensions over the course of day-to-day interaction and over the course of a usual week.

**Hypothesis.** Brown and Moskowitz hypothesized that they would not find simple stability in personality traits but would, rather, find them to follow predictable cycles over the course of day-to-day interaction over the week.

**Participants.** Researchers recruited 72 participants between the ages of 19 and 63.

**Procedure.** The participants were asked to complete a detailed one-page personality form following every social interaction that lasted longer than 5 minutes for 20 days. The form measured aspects of personality, including dominance, submissiveness, agreeableness, quarrelsomeness, agency, and communion (getting along with others). The participants were also beeped with a pager three times a day on weekends and twice a day on weekdays, at which point they also completed the form.

**Results.** Brown and Moskowitz found that scores on the personality measures were quite variable but that there were predictable cycles of scores. For example, dominance, submissiveness, agreeableness, and quarrelsomeness scores rose during the week and fell during the weekend. General dimensions of personality showed opposite patterns, with agency rising over the week and communion falling. Finally, extroverts showed a daily pattern of exhibiting more and more extroversion as the day went on and especially into the evening (likely due to a busy social life).

**Conclusions.** Personality varies quite a bit from social interaction to social interaction, clearly suggesting that it is influenced by social circumstances. As well, there appear to be predictable daily and weekly cycles of personality characteristics. Brown and Moskowitz suggest that we should turn our attention away from the search for stability in basic personality traits and look, instead, for predictable patterns in the expression of personality.

---

individuals. Someone might characterize one political figure as energetic and forward-looking and another as tough and patriotic, for example. Such characterizations present specific ideas about a person's *disposition*—the way that person is likely to behave across a wide range of circumstances and situations as well as over time (see *Introduction to Research Basics*). Traits can be placed on a continuum, so a person can be extremely shy, very shy, shy, or mildly shy, for example. For some personality theorists, traits are the elements of which personality is made.

Types emerge when personality theorists combine several related traits into one category. **Types**, therefore, are personality categories in which broad collections of traits are loosely tied together and interrelated.

We'll examine the trait and type theories of Gordon Allport, Raymond Cattell, and Hans Eysenck, as well as a newer model of traits—the Five Factor Model.

**TYPES**

Personality categories in which broad collections of traits are loosely tied together and interrelated.

### ALLPORT'S PERSONAL DISPOSITION THEORY

The distinguished psychologist Gordon Allport (1897–1967) suggested that each individual has a unique set of personality traits, which he called *personal dispositions*. Allport counted several thousand descriptive trait names in an English-language dictionary, and these traits have formed the basis for the way Allport and other people have studied traits.

Allport divided traits into three categories: cardinal, central, and secondary. *Cardinal traits* are so dominant that a person's entire life revolves around that trait, as with Snape in the Harry Potter books. Most people do not have a cardinal trait, but those who do have one are guided by a single ruling passion. For example, a clergyman's cardinal trait may be intense belief in and devotion to God. His entire life revolves around this passion. Some words in the English language stem from people (real or fictional) who possessed a cardinal trait, for instance, *sadism* (from the Marquis de Sade), *narcissism* (from Narcissus), and *Scrooge* (from Dickens's character).

Although most people do not have a cardinal trait, each of us has about 5 to 10 *central traits*, or qualities that characterize our daily interactions. To understand a person, we should look at the *pattern* of that person's central traits. Two people could possess the same set of traits, such as self-control, apprehension, tension, self-assertiveness, forthrightness, and practicality, but the manner in which one woman's self-control relates to her apprehension, tension, and so on may be quite different from the way another woman's self-control relates to these other central traits.

*Secondary traits* are characteristics that are exhibited in response to specific situations. For example, a person may have a secondary trait of xenophobia—a fear and intolerance of strangers or foreigners. Secondary traits are more easily modified than central traits and are not necessarily exhibited daily. Also, people have many more secondary traits than central traits.

Everyone has different combinations of traits, which is why Allport claimed that each person is unique. To identify a person's traits, Allport recommended an in-depth study of that individual through an analysis of personal diaries, letters, and interviews over a lengthy period of time.

▲ Gordon Allport argued that people can be described by three categories of personality traits.

## CATTELL'S TRAIT THEORY

Allport's study of traits was based mostly on non-mathematical procedures, including common sense. In contrast, Raymond B. Cattell (1905–1998) used the technique of *factor analysis*—a statistical procedure in which psychologists analyze groups of variables (factors) to detect which are related—to show that groups of traits tend to cluster together. Thus, researchers find that people who describe themselves as warm and accepting also tend to rate themselves as high in nurturance and tenderness and low in aggression, suspiciousness, and apprehensiveness. Researchers also see patterns within professions. For example, artists may see themselves as creative, sensitive, and open; accountants may describe themselves as careful, serious, conservative, and thorough-minded. Cattell termed obvious, day-to-day traits *surface traits*, and he called higher-order, "deep" traits *source traits*.

Cattell used the factor analysis process to extract 35 specific traits. These 35 can be broken down into 23 normal and 12 abnormal primary source traits. (Sixteen of the normal traits are the basis for Cattell's personality test, which is described on p. 444.) Through additional factor analysis, Cattell identified eight second-order traits. The most powerful of these is the extroversion–introversion dimension, which also appears in Eysenck's theory and in the Five Factor Model.

## EYSENCK'S FACTOR THEORY

Whereas Allport and Cattell focused on traits, Hans Eysenck (1916–1997) focused on higher levels of trait organization, or what he called *types*. Each type incorporates lower-level elements (traits), and each trait incorporates still-lower-order qualities (habits). Eysenck (1970) argued that all personality traits could be grouped under three basic bipolar dimensions: extroversion–introversion (E), neuroticism–emotional stability (N), and psychoticism–superego function (P).

*Extroverts* are sociable and impulsive, and they enjoy new and exciting experiences, including meeting new people. In contrast, *introverts* are unsociable and

▲ Woody Allen's film persona is usually high in neuroticism.

cautious, prefer routine activities, and do not enjoy meeting new people. People who score high on *neuroticism* (N) are not necessarily pathological, but they do have high levels of anxiety, tend to overreact emotionally, and experience difficulty calming down after emotional arousal. They frequently complain of physical difficulties, such as headache or back pain, and are often overly concerned about matters they cannot change. People who score low on this scale are *emotionally stable* and are able to control their feelings. They are often spontaneous, genuine, and warm. Eysenck's third factor, psychoticism, is sometimes called tough- or tender-mindedness. Again, high scores on *psychoticism* (P) do not necessarily indicate psychopathology, but they do suggest a person who is cold, self-centred, non-conforming, hostile, aggressive, and suspicious. People who score low on this dimension (toward the superego function) tend to be altruistic, highly socialized, caring, cooperative, and conventional.

Eysenck argued that personality has a biological basis; he also believed that learning and experience help shape an individual's behaviour. For example, he said that introverts and extroverts experience different levels of arousal in the cortex of the brain. Accordingly, persons of each type seek the amount of stimulation necessary to achieve their preferred level of arousal. For example, a person who prefers a low level of arousal, in which stimulation is less intense, might become a librarian; a person who prefers a high level of arousal might become a race-car driver. Many people who prefer high levels of arousal might be characterized as sensation seekers; they climb mountains, ride dirt bikes, gamble, and take drugs.

## THE FIVE FACTOR MODEL

Because trait and type theories follow a common sense approach, researchers today still find them attractive. However, rather than speaking of hundreds of traits or of a few types, many theorists agree that there are five broad trait categories. These categories have become known as the Five Factor Model or the Big Five (McCrae & Costa, 1999):

- *Extroversion–introversion*, or the extent to which people are social or unsocial, talkative or quiet, affectionate or reserved
- *Agreeableness–antagonism*, or the extent to which people are good natured or irritable, courteous or rude, flexible or stubborn, lenient or critical
- *Conscientiousness–undirectedness*, or the extent to which people are reliable or undependable, careful or careless, punctual or late, well organized or disorganized
- *Neuroticism–stability*, or the extent to which people are worried or calm, nervous or at ease, insecure or secure
- *Openness to experience*, or the extent to which people are open to experience or closed, independent or conforming, creative or uncreative, daring or timid

▼ Sensation seekers strive to maintain a high level of arousal by engaging in stimulating (and even dangerous) activities.

Although dozens of traits can describe people, researchers think of the five factors as "supertraits," the important dimensions that characterize every personality (McCrae & Costa, 1999). Research has supported the idea of the Five Factor Model (Busato et al., 1999) and shown the stability of the categories (Borkenau & Ostendorf, 1998); in addition, the Five Factor Model holds up cross-culturally (Costa & McCrae, 1998; McCrae et al., 1998; McCrae et al., 2000; Trull & Geary, 1997). Some research suggests there may be genetic influences on the categories (see *Brain and Behaviour*). Finally, the Five Factor Model may help us understand children's personalities (Shiner, 1998), although little research has been conducted on children and personality development. A useful way to think about the "Big Five" personality factors is provided through the seminal research of Ross Broughton (1987, 1990) of the University of

## The Genetics of Personality Traits

The ideal of a biological basis for personality is widely debated, but a growing body of evidence indicates that some traits or dispositions have a genetic basis. Researchers in the area of behaviour genetics attempt to identify genetic influences, determining the proportion of a trait that is determined by heredity and what is due to environment (Segal & MacDonald, 1998). Common methods include assessing people with various degrees of biological relationship to determine how much variation in a trait is genetic. For example, a common method involves administering a personality inventory to both identical and fraternal twins. For traits with a genetic basis, the relationship is higher in identical than in fraternal twins.

Research on the heritability of personality traits has concentrated on the traits of the Five Factor Model, and each of these five traits shows some heritability (Loehlin, 1992; Loehlin et al., 1998; Plomin & Caspi, 1999). Heritability is a measure of how much of the variation in a trait is due to genetics and is expressed as a proportion or percentage. Estimates of these numbers vary from study to study, but the studies that examine genetics and personality traits typically show some degree of heritability higher than zero, which suggests some degree of genetic contribution. Figure 12.2 shows the range of estimates for genetics in the personality factors in the Five Factor Model.

Behaviour genetics studies do not directly measure genes. To determine the genetic basis for any trait, researchers must establish exactly how genes affect the behaviours in the personality trait. That is, researchers must establish a link between specific gene locations and a given behaviour that is part of a personality trait. (For a review of heritability go to Chapters 2 and 8.) Louis Schmidt of McMaster University and his colleagues (Schmidt et al., 2002), using this approach, found an association between the personality traits of shyness and aggressiveness gene receptors for the neurotransmitters dopamine and serotonin.

These studies in molecular genetics are a necessary component in establishing how genetics influences personality traits. Robert Plomin and Avshalom Caspi (1999, p. 262)

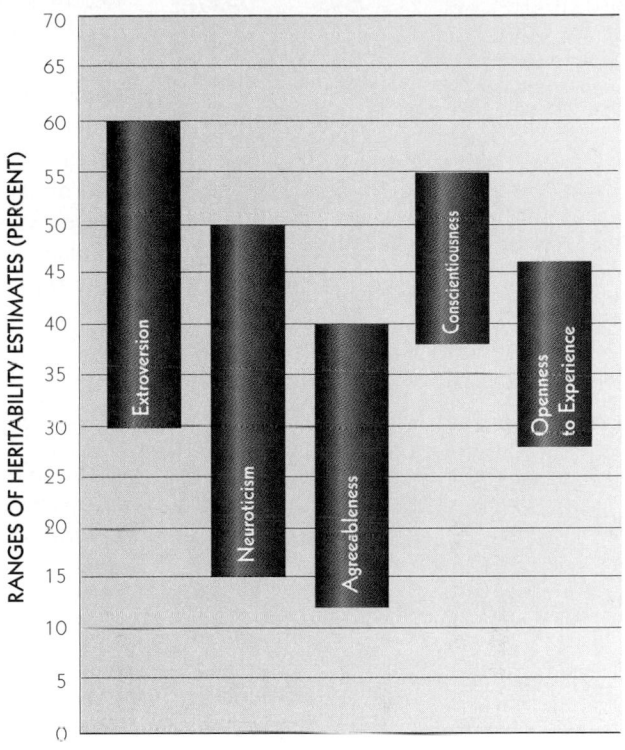

**FIGURE 12.2**

**Estimates for the Heritability of Personality Traits in the Five Factor Model Range from Low to Moderate**

described the difficulties of the task of finding the genetic basis of personality: "The goal is not to find the gene for a particular personality trait, but rather some of the many genes that make contributions of varying effect sizes to the variance of the trait." Some genes may make very small contributions, and their effects will be difficult to determine, even with advances in gene mapping, but research has made a promising start in this difficult task.

Winnipeg. Broughton argues that each personality factor represents a prototype or ideal personality component. His research suggests that we analyze our own and other people's personalities by estimating how close to or distant from each personality prototype they are. His approach can also be used to track development of children's personality systems. In this area, Broughton has shown that preschool and early grade-school children use only one personality factor (good–bad) and the full five-factor structure emerges beginning in the early elementary-school grades (Broughton, Boyes, & Mitchell, 1993).

**REVIEW**

> Identify three behavioural concepts used to explain personality development. pp. 426–427

> Distinguish between a *trait* and a *type*. pp. 428–429

> Trace the development of the Five Factor Model, beginning with Cattell's theory and including Eysenck's theory. pp.429–430

**THINK CRITICALLY**

> Many psychologists accept the basic idea of the Five Factor Model but think the list should include six, seven, or possibly four factors. Does the Five Factor Model have the right number and assortment of factors? Are five dimensions too many or not enough to characterize individual differences in personality? Explain your reasoning.

> How does evolution explain the existence of various personality traits such as neuroticism and psychoticism?

**APPLY PSYCHOLOGY**

> Describe your best friend and yourself in terms of the five factors from the Five Factor Model of personality. What are the similarities and differences? If you were to use the same traits to characterize someone whom you dislike, what differences would emerge?

The Five Factor Model is easily understood (Sneed, McCrae, & Funder, 1998) and has been adapted to psychological assessment (Matthews et al., 1998). However, not all researchers agree on the categories (Almagor, Tellegen, & Waller, 1995; Benet-Martinez & Waller, 1997), and certain elements of personality are not well identified by the Five Factor Model (Schinka, Dye, & Curtiss, 1997).

Like other trait theories, the Five Factor Model is a description but not an explanation of personality. In describing broad traits, these approaches lose some ability to predict behaviour and why it occurs. Individual behaviour is affected by situation and context (Schmit & Ryan, 1993). Knowing that one person in the Brazilian rain forest and another in London are both high in anxiety is descriptive, but these two people will almost certainly not express their anxiety in similar ways. Therefore, the knowledge of their status on this personality trait will not allow predictions about their behaviour.

# Humanistic Approaches: The Search for Psychological Health

Some psychologists have objected to psychodynamic, behavioural, and type theories because they believe that these approaches have *dehumanized* people, describing them as being a prisoner of their unconscious (Freud and Jung), little different from other animals (Skinner), or best understood by measuring their types and traits (Cattell and Eysenck). These psychologists, led by Abraham Maslow and Carl Rogers, attempted to humanize the study of personality by focusing on humans' unique qualities. Humanistic theorists are interested in people's conceptions of themselves and what they would like to become. In general, *humanistic theories* assume that people are motivated by internal forces to achieve personal goals. Humanistic psychology focuses not on maladjustment or abnormal behaviour but on well-adjusted individuals who are basically decent (although some of their specific behaviours may not be). Moreover, humanistic theories enable theoreticians and practitioners to make predictions about specific behaviours.

Humanistic theories usually take a *phenomenological approach* because they focus on the individual's unique experiences with and ways of interpreting the things and people in the world (phenomena). These approaches are more likely to examine immediate experiences than past ones and are more likely to deal with an individual's perception of the world than with a therapist's perception of the individual. Finally, they focus on self-determination; the theories assert that people carve their own destinies, from their own vantage points and in their own ways. For these reasons, many psychologists regard Alfred Adler as the first humanistic theorist.

## MASLOW AND SELF-ACTUALIZATION

No single individual is more closely associated with humanistic psychology than Abraham Maslow (1908–1970). In Chapter 9, we examined Maslow's theory of motivation, which states that human needs are arranged in a step-by-step hierarchy. Lower needs—for food and water, for example—are powerful and drive people toward fulfilling them. In the middle are the needs for safety, belongingness, and self-esteem. At the top step is **self-actualization,** or the need to realize one's full human potential. The higher a need is in the hierarchy, the more distinctly human it is.

As a humanist, Maslow focused on psychologically healthy people rather than disturbed individuals. He studied both living and historical people whom he believed were self-actualizing and found that these people differed from the rest of the population on several important characteristics. Self-actualizing people, who

**SELF-ACTUALIZATION**

The process of growth and the realization of individual potential; in the humanistic view, a final level of psychological development in which a person attempts to minimize ill health, be fully functioning, have a superior perception of reality, and feel a strong sense of self-acceptance.

make up a very small percentage of all people, have a more efficient perception of reality—they are not easily fooled by phony people; they accept themselves, others, and nature; they are spontaneous, simple, and natural; they are problem centred rather than person centred—a good idea is a good idea regardless of who thought of it first; they are able to feel comfortable when they are alone, but they genuinely like at least some people; they are autonomous and are unmoved by either flattery and unjust criticism; they are almost childlike in their continual appreciation of the world around them; they have high levels of what Adler called *social interest*, or a genuine concern and caring for all people; they enjoy profound interpersonal relations; they can clearly discriminate between ends and means—they recognize that a desirable end product does not justify unlawful means to attain it; they have a philosophical sense of humour and are not amused by contrived stories; they are creative in the broad meaning of the term—a hand-picked bouquet of flowers may be more creative than a popular work of art; and they have the ability to transcend a particular culture—they don't do things merely because "everyone else is doing it." Maslow believed that each of us has the potential for self-actualization, but to reach that stage of psychological health we must have our lower-level needs at least mostly satisfied.

Critics of Maslow find his notions too fuzzy and view his approach to psychology as romantic and not fully developed. Also, his theory is virtually untestable because he provided little explanation of the nature of self-actualizing tendencies. Carl Rogers formulated a more complete and scientific humanistic approach to personality.

▲ Abraham Maslow believed that human beings are only able to attain self-actualization after their lower needs have been met.

## ROGERS AND SELF THEORY

Carl Rogers (1902–1987) began to formulate his personality theory during the first years of his practice as a clinician in Rochester, New York. He listened to thousands of patients and was among the first psychologists to tape-record and transcribe his interactions with patients. What Rogers' patients said about their experiences, their thoughts, and themselves led him to make three basic assumptions about behaviour: (1) behaviour is goal-directed; (2) people have the potential for growth; and (3) how individuals see their world determines how they will behave.

Rogers believed that personal experiences provide an individual with a unique and subjective internal frame of reference and world view. He believed that **fulfilment**—an inborn tendency directing people toward actualizing their essential nature and thus attaining their potential—is the force that motivates personality development. However, people do not move inevitably toward fulfilment. Like a seed that reaches its potential only if certain conditions are present, people attain self-fulfilment only if they have experienced three essential conditions. For a seed, those conditions might be water, fertile soil, and sunlight. For humans, the necessary and sufficient conditions for growth are *empathy* and *unconditional positive regard* received in a relationship with a *congruent* partner or therapist. You experience empathy when you perceive that another person accurately senses your feelings; you receive unconditional positive regard when you sense that another person accepts you completely and unconditionally; and both these conditions must be received from a partner who is congruent, or psychologically healthy.

**THE SELF-CONCEPT AND THE IDEAL SELF.** Rogers' theory of personality is structured around the concept of the **self**—the view that you have of yourself and of your relationships to other people and to various aspects of life. Your *self-concept* is how you see your own behaviour and internal characteristics. In addition to your self-concept, you have a picture of what you would like to be, that is, your **ideal self**. Incongruence, or psychological stagnation, exists when your ideal self is greatly inflated and severely out of line with your self-concept. According to Rogers, people are generally happy when there is agreement between their self-concept and their

▲ Carl Rogers believed that the personality was structured around a person's view of the self.

FULFILMENT

In Rogers' theory of personality, an inborn tendency directing people toward actualizing their essential nature and thus attaining their potential.

SELF

In Rogers' theory of personality, the perception an individual has of himself or herself and of his or her relationships to other people and to various aspects of life.

IDEAL SELF

In Rogers' theory of personality, the self a person would ideally like to be.

ideal self. Great discrepancies between the two selves create unhappiness, dissatisfaction, and, in extreme cases, maladjustment. These discrepancies are seen by the individual—not by another person. Rogers stressed that each person evaluates her or his own situation using a personal (internal) frame of reference, not the external framework that would be provided by society or others.

When your self-concept and ideal self are congruent, you will move naturally toward *self-actualization*, that is, toward becoming fully functioning. People who are fully functioning have a clear perception of reality and feel a strong sense of self-acceptance. When your self-concept is not what you would like it to be, you may become anxious. Rogers saw anxiety as useful because it motivates people to try to actualize their best selves, to become all they are capable of being.

**PSYCHOLOGICAL STAGNATION.**    People with rigid self-concepts guard themselves against potentially threatening feelings and experiences. Rogers suggested that such people become unhappy and psychologically stagnant when they are unable to fit new types of behaviour into their existing self-concepts. They then distort their perceptions of their behaviour to make these perceptions compatible with the self-concept. A man whose self-concept includes high moral principles, rigid religious observance, and strict self-control, for example, might become anxious when he feels greed; such a feeling is inconsistent with his self-concept. To avoid anxiety, he denies or distorts what he is truly experiencing. He may deny that he feels greed, or he may insist that he is entitled to the object he covets.

**THE FULLY FUNCTIONING PERSON.**    People who have received empathy and unconditional positive regard from a congruent, healthy partner develop healthy self-concepts and will move in a positive direction, toward becoming a fully functioning person. Rogers suggested several characteristics of the fully functioning person.

Such people are in a constant state of change; they welcome new experiences and have little reason to deny or distort their view of self. They allow even unpleasant and repugnant experiences to come to awareness, because they see each new experience as an opportunity to learn and to grow. They trust in their organismic self, which means that they act on deeply felt emotions such as love, disgust, joy, anger, fear, and so on. They do not waste time in wishful thinking and have a clear perception of their own values. Finally, fully functional people establish harmonious relations with others. Because they like themselves, they behave in likeable ways, which in turn makes it easier for other people to like them.

## POSITIVE PSYCHOLOGY

As humanistic psychologists contend, psychology has tended to concentrate on problems and maladjustment to the neglect of studying positive human qualities. Although humanistic psychology focused on positive factors such as self-actualization, congruence, and fulfilment, the humanistic movement did not generate a body of research to provide confirmation for its contentions (Seligman & Csikszentmihalyi, 2000). The developing field of *positive psychology* attempts to include well-being, contentment, hope, optimism, and happiness, but researchers in this field strive to collect information using scientific research methods. Martin Seligman and Mihaly Csikszentmihalyi (pronounced CHICK-sent-me-high-ee) (2000, p. 7) explain the emphasis of this developing field: "Psychology is not just a branch of medicine concerned with illness or health; it is much larger. It is about work, education, insight, love, growth, and play. And in this quest for what is best, positive psychology does not rely on wishful thinking, faith, self-deception, fads, or hand waving; it tries to adapt what is best in the scientific method to the unique problems that human behavior presents to those who wish to understand it in all its complexity."

Subjective well-being—happiness—has been a topic of research in the field of positive psychology. Although it surprises some people, results indicate that people are generally happy (Diener, 2000; Myers, 2000). These findings apply to people in countries throughout the world, including people living in conditions of poverty and disease that would seem to make happiness difficult to attain (Diener, 2000). Rather than concentrating on who is happy, positive psychology focuses on the processes that influence subjective well-being. Adaptation is one such process. People adapt to unfortunate circumstances, but they also adapt to prosperity, so personal evaluations of well-being remain fairly stable. Personality is another factor in happiness, and culture also exerts influences in the values and goals people set and are able to attain. Ed Diener (2000) has called for the development of a measurement of subjective well-being that can apply on a national level so that researchers can compare happiness not only among people but also across cultures.

People tend to be happier when they are involved with family, friends, and community and when they are productive. According to Csikszentmihalyi (1997), when people become deeply engaged in some activity, they may experience the phenomenon of *flow*. Flow occurs when a person's skills are engaged in overcoming a challenge they can meet. When people are engaged in an activity, they feel less self-conscious, more in control, and more confident. From Csikszentmihalyi's view, happiness follows from flow, from engagement—whether a person is a physician or a clerk in a department store. Csikszentmihalyi argues that each of us can transform our lives, find flow, and then achieve happiness by complete engagement with what we do and those we do it with.

Happiness is only one of the topics in positive psychology. This area also includes research into optimism, wisdom, creativity, and giftedness. At this point, positive psychology has asked important questions but leaves many others without answers. For example, research needs to address the development of engagement, the role of genetics and biology in positive states, and the benefits of positivity.

▲ Optimistic people are able to maintain a positive outlook, even under difficult circumstances.

**Be an ACTIVE LEARNER**

**REVIEW**
> What does self-actualization mean in the context of Maslow's and Rogers' personality theories? pp. 432–433
> How do empathy and unconditional positive regard contribute to fulfilment? p. 433
> How does the area of positive psychology differ from humanistic psychology? What do the two fields share? pp. 434–435

**THINK CRITICALLY**
> What do you think is the most important way humanistic theory differs from Freudian theory?
> What are the problems and challenges of research investigations of the concept of *flow*?

**APPLY PSYCHOLOGY**
> Do you know anyone who matches the characteristics of the self-actualizing person? Describe that person.

## Cognitive Approaches to Personality

Recently, cognitive approaches to personality theory have gained acceptance among many psychologists. Cognitive theorists generally reject the broad theories of Freud, Adler, and Jung that were based largely on experiences during therapy. Cognitive theorists also find problems with the behaviourists, especially the early behaviourists, who were single-minded in their belief that psychology should limit itself to only observable, measurable behaviour. But human beings clearly have an inner mental and psychic life; they think about things and react emotionally, and those thoughts and reactions are not always evident in observable behaviour. In important ways, cognitive approaches to personality appeared as a reaction not only to psychodynamic and behavioural theories but also to trait and type theories, as well as to humanistic theories.

Cognitive theories emphasize the interaction of thoughts and behaviour. They consider the uniqueness of human beings, especially of their thought processes, and assume that human beings are decision makers, planners, and evaluators of their own behaviour. Rather than viewing people as having stable traits, cognitive approaches assume that people are fluid and dynamic in their behaviour and responses to the world. Many contemporary cognitive therapists claim that people can change their behaviour, their conceptions of themselves, and thus their personalities, if they change their thoughts.

## KEY COGNITIVE CONCEPTS

From a cognitive point of view, the mere association of stimuli and responses is not enough for conditioning and learning to occur in human beings; thought processes also have to be involved. Thought and behaviour affect each other. According to cognitive theory, whether a person exhibits learned behaviour depends on the situation and personal needs at a particular time. If thought and behaviour are closely intertwined, then when something affects the person's thoughts, it should also affect his or her behaviour.

One of the key elements of the cognitive approach to personality is the idea that people develop self-schemata. As we saw in Chapters 6 and 10, a *schema* is a conceptual framework by which people make sense of the world. Self-schemata (*schemata* is the plural of *schema*) are collections of ideas and bits of self-knowledge that organize people's thoughts about themselves. They are often global themes that help individuals define themselves. A man's self-schemata may comprise one self-schema that involves exercise, another that concerns his wife, and still others that are about work, family, and religious feelings. Cognitive researchers assert that people's self-schemata help shape their day-to-day behaviour. They may affect people's adjustment, maladjustment, and ability to regulate their own behaviour. Thus, someone who has a self-schema for being in control of her emotions may find the death of a loved one a challenge to normal day-to-day coping mechanisms.

Over the years, a number of cognitive theories have been developed, dealing with how people perceive themselves and their relationship with the world. Like their behaviourist colleagues, cognitive psychologists have reacted against psychoanalytic and humanistic theories, which they deem difficult or impossible to verify scientifically. Several cognitive theories have attempted to account for specific behaviours in specific situations. Because these cognitive concepts are far better defined than those in psychodynamic and humanistic theories, they are easier to test. We will consider three such concepts from cognitive personality theories next: Julian Rotter's concept of locus of control, Albert Bandura's concept of self-efficacy, and Walter Mischel's concept of cognitive social learning. Each of these concepts is an integral part of these theorists' cognitive personality theories.

## ROTTER AND LOCUS OF CONTROL

Patients who seek the help of a therapist frequently say they feel "a lack of control." Often the task of therapy is to help clients realize what forces are shaping events and what they can do to gain a sense of control. One widely studied cognitive–behavioural concept that therapists often make use of is locus of control, introduced in the 1950s and systematically developed by Julian Rotter and Herbert Lefcourt. *Locus of control* involves the extent to which individuals believe that a reinforcer or an outcome is contingent on their own behaviour or personal characteristics rather than being a function of external events not under their control or simply unpredictable (Lefcourt, 1992; Rotter, 1990). Rotter focused on whether people place their locus of control inside themselves (internal) or in their environments (external). Locus of control influences how people view the world and how they identify the causes of success or failure in their lives. In an important way, locus of control reflects people's personalities—their views of the world and their reactions to it.

To examine locus of control, Rotter developed an inventory consisting of a series of statements about oneself and other people. To determine whether your locus of control is internal or external, ask yourself to what extent you agree with the statements in Table 12.4. People with an internal locus of control (shown by

| TABLE 12.4 | Statements Reflecting Internal versus External Locus of Control | |
|---|---|---|

| Internal Locus of Control | | External Locus of Control |
|---|---|---|
| People's misfortunes result from the mistakes they make. | versus | Many of the unhappy things in people's lives are partly due to bad luck. |
| With enough effort, we can wipe out political corruption. | versus | It is difficult to have much control over the things politicians do in office. |
| There is a direct connection between how hard I study and the grade I get. | versus | Sometimes I can't understand how teachers arrive at the grades they give. |
| What happens to me is my own doing. | versus | Sometimes I feel that I don't have enough control over the direction my life is taking. |

their choice of statements) feel a need to control their environment. They are more likely to engage in proactive behaviour, such as preventive health measures and dieting, than are people with an external locus of control. People who endorse most, but not all, of the internal statements have the highest level of health—those who endorse all of the internal items feel anxious and guilty because they see themselves as responsible for everything, even the things they actually cannot control, and those who endorse most of the external statements feel little responsibility for their actions.

Locus of control is associated with differences in many behaviours, including those important to school and achievement. University and college students characterized as internal are more likely than others to show high academic achievement (Lefcourt & Davidson-Katz, 1991). In contrast, people with an external locus of control believe they have little control over their lives. A university or college student characterized as external may attribute a poor grade to a lousy teacher, feeling there was nothing he or she could have done to get a good grade. They are more likely than those with an internal locus of control to procrastinate on a project (Janssen & Carton, 1999). External locus of control is also associated with high levels of competitiveness but lower grade-point averages (Frederick, 2000). Individuals who develop an internal locus of control, on the other hand, feel that hard work will allow them to make their best grades. In general, such people report less stress in their lives (Carton & Nowicki, 1994; Carton, Nowicki, & Balser, 1996).

People develop expectations based on their beliefs about the sources of reinforcement in their environment. These expectations lead to specific behaviours. Reinforcement of these behaviours in turn strengthens expectancy and leads to increased belief in internal or external control (see Figure 12.3). Not surprisingly, in therapeutic situations where self-esteem is an issue, psychologists often seek to bolster a client's self-esteem by helping the person recognize the things she or he can control effectively (Betz, 1992).

Locus of control integrates personality theory, expectancy theories, and reinforcement theory. It describes several specific behaviours but is not comprehensive enough to explain all, or even most, of an individual's behaviour.

INTERNAL LOCUS OF CONTROL

EXTERNAL LOCUS OF CONTROL

**FIGURE 12.3**
**Locus of Control**

A person's general expectations about life are determined in a three-part process: specific expectancies result in specific behaviours, which are reinforced. This cycle eventually leads to a general expectancy about life, which underlies either an internal or an external locus of control.

## BANDURA AND SELF-EFFICACY

Albert Bandura, a psychology professor at Stanford, developed one of the most influential cognitive theories of personality. His conception of personality began with observational learning theory and the idea that human beings observe, think about, and imitate behaviour, which accounts for learning both acceptable and unacceptable behaviours (see *Psychology in Action*). Bandura has played a major role in reintroducing thought processes into learning and personality theory.

Bandura argued that people's expectations of mastery and achievement and their convictions about their own effectiveness determine the types of behaviours they will engage in and the amount of risk they will undertake (Bandura, 1977a). He used the term **self-efficacy** to describe a person's belief about whether he or she can successfully engage in and execute a specific behaviour. Judgments about self-efficacy determine how much effort people will expend and how long they will persist in the face of obstacles (Bandura, 2001).

A strong sense of self-efficacy allows people to feel free to influence and even create the circumstances of their own lives. Also, people's perceived self-efficacy in managing a situation heightens their sense that they can control it (Conyers, Enright, & Strauser, 1998). Thus, people who have a high level of self-efficacy are more likely than others to attribute success to variables within themselves rather than to chance factors, making them more likely to pursue their own goals (Bandura, 1999, 2000). Because people can think about their motivation, and even their own thoughts, they can effect changes in themselves, persevere during tough times (Sterrett, 1998), and do better at difficult tasks (Stajkovic & Luthans, 1998).

Bad luck or non-reinforcing experiences can damage a developing sense of self-efficacy. Observation of positive, prosocial models during the formative years, on the other hand, can help people to develop a strong sense of self-efficacy that will encourage them in directing their own lives. Bandura's theory allows individual flexibility in behaviour. People are not locked into specific responses to specific stimuli, as some strict behaviourists might assert. According to Bandura, people choose the behaviours they will imitate, and they are free to adapt their behaviour to any situation. Self-efficacy both determines and flows from feelings of self-worth. Thus, people's sense of self-efficacy may determine how they present themselves to other people. For example, a man whom others view as successful may not share that view, whereas a man who has received no public recognition may nevertheless consider himself a capable and worthy person; each of these men will present himself as he sees himself (as a failure or as a worthy person), not as others see him.

Bandura's theory is optimistic. It is a long way from Freud's view, which argues that conflicting biologically based forces determine human behaviour. It is also a long way from a strict behavioural theory, which suggests that environmental contingencies shape behaviour. Bandura believes that human beings have choices, that they direct the course of their lives. He also believes that society, parents, experiences, and even luck help shape the life course.

**GENDER AND SELF-EFFICACY.** In Bandura's view, gender has a major impact on personality through modelling and observational learning. Boys and girls receive different rewards for gender-typed behaviours—girls tend to be reinforced for behaviours considered to be feminine, boys for behaviours considered to be masculine. Girls and boys also have the experience of observing women and men who receive rewards for gender-typical behaviours and punishments for behaviours that are not typical of their gender (Bussey & Bandura, 1999). Their environment is filled with stereotypical models in the family, schools, and media. This stereotyping has effects on self-efficacy in women and men.

Self-efficacy is specific to any given activity, and people tend to have higher self-efficacy for activities that are gender-typed for their gender. However, women show lower expectancies for success on a masculine task than on a feminine or neutral

SELF-EFFICACY

A person's belief about whether he or she can successfully engage in and execute a specific behaviour.

## Seeing Violence, Doing Violence

You and a group of your friends walk out of a club late one night and see two people involved in a fight in the parking lot. How do you infer the reasons for their behaviour? For Freud, aggression was one of the basic drives that underlie personality; he saw aggression as an instinctive force. In Freudian theory, expressing aggression could be cathartic, leading to "getting it out of your system." For Bandura, aggression is learned through observation and thus far from inevitable. In his view, seeing violence leads to doing violence. Rather than getting it out of your system, performing violence makes it more likely that such behaviour will be repeated. These two views lead to very different predictions about the influence of observing violence.

In modern society, you have many opportunities to see violence, and the electronic media offer many times more opportunities than does real life. The power of the media to teach violence has been a topic of research since the 1960s (Bandura, Ross, & Ross, 1963). That research has indicated a positive relationship: Seeing violence on television and in the movies makes children and adults more likely to do violence (Villani, 2001; Johnson et al., 2002).

The effects of observing violence are stronger for younger than for older children, and preschool children are affected most strongly (Villani, 2001). Television affects young children more than other media because young chil-

dren are exposed to television more than any other medium. Children see about 10 000 acts of violence on television each year, and 38 percent of such acts were committed by an attractive person. According to Bandura, the attractiveness and power of the model are factors in observational learning, so the current television depictions of violence have a great deal of power to do harm.

Another distressing trend in media violence is the connection between violence and sexuality. This connection occurs in movies but is especially prominent in music videos (Villani, 2001) and on the Internet (Barron & Kimmel, 2000). The combination of violence and sex not only connects the two through association but also desensitizes viewers to occurrences of sexual violence. The presentation of sexual violence should lead to a high occurrence of such violence, and this prediction is confirmed by the results of a survey of adolescent girls that showed that dating violence is very common—20 percent of young women in the survey reported that they had experienced some type of dating violence (Silverman et al., 2001).

Tannis Williams of the University of British Columbia conducted a detailed content analysis of North American television programming (Williams, Zabrack, & Joy, 1982) and found that there was an average of 9.0 acts of physical aggression and 7.8 acts of verbal aggression per program hour. Williams (1985) was also able to show that when television first became available in a small town, the level of schoolyard violence increased over the first year. Another study offers some hope for a strategy to control the influence of media violence. Reducing the time children spent watching television and playing video games decreased their aggressive behaviour (Robinson, 2001). Children in one elementary school participated in a six-month program to decrease their television and video game usage. Children were rated by their peers and parents to assess their aggression. Decreased television and video game use was associated with lower peer ratings of aggression and lower ratings of verbal aggression on the playground. This result suggests that seeing less violence leads to doing less violence (Anderson & Bushman, 2002).

And the answer is at the tip of our fingers—turn off the television.

task, but this bias does not occur in men (Beyer, 1998). Thus, the many messages that women receive about the limits on their achievement affect their self-efficacy, which may have major effects on their choices in coursework and careers (Betz & Fitzgerald, 1987; Bussey & Bandura, 1999). For example, girls who believe that girls are not good at math will not enrol in advanced mathematics courses and will not consider careers in engineering.

## MISCHEL'S COGNITIVE–AFFECTIVE PERSONALITY SYSTEM

Like Bandura, Walter Mischel claims that thought is crucial in determining human behaviour and that both past experiences and current reinforcement are important. However, Mischel is an *interactionist*—he focuses on the interaction between people's stable personality traits and the situation (Mischel, 1999). Mischel and other cognitive theorists argue that people respond flexibly to various situations. They change their responses on the basis of their past experiences and their current assessment of the present situation (Brown & Moskowitz, 1998). This process of adjustment is called *self-regulation*. For example, people make subtle adjustments in their tone of voice and overt behaviour (aspects of their personality), depending on the context in which they find themselves. Those who tend to be warm, caring, and attentive, for example, can in certain situations become hostile and dismissive.

Mischel believes that behaviours are relatively inconsistent from one situation to another, but they have some consistency over time. He and Yuichi Shoda (Mischel & Shoda, 1998, 1999) suggest that relatively permanent personal dispositions interact with cognitive–affective units to produce behaviour. Cognitive–affective personality units include *competencies* (what people know and can do), *encoding strategies* (the way they process, attend to, and select information), *expectancies and beliefs* (their prediction of the outcomes of their actions), *personal goals and values* (the importance they attach to various aspects of life), and *affective responses* (their feelings and emotions as well as the affects that accompany physiological responses).

Mischel has had a great impact on psychological thought because he has challenged researchers to consider the idea that traits alone cannot predict behaviour. The context of the situation must also be considered—not only the immediate situation but also the culture in which a person lives and was raised, as well as other variables such as the gender and age of the person whose behaviour is being predicted. Day-to-day variations in behaviour should not be seen as aberrations, but rather as meaningful responses to changing circumstances (Brown & Moskowitz, 1998). Mischel's view of personality takes situation and culture into account, but most theories of personality do not, making them subject to criticisms of inflexibility and cultural bias. Next, we turn to a consideration of the effects of culture on personality.

Building Table 12.2 presents an overall summary of the theories presented in this chapter.

# Personality in Cultural Context

Like other behaviours, personality must be viewed in cultural context. The fact that Freud's patients were primarily from a certain segment of Austrian society has wide implications. Freud developed a theory from dealing with a particular group of patients whose day-to-day behaviour, personalities, and problems were shaped by the culture in which they lived. In addition, Freud's own interpretation of his patients' behaviour was influenced by the culture. *Culture,* as we have seen, refers to the norms, ideals, values, rules, patterns of communication, and beliefs adopted by a group of people. Within a culture, there may be different social classes, but all of the people have the same basic set of norms.

Cultural differences between countries are still apparent. For example, people in England, Spain, France, Germany, China, and Turkey have distinctly different value systems, lifestyles, and personalities. Modes of dress and attitudes about work, family, and religion all differ. Culture is significant because it shapes how people raise

**BUILDING TABLE 12.2** Psychodynamic, Behavioural, Trait and Type, Humanistic, and Cognitive Approaches to Personality

| Approach | Major Proponent | Core of Personality | Development | Structure of Personality | Cause of Problems |
|---|---|---|---|---|---|
| Psychodynamic | Sigmund Freud | Maximizes gratification while minimizing punishment or guilt; instinctual unconscious urges direct behaviour | Five stages: oral, anal, phallic, latency, genital | Id, ego, superego | Imbalances between the id, ego, and superego, resulting in fixations |
| Behavioural | B. F. Skinner | Patterns of behaviours learned through experience with the environment | Process of learning new responses | Responses | Faulty or inappropriate behaviours learned through experience with the environment |
| Trait and Type | Raymond Cattell<br><br>Hans Eysenck | Organizes responses in characteristic modes | Genetic factors and learning | Traits and types | Having learned faulty or inappropriate traits |
| Humanistic | Carl Rogers | Self | Actualizes, maintains, and enhances the experiences of life through the process of self-actualization | Incongruence between self and concept of ideal self | Process of cumulative self-actualization and development of sense of self-worth |
| Cognitive | Several, including Rotter, Bandura, and Mischel | Responses determined by thoughts | Ways of thinking and acting In response to a changing environment | Inappropriate thoughts or faulty reasoning | Process of thinking about new responses |

their children, what values they teach, and what family life is like. However, the role of culture in personality is controversial.

Some researchers have focused on the differences among cultures, concentrating on the obvious ones. Western societies value competitiveness, autonomy, and self-reliance, and Western conceptions of personality focus on the individual. In contrast, many non-Western cultures value interdependence and cooperation; they also focus more on group dynamics in constructing conceptions of personality. For developing adolescents, one culture may value conformity to rules, strict adherence to religious values, and obedience to parental authority. Another culture may stress independence of thought, experimentation, and less reliance on parental authority. Even within Canadian culture, there are significant variations in values and social norms among various ethnic and cultural groups.

These sorts of cultural differences have obvious effects on behaviour, but do they affect personality? The answer to that question depends in part on the definition of personality. Some researchers have searched for differences in behaviours that relate to cultural variations. For example, the difference between independence and interdependence is consistent with the individualistic versus collectivist difference. Some cultures value conformity and

▲ Collectivist cultures emphasize interdependence and cooperation.

**Be an**
**ACTIVE**
**LEARNER**

**REVIEW**
> What is locus of control? p. 436
> What is self-efficacy? p. 438
> Why is Mischel called an inter-
   actionist? p. 439
> In what sense is personality common across cul-
   tures, and in what sense does it vary? pp. 440–442

**THINK CRITICALLY**
> What are some possible explanations a cognitive
   psychologist might offer for the constancy of
   personality?
> What factor would an internal locus of control
   play in the experience of negative emotion?
> Are there differences in personalities within dif-
   ferent ethnic groups in Canada?

**APPLY PSYCHOLOGY**
> Have you experienced any change in your self-
   efficacy since beginning university or college? For
   what tasks or skills? Has the change been positive?

**ASSESSMENT**

Process of evaluating individual
differences among human beings
by means of tests, interviews,
observations, and recordings of
physiological processes.

pleasing the family and social group, whereas others emphasize personal achievement and "doing your own thing." Nor are all individualistic or collectivist cultures the same; American individualism varies from Canadian individualism, which in turn varies from Swedish individualism (Triandis & Gelfand, 1998). Differences between individuals in collectivist versus individualist cultures have a great deal of research support. For example, conformity is higher among individuals from collectivist than individualist cultures (Bond & Smith, 1996; Kim & Markus, 1999).

Rather than exploring differences among cultures, some personality researchers contend that culture makes very little contribution to personality traits. These researchers tend to see personality as the expression of biological traits and look for the commonalities across cultures, searching for the underlying dimensions of personality that all humans share (McCrae & Costa, 1997; McCrae et al., 2000). This line of research has also been successful. Using the Five Factor Model as their basis, researchers have found this factor structure in many different cultures around the world.

Do these results mean that people in different cultures have the same personalities? Not exactly. The results mean that people's personalities can be analyzed in terms of the same factors but not that people in different cultures have the same scores on these factors. Indeed, average scores for personality traits vary substantially across cultures (Lynn & Martin, 1997). For example, people in China score much lower on the trait of extroversion than do people in Canada; individuals in Italy score in between. In some cultures, women score higher in extroversion than men, but in most, men's scores are higher than women's. In all cultures, individual variation is large. The search for commonalities does not mean that personality researchers will lose interest in the individual.

The search for differences and similarities in personality depends on measuring personality and personality traits. This goal has been part of psychology from the early years, and the large variety of personality assessments is our next topic of discussion.

## Personality Assessment

When you think to yourself that your neighbour is a fun-loving guy, that your mom is an affectionate person, or that your brother is politically skilful, you are making assessments of their personalities. Most people make these types of evaluations, but psychologists approach assessment in a more thorough and systematic way.

**Assessment** is the process of evaluating individual differences among human beings by means of tests, interviews, observations, and recordings of physiological processes. Psychologists who conduct personality assessments usually have one of two goals. They seek to evaluate personality in order either to explain behaviour or to diagnose and classify people with behavioural problems. Psychologists who are motivated by the first goal have developed hundreds of personality tests, which can be grouped according to the personality theory that prompted their development. Psychologists who want to diagnose psychopathology use some of the same tests that personality researchers do, but they also have other tests that are oriented toward specific types of psychopathologies. Rather than relying on a single test, clinicians often use information from a battery of tests to make their diagnosis. The purpose of the testing determines the types and numbers of tests administered, but personality tests fall into two major types—projective tests and personality inventories.

### PROJECTIVE TESTS

The fundamental idea underlying the use of projective assessment techniques is that a person's unconscious motives direct daily thoughts and behaviour, a belief that can be traced back to Freud's theory of personality. To uncover a person's unconscious motives, psychologists have developed **projective tests**—devices or instruments used to assess personality by showing examinees a standard set of ambiguous stimuli and asking people being tested to respond to the stimuli in their own way. The examinees are assumed to use the defence mechanism of projection and to impose their unconscious feelings, drives, and motives onto the ambiguous stimuli. Such tests can be used by personality researchers but are more often clinical tools used to diagnose problems, most often by clinicians with a psychodynamic orientation. Projective tests are used when it is important for an examiner to uncover a hidden or unconscious motivation. They do not have the rigorous development on standardized scoring procedures associated with IQ tests, and they are less reliable than personality inventories—nevertheless, they help complete a picture of psychological functioning.

**THE RORSCHACH INKBLOT TEST.** A classic projective test is the Rorschach Inkblot Test (see Figure 12.4). The test taker sees 10 inkblots, one at a time. The blots are symmetrical, with a distinctive form; five are black and white, two also have some red ink, and three have various pastel colours. Examinees tell the clinician what they see in the design, and a detailed report of the response is made for later interpretation. Aiken (1988, p. 390) reports a typical response:

> My first impression was a big bug, a fly maybe. I see in the background two face-like figures pointing toward each other as if they're talking. It also has a resemblance to a skeleton—the pelvis area. I see a cute little bat right in the middle. The upper half looks like a mouse.

The examiner usually prompts the examinee to give additional information, such as "Describe the face-like figures." Although norms are available for responses, skilled interpretation and good clinical judgment are necessary in order to place an individual's responses in a meaningful context. Long-term predictions can be formulated only with great caution (Exner, Thomas, & Mason, 1985) because of a lack of substantive supporting research (Garb, Florio, & Grove, 1998).

**THE THEMATIC APPERCEPTION TEST.** The Thematic Apperception Test (TAT) is much more structured than the Rorschach. (The TAT was discussed in Chapter 9 as one way to assess a person's need for achievement.) It consists of black-and-white pictures, each depicting one or more people in an ambiguous situation; examinees are asked to tell a story describing the situation. Specifically, they are asked what led up to the situation, what will happen in the future, and what the people are thinking and feeling. The TAT is particularly useful as part of a battery of tests to assess a person's characteristic way of dealing with others and of interacting with the world.

To some extent, projective tests have a bad reputation among psychologists who are not psychodynamically oriented. Most argue that the interpretation of pictures is too subjective and prone to error. Practising clinicians, even those who use projective tests, often rely more heavily on personality inventories to assess people with problems, and personality researchers rarely use projective techniques.

## PERSONALITY INVENTORIES

Next to intelligence tests, the most widely given tests are *personality inventories*, generally consisting of true/false or multiple-choice questions to which people respond. The aims of personality inventories vary, but the major approaches to personality have generated assessments, each

PROJECTIVE TESTS

Devices or instruments used to assess personality, in which examinees are shown a standard set of ambiguous stimuli and asked to respond to the stimuli in their own way.

**FIGURE 12.4**
**The Rorschach Inkblot Test**

In a Rorschach Inkblot Test, the psychologist asks a person to describe what he or she sees in an inkblot such as this one. From the person's descriptions, the psychologist makes inferences about the person's drives, motivations, and unconscious conflicts.

▼ The Thematic Apperception Test is a projective test that involves interpreting people's interpretations to photographs that depict vague themes.

tied to its theoretical basis. Well-constructed personality tests turn out to be valid predictors of performance in a wide array of situations, including school, work, and personal interactions; this is true for people of various ethnicities and minority status groups (Hogan, Hogan, & Roberts, 1996).

The Myers–Briggs Type Indicator (MBTI; Myers, 1962) is a test based on Jung's theory of personality. Jung proposed that each individual favours specific modalities, or ways of dealing with and learning about the world; the preferred modalities define personality type. The MBTI asks people to choose between pairs of statements that deal with preferences or inclinations and scores the responses so that the test taker is characterized as predominantly at one pole or another on four distinct dimensions: extroversion–introversion (E or I), sensing–intuition (S or N), thinking–feeling (T or F), and judging–perceptive (J or P). The MBTI is a quick and easy way to gather information about personality, but its uses are limited. This test was developed using students in grades 4 through 12 and is best used for individuals in that age range. The MBTI has been used to predict romantic attraction and relationship stability (Hester, 1996) and academic success (Schurr et al., 1997). John Hunsley and Catherine Lee of the University of Ottawa, however, caution that the psychometric properties of the MBTI are uncertain and it should be used with caution in clinical and employment settings (Hunsley, Lee, & Wood, 2003).

Trait theories of personality have generated the majority of personality inventories. These tests require test takers to respond to many items (often more than 100 and sometimes more than 500) that are measurements of the personality traits in the theory. These items have been created and tested on groups of people such that the responses reflect not only the traits in each theory but also a comparison among individuals. The process allows an assessment of how people vary along these dimensions of personality.

One trait test, the Sixteen Personality Factor Test (16 PF), was developed by Raymond Cattell (1949). Using the technique of factor analysis, Cattell constructed a test of personality traits that fits with his theory of personality. People taking this test respond to 187 items, choosing one of three choices for each item. The scoring results in a score for each of the 16 factors, so test administrators can compare the person being tested to others on each dimension. Table 12.5 lists the 16 factors included in Cattell's 16 PF and the descriptors for each dimension. In contrast to the many traits in the 16 PF, Hans Eysenck conceptualized personality as consisting of only the three broad factors called types—extroversion, neuroticism, and psychoticism. The Eysenck Personality Questionnaire (Eysenck & Eysenck, 1993) includes scales that measure each of these types.

The Five Factor Model (or Big Five model) of personality has also prompted the development of a personality inventory, the Revised NEO-Personality Inventory (NEO-PI-R; Costa & McCrae, 1995). This personality inventory consists of 240 items, which yield measures on the five factors proposed by the theory as well as six traits related to each of the five factors. The test can be used in research as well as in clinical diagnosis and has generated a large body of research. For example, Sampo Paunonen (2003) at the University of Western Ontario has demonstrated the effectiveness of using the Big Five model to predict behaviour. Paunonen's colleague at the University of Western Ontario, Douglas Jackson, has done research that indicates that there may be a sixth factor in addition to the Big Five (Jackson & Tremblay, 2002). His six-factor solution includes, extroversion, agreeableness, openness to experience, independence, methodicalness, and industriousness.

Humanistic personality theory prompted the development of the Personal Orientation Inventory (POI), based on Maslow's theory of personality (Shostrom, 1974). This test is oriented toward assessing self-actualization. The POI consists of 150 items to which people must choose one of two alternatives, such as (a) "Two people can get along best if each concentrates on pleasing the other" versus (b) "Two people can get along best if each person feels free to express himself." The

**TABLE 12.5** *For the Active Learner:* **The Sixteen Personality Factor Assessment**

Place an X on each of the lines to indicate where you think you would rate on each of the following dimensions if you took Cattell's Sixteen Personality Factor Test. (Cattell, 1949)

| Low Description | High Description |
| --- | --- |
| Reserved | Outgoing |
| Less intelligent | More intelligent |
| Affected by feelings | Emotionally stable |
| Humble | Assertive |
| Serious | Happy-go-lucky |
| Expedient | Conscientious |
| Shy | Venturesome |
| Tough-minded | Tender-minded |
| Trusting | Suspicious |
| Practical | Imaginative |
| Forthright | Astute |
| Self-assured | Apprehensive |
| Conservative | Experimenting |
| Group-dependent | Self sufficient |
| Undisciplined self-conflict | Controlled |
| Relaxed | Tense |

items are scored in terms of 2 major scales and 10 subscales. Higher scores indicate agreement with self-actualizing values.

One of the most widely used and researched personality tests is the Minnesota Multiphasic Personality Inventory–2nd Edition (the MMPI–2). Unlike the personality inventories designed to assess personality in terms of various theories, the MMPI was designed as a diagnostic instrument. The MMPI–2 consists of 567 true/false statements that focus on the test taker's attitudes, feelings, motor disturbances, and bodily complaints.

Generally, the MMPI–2 is used as a screening device or diagnosis for behaviour problems or psychopathology. Its norms are based on the profiles of thousands of normal people and smaller groups of psychiatric patients. Each scale compares test takers' responses to those of the normal people and the psychiatric patients. In general, a score significantly above normal may be considered evidence of psychopathology. The test has built-in safeguards to detect people who are not responding truthfully to the items. Interpretation of the MMPI–2 generally involves looking at patterns of scores, rather than at a person's score on a single scale.

Students who want to know about their personalities are often anxious to take the MMPI. Generally, psychologists discourage students from doing so; the test is designed to diagnose pathological problems, making it unsuitable for students interested in learning about testing or their own personalities. The other personality tests are typically better choices than the MMPI.

**Be an ACTIVE LEARNER**

**REVIEW**
> What are the two major goals of personality assessment? p. 442
> What is the goal of a projective test? p. 443

**THINK CRITICALLY**
> Do you think that projective tests such as the TAT and the Rorschach Inkblot Test can achieve their goal? Explain your answer.
> What aspects of personality do you think a personality test might be unable to characterize? Why?

**APPLY PSYCHOLOGY**
> Lay out the basic plans for constructing a personality test, including the type of test, the format of the questions, and the type of scoring you would use.

# Summary and Review

## WHAT IS PERSONALITY?

### How do psychologists define personality?

> *Personality* is a set of relatively enduring behavioural characteristics (including thoughts) and internal predispositions that describe how a person reacts to the environment. **p. 414**

**KEY TERM**

personality, p. 414

## PSYCHODYNAMIC THEORIES

### What fundamental assumptions about human behaviour and the mind underlie Freud's theory?

> Freud's structure of the mind includes three levels: *consciousness, preconscious,* and *unconscious.* The primary structural elements of the mind and personality—the id, the ego, and the superego—are three forces that reside, completely or partially, in the unconscious. The *id,* which works through the pleasure principle, is the source of human instinctual energy. The *ego* tries to satisfy instinctual needs in accordance with reality. The *superego* is the moral aspect of mental functioning. **pp. 415–416**

> Freud described the development of personality in terms of five consecutive stages: oral, anal, phallic, latency, and genital. In the *oral stage,* newborns' and young children's instincts are focused on the mouth—their primary pleasure-seeking centre. In the *anal stage,* children learn to control the immediate gratification obtained through defecation and become responsive to the demands of society. In the *phallic stage,* children obtain gratification primarily from the genitals. During this stage, children pass through the *Oedipus complex,* which occurs somewhat differently in boys and girls, but results in identification with the same-sex parent. In the *latency stage,* sexual urges are inactive. The *genital stage,* Freud's last stage of personality development, is that in which the sexual conflicts of childhood resurface (at puberty) and are resolved (in adolescence). The energy for personality comes from the instincts of sex (*libido*) and aggression. **pp. 416–420**

### What is the fundamental function of all of Freud's defence mechanisms?

> For Freud, the most important *defence mechanism* (a defence against anxiety caused by drives toward sex and aggression) was *repression*—in which people block anxiety-provoking feelings from conscious awareness and push them into the unconscious. Other defence mechanisms, such as *rationalization, fixation, regression, projection, reaction formation, displacement, denial,* and *sublimation,* are ways to reduce anxiety by distorting one's perceptions of reality. Defence mechanisms allow the ego to deal with anxiety. **pp. 420–421**

### How did Adler and Jung differ from Freud in their views of personality?

> Adler and Jung modified some of the basic ideas of Freud; these theorists usually attributed a greater influence to cultural and interpersonal factors than did Freud. Adler broke with Freud and argued that Freud overemphasized sex and ignored social issues, formulating the concept of *social interest* as a foundation of his view of personality. Adler theorized that people strive for superiority or success. This tendency is often prompted by feelings of inferiority. According to Adler, individuals develop a lifestyle that allows them to express their goals in the context of human society. **pp. 421–424**

> Jung emphasized unconscious processes as determinants of behaviour and believed that each person houses past events in the unconscious. The *collective unconscious* is a shared collection of *archetypes,* emotionally charged ideas and images that have rich meaning and symbolism and are inherited from one's ancestors. **p. 425**

**KEY TERMS**

consciousness, p. 415; preconscious, p. 415; unconscious, p. 415; id, p. 415; ego, p. 416; superego, p. 416; oral stage, p. 418; anal stage, p. 418; phallic stage, p. 418; Oedipus complex, p. 418; latency stage, p. 419; genital stage, p. 419; libido, p. 419; defence mechanism, p. 420; repression, p. 420; rationalization, p. 420; fixation, p. 420; regression, p. 420; projection, p. 420; reaction formation, p. 420; displacement, p. 421; denial, p. 421; sublimation, p. 421; social interest, p. 423; collective unconscious, p. 425; archetypes, p. 425

## SKINNER AND BEHAVIOURAL ANALYSIS

### What are the important aspects of behavioural approaches to personality?

> The behavioural approach to personality centres on learning principles, such as reinforcement and punishment. These principles allow behavioural researchers to determine which behaviours increase and which behaviours decrease in frequency. For behaviourists, the structural unit of personality is the response. Behavioural psychologists try to discover behaviour patterns. **p. 426**

### Describe Skinner's view of personality.

> According to Skinner, personal learning history is the foundation of stable patterns of behaviour, the basis of personality. However, Skinner used not only behavioural

learning principles but also the concepts of natural selection and evolution of culture to explain personality. **pp. 426–427**

## TRAIT AND TYPE THEORIES: STABLE BEHAVIOURAL DISPOSITIONS

**Distinguish between a trait and a type.**

> A *trait* is any readily identifiable stable quality that characterizes how an individual differs from others; a *type* is a personality category in which a broad collection of traits are loosely tied together and interrelated. A person can be said to *have* a trait or to *fit* a type.   **pp. 427–428**

**Describe the ideas of Allport, Cattell, and Eysenck regarding traits.**

> Allport argued that if you know a person's traits, it is possible to predict how he or she will respond to stimuli. Cardinal traits are enduring characteristics that determine the direction of a person's life. Central traits are the qualities that characterize a person's daily interactions. Secondary traits are characteristics that are exhibited in response to specific situations. Cattell used the technique of factor analysis to show that groups of traits tend to cluster together. Cattell called obvious, day-to-day traits surface traits and higher-order, "deep" traits source traits. Eysenck focused on types, which are higher levels of trait organization. Eysenck argued that all personality traits can be grouped under three basic dimensions: emotional stability, introversion–extroversion, and psychoticism.   **pp. 428–430**

**What is the Five Factor Model?**

> Although dozens of traits exist, researchers think of the Five Factor Model as consisting of "supertraits," the important dimensions that characterize every personality. The five dimensions are extroversion–introversion, or the extent to which people are social or unsocial; agreeableness–antagonism, or the extent to which people are good-natured or irritable; conscientiousness–undirectedness, or the extent to which people are reliable or undependable; neuroticism–stability, or the extent to which people are nervous or at ease; and openness to experience, or the extent to which people are independent or conforming.   **pp. 430–432**

**KEY TERMS**

trait, p. 427; types, p. 428

## HUMANISTIC APPROACHES: THE SEARCH FOR PSYCHOLOGICAL HEALTH

**What are the motivating forces of personality development, according to Maslow's and Rogers' theories?**

> In Maslow's theory, *self-actualization* is the process of realizing one's innate human potential to become the best one can be. The process of realizing potential, and of growing, is the process of becoming self-actualized. **pp. 432–433**

> The humanistic approach of Rogers states that *fulfilment* is the motivating force of personality development. Rogers focuses on the concept of *self*; the *ideal self* is the self a person would ideally like to be. For personal growth, people must experience a relationship that includes empathy, congruence, and unconditional positive regard.   **pp. 433–434**

**What is positive psychology?**

> Positive psychology is a new movement within psychology that focuses on positive human characteristics such as happiness, optimism, and flow. In contrast to the traditional humanist movement, positive psychology seeks to integrate an emphasis on positive characteristics and behaviours with research that confirms the existence and benefits of these qualities.   **pp. 434–435**

**KEY TERMS**

self-actualization, p. 432; fulfilment, p. 433; self, p. 433; ideal self, p. 433

## COGNITIVE APPROACHES TO PERSONALITY

**What are the key ideas of the cognitive approach to personality?**

> The cognitive approach emphasizes the interaction of a person's thoughts and behaviour. Cognitive views assert that people make rational choices in trying to predict and manage events in the world. One important concept in the cognitive approach is the idea that people develop self-schemata—collections of ideas and bits of self-knowledge that organize how a person thinks about himself or herself.   **pp. 435–436**

> Locus of control, according to Rotter, is the extent to which individuals believe that a reinforcement or an outcome is contingent on their own behaviour or personal characteristics, rather than not being under their control or being unpredictable. People with an internal locus of control feel in control of their environment and future; people with an external locus of control believe that they have little control over their lives.   **pp. 436–437**

> *Self-efficacy*, in Bandura's theory, is a person's belief about whether he or she can successfully engage in and execute a specific behaviour. Judgments about self-efficacy determine how much effort people will expend to achieve a goal and how long they will persist in the face of obstacles. A strong sense of self-efficacy allows people to feel free to influence and even construct the circumstances of their lives.   **pp. 438–439**

> Cognitive theories of personality have reintroduced thought into the equation of personality and situational variables. They focus on how people interpret the situations in which they find themselves and then alter their behaviour. Mischel argues that people adjust their responses based on their past experiences and their assessment of the current situation. This process of adjustment is called self-regulation.   **p. 440**

**KEY TERM**

self-efficacy, p. 438

## PERSONALITY IN CULTURAL CONTEXT

**What are the effects of culture on personality?**

> Personality theories all developed within a cultural context, but culture was not considered as a factor in personality theory until recently. Some psychologists look for differences in personality from culture to culture, such as variance across the individualistic–collectivist dimension, and others search for the universal traits in personality. **pp. 440–442**

## PERSONALITY ASSESSMENT

**What is the process and what are the uses of personality testing?**

> *Assessment* is the process of evaluating individual differences among human beings by means of tests, interviews, observations, and recordings of physiological processes. Psychologists use personality tests as part of an assessment process. Some psychologists use personality tests to understand personality, and others use these tests to diagnose psychopathology. **p. 442**

**What is a projective test?**

> *Projective tests* such as the Rorschach Inkblot Test and the TAT ask examinees to respond to ambiguous stimuli in their own way. Examinees are thought to project unconscious feelings, drives, and motives onto the ambiguous stimuli. **pp. 442–443**

**What are personality inventories?**

> Personality inventories are tests consisting of questions to which test takers respond. The responses are scored, yielding assessments of personality according to the traits measured by the specific tests. Many tests are based on various theories of personality, such as the 16 PF and the NEO-PI-R. The MMPI–2 is a personality test that is used for diagnosis of psychopathology. **pp. 443–445**

**KEY TERMS**

assessment, p. 442; projective tests, p. 443

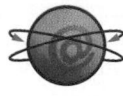 Take advantage of the multimedia resources available with this text! Follow the marginal icons to access the interactive modules on the *HandsOnPsych* CD-ROM; log on to *MyPsychLab* to explore the ebook, study aids, and other online resources; and visit the Companion Website at **www.pearsoned.ca/lefton** for additional exercises and links.

# 13 Social Psychology

Think about it—do you really need other people? Generally we seem to be a bit divided on this question. On one hand we want to feel independent, that our accomplishments are our own. But on the other hand few of us choose to live an isolated life away from all human contact. Besides, how would we keep track of our achievements if there were no other people around to compare ourselves to? The most memorable moments of our lives inevitably involve other people—friends, family, or just fellow human beings. The simple presence of others can spur us to higher levels of performance or can provide us with the encouragement and support we need to remain clear about who we are and where we are going. There is an old song refrain that states, "Ya gotta have friends," but this view is balanced by the rather depressing quote from the philosopher Jean-Paul Sartre that "Hell is other people." For each person reality differs, generally falling somewhere between these two extremes.

In this chapter, we examine the social world of interactions among individuals and within groups. We will see that other people affect each individual's attitudes and self-perceptions and exert powerful influences on individual behaviour. *Brain and Behaviour* explores what happens when people are unable to seek social interaction.

**Social psychology** is the study of how individuals influence and are influenced by the thoughts, feelings, and behaviours of others—it is the scientific study of how we think about and interact with other people.

These concepts help psychologists understand behaviour that occurs when more than one person is involved—that is, social behaviour. Human beings are social organisms; we live with, work with, and seek out others—and social psychologists examine both how others shape our behaviour and how we, in turn, shape theirs. Let us first look at how individual attitudes are affected by other people.

## Attitudes: Deeply Held Feelings and Beliefs

**Attitudes** are long-lasting patterns of feelings and beliefs about other people, ideas, or objects that are based in a person's past experiences and shape his or her future behaviour. They are usually evaluative and serve certain functions, such as guiding new behaviours and helping the individual interpret the world efficiently (Eagly & Chaiken, 1993). Attitudes are shaped by how a person perceives other people, how others perceive him or her, and how the person *thinks* others see him or her. Think

## BRAIN AND Behaviour

### Social Phobia

Human beings are social creatures. There is no doubt that we are all influenced by the thoughts, feelings, and behaviours of others, just as we influence others ourselves. For most, these ongoing interactions with others provide satisfaction and pleasure. However, for some, social situations are unbearable; situations where these individuals feel that others might scrutinize them are either avoided or endured with suffering. Such individuals suffer from social phobia, a disorder in which the prominent symptom is fear of negative evaluation. Although some discomfort or anxiety is not unusual when faced with an unfamiliar or stressful experience (such as public speaking), the intensity of anxiety experienced by an individual with social phobia is extreme and disproportionate to the event itself. In its most severe form, social phobia restricts social interaction, limiting achievement and eroding self-esteem. Individuals suffering from social phobia desire social affiliation and social approval but their fear of rejection overrides their need for social interaction. They have the capacity to form attachments and to maintain relationships but appear to perceive social situations as too "risky" (Stein, 1998) and therefore refrain from the social contact they long for.

Only in the last decade or so have researchers begun to consider the neurobiology of this debilitating social disorder. The tendency for excessive shyness or a tendency toward fearfulness has been shown to have a heritable component (Kagan, Reznick, & Snidman, 1987; Robinson et al., 1992). Likewise, social phobia also appears more frequently in first-degree relatives (Mannuzza et al., 1995). What is unclear is what exactly is inherited when an individual inherits social phobia. Recent research suggests that social phobics may inherit the genetic tendency to fear negative evaluation. Conjoint research at the University of British Columbia and University of California San Diego (Stein, Jang, & Livesley, 2002) suggests that fear of negative evaluation is moderately heritable. In this research, a sample of 437 twin pairs (245 monozygotic and 192 dizygotic) was recruited in Vancouver. Each twin completed a packet of questionnaires, including a brief Fear of Negative Evaluation Scale. Results from this study suggest that genetic influences account for about 42 percent of the symptoms observed in social phobia. Moreover, it is the fear of negative evaluation that appears linked to other anxiety-related personality variables.

Using this research as an example, it is once again important to underscore that nature and nurture are inextricably linked. Genes and environment work in tandem. Genes, in fact, drive social behaviours that may appear to be entirely environmental. Conversely, environment serves to alter genetic influence in important, and largely unknown, ways.

of a time when you were discussing with friends a movie you had just seen. You may recall offering your view somewhat tentatively and even adjusting it as you were speaking in response to the comments, facial expressions, and body postures of your friends, or you may have been more sure of your position and therefore stuck by your opinions in response to the reactions of others.

## DIMENSIONS OF ATTITUDES

Football fans are often fanatical in their attitudes; their enthusiasm is earnest and they often back up their feelings with visible support for the team. Many people are ardently committed to a political position. While many people are vehemently opposed to the Liberal party, there are many who espouse their political views. People's feelings and beliefs about politics, or any other subject, are a crucial part of their attitudes. Attitudes have three dimensions—cognitive, emotional, and behavioural— each of which serves a specific purpose.

The *cognitive dimension* of an attitude consists of thoughts and beliefs. When someone forms attitudes about a group of people, a series of events, or a political philosophy, the cognitive dimension of those attitudes serves a function by helping the person categorize, process, and remember the people, events, and philosophy. The *emotional dimension* of an attitude involves evaluative feelings, such as like or dislike. For example, some people feel excited when in a large crowd while others may feel apprehensive or afraid. The *behavioural dimension* of an attitude determines how people actually show their beliefs and evaluative feelings (Eagly, 1992), such as by voting in accordance with their political beliefs or attending folk concerts. Behaviourally, attitudes function to shape specific actions. Individuals do not always publicly display their attitudes, of course, especially when the attitudes are not yet firmly established or when attitudes and behaviours are inconsistent. For example, many more people cognitively and emotionally were opposed to the war in Iraq than gave their time, energy, or money to organizations speaking out against the war.

When people have very strongly held attitudes about a specific topic, they are said to have a *conviction*. Once people form a conviction, they think about it and become involved with it (which makes convictions long lasting and resistant to change). This is especially true of religious and political convictions. (For example, despite carbon dating evidence to the contrary, many people believe the Shroud of Turin is older than it really is.) Once people have adopted a belief, it functions to justify a wide range of behaviours and to interpret new information about events.

What variables determine how attitudes are formed, displayed, or changed? Why are some attitudes hard to modify and others relatively easy? We will take up each of these questions in the following sections, beginning at the beginning—with attitude formation.

## FORMING ATTITUDES

Though it someday may be discovered that there is a genetic predisposition to develop one type of attitude over another, the most common current position is that attitudes are formed through learning that begins early in life. Thus, psychologists rely on learning theories to explain how children form attitudes. Three learning theory concepts that help explain attitude formation are classical conditioning, operant conditioning, and observational learning (see Chapter 5 for a review and detailed explanation of these concepts).

The association of people, events, and ideologies with certain attitudes often goes unnoticed because it happens so effortlessly. However, such associations can

▲ In response to strongly held political views, many individuals took part in peace rallies protesting the war in Iraq.

**Social Psychology I**

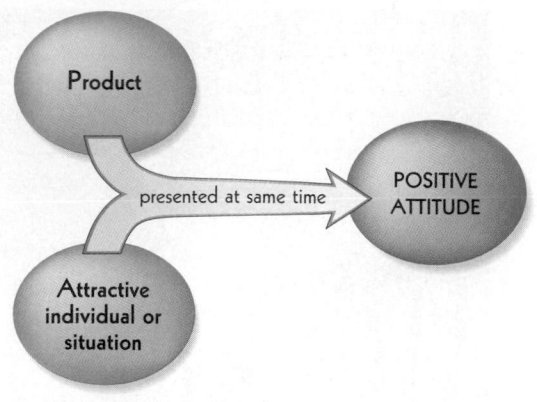

## FIGURE 13.1
### Classical Conditioning in Attitude Formation

In attempting to create positive attitudes toward a product or idea, advertisers use classical conditioning techniques. They pair the product or idea with an attractive, desirable individual or situation to evoke a positive response.

**HandsOnPsych**
Version 2.0

**Social Psychology I**

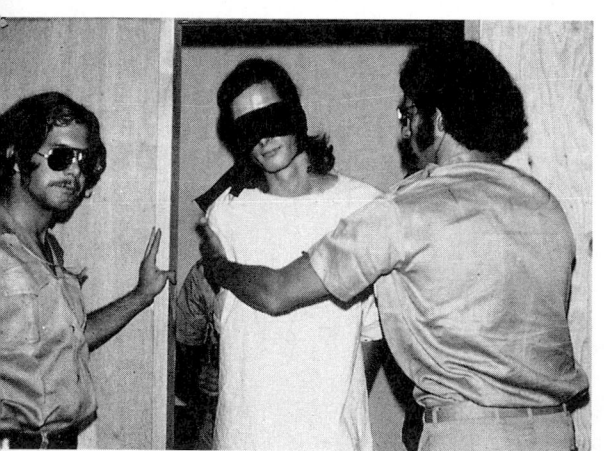

▼ In studies that came to be known as the Stanford Prison Experiment, researchers asked normal, well-adjusted students to dress and act as prisoners and guards.

shape children's views of and emotional responses to the world, thereby forming the basis of their future attitudes as adults. (See Figure 13.1 for an application of this process to attitude formation in adults.) For example, suppose a parent never has a good word to say about the Alberta Conservative party ("red-necked right-wingers" and so on). *Classical conditioning* pairs the formerly neutral stimulus (the Alberta Conservative party) with an unconditioned stimulus (derogatory comments). Because derogatory comments naturally elicit negative feelings, the resulting negative feelings can be considered an unconditioned response. If a child overhears such remarks repeatedly, the Alberta Conservative party eventually will evoke a response of negative feelings (now a conditioned response) in the child.

A key principle of *operant conditioning* is that reinforced behaviours are likely to recur; this principle helps explain how attitudes are maintained over time. In socializing their children, parents express approval for and reinforce ideas and behaviours consistent with their own "correct" view of the world. Such approval and reinforcement help children adopt their parents' attitudes.

According to the concept of *observational learning*, people establish attitudes by watching the behaviour of those they consider significant and then imitating that behaviour. The new attitudes people learn eventually become their own. Suppose that a young girl sees her father react angrily to a TV news story that contradicts a tenet of the family's religious faith. The next time the child hears a similar argument, she will be likely to mimic her father's attitude, which may affect her own attitude.

### DOES BEHAVIOUR DETERMINE ATTITUDES?

Is it possible that your attitudes don't determine your behaviour, but just the opposite—that your behaviour shapes your attitudes? Mounting evidence argues that to a certain extent this is the case. People often develop positive attitudes toward a charity after making a contribution, however small. In weight control programs, alcohol abstinence programs, and many therapy groups, facilitators try to change behaviours (get people to abstain from alcohol, for example) with the idea that positive attitudes about a new life will *follow* changes in behaviour.

A dramatic demonstration of attitudes resulting from behaviours occurred in the 1970s. In studies that came to be known as the Stanford Prison Experiment (Haney, Banks, & Zimbardo, 1973; Zimbardo, Maslach, & Haney, 2000), researchers asked normal, well-adjusted college students to dress and act as prisoners or guards. Guards were given uniforms, billy clubs, and whistles; prisoners were given prison jumpsuits and were locked in cells. Within a few days, "guards" were harassing and degrading "prisoners." Prisoners were caving in and becoming obedient, and many were suffering intense psychological pain. The experiment was aborted after a week. The study showed that an individual could play a role—guard or prisoner—and quickly adapt to that role, develop attitudes that were consistent with it, and become actively committed to the attitudes associated with that role. This research study, with its shocking result, would not be conducted today because of ethical considerations.

### PERSUASION: CHANGING ATTITUDES

Television is one of the prime ways that politicians and marketing executives try to change our attitudes. They know that since attitudes are learned, they can be changed or replaced. Changed attitudes may impel a person to do almost anything—from voting Liberal, to trying a new brand of soap, to undergoing a religious conversion, to becoming a fan of opera. In the 1950s, Carl Hovland was one of the first social psychologists to identify key components of attitude change: the communicator, the communication, the medium, and the audience.

THE COMMUNICATOR.   To be persuasive, a communicator—the person trying to effect attitude change—must project integrity, credibility, and trustworthiness. If people don't respect, believe, or trust the communicator, they are unlikely to change their attitudes. Communicators with "mature" faces have more influence (Berry & Landry, 1997). Researchers also have found that the perceived power, prestige, celebrity, prominence, modesty, and attractiveness of the communicator are extremely important (Dillard & Pfau, 2002). Credibility is also an important characteristic. A credible communicator is perceived as a trustworthy expert. For example, a spokesperson at Health Canada has a greater ability to change your views about cigarette smoking in the workplace than does a local school board member. Information received from friends is considered to be more influential than information from the communications media. Communicators who share characteristics with their audience are more persuasive than communicators who are seen as different from their audience. So a teenager is more likely to follow a close friend's advice on the use of condoms than that of an unknown public health official (Jaccard et al., 1990).

▲ Communications that arouse fear are effective in motivating attitude change, especially when they focus on health issues and the communicator does not overdo the fear appeal.

THE COMMUNICATION.   A clear, convincing, and logical argument is the most effective tool for changing attitudes—especially attitudes with strong emotional content, such as those concerning capital punishment or legalized abortion (Millar & Millar, 1990). This is especially true in Canadian culture, where appeals to logic and reason are more prevalent than in Japan, for example, where appeals to authority and tradition are more common.

Communications that arouse fear are effective in motivating attitude change, especially when health issues are concerned and the communicator does not overdo the fear appeal (Sturges & Rogers, 1996). For example, think of some of the anti-smoking messages you've seen on television. What techniques do they use to induce fear? Fear works; university and college students who come to fear AIDS are more likely to use condoms (Boyd & Wandersman, 1991), and fear of cancer can be motivating in some situations (Wandersman & Hallman, 1993). In fact, research is now beginning to show that negative information tends to influence people more strongly than comparably extreme positive information (Ito, Larsen, Smith, & Cacioppo, 1998). This is particularly true if the report of dire consequences also includes something that people can do to avoid the danger (Gleicher & Petty, 1992).

Researchers have also found that if people hear a persuasive message often enough, they begin to believe it, regardless of its validity. Repeated exposure to certain people or situations can also change attitudes (Bornstein, 1989). For example, after seeing TV commercials showing the Energizer Bunny outperforming other brands, a viewer may change his or her attitude toward the product from neutral to positive. Similarly, someone who is seen frequently is more likely to be viewed positively than is someone who is seen less frequently; this is called the *mere exposure effect*.

THE MEDIUM.   The way in which communication is presented—its medium—influences people's receptiveness to attitude change. Today, one of the most common avenues for attempts to change attitudes is the mass media, particularly television. After all, the goal of TV commercials is either to change or to strengthen people's behaviour. Commercials exhort viewers to drink Pepsi instead of Coke, to say no to drugs, or to vote Liberal instead of NDP. Research shows that TV advertising is one of the most influential media of attitude change in the Western world; this is no surprise, given that in the average household the television is on for more than four hours every day.

Nevertheless, face-to-face communication often has more impact than communication through television or in writing. Thus, even though candidates for public office rely heavily on TV, radio, and printed ads, they also try to meet people face to face, sometimes taking to the road to bring their message directly to the people.

THE AUDIENCE.    Attitude changes can occur. However, openness to attitude change is in part age- and education-related. People are most susceptible to attitude change in their early adult years (Ceci & Bruck, 1993); susceptibility to change drops off in later years. People of high intelligence are less likely to have their opinions changed, and people with high self-esteem tend to be similarly unyielding (Rhodes & Wood, 1992).When a friend tries to change a person's attitudes, attitude change is far more likely (Cialdini, 2001).

Attitude change is complicated, and researchers have shown that a number of other variables are also important. For example, attitude change is more likely when the targeted attitude is not too different from an existing one (McCaul, Jacobson, & Martinson, 1998); it is also more likely when the audience is not highly involved with a particular point of view (Johnson & Eagly, 1989). Research also shows that people who positively anticipate a new idea or who feel that others around them are inclined to change their views are likely to exhibit attitude change (Cialdini, 2001). The extent of attitude change can also be affected by prevalent attitudes in a particular region of the country, as was seen in the most recent referendum on separation in Quebec.

Changing attitudes, and ultimately behaviour, can be difficult if people have well-established habits or are highly motivated in the opposite direction. Consider attitudes toward smoking. Although most people generally believe in the serious health consequences of smoking, 30 percent of Canadians still smoke. Getting people to stop smoking—or to not start—takes more than fostering positive attitudes about health; it also requires instilling a new habit in people and removing an old one. Education can be helpful, as can devices to help people remember not to smoke (such as warning buzzers or strings on fingers); nevertheless, smoking behaviour, once established, is hard to stop due to physical addiction and psychological dependence.

*Psychology in Action* shows some reliable techniques that have been used for decades to influence attitudes, change behaviours, and obtain favours.

COGNITIVE APPROACHES: THE ELABORATION LIKELIHOOD MODEL. Decades of research have identified the components of attitude change. However, researchers only recently have begun to focus on what happens cognitively to individuals whose attitudes are being changed. Various theories attempt to understand individuals' thought processes so as to be able to predict actual attitude change. One such theory, proposed by Richard Petty and John Cacioppo (1985), suggests that people generally want to have valid attitudes and beliefs that will prove helpful in the face of day-to-day challenges and problems (Petty & Wegener, 1999). This theory is called the **elaboration likelihood model**—a view of attitude change suggesting that it can be accomplished via two routes: central and peripheral. (See Figure 13.2 for an overview of this model.)

The *central route* emphasizes the content of the message; conscious, thoughtful consideration; and elaboration of arguments concerning a particular issue. Attitude change via this route depends on how effective, authoritative, and logical a communication is. Confronted with scientific evidence on the effects of second-hand smoke on people's health (especially the prevalence of respiratory diseases), most people conclude through the central route that second-hand smoke is in fact detrimental to health. That is, unless they are highly motivated to believe otherwise, they conclude that the scientific arguments against smoking are too strong to refute.

ELABORATION LIKELIHOOD MODEL

A theory suggesting that there are two routes to attitude change: central, which focuses on thoughtful, elaborative considerations, and peripheral, which focuses on less careful, more emotional, and even superficial considerations.

## Techniques to Induce Attitude Change

How do people influence one another? What techniques promote attitude change? Many people apply principles of social psychology in their work. They influence people regularly by using social psychology techniques such as the foot in the door, the door in the face, the ask-and-you-shall-be-given approach, lowballing, modelling, and incentives. If you understand these techniques, you can both use them and see them coming when others are trying to use them on you. Imagine you are going to ask your parents for some money to get you through to the end of the month. How would you go about it?

### Foot-in-the-Door Technique

To get someone to change an attitude or grant a favour, begin by asking for a small attitude change or a small favour. In other words, get your foot in the door. Ask to borrow a quarter today, a dollar next week, and money to supplement your meagre income within a month.

The essence of the foot-in-the-door technique is that a person who grants a small request is likely to comply with a larger request later. However, it works only if the person first grants the small favour, and it works best if there is some time between the first, small request and the later, large one. A person who says no to the first favour may find it even easier to say no to subsequent ones (Kilbourne, 1989).

### Door-in-the-Face Technique

To use the door-in-the-face technique, first ask for something outrageous; then later ask for something much smaller and more reasonable. Ask your parents for $2000; after being turned down, ask to borrow $200. Your parents may be relieved to grant the smaller favour.

The door-in-the-face technique appears to work because people do not want to be seen as turning someone down twice, and it works best if there is little time between requests. To look good and maintain a positive self-image, people agree to the lesser of two requests.

### Ask-and-You-Shall-Be-Given Technique

When people ask for money for a good cause, whether the request is large or small, they usually will get a positive response. Ask someone who has given before and the request is even more likely to be granted (Doob & McLaughlin, 1989), especially if the person is in a good mood (Forgas, 1998). Fundraisers for universities, churches, and museums know that asking usually will get a positive response. Research indicates that asking in an unusual way can pique a person's interest, turn the potential donor aside from his or her well-rehearsed script of saying no, and increase the likelihood of giving (Santos, Leve, & Pratkinis, 1994). So, wait for your parents to be in a good mood and then sing your request to them!

### Lowballing Technique

Lowballing is a technique by which a person is influenced to make a decision or commitment because of the low stakes associated with it. Once the decision is made, the stakes may increase; but the person will likely stick with the original decision. For example, if your parents agree to lend you $200 and you then sadly start to list all the essential things you must have to succeed in school, they may continue to agree while you work the request up to $400. Lowballing works because people tend to stick to their commitments, even if the stakes are raised. Changing one's mind may suggest a lack of good judgment, may cause stress, and may make the person feel as if he or she is violating an (often imaginary) obligation.

### Modelling

Showing good behaviour, such as conserving energy or saying no to drugs, to someone else increases the likelihood that the person will behave similarly. The person being observed is a model for the desired behaviour. Modelling, which is examined in Chapter 5, is a powerful technique for influencing behaviours and attitudes by demonstrating those behaviours and expressing those attitudes. Talk to your parents about all the work hours you have had to turn down due to the demands of studying.

### Incentives Technique

Nothing succeeds better in eliciting a particular behaviour than a desired incentive. Offering a 16-year-old use of the family car for setting the dinner table every night usually results in a neatly set dinner table. Figure out what your parents might want from you (more phone calls or e-mails, or better grades) and see if you can give them some of what they want as a bonus for them helping you out financially. Behaviour changes occur—the person is doing it for an incentive—but attitude changes may not follow—the 16-year-old sets the table, but still hates doing so.

FIGURE 13.2

Elaboration Likelihood
Model

According to the elaboration
likelihood model, attitude change
can occur through the central route
or the peripheral route.

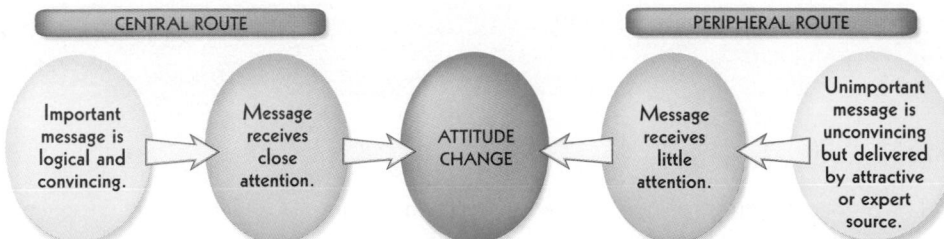

The *peripheral route* emphasizes a more superficial, less careful, and more emotional evaluation of the message. This route has an indirect but nevertheless powerful effect, especially when there are no convincing or strong arguments that can motivate the use of the central route. This is what happens frequently with political messages (DeBono, 1992; Petty et al., 1993). Former Toronto mayor Mel Lastman used emotion-laden language to get his message across. Unfortunately, he often relied overly much on emotion at the expense of facts. For example, in an effort to revive the flagging tourism trade in the midst of the SARS crisis, Lastman inadvisably raged emotionally at the renowned World Health Organization for having raised a travel advisory about Toronto, saying, among other things, "I don't know who this group is. I've never heard of them before!"(CNN, 2003). Whether a person accepts a message through the peripheral route depends on how the person perceives its tone, its delivery, and its similarity to well-established personal attitudes, and on the characteristics of the communicator. Think of an infomercial that you may have seen on television that attempts to sell exercise equipment. Such commercials often make their pitch while featuring attractive models and an upbeat, eager (and trim) audience. You may believe the evidence presented only because a convincing, seemingly honest, and fit person has expressed confidence in the product. The attitude change you may show—a desire to buy the product—often stems largely from emotional or personal rather than logical arguments and therefore may not be long lasting (Petty et al., 1993).

The key idea of the elaboration likelihood model is that sometimes people form or change attitudes because of thoughtful, conscious decisions (central route) or because of more superficial, emotional, and quick ideas or feelings (peripheral route). The central route is used when people have the ability, time, and energy to think through arguments carefully; the peripheral route is more likely to be used when decisions are less important, motivation is low, time is short, or the ability to think through arguments is impaired (Petty et al., 1994).

▼ Former Toronto mayor Mel Lastman often relied on emotion-laden language to attain media attention.

## SEARCHING FOR COGNITIVE CONSISTENCY

People often try to maintain consistency among their various attitudes and between their attitudes and their behaviour. *Consistency* refers to a high degree of coherence among elements of behaviour and mental processes; such coherence leads to orderly living and enables people to make decisions about their future behaviour without having to filter out numerous alternatives.

COGNITIVE DISSONANCE.    Imagine the dilemma faced by a scientist who smokes cigarettes and who finds through her research that cigarettes do indeed cause cancer. As a scientist, she must find the physical evidence compelling; as a smoker, she recognizes that she has smoked for years, feels fine, and has a 92-year-old grandmother who still smokes. How does she reconcile these opposing facts? Moreover, what further confusion would she suffer if she learned that a chest X-ray found that her grandmother's lungs are totally clear?

When people's various attitudes conflict with one another or when their attitudes conflict with their behaviour, they feel uncomfortable. Leon Festinger

(1919–1989) called this feeling of tension **cognitive dissonance**—the state of mental discomfort that results when a discrepancy exists between two or more of a person's beliefs or between a person's beliefs and overt behaviour. Based on the premise that people seek to reduce such dissonance, Festinger (1957) proposed a *cognitive dissonance theory*. According to the theory, when people experience conflict among their attitudes (see Figure 13.3) or between their attitudes and their behaviour, they are motivated to change either their attitudes or their behaviour. Cognitive dissonance theory also may be considered to be a type of motivation theory, because it suggests that people become energized by their cognitive dissonance (Tesser, 2001). Consider an example of behaviour–attitude conflict. Suppose you are a strong proponent of animal rights. You support your local animal rights organization and Greenpeace, refrain from eating meat, and are repulsed by fur coats. Then you win a raffle and are awarded a stylish black leather coat. Wearing the coat goes against your beliefs, but it feels good, you know it looks great on you, and all of your friends admire it. According to cognitive dissonance theory, you are experiencing conflict between your attitudes (animal rights) and your behaviour (wearing the coat). To relieve the conflict, you either will stop wearing the coat or will modify your attitude (leather becomes a more acceptable choice). People choose the most direct method (the one that is easiest) to reduce dissonance (Stone et al., 1997). Psychologists have devised measures for a person's preference for consistency (Cialdini, Trost, & Newsom, 1995), but not all people are consistent, nor do all psychologists suggest that consistency is important.

**SELF-PERCEPTION THEORY.** Social psychologist Daryl Bem (1972) claims that people do not change their attitudes because of internal states such as dissonance. He has proposed **self-perception theory**—an approach to attitude formation in which people are assumed not to know what their attitudes are until they examine their behaviour. Bem argues that people infer their attitudes and emotional states from their behaviour. First they search for an external explanation; if no such explanation is available, they then turn to an internal one. That is, people simply look at their behaviour and say, "I must have liked this if I behaved this way." For example, if you are angry when a salesperson calls you at home but respond to the call in a warm and polite manner, you may infer that you liked the product or the salesperson (or at least that you didn't hate it as much as you thought you might). See Figure 13.4 for a comparison of the traditional view of attitude formation and Bem's view.

COGNITIVE DISSONANCE
[COG-nuh-tiv DIS-uh-nins]
The state of discomfort that results when a discrepancy exists between two or more of a person's beliefs or between a person's beliefs and overt behaviour.

SELF-PERCEPTION THEORY
An approach to attitude formation in which people are assumed to infer their attitudes based on observations of their own behaviour.

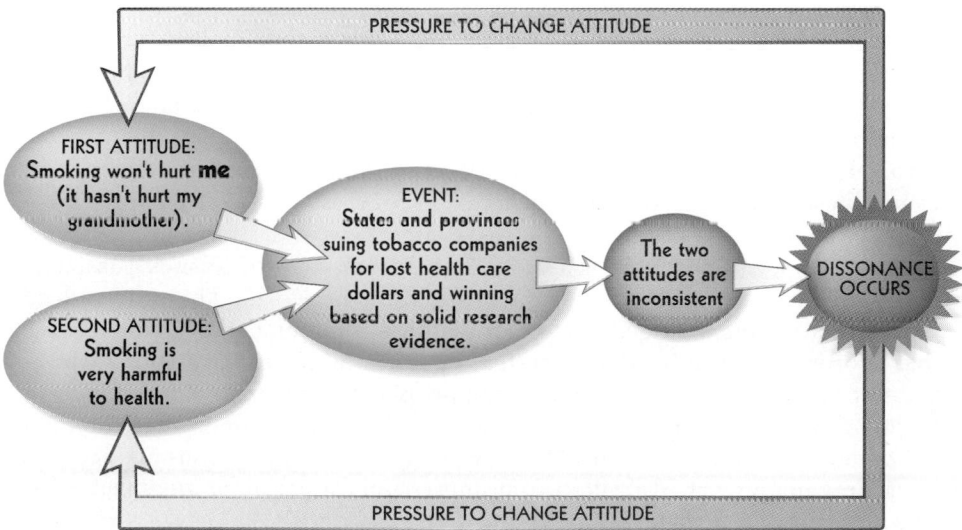

FIGURE 13.3
**Cognitive Dissonance**

A person often holds conflicting attitudes or behaves in ways that are inconsistent with his or her attitudes. When an event challenges one of those attitudes or the behaviour, the person is motivated to change the attitude or behaviour because of cognitive dissonance.

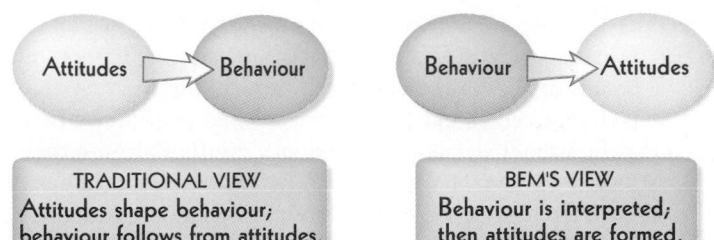

**FIGURE 13.4**
**Two Views of Attitudes**

Does behaviour follow from attitudes (the traditional view), or do attitudes follow from behaviour (Bem's view)?

TRADITIONAL VIEW
Attitudes shape behaviour; behaviour follows from attitudes.

BEM'S VIEW
Behaviour is interpreted; then attitudes are formed.

---

**Be an ACTIVE LEARNER**

**REVIEW**
> Do attitudes predict behaviour, or is it the other way around? Explain your answer. pp. 453–454
> What are the most salient qualities of the communicator that can change attitudes? p. 455
> What is the fundamental idea of the elaboration likelihood model? pp. 456, 458
> What is reactance theory? p. 460

**THINK CRITICALLY**
> Under what conditions are attitudes most likely to predict behaviours? Can you think of examples of attitudes that will not predict future behaviours?
> What can people do as individuals to help them avoid the "spin" put on stories from television and print media?

**APPLY PSYCHOLOGY**
> If you were a sales manager, what would you tell your salespeople to do to appear, and in fact be, more credible to customers?

---

**REACTANCE**

A pattern of feelings and subsequent behaviours aimed at re-establishing a sense of freedom when there is an inconsistency between a person's self-image as being free to choose and the person's realization that someone is trying to force him or her to choose a particular alternative.

**SOCIAL COGNITION**

The thought processes involved in making sense of events, other people, oneself, and the world in general by analyzing and interpreting them.

**IMPRESSION FORMATION**

The process by which a person uses the behaviour and appearance of others to infer their internal states and intentions.

---

**REACTANCE THEORY.** Leading a consistent and coherent life with a clear set of attitudes may be satisfying, but attitudes are often challenged. Have you ever been ordered to do something and found that you wanted to do exactly the opposite? According to social psychologist Jack Brehm (1966), whenever people feel that their freedom of choice is being unjustly restricted, they are motivated to re-establish that freedom. Brehm calls this form of negative influence reactance. **Reactance** is the negative response evoked when there is an inconsistency between a person's self-image as being free to choose and the person's realization that someone is trying to force him or her to choose a particular alternative.

Reactance theory focuses on how people re-establish a feeling that they have freedom of choice. Often, forbidden activities become attractive; choosing the forbidden may boost an individual's sense of autonomy. For example, an adolescent who is told he cannot be friends with a particular person may seek out that person more often. When coercion is used, resistance follows. According to reactance theory, the extent of reactance is directly related to the extent of the restriction on freedom of choice. If a person does not consider the choice very important and if the restriction is slight, little reactance develops. The wording or delivery of the restriction also affects the extent of reactance. People who are told they *must* respond in a certain way are more likely to react negatively than if they merely receive a suggestion or are given a relatively free choice.

## Social Cognition: The Impact of Thought

On meeting someone for the first time, you might say, "I really hit it off with him!" or "I can't put my finger on why, but she irritates me." Often, first impressions are based on nothing more than the other person's appearance, body language, and speech pattern. Yet these impressions can have lasting effects. Such individual impressions form one aspect of social cognition.

**Social cognition** is the process of analyzing and interpreting events, other people, oneself, and the world in general. It focuses on social information in memory, which affects judgments, choices, evaluations, and, ultimately, behaviour (Fiske, 1992). Social cognition is a useful and pragmatic process in which people often use mental shortcuts to help them organize the world. The process often begins with attempts to understand other people's communications, which can be verbal (words) or nonverbal (looks, gestures, body movements, and other means of expression), and to form impressions of the people. The process by which a person uses the behaviour and appearance of others to infer their internal states and intentions is known as **impression formation**; sometimes the impressions are accurate, but certainly not always. We will look at impression formation in more depth later in this section, when we study attribution.

## ORGANIZING THE WORLD USING MENTAL SHORTCUTS

We saw earlier that people use their attitudes to help them make decisions and organize their lives. In a related way, using mental shortcuts helps people process information and decreases the information overload. People seek to be "cognitive misers," processing information superficially unless they are motivated to do otherwise. According to Susan Fiske (1992, p. 879), "Social cognition operates in the service of practical consequences." To help themselves make decisions people develop pragmatic rules of thumb.

One rule of thumb is *representativeness*; individuals or events that appear to be representative of other members of a group are quickly classified as such, often despite a complete lack of evidence. If you see a six-foot-six 19-year-old, you are likely to think that he plays basketball—without knowing anything else about him, let alone his interests or abilities. Another rule of thumb is *availability*; the easier it is to bring to mind instances of one category, type, or idea, the more likely it is that the category, type, or idea will be used to describe an event. Politicians associate memorable images and ideas—often stark, vivid ones—with themselves or their opponents. Few Canadians have forgotten the image of Stockwell Day on a Jet Ski. The more vivid the image, the more likely this will be available and remembered by voters. Still another rule of thumb is the *false consensus effect*; people tend to believe that others agree with them. Whatever their view on a politician or a social issue, people believe that most other people believe the way they do. The last rule of thumb is *framing*; the way in which information is organized and the context in which it is presented to people helps determine whether people are likely to accept it easily, ignore it, or reject it. Consider the different impacts of these two public health warnings: "95 percent of the population will not be affected by the disease and only 5 percent will become seriously ill" and "Due to the disease, 5 percent of you will become seriously ill, although the rest of you will be unaffected." When other people's behaviour fits neatly into a person's conceptions of the world, the individual can use little effort to make judgments about it. One of the most powerful ways of sending easily interpreted signals is nonverbal communication.

## ASSESSING THE WORLD BY USING NONVERBAL COMMUNICATION

Impression formation often begins with **nonverbal communication**, the communication of information by physical cues or actions that include gestures, tone of voice, vocal inflections, and facial expressions. When a person irritates you, it may be a shrill laugh, a grimace, or an averting of the eyes that generates your bad feelings—not the words the person uses. Nonverbal communication is difficult to suppress and is easily accessible to observers (DePaulo & Friedman, 1998). Three major forms of nonverbal communication are facial expressions, body language, and eye contact.

**FACIAL EXPRESSIONS.**   Many of the conclusions we draw about other people are based on their facial expressions. Most people, across cultures, can distinguish six basic emotions in the facial expressions of other people: happy, sad, angry, fearful, surprised, and disgusted (Kupperbusch et al., 1999). A simple expression such as a smile, for example, gives others a powerful cue about a person's truthfulness. Research shows that when a person smiles, both the smile and the muscular activity around the eyes help determine whether the person is telling the truth or is smiling to mask another emotion (Ekman & Keltner, 1997).

**BODY LANGUAGE.**   People also convey information about their moods and attitudes through body positions and gestures—**body language**. Movements such as crossing the arms, lowering the head, and standing rigidly can communicate negative

**NONVERBAL COMMUNICATION**
The communication of information by cues or actions that include gestures, tone of voice, vocal inflections, and facial expressions.

**BODY LANGUAGE**
Communication of information through body positions and gestures.

In some non-Western cultures, making direct eye contact may be a sign of disrespect, arrogance, or even a challenge.

attitudes. On the other hand, when a server in a restaurant moves close to the table and makes direct eye contact, tips increase (Lynn & Mynier, 1993). Aspects of body language differ with culture and gender. For example, in Canada, the energetic and forceful way younger people walk makes them appear sexier, more carefree, and happier than older people (Montepare & Zebrowitz-McArthur, 1988). A pensive, reflective posture or a deferential movement or head position might signal composure, confidence, and status in Japan (Matsumoto & Kudoh, 1993). Gestures also have different meanings in different societies. For example, the okay sign (a circle formed with the thumb and forefinger) is a rude gesture referring to sexual acts in many cultures. Research also shows that in Western cultures, women are sometimes better than men at communicating and interpreting nonverbal messages, especially facial expressions (Graham & Ickes, 1997). Women are more likely to send nonverbal facial messages but are also more cautious in interpreting nonverbal messages sent to them by men. It turns out, though, that while women may be more accurate than men at interpreting social cues, the advantage is small; furthermore, women cannot intuit, any more than men, the specific content of another person's thoughts (Graham & Ickes, 1997).

EYE CONTACT.   Another form of nonverbal communication is *eye contact*. The eyes convey a surprising amount of information about feelings. A person who is looking at you may glance briefly or stare; you may glance or stare back. You would probably gaze tenderly at someone you were fond of but avoid eye contact with someone you did not trust or like or did not know well. Frequent eye contact between two people may indicate that they are sexually attracted to each other.

People tend to judge others based on the eye contact they engage in, making inferences (attributions) about others' internal motivations from the degree of eye contact. Canadians generally prefer modest amounts of eye contact rather than constant eye contact or none at all. Job applicants, for example, are rated more favourably when they make moderate amounts of eye contact; speakers who make more rather than less eye contact are preferred; and witnesses testifying in a court trial are perceived as more credible when they make eye contact with the attorney (DePaulo, 1992). However, all this is true only in Western cultures, which foster an individualistic stance; in some non-Western cultures—for example, Japan—making direct eye contact may be a sign of disrespect, arrogance, or even a challenge.

## INFERRING THE CAUSES OF BEHAVIOUR: ATTRIBUTION

If you see people standing in line at a bus stop, you can be fairly certain that they wish to take a bus. Similarly, if you saw a man at the bus stop reading the Muslim holy book, the Koran, you might infer that he is a devout Muslim. In getting to know others, people often infer the causes of their behaviour. When they do, they are making attributions. **Attribution** is the process by which a person infers other people's motives and intentions by observing their behaviour. It turns out that attributions are not just cognitive processes but also communicative acts (Malle et al., 2000). Through attribution, people decide how they will react toward others, in an attempt to evaluate and make sense of their social world. Attribution may seem like a fairly straightforward process based on common sense. However, it must take into account internal as well as external causes of behaviour. Someone making an *internal attribution* thinks the behaviour comes from within the person, from the individual's personality or abilities. Someone making an *external attribution* believes that person's behaviour is caused by outside events, such as the social situation or luck.

People can be mistaken when they infer the causes of another person's behaviour. Suppose the man you saw reading the Koran is actually a Catholic taking a world religions class that uses the book as a text. In that case, your original

ATTRIBUTION

The process by which a person infers other people's motives and intentions by observing their behaviour.

HandsOnPsych
Version 2.0

**Social Psychology I**

attribution (that he is a Muslim) was wrong. It is also easy to see that culture shapes attributions; Morris and Peng (1994) found that accounts of certain crimes in English-language newspapers were *dispositional* (based on internal attributions) in tone, but that Chinese newspapers were more *situational* (based on external attributions) in their explanations of the same crimes.

To learn more about attribution, researchers have attempted to conceptualize the process. Harold Kelley's (1972, 1973) theory of attribution suggests that people use three criteria to decide whether the causes of a behaviour are internal or external: *consensus, consistency*, and *distinctiveness* (see Figure 13.5). According to Kelley, to infer that someone's behaviour is caused by internal characteristics, you must believe that (1) few other people in the same situation would act in the same way (low consensus), (2) the person has acted in the same way in similar situations in the past (high consistency), and (3) the person acts in the same way in different situations (low distinctiveness). To infer that a person's behaviour is caused by external factors, you must believe that (1) most people would act that way in that sort of situation (high consensus), (2) the person has acted that way in similar situations in the past (high consistency), and (3) the person acts differently in other situations (high distinctiveness).

To see how Kelley's theory works, suppose that a man in an office gets into an argument with his supervisor, but other people in the same office do not enter into the discussion (low consensus). Also suppose that the man has argued about the same issue on other occasions (high consistency). Finally, assume that he argues with everybody (low distinctiveness). In such a case, people would no doubt attribute the argument to the individual's personality; the man is simply argumentative. Now suppose that (1) many of the man's co-workers join in and support him in the debate (high consensus), (2) the man has argued about the same issue in the past (high consistency), but (3) he does not argue in other situations (high distinctiveness). People would then be more likely to attribute the argument to situational factors, such as a disagreement over handling a particular file.

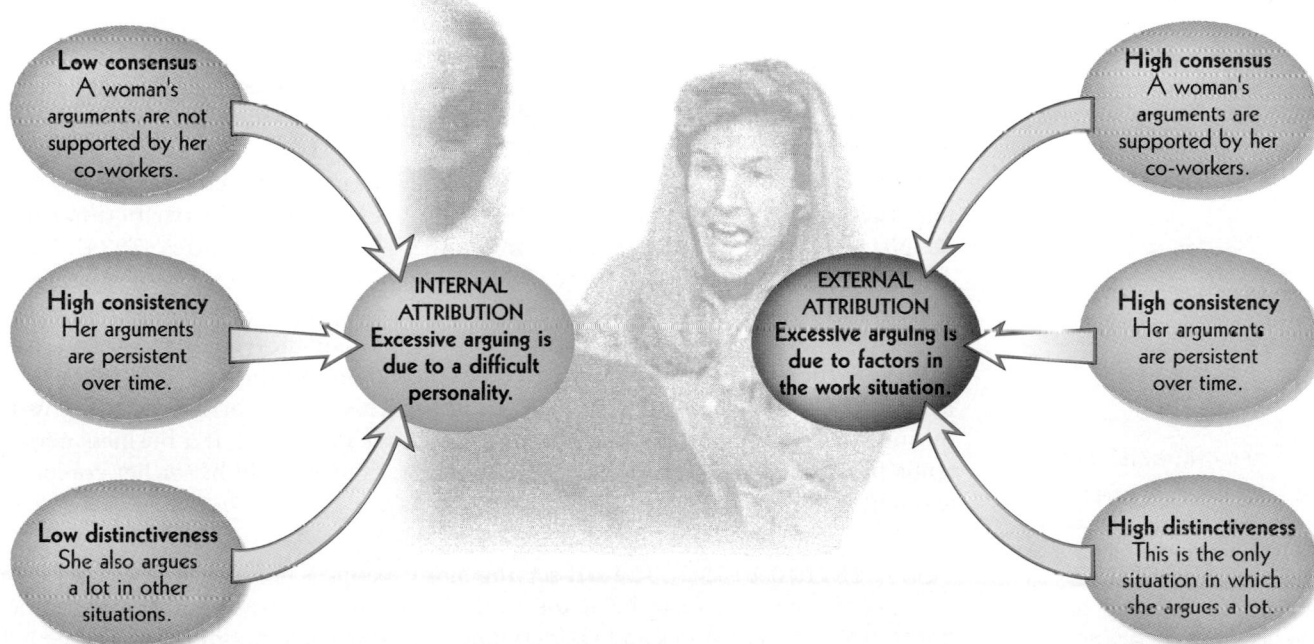

Why do people make attributions? What motivates a person to want to know the causes of other people's behaviour? The accepted explanation is that individuals engage in the process of attribution to maintain a sense of control over their environment. It helps people feel competent and masterful, because they think that knowledge about the causes of behaviour will help them control and predict similar events in the future. People also make attributions to make sense of their world quickly. If a person's behaviour fits in with a pattern already observed, why analyze it in depth? People are quick to make causal attributions if the behaviour being observed is not unusual.

**ERRORS IN ATTRIBUTION.** Residents of Garrison Keillor's Lake Wobegon, Minnesota, are strong women, good-looking men, and children who are all above average. Like Keillor's fictional characters, most of us tend to see ourselves in flattering ways—we often have unrealistically positive views of our abilities and perceptions of our control of the world. Wobegoners, like the rest of us, tend to see themselves and the rest of their peer group as above average (Klar & Giladi, 1997). These perceptions are often self-enhancing and even egocentric (Farwell & Wohlwend-Lloyd, 1998). Social psychologists have found that people are often especially error-prone or biased in their attributions concerning the behaviours of others. Sometimes they make errors because they use mental shortcuts that are not accurate. Two common types of errors that have been identified are the fundamental attribution error and the actor–observer effect.

## FUNDAMENTAL ATTRIBUTION ERROR

The tendency to attribute other people's behaviour to dispositional (internal) causes rather than situational (external) causes.

When people commit the **fundamental attribution error**, they assume that other people's behaviour is caused by internal dispositions and underestimate situational influences. For example, we observe a man who loses his temper in a restaurant and we assume that he is hot-tempered; however, the truth is that he was kept waiting for his table, treated rudely by the staff, served the wrong entree, and then overcharged for his meal. We observe the behaviour of others and tend to discount or not pay attention to the circumstances (Sabini, Siepmann, & Stein, 2001).

## ACTOR–OBSERVER EFFECT

The tendency to attribute the behaviour of others to dispositional causes but to attribute one's own behaviour to situational causes.

The **actor–observer effect** is the tendency to attribute the behaviour (especially failings) of others to dispositional causes but to attribute one's own behaviour to situational causes. An individual knows himself or herself in many situations and observes much variety in day-to-day behaviour; outside observers, on the other hand, have less information to go on and are more likely to make dispositional attributions. If you fail an exam, you may blame it on your roommate, whose radio prevented you from concentrating on your studies. When someone else fails an exam, you may wonder about that person's ability.

Errors in attribution are often judgments made in a limited context with limited knowledge and they tend to focus solely on the person or the situation. However, attributions must also consider whether a behaviour is intentional or unintentional to be thorough (Malle et al., 2000). Often they do not help people cope any better—they simply assign blame (Weisberg et al., 2001). Errors in attribution cause people to blame rape victims, for example (Bell, Kuriloff, & Lottes, 1994). Some errors in attribution come from the fact that people generally perceive themselves as having more positive traits than others and as being more flexible in their ability to adapt (Sande, Goethals, & Radloff, 1988). This tendency has been seen cross-culturally (but often does not exist to the same extent in other cultures (Bersoff & Miller, 1993; Matsumoto, 1994; Takaku, 2000). This has important implications in business relationships, where goodwill and trust are important; if a business person tends to see others as less (or more) flexible than the people in his or her company, this may alter a negotiation in a fundamental way.

## SELF-SERVING BIAS

People's tendency to evaluate their own positive behaviours as being due to their own internal traits and characteristics, but to blame their failures and shortcomings on external, situational factors.

**SELF-SERVING BIAS.** The **self-serving bias** is people's tendency to evaluate their own positive behaviours as being due to their own internal traits and characteristics but to blame their failures and shortcomings on external, situational factors. People may develop a self-serving bias because it helps meet their need for self-esteem. This bias can be seen as an adaptive response that helps people deal with their limitations and gives them the courage to venture into areas they normally might not explore. People also make such attributions about themselves to help maintain a sense of balance by resolving inconsistencies between old and new information about themselves (Higgins & Snyder, 1990). Often, a person who makes an excuse about some negative personal behaviour has shifted the cause of the behaviour to a less central element of personality or to situational factors. This behaviour results in enhanced image building and a sense of control. Furthermore, a self-serving bias allows people to present themselves to others in a positive light (Celuch & Slama, 1995). The self-serving bias is more common in men than in women and in Western than in non-Western cultures (Higgins & Bhatt, 2000).

Errors in attribution contribute to the self-serving bias. People tend to take credit for their successes but to blame others for their failures; that is, people assume that good things happen to them because they deserve it and that bad things happen to them because they have had bad luck. The combination of attribution errors and self-serving bias helps some people maintain self-esteem and appear competent. Such an attitude, however, may inhibit people from having realistic goals, thus setting them up for disappointment.

The impact of errors in attribution and the self-serving bias can be seen in society at large. For example, Claude Steele has asserted that whenever members of minority groups concentrate on scholastic tasks, they worry too much about the risk of confirming their group's negative stereotype (Steele, 1997; Osborne, 1997; Aronson, Quinn, & Spencer, 1998). This burden may drag down their performance through what Steele calls *stereotype threat*. Stereotype threat probably occurs in part because a situational, academic pressure threatens global self-esteem; people fear being reduced to a stereotype (for example, a dithery old lady) and then stop trying and ultimately do worse because of the fear (van Laar, 2001). This behaviour—no longer trying—is referred to as *disidentification*; it suggests that there was once a relationship between academic success and self-esteem, but it no longer exists. Unless minorities (for example, older adults and First Nations people) are resilient to such threats, their performance is likely to suffer (Steele, 1997). People constantly assess the reasons for other people's behaviour in order to make judgments about them. Most people also regularly reflect on their own behaviour and in doing so form self-perceptions. Of course, not everyone forms attributions in the same way, and some people, especially in some cultures, are more likely to be sensitive to situational causes of behaviour. For example, people in East Asian cultures are less likely to attach traits to an individual and thus consider situational variables more than people in Western cultures do (Choi, Nisbett, & Norenzayan, 1999; Hinton, 2000). Recent research by Greenwald shows that people's views of others and themselves are modifiable. If you change the social context, change the associations, and present to individuals examples of people or situations that are admired or valued and tie those to neutral or even negatively viewed people or events, the new associations tend to take hold (Dasgupta & Greenwald, 2001; Greenwald et al., 2002). Greenwald concludes that people's near-automatic attitudes can be modified and can help buffer them from the negative effects of disappointment or failure (Greenwald & Farnham, 2000). This becomes important in studying prejudice, our next topic.

## PREJUDICE: THE DARKER SIDE OF ATTITUDES

People's ideas, about themselves and others, help define who they are, how they view the world, and ultimately how they behave. But what happens when the ideas, values, or activities of another person or another group of people are different from yours? What happens when you do not know the other group of people well, or at all? Why do some people form negative evaluations of certain groups, such as Aboriginal

**Social Psychology I**

# INTRODUCTION TO Research Basics

## Self-Perceptions Depend on Your Cultural Context

Psychologists know that men and women perceive themselves differently. How do self-perceptions vary among different groups of people in Canada?

In studies conducted in Western cultures, it is routinely found that people adopt a self-serving bias, rating their own actions more positively than the actions of others, even though others would rate the behaviours as indistinguishable. Interestingly, this self-serving bias is not found among Asian samples. It is argued that this difference is due to a Western orientation toward individualism and an Asian orientation toward collectivism (where the individual is regarded as part of a group). Steven Heine and Darrin Lehman at the University of British Columbia (Heine et al., 2001) examined whether this cultural difference was evident in how participants reacted to failure.

**Design.** Heine and Leman ran a comparative study looking at how Japanese as opposed to Western students responded when given a second chance on a task after receiving negative feedback about their first performance on that task.

**Hypothesis.** The researchers hypothesized that when Western participants thought they had done poorly on the first task they would be motivated by self-enhancement to downplay the importance of the task and would therefore make less effort on their second attempt at the task, whereas Japanese participants would be motivated to improve themselves and would thus try harder on the second attempt at the task.

**Participants.** Sixty-two Canadian participants were introductory psychology students at the University of British Columbia. Seventy-seven Japanese participants were introductory psychology students at Kyoto University.

**Procedure.** Participants were told that the purpose of the study was to assess the relationship between creativity and emotional intelligence. This was not true. The actual purpose of the experiment was to assess response to a second task following a perceived initial poor first attempt. Therefore, this study involved **deception**, as this was the only way to consistently be sure that participants received initial negative feedback.

The study began with the participants completing a version of a creativity test, the Remote Associates Test (RAT). Participants were shown three words and were asked to generate the one word that related to the other three (e.g., *sleep*, *fantasy*, and *day* all relate to the word *dream*). Upon completion, participants were asked to score their own performance on this measure. Once they had scored their performance they were asked to place their results in an envelope so that the experimenter would not see it. This was done to ensure that the participants believed their test results to be private (this in turn allowed their reaction to be entirely

up to them). In fact, the difficulty of the test and the norms they compared their scores to were fixed in advance so that regardless of their actual performance students appeared to do very poorly on the test.

Participants were then asked to move to a computer to complete the last "test." The computer then "froze" (by plan) and the research assistant explained that he or she would have to get help. Before leaving, however, the research assistant gave each participant another copy of the first test (this time a fair one) and said that if they wanted to they could complete a second test while they waited. Upon returning, the research assistant explained the true nature of the study.

**Results.** Canadian participants tended to discount the initial negative feedback and made few changes in their strategies on the subsequent task, whereas Japanese participants more readily accepted the negative feedback as relevant to their performance and tried harder the second time they got to try the task.

**Conclusions.** The results of this study likely reflect different cultural approaches to self-concept. The Canadian participants' independent approach to self-conceptualization appeared to cause a need to justify or rationalize their failures, whereas the Japanese participants appeared to be more open to criticism and used this criticism to identify areas where self-improvement was needed. Overall, the researchers argued that people from the two cultures share similar goals in wanting to do their best. Beyond this, however, they suggest that these two groups use different strategies to attain their goals of excellence. From this study it appears that Japanese participants are motivated by self-criticism, working harder when focusing on their shortcomings, whereas North Americans are motivated by self-enhancement, working harder when focusing on their strengths (Heine et al., 2001).

people, Asians, Jews, or lesbians and gay men? In this section, we will explore the darker side of attitudes and attributions about others—prejudice—and how it can be prevented.

**Prejudice** is a negative evaluation of an entire group of people that is typically based on unfavourable (and often wrong) ideas or stereotypes about the group (Nelson, 2002). It is usually based on a small sample of experience with an individual from the group being evaluated, or even on no experience. **Stereotypes** are fixed, overly simple, often incorrect, and often negative ideas about traits, attitudes, and behaviours attributed to groups of people; stereotypes assume that all members of a given group are alike. Among others, people hold stereotyped ideas about First Nations people, stepmothers, dentists, and people from Alberta; the stereotypes, often shared by many people, can lead to prejudice. Worldwide prejudice includes the Taliban's suppression of women, "ethnic cleansing" in Bosnia, the Hutus versus the Tutsis in Burundi, white North Americans versus Aboriginal peoples, and the list goes on and on.

▲ Children are less often the focus of racial bias.

Prejudice, as an attitude, is composed of a cognitive belief (all Xs are stupid), an emotional element (I hate those Xs), and often a behaviour (I am doing everything I can to keep those Xs out of my neighbourhood). Mark Zanna (1994) of the University of Waterloo asserts that stereotypes, symbolic beliefs, emotions, and past experiences with the group are *all* essential components of prejudice. When prejudice is translated into behaviour, it is called **discrimination**—behaviour targeted at individuals or groups with the aim of holding them apart and treating them differently. Stereotyping promotes prejudice and prejudice promotes discrimination. You can think of discrimination as prejudice in action. Table 13.1 shows all of the possible interactions between prejudice and discrimination. One common type of discrimination is *sexism* (prejudice based on gender), which involves accepting the strong and widely held beliefs of rigid gender-role stereotyping (examined in Chapter 11). Overt discrimination based on gender is illegal but still exists, and many people's expectations for women are still based on old stereotypes about gender (Eagly & Steffen, 2000; Goodwin & Fiske, 2001). Fiske asserts that gender—with all that goes with one's views of gender—dominates the perception of another person (Zemore, Fiske, & Hyun-Jeong, 2000).

DECEPTION

Misleading research participants as to the nature or purpose of an experiment or condition in order to study a particular response. Is strictly limited for ethical reasons.

PREJUDICE

Negative evaluation of an entire group of people, typically based on unfavourable (often incorrect) ideas or stereotypes about the group.

STEREOTYPES

Fixed, overly simple, often incorrect, and often negative ideas about traits, attitudes, and behaviours attributed to groups of people.

DISCRIMINATION

Behaviour targeted at individuals or groups with the aim of holding them apart and treating them differently.

---

**TABLE 13.1** **Prejudice and Discrimination**

Prejudice and discrimination interact in such a way that one can be evident without the other.

|  | Presence of Prejudice | Absence of Prejudice |
|---|---|---|
| **Presence of Discrimination** | An employer believes that non-whites cannot do quality work and does not promote them, regardless of their performance. | An employer believes that all people can do quality work but does not promote minorities because of long-held company policies. |
| **Absence of Discrimination** | An employer believes that non-whites cannot do quality work but promotes them on the basis of their performance rather than following preconceived ideas. | An employer believes that all people can do quality work and promotes people on the basis of their performance on the job. |

Sometimes people are prejudiced but do not show that attitude in their behaviour; that is, they do not discriminate. Merton (1949) referred to such individuals as *cautious bigots* (unlike true bigots, who *do* discriminate). People sometimes show *reverse discrimination*, bending over backward to treat an individual more positively than they should, solely to counter their own pre-existing biases or stereotypes (Chidester, 1986). That is, someone prejudiced toward First Nations people may be overly solicitous toward a First Nations person and may evaluate the person favourably on the basis of standards different from those used for others. This, too, is discrimination. In the end, people who hold stereotypes and discriminate are at risk for maladaptive behaviours that are often at odds with society (Wheeler, Jarvis, & Petty, 2001).

A related behaviour is *tokenism*, in which prejudiced people engage in superficially positive and trivial actions toward members of a group they dislike. A male executive may make a token gesture toward the women on his staff, or a manager may hire a token Asian. By engaging in tokenism, a person often attempts to put off more important actions, such as changing overall hiring practices. In this person's mind, the trivial behaviour justifies the idea that he or she has done something for the disliked group. Tokenism has negative consequences for the self-esteem of the person to whom it is applied, and it perpetuates discrimination by suggesting that only one member of the disliked group was good enough to be given a job. In the end, social psychologists generally conclude that stereotyping promotes prejudice, and that prejudice promotes discrimination.

**WHAT CAUSES PREJUDICE?**   The causes of prejudice cannot be summarized with a simple explanation. Like so many other human behaviours, prejudice is a cross-cultural phenomenon (Pettigrew et al., 1998); it has multiple causes and can be examined within an individual, between individuals, within a group, or within society (Duckitt, 1992). We will consider four theories to explain prejudice: social learning theory, motivational theory, cognitive theory, and personality theory.

According to *social learning theory*, children *learn* to be prejudiced; they watch parents, other relatives, teachers, peers, and neighbours engage in acts of discrimination, which often include stereotyped judgments and racial slurs; they then incorporate those ideas into their own behavioural repertoire. After children have observed such behaviours, they are then reinforced (operant conditioning) for exhibiting similar behaviours. Thus, through imitation and reinforcement, a prejudiced view is transmitted from one generation to the next.

We saw in Chapter 9 that people are motivated to succeed, to get ahead, and to provide for basic as well as high-level emotional needs. If people are raised to compete against others for scarce resources, this competition can foster negative views of competitors. Lynne Jackson and Victoria Esses (2000) at Ryerson Polytechnic University have shown that Canadians' desire to empower new immigrants is lessened by a desire to maintain an economic discrepancy between themselves and the immigrants. Kenneth Dion (2001) of the University of Toronto found similar patterns when he examined the experiences of immigrants looking for housing through the Housing New Canadian project.

*Motivational theory* asserts that individuals learn to dislike specific individuals (competitors) and then generalize that dislike to whole classes of similar individuals (races, religions, or cultures). Gordon Allport asserted that the arousal of competition followed by erroneous generalizations creates specific prejudice toward minority groups (Allport, 1979; Gaines & Reed, 1995). This helps make minorities that are seen as economic competitors into scapegoats—for example, Jews in Nazi Germany and Japanese Canadians during the Second World War. Research conducted with children, adolescents, and adults shows that people who are initially seen as friends or as neutral others are sometimes treated badly when turned into competitors.

*Cognitive theorists* assert that people think about individuals and their groups of origin as a way of organizing the world. Cialdini (1993) argues that there are so many events, circumstances, and changing variables in their lives that people cannot analyze all of the relevant data about any one thing easily. People thus devise mental shortcuts to help them make decisions. One of those shortcuts is to stereotype individuals and the groups they belong to—for example, all French Canadians, all homeless people, all men, all lawyers. Research shows that people use such shortcuts to socially categorize individuals on traits such as athleticism, intelligence, gender, and ethnicity, and that they develop illusory correlations about social groups and their behaviours (Schaller, 1991; Spears & Haslam, 1997; Stone, Perry, & Darley, 1997). An *illusory correlation* is an unsubstantiated and incorrect correlation between two events or situations that appear, by inference, to be related. By devising such shortcuts in thinking, people develop ideas about who is in an *in group*—that is, who is a member of a group to which those people belong or want to belong. The division of the world into groups labelled "in" versus "out" or "us" versus "them" is known as **social categorization**. Not only do people divide the world into in groups and out groups, but they tend to see themselves and other members of an in group in a favourable light; doing so bolsters their self-esteem and occurs almost automatically (Fiske, 1998).

As we saw earlier in this chapter, when judging other people, individuals make fundamental attribution errors. They assume that other people's behaviour is caused by internal dispositions—which may not be true—and that other people are all alike, at least most of the time (Lambert, 1995). They underestimate situational influences and overestimate dispositional influences on other people's behaviour, and then they use those behaviours as evidence for their attitudes (prejudices). Thus, hostilities between Arabs and Israelis in the Middle East, Catholics and Protestants in Ireland, and blacks and whites in South Africa are perpetuated.

Researchers such as Susan Fiske (1998) assert that when people develop stereotypes about groups—who's in and who's out—the stereotype and the prejudice that follows is a more complex affair than previously thought. For example, there are groups that some people like but do not respect, or vice versa. In some circles, the traditional housewife is liked but not respected; similarly, militant feminists may be respected but not liked. This duality of liking/respecting may translate into complex social behaviours such as sexism and racism in which individual members of a given group are treated benevolently while the group as a whole is treated with hostility (Glick & Fiske, 1997; Glick et al., 1997; Monteith, Zuwerink, & Devine, 1994).

*Personality psychologists* and evolutionary approaches have their supporters as well. Fiske (2000) argues that we must pay attention not only to cultural factors but also to potential evolutionary ones that assert that a person who develops a prejudice has a "prejudice-prone personality." In fact, some personality tests examine the extent to which people are likely to be prejudiced. For example, one common personality type is the *authoritarian personality*. Authoritarian people may have been fearful and anxious as children and may have been raised by cold parents who withheld love and regularly used physical punishment. Bob Altemeyer (1996, 1999) of the University of Manitoba has studied authoritarianism extensively and has shown that, in addition to having its roots in experiences of fear and aggression, it is related to early experiences with parents and religious activities that promote a strong reverence for authority. To gain control and mastery as adults, such individuals become aggressive and controlling over others. They see the world in absolutes—good versus bad, black versus white. They also tend to blame others for their problems and to become prejudiced toward those people (Adorno et al., 1950). The relationship between personality and prejudice has its roots in psychoanalytic theory and is hotly debated.

**HOW TO REDUCE AND ELIMINATE PREJUDICE.** To reduce and eliminate prejudice, people can teach rational thinking, try to judge others based on their

**Be an**

**ACTIVE LEARNER**

**REVIEW**

> Identify key characteristics of nonverbal communication. pp. 461–462
> Describe the fundamental difference between internal and external attribution in interpreting the causes of behaviour. pp. 462–463
> Describe the actor–observer effect. p. 464
> How do psychological theories explain the development of prejudice? pp. 468–469
> How do you describe social categorization? p. 469

**THINK CRITICALLY**

> Can you describe any useful functions that errors in attribution have served for you or a friend in the last few months? Have such errors helped someone feel more intelligent, more worthwhile, or less at fault?
> Negative behaviours, especially in a small group, are high in distinctiveness. What does this suggest will happen when the negative behaviours occur in a minority ethnic group?

**APPLY PSYCHOLOGY**

> In Canada, prejudice has been instrumental in the poor treatment of First Nations people, women, the aged, gays and lesbians, and many minority groups. What are some effective techniques (not necessarily governmental policies) that can be used to help eliminate prejudice, correct previous injustices, and make for a more tolerant society?
> Devise a program that could be run in a club, house of worship, or social group that could help break down the idea of "us" versus "them."

**HandsOnPsych**
Version 2.0

**Social Psychology II**

**SOCIAL INFLUENCE**

The ways in which people alter the attitudes or behaviour of others, either directly or indirectly.

**CONFORMITY**

People's tendency to change attitudes or behaviours to be consistent with other people or with social norms.

behaviour, promote equality, and avoid labels that perpetuate stereotypes (Jussim et al., 1995). Research shows that once people have worked on a community project with a member of a different culture, lived with a member of a different culture, lived with a person of a different race, or prayed with members of a different religious faith, their emotional views of them as individuals change (Pettigrew, 1997). While some individuals use race or ethnicity as a categorizing variable, it turns out that as little as a few minutes exposed to an individual who is grouped by some other category—such as religion, political party, or on which side of a social issue a person aligns—can change an individual's use of social categorization and ultimately their definition of "us" and "them" (Kurzban, Tooby, & Cosmides, 2001).

A society can pass laws that mandate equal treatment for all people—for example, those that forbid discrimination in the workplace or in the housing market. Such laws generally reflect changing beliefs (Bobo & Kluegel, 1997). Voters can elect officials on the basis of their competence, throw them out of office on the basis of their incompetence, and make gender-neutral judgments of performance. Governor general Adrienne Clarkson is judged by her performance, not by her gender. Svend Robinson, widely perceived as a highly principled politician due to his integrity and character, has the ability to transform people's views of the role of homosexuals in our society (Sigelman, 1997).

## Social Interactions: The Power of People and Situations

How you initiate a conversation with someone you haven't met before is a task all of us have had to deal with. When people interact with one another, complex new realms of possibility open up. Day-to-day social interactions can be exceedingly complex and are affected by many variables.

### SOCIAL INFLUENCE

Parents try to instill specific values in their children. An adolescent may admire the hairstyle or mannerisms of an attractive peer and decide to adopt them. Adoring fans emulate the behaviour or appearance of a rock star or top athlete. Religious leaders exhort their followers to live in certain ways. Social interactions affect individual behaviour in profound ways; when people are members of a group, their social interactions are often even more striking than their individual behaviour.

**Social influence** refers to the ways in which people alter the attitudes or behaviour of others, either directly or indirectly. Studies of social influence have focused on two topics: conformity and obedience.

CONFORMITY.  When someone changes attitudes or behaviours to be consistent with other people or with social norms, the person is exhibiting **conformity**; he or she is trying to fit in. The behaviours the person may adopt include positive, prosocial behaviours such as wearing seatbelts, volunteering time and money for a charity, or buying only products that are safe for the environment. Sometimes, however, people conform to counterproductive, anti-social behaviours, such as drug abuse or mob violence.

People conform to the behaviours and attitudes of their peer or family groups. A successful young executive may wear conservative dark suits and drive a BMW to fit in with office colleagues. Similarly, the desire to conform can induce people to do

things they might not do otherwise. An infamous example is the My Lai massacre, in which American soldiers slaughtered Vietnamese civilians during the Vietnam War. While several factors account for the soldiers' behaviour (including combat stress, hostility toward the Vietnamese, and obedience to authority), the soldiers also yielded to extreme group pressure. The few soldiers who refused to kill the civilians hid that fact from their comrades. One soldier even shot himself in the foot to avoid taking part in the slaughter.

Groups strongly influence conformity. Solomon Asch (1907–1996) found that people in a group adopt the values and standards set by the group. Examples of conformity to group standards range from an individual refraining from speaking during a public address to a whole nation discriminating against a particular religious or ethnic group. Studies also show that individuals conform to group norms even when they are not pressured to do so. Consider what happens when an instructor asks a class of 250 students to answer a relatively simple question, but no one volunteers. When asked, most students will report that they did not raise their hand because no one else did. Asch (1955, p. 6) stated:

> The tendency to conformity in our society [is] so strong that reasonably intelligent and well-meaning young people [being] willing to call white black is a matter of concern. It raises questions about our ways of education and about the values that guide our conduct.

Imagine this situation: You have agreed to participate in an experiment. You are seated at the end of a table next to four other students. The experimenter holds up a card and asks each of you to pick which of two lines is longer, A or B. You quickly discover that the task is simple. The experimenter holds up successive pairs of lines and each participant correctly identifies the longest. But, after several rounds, you notice that the first person has chosen line A instead of line B, though B is obviously longer. You are surprised when the second person also chooses line A, then the third, then the fourth. Your turn is next. You are sure that line B is longer but the four people before you have all chosen line A. What do you do?

In 1951, Asch performed a similar experiment to explore conformity. Seven to nine individuals were brought into a room and asked to judge which of three lines matched a standard (see Figure 13.6). However, only *one* group member—the naive participant—was unaware of the purpose of the study. The others were collaborators of the researcher, and they deliberately gave false answers to try to influence the naive participant. Each naive participant took part in several conformity trials. Asch found that approximately two-thirds of naive participants went along with the group at least once, even though the majority answer was obviously wrong and even though the group exerted no explicit, or directly observable, pressure on that person.

**FIGURE 13.6**

**Asch's Classic Study of Conformity**

Participants were shown cards like these and asked to choose the line on the lower card that was the same length as the line on the upper card. The confederates deliberately chose incorrect answers to see if the unsuspecting participant would go along with the majority.

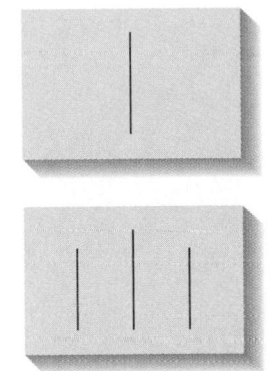

It turns out that the relative number of individuals purposely giving wrong answers is a critical variable. When 1 or 2 individuals pick the wrong line, the tendency to conform is considerably less than when 10 do. Another important variable is whether there are any dissenting votes. If even 1 of 15 people disagrees with the other participants, the naive participant is more likely to choose the correct line.

How do groups influence individual behaviour? One conformity variable is the *amount of information* provided when a decision is to be made. When people are uncertain of how to behave in ambiguous situations, they seek the opinions of others. For example, people who are unsure of which of several utensils to use at a formal dinner often will look to see which fork other people are using. People tend to conform to those they like and those who are similar to them.

Another important variable that affects the degree of conformity is the *relative competence* of the group. People are more likely to conform to the decision of a group if they perceive its members as being more competent than they themselves are. This pressure becomes stronger as group size increases. A first-year student in a large class of first-, second-, and third-year students may not answer even a simple question if no one else speaks up because he or she assumes that his or her classmates are more competent.

*Position within a group* also affects individual behaviour. A person who confidently believes that a group holds them in high esteem will respond independently. If they are insecure about their status they may respond as the group does because they fear losing status.

The *public nature of behaviour* also determines people's responses. Individuals are more willing to make decisions that are inconsistent with those of their group when the behaviour is private. In a democracy, for example, voting is done privately so as to minimize group pressure on how individuals vote.

Why do people tend to conform? Several theories have attempted to explain this phenomenon. The *social conformity approach* states that people conform to avoid the stigma of being wrong, deviant, out of line, or different from others. According to this view, people want to do the right thing, and people define as right whatever is generally accepted (Festinger, 1954). Another explanation for why individuals in a group conform—or don't conform—is *attribution*. When a person can identify reasons for other people's behaviour and strongly disagrees with those reasons, conformity disappears (Ross, Bierbrauer, & Hoffman, 1976). The issue of *independence* also helps explain conformity (or lack of it). Although most people would like to be independent, independence is risky. People in a group may have to face the consequences of their independence, such as serious disapproval, peer pressure to conform, being seen as deviant, becoming less powerful, or simply being left out. Finally, conformity is partly a matter of *expediency*; conforming conserves mental energy. Recall Cialdini's (1993) argument that people face too many events, circumstances, and changing variables to be able to analyze all the relevant data. People therefore need shortcuts to help them make decisions. It is efficient and easy for people to go along with others whom they trust and respect, especially if key elements of a situation fit in with their views.

It is important to recognize that not everyone conforms to group pressures all the time. Both everyday experience and research show that *dissenting opinions* help counteract group influence and conformity. Even one or two people in a large group can seriously influence decision making. Moreover, when group decision making occurs, a consistent opposing voice (think of South African leader Nelson Mandela, or French President Jacques Chirac in opposition to the War on Iraq) can exert substantial influence and foster a sense of liberation, even when the opposition is devoid of power or status (Kitayama & Burnstein, 1994). Not surprisingly, analysis of cross-cultural studies shows that countries with collectivist cultures exhibit more conformity than do countries with individualistic cultures (Cialdini et al., 2001).

**OBEDIENCE AND MILGRAM'S STUDY.** **Obedience** is compliance with the orders of another person or a group of people. The studies on obedience by Stanley Milgram (1933–1984) are classic, and his results and interpretations still generate debate. Milgram's work focused on the extent to which an individual will obey a person in authority. His studies showed that ordinary people were remarkably willing to comply with those they saw as legitimate authority figures.

Imagine that you are one of the participants in Milgram's 1963 study at Yale University. You and a man you do not know are brought into a laboratory and are told that you will be participating in an experiment on the effects of punishment on paired-associate learning. You draw lots to determine who will be the teacher and who will be the learner. The drawing is actually rigged so that you will be the teacher and the man (who is collaborating with the experimenter) will be the learner.

The learner/collaborator is taken to an adjoining room, where you cannot see him. You are shown a shock-generating box containing 30 switches, with labels that range from "15 Volts: Slight Shock" to "420 Volts: Danger: Severe Shock" to "450 Volts: XXX." You are told that the learner will be given a test, and that you will listen to his answers and punish him when he is incorrect. Your job is to shock the learner by flipping one of the switches every time he makes an error on the test.

As the test continues, the experimenter and an assistant, both wearing white lab coats, encourage you to increase the shock voltage by one level each time the learner makes a mistake. As the shock level rises, the learner/collaborator screams as if he is suffering increasing pain. When the intensity reaches the point of intense shock (255 to 300 volts), the learner stops responding vocally to the test stimulus and pounds on the walls of the booth. The experimenter tells you to treat the learner's lack of vocal response as an error and to continue increasing the levels of shock. What would you do?

This was the basic scenario of the Milgram study. As you may have guessed by now, the learner/collaborators were not actually receiving shocks; they were only pretending to be in pain, but the participants believed that they were delivering actual shocks. As Figure 13.7 shows, 65 percent of the participants continued to shock the learner until they had delivered shocks at all levels. However, not all of Milgram's participants were obedient. Moreover, in a follow-up study, the presence of another "teacher" who refused to participate reduced the probability of obedience to as little as 10 percent (Milgram, 1965; Powers & Geen, 1972). These data suggest that obedience is sensitive to both authority and peer behaviour. The fact that an individual's ability to resist coercion improves in the presence of an ally who also resists indicates the importance of other social influences on behaviour.

Did conducting the study at the prestigious Yale University influence the participants? Milgram (1965) suggested that his experiment might have involved a particular type of experimental bias—*background authority*. To investigate the issue, Milgram conducted a second study in an office building in Bridgeport, Connecticut. Participants were contacted by mail and had no knowledge that Milgram or his associates were from Yale. In this second study, 48 percent of the participants, as compared with 65 percent at Yale, delivered the maximum level of shock. Although this was not a big difference, Milgram inferred that the perceived function of an institution could induce obedience in participants. Moreover, an institution's qualitative position within a category (for example, a prestigious versus a little-known university) may be less important than the type of institution it is (for example, a university rather than an office building; Rochat, Maggioni, & Modigliani, 1999).

OBEDIENCE

Compliance with the orders of another person or a group of people.

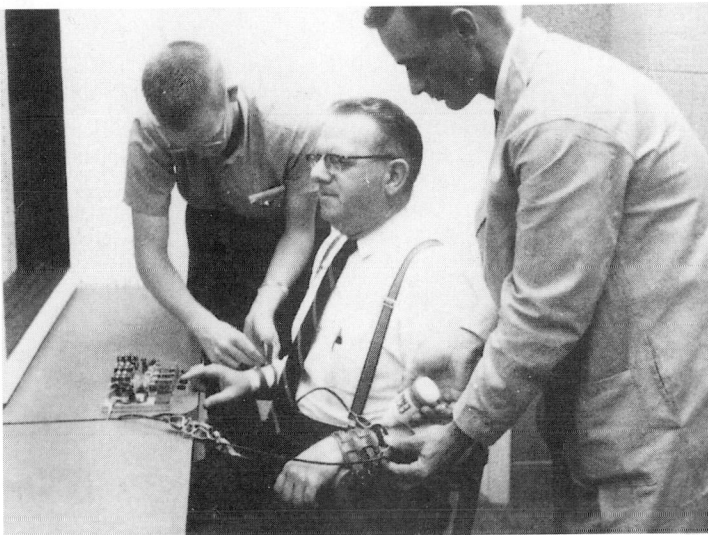

▲ Milgram's work focused on the extent to which an individual will obey. His studies showed that ordinary people were remarkably willing to comply with the wishes of others, especially if they saw the others as legitimate authority figures.

FIGURE 13.7
Milgram's Obedience Study
(Based on data from Milgram, 1963.)

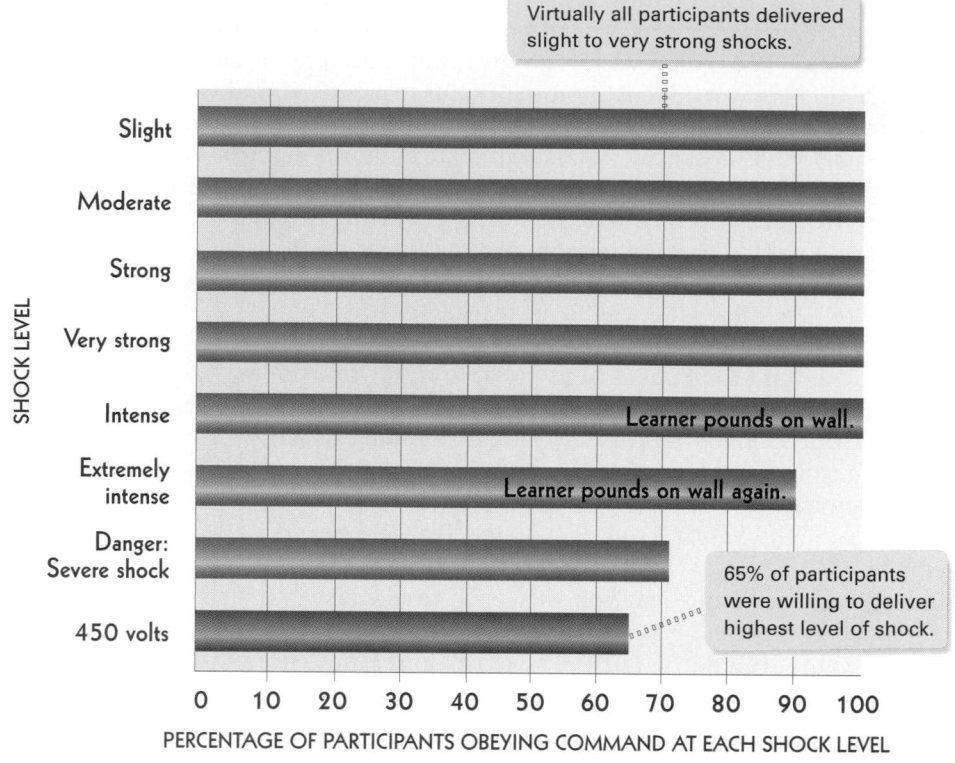

EXPLAINING MILGRAM'S RESULTS.   Why did so many participants in Milgram's experiments obey the wishes of the authority figure? One reason is that they were volunteers. Volunteers often bring undetected biases to an experimental situation, and one such bias is a willingness to go along with authority. When instructed to shock, Milgram's participants did what they were told (Blass, 2000). Another explanation derives from learning theories. Children learn that authority figures, such as teachers and parents, know more than they do and that taking their advice generally proves beneficial. As adults, they maintain those beliefs and apply them to authority figures such as employers, judges, government leaders, and so on. Cialdini (1993) also notes that obedience has practical advantages, such as helping people make decisions quickly: "It is easy to allow ourselves the convenience of automatic obedience. . . . We don't have to think, therefore we don't" (p. 178).

Researchers repeated Milgram's methods, and the results of one study suggest that obedience to authority is not specific to Western cultures (Shanab & Yahya, 1978). People tend to obey those in authority, and such obedience is even more highly valued in many non-Western cultures. Students at the University of Jordan participated in a similar study; as in the original Milgram study, about 65 percent were willing to give high levels of shock to other students. Milgram's findings apply to men and women, old and young; they show that the social world and people's interactions within it are strongly affected by others.

In any study of social influence, researchers worry about ethics, and Milgram's experimental methods certainly raised ethical issues. The primary issue was one of deception and potential harm to those who participated. Obtaining unbiased responses in psychological research often requires deceiving naive participants. To ensure that participants do not have any lasting ill effects, researchers debrief them after the experiment. **Debriefing** is informing participants about the true nature of the experiment after its completion, including an explanation of hypotheses, methods, and expected or potential results. Researchers debrief participants *after* the experiment to preserve the validity of the responses while taking ethical considerations into

DEBRIEFING

Informing participants about the true nature of an experiment after its completion.

account. Of course, debriefing must be done clearly and with sensitivity, especially in studies such as Milgram's, which could affect a participant's self-concept and self-esteem.

Milgram's participants were fully debriefed and shown that they had not harmed the other person. Nevertheless, critics argued, the participants came to realize that they were capable of inflicting severe pain on other people. Milgram therefore had a psychiatrist interview a sample of his obedient participants a year after the study. He claimed that no evidence of psychological trauma or injury was found. Moreover, one study reported that participants viewed participation in the obedience experiment as a positive experience. They did not regret having participated; nor did they report any short-term negative psychological effects (Ring, Wallston, & Corey, 1970). Nevertheless, today, due to ethical constraints that are now in place, Milgram's research and its variations would not be allowed in research laboratories.

Studies of social influence, especially conformity and obedience studies, show us that people exert powerful influences on individuals and that those influences are even greater when a group exerts them (Blass, 1999, 2000). Let's look at the effects of groups on individual behaviour and how individuals behave within groups.

## GROUPS: SHARING COMMON GOALS

In appealing to people's desire to be part of a group, credit card companies employ psychological principles to sell their products and engender loyalty. For example, to make the Visa cardholders' group as attractive as possible, the company has run magazine ads featuring all of the places cardholders can go that only accept Visa. Who wouldn't want to be a part of such a special elite group?

Membership does confer certain advantages, which is why people belong to all kinds of groups. There are formal groups, such as the Canadian Psychological Association, and informal ones, such as a lunch group of co-workers. A **group** can be either a large number of people working toward a common purpose or a small number of people (even two) who are loosely connected by some common goals or interests. As already discussed, we tend to sort people into groups. An *ingroup* is a group that an individual belongs to or identifies with. An *outgroup* is a group that an individual neither belongs to nor identifies with. Not surprisingly, people favour those in their ingroup. By joining a group, people indicate that they agree with or have a serious interest in its purpose. If a major function of the Canadian Cancer Society is to raise money for cancer research, a person's membership indicates an interest in finding a cure for cancer. It generally has been thought that groups function well and enhance performance; research shows, however, that such effects of groups are modest and that the larger effect that emanates from a group is a sense of cohesion, solidarity, and commitment to a task (Mullen & Copper, 1994).

**SOCIAL FACILITATION.**   Individual behaviour is affected not only by membership in a group but also by the mere presence of a group. **Social facilitation** is a change in performance that occurs when people believe they are in the presence of other people. For example, an accomplished athlete practising his or her sport may do better when other people are watching. A person who is less accomplished, however, may do worse when other people are watching. Research studies that examine people's performance at various tasks—for example, keyboard data entry—show this effect (Aiello & Kolb, 1995).

How the presence of others changes a person's behaviour, and whether it changes the behaviour for better or worse, is illustrated in Figure 13.8. This figure is based on Robert Zajonc's (1965) *drive theory of social facilitation*. According to Zajonc, the presence of others produces heightened arousal, which leads to a greater likelihood that an individual will exhibit a particular response (Jackson & Latané, 1981; Zajonc, 1965).

**GROUP**

Two or more individuals who are loosely or cohesively related and who share some common characteristics and goals.

**SOCIAL FACILITATION**

A change in performance that occurs when people believe they are in the presence of other people.

FIGURE 13.8
## Social Facilitation

The presence of others may either help or hinder a person's performance. The presence of others heightens arousal, and heightened arousal leads to better performance on tasks a person is good at and worse performance on difficult tasks.

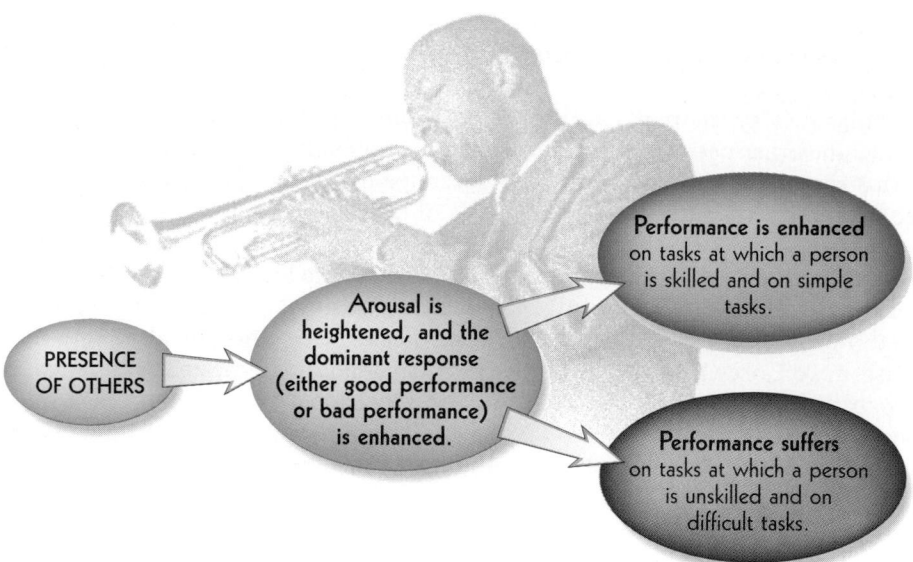

PRESENCE OF OTHERS

Arousal is heightened, and the dominant response (either good performance or bad performance) is enhanced.

Performance is enhanced on tasks at which a person is skilled and on simple tasks.

Performance suffers on tasks at which a person is unskilled and on difficult tasks.

However, the exact nature of this heightened arousal is a source of some debate. One theory of social facilitation suggests that fear of evaluation—not the mere presence of people—brings about changes in performance (see Innes & Young, 1975). If an auto mechanic knows that a customer is watching him repair an engine, he is likely to increase his work speed to convince the observer of his efficiency and professionalism. Bond and Titus (1983) suggest that the effects of social facilitation are often overestimated. They caution that a model of social facilitation must take into account the actual and believed presence of observers, as well as the perceived importance of the evaluation by the perceived observers. Thus, being evaluated by a friend has a different effect than being evaluated by a superior or even a stranger (Buck et al., 1992).

**SOCIAL LOAFING.**    A decrease in an individual's effort and productivity as a result of working in a group is known as **social loafing**. Suppose you and several fellow students are working on a group project for one of your classes. Would you expend as much effort as a member of the group as you would have expended if you had had to complete a project on your own? Research confirms the social loafing effect—you probably would not work as hard in the group. In an experiment in which individuals were instructed to clap their hands and cheer, they clapped and cheered less loudly when they were part of a group (Latané, Williams, & Harkins, 1979).

Most psychologists claim that social loafing occurs when individual performance within a group cannot be evaluated; that is, poor performance may go undetected, and exceptional performance may go unrecognized. Consequently, people feel less pressure to work hard or efficiently. One study showed that as group size increased, individual members believed their own efforts were more dispensable—the group could function without their help. "Let George do it" became the prevailing attitude (Kerr & Bruun, 1983). Such findings are evident cross-culturally; even Japanese students, who come from a society that stresses cohesion and group cooperation, worked less hard when they were working together than when working alone (Kugihara, 1999).

Social loafing is minimized when the task is attractive and rewarding and the group is cohesive and committed to high task performance (Karau & Williams, 2000). It is also less apparent when a group is small, when the members know one another well, and when a group leader calls on individuals by name or lets it be known that individual performance may be evaluated (Williams, Harkins, & Latané, 1981). Some researchers have noted decreased social loafing when individuals have

SOCIAL LOAFING

A decrease in productivity that occurs when an individual works in a group instead of alone.

the opportunity to assess their own performance relative to an objective standard or relative to other people's performance, even though no one else is evaluating them (Harkins & Szymanski, 1988; Szymanski & Harkins, 1993). As with so many other social phenomena, a wide array of variables can alter the extent of social loafing; yet researchers conclude that social loafing is a robust phenomenon that occurs across a wide variety of tasks and situations (North, Linley, & Hargreaves, 2000).

GROUP POLARIZATION.   People in groups may be willing to adopt behaviours slightly more extreme than their individual behavioural tendencies. They may be willing to make decisions that are risky or even daring. Some early research on group decision making focused on the willingness of individuals to accept more risky alternatives when other members of the group did so; this research described such individuals as making a *risky shift* in their decisions.

In a group, individuals initially perceive themselves as being more extreme than the other members of the group. They also believe that they are more fair, more right-minded, more liberal, and so on. When they discover that their positions are not very different from those of others in the group, they shift, or become *polarized*, to show that they are even more right-minded, fairer, or more liberal. They also may become more assertive in expressing their views. Shifts or exaggerations that take place among group members after group discussions are referred to as **group polarization** (Zuber, Crott, & Werner, 1992).

A *persuasive argument* explanation of the polarization phenomenon asserts that people tend to become more extreme after hearing views similar to their own. A person who is mildly liberal on an issue becomes even more liberal, more polarized. The explanation therefore suggests that people in a group often become more wedded to their initial views instead of becoming more moderate. If other people in the group hold similar views, that may polarize them even more. The effects of group polarization are particularly evident among juries. After group discussion, jury members are likely to return to their initial views and argue for them more strongly. Thus, individual jury members with an initially doubting view toward a witness will have even deeper doubts after group discussions.

Another explanation for group polarization is *diffusion of responsibility*—the feeling of individual members of a group that they cannot be held responsible for the group's actions. If a church youth group makes a decision to invest money, for example, no single individual is responsible. Diffusion of responsibility may allow the members to make far more extreme investment decisions as a group than they would individually.

*Social comparison* also may play a role in group polarization. People compare their views with the ideas of others whom they respect and who may hold more extreme attitudes than they do. Feeling as right-minded as their colleagues, they become at least as liberal or as conservative as their peer group—they polarize their views.

GROUPTHINK.   Studies of decision making in government have often focused on the concept of **groupthink**—the tendency of people in a group to seek agreement with one another when reaching a decision, rather than effectively evaluating the options. Groupthink occurs when group members reinforce shared beliefs in the interest of getting along rather than effectively evaluating alternative solutions to the problem. The group does not allow its members to disagree, accept dissenting opinions, or evaluate options realistically (Janis, 1983). Groupthink discredits or ignores information not held in common, and thus cohesive groups are more likely to exhibit it (Mullen et al., 1994). See Figure 13.9 for a summary of the factors leading to groupthink.

Studies of history and government offer several examples of groupthink resulting in defective decision making, including the ill-fated decision to launch the space shuttle *Challenger* against the advice of engineers on the launch team (Moorhead,

**GROUP POLARIZATION**
Exaggeration of individuals' pre-existing attitudes as a result of group discussion.

**GROUPTHINK**
The tendency of people in a group to seek agreement with one another when reaching a decision, usually prematurely.

FIGURE 13.9
Groupthink: Development
and Results

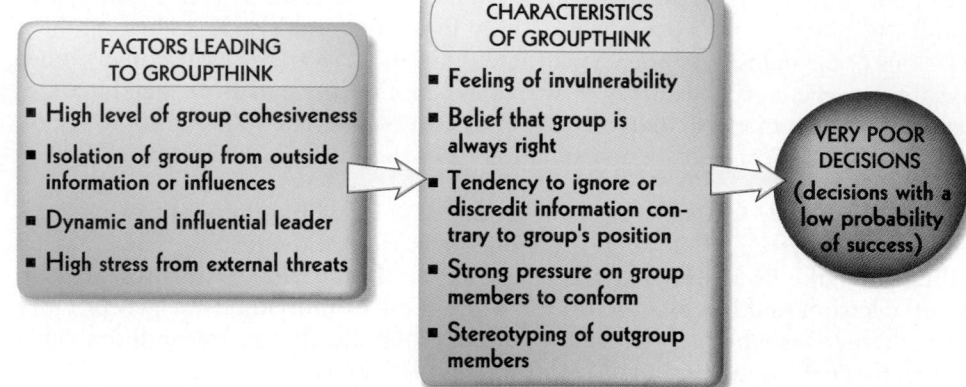

Ference, & Neck, 1991). Another example of groupthink was the calling of the budget vote in the House of Commons that brought down the Joe Clark government. In hindsight, it is clear that the Progressive Conservatives did not have enough support to pass the budget, but at the time they seemed certain that all would go well with the vote. This groupthink proved to be costly, as Joe Clark was forced to resign after having served only nine months as prime minister and Pierre Trudeau and the Liberals regained power in the election that followed.

Social psychologist Ivan Steiner (1982) suggests that groupthink occurs when members' overriding concern is to maintain group cohesiveness and harmony. Maintaining cohesiveness helps individuals believe that the group cannot make mistakes. In addition, strong leaders often insulate a group from information or from other people to keep the group thinking along the same line (McCauley, 1989; Pratkinis & Turner, 1999; Raven, 1998).

Despite the intuitive appeal of the groupthink concept, however, research support for it is limited (Paulus, 1998). Nevertheless, Aldag and Fuller (1993) assert that despite its lack of empirical support, groupthink is a defective process that people should guard against. They argue that groupthink can happen and that research into leaders, committees, and technology needs to focus on the variables that may create it or help defend against it (Shelton, 2000).

UNRESTRAINED GROUP BEHAVIOUR. The presence of other people can arouse people (social facilitation), can make them less active (social loafing), can cause them to make extreme decisions (group polarization), or can lead to consensus-making poor decisions (groupthink). So, when placed in a group, normally thoughtful people have been known to take part in bad decision making and even very irrational behaviours. Consider mob violence. When people engage in a riot, looting, or a beating, individuals explain their behaviour not in terms of individual responsibility but as a group decision.

A key component of unrestrained behaviour such as mob violence is *anonymity*. Anonymity produces a lack of self-awareness and self-perception that leads to decreased concern with social evaluation. When people have fewer concerns about being evaluated, they are more willing to engage in inappropriate or irrational behaviours. When there is violence or illegal drug use among a crowd at a rock concert, people feel less responsible. The view that no single individual can be held responsible for the behaviour of a group arises out of **deindividuation**—the process by which individuals lose their self-awareness and distinctive personalities in the context of a group and may engage in anti-normative behaviour (Diener et al., 1980). Deindividuation (and its accompanying arousal) can lead to shifts in people's perceptions of how their behaviour will be viewed—and thus to less controlled, less self-conscious, or less careful decisions about behaviour. With deindividuation, people alter their thoughts about decisions. The riot on Toronto's Yonge

DEINDIVIDUATION

The process by which individuals in a group lose their self-awareness and concern with evaluation and may engage in anti-normative behaviour.

478

Street following the Blue Jays' World Series win is a Canadian example of deindividuation. Similar behaviour occurred a number of years ago during the Regatta in Kelowna, British Columbia, when large numbers of partiers moved through the downtown area overturning cars and causing other damage after the formal festivities ended.

Groups such as the military, prisons, and cults use deindividuation to encourage their members to conform. In boot camp, military recruits are made to feel that they are there to serve the group, not their conscience. In prisons, inmates are made to wear uniforms and cut their hair short and are assigned numbers. With their unique personality stripped away, they are no longer treated as individuals and are made to behave as members of one large prison group. A cult persuades members to go along with group beliefs and acquire a sense of obligation to the group by asking individual members to perform increasingly taxing services on the group's behalf. In the end, an individual's behaviour in a group often becomes distorted, more extreme, and less rational; the group leads members to feel less accountable for their own actions. Researchers are increasingly asserting that people's interpretation of the setting in which they find themselves holds the key to understanding deindividuated behaviour.

▲ Groups such as the military, prisons, and cults encourage their members to conform and behave as members of the larger group.

## AGGRESSION AND VIOLENCE: THE DARK SIDE OF HUMAN BEHAVIOUR

Our social interactions with people are sometimes quite inconsequential; we say hello to others as we pass them on the street, for example. Other times our interactions affect family or work relationships, such as when we recognize kindness or good work in our family or co-workers. But social interactions also include the dark side of people's behaviours, including their aggressive and violent acts—children and adults kill cats, set fires, and engage in acts of terror. People strike out at others, behave aggressively and violently, and the cause often is not apparent or justified. As we will see in this section, social interactions are shaped by a wide array of events in people's lives.

When people feel unable to control situations that affect their lives, they may become frustrated, angry, and aggressive. Social psychologists define **aggression** as any behaviour designed to harm another person or thing. An aggressive person may attempt to harm others physically through force; to harm them verbally through gossip, rumours, or irritating comments; or to harm them emotionally by withholding attention or love. On a larger scale, whole countries attempt to harm others through economic sanctions or by acts of war. Three major theoretical explanations for aggressive behaviour focus on acquired drives, and on cognitive psychological and biological influences.

**ACQUIRED DRIVES.** As discussed in *Point/Counterpoint*, some psychologists believe that many aspects of behaviour, including aggression, are inborn (see DiLalla & Gottesman, 1991); however, most psychologists, the Canadian Psychological Association (1998), and the American Psychological Association (1990) do not agree. Those who believe that people are genetically predisposed toward aggression are termed *nativists*. An early nativist was Freud, who suggested that people have a destructive desire to release aggression against themselves, a death instinct he called *thanatos*. However, Freud never fully developed this concept, and today his conceptualization of the death instinct is not widely accepted.

Another nativist was the ethologist and Nobel laureate Konrad Lorenz (1903–1989), who investigated aggressive behaviour through

**HandsOnPsych**
Version 2.0

**Social Psychology II**

AGGRESSION
Any behaviour designed to harm another person or thing.

▼ Unrestrained individual behaviours more commonly occur in groups where people feel both anonymous and able to relinquish responsibility for their actions.

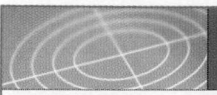
## Is Aggression Socially or Biologically Produced?

**POINT:** We are "wired" by biology to be aggressive when necessary.

**COUNTERPOINT:** Our aggressive tendencies are learned through social interaction and are not a biological "fact."

When we watch the Academy Award–winning movie *Gladiator,* are we fulfilling a basic human need? Is Russell Crowe exhibiting an inborn biological tendency when he battles for freedom in the Coliseum? It is widely held by many people that human beings are aggressive and that this is an inborn, biologically based capacity. It is part of our human nature. Or is it? The joining together of social psychology and brain science hopes to make sense of how the brain controls cognitive processes such as memory and attention, which in turn influence social behaviours such as self-control, aggression, and attitudes. In the end, social psychologists are developing what some call *social cognitive neuroscience* and it speaks directly to aggressive behaviours.

Some psychologists believe that many aspects of behaviour, including aggression, are inborn (DiLalla & Gottesman, 1991), but most psychologists (APA, 1990) do not agree. Evolutionary theorists support this biological view—at least to some extent. They argue that sexual jealousy, for instance, is a factor in homicidal violence among young men (Starzomki & Nussbaum, 2000). The jealousy of a young man is a consequence of his evolved tendencies to be proud of his offspring of his chosen mate (Wilson & Daly, 1998). While there is anecdotal evidence for male pridefulness, little firm evidence shows an evolutionary link for violence because indiscriminate violence is more of a problem than a benefit to both individuals and to the groups to which they belong.

However, studies of monozygotic twins show that reported aggressiveness is a heritable trait. When one identical twin is aggressive, studies suggest that the other twin is also aggressive. Yet not all research in this field shows consistent results (Miles & Carey, 1997). Geen (1998) argues that there are just too many conflicting results and too many definitions of aggression to make firm conclusions possible. Nevertheless, Niehoff (1999) concludes that heritability, along with neurochemistry, plays a role in human aggression.

What about raging hormones? We know that, in animals, hormones such as testosterone organize and activate aggressive behaviours. For humans, the data are a bit murkier. Many investigators argue that testosterone plays an important or significant role in human aggression; other research shows that it produces only some activation effects (McCaul, Gladue, & Joppa, 1992). So in some cases we find that teenage boys who are viewed as *rebellious* often have higher levels of testosterone than other boys; but testosterone levels do not vary among aggressive and nonaggressive boys (Constantino et al., 1993). It also turns out that testosterone often rises *after* (not before) competitive or aggressive behaviour—that is, rising testosterone may be a result rather than a cause of competitive and aggressive behaviour. Thus, no simple causal relationship exists between aggression and androgens in human males. Hormonal activity may predispose individuals to competition and aggression, but it does not determine this behaviour.

Whether aggression is inhibited or expressed depends on the organism's previous experiences and current social context—for example, whether it has been raised in a hostile environment or is currently being provoked (Lore & Schultz, 1993). While most social psychologists are attempting to sort out the cultural variables that prompt aggression—such as viewing or listening to violence portrayed by the media—those who study brain and behaviour find links in biology. Evolutionary history, genetic inheritance, and hormones may contribute to the base level of aggressiveness in human beings (Miczek et al., 2001). It is generally accepted that there is some biological predisposition for violence among people (Dobash & Dobash, 1998). But in the end, the research does not show—by any stretch of the imagination—that biology *determines*, or causes, aggressive behaviour in human beings.

naturalistic observation. He noted that although animals of the same species fight with one another, they often use signals that tell them to avoid fighting or to stop fighting well before serious injury or death occurs. According to Lorenz (1964), aggression is instinctive and spontaneous; the aggressive instinct serves to maximize the use of food, space, and resources. Lorenz stressed the social implications of people's aggressive instincts, focusing on their adaptive values.

Both animals and human beings can be aggressive; whether that aggression is inhibited or expressed depends on the organism's previous experiences and current social context, such as whether the organism is being provoked or whether it has been raised in a hostile environment (Lore & Schultz, 1993).

An explanation for aggressive behaviour is that it results when goal-directed behaviour has been frustrated—this is the *frustration–aggression hypothesis*, initially proposed by Dollard and colleagues (1939). This theory relies on observations demonstrating that people involved in everyday goal-oriented tasks often become aggressive or angry when frustrated. For example, ordinarily you may be unlikely to become upset if another car pulls out into traffic in front of you. However, if you are in a hurry to get to work, you might honk or mutter angrily at the other driver.

Berkowitz (1964) examined the evidence for the frustration–aggression hypothesis and proposed a modified version of it. He suggested that frustration creates a *readiness* for aggressive acts rather than producing actual aggression. He showed that even when frustration is present, certain events must occur or certain conditions must exist before aggression results; for example, someone embroiled in a heated argument might be more likely to become aggressive if there is a weapon lying on a nearby table. In a later reformulation, Berkowitz (2000) suggested that frustrations generate aggressive inclinations to the extent that they arouse negative feelings in the frustrated individual (Berkowitz, 1990). Berkowitz's conception accounts for the instances when frustrated people don't become aggressive. Although many psychologists find the frustration–aggression hypothesis too simplistic, it is useful, in part because it has led to other research that helps describe behaviour—for example, cognitive theory.

COGNITIVE PSYCHOLOGY.     A tendency to violence is not inherited (see Table 13.2); rather people actively engage in thoughts that lead them to violent behaviours, according to cognitive psychologists. What thoughts go through people's minds when they engage in road rage? What possesses people to engage in mob violence? Leonard Eron (1987) conducted a 22-year longitudinal study of aggression. He tracked the entire third-grade population (870 students) of Columbia County, a semi-rural area in New York State. Eron's work probed the influences in children's lives that cause them to *interpret* the world in a way that makes them aggressive. He reasoned that an aggressive child responds to the world with combativeness because the child has internalized aggressive ideas. These children saw the world as a violent place and responded accordingly. Eron (1987, p. 441) argued: "It was what the subjects were saying to themselves about what they wanted . . .

TABLE 13.2    **A Tendency to Violence Is Not Inherited**

Scientific groups, including the Canadian and American Psychological Associations, have adopted a statement called the Seville Statement on Violence, which asserts that the use of scientific data to support war is wrong and is based on erroneous assumptions.

**The following statements are scientifically incorrect:**

We have inherited a tendency to make war from our animal ancestors.

War or any other violent behaviour is programmed into our human nature.

Through the course of human evolution, aggression, more than any other characteristic, has been programmed into human behaviour.

Humans have a violent brain.

War is caused by instinct or any other specific inborn motivation.

Adapted from the Seville Statement on Violence (APA, 1994)

what might be an effective or appropriate response . . . that helped determine how aggressive they are today."

Researchers today are examining how stimuli in an individual's environment may bring forth thoughts and emotional responses that lead to aggressive behaviour (Bushman & Geen, 1990). Stimuli that have been examined include difficult personal situations and frustrating social conditions. Such views have led researchers to believe that harsh, punitive parenting leads to aggressiveness and negativity. Aggressive children see others as hostile to them, and they respond in kind.

A key cognitive variable that may predispose people to aggression is their self-esteem. Conventional wisdom has held that people with low self-esteem—unfavourable overall impressions of themselves—are more likely to be violent and aggressive. However, a review of research shows that crime, violence, and aggression are not *caused by* low self-esteem (or, for that matter, by high self-esteem). According to Roy Baumeister (Bushman & Baumeister, 1998), aggression is caused by *threats* to a person's level of self-esteem. When their views of themselves (however high or low) are threatened or contradicted, people become aggressive. This view suggests that those who fail to adjust their self-appraisal—despite evidence of the correctness of the new view—may become aggressive. There are some strong direct implications of such an idea. Western society places a strong emphasis on helping develop individuals' self-esteem. But development of self-esteem doesn't protect individuals from threats to it. Baumeister suggests that societal pursuit of high self-esteem for everyone may end up doing considerable harm, given the fact that it is impossible to insulate everyone from threats to self-esteem! As yet there is little research on how threats to self-esteem affect aggression, but the idea has considerable interest. Perhaps it derives from previous experience and people are set up to be aggressive.

What happens when you are provoked by a co-worker at the office and then go immediately home? Do you argue with a housemate? If you go to a rousing, exciting football game and are then confronted by road rage on the way home, how do you respond? Zillman (1994) proposed the *excitation transfer theory*. He argued that excitation (arousal) dissipates slowly and that excitation that is stirred up in a specific situation can transfer to situations afterward. He reasoned that emotional reactions may come from a previous event. He claimed that aggression is most likely to occur when we are not aware of surplus (leftover) arousal and we misattribute the source of our current arousal to present events rather than previous ones. So when someone cuts you off while you drive home from an exciting game, you misattribute your current arousal to the bad driver and become aggressive.

Excitation transfer theory also relates to the effects of television violence. A stimulus such as high-violence television programs produces a high level of excitation, and it may take a long time for the excitation to decay or lessen. The outcome: aggressive behaviour—let's look at the evidence.


**TELEVISION VIOLENCE.** Exposure to television, with its stylized view of the world, may have negative consequences. Exposure to violence on television has been likened to a public health epidemic; violence is portrayed on city streets, in rural communities, and on the worldwide stage. Its presence is almost commonplace; nowhere are violence and aggression, especially sexual aggression, more prevalent than on television (MacKay & Covell, 1997). And most Canadian children ages 2 to 11 spend more hours watching television (an average of almost 15.5 hours a week) than in any other activity except sleep; they are also often indiscriminate viewers (Statistics Canada, 2001).

The fact that television portrays so much aggressive behaviour concerns parents and educators as well as social psychologists. Half of all prime-time TV characters are involved in violent activity of some kind; about one-tenth kill or are killed; the perpetrators of these crimes go unpunished in nearly three-quarters of violent scenes. Sixty percent of television programs contain violence—and that violence is often glamorized (Bushman & Phillips, 2001; Smith et al., 1998). Moreover, about 20 percent of males appearing on TV shows are employed in law enforcement, whereas less than 1 percent of adult men are so employed in the real world. Although the overall amount of violence shown on television is staggering, some programs clearly account for a disproportionate number of violent acts.

Research generally supports the contention that viewers who frequently watch violent programs on television are more likely to be aggressive than are viewers who see less TV violence (Anderson & Bushman, 2002; Johnson et al., 2002; Villani, 2001). Further, children exposed to large doses of TV violence are less likely to help a real-life victim of violence, and viewers of violence are less sympathetic to victims than are non-viewers (Villani, 2001). Viewers of violence also are more fearful of becoming victims of violent

▲ Research suggests that children who play violent video games may act more aggressively as they get older.

acts. Children who play violent video games also seem to act more aggressively at later ages (Anderson & Dill, 2000; Brooks, 2000), and even infants can become fearful from watching television (Meltzoff, 1988). According to Stacy Smith and her colleagues (1998), who conducted the National Television Violence Study, violence on television hasn't changed appreciably in decades—neither its overall prevalence nor how it is presented has changed much. How does watching violence on television affect viewers? Smith and her colleagues describe some of the key effects of viewing violence on television:

- It weakens viewers' inhibitions.
- It may suggest new ideas and techniques to the uninitiated.
- It may activate or stimulate existing aggressive ideas and behaviours.
- It desensitizes people, reducing their overall emotional sensitivity to violence.
- It introduces a fear of being a victim of violence.

Of course, television can also have positive effects on children (Henry et al., 2000). Children exposed to shows such as *Sesame Street* and *Mister Rogers' Neighborhood*, which focus on topics such as sharing and caring, are thought to encourage more prosocial behaviour with other children. Still, watching too much television has a deleterious impact on children's reading comprehension skills (Koolstra, van der Voort, & van der Kamp, 1997).

Research on the effects of television and other media is tricky. Often the effects are subtle because potential influences—violence, sex, and education—are sometimes combined in one program. Some assert that children are "protected" from the effects of violence by knowledge that what they see is not real (Davies, 1997); research, however, indicates that even adults blend the fictional portrayals of characters on television into their views of real people (Murphy, 1998). In the end, the data are fairly clear: TV programming, for better or worse, can affect children (and adults). How, when, and how often information is conveyed to children ultimately have important social implications (Calvert, 1998). Social psychologists interested in public policy suggest requiring that every TV station broadcast at least a certain amount of educational programming for children and establishing controls to protect children from advertising that exploits their special vulnerability (Smith et al., 1998).

▲ Men are more physically aggressive than women but both men and women use verbal aggression and threats. Women in many cultures have been raised with values that make them feel guilty if they cause physical pain; men have not been raised with these values, at least not to the same extent.

**HandsOnPsych**
Version 2.0

**Social Psychology II**

*Be an*
**ACTIVE LEARNER**

**REVIEW**
> What are the key findings of Milgram's study? pp. 473–474
> How do social facilitation and social loafing differ? pp. 475–476
> Identify the social variables that are important in explaining unrestrained group behaviour. pp. 478–479
> Why might not getting what one wants sometimes lead to aggression? pp. 479–481

**THINK CRITICALLY**
> Is it possible to shape society to make people less aggressive?
> Some advertisers and local television stations dropped ABC's *Politically Incorrect* after host Bill Maher referred to some past U.S. military actions as "cowardly." Did his dissent influence society?

**APPLY PSYCHOLOGY**
> Devise a system, a program, or a plan to help people feel less pressure to conform to group norms and more likely to make choices based on their own conscience.

**GENDER DIFFERENCES IN AGGRESSION.** Many people believe that men are naturally more aggressive than women. They refer to aggressive contact sports such as football and boxing, the aggressive behaviour of men in business, the overwhelming number of violent crimes committed by men, and the traditional view that men are more likely than women to be ruthless and unsympathetic. It is also generally accepted that "more masculine" people (whether men or women) are more aggressive, and this attitude is reflected in children's toys (Dietz, 1998), on television (Browne, 1998), and in viewing behaviour (Wright et al., 2001). But are men really more aggressive than women?

Many have observed that men are more *physically* aggressive than women (Harris & Knight-Bohnhoff, 1996). But Crick and Rose (2000) found that both men and women use *psychological* aggression such as verbal abuse and angry gestures. For example, some girls use indirect aggression with peers; they instigate fights and conflicts among friends or family members or perhaps spread false stories (Owens, Shute, & Slee, 2000; Walker, Richardson, & Green, 2000). One interpretation of this finding suggests that the differences in aggression that appear between boys and girls, and men and women, are directly related to the perceived consequences of the aggression. Women in many cultures have been raised with values that make them feel especially guilty if they cause physical pain; men have not been raised with those values, at least not to the same extent. In addition, women are more vulnerable to physical retaliation than men are. So women are more likely than men to use relationship or indirect aggression, which does harm but carries less risk of physical retaliation. However, situations involving insults and con- descending treatment provoke women more than men (Bettencourt & Miller, 1996), and when women feel justified and protected from retaliation, they can be as aggressive as men (Brannon, 2002).

Research supports the idea that the context and situation in which people find themselves alter the nature and extent of aggression in men and women toward individuals of their own and the other gender (Crick & Rose, 2000). The research picture is complicated, and some important and subtle effects occur. For example, research shows that the age at which aggression occurs varies in men and women; girls develop aggressive behaviours in adolescence, while boys do so earlier (Werner & Crick, 1999). Furthermore, early-maturing girls are at higher risk for psychological problems and aggressive behaviours (Loeber & Stouthamer-Loeber, 1998). Some social behaviours may be genetically programmed and may have an evolutionary basis, but the weight of the evidence leans toward socialization by society. Psychologists are just beginning to assess the important issues involving gender and the developmental course of aggression.

## PROSOCIAL BEHAVIOUR

On September 11, 2001, hundreds of people in and around the World Trade Center helped others escape. Some of these individuals were helping co-workers, but many rendered aid to strangers, often risking their own lives to do so. Canadians from Whitehorse to Gander immediately opened their homes and communities to strangers travelling on planes that were destined for the United States but grounded when American airspace was closed. Canadians moved to offer aid and comfort in a multitude of significant and minor ways. Many people opened their homes to Americans stranded in their cities, while others donated food, money, and supplies to those marooned in Canada and to those more directly affected in New York City and Washington, D.C. In Prince Edward Island, Cheryl Boyle and her friends baked more than 200 apple pies and sent them to a restaurant serving relief workers at Ground Zero. Psychologists have long studied instances of people rendering help. For example, if you are walking down the street with a bag of groceries and you drop them, what is the likelihood that someone will help you pick them up? Psychologists who try to find out when, and under what conditions, someone will help a stranger are examining the likelihood of **prosocial behaviour**—behaviour that benefits someone else or society but that generally offers no obvious benefit to the person performing it and may even involve some personal risk or sacrifice.

**ALTRUISM: HELPING WITHOUT REWARDS.**   Why does Peter Beneson, founder of Amnesty International, devote so much time and effort to helping "prisoners of conscience" around the world? What compelled Mother Teresa to wander Calcutta's streets and attend to the wounds and diseases of people no one else will touch? Why did Oskar Schindler risk his life to save 1100 Jews from the Nazi death camps during the Second World War?

**Altruism** consists of behaviours that benefit other people and for which there is no discernible extrinsic reward, recognition, or appreciation (Quigley, Gaes, & Tedeschi, 1989; Toch, 2001). The key is that rewards are not part of the altruism equation. Although many prosocial behaviours involve rewards and altruistic behaviours are prosocial, altruistic behaviours are done without any expectation of reward. But isn't the feeling of well-being after performing an altruistic act a type of reward?

Many behaviourists contend that an element of personality directs people to seek social approval by helping. According to this view, people with a high need for achievement are more likely than others to be helpful, and people may continue to be helpful because the positive consequences of their actions are self-reinforcing (Batson et al., 1991; Puffer, 1987). From a behavioural view, intrinsically rewarding activities become powerful behaviour initiators; thus, when you have a relationship with a person, the person's affection and approval make you more likely to be caring and helpful (Batson, 1990). Further, once kindness and helpfulness become well established and even routine, individuals are more likely to help others, such as the homeless, disadvantaged senior citizens, and orphans.

Other theorists argue that biological drives underlie altruistic behaviour. Consider the following scenario. An infant crawls into a busy street. A truck is approaching. The infant's mother darts in front of the oncoming vehicle and carries her child to safety. Most people would say that love impelled the mother to risk her life to save the child. Sociobiologists would argue that the mother committed her selfless deed so her genes would be passed on to another generation.

The idea that people are genetically predisposed toward certain behaviours was described by Edward Wilson, a Harvard University zoologist, in his 1975 book *Sociobiology: A New Synthesis*. Wilson argued that biological, genetic factors underlie all behaviour. But he went one step further. He founded a new field, **sociobiology**, based on the premise that even day-to-day behaviours are determined by the process of natural selection—that social behaviours that contribute to the survival of a species are passed on via the genes from one generation to the next. Natural selection accounts for the mechanisms that have evolved to produce altruistic behaviours (Crawford & Anderson, 1989). For the sociobiologist, genetics is the key to daily behaviour.

**Social Psychology II**

Psychologists hotly debate sociobiological theory, because it places genetics in a position of primary importance and minimizes the role of learning. Most psychologists feel strongly that learning plays a key role in the day-to-day activities of human beings. People *learn* to love, to become angry, to help or hurt others, and to develop relationships with those around them. Although sociobiology is too fixed and rigid for most psychologists, it does raise interesting questions about the role of biology and genetics in social behaviour.

Behavioural theories and sociobiology are two ways of explaining why people help others. People don't always help, however. One important area of research seeks to explain why.

**BYSTANDER APATHY: FAILING TO HELP.** The study of helping behaviour has taken some interesting twists and turns. For example, psychologists have found that in large cities, where potentially lethal emergencies (accidents, thefts, stabbings, rapes, and murders) occur frequently, people often exhibit bystander apathy—they watch, but seldom help. *Bystander apathy* is the unwillingness of witnesses to an event to help; this unwillingness increases with the number of observers, a fact that has been termed the **bystander effect**. In a well-known horrific incident in New York City in 1964, Kitty Genovese was walking home when a man approached her with a knife. A chase ensued, during which she screamed for help. He stabbed her, and she continued to scream. When lights came on in nearby buildings, the attacker fled. However, when he saw that no one was coming to his victim's aid, he returned and stabbed her again. The assault lasted more than 30 minutes and was heard by 38 neighbours, yet no one came to the victim's aid or called the police. This is a classic case of bystander apathy because, in every case, each witness said he or she thought someone else would help.

Bibb Latané and John Darley (1970) investigated bystander apathy in a long series of studies. They found that in situations requiring uncomfortable responses, people must choose between helping and standing by apathetically. They must decide whether to introduce themselves into a situation, especially when there are other bystanders. But they first have to decide what is going on (is this an emergency or not?) and often are misled by the *apparent* lack of concern among other bystanders to conclude that nothing bad is really going on after all—so they don't help. Latané and Darley reasoned that when people are aware of other bystanders in an emergency situation, they also may be less likely to help because they experience *diffusion of responsibility* (the feeling that they cannot be held responsible). To test their hypothesis, the researchers brought college students to a laboratory and told them they were going to be involved in a study of people who were interested in discussing college life in New York City. They explained that, in the interest of preserving people's anonymity, a group discussion would be held over an intercom system rather than face to face, and that each person in the group would talk in turn. In fact, in each experimental session there was only one true participant. Assistants who worked for the researchers prerecorded all of the other conversations.

The independent variable was the number of people the naive participant thought were in the discussion group. The dependent variable was whether and how fast the naive participant reported as an emergency an apparently serious seizure affecting one of the "other participants." The future "seizure victim" spoke first; he talked about his difficulties in adjusting to college and mentioned that he was prone to seizures, particularly when studying hard. Next, the naive participant spoke. Then came the prerecorded discussions by assistants. Then the "seizure victim" talked again. After a few relatively calm remarks, his speech became increasingly loud and incoherent; he stuttered and indicated that he needed help because he was having "a-a-a real problem—er—right now and I—er—if somebody could help me out it would—it would—er—er sh-sure be good." At this point, the experimenters began timing the speed of the naive participant's response.

Each naive participant was led to believe that his or her discussion group contained two (participant and victim), three (participant, victim, and one other person), or six (participant, victim, and four other people) people. That is, in the two-person group, participants believed they were the only bystander; in the three-person group, they thought there was one other bystander. When participants thought they were the only bystander, 85 percent of them responded before the end of the seizure. If they thought there was only one other bystander, 62 percent of the participants responded by the end of the seizure. When participants thought there were four additional bystanders, only 31 percent responded by the end of the seizure (see Figure 13.10).

In general, research has shown that bystanders will help under some conditions—much has to do with the character and characteristics of the bystander (Laner, Benin, & Ventrone, 2001). For one thing, people's self-concepts and previous experiences affect their willingness to intercede. Bystanders who see themselves as being especially competent in emergencies (such as doctors and nurses) are likely to help a victim regardless of the number of people present (Pantin & Carver, 1982). If the person who needs help has a relationship with the person who can offer help, help is more likely to be given (Batson, 1990). Research in cities of various sizes shows that people who live in small communities are more likely to help (Levine et al., 1994). Also, personality characteristics of the individual involved in a bystander situation are important. Men respond more often than women (Salminen & Glad, 1992). Tice and Baumeister (1985), however, found that participants with a high degree of masculinity were less likely to respond. They contended that highly masculine subjects might be especially fearful of embarrassment. In Western cultures, the personality characteristics of men, in general, emphasize strength and aggression rather than sensitivity and nurturing. This finding is supported by work showing that women are more likely than men to help friends, and that when women do so, they do it in a nurturing rather than in a problem-solving way (Belansky & Boggiano, 1994).

## RELATIONSHIPS AND ATTRACTION

Some people feel that they are living a life that is predetermined and that relationships with others—especially love relationships—are a part of their personal destiny. It turns out that people who believe in romantic destiny—that people are meant for each other—tend to have long relationships, if they let a relationship begin in the first place (Knee, 1998). But relationships with friends, lovers, and spouses are intricate. What is it about your friends that attracts you and makes you want to maintain a relationship with them in the first place? We saw in Chapter 11 that people develop relationships to fulfil their needs for warmth, understanding, and emotional security. Psychologists also know that people are attracted to those who live or work near them, whom they consider good looking, who share their attitudes, and with whom they spend time. Social psychologists in particular study **interpersonal attraction**, the tendency of one person to evaluate another person (or a symbol or image of another person) in a positive way.

**PROXIMITY.** People are more likely to develop a relationship with a neighbour than with someone who lives several blocks or kilometres away. Three decades of research show that the closer people are geographically—whether this means where they work or where they live—the more attracted they will be. A simple explanation is that they are likely to see each other more often, and repeated exposure leads to familiarity, which leads to attraction. Another reason is that attraction is facilitated by the anticipation of a relationship with someone encountered frequently. In addition, if people are members of the same group, such as a club, a volunteer

**FIGURE 13.10**
**The Bystander Effect**

In a classic bystander apathy study, as the number of people in the group increased, the willingness of the naive participant to inform the experimenter that the victim had suffered a seizure decreased. (From Latané & Darley, 1970.)

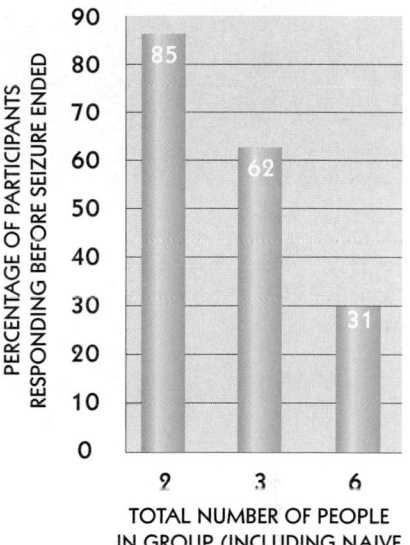

PERCENTAGE OF PARTICIPANTS RESPONDING BEFORE SEIZURE ENDED

TOTAL NUMBER OF PEOPLE IN GROUP (INCLUDING NAIVE PARTICIPANT AND VICTIM)

**HandsOnPsych**
Version 2.0

**Social Psychology II**

INTERPERSONAL ATTRACTION
The tendency of one person to evaluate another person (or a symbol or image of another person) in a positive way.

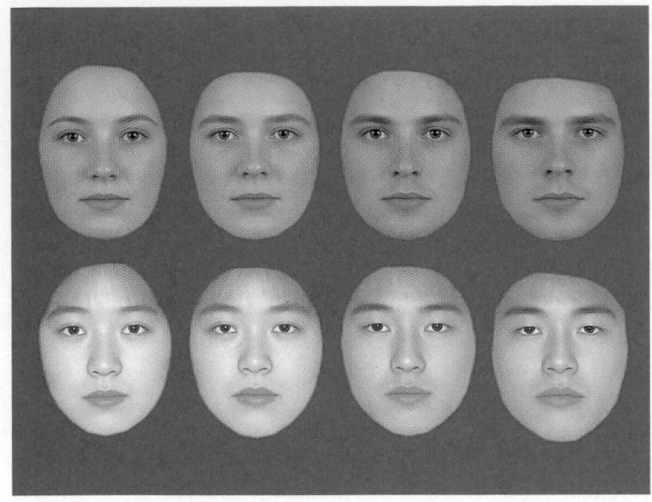

▲ Look at these two sets of faces. In each group, which face appeals to you more—the feminized or the masculinized?

organization, or a class, they perceive themselves as sharing the same feelings, attitudes, and values as others in the group. That perception leads to attraction.

**PHYSICAL ATTRACTIVENESS.** Within seconds of seeing a person, you are able to decide if they are attractive to you (Locher et al., 1993). Research shows that people feel more personal regard and ascribe more power, status, and competence to individuals they find physically attractive than to those they don't; we saw this earlier when we discussed who could best change people's attitudes (Feingold, 1992a, 1992b). Interestingly, Karen and Kenneth Dion and Anita Pak (1990) of the University of Toronto found that this tendency is *less* pronounced among individuals involved in collectivist cultures (such as the Toronto Chinese community) than among individuals involved in individualistic cultures.

Attractiveness is affected by subtle but powerful variables. For example, in a recent study both men and women were shown facial images of Caucasian and Japanese females and males that had been "feminized" or "masculinized" by a computer (Perrett et al., 1998). Both Caucasian and Japanese participants preferred and rated as most attractive the faces that were feminized. The researchers suggested that computer alteration of men's faces to make them slightly feminine makes them appear less menacing and softens other features that are associated with negative traits. The researchers assert that more feminine faces appear younger and that people's preferences for young faces are correlated with their preference for feminized faces. Such results are probably no surprise to Leonardo DiCaprio's agent.

Volumes of research show that people are attracted romantically, at least at first, to those whom they find physically attractive (Langlois, Roggman, & Musselman, 1994). People judge an attractive individual to have more positive traits and characteristics than an unattractive one, especially when appearance is the first information provided (DeSantis & Kayson, 1997). People feel more personal regard for and ascribe more power, status, and competence to individuals they find physically attractive than to those they don't; this affects who can best change people's attitudes (Feingold, 1992a; Fiske, 2001). Attractive people are granted more freedom and are perceived as being fairer and healthier than unattractive people (Cherulnik, Turns, & Wilderman, 1990; Kalick et al., 1998). For example, attractive university and college professors are seen as better teachers and are less likely to be blamed by a student who receives a failing grade in a course (Romano & Bordieri, 1989). But such findings about attractiveness are a distinctly Western phenomenon; ideas about attractiveness may differ cross-culturally (Matsumoto & Kudoh, 1993). For example, for more than a thousand years Chinese women endured the suffering of footbinding in the name of beauty. Yet a study by Cunningham and colleagues (1995) found that Asian, Latino, and white judges of what was attractive were consistent in their judgments: faces with neonate large eyes, greater distance between eyes, and small noses; sexually mature, narrower female faces with smaller chins; expressive, higher eyebrows, dilated pupils, larger lower lips, larger smiles, and well-groomed, full hair. Yet some cultural differences persist, while some change over time. In our culture, thin is the standard. In Hawaiian culture of the past century, fat was considered desirable. A few hundred years ago, European culture held a similar view. Westerners wear earrings; many women in India also wear nose rings. Thus, though some standards of beauty appear consistent throughout the world, certain elements can vary according to place and time period.

**LIKING THOSE WHO SHARE THE FEELING AND WHO HOLD SIMILAR ATTITUDES.** Learning theorists contend that people are attracted to and form relationships with those who give them positive reinforcement and that people dislike those who punish them. The basic idea is simple: You like the people who like you (Katz & Beach, 2000). Moreover, if you like someone, you tend to assume (sometimes incorrectly) that the other person likes you in return and that the two of you share similar qualities. This tendency is especially prevalent in people who need social approval (Jacobs, Berscheid, & Walster, 1971).

Another attribute that affects the development of relationships is real or perceived similarity in attitudes and opinions. If you perceive someone's attitudes as similar to your own, there is an increased probability you will like that person. Having similar values, interests, and background is a good predictor of friendship (e.g., Miller, 1990). Similarly, voters who agree with the views of a particular political candidate tend to rate that person as more honest, friendly, and persuasive than the politicians with whom they disagree. Researchers also have found that, conversely, if you already like someone, you will perceive that person's attitudes as being similar to your own. For example, voters who like a particular political candidate, perhaps because the candidate is warm-hearted or physically attractive, will tend to minimize their attitudinal differences.

That you like those who like you is explained by cognitive consistency theory, which suggests that sharing similar attitudes reduces cognitive dissonance (the phenomenon we examined earlier). In your natural inclination to avoid dissonance, you are attracted to those you believe share similar attitudes; shared attitudes in turn lead to attraction and liking. Learning theories also suggest that you like people with similar attitudes because similar attitudes are reinforcing to you.

**INTIMATE RELATIONSHIPS AND LOVE.**   In **intimacy** each person is willing to self-disclose and to express important feelings and information to the other person; in response, the other person usually acknowledges the first person's feelings, making each person feel valued and cared for (Katz & Beach, 2000). Research shows that self-disclosure tends to be reciprocal; people who disclose themselves to others are usually recipients of intimate information (Collins & Miller, 1994). When people self-disclose they validate each other; that is, they accept each other's positive and negative attributes. Although such self-disclosure is important, revealing secrets and intimate information is not always beneficial to individuals (Kelly & McKillop, 1996).

Most research on intimate relationships focuses on marriage rather than friendships, but some research exists on communication, affection, consideration, and self-disclosure between friends. However, important individual and gender differences in friendships have been identified (Reeder, 2000). For example, women more than men incorporate close relationships into their view of themselves and let those views affect their thoughts and behaviours (Cross & Madson, 1997). Women more than men evaluated same-sex friendships very positively (Veniegas & Peplau, 1997). Furthermore, in relationships, men are more self-disclosing with a woman than they are with another man; in general, men are less likely to be self-disclosing and intimate than are women (Dindia & Allen, 1992), but men are more self-disclosing with a woman than with another man. On the whole, however, psychologists know much more about intimate relationships that involve sex, love, and marriage (Stewart, Stinnett & Rosenfeld, 2001).

Love, emotional commitment, and sex are the parts of intimate relationships that most people think of when they hear the word *intimacy*. People in love relationships often express feelings in unique ways—they give flowers, take moonlit walks, write lengthy letters, and have romantic dinners. According to psychologists, love has psychological, emotional, biochemical, and social factors. Consider this array of definitions of *love*:

INTIMACY

A state of being or feeling in which each person is willing to self-disclose and to express important feelings and information to the other person; such behaviours are usually reciprocated.

## Be an
# ACTIVE
# LEARNER

**REVIEW**
> What is the primary explanation for the bystander effect? p. 486
> Are bystanders indifferent or inhibited? Why? pp. 486–487

**THINK CRITICALLY**
> Provide a psychological explanation of why you probably will like someone whose attitudes you perceive as similar to your own. Why might that person be able to influence you to do things you might otherwise not do?
> Do you think that some people create situations that make them ultimately feel lonely? Explain your answer.

**APPLY PSYCHOLOGY**
> Psychologists know that people like those who are similar to themselves. What psychological principles could you call on to increase the likelihood that you will get a job or be promoted in the job you are in?
> Make a list of those things that would attract you to someone else romantically. Then make a list of those things that you would see as a turnoff. Are they polar opposites, for example, good-looking versus ugly? Which dimensions are opposites? Why?

- Fromm (1956) focused on the idea that mature love is possible only if a person achieves a secure sense of self-identity. He said that when people are in love, they become one and yet remain two individuals.
- Heinlein (1961) wrote that love "is a condition in which the happiness of the other person is essential to your own."
- Branden (1980) suggested that love is "a passionate spiritual, emotional, sexual attachment . . . that reflects a high regard for the value of each other's person."
- Tennov (1981) believed that the ultimate state of romantic love is one called "limerance": a head-over-heels involvement and preoccupation with thoughts of the loved one.

## EVOLUTION AND SOCIAL PSYCHOLOGY

Throughout this chapter we have been considering the various personal and situational variables that create social behaviours. But evolutionary theory argues that this is only part of the story; our genes have changed over time (adapted) to reflect environmental and breeding dynamics. From an evolutionary view, our social behaviour reflects smart adaptations to survive in groups both large and small. Remember that evolutionary theory asserts that behaviour is a product of the mix between evolved psychological mechanisms and social and physical environments. The adaptations that people make are meant to solve problems of survival and reproduction, and getting along in groups and forming interpersonal relationships are important for survival. Thus men are attracted to those women whom they see as fertile, good reproductive hosts; and women are attracted to men who will be good providers (Hinsz, Matz, & Patience, 2001). Indeed, social relationships are at the core of evolved psychological mechanisms because friendships, alliances, close relationships, and sexual behaviour are at the root of reproduction. It follows that men and women differ genetically, and in social behaviours, because of evolved psychological adaptations, and evolutionary psychologists hold that men and women value different characteristics in mates. As Buss and Kenrick (1998) put it, beauty is in the eyes and adaptations of the beholder. And so are violence and aggression; when a man sees a threat to his spouse or family, his natural evolved instinct gives rise to aggression and protective mechanisms, but people must restrain their aggressive impulses toward members of their families and others in their social group.

In the end, evolutionary psychology may be a unifying theory for social psychological phenomena. The research is still being done, and evolutionary theory is hard to test, but data from many areas come together to support this approach.

# Summary and Review

## ATTITUDES: DEEPLY HELD FEELINGS AND BELIEFS

### What is social psychology?

> *Social psychology* is the scientific study of how people think about, interact with, influence, and are influenced by the thoughts, feelings, and behaviours of others. **p. 452**

### What is the relationship between attitudes and behaviour?

> *Attitudes* are long-lasting patterns of feelings and beliefs about other people, ideas, or objects, which are based in people's experiences and shape their future behaviour. Attitudes are usually evaluative and have cognitive, emotional, and behavioural dimensions, each of which serves a function. Attitudes are formed early in life, through learning processes. Social psychologists can assess people's attitudes, but whether those attitudes predict behaviour depends on a number of variables including attitude strength, vested interest, specificity of attitudes, and accessibility of attitudes. **pp. 452–454**

### What are the key components of attitude change?

> There are four key components of attitude change: the communicator, the communication, the medium, and the audience. Each of these affects the extent of change that may take place. The *elaboration likelihood model*, proposed by Petty and Cacioppo, asserts that there are two routes to attitude change: central and peripheral. The central route emphasizes rational decision making; the peripheral route, which is more indirect and superficial, emphasizes emotional and motivational influences. **pp. 454–458**

> Cognitive explanations of attitudes and attitude change include cognitive dissonance and reactance theory. *Cognitive dissonance* is the state of mental discomfort that results when an individual maintains two or more beliefs, attitudes, or behaviours that are inconsistent with one another. *Reactance* is the negative response evoked when there is an inconsistency between a person's self-image as being free to choose and the person's realization that someone is trying to force him or her to choose a particular alternative. **pp. 458–460**

#### KEY TERMS

social psychology, p. 452; attitudes, p. 452; elaboration likelihood model, p. 456; cognitive dissonance, p. 459; self-perception theory, p. 459; reactance, p. 460

## SOCIAL COGNITION: THE IMPACT OF THOUGHT

### What is social cognition?

> *Social cognition* is the process of analyzing and interpreting events, other people, oneself, and the world in general. Often, to save time, people use mental shortcuts to make sense of the world, developing rules of thumb. **p. 460**

### What are nonverbal communication and attribution theory?

> *Nonverbal communication* is the communication of information by cues or actions that include gestures, tone of voice, vocal inflections, and facial expressions. These sources of information help people make judgments about other people and about events in the world. **pp. 461–462**

> *Attribution* is the process by which someone infers other people's attitudes, beliefs, motives, or intentions from observing their behaviour and deciding whether the causes of the behaviour are dispositional (internal) or situational (external). Attribution helps people make sense of the world, organize their thoughts quickly, and maintain a sense of control over the environment. It helps people feel competent and masterful because it helps them predict similar events in the future. **pp. 462–463**

### Describe the most common attribution errors.

> Two of the most common errors in attribution are the fundamental attribution error and the actor–observer effect. The *fundamental attribution error* is the tendency to attribute other people's behaviour to dispositional rather than situational causes. The *actor–observer effect* is the tendency to attribute the failings of others to dispositional causes but to attribute one's own failings to situational causes. Sometimes these errors occur because of a *self-serving bias*, that is, people's tendency to ascribe their positive behaviours to their own internal traits but their failures and shortcomings to external, situational factors. **pp. 464–465**

### Define prejudice, and identify the theories that explain it.

> *Prejudice* is a negative evaluation of an entire group of people. Prejudice is typically based on *stereotypes*—fixed, overly simple, and often erroneous ideas about traits, attitudes, and behaviours of groups of people; members of a group are assumed to be all alike. Prejudice often leads to *discrimination*, behaviour targeted at individuals or groups with the aim of holding them apart and treating them differently. Prejudice has multiple causes and can be accounted for, at least to some extent, by social learning theory, motivational theory, cognitive theory, and personality theory. **pp. 467–469**

#### KEY TERMS

social cognition, p. 460; impression formation, p. 460; nonverbal communication, p. 461; body language, p. 461; attribution, p. 462; fundamental attribution error, p. 464; actor–observer effect, p. 464; self-serving bias, p. 464; deception, p. 467; prejudice, p. 467; stereotypes, p. 467; discrimination, p. 467; social categorization, p. 469

## SOCIAL INTERACTIONS: THE POWER OF PEOPLE AND SITUATIONS

**Explain social influence and conformity.**

> *Social influence* refers to the ways people alter the attitudes or behaviour of others, either directly or indirectly. Social influence is easily seen in studies of conformity. *Conformity* occurs when a person changes attitudes or behaviours so that they are consistent with those of other people or with social norms.　**pp. 470–471**

**What is obedience, and what did Milgram's studies of obedience demonstrate?**

> *Obedience* is compliance with the orders of another person or group of people. Milgram's studies demonstrated that an individual's ability to resist coercion is limited, although the presence of an ally who refuses to participate reduces obedience, which underscores the importance of social influences on behaviour.　**pp. 473–474**

**What are social facilitation and social loafing?**

> *Social facilitation* is a change in a person's behaviour that occurs when people believe they are in the presence of other people. The change can be either positive or negative. *Social loafing* is a decrease in an individual's effort and productivity as a result of working in a group. **pp. 475–476**

**Identify three processes that may occur in group decision making that may or may not be helpful.**

> Processes that may affect group decision making, positively or negatively, include *group polarization*, the exaggeration of pre-existing attitudes as a result of group discussion; *groupthink*, the tendency of people in a group to seek concurrence with one another; and *deindividuation*, the process by which the individuals in a group lose their self-awareness, self-perception, and concern with evaluation and ultimately may engage in anti-social, anti-normative behaviour.　**pp. 477–479**

**Describe aggression, prosocial behaviour, and the bystander effect.**

> *Aggression* is viewed by social psychologists as any behaviour intended to harm another person or thing. *Prosocial behaviour* exhibits itself in *altruism*, behaviours that benefit someone else or society but that generally offer no obvious benefit to the person performing them. In contrast, the *bystander effect* is the unwillingness of witnesses to an event to help, especially when there are numerous observers.　**pp. 479–487**

**Define interpersonal attraction.**

> *Interpersonal attraction* is the tendency of one person to evaluate another person (or a symbol or image of another person) in a positive way. The process of attraction involves the characteristics of both the people involved and the situation. People give more personal regard and ascribe more power, status, and competence to people they find attractive than to those they don't. **pp. 487–488**

**Define friendship and love, and distinguish between them.**

> Reciprocity, closeness, and commitment between people who see themselves as equals are essentials of friendship. Love usually involves the idealization of another person. People see their loved ones in a positive light, care for them, and are fascinated with them; love also involves trust and commitment.　**pp. 481–484**

**KEY TERMS**

social influence, p. 470; conformity, p. 470; obedience, p. 473; debriefing, p. 474; group, p. 475; social facilitation, p. 475; social loafing, p. 476; group polarization, p. 477; groupthink, p. 477; deindividuation, p. 478; aggression, p. 479; prosocial behaviour, p. 489; altruism, p. 485; sociobiology, p. 485; bystander effect, p. 486; interpersonal attraction, p. 487; intimacy, p. 489

---

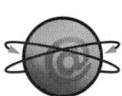

Take advantage of the multimedia resources available with this text! Follow the marginal icons to access the interactive modules on the *HandsOnPsych CD-ROM*; log on to *MyPsychLab* to explore the ebook, study aids, and other online resources; and visit the Companion Website at **www.pearsoned.ca/lefton** for additional exercises and links.

# 14 Stress and Health Psychology

Peter was worried. His parents didn't think he was getting good enough grades at school and he wasn't sure he could do any better. His girlfriend Lise was going to leave him because he couldn't spend enough time with her. His friends weren't calling because he could never think of anything interesting to do. He was concerned with the demands his professors were making on him because he just couldn't keep up. He was anxious that he would be fired because he had had to get someone to cover two of his shifts while he finished two papers.

In reality, Peter's parents were proud of his efforts, his girlfriend was preoccupied with her own workload but happy with him, and his friends were busy with final exams but planning to include him in celebrations for term end. All of his professors as well as his boss were happy with his work. What was the problem? Why was Peter so wrong? To those who knew him best Peter seemed irritable at times but generally calm and capable. He never expressed his worry or frustrations about the competing demands being made on him. But inside Peter the pressure was building.

Psychologists have labelled Peter and others like him as having "Type D" or "distressed type" personalities (Denollet, 2000). These are people who are negative thinkers and who worry about every detail; they are reluctant to vent their negative feelings and tend to view the glass as "half empty" rather than "half full." Studies have shown that Type Ds are four times more likely to suffer heart disease than are more positive thinkers. People with anxious, gloomy, worried outlooks are at risk. So what can Peter do? A personality isn't a disease. Can it be changed? Can Peter do anything to reduce his level of stress and therefore improve his chances for a healthier outcome? These are topics we will consider in this chapter.

The notion that stress is a problem for modern life is not even controversial—everyone accepts the inevitability of stress. You face a variety of stressors: studying for multiple exams in the same week, juggling studies and a part-time job, getting along with a difficult roommate in cramped quarters. Stressors, from filing tax returns to the loss of loved ones, are a reality for everyone. People can deal with stressors in either positive or negative ways; unfortunately, many don't cope effectively, and some take their frustrations out on others.

In this chapter, we examine the nature of stress, discuss how to cope with it, and look at the interrelationship of health and stress. We also look at how learned skills and personality work together to influence the ability to cope with stress in day-to-day life.

## Stress

Losing your temper with co-workers or friends, pounding your fists on a table, refusing to discuss a problem, and relying on alcohol each night are signs of stress. Stress can be handled in more positive ways, such as scheduling time more effectively, getting enough sleep, or exercising. One person may have a high-pressure job that affects her social life and causes regular migraines. A co-worker may manage the same amount of stress in more positive ways, without suffering negative health consequences. Such examples illustrate an important point: Different people evaluate and handle stress in different ways.

### WHAT IS STRESS?

The definition of stress depends on whose theory you follow. Theorists and researchers have defined stress in terms of external forces, internal responses, and an interaction of the two. According to Hans Selye, one of the first researchers to consider its effects, **stress** is a nonspecific response to real or imagined challenges or threats. Theorists who consider stress as a response define a **stressor** as an environmental stimulus that affects an organism, producing physical and psychological effects such as physical arousal and psychological tension and anxiety. According to Richard Lazarus, stress results from a cognitive appraisal of situations involving challenges or threats. According to this view, not all people view a situation in the same way; *a person must appraise a situation as stressful for it to be stressful.*

### CAUSES OF STRESS

Most of us have left a term paper until the last minute. As we scramble through the library trying to find appropriate references, we begin to realize that most of the sources for our project are signed out and that several other students also are looking for the few remaining relevant books and journals. How do we feel? There are four broad types of situations that cause stress: frustration, conflict, pressure, and challenge.

FRUSTRATION.    When people are hindered from meeting their goals, they often feel frustrated. **Frustration** is the emotional state or condition that results when a goal—work, family, or personal—is thwarted or blocked. When people believe that they cannot achieve a goal (often because of situations beyond their control), they may experience frustration. When you are unable to obtain a summer job because of a lack of experience, it can cause feelings of frustration. When a grandparent becomes ill, you may feel helpless; this can cause frustration. When there is an environmental threat over which people have no control, frustration is often the result (Hallman & Wandersman, 1992).

**Personality and Health**

STRESS

A nonspecific response to real or imagined challenges or threats.

STRESSOR

An environmental stimulus that affects an organism, producing physical and psychological effects such as physical arousal and psychological tension and anxiety.

FRUSTRATION

The emotional state or condition that results when a goal—work, family, or personal—is thwarted or blocked.

Some frustrations are externally caused. Examples are time lost in rush hour traffic or your grandparent's illness. Specific people cause other frustrations; your boss may be unfair in his appraisal of you, or your child or roommate may watch television while you are trying to study. You can sometimes alleviate the frustration of dealing with other people by taking some action; this action, however, may place you in conflict, another type of stress.

CONFLICT.  When people must make difficult decisions, they may be in a state of conflict. **Conflict** is the emotional state or condition in which people have to make difficult decisions about two or more competing motives, behaviours, or impulses. Consider the difficult decisions of American draftees who did not want to fight in the Vietnam War but also did not want to flee to Canada or face imprisonment. Or what happens if a person's goals and needs conflict—if a student must choose between two equally desirable academic courses, both of which will advance the student's career plans but which meet at the same hour?

One of the first psychologists to describe and quantify such conflict situations was Neal Miller (1944, 1959). Miller developed hypotheses about how animals and human beings behave in situations that have both positive and negative aspects. In general, he described three types of conflicts that result when situations involve competing demands: approach–approach conflicts, avoidance–avoidance conflicts, and approach–avoidance conflicts.

**Approach–approach conflict** is the conflict that results when a person must choose between two equally attractive alternatives or goals (for example, two wonderful job offers). Approach–approach conflict generates discomfort and a stress response; however, people usually can tolerate it because either alternative is pleasant. **Avoidance–avoidance conflict** is the conflict that results from having to choose between two equally distasteful alternatives or goals (for example, paying your taxes or facing prosecution). **Approach–avoidance conflict** is the conflict that results from having to choose an alternative or goal that has both attractive and repellent aspects. Studying for an exam, which can lead to good grades but is boring and difficult, is an approach–avoidance situation. As Figure 14.1 shows, any of the three types of conflict situations will lead to a different degree of stress. Miller developed principles to predict behaviour in conflict situations, particularly in approach–avoidance situations: (1) the closer a person is to a goal, the stronger the tendency is to approach the goal. (2) When two incompatible responses are available, the stronger one will be expressed. (3) The strength of the tendency to approach or avoid is correlated with the strength of the motivating drive. (Thus, someone on a diet who is considering a hot fudge sundae may yield to temptation if desire for the sundae is stronger than the desire to lose weight.) People regularly face conflict situations that may cause them to become anxious. Moreover, if conflicts affect day-to-day behaviour, people may exhibit symptoms of maladjustment.

PRESSURE FROM WORK, TIME, AND LIFE EVENTS.  Arousal and stress may occur when people feel **pressure**—the emotional state or condition resulting from the real or imagined expectations of others for certain behaviours or results. Although individual situations differ, pressure is common to almost everyone. Most of the time, it is associated with work, a lack of time, and life changes.

Work that is either overstimulating or understimulating can cause stress. Work-related stress also can come from fear of being let go or retired, of being passed over for promotion, or of organizational changes. In addition, the physical work setting may be too noisy, crowded, or isolated. Work-related pressure from deadlines, competition, and professional relationships (to name just a few possibilities) can cause a variety of physical problems. People suffering from work stress may experience migraines, sleeplessness, hunger for sweets, overeating, and intestinal distress. Stress

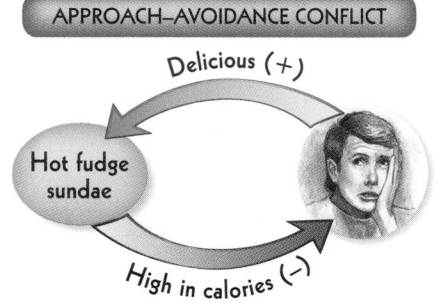

**FIGURE 14.1**
**Three Types of Conflict**

In approach–approach conflict, people have to choose between equally appealing alternatives. In avoidance–avoidance conflict, people have to choose between equally distasteful alternatives. In approach–avoidance conflict, people are faced with a single alternative that is both appealing and distasteful.

CHALLENGE

The emotional state that results when circumstances change in a way that requires action or effort.

at work often leads to an impaired immune system, which in turn leads to illness, resulting in lost efficiency and absenteeism (Levi, 1990). Stress at work also often "spills over" to non-work hours and may lead to other problems such as alcoholism (Grunberg, Moore, & Greenberg, 1998).

Individuals with high-stress jobs, particularly where the stress is constant and the stressors are beyond the individual's control, show the effects most dramatically. Air traffic controllers and surgeons, for example, are responsible for the lives of other people every day and must be alert and organized at all times. If they work too many hours without relief, they may make a fatal mistake. Other examples of high-stress jobs are social workers, customer service agents, waiters and waitresses, and emergency workers.

Lack of time is another common source of stress. Everyone faces deadlines: Students must complete papers and tests on time, auto workers must keep pace with the assembly line, and taxpayers must file their returns by April 30. People have only a limited number of hours each day in which to accomplish tasks; therefore, many people carefully allocate their time to reduce time pressure. They may establish routines, make lists, set schedules, leave optional meetings early, and set aside leisure time in which to rid themselves of stressful feelings. If they do not handle time pressures successfully, they may begin to feel overloaded and stressed.

**CHALLENGE.** Typically we think of a stressful event as something that threatens us in some way. But stressful events can also be happy, positive events. It is easy to understand why threats produce stress, but why do **challenges** cause stress? Think back to your high-school graduation. It was no doubt a turning point in your life. You were probably excited to be leaving school but were probably also experiencing stress due to the many decisions about your future that were now going to have to be made. Many of the changes you planned were positive but nonetheless required focus and effort. This shift from what we know and can predict is in itself stressful. So stress doesn't have to be a bad thing. It can serve to motivate each of us to strive for great things.

These four aspects of stress share a commonality: They affect us physiologically. When an individual experiences stress, there is a characteristic physiological reaction within the body that has important short-term and long-term implications. Hans Selye's model is probably the best-known account of these important physical processes.

## STUDYING STRESS: FOCUS ON PHYSIOLOGY

**SELYE'S GENERAL ADAPTATION SYNDROME.** Working first at McGill University and then at the University of Montreal, Hans Selye (1907–1982) systematically studied stressors and stress. Selye (1956, 1976) conceptualized people's responses to stress in terms of a *general adaptation syndrome*. (A *syndrome* is a set of responses; in the case of stress, these responses include behaviours and physical symptoms.) Selye's work initiated thousands of studies on stress and stress reactions, and Selye himself published more than 1600 articles on the topic.

According to Selye, people respond to any stressor similarly, regardless of the type of stressor. This response occurs in three stages: (1) an initial short-term stage of alarm, (2) a longer period of resistance, and (3) a final stage of exhaustion (see Figure 14.2). During the *alarm stage*, people experience increased physiological arousal. They become excited, anxious, or frightened. Bodily resources are mobilized. Metabolism speeds up dramatically, heart rate increases, and blood is diverted

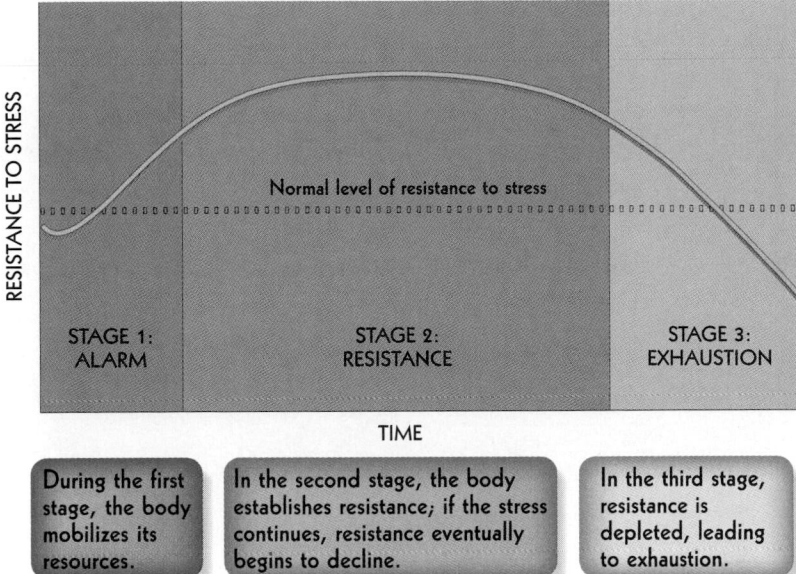

FIGURE 14.2
Selye's General Adaptation
Syndrome

According to Hans Selye, a person's
response to a stressor can be
divided into three stages: alarm,
resistance, and exhaustion.

RESISTANCE TO STRESS

Normal level of resistance to stress

STAGE 1:
ALARM

STAGE 2:
RESISTANCE

STAGE 3:
EXHAUSTION

TIME

During the first stage, the body mobilizes its resources.

In the second stage, the body establishes resistance; if the stress continues, resistance eventually begins to decline.

In the third stage, resistance is depleted, leading to exhaustion.

from the skin and extremities to the brain and internal organs (Selye, 1976). (The responses involve activation of the sympathetic nervous system; see Chapter 2.)

When stress continues, people's responses change. Because people cannot remain highly aroused for very long, *resistance* occurs. During this stage, physiological and behavioural responses become more moderate (but still elevated) and sustained. People in the resistance stage may appear normal, but their physiological responses are not. They continue to operate at a heightened level, and they are often irritable, impatient, and easy to anger; they may experience loss of appetite, sleep problems, headaches, or hormone imbalances. This stage can persist for a few hours, several days, or even years, although eventually resistance begins to decline.

The final stage is *exhaustion*. Stress saps psychological and physical energy; adaptability is depleted. If people don't reduce their level of stress, they can become so exhausted physically, mentally, and emotionally that they give up. Selye believed that serious illness or even death could occur in the exhaustion stage.

This view of stress predicts that any event that requires adaptation is stressful and that illness and stress are linked; that is, stress can make people sick. To test the link between stress and illness, researchers must have ways to measure stress, and several assessments of stress have been created.

**THE HOLMES–RAHE SCALE.** Among the many researchers inspired by Selye to study stressors and refine the theory were Thomas Holmes and Richard Rahe. Their basic assumption was that stressful life events, especially those occurring in combination, damage health (Holmes & Rahe, 1967; Rahe, 1989). *Stressful life events* are prominent events in a person's life that necessitate change; this change requires adaptation, which is the source of stress. Even positive events, such as getting a new job, can produce stress.

To test their assumption, the researchers devised the Social Readjustment Rating Scale—basically a list on which individuals circle significant life events (changes) that they've recently experienced (Table 14.1 shows part of this scale). Holmes and Rahe developed a rating for each of the life events. The death of a spouse, divorce, and serious illness rate high as stressors; changes in eating or sleeping habits or vacations rate lower but still require some adaptation. A person taking the test indicates the number of events experienced, typically within the past year. A person's total score reflects the cumulative impact of stressful life events and, according to Holmes and Rahe, provides an index of the likelihood of the person

▲ Hans Selye argued that the physiological response to stress occurred in three stages.

**TABLE 14.1** *For the Active Learner:* **A Portion of the Holmes–Rahe Social Readjustment Rating Scale**

Check the events that have happened to you within the past 18 months.

| | Rank | Life Event | Value | | Rank | Life Event | Value |
|---|---|---|---|---|---|---|---|
| ☐ | 1 | Death of spouse | 100 | ☐ | 25 | Outstanding personal achievement | 28 |
| ☐ | 2 | Divorce | 73 | ☐ | 26 | Spouse begins or stops work | 26 |
| ☐ | 3 | Marital separation | 65 | ☐ | 27 | Begin or end school | 26 |
| ☐ | 4 | Jail term | 63 | ☐ | 28 | Change in living conditions | 25 |
| ☐ | 5 | Death of close family member | 63 | ☐ | 29 | Revision of personal habits | 24 |
| ☐ | 6 | Personal injury or illness | 53 | ☐ | 30 | Trouble with boss | 23 |
| ☐ | 7 | Marriage | 50 | ☐ | 31 | Change in work hours or conditions | 20 |
| ☐ | 8 | Fired at work | 47 | ☐ | 32 | Change in residence | 20 |
| ☐ | 9 | Marital reconciliation | 45 | ☐ | 33 | Change in schools | 20 |
| ☐ | 10 | Retirement | 45 | ☐ | 34 | Change in recreation | 19 |
| ☐ | 11 | Change in health of family member | 44 | ☐ | 35 | Change in church activities | 19 |
| ☐ | 12 | Pregnancy | 40 | ☐ | 36 | Change in social activities | 18 |
| ☐ | 13 | Sex difficulties | 39 | ☐ | 37 | Loan for lesser purchase (under $10 000) | 17 |
| ☐ | 14 | Gain of new family member | 39 | ☐ | 38 | Change in sleeping habits | 16 |
| ☐ | 15 | Business readjustment | 39 | ☐ | 39 | Change in number of family get-togethers | 15 |
| ☐ | 16 | Change in financial state | 38 | ☐ | 40 | Change in eating habits | 15 |
| ☐ | 17 | Death of a close friend | 37 | ☐ | 41 | Vacation | 13 |
| ☐ | 18 | Change to different line of work | 36 | ☐ | 42 | Christmas | 12 |
| ☐ | 19 | Change in number of arguments with spouse | 35 | ☐ | 43 | Minor violations of the law | 11 |
| ☐ | 20 | Mortgage or loan for major purchase | 31 | | | | |
| ☐ | 21 | Foreclosure of mortgage or loan | 30 | | | | |
| ☐ | 22 | Change in responsibilities at work | 29 | | | | |
| ☐ | 23 | Son or daughter leaving home | 29 | | | | |
| ☐ | 24 | Trouble with in-laws | 29 | | | | |

Add the points for each of the events you checked. Totals of more than 300 elevate the risk of health problems; totals below 150 reflect low risk.

(Holmes & Rahe, 1967)

▼ Even positive life events, such as getting married, may cause stress.

suffering stress-related illness in the next two years. According to Holmes and Rahe, a person who scores above 300 points will be much more likely to suffer a stress-induced physical illness than a person whose score is below 150.

Although widely used, the Holmes–Rahe scale has been sharply criticized for a number of reasons. First, most people whose scores are high do not get sick. Even people who accumulate many points are not destined to develop any illness, and most do not. That is, the relationship between life events and illness is far from perfect. Another criticism stems from the fact that the scale was based on a study of young male navy personnel, whose characteristics do not necessarily match those of the general population, especially older people, women, and low-income individuals (Shalowitz et al., 1998). In addition, the inclusion of major life events is not a comprehensive way to conceptualize stress. The Undergraduate Stress Questionnaire (Crandall, Preisler, & Aussprung, 1992) is an alternative that includes events common in the lives of university and college students. The Undergraduate Stress Questionnaire appears in Table 14.2.

**TABLE 14.2** *For the Active Learner:* **Undergraduate Stress Questionnaire**

Has this stressful event happened to you at any time during the last two weeks? If it has, please check the space next to it. If it has not, please leave the space blank.

- [ ] Lack of money
- [ ] Someone broke a promise
- [ ] Death (family member or friend)
- [ ] Dealt with incompetence at the registrar's office
- [ ] Can't concentrate
- [ ] Had a lot of tests
- [ ] Thought about unfinished work
- [ ] Someone did a "pet peeve" of yours
- [ ] It's finals week
- [ ] Lived with boyfriend/girlfriend
- [ ] No sleep
- [ ] Applied to graduate school
- [ ] Felt need for transportation
- [ ] Sick, injury
- [ ] Bad haircut today
- [ ] Victim of a crime
- [ ] Had a class presentation
- [ ] Job requirements changed
- [ ] Applied for a job
- [ ] Assignments in all classes due the same day
- [ ] Fought with boyfriend/girlfriend
- [ ] No time to eat
- [ ] Have a hard upcoming week
- [ ] Felt some peer pressure
- [ ] Lots of deadlines to meet
- [ ] Went into test unprepared
- [ ] Worked while in school
- [ ] Arguments, conflict of values with friends
- [ ] Had a hangover
- [ ] Problems with computer

- [ ] Lost something (especially wallet)
- [ ] Death of a pet
- [ ] Bothered by having no social support from family
- [ ] Performed poorly at a task
- [ ] Did worse than expected on test
- [ ] Problem getting home from bar when drunk
- [ ] Used a fake ID
- [ ] Had an interview
- [ ] Had projects, research papers due
- [ ] Did badly on a test
- [ ] Can't finish everything you needed to do
- [ ] Heard bad news
- [ ] No sex for a while
- [ ] Someone cut ahead of you in line
- [ ] Had confrontation with an authority figure
- [ ] Maintained a long-distance relationship with boyfriend/girlfriend
- [ ] Crammed for a test
- [ ] Parents getting divorce
- [ ] Dependent on other people
- [ ] Feel unorganized
- [ ] Broke up with boyfriend/girlfriend
- [ ] Tried to decide on major
- [ ] Feel isolated
- [ ] Had roommate conflicts
- [ ] Chequebook didn't balance
- [ ] Visit from a relative and entertaining them

- [ ] Decision to have sex is on your mind
- [ ] Car/bike broke down, flat tire, etc.
- [ ] Parents controlling with money
- [ ] Couldn't find a parking space
- [ ] Noise disturbed you while trying to study
- [ ] Someone borrowed something without permission
- [ ] Had to ask for money
- [ ] Got a traffic ticket
- [ ] Talked with a professor
- [ ] Change of environment (new doctor, dentist, etc.)
- [ ] Exposed to upsetting TV show, book, or movie
- [ ] Got to class late
- [ ] Erratic schedule
- [ ] Found out boyfriend/girlfriend cheated on you
- [ ] Can't understand your professor
- [ ] Tried to get into your major or university/college
- [ ] Missed your period and waiting
- [ ] Coping with addictions
- [ ] Registration for classes
- [ ] Stayed up late writing a paper
- [ ] Property stolen
- [ ] Someone you expected to call did not
- [ ] Holiday
- [ ] Sat through a boring class
- [ ] Favourite sporting team lost
- [ ] Thought about future

Count the number of check marks. Students with higher scores are more likely to need health care (as measured by going to the student health centre or infirmary) than students with lower scores.

Did this stress inventory do a better job of capturing the stress in your life than Holmes and Rahe's Social Readjustment Rating Scale?

(Crandall, Preisler, & Aussprung, 1992)

As many items on the Undergraduate Stress Questionnaire reflect, the stressors faced by most people are seldom major events or crises; people experience stress from day-to-day irritations and difficulties. These irritations and their effects are more closely related to the conceptualization of stress put forth by Richard Lazarus.

**LAZARUS AND STRESS.**   This broad definition recognizes that everyone experiences stress at times, but also that stress is an interpreted state; it is a response by an individual. Richard Lazarus (1993), a leader in the study of emotion and stress, asserts that people *actively negotiate* between the demands of the environment (stressors) and personal beliefs and behaviours. Therefore, stress is the result of an interaction of events and people's evaluation of those events. Cognitive researchers refer to this active negotiation as *cognitive appraisal*. Sometimes the arousal that stressors bring about initiates positive actions; sometimes its effects are detrimental. Thinking, "I can't possibly handle this!" is likely to lead to a less positive response than is thinking, "This is my chance to really show my stuff!" (Lyubomirsky & Tucker, 1998). See Figure 14.3 for an overview of the responses that occur after a cognitive appraisal has identified an event as a stressor.

What influences an individual's cognitive appraisal, determining whether a particular event will be stressful? The answer lies in the extent to which the person is familiar with the event, how much she or he has anticipated the event, and how much control she or he has over the event and the response to it. For example, the first day of a new course brings excitement and some apprehension about the instructor's expectations and whether the time commitment for the course will be burdensome; the second or third time the class meets is usually much less worrisome. When people can predict events and are familiar with them, they feel more in control, more confident that they can have some impact on the future. That is, when people appraise that they have the resources to cope with an event, that event is not a threat. When people believe that they lack the resources to cope with a threat, they experience stress. This view of stress includes a wider variety of potential stressors plus individual evaluation of these events. The concept of hassles—inconveniences and annoyances in everyday life—captures this view better than major life events and has led to the development of an alternative assessment.

**THE HASSLES SCALE.**   Even routine life events can cause stress. Indeed, Lazarus and his colleagues propose that routine events are more closely related to the experience of stress and physical problems than are major life events. Lazarus and his colleagues (Kanner et al., 1981) developed an assessment, the Hassles Scale, that is oriented toward measuring these events. People completing this assessment respond to 117 potential hassles, rating each according to how much the situation is a hassle.

FIGURE 14.3

**The Effect of Cognitive Appraisal on Responses to Stressors**

Depending on how a potential stressor (for example, entering a tied game in overtime) is evaluated, its impact can vary emotionally, physiologically, and behaviourally.

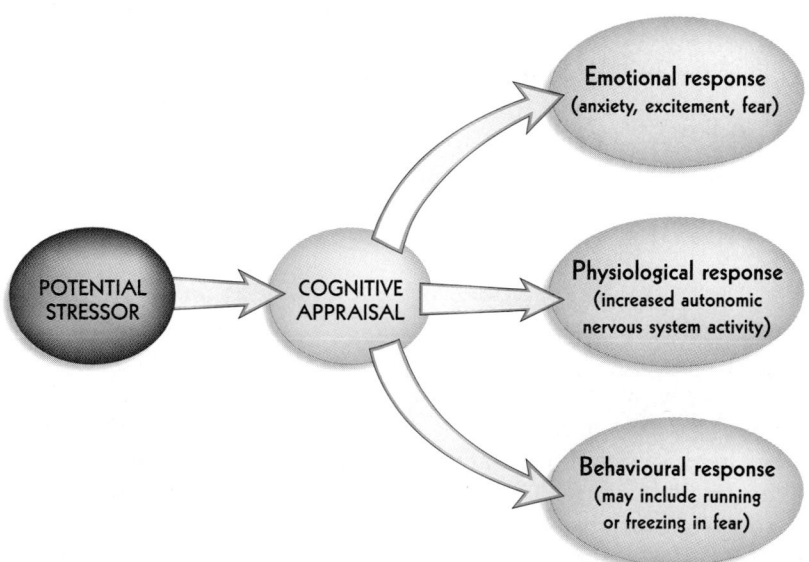

A later, streamlined revision of this scale contains only 53 items (DeLongis, Folkman, & Lazarus, 1988). Table 14.3 presents the 10 daily hassles most frequently cited as sources of stress. According to research, daily hassles are more strongly correlated with physical and psychological health than are major life events. Both major life events and daily hassles relate to health, but in somewhat different ways (Cassidy, 2000). In addition, hassles affect the quality of intimate relationships (Tesser & Beach, 1998) and symptoms such as headaches (Fernandez & Sheffield, 1996). Therefore, the concept of hassles adds to the explanation of the relationship between stress and health.

## SOURCES OF STRESS

Researchers have taken both life events and hassles approaches to studying the impact of stressors. As a result, researchers have examined a variety of situations, ranging from war and earthquakes to traffic congestion and deadlines.

| TABLE 14.3 | Life's Little Hassles— The Top 10 |
|---|---|
| 1. | Concerns about weight |
| 2. | Health of a family member |
| 3. | Rising prices of common goods |
| 4. | Home maintenance |
| 5. | Too many things to do |
| 6. | Misplacing or losing things |
| 7. | Yard work or outside home maintenance |
| 8. | Property, investments, or taxes |
| 9. | Crime |
| 10. | Physical appearance |

**CATASTROPHES AND STRESS.** Throughout history, there have been many *catastrophes*—events of massive proportion and destruction—that have affected people and communities profoundly. Catastrophes can be either natural disasters, such as earthquakes and hurricanes, or events with a human origin, such as airplane crashes and terrorist attacks.

How do people respond to catastrophes? How do people cope with stressors of such magnitude? It turns out that people are amazingly resilient (a topic we'll consider later), but the impact of a catastrophe—of a natural disaster, war, or traumatic event—can be long lasting (see *Psychology in Action*). Mental health practitioners see many clients who continue to suffer long after an event that has changed their lives. For example, in 1989 a group of U.S. Army veterans returned with several therapists to Vietnam, where they had waged war more than two decades earlier. This time, however, their mission was not to fight an enemy but to heal their own psychological wounds. One veteran reported that he had been haunted for years by nightmares of his combat experiences. This severe stress-related disorder is termed **post-traumatic stress disorder (PTSD)**—a psychological disorder that may become evident after a person has undergone severe stress caused by some type of disaster. The likelihood that a person will experience PTSD at some time during his or her life is about 8 percent (Kessler et al., 2003). Common symptoms of PTSD are vivid, intrusive recollections or re-experiencing of the traumatic event and occasional lapses of normal consciousness (Morgan et al., 1998). People may develop anxiety, depression, or exceptionally aggressive behaviour; they may avoid situations that resemble the traumatizing events. Such behaviours may eventually interfere with daily functioning, family interactions, and health.

Although most veterans of the Vietnam War did not develop PTSD, thousands did. Decades later, these individuals still endure sleep problems, relive painful experiences, have difficulty concentrating, and experience feelings of panic and alienation (Kagan et al., 1999). Initially, combat veterans were diagnosed with PTSD, and the disorder was considered to be confined mostly to men. But others who experienced traumatic events were considered and found to suffer from similar symptoms. Now a wide variety of experiences are recognized to raise the risk for PTSD. Veterans are at elevated risk (Hankin et al., 1999; Keane, 1998; Rosebush, 1998; Ursano et al., 1995), but victims of all types of trauma, especially those who are the victims of violence, are at risk (Dohrenwend, 2000). Divers trying to recover the wreckage and bodies of victims of Swissair flight 111 in Peggy's Cove suffered symptoms of PTSD after a prolonged period of gruesome work.

**POST-TRAUMATIC STRESS DISORDER (PTSD)**

Psychological disorder that may become evident after a person has undergone extreme stress caused by some type of disaster; common symptoms include vivid, intrusive recollections or re-experiences of the traumatic event and occasional lapses of normal consciousness.

## Psychology in the Aftermath of Human Disaster

Following any major disaster, survivors and observers are left wondering why some survived when others did not. *Survivor guilt* is a term used to describe the feelings of some that emerge alive from a disaster that took the lives of others. Although irrational, these survivors blame themselves for surviving the fate of those who died. Survivors suffer from guilt and self-blame, which may result in either adaptive or maladaptive coping as individuals struggle to address feelings of powerlessness and loss (Garwood, 1996). Those with survivor guilt experience chronic and diffuse anger, anxiety, sleep disturbances, flashbacks, hypervigilance (constant alertness), and depression.

Such guilt reactions are particularly salient when disasters have been deliberately caused by other human beings, such as through war or terrorism. The tragic events of September 11, 2001, in the United States have once again raised the spectre of survivor guilt in the public consciousness.

The Nazi attempt to annihilate the Jewish people, resulting in the murder of 6 million individuals, is one of the worst atrocities of all time. An ongoing research project by Peter Suedfeld and his colleagues (1997, 1998a, 1998b, 2000, 2003) at the University of British Columbia has been attempting to answer the many psychological questions that arise following human-produced disaster. The Holocaust has left us with many psychological questions that Suedfeld and many others (Dimsdale, 1974; Garwood, 1996; Krell & Sherman, 1997; Langer, 1991; McCann & Pearlman, 1990) have been attempting to answer.

Suedfeld, Fell, and Krell (1998a) suggest that the majority of survivors suffer no long-lasting distress and further cite evidence to demonstrate that the majority of Holocaust survivors, even young children released from death camps, go on to establish fairly normal lives in which they experience general contentment. Most survivors have a positive and powerful desire to bear witness to the events they were part of and to remember those who did not survive. Others, however, become unable to escape the past, paying penance through irrational and unending guilt. They tell themselves agonizingly and repeatedly: "It should have been me," "I should have done more," "I have no right to be happy when others are dead," and so on.

What differentiates a positively adapting survivor from one who is suffering from overpowering guilt? Suedfeld (2000) reports that survivors were more likely to report external factors, such as luck or help from others, as a reason for their survival than were age-matched Jewish respondents who had not directly experienced Nazi persecution. In contrast, internal factors such as determination or strength of will were less likely to be cited as reasons for survival. It may be that overcoming the belief that one has little control in the outcome of one's life may have a role to play in the acquisition or mastery of survivor guilt.

In the final analysis, Suedfeld pays tribute to "the hardiness and resilience of the survivors . . . emphasizing the strengths and positive characteristics of human beings" (2003, p. 6).

An increasing number of studies are focusing on the psychological aftermath of natural disasters such as earthquakes, tornadoes, and floods (Wang et al., 2000), as well as on the impact on survivors of traumatic events such as the displacement of refugees (Weine et al., 2001) and refugee children (Ajdukovic & Ajdukovic, 1998), severe accidents (Schnyder et al., 2001), and cancer (Kahana, Deimling, & Bowman, 2000). Peter Suedfeld and others have studied the impact of the Second World War on survivors (Suedfeld, 2000, 2003; Yehuda et al., 1998).

Despite the initial emphasis on men, women have been found to be more susceptible to PTSD than men (Stein, Walker, & Forde, 2000). Rape and other violence at the hands of intimate partners such as boyfriends or husbands, and sexual abuse during childhood are all experiences that elevate the risk for PTSD, and women are more likely than men to have such experiences (Golding, 1999).

**UNHEALTHY ENVIRONMENTS AND STRESS.** Some environments may be hazardous to people's health. A neighbourhood environment may contain many factors that contribute to stress. Certainly toxins and pollution are stressors that also carry health risks, but even without such obvious health threats, certain neighbourhoods contain elements that produce stress. Many of these factors revolve around poverty and the communities in which poor people live. People in *low socio-economic groups* often live in overcrowded and substandard housing, lack access to services such as banks and stores, experience high noise levels, and live with the threat of crime and violence (Taylor, Repetti, & Seeman, 1997). These situations often combine to produce the type of stressors called hassles, such as having trouble cashing a cheque, and the type of life events that are related to PTSD, such as witnessing or being the victim of violence. Research indicates that the chance of witnessing violence is especially high for children living in a poor, inner-city neighbourhood, and this experience is related to stress and anxiety (Cooley-Quille et al., 2001).

Even people who are wealthy do not escape the stresses of urban living. Eric Graig (1993) formulated the term *urban press* to describe the multitude of factors that combine in modern urban life. These factors include crowding, pollution, noise, commuting stress, and fear of crime. Graig argues that these factors are a constant presence for city dwellers, and their combination produces a level of stress that is not accounted for by each stressor considered individually.

These environments can be detrimental in several ways—when safety is threatened, when the environment prevents people from forming social ties, and when conflicts occur in schools, in families, and on the street. Any or all of them can affect physiology and health. Thus, people who live in poverty are at higher risk for stress, anxiety, and associated health consequences.

Although unhealthy environments produce stress, the evolutionary point of view hypothesizes that environmental stress may not be all bad. In this view, environmental stress is a force for selection and evolution (Hoffmann & Hercus, 2000). For example, the presence of chemical pesticides has produced changes in some insect species so that they are resistant to these chemicals. The environmental stressors in modern city life may act similarly, providing a means of rapid evolution as a way to adapt to these stressful conditions.

**DISCRIMINATION AND STRESS.** Discrimination is an all-too-common experience, and people perceive that they are discriminated against on the basis of ethnicity, sex, and sexual orientation. A survey of Canadians showed that 7 percent of participants said they had been the target of discrimination in the previous 12 months (Canadian Human Rights Commission, 1979). In addition, there was a substantial relationship between perception of discrimination and mental health problems.

Discrimination and unfair treatment are factors in feeling stressed, and the combination of discrimination with poverty showed a potent effect in producing distress in a study of African Americans (Schultz et al., 2000). See *Introduction to Research Basics* for a discussion on how stress from discrimination affects individuals from Aboriginal backgrounds. Language problems and the lack of familiarity with the culture can make daily tasks into hassles. Immigrants are more likely than native-born people to be poor and affected by the stressors related to poverty. A

▲ Following the crash of Swissair flight 111 in Peggy's Cove, Nova Scotia, many of the rescue and recovery workers given the task of finding victims' bodies and debris from the crash suffered symptoms of PTSD.

## Racism and Reactivity

Research has established that prejudice is typically a significant source of stress and negatively impacts quality of life. Testing a sample of residents of Prince George, British Columbia, researchers Alex Michalos of the University of Northern British Columbia and Bruno Zumbo of the University of British Columbia (2001) investigated the relationship between levels of ethnic or cultural diversity, social cohesion, and prejudice and quality of life.

**Design.** The study had a *quasi-experimental design* that constructed the independent variable, based on participants' self-reports, as Aboriginal, non-Aboriginal visible minority, or anything else. The researchers measured several dependent variables, including preference for one's own ethnic group, perception of the fairness of treatment of minorities, and general quality of life.

**Hypothesis.** Ethnic or cultural diversity, differences in social cohesion, and/or prejudice affect perceptions about quality of life.

**Participants.** Seven hundred and forty-three residents of Prince George participated in the research. Participants were divided into three roughly distinct groups composed of individuals self-identified as Aboriginal, non-Aboriginal visible minority, and other.

**Procedure.** Ten-page questionnaires were mailed to a random sample of households in Prince George. These questionnaires contained items asking participants about their cultural or ethnic backgrounds, their cultural/ethnic relations, their preferences and experiences, and their satisfaction with particular domains of their lives (for example, job satisfaction, relationships). The questionnaire also contained two pages of demographic questions.

**Results.** On all significant comparisons, participants with Aboriginal backgrounds reported a generally lower quality of life than did those in either of the other two groups. The quality of life scores in the other two groups were almost identical. Members of the largest group tended to be the most prejudiced and the most optimistic, whereas people with Aboriginal backgrounds tended to be the least optimistic and the least prejudiced. People in the non-Aboriginal visible minority background tended to fall between the other two groups.

**Conclusions.** Differences in quality of life experienced by those in the Aboriginal group could not be attributed to differences in socio-economic background. Rather, these differences were largely attributable to differences in life satisfaction within particular domains and, to a lesser extent, to cultural/ethnic attitude measures such as personal fair treatment. In spite of the negative aspects of prejudice, it would appear from this research that identifying with a particular ethnic group can provide the kind of support that protects individuals from the stresses that can arise from inclusion in a stigmatized visible minority group.

study conducted in Toronto by Ken and Karen Dion (Dion, Dion, & Pak, 1992) explored the factors involved in predicting the level of stress experienced by new members of the local Chinese community. The data showed that the more successful and more adapted the immigrants were to Canadian life, the less stress they experienced. Stress levels are also significantly lower if immigrants can settle into a community of people from their own cultural background (Baker, 1993).

Sexist discrimination is also a stressor. Women are the targets of sexist discrimination and harassment much more often than men are, and these experiences produce stress (Klonoff, Landrine, & Campbell, 2000). Indeed, women who experience a high level of sexist discrimination feel its effects in terms of physical symptoms, whereas women whose experience of sexist discrimination is low report stress levels similar to men's. For some women, discrimination is a significant factor in their lives.

Gays, lesbians, and bisexuals also experience discrimination because of their sexual orientation (DiPlacido, 1998). Indeed, having any sexual orientation other than heterosexual is a stigma in our culture. Gays, lesbians, and bisexuals are a minority group and subject to stress from discrimination. Any such individuals who decide to reveal their sexual orientation often experience conflict; research indicates that this conflict may have no stress-free resolution. Revealing a gay or lesbian sexual orientation puts a person in a position of facing discrimination, but being "in the closet" is also stressful (Cole et al., 1996). For those who are not heterosexual, either choice potentially brings stress.

**PERSONAL FACTORS AND STRESS.** People who experience catastrophic events and the stressors associated with poverty may also face stress from personal factors. People who experience no catastrophe and only minor stress from the environment still have stress from the workplace, personal relationships, and time pressure. Stress is an unavoidable part of life.

Workplaces are environments and may contain environmental stressors such as toxins, noise, and crowding. However, work presents an additional array of stressors. People tend to think of executives who make many important decisions as experiencing a great deal of stress, but research indicates that the freedom to make decisions actually *decreases* a job's stress (de Jonge et al., 2000; Karasek, 1979). Instead, high-stress jobs tend to be the ones that impose high demands on workers but give them little latitude to make decisions or to exert control. The types of jobs that are high in stress include middle-level managers, inner-city high-school teachers, customer service agents, waiters and waitresses, and emergency workers. These jobs combine high demands and low decision-making power; this combination tends to create stress for workers.

A number of additional factors associated with work can produce stress. Demanding jobs are not necessarily stressful; when workers feel in control of the important aspects of their jobs, they may see high demands as a challenge. Alternatively, when workers experience high demands and low control on the job, they are more likely to feel stressed than challenged (Cheng et al., 2000). Workers who feel many constraints, who work at night, who work a lot of overtime, and who are under constant deadline pressure experience increased stress (Ettner & Grzywacz, 2001). When workers feel adequately rewarded for their job performance, they are less likely to feel stressed than workers who feel that their rewards are not proportional to their efforts on the job (de Jonge et al., 2000).

The dangers of low-level jobs apply to men as well as to women (Wamala et al., 2000). A specific comparison of female managers and female clerks showed that the clerks evaluated stressors as more severe, less controllable, and more distressing than did the managers (Long, 1998). These results point to low-level rather than high-level jobs as stressful. However, even high-level jobs can be stressful. A study of physicians indicated that both male and female doctors felt stressed by the time pressure of keeping up with scheduled appointments and the amount of work they were required to do (Rout, 1999). Therefore, all types of jobs have stressful components, and very few people escape on-the-job stress. Despite the many possibilities for stress on the job, being without a job or being uncertain about continued employment is even more stressful (Ferrie et al., 2001).

Personal relationships are a potential source of stress, both at work and at home. At work, interactions with co-workers can be sources of satisfaction or stress (Monnier et al., 1998). Support from supervisors and co-workers can make a critical difference in the experience of stress on the job; supportive relationships are positive factors in work and life satisfaction. Co-workers who are harassing or violent create workplace problems that produce stress not only for the targets of these unacceptable behaviours but also for the entire staff (Bennett & Lehman, 1999).

Work stress and personal relationships also intersect in the challenge of balancing job and family commitments. This balancing act is a major source of stress, especially for women. Traditionally, women have been the primary caregivers for children and family. As women have entered the workforce, they have also kept the caregiver role, creating difficulties in fulfilling both roles (Hochschild,

▲ Deadlines, exams, and schoolwork may be sources of stress for adolescents.

1997; Williams, 2000). Men who work long hours sacrifice family time, and their children feel this choice even more sharply than their wives do (Crouter et al., 2001). Men who have become more involved in family life and wish to devote more time to home and family experience problems in justifying this choice to their employers (Hochschild, 1997). These men are in a position similar to that of employed women who feel the time bind and conflict of balancing family and work demands.

Marriage is celebrated as a positive event in many cultures. Nonetheless, adjusting to married life means becoming familiar with new experiences, responding in new ways, and having less control over many aspects of day-to-day life—all of which can be stressful. Even among couples married for years, daily hassles increase stress between partners (Harper, Schaalje, & Sandberg, 2000). Also, at times, marriage involves interpersonal conflict, which may produce stress. One partner may not be fulfilling obligations or may be preoccupied in some way, causing the spouse to feel left out; both possibilities may bring about stress and even health problems (Tesser & Beach, 1998). One prominent source of stress for many couples is conflict over household chores; men's lower contribution to household work is a significant source of stress for women (Bird, 1999). Stresses in marriage are certainly problems, but ending a marriage creates even more stress (McKelvey & McKenry, 2000).

Lack of time is another common source of stress. Everyone faces deadlines: Students must complete tests before class ends, auto workers must keep pace with the assembly line, and taxpayers must file their returns by April 30. People have only a limited number of hours each day in which to accomplish tasks, and people who work long hours often have no time for leisure and family. If people do not handle time pressure successfully, they may begin to feel overloaded and stressed. Employees mention time pressure constraints as a source of stress in several different work settings (Rout, 1999; Teuchmann, Totterdell, & Parker, 1999). One possibility for more time is flexible or fewer hours spent working, but most people are unwilling to take that option, even when their workplace offers it (Fast & Frederick, 1996).

Stress affects children as well as adults. Children are much less able to change or control the circumstances in which they find themselves (Band & Weisz, 1988). They often experience stress in school, and an abusive or neglectful home life may produce symptoms of PTSD in children. In fact, Bruce Perry (1994), the former Provincial Medical Director in Children's Mental Health for the Alberta Mental Health Board, has shown that early experience with PTSD can have neurological effects on young children. Children often respond to stress with some type of physical reaction, a headache, a stomach ache, or apathy (Walker et al., 2001).

▼ Stress can affect a person's behaviour, making responses disorganized and ineffective.

## RESPONSES TO STRESS

People respond to stress on physiological as well as on behavioural and psychological levels, and individuals vary in their responses on each of these levels. The basic idea underlying the work of many researchers is that stress activates physiological responses that can result in disease. Psychologists who study stress typically divide the stress reaction into physiological and behavioural components.

**THE PHYSIOLOGY OF STRESS.** Researchers such as James, Lange, and Cannon (discussed in Chapter 9) studied emotions, focusing on when an emotion was felt in response to a stressful incident—during or after the actual event. *Physiologically*, the stress response is characterized by arousal of the sympathetic division of the autonomic nervous system (see Chapter 2, p. 58). This arousal consists of a host of changes, including increased heart rate, faster but shallower breathing, higher blood pressure, sweating palms, and dilation of the pupils. This array of physiological changes begins in the brain, with the activation of the pituitary gland and the hypothalamus. This action produces the release of a hormone that stimulates the adrenal glands, located above the kidneys. These glands release several hormones related to stress, including cortisol and epinephrine, each of which produces specific effects. The action of epinephrine produces the variety of physiological reactions associated with stress. Cortisol allows for the mobilization of energy reserves and decreases in inflammation. Figure 14.4 shows these responses. This arousal of the sympathetic division of the autonomic nervous system mobilizes the body for fight or flight, preparing for a physiological response to a stressor. It may be that this response was more adaptive in our evolutionary history than it is today; cortisol and epinephrine and the reactions they provoke have been implicated in the health risks related to stress.

**BEHAVIOUR AND STRESS.** *Behaviourally*, stress and arousal are related. As we saw in Chapter 9, Canadian psychologist Donald Hebb (1972), who worked at McGill University and passed away in 1985, argued that effective behaviour depends on a person's state of arousal. When people are moderately aroused, they behave with optimal effectiveness. When they are underaroused, they lack the stimulation to behave effectively. Overarousal tends to produce disorganized and ineffective behaviour, particularly if the tasks people undertake are complex. (Figure 14.5 shows the effects of arousal on task performance.)

A moderate level of stress and the arousal that accompanies it may be unavoidable and even desirable. Arousal keeps people active and involved. It impels students to study, athletes to excel during competition, and workers to perform better on the job. In short, some levels of stress and arousal can be beneficial, helping people achieve their potential. On the other hand, some levels of stress are related to a variety of diseases.

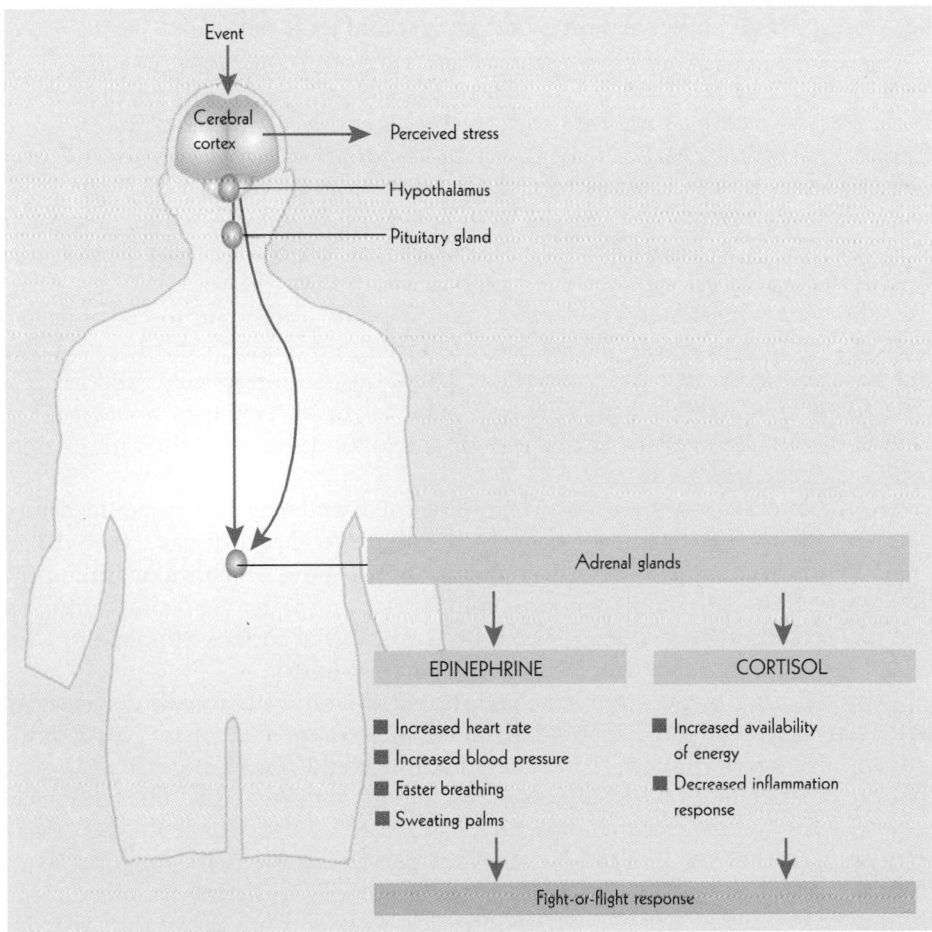

**FIGURE 14.4**
**Physiological Reactions to Stress**

Perceiving stress initiates a cascade of effects, including in the nervous system and hormones.

FIGURE 14.5

## Effects of Arousal on Task Performance

When arousal is low, task performance is poor or nonexistent. Performance is usually best at moderate levels of arousal. High levels of arousal usually improve performance on simple tasks but impair performance on complex tasks (such as surgery).

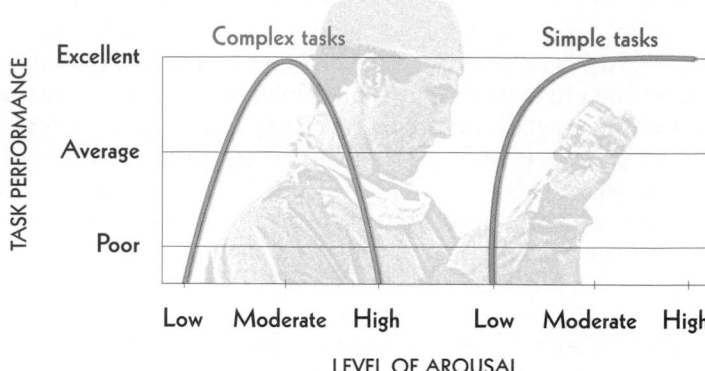

## STRESS AND HEALTH

Mothers, grandmothers, and self-help books have long advised people to reduce their levels of stress to keep from getting sick, and research now supports their advice. Stress prompts a variety of physical responses, but its effect on the development of disease is not direct; rather, stress responses cause a range of physiological reactions that can initiate various disease processes. Therefore, stress has a relationship to many diseases, including the five major causes of death in Canada: heart disease, cancer, stroke, lung disease, and accidental injuries. However, researchers have been most interested in the link between stress and heart disease. Stress elevates blood pressure, but that increase is temporary; the underlying *cause* of hypertension is currently unknown. Stress can be a problem for people with hypertension, but it is not the cause of hypertension. Therefore, the link between stress and heart disease is not obvious and quite complex.

**HEART DISEASE AND STRESS.** Heart disease and high blood pressure account for more than half of the total deaths each year in Canada. In 2000, 76 476 Canadians died of heart attacks or related circulatory issues (Statistics Canada, 2003). The coronary arteries furnish the blood supply to the heart muscle, and when those arteries are blocked, the heart muscle no longer gets blood, precipitating a heart attack. The most common underlying cause is the buildup of deposits inside the coronary arteries, which restricts blood flow.

The behavioural factors related to this physiological condition have been the subject of intensive research, and several behaviours relate to the disease process that results in coronary artery blockage. Therefore, both physicians and psychologists accept that lifestyle factors are important to the development of heart disease. One of the first attempts to link behaviour and heart disease was the formulation of the Type A behaviour pattern.

In the late 1950s, physicians Meyer Friedman and Ray Rosenman identified a pattern of behaviour that they believe contributes to heart disease; they called it Type A behaviour (Friedman & Rosenman, 1974). **Type A behaviour** is the behaviour pattern of individuals who are competitive, impatient, hostile, and always striving to do more in less time. **Type B behaviour** is the pattern exhibited by people who are calmer, more patient, less hurried, and less hostile.

Early studies of the Type A behaviour pattern showed a positive association with heart disease; that is, Type A individuals were more likely than Type B individuals to have heart attacks. The concept became well known, and people accepted that the combination of Type A behaviours significantly increased the risk for heart disease. More recent research, however, casts doubt on the concept. This research suggests that the overall Type A behaviour pattern is not a risk for heart disease (Johnsen, Espenes, & Gillard, 1998; Lilla et al., 1998). Criticisms include the applicability of the concept to Western culture and to men more than to other groups.

## TYPE A BEHAVIOUR

Behaviour pattern characterized by competitiveness, impatience, hostility, and constant efforts to do more in less time.

## TYPE B BEHAVIOUR

Behaviour pattern exhibited by people who are calmer, more patient, and less hurried than Type A individuals.

Heart disease is a leading cause of death across the world, but the Type A behaviour pattern fits middle-aged North American businessmen better than other people. Women exhibit Type A behaviour, but some evidence suggests that this behaviour pattern does not relate to heart disease in women (Orth-Gormér, 1998).

Researchers began to examine components of the Type A behaviour pattern for their toxic effects and found that hostility and anger relate to the development of heart disease (Madigan, Dale, & Cross, 1997; Morren, 1998). Feelings of suspiciousness, mistrust of others, and thinking the worst of people are associated with increased risk for coronary heart disease. Anger is associated with increased blockage of arteries in women (Matthews et al., 1998). Anger and anxiety are also associated with death from cardiovascular disease (Suinn, 2001). In addition, both the experience of anger and its expression are related to heart disease. That is, even people who only experience the emotion of anger and do not express it are at increased risk. To examine your own behaviours and attitudes that relate to heart disease risk, answer the questions in Figure 14.6.

**FIGURE 14.6**
**For the Active Learner: Estimating Risk Factors for Heart Disease**

Rate the following statements according to how each applies to you. Write the number that represents your rating in the blank to the left of each statement. Use the same scale for both sets of questions.

| 1 | 2 | 3 | 4 | 5 | 6 | 7 |
|---|---|---|---|---|---|---|
| Not at all | | | Sometimes | | | All the time |

**Set 1**

___ I get impatient when people do things slowly.

___ I experience a lot of time pressure.

___ I feel the pressure to get ahead and succeed.

___ I do many things fast—talking, walking, eating, and so forth.

___ People consider me short-tempered.

___ I work long hours.

___ I often want to (and sometimes actually do) finish other people's sentences.

___ I think that it is important to acquire a lot of money and possessions.

___ I often lose my temper.

___ I hate to stand in line.

___ It is not necessary for others to impose deadlines; I set them for myself.

**Set 2**

___ People seem to annoy me intentionally.

___ I often raise my voice.

___ Many situations make me angry.

___ I expect the worst from people, and that's what usually happens.

___ Although I often feel angry, I try to hide these feelings.

___ I have a "short fuse" when it comes to tolerating incompetence.

___ Being caught in slow traffic frustrates me so much that I want to yell at the other drivers (and sometimes, I do).

___ It's not wise to trust people.

___ Sometimes I think people single me out for bad treatment.

___ I try to control my temper, but I often lose it.

___ I express my anger physically by hitting, kicking, slapping, or throwing things.

If you rated many of the statements in Set 1 with 6s or 7s, then you have characteristics consistent with the Type A behaviour pattern.

If you marked 6s or 7s to many of the items in Set 2, your responses indicate that you experience a lot of hostility and anger, and you tend to express or suppress these feelings.

Although the Type A behaviour pattern is popularly associated with the development of heart disease, the experience and expression of anger have a much stronger relationship. So, indications of Type A behaviour based on the first set of questions do not elevate your behavioural risk of coronary heart disease as much as high ratings on the second set.

The link between anger and heart disease may come about through the physiological changes that occur in response to this emotion, which is the same as the stress response—activation of the sympathetic division of the autonomic nervous system. However, hostility and anger are not the same as stress. Therefore, the experience of stress relates to the development of heart disease, but the relationship is complex. For people who have coronary heart disease, however, the experience of stress increases the chances of sudden heart attack (Bosma et al., 1998) and fatal heart attack (Niaura & Goldstein, 1995). Therefore, several lines of research have linked stress and heart disease.

Another link between heart disease and stress has become apparent from a situation generated by world politics. Following the collapse of the Soviet Union, heart disease deaths skyrocketed in Russia and in countries that had been under the control of the Soviet Union. Stress has been implicated in this epidemic (Stone, 2000; Weidner, 2000). Some researchers argue that when communism collapsed, people felt optimistic for a better life that did not happen. Instead, people experienced uncertainty and economic turmoil that translated into feelings of stress, pessimism, and depression. The incidence of heart disease rose dramatically and life expectancy decreased, especially among middle-aged men. Researchers examined other behavioural factors that related to heart disease, such as diet and smoking, but found few differences between people in Eastern and Western Europe. Yet their heart disease death rates were dramatically different. Now researchers are concentrating on stress and depression as a source of difference. This emphasis highlights the involvement of stress and psychological factors in the development of heart disease and the importance of considering the cultural context of health and disease.

STRESS AND INFECTIOUS DISEASE.    Does it seem as if you always get a cold just after final exams are over? Do you feel as though the stress makes you vulnerable to all types of infections? That feeling may be correct. Stress is related to the development of disease through its effect on the immune system, the body's defence against infection. The immune system is a complex network of specialized cells and organs that has evolved to defend the body against attacks by "foreign invaders"—bacteria, viruses, and fungi. These specialized cells and organs are able to distinguish these foreign invaders from the body's own cells and tissues. The recognition of cells that are not part of the body prompts immune system reactions that locate, identify, and obliterate the invaders. As part of the immune response, the system acquires a way to fight against reinfection, called immunity. Thus, exposure to the same infectious agent causes a rapid immune system response and protection against reinfection—the body has acquired immunity against that specific infectious agent. For example, there are hundreds of variations on the virus that produces colds; we never get the same cold twice, but we can get a new version any time. The immune system also has cells that fight infection in more general ways, protecting against a wide range of infections.

We are exposed to many infectious agents daily, and sometimes our immune systems are not 100 percent effective. When they are not, we can get sick. The reason that some people get sick and others do not may relate to the efficiency of their immune systems. When researchers discovered that the immune system responds to behaviours and events through connections with the nervous system, the field of psychoneuroimmunology was born (Ader & Cohen, 1975). **Psychoneuroimmunology** is an interdisciplinary area of study that includes behavioural, neurological, and immune factors and their relationship to the development of disease (see *Brain and Behaviour*). A basic finding from this field shows that events affecting the immune system make people more vulnerable to disease (Herbert et al., 1994; Sher, 1998).

Sheldon Cohen and his colleagues (Cohen, 1996; Cohen et al., 1998) have demonstrated that stress makes people more vulnerable to infection from the common cold. Cohen conducted a series of experiments in which he assessed the level of

PSYCHONEUROIMMUNOLOGY
[SYE-ko-NEW-ro-IM-you-NOLL-oh-gee]

An interdisciplinary area of study that includes behavioural, neurological, and immune factors and their relationship to the development of disease.

## Psychoneuroimmunology

The immune system is responsible for fighting foreign invaders in the body, much like an army defending against bacteria, viruses, and fungi that should not cross the border—the skin—and enter the body. For many years, experts believed that the immune system operated independently of the nervous and endocrine systems, performing its functions under its own directions rather than communicating with any other system. However, researchers demonstrated that the immune system can be conditioned by pairing an unconditioned stimulus (an injection of a drug that decreases immune system response) and a conditioned stimulus (the presentation of a water and saccharine solution) (Ader & Cohen, 1975). The result of the injection was an unconditioned response (a decrease in immune function) in the rats that received the immune-suppressant drug, and the conditioning was demonstrated when the immune suppression response appeared in response to the saccharine solution. This finding suggests that the immune and nervous systems interact.

The suggestion of an interaction between the immune and nervous systems prompted the development of psychoneuroimmunology (PNI), an interdisciplinary area of study that includes behavioural, neurological, and immune factors and their relationship to the development of disease. The endocrine system was soon included in the area, and researchers began to investigate this interaction among systems. One pathway is through chemicals called cytokines, which are messenger molecules in the immune system (Glaser et al., 1999). The hormones released by sympathetic nervous system arousal produce changes in cytokines, so activity in the brain affects both sympathetic nervous system activity and the messenger system for the immune system.

Research in the area of psychoneuroimmunology indicates that stressors decrease a wide variety of immune system responses and affect the risk for infectious disease (Cohen, 1996), wound healing (Marucha, Kiecolt-Glaser, & Favagehi, 1998), and recovery from surgery (Kiecolt-Glaser et al., 1998). The degree of change is typically small, which suggests that stressors are not a major source of decrease in immune system response (Ader, 2001). However, many people have immune system problems, including people under chronic stress and those with immune disorders such as HIV. For people with compromised immune systems, additional stressors could make a significant difference for immune system functioning and the ability to fight disease (Glaser et al., 1999). For people with healthy immune systems, chronic stress can have a cumulative effect, which may explain the increased number of visits to the infirmary at the end of each school semester.

---

people's stress and their moods, made sure they were healthy, and then exposed them to a combination of cold viruses. Only one-third of the people developed colds, but those who reported high stress and negative moods were much more likely to get sick than those who reported low levels of stress and positive moods.

The participants' perceptions were important, but their experience of stressful life events was an independent risk. In addition, Cohen's studies indicate that the duration of the stress may be more important than the severity in decreasing immune system function. A study on the same topic, using a naturalistic setting, confirmed the relationship between stress and vulnerability to infection with cold viruses (Takkouche, 2001). Therefore, the amount, duration, and perception of stress are all important factors in vulnerability to infection.

STRESS AND HEALTH-RELATED BEHAVIOURS. Stress has another route through which it can influence health—through behaviours that increase the risk for disease and death. We examined how stress may be related to the development of heart disease through responses mediated by activation of the sympathetic nervous system and the development of infectious disease through its effect on the immune system. However, stress also affects how people behave, including behaviours that can damage or enhance health (Schneiderman et al., 2001). For example, many people claim that smoking helps them cope with stress. Whether or not this belief is accurate, smoking is related to the development of heart disease, cancer, and chronic

> How do Selye's and Lazarus's views of stress differ? pp. 499–502

> What are the symptoms of post-traumatic stress disorder, and what types of events produce this disorder? p. 503

> How can stress cause disease? pp. 510–514

> What connection exists among the immune system, behaviour, and health? p. 512

**Be an ACTIVE LEARNER**

**THINK CRITICALLY**

> Are children or adults more vulnerable to post-traumatic stress disorder?

> Evaluate the sources of stress experienced by a 24-year-old single factory worker who is the mother of two preschool children.

**APPLY PSYCHOLOGY**

> Assess the amount of stress in your life and how you think it relates to your health. Does the concept of hassles or of life events best define your stress?

**COPING**

Process by which a person takes some action to manage, master, tolerate, or reduce environmental or internal demands that cause or might cause stress and that tax the individual's inner resources.

**RESILIENCE**

The extent to which people are flexible and respond adaptively to external or internal demands.

lung disease. These three diseases are among the leading causes of death in Canada and many other countries. Thus, this indirect link between stress and disease takes a substantial health toll.

Relief from stress is also one of the reasons people give for drinking alcohol, and alcohol is a risk for some types of cancer as well as a significant risk for accidents. Stress also influences eating, which can be either a positive or negative factor for health. Stressed people tend to eat a less healthy diet, and dietary factors are involved in heart disease and many types of cancers (Baum & Posluszny, 1999). Therefore, stress has several routes through which it can affect health. The extent to which stress will result in disease is moderated by successful coping.

# Coping

Everyone needs a way to cope with stress, and most people use a variety of strategies. People may not be aware that they choose among various ways to cope, but they do. However, most people imagine that they could choose ways to cope more effectively, and they are correct. Coping strategies need to be tailored to the individual and the situation—and some strategies are better than others.

## WHAT IS COPING?

In general, *coping* means dealing with a situation. However, for a psychologist, **coping** is the process by which a person takes some action to manage, master, tolerate, or reduce environmental and internal demands that cause or might cause stress and that will tax the individual's inner resources. This definition of coping involves five important assumptions. First, coping is constantly changing and being evaluated and is therefore a process or a strategy. Second, coping involves managing situations, not necessarily bringing them under complete control. Third, coping is effortful; it does not happen automatically. Fourth, coping aims to manage cognitive as well as behavioural events. Finally, coping is learned.

There are many types of coping strategies, and people tend to use a variety. Coping begins with the reaction to stress at the physiological level. People's bodies respond to stress with specific reactions, including changes in hormone levels, in autonomic nervous system activity, and in the levels of neurotransmitters in the brain. Effective coping strategies are developed when people learn new ways of dealing with their vulnerabilities.

## FACTORS THAT INFLUENCE COPING

People vary enormously in their ability to cope with stressors, and some of that variation is due to personal resources that contribute to **resilience**, the extent to which people are flexible and respond adaptively to external or internal demands.

A person who is resilient is said to be less vulnerable to stressors (Zuckerman, 1999). Factors that influence coping include personal resources, a sense of control, and social support.

Personal resources include a variety of factors, ranging from money to good health. Money and other material resources can be an important factor in dealing with both daily hassles, such as car problems, and life events, such as changing residence. Social skills and knowledge are also personal resources that affect coping. People who are socially skilled are better at getting along with others and are at ease in social situations. These individuals are less likely to feel stressed by having to attend a social gathering or make a speech than individuals who are less socially skilled. Knowledge is an important resource. A person who knows about automobile transmissions, for example, may not need the money that someone with less knowledge requires to get the transmission fixed. Being healthy is an obvious advantage in coping with stressors; healthy people have more energy and are able to endure the physical demands imposed by the stress response.

A sense of being in control is also important in resilience and coping. People who believe that they can control important factors in their lives have an internal (rather than an external) locus of control. As we explored in Chapter 12, people who have an internal locus of control have advantages over those who have an external locus of control, and coping with stress is one of those advantages. People who believe that they can exert control over important events and conditions in their lives have advantages, even if the things they control are minor and even if the control is only an illusion and not real. Two classic experiments demonstrated the importance of control, over even minor details. Ellen Langer and Judith Rodin (1976) demonstrated how important control could be by manipulating the amount of control residents exerted over their new rooms in a retirement home. The new residents of one floor were asked about their schedules, were encouraged to arrange the furniture to their liking, and were given a plant, which they were told was their responsibility to care for. The new residents of another floor lived in similar rooms but were not given choices or encouraged to make decisions. They also received a plant, but the staff cared for it. Those residents who had more control were happier and healthier than the comparison residents, and these advantages persisted over time (Rodin & Langer, 1977). These studies show that controlling even small details can be beneficial.

Feeling in control is a positive state of mind that leads to optimism, which has a positive relation to health. Even more interesting, the feeling of being in control does not have to be reality based to be effective; even the *illusion of control* can exert a positive effect on mental and physical health (Taylor et al., 2000). When people feel in control of their health and factors that relate to their health, they adopt more healthy behaviours, maintain better social relationships, and possibly have healthier immune systems. The personal belief in control, even if it is not entirely reality based, is healthy when this belief prompts people to behave in health-promoting ways (Peterson, 2000).

Feeling in control is the opposite of learned helplessness. People who experience learned helplessness find that rewards and punishments are not contingent on their behaviour, and they learn not to try to cope. Because they are young, children are less likely to have well-developed coping skills and are especially vulnerable to learned helplessness (Hilsman & Garber, 1995). Faced with poor coping skills and a loss of control, both children and adults stop responding (Job & Barnes, 1995). (We examined learned helplessness in Chapter 5.)

Exposure to stressful conditions is not sufficient to produce a stressed individual. Some children are separated from their parents by war and live among strangers and yet grow up to be healthy, happy adults (Palmer, 2000). Some adolescents live in poverty with the threat of violence and manage to function effectively (D'Imperio, Dubow, & Ippolito, 2000). Some people are resilient to trauma and stress. The feelings of control, self-worth, and optimism are related to resilience (Dumont & Provost, 1999).

Studies on the development of resilience have focused on children and adolescents, and those studies tend to show that children often experience many short-term problems when they are separated from their parents under traumatic circumstances, but they may still grow up to be well adjusted and capable (Palmer, 2000). One key factor in resilience is a close, supportive relationship. The experience of good parenting early in life conveys some protection against stress, but other types of supportive experiences may also be important. For example, a group

▲ Social skills are personal resources that influence coping.

of Aboriginal students who were attending college related their stories about the factors in their lives that allowed them to go to college (Montgomery et al., 2000). For many, tribal traditions and feeling that they were part of the Aboriginal community were related to their resiliency and success. Social support is a repeated theme in developing a sense of resiliency, and it is also an important coping resource.

**Social support** consists of the comfort, recognition, approval, and encouragement available from other people, including friends, family members, and co-workers. Even animals can provide social support (Siegel, 1990). People provide social support in the form of emotional support, but they can also contribute material resources such as money and knowledge and advice. All of these forms of social support enhance the ability to deal with stress.

People receive social support from friends and family, but being part of a network includes obligations to provide support as well as opportunities to receive support. Providing social support can be stressful, so being part of a social network has costs as well as benefits. The benefits outweigh the costs, but not always equally for women and men. Women tend to have larger social networks, which may overburden them with providing support (Orth-Gomér, 1998) but which also offer the benefits of variety and accessibility.

In addition to (and sometimes in place of) friends and family, group therapy (to be examined in Chapter 16) and support groups can be effective in managing stress. In group therapy and in support groups, other people who are in a similar situation can offer concern, advice, and emotional support. Therefore, people who do not have social support can find ways to obtain it, which suggests that people can find ways to develop coping skills and strategies.

## COPING STRATEGIES

Stress is a universal experience, and everyone uses some techniques to make levels of stress more manageable. All people do not use the same techniques, even if they find themselves in similar situations, and some people are much more effective in coping than others are. That is, some people use coping strategies more effectively than other people do.

**Coping strategies** are the techniques people use to deal with the stress of changing situations. Effective coping requires that people have a variety of strategies and make appropriate choices about when to use them. No single strategy is bad or good, but some strategies tend to be more effective than others. For example, some coping strategies involve actively dealing with the stressor, whereas other strategies are more passive. Passive coping strategies include refusing to accept the reality of the problem, trying to ignore the problem, avoiding the situation, engaging in distracting activities, or sleeping more than usual.

These approaches sound ineffective and even potentially dangerous, but under some circumstances they can work. For example, avoiding an unpleasant person may be an effective way to cope with that person. However, this coping strategy is effective in a limited number of situations and will be disastrous in others. For example, avoiding a person with whom one must work is not an effective way to deal with a difficult colleague. Also, failing to accept the possibility that one is ill and avoiding medical care can be fatal.

Psychologists usually accept active coping strategies as being more effective than passive ones, but some types of active coping are not necessarily the best choices. For example, using drugs or alcohol requires active effort, but this activity is not oriented toward solving the problem. Thus, this type of active coping is not a good strategy. One way to conceptualize active coping is to divide the strategies into emotion-focused strategies and problem-focused strategies. Both are active ways to deal with stressful situations, but the two types of strategies are very different. *Emotion-focused coping* concentrates on managing the feelings that accompany stress and trying to find ways to feel better, including focusing on and expressing emotions, reinterpreting the event in a positive way, finding comfort in religion, and seeking social support. *Problem-focused coping* concentrates on doing something about the situation, including taking action to get rid of the problem, making a plan about what to do, and putting aside other activities to concentrate on the problem. Researchers initially believed that some people tend to choose one approach and use that strategy in many situations. Researchers hypothesized that women choose emotion-focused strategies and men select problem-focused approaches. This stereotypical view is not accurate. Both women and men use both emotion-focused and problem-focused strategies (Porter & Stone, 1995).

In the selection of coping strategy, situation is more important than gender. For example, a woman who deals with problems with her husband through emotional confrontation might be less likely to deal with problems with her supervisor in the same way. Following nationality stereotypes, researchers hypothesized that Indian and Canadian students would differ in their levels of stress, attitudes about life, and preferred coping strategies (Sinha, Willson, & Watson, 2000). The students living in India did prefer emotion-focused coping more than the Canadian students did, especially in their tendency to reappraise their stresses in a positive way. Otherwise, the students in both countries were similar in levels of stress and attitudes about life, demonstrating both the influence of culture and the importance of situation in stress and coping—the situation of being a student involves similar stressors in many cultures.

EMOTION-FOCUSED COPING. When you have a problem (or just a bad day), is your first thought to talk to a friend or partner to help you ease those feelings of stress? If so, you are using emotion-focused coping. Women tend to use the strategy of seeking social support more than men do, but this tendency may relate to their relationship styles and the availability of support in their social network. In addition, seeking social support can be an adaptive strategy (Taylor et al., 2000).

▼ Writing about stress and trauma is an emotion-focused coping technique that can be effective.

In addition to seeking social support, another emotion-focused technique that can be very effective is writing about stresses and trauma. James Pennebaker (1997; Pennebaker & Graybeal, 2001) has researched the benefits of writing about problems. Pennebaker asked students to write about a traumatic event for 20 minutes for 3 consecutive days and compared these participants to other students who wrote about trivial events. Those students who wrote about stresses and problems experienced better health; these findings prompted additional research, which confirmed the benefits of writing about emotional events. Improvements include a wide variety of benefits, from better immune system functioning to better grades. Pennebaker believes that the benefits come from helping people think differently about their stresses and traumas and not from merely "getting it out in the open." Talking about problems is the basis for many psychological treatments (see Chapter 16), but writing as a coping technique has a much shorter history but comparable effectiveness (Pennebaker & Graybeal, 2001).

Therefore, some emotion-focused coping strategies are effective ways to deal with some stressors. However, problem-focused coping is usually a better choice as a coping strategy.

PROBLEM-FOCUSED COPING. Most psychologists recommend problem-focused coping for managing stress. This strategy has the goal of solving or managing the problem that is producing stress, and includes approaches for planning and resolving problems, gathering information, making decisions, and obtaining resources to deal with the problem (Folkman & Moskowitz, 2000).

▲ Exercise is an effective emotion-focused coping technique.

PROACTIVE COPING

Taking action in advance of a potentially stressful situation to prevent it, modify it, or prepare for it before it occurs.

These strategies require an active, task-oriented approach, which is associated with effective problem solving and decision making in many domains other than stress. People who use these strategies tend to feel that they can effectively solve a problem with a stressor, so they have a high sense of self-efficacy for the problem. As we saw in Chapter 12 (p. 439), a sense of self-efficacy is important, and this concept applies to stress situations (Ingledew, Hardy, & Cooper, 1997). In addition, people with an internal locus of control tend to choose problem-focused coping; such individuals believe that they can control important aspects of their lives (see Chapter 12) and attempt to control their stress. Thus, some individuals are more likely to use problem-focused coping, at least in some situations, and these individuals tend to be effective problem solvers.

Not only do problem-focused strategies tend to be more likely to solve stress-related problems, but some research indicates that people who use this strategy tend to have a more positive outlook (Folkman & Moskowitz, 2000), experience fewer symptoms of illness (Soderstrom et al., 2000), and show better immune system functioning (Stowell, Kiecolt-Glaser, & Glaser, 2001). Therefore, this approach has advantages over emotion-focused coping. Figure 14.7 compares the two approaches and also includes another strategy—proactive coping.

PROACTIVE COPING. If you know that you are going to have a challenging semester next fall, you might try to get a full-time job over the summer so that you'll only need to work part-time when school starts. By doing so (whether you think of it that way or not), you are already coping with your tough fall semester. You are practising **proactive coping**; you are anticipating a problem and taking action to avoid or decrease its impact.

FIGURE 14.7
Coping Strategies and Their Effects

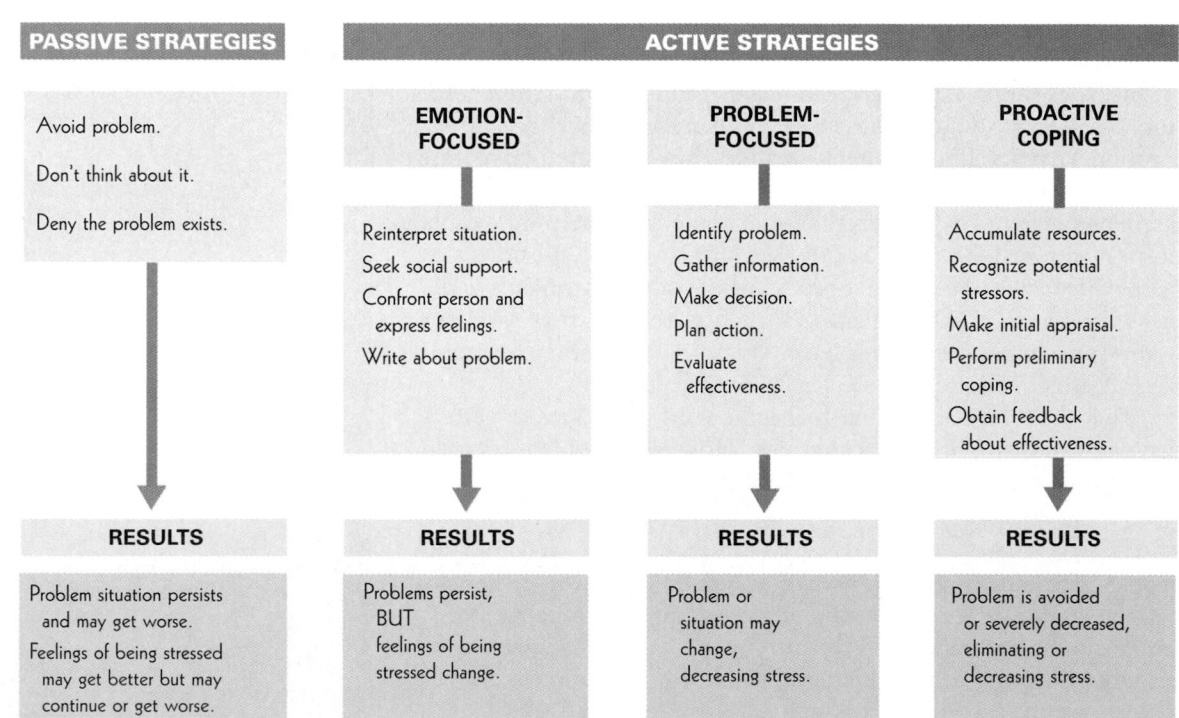

| PASSIVE STRATEGIES | ACTIVE STRATEGIES | | |
|---|---|---|---|
| | EMOTION-FOCUSED | PROBLEM-FOCUSED | PROACTIVE COPING |
| Avoid problem. Don't think about it. Deny the problem exists. | Reinterpret situation. Seek social support. Confront person and express feelings. Write about problem. | Identify problem. Gather information. Make decision. Plan action. Evaluate effectiveness. | Accumulate resources. Recognize potential stressors. Make initial appraisal. Perform preliminary coping. Obtain feedback about effectiveness. |
| RESULTS | RESULTS | RESULTS | RESULTS |
| Problem situation persists and may get worse. Feelings of being stressed may get better but may continue or get worse. | Problems persist, BUT feelings of being stressed change. | Problem or situation may change, decreasing stress. | Problem is avoided or severely decreased, eliminating or decreasing stress. |

Lisa Aspinwall and Shelley Taylor (1997) have described proactive coping as a five-stage process. First, we accumulate resources, mustering time, money, and social support and managing current situations. Next, we recognize that a stressful event is coming. Third, we appraise the event for its difficulty and its potential impact. Fourth, we engage in preliminary coping, to see what we can do now to prevent or minimize a threat. And last, we elicit and use feedback to assess whether we have averted a future stressor.

Using this active approach, some stressors can be avoided and others can be modified so that they are not so stressful; thus, people can lessen or eliminate the potential impact of stress. However, the process of proactive coping requires effort, so people need to be reasonable in choosing which situations to manage and which to allow to develop. Therefore, choosing a strategy is important for effectively managing stress.

EFFECTIVE COPING. Both emotion-focused and problem-focused coping can be successful, and both can fail. Proactive coping can prevent or decrease stress but requires time and effort. Therefore, selecting the appropriate strategy is critically important for managing stress. Emotional confrontation is obviously a strategy that needs to be chosen with much care; inappropriate choices may be not only ineffective but also dangerous. Seeking social support or writing about a distressing experience are better choices to manage the emotions generated by stress. Some research indicates that people who have to deal with chronic pain as a daily stressor rely first on problem-focused coping, but when that strategy fails, they resort to emotion-focused efforts to manage the stress (Tennen et al., 2000). Their approach may be similar to the one used by many people—use a variety of strategies; if the first strategy is not effective, change to an alternative.

This picture portrays people as flexible and effective in dealing with the stressors in their lives, but this picture is not true for everyone, and some people need help in learning to cope with stress. Biofeedback, relaxation techniques, and meditation are effective for some people in helping manage the physical responses that accompany stress (see Chapter 4, pp. 147–149, for a description of biofeedback and meditation).

The process of **stress inoculation** is a therapeutic technique developed to help people cope with stress. This approach combines cognitive and behavioural techniques to improve coping (Meichenbaum & Cameron, 1983). Stress inoculation is based on the same principle as inoculation against a disease: It introduces a low, harmless level of stress and provides people with practice in using coping skills so that when threatening stress comes along, they will know how to cope—they have become immune to stressors. This process involves three stages:

1. *Conceptualization.* People develop an understanding of the stress process and their specific problems.
2. *Skills acquisition and rehearsal.* People learn relaxation and imagery techniques that are incompatible with stress and anxiety; they learn how to reinterpret stressors and regulate their feelings.
3. *Follow-through.* People apply their acquired coping skills to problems in a natural context; that is, they practise the techniques they have learned in the second stage.

This program provides training in a number of coping techniques, giving people a variety of strategies to manage stress. It can help people who have not devised effective strategies on their own.

In addition to having a variety of strategies to manage stress, people are better equipped to deal with the inevitable stressors of life if they lead a healthy lifestyle. However, a healthy lifestyle is important for much more than effective coping. Behaviours that relate to health are part of the area of health psychology, a relatively new field within psychology, which we will discuss next.

STRESS INOCULATION
[in-OK-you-LAY-shun]
Procedure of teaching people ways to cope with stress and allowing them to practise in realistic situations so they will develop "immunity" to stress.

Be an
ACTIVE
LEARNER

REVIEW
> What factors influence coping in a beneficial way, and what factors diminish the ability to cope? pp. 514–516
> What are the advantages and disadvantages of emotion-focused and problem-focused coping? pp. 517–518
> What is proactive coping? pp. 518–519

THINK CRITICALLY
> In what types of situations will emotion-focused coping be the best strategy?
> Contrast women's and men's styles of emotion-focused coping.

APPLY PSYCHOLOGY
> Keep a stress diary for a week to record your stressors and how you coped with each one, and then analyze how you could improve your coping strategies.

# Health Psychology

At least half of all premature deaths in Canada are the result of unhealthy lifestyles. In the past, infectious diseases such as influenza, tuberculosis, and pneumonia were among the leading causes of death. Today, the leading causes of death in Canada—heart disease, cancer, stroke, lung disease, and accidents—relate to behavioural and environmental variables. Psychologists believe that there is a direct relationship between people's health and their behaviour. **Health psychology** is the subfield of psychology concerned with the use of psychological ideas and principles to enhance health, prevent illness, diagnose and treat disease, and improve rehabilitation. It is an action-oriented discipline that assumes that people's ideas and behaviours contribute to the onset and prevention of illness. A closely related field, behavioural medicine, integrates behavioural science with biomedical knowledge and techniques; it is narrower in focus than health psychology.

Traditionally, physicians have considered health to be the absence of disease. A person who was not experiencing adverse effects from an infection, injury, or abnormal condition of some kind was considered healthy. Now, however, physicians and psychologists acknowledge that health is not just the absence of disease but must take into account a person's total social, physical, and mental well-being. This new orientation gives health psychology a focus on the positive—health promotion. Health and wellness are seen as conditions people can actively pursue by eating well, exercising regularly, and managing stress effectively (Baum & Posluszny, 1999). Unlike medicine, which focuses on specific diseases, health psychology looks at the broad effects of thoughts and behaviours on fundamental psychosocial mechanisms that affect health and disease. In addition, researchers focus on the positive effects of health-promoting behaviours as well as the dangers of risky behaviours.

## VARIABLES THAT AFFECT HEALTH AND ILLNESS

We can set a positive tone for our lives, enhance feelings of belonging, and see the bright side of things. We can laugh at things and wear "rose-coloured glasses" to help ward off the impact of negative or difficult life events (Kuiper & Martin, 1998). Our attitudes and outlook affect health and illness, and they in turn are affected by complex interrelationships among many events (Cohen, 1996; Lefcourt & Thomas, 1998). But health is also affected by behaviours. Research has demonstrated that health-related behaviours have a large influence not only on health but also on life expectancy.

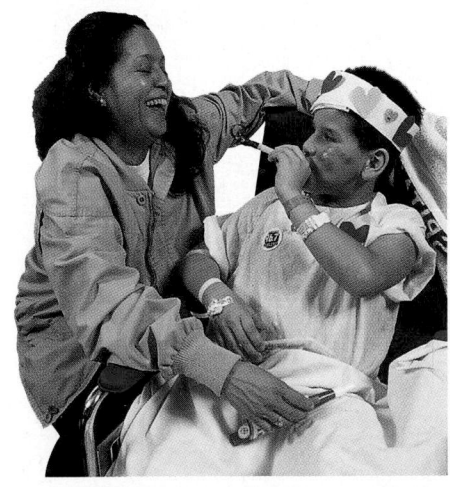

▼ Positive experiences and outlook can be important in health, illness, and recovery.

**HEALTH-RELATED BEHAVIOURS.** In 1965, researchers in Alameda county, California, began a study on health practices and social variables that continues today (Berkman & Breslow, 1983). The study began with nearly 7000 adults who were questioned about their health practices. Results indicated that five of those behaviours showed a strong relationship to health and life expectancy: (1) getting seven or eight hours of sleep daily, (2) drinking alcohol in moderation or not at all, (3) not smoking cigarettes, (4) exercising regularly, and (5) maintaining a weight near the prescribed ideal.

Follow-ups over the years have indicated that people who practise zero to two of these five behaviours are about three times more likely to be sick or die than people who practise all five. These behaviours reflect typical advice for maintaining a moderate and healthy lifestyle, and the Alameda County Study demonstrated the validity of such advice—how important behaviour can be in determining health. Since the beginning of that study, research evidence has grown that connects the failure to perform these behaviours to the leading causes of death.

For example, people engage in a whole range of self-destructive, health-impairing behaviours. About 28 percent of Canadians still smoke cigarettes, despite massive evidence that smoking causes and ultimately leads to premature deaths (Health Canada, 1999). Cigarette smoking is related to increased risks for heart disease, cancer, stroke, and lung disease—the four leading causes of death in Canada. Indeed, tobacco use is the most damaging health habit, related to more preventable deaths than any other single behaviour. Health psychologists are involved in research concerning why people begin to smoke and the difficulties they have in quitting so that they can devise more effective programs to help decrease this health-threatening behaviour.

Canadians also eat too much of the wrong things, and a high-fat diet contributes to heart disease, cancer, and stroke (Health Canada, 1999). The typical Canadian diet is too high in fat and too low in fruits, vegetables, and grains. This typical diet is a factor in obesity, and more than 50 percent of Canadians report that they are taking action to try to reduce fat in their diets (Health Canada, 1999). Health psychologists research eating and weight control as well as devise programs to help individuals and communities adopt healthier eating habits.

Health psychologists also recognize the value of exercise in promoting health, recognizing that Canadians are too sedentary to be healthy. A sedentary lifestyle is related to heart disease and stroke as well as to some types of cancers and, of course, obesity. People who exercise regularly have better overall health and more effective immune systems, are better at coping with stress, and live longer than people who are sedentary (Baum & Posluszny, 1999). About 50 percent of Canadians report engaging in no regular physical activity at all (Health Canada, 1999). As computers and video games become preferred entertainment for children, the trend toward a sedentary lifestyle applies to children as well as adults. Finding ways to boost physical activity is one challenge that faces health psychologists.

PREVENTING AIDS.   Educating people about prevention and wellness and discovering the variables that affect health are central goals of health psychologists. The focus on disease prevention led health psychologists to be involved in the AIDS (acquired immune deficiency syndrome) epidemic from its beginning. AIDS is caused by the human immunodeficiency virus (HIV), an infectious disease transmitted through bodily fluids. The serious worldwide AIDS epidemic is still continuing, and the disease kills thousands of people in Canada each year. (See Figure 14.8 for Canada and worldwide mortality rates.) Despite the developing knowledge about the virus and its methods of infection, no vaccine exists to prevent its transmission. A combination of drugs can help infected people manage the disease, but no cure exists.

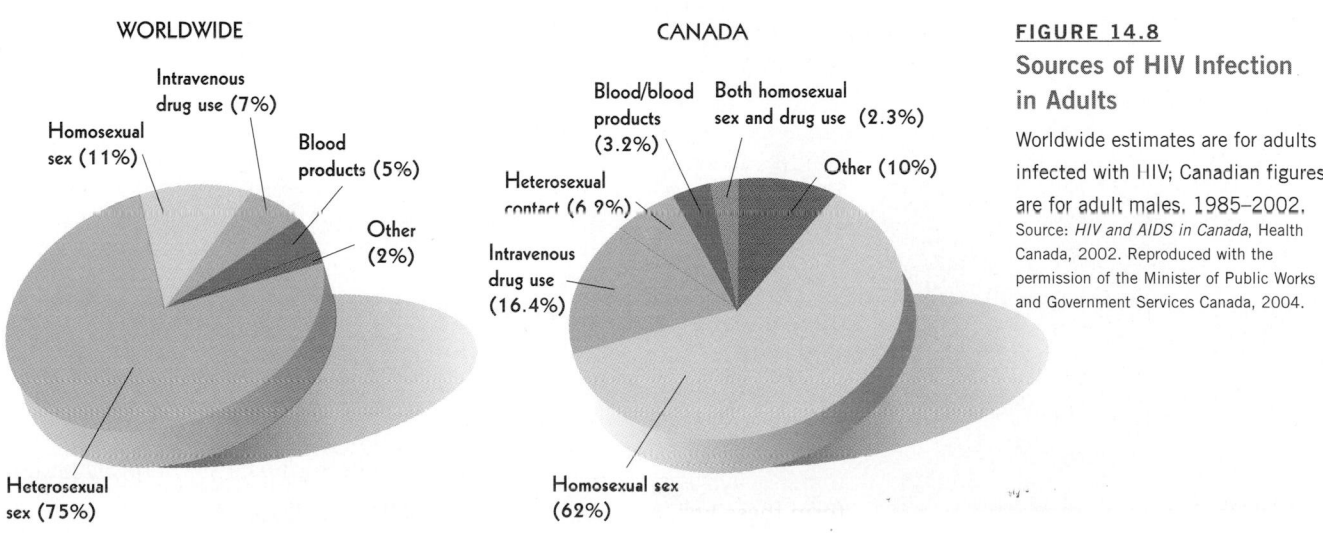

**FIGURE 14.8**

**Sources of HIV Infection in Adults**

Worldwide estimates are for adults infected with HIV; Canadian figures are for adult males, 1985–2002.
Source: *HIV and AIDS in Canada*, Health Canada, 2002. Reproduced with the permission of the Minister of Public Works and Government Services Canada, 2004.

The primary modes of transmission of the virus are behavioural; that is, risky behaviours spread HIV infection. High-risk behaviours are those that directly expose a person to the blood or semen of others who are likely to have been exposed to the virus—in other words, to others who are likely to have engaged in high-risk behaviours. Those behaviours include having sex with many partners, having sex with a man who has had sex with other men, and injection drug use. During the early years of the epidemic, AIDS was associated with gay men, and many people developed the belief that heterosexuals were not at risk. That belief is incorrect; heterosexuals who have had sexual contact with carriers of AIDS are at significant risk.

In Canada, about 19 percent of known cases of AIDS are contracted through heterosexual sex (Health Canada, 2002). However, according to the Centers for Disease Control and Prevention, heterosexual sex accounts for 75 percent of reported AIDS cases in other parts of the world. Everywhere, adolescents are at especially high risk because they, more than adults, are likely to engage in unprotected sexual activity, and they have some of the highest rates of sexually transmitted diseases, including HIV.

Health psychologists are involved in preventing the spread of HIV infection through attempts to change risky behaviours. An extensive education campaign transmitted information about HIV infection and the dangers of high-risk behaviours, but this campaign was not sufficient to alter risky behaviours. People who understand the risks still engage in risky behaviour (Helweg-Larsen & Collins, 1997). Additional strategies are necessary to change behaviour. An example of such a strategy involves condom use. Research shows that the most effective way to get men and women to use condoms is not through fear but through engendering positive attitudes about condoms—that others will accept and like condoms and that carrying and using condoms are positive and rewarding behaviours (Sheeran, Abraham, & Orbell, 1999).

**BARRIERS TO ADOPTING HEALTH-PROMOTING BEHAVIOURS.** People usually know about healthy lifestyles, but they are stuck with habits that increase their risks for disease and death. It's easy to fall into bad habits, and it's often difficult to change. Social circumstances and personal attitudes make change difficult. For example, eating a healthy diet can be a challenge. Billions of dollars are spent on advertising for fast foods and junk foods (poor dietary choices) to generate a desire for these foods. Even if people prefer healthy foods, fast-food restaurants and vending machines offer few good nutritional choices. Sometimes it is easier to make bad choices than good ones. Thus, environmental circumstances can push people toward an unhealthy diet.

Personal habits of thinking also perpetuate poor health choices. Many people mistakenly believe that risky behaviours will harm others but not them; that is, people have an *optimistic bias* (Weinstein, Rothman, & Sutton, 1998). This biased way of thinking allows people to continue risky behaviour, even if they have an intellectual understanding of the dangers. This "magical thinking" resembles teenagers' belief in the personal fable—they are so special and unique that risky behaviours (unsafe sex, alcohol consumption, or cigarette smoking) that might harm other people will not harm them. These cognitive distortions allow people to continue unsafe behaviours. Health psychologists must work against these thought patterns in helping people adopt healthier behaviours.

▼ Vending machines are often a barrier to healthy eating.

## THE PSYCHOLOGY OF BEING SICK

When people experience symptoms that may indicate illness, they must decide what to do. Should they continue with their regular activities, treat the symptoms themselves, or seek medical care? Most people prefer not to be sick, and the thought of a disease that impairs day-to-day functioning is threatening. These factors make people reluctant to seek medical care, and being sick changes many factors in people's lives. Health psychologists are concerned not only with the links between stress and illness but with how people cope with illness when it occurs.

**SEEKING MEDICAL CARE.** When do people seek medical care? What variables prompt a person to get help? Most people avoid medical care and advice except when they judge it to be necessary. The presence of visible symptoms (rashes, cuts, swellings, or fever) that are threatening, painful, or persistent are all important factors in the decision to seek professional help. Painful symptoms alone will not necessarily motivate people to seek medical care. For example, a cut or burn can be very painful, but if the injury is not judged to be serious, people tend to treat themselves rather than seek help. Visible symptoms, rather than those not readily visible, are more likely to prompt a search for medical care. However, if the symptom does not persist or if the person believes that the symptom does not indicate a serious condition, the person will not seek medical care.

People are more willing to seek medical help when they believe it will lead to a cure, and they are especially reluctant when the potential diagnosis is a dreaded one. For example, people avoid cancer screenings, partly because cancer is such a dreaded disease. In addition, people try to find the least threatening explanation for a symptom—the headache must be due to a stressful day and not to brain cancer. All these tendencies point to a great deal of personal reluctance in seeking medical care (Brannon & Feist, 2000).

There are gender differences in people's willingness to seek medical attention. The female gender role is more compatible with seeking help, and women seek medical help more than men do (Waldron, 1997). Women often visit physicians not for reasons of ill health but for consultation regarding birth control, pregnancy, and childbirth; women do, however, report more distress and symptoms of illness than men do.

Being strong and invincible is part of the male gender role, and men may perceive seeking health care as a sign of weakness or vulnerability. Ironically, men have a shorter life span than women do, so their tendency to avoid health care may not serve them well. A dramatic gender difference in life expectancy comes from men's higher rate of heart disease during middle age, leading to premature death. (Women also die of heart disease, but at older ages.) Heart disease may produce few noticeable symptoms, and men's avoidance of health care allows their heart disease to go undiagnosed and untreated—a potentially fatal situation.

Major cultural differences exist in making decisions about seeking health care, and people tend to do so in a manner that is consistent with their cultural conceptions of appropriate care. Most people in Canada and other Western countries have beliefs about the causes of and cures for disease that are compatible with Western medicine and expect to seek help from physicians and go to the hospital for certain treatments. Other views of health and disease vary drastically from those of traditional Western medicine, leading people to seek different practitioners and health-care settings. For example, traditional Chinese medicine is oriented toward understanding the body's vital energy, blood, and body fluids and maintaining a balance in the flow of these essential elements (Takeichi & Sato, 2000). This holistic concept of health has become attractive to a growing number of people in Canada, the United States, and Great Britain. They are seeking health care from alternative sources, and the *Point/Counterpoint* feature presents the controversy over choosing between traditional and alternative medicine.

Large, ethnically diverse societies such as Canada, the United States, and Great Britain are faced with providing health care to people who have a variety of beliefs about the nature of health and illness, some of which differ sharply from the views of traditional practitioners (McLaughlin & Braun, 1998). Indeed, these practitioners provide health care that is compatible with the beliefs of those who seek their care, thus producing situations that boost healing: Patients trust and will follow the directions of these health-care providers (Applewhite, 1995; Kim & Kwok, 1998; Lowery, 1998).

Seeking health care from practitioners associated with specific ethnic groups is more common among immigrants and older people (Applewhite, 1995), but people tend to hold beliefs about health and illness that include what constitutes appropriate treatment. These beliefs may continue, even among those who accept the cultural values of their adopted countries. In such situations, people often seek health care from a combination of practitioners—those traditional to their society plus traditional Western physicians (Applewhite, 1995; Kim & Kwok, 1998). This combination of sources for health care is similar to individuals who seek alternative health care.

**THE SICK ROLE.**   When people seek medical care and receive a diagnosis, they are expected to follow medical advice and try to get well. When they try to recover, they are adopting a *sick role*. For most people, this means taking specific steps to get well, relieving themselves of normal responsibilities, and realizing that they are not at fault for their illness. When they are in the hospital, they give the responsibility for their care to physicians and nurses. The situation of relinquishing personal control may create a feeling of helplessness that adds stress to the experience of being ill.

Sickness is generally seen as a temporary state, so people are expected to work toward getting well—taking medication, sleeping, and, especially, complying with medical advice. This view fits well with diseases from infection, which are typically temporary. Chronic diseases, on the other hand, do not have cures. These diseases include heart disease, diabetes, most types of cancer, asthma, and many other conditions that can be managed but not cured. This difference creates problems for people with these disorders—they cannot get well, they may have to (or want to) continue with normal responsibilities, but following medical advice is critically important. To manage their chronic illness, they must comply with medical advice.

**COMPLIANCE WITH MEDICAL ADVICE.**   Getting people to adhere to health regimens or to follow their physicians' advice has long been a focus of health psychologists because it is a persistent problem for medical treatment. People have trouble in following all types of medical recommendations. Some difficulties originate in communication problems between practitioner and patient—when patients do not understand practitioners' recommendations, they cannot follow them (Baum & Posluszny, 1999). Other problems occur when patients stop taking their medications when they begin to feel better. Another type of noncompliance problem comes from the failure to follow a healthy lifestyle, including eating a healthy diet, getting enough exercise, avoiding tobacco, drinking alcohol in moderation or not at all, getting enough sleep, and having medical checkups and screening tests.

People are more likely to comply with recommendations about treatments designed to cure a disease than with prevention efforts (DiMatteo, 1994). That is, people will comply with specific recommendations such as "Take 3 tablets a day for 10 days," but they are less likely to adhere to general recommendations aimed at improving overall health conditions, such as quitting smoking or getting more exercise. Overall, noncompliance is around 50 percent, which means that half of all people who receive medical advice fail to follow it in some way.

Compliance with medical advice has some relationship with the severity of the problem, but the patient's perception of the severity is what matters, not the medical

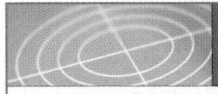
## Does the Use of Alternative Medicine Prevent People from Seeking Effective Traditional Care?

**POINT:** There is a lack of evidence that alternative medicine is effective.

**COUNTERPOINT:** Alternative medicine offers valuable benefits that have advantages over traditional medicine.

The growing popularity of alternative medicine has sparked a heated debate. On one side of the debate is traditional medicine, which represents the majority of treatment in developed countries. Traditional practitioners believe that modern medicine offers the best treatments for medical problems (Ziel, 1999). Indeed, medical advances have resulted in treatment that is more effective than that of any time in the past. Modern medicine is much more than bedside manner, and more than at any point in history, medicine promises cures for diseases that have been disabling and even fatal in the past. Advocates of traditional medicine believe that the best chances for recovery come through diagnosis, drugs, and surgery and that alternative treatments are unproven or even dangerous.

However, the advent of technological medicine and the growth of managed medical care have resulted in the loss of personal relationships and trust between patient and physician. This loss is seen as the main reason that prompts people to seek alternative medical care; people who feel that their doctor doesn't listen to or care about them seek care that seems more accessible and personal (Holland, 1999).

Alternative medicine encompasses a wide variety of treatments. Exercise and dietary programs are considered to be alternative but are part of traditional medical recom-

mendations for many conditions such as diabetes. Other treatments such as herbal remedies, massage therapy, and meditation fit into the alternative category but have many adherents (Ernst, 2000). Indeed, the number of people who seek alternative medical care has grown in recent years, not only in Canada but also in many countries.

Research on people who seek alternative care reflects a picture of users who are well educated with high incomes—people who could afford any type of care but choose alternative therapies (Astin, 1998). But they also seek traditional medical care and use alternative sources in addition to traditional ones in a pattern that can be described as *complementary* rather than *alternative*. Only 4.4 percent use alternative medicine exclusively. People who seek alternative care are more likely to have problems that are resistant to traditional medical care, such as back pain, chronic pain, allergies, and headaches. Those who seek alternative treatment tend to be satisfied with the treatment and report relief from their symptoms. Some who use alternative medicine fit the "new age" stereotype of having belief in the power of holistic healing and herbal medicine, but most who seek alternative medicine pick and choose among available treatments and do not limit their care to traditional medicine.

practitioner's view. If an illness causes pain or discomfort, people are more likely to comply with a regimen of treatment to alleviate the discomfort. People are more receptive to medical treatment when it is specific, simple, and easy to do, when it has minimal side effects, and when it brings relief they can see quickly (Ley, 1997).

Compliance with a health-care regimen is increased when the regimen is tailored to the person's lifestyle and habits. Patients are more likely to follow the advice of a practitioner whom they like and trust than one whom they find uncaring and uncommunicative. Written agreements between practitioners and clients can be helpful in detailing the responsibilities and commitments of each; clients who sign such an agreement are more likely to adhere to their commitment than clients who agree but do not sign an agreement.

Health psychologists have found clients more likely to adhere to treatments when a physician's influence and the family support systems are substantial. Social support from family and friends turns out to be especially effective in getting even very sick people to comply with guidelines for treatment (DiMatteo & DiNicola, 1982). However, compliance is far from perfect, even under the best conditions, and this problem remains persistent for health psychologists who want to help practitioners provide better health care.

## HEALTH PSYCHOLOGY AND HEALTHIER LIFESTYLES

Health psychologists focus on research to help them understand health-related behaviours, and they devise and implement interventions to bring about changes for healthier lifestyles. The interventions may take the form of individual programs for people with health-impairing behaviours or health problems, but some interventions are aimed at groups and even entire communities.

Health psychologists recommend preventive programs in the workplace to educate people about ways to manage stress and about other positive behaviours that can enhance and prolong life. They frequently conduct stress management workshops to help managers and workers cope with increasing pressures and heavy workloads; they are also involved in helping people quit smoking, control their alcohol intake, follow exercise programs, make healthy dietary choices, and practise safer sex. Let's examine three ways of dealing with health problems: pain management, workplace stress management, and the nationwide campaign to promote condom use.

**PAIN MANAGEMENT.** We all experience pain, but that experience is usually brief and does not present a problem for daily functioning. People with chronic headache, arthritis, back problems, or many types of cancers must live with pain that does cause problems for their daily lives. Psychologists work to help such individuals manage this pain. Severe and disabling pain can take three forms: (1) *chronic pain* is long-lasting and ever present, such as the pain caused by arthritis; (2) *periodic pain* comes and goes, such as headache pain; (3) *progressive pain* is ever present and increases in severity as the illness progresses, such as cancer-related pain. Drugs, surgery, or other medical interventions are usually part of treatment for chronic pain, but behavioural techniques can also offer relief.

Pain management programs usually work on two fronts: They try to reduce suffering, the negative emotional experience that accompanies pain, while also decreasing the physical aspects of pain. A number of behavioural treatments have been used to manage pain, including hypnosis and biofeedback (examined in Chapter 4), behaviour modification, and cognitive therapy. Behaviour modification uses learning principles (see Chapter 5) to teach people new effective behaviours, to help them unlearn maladaptive behaviours, and to train those around them not to reward pain behaviours (McCracken, 1997). For example, a person with back pain might be rewarded for performing normal activities and ignored for complaining about how much his back hurts. In addition, the person might be taught to relax as a coping strategy rather than becoming tense, focusing on the pain, and thus making it worse.

A review of studies on behaviour modification for back pain indicates that these techniques are effective in increasing the level of patients' physical activity and in decreasing use of medications (Compas et al., 1998). Chapter 16 looks into the use of cognitive therapy to help people acquire new thoughts, beliefs, and values, which can also be helpful in managing pain.

**WORKPLACE WELLNESS PROGRAMS.** People care about stress management, and health psychologists have devised many techniques that can be applied to stress management. Employers are concerned about the effects of stress on their employees. Work site stress is one of the major sources of stress and it decreases work effectiveness and increases health-care costs to employers (Stein, Karel, & Zuidema, 1999). Employers are interested in having healthier employees in order to decrease the payments they make for employees' health care, so some companies offer employees workplace wellness programs.

Such programs may include one or many components; smoking cessation programs are a common choice because smoking relates to so many health problems. However, relaxation or other stress management techniques are also common (Hobfoll & Shirom, 2001). The programs usually involve inducements for employee participation, and effective programs are voluntary rather than required. The results are fewer workdays lost to illness and lower health-care costs. An example of such a program targeted secondary school teachers, who participated in a work site stress management program (Lapp & Attridge, 2000). The program had educational, stress management, and strategy-building components and lasted nine months. Before the program, one-third of the teachers reported high levels of stress, and the intervention had a positive impact in helping these teachers reduce their levels of stress.

**COMMUNITY INTERVENTIONS.** To manage existing health problems and help prevent disease, behavioural interventions are necessary and important. Individual and workplace programs can reach many people, but wide-scale campaigns are necessary to reach enough people to improve life expectancy for a community or for a nation. Health psychologists know that many problem behaviours can be modified, but they also know that traditional information campaigns are not very effective in changing behaviour.

The "safer-sex" campaign is an example of an attempt to change behaviour in order to decrease health risks. Such campaigns use a variety of approaches that target the entire society as well as smaller risk groups. When researchers discovered that HIV infection was transmitted through contact with blood or semen, one of the prevention strategies was to increase condom use. Initially, the target was gay men because their rate of HIV infection was very high compared to that of other groups (Health Canada, 2002). That campaign took many forms, educating people about the dangers of HIV infection and the behaviours that are risky. As psychologists know, education is not an adequate intervention, and the campaign was extended to include persuasive techniques to increase condom use and overcome the barriers to it (Perloff, 2001). This campaign was at least somewhat successful. Indeed, gay men changed their sexual behaviour and condom use, and their rate of HIV infection slowed more than that of other groups (CDC, 2001).

Other groups, including heterosexuals, became the targets of the campaign to increase condom use. Messages about condom use appeared in a variety of settings, from school-based sexuality education programs that provided condoms, to TV public service announcements in which entertainment personalities advocated condom use. Teenagers and young adults were the primary targets because their rate of infection from sexually transmitted diseases is higher than that of older individuals (Kaplan et al., 2001). Among adolescents, condom use has increased significantly over the past two decades, suggesting that a massive nationwide health campaign oriented toward changing behaviour can have some success.

Unfortunately, recent research has shown that continued efforts are required to maintain condom use. Heterosexuals encounter a number of relationship issues, such as lack of trust and suspicion, that make requests for condom use difficult (Gavin, 2000), and the growing availability of treatment for HIV-infected people has created a climate of acceptance of risky sex among gay men (Williams, Elwood, & Bowen, 2000).

Therefore, continued efforts are required to maintain behaviour changes, even when people understand and accept the value of their health-protective behaviours. Condom use and sexual behaviour are not exceptions; people have a tendency to quit exercise programs, regain lost weight, and relapse into smoking after they have quit. Maintaining a healthy lifestyle is a personal challenge, also creating a challenge for health psychologists.

## HEALTH PSYCHOLOGY AND THE FUTURE

At the beginning of this chapter, we considered the idea that stress has biological, psychological, and social components, but so does health. A number of biological, behavioural, and social factors intersect to

▼ Health campaigns aimed at reducing the spread of HIV infection have been effective in changing risky behaviours.

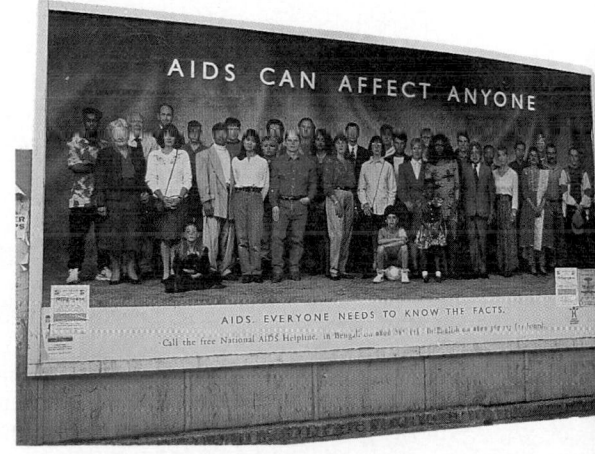

determine each person's state of wellness, including genetics, biological endowment, education, social support, health habits, and medical care.

Whether studying stress and its causes and treatment or looking at ways to improve health, psychologists are taking a prosocial, action-oriented approach. In many ways, the study of stress and health can be considered the future of the discipline. If people can learn to manage their stressors and adopt a healthy lifestyle, they may be able to avoid many psychological and physical problems, function at a higher and more effective level, and live longer and healthier lives.

Created in the 1970s, health psychology has a short history, but during this time it has managed to draw from research and applied areas of psychology, including biopsychology, learning, motivation, emotion, personality, developmental, social, and clinical psychology (Brannon & Feist, 2000). In addition, health psychology has integrated information from disciplines outside psychology, such as sociology and various areas of medicine, including neurology and immunology. This integration has moved psychology to a more prominent place in health care. As practitioners in health care come to accept the value of psychological contributors to health and disease and psychologically based interventions, the field of health psychology will continue to grow.

# Summary and Review

## STRESS

### How has stress been defined and measured?

> Frustration, conflict, pressure, and challenge are all situations that cause stress. *Frustration* is experienced when people are thwarted from meeting a goal. *Conflict* is experienced when a person has two or more competing motives, behaviours, or impulses and is forced to choose one. *Pressure* is experienced when a person experiences a real or imagined emotional state that can be attributed to the expectations of others. *Challenge* is experienced when a person experiences an emotion resulting from a changed situation that requires action of some type. pp. 496–498

> *Stress* was defined by Selye as a nonspecific emotional response to real or imagined challenges or threats. He characterized stress responses as a general adaptation syndrome with three stages: alarm, resistance, and exhaustion. Physiological arousal is heightened during alarm and resistance. If people do not relieve their stress, they experience exhaustion. *Stressors* are environmental

stimuli that affect an organism in either physically or psychologically injurious ways. Life events scales, such as the Holmes–Rahe scale, measure stress as life events that require change and adaptation.    pp. 498–500

> According to Lazarus, stress is an interaction of stressors and a cognitive appraisal of threat in the situation. Whether a situation is stressful or not depends on a person's appraisal of the situation. The Hassles Scale is an alternative way to assess stress based on the concept that everyday annoyances are more important stressors than life events.    pp. 502–503

### What are the major causes of and responses to stress?

> Stress can come from catastrophes, such as natural disasters and events of human origin, that may produce *post-traumatic stress disorder* (PTSD). Stress can also originate in unhealthy environments such as poverty, or in discrimination based on ethnicity, gender, or sexual orientation. Personal factors such as jobs and relationships can produce satisfaction or stress.    pp. 503–508

> Responses to stress occur on the physiological level in terms of arousal of the sympathetic nervous system and on the behavioural level. **pp. 508–509**

### How is stress related to disease?

> *Type A behaviour* is the behaviour pattern of individuals who are competitive, impatient, hostile, and always striving to do more in less time. The overall Type A behaviour pattern is not related to the development of heart disease, but the elements of anger and hostility seem to be. **p. 510**
> The field of *psychoneuroimmunology* studies how stress can decrease the function of the immune system, which increases vulnerability to infectious disease. In addition, stress tends to alter behaviour in ways that affect health-related behaviours. **pp. 512–514**

**KEY TERMS**

stress, p. 496; stressor, p. 496; frustration, p. 496; conflict, p. 497; approach–approach conflict, p. 497; avoidance–avoidance conflict, p. 497; approach–avoidance conflict, p. 497; pressure, p. 497; challenge, p. 498; post-traumatic stress disorder (PTSD), p. 503; Type A behaviour, p. 510; Type B behaviour, p. 510; psychoneuroimmunology, p. 512

## COPING

### What factors influence coping?

> A sense of personal control, even if it is an illusion, is a positive factor in coping. Social support also increases coping ability. People who cope, despite a great deal of stress, have a high level of *resilience*. **pp. 514–516**

### Distinguish various forms of coping.

> *Coping* is the process by which a person takes some action to manage, master, tolerate, or reduce environmental and internal demands that cause or might cause stress and that tax the individual's inner resources. *Social support* can provide a buffer against stress. *Coping*

*strategies* are the techniques people use to change stressful situations. **p. 516**

> People use both passive and active strategies to cope. Active coping strategies can be emotion-focused or problem-focused. *Proactive coping* is taking action in advance of a potentially stressful situation to prevent it or modify it before it occurs. Typically, active strategies are better than passive ones, and problem-focused strategies are more effective than emotion-focused ones, but all coping strategies can be effective in some situations. Therefore, people must learn a variety of coping strategies and how to effectively employ them. *Stress inoculation* is a therapy technique that teaches people how to cope more effectively. **pp. 516–519**

**KEY TERMS**

coping, p. 514 resilience, p. 514; social support, p. 516; coping strategies, p. 516; proactive coping, p. 518; stress inoculation, p. 519

## HEALTH PSYCHOLOGY

### What is the role of health psychology?

> *Health psychology* uses psychological ideas and principles to help enhance health, prevent illness, diagnose and treat disease, and rehabilitate people. Health psychology is an action-oriented discipline that emphasizes preventive health measures as well as interventions directed at existing conditions. **pp. 520–523**
> Health psychologists also work to help people who are ill, trying to understand the factors that relate to seeking medical care and compliance with medical advice. **pp. 523–525**
> Health psychologists are involved in promoting healthy behaviour for individuals, such as pain management programs; for workplaces, such as stress management programs; and for communities, such as the AIDS prevention campaign that focuses on condom use and safe sex. **pp. 526–527**

**KEY TERM**

health psychology, p. 520

---

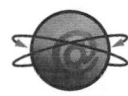 Take advantage of the multimedia resources available with this text! Follow the marginal icons to access the interactive modules on the *HandsOnPsych* CD-ROM; log on to *MyPsychLab* to explore the ebook, study aids, and other online resources; and visit the Companion Website at **www.pearsoned.ca/lefton** for additional exercises and links.

# 15 Psychological Disorders

A young woman was found wandering aimlessly beside a highway in northern Ontario. She had no memory of who she was or where she came from. She was bright, articulate, and well spoken. She was concerned that she couldn't recall any memories but was otherwise calm and anxious to help authorities unravel the mystery of her identity. When authorities began to look for clues, they discovered her name was Chelsea and that her older sister had reported her missing from a small town in Manitoba several weeks before. Prior to her disappearance, Chelsea had been under tremendous stress; she had witnessed her father brutally beat her mother. Her mother was on life-support in the critical care unit of the local hospital. Her father was in jail but police were going to have to release him unless Chelsea was prepared to press charges on her mother's behalf and then testify against him. Even when authorities gave Chelsea the information they had uncovered, she was unable to associate those events as her own experiences. Chelsea had no memory of her life prior to being picked up on the highway, nor could she account for her whereabouts between the time she had left Manitoba and had been discovered in Ontario.

Is this possible? Or is this just a tale for soap opera fans? Although very rare, this type of disorder, called *dissociative fugue*, can occur outside of television. Generally, people with dissociative fugue experience a traumatic event and lose their memories of their entire life, including their sense of personal identity. Chelsea's case is not typical of dissociative fugue as many who suffer this disorder actually adopt another identity to replace the one with which they have lost touch. In this chapter we will examine unusual disorders as well as more common disorders. We will discuss what differentiates the typical from the atypical.

# What Is Abnormal Behaviour?

▲ Sometimes the line between eccentricity and abnormality is difficult to draw.

Bankview is an older neighbourhood in Calgary made up of houses and apartment buildings. Until he lost parts of his feet to frostbite, a man known as the Bankview Bottle Picker (shown in the photograph) lived beside a park under the overhang of an apartment garage. He slept on an old mattress and kept warm in the winter months with a large collection of blankets and old sleeping bags he had found in various dumpsters in the area. When interviewed from time to time by the local media he refused to discuss his past but was open about the fact that he drank excessively and spent his days collecting bottles and cans in neighbourhood garbage cans and bins that could be cashed in to buy alcohol. Many local residents made a point of putting any bottles or cans they were throwing out beside their garbage cans in order to make it easier for the Picker to find them. He refused offers of more substantial assistance and he and the neighbourhood residents basically got used to their unusual relationship.

Is this behaviour abnormal? To some extent, it depends on where you live, because every society has its own definition of abnormal behaviour. In Russia, for example, people were once regularly placed in mental institutions for homelessness or political dissent. Generally, however, behaviour classified as abnormal is more than odd. In any single year, between 15 and 25 percent of adults worldwide meet the criteria for having a mental disorder, that is, they exhibit symptoms of abnormality (Kessler, 2000).

## A DEFINITION

**ABNORMAL BEHAVIOUR**

Behaviour characterized as not typical, socially unacceptable, distressing, maladaptive, and/or the result of distorted cognitions.

**Abnormal behaviour** is behaviour characterized as (1) not typical, (2) socially unacceptable, (3) distressing, (4) maladaptive, and/or (5) the result of distorted cognitions. Let's consider these five distinguishing characteristics in turn.

First, abnormal behaviour is *atypical*. Many behaviours are unusual; however, abnormal behaviours tend to be so unusual as to be statistically rare. For example, you would not consider ear or body piercing among teenagers to be abnormal, because the practice is fairly common today. However, washing one's hands every few minutes during the day until they are raw is atypical. Of course, not all atypical behaviour is necessarily abnormal. The athleticism of Wayne Gretzky is statistically uncommon but not abnormal and Einstein's rare genius was considered atypical. On the other hand, most people would not hesitate to label drug abuse as abnormal behaviour, even though it is not as unusual as it once was.

Second, in addition to being atypical, abnormal behaviour is also often *socially unacceptable*. To some degree, ideas about what is normal and abnormal vary according to cultural values, which are in a constant state of flux. What is acceptable in one culture may be labelled unacceptable in another. Similarly, behaviour that was considered unacceptable 25 years ago, such as males wearing earrings or colouring their hair, may be considered acceptable today. A behaviour that is judged abnormal, however, is one that is unacceptable to society in general.

Third, a person's abnormal behaviour often causes *distress* to that person or to those around the person. While feelings of anxiety or distress are normal in many situations, prolonged anxiety (distress) may result from abnormal behaviour. You may feel anxious while you are preparing to speak in front of a group; however, constant, unrelenting anxiety, the avoidance of any situation that might require simply interacting with other people, and fear of people in general suggest a problem.

Fourth, abnormal behaviour is usually *maladaptive*, or self-defeating to the person exhibiting it. Maladaptive behaviour, such as drug abuse, is harmful and nonproductive. It often leads to more misery and prevents people from making positive changes in their lives.

Last, abnormal behaviour is often the result of *distorted cognitions* (thoughts). For example, a young man with distorted cognitions may falsely believe that people are out to get him. A woman suffering from distorted cognitions associated with major depression may believe that she is worthless, stupid, and unlovable.

In recent years, psychologists have begun to describe behaviour in terms of *maladjustment* rather than *abnormality*. The distinction is important because it implies that maladaptive behaviour can, with treatment, be adjusted and become adaptive and productive. The term *maladjustment* also emphasizes specific behaviours rather than labelling the entire person.

Using the sociocultural approach (described on p. 535), researchers such as Thomas Szasz go so far as to say that maladjustment and mental illness are socially constructed and defined—abnormal behaviours are whatever a society fails to accept. Szasz argues that there is, in fact, a myth of mental illness; according to him, once a practitioner labels a person as "abnormal," the person starts to act that way (Szasz, 1984, 1987). The patient confirms the therapist's expectations about his or her abnormality, even when the expectations may not reflect the patient's real condition. In Szasz's view, a patient in therapy creates situations that lead to behaviours that the therapist has predicted. This phenomenon is called the *self-fulfilling prophecy*, the creation by the therapist of the expected behaviours. The phenomenon of the self-fulfilling prophecy is one of the drawbacks of diagnosis and labelling. Giving a person or the person's behaviour a label or tag rarely helps; in Szasz's view, "mental illness" is a label that serves no good purpose. However, people *do* suffer from behaviour problems, and labelling is part of the process of diagnosis and treatment. Labels have negative consequences, but they also have the advantage of allowing researchers to categorize and research these problems and allowing people who receive a diagnosis to identify and understand their behaviour.

To summarize, abnormal behaviour is characterized as atypical, socially unacceptable, distressing, maladaptive, and/or the result of distorted cognitions. There are, of course, exceptions to this definition. Nevertheless, this definition provides psychologists with a solid framework from which to explore abnormal behaviour and its treatment.

## PERSPECTIVES ON ABNORMALITY

On July 26, 1997, Victoria Hamm, a 30-year-old Drumheller mother, suddenly killed her two-and-a-half-year-old son, Christopher, and nearly killed herself. Her life had not been an easy one. Her parents had divorced when she was a youth and her new stepfather had abused her physically and sexually. She had used drugs and her own first marriage had ended in divorce after a year. Things seemed to straighten out for her when she met her common-law husband. They were together for four years before she had Christopher. Victoria suffered from postpartum depression following her son's birth. When Christopher was about two years old, she began to sink deeper and deeper into depression, becoming convinced that the world was far too dangerous or scary a place for her child. She decided that she would have to kill herself and Christopher to spare him the nasty existence she believed the world offered. As a result of the testimony of a forensic psychologist, Dr. Julio Arboleda-Florez, who stated that the depression had so changed Victoria that she was not fully aware of the consequences of her actions, she was acquitted of murder charges.

Before prescribing treatment or deciding on issues of responsibility, mental health practitioners want to know why a person is maladjusted, because establishing the cause of a disorder can sometimes help define a treatment plan. Therefore, practitioners often turn to theories and models that attempt to explain the causes of abnormality. A **model** is a guideline, perspective, or approach that helps scientists discover relationships among data; it uses a structure from one field to help describe data in another. Psychologists use models to make predictions about behaviour. An

**MODEL**

A guideline, perspective, or approach derived from data in one field and used to help describe data in another field.

attempt to explain a school phobia as at least partially due to attachment issues is one example of a model that allows for the design of possible treatments. These models form the basis of **abnormal psychology**, the field of psychology concerned with the assessment, treatment, and prevention of maladaptive behaviour. Several models help explain abnormal behaviour: medical–biological, psychodynamic, humanistic, behavioural, cognitive, sociocultural, and evolutionary.

**MEDICAL–BIOLOGICAL MODEL.** Thousands of years ago, people believed that abnormal behaviour was caused by demons that invaded an individual's body. The "cure" often involved a surgeon performing *trephination*—drilling a hole into the skull to allow the evil force to escape. Even as recently as a few hundred years ago, people with psychological disorders were caged and treated like animals. Early reformists, such as French physician Philippe Pinel, advocated the medical model and proposed that abnormal behaviour could be treated and cured, like an illness. When scientists showed that syphilis could cause mental disorders, the medical model gained even greater acceptance and led to more humane treatment and better conditions for those with psychological disorders.

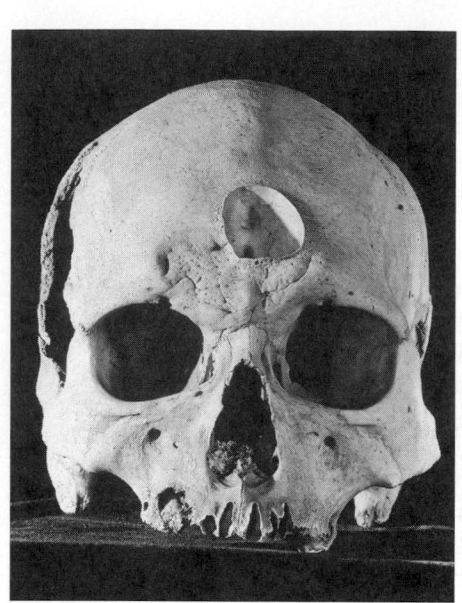

▲ This skull shows that *trephination* was practised for thousands of years.

The *medical–biological model* of abnormal behaviour focuses on the biological and physiological conditions that cause abnormal behaviours. This model deals with a range of mental ailments, such as those caused by mercury poisoning or viral attacks on brain cells. It focuses on genetic abnormalities, problems in the central nervous system, and hormonal changes. It also helps explain and treat substance abuse problems and schizophrenia, two disorders that may have a strong biological component. Proponents of the medical–biological model might explain the Bankview Bottle Picker's lifestyle as resulting from a chemical or hormonal imbalance that alters judgment.

Many of the terms and concepts used in psychology and psychiatry are borrowed from medicine; they include *treatment*, *case*, *symptom*, and *syndrome*, as well as *mental illness*. The medical model assumes that abnormal behaviour, like other illnesses, can be diagnosed, treated, and often cured. This approach has not gone unchallenged, however. Its critics say that it does not take advantage of other psychological insights, such as those derived from cognitive or behavioural models. A major—but not surprising—disadvantage of the medical model is that it emphasizes drug treatment and often involves hospitalization rather than solving psychological problems by psychological means.

**THE PSYCHODYNAMIC MODEL.** The *psychodynamic model* of abnormal behaviour is loosely rooted in Freud's theory of personality (discussed in Chapter 12). This model assumes that psychological disorders result from anxiety produced by unresolved conflicts and forces that lie outside a person's awareness. It asserts that maladjustment occurs when a person's ego is not strong enough to balance the demands of the id, the superego, and the outside world. According to the psychodynamic model, maintaining a healthy, functioning personality is a careful balancing act of satisfying these often conflicting demands. Thus, even seemingly healthy people are vulnerable to maladjustment. A homeless person's talking to himself might be explained as loneliness, despair, or anger turned inward, traceable to personality development during childhood.

**THE HUMANISTIC MODEL.** Like the psychodynamic model, the *humanistic model* of abnormal behaviour assumes that inner psychic forces are important in establishing and maintaining a fulfilling lifestyle. Unlike psychodynamic theorists, however, humanists believe that people have a good deal of control over their lives. The humanistic model focuses on individual uniqueness and decision making. Maladjustment occurs when people's needs are not met; either they are unable to fulfil their needs or some circumstance prevents them from doing so. In the case of a homeless person, many needs may be unfulfilled; the person may lack food and shelter, putting the person in the situation of concentrating on these needs. Thus, a homeless person's abnormal behaviour may be determined by the circumstances of living on the street rather than by internal, personal factors.

**THE BEHAVIOURAL MODEL.**    The *behavioural model* of abnormal behaviour states that such behaviour is learned. Behavioural theorists assume that events in a person's environment selectively reinforce or punish various behaviours and, in doing so, shape personality and may create maladjustment. They thus contend, for example, that an abusive husband may have learned to assert dominance over women through physical abuse because physical force has been effective in allowing him to dominate women. Two fundamental assumptions of behavioural (learning) theorists are that disordered behaviour can be reshaped and that more appropriate, worthwhile behaviours can be substituted through traditional learning techniques (see Chapter 5). Proponents of the behavioural model might explain a man's homelessness by hypothesizing that he did not find significant reinforcers in the work world and felt he could take care of himself and manage better by living on the streets.

**THE COGNITIVE MODEL.**    The *cognitive model* of abnormal behaviour asserts that human beings engage in both prosocial and maladjusted behaviours because of their thoughts. As thinking organisms, people decide how to behave; abnormal behaviour is based on false assumptions or unrealistic coping strategies. Practitioners with a cognitive perspective treat people with psychological disorders by helping them develop different ways of thinking about problems and new values. A cognitive theorist might assume that maladjusted people have developed ideas about the world that made them want to withdraw; these ideas might be irrational and might have led to abnormal behaviours.

**THE SOCIOCULTURAL MODEL.**    According to the *sociocultural model* of abnormal behaviour, people develop abnormalities within and because of a context—the context of the family, the community, and the society. Cross-cultural researchers have shown that personality development and psychological disorders reflect the culture and the stressors in the society. Relying heavily on the learning and cognitive frameworks, the sociocultural model focuses on cultural variables as key determinants of maladjustment.

As researchers examine the frequency and types of disorders that occur in different societies, they also note some sharp differences between societies. In China, for example, depression is relatively uncommon, but stress reactions manifested in the form of physical ailments are frequent. Canadians and Europeans report guilt and shame when they are depressed; depressed individuals in Africa, on the other hand, are less likely to report these symptoms but more likely to report somatic (physical) complaints. Certain disorders seem highly culture-specific; for example, *amok* (as in "running amok") is a disorder that is characterized by sudden rage and homicidal aggression and is seen in some Asian countries, including Malaysia and Thailand. Brought on by stress, sleep deprivation, and alcohol consumption, the behaviour can be broken down into a series of stages. Researchers now recognize that some disorders are specific to a culture.

**THE EVOLUTIONARY MODEL.**    According the *evolutionary model*, abnormal behaviour may arise from several types of circumstances. The evolutionary view hypothesizes that humans evolved in a specific type of environment, and that humans are best suited to function in similar environments. Modern societies are not like that ancestral environment, so maladjustments may represent behaviour that was normal at some point in evolutionary history but is not today (Cosmides & Tooby, 1999). Some behaviour problems are adaptive behaviours taken too far, such as fear of heights or snakes. These fears likely kept people out of trouble in the distant past, but today they may produce problems. Another source of maladjustment comes from the many genetic defects that all humans have; these defects do not produce problems in all environments, but in some circumstances, they do. When built-in mechanisms do not perform their adaptive function, they may instead produce harmful dysfunctions (Wakefield, 1999). The criterion of producing harm is one that evolutionary psychologists use to identify a behaviour as abnormal.

**WHICH MODEL IS BEST?** Each of the models we've examined—medical–biological, psychodynamic, humanistic, behavioural, cognitive, sociocultural, and evolutionary—looks at maladjustment from a different perspective. Some psychologists hold to one model and use it to analyze all behaviour problems, but other psychologists believe that different models seem to explain different disorders. For phobias (unreasonable fears), learning theory explains the cause and prescribes an effective course of treatment. For schizophrenia, medical–biological theory clarifies a significant part of the problem. Consequently, many psychologists use an *eclectic approach,* choosing the model that seems to fit the problem. Other psychologists prefer a *biopsychosocial approach*, which acknowledges that a combination of biological, psychological, and social factors shape behaviour. This approach differs from an eclectic approach in its combination of influences; the eclectic approach promotes a selection among discrete models.

**BE A CRITICAL THINKER.** People have developed a whole range of ideas about abnormality, and a veil of misunderstanding still surrounds mental illness in many people's minds. For example, many individuals still think that a mental illness is "forever" and incurable. They sometimes worry that those diagnosed as mentally ill are dangerous, violent, or out of control, behaving bizarrely and wildly different from normal people. The truth is, of course, that more people recover from mental illness than do not, few people with mental illness are violent, and most people with mental illnesses suffer quietly and bear their pain privately. Treatment with therapy, drugs, and love and care from family members and friends helps in managing these illnesses.

As you examine each psychological disorder presented in this chapter, think about whether you favour one model of maladjustment over another. Do you have a cognitive bent, or do you favour a more psychodynamic approach? Perhaps you take a more behavioural view, or the biopsychosocial model represents a combination you like. Regardless of a practitioner's predisposition, it is important that symptoms be carefully evaluated so that proper diagnoses can be made. People who are suffering need appropriate help, and a wide variety of treatments is available.

Next, we consider a system that has been developed to help practitioners make diagnoses. The system is presented in *The Diagnostic and Statistical Manual of Mental Disorders*.

**HandsOnPsych**
Version 2.0

**Psychopathology**

## DIAGNOSING MALADJUSTMENT: THE *DSM–IV–TR*

Ask psychologists and psychiatrists to describe or explain some of your more interesting relatives and they are likely to indicate that they are odd but not mentally ill. Trying to sort out odd or idiosyncratic from mentally ill by diagnosing maladjusted behaviour is a complicated process.

**DIAGNOSTIC AND STATISTICAL MANUAL OF MENTAL DISORDERS.** Most Canadian psychologists and psychiatrists use a system for diagnosing maladjusted behaviour called the *Diagnostic and Statistical Manual of Mental Disorders (DSM)*, devised by the American Psychiatric Association. The current edition of the manual is the fourth, the *DSM–IV–TR*, published in 2000. Its goals are (1) to improve the reliability of diagnoses by categorizing disorders according to observable behaviours, and (2) to ensure that the diagnoses are consistent with research evidence and practical experience (Widiger et al., 1991) but many critics claim that the system is less successful than intended (Kutchins & Kirk, 1997). The system designates 16 major categories of maladjustment and more than 200 subcategories. (Table 15.1 lists some of the major classifications.) The *DSM* also cites the **prevalence** of each disorder—the percentage of the population displaying the disorder during any specified period. For most psychological disorders, researchers also know the lifetime prevalence—the statistical likelihood that a person will develop the disorder during his or her lifetime.

PREVALENCE

The percentage of a population displaying a disorder during any specified period.

An important feature of the *DSM–IV–TR* is that diagnostic information for any individual is laid out on five different dimensions. The *DSM–IV–TR* refers to these dimensions as axes; the manual thus uses what is called a *multiaxial* system, and an individual receives a diagnosis on each of five axes. Axis I describes the *major disorders* themselves. Axis II describes *personality disorders and mental retardation*. Axis III describes *current medical conditions* that might be pertinent to understanding or managing the individual's mental disorder—for example, restricted activity due to heart disease may be a relevant factor for depression. Axis IV, *psychosocial or environmental problems*, refers to life stresses or familial support systems that may or may not facilitate a person's treatment or recovery. These include economic, job, or educational problems. Finally, Axis V comprises a *global assessment of functioning*, which reports the clinician's overall assessment of the client's functioning in the psychological, social, and occupational domains of the client's life in the past year. For example, a client might be said to have some mild symptoms such as insomnia and occasional truancy from school but, in general, be functioning pretty well. These five axes, when viewed together, help a clinician fully describe the nature of a person's maladjustment. It is important to note that there may not be an assessment on a particular axis. For example, there may be no medical condition to report on Axis III. Table 15.2 describes the axes of the *DSM–IV–TR*.

You might think that such a diagnostic manual would be straightforward, like an encyclopedia of mental disorders. However, because it was written by committees, the *DSM* represents various points of view, biases, and compromises; therefore, it has met with resistance and engendered controversy. Some take issue with the way the *DSM* groups disorders based on symptoms rather than causes. This

---

**TABLE 15.1**  Major Classifications of the *Diagnostic and Statistical Manual of Mental Disorders*, Fourth Edition (TR)

Disorders First Diagnosed in Infancy, Childhood, and Adolescence

Delirium, Dementia, and Other Cognitive Disorders

Substance-Related Disorders

Schizophrenia and Other Psychotic Disorders

Mood Disorders

Anxiety Disorders

Somatoform Disorders

Factitious Disorders

Dissociative Disorders

Sexual and Gender Identity Disorders

Eating Disorders

Sleep Disorders

Impulse Control Disorders

*Note: Each classification is further broken down into subtypes.*

**TABLE 15.2    The Axes of the *DSM–IV–TR***

| Axis | Description |
|------|-------------|
| Axis I | Symptoms that cause distress or significantly impair social or occupational functioning |
| Axis II | Personality disorders—personality patterns that are so pervasive, inflexible, and maladaptive that they impair interpersonal or occupational functioning |
| Axis III | Medical conditions that may be relevant to the understanding or treatment of a psychological disorder |
| Axis IV | Psychosocial and environmental problems (such as negative life events and interpersonal stressors) that may affect the diagnosis, treatment, and prognosis of psychological disorders |
| Axis V | Global assessment of functioning—the individual's overall level of functioning in social, occupational, and leisure activities |

*Source: Adapted from* Diagnostic and Statistical Manual of Mental Disorders, *Fourth Edition, American Psychiatric Association, 1994.*

feature results in a diagnostic system without a theoretical basis. Others argue that it is too complex, with too many categories and symptoms that overlap among the categories. Some say that, despite its complexity, questions remain about the reliability of its diagnoses for many disorders (Nathan & Langenbucher, 1999). Some have criticized those who formulated the *DSM* for using political rather than scientific criteria in determining what disorders are included (Kutchins & Kirk, 1997). Some have concerns about potential gender bias against women (e.g., Hartung & Widiger, 1998). Many psychologists are unhappy with the use of psychiatric terms that perpetuate a medical rather than a behavioural model. Finally, a few psychologists maintain that the *DSM* pathologizes everyday behaviours and allows some practitioners to take advantage of its legitimization of the psychiatric terms for political and monetary gain (Kutchins & Kirk, 1997). Therefore, the *DSM* is the most widely accepted classification system for mental disorders, but many object to its widespread use.

DIVERSITY AND DIAGNOSES.    The *DSM* is by no means the final word in diagnosing maladjustment, and its reliability is not completely known; rather, it is a developing system of classification. *DSM–IV–TR* includes instructions to clinicians to be more sensitive to issues of diversity and examples of syndromes that are specific to various cultures. Not all ethnic groups exhibit symptoms of every disorder; nor do all members of one ethnic group have an equal likelihood of exhibiting specific symptoms.

Research shows that the likelihood of a specific diagnosis is indeed related to ethnicity (for a specific example, see *Introduction to Research Basics*). For example, Asians receive more diagnoses of schizophrenia than do whites (Paradis, Hatch, & Friedman, 1994), despite the fact that Asians in general do not seek mental health services as often as whites do (Uba, 1994). In the United States, Hispanic Americans receive fewer diagnoses of schizophrenia than do whites (Flaskerud & Hu, 1992). Similarly, Koreans are more likely to be diagnosed as depressed than are people in Taiwan, the Philippines, the United States, or Canada (Crittenden et al., 1992). The rates of a specific disorder in a particular country probably reflect racial, religious, and cultural biases; they especially reflect the specific culture-bound symptomatology that a society considers normal. As suggested earlier, various cultures allow for, and perhaps encourage, specific symptomatology. Culture and its effects on clinical

## Cross-cultural Factors in a Diagnosis

A mother brought her 12-year-old daughter to the emergency room of a hospital because the girl seemed ill. Her diagnosis and treatment constituted an interesting case that Jason Takeuchi (2000) presented as a case study to illustrate the influence that culture has on abnormal behaviour and the diagnosis of mental disorders.

**Design.** A **case study** is a descriptive study that includes an intensive examination of one person. This approach allows an intensive study of a single case, usually chosen for its interesting or unique characteristics.

**Hypothesis.** Ethnicity has an impact on the expression of abnormal behaviour as well as on diagnosis and the types of treatment approaches that are successful.

**Participant.** Takeuchi described the case of this 12-year-old girl, whom he called C. C.'s father was from the United States and her mother was from Tonga, in the South Pacific. C. was born and lived in the US, but her mother maintained close ties with her family and the cultural traditions of Tonga.

**History.** During the two weeks prior to the emergency room visit, her mother said that C. became progressively preoccupied, isolated, and "spacey." Before that time, C.'s mother had been in Tonga taking care of C.'s grandfather, who had subsequently died.

**Procedure.** During the initial interview, C. expressed fear that she would harm herself, and subsequent conversations revealed hallucinations and claims that ghosts were after her, trying to harm her, including the ghost of her recently deceased grandfather. Her thought processes were disorganized, and her emotional reactions were not always appropriate to the situation.

The interpretation of C.'s symptoms varies according to the cultural perspective of the person making the diagnosis. According to psychiatric diagnosis in the US, C. exhibited seriously abnormal behaviour, which would likely result in prolonged treatment with psychoactive drugs and possibly psychotherapy. According to the cultural beliefs of Tonga, her grandfather's ghost could be haunting C. This condition is known as *fakamahaki*, which includes hearing the voices of dead relatives. Both her mother and her grandmother reported that they had experienced *fakamahaki* and had been cured by native healers who applied a specified course of herbs and rituals.

**Outcome.** An interesting part of this case study was the fact that C. received both diagnoses and both treatments. She was confined to a psychiatric facility and treated with base psychoactive drugs and psychotherapy, which were only partially effective in bringing about a decrease in her symptoms. Then her mother took her to Tonga, where she underwent treatment from a native healer. This treatment was more effective. C.'s acceptance of the treatment, belief in its effectiveness, and her family's cultural values were important in its success.

In many ways, C. appeared to be completely acculturated to Western society, but her close relationship with her Tongan relatives and acceptance of Tongan cultural values made a difference for both the expression of her symptoms and the effectiveness of her treatment. This case study provides a valuable lesson to psychiatrists and psychologists about the importance of taking culture into account in decisions concerning diagnosis and treatment. However, the uniqueness of the case does not allow generalization of these findings to others, which is a limitation of the case study method.

---

diagnosis and treatment plans are underresearched and constitute an important area of concern for practising psychologists. The Canadian Psychological Association and the American Psychological Association (1993) state that practitioners must:

- Recognize cultural diversity.
- Understand the role of culture and ethnicity in development.
- Help clients understand their own sociological identification.
- Understand how culture, race, gender, and sexual orientation interact to affect behaviour.

In the remainder of this chapter, we will explore some of the most important disorders described in *DSM–IV–TR* and their consequences. We begin with anxiety disorders.

CASE STUDY

A descriptive study that includes an intensive examination of one person.

## Be an ACTIVE LEARNER

**REVIEW**

> If you accept the medical–biological model of abnormal behaviour, what factors would you take seriously that those who accept the behavioural model would find unimportant? p. 534

> What are the differences in the psychodynamic, humanistic, and evolutionary views of abnormal behaviour? Are there any similarities? pp. 534–536

> What are the goals of the *DSM*, and what are its potential advantages and disadvantages? pp. 536–538

**THINK CRITICALLY**

> Try to "think outside the box" of your culture and analyze what behaviours are accepted as normal that might be considered abnormal for a visitor from another country or another world.

> A medical model assumes that people who suffer from a psychological disorder have no more control over their problem than do people who suffer from cancer. What do you think are the implications of such an assumption for the diagnosis and treatment of mental illnesses?

**APPLY PSYCHOLOGY**

> Make a list of behaviours that you consider abnormal but have observed on your campus. Keep this list and try to classify these behaviours according to the *DSM*.

**ANXIETY**

A generalized feeling of fear and apprehension that may be related to a particular situation or object and is often accompanied by increased physiological arousal.

▼ Karen Horney conceptualized anxiety as a central factor in both normal and abnormal behaviour.

# Anxiety Disorders

Everyone experiences anxiety, just as everyone experiences stress. Most people feel anxious in specific situations, such as before taking an exam, competing in a swim meet, or delivering a speech. Although anxiety can be a positive, motivating force, its effects also can be debilitating; left untreated, chronic anxiety eventually may impair a person's health. Those who have had serious enough anxiety problems to have been hospitalized are at increased risk for suicide (Allgulander, 1994). Anxiety disorders are so common in the general population that they warrant special consideration. Research into them, however, is not extensive, and there is a genuine lack of research on special populations or ethnic groups (Lee, Lei, & Sue, 2001). What has emerged in recent years has been the finding that at least some anxiety-related traits may have a genetic basis, and that symptoms sometimes can be alleviated through various drugs that facilitate serotonin transmission (Lesch et al., 1996). Let's look at the scope of the disorders.

## DEFINING ANXIETY

Karen Horney (pronounced HORN-eye), a neo-Freudian renowned for her work on anxiety, described it as the central factor in both normal and abnormal behaviour (Horney, 1937). **Anxiety** is a generalized feeling of fear and apprehension that may be related to a particular situation or object and is often accompanied by increased physiological arousal. Horney considered it a motivating force, an intrapsychic urge, and a signal of distress. She also argued that anxiety underlies many forms of maladjustment. She believed that maladjustment occurs when too many defences against anxiety pervade the personality.

Freud, in contrast, saw anxiety as the result of constant conflict among the id, ego, and superego; he called nearly all forms of behaviour associated with anxiety *neurotic*. Freud's term *neurosis* has made its way into everyday language, to the point where nonpsychologists tend to describe any quirky or annoying behaviour as neurotic. Anxiety (and what Freud called neurotic behaviour) refers to a wide range of symptoms, including fear, apprehension, inattention, heart palpitations, respiratory distress, and dizziness. The term *neurosis* was once part of the *DSM* and diagnostic terminology, but it was removed and is no longer part of the official terminology that describes abnormal behaviour. People also use the term *free-floating anxiety* to describe persistent anxiety not clearly related to any specific object or situation and accompanied by a sense of impending doom. This term also dates back to psychodynamic theories of abnormal behaviour and is not part of current terminology.

Psychologists recognize that anxiety is an important symptom of maladjustment—not necessarily the cause. Thoughts, environmental stimuli, or perhaps some long-standing and as yet unresolved conflict causes apprehension, fear, and its accompanying autonomic nervous system arousal. Feelings of not being able to control a situation are common to both children's and adults' anxiety. Some researchers speculate that childhood anxiety and a perceived sense of lack of control may lead to similar, if not identical, feelings in adulthood, which may result in a disorder (Chorpita & Barlow, 1998).

During the 1980s, research on anxiety disorders increased dramatically, partially prompted by the recognition that these disorders were very common and not always diagnosed (Cox & Taylor, 1999). Several different types of anxiety disorders appear in the *DSM*, including generalized anxiety disorder, phobias, and obsessive–compulsive disorder.

## GENERALIZED ANXIETY DISORDER

**Generalized anxiety disorder** is an anxiety disorder characterized by persistent anxiety occurring on more days than not for at least six months, sometimes with increased activity of the autonomic nervous system, apprehension, excessive muscle tension, and difficulty in concentrating. In addition to such excessive anxiety, people with generalized anxiety disorder find it difficult to control the anxiety they experience, so anxiety is a persistent problem in their lives. In addition, people with generalized anxiety disorder show impairment in at least three of six areas of functioning. These areas include three types of symptoms related to vigilance—restlessness or feeling "on edge," difficulty in concentrating, and irritability or impatience. Other symptoms include being easily fatigued, but another symptom is sleep difficulties or disturbances. Muscle tension and the inability to relax are the last set of symptoms. The *DSM* states that a person must show persistent anxiety that is not specific to one situation to be diagnosed with generalized anxiety disorder.

People with generalized anxiety disorder feel anxious almost constantly, even though nothing specific seems to provoke their anxiety. Expressed fears often revolve around health, money, family, or work. Unable to relax, they have trouble falling asleep; they tend to feel tired and have trouble concentrating. They often report excessive sweating, headaches, and insomnia. They are tense and irritable, have difficulty making decisions, and may hyperventilate (Kendall, Krain, & Treadwell, 1999).

GENERALIZED ANXIETY DISORDER

An anxiety disorder characterized by persistent anxiety on more days than not for at least six months, sometimes with autonomic hyperactivity, apprehension, problems with motor tension, and difficulty in concentrating.

**HandsOnPsych**
Version 2.0

**Psychopathology**

## PHOBIC DISORDERS

Do you know someone who is petrified at the thought of an airplane ride, who avoids crowds at all cost, or who shudders at the sight of a harmless garden snake? That person may suffer from a **phobic disorder**—an anxiety disorder involving an excessive, unreasonable, and irrational fear of, and consequent attempt to avoid, specific objects or situations. People with phobic disorders exhibit avoidance and escape behaviours, show increased heart rate and irregular breathing patterns, and report thoughts of disaster and severe embarrassment. Many psychologists agree that, once established, the relief a person derives from escaping or avoiding the feared situation maintains phobias. Fear alone does not distinguish a phobia; both fear and avoidance must be evident.

One key to diagnosing a phobic disorder is that the fear must be excessive and disproportionate to the situation. Most people have fears, some of which can be adaptive. Phobias, however, are not normal fears, and they are not adaptive. For example, many people fear heights, but this fear is not usually phobic—heights can be dangerous. Most people who fear heights would not avoid visiting a friend who lived on the top floor of a tall building; a person with a phobia of heights would, however. Fear alone does not distinguish a phobia; both fear and avoidance must be evident.

Mild phobic disorders occur in about 7.5 percent of the population. They are, in fact, relatively common in well-adjusted people. Severe, disabling phobias occur in less than 0.05 percent of the population, typically in patients with other disorders. Phobias occur most frequently between the ages of 30 and 60 and occur about equally in men and women. There are an infinite number of objects and situations toward which people become fearful. Because of the diversity and number of phobias, *DSM* classifies three basic kinds: agoraphobia, social phobia, and specific phobia.

PHOBIC DISORDERS

Anxiety disorders characterized by excessive, unreasonable, and irrational fear of, and consequent attempt to avoid, specific objects or situations.

**AGORAPHOBIA.** **Agoraphobia** is an anxiety disorder characterized by a marked fear and avoidance of being alone or isolated in open and public places from which escape might be difficult or embarrassing. This phobia is accompanied by avoidance behaviours that eventually may interfere with normal activities. It can become so debilitating that it prevents the individual from going into a space from which escape might be difficult or awkward (for example, airplanes or tunnels) or from being in crowds. People with a severe case may decide never to leave their home,

AGORAPHOBIA
[AG-or-uh-FOE-bee-uh]

An anxiety disorder characterized by fear and avoidance of being alone or isolated in open and public places from which escape might be difficult or embarrassing.

▲ Agoraphobia often leads to people isolating themselves in their homes.

fearing that they will lose control, panic, or cause a scene in a public place. Agoraphobia is often brought on by stress, particularly interpersonal stress. It is far more common in women than in men (5.8 percent versus 2.8 percent; Kessler et al., 1994).

Symptoms of agoraphobia are hyperventilation, extreme tension, and even cognitive disorganization. Agoraphobia may occur alone but people with agoraphobia often suffer from severe panic attacks. *Panic attacks* are characterized as acute anxiety, accompanied by sharp increases in autonomic nervous system arousal, that is not triggered by a specific event; persons who experience such attacks often avoid the situations that are associated with them, thus perpetuating the agoraphobia (McNally, 1994). Some cognitive psychologists think of a panic attack as a "fear of fear"; attempting to avoid anxiety because they are so sensitive to it and its symptoms, people may panic while trying to avoid the symptoms of being fearful (McNally et al., 1997; Zuckerman, 1999). About 24 percent of people who experience panic disorders (including those with agoraphobia) also have some type of depressive disorder and about 10 to 20 percent have alcohol-related problems (Cox & Taylor, 1999).

Agoraphobia is complicated, incapacitating, and extraordinarily difficult to treat. According to Freud and other psychoanalysts, traumatic childhood experiences may cause people to avoid particular objects, events, and situations that produce anxiety. Freudians speculate that as young children, agoraphobics may have feared abandonment by a cold or nonnurturing mother, and the fear has generalized to a fear of abandonment or helplessness. Most researchers today find Freudian explanations of phobic behaviour unconvincing. Contemporary researchers have searched for events that initiate panic attacks and the development of agoraphobia in the individual's learning history, family experiences, and genetics (Zuckerman, 1999). Despite much research, no simple cause for the disorder has yet been found.

SOCIAL PHOBIA
[FOE-bee-uh]

An anxiety disorder characterized by fear of, and a desire to avoid, situations in which the person might be exposed to scrutiny by others and might behave in an embarrassing or humiliating way.

**SOCIAL PHOBIA.** Whereas a person with agoraphobia may avoid all situations involving other people, a person with a social phobia tends to avoid situations involving possible exposure to the scrutiny of other people. A **social phobia** is an anxiety disorder characterized by fear of, and a desire to avoid, situations in which one might be exposed to scrutiny by others and might behave in an embarrassing or humiliating way. A person with a social phobia avoids eating in public or speaking before other people. Such a person also avoids evaluation by refusing to deal with people or situations in which evaluation and a lowering of self-esteem might occur (Williams, Kinney, & Falbo, 1989; Hackmann, Clark, & McManus, 2000). Social phobia is more than being shy, as shy individuals don't astutely avoid circumstances that make them uncomfortable or self-conscious. Social phobia disrupts normal living and social relationships. The dread of attending a social function can begin weeks in advance and lead to debilitating symptoms.

SPECIFIC PHOBIA

An anxiety disorder characterized by irrational and persistent fear of a specific object or situation, along with a compelling desire to avoid it.

**SPECIFIC PHOBIA.** A **specific phobia** is an anxiety disorder characterized by irrational and persistent fear of a specific object or situation, along with a compelling desire to avoid it. Most people are familiar with specific phobias; see Table 15.3 for some examples. Among specific phobias are *claustrophobia* (fear of closed spaces), *hematophobia* (fear of the sight of blood), and *acrophobia* (fear of heights). Many specific phobias develop in childhood, adolescence, or early adulthood. Most people who have fears of heights, small spaces, water, doctors, or flying can calm themselves and deal with their fears, but those who cannot (true phobics) often seek the help of a psychotherapist when the phobia interferes with their health or day-to-day functioning. Treatment using behaviour therapy is typically effective.

| TABLE 15.3 | Some Specific Phobias |
| --- | --- |

Acrophobia (fear of high places)

Ailurophobia (fear of cats)

Algophobia (fear of pain)

Aquaphobia (fear of water)

Astraphobia (fear of storms, thunder, and lightning)

Barophobia (fear of gravity)

Claustrophobia (fear of enclosed places)

Cynophobia (fear of dogs)

Gymnophobia (fear of nudity)

Hematophobia (fear of blood)

Mysophobia (fear of contamination)

Nyctophobia (fear of darkness)

Peladophobia (fear of bald people)

Phonophobia (fear of one's own voice)

Thanatophobia (fear of death)

Xenophobia (fear of strangers)

Zoophobia (fear of animals)

## OBSESSIVE–COMPULSIVE DISORDERS

Being orderly and organized is an asset for most people in today's fast-paced, complex society. However, when orderliness becomes a driving concern, a person may be suffering from an obsessive–compulsive disorder. An **obsessive–compulsive disorder** is an anxiety disorder characterized by persistent and uncontrollable thoughts and irrational beliefs (obsessions) that cause performance of intrusive and inappropriate compulsive rituals that interfere with daily life. The unwanted thoughts, urges, and actions of people with obsessive–compulsive disorders focus on maintaining order and control. About 2 percent of the population suffer from obsessive–compulsive disorders. Of those with the disorder, about 20 percent have only obsessions or compulsions; about 80 percent have both.

People with obsessive–compulsive disorders combat anxiety by carrying out ritual behaviours that reduce tension; they feel that they have to *do* something. If they do not perform these compulsive acts, they may develop severe anxiety. Their thoughts have extraordinary power to control actions. For example, a person obsessed with avoiding germs may wash his hands a hundred times a day and may wear white gloves to avoid touching contaminated objects. A person obsessed with punctuality may become extremely anxious if she happens to arrive late for a dinner date. Adolescents with obsessive–compulsive disorders tend to wash and rewash, check, count, repeat, touch, and straighten their environment (March, Leonard, & Swedo, 1995). A person may compulsively write notes about every detail of every task before permitting himself to take any action. Here is an account of fairly severe obsessive–compulsive behaviour:

> I used to write notes to remind myself to do a particular job, so in my mind there was a real risk that one of these notes might go out of the window or door . . . My fear was that if one of these papers blew away, this would cause a fatality to the person carrying out my design project . . . I found it difficult to walk along the street, as every time I saw paper I wondered if it was some of mine. I had to pick it all up, unless it was brown chocolate paper, or lined paper, which I didn't use. And before I got on my bike, I checked that nothing was sticking out of my pockets and got my wife to recheck . . . I couldn't smoke a cigarette without taking it to bits and checking there

OBSESSIVE–COMPULSIVE DISORDER

An anxiety disorder characterized by persistent and uncontrollable thoughts and irrational beliefs (obsessions) that cause performance of intrusive and inappropriate compulsive rituals that interfere with daily life.

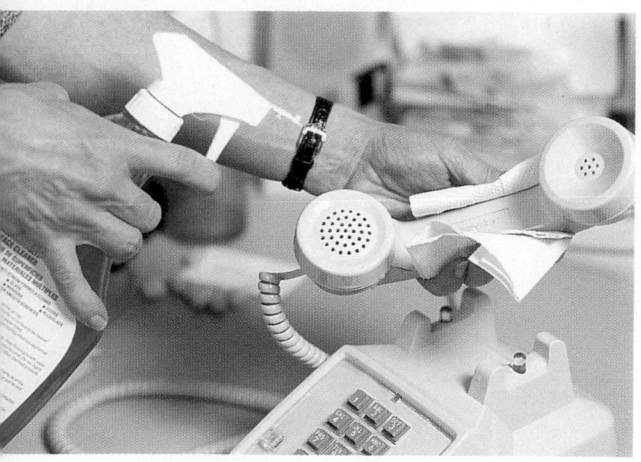

▲ An obsession with avoiding "germs" and a compulsion to disinfect is a common form of obsessive–compulsive disorder.

was no document between the paper and tobacco. I couldn't even have sex because I thought a piece of paper might get intertwined into the mattress. (Melville, 1977, pp. 66–67)

Freud and other psychodynamic theorists believed that obsessive–compulsive disorders come largely from difficulties during the anal stage of development, when orderliness and cleanliness are often stressed. Learning theorists argue that bringing order to a person's environment reduces uncertainty and risk and thus is reinforcing. Because reinforced behaviours tend to recur, these behaviours become exaggerated during times of stress.

Biopsychologists have identified brain structures involved with obsessive–compulsive disorder. Studies that involve imaging the brain indicate that several parts of the brain are involved, including parts of the frontal lobe of the cerebral cortex, the basal ganglia, and the amygdala (Szeszko et al., 1999). Both the functioning and the structure of the area of the frontal lobes just behind the eyes and the amygdala (under the temporal lobes) are affected in individuals with obsessive–compulsive disorder. This evidence leads some neurologists to define obsessive–compulsive disorder as a brain disorder with behavioural symptoms (Micallef & Blin, 2001).

Practitioners report that full-blown and dramatic cases of obsessive–compulsive disorders are relatively rare. Treatment often includes drugs (such as Anafrinil, Prozac, or Zoloft; see Chapter 16) combined with relaxation exercises (March, Leonard, & Swedo, 1995) and cognitive behaviour therapy (Abramowitz, 1998). Such treatment helps change ideas about stress and the consequences of anxiety. Family support and family psychotherapy are also helpful; families are taught that they should neither encourage the behaviours nor participate in the person's rituals. In fact, research shows that when clients are given training to refrain from compulsive behaviours after exposure to anxiety-producing ideas, people, or events, the training decreases compulsive acts and associated anxiety (Marks et al., 1986). Today self-help groups are also part of successful treatments. Although most people improve, even without treatment, over a period of five years or more, people who develop obsessive–compulsive disorder before the age of 20 are less likely to improve (Skoog & Skoog, 1999).

*Be an*
## ACTIVE LEARNER

**REVIEW**
> How does agoraphobia differ from the other phobias? pp. 542–543
> Identify the central elements of obsessive–compulsive disorder. pp. 543–544

**THINK CRITICALLY**
> Evolutionary psychologists argue that a value for cleanliness and disgust over filth are adaptive. How would evolutionary psychology explain obsessive–compulsive disorder, which is clearly not adaptive?

**APPLY PSYCHOLOGY**
> What situations do you fear? How do your fears differ from phobias?

# Mood Disorders

Everyone experiences dark moods at one time or another. Ending a long-term intimate relationship, feeling overwhelmed during final exams, mourning the death of a close friend, and experiencing serious financial problems can all be sources of sad moods. In fact, we often refer to *depression* as feeling sad or lonely. But when people become so depressed or sad that a change occurs in their outlook and overt behaviour, they may be suffering from *clinical depression*, a term that has a specific meaning for psychologists. Depression is considered to be a type of mood disorder. Mood disorders, which include bipolar disorder and depressive disorders, may sometimes be triggered by a specific event, although for many individuals the symptoms develop with no apparent cause.

### DEPRESSIVE DISORDERS

Depression is sometimes referred to as the common cold of psychological disturbances. This is an apt metaphor because it serves not only to underscore its prevalence but also to indicate the trivializing of its impact on those affected. Statistics Canada (2003) noted that, at any time, about 1.12 million Canadians suffer from this disabling disorder. Many of those people are misdiagnosed or undiagnosed and are not receiving treatment, despite its availability (Hirschfeld et al., 1997).

In his 1990 memoir, *Darkness Visible*, American novelist and Pulitzer Prize winner William Styron described his state of mind during a period of depression:

> He [a psychiatrist] asked me if I was suicidal, and I reluctantly told him yes. I did not particularize—since there seemed no need to—did not tell him that in truth many of the artifacts of my house had become potential devices for my own destruction: the attic rafters (and an outside maple or two) a means to hang myself, the garage a place to inhale carbon monoxide, the bathtub a vessel to receive the flow from my opened arteries. The kitchen knives in their drawers had but one purpose for me. Death by heart attack seemed particularly inviting, absolving me as it would of active responsibility, and I had toyed with the idea of self-induced pneumonia—a long frigid, shirt-sleeved hike through the rainy woods. Nor had I overlooked an ostensible accident, à la Randall Jarrell, by walking in front of a truck on the highway nearby . . . Such hideous fantasies, which cause well people to shudder, are to the deeply depressed mind what lascivious daydreams are to persons of robust sexuality. (p. 52)

Depressed people are more than simply blue or sad. As Styron reveals, depression is debilitating, overwhelming, and dangerous. **Depressive disorders** are mood disorders in which people show extreme and persistent sadness, despair, and loss of interest in life's usual activities on a day-to-day basis. **Major depressive disorder** (or clinical depression) is characterized by loss of interest in almost all of life's usual activities; a sad, hopeless, or discouraged mood; sleep disturbance; loss of appetite; loss of energy; and feelings of unworthiness and guilt. Someone experiencing major depressive disorder is not merely experiencing fleeting anxiety or sadness, although this disorder may be triggered by a specific event, such as the loss of a loved one, a job, or a home. Sufferers show at least some difficulties with social and occupational functioning, although their behaviour is not necessarily bizarre.

**SYMPTOMS.** The symptoms of major depressive disorder include poor appetite, insomnia, weight loss, loss of energy, feelings of worthlessness and intense guilt, inability to concentrate, and sometimes thoughts of death and suicide (Zuckerman, 1999). Depressed people have a gloomy outlook on life, an extremely distorted view of their problems, a tendency to blame themselves, and low self-esteem. They often withdraw from social and physical contact with others. Every task seems to require a great effort, thought is slow and unfocused, and problem-solving abilities are impaired. Individuals may display certain physical problems as well; for example, decrease in bone density and heightened risk of osteoporosis occur in those who suffer from depression, and depression is associated with abnormal brain activity in the frontal lobes and with immune system problems (Leonard, 2001; Schweiger et al., 1994; Videbech, 2000).

Depressed people may also have **delusions**—false beliefs that are inconsistent with reality but are held in spite of evidence that disconfirms them. Delusions may induce feelings of guilt, shame, and persecution. Seriously disturbed people show even greater disruptions in thought and motor processes and a total lack of spontaneity and motivation. Such people typically report that they have no hope for themselves or the world; nothing seems to interest them. They are often extremely self-critical (Blatt, 1995). Some feel responsible for serious world problems such as economic depression, disease, or hunger. They report strange diseases and may insist that their body is disintegrating or that their brain is being eaten from the inside out. Most people who exhibit symptoms of major depressive disorder can describe their reasons for feeling sad and dejected; however, they may be unable to explain why their response is so deep and so prolonged.

**DEPRESSIVE DISORDERS**
General category of mood disorders in which people show extreme and persistent sadness, despair, and loss of interest in life's usual activities.

**MAJOR DEPRESSIVE DISORDER**
Depressive disorder characterized by loss of interest in almost all of life's usual activities; a sad, hopeless, or discouraged mood; sleep disturbance; loss of appetite; loss of energy; and feelings of unworthiness and guilt.

**DELUSIONS**
False beliefs that are inconsistent with reality but are held in spite of evidence that disproves them.

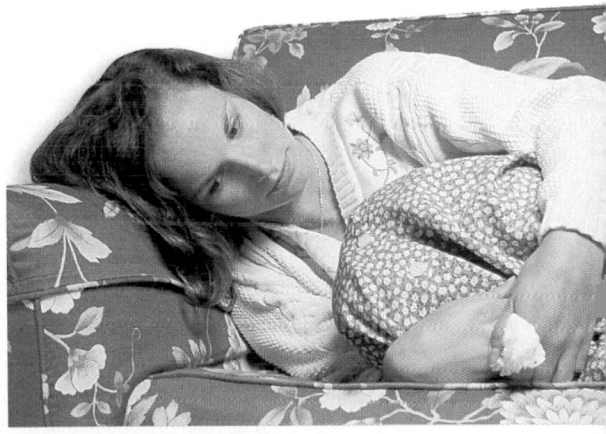

▼ Depressed people are more than sad—depression is a debilitating disorder.

Psychologists say that many people suffering from major depressive disorder are poor at reality testing. *Reality testing* is a person's ability to judge the demands of the environment accurately and to deal with those demands. People who are poor at reality testing are unable to cope with the demands of life in rational ways because their reasoning ability is grossly impaired.

**ONSET AND DURATION.**    A major depressive episode can occur at any age, but most people who experience these episodes usually undergo the first one before age 40. Symptoms are readily apparent and may last for days, weeks, or even months. One form of depressive disorder, seasonal affective disorder, discussed in *Psychology in Action*, is cyclical, with levels of depression rising and falling seasonally. Because so many different circumstances can be involved, the extent of depression varies dramatically from individual to individual. Episodes may occur once or many times. Sometimes a depressive episode may be followed by years of normal functioning—followed by two or three brief incidents of depression a few weeks apart. Stressful life events are sometimes predictors of depression (Mazure et al., 2000). Major depressive disorder is not exclusively an adult disorder; researchers find evidence of it in children and adolescents (Lewinsohn et al., 1999). When children suffer from depression, they often have other symptoms, especially anxiety and loneliness.

**PREVALENCE.**    According to Statistics Canada, major depressive disorder strikes about 1.3 million Canadians each year; around the world, depression imposes an enormous burden of disease to additional millions (Kessler, 2000). Women are twice as likely as men to be diagnosed as depressed and are more likely to express feelings of depression openly (Culbertson, 1997; Sprock & Yoder, 1997). Women's higher rate of depression appears in many (but not all) cultures around the world. The reasons for this gender difference are not clear, but Susan Nolen-Hoeksema and her colleagues (Nolen-Hoeksema, 2000; Nolen-Hoeksema, Larson, & Grayson, 1999) hypothesize that girls and women have more negative experiences as well as lower feelings of mastery, and they engage in rumination in response to negative events and feelings. *Rumination* is the process of dwelling on and analyzing problems and negative feelings. As Figure 15.1 shows, this coping style tends to prolong negative feelings and to increase depression.

Depression varies with age, and people between ages 25 and 45 are most vulnerable (Ingram, Scott, & Siegle, 1999). According to several studies, Canadians born since 1950 are more likely to be depressed than their grandparents or great-grandparents were (Lewinsohn et al., 1993). These changes may be due to changes in diagnosis or reporting frequency, but the difference may be mostly due to the method of study rather than increases in the risks for depression (Stassen, Ragaz, & Reich, 1997). Martin Seligman (1988) suggests that the increased incidence of depression stems from too much emphasis on the individual, coupled with a loss of faith in supportive institutions such as family, country, and religion. Some research (Oliver & Novak, 1993) supports the notion that the type of alienation Seligman describes is related to depression. Examining the rates of mood disorders in countries around the world, industrialized countries show higher rates than developing countries (WHO International Consortium in Psychiatric Epidemiology, 2000), but this difference may reflect better access to mental health services in developed countries. However, depression is a worldwide problem not restricted to industrialized, individualistic cultures. It is a leading cause of disability worldwide, affecting more than 300 million people (Holden, 2000).

**CLINICAL EVALUATION.**    How does a practitioner know if a person is suffering from major depressive disorder? Diagnosis for depression (or any other mental disorder) should include a complete clinical evaluation, which comprises three parts: a

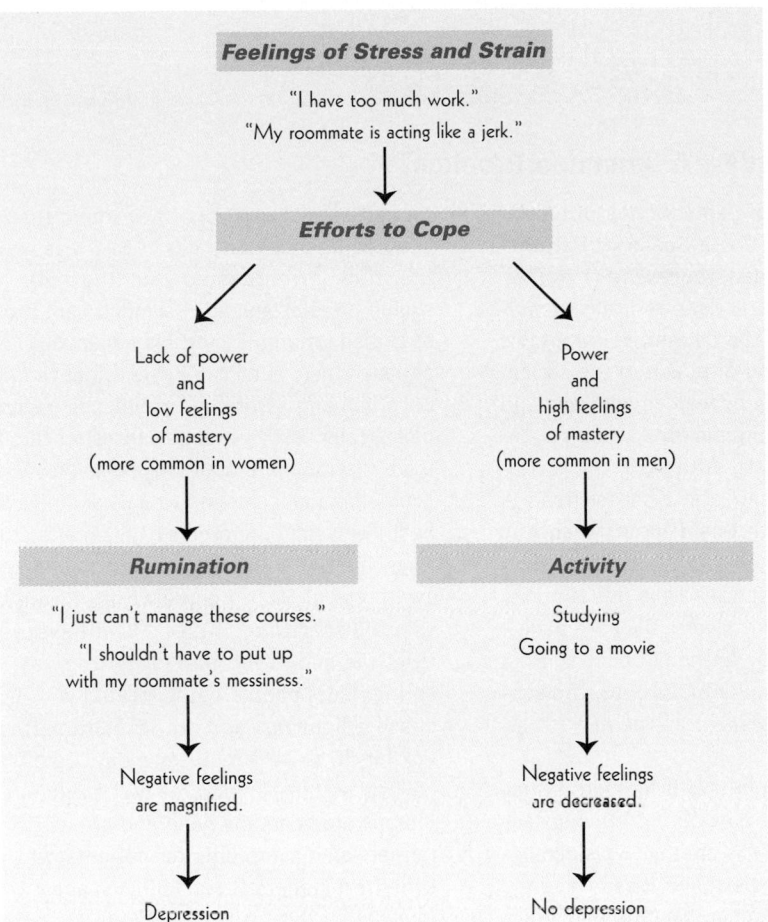

**FIGURE 15.1**

**How Stress, Feelings of Mastery, and Rumination Influence Depression**

Susan Nolen-Hoeksema (2000) and her colleagues hypothesize that rumination increases feelings of depression. Women are more likely than men to experience low power and feelings of low mastery, which magnify rumination and depression.

physical examination, a psychiatric history, and a mental status examination. The *physical examination* is done to rule out thyroid disorders, viral infection, and anemia—all of which cause a slowing down of behaviour. A neurological check of coordination, reflexes, and balance is part of this exam, to rule out brain disorders. The *psychiatric history* attempts to trace the course of the apparent disorder, genetic or family factors, and past treatments. Finally, the *mental status examination* scrutinizes thought, speaking processes, and memory; it includes interviews and may include tests for psychiatric symptoms (such as the MMPI–2) and projective tests (such as the TAT) (see Chapter 12 for information about these tests).

One reason for the extensive clinical evaluation is the importance of distinguishing between major depressive disorder and dysthymic disorder. In *dysthymic disorder*, people experience a chronic depressed mood for more days than not for a period of at least two years, but this reaction is mild compared to major depressive disorder. Along with depressed mood, people with dysthymic disorder experience poor appetite, insomnia, low self-esteem, and feelings of hopelessness. This disorder often goes undiagnosed and untreated; people begin to accept this mood as part of their typical personality. Dysthymic disorder spreads a thin veil of sadness over a person's life; individuals with the disorder are less likely to marry and more likely to divorce and are often underemployed or unemployed. They report being self-critical, take little interest in life's activities, and show occupational and social impairment. Dysthymic disorder is not as severe as major depressive disorder but lasts longer and often occurs alongside it; clinicians often diagnose dysthymic disorder in persons who were initially seeking help for a major depressive episode.

## Seasonal Affective Disorder: A Canadian Problem?

In the *DSM–IV–TR,* a diagnosis of depression or of bipolar disorder can have the specifier "With Seasonal Pattern" applied to it. This specifier is added whenever a characteristic pattern of depression regularly rises and falls at various times of the year. Typically, the depressive symptoms worsen in either fall or winter and diminish in the spring. This disorder varies with latitude as well as with age and sex, with latitudes further from the equator, younger people, and women at higher risk. Although the "With Seasonal Pattern" qualifier is new, the disorder itself is not. Most people are familiar with this disorder when it is called by its better known name, *seasonal affective disorder* (SAD). Probably because most Canadians live at northern latitudes with low winter light levels, they are at risk for SAD. In a study conducted by Anthony Levitt and his colleagues (2000) at the University of Toronto, the seasonal subtype was found to represent 11 percent of all individuals with major depression.

SAD differs from depression in that it includes symptoms such as overeating, usually involving cravings for sweets and carbohydrates, as well as apathy, oversleeping, and weight gain. People also experience loss of energy, anxiety, and irritability; have difficulty concentrating; experience bouts of crying; and suffer from headaches and fatigue. There is some question about whether people without other forms of depression suffer SAD. Recent research (Harmatz et al., 2000) suggests that significant seasonal variation in mood occurs in individuals never diagnosed as depressed; this effect was particularly noticeable in women. So it appears that individuals in high-risk groups, who are not at risk for depression, may in fact be at risk for SAD.

The causes of SAD are not well understood. It is thought that genetics may predispose a person to vary production of serotonin (an important neurotransmitter in the regulation of mood) seasonally. It is also thought that diminished sunlight may trigger the symptoms associated with SAD. It may be that lower light levels disrupt circadian rhythms and that this disruption in turn affects hormone production. However, when John Haggarty and his colleagues (2001) at the University of Western Ontario per-

formed a meta-analysis, they found that the relationship between latitude and rates of SAD was weak and, based on this finding, suggested that the light level hypothesis should be re-examined. Raymond Lam, from the University of British Columbia, and his colleagues (2000) argue that although there is considerable evidence to support both the circadian and serotonin hypotheses, recent data argue for biologically heterogeneous causes for the disorder. That is, there may be more than one cause of SAD. For example, it is possible that some individuals are more sensitive to lower light levels than are others (Guillemette et al., 1998).

Effective treatments exist to eliminate or reduce the symptoms of SAD. People with SAD are typically treated with full-spectrum ("white") light therapy in an attempt to reset the body's internal clock from late in the fall until spring. Most people being treated with light therapy purchase a light box and sit 45 centimetres in front of the box for 30 to 120 minutes a day. Data from Lam and his colleagues (2001) indicate that clinical responses to light therapy are generally good and are associated with reduction of some symptoms for patients diagnosed with SAD. Other researchers (Lee, 1996) suggest that the dose and intensity of the light is related to the alleviation of symptoms. Medium-intensity light (1700 to 3500 lux) twice a day, morning and evening, was found to be most effective at reducing symptoms. People with SAD may also take antidepressants to treat the depressive symptoms during the fall and winter months.

## CAUSES OF MAJOR DEPRESSIVE DISORDER

Although major depression is "the common cold of mental disorders," its cause is not understood. Identifying the cause is difficult because several different theories exist, and all have research support. However, the research does not present a coherent picture; instead, results are complex and mixed, leading prominent researcher Marvin Zuckerman (1999) to propose that more than one theory may be necessary to explain all cases of depression. Let's consider the leading theories and the research support and problems with each, bearing in mind that Zuckerman may be correct, and depression may have more than one cause.

**BIOLOGICAL THEORIES.**  Both genetics and neurotransmitters have been implicated as biological factors that underlie depression. Children of depressed parents are more likely than other children to be depressed; further, twin studies indicate that genetic factors play a substantial role in depression (Barondes, 1998; Kendler et al., 1992; Kendler, Neale, Kessler et al., 1993). However, depression is not caused by a single gene, and finding multiple gene locations is a complex task (Zuckerman, 1999). In addition, the process through which genes affect behaviour must be demonstrated. In the case of depression, genetics may affect neurotransmitters (Dikeos et al., 1999).

Neurotransmitters held within vesicles in one neuron are released, move across the synaptic space, and attach themselves at a binding site at an adjacent neuron (see Chapter 2). The receptors have binding sites for particular neurotransmitters. This is an important point, because a specific neurotransmitter can and will influence only those neurons that have receptors for it. Four of the key neurotransmitters in the brain are dopamine, norepinephrine, epinephrine, and serotonin, all of which are categorized chemically as *monoamines*.

When monoamines are released but do not bind to the next neuron, researchers find that people report feeling depressed. Such neurotransmitters are then either neutralized or taken back up by the neuron that released it, in a process called *reuptake*. (Again, see Chapter 2 for a review of this process.) When a person is given drugs that do not allow the neurotransmitters to be neutralized or restored to the releasing cell, the neurotransmitter is more likely to bind, and depression lifts. The *monoamine theory of depression* suggests that major depression results from a deficiency of monoamines or inefficient monoamine receptors (Mann et al., 1996; Soares & Mann, 1997). This theory is supported by the effectiveness of antidepressant drugs, which affect the availability of monoamines.

However, part of the problem in accepting neurotransmitters as the underlying cause of depression is the length of time required for these drugs to take effect—depressed people must take antidepressant drugs for several weeks before they start to feel relief of their symptoms, but blood tests show that the drugs are available in the body after a few days. In addition, these drugs are not effective for some individuals, and researchers are beginning to question the adequacy of the monoamine theory of depression (Hindmarch, 2001). The inconsistency of findings points to the possibility that Zuckerman (1999) mentioned: multiple causes of depression. Another type of explanation for depression comes from learning and distorted ways of thinking.

**LEARNING AND COGNITIVE THEORIES.**  Learning and cognitive theorists argue that learning and thoughts underlie depression. Peter Lewinsohn (1974) developed a view that people who fail to receive reinforcement are deprived of pleasure and thus become depressed. Other people find them unpleasant to be with and avoid them, thus perpetuating an environment with little reinforcement (Lewinsohn & Talkington, 1979). Lewinsohn stresses that depressed people often lack the social skills needed to obtain reinforcement, such as asking a neighbour or friend for help with a problem. See Figure 15.2 for details of Lewinsohn's view. A modification of this view incorporates the impact of stressful life events and cognition, making the model no longer strictly a learning explanation of depression (Ingram, Scott, & Siegle, 1999).

Psychiatrist Aaron Beck proposed another influential theory that explains depression in terms of thought processes. Beck (1967) suggested that depressed people already have negative views of themselves, the environment, and the future,

FIGURE 15.2
**Lewinsohn's View of Depression**

According to Lewinsohn (1974), some people have few reinforcers available in the environment. This lack of reinforcers causes depression, which then leads to even fewer reinforcers.

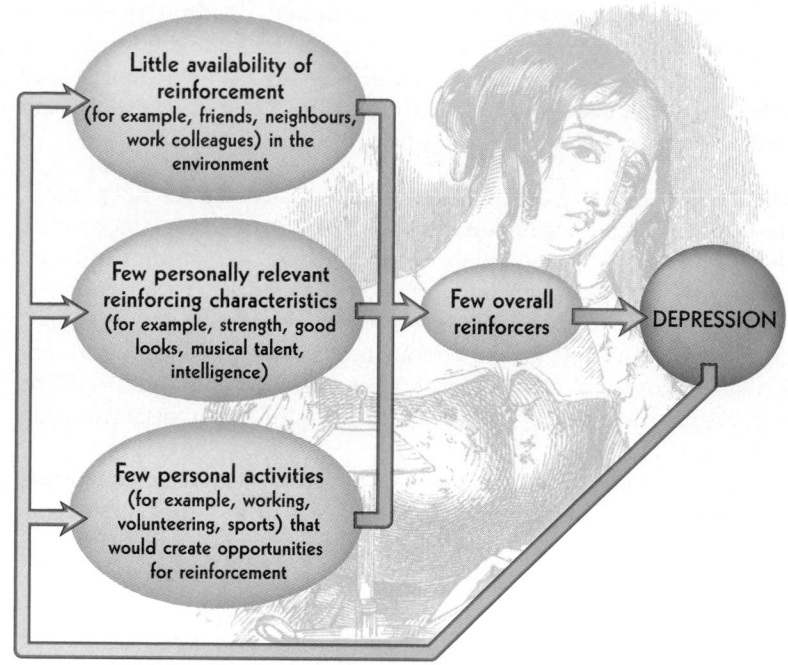

and these views cause them to magnify their errors. This way of thinking forms a schema that is the basis for depression. Depressed people compare themselves to other people, usually unfairly; when they come up short, they see the difference as disastrous. They see the human condition as universally wretched and view the world as a place that defeats positive behaviour. Their poor self-concept and negative expectations about the world lead to depression.

These cognitive distortions may occur in adolescents as well as adults, and research indicates that adolescents who have a negative, fatalistic view of the world are at greatly increased risk for depression (Roberts, Roberts, & Chen, 2000). Research also supports Beck's view that depressed people have more negative thoughts about themselves, the future, and the world in general and that this tendency to interpret the world in negative terms is a stable way to process information (Ingram et al., 1999). These tendencies exist and are activated under situations of stress.

According to Beck, cognitions underlie depression and perpetuate it by causing poor judgments, which feed back into negative cognitions. Beck's theory is influential among psychologists for two reasons: First, it is consistent with the notion that depression stems from ways of thinking. Second, it acknowledges the interaction of the cognitive schema that underlies depression with environmental variables such as stress.

**LEARNED HELPLESSNESS.** What would you do if you failed every exam you took, regardless of your efforts? What happens when a person's hopes and dreams are constantly thwarted, regardless of her or his behaviour? The result may be **learned helplessness**—the behaviour of giving up or not responding, exhibited by people and animals exposed to negative consequences or punishment over which they feel they have no control.

Seligman (1976) has suggested that people's beliefs about the causes of their failures determine whether they will become depressed. When they attribute their failures to unalterable conditions within themselves ("my own weakness, which is unlikely to change"), their self-esteem is diminished (Maddux & Meier, 1995). People who develop learned helplessness feel that they cannot change highly

**LEARNED HELPLESSNESS**

The behavior of giving up or not responding, exhibited by people and animals exposed to negative consequences or punishment over which they feel they have no control.

aversive life events (Abramson, Metalsky, & Alloy, 1989). That is, when people come to believe that outcomes are unrelated to anything under their control, they develop learned helplessness and become pessimistic rather than optimistic. For example, a man who comes to believe that his effort to meet new people by being outgoing and friendly never works may stop trying. Eventually, he will choose not to respond to the environment because he has learned that his behaviour makes no difference (Peterson & Seligman, 1984). According to Seligman, the major cause of learned helplessness is a person's (or animal's) belief that its response will not affect what happens to it in the future. The result of this belief is anxiety, depression, and, eventually, nonresponsiveness. The opposite of learned helplessness is *learned optimism*—a sense that the world has positive outcomes, which leads people to see happy things in their lives (Seligman, 1991; Seligman & Csikszentmihalyi, 2000). Seligman asserts that *learning* is key to developing a sense of hopelessness or optimism. Seligman (1988) argues that the environment, not genetics, is the cause of pessimism, depression, and helplessness, especially when people believe that they are responsible for long-standing failures in many areas of their lives.

**THE BIOPSYCHOSOCIAL MODEL.** Many variables determine whether an individual will develop depression, or any other disorder, for that matter. Some factors, including genetic history, brain chemistry, cognitions, stress, and family environment, make some people more vulnerable than others. **Vulnerability** is a person's diminished ability to deal with demanding life events. The more vulnerable a person is, the less environmental stress or other factors (such as anxiety) are needed to initiate depression. This is the vulnerability–stress hypothesis, sometimes termed the *diathesis–stress model.*

The diathesis–stress model hypothesizes that mental disorders occur when people with vulnerability encounter stressful situations. That is, disorders develop from the combination of factors. The vulnerability may be due either to biological factors or learned tendencies, but vulnerable people develop problems at lower levels of stress than do less vulnerable people (Zuckerman, 1999). For example, a person with a genetic vulnerability for depression will not necessarily become depressed, but experiences such as parental divorce or death will be more likely to result in depression for this individual than for one with no genetic vulnerability for depression. The concept of vulnerability also applies to another type of mood disorder—bipolar disorder.

## BIPOLAR DISORDER

Canadian actors Margot Kidder and Jim Carrey, writers Margaret Laurence and Timothy Findley, and ballerina Karen Kain all have at least two things in common: artistic talent and a diagnosis of bipolar disorder. People who suffer from bipolar disorder experience depression similar to major depression, but they also experience the opposite feelings—excitement, confidence, and euphoria. **Bipolar disorder**, which was originally known as *manic–depressive disorder*, gets its name from the fact that people with this disorder experience behaviour that varies between two extremes: mania and depression. The *manic phase* is characterized by rapid speech, inflated self-esteem, impulsiveness, euphoria, and decreased need for sleep. People in the manic phase are easily distracted, get angry when things do not go their way, and seem to have boundless energy. A person in the *depressed phase* is moody and sad, with feelings of hopelessness. People with bipolar disorder cycle between these two mood extremes.

Bipolar disorder is much less common than major depression. Only about 1 percent of the population develops this disorder (Canadian Mental Health Association, 2002a), but that percentage means that about 200 000 Canadians suffer from bipolar disorder. Men and women are equally likely to be affected. People who suffer from bipolar disorder are often in their late twenties before they begin to

VULNERABILITY
A person's diminished ability to deal with demanding life events.

BIPOLAR DISORDER
Mood disorder originally known as manic–depressive disorder because it is characterized by behaviour that vacillates between two extremes: mania and depression.

Be an
## ACTIVE
## LEARNER

**REVIEW**
> What are the essential charac-
teristics of major depression?
pp. 545–546
> What evidence supports each
of the theories of depression? pp. 549–551
> Identify the characteristics that distinguish bipo-
lar disorder from major depression. pp. 551–552

**THINK CRITICALLY**
> Women are diagnosed with major depression at a
2-to-1 ratio compared to men in Canada and
many other countries. In some societies, however,
rate of diagnosis is similar for men and women.
What are the implications of these differing rates
of diagnoses for major depression?
> People often believe that mental disorders lead to
unusual thought processes, which boost creativity.
Most people diagnosed with mental disorders are
not as creative as normal people, but a disproportionate number of creative people have been diagnosed with bipolar disorder. What characteristics
of this disorder might relate to creativity?

**APPLY PSYCHOLOGY**
> Visit the Web site for the National Depression and
Manic Depressive Association at www.ndmda.org
to learn more about these disorders. The Web site
includes a screening for bipolar disorder.
Complete this screening to help you understand
how your behaviour matches (and fails to match)
the symptoms of bipolar disorder.

DISSOCIATIVE DISORDERS
Psychological disorders characterized by a sudden but temporary
alteration in consciousness,
identity, sensorimotor behaviour,
or memory.

manifest the symptoms, and the disorder often continues throughout their lives. Bipolar disorder may go unrecognized and be underdiagnosed in children and adolescents (Geller & Luby, 1997).

People with bipolar disorder may be relatively stable for a few days, weeks, or months between episodes of excitement and depression, or they may rapidly cycle between the two moods. The key component of bipolar disorder is the shift from excited states to depressive states of sadness and hopelessness. The disorder seems to have a biological basis with a substantial genetic component (Zuckerman, 1999). People with bipolar disorder often respond fairly well to drug treatment, especially to lithium and other newer drugs, which we'll discuss in Chapter 16 (Barondes, 1998; Post et al., 1998). Although those who take the appropriate medications for the disorder respond fairly well, many refuse to medicate themselves because it means forgoing the "highs" of the manic episodes. As many as 50 percent of individuals who suffer from bipolar disorder also exhibit maladaptive behaviours or personality traits, such as obsessions and compulsions or extreme dependence or narcissism (Peselow, Sanfilipo, & Fieve, 1995). Table 15.4 lists the signs and symptoms of mania and depression in bipolar disorder.

Depressive and bipolar disorders leave people unable to cope effectively on a day-to-day basis. Dissociative disorders, which will be discussed next, can be even more disruptive.

## Dissociative Disorders

If you watch daytime TV dramas, you see dissociative disorders more often than psychologists and psychiatrists do. These disorders are much more common in fictional plots than in reality. **Dissociative disorders** are psychological disorders characterized by a sudden but temporary alteration in consciousness, identity, sensorimotor behaviour, or memory. Although relatively rare, these disorders are easily identifiable. They include dissociative amnesia and dissociative identity disorder.

| TABLE 15.4 | Bipolar Disorder: Cycles of Mania and Depression | |
|---|---|---|
| | **Manic Behaviour** | **Depressive Behaviour** |
| **Emotional Characteristics** | Elation, euphoria | Gloominess, hopelessness |
| | Extreme sociability, expansiveness | Social withdrawal |
| | Impatience | Irritability |
| | Distractibility | |
| | Inflated self-esteem | |
| **Cognitive Characteristics** | Desire for action | Indecisiveness |
| | Impulsiveness | Slowness of thought |
| | Talkativeness | Obsessive worrying about death |
| | Grandiosity | Negative self-image |
| | | Delusions of guilt |
| | | Difficulty in concentrating |
| **Motor Characteristics** | Hyperactivity | Fatigue |
| | Decreased need for sleep | Difficulty in sleeping |
| | Sexual indiscretion | Decreased sex drive |
| | Increased appetite | Decreased appetite |
| | | Decreased motor activity |

## DISSOCIATIVE AMNESIA

**Dissociative amnesia** (formerly called *psychogenic amnesia*) is a dissociative disorder characterized by the sudden and extensive inability to recall important personal information, usually information of a stressful or traumatic nature. The memory loss is too extensive to be explained as ordinary forgetfulness; it may be loss of all information about personal identity or only selective portions.

Dissociative amnesia is not the same as amnesia due to head injury. When people receive a blow to the head or an electric shock severe enough to produce unconsciousness, they often experience some memory loss. This organically based memory loss typically occurs from the point of injury backward and may include loss of all personal memory. People with this type of memory loss typically find that their memories return gradually, and memory loss rarely persists for more than a few days or weeks. Dissociative memory, on the other hand, may be selective, only affecting certain types of memory; it is usually associated with traumatic events, but does not stem from a physical medical condition. Dissociative amnesia can suddenly disappear, and the person's memory returns. Often, dissociative amnesia is brought on by a traumatic incident involving the threat of physical injury or death. Unlike its portrayal on daytime television, dissociative amnesia occurs most often during wars or natural disasters.

## DISSOCIATIVE IDENTITY DISORDER: MULTIPLE PERSONALITY

Another form of dissociative disorder, often associated with dissociative amnesia but presenting a dramatically different kind of behaviour, is **dissociative identity disorder**, historically known as *multiple personality disorder*. Dissociative identity disorder is characterized by the existence within an individual of two or more distinct personalities, each of which is dominant at different times and directs the individual's behaviour at those times. The personalities of the person with the disorder often have different names, and their identities may differ quite sharply from the person's principal identity. A person with dissociative identity disorder usually cannot recall what occurs when one of the alternate personalities is controlling his or her behaviour. Each personality has unique traits, memories, and behavioural patterns. For example, one personality may be adaptive and efficient at coping with life, while another may exhibit immature, maladaptive behaviour. Some people's alternate personalities are of the other sex. Each of the alternate personalities is sometimes aware of the other ones (Putnam & Carlson, 1998; Steinberg, 1995). Each personality, when active, acknowledges that time has passed but cannot account for it. The switch from one personality to another is usually brought on by stress.

Cases of dissociative identity disorder began to receive a great deal of publicity during the 1950s, but symptoms consistent with this disorder appeared in a case reported in 1815 (Hacking, 1997). The disorder was not recognized as a diagnosis in the *DSM* until 1980, and it was considered very rare. During the 1980s, thousands of cases were identified, and controversy ensued (see *Point/Counterpoint* on page 554). Despite its common portrayal in fiction, dissociative identity disorder remains poorly understood and controversial.

# Schizophrenia

Schizophrenia is considered the most devastating, puzzling, and frustrating of all mental disorders; people with this disorder lose touch with reality and are often unable to function in a world that makes no sense to them. The word *schizophrenia* comes from two Greek words that together mean "split mind," and the split refers to the fragmentation of thought processes. (A caution—schizophrenia is *not* split or multiple personality. People sometimes confuse the notion of a "split mind" with

**DISSOCIATIVE AMNESIA**
Dissociative disorder characterized by the sudden and extensive inability to recall important personal information, usually of a traumatic or stressful nature.

**DISSOCIATIVE IDENTITY DISORDER**
Dissociative disorder characterized by the existence within an individual of two or more distinct personalities, each of which is dominant at different times and directs the individual's behaviour at those times; commonly known as *multiple personality disorder*.

**HandsOnPsych**
Version 2.0

**Psychopathology**

## Is Multiple Personality Disorder a Legitimate Diagnosis of Mental Disorder?

**POINT:** Multiple personality disorder is created by therapists and is not a naturally occurring mental disorder.

**COUNTERPOINT:** Multiple personality disorder is a legitimate diagnosis that identifies people with a specific mental disorder.

The publication of *The Three Faces of Eve* and *Sybil* and the movies based on these books caught the imagination of the public and sparked interest in multiple personality disorder. The disorder was considered rare, and most therapists had never seen a client whom they identified as having multiple personalities. That situation changed during the 1980s, when thousands of cases were identified and treated (Acocella, 1999). This explosion of cases coincides with the recognition of the problem of child sexual abuse, and most cases of multiple personality disorder were identified as people who had been abused as children. Sybil is the most famous psychiatric patient in history and provides a model for multiple personality disorder. Her history includes physical and sexual abuse, leading to the hypothesis that abuse was a risk factor for multiple personality disorder.

Some researchers contend that the thousands of people (mostly women) who were diagnosed with multiple personality disorder received invalid diagnoses; these women did not have this disorder. Instead, these patients exhibited symptoms suggested by their therapists and created by hypnosis and psychoactive drugs administered by therapists (Acocella, 1999) or, according to Nick Spanos who worked at Carleton University before his death, these patients enacted the role of multiple personality learned from the media (Lilienfield et al., 1999; Spanos, 1994). Either view casts doubt on the validity of multiple personality disorder, contending that the symptoms are either implanted by therapists or created by patients playing a role.

Other researchers consider multiple personality disorder (now called *dissociative identity disorder*) a legitimate diagnosis and contend that the critics are doing a disservice to people with this disorder (Gleaves, 1996). These authorities consider multiple personality disorder as a response to traumatic experiences during childhood that led to the creation of separate facets of personality, each of which functions independently to cope with specific types of stressors. They propose that the disorder is often misdiagnosed, and that it is not as rare as researchers initially believed (Murray, 1994). Some researchers who hold this view acknowledge that it is possible for therapists to create symptoms of multiple personality disorder, but that the disorder is also real in some cases (Ross, 1999). These researchers argue that multiple personality consists of more than patients' acting on therapists' suggestions.

In a survey of mental health care professionals (Hayes & Mitchell, 1994), 24 percent expressed scepticism about the diagnosis of multiple personality disorder. In addition, these professionals said that multiple personality disorder poses more of a diagnostic problem than other disorders, such as schizophrenia. These findings suggest that the controversy over multiple personality disorder has affected psychologists and psychiatrists, and the prevailing belief is that more research is necessary to resolve this controversy.

---

**SCHIZOPHRENIC**
[SKIT-soh-FREN-ick]
**DISORDERS**

A group of psychological disorders characterized by a lack of reality testing and by deterioration of social and intellectual functioning and personality, beginning before age 45 and lasting at least six months.

dissociative identity disorder, which is characterized by the existence of two or more distinct personalities within one person.) In 1911, when one of the most influential psychiatrists of the time, Eugen Bleuler, coined the term *schizophrenia,* he recognized that the symptoms include seriously disorganized thinking, perceptions, emotions, and actions.

A person with schizophrenia is said to have a schizophrenic disorder; this is because schizophrenia is really a variety of disorders. **Schizophrenic disorders** are a group of disorders characterized by fragmented thought and by deterioration of social and intellectual functioning. The symptoms must begin before age 45, and some disturbances in behaviour must last at least six months, with symptoms persisting for at least one month. People diagnosed as having a schizophrenic disorder often show serious personality disintegration. They match the definition of **psychotic**—suffering from a gross impairment in reality testing that is wide-ranging and interferes with their ability to meet the ordinary demands of life.

Schizophrenia usually begins slowly, with more symptoms developing as time passes. It affects 1 out of every 100 people in Canada, which means that in any given year, about 220 000 people in Canada have schizophrenia (Canadian Mental Health Association, 2002b). Women and men are equally likely to be affected. The disorder is associated with more lengthy hospital stays than most other conditions, so people with schizophrenia account for a larger percentage of people in mental hospitals than those with other mental disorders (Cano et al., 1996). The diagnosis is applied more frequently to those in lower socio-economic groups, even when symptoms are similar (Cano et al., 1996; Nathan & Langenbucher, 1999). This finding suggests that diagnosis is biased, and a study of bias among clinicians making diagnoses confirms this view (Trierweiler et al., 2000).

## ESSENTIAL CHARACTERISTICS OF SCHIZOPHRENIC DISORDERS

People with schizophrenic disorders display sudden significant changes in thought, perception, mood, and overall behaviour. How they think about themselves, social situations, and other people—their social cognition—becomes seriously distorted (Penn et al., 1997). Those changes are often accompanied by distortions of reality and an inability to respond with appropriate thoughts, perceptions, or emotions. Schizophrenia is characterized by both positive and negative symptoms. *Positive symptoms* are those that people with schizophrenia experience and normal people do not—for example, delusions or hallucinations. *Negative symptoms* are behaviours that occur normally but are absent in people with schizophrenia—for example, an inability to experience pleasure. Not all of the symptoms of a schizophrenic disorder are necessarily present in any given person, although many are often seen together.

**THOUGHT DISORDERS.**   One of the first signs of schizophrenia is difficulty maintaining logical thought and coherent conversation. People with schizophrenic disorders show disordered thinking and impaired memory (Hooley & Candela, 1999). They may also suffer from *delusions,* incorrect beliefs. For example, delusions of persecution cause the person to believe that someone or something is trying to harm him or her. Such delusions are often accompanied by delusions of grandeur, which cause the person to believe that he or she is particularly important—important enough to be the target of persecution. Some people with schizophrenia take on the role of an important character in history (for example, Jesus Christ or the Queen of England) and imagine that people are conspiring to harm them. Delusional thought is often apparent in schizophrenics' speech, in which sentence structure, words, and ideas become jumbled and disordered, creating a "word salad" of thoughts. Thus, a schizophrenic person might be heard to say, "Your highness, may I more of some engine to my future food, for his lowness." Memory is seriously disturbed, especially working memory (Schooler et al., 1997). Recall that working memory holds information for a brief period so that further processing can take place and allow a person to respond as a task demands. It is not surprising that when a system that is so important to thought and language fails, both thought and speech patterns become disorganized and often incoherent.

**PERCEPTUAL DISORDERS.**   Another sign of schizophrenic disorders is the presence of *hallucinations*—compelling perceptual (visual, tactile, olfactory, or auditory) experiences that occur without any actual physical stimulus. Auditory hallucinations are the most common. Hallucinations have a biological basis; they are caused by abnormal brain responses (Shergill et al., 2000). The person reports hearing voices originating outside his or her head, which may comment on the person's behaviour or direct the person to behave in certain ways. For example, convicted murderer David Berkowitz (known to the media as Son of Sam) claimed that he was following the orders of his neighbour's dog, which told him to kill.

**EMOTIONAL DISORDERS.**   One of the most striking characteristics of schizophrenia is the display of *inappropriate affect*—emotional responses that are not appropriate in the circumstances. A person with schizophrenia may become upset and cry when her favourite food falls on the floor, yet laugh hysterically at the death of a close friend or relative. Some people with schizophrenia display no emotion (either appropriate or inappropriate) and seem incapable of experiencing a normal range of feeling. Their affect is constricted, or *flat*. Their faces are blank and expressionless, even when they are presented with a deliberately provocative remark or situation. Other people with schizophrenia exhibit *ambivalent* affect. They go through a wide range of emotional behaviours in a brief period, seeming happy one moment and dejected the next.

## TYPES OF SCHIZOPHRENIA

People with schizophrenia display a variety of symptoms, but the *DSM–IV–TR* classifies schizophrenia into five types: paranoid, catatonic, disorganized, residual, and undifferentiated. Each of these has different symptoms and diagnostic criteria (see Table 15.5).

PARANOID [PAIR-uh-noid]
TYPE OF SCHIZOPHRENIA
Type of schizophrenia characterized by hallucinations and delusions of persecution or grandeur (or both), and sometimes irrational jealousy.

**THE PARANOID TYPE.**   People with the **paranoid type of schizophrenia** may seem quite normal, but their thought processes are characterized by hallucinations and delusions of persecution or grandeur (or both). Their delusions are often organized around a theme, and the hallucinations (which are most often auditory) are typically related to this theme. For example, a paranoid schizophrenic may have the delusion that Martians have implanted a radio receiver in his brain and may hallucinate hearing messages telling him to stop those who are polluting the environment or Martians will destroy the earth. They may believe certain world events are particularly significant to them. If, for example, the prime minister of Canada makes a speech deploring pollution, the paranoid schizophrenic person may believe that the prime minister is referring specifically to his behaviour and confirming the messages from the Martians to act against polluters.

| **TABLE 15.5** | **Types and Symptoms of Schizophrenia** |
|---|---|
| **Type** | **Symptoms** |
| **Disorganized** | Frequent incoherence; disorganized behaviour; blunted, inappropriate, or silly affect |
| **Paranoid** | Delusions and hallucinations of persecution or grandeur (or both) and sometimes irrational jealousy |
| **Catatonic** | Stupor in which there is a negative attitude and marked decrease in reactivity to the environment, or an excited phase in which there is agitated motor activity not influenced by external stimuli and which may appear or disappear suddenly |
| **Residual** | History of at least one previous episode of schizophrenia with prominent psychotic symptoms but at present a clinical picture without any prominent psychotic symptoms; continuing evidence of the illness, such as inappropriate affect, illogical thinking, social withdrawal, or eccentric behaviour |
| **Undifferentiated** | Prominent delusions, hallucinations, incoherence, or grossly disorganized behaviour, which do not meet the criteria for any other types or which meet the criteria for more than one type |

Paranoid schizophrenics may be alert, intelligent, and responsive. In addition, they may be secretive concerning their delusions and hallucinations, which makes them difficult to detect and diagnose. However, their delusions and hallucinations impair their ability to deal with reality, and their behaviour is often unpredictable and sometimes hostile. The relatively low level of cognitive impairment leads people with the paranoid type of schizophrenia to have a better chance of recovery than do people with other types of schizophrenia.

**THE CATATONIC TYPE.** The **catatonic type of schizophrenia** is characterized either by displays of excited or violent motor activity or by stupor. That is, there are actually two subtypes of the catatonic type of schizophrenia—excited and withdrawn—both of which involve extreme overt behaviour. *Excited* catatonic schizophrenics show excessive activity. They may talk and shout almost continuously and engage in seemingly uninhibited, agitated, and aggressive motor activity. These episodes usually appear and disappear suddenly. *Withdrawn* catatonic schizophrenics tend to appear stuporous—mute and basically unresponsive. Although they occasionally exhibit some signs of the excited type, they usually show a high degree of muscular rigidity. They are not immobile, but they speak, move, and respond very little, although they are usually aware of events around them. Withdrawn catatonic schizophrenics may use immobility and unresponsiveness to maintain control over their environment; their behaviour relieves them of the responsibility of responding to external stimuli.

**THE DISORGANIZED TYPE.** The **disorganized type of schizophrenia** is characterized by severely disturbed thought processes, frequent incoherence, disorganized behaviour, and inappropriate affect. People with this type of schizophrenia may exhibit bizarre emotions, with periods of giggling, crying, or irritability for no apparent reason. Their behaviour can be silly or even obscene. They show a severe disintegration of normal personality, a total lack of reality testing, and often poor personal hygiene.

**RESIDUAL AND UNDIFFERENTIATED TYPES.** People who show symptoms attributable to schizophrenia but who remain in touch with reality are said to have the **residual type of schizophrenia**. Such people show inappropriate affect, illogical thinking, eccentric behaviour, or some combination of these symptoms. They have a history of at least one previous schizophrenic episode.

Sometimes it is difficult to determine which category a specific person best fits into (Gift et al., 1980). Some people exhibit all the essential features of schizophrenia—prominent delusions, hallucinations, incoherence, and grossly disorganized behaviour—but do not fit neatly into the category of paranoid, catatonic, disorganized, or residual. Individuals with these characteristics are said to have the **undifferentiated type of schizophrenia**.

## CAUSES OF SCHIZOPHRENIA

What causes people with schizophrenia to lose their grasp on reality with such devastating results? Are people born with schizophrenia, or do they develop it as a result of painful childhood experiences? Researchers take markedly different positions on these questions. Biologically oriented psychologists focus on genetics, brain structures, and chemicals in the brain; their basic argument is that schizophrenia is a brain disease. Psychodynamic and learning theorists argue that a person's environment and early experiences cause schizophrenia. The arguments for each approach are compelling, but most theorists adopt a *diathesis–stress model*, asserting that schizophrenia is the result of a combination of genetic predisposition or biological vulnerability, which interacts with life situations to produce schizophrenia. Let's look at the evidence.

▲ Russell Crowe portrays the mathematician John Nash in the movie *A Beautiful Mind*. Professor Nash has battled schizophrenia for many years.

CATATONIC [CAT-uh-TONN-ick] TYPE OF SCHIZOPHRENIA
Type of schizophrenia characterized either by displays of excited or violent motor activity or by stupor.

DISORGANIZED TYPE OF SCHIZOPHRENIA
Type of schizophrenia characterized by severely disturbed thought processes, frequent incoherence, disorganized behaviour, and inappropriate affect.

RESIDUAL TYPE OF SCHIZOPHRENIA
A schizophrenic disorder in which the person exhibits inappropriate affect, illogical thinking, and/or eccentric behaviour but seems generally in touch with reality.

UNDIFFERENTIATED TYPE OF SCHIZOPHRENIA
A schizophrenic disorder that is characterized by a mixture of symptoms and does not meet the diagnostic criteria of any one type.

**BIOLOGICAL FACTORS.** Substantial evidence suggests that biological factors play some role in schizophrenia, producing a predisposition to develop the disorder. People born with that predisposition have a greater probability of developing schizophrenia than do other people, given similar circumstances. When one parent has schizophrenia, the probability that an offspring will develop the disorder is between 3 and 14 percent. If both parents have schizophrenia, their children have about a 35 percent probability of developing this disorder. It is now generally accepted that schizophrenia runs in families; the children and siblings of people with schizophrenia are more likely to exhibit maladjustment and schizophrenic symptoms than are other people (Kety et al., 1994). Researchers have been looking for a gene that might carry specific traits associated with schizophrenia, but no single gene seems likely to be the cause of schizophrenia (Zuckerman, 1999).

If schizophrenia were totally genetic, the likelihood would be 100 percent that identical (monozygotic) twins, who have identical genes, would both manifest the disorder if one did. This kind of estimate of the degree to which a condition or trait is shared by two or more individuals is referred to as a **concordance rate**. However, studies of schizophrenia in identical twins show concordance rates that range from 15 to 86 percent, averaging around 48 percent (Gottesman, 1991). This figure suggests that factors other than genetics are involved. In one important study, analysis of brain structures showed subtle but important brain abnormalities in a schizophrenic individual whose identical twin did not show the abnormality. Such studies support the hypothesis that non-genetic factors must exert an important influence related to schizophrenia and are critical in its development (DiLalla & Gottesman, 1995). Nevertheless, most researchers agree that genetic background is a fundamental factor in the disorder. The concordance rate for schizophrenia in identical twins is 48 percent, compared to 17 percent for fraternal twins. Moreover, identical twins reared apart from their natural parents and from each other show a higher concordance rate than do fraternal twins or controls (Cornblatt, Green, & Walker, 1999).

The development of anti-schizophrenic drugs (formerly called anti-psychotics) contributed to a better understanding of the biochemistry of the disorder. Researchers today readily acknowledge that neurotransmitters and their actions are involved in schizophrenia. An early view of neurotransmitter involvement was the *dopamine theory of schizophrenia*. This theory asserts that too much of the neurotransmitter dopamine or too much activity at dopamine receptors causes schizophrenia. Neuroleptic drugs, the drugs that control symptoms of schizophrenia, block dopamine sites and decrease the disturbed thought processes and hallucinations characteristic of schizophrenia; drugs that stimulate the dopamine system (such as amphetamines) aggravate existing schizophrenic disorders. Dopamine receptors are considered to be major sites of biochemical disturbances in the brain (Fang, 1996; Masotto & Racagni, 1995). Further research revealed that there are subtypes of dopamine receptors and neuroleptic drugs that bind to the specific receptors that most likely inhibit schizophrenic symptoms, especially positive symptoms (O'Connor, 1998). Neuroleptic drugs also affect other neurotransmitters, and the neurotransmitters glutamate and GABA have both been implicated in schizophrenia (Cornblatt, Green, & Walker, 1999).

Biochemistry is not the whole story—if it were, drugs would fully control symptoms of schizophrenia. Unfortunately, this is not the case, and researchers have also looked for differences in brain structures between people with and without schizophrenia (see *Brain and Behaviour*).

In sum, researchers now assert that genetic, biochemical factors and brain abnormalities are all associated with schizophrenia. While many stress factors (which are the focus of environmental researchers) may contribute to schizophrenia, a biological component seems to be essential.

**ENVIRONMENTAL FACTORS.** Some psychologists believe that, in addition to genetic factors, environmental interactions determine the onset and development of

---

**CONCORDANCE RATE**

The degree to which a condition or trait is shared by two or more individuals or groups.

## "It's All In Your Head"

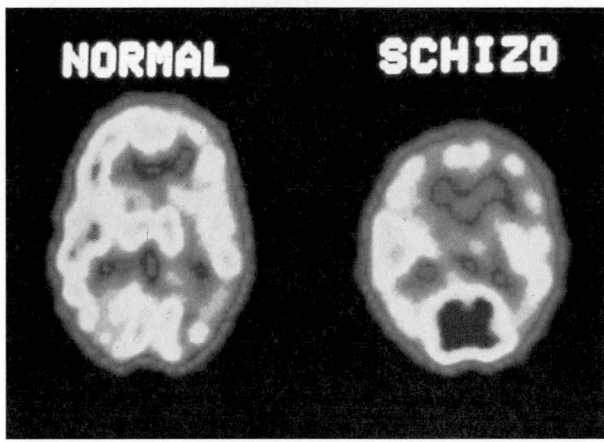

People who show evidence of psychological distress are sometimes told to "snap out of it" because "it's all in your mind." The development of brain imaging technology and the study of brain function in people with various mental disorders have led to a revision of the old saying: "It's all in your head."

Brain imaging studies of people with obsessive–compulsive disorder have found some structural differences in the frontal lobes of the cerebral cortex, but larger functional differences (Szeszko et al., 1999). The areas most strongly affected are the frontal lobes, in the area just behind the eyes; the anterior cingulate, the front part of a structure just underneath the cerebral cortex; and the basal ganglia, a group of forebrain structures underneath the cerebral cortex. These structures appear in Figure 15.3. These areas show increased metabolism when people with this disorder are provoked into showing symptoms, for example, when someone with an obsession with germs is holding a dirty towel. Metabolism becomes more normal with treatment.

Many structures implicated in obsessive–compulsive disorder are believed to be involved in major depression (Videbech, 2000). Brain imaging studies show that parts of the prefrontal cortex, the anterior cingulate, and parts of the basal ganglia are involved in depression, but blood flow and metabolic activity levels are lower in depressed than non-depressed people (whereas activity is higher in people with obsessive–compulsive disorder). When depressed people are treated with drugs in psychotherapy, changes occur in their brains that suggest that both types of treatments are similar at the brain level (Sackeim, 2001).

Brain imaging and autopsy studies show physical differences associated with schizophrenia. For example, the ventricles (hollow areas in the brain that are normally filled with fluid) are enlarged in some people with schizophrenia (Cornblatt, Green, & Walker, 1999; Raz & Raz, 1990). People with schizophrenia also have larger spaces (sulci) between the ridges (gyri) in their brains. Furthermore, some brain structures, notably the frontal lobes, show reduced blood flow and functioning in schizophrenics (Longworth, Honey, & Sharma, 1999). These differences were interpreted to indicate degeneration of the brain, but more recent views cast these differences as developmental differences in the brains of schizophrenics. That is, these brain structures exist before the diagnosis of schizophrenia (Cornblatt, Green, & Walker, 1999). The underlying cause of these structural differences in the brains of people with schizophrenia is not clear; genetics could be the cause, but prenatal exposure to viruses and birth trauma have also been implicated.

In some specific ways, the brains of people with mental disorders function differently than those of people without disorders. However, these findings do not indicate that mental disorders are all "in your head." That is, these differences in brain function are not necessarily the underlying basis of these disorders. To understand mental disorders, researchers must learn how genetic factors affect brain structure and function as well as how stressors, personal learning history, and culture interact with biological factors to produce problems. These mental disorders involve both nurture and nature.

### FIGURE 15.3
### Brain Structures Involved in Anxiety and Mood Disorders

Several brain structures are involved in both anxiety and mood disorders, but their activation levels differ from these disorders. The anterior cingulate and basal ganglia are more active during anxiety reactions but less active during depression.

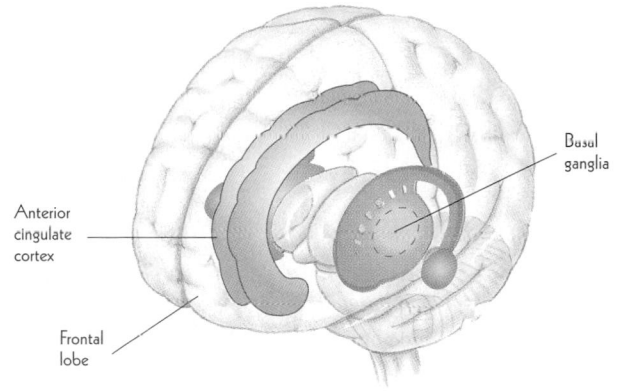

Basal ganglia

Anterior cingulate cortex

Frontal lobe

FIGURE 15.4
**The Vulnerability–Stress View of Schizophrenia**

According to the vulnerability–stress view of schizophrenia, the environment triggers behaviours in people who are predisposed to schizophrenia.

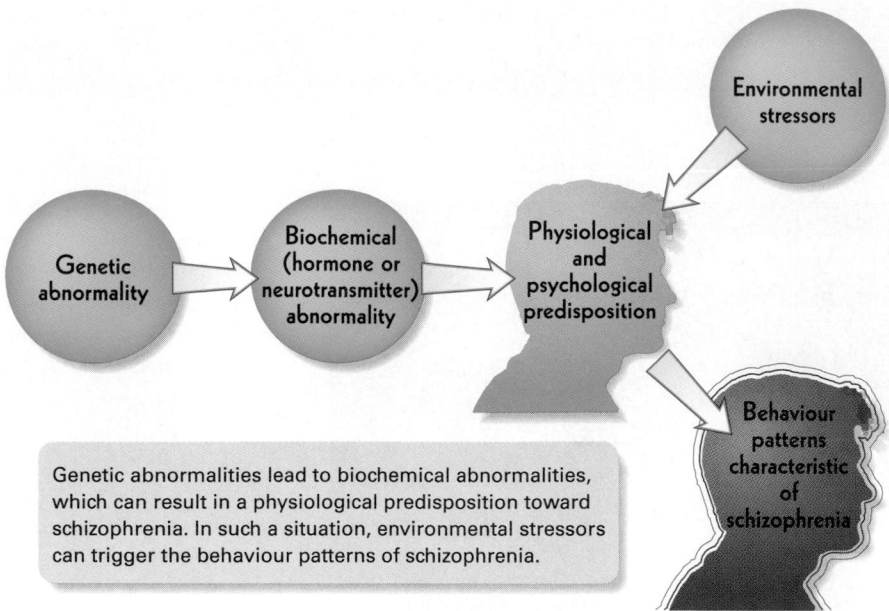

Genetic abnormalities lead to biochemical abnormalities, which can result in a physiological predisposition toward schizophrenia. In such a situation, environmental stressors can trigger the behaviour patterns of schizophrenia.

**DOUBLE BIND**

A situation in which an individual is given two different and inconsistent messages.

schizophrenia (see Figure 15.4). Behavioural explanations of schizophrenia are based on traditional learning principles (explored in Chapter 5). The behavioural approach argues that faulty reinforcement and extinction procedures, as well as social learning processes, can account for schizophrenia. Imagine a child brought up in a family where the parents constantly argue, where the father or the mother is alcoholic, and where neither parent shows much affection for the other parent or for anyone else. Lidz (1973) argues that children who grow up in homes where they receive no reinforcement for showing interest in events, people, and objects in the outside world may become withdrawn and begin to exhibit schizophrenic behaviour. Growing up in such an emotionally fragmented environment may predispose individuals to emotional disorders and even schizophrenia (Miklowitz, 1994; Walker et al., 1983).

Even in families in which there is no alcoholism or much marital conflict, parents sometimes confuse their children or have difficulty communicating effectively. Research indicates that the emotional tone in families affects the developmental course and severity of a member's schizophrenia. When families have an interaction style characterized by hostility, criticism, emotional overinvolvement, and a lack of boundaries (overintrusiveness), their level of *expressed emotions* is said to be high. People with schizophrenia who return to families in which there are high levels of expressed emotion have a higher relapse rate than that those from families with low levels of expressed emotion (Widiger & Sankis, 2000). In addition, parents can place their children in a situation that offers inconsistent messages, a **double bind**. Initially described by Bateson as an explanation for the causes of schizophrenia (Bateson et al., 1956), double bind usually occurs between individuals with a strong insecure emotional attachment, such as a child and a parent (Mishler & Waxler, 1968). For example, a parent may present a gift and teasingly say, "No, you may not have this," while smiling and giving other nonverbal assurances that the individual may have the gift. Most children understand that the parent is teasing. However, not all children will understand, and not all situations are so clearly cued. And research shows that people with schizophrenia are less accurate at interpreting emotional communications than are control participants (Fagan & Silverthorn, 1998). Games and ineffective communication of this kind, if frequent, may shape an environment of confusion conducive to the development and maintenance of schizophrenia. However, what Bateson saw as a cause of schizophrenia may be more a pattern of a lack of communication skills, especially during stressful periods (Docherty, Hall, & Gordinier, 1998).

According to learning theory, a person who receives a great deal of attention for behaviours is likely to continue those behaviours, even bizarre ones. People who fail to develop effective social skills are more at risk for bizarre behaviours (Mueser et al., 1990). Other learning theories suggest that bizarre behaviour and thoughts are themselves reinforcing because they allow the person to escape from both acute anxiety and an overactive autonomic nervous system.

**NATURE AND NURTURE.** The development of schizophrenia does not occur through any simple mechanism—both biology and environment are involved. Some people, because of family environment, genetic history, or brain chemistry, are more vulnerable than others. As with mood disorders, *vulnerability* is a person's diminished ability to deal with demanding life events. The more vulnerable a person is, the more likely the person will experience a schizophrenic episode as a reaction to difficult events.

To summarize, although the exact causes of schizophrenia are still unknown, the development of this disorder is likely to be due to a set of factors. These factors include a genetic component. This component may underlie the neurochemical functions associated with schizophrenia. These biological vulnerabilities do not produce schizophrenia by themselves; environmental events contribute to the development of the disorder. Early childhood relationships filled with mixed emotional messages, poor communication, and even abuse may leave biologically vulnerable children at high risk for schizophrenia.

**Be an ACTIVE LEARNER**

**REVIEW**
> What symptoms allow a diagnosis of dissociative identity disorder rather than dissociative amnesia? p. 553
> What are the thought, perceptual, and emotional disorders associated with schizophrenia? pp. 555–556
> What are the different types of schizophrenia? pp. 556–557
> What biological factors contribute to vulnerability for schizophrenia? What environmental factors contribute? pp. 558, 560

**THINK CRITICALLY**
> People tend to confuse dissociative personality disorder (multiple personality) with schizophrenia, probably because schizophrenia is often described as "split personality." In what sense is the personality "split" in schizophrenia?
> How likely would it be for a homeless person to be diagnosed as schizophrenic? Explain.

**APPLY PSYCHOLOGY**
> Watch an episode of *The X-Files* and analyze character Fox Mulder for symptoms of the paranoid type of schizophrenia.

# Personality Disorders

Disorders such as phobias, obsessive–compulsive disorder, depression, dissociative personality disorder, and schizophrenia are among those on Axis I of the *DSM* classification system. The disorders on Axis II are **personality disorders**. These disorders apply to people who exhibit inflexible and long-standing maladaptive behaviours that typically cause stress and social or occupational difficulties. Often these disorders begin in childhood or adolescence and persist throughout adulthood. People with personality disorders are easy to spot but difficult to treat. Paul Bernardo, who was declared a dangerous offender and convicted of the rapes and murders of several young women in southern Ontario, has been diagnosed as having a personality disorder.

Categorizations of personality disorders are more controversial than those of the disorders on Axis I of *DSM*, in terms of both their reliability and their validity. The line separating normal from abnormal behaviour, as well as the characteristics of each class of disorder, sometimes can be blurry, which may lead to problems in reliably placing an individual in one category (Nathan & Langenbucher, 1999). Consistent with this view, a person with a personality disorder is often at high risk for other disorders; thus it is not uncommon for an individual to exhibit symptoms of two disorders simultaneously.

People with personality disorders are divided into three broad classes: (1) those whose behaviour appears odd or eccentric, (2) those whose behaviour is dramatic, emotional, and erratic, and (3) those who are fearful or anxious. We'll consider six specific personality disorders: paranoid, borderline, histrionic, narcissistic, antisocial, and dependent.

People with *paranoid personality disorder* experience odd or eccentric behaviour with unwarranted feelings of persecution; they mistrust almost everyone. They are hypersensitive to criticism and have a restricted range of emotional responses. They have strong fears of being exploited and of losing control and independence.

**PERSONALITY DISORDERS**
Psychological disorders characterized by inflexible and long-standing maladaptive behaviours that typically cause stress and/or social or occupational problems.

▲ Individuals diagnosed with narcissistic personality disorder have a grandiose sense of self-importance.

ANTI-SOCIAL PERSONALITY DISORDER

Personality disorder characterized by egocentricity, behaviour that is irresponsible and that violates the rights of other people, a lack of guilt feelings, an inability to understand other people, and a lack of fear of punishment.

Sometimes they appear cold, humourless, and even scheming. As you might expect, people with paranoid personality disorder are suspicious and seldom able to form close, intimate relationships with others.

Fitting into the second behaviour classification, individuals with *borderline personality disorder* have trouble with relationships; they show a pattern of instability in interpersonal relationships, self-image, and affect. In addition, they are often impulsive. They are sometimes suicidal; they report feelings of emptiness and are sometimes inappropriately angry. Easily bored and distracted, such individuals fear abandonment. Individuals with borderline personality disorder often sabotage or undermine themselves just before a goal is to be reached— for example, by dropping out of school just before graduation.

Fitting into the second broad class, because of their dramatic, emotional, and erratic behaviours, are those people with *histrionic personality disorder*. Individuals with this disorder seek attention by exaggerating situations in their lives. They have stormy personal relationships, are excessively emotional, and demand constant reassurance and praise.

Closely related to histrionic personality disorder, and also classified in the second class, is *narcissistic personality disorder*. People with this disorder have an extremely exaggerated sense of self-importance, expect favours, and need constant admiration and attention. They show little concern for others, and they react to criticism with rage, shame, or humiliation.

Perhaps the most widely recognized personality disorder in the second class is anti-social personality disorder. People with **anti-social personality disorder** are self-centred and irresponsible, violate the rights of other people (through lying, theft, cheating, or other violations of social rules), lack guilt feelings, are unable to understand other people, and do not fear punishment. Individuals with this disorder may be superficially charming, but their behaviour is destructive and often reckless.

As many as 3 percent of all individuals may be candidates for diagnosis of anti-social personality disorder. Men are much more likely than women to receive this diagnosis, even when they both show similar symptoms (Nathan & Langenbucher, 1999). Researchers are exploring the possibility of a biological component in anti-social personality disorder, and some evidence for brain differences and genetic influence has appeared. A brain imaging study showed that people with anti-social personality disorder have less brain tissue in their frontal lobes (Raine et al., 2000). This structure is involved in planning and impulse control, abilities that present problems for people with anti-social personality disorder. This study also confirmed a difference in nervous system response; people with anti-social personality disorder do not show normal autonomic nervous system reactions to fear and surprise. As a result of experiencing abnormal reactions to these emotions, people with anti-social personality disorder do not learn to associate fear or anxiety with unacceptable behaviour (Patrick, 1994). Thus their biological differences interact with the environment to produce these symptoms of the disorder.

Interaction between biology and environment may also occur through parents' interactions with children. Parental neglect and abuse are important risks for anti-social personality disorder, and one study suggests that children with an anti-social parent interacted with their adoptive parents in more negative ways than children with no genetic risk (Ge et al., 1996). The biological roots of anti-social personality disorder clearly interact with family and social circumstances to prompt the development of anti-social personality disorder.

Fitting into the third behavioural classification are those acting fearful or anxious—individuals with *dependent personality disorder*. Such people are submissive and clinging; they let others make all important decisions in their lives. They try to appear pleasant and agreeable at all times. They act meek, humble, and affectionate in order to keep their protectors. Battered wives often receive diagnoses of dependent personality disorder, which may result from the mistreatment they receive and their strategy for coping (or possibly because of stereotyping and diagnostic bias). Overprotective, authoritarian parenting seems to be a major initiating cause of dependency (Bornstein, 1992).

# Violence and Mental Disorders

The media have linked mental disorders and violence. Movies show mentally disturbed individuals who "snap" and go on homicidal rampages. Television presents stories of seemingly ordinary people who are, in reality, crazed killers. News stories tend to sensationalize coverage of people with mental disorders who have committed crimes (Smellie, 1999). These images are powerful in shaping opinions about people with mental disorders and add to the stigma of having such a problem (Link, Phelan et al., 1999). Is there any truth to the association of mental disorders and violence? Are people with mental disorders more likely than others to be violent?

Most people who have mental disorders are not violent, and most people who commit violence do not have a mental disorder. However, some mental disorders are associated with a greater likelihood of committing violent acts.

## DIAGNOSES ASSOCIATED WITH VIOLENCE

Several diagnoses are associated with increased risk for violence. In general, the more serious disorders carry a greater risk, and people who have delusions may be at specific risk (Nathan & Langenbucher, 1999). For example, in the manic phase of bipolar disorder, people can be impatient and easily angered. This anger may become violence. People who question the plans and capabilities of a person experiencing a manic episode may be the target for a violent reaction.

People with schizophrenia are also risks for violence, especially those with the paranoid type. An extreme example of violence among schizophrenics is Theodore Kaczynski, the serial killer more commonly known as the Unabomber, who was diagnosed as paranoid schizophrenic. His paranoia focused on technology, and his violence was directed toward those who were involved with technology. Such delusions of persecution make people with paranoid schizophrenia suspicious, and they feel the need to protect themselves against what they see as real danger (Link, Monahan et al., 1999). When paranoid schizophrenics react to these "dangers," their actions are difficult for others to understand and anticipate because the danger is a delusion. Nevertheless, the actions that they take for protection may be harmful, even deadly, to someone who has accidentally said or done the wrong thing. Research on people discharged from mental institutions indicates that the threat of violence is elevated, but not as strongly related to the experience of threatening delusions as previously believed (Appelbaum, Robbins, & Monahan, 2000).

Most schizophrenics who are violent are not killers, but young adults with schizophrenia account for a disproportionate amount of community violence (Arseneault et al., 2000). However, young adults with alcohol- or drug-dependency problems are more likely than schizophrenics to be involved in violent crimes. Substance abuse alone is a risk for violence, but the combination of alcohol or drug use with other mental disorders additionally elevates risks for violence (Nathan & Langenbucher, 1999).

Individuals with anti-social personality disorder may be violent; in addition, they do a great deal of damage by nonviolent criminal and amoral behaviour (Zuckerman, 1999). Their disregard for the welfare of others and their resistance to change make people with anti-social personality disorder risks to others. When

*Be an*
**ACTIVE LEARNER**

**REVIEW**
> Identify the distinguishing characteristics of a person diagnosed with an anti-social personality disorder. p. 562

**THINK CRITICALLY**
> Some critics have argued that personality disorders seem like exaggerations of gender and ethnic stereotypes. Think about these six personality disorders according to both kinds of stereotypes. Do you think that these stereotypes influence clinicians who make these diagnoses?

**APPLY PSYCHOLOGY**
> From your limited understanding of personality disorders, you may believe that a person you know has some of the traits of this disorder. Think of the behaviours that have led to this theory. What harm has this person done to others? How has this person avoided punishment?

these individuals are violent, they feel no compassion or remorse. Extreme examples of anti-social personality disorder are infamous Canadian murderers Paul Bernardo and Clifford Olson. These men showed little emotion related to their horrific crimes.

Despite the possibility that killers such as Bernardo and Olson meet the criteria for anti-social personality disorder, they would not meet the legal definition of insanity. Indeed, most people with mental disorders who commit violence do not meet that definition. The concept of insanity is not a psychological one; its definition is legal. *Insanity* refers to a condition that excuses people from responsibility and protects them from punishment. From the legal point of view, a person cannot be held responsible for a crime if, at the time of the crime, the person lacked the capacity to distinguish right from wrong or to obey the law.

The *legal model* of abnormal behaviour defines such behaviour strictly in terms of guilt, innocence, and sanity. Consider Dorothy Joudrie, a Calgary women who was charged with shooting her husband, Earl. Dorothy, who had been an alcoholic for many years, had been beaten by her husband over a prolonged period, though the beatings had stopped 18 years before the shooting. Claiming she had no memory of the incident, Dorothy shot Earl six times at close range with a small-calibre handgun. She seemed unaware of her actions and even Earl said that she looked and sounded very calm during the shooting. At her trial, all of the psychiatrists, even those called by the prosecution, agreed that Dorothy has been in a dissociative state at the time of the shooting. Based on this evidence the jury found her not criminally responsible for her actions. She was placed in a mental hospital and released within a year, though she continued to undergo treatment until her death.

Most people overestimate how often such pleas are made. The truth is that only about 1 percent of all felony defendants use an insanity defence—and the plea is successful only about one-quarter of the time (Lymburner & Roesch, 1999). Despite media portrayals of the insanity defence as a mainstay of the legal system that frees guilty people, people who "get away with murder" by using the insanity plea are more common in fiction than in courtrooms. Even when the insanity plea is successful, the person rarely walks out of the courtroom a free person; such people generally are confined to mental hospitals. People with mental disorders are more likely to be a danger to themselves than to others. That is, violence among people with mental disorders is more likely to be suicide or a suicide attempt than assault or homicide. Depressed people feel hopeless, and their feelings of endless misery lead to thoughts of and attempts at suicide. Each day, about 10 people in Canada commit suicide, amounting to more than 3700 Canadians each year (Health Canada, 1994). However, many more people attempt than commit suicide. *Attempters* try to commit suicide but are unsuccessful. They tend to be young, impulsive, more often women than men, and more likely to make non-fatal attempts such as making only shallow cuts on the wrists. *Completers* succeed in taking their lives. They tend to be white, male, and older, and they use highly lethal techniques of self-destruction, such as guns. Alcohol or drug abuse increases the risk for violence associated with mental disorders, and this increase applies to suicide. Although estimates vary with age and gender, there are an estimated 10 to 25 attempted suicides for every completion. Table 15.6 presents some of the many myths about suicide and counters them with facts.

Who commits suicide? More than four times as many men as women actually complete suicides. Among adolescents, suicide is the second leading cause of death (after accidents) compared to adults, where it is the ninth leading cause of death; 1 out of every 1000 adolescents attempts suicide each year (Health Canada, 1994). The elderly, the divorced, and former patients with psychological disorders have a higher likelihood than others of attempting and committing suicide. Alcoholics have a high rate of suicide; First Nations

▼ Suicide deeply affects the friends and families of those who take their own lives.

## TABLE 15.6 Myths and Facts about Suicide

| Myth | Core Components |
|------|-----------------|
| 1. Suicide happens without warning. | 1. Suicidal individuals give many clues; 80 percent have to some degree discussed with others their intent to commit suicide. |
| 2. Once people become suicidal, they remain so. | 2. Suicidal persons remain so for limited periods—thus the value of restraint. |
| 3. Suicide occurs almost exclusively among affluent or very poor individuals. | 3. Suicide tends to occur in the same proportion at all economic levels of society. |
| 4. Virtually all suicidal individuals are mentally ill. | 4. This is not so, although most are depressed to some degree. |
| 5. Suicidal tendencies are inherited or run in families. | 5. There is no evidence for a direct genetic factor. |
| 6. Suicide does not occur in primitive cultures. | 6. Suicide occurs in almost all societies and cultures. |
| 7. In Japan, ritual suicide is common. | 7. In modern Japan, ritual suicide is rare; the most common method is barbiturate overdose. |
| 8. Writers and artists have the highest suicide rates because they are "a bit crazy to begin with." | 8. Physicians and police officers have the highest suicide rates; they have access to the most lethal means, and their work involves a high level of frustration. |
| 9. Once a person starts to come out of a depression, the risk of suicide dissipates. | 9. The risk of suicide is highest in the initial phase of an upswing from the depth of depression. |
| 10. People who attempt suicide fully intend to die. | 10. People who attempt suicide have diverse motives. |

(Meyer & Salmon, 1988)

people do, as well, partly because alcoholism is more common in this group than in many others (Murphy et al., 1992; Young & French, 1993). However, drugs and alcohol only account for some of the increased risk observed in certain high-risk groups. People who have been suffering from major depression are more likely to attempt suicide while they are recovering, when their energy level is higher, than at the depths of depression; during the worst part of a depressive episode, a person is usually too weak, divided, and lacking in energy to commit suicide. Although only 15 percent of depressed people are suicidal, most suicide-prone individuals are depressed.

Two segments of Canadian society at increased risk for suicide are Aboriginal people and urban street youth. Sean Kidd (2003a, 2003b) and Michael Kral (Kidd & Kral, 2002; Kral, Burkhardt, & Kidd, 2002) at the University of Windsor have suggested that the feelings of worthlessness, loneliness, and hopelessness experienced by homeless street youth in both Toronto and Vancouver contribute to the high rates of suicide found among street youth. In northern, isolated aboriginal communities, such as Pikangikum, Ontario, the suicide rate has been found to be as high as seven to eight times that for the general population (Health Canada, 2000). These dismal findings are not limited to the North. The Siksika Nation, in southern Alberta, also has a suicide rate that far exceeds that found in the general population. Here, too, a general lack of social control in light of radical economic change, resettlement, isolation, and breakdown of immediate and extended families

## Preventing Suicide

Most individuals who attempt suicide really want to live. However, their sense of hopelessness about the future tells them that death is the only way out. Feelings of despair underlie suicide attempts, but alcoholism and alcohol use, drug abuse, and emotional isolation increase the risk (Maris & Silverman, 1995). People who attempt or complete suicide typically give some warnings before their attempts. Knowing these signs permits family and friends to understand the depth of pain the person is experiencing and prepares them to intervene. The following warning signs are signals of danger for anyone, especially when appearing in combination:

- Depression
- Verbal statements such as "You'd be better off without me" or "Maybe I won't be around any more . . ."
- Expressions of hopelessness, helplessness, or a combination of the two
- Daring and risk-taking behaviour that is not typical of the person
- Personality changes such as withdrawal, aggression, or moodiness
- Giving away prized possessions
- Lack of interest in the future

Direct threats or statements are the most serious signal, and *when a person makes a suicide threat, always take that threat seriously.* If you know someone you think may be considering suicide, here are some steps you can take:

- Remember that the most important thing is to listen. Say that you understand the person's feelings but do not agree with the suicide plans.
- Talk with the person about your concerns, and show that you care and want to help.
- Do not act shocked or judge the person.
- Ask the person direct questions about their suicidal thoughts and behaviours. The more detailed their plan, the greater the immediate risk.
- Do not leave the person alone.
- Do not agree to secrecy. Resist the person's attempts to force you to remain quiet, and tell relatives, friends, or a counsellor.
- Get professional help—even if the person resists. Assist the person in finding a qualified psychologist, psychiatrist, or counsellor who can help.

(Charles, 1991) can account for high suicide rates. As reported by University of British Columbia's Rod McCormick (2000), high levels of anomie (feeling cut off from society) characterize many Aboriginal communities as well as many homeless youth.

In some Aboriginal communities as well as in the community of homeless youth, alcohol and drug abuse are often factors that account for higher rates of suicide (Kettl & Bixler, 1993; Yoder, Whitbeck, & Hoyt, 2003). However, individuals in both groups are more likely to have experienced physical, emotional, and/or sexual abuse and are more likely to have chaotic family backgrounds than are people in the general population. Because high suicide rates are not observed in all Aboriginal communities or among all urban street youth, there are clearly important factors involved in determining who will succumb to the hopelessness that characterizes some of the individuals in these communities. Clearly, solutions to this problem will not be solely psychological, but also will require economic and societal intervention.

# VIOLENCE AS A RISK FOR DEVELOPING MENTAL DISORDERS

Only a few mental disorders increase the likelihood that a person will be violent, but being the target of violence increases the risk for many disorders. The experience of violence that has the greatest potential for harm is violence toward children. **Child abuse** is the physical, emotional, or sexual mistreatment of a child. This problem is a large one—more than 80 000 children in Canada are the victims of abuse or neglect each year (Health Canada, 2001). Girls are more often targets than are boys, especially of sexual abuse (Molnar, Buka, & Kessler, 2001). Children who are the victims of sexual abuse are at elevated risk for post-traumatic stress disorder, depression, suicide, and sexual problems during adulthood as well as for growing up to be abusers themselves (Oddone-Paolucci, Genuis, & Violato, 2001). Childhood victims of abuse and neglect are at greater risk of developing mood disorders and anti-social personality disorder than are children who are not abused (Horwitz et al., 2001). Abused girls show an increased risk for alcohol abuse problems as adults, but abused boys do not.

Child abusers usually do not have any diagnosable mental disorder; only about 5 percent of child abusers exhibit symptoms of very disturbed behaviour. Most abusive parents seem quite normal by typical social standards, and sometimes they are prominent members of their communities. Most psychologists and social workers consider child abuse to be an interactive process involving incompetent parenting, environmental stress, and poor child management techniques. Although their behaviour does not necessarily signal mental disorders for the abusers, it can produce both short-term and long-term problems for the abused children.

Other forms of violence within families also create mental health problems, such as violence between intimate partners (husbands and wives or boyfriends and girlfriends). *Intimate partner violence* is also known as spouse abuse and domestic violence. This type of violence is a common occurrence throughout the world (Heise, Ellsberg, & Gottemoeller, 1999). Both men and women do violence to each other, but women are more likely than men to be harmed—about one-third of all women in the world have been physically abused in some way. Partner violence is more likely to occur in couples and in societies in which gender roles are rigid and inflexible and when women have little power and few resources. Partner violence poses a substantial risk for post-traumatic stress disorder and depression. Indeed, some researchers believe that women's higher rate of depression is largely due to their victimization by childhood sexual abuse, partner violence, and rape (Golding, 1999).

These negative effects are not limited to violence between spouses; a survey of teenage girls (Silverman et al., 2001) found that 20 percent reported some experience of violence from a boyfriend. Those girls were at increased risk for a variety of problems, including suicide, eating disorders, and substance abuse. Those who perpetrate partner violence may have some mental disorder, but most do not; they are exerting rational and often effective attempts to control their partners.

Rape is also a form of violence that women experience more often than men. **Rape** is forcible sexual assault on an unwilling partner. The legal definition of rape varies, but it is generally being broadened to include any sexual assault (usually intercourse) that occurs without freely given consent. People tend to think of rape as a violent attack by a stranger, but most cases of rape involve individuals who are acquainted. That is, *date rape* or *acquaintance rape* is more common than stranger rape. Studies of high-school girls (Silverman et al., 2001), college women (Koss, Gidycz, & Wisniewski, 1987), and women from the general population (Tjaden & Thoennes, 2000) indicate that around 20 percent have been the targets of some type of

**CHILD ABUSE**

Physical, emotional, or sexual mistreatment of a child.

**RAPE**

Forcible sexual assault on an unwilling partner.

▼ Often perpetrators of child abuse appear to be quite normal socially; however, their behaviour can produce both short-term and long-term problems for the abused children.

### Be an
### ACTIVE
### LEARNER

**REVIEW**

> What diagnoses are associated with an increased risk for violence? pp. 563–564
> How does the legal definition of insanity differ from the psychological definition of mental disorders? p. 564
> What diagnoses are more likely for people who are the victims of violence? pp. 567–568

**THINK CRITICALLY**

> Analyze the role of the media in the connection between mental illness and violence. How could the media become a positive factor in decreasing the stigma associated with mental disorders?
> Describe the key aspects of a preventive program to help decrease child abuse.

**APPLY PSYCHOLOGY**

> Make a plan for the action you would take if a friend or relative showed the warning signs of suicide. Think about specific things you would say, and find sources for professional help on your campus and in your community.
> Most colleges have a rape prevention program, but what steps can colleges take to make these programs more effective?

sexual violence; around 15 percent have been raped. In some ways, knowing the person who commits rape is an additional trauma—the person is known and trusted. In Canada in 2001, there were nearly 25 000 reported cases of sexual assault, though that number may be greatly underreported (Canadian Centre for Justice Statistics, 2002). Twenty-nine percent of Canadian female undergraduates reported incidents of sexual assault that occurred in dating relationships (DeKeseredy & Kelly, 1993). Rape perpetrated by intimate partners and acquaintances is less likely to be reported and less likely to be prosecuted than stranger rape (Koss, 2000). Thus, rape victims may feel victimized by the experience of rape and again by the failure of the justice system. Men are victims of sexual violence less often than women; around 3 percent of men are the victims of attempted or completed rape (Tjaden & Thoennes, 2000). When men are the victims of sexual violence, their experience is similar: They are likely to be raped by an intimate, they are not likely to report the incident, and they are likely to feel additionally victimized by their experience with the justice system.

The most common effect of rape on victims' mental health is post-traumatic stress disorder. Indeed, the *DSM–IV–TR* mentions rape as one of the events that may cause PTSD. In addition, rape victims are at increased risk for anxiety disorders, depression, suicide, and substance abuse disorders (Boudreaux et al., 1998).

Similar to other perpetrators, rapists are not likely to have a disorder that fits into any diagnostic category in the *DSM*. Men (and women) with anti-social personality disorder are more likely than other men to do harm to others, including through sexual violence, but the majority of rapists does not fit into this classification. Ten percent of men admit that they have committed acquaintance rape, and 24 percent of men admit that they have used force or other tactics that would meet the criteria for rape (Rubenzahl & Corcoran, 1998); these percentages are much higher than the estimates for anti-social personality disorder, indicating that most men who commit acquaintance rape do not have this disorder.

Circumstances, social setting, and attitudes can be factors in rape. For example, substance use and abuse increase the risk. Men who admit to perpetrating acquaintance rape are more likely than sexually active, non-aggressive men to use drugs or alcohol (Ouimette, 1997). Alcohol use also makes women more vulnerable to acquaintance rape (Ullman, Karabatsos, & Koss, 1999). Thus, substance use is a risk for rape for both victim and perpetrator. Men who commit acquaintance rape are also more likely than other men to find sexual aggression attractive, to have attitudes that support violence, to have many sexual partners, and to see relationships with women as a contest (Malamuth, 1996). Their attitudes differ from those of other men in ways that allow them to commit sexual violence, but most are not mentally ill.

# Summary and Review

## WHAT IS ABNORMAL BEHAVIOUR?

**Define abnormal behaviour, and describe the major perspectives that try to explain it.**

> *Abnormal behaviour* is behaviour that is not typical but is socially unacceptable, distressing, maladaptive, and/or the result of distorted cognitions, and *abnormal psychology* is the field of psychology concerned with the assessment, treatment, and prevention of maladaptive behaviour.   pp. 532–533

> Different *models* provide alternatives for understanding abnormal behaviour. The medical–biological model focuses on the biological and physiological conditions that initiate abnormal behaviours. The psychodynamic model focuses on unresolved conflicts and forces of which a person may be unaware. The humanistic model assumes that people naturally move toward health, so maladaptive behaviour is the result of some force that prevents this movement. The behavioural model states that abnormal behaviour is caused by faulty or ineffective learning. The cognitive model looks at people's ideas and thoughts. The sociocultural model examines abnormalities within the context of culture, the family, the community, and society. The evolutionary model sees abnormal behaviour as potentially adaptive in evolutionary history but not in modern society. The biopsychosocial model holds that biological, personal, and social forces all influence the expression of abnormal behaviour. pp. 533–536

**What are the goals of the *DSM*, and what are its advantages and disadvantages?**

> The *DSM–IV–TR* is the latest edition of the *Diagnostic and Statistical Manual of Mental Disorders*, the manual that mental health practitioners use to diagnose and classify mental disorders. It describes behaviour in terms of its characteristics and its *prevalence* and uses what is called a multiaxial system. Its goals are to improve the reliability of diagnoses and to provide a standardized system for diagnosis. Some psychologists applaud the *DSM* for its recognition of social and environmental influences on behaviour; others take issue with how it creates diagnoses based on political rather than research or theoretical criteria.   **pp. 536 539**

### KEY TERMS

abnormal behaviour, p. 532; model, p. 533; abnormal psychology, p. 534; prevalence, p. 537; case study, p. 539

## ANXIETY DISORDERS

**What are the chief characteristics of anxiety disorders?**

> *Anxiety* is a generalized feeling of fear and apprehension, which is often accompanied by increased physiological arousal and may or may not be related to a specific event or object.   **p. 540**

> *Generalized anxiety disorder* is characterized by persistent anxiety of at least six months' duration. It can include increased physiological arousal, excessive muscle tension, and vigilance. Irrational fear and avoidance of certain objects or situations characterize a *phobic disorder*, including *agoraphobia* (with and without panic attack), *social phobia*, and *specific phobia*.   **p. 542**

> Individuals with *obsessive–compulsive disorder* have persistent and uncontrollable thoughts and irrational beliefs, which cause them to perform compulsive rituals that interfere with normal daily functioning. The focus of these behaviours is often on maintaining order and control.   **pp. 543–544**

### KEY TERMS

anxiety, p. 540; generalized anxiety disorder, p. 541; phobic disorders, p. 541; agoraphobia, p. 541; social phobia, p. 542; specific phobia, p. 542; obsessive–compulsive disorder, p. 543

## MOOD DISORDERS

**What are the characteristics of the major mood disorders, and what theories account for these disorders?**

> People diagnosed with *depressive disorders* such as *major depressive disorder* have a gloomy outlook on life, slow thought processes, loss of appetite, sleep problems, *delusions* such as an exaggerated view of current problems, loss of energy, and a tendency to blame themselves. pp. 544–546

> The monoamine theory of depression suggests that major depression results from deficient monoamines or inefficient monoamine receptors. This theory is based on the finding that antidepressant drugs work by blocking reuptake of monoamines, thus keeping people from being depressed. Learning theorists argue that reinforcement patterns and social interactions determine the course and nature of depression. Cognitive theorists hypothesize that depressed people have thoughts that perpetuate their negative mood. *Learned helplessness* produces feelings consistent with the experience of depression.   **pp. 548–551**

> *Vulnerability* is a person's diminished ability to deal with demanding life events. The more vulnerable a person is, the fewer environmental stressors are needed to initiate a depressive episode. **p. 551**

> *Bipolar disorder* gets its name from the fact that people with this disorder show behaviour that vacillates between two extremes: mania and depression. **pp. 551–552**

**KEY TERMS**

depressive disorders, p. 545; major depressive disorder, p. 545; delusions, p. 545; learned helplessness, p. 550; vulnerability, p. 551; bipolar disorder, p. 551

## DISSOCIATIVE DISORDERS

### Characterize dissociative disorders.

> *Dissociative disorders* are disorders characterized by a sudden but temporary alteration in consciousness, identity, sensorimotor behaviour, or memory. These disorders include *dissociative amnesia* and *dissociative identity disorder*. These disorders are not well understood and are controversial, with some authorities believing that they do not actually exist. **pp. 552–553**

**KEY TERMS**

dissociative disorders, p. 552; dissociative amnesia, p. 553; dissociative identity disorder, p. 553

## SCHIZOPHRENIA

### Identify the essential characteristics of the major types of schizophrenia.

> Schizophrenia is a group of disorders characterized by a lack of reality testing and by deterioration of social and intellectual functioning. Individuals with *schizophrenic disorders* often show serious personality disintegration, with significant changes in thought, mood, perception, and behaviour, which matches the definition of *psychotic*. Positive symptoms are those present in people with schizophrenia but not in normal people, for example, hallucinations; negative symptoms relate to behaviours that people with schizophrenia lack but normal people have, for example, an inability to experience pleasure. **pp. 553–556**

> People with the *paranoid type of schizophrenia* experience delusions of persecution—beliefs that there are plots to harm them. They also often experience delusions of grandeur as well as hallucinations. Their paranoia may make them secretive, so their behaviour may seem normal, but their thought processes are not. There are actually two subtypes of the *catatonic type of schizophrenia*: excited and withdrawn. Severely disturbed thought processes characterize the *disorganized type of schizophrenia*. People with this type of schizophrenia have hallucinations and delusions and are frequently incoherent. People who show symptoms attributable to schizophrenia but who remain in touch with reality are diagnosed as having the *residual type of schizophrenia*.

Some people exhibit all the essential features of schizophrenia but do not fall clearly into any one of the other categories; these individuals are classified as suffering from the *undifferentiated type of schizophrenia*. **pp. 556–557**

**What has research revealed about the causes of schizophrenia?**

> The *concordance rate* is the likelihood that two groups or biologically related individuals show the same trait. Research into schizophrenia shows higher concordance rates for identical twins than for fraternal twins, which suggests that schizophrenia has a genetic component. **p. 558**

> The dopamine theory of schizophrenia asserts that too much dopamine or too much activity at dopamine receptors causes schizophrenia. The effectiveness of anti-schizophrenic drugs that decrease dopamine activity supports this view. **p. 558**

> A family environment that lacks good communication and sends mixed messages can create a *double bind*, which is one situation that increases vulnerability for schizophrenia. Other factors include genetic history and brain chemistry. In vulnerable individuals, low levels of environmental stress or other disorders can precipitate a schizophrenic episode. **pp. 560–561**

**KEY TERMS**

schizophrenic disorders, p. 554; psychotic, p. 555; paranoid type of schizophrenia, p. 556; catatonic type of schizophrenia, p. 557; disorganized type of schizophrenia, p. 557; residual type of schizophrenia, p. 557; undifferentiated type of schizophrenia, p. 557; concordance rate, p. 558; double bind, p. 559

## PERSONALITY DISORDERS

### What are the chief characteristics of six key personality disorders?

> People who have unwarranted feelings of persecution and who mistrust almost everyone are said to be suffering from the type of *personality disorder* called paranoid personality disorder. Those with borderline personality disorder have unstable interpersonal relationships, self-image, and affect and are often impulsive and easily distracted. Dramatic, emotional, and erratic behaviours are characteristic of the histrionic personality disorder. The narcissistic personality disorder is characterized by an extremely exaggerated sense of self-importance, an expectation of special favours, and a constant need for attention; people with the disorder show a lack of concern for others and react to criticism with rage, shame, or humiliation. The *anti-social personality disorder* is characterized by behaviour that is irresponsible and destructive and violates the rights of others; persons with anti-social personality disorder experience little guilt or empathy for others. Submissive and clinging behaviours are characteristic of people with a dependent personality disorder. **pp. 561–563**

## VIOLENCE AND MENTAL DISORDERS

### What diagnoses are associated with increased risk for violence?

> The association between mental disorders and violence is not as strong as the popular perception of it, but some disorders increase the risk for violence. More serious disorders are the highest risks, including schizophrenia, bipolar disorder, depression, and anti-social personality disorder. People with mental disorders are more likely to harm themselves than others. **pp. 563–564**

> Most depressed people do not attempt suicide, but most people who attempt suicide are depressed. Many people think about suicide, but most do not make an attempt.

Many more people attempt suicide than commit suicide. More than 3700 people commit suicide each year in Canada, and all of these deaths are preventable. **pp. 564–566**

### How does violence relate to the risk of developing mental disorders?

> Victims of *child abuse*, domestic violence, and *rape* are at increased risk for a variety of mental disorders, including post-traumatic stress disorder, depression, substance abuse, and anxiety disorders. **pp. 567–568**

> People who commit violence may have mental disorders, but most do not fit into any of the current diagnostic categories. **pp. 567–568**

**KEY TERMS**

child abuse, p. 567; rape, p. 567

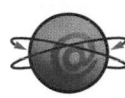

Take advantage of the multimedia resources available with this text! Follow the marginal icons to access the interactive modules on the *HandsOnPsych* CD-ROM; log on to *MyPsychLab* to explore the ebook, study aids, and other online resources; and visit the Companion Website at **www.pearsoned.ca/lefton** for additional exercises and links.

# 16 Therapy

Rob has been experiencing a lot of despair lately for reasons he cannot seem to figure out. That along with the fact that he was losing sleep and weight and engaging in serious alcohol use on weekends indicated that he needed help. And help was not far away. It came from his company's in-house nurse, who referred him to a psychologist who was part of an extended care plan set up for his company. Early on, the psychologist had Rob go for a physical checkup; after consultation with the psychologist, the physician felt that Rob should take an antidepressant for a short time to combat his depression. Prozac was prescribed—and it helped a great deal. In fact, within 10 days Rob's mood started to lift, which made his weekly session with his therapist much easier. Problems came into sharper focus. His energy was greater. Rob started to see his issues clearly and even started to mend a strained relationship with his father and brother. The struggle from the depths of despair to recovery was long and tough, though. It involved months of therapy dealing with diverse issues, including self-esteem, distorted ideas about work demands, and his relationship with his dad and brother.

Was it the psychological therapy that helped, or was it the drug? The truth is that it was probably a combination of the drug therapy and the psychotherapy that helped Rob to move ahead. Would one have worked without the other? Perhaps—but the combination turned out to be extremely effective. Many researchers think that this is the key to therapy, but others insist on approaches involving only psychotherapies or only drug therapies. A great deal depends on the disorder.

FIGURE 16.1
Types of Treatment

A 1993 study of nearly 23 million people with mental health or substance abuse problems showed that such people seek help from a variety of sources.
(Adapted from Narrow, Regier, & Rae, 1993.)

Psychiatrists, clinical psychologists, psychiatric social workers, other trained mental health counsellors

Friends, family members, self-help groups

37.5%

39.7%

11.7%

11.1%

General medical doctors

Clergy, family service agencies, welfare workers, ethnic healers

**HandsOnPsych**
Version 2.0

**Treatment**

PSYCHOTHERAPY
[SYE-ko-THER-uh-pee]

The treatment of emotional or behavioural problems through psychological techniques.

In some important ways therapy is changing; people are relying more and more on drugs for the treatment of anxiety and depression. However, many psychologists think that professionals involved in the mental health area pathologize people's problems and overdiagnose them as psychological disorders (Kutchins & Kirk, 1997) and that they overmedicate patients (Valenstein, 1998). The reality is that the causes of people's disorders—the initiators of unhappiness—are not usually biological. When people have marital problems, let work relationships get to them, or start to view the world too rigidly, help from a therapist—not a drug—is usually more effective. Overall mental health and therapy is complicated by two facts today. First, cuts to the health-care system are putting pressure on practitioners to find fast, efficient cures that are helpful but also less costly. Second, some disorders, especially disorders such as depression, often are undiagnosed and therefore remain untreated (Hirschfeld et al., 1997). Let's look at the available therapies and sort out the issues to determine what works best, and when.

## Therapy Comes in Many Forms

Many sources and types of treatment are available for people who are having difficulty coping with their problems (see Figure 16.1). When a person seeks help from a physician, mental health counselling centre, or drug treatment centre, an initial working diagnosis is necessary. Does the person have medical problems? Should the person be hospitalized? Is the person dangerous? If psychotherapy is in order, what type of practitioner is best suited for the person? There are two broad types of therapy: biologically based therapy and psychotherapy.

### BIOLOGICALLY BASED THERAPY AND PSYCHOTHERAPY

Biologically based therapy traditionally has been called *somatic therapy*; this term refers to treatment of psychological disorders by means of treatments for the body, including therapy that affects hormone levels and the brain. For example, severely depressed individuals may need antidepressants; those diagnosed as having schizophrenia may need anti-psychotic drugs; those with less severe disorders may be advised to change their diet and exercise more, because exercise has mood-enhancing effects for many disorders (Tkachuk & Martin, 1999). We will examine some of these biological therapies later in this chapter, but first, we will explore the broad array of psychological therapies that are available for people suffering from life problems or maladjustment.

**Psychotherapy** is the treatment of emotional or behavioural problems through psychological techniques. It is a change-oriented process, sometimes fairly emotional, whose goal is to help individuals cope better with their problems and achieve more emotionally satisfying lifestyles. Psychotherapy accomplishes its goal by teaching people how to relieve stress, improve interpersonal communication, understand previous events in their lives, and/or modify their faulty ideas about the world. Psychotherapy helps people improve their self-image and adapt to new and challenging situations.

Of course, different cultures perceive different outcomes as optimal. Thus, in Canada, enhancing self-esteem through accomplishment may be seen as an optimal goal of psychotherapy. In Asia, an outcome that improves family harmony may enhance self-esteem, even though achieving that goal means working for collective rather than personal good.

## IS PSYCHOTHERAPY NECESSARY AND EFFECTIVE?

The mass media and the images they present to the public often shape the reputation of psychotherapy. Talk show psychiatrist Frasier Crane on *Frasier* bumbles through his own life. These images, as well as talk show pop psychology, make many ask, "Is psychotherapy really necessary or effective?" Some researchers note that many clients could outgrow or otherwise find relief from their symptoms without psychotherapy. Others assert that psychotherapy is more art than science. Still others believe that psychotherapy provides only temporary relief. Recall from Chapter 1 that both psychologists (generally a Ph.D. in psychology) and psychiatrists (medical physicians) can offer psychotherapy but that only psychiatrists can prescribe drug therapies. Let's consider some of these arguments.

▲ Talk show psychiatrist Frasier Crane of the TV series *Frasier* bumbles through his own life. These images presented by the mass media often shape the public's perception of psychotherapy.

**PLACEBO EFFECTS.**    A **placebo effect** is a therapeutic change that occurs as a result of a person's expectations of change rather than as a result of any specific treatment. Is the benefit of psychotherapy largely a placebo effect? Physicians report that people sometimes experience relief from their symptoms when they are given sugar pills and are told that the pills are medicine. In much the same way, some patients in psychotherapy may show relief from their symptoms simply because they have entered therapy and now are committed to and expect change. For some people, just the attention of a therapist and the chance to express their feelings can be therapeutic.

The placebo effect complicates research on therapy effectiveness. Researchers must determine if the improvements they observe are the result of people's expectancy or real benefits of the therapy. The double-blind technique allows researchers to distinguish between improvement produced by expectancy versus that produced by therapy. The **double-blind technique** is a procedure in which neither the experimenter nor the participants know who is in the control and experimental groups. It helps eliminate any potential bias on the part of experimenters or participants by reducing the experimental **demand characteristics**, elements of an experimental situation that might cause a participant to perceive the situation in a certain way or become aware of the purpose of the study and thus bias the participant to behave in a certain way and in so doing distort results.

Using the double-blind technique, a researcher assigns some participants to a control condition in which they receive a placebo rather than actual treatment, whereas the participants assigned to the experimental group receive treatment believed to be effective. The participants do not know which group they are in, and neither do the researchers. This "blinding" of both participants and researchers prevents expectancy from contaminating the results. For example, participants in the control group might receive a pill with inactive ingredients whereas those in the experimental group receive a new drug for depression. Both groups receive pills that look the same, so the placebo effect and demand characteristics apply to both equally; they have similar expectancies for effectiveness. The researchers who dispense the pills have no way to convey different expectancies to the participants in the experimental group because they too are "blind" to the conditions. Thus, any improvement that the experimental group shows can be attributed to the treatment effect rather than the placebo effect. Double-blind studies are the best technique for demonstrating therapy effectiveness. Research studies that compare traditional psychotherapies with placebo treatment show that the therapies are consistently more effective (Kazdin, 2001).

**RESEARCH ON PSYCHOTHERAPY.**    In 1952, an important paper by Hans Eysenck challenged the effectiveness of psychotherapy, claiming that it produces no greater change in maladjusted individuals than do naturally occurring life experiences.

PLACEBO [pluh-SEE-bo] EFFECT

A therapeutic change that occurs as a result of a person's expectations of change rather than as a result of any specific treatment.

DOUBLE BLIND TECHNIQUE

A research technique in which neither the experimenter nor the participants know who is in the control and experimental groups.

DEMAND CHARACTERISTICS

Elements of an experimental situation that might cause a participant to perceive the situation in a certain way or become aware of the purpose of the study and thus bias the participant to behave in a certain way, and in so doing, distort results.

Thousands of studies attempting to investigate the effectiveness of therapy followed. These studies showed what clients and therapists have known for decades: that Eysenck was wrong. Analyses of large amounts of data using sophisticated statistical techniques found psychotherapy effective (Bachar, 1998; Smith, Glass, & Miller, 1980; Tritt et al., 2000). Although some psychologists continue to challenge the effectiveness of psychotherapy, most are convinced that it is effective with a wide array of clients (e.g., Kazdin, 2000; Lindfors et al., 1995; Seligman, 1995). The effectiveness of therapy and people's speed of response vary with the type of problem—for example, anxiety and depression respond more rapidly than do personality disorders (Kopta et al., 1994). Table 16.1 presents some generally recognized signs of good progress in therapy.

Is one type of therapy more effective than another? Many researchers contend that most psychotherapies are equally effective; that is, regardless of the approach a therapist uses, the results are often the same (Wampold et al., 1997). However, some newer and trendier approaches—ones that often appear in popular magazines—tend to be less reliable and reflect a culture that is fascinated with novelty. Some therapists do not pay attention to known data, and some therapists—often those with little training—do their clients a disservice by ignoring the facts and looking for an unusual or easy way out. But if most of the traditional therapies are effective, there must be some common underlying component that makes them successful. Both the Canadian Psychological Association and many individual researchers are seeking to systematize research strategies to investigate effectiveness; this research will lead to a clearer picture of which approaches are best for certain disorders, for clients of various ages, and for particular types of clients (Chambless & Hollon, 1998; Kazdin 2001). Furthermore, researchers are suggesting ways to validate therapy research in the laboratory and the real world (Goldfreid & Wolfe, 1998) for problems as diverse as family conflict and cocaine addiction (Van Horn & Frank, 1998).

## WHICH THERAPY, WHICH THERAPIST?

Before 1950, there were about 15 types of psychotherapy; today, there are hundreds. Some focus on individuals, some focus on groups of individuals (group therapy), and

---

**TABLE 16.1**     Signs of Good Progress in Therapy

The client is providing personally revealing and significant information.

The client is exploring the meanings of feelings and events.

The client is exploring material avoided earlier in therapy.

The client is expressing significant insight into personal behaviour.

The client's method of communicating is active, alive, and energetic.

There is a valued client–therapist working relationship.

The client feels free to express feelings toward the therapist—either positive or negative.

The client is expressing feelings outside of therapy.

The client is moving toward a different set of personality characteristics.

The client is showing improved functioning outside of therapy.

The client indicates a general state of well-being, positive feelings, and positive attitudes.

Source: Mahrer & Nadler, 1986.

others focus on families (family therapy). Some psychologists even deal with whole communities; these *community psychologists* focus on helping individuals, groups, and communities develop a more action-oriented approach to individual and social adjustment. A therapist's training usually will determine the type of treatment approach he or she takes. Rather than using just one type of psychotherapy, many therapists take an *eclectic approach*—that is, they combine several different techniques in their treatment.

A number of systematic psychotherapeutic approaches are in use today. Each can be applied in several formats—with individuals, couples, or groups—and each will be defined and examined in greater detail in later sections of this chapter. Some practitioners use *psychodynamically based approaches*, which loosely or closely follow Freud's basic ideas. These therapists' aim is to help patients understand the motivations underlying their behaviour. They assume that maladjustment and abnormal behaviour occur when people do not understand themselves adequately. Practitioners of *humanistic therapy* assume that people are essentially good—that they have an innate disposition to develop their potential and to seek beauty, truth, and goodness. This type of therapy tries to help people realize their full potential and find meaning in life. In contrast, *behaviour therapy* is based on the assumption that most behaviours, whether normal or abnormal, are learned. Behaviour therapists encourage their clients to learn new adaptive behaviours. Growing out of behaviour therapy and cognitive psychology (see Chapters 1 and 7) is *cognitive therapy*, which focuses on changing a client's behaviour by changing his or her thoughts and perceptions.

Most of the therapy approaches that we will discuss adopt a single theoretic point of view that guides research and practice. Certainly one example will be psychoanalysis, which prescribes a clear set of guidelines for therapy and its process. However, a new approach called *psychotherapy integration* has developed. Psychotherapy integration is not a single-theory approach, but rather open to integrating diverse theories and techniques.

Psychotherapy integration is more than an eclectic approach (a bit of this and a bit of that) because the goal is to integrate theories to solve problems. Research on psychotherapy integration is relatively scarce, however, because hypotheses from these new points of view are difficult to generate. Arkowitz (1997) argues that psychotherapy integration does not try to develop one, overarching view of therapy, but rather suggests that it is a way of thinking about and doing psychotherapy that reflects an openness to points of view other than the one with which a therapist is most familiar. In some important ways, psychotherapy integration is a process, a way of thinking, and it may help psychologists define the future of psychotherapy. Another ongoing development that may prove a better avenue to explore is research on prevention of disorders, discussed in *Introduction to Research Basics*.

The effectiveness of the different kinds of therapies varies with the type of disorder being treated and the goals of the client. Research to discover the best treatment method often focuses on specific disorders, such as depression. Conclusions from such studies are usually limited to recommending a specific method as effective for a specific problem. For example, cognitive behaviour therapy has a good success rate for people with phobias or depression, but it is less successful for those with schizophrenia. Long-term group therapy is more effective than short-term individual therapy for people with personality disorders. Behaviour therapy is usually the most effective approach with children, regardless of the disorder.

An individual can receive effective treatment from a variety of therapists. One therapist might focus on the root causes of maladjustment. Another might concentrate on eliminating symptoms: sadness, anxiety, or alcohol abuse. Besides the therapeutic approaches, personal characteristics of the therapists themselves can affect treatment; among these characteristics are ethnicity, personality, level of experience, and degree of empathy. Moreover, as outlined in Table 16.2 on page 579, psychotherapeutic practitioners have diverse types and levels of training. Practitioners

## Prevention Instead of Treatment? Is Our Research Starting in the Right Direction?

This *Introduction to Research Basics* box is slightly different from the others that have appeared so far in this book. So far, we have shown you examples of what researchers do once they get down to the business of designing and conducting studies. In this box, we want to do what all researchers must do from time to time—step back and critically evaluate whether you are actually studying the right sorts of things at all.

When psychologists conduct research, they often have set a research agenda. They might ask: What is the best therapy for anorexia nervosa? What is the optimal number of sessions for therapy to be effective? Or perhaps they seek to know whether combination treatments of drugs and talking therapy work better than either drugs or talking therapy alone. But *before* a research agenda can be set, scientists must establish what needs to be studied, discovered, or examined. Such was the case with prevention science; psychologists were not sure that mental disorders could be prevented or how to study their prevention. For example, can depression be prevented the way you prevent a child from being exposed to a cold virus?

Innovative and promising work has been done in prevention, and psychologists have recently reconsidered their reluctance to study this possibly important area. Researchers and practitioners have begun to map out a new field for research, have helped set a research agenda, and are suggesting that psychological disorders can be averted. Nancy Jonah (1996) at Health Canada in parallel with David Reiss and Richard Price (1996) outlined that research agenda. To help *prevent mental disorders*, they first argue that we need

to do research to learn (1) how we reduce the risk of developing a disorder, and (2) what protective factors people can develop to assist them when their level of risk is high. For example, can we reduce the likelihood that a person will be among people who themselves are disordered, alcoholic, or ineffective communicators? Second, they assert that research is necessary on how to *identify pre-clinical cases* so that full-blown disorders can be prevented. Third, they argue that research is necessary into how one disorder often leads to another and is associated with another. For example, a disorder such as social phobia might lead to other symptoms, perhaps panic attacks and then agoraphobia—psychologists need to know what precedes what.

From a research perspective, the key is that prevention research offers the possibility of new insights into the development of disorders, the mechanisms that cause disorders, and the social and community context in which disorders develop. This is a tall order, but the research process first requires agenda setting. Reiss and Price and their colleagues who work in the prevention field are challenging researchers to do this work to help better the human condition. Prevention science requires a unique combination of scientist and practitioner (Goldfried & Wolfe, 1996). It also requires an active collaboration among psychologists, but such work may bridge an important gap in the field's understanding of psychological disorders and their treatment. By stopping and reconsidering our direction of study, we can possibly discover whole new areas and techniques that can benefit many people.

---

with lower levels of training often work with a clinical psychologist or psychiatrist as part of a team that offers mental health services to clients.

Although there are differences among the various psychotherapies and therapists, there are also some commonalties. In all of the therapies, clients usually expect a positive outcome, which helps them strive for change. Figure 16.2 presents an overview of outcomes when psychotherapy is combined with efforts to change. In addition, clients receive attention, which helps them maintain a positive attitude. Moreover, no matter what type of therapy is involved, certain characteristics must be present in both the therapist and the client for therapeutic changes to occur. For example, good therapists communicate interest, understanding, respect, tact, maturity, and ability to help. They respect their clients' ability to cope with their troubles (Fischer, 1991). They use suggestion, encouragement, interpretation, examples, and perhaps rewards to help clients change or rethink their situations. But clients must be willing to make some changes in their lifestyles and ideas. A knowledgeable, accepting, and objective therapist can facilitate behaviour changes, but the client is the one who makes the changes (Lafferty, Beutler, & Crago, 1989).

| Type of Practitioner | Degree | Years of Education Beyond Undergraduate Degree | Activities |
|---|---|---|---|
| Clinical or counselling psychologist | Ph.D. (Doctor of Philosophy) or Psy.D. (Doctor of Psychology) | 5–8 | Diagnosis, testing, and treatment using a wide array of techniques, including insight and behaviour therapy. Cannot prescribe medication. |
| Psychiatrist | MD (Doctor of Medicine) | 8 | Biomedical therapy, diagnosis, and treatment, often with a psychoanalytic emphasis |
| Social worker | MSW (Master of Social Work) | 2 | Family therapy or behaviour therapy, often in community-based settings such as hospitals |
| Psychiatric nurse | BSN (Bachelor of Science in Nursing) or MA (Master of Arts) | 0–2 | Inpatient psychiatric care, supportive therapy of various types |
| Counsellor | MA (Master of Arts, often in counselling) | 2 | Supportive therapy, family therapy, vocational readjustment, alcoholism and drug abuse counselling |

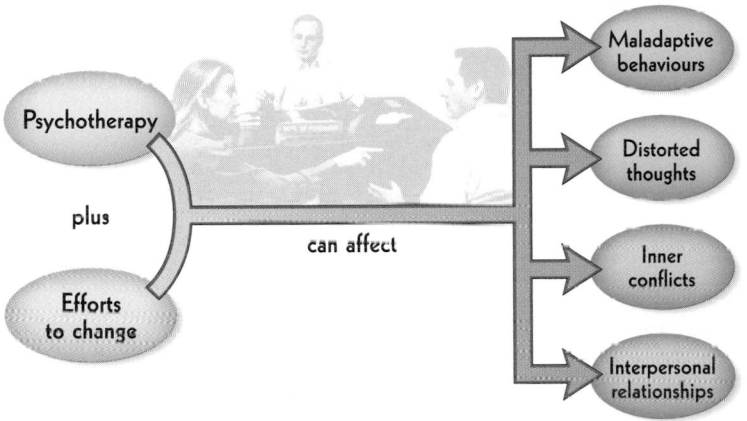

**FIGURE 16.2**
**Goals of Psychotherapy**

An important goal of psychotherapy is engaging the client in the process of change. Once initiated, psychotherapy, along with efforts to change, can affect a host of problems, including specific maladaptive behaviours, distorted thoughts, inner conflicts, and interpersonal relationships.

In general, the therapist and client must form an alliance to work together purposefully (Howe, 1999); such alliances are formed more readily if the therapist and client share some values (Kelly & Strupp, 1992), including those concerned with religious, political, and family views.

To better understand the issues involved in psychotherapy, in the next sections we will look more closely at the four major psychotherapeutic approaches: psychodynamic, humanistic, behaviour, and cognitive therapies. Then we will examine group therapy and the biologically based approaches. But first, let's look at the crucial variables of gender and culture.

## CULTURE AND GENDER IN THERAPY

Throughout this book we have been emphasizing the role of culture in psychology, stressing that a person's vantage point and world view affect his or her thoughts and behaviour. In no place is this more vital than in therapy. When a person seeks help for problems large and small, both the therapy process and the outcome are affected by the client's ethnicity. To be effective, care must be culturally congruent—there must be a sensitivity and match between the therapist and client (Zoucha &

Hustead, 2000). This means that the therapist should either be of the same culture as the client or be aware of, and sensitive to, the cultural norms and practices of the client.

At a minimum, psychologists respect *multiculturalism*—the acceptance and celebration of distinct cultural heritages—and it continues to be the prevailing organization through which ethnic identity and social problems are examined. However, practitioners and scholars also know that therapists must look beyond the distinct margins of a specific culture (such as Vietnamese, French, Bosnian) and see individuals as made up of a confluence of different influences. This view, *transculturalism*, recognizes that a woman with an Asian family heritage may embrace Western values of independence and individuality and be a single mother who runs a business. Transculturalism reflects changes that have occurred throughout the world due to globalization, increased mobility, improved communications systems (including the Internet), and intermarriage. Therapists need to be well informed about clients' backgrounds and provide interventions based on and using cultural symbols, rituals, and metaphors that are meaningful to the client (Witzum & Buchbinder, 2001).

So, for example, in traditional Asian cultures, the *family* is the primary source of emotional support. The most important family relationship is not the husband–wife–children relationship but rather the parent–child relationship. A person is defined by her or his roles in the family, including parent roles, grandparent roles, and child roles.

▲ In traditional Asian cultures, the family is the primary source of emotional support. The most important family relationship is the parent–child relationship.

Children of any age, including adult children, are expected to maintain a deferential and respectful relationship to their elders. These roles and the consequent responsibilities provide emotional support for individual family members. The therapeutic alliance must respect the family, its life cycle, and its traditions and recognize the types of problems presented to practitioners (Tempo & Saito, 1996). See *Psychology in Action* for a more specific application of cultural values to therapeutic intervention. Often, emphasizing family bonds—perhaps through family therapy—is an effective technique, as is relying on traditional and familiar Asian philosophical traditions.

Within a culture, therapists need to recognize that culture, even popular culture, is powerful and can be used as a tool to influence clients and help them explore their values and goals (Oliver, 2000). It also helps therapists to realize that various communities have constraints and prohibitions against self-disclosure, or an alternate view of appropriate responses to domestic violence (Thomas, 2000). Some Arab cultures are strongly patriarchal and resistant to emotional exploration and more likely to value and adapt to therapies that are cognitive in nature (Chaleby, 2000). Han Li and Annette Browne (2000) of the University of Northern British Columbia have found that Asian Canadians underuse mainstream mental health services. Their interviews revealed that this may, in part, be due to the belief that mental illness is serious and untreatable or that the problem is somatic (physical) and not psychological.

Client variables are also potent—evidence shows that there are both gender and ethnic differences in the way people respond to drugs that treat anxiety and depression (Lin, 2001; Melfi et al., 2000; Smith, Mendoza, & Lin, 1999) as well as cultural effects on maintaining commitment to medical advice and therapeutic drug usage (Kemppainen et al., 2001). Men and women respond to therapy differently (Philpot, 2001; Scher, 2001), and one's ethnicity—the therapist's and the client's—is an important variable and must be studied, valued, and taken into account in the therapeutic milieu (LaRoche, 1999). And last, culture is dynamic, contextual, and even political; stereotypes and oversimplifications abound (Romero, 2000). Therapists must recognize that all Asian men, Orthodox Jews, feminists, or immigrants are not the same and that therapists' own cultural values and preconceived ideas may be oppressive to their clients and constrain the effectiveness of therapy

## Aboriginal Health and Wellness: Spiritual and Community Healing

Openness toward and understanding of cultural beliefs, a demonstrated respect for those beliefs, and the establishment of a solid basis of mutual trust are keys to effective counselling. Carrie Heilbron and Mary Alice Julius Guttman (2000) at the University of Toronto and Rod McCormick (2000) at the University of British Columbia suggest that traditional Aboriginal healing ceremonies have a strong spiritual component that has much to offer the healing process for both Aboriginals (First Nations, Métis, Inuit, and native Canadians) and non-Aboriginals. The disconnection from cultural values experienced by Aboriginal peoples is in large measure the result of devastating attempts at assimilation and cultural genocide by the mainstream society. There is therefore a strong belief among Aboriginal elders that reconnecting to culture, community, and spirituality is healing for Aboriginal people, that there is a link between cultural dislocation and sickness.

Therapy with Aboriginal people often fails because cultural and traditional beliefs are not addressed. Effective counsellors need to understand the importance of traditional healing beliefs and practices (LaDue, 1994). Therapeutic effectiveness is increased when traditional ceremonies and

beliefs are included in the counselling setting. Heilbron and Guttman (2000) argue that sharing traditional values in a story format as well as addressing both community and individual healing serves to enhance outcome for many Aboriginal clients. Of course, not all Aboriginal people adhere to such traditional beliefs and it is therefore important for counsellors to be open to providing options about whether patients wish to participate in cultural ceremonies and practices.

Non-Aboriginal counsellors usually lack experience with Aboriginal traditional ceremonies and must therefore be willing to adopt a more passive role during traditional ceremonies and to defer to elders or Aboriginal healers performing the healing practices. Another effective way to show respect for, and faith in, the role of traditional ceremonies is to include an Aboriginal co-leader who establishes the connection to the traditional ceremonies and beliefs.

A collectively oriented culture provides meaning to its members through family, community, and cultural values. Heilbron and Guttman (2000) suggest that community interconnectedness and healing is an integral part of the therapeutic process and argue that it may therefore be necessary for the community to become involved in treating the group, involving friends, relatives, or other members of the community (Connors, 1993). For many mainstream counsellors, this means a move away from culture-bound interventions that focus mainly on individual change, where individuals seek meaning on their own (McCormick, 1998).

Programs that work stress traditional values, spirituality, and activities that enhance self-esteem. Successful programs, organized using Aboriginal values and approaches, have been used to treat substance abuse (McCormick, 2000), sexual abuse (Heilbron & Guttman, 2000), and other presenting issues, such as experiencing prejudice (Malone, 2000). A review of successful programs has led to the view that mainstream psychological techniques could be enhanced if fused with Aboriginal values and approaches (Anderson, 1992). Non-Aboriginal people as well as Aboriginal people stand to gain from the integration of the spirituality and healing wisdom of Aboriginal approaches with the more common approaches used in the dominant culture.

(Laird, 2000). Karen Grant and her colleagues (2001) at the City University in Vancouver developed a "co-therapy" approach to treating families that involves the assistance of settlement counsellors in providing immigrant and ethnic families with therapeutic support.

Not only is ethnicity important, but a person's gender turns out to be significant. Women seek out therapy more often than do men, and they respond differently to talking therapy (Romans, 2001) and to drug therapy (Martenyi et al., 2001). Therapists need to be aware of gender roles and expectations related to gender roles (Papp, 2000; Scher, 2001). For example, therapists must also consider the way men and women talk about themselves, others, and situations. Linguist Deborah Tannen (2001) has studied language and social interactions among men and women and convincingly argues that men and women talk differently; while both try to be open and communicative, men tend to give *reports* while women try to establish *rapport*. Tannen further argues that people in therapeutic and family relationships feel an ability to say things that are heard quite differently than intended. So, she argues, mothers who offer help are often heard to be offering criticism. "Oh, your hair would be so cute if it were short" may be heard by a daughter as "You look terrible." In a therapeutic relationship, a therapist must hear what clients say and the messages that they actually intend to deliver. They must also realize that they and their clients may have experienced gender bias in their families that affect their gender assumptions (Atwood, 2001). This is compounded by ethnicity—Asian men view masculinity differently than do European or Canadian men (Sue, 2001), as do Latinos (Casas et al., 2001), and women view it differently still. Gay men and lesbians bring still another view to gender roles and the therapeutic situation (Biaggio et al., 2000; Gainor, 2000).

Differences occur between men and women in a variety of domains; for example, men and women tend to report similar alcohol-related psychosocial problems, but women are more likely to be diagnosed as suffering from depression and men diagnosed with anti-social personality disorder (Parks et al., 2001). Again, the differences between men and women become compounded by ethnicity; African-American women are seen first as women, and then considered as African American—with each designation connected to certain biases (Williams, 2000). As with ethnicity, therapists must come to understand how their own personal gender socialization affects therapy (Brooks, 2000), avoid stereotypes, and recognize the diversity of men's and women's experiences (McMahon & Luthar, 2000).

## BRIEF THERAPY

Professionals and patients have been forced by health-care systems and health insurance companies into a model that, for economic reasons, is often short, focused—and sometimes especially effective (Cummings, Budman, & Lawrence, 1998). The model rejects many of the traditional ideas of various therapies. Its proponents reject the idea that any one therapeutic approach can help all people with any behavioural or emotional problem. It rejects the belief that a person's unconscious or life history *must* be understood fully before the client can end therapy. Finally, it disavows the idea that the therapist and the client have to resolve past or future psychological problems during psychotherapy sessions.

Sometimes termed *brief therapy*, this therapeutic approach is based on a blend of psychotherapeutic orientations and skills (Cummings, 1986). A basic goal is to give clients what they need; the therapy therefore focuses on treating clients' problems efficiently and getting clients back on their own as quickly as possible. The time frame varies from therapist to therapist and client to client, but 6 weeks is common and 16 to 24 weeks is considered lengthy. One of its objectives is to save clients time and money. Although insurance companies or health-care systems may place limits on the number of sessions they will cover for a given individual, clients may remain in therapy longer if they feel the need and are willing and able to continue to pay. They also can return if they need help in the future. The

▼ The goals of therapy are established and agreed upon by the client and the therapist.

key distinction of this changing approach to therapy is that more and more therapists are thinking in terms of *planned* short-term treatments (Messer & Wachtel, 1997).

The therapist makes sure that treatment begins in the first session of brief therapy. He or she strives to perform an *operational diagnosis* that answers this question: Why is the client here today instead of last week, last month, last year, or next year? The answer indicates to the therapist the specific problem for which the client is seeking help. Also in the first session, "each client forms a therapeutic contract with their therapist" (Cummings, 1986; Goulding, 1990). The goals of therapy are established and agreed on by the client and the therapist, and the therapy is precise, active, and directive, with no unnecessary steps (Clarkin & Hull, 1991; Lazarus & Fay, 1990).

Published research on brief therapy is encouraging, suggesting that the therapy is effective and that its effects are long-lasting (e.g., Kush & Fleming, 2000). Research has been limited to relatively few clients with a narrow range of problems. Nonetheless, researchers have found brief therapy to be effective when treatment goals and procedures are tailored to the client's needs and the time available. It can be especially effective with couples (Donovan, 1998) and when combined with cognitive restructuring (Ellis, 1990).

Brief therapy is not a cure-all. As with all therapies, its aim is to help relieve clients' suffering, and it is effective with some clients and with some problems some of the time (Hempill & Littlefield, 2001; Stalker, Levene, & Coady, 1999). Further research on brief therapy is being conducted now, and its future will depend on the results of that research.

## Psychoanalysis and Psychodynamic Therapies

**Psychoanalysis** is a lengthy insight therapy developed by Sigmund Freud that aims at uncovering conflicts and unconscious impulses through special techniques, including free association, dream analysis, and transference. Many other psychologists use a therapy loosely connected to or rooted in Freudian theory. These psychologists refer to their therapies as **psychodynamically based therapies**—therapies that use approaches or techniques derived from Freud, but that reject or modify some of the elements of Freud's theory.

Sigmund Freud believed that the exchange of words in psychoanalysis causes therapeutic change. According to Freud (1966, p. 21):

> The patient talks, tells of his past experiences and present impressions, complains, and expresses his wishes and his emotions. The physician listens, attempts to direct the patient's thought-processes, reminds him, forces his attention in certain directions, gives him explanations and observes the reactions of understanding or denial thus evoked.

Freud's therapy is an **insight therapy**—a therapy that attempts to discover relationships between unconscious motivations and current abnormal behaviour. Insight therapy has two basic assumptions: (1) that becoming aware of one's motivations helps one change and become more adaptable, and (2) that the causes of maladjustment are unresolved conflicts that the person was unaware of and therefore unable to deal with. The goal of insight therapy is to treat the causes of abnormal behaviours rather than the behaviours themselves. In general, insight therapists try to help people see life from a different perspective so that they can choose more adaptive behaviours.

**HandsOnPsych**
Version 2.0

**Treatment**

PSYCHOANALYSIS
[SYE-ko-uh-NAL-uh-sis]
A lengthy insight therapy developed by Sigmund Freud that aims at uncovering conflicts and unconscious impulses through special techniques, including free association, dream analysis, and transference.

PSYCHODYNAMICALLY [SYE-ko-dye-NAM-ick-lee] BASED THERAPIES
Therapies based loosely on Freud's psychoanalytic theory, using a part of that approach but rejecting or modifying some of its elements.

INSIGHT THERAPY
Therapy that attempts to discover relationships between unconscious motivations and current abnormal behaviour in order to change that behaviour.

▲ In traditional psychoanalysis, the patient lies on a couch and the therapist sits in a chair out of the patient's view. This is a photo of Freud's office where he saw patients.

FREE ASSOCIATION

A psychoanalytic technique in which a person reports to the therapist his or her thoughts and feelings as they occur, regardless of how trivial, illogical, or objectionable their content may appear.

DREAM ANALYSIS

A psychoanalytic technique in which a patient's dreams are interpreted and used to provide insight into the individual's unconscious motivations.

INTERPRETATION

In Freud's theory, the technique of providing a context, meaning, or cause of a specific idea, feeling, or set of behaviours; the process of tying a set of behaviours to its unconscious determinant.

RESISTANCE

In psychoanalysis, an unwillingness to cooperate by which a patient signals a reluctance to provide the therapist with information or to help the therapist understand or interpret a situation.

## GOALS OF PSYCHOANALYSIS

Many individuals who seek psychotherapy are unhappy with their behaviour but are unable to change it. As we saw in the discussion of Freud's theory of personality (Chapter 12), Freud believed that conflicts among a person's unconscious thoughts and processes produce maladjusted behaviour. The general goal of psychoanalysis is to help patients understand the unconscious motivations that direct their behaviour. Only when they become aware of those motivations can they begin to choose behaviours that lead to more fulfilling lives. In psychoanalysis, patients are encouraged to express healthy impulses, strengthen day-to-day functioning based on reality, and perceive the world as a positive rather than a punishing place.

## TECHNIQUES OF PSYCHOANALYSIS

In general, psychoanalytic techniques are geared toward the exploration of early experiences. In traditional psychoanalysis, the patient lies on a couch and the therapist sits in a chair out of the patient's view. Freud used this arrangement in his office in Vienna and believed that it would allow the patient to be more relaxed and feel less threatened than if the therapist was in view. Today, however, many followers of Freud prefer face-to-face interactions with patients.

Two major techniques used in psychoanalysis are free association and dream analysis. In **free association**, the patient is asked to report whatever comes to mind, regardless of how disorganized it might be, how trivial it might seem, or how disagreeable it might feel. A therapist might say, "I can help you best if you say whatever thoughts and feelings come to your mind, even if they seem irrelevant, immaterial, foolish, embarrassing, upsetting, or even if they're about me, even very personally, just as they come, without censoring or editing" (Lewin, 1970, p. 67). The purpose of free association is to help patients learn to recognize connections and patterns among their thoughts and to allow the unconscious to express itself freely.

In **dream analysis**, patients are asked to describe their dreams in detail; the dreams are interpreted and used to provide insight into unconscious motivations. Sometimes lifelike, sometimes chaotic, sometimes incoherent, dreams at times may replay a person's life history and at other times may venture into the person's current problems. Freud believed that dreams represent some element of the unconscious seeking expression. Psychodynamically oriented therapists see much symbolism in dreams; they assert that the content of a dream hides its true meaning.

Many therapists use patients' dreams to gain insight into patients' current problems. The goal of dream analysis is to help therapists reveal patients' unconscious desires and motivations by discovering the meaning of their dreams.

Both free association and dream analysis involve the therapist's interpretation. **Interpretation**, in Freud's theory, is the technique of providing a context, meaning, or cause of a specific idea, feeling, or set of behaviours; it is the process of tying a set of behaviours to its unconscious determinant. With this technique, the therapist tries to find common threads in a patient's behaviour and thoughts. Patients' use of *defence mechanisms* (ways of reducing anxiety by distorting reality, examined in Chapter 12) is often a sign of an area that may need to be explored. For example, if a male patient avoids the subject of women, invariably deflecting the topic with an offhand remark or a joke, the therapist may wonder if some kind of defensive avoidance is going on. The therapist then may encourage the patient to explore his attitudes and feelings about women in general and about his mother in particular.

Two processes are central to psychoanalysis: resistance and transference. **Resistance** is an unwillingness to cooperate by which a patient signals a reluctance to provide the therapist with information or to help the therapist understand or interpret a situation, sometimes to the point of belligerence. For example, a patient disturbed by her analyst's unsettling interpretations might become angry and start resisting treatment by missing appointments or failing to pay for therapy. Analysts usually interpret resistance as meaning either that the patient wishes to avoid discussing a particular subject or that an especially difficult stage in psychotherapy has been reached. To minimize resistance, analysts try to accept patients' behaviour. When a therapist does not judge but merely listens, a patient is more likely to describe feelings thoroughly.

In transference, patients transfer feelings from earlier relationships to the therapist. **Transference** is a psychoanalytic phenomenon in which a therapist becomes the object of a client's emotional attitudes about an important person in the client's life, such as a parent. For example, if a client's therapist is a man and the client becomes hostile toward the therapist, a psychoanalyst would say that he is acting as though the therapist were his father; that is, he is directing attitudes and emotional reactions from that earlier relationship toward the therapist (Butler & Strupp, 1991). The importance of transference is that the psychotherapist will respond differently so that the client can experience the conflict differently, which will lead him to a better understanding of the issue. By permitting transference, the therapist gives patients a new opportunity to understand their feelings and can guide them in the exploration of repressed or difficult material. The examination of thoughts or feelings that previously were considered unacceptable (and therefore often were repressed) helps patients understand and identify the underlying conflicts that direct their behaviour.

Psychoanalysis, with its slowly gained insights into the unconscious, is a gradual and continual process. Through their insights, patients learn new ways of coping with instinctual urges and develop more mature means of dealing with anxiety and guilt. The cycle of interpretation, resistance to interpretation, and transference occurs repeatedly in the process of psychoanalysis and sometimes is referred to as **working through.**

## CRITICISMS OF PSYCHOANALYSIS

Freud's theory has not been universally accepted; even his followers have disagreed with him. One group of psychoanalysts, referred to as *ego analysts* or *ego psychologists*, has modified some of Freud's basic ideas. *Ego analysts* are psychoanalytic practitioners who assume that the ego has greater control over behaviour than Freud suggested and who are more concerned with reality checking and control over the environment than with unconscious motivations and processes. Like Freud, ego analysts believe that psychoanalysis is the appropriate method for treating patients with emotional problems. Unlike Freud, however, they assume that people have voluntary control over whether, when, and in what ways their biological urges will be expressed.

A major disagreement between ego analysts and traditional psychoanalysts has to do with the role of the id and the ego. (Recall from Chapter 12 that the id operates on the pleasure principle, while the ego operates on the reality principle and tries to control the id's impulsive behaviour.) A traditional Freudian asserts that the ego grows out of the id and controls it—but an ego analyst asserts that the ego is independent of the id, controls memory and perception, and is not in constant conflict with the id. Whereas traditional psychoanalysts begin by focusing on unconscious material in the id and only later try to increase the patient's ego control, ego analysts try to help clients develop stronger egos. They may ask a client to assertively take control of a situation—to let reason, rather than feeling, guide a specific behaviour pattern. From an ego analyst's point of view, a weak ego may cause maladjustment by its failure to perceive, understand, and control the id. Thus, by learning to master and develop their egos—including moral reasoning and judgment—people gain greater control over their lives.

TRANSFERENCE
A psychoanalytic phenomenon in which a therapist becomes the object of a patient's emotional attitudes about an important person in the patient's life, such as a parent.

WORKING THROUGH
In psychoanalysis, the repetitive cycle of interpretation, resistance to interpretation, and transference.

Critics of psychoanalysis contend that the approach is unscientific, imprecise, and subjective; they assert that psychoanalytic concepts such as id, ego, and superego are not linked to real things or to day-to-day behaviour. Other critics object to Freud's biologically oriented approach, which suggests that a human being is a mere bundle of energy caught in conflict and driven toward some hedonistic goal. These critics ask: Where in this approach does human free will come in? Also, elements of Freud's theory are untestable, and some are sexist. For example, Freud conceived of men and women in prescribed roles; most practitioners today find this idea objectionable.

Aside from these criticisms, the effectiveness of psychoanalysis is open to question. Research shows that psychoanalysis is more effective for some people than for others. It is more effective, for example, for people with anxiety disorders than for those diagnosed as schizophrenic. In addition, younger patients improve more than older ones. In general, studies show that psychoanalysis can be as effective as other therapies, but no more so (Kazdin, 2000, 2001).

Psychoanalysis does have certain disadvantages. The problems addressed in psychoanalysis are difficult, and a patient must be highly motivated and articulate to grasp the complicated and subtle relationships being explored. Further, because traditional psychoanalysis involves meeting with an analyst for an hour at a time, five days a week, for approximately five years, psychoanalysis is typically extremely costly. Many people who seek therapy cannot afford the money or the time for this type of treatment.

Building Table 16.1 presents a summary of the key components of the psychoanalytic view of therapy. Humanistic therapies, which we will examine next, are neither as time-consuming nor as comprehensive in their goals as is psychoanalysis.

## Humanistic Therapies

Humanistic therapies, unlike psychoanalytic therapies, emphasize the uniqueness of the human experience, the ability to reflect on conscious experience, and the idea that human beings have free will to determine their destinies.

Humanistic psychologists tend to focus on the present and future rather than on the past and assert that human beings are conscious, creative, and born with an innate desire to fulfil themselves. To some extent, humanistic approaches, being insight-oriented, are an outgrowth of psychodynamically based insight therapies: Humanistic therapies help basically healthy people understand the causes of their behaviour, both normal and maladjusted, and take responsibility for their futures by promoting growth and fulfilment. Client-centred therapy is a type of humanistic therapy that focuses on such self-determination. Building Table 16.2, on page 589, presents a summary of the key components of both psychoanalytic and humanistic therapies.

| BUILDING TABLE 16.1 | Key Components of Psychoanalytic Therapy | | | | | |
|---|---|---|---|---|---|---|
| Therapy | Nature of Psychopathology | Goal of Therapy | Role of Therapist | Role of Unconscious Material | Role of Patient's Insights | Techniques |
| Psychoanalytic | Maladjustment reflects inadequate conflict resolution and fixation in early development. | Attainment of maturity, strengthened ego functions, reduced control by unconscious or repressed impulses. | An *investigator*, uncovering conflicts and resistances. | Primary in classical psychoanalysis; less emphasized in ego analysis. | Includes not solely intellectual understanding but also emotional experiences. | Analyst takes an active role in interpreting the dreams and free associations of patients. |

# CLIENT-CENTRED THERAPY

**Client-centred therapy,** or *person-centred therapy*, is an insight therapy that seeks to help people evaluate the world and themselves from their own perspective. Carl Rogers (1902–1987) first developed client-centred therapy. Rogers was a quiet, caring man who turned the psychoanalytic world upside-down when he introduced his approach. He focused on the person, listening intently to his clients and encouraging them to define their own "cures." Rogers saw people as basically good, competent, social beings who move forward and grow. He believed that people move toward their ideal selves throughout life, maturing into fulfilled individuals through the process of self-actualization. He believed that to reach one's full potential, a person must be involved in a relationship that includes unconditional positive regard, congruence, and empathy (to be discussed in a few paragraphs). When people lack this experience in their lives, client-centred therapy can provide it.

Rogerian therapists hold that problem behaviours occur when the environment prevents a person from developing his or her own innate potential. If children are given love and reinforcement only for their achievements, for example, as adults they may see themselves and others almost solely in terms of achievement. Rogerian treatment involves helping people evaluate the world from their own perspective and improve their self-regard. A Rogerian therapist might treat a client by encouraging him to explore his past goals, current desires, and expectations for the future, and then asking whether he can achieve what he wants through a new relationship with a woman or even at work. Table 16.3 presents the basic assumptions underlying Rogers' approach to treatment.

**TECHNIQUES OF CLIENT-CENTRED THERAPY.** The goal of client-centred therapy is to help clients discover their ideal selves and reconcile this ideal with their real selves. The use of the word *client* rather than *patient* is a key aspect of Rogers' approach to therapy (*patient* connotes a medical model). In psychoanalysis, the therapist *directs* the "cure" and helps patients understand their behaviour; in client-centred therapy, the therapist *guides* clients and helps them realize what they feel is right for themselves. Clients are viewed as the experts concerning their own experience.

The therapist must have certain characteristics for therapy to be successful. The three essential characteristics are unconditional positive regard, congruence, and empathy (Rogers, 1957). A basic tenet of client-centred therapy is that the therapist must show *unconditional positive regard*—be an accepting person who projects positive feelings toward clients. To counteract clients' negative

**CLIENT-CENTRED THERAPY**
An insight therapy, developed by Carl Rogers, that seeks to help people evaluate the world and themselves from their own perspective by providing them with a nondirective environment and unconditional positive regard. Also known as *person-centred therapy*.

**HandsOnPsych**
Version 2.0

**Treatment**

▼ Carl Rogers' client-centred therapy, or person-centred therapy, is an insight therapy that seeks to help people evaluate the world and themselves from their own perspective.

| TABLE 16.3 | Rogers' Assumptions about Human Beings |
|---|---|

1. People are innately good and are effective in dealing with their environments.

2. Behaviour is purposeful and goal-directed.

3. Healthy people are aware of all their behaviour; they choose their behaviour patterns.

4. A client's behaviour can be understood only from the client's point of view. Even if a client has misconstrued events in the world, the therapist must understand how the client sees those events.

5. Effective therapy occurs only when a client modifies his or her behaviour, not when the therapist manipulates it.

experiences with people who were unaccepting, and who thus have taught them to think that they are bad or unlikeable, client-centred therapists accept clients as they are, with good and bad points; they respect them as individuals.

*Congruence* is the second necessary component of client-centred therapy. This term refers to being real or genuine. Rogers believed that therapists must be more than accepting; they must be honest and aware of their own feelings. Counsellors' congruence allows them to communicate more effectively and to help clients become more aware and open.

*Empathic listening*, whereby therapists sense how their clients feel and communicate these feelings to clients, is a final condition for client growth. Therapists help clients organize their thoughts and ideas simply by asking the right questions, by giving neutral responses to encourage the client to continue, and by reflecting back the clients' feelings. (That is, the therapist may *paraphrase* a client's ideas, ask the client to clarify and *restate* ideas and feelings in other words, or *reflect* back what the client has just said so that the person can hear his or her own words again.) Even a small physical movement, such as a nod or gesture, can help clients stay on the right track. The client learns to evaluate the world from a personal vantage point, with little interpretation by the therapist.

The combination of acceptance and recognition of clients' emotions, expression of genuine feelings, and listening to clients' problems with empathy form the essentials of the therapeutic relationship. Client-centred therapy can be viewed as a consciousness-raising process that helps people expand their awareness so as to construct new meanings. Initially, clients tend to express the attitudes and ideas they have adopted from other people, are defensive, and show ineffective, disorganized behaviour. A client might say, "I should be making top sales figures," implying "because my father expects me to be a success." As therapy progresses and she experiences the empathy, congruence, and unconditional positive regard of the therapist, the client will begin to use her own ideas and standards when evaluating herself (Rogers, 1951). As a result, she may adjust her ideal self so that it is more in line with her own (rather than her father's) goals, or her behaviour may change so that her sales figures climb. Such change allows her to begin to talk about herself in more positive ways and to try to please herself rather than others, part of the process of constructing new meanings. She may say, "I'm satisfied with my sales efforts," or "Since I've started rethinking my goals, my sales figures have improved," reflecting a more positive, more accepting attitude about herself. Successful therapy results in clients who are less defensive, more congruent, and more open to new experiences (Rogers, 1980). As this client begins to feel better about herself, she will eventually suggest to the therapist that she feels ready to deal with the world and may be ready to leave therapy.

**CRITICISMS OF CLIENT-CENTRED THERAPY.** Client-centred therapy is acclaimed for its focus on the therapeutic relationship. No other therapy makes clients feel so warm, accepted, and safe. These are important characteristics of any therapy, but critics argue that they may not be enough to bring about long-lasting change.

Critics of client-centred therapy assert that lengthy discussions about past problems do not necessarily help people with their present difficulties and that an environment of unconditional positive regard may not be enough to bring about desired behaviour changes. They believe that this therapy may be making therapeutic promises that cannot be fulfilled and that it focuses on concepts that are hard to define, such as self-actualization.

Be an
**ACTIVE LEARNER**

**REVIEW**
> Define *resistance* and *transference*. pp. 584–585
> What basic criticism of psychoanalysis do ego analysts offer? p. 585
> What is the major disagreement between ego analysts and traditional psychoanalysts on the roles of the id and the ego? p. 585
> Identify the disadvantages of psychoanalysis. p. 586
> Why is Rogers' form of therapy called *client-centred*? p. 587
> What is the fundamental aim of client-centred therapy? pp. 587–588

**THINK CRITICALLY**
> Why do you think most practitioners feel that psychoanalysis is not the most appropriate treatment for marital problems?
> What are the implications of a theory of therapy based on the assumption that people are drawn toward growth fulfilment, as Rogers assumed?
> Why do you think client-centred therapy might be viewed as a consciousness-raising process?

**APPLY PSYCHOLOGY**
> If you were a psychologist training others, how might you help them communicate acceptance and recognition of clients' emotions?

**Key Components of Psychoanalytic and Humanistic Therapies**

| Therapy | Nature of Psychopathology | Goal of Therapy | Role of Therapist | Role of Unconscious Material | Role of Patient's Insights | Techniques |
|---|---|---|---|---|---|---|
| Psychoanalytic | Maladjustment reflects inadequate conflict resolution and fixation in early development. | Attainment of maturity, strengthened ego functions, reduced control by unconscious or repressed impulses. | An *investigator*, uncovering conflicts and resistances. | Primary in classical psychoanalysis; less emphasized in ego analysis. | Includes not solely intellectual understanding but also emotional experiences. | Analyst takes an active role in interpreting the dreams and free associations of patients. |
| Humanistic | Incongruity between the real self and the potential, desired self; overdependence on others for gratification and self-esteem. | To foster self-determination, release human potential, expand awareness. | An empathic person, in honest encounter with client, sharing experience. | Emphasis is primarily on conscious experience. | There is more emphasis on how and what questions than why questions. | Help client to see the world from a different perspective and to focus on the present and the future instead of the past. |

# Behaviour Therapy

Behaviour therapy has assumptions and goals that differ from those of psychodynamic and humanistic therapies. It has become especially popular in the past three decades for three principal reasons. First, people sometimes have problems that may not warrant an in-depth discussion of early childhood experiences, an exploration of unconscious motivations, a lengthy discussion of current feelings, or a resolution of inner conflicts. Examples of such problems are fear of heights, anxiety about public speaking, marital conflicts, and sexual dysfunction. In these cases, behaviour therapy may be more appropriate than psychodynamically based or humanistic therapies. Second, behaviour therapy has become popular because health-care systems are seeking quicker, less expensive solutions to everyday problems. Last, behaviour therapy can be very effective. As you will see, this type of therapy is very focused on changing current behaviour and on designing solutions to problems.

## GOALS OF BEHAVIOUR THERAPY

**Behaviour therapy** is a therapy based on the application of learning principles to human behaviour. Also called *behaviour modification*, it focuses on changing overt behaviours rather than on understanding subjective feelings, unconscious processes, or motivations. It uses learning principles to help people replace maladaptive behaviours with more effective ones. Behaviour therapists assume that people's behaviour is influenced by changes in their environment, in the way they respond to that environment, and in the way they interact with other people. Unlike psychodynamically based therapies, behaviour therapy does not aim to discover the origins of a behaviour; it works only to alter it. For a person with a nervous twitch, for example, the goal would be to eliminate the twitch, not to uncover its psychological origins. Thus, behaviour therapists treat people by having them first unlearn old, faulty behaviours and then learn new, more acceptable or effective ones.

Behaviour therapists do not always focus on the problems that caused the client to seek therapy. If they see that the client's problem is caused by some other

**Treatment**

**BEHAVIOUR THERAPY**

A therapy based on the application of learning principles to human behaviour that focuses on changing overt behaviours rather than on understanding subjective feelings, unconscious processes, or motivations. Also known as *behaviour modification*.

situation, they may focus on changing that situation. For example, a man may seek therapy because of a faltering marriage. However, the therapist may discover that the marriage is suffering because of the client's frequent and acrimonious arguments with his wife, each of which is followed by a period of heavy drinking. The therapist then may discover that both the arguments and the drinking are brought on by stress at work, aggravated by the client's unrealistic expectations regarding his performance. In this situation, the therapist may focus on helping the client develop standards that will ease the original cause of the problem—the tension felt at work—and that will be consistent with the client's capabilities, past performance, and realistic likelihood of future performance.

Unlike psychodynamic and humanistic therapies, behaviour therapy does not encourage clients to interpret past events to find their meaning. Although a behaviour therapist may uncover a chain of events leading to a specific behaviour, that discovery generally will not prompt a close examination of the client's early experiences.

When people enter behaviour therapy, many aspects of their behaviour may change, not just those specifically being treated. Thus, a woman being treated for extreme shyness may find not only that the shyness decreases but also that she can engage more easily in discussions about emotional topics and can perform better on the job. Behaviourists argue that once a person's behaviour has changed, it may be easier for the person to manage attitudes, fears, and conflicts.

Behaviourists are dissatisfied with psychodynamic and humanistic therapies for three basic reasons: (1) those therapies use concepts that are almost impossible to define and measure (such as the id and self-actualization); (2) some studies show that patients who do not receive psychodynamic and humanistic therapies improve anyway; and (3) once a therapist has labelled a person as abnormal, the label itself may lead to maladaptive behaviour. (Although this is true of any type of therapy, psychodynamic therapy tends to use labels more than behaviour therapy does.) Behaviour therapists assume that people display maladaptive behaviours not because they are abnormal but because they are having trouble adjusting to their environment; if they are taught new ways of coping, the maladjustment will disappear. A great strength of behaviour therapy is that it provides a coherent conceptual framework.

However, behaviour therapy is not without its critics. Most insight therapists, especially those who are psychodynamically based, believe that if only overt behaviour is treated, symptom substitution may occur. **Symptom substitution** is the appearance of one overt symptom to replace another that has been eliminated by treatment. Thus, insight therapists argue that if a therapist eliminates a nervous twitch without examining its underlying causes, the client will express the underlying disorder by developing some other symptom, such as a speech impediment. Behaviour therapists, on the other hand, contend that symptom substitution does not occur if the treatment makes proper use of behavioural principles. Research shows that behaviour therapy is at least as effective as insight therapy and in some cases more effective (Kazdin, 2000, 2001).

Behaviour therapists use an array of techniques, often in combination, to help people change their behaviour; chief among these techniques are operant conditioning, counterconditioning, and modelling. A good therapist will use whatever combination of techniques will help a client most efficiently and effectively—so, in addition to using several behavioural techniques, a behaviour therapist may use some insight techniques. The more complicated the disorder being treated, the more likely it is that a practitioner will use a mix of therapeutic approaches.

Behaviour therapy usually involves three general procedures: (1) identifying the problem behaviour and its frequency by examining what people actually do; (2) treating a client with treatment strategies that are individually tailored to the client, perhaps by re-education, communication training, or some type of counterconditioning; and (3) continually assessing whether there is a behaviour change. If the client exhibits a new behaviour for several weeks or months, the therapist concludes that treatment was effective. Let's now explore the three major behaviour therapy techniques: operant conditioning, counterconditioning, and modelling.

SYMPTOM SUBSTITUTION

The appearance of one overt symptom to replace another that has been eliminated by treatment.

## OPERANT CONDITIONING

Operant conditioning procedures are used with different people in different settings to achieve a wide range of desirable behaviours, including increased reading speed, improved classroom behaviour, and the maintenance of personal hygiene. As we saw in Chapter 5, operant conditioning to establish new behaviours often depends on a *reinforcer*—any event or circumstance that increases the probability that a particular response will recur. A client could employ operant conditioning to help herself adopt more positive responses toward herself. For example, she could ask her boyfriend to praise her every time she honours her own best judgment or is honest about her feelings.

One of the most effective uses of operant conditioning is with children who are anti-social, slow to learn, or in some way maladjusted. Operant conditioning is also effective with patients in mental hospitals. Ayllon and Haughton (1964), for example, instructed hospital staff members to reinforce patients for psychotic, bizarre, or meaningless verbalizations during one period and for neutral verbalizations (such as comments about the weather) during another. As expected, the relative frequency of each type of verbalization increased when it was reinforced and decreased when it was not reinforced (see Figure 16.3).

**TOKEN ECONOMIES.**   One way of rewarding adaptive behaviour is with a **token economy**—an operant conditioning procedure in which individuals who engage in appropriate behaviour receive tokens that they can exchange for desirable items or activities. In a hospital setting, for example, some rewards might be candy, new clothes, games, or time with important people in the patients' lives. The more tokens people earn, the more items or activities they can obtain. Token economies have also been effective in school settings. Teachers who use a token economy often keep track of tokens openly and reward students publicly.

Token economies are used to modify behaviour in social settings, usually with groups of people. They aim to strengthen behaviours that are compatible with social norms. For example, a patient in a mental hospital might receive tokens for cleaning tables, helping in the hospital laundry, and maintaining certain standards of personal hygiene and appearance. The level of difficulty of the behaviour or task determines the number of tokens earned. Thus, patients might receive 3 tokens for brushing their teeth but 40 tokens for engaging in helping behaviours.

**TOKEN ECONOMY**

An operant conditioning procedure in which individuals who engage in appropriate behaviour receive tokens that they can exchange for desirable items or activities.

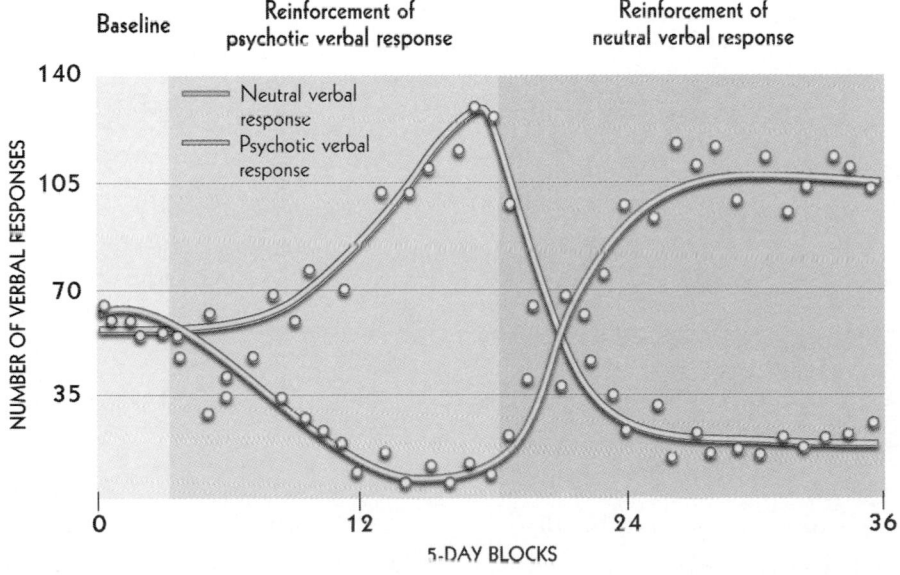

**FIGURE 16.3**

**Reinforcement Increases Desired Behaviours**

A study by Ayllon and Haughton (1964) found that reinforcement affected the frequency of psychotic and neutral verbal behaviour in hospitalized patients.

Ayllon and Azrin (1965) monitored the performance of a group of hospitalized patients who were involved in doing simple work tasks for 45 days. They found that when tokens (reinforcement) were contingent on performance, the patients produced about four times as much work per day as when tokens were not delivered. (See Figure 16.4, in which some of the researchers' results are presented.) Token economies become especially effective when combined with other behavioural techniques (Miller, Cosgrove, & Doke, 1990). We will examine two of these techniques next—extinction and punishment first, followed by time out.

**EXTINCTION.**  As we saw in Chapter 5, if reinforcers are withheld, extinction of a behaviour will occur. Suppose a six-year-old girl refuses to go to bed at the designated time. When she is taken to her bedroom, she cries and screams violently. If the parents give in and allow her to stay up, they are reinforcing the crying behaviour: The child cries and the parents give in. A therapist might suggest that the parents stop reinforcing the crying behaviour by insisting that their daughter go to bed and stay there. Chances are that the child will cry loudly and violently for two or three nights, but the behaviour will eventually be extinguished (Williams, 1959).

**PUNISHMENT.**  Another way to decrease the frequency of an undesired behaviour is to punish it. Punishment often involves the presentation of an aversive stimulus. In the laboratory, researchers might use slight electric shocks to get adult participants to stop performing a specific behaviour. As we saw in Chapter 5, a serious limitation of punishment as a behaviour-shaping device is that it suppresses only existing behaviours; it cannot be used to establish new, desired behaviours. Thus, punishment for undesired behaviours is usually combined with positive reinforcement for desired behaviours.

Research also shows that people, especially young people, imitate aggression. Thus, a child (or institutionalized person) in therapy may strike out at the therapist who administers punishment in an attempt to eliminate the source of punishment, sometimes inflicting serious injury. Punishment can also bring about generalized aggression. This is especially true for prison inmates, whose hostility is well recognized, and for class bullies, who are often the children most strictly disciplined by their parents or teachers. Skinner (1988) believed that punishment is harmful; he advocated non-punitive therapeutic techniques, which might involve developing

**FIGURE 16.4**

**Token Economies Change Performance Effectively**

Ayllon and Azrin (1965) found that tokens increased the total number of hours worked per day by a group of 44 patients.

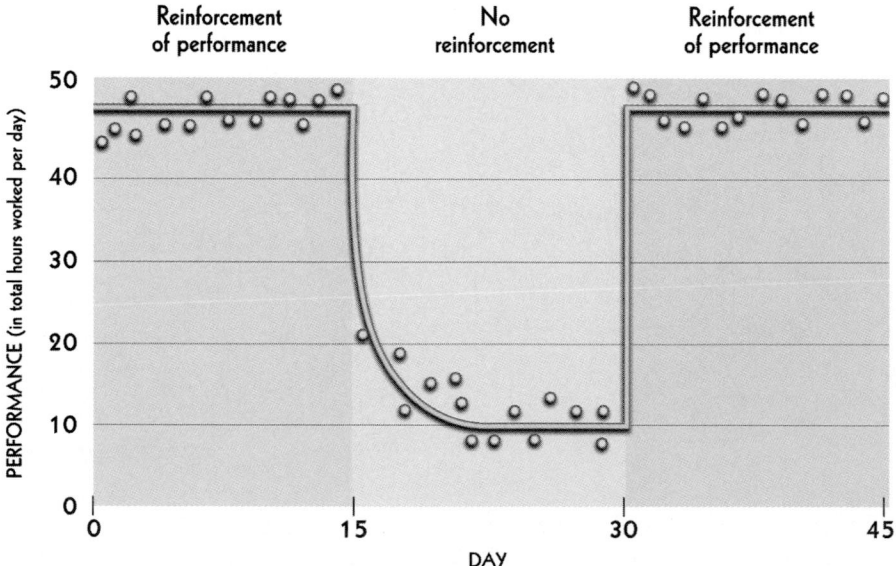

strong bonds between clients and therapists and reinforcing specific prosocial activities. In general, procedures that lead to a perception of control on the part of a client are much more likely to lead to the extinction of undesired behaviour.

**TIME OUT.** As we saw in Chapter 5, **time out**—the physical removal of a person from sources of reinforcement in order to decrease the occurrence of undesired behaviours—is an effective operant conditioning procedure. Suppose a boy throws a temper tantrum each time he wants a piece of candy, an ice-cream cone, or his little brother's toys. With the time-out procedure, whenever the child misbehaved, he would be placed in a restricted area away from the rest of the family, without sweets, toys, television, or other people. He would be required to stay in the restricted area (such as a chair or a time-out room) for a short period, such as 5 or 10 minutes depending on the age of the child; if he left the area, more time would be added. Not only would the child not get what he wanted, he also would be removed from any potential source of reinforcement. Time out is used principally with children; it is especially effective when it is combined with positive reinforcers for appropriate behaviour and is administered by a knowledgeable parent or child-care specialist (Crespi, 1988). There are opponents to the use of time out. Gabor Maté (2003), a Vancouver physician and writer, argues that time outs directly threaten a child's sense of security in their relationship with their parents, breed hostility, and should therefore never be used.

## COUNTERCONDITIONING

A second major technique of behaviour therapy is **counterconditioning**—a process of reconditioning in which a person is taught a new, more adaptive response to a familiar stimulus. For example, anxiety is one of the first responses people show when they are maladjusted, fearful, or lacking in self-esteem. If a therapist can condition a person to respond with something other than anxiety—that is, *counterconditioning* the person—a real breakthrough will be achieved, and the person's anxiety will be reduced.

Joseph Wolpe (1915–1997) was one of the initial proponents of counterconditioning. His work in classical conditioning, especially in situations in which animals show conditioned anxiety responses, led him to attempt to inhibit or decrease anxiety as a response in human beings. His therapeutic goal was to replace anxiety with some other response, such as relaxation, amusement, or pleasure.

Behaviour therapy using counterconditioning begins with a specific stimulus (S1), which elicits a specific response (R1). After the person undergoes counterconditioning, the same stimulus (S1) should elicit a new response (R2) (Wolpe, 1958). There are two basic approaches to counterconditioning: systematic desensitization and aversive counterconditioning.

**SYSTEMATIC DESENSITIZATION.** **Systematic desensitization** is a three-stage counterconditioning procedure in which people are taught to relax when presented with stimuli that formerly elicited anxiety. First the client learns how to relax; then the client describes the specific situations that arouse anxiety; finally the client, while deeply relaxed, imagines increasingly vivid scenes of the situations that elicit anxiety. In this way, the client is gradually, step by step, exposed to the source of anxiety, usually by imagining (while relaxed) a series of progressively more fearful or anxiety-provoking situations. With each successive experience, the client learns relaxation rather than fear as a response. Eventually, the client actually approaches the real-life situation.

Flying in an airplane, for example, is a stimulus situation (S1) that can bring about an inappropriate fear response (R1). With systematic desensitization therapy,

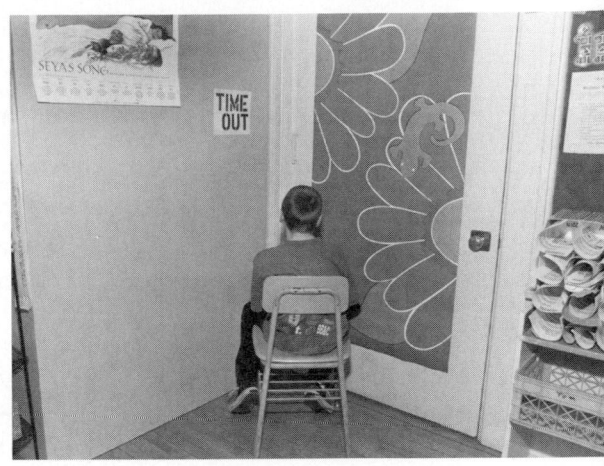

▲ Although using time out at all is controversial, it should never be used unless combined with positive reinforcers for desired behaviours.

TIME OUT

A punishment procedure in which a person is physically removed from sources of reinforcement in order to decrease the occurrence of undesired behaviours.

COUNTERCONDITIONING

A process of reconditioning in which a person is taught a new, more adaptive response to a familiar stimulus.

SYSTEMATIC DESENSITIZATION

A three-stage counterconditioning procedure in which people are taught to relax when presented with stimuli that formerly elicited anxiety.

the idea of flying (S1) eventually can elicit a response of curiosity or even relaxation (R2). The therapist first might ask the relaxed client to imagine sitting in an airplane on the ground, then to imagine the airplane taxiing, and eventually to imagine flying though the billowing clouds. As the client practises relaxation while imagining the scene, he or she becomes able to tolerate more stressful imagery and eventually may perform the imagined behaviour—in this case, flying in an airplane. Eventually, practising and becoming desensitized in real-world situations produces the most lasting effects (Hoffart, 1996). For example, if therapists combine systematic desensitization with changing people's ideas about the world—cognitive therapy, which we examine later in this chapter—they find that people cope better. Through systematic desensitization and cognitive therapy, people can lose their fears of flying.

Systematic desensitization is most successful for people who have problems such as impulse control or who exhibit forms of anxiety, such as phobias. It is not especially effective for people who exhibit serious psychotic symptoms; nor is it the best treatment for situations involving interpersonal conflict.

**AVERSIVE COUNTERCONDITIONING.**   Before therapy, some clients often do not avoid a stimulus that prompts inappropriate behaviour. This is where aversive counterconditioning, another form of counterconditioning, can be used. **Aversive counterconditioning** is a counterconditioning technique in which an aversive or noxious stimulus is paired with a stimulus that elicits the initial undesired behaviour so that the client will adopt a new, more worthwhile behaviour in response to the familiar stimulus and thus cease the undesired behaviour. As with systematic desensitization, the objective is to teach a new response to the original stimulus. A behaviour therapist might use aversive counterconditioning to teach an alcoholic client to avoid alcohol. The first step might be to teach the person to associate alcohol (the original stimulus) with the sensation of nausea (a noxious stimulus). If verbal instruction is not enough, the therapist might administer a drug that causes nausea whenever alcohol is consumed (the *undesired* behaviour). The goal is to make the drinking of alcohol unpleasant. Eventually, the treatment will make the client experience nausea just at the *thought* of consuming alcohol, thus causing the client to avoid alcohol (the new *desired* behaviour). This approach is limited, of course, by the ability of the client to realize that it was the drug and not the alcohol that made him or her sick.

## MODELLING

Both children and adults learn behaviours by watching and imitating other people—in other words, by observing models. Children learn table manners, toilet behaviour, and appropriate responses to animals by observing and imitating their parents and other models. Similarly, the music you listen to, the styles of clothing you wear, and the social or political causes you support are determined, in part, by the people around you.

According to Albert Bandura (1977a), as part of behaviour therapy, modelling is most effective in three areas: (1) teaching new behaviour, (2) helping to eliminate fears, especially phobias, and (3) enhancing already existing behaviour. By watching the behaviour of others, people learn to exhibit more adaptive and appropriate behaviour. Bandura, Blanchard, and Ritter (1969), for example, asked people with snake phobia to watch other people handling snakes. Afterwards, the watchers' fear of snakes was reduced.

One problem with modelling is that people may observe and imitate the behaviour of inappropriate models. We saw in Chapter 13 that people imitate violent behaviours they have observed on television and in movies. Further, many adolescents

**AVERSIVE COUNTERCONDITIONING**

A counterconditioning technique in which an aversive or noxious stimulus is paired with a stimulus that elicits an undesired behaviour so that the client will adopt a new, more worthwhile behaviour in response to the familiar stimulus and thus cease the undesired behaviour.

▼ Children learn a host of behaviours by observing and imitating their parents and other models.

become involved in abuse of alcohol and other drugs because they imitate their peers. Such imitation often occurs because of faulty thinking about situations, people, or lifelong goals. When people have developed a faulty set of expectations that guide their behaviour, cognitive therapy may be in order.

Building Table 16.3 presents a summary of the key components of the psychoanalytic, humanistic, and behavioural views of therapy.

## Cognitive Therapy

Behaviour therapy and cognitive therapy have been heavily influenced by health-care systems and managed care. A managed care organization usually controls the reimbursement of therapists and thus intervenes between a client and a therapist to make rulings about questions such as these: Does this problem qualify for reimbursement? What technique should be used to treat this client? Is this clinician the appropriate therapist for this client? Many psychologists see managed care as a crisis, a nightmare, and the downfall of psychotherapy (Fishman & Franks, 1997). Behaviour therapists and cognitive therapists, however, more than other therapists, have become allies of managed care organizations because of the close alignment of their shared goals, especially the goal of efficiency.

According to cognitive therapists, wrong, distorted, or underdeveloped ideas and thoughts often prevent a person from establishing effective coping strategies. Growing out of behaviour therapy and the developing study of cognitive psychology, *cognitive therapy* focuses

**Be an ACTIVE LEARNER**

**REVIEW**
> Identify the fundamental reasons behaviourists are dissatisfied with psychodynamic and humanistic therapies. p. 590
> For what disorders is the behaviour therapy technique of operant conditioning especially effective? pp. 591–593
> Explain what happens in a time out. p. 593

**THINK CRITICALLY**
> How would a behaviour therapist's approach to assisting a person suffering from low self-esteem differ from that of a humanistic therapist?
> Why do you think modelling is especially effective in the treatment of phobias?
> Do you think that the appearance of one overt symptom to replace another that has been eliminated by treatment—symptom substitution—is a sufficient reason to discredit behaviour therapy? Explain your answer.

**APPLY PSYCHOLOGY**
> To achieve optimal results, in what ways should health-care systems be permitted to determine the best type and duration of therapy for a client?
> Is it possible to design a time-out procedure for an adolescent who will not keep his or her clothes clean? What specific procedures might you put in place?

## BUILDING TABLE 16.3   Key Components of Psychoanalytic, Humanistic, and Behaviour Therapies

| Therapy | Nature of Psychopathology | Goal of Therapy | Role of Therapist | Role of Unconscious Material | Role of Patient's Insights | Techniques |
|---|---|---|---|---|---|---|
| Psychoanalytic | Maladjustment reflects inadequate conflict resolution and fixation in early development. | Attainment of maturity, strengthened ego functions, reduced control by unconscious or repressed impulses. | An *investigator*, uncovering conflicts and resistances. | Primary in classical psychoanalysis; less emphasized in ego analysis. | Includes not solely intellectual understanding but also emotional experiences. | Analyst takes an active role in interpreting the dreams and free associations of patients. |
| Humanistic | Incongruity between the real self and the potential, desired self; overdependence on others for gratification and self-esteem. | To foster self-determination, release human potential, expand awareness. | An empathic person, in honest encounter with client, sharing experience. | Emphasis is primarily on conscious experience. | There is more emphasis on how and what questions than why questions. | Help client to see the world from a different perspective and to focus on the present and the future instead of the past. |
| Behaviour | Symptomatic behaviour stems from faulty learning or learning of maladaptive behaviours. | To relieve symptomatic behaviour by suppressing or replacing maladaptive behaviours. | A helper, helping client unlearn old behaviours and learn new ones. | Not concerned with unconscious processes. | Irrelevant and unnecessary. | Clients learn new responses, establish new behaviours, and eliminate faulty or undesirable ones. |

on changing a client's behaviour by changing his or her thoughts and perceptions. Cognitive therapy is derived from three basic propositions: (1) cognitive activity affects behaviour, (2) cognitive activity can be monitored, and (3) behaviour changes can be effected through cognitive changes. Cognitive psychologists have had a profound impact in many areas of psychology, especially in therapy. In the past, behaviour therapists were concerned only with overt behaviour; today, many incorporate thought processes into their treatments. For this reason, their work is often called *cognitive behaviour therapy*. Researchers now suggest that thought processes may hold the key to managing many forms of maladjustment, including disorders such as obsessive–compulsive disorder (Abramowitz, 1998).

Therapists who use *cognitive restructuring* (cognitive therapy) are interested in modifying the faulty thought patterns of disturbed people (Mahoney, 1977). This type of therapy is effective for people who have attached overly narrow or otherwise inappropriate labels to certain behaviours or situations; for example, such a person may believe that sex is dirty or that assertiveness is unwomanly. Whenever presented with a situation that involves sex or assertiveness, the person will respond in a way that is determined by his or her thoughts about the situation rather than by the facts of the situation.

Cognitive therapy typically focuses on current behaviour and current thoughts. It is not especially concerned with uncovering forgotten childhood experiences, although it can be used to alter thoughts about those experiences. University of Calgary's Keith Dobson (2001) and his colleague Kate Hamilton (Hamilton & Dobson, 2002a, 2002b) have demonstrated the effectiveness of cognitive therapy with depressed patients. Cognitive therapy has also been used effectively to assist in weight loss, bulimia, excessive anger, and adolescent behaviour problems (e.g., Bruce, Spiegel, & Hegel, 1999; Mohr et al., 2000). When cognitive restructuring is combined with other psychological techniques, such as reinforcement, which help a person make behavioural changes, results are even more impressive (Wilson et al., 1999).

Cognitive therapy is derived from three basic propositions:

- Cognitive activity affects behaviour.
- Cognitive activity can be monitored.
- Behaviour changes can be effected through cognitive changes.

## RATIONAL–EMOTIVE THERAPY

The best-known cognitive therapy is **rational–emotive therapy**—a cognitive behaviour therapy that emphasizes the importance of logical, rational thought processes. Researcher Albert Ellis developed this therapy more than 30 years ago. Most behaviour therapists assume that abnormal behaviour is caused by faulty and irrational *behaviour* patterns. Ellis and his colleagues, however, assume that it is caused by faulty and irrational *thinking* patterns (Ellis, 1970, 1999a; Dryden & Ellis, 2001). They believe that if faulty thought processes can be replaced with rational ones, maladjustment and abnormal behaviour will disappear.

According to Ellis, psychological disturbance is a result of events in a person's life that give rise to irrational beliefs leading to negative emotions and behaviours. Moreover, these beliefs are a breeding ground for further irrational ideas (Dryden & Ellis, 1988). Ellis (1988, 1999b) argues that people make formal demands on themselves and on other people, and they rigidly hold on to them no matter how unrealistic and illogical they are. See Figure 16.5 to see this sequence of events.

Thus, a major goal of rational–emotive therapy is to help people examine the past events that produced the irrational beliefs (Ellis, Shaughnessy, & Mahan, 2002). Ellis, for example, tries to focus on a client's basic philosophy of life and how it is self-defeating. He thus tries to uncover the client's thought patterns and help the client recognize that the underlying beliefs are faulty. Table 16.4, on page 598, lists 10 irrational assumptions that, according to Ellis, cause emotional problems and

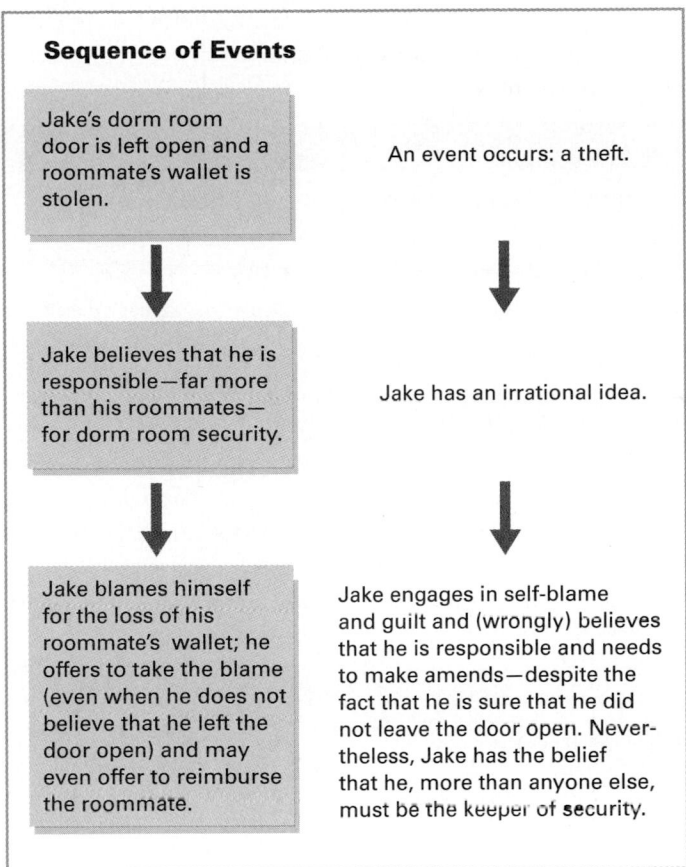

**Sequence of Events**

Jake's dorm room door is left open and a roommate's wallet is stolen.

An event occurs: a theft.

↓

Jake believes that he is responsible—far more than his roommates—for dorm room security.

Jake has an irrational idea.

↓

Jake blames himself for the loss of his roommate's wallet; he offers to take the blame (even when he does not believe that he left the door open) and may even offer to reimburse the roommate.

Jake engages in self-blame and guilt and (wrongly) believes that he is responsible and needs to make amends—despite the fact that he is sure that he did not leave the door open. Nevertheless, Jake has the belief that he, more than anyone else, must be the keeper of security.

**FIGURE 16.5**

**The Foundations of Irrational Behaviours**

From Albert Ellis's view, irrational beliefs about events in people's lives cause emotional distress and maladjustment. Jake has a careless roommate (or even a careless friend) who leaves a dorm room open; a roommate's wallet disappears. Jake's wrongheaded belief that he alone has to take responsibility for dorm room security leads to unhappiness and anxiety.

maladaptive behaviours. They are based on people's needs to be liked, to be competent, to be loved, and to feel secure. When people place irrational or exaggerated value on these needs, the needs become maladaptive and lead to emotional disturbance, anxiety, and abnormal behaviour. If rational–emotive therapy is successful, the client adopts different behaviours based on new, more rational thought processes. Research supports the effectiveness of the approach (Abrams & Ellis, 1994; Haaga & Davison, 1993), and Ellis (2001) asserts that rational–emotive therapy has broad applications in both therapy and classroom settings.

## BECK'S APPROACH

Another cognitive therapy that focuses on irrational ideas is that of Aaron Beck (1963). As we saw in Chapter 15, Beck's theory assumes that depression is caused by people's distorted cognitive views of reality, which lead to negative views about the world, themselves, and the future, and often to gross overgeneralizations. For example, people who think they have no future—that all of their options are blocked—and who undervalue their intelligence are likely to be depressed. Such individuals form appraisals of situations that are distorted and based on insufficient (and sometimes wrong) data. The goal of therapy, therefore, is to help them develop realistic appraisals of the situations they encounter and solve problems (Beck, 1991). The therapist acts as a trainer and co-investigator, providing data to be examined and guidance in understanding how cognitions influence behaviour (Beck & Weishaar, 1989).

According to Beck (1976), a successful client passes through four stages in the course of correcting faulty views and moving toward improved mental health: "First, he has to become aware of what he is thinking. Second, he needs to recognize what thoughts are awry. Then he has to substitute accurate for inaccurate judgments. Finally, he needs feedback to inform him whether his changes are correct" (p. 217).

| TABLE 16.4 | Ellis's Outline of 10 Irrational Assumptions |
|---|---|

1. It is a necessity for an adult to be loved and approved of by almost everyone for virtually everything.

2. A person must be thoroughly competent, adequate, and successful in all respects.

3. Certain people are bad, wicked, or villainous and should be punished for their sins.

4. It is catastrophic when things are not going the way one would like.

5. Human unhappiness is externally caused. People have little or no ability to control their sorrows or to rid themselves of negative feelings.

6. It is right to be terribly preoccupied with and upset about something that may be dangerous or fearsome.

7. It is easier to avoid facing many of life's difficulties and responsibilities than it is to undertake more rewarding forms of self-discipline.

8. The past is all-important. Because something once strongly affected someone's life, it should continue to do so indefinitely.

9. People and things should be different from the way they are. It is catastrophic if perfect solutions to the grim realities of life are not immediately found.

10. Maximal human happiness can be achieved by inertia and inaction or by passively and without commitment "enjoying oneself."

Source: Ellis & Harper, 1961.

## MEICHENBAUM'S APPROACH

Some researchers, among them Donald Meichenbaum, Professor Emeritus at the University of Waterloo, believe that what people say to themselves determines what they will do. Therefore, a key goal of therapy is to change the things people say to themselves. According to Meichenbaum, the therapist has to change the client's appraisal of stressful events and the client's use of self-instructions, thus normalizing his or her reactions (Meichenbaum, 1993).

A strength of Meichenbaum's theory is that self-instruction can be used in many settings for many different problems (Dobson & Block, 1988). It can help people who are shy or impulsive, people with speech impediments, and even those who are schizophrenic (Meichenbaum, 1974; Meichenbaum & Cameron, 1973). Rather than attempting to change their irrational beliefs, clients learn a repertoire of activities they can use to adjust their behaviour when it seems problematic. For example, they may learn to conduct a private monologue in which they work out adaptive ways of thinking and coping with situations. They can then discuss with a therapist the quality and usefulness of these self-instructional statements. They may learn to organize their responses to specific situations in an orderly, more easily exercised set of steps.

Building Table 16.4 provides an overall summary of the psychoanalytic, humanistic, behavioural, and cognitive approaches to individual therapy.

Cognitive therapy in its many forms has been used with adults and children, and with specialized groups such as women and the elderly. It can be applied to such problems as anxiety disorders, marital

*Be an*
**ACTIVE LEARNER**

**REVIEW**
> What is the basic idea behind cognitive therapy? pp. 595–596
> According to Ellis, what are the consequences of developing irrational beliefs? p. 596
> Compare rational–emotive therapy and Beck's approach to cognitive therapy. pp. 596–597

**THINK CRITICALLY**
> What do you think people say to themselves that brings about dysfunctional behaviour? How can therapy change that conversation?

**APPLY PSYCHOLOGY**
> What irrational belief can you identify in a friend or family member who suffers from some psychological condition? Make a list of the top three things you think guide this person's behaviour in maladaptive ways.

**BUILDING TABLE 16.4** — Key Components of Psychoanalytic, Humanistic, Behaviour, and Cognitive Therapies

| Therapy | Nature of Psychopathology | Goal of Therapy | Role of Therapist | Role of Unconscious Material | Role of Patient's Insights | Techniques |
|---|---|---|---|---|---|---|
| Psychoanalytic | Maladjustment reflects inadequate conflict resolution and fixation in early development. | Attainment of maturity, strengthened ego functions, reduced control by unconscious or repressed impulses. | An *investigator*, uncovering conflicts and resistances. | Primary in classical psychoanalysis; less emphasized in ego analysis. | Includes not solely intellectual understanding but also emotional experiences. | Analyst takes an active role in interpreting the dreams and free associations of patients. |
| Humanistic | Incongruity between the real self and the potential, desired self; overdependence on others for gratification and self-esteem. | To foster self-determination, release human potential, expand awareness. | An empathic person, in honest encounter with client, sharing experience. | Emphasis is primarily on conscious experience. | There is more emphasis on how and what questions than why questions. | Help client to see the world from a different perspective and to focus on the present and the future instead of the past. |
| Behaviour | Symptomatic behaviour stems from faulty learning or learning of maladaptive behaviours. | To relieve symptomatic behaviour by suppressing or replacing maladaptive behaviours. | A helper, helping client unlearn old behaviours and learn new ones. | Not concerned with unconscious processes. | Irrelevant and unnecessary. | Clients learn new responses, establish new behaviours, and eliminate faulty or undesirable ones. |
| Cognitive | Maladjustment occurs because of faulty, irrational thought patterns. | To change the way clients think about themselves and the world. | A trainer and co-investigator, helping the client learn new, rational ways to think about the world. | Little or no concern with unconscious processes. | Irrelevant to therapy but may be used if they do occur. | Clients learn to think situations through logically and to reconsider many of their irrational assumptions. |

difficulties, chronic pain, and (as is evident from Beck's and Dobson's work) depression. Cognitive therapy continues to make enormous strides. It is influencing an increasing number of theorists and practitioners who conduct both long-term therapy and brief therapy.

# Group Therapy

When several people meet as a group to receive psychological help, the treatment is referred to as **group therapy**. This technique was introduced in the early 1900s and has become increasingly popular since the Second World War. One reason for its popularity is that the demand for therapists exceeds the number available. Individually, a therapist can see up to 40 clients a week for one hour each, but in a group the same therapist might see 8 to 10 clients in just one hour. Another reason for its popularity is that the therapist's fee is shared among the members of the group, making group therapy less expensive than individual therapy.

Group therapy also can be more effective than individual therapy because the social pressures that operate in a group can help shape the members' behaviour. In addition, group members can be useful models of behaviour for one another, and they can provide mutual reinforcement and support. However, it is important to note that group therapy does not generally allow for the in-depth individual

**GROUP THERAPY**

A psychotherapeutic process in which several people meet as a group with a therapist.

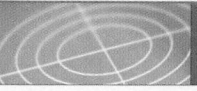 

## Can Alcoholics Become Controlled Drinkers?

**POINT:** Alcoholism is a disease that can be treated only through complete and total abstinence.

**COUNTERPOINT:** Some people with alcohol-related disorders can be taught to control their drinking; abstinence is not required.

Alcohol and drug abuse problems are among the most common that practitioners face, and there is no consensus on treatment goals.

On one hand, some psychologists argue that the goal of treatment must be total, complete, and permanent abstinence from alcohol. This position has been popularized by Alcoholics Anonymous (AA) and has become the most prominent approach among those therapists who treat alcoholism. From AA's point of view, once a person has crossed the line from heavy drinking to irresponsible alcoholic drinking, there seems to be no turning back—an alcoholic will never be able to control his or her drinking for any significant duration. Alcoholics must become abstinent—staying away from alcohol completely. Abstinence is a difficult treatment goal; only 15 percent of all alcoholics seen in treatment facilities are abstinent for at least five years.

Some therapists, on the other hand, contend that controlled, moderate drinking is an attainable treatment goal. Through training oriented toward teaching problem

drinkers to pace their drinking and limit their alcohol intake, proponents argue that problem drinkers can become social drinkers.

Is controlled drinking an attainable goal for problem drinkers? Many individuals who develop drinking problems modify their alcohol abuse habits without professional help, which suggests that people can learn to control their problem drinking (Sobell, Cunningham, & Sobell, 1996). Controlled drinking becomes less likely the more severe the degree of alcohol-related problems; people who have been heavy, long-term drinkers are not good candidates for controlled drinking. The duration and extent of abusive drinking predict who best can control their drinking (Rosenberg, 1993).

If a person is a long-term alcoholic, the likelihood that controlled drinking will be attainable is unlikely. In this case, abstinence is the most reliable goal. Others who have experienced problems with alcohol may be able to learn to be moderate drinkers, and for these individuals, controlled, moderate drinking is a reasonable treatment goal.

▲ When several people meet as a group to receive psychological help from a therapist, the treatment is referred to as group therapy.

counselling necessary for more severe disorders and is therefore not always the ideal therapeutic choice. See *Point/Counterpoint* for further discussion of this issue with respect to the prominent support group Alcoholics Anonymous.

### TECHNIQUE AND FORMATS

The techniques used in group therapy are determined largely by the nature of the group and the orientation of its therapist. The group may follow a psychoanalytic, client-centred, Gestalt, behavioural, or other approach. No two groups are alike, and no two groups deal with individual members in the same way.

In traditional group therapy, 6 to 12 clients meet on a regular basis (usually once a week) with a therapist in a clinic or hospital or in the therapist's office. Generally, the therapist selects members on the basis of what they can gain from and offer to the group. The goal is to construct a group whose members are compatible (though not necessarily the same) in terms of age, needs, and problems. The duration of group therapy varies; it usually takes longer than 6 months, but there are a growing number of short-term groups that meet for fewer than 12 weeks (Rose, 1999; Rycroft, 2001). The format of traditional group therapy varies, but generally each member describes her or his problems to the other members, who in turn relate their experiences with similar problems and how they coped with them. This gives individuals a chance to express their fears and anxieties to people who are warm and accepting; each member eventually realizes that everyone has emotional problems. Group members also have opportunities to role play (try out) new behaviours in a safe environment. In a mental health centre, for example, a therapist might help members relive past traumas and cope with their continuing fears. Sometimes the therapist is directive in helping the group cope with a problem. At other times the therapist allows the group to resolve a problem independently Finally, in group therapy, members can exert pressure on an individual to behave in more appropriate ways.

## FAMILY THERAPY

**Family therapy** is a special form of group therapy in which two or more people who are committed to each other's well-being are treated together in an effort to change the ways they interact. (Marital, or couples, therapy is thus a subcategory of family therapy.) A *family* is defined as any group of people who are committed to one another's well-being, preferably for life (Bronfenbrenner, 1989, 1999). Today's therapists recognize that families are often nontraditional; blended families and single-parent families are very common, for example. Different kinds of families are shaping the way people respond to the world and must be considered as part of the cultural context in which psychologists view behaviour. And even for traditional families, life has grown more complicated by the increasing need to juggle work and family responsibilities and cope with societal problems.

With families facing new kinds of problems, family therapy is now used by a large number of practitioners, especially social workers. From a family therapist's point of view, the real focus of family therapy is the family's structure and organization. While family members may identify one person—perhaps a delinquent child—as the problem, family therapists believe that in many cases that person may simply be a scapegoat. The so-called problem member diverts the family's attention from structural problems that are difficult to confront. Any clinician who works with a person who has some type of adjustment problem must also consider the impact of this problem on the people with whom that individual interacts.

Sometimes family therapy is called *relationship therapy* because relationships are often the focus of the intervention, especially with couples (Jacobson et al., 2000; Johnson & Lebow, 2000; Lawrence et al., 1999). Research indicates that, like other forms of therapy, family therapy and marital (couples) therapy are effective (Behr, 2000). However, because of the myriad of variables operating within families, such research is complicated, to say the least (Villeneuve, 2001).

Family therapists often attempt to change *family systems*. This means that treatment takes place within the dynamic social system of the marriage or the family (Fraenkel & Pinsof, 2001; Hoffman, Fruzzetti, & Swenson, 1999). Therapists assume that there are multiple sources of psychological influence: Individuals within a family affect family interactions, and family interactions affect individuals; the family is thus an interactive system (Sturges, 1994). For example, in a family situation where the mother is mainly responsible for monitoring an adolescent's behaviour and disciplining misbehaviour, the mother and adolescent may be locked in conflict. The father may be adding to this conflict by criticizing the mother's apparent lack of control while trying to act like a friend (rather than a parent) to the adolescent. This type of situation can produce tension and conflict that steadily worsens unless systematic changes are made to the functioning of the entire family system. The family systems approach has become especially popular in schools of social work, departments of psychology, and even in schools of medicine, where patients are often seen in a family setting. A useful technique in family therapy is to *restructure* the family's interactions. If a son is responding passively to his domineering mother, for example, the therapist may suggest that the son be assigned chores only by his father.

A type of therapy in which two or more people who are committed to one another's well-being are treated at once, in an effort to change the ways they interact.

An issue that often emerges in family therapy is how all members of the family can become enmeshed in one member's problem—for example, depression, alcoholism, drug abuse, or anxiety disorder. Such involvement often becomes devastating for the whole family. This problem is termed *codependence*. Practitioners often see patients with alcoholism or cocaine addiction whose friends or family members are codependent. Codependence is not a disorder in the *DSM–IV–TR*. In fact, the families of people with problems such as substance abuse have gone relatively unnoticed. But practitioners who treat whole families, not just the person suffering from maladjustment, view codependence as an additional type of adjustment problem—not for the patient but for the patient's family and friends.

The codependents—the family members or friends—are often plagued by intense feelings of shame, fear, anger, and pain; they cannot express those feelings, however, because they feel obligated to care for the person suffering from the disorder or addiction. Codependent children may believe that their job is to take care of their maladjusted parents. Codependent adults may strive to help their maladjusted spouses, relatives, or friends with their problems. They often think that if they were perfect, they could help the maladjusted individual. In some cases, people actually *need* the person to stay disordered; family members sometimes unconsciously want a member with a problem to remain dependent on them so that they can remain in a controlling position.

Some researchers believe the family systems approach to be as effective as individual therapy—and more effective in some situations (Ford et al., 1998). Not all families profit equally from such interventions, however. Family therapy is difficult with families that are disorganized. Younger couples and families seem to have better outcomes. When depression is evident, outcomes are not as good (Lebow & Gurman, 1995). In addition, some family members may refuse to participate or drop out of therapy; this almost always has negative consequences (Prinz et al., 2001).

Family therapy is eclectic, borrowing from many schools of therapy and treating a broad range of families and problems (Guerin & Chabot, 1997). Family therapists join with families in helping them change because they acknowledge and recognize that change of one sort or another is inevitable in a dynamic system. They further assert that only a small change for the better is necessary to make a big difference. Most family therapists assert that clients have the strength and resources to change and that people don't need to understand the origins of a problem to solve it. Last, there is no *one* solution to family problems—especially given today's complicated families (Selekman, 1993).

**Be an ACTIVE LEARNER**

**REVIEW**

> Why do therapists feel that group therapy can sometimes be more effective than individual therapy? p. 599
> What is a codependent person? p. 602

**THINK CRITICALLY**

> Why do you think that having several people in treatment together makes such a difference? Isn't getting a great deal of one-on-one attention—individual therapy—likely to produce superior results? Explain your answer.
> Why do you think that researchers believe the family systems approach is as effective, or even more effective, than other approaches to therapy?
> Why do you think that codependent people are often plagued by intense feelings of shame, fear, anger, and pain, and they cannot express those feelings?

**APPLY PSYCHOLOGY**

> As an adult, is group therapy for you? Why do you think it would be more or less influential in your life than individual therapy?

## Biologically Based Therapies

Do some people have pre-existing brain abnormalities that make them susceptible to alcohol or other drug abuse? Are there inborn mechanisms that create such drug abuse? Are these evolved mechanisms? Evolutionary psychologists think that they are evolved mechanisms gone awry. Indeed, evolutionary psychologists assert that in therapy one must take into consideration the way the brain has evolved and consider both drug and talking therapies to overcome the limitations that may have developed (Bailey, 2000; Troisi & McGuire, 2000).

When a person seeks a therapist for help with a psychological problem—whether it has a biological basis or not—the usual approach involves some form of talking therapy that may be based on psychodynamic, humanistic, behavioural, or cognitive theories. For some patients, however, talking therapy is not enough. Some may be too profoundly depressed; others may be exhibiting symptoms of bipolar disorders (manic depression) or schizophrenia; still others may need hospitalization because they are suicidal. This is where biologically based therapies enter the picture. These therapies often involve medication, hospitalization, and physicians. They are generally used in combination with traditional forms of psychotherapy. Most practitioners and theoreticians believe that the most effective treatment is drugs in combination with psychotherapy (Guimon et al., 2001). Biologically based therapies exist as drug therapy (often used), electroconvulsive therapy (occasionally used), and psychosurgery (rarely used).

## DRUG THERAPY

People often need to take drugs to alleviate emotional problems. Drug therapy is an important form of treatment, especially for anxiety, depression, and schizophrenia. (See Figure 16.6 for recent trends in the use of drugs in treating depression.) It is the most widely used biologically based therapy, and it is effective when used correctly and carefully. Drug therapy is sometimes used in combination with traditional talking therapy. Clinicians who recommend drug therapy must be aware of several key issues. Dosages are especially important and must be monitored; too much or too little of certain drugs is dangerous. Long-term use of many drugs is ill advised. Further, no drug will permanently cure the maladjustment of people who are not coping well. Last, physicians and psychiatrists must be sensitive to the issues of overmedication and long-term dependency on drugs.

In the past decade, clinical psychologists have been lobbying for the legal right to write prescriptions for a limited class of drugs. The argument is that patients would benefit by the better integration of medications and psychological techniques (Hines, 1997; Tuckman, 1996), but this is a controversial proposition even among psychologists (Tasman, Riba, & Silk, 2000). Those who do support the idea recognize that additional training would be necessary and a licensing authority would need to be instituted (Klusman, 1998). This debate continues among physicians and psychologists as well as medical licensing boards. Provincial colleges of psychologists in Canada are watching this American debate with interest.

When physicians (often psychiatrists) do administer drugs, people may experience relief from symptoms of anxiety, mania, depression, and schizophrenia. Drugs for the relief of mental problems are sometimes called *psychotropic drugs*; they are usually grouped into four classes: anti-anxiety drugs, antidepressant drugs, anti-mania drugs, and anti-psychotic drugs.

**ANTI-ANXIETY DRUGS.**   Anti-anxiety drugs, or tranquilizers (technically, *anxiolytics*), are mood-altering substances. Librium, Xanax, and Valium are trade names of the most widely prescribed anti-anxiety drugs. Widely used in Canada (and probably overprescribed), these drugs reduce feelings of stress, calm patients, and lower excitability. When taken occasionally to help a person through a stressful situation, such drugs are useful. They can also help moderate anxiety in a person who is extremely anxious, particularly when the person is also receiving some form of psychotherapy. However, long-term use of anti-anxiety drugs without some adjunct therapy is usually ill advised. Today, physicians are wary of patients who seek anti-anxiety drugs for management of daily stress; they worry about substance abuse and an overreliance on drugs to get through the day.

**ANTIDEPRESSANT DRUGS.**   As their name suggests, antidepressants (technically, *thymoleptics*) are sometimes considered to be mood elevators. They work by altering the level of neurotransmitters in the brain. With the wide availability of antidepressants, it is surprising that half of those who have been depressed for more than 20 years have never taken an antidepressant (Hirschfeld et al., 1997). Depression often goes undiagnosed and is definitely undertreated.

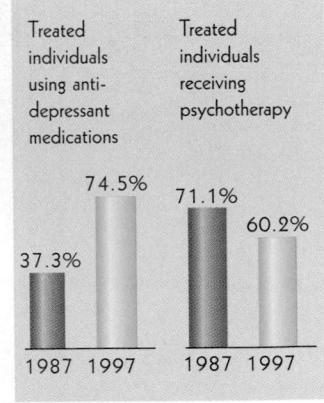

**FIGURE 16.6**
**Trends in Treatment of Depression**

More people receive drug treatment for depression than ever before. Note the decline in psychotherapy (Olfson et al., 2002).

Source: Journal of the American Medical Association.

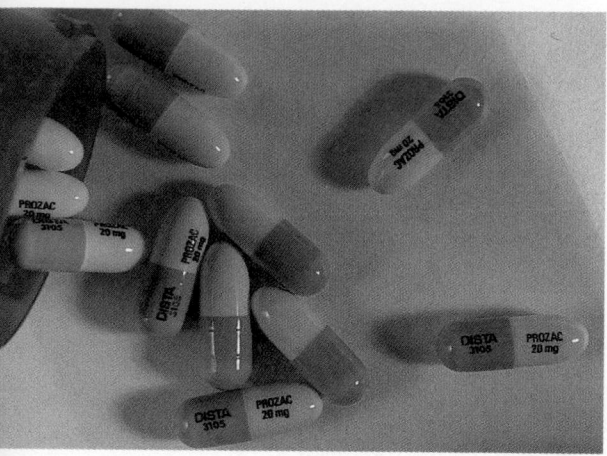

▲ Drug therapy is an important form of treatment, especially for anxiety, depression, and schizophrenia.

One kind of antidepressant, selective serotonin reuptake inhibitors (SSRIs), blocks the reuptake of serotonin. SSRIs work by prolonging the time that serotonin stays in a synapse. According to researchers, when a key neurotransmitter like serotonin is released but does not bind to receptors on the next neuron, the person experiences symptoms of depression. After release, the neurotransmitter is either neutralized in the synapse or taken back up by the neuron that released it, in a process called *reuptake*. SSRIs do not allow the neurotransmitter to be neutralized or restored to the releasing cell; thus, it stays in the synapse longer, where it is more likely to bind, and depression is averted. Drugs such as Prozac, Zoloft, and Paxil are SSRIs. These drugs account for 60 percent of antidepressant sales in Canada. *Brain and Behaviour* discusses the success of Prozac.

A newer type of antidepressant, serotonin and norepinephrine reuptake inhibitors (SNRIs), block the reuptake of serotonin and norepinephrine. These drugs, which include Effexor and Remeron, are effective at treating depression and the associated symptoms of anxiety.

Extremely depressed people who take such antidepressants often become more optimistic and redevelop a sense of purpose in their lives after taking antidepressants for about four weeks. These medications allow many people to function outside a hospital setting. Antidepressants also include two other major categories of drugs: tricyclics and monoamine oxidase (MAO) inhibitors. Both types of drugs are potent. The tricyclics (named for their chemical structure) act like SSRIs and SNRIs to block neurotransmitter reuptake, but MAO inhibitors work by breaking down monoamine oxidase, an enzyme that destroys the neurotransmitters. Tricyclics are prescribed much more often than MAO inhibitors because they pose less danger of medical complications. (Patients on MAO inhibitors have to adhere to special diets and some other restrictions to prevent adverse physical reactions to the drugs.)

Research on the effectiveness of antidepressant drugs is contradictory. Some researchers assert that these drugs have strong effects; others report only modest help from the drugs (Greenberg et al., 1992; Schulberg & Rush, 1994). Research using double-blind procedures and carefully controlled conditions continues, especially with drugs that have specific actions on depressive behaviours (Palatnik et al., 2001; Schmitz et al., 2001). The impact of new research findings will be profound because there are a great number of people with depressive disorders.

**ANTI-MANIA DRUGS.** Lithium carbonate has long been used as an effective anti-mania drug (like antidepressants, technically, a *thymoleptic*) and has come into wide use for patients with bipolar (manic–depressive) disorder because it relieves the manic symptoms. Psychiatrists find that when clients take a daily maintenance dose, lithium is especially helpful in warding off episodes of mania. The dosage of any drug is important, but in the case of lithium it is vital. Too much produces noxious side effects; too little has no effect. No drug will cure all individuals with bipolar disorder of all their symptoms and solve all their problems (for example, lithium is less effective with young patients); in general, however, lithium allows some patients to cope better, to control their symptoms, and to seek other therapies that allow them to manage their lives in the most productive way possible (Moncrieff, 1997). The same is true of other drugs in this class, including valproic acid, or valproate.

**ANTI-PSYCHOTIC DRUGS.** Anti-psychotic drugs (technically, *neuroleptics*) are used mainly for people who suffer from the disabling disorder schizophrenia. These drugs reduce hostility and aggression in violent patients. They also reduce delusions and allow some patients to manage life outside a hospital setting.

Most of the anti-psychotic drugs prescribed are phenothiazines; one of the most common is chlorpromazine (Thorazine). However, a number of other anti-psychotic

## A Best-selling Medication—Prozac

Since its introduction in 1987, about 31 million people have taken the drug Prozac. Along with two other drugs, Zoloft and Paxil, which are similar to Prozac in chemical makeup, this "wonder drug" is so popular that pharmacies need whole shelves to stock a one-week supply. Prozac is a member of the selective serotonin reuptake inhibitor (SSRI) family, as are Zoloft (sertraline) and Paxil (paroxetine). Yearly sales of such drugs total more than $4 billion.

Many people who take Prozac and its sister medications feel better—symptoms of depression lift, appetite returns, and the outlook seems less bleak (Rahola, 2001). People who take the drug feel so much better that they do better in their work and their relationships, and life seems to turn around. The drugs decrease the likelihood of new episodes of depression and work well for older adults, adolescents, and even children (Geller et al., 2001; Schmitz et al., 2001; Yohannes, Connolly, & Baldwin, 2001). The number of side effects from drugs like Prozac is small compared to drugs used earlier. Those drugs had potent side effects—increased heart rate, increased blood pressure, nausea, and sleepiness, to name a few. So, one reason why Prozac has been so successful is that it is relatively free of serious side effects, but it is not totally without them.

Researchers have long known that drugs that affect the reuptake of monoamines (serotonin, dopamine, norepinephrine, and epinephrine) can lighten some depressive symptoms. However, the runaway success of Prozac has startled practitioners and researchers alike. They are also puzzled because

not everyone who takes Prozac feels better. Furthermore, Prozac does have side effects, including a diminution of sexual appetite. Originally intended to be taken for short durations—six months or so—Prozac is now being taken for years on end. Are people staying on the drug too long? Researchers are wondering if the drug (like many others) is being overprescribed and is not especially effective (Glenmullen, 2001; Kirsch & Sapirstein, 1999). How many people who take the drug actually need it? How many were not properly diagnosed?

The effects of this class of drugs are so quickly evident, and the side effects so few, that psychologists worry that the original problems—low self esteem or depression over a bad relationship, for example—may not get the attention they deserve. SSRIs have an important place in the treatment of people with various disorders, but most psychologists feel that they should be part of a full treatment program that also involves short-term or perhaps even long-term psychotherapy.

Some researchers have questioned whether depression, schizophrenia, and a host of other disorders can be explained solely on the basis of brain chemistry (Valenstein, 1998). They argue that easy explanations and quick fixes with drugs are rarely the complete answer to psychological problems. Will new drugs evolve that will be better, more refined, and more potent than today's SSRIs? The answer is undoubtedly yes. Will drugs alone solve people's psychological problems? The answer is surely no. Are they part of a solution for some people? The answer is unquestionably yes.

drugs (sometimes called "atypical anti-psychotics") have been introduced in the past decade. One of these, clozapine (Clozaril), has been shown to be especially effective but can have severe side effects. Even newer anti-psychotic drugs, such as risperidone (Risperdal), are safer than either chlorproazine or clozapine, and they also may be tolerated better.

Anti-psychotic drugs are often very effective in treating certain symptoms of schizophrenia, particularly hallucinations and delusions; unfortunately, they may not be as effective for other symptoms, such as reduced motivation and emotional expressiveness. As with antidepressants, dosages of anti-psychotic drugs are crucial. Further, if patients are maintained on anti-psychotic drugs for too long, other problems can emerge. One such problem is *tardive dyskinesia*—a central nervous system disorder characterized by involuntary, spasmodic movements of the upper body, especially the face and fingers, and including leg jiggling and tongue protrusions, facial tics, and involuntary movements of the mouth and shoulders (Fleischacker, Lemmens, & van Baelen, 2001). See Table 16.5 for a detailed listing of some common drugs used to treat psychiatric disorders.

For many, drug therapy is the answer. But the majority of drug treatments involve drugs that may have irritating, or even dangerous, side effects. Moreover, drugs do not solve an individual's personal difficulties. The choice to use a drug

## TABLE 16.5    Drugs Commonly Used to Treat Psychiatric Disorders

| Effect Group | Chemical Group | Generic Name | Trade Name | Common Function | Side Effects |
|---|---|---|---|---|---|
| Anti-anxiety (anxiolytic) | Benzodiazepines | Diazepam<br>Chlordiazepoxide<br>Alprazolam<br>Clonazepam | Valium<br>Librium<br>Xanax<br>Klonapin | Increases neuro-transmission of GABA | Addictive, fatal when mixed with alcohol, slurred speech, dry mouth, lightheadedness, diminished motor control. May cause "rebound anxiety" at a more intense level than prior to medication |
| | Nonbenzodiazepine | Buspirone | Buspar | As above | Not addictive, takes longer to be effective |
| Antidepressant (thymoleptic) | Tricylics | Amitriptyline<br>Imipramine<br>Nortriptyline<br>Desipramine<br>Doxepin<br>Clomipramine | Elavil<br>Tofranil<br>Pamelor<br>Norpramin<br>Sinequan<br>Anafranil | Block reuptake of serotonin and norepinephrine | Dry mouth, dizziness, blurred vision, weight gain |
| | Monoamine oxidase inhibitors | Phenelzine<br>Tranylcypromine | Nardil<br>Parnate | Blocks the breakdown of norepi nephrine and serotonin, making more available for transmission | Dangerous rise in blood pressure if patient does not follow dietary restrictions |
| | Serotonin norepineph-rine reuptake inhibitors | Mirtazapine<br>Venlafaxine HCl | Remeron<br>Effexor XR | Blocks the reuptake or reabsorption of serotonin and norepi-nephrine | Weight gain, drowsiness, dry mouth, nausea |
| | Serotonin reuptake inhibitors | Fluoxetine<br>Sertraline<br>Paroxetine<br>Fluvoxamine | Prozac<br>Zoloft<br>Paxil<br>Luvox | Blocks the reuptake or reabsorption of only serotonin | Nausea, insomnia, diarrhea, headache, anxiety, loss of sexual desire or response |
| Anti-manic (thymoleptic) | Lithium carbonate | Lithium | Eskalith<br>Lithonate<br>Lithobid | Uncertain | Weight gain, tremors, dry mouth, thirst, toxic at high levels, excessive urination, fatigue |
| | GABA agonist | Valproic acid | Depakene | Better for fast-cycling disorders | |
| Anti-psychotic (neuroleptic) | Phenothiazines | Chlorpromazine<br>Trifluoperazine<br>Fluphenazine<br>Thioridazine | Thorazine<br>Stelazine<br>Prolixin<br>Mellaril | Block neurotransmis-sion of dopamine, effects positive symptoms | Sedation, constipation, dry mouth, blurred vision, cardiac irregularities, tremors and muscle spasms, restless-ness, a shuffling gait. |
| | Atypical anti-psychotic | Clozapine<br>Risperidone | Clozaril<br>Risperdal | | Can produce permanent Parkinson's-like motor disorders involving shaking, loss of voluntary muscle control, and stiff muscles |

protocol for psychological problems must always involve a careful analysis of the potential cost to the individual if they take the drug weighed against any potential benefit.

**PSYCHOSURGERY**
Brain surgery used in the past to alleviate symptoms of serious mental disorders.

## PSYCHOSURGERY AND ELECTROCONVULSIVE THERAPY

**Psychosurgery** is brain surgery; it was used in the past to alleviate symptoms of serious mental disorders. A particular type of psychosurgery commonly performed in the 1940s and 1950s was the *prefrontal lobotomy*, in which a surgeon would sever parts of the brain's frontal lobes from the rest of the brain. The frontal lobes were thought to control emotions; their removal destroyed connections within the brain, making patients calm and passive. Patients lost the symptoms of their mental disorders, but they also became unnaturally calm and completely unemotional. Some became unable to control their impulses, and an estimated 1 to 4 percent of patients died from the operation.

Today, despite advances in technology and in the precision of the operation, psychosurgery is rare, for three reasons: First, drug therapy has proved more effective than surgical procedures. Second, the long-term effects of psychosurgery are questionable. Third, and most important, the procedure is irreversible and therefore morally objectionable to most practitioners and to patients and their families. Its widespread use during the 1940s and 1950s is considered by many to have been a serious mistake.

**Electroconvulsive therapy (ECT)**, once widely employed to treat depressed individuals, is a therapy for severe mental illness in which an electric current is briefly applied to the head in order to produce a generalized seizure (convulsion). The duration of the shock is less than a second, and patients are treated in 3 to 12 sessions over several weeks. In the 1940s and 1950s, ECT was routinely given to severely disturbed patients in mental hospitals. Unfortunately, it was often used on patients who did not need it or administered by physicians who wished to control difficult patients. Today, ECT is not a widely used treatment. According to the National Institutes of Health, fewer than 2.5 percent of all psychiatric hospital patients are treated with ECT.

Is ECT at all effective? Could drug therapy or traditional psychotherapy be used in its place? ECT is effective in the short-term management of severely depressed individuals, those suffering from extreme episodes of mania, and people with psychotic depression (Flint & Rifat, 1998; Rohland, 2001); it is sometimes used when a particular patient is at risk of suicide (Cohen, Tyrrell, & Smith, 1997). It is effective and safe (Glass, 2001; McCall et al., 2001); however, its effects are only temporary if it is not followed by drug therapy and psychotherapy (American Psychiatric Association, 2001). Generally speaking, ECT should be used as a last option, when other forms of treatment have been ineffective and when a patient does not respond to medications (Prudic, Olfson, & Sackheim, 2001). ECT is not appropriate for treating schizophrenia or for managing unruly behaviours associated with other psychological disorders.

The risk of death during the administration of ECT is low (Coffey et al., 1991), but there are side effects including memory loss (Lisanby et al., 2000; Prudic, Peyser, & Sackheim, 2000). In addition, ECT frightens some patients. If practitioners determine that ECT is warranted, the law requires (and medical ethics demand) that the patient be given the option to accept or reject the treatment—as is true for *any* treatment.

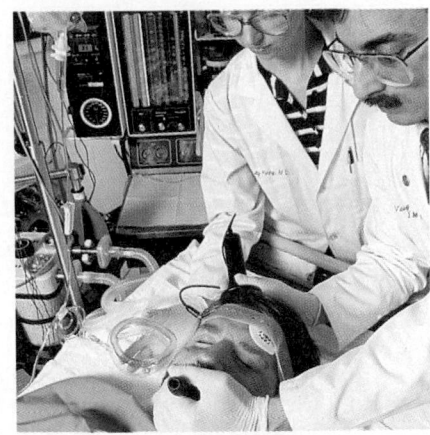

▲ Electroconvulsive therapy, once widely used with depressed patients, is a treatment for severe mental illness in which an electric current is briefly applied to the head to produce a generalized seizure.

ELECTROCONVULSIVE
[ee-LECK-tro-con-VUL-siv]
THERAPY (ECT)

A treatment for severe mental illness in which an electric current is briefly applied to the head in order to produce a generalized seizure.

**Be an ACTIVE LEARNER**

**REVIEW**
> What are the major classes of psychotropic drugs, and for which disorders or conditions is each effective? pp. 603–605
> What are selective serotonin reuptake inhibitors? How do they work? p. 604

**THINK CRITICALLY**
> Drugs take a while before they start to work. What does this imply for individuals who take the drugs? How might the delay impede performance in therapy?
> If drug therapy is so effective, why aren't more people being treated in this way?
> What are the ethical implications of the use of psychosurgery and electroconvulsive therapy (ECT)?

**APPLY PSYCHOLOGY**
> Devise a policy solution to the problem of the overprescription of medications, especially antidepressants.

# Summary and Review

## THERAPY COMES IN MANY FORMS

### What is the essential difference between biologically based therapy and psychotherapy?

> Two broad types of therapy are biologically based therapy and psychotherapy. Biologically based therapy refers to treatment of emotional or behavioural problems by treating the body. *Psychotherapy* is treatment through psychological techniques. **pp. 574–575**

### What is the placebo effect in therapy?

> A *placebo effect* is a nonspecific therapeutic change that occurs as a result of a person's expectations of change rather than as a direct result of a certain treatment. However, any long-term therapeutic effects come from the client's and therapist's efforts. **p. 575**

**KEY TERMS**

psychotherapy, p. 574; placebo effect, p. 575; double-blind technique, p. 575; demand characteristics, p. 575

## PSYCHOANALYSIS AND PSYCHODYNAMIC THERAPIES

### According to psychoanalytic theory, what causes maladjustment, and what processes are involved in treatment?

> *Insight therapies*, which include *psychodynamically based therapies*, assume that maladjustment and abnormal behaviour are caused by people's failure to understand their own motivations and needs. Insight therapists believe that once patients understand the motivations that produce maladjusted behaviour, the behaviour can be changed. **p. 583**
> According to Freud, conflicts among a person's unconscious thoughts and processes produce maladjusted behaviour. Classical Freudian *psychoanalysis* often involves a process of *free association, dream analysis, interpretation, resistance,* and *transference*; the repetitive cycle of interpretation, resistance, and transference is referred to as *working through*. **pp. 583–584**

### What are the basic criticisms of psychoanalysis?

> Ego analysts are psychoanalytic practitioners who are often critical of classical Freudian analysis and believe that the ego has greater control over behaviour than Freud suggested. They are more concerned with a client's reality testing and control over the environment than with unconscious motivations and processes. **p. 585**
> Some critics of psychoanalysis contend that the approach is unscientific, imprecise, and subjective. Other critics object to Freud's biologically oriented approach, which suggests that a human being is a mere bundle of energy caught in conflict and driven toward some hedonistic goal. Further, many elements of Freud's theory are sexist or untestable. **p. 586**

**KEY TERMS**

psychoanalysis, p. 583; psychodynamically based therapies, p. 583; insight therapy, p. 583; free association, p. 584; dream analysis, p. 584; interpretation, p. 584; resistance, p. 584; transference, p. 585; working through, p. 585

## HUMANISTIC THERAPIES

### Briefly describe the focus of client-centred therapy.

> *Client-centred therapy* aims to help clients realize their full potential by forming a therapeutic relationship with a counsellor. To be effective, the therapist must convey unconditional positive regard, show congruence, and practise empathic listening so that clients can become less defensive, more open to new experiences, and more fulfilled. **pp. 587–588**

**KEY TERM**

client-centred therapy, p. 587

## BEHAVIOUR THERAPY

### Identify the basic assumptions and techniques of behaviour therapy.

> *Behaviour therapy*, or behaviour modification, is a therapy based on the application of learning principles to human behaviour. It focuses on changing overt behaviours rather than on understanding subjective feelings, unconscious processes, or motivations. It attempts to replace undesirable behaviours with more adaptive ones. **p. 589**
> Techniques of behaviour therapy include *token economies, time out,* and *counterconditioning. Systematic desensitization* is a three-stage counterconditioning procedure in which a person is taught to relax while imagining increasingly fearful situations. **pp. 591–594**
> As part of behaviour therapy, modelling is especially effective in three areas: (1) teaching new behaviour, (2) helping to eliminate fears, especially phobias, and (3) enhancing already existing behaviour. **pp. 594–595**

**KEY TERMS**

behaviour therapy, p. 589; symptom substitution, p. 590; token economy, p. 591; time out, p. 593; counterconditioning, p. 593; systematic desensitization, p. 593; aversive counterconditioning, p. 594

## COGNITIVE THERAPY

### What are the basic propositions that guide cognitive therapy?

> The three basic propositions of cognitive therapy are that (1) cognitive activity affects behaviour, (2) cognitive activity can be monitored, and (3) behaviour changes can be effected through cognitive changes.   **p. 596**

> *Rational–emotive therapy* emphasizes the role of logical, rational thought processes in behaviour. It assumes that faulty, irrational thinking patterns are the cause of abnormal behaviour.   **p. 596**

**KEY TERM**

rational–emotive therapy, p. 596

## GROUP THERAPY

### What is group therapy, and what is the function of family therapy?

> *Group therapy* is therapy used to treat several people simultaneously for emotional and behaviour problems. The techniques used in a therapy group are determined by the nature of the group and the orientation of its therapist.   **pp. 599–601**

> *Family therapy* attempts to change family systems, because individuals affect family processes and family

processes affect individuals. Treatment takes into account that a family is a dynamic social system.   **p. 601**

**KEY TERMS**

group therapy, p. 599; family therapy, p. 601

## BIOLOGICALLY BASED THERAPIES

### What are the major types of biologically based therapies and the major classes of psychotropic drugs?

> Drugs for the relief of mental problems are usually grouped into four classes: anti-anxiety drugs, anti-depressant drugs, anti-mania drugs, and anti-psychotic drugs. Such drugs often work by altering the level of a key neurotransmitter in the brain.   **pp. 603–605**

> The major biologically based therapies are psychosurgery, electroconvulsive therapy, and drug therapy. *Psychosurgery* (brain surgery) is an infrequently used method of treatment used to alleviate symptoms of serious mental disorders. *Electroconvulsive therapy* (ECT) is a treatment for severe mental illness in which a brief application of electricity to the head is used to produce a generalized seizure.   **pp. 603, 606–607**

**KEY TERMS**

psychosurgery, p. 606; electroconvulsive therapy (ECT), p. 607

---

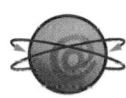

Take advantage of the multimedia resources available with this text! Follow the marginal icons to access the interactive modules on the *HandsOnPsych* CD-ROM; log on to *MyPsychLab* to explore the ebook, study aids, and other online resources; and visit the Companion Website at **www.pearsoned.ca/lefton** for additional exercises and links.

In the 1930s one of the most famous experiments in industrial/ organizational psychology took place. The Hawthorne experiments were conducted at Western Electric's Hawthorne plant (Roethlisberger & Dickson, 1939). Although the findings of these experiments continue to be a source of debate, their historical significance to the study of human behaviour at work is unquestionable.

Five women were placed in a room where they were to proceed with their work of assembling telephone relays. They were isolated so that the conditions for their work could be carefully controlled and their behaviour could be monitored. Meticulous records were kept regarding the conditions in the room, including variables such as temperature and humidity, as well as what each woman ate at mealtimes, how much she slept, as well as each woman's feelings about her experience. At specified intervals, their working conditions were altered and output following the changes was noted. For example, shorter rest periods, longer but fewer rest periods, group incentive pay, a five-day week, and even a reversion to original work conditions, occurred over the course of the experiment. Data were collected over two and a half years.

What did the researchers find? To the surprise of almost everyone, every single change (except one in which the women had to work in near darkness) resulted in increased output. That is, production continued to increase over the duration of the experiment, no matter what the change. Why? There are a number of theories, many of which will be discussed in this chapter, but the most commonly cited effect is what has become known as the *Hawthorne effect*. Simply paying attention to the women increased their feelings of self-worth and motivation, resulting in increased output. Of course, creating a sense of group unity and giving them control over their work environment was also important.

APPLIED PSYCHOLOGY

The branch of psychology that uses psychological principles to help solve practical problems of everyday life.

These early experiments, and others like them, paved the way for a new field in psychology. This chapter will highlight the concepts and theories important to this area: industrial/organizational psychology. **Applied psychology** is the branch of psychology that uses psychological principles to help solve practical problems of everyday life—whether those problems come up on the job, at school, or on the playing field. Consider hockey, for example. Applied psychologists examine how the basics of behaviour, such as learning and memory, affect athletic activities. They also consider how coaches can motivate athletes to perform their best by using common psychological concepts to help them visualize possibilities, overcome obstacles, and achieve fulfilment. To a great extent, applied psychologists help people manage their own behaviour better. Whether you are the coach of the Calgary Flames, the regional director of the Red Cross, or a corporate manager making human resources decisions, the principles of applied psychology go a long way.

In this chapter, we consider an array of fields that apply psychology to modern life. We begin with the workplace because that is where psychological principles have been studied and applied longest and most systematically—going as far back as John B. Watson, who applied psychology to a Maxwell House coffee advertising campaign in 1915.

## Industrial/Organizational Psychology

Work consumes a high proportion of a person's waking hours, and how we work, where we work, and why we work are important questions. Increased global competition, changes in information technology, and industrial re-engineering are fast changing the world of work. As productivity has become increasingly important to business, industrial/organizational psychology has grown in importance.

INDUSTRIAL/ORGANIZATIONAL (I/O) PSYCHOLOGY

The study of how individual behaviour is affected by the work environment, by co-workers, and by organizational practices.

**Industrial/organizational (I/O) psychology** is the study of how individual behaviour is affected by the work environment, by co-workers, and by organizational practices. It is the study of people not only in industry but in government, hospitals, universities, and non-profit organizations. I/O psychologists study behaviour in large and small businesses—from small biotech startups to large multinational corporations. In all of these environments, key concerns are how well individuals perform their duties and relate to one another; I/O psychology is increasingly being applied to address those concerns through provision of research-based answers to pressing organizational problems (Cascio, 1995). Large companies have I/O psychologists on site, working in their human resources departments, and small companies hire them as consultants.

I/O psychologists pay close attention to the type of company in which they work, because companies vary in their organizational structures, and worldwide companies vary even more. Given today's increasingly global economy, I/O psychologists must take into account global multicultural differences among organizations. Many companies reflect an organizational structure that in turn reflects their society. Asian companies—in Korea, for example—often reflect a family orientation, where people work hard for the good of the entire family. This affects hiring decisions, firing, promotions, hierarchies, and the general work ethic. Culture especially affects how decisions are made; in Japan, for example, plans for new ideas are often drafted from the bottom up, rather than emanating from higher levels of an organization as they often do in Canada. The entire corporate mindset may vary from culture to culture, and from company to company within each culture. Some companies, especially those in Latin American countries, are extremely hierarchical in nature, according high respect to authority figures; some companies in developing countries are more loosely organized in terms of who does what; in North America, there is often some flexibility as to who is allowed to assume various roles.

In general, I/O psychology can be divided into four broad areas: human resources psychology, motivation and job performance, job satisfaction, and leadership.

*Human resources psychology* focuses on the personnel functions of placing people in their jobs, training them, promoting, determining benefits, and evaluating performance. Such functions take place both before people begin to work for an organization and as an ongoing process within the organization. *Motivation and job performance* is a key area for I/O psychologists; they study not only rewards and success at work but also workers' influence on management and management's concerns about itself. *Job satisfaction* and other aspects of happiness at work are concerns of workers and employers alike. Finally, the study of *leadership* focuses on the key attributes of leaders—people who influence other people's behaviour toward the attainment of agreed-upon goals.

## HUMAN RESOURCES PSYCHOLOGY

Human resources, or personnel, psychologists are involved in a broad array of activities related to employment—from helping employers choose among prospective job candidates, to determining compensation packages, to facilitating on-the-job training, to arranging termination programs when businesses must downsize. To help organizations succeed, human resources psychologists must consider the internal conditions of an organization (its size, structure, and business strategies) as well as external conditions (legal, social, political, cultural) (Jackson & Schuler, 1995). Among the most important tasks is helping organizations select among well-trained, qualified candidates for specific positions. Today, finding the right people for jobs occurs within the overall context of an organization's *strategic planning*. This high-level planning, which is finalized at the top levels of the organization, includes forecasting the organization's future needs, establishing specific objectives, and implementing programs to ensure that appropriate people will be available when needed (Jackson & Schuler, 1990).

**JOB ANALYSES.** An important step in the strategic planning process is ensuring that there are well-qualified personnel to fill all of the company's needs. Companies often prepare **job analyses**—careful descriptions of the various tasks and activities that are required for employees to do their jobs, along with the necessary knowledge, skills, and abilities. Thus, there is an analysis of *what* gets done and *how* it gets done. This means specifying performance criteria—behaviours—that are required of employees. For example, a computer programmer might be expected to write code, debug the code of other programmers, and evaluate the efficiency of the code. Job analysis also means enumerating the qualifications for employment. For example, a computer programmer might need a college degree in computer science, two or three years of experience, and top-notch hands-on computing skills.

A *functional job analysis*, sometimes called an FJA, describes each type of work and the level of complexity of each job. An FJA is appealing to I/O psychologists because—like operationally defined behaviour in a research study—it is concrete, observable, and measurable. In an FJA there are three hierarchies of worker functions, and in each hierarchy there is an analysis of what gets done and how. In most jobs, workers have to deal with data (information), people (co-workers, subordinates, or customers), and things (objects). Within each of these types of work there are various levels of complexity. With data, individuals may have to compare, contrast, or copy data; on a more complex level, they also may have to analyze or synthesize data from different sources. With people, individuals may have to take instructions, help others, or serve others; on a more complex level, they may have to supervise, instruct, negotiate with, or mentor other people. With things, individuals may handle, carry, sort, or tend; on a more complex level, they may be altering, preparing, or fixing equipment.

JOB ANALYSES
Careful descriptions of the various tasks and activities that are required for employees to do their jobs, along with the necessary knowledge, skills, and abilities; such analyses describe what gets done and how it gets done.

Human resource psychologists must identify the right people for specific positions.

There are other ways to measure what a job is, what gets done on a job, and who is best suited to specific work. For example, the *position analysis questionnaire* is widely used to ask those who know the job best to analyze their own jobs. On this questionnaire, workers fill out up to 194 statements describing a given job (McCormick, Jeanneret, & Mecham, 1972). The position analysis questionnaire has questions in six major areas: information sources (where the worker gets data from), mental processes (what decision making is required), work output (what physical work is required), relationships with others (communication skills), job context (physical working conditions), and other (licensing, criticality of position, special clothes, etc.).

The FJA and the position analysis questionnaire are widely used instruments, but there are many other such tests and analysis instruments, and most of them work equally well (Levine et al., 1983). All have a similar goal: Employers need to ensure that jobs are appropriate and have the correct scope. A job should not be too big or encompass too many tasks; nor should it be too limiting and so focused that it becomes boring and repetitive. Ideally, jobs should allow employees some level of responsibility for and control over how they do their work. Two of the key tasks of an I/O psychologist are balancing the scope and complexity of jobs and helping employers create jobs that will be motivating.

**SELECTION PROCEDURES.** Employers want to hire individuals who will enjoy their work, suit the company's needs, and be productive. I/O psychologists develop specific selection procedures, including tests, to produce the best match between employers and employees. The selection procedures for jobs with large firms are often complicated and time-consuming.

*Selection procedures* have one basic goal—predicting the success of job candidates to help an employer determine which candidates to hire and which to reject. Employers and researchers use application forms, interviews, work samples, and tests to make comparisons between people looking for a job. Subtle factors can be at work in selection procedures, and evaluators have to pay particular attention to these factors—for example, to guard against the influence of their own moods (Baron, 1993), an applicant's expensive clothes or unattractive looks, and other non–job-related characteristics that have nothing to do with an applicant's true capabilities (Forsythe, 1990).

There exists a wide range of selection methods that involve everything from tests of mental ability to peer rating, examination of experience, interests, and even handwriting. But research shows that the best measures to help employers decide who to hire are mental ability tests, work sample tests, and integrity tests—and when these are combined, employers are even more likely to choose a candidate that will work out well (Schmidt & Hunter, 1998).

*Tests of general mental ability* come in many forms and test many abilities; most are paper-and-pencil tests and can be administered in groups or individually. They can focus on measures of general or specific abilities; intelligence tests are widely used measures of general ability in jobs that require high-level cognitive skills. Other standardized cognitive tests, such as those for general ability and specific verbal or mathematical knowledge, are good predictors of both academic success and certain types of job performance (Ree, Earles, & Teachout, 1994; Schmidt, Onex, & Hunter, 1992). However, an important question for I/O psychologists is whether such tests (or any tests for that matter) are the *best* predictors of job performance (or even if they are *valid, sufficient* predictors). This question has become especially important because of a large number of lawsuits filed by those who argue that the tests discriminate against them. *Introduction to Research Basics* addresses this issue of equal employment opportunity further.

▼ Employers want to hire individuals who will enjoy work, suit the company's needs, and be productive.

## Does a "Similar-to-Me" Effect Exist in Job Interviews and, If So, Is That Necessarily a Bad Thing?

Surprisingly little empirical data exist about gender, minority group status, and interview outcomes. Most research has been done with university and college students, with simulated interviews and involved questionnaires rather than real-life observations of job interviews.

One of the problems associated with interviews is that of *rater bias*. In particular, researchers have identified the *"similar-to-me effect."* Interviewers prefer candidates who share their own age, race, socio-economic background, and attitudinal characteristics. Greg Sears at McMaster University and Patricia Rowe at the University of Waterloo (2003) have shown that similarity in personality is also a factor that positively influences interviewer judgment.

**Design.** A repeated measures design was used in this study (where each participant responds to each of the conditions of interest in the study). This means that all participants viewed and responded to videotaped interviews with two types of job applicants for the position of residence don—one that matched them on a number of key personality and personal variables, and one that did not match them on the chosen key variable of conscientiousness.

**Hypothesis.** Specifically, Sears and Rowe set out to test their hypothesis that the more similar a job applicant was

considered to the interviewer in terms of conscientiousness (a personality trait), the higher the applicant would be ranked by the interviewer.

**Participants.** Forty male undergraduate psychology students participated in this study. They were pre-tested and only those who scored either high or low on a personality measure of conscientiousness were included in the actual study (20 of each).

**Results.** After observing each of the applicants (one matched to their own level of conscientiousness, either high or low, and the other not), participants were asked to rate each of the applicants in terms of how they felt about each applicant (affect), how competent they believed each applicant to be, and how suitable they believed each applicant to be for the job. Results indicated partial support for the existence of a similar-to-me effect for the personality variable of conscientiousness. Participants did *not* show a preference for the more similar to them applicant in terms of their stated feelings toward the applicant (that is, they did not say they liked the similar applicant more). They *did*, however, consistently rate the more similar applicant as more competent than the less similar applicant, showing a clear similar-to-me effect. Finally, the ratings of job suitability suggested a partial similar-to-me effect that showed that highly conscientious participants rated the matching highly conscientious applicant as more suitable for the job than the low conscientious applicant. This sort of similar-to-me effect was not found for low conscientiousness participants.

**Conclusions.** Sears and Rowe acknowledge that the similar-to-me effect shown here could be problematic in some interview settings but go on to suggest that, especially in terms of positive factors such as conscientiousness, it's possible the similar-to-me effect might not be so much a bias as an asset if solidly competent and highly conscientious interviewers are used to search for those kinds of potential employees.

---

*Work samples* are hands-on simulations of all or part of a job's tasks. Depending on the job, there may be tests of spatial abilities (for air traffic controllers), perceptual accuracy (stenographers, proofreaders), or motor abilities (firefighters). Each test is used to help the employer determine whether a job candidate's abilities match the job's requirements. Tests of managerial ability, which sometimes present the applicant with a simulated in-box to sort through, also have been devised and have proved successful at indicating who will be a good manager (Berman & Miner, 1985).

One type of test that has seen significantly increased use across different kinds of jobs is the *test of integrity*. Some such tests focus on attitudes about theft, including rationalizations about "acceptably" small amounts of on-the-job theft. Other tests examine integrity more indirectly, by looking at characteristics such as dependability, conscientiousness, and thrill seeking. Finally, tests such as the MMPI–2, which screens for maladjustment, are also used to reveal people of low integrity. Although such tests are controversial—many feel that individuals may be misdiagnosed or wrongly classified as lacking integrity—their usage is on the increase, and they are seen as an alternative that is better than not testing at all (Camara & Schneider, 1994; Sackett, 1994, 2001, 2003).

Although, when taken in combination, mental ability, work samples, and integrity are good predictors, there are others that are important. We live in a fast-changing service-based economy, in which jobs in the service sector account for about 79 percent of all employment. The rise of the Internet and Internet sales over the last five years shows how an economy and job requirements can rapidly change the life of a business. Thus, many employers want their employees to be able to provide high-quality customer service and to be creative, adaptable, resilient, empathic, and understanding with customers—and technologically adept. Since these abilities are now being considered important as job qualifications (Cascio, 1995), it is not surprising that the use of tests to measure elements of personality in the workplace has increased markedly in the last decade. Several million such tests are administered yearly. Personality tests are used more to find specific behaviour patterns that are well suited to a type of job than to screen out people who may be abnormal (Hogan, Hogan, & Roberts, 1996). For example, some people who exhibit Type A behaviour patterns do better at some types of high-pressure work, such as being a commodities trader, than at others, such as meticulously checking a manuscript for typographical errors (Lee, Ashford, & Bobko, 1990). Tests of personality and interests, however, are difficult to correlate with job performance; for example, outgoing individuals may be good salespeople, but quiet, introspective individuals often can be just as persuasive. What all this boils down to is that to be fair and hire the best possible candidates, employers should make sure that their human resources departments use structured interviews because they are a more reliable and valid selection procedure (Campion, Palmer, & Campion, 1998).

Tests are just one way to gather information about applicants. Biographical data can help paint an accurate picture of an individual, as can work samples, letters of recommendation, and exercises in which job candidates take part in general discussions about work. Interviews can be important in determining the fit of an applicant with a position—but research shows that interviewers often make final decisions about applicants within the first minutes of an interview! Also, sometimes interviewers' judgments are based more on negative information provided than on positive information. Structured interviews—in which each applicant is asked the same questions in a certain way, in a certain order, and in the same manner—work better than do unstructured interviews (Arvey & Campion, 1982).

**EDUCATION AND TRAINING.** Imagine you landed a new job; now you are faced with "learning the business." It is a process of training and education whereby organizations systematically teach employees skills to improve their job performance. Most corporations offer systematic training, which typically begins by educating employees about the organization and its goals. Walt Disney World's Disney University offers world-class training ranging from computer applications to culinary arts. Using first-tier faculty, self-paced courses, and distance education, Disney U. trains its workers to be top flight, upbeat, and service oriented. They recognize that people are at the core of their business, and a well-educated workforce is essential. Disney, like all employers, recognizes that a new employee may also need to learn specific skills, such as how to use a particular computer animation program. The increasing amount of information required in today's fast-changing workplace makes employers especially concerned that employees have the necessary knowledge to perform their jobs. To help ensure this, knowledge must be defined in job-relevant terms, a classification of knowledge areas that are relevant to the job must be identified, and evidence of the comprehensiveness of the new knowledge system must be gathered (Costanza, Fleishman, & Marshall-Mies, 1999).

At the Royal Military College of Canada, one of the primary roles of personnel selection officers is to train military personnel, assisting soldiers as well as navy and air personnel make the transition from civilian to military life (Lamerson, 2002). In fact, Ronald Holden of Queens University (Holden & Scholtz, 2002) has developed the Holden Psychological Screening Inventory (HPSI) scales to screen for psychological maladjustment, therefore predicting those individuals most amenable to training and those least likely to succeed.

▲ Training programs often use on-the-job procedures to teach specific skills, such as how to use a computer.

A variety of methods is available for education and training. Among the most common are lectures, films, and videotapes. Self-paced instructional materials are often used. Training programs may also include discussion groups, simulations, and on-the-job demonstrations. Letting employees observe others so that they can imitate them is particularly effective. However, some people respond better than others to any training method. A training program can involve an apprenticeship or a mentoring relationship, with regular performance appraisals made by a more experienced or higher-ranking employee. Finding female mentors for women has sometimes been difficult because of smaller numbers of women in upper management.

Even seasoned employees need education and retraining. In large organizations, education is an ongoing process, as new products and technologies are introduced. I/O psychologists typically break down a training program into a series of learning objectives. Because it provides very specific goals for knowledge and skill acquisition, this method of training can be a particularly effective way to help employees identify their strengths and weaknesses. It also helps employees pinpoint specific obstacles to overcome and opportunities for improvement.

Training may be as simple as reviewing a new tool or procedure—as in introducing an executive to the Internet, teaching a secretary a new word-processing program, or working with custodians to promote recycling efforts. It may also be an elaborate process that takes place on the job and involves the employee's active participation—perhaps in programming a robot or pitching a product to clients. Training may include repetitive practice, particularly with highly technical equipment. It often involves moving from a classroom or meeting room to the actual workplace. Last, good training usually includes feedback, so that employees can learn whether they have successfully acquired the new skill or knowledge.

I/O psychologists assign great importance to education and training because business or organizational success requires well-informed employees. To help ensure good education and training, researchers attempt to determine what constitutes good work performance. That is, they begin with the desired outcome and work backward to determine how employees should be trained. I/O psychologists evaluate the effectiveness of recent training by examining employees' work products or test results immediately after the training procedure. Results are, after all, what employers are interested in. Effective education and training produce improvements in employees' ability to deliver results, whether in the form of better-quality products, clearer communications, or more effective supervision.

**PERFORMANCE APPRAISAL.** Have you ever been evaluated by an employer? Bosses are sometimes good at appraising work, but they also may overlook your best efforts and remember your mistakes, or they may not accurately convey how they feel about your performance. What makes a boss good at evaluating employees?

The process by which a supervisor periodically evaluates job-relevant strengths and weaknesses of a subordinate is called **performance appraisal**. Performance appraisals are especially important because they often are used to determine salaries, layoffs, firings, transfers, and promotions (Harris, Gilbreath, & Sunday, 1998). Researchers have tried to find ways for them to do it more systematically.

The problem with performance appraisals is that they often are done inaccurately by people with few skills in evaluation and with few diagnostic aids. Supervisors generally report that they dislike conducting appraisals. They don't like to review their subordinates, and many acknowledge that they do not have strong evaluative skills. Further, supervisors have just as many inappropriate biases as anyone else (Swim et al., 1989), including the tendency to make attribution errors (pointed out in Chapter 13). Even when performance appraisals are done well, research shows that people's pay is more often associated with the quantity of their work than with its quality (Jenkins et al., 1998).

There are ways to do appraisals well. The first thing to consider is the criteria, or standards, on which a worker should be judged. There is usually no single performance criterion, no comprehensive yardstick, by which to evaluate a worker.

Second, a worker's quantity of work is often important, but so is its quality. Also, relationships with other workers often affect performance. Researchers have devised scales to measure performance variables such as sales volume, relationships with customers, and quality of interworker communication; these scales can be helpful diagnostic tools. But because skills often overlap, composite scales have had to be devised. None has proved totally satisfactory.

Because of the "soft" nature of some performance criteria, such as how well people "get along," most I/O psychologists recommend focusing on the best available criteria. This means giving first attention to those elements that *best* describe satisfactory performance, recognizing that many criteria can be used. For example, a manager would look first at "measurables," such as a salesperson's sales volume, a keyboarder's number of words or characters typed, a bank teller's number of shortages, or a nursery worker's number of saplings planted. The manager would then assess other elements of performance that may be important, such as customer relations or co-worker communication.

Performance appraisals need objective measures. Managers often compare employees, ranking them from best to worst or rating them in percentile groups (the top 10 percent, the next 20 percent, and so on). Such ratings help differentiate among employees, but they sometimes fall short of fairness. What if workers doing the same job are evaluated by different supervisors, one of them easygoing and the other demanding? What if supervisors use, even if unintentionally, subjective, "soft" criteria, such as how friendly they feel employees are? Might that discriminate against workers who don't have personal interests in common with the supervisors?

Even when using objective measures, certain problems arise; these include leniency, central tendency, the halo effect, and lack of reliability. Some raters always judge people with *leniency,* giving them higher evaluations than they actually deserve. The rater may simply want to be liked, may want to avoid confrontation, or may want to have the employee's positive evaluation reflect well on himself or herself. Other raters always judge people "about average," giving them a *central* rating. These raters are unwilling to rank people very high or very low but give "safe" judgments that are unlikely to raise eyebrows. The *halo effect* occurs in job performance appraisals when a rater is unable to discriminate among the many discrete parts of a job. Thus, a good first impression or good work on one part of a job may lead to a high rating on later work or on other parts of the job—regardless of the quality of performance in that case. *Reliability* refers to the consistency of observations. Good raters consistently rate similar work in similar ways; others,

**PERFORMANCE APPRAISAL**

The process by which a supervisor periodically evaluates the job-relevant strengths and weaknesses of a subordinate.

however, deviate in their ratings from one occasion to the next and from one employee to the next, based on factors that are hard to quantify, such as a worker's unique ability to perform well in a team.

Most companies require periodic evaluations, so if a reluctant manager does them as infrequently as possible and in a cursory manner, they must be taught how do them objectively and with skill. Good-faith evaluations leave employees feeling appreciated and comfortable with the system (Tziner & Murphy, 1999).

## MOTIVATION AND JOB PERFORMANCE

I/O psychologists help people work together in organizations; they work at understanding the emotional and social needs of employees, and they help organizations motivate management and workers. One obvious motivator is the fact that people need money to live. But both employers and psychologists know that different people are motivated by different things. Monetary rewards are important, of course—but so is praise for success. Such values are very much culturally determined; the value placed on hard work varies from culture to culture. Some cultures stress a person's duties to contribute to society; others stress a person's right to meaningful work; still others stress a person's need for happiness at work. I/O psychologists study especially carefully the impact of rewards and success within the context of culture.

When Hofstede (1983) examined attitudes in more than 50 countries, he found that organizations and culture varied on four main dimensions. *Power distance* is the extent to which there is a rigid hierarchy, or pecking order, in a company, limiting employees' independence of action. *Uncertainty avoidance* is a lack of tolerance for ambiguity or uncertainty in the workplace, which may be found in risk-averse countries such as Japan and Greece. Cultures varied in the extent to which they valued *individualism* as opposed to the collective good of the organization. Finally, Hofstede found that emphasis on work goals as opposed to interpersonal goals, a trait he labelled *masculinity*, also varied from culture to culture. Not surprisingly, Hofstede found that most Western companies fostered a combination he called independent individualism; Asian companies fostered collectivism; and some other societies fostered unique combinations. Israel, for instance, fosters dependent collectivism (high power distance, low individualism). These cultural values will affect people's needs and goals, what they value, what they consider equitable, and how they can be managed most effectively.

In Western culture, job performance generally is affected by *intrinsically motivated behaviour*—behaviour engaged in strictly because it brings pleasure. Recall that when intrinsically motivated behaviours are constantly reinforced with direct external rewards (such as money), productivity often drops. Money often is not that important to job performance. A well-paid plumber may find plumbing work tedious and unfulfilling, whereas a lower-paid clerical worker who finds the job important and challenging will perform well and be given increased responsibilities. With the help of I/O psychologists' theoretical work, employers can find ways to motivate employees to be more productive (and thus to provide companies with more profits).

**NEED AND GOAL-SETTING THEORY.** Workers often will perform difficult tasks for long hours, not for pay or for food or for praise, but merely to reach a goal or to compare their present performance with new performance. Mountain climbers tackle a new peak "because it's there." **Goal-setting theory** asserts that setting specific, clear, attainable goals for a given task will lead to better performance. In running or biking, for example, you challenge yourself to run or ride harder and longer—not to break records for your age group, but to meet artificial goals you have set for yourself.

Goal-setting theory states that goals work best when they are somewhat challenging but attainable and personally agreed to by a worker. Goals work especially

GOAL-SETTING THEORY
A theory that asserts that setting specific, clear, attainable goals for a given task will lead to better performance.

FIGURE 17.1
Goal-setting Theory

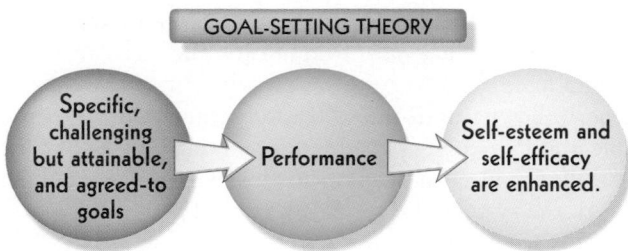

well when they enhance a worker's sense of self-esteem or self-efficacy. For example, if a sales manager and her staff agree to a 50 percent increase in annual sales, rather than an unrealistic 200 percent increase, chances are that the sales staff will perform well (see Figure 17.1).

Goal-setting theory can account for some work behaviours, but it cannot explain why people will work on projects for years, at low pay, or under difficult conditions. More fully developed expectancy theories take the next step forward—explaining the motivation for this type of performance.

**EXPECTANCY THEORIES.**    A successful employer–employee relationship relies on many factors beyond economic motivation. **Expectancy theories**, which we discussed in Chapter 9, suggest that a worker's effort and desire to maintain goal-directed behaviour (in other words, to work) is determined by expectations regarding the outcomes of that behaviour.

One expectancy theory, proposed by Victor Vroom (1964), suggests that both motivation and ability determine job performance. Vroom's proposal is considered an expectancy theory because it states that motivation is determined by what people expect to experience in performing a task—a rewarding outcome or a frustrating one. Vroom's theory holds that motivation results from a three-part equation made up of expectancy, instrumentality, and valence. *Expectancy* is the belief that hard or extra work will lead to good or improved performance; *instrumentality* refers to a worker's belief that good performance will be rewarded; and *valence* refers to the value placed on the rewards that are offered. A person who is awarded a big raise but later gets the cold shoulder from co-workers because of it may then give the raise lower valence.

It turns out that ability, effort, *and* role perceptions—the ways people believe they should be doing their jobs—are the key variables that determine performance (see Figure 17.2). Edward Lawler and Lyman Porter (1967) believed that workers must fully understand the nature of their positions and exactly what is required of them. Too often, people fail not because of lack of effort or ability, but because they do not know what is expected of them or how to achieve a sense of control or power in the organization. So an employee may burn a great deal of midnight oil, but if he or she has misread what it really takes to succeed in the organization (say, teamwork rather than long hours), performance may not be rated highly.

Today, researchers claim that the motivation to work can be explained more by integrative theories that focus on goals, experiences, and thoughts (Locke & Latham, 1990a). Daniel Skarlicki at the University of British Columbia (Klammer, Skarlicki, & Barclay, 2002; Skarlicki & Latham, 1995) argues that organizational citizenship behaviour (OCB) is critical because it relates not just to the functioning of the organization but to individual performance as well. OCBs are those employee behaviours that further the goals of the organization but that are not recognized by the formal reward system of the organization. In other words, employees help the organization without getting payment or promotion or any other type of tangible reward. Therefore, identifying what motivates such behaviours is of critical importance to organizations.

EXPECTANCY THEORIES
Theories that suggest that a worker's effort and desire to maintain goal-directed behaviour (to work) is determined by expectancies regarding the outcomes of that work.

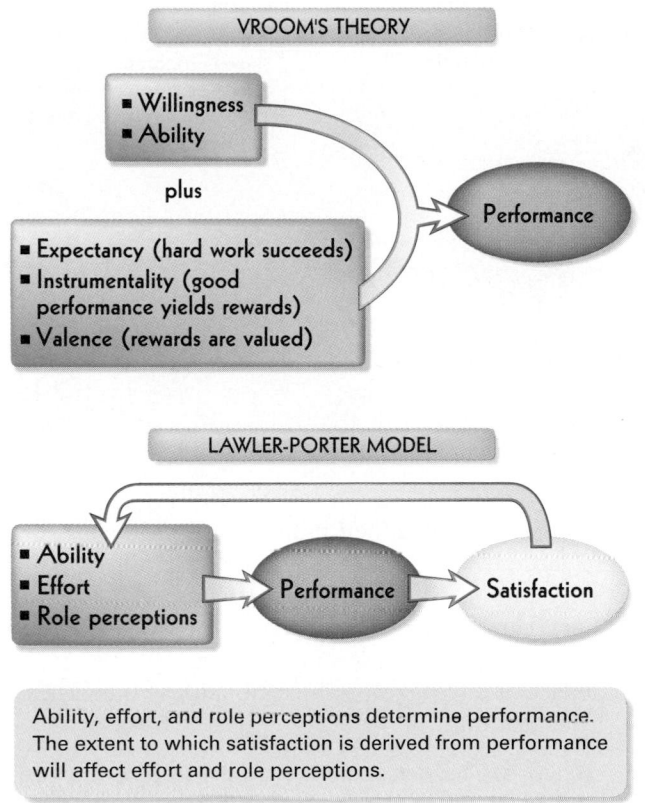

FIGURE 17.2
Expectancy Theories

**VROOM'S THEORY**

- Willingness
- Ability

plus

- Expectancy (hard work succeeds)
- Instrumentality (good performance yields rewards)
- Valence (rewards are valued)

Performance

**LAWLER-PORTER MODEL**

- Ability
- Effort
- Role perceptions

Performance → Satisfaction

Ability, effort, and role perceptions determine performance. The extent to which satisfaction is derived from performance will affect effort and role perceptions.

When people receive incentives, when they think their contributions are important, and when the effort required of them is not excessive, productivity tends to be high (Shepperd, 1993). When performance is high, job satisfaction is likely; job satisfaction then increases the employee's commitment to the organization and its goals.

**EQUITY THEORY.** Being treated fairly is a prime concern for almost everyone. People want to be compensated for their work, to earn as much as they can, and most feel that they are worth more than they are paid. As radio personality and author Garrison Keillor implied when he described the inhabitants of Lake Wobegon, most people feel that they are "above average." But what happens when people feel that they are being treated unfairly?

In I/O psychology, **equity theory** asserts that what people bring to a work situation should be balanced by what they receive compared with other workers; thus, workers' input (what they bring or do) should be balanced by their compensation (what they receive). If input and compensation are not balanced, people will adjust their work level and potentially their job satisfaction accordingly. According to equity theories, each individual privately weighs the balance between input and compensation and compares this ratio to other people's input/compensation ratio. When people perceive that the ratios are similar, people are relatively happy. Thus, if a colleague's workloads and talent are compensated at a certain level, and other workers feel similarly compensated, their ratios are about equal.

What if a person feels that his or her ratio is way out of balance? In such cases (especially in cases of underpayment), people may slow down their work behaviour and gripe and groan, and the quality of work often decreases (see Figure 17.3). If inequities exist, people will choose one of several alternatives to alter the situation (Berg, 1991; Greenberg, 1990; Summers & Hendrix, 1991). Hellriegel and Slocum (1992) assert that people have choices when they feel that an inequity exists:

**EQUITY THEORY**

In I/O psychology, the theory that suggests that what people bring to a work situation should be balanced by what they receive compared with other workers; thus, input should be balanced by compensation, or rewards, or workers will adjust their work level and potentially their job satisfaction accordingly.

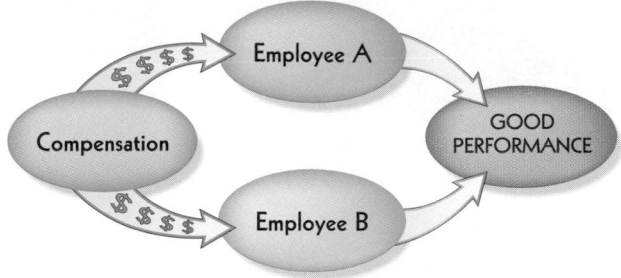

If two employees receive equal compensation for similar performance levels, they will tend to continue to exert the same effort.

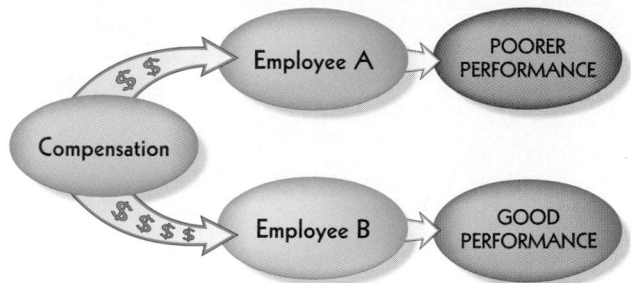

In contrast, if two employees who exert the same effort and show comparable levels of performance receive unequal compensation, the employee who receives the lower reward is likely to exert less effort. His or her performance may suffer.

**FIGURE 17.3**
**Equity Theory**

- They can increase their inputs to justify higher rewards (when they feel over-rewarded).
- They can decrease their inputs to compensate for low rewards.
- They can change their rewards through legal actions, illegal actions (stealing company assets), or leaving early.
- They can distort reality by rationalizing inequities, and thus feel better.
- They can quit.

There are hidden costs of inequity in pay and benefits. When Greenberg (1990) examined employee theft rates in manufacturing plants after pay cuts, he found higher rates of theft than before pay reductions. When supervisors explained the basis for pay cuts to workers, feelings became less bruised, ratios were not perceived as being so out of kilter, and the theft rate decreased. A key finding of this study was that when management explains the nature of pay shifts, the perception of inequity is minimized.

**SELF-EFFICACY AND WORK.**   How well you believe that you will be able to execute a series of actions required to deal with a situation is your self-efficacy. People who view themselves as having high degrees of self-efficacy turn out to do better at work than others. This turns out to be especially true for easier tasks. When tasks are especially complicated or difficult, even people with a great deal of confidence don't do well (Stajkovic & Luthans, 1998). This leads researchers to some practical suggestions for employers: Managers should provide accurate descriptions of work to be performed; employees should be given clues as to what techniques should be used to complete tasks; employers should provide tasks that employees can accomplish to enhance worker self-efficacy; and contingencies and rewards should be timed to enhance a worker's self-efficacy. In the end, goals—their content and form—and the rewards associated with them, when well formed, can act to enhance self-efficacy and performance (Audia, Kristof-Brown, & Locke, 1996; Locke, 1996; Latham, Daghighi, & Locke, 1997).

**MOTIVATION MANAGEMENT: THREE APPROACHES.**   Recognizing the complexity of motivation management, I/O psychologists have developed three basic approaches to motivation in the workplace: paternalistic, behavioural, and participatory. The fundamental idea of the *paternalistic approach* to motivation is that a company takes care of its employees' needs and desires in a fatherly manner. Early in the twentieth century, this approach was common in the mining companies and lumber and paper mills in the West, which provided housing, schools, recreation, and churches for employees. This approach is common today in some Japanese companies, which promote lifelong employment and support employees' needs, from recreation to drug rehabilitation. Nevertheless, such approaches are contrary to many Western psychologists' views on behaviour. Instrumental (operant) conditioning studies show that for a behaviour (such as work) to be established and maintained—at least in Western cultures—reinforcement must be contingent on performance. In a paternalistic system all employees, productive as well as nonproductive, are given reinforcement if they fulfil their roles as workers. Reinforcement without the need for performance does not encourage people to work hard, as equity theory predicts.

*Behavioural approaches* to motivation assume that people will work only if they receive tangible rewards for specific task performance. Examples include paying a factory worker by the piece and a typist by the page. In such a system, hard-working employees obtain more rewards—commissions, salary increases, bonuses, and so on—because they produce more; but little attention is paid to the emotional needs of workers. In the end, goal-setting theory and, to some extent, expectancy theory predict that this situation will not work.

▲ The participatory approach to motivation is based on the belief that individuals who have a say in the decisions that affect their work lives are motivated to work harder and smarter.

The *participatory approach* to motivation is based on the belief that individuals who have a say in the decisions that affect their lives are motivated to work harder and smarter. Participation, it is argued, provides a setting in which managers and employees can exchange information to solve problems (Tjosvold, 1987). Supporters of this approach believe that a sense of competence and self-determination is likely to increase individuals' levels of motivation (Deci, 1975). *Quality circles*, in which workers at all levels meet to discuss ways to improve product quality and promote excellence, constitute one technique employers use to involve workers in the management process (Matsui & Onglatco, 1990).

Many variables affect the success of participatory programs: the work setting, the individuals involved, the kinds of decisions to be made, and the hiring policies, for example. When truly participatory approaches are followed, there are positive effects on workers' values, thoughts, and motivation. These changes lead to less conflict among workers, increased productivity, and better overall job performance (see Figure 17.4). When workers feel comfortable and involved with their work and their organization, they are more likely to be spontaneous, to help co-workers, to protect the organization, and so on. Many of these behaviours depend on the employees feeling positive about the work environment and having a good attitude at work (George & Brief, 1992).

## JOB SATISFACTION

If you have a positive view of your abilities and feel competent and in control (at least most of the time), chances are good that you will like your job and that you will feel satisfied (Judge et al., 1998). It is important to realize that job satisfaction is different from job motivation. Motivation is always shown in behaviour; job satisfaction (a person's attitude about the work and workplace) may not be shown in behaviour. A tired, bored, overworked electrician may feel discouraged and angry—and may even hate her job—but still be motivated to work. Her motivation may stem from the high pay she receives, from her sense of obligation to get the job done, or from some other source. Thus, although her job satisfaction is low, it does not affect her performance. In general, however, a satisfied worker is a high-performing worker who will remain in the organization. This is why organizations want I/O psychologists to identify the sources of job satisfaction. For example, at Lakehead University, Andrea Kohan and Brian O'Connor (2002) have found that for police officers self-esteem is a critical component of not only job satisfaction but *life satisfaction*. Those with job stress reported experiencing negative affect and were more likely to have alcohol-related problems.

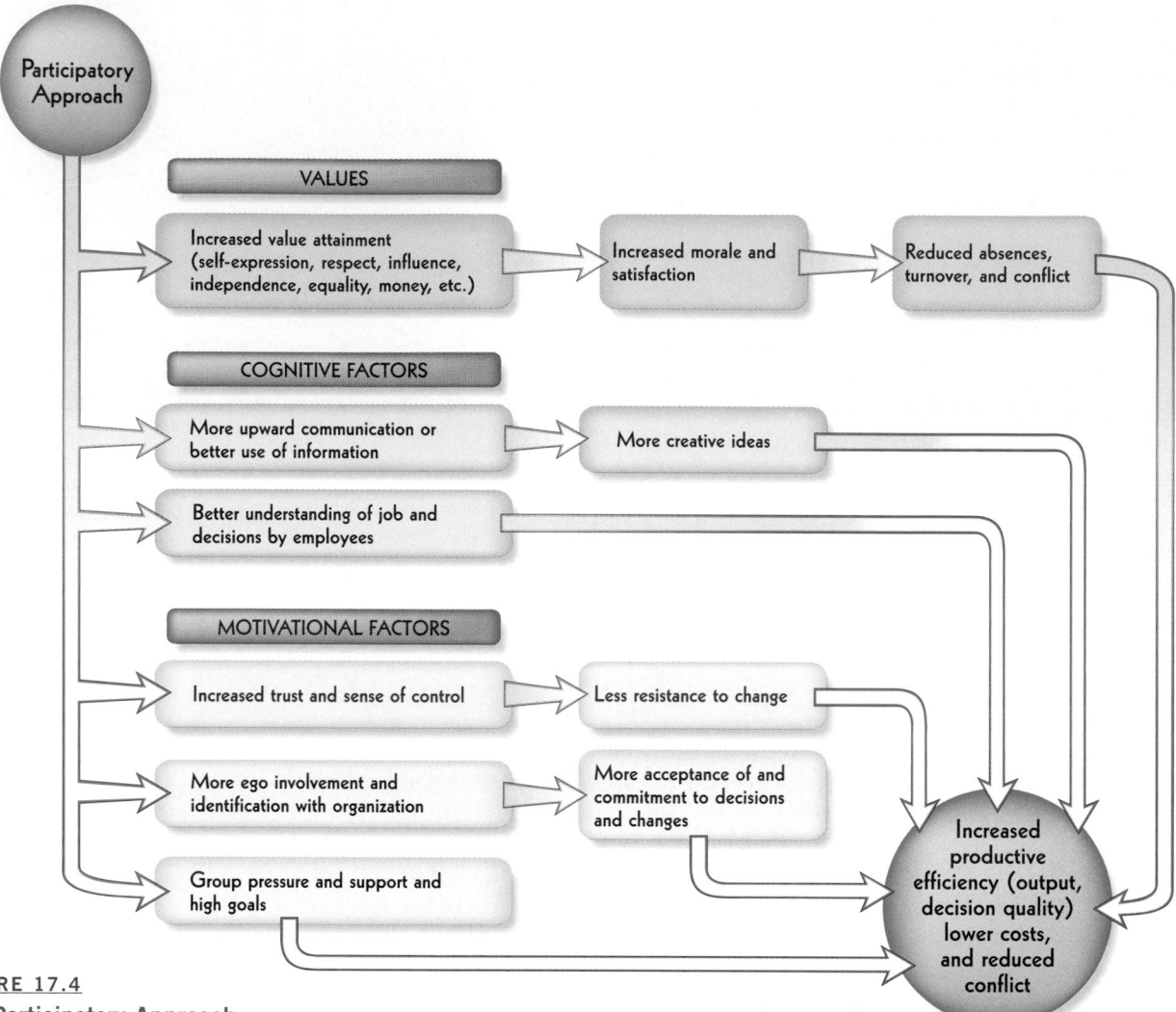

**FIGURE 17.4**
**The Participatory Approach to Motivation Leads to Increased Work Effectiveness**

There are probably more sources of job satisfaction than can be listed here, but they cluster in five basic categories: the work itself, the perceived rewards of the work, the quality of supervision, the support of co-workers, and the work setting. These categories, with examples of each, are presented in Table 17.1. The overall level of satisfaction depends on the extent to which people feel that their expectations for satisfaction are matched by their actual feelings of satisfaction.

Pay and benefits have an impact on job satisfaction, to be sure. But workplace support and feelings about the work environment have an even greater impact. A person's dispositions—his or her personality—also affect job satisfaction. Mood and emotions experienced at work affect job satisfaction. The key here is that a mood, a bad day, a difficult challenge, or a disagreeable co-worker may—but also may not—affect a person's job satisfaction. Moods and emotions at work are not equated with job satisfaction (Brief & Weiss, 2002). Stephanie Cote and Laura Morgan (2002) at the University of Toronto suggest that emotional regulation is also important in determining job satisfaction. Individuals who suppress negative emotions have low job satisfaction and are more likely to quit.

One potential way to maximize and foster job satisfaction is having people work in teams. Today, more than ever before, companies are relying on teams of workers to accomplish complex tasks. Surprisingly, as teamwork has increased, research on what makes a good team, how teams work, and how to best use teams

| TABLE 17.1 | Key Factors Related to Job Satisfaction |
| --- | --- |
| **Area** | **Factors** |
| The work itself | The work is interesting. |
| | The work is perceived to be challenging. |
| | There are opportunities to apply one's own judgment. |
| | There is some degree of autonomy. |
| Perceived rewards | There is adequate recognition. |
| | The pay is adequate and equitable. |
| | The work contributes to self-esteem and self-efficacy. |
| | There are opportunities for advancement. |
| Quality of supervision | Supervisors offer encouragement, support, and help (Huebner, 1994). |
| Support from co-workers | There are opportunities to interact socially and in teams. |
| | Co-workers are supportive and compatible. |
| The work setting | There is job security. |
| | The work environment is viewed positively (it is seen as pleasant, attractive, and comfortable). |
| | There are opportunities to influence company policy and procedures. |
| | Adequate information and equipment are available. |

has decreased (Ilgen, 1999). Teams are groups of two or more people who work interdependently toward some common goal. The idea behind teams is that many tasks cannot be accomplished by a single person but require the skills and abilities of more than one person (Cannon-Bowers & Salas, 1998). When teams are put together carefully, job satisfaction is bound to increase. Workers enjoy collaborating with their colleagues toward a shared goal. Identifying the shared goals—such as developing the best precision-drilling-systems device—and setting up the teams often require the leadership that comes from managers.

## LEADERSHIP

The Borg, in the popular television series *Star Trek*, tells its enemies that "resistance is futile." The Borg tries not to lead, but to dominate. In organizations large and small leaders try to persuade, encourage, and inspire. They try to build cohesion and goal-oriented teamwork. In every organization, some individuals emerge as *leaders*—people who influence other people's behaviour toward the attainment of agreed-upon goals. But there is no "right" type of leader; in fact, leadership styles fluctuate widely in popularity from autocratic leaders who might say "My way or the highway" to leaders who are democratic and might say "Let's decide this together."

Informal leaders may emerge spontaneously in any group, or higher management may choose them formally. Leaders are expected to help further the purposes of their organization. Thus, one of their primary roles is to persuade and motivate employees to perform at a high level. It is important to note, however, that not all managers are leaders; nor are all leaders managers. What makes for truly effective leadership is thus important but not clearly understood, so it should be no surprise that I/O psychologists have studied it intensively.

In some ways we all know a great deal about leadership; in other ways, we can see daily that our national leaders are often quite fallible, make mistakes, and fail to lead effectively. Can we choose a good leader? Can we forecast leadership? Why do some leaders succeed and others fail? The study of leadership has gone through three major phases, each with a characteristic focus: traits, behaviours, or situations. The right combination of these elements ultimately describes an effective leader.

▲ The Governor General, Her Excellency the Right Honourable Adrienne Clarkson, has many of the characteristics of a strong leader.

**TRAIT THEORIES OF LEADERSHIP.** The specific personality traits of individual organizational leaders were studied intensively in the early 1950s and are receiving increased attention again. This research tries to isolate the characteristics that make individuals good or poor leaders (Northouse, 2001); for example, are good leaders intelligent, self-confident, determined, sociable, and capable of demonstrating integrity? However, the trait approach troubles some researchers. Leaders cannot be universally characterized by traits such as assertiveness, self-confidence, or drive. Many business leaders are assertive, but many others are not. In fact, individual differences among leaders are extreme. Although an individual leader's personality traits will tell psychologists something about leadership, the differences among leaders tend to be greater than the similarities. One reason that studies are unable to find a common denominator is that each leader and each organization has different goals. For example, results from a recent study conducted at the Royal Military College of Canada (Bradley et al., 2002) suggest that in the military good leaders are dominant and have high levels of energy and a strong internal locus of control. In contrast, researchers recognize that a key, and sometimes defining, trait of effective business leaders is *flexibility*—the ability to adapt to a rapidly changing workplace, organization, and global economy. Other key traits are intelligence, maturity, inner motivation, and being employee-focused.

**LEADERSHIP BEHAVIOURS.** Another focus of research in leadership is specific leadership behaviours. Many research studies try to find characteristic ways in which leaders interact with other members of their organizations. Whether a leader is employee-oriented or task-oriented has to do with how the leader chooses to influence behaviour. An employee-oriented leader acts so as to maintain and enhance individual employees' feelings of self-worth or self-esteem. Such leaders try to empower employees and co-workers and make them feel valued and important. A task-oriented leader focuses on getting the job done efficiently and quickly, with as little effort as possible.

Leadership styles are sometimes related to gender, with women being more employee-oriented and men being more task-oriented (Eagly & Johnson, 1990). Recent studies show that the gender of the leader and of the followers has other important effects. For example, female leaders or managers tend to be evaluated as positively as their male counterparts. However, when they behave in stereotypically male ways, they are devalued—especially if the evaluators are men (Eagly, Makhijani, & Klonsky, 1992).

Further research has confirmed that behavioural differences among leaders are great and that a leader's behaviour is determined by personal traits, by overall orientation (employee or task), and sometimes by the group of people being led. Some groups of individuals have characteristics that demand an employee orientation on the leader's part. For example, an underpaid, overworked, but dedicated social worker may have a great need for self-esteem, feel that his work is worthwhile, but also know that he is underpaid. A supervisor must motivate this person not with authoritarian task-oriented directions but with concern for his need for self-worth. Highly paid executives, however, may be more easily motivated by a task-oriented approach, because they recognize that their salaries reflect their higher levels of creativity and productivity. Job performance, job satisfaction, and the way a worker is treated are closely related. In motivating workers, leaders must consider their own personal traits, the various possible behaviours they might use to influence others, and the conditions in which they and their co-workers work.

**SITUATIONAL LEADERSHIP THEORY.** Many researchers have shifted from investigating leader behaviour to investigating the *situations* in which these behaviours are performed. Some situations lend themselves to leadership, and even to specific forms of leadership; others call for little leadership. Thus, a warm, friendly, employee-oriented leader (or supervisor) is generally very useful for a group of service workers. But if the organization encounters financial trouble and its workers must be laid off, with the supervisor having no control over who is let go, the climate of uncertainty may undermine the usefulness of the warm and friendly approach. To continue functioning, the organization then may have to find a task-oriented leader who is trusted for his or her integrity and fairness.

**THEORIES OF LEADERSHIP EFFECTIVENESS.** A number of interacting factors determine the most effective style of leadership for a given situation. Effective leaders may simply be those who are best at perceiving the current goals and needs of their organization and fitting their style to those needs. A major theory that accounts for leadership effectiveness is *Vroom's leadership model.*

Victor Vroom and his colleagues Phillip Yetton and Arthur Jago focused on the various ways in which leaders may make decisions in organizations. As part of this leader-participation model, Vroom created a flowchart for determining the amount of advice a leader should seek, depending on the task to be accomplished. A leader can make an authoritarian decision and simply announce it; a leader can present a problem, solicit advice, and then make the final decision; or a leader can allow other people to make the decision. As a leader's use of authority increases, the freedom of others in the group decreases. That is, when a manager makes a decision and announces it, subordinates and co-workers have little freedom of choice; this style of leadership is called *boss-centred* (Vroom, 1974; Vroom & Jago, 1995; Vroom & Yetton, 1973). According to Vroom's leadership model, each time a decision is to be made, managers can ask themselves a series of questions to arrive at the best possible leadership approach for the situation. For example, a prototypical question is "Is the quality of the final result important?" (The answer had better be yes!)

The strength of Vroom's model is that it recognizes that leaders have options—that they can choose how to behave in light of their previous experiences and knowledge and the current situation or conditions (Vroom, 1997). Vroom's model has received some research support, but its practical implications in the workplace have not been evaluated systematically. It emphasizes the important role of situational variables in determining which leadership approach is most appropriate at any given time.

**TRANSFORMATIONAL LEADERSHIP.** If one person took an organization or company and provided it with direction, a new vision, and a sense of purpose, that person would be considered a first-rate leader. Such leaders are hard to find, but occasionally someone emerges who is considered to be charismatic, having extraordinary effects on followers. These leaders are often called **transformational leaders;** they provide inspiration, intellectual stimulation, and individual care to followers and are able to draw extra creativity and effort out of organization members (Bass, 1985, 1990, 1997). Often such individuals do not have formal authority based on their position; because of their personality, style, and interpersonal skills, however, they seem to be able to influence and empower others. Transformational leaders have a strong sense of moral purpose, have an aura of authority and dignity, and define people's roles in terms of their own ideological values. Such leaders often have a strong vision, use unconventional techniques or ideas to frame their vision for the future, and communicate extreme confidence in their own abilities to lead and solve problems. Pierre Trudeau was a transformational leader. He was prime minister of Canada, led the country through good and bad times, never lacked confidence, and always inspired commitment and loyalty in his followers.

Transformational leaders often take advantage of organizational weaknesses and create opportunities to recreate, or transform, an organization and its employees or constituents. Such leaders are often able to create a willingness on the part of

**TRANSFORMATIONAL LEADER**
A charismatic leader who inspires and provides intellectual stimulation to recreate an organization.

▲ Pierre Elliott Trudeau was a transformational leader who acted daringly and decisively and was an empowering inspiration to others.

employees to go along with their ideas and a reluctance to criticize their ideas or them by creating situations that allow them to be seen as charismatic—such individuals can manage impressions well (Gardner & Avolio, 1998). A transformational leader inspires followers to rank organizational goals above self-interest. Some researchers assert that charisma isn't needed but that transformational leaders can be effective using inspiration, intellectual stimulation, and individual consideration (Barbuto, 1997). With such leadership, the members of an organization adopt new values, ideas, and ways of operating (Sosik, Kahai, & Avolio, 1998). When new values are adopted, new levels of performance are often expected. Many feel that transformational leaders are born, not made, and are individually unique. Bernard Bass (2001) asserts that the unique combination of three types of intelligence—cognitive, social, and emotional—contributes to transformational leadership. In the end, we still are not sure that transformational skills can be learned.

**WHAT CONSTITUTES EFFECTIVE LEADERSHIP?**   Psychologists' knowledge of how people influence and manage others has grown dramatically. Researchers now know that effective leadership depends not only on personal traits and specific techniques or behaviours, but also on the situation. Workers may exaggerate a boss's leadership effectiveness if they are productive and happy (Shamir, 1992). Thus, leadership, workers' perceptions of leadership, and motivation are interrelated.

Although the research is complex and not unanimous, several ideas are widely agreed on (Bass, 1998; McGill & Slocum, 1998; Ross & Offermann, 1997). To be an effective leader, follow these guidelines:

- Know the job, and be practical in decision making.
- Be an active leader—passive leadership is not effective.
- Set up effective personnel selection policies—good selection procedures help establish a favourable working situation.
- Act in ways consistent with the organization's vision—this builds a strong organization.
- Foster listening among all levels of employees.
- Create an organization that allows for choices.
- Be sensitive to worker motivation, satisfaction, and performance—be nurturing.

Through carefully conducted I/O research, psychologists can help organizations more effectively meet their goals by seeking out effective leaders who can persuade, motivate, build confidence, and create a better workplace with more satisfied workers and stockholders (Hogan, Curphy, & Hogan, 1994).

## Human Factors and Ergonomics

When those of us old enough to remember what banking was like before automated teller machines stand at an ATM, we often recall how frustrating it was to wait in line for 10 minutes to see a teller. At first, banks designed more efficient, roped-off waiting "stream" lines and even electronic client directing systems. Now we can bank at our convenience through a machine. In addition, by phone or Internet we can check our balance, move money between accounts, and pay bills—all rather easily. Applied psychologists who study human factors have played an important role in streamlining banking experiences as

**Be an ACTIVE LEARNER**

**REVIEW**
> Discuss the focus and scope of the work of an I/O psychologist. pp. 612–613
> What is a job analysis? pp. 613–614
> What are the goals of selection procedures in human resources departments? p. 614
> What are performance appraisals? pp. 617–619
> Describe the elements of transformational leadership. p. 627

**THINK CRITICALLY**
> Ability, effort, *and* role perceptions are supposed to be the key variables that determine job performance. Can you think of any others?
> If you were the boss of a corporation, how would you determine workplace dress codes? Why?
> In what ways might a company benefit from assigning employees to work in teams rather than independently?
> If you became a transformational leader, would you have to create a "new" organization, that is, redefine the current one from scratch?

**APPLY PSYCHOLOGY**
> Imagine you have been assigned to develop a training manual to help employees learn about a particular company's culture and ways of operating. Write a paragraph to motivate employees to become part of the company culture.
> If you were the head of human resources and had to choose a new corporate president, do you think you would choose someone very different from one whom stockholders, who are concerned about profits, would choose? Why or why not?

well as many other day-to-day routines. Donald Norman, a psychologist who has studied applied issues, wrote a best-selling book that is worth a look: *Design of Everyday Things* (1990). Entertaining and enlightening reading, it focuses on how clever machines are making life easier.

**Human factors** is the study of the relationship of human beings to machines and to workplaces and other environments. A human factors psychologist might focus on the creation of health-care products for use by the handicapped, on the design of cooking utensils or educational products, on the interaction of cellphone use and driving, or on the interaction of robots and people. The photos below show various controls that adjust automobile seats. As you can see, not all are equally well designed. From a human factors view, the controls in photo (b) are the most effective; those in photo (d) are the least effective. Most human factors research focuses on the work environment, especially in the areas of efficiency and safety.

## EFFICIENCY

In the work environment, researchers have examined workers' ability to operate machines effectively. Much of this research centres on **ergonomics**—the study of the fit between human anatomy or physiology, the demands of a particular task or piece of equipment, and the environment in which the task occurs. Human factors researchers seek to develop person–machine interfaces that minimize frustration and errors, maximize output, and are reliable. Such researchers have focused on studying machines and interfaces to ensure that speed and accuracy of work are optimized and that workplaces minimize fatigue and stress (Westgaard, 2000).

A key difference between a human factors researcher and an I/O psychologist is that the I/O researcher might examine what can be done to the human being to change his or her behaviour to improve efficiency. A human factors researcher, on the other hand, will look at what can be changed about the machine, computer, or interface. It is often easier to change a machine than to change a human being!

In the early part of the twentieth century, working with machinery meant reading dials, turning wheels, and lifting equipment. Today, working with machinery often means operating a computer, monitoring computer-controlled devices, programming equipment, and working in teams with other highly skilled employees. If equipment is to be properly controlled, dials, computer screens, and display devices have to be designed to minimize errors. For example, a pilot must be able to read a computer screen accurately, under all possible conditions, in order to land a plane safely; a nuclear power plant operator must be able to read the temperature of nuclear devices. Computer displays are everywhere. You often type at a computer, pay a restaurant cheque at a computer-controlled cash register, and bank at ATMs. Well-designed machines and computer interfaces minimize errors; but the ability to create good interfaces depends on knowledge of how human beings see, manipulate, and interact with the machine. This means studying

▼ Not all automobile seat adjusters are equally well designed.

**(a)**

**(b)**

**(c)**

**(d)**

perception, human information processing, and complex decision making (Sommerich, Joines, and Psihogios, 2001). The ATM is an example of an interface that has been studied well by human factors researchers. Most banks have ATMs that are easy to operate. However, the ATM at a bank next door may have a confusing, gaudy interface, and many users can be observed to kick the machine, curse, and lose their cards. Usually the human factors psychologist can take the credit for a well-designed interface that minimizes errors, confusion, and angry customers.

Many jobs are complex and require advanced technology. In industries such as auto manufacturing, for instance, robotic equipment has been programmed to do many tasks that human beings once did. These devices must be designed effectively to duplicate the abilities of human beings. Much of the work of robotics engineers is dedicated to making sure that robots are both effective and safe.

Even the tools of carpenters, tailors, and technicians can be designed using the principles of human factors. For example, what is the best weight for a hammer? How tall should a drill press be? Today, computer keyboards have been designed to be easy to type on, to minimize typing errors, and to reduce carpal tunnel syndrome. The human factors psychologists who design such keyboards try to meet the important human factors considerations of accuracy, productivity, and safety.

## BEHAVIOUR-BASED SAFETY

The goal of any safety practice is injury prevention. In *behaviour-based safety*, effective safety management refers to a wide range of programs that focus on changing the behaviour of workers *and* companies to prevent occupational injuries and illnesses. A good safety culture within a company minimizes shortcuts and rule violations, encourages open communication among workers and management, and thus reduces the probability of on-the-job injuries. In fact, the failure of employees and management to communicate about safety issues is in itself a safety issue—safety is more than just common sense, and it is more than just a way to shift responsibility to workers alone (Geller, 2001a, 2001b).

Geller (2001c) argues that corporations must develop cultures that value and reinforce safety; that safety has to be part of the work ethic; that it is a process of continuous development; and that companies must develop a total safety culture. Human factors research can contribute to making work environments not only efficient but also safe. Many industrial accidents occur despite attempts to protect workers' safety; human factors research can help reduce accidents through design improvements. Human factors psychologists can also help estimate how quickly people become fatigued and then can design work schedules that optimize the safe use of potentially dangerous equipment. Such psychologists can help promote safety through programs that improve people's attitudes about safety and therefore promote safer work behaviour. Only when workers believe that the company values their safety are they likely to make safety-promoting changes.

It is often easier to design a safe, or nearly safe, work environment than to influence workers to work safely. Researchers classify efforts to design safe work environments into three categories (Sanders & McCormick, 1993): *exclusion designs* make it impossible for a specific error to occur; *prevention designs* make it difficult though not impossible for an error to happen; *fail-safe designs* do not reduce the likelihood of an accident, but do lessen its consequences should it occur. For a nuclear power plant, human factors psychologists might develop prevention designs that greatly decrease the likelihood of a nuclear accident (or so they hope). In efforts to ensure safe work environments, the federal government has enacted the Occupational Safety and Health Act (OSHA), which establishes standards for health and safety in the workplace. These standards function as prevention designs. Workers must accept safety standards before they can be effective, and the government really does not have adequate staff to regulate, enforce, or inspect all places of business. Since OSHA was enacted, however, the death rate from workplace accidents has been cut in half.

Research in several other subdisciplines in psychology has also helped establish and maintain workplace safety. *Perceptual research* investigates topics such as which light levels are appropriate for reading computer screens. Which colour is most visible in the dark? (Yellow.) Is it easier to see white letters on a dark background, or the reverse? (White letters on dark backgrounds are easier.) *Environmental research* (which we'll examine in more detail later) has focused on variables such as temperature and noise. When the temperature or noise level is too high, performance decreases. Moderate temperatures and noise levels improve both efficiency and safety. Warnings, labels, and compliance techniques are also helpful in establishing safety. Environmental research reveals that signs and warnings help motivate people to follow regulations. Specific instructions for a specific user—for example, using that person's name as part of the instructions—work better still. Labels are especially effective when the user has to remove a warning label before using a machine (Duffy, Kalsher, & Wogalter, 1993). Even if people are given specific warnings about equipment safety and clear directions, incentives and proper reinforcements boost compliance; this is the domain of learning and social psychologists, who study how reinforcements and social influence can be used to induce worthwhile and helpful behaviours

**Be an ACTIVE LEARNER**

**REVIEW**
> What does "human factors" mean? p. 629
> What is the most effective approach for ensuring that people will take safety precautions? p. 630
> What steps can a company or a management team take to help ensure the safety of employees? pp. 630–631

**THINK CRITICALLY**
> What might community organizations do to facilitate the health, safety, and effectiveness of shift workers?

**APPLY PSYCHOLOGY**
> Imagine you are the boss of a company that is developing safety manuals to help employees learn to operate machinery safely. Write a paragraph to motivate an employee to become part of a safety team.
> If you were designing a new kind of scanner at a supermarket checkout, what would you do to make it efficient *and* accurate?

## Psychology and the Law

In the workplace, as elsewhere, the laws that govern society help regulate both public and private behaviour. Among other things, laws determine how people make fair hiring or firing decisions and how old individuals have to be to work in the first place. To some extent, laws determine whom people can marry and when. People's thoughts and behaviours shape laws, and laws in turn shape people's behaviours; there is a reciprocal relationship in which each affects the other. The interface between the law and psychology is thus as complex as are people and the legal system.

The interaction between the fields of psychology and law has greatly increased over the past few decades in overlapping areas. *Legal psychology* is the field that conducts empirical research on psychological issues important to the legal system, such as eyewitness accuracy, police selection, decision making by juries, and legal assumptions about human behaviour relevant to the rights of defendants, victims, children, and mental patients. *Forensic psychology* focuses on legally relevant clinical areas where psychologists act as expert witnesses and consultants, as in the insanity defence, competency to stand trial, and commitment to mental hospitals. Forensic psychologists might help a judge decide which parent should have custody of the children or evaluate the victim of an accident to determine if he or she endured psychological or neurological damage. In criminal cases, forensic psychologists might evaluate a defendant's mental competence to stand trial. Some forensic psychologists counsel inmates; others counsel the victims of crimes and help them prepare to testify, cope with emotional distress, and resume their normal activities. *Psychological jurisprudence* is the study of efforts to develop a philosophy of law and justice based on psychological values.

As discussed further in *Psychology in Action*, psychologists play several roles in the legal system: researchers, policy or program

▼ Psychologists often serve as expert witnesses in court.

## The Law and I/O Psychology—A Dynamic Tension

The Canadian Charter of Rights and Freedoms holds that it is illegal to discriminate against individuals or groups of people on the basis of race, gender, or disability. Systematic discrimination is said to occur when any group or groups protected under the Charter are adversely affected by employment practices (Cronshaw, 1991). Supreme Court of Canada decisions have taken this further (*Bhinder v. CN Rail*, 1985; *Ontario Human Rights Commission and O'Malley v. Simpson-Sears*, 1985), indicating that these provisions apply not only to direct discrimination (for example, refusal to hire someone because she is a woman) but also to indirect discrimination (for example, the establishment of or a change in business practices that unintentionally adversely affects a protected group, such as the way Sunday store openings might affect persons with particular religious views). At a minimum, employers are required to demonstrate that their hiring and job performance criteria reflect bona fide occupational qualifications (BFOQs). It should come as no surprise that I/O psychologists are often called in to ensure that the guidelines used to select and promote employees are based on truly job-related knowledge and skills, or BFOQs.

I/O psychologists may be hired as expert witnesses by individuals who file suit against employers; in this capacity, they help the aggrieved individuals establish that employers engaged in bias, discrimination, and/or unfair practices. They sometimes assert that the validity of a particular employment criterion (such as attractiveness and youthfulness for flight attendants) is questionable. Of course, employers hire their own expert witnesses. In court, these I/O psychologists testify to the validity, reliability, and predictability of various tests and selection procedures.

In addition to concern over direct and indirect discrimination, the Supreme Court rulings also require that employers make reasonable accommodations for employees who have disabilities but are otherwise qualified to perform various jobs. That is, for potential or current employees who may fall short of a job requirement that has been properly identified as a BFOQ, employers may be expected to try to make accommodations in order to make the job more accessible. This can be a simple matter of making the office and equipment (for example, desks) wheelchair accessible or it can be a more complex issue. As expert witnesses in these legal cases, I/O psychologists help the courts answer questions like these: What exactly is a disability? (Is an employee with attention deficit/hyperactivity disorder (ADHD) "disabled"?) What exactly is a reasonable accommodation? (Should such an employee be given extended deadlines?) What tests should be used to decide whether an employee is disabled? (Who says the employee has ADHD? Is he or she "self-diagnosed"?) What if psychologists and medical doctors disagree about a person's disability?

Psychologists who are willing and qualified to act as expert witnesses are also in high demand. There is a dynamic and healthy tension between the law and psychology—with lawyers wanting psychologists to be more precise and psychologists wanting lawyers to show that they understand the complexity of human functioning. Psychological science has much to offer individuals, employers, and the courts. Like medical diagnoses, legal judgments are sometimes less precise than either employers or employees would like. With each passing year, however, psychological research is helping to sharpen the decision-making rules and to bring legal criteria into focus.

evaluators, advocates, and expert witnesses. As an area of research, psychology and law is concerned both with looking at legal issues from a psychological perspective (for example, how juries decide cases) and with looking at psychological questions in a legal context (for example, how jurors assign blame or responsibility for a crime). As *researchers*, psychologists help determine why individuals behave in ways that are unacceptable to society. For instance, psychologists do basic research on intelligence, personality, mathematical ability, and the role of genetics in determining aggressiveness, to name just a few areas. This basic research often helps solve some very practical problems. For example, some psychologists develop tests to determine who is mentally ill and who is capable of standing trial, as well as tests to evaluate truthfulness and integrity among defendants and witnesses. Other psychologists look for the causes of aggressiveness in order to develop programs to avert it among accused criminals and to help convicted criminals channel their aggressive energy productively.

Psychologists often serve as *policy or program evaluators*, who help governments and other institutions determine whether various policies, agencies, or programs actually work. For example, psychologists interpret what remedial education has accomplished and whether IQ testing has been valid. When legislators wonder whether early intervention programs (designed to assist children in "at risk" family settings) are making a difference, they turn to psychologists. When new laws calling for equal educational opportunities for the handicapped were being considered, lawyers and judges turned to psychologists for insight into how well various programs might work.

Psychologists are also often asked to be *advocates* for individuals and society, helping to shape social policy in such areas as minority, remedial, and gifted education. When provincial and federal governments seek to trim budgets of social programs affecting children, they turn to psychologists to ascertain what the impact for the future might be. Boards of education consult psychologists to determine how best to assist exceptional students. Psychologists advise government agencies at all levels on how to help those who suffer post-traumatic stress after a flood, ice storm, or other disaster and on how to respond more effectively to such disasters in the future.

Finally, psychologists often serve as *expert witnesses*, bringing their knowledge to the courts as consultants. They do not try to address legal issues directly or to make the ultimate decisions for the courts. Psychologists help the courts in their area of competence—psychology. Psychologists often have been asked to determine who is a good eyewitness (we examined this topic in Chapter 6). They also address specific questions like these: Is this person insane? What are the implications of a divorce on this child? Is this person competent to stand trial?

Psychologists can help determine whether there was any link between a person's mental state or problem and a crime that occurred. From a legal standpoint, a person who deliberately plans a crime is more accountable than one who commits one accidentally. In many jurisdictions, when an accused person is convicted of a serious crime, a jury can judge the person "guilty, but mentally ill." This verdict is seen by many as a reasonable alternative because it reduces the frequency of findings of "not guilty by reason of insanity" (which many find unsatisfying), encourages treatment for the seriously mentally ill, and takes a potentially dangerous offender off the street.

There is, of course, an uneasy alliance between the legal and the psychological professions (Melton et al., 1987). Lawyers assert that psychology is an inexact, or "fuzzy," science and that psychologists should not be allowed to testify as expert witnesses. Psychologists argue that lawyers always want simple answers to complicated human questions and insist on seeking facts even when theories may best describe the truth. In the area of child custody, for example, psychologists are asked to testify in a divorce settlement as to who would be the best custodian of the children and what the psychological consequences of living with one parent or the other will be for a child. But because the legal system is adversarial, each side is likely to have a psychologist testifying that the children will do best with the parent who hired him or her. In fact, there may be no right or wrong answer in some cases. Answers to various legal questions are not usually clear or definitive. One exception to this general observation is the increased use of DNA samples. Increasingly, forensic psychologists are using a fairly exact method for identifying the perpetrators of crimes. The use of DNA in forensic psychology is discussed in *Brain and Behaviour*.

## Forensic Psychology—DNA and the Law

In a small town in Ontario in October 1998, a teenager was attacked, brutally beaten, and violently and repeatedly raped. There was no suspect; there were no leads. In the fall of 2001, the Centre of Forensic Sciences in Toronto contacted the regional police; the Centre had a match between the 1998 crime profile and a recently submitted convicted offender profile. The police had the evidence they needed. The man pleaded guilty to the 1998 attack and was sentenced to five years in jail. The crime-solving power of DNA technology provided the evidence necessary to capture and convict this predator.

DNA, or deoxyribonucleic acid, is the primary building block of an individual's genetic makeup. Testing can establish the identity of the person from whom cellular material is taken. DNA is contained in blood, semen, skin cells, tissue, organs, muscle, brain cells, bone, teeth, hair, saliva, mucus, perspiration, and fingernails, among other things. DNA analysis is a powerful tool because every person's DNA is different from every other individual's. DNA analysis can be likened to fingerprint analysis. If enough of the identifying features are the same between the DNA of a suspect and some evidence found on an injured person or at the scene of a crime, the DNA fingerprint is determined to be a match.

Today, police and Crown attorneys are preserving biological evidence from crime scenes such as hairs and mucus to prove a defendant's guilt. Police and prosecutors routinely take into account evidence that may rely on DNA. Thus, for example, the saliva on the stamp of a letter containing anthrax could be compared with a potential perpetrator's saliva sample at a later date. The Criminal Code of Canada requires that offenders provide a biological sample for analysis and entry into the Data Bank's Convicted Offender Index. These data are then entered into a database system known as CODIS (Combined DNA Index System). CODIS (developed by the FBI and U.S. Department of Justice) links forensic laboratories across Canada and around the world. This DNA index of individuals is a database of universally recognized, standardized DNA profiles that can be accessed by law enforcement officers worldwide and used to cross-reference DNA evidence obtained at the scene of the crime.

The National DNA Data Bank is giving investigators much needed evidence for current as well as stale investigations, helping to solve violent crime. Importantly, such DNA data are also being used to exonerate innocent prisoners for crimes they did not commit. David Milgaard and Guy Paul Morin are two such individuals. Convicted in 1969 for the rape and murder of Gail Miller in Saskatoon, Saskatchewan, Milgaard maintained his innocence throughout his incarceration. Based on fresh evidence, Milgaard was released in 1992 and cleared by DNA evidence in 1997. He was awarded $10 million for his wrongful conviction. Guy Paul Morin was sentenced to life in prison in 1992 for the murder of nine-year-old Christine Jessop in Queensville, Ontario. It was not until 1995 that sophisticated DNA testing exonerated Morin and he was released from prison. He received a $1.25 million settlement for his wrongful conviction.

# Environmental Psychology

In a small community near Calgary, a rainstorm caused a sewage holding pond to overflow into the local water system and into a small lake nearby. Children occasionally swim in this lake, and people regularly catch fish there. The reaction of the neighbourhood was swift; people became alarmed about their health and welfare. Signs went up warning people to stay away from the lake. The phone lines hummed, the press was brought in, and the local environmental control agency sprang into action. In the end, the spill turned out to be very localized, the levels of toxins were low, and no one was hurt. From an applied psychologist's point of view, however, the mobilization of the residents in the neighbourhood was classic. People became empowered, discussions ensued, and people were energized. Individuals who had never met one another started sharing ideas, and people who had never given much thought to sewage treatment systems became knowledgeable and outspoken on the subject.

A particular group of applied psychologists, known as environmental psychologists, study how physical settings such as people's homes and neighbourhoods affect behaviour. They are interested in issues such as the effects of crowding, how personal space can be changed to meet changing needs, and group reactions to environmental threats. These psychologists examine not only whole neigh-bourhoods but also smaller groups. **Environmental psychology** is the study of how physical settings affect human behaviour and how people change their environment, often to make it more comfortable and acceptable. Environmental psychologists focus on human interactions with the environment; they recognize that people are affected by the environment in which they live, work, and play and that the environment is affected by human behaviour. To better understand the impact of environmental psychology, you might want to look at the work of University of Victoria's Robert Gifford (2002). He has researched ways in which urban living and design, learning, response to hazardous situations, the media, and so on have been positively affected by applied environmental psychology. Today, the field of environmental psychology has expanded to embrace the idea that human beings affect and to a great extent can control environmental quality for future generations. Behavioural interventions are now being designed to preserve and protect the environment (e.g., Dwyer et al., 1993; Porter, Leeming, & Dwyer, 1995). Because of the large number of variables that enter into studies in environmental psychology, the field has become multidisciplinary, encompassing research from many other fields, such as architecture, geography, and sociology (Stokols, 1995).

Environmental psychologists often conduct studies and consult for institutions, such as governments, schools, hospitals, churches, and museums. For example, consider the design of a nursing station in a hospital. The station is the centre of activity on each floor, and in traditional hospital floor plans it usually is placed at the junction of two long corridors. An alternative is to place it at the hub of a wheel-like arrangement of rooms (a radial design). Most of the patient rooms then will be closer to the nursing station, and nurses can reach them faster and more efficiently. When Trites and his colleagues (1970) investigated worker satisfaction with different hospital designs, they found a distinct preference for the radial design. That result led to the redesign of many hospital floors with positive results (Ittelson & O'Hanlon, 1976; Proshansky & O'Hanlon, 1977). The work space of a hospital or any semi-public space is crucial. When museums are redesigned to allow for great interactivity, multisensory stimulation, and dynamic displays, visitors are more immersed in exhibits—again, design affects how people use and appreciate space (Harvey et al., 1998).

▲ Environmental psychology is the study of how physical settings affect human behaviour. Environmental psychologists are interested in issues such as group reactions to environmental threats.

**ENVIRONMENTAL PSYCHOLOGY**

The study of how physical settings affect human behaviour and how people change their environment.

## ENVIRONMENTAL VARIABLES

The environment includes not only the shape of a building, the layout of a hospital floor or a dormitory, or the arrangement of buildings in a housing development or shopping mall. It also includes variables such as furniture and fixtures, climate, noise level, and the number of people per square metre. Environmental psychologists study the relationships among many variables. Whether a room is perceived as crowded, for example, depends not only on the number of people in it but also on the room's size and shape, furniture layout, ceiling height, number of windows, wall colours, and lighting—as well as on the time of day (Devlin, 1992). Researchers who look at global environmental systems such as cities, communities, and neighbourhoods must consider all of these variables and more. Three of the environmental variables that are easiest to control in order to promote people's well-being are temperature, noise, and environmental toxins.

**TEMPERATURE.**   Very hot or very cold climates can cause behavioural effects that range from annoyance to inability to function. Construction workers in Canada's

North, for example, would never survive the winter without proper shelter, heating, and warm clothes; workers in the southern United States would be far less productive without air conditioning during the summer and in particular areas would not survive without proper shelter and water.

Environmental variables that impair work performance are considered to be stressors. As we saw in Chapter 14, a **stressor** is a stimulus that affects an organism in physically or psychologically injurious ways and usually elicits feelings such as anxiety, tension, and physiological arousal. Temperature can be a stressor that affects many behaviours, including academic performance, driving an automobile, and being attracted to others. In general, performance is optimal at moderate temperatures and becomes progressively worse at high or low temperatures.

When the temperature rises and people become uncomfortable, they are more likely to make risky decisions and to behave erratically and less likely to be accurate (Kudoh et al., 1991). Research shows that as temperature rises (up to a point where *any* activity is too much given the heat), aggressive feelings and aggression increase (Anderson, Anderson, & Deuser, 1996). In hotter regions of the world, people show more aggression; hotter years, months, and days all have been associated with more aggressive behaviours, such as murders, riots, and spouse abuse (Anderson, 1989). Laboratory research on temperature can never be identical to situations in a real-life setting; therefore, ongoing field-based work is likely to provide better evidence about the exact nature of a relationship between heat and aggression (Anderson & Anderson, 1998; Anderson & DeNeve, 1992).

**NOISE.**   Another environmental variable that often affects human behaviour is *noise*—unwanted sound. Noise is a stressor that can overstimulate people—they become uncommonly aroused—and often leads to poor work performance and social functioning.

Some noises are almost always present: the buzzing of fluorescent lights, the humming of refrigerators, the banging of doors as they open or close, the chirping of birds, the sounds of moving cars, and the murmur of people talking. Although some of these sounds may be unwanted, they are usually not too disruptive; nor are they stressors. They rarely raise levels of arousal or interfere with daily activities.

However, an unpredictable and intermittent noise of moderate intensity, such as a train whistle, can impair performance on tasks that involve sustained attention or memory. And if noise raises physiological arousal to very high levels, it may impair performance in general and even cause hearing damage (see Chapter 3). Thus, noise acts as a stressor when it interferes with communication, raises physiological arousal, or is so loud that it causes pain. More commonly, noise simply interferes with the ability to concentrate, learn, and remember—thus, it induces stress (Evans, Hygge, & Bullinger, 1995).

**ENVIRONMENTAL TOXINS (POLLUTANTS).**   As you drive into a congested city such as Windsor, Toronto, or Vancouver, it is distressing to see how the skyline is at once beautiful and polluted with airborne toxins. These toxins include an array of chemicals and substances such as carbon monoxide and sulphur that fill the air from automobiles and from the burning of high-sulphur coal and oil in industrial cities. Nearly any airborne substance, whether an industry-based chemical or a naturally occurring substance such as pollen, can trigger respiratory problems and result in deleterious work performance and health consequences. Airborne toxins, which are often deeply breathed and absorbed by the lungs, can impair motor tasks that involve reaction time, as well as affect long-term health; for example, even in cities that meet federal standards for clean air, the risk of premature death is 3 to 8 percent higher than in the cleanest areas.

## CROWDING

Prisons are places where crowding can become a very serious issue, as more and more prisoners are held in a fixed amount of space. A key environmental variable that has a profound impact on individual and group behaviour is simply the number of people that are around. In some situations that involve many people, you may feel closed in and crowded. In other situations, the excitement of a crowd may be exhilarating. It generally is not the size of a space or the number of people that causes you to feel crowded; rather, **crowding** is the *perception* that your space is too limited. Thus, crowding is a psychological state affected by individual and cultural differences. When people feel crowded, their sense of well-being is threatened and day-to-day behaviours are affected (Evans et al., 2000). The Canadian Space Agency is interested in psychological research in the areas of both social psychology and environmental psychology, funding Canadian researchers studying the interaction of multicultural groups as well as the effects of isolation and confinement. Peter Suedfeld and his colleagues (2003; Suedfeld & Steel, 2000) at the University of British Columbia are investigating the effects of extreme and unusual restricted environments on astronauts. Specifically, they have reported on the psychological stresses related to living in encapsulated environments for long durations. These effects include monotony, lack of privacy, and crowding.

▲ Crowding is the perception that personal space is too limited. Thus, crowding is a psychological state.

CROWDING

The perception that one's space is too limited.

**PERSONAL SPACE.** Both social density and spatial density affect crowding. *Social density* is the number of people in a given space; *spatial density* is the amount of space allocated to a fixed number of people. For example, in an empty theatre a person might feel lonely; but in a full, or even half-full, theatre the same person might feel crowded (social density). In contrast, eight people may feel comfortable in a large modern elevator, but the same eight people might feel intolerably cramped in a small old-fashioned elevator (spatial density). Researchers must be careful to separate the variables of social and spatial density (Baum, 1987).

In 1973, Valins and Baum conducted a study on the effects of architectural design in dormitories. The dormitories were of two designs: (1) corridors with long hallways, 2 people per room, 34 people per floor, and a shared bathroom and lounge; or (2) suites, with 4 or 6 students sharing a bathroom and lounge, and several suites per floor (see Figure 17.5). The actual square footage per student was about the same in both types of dormitories, but 67 percent of corridor residents found their living space crowded, compared with only 25 percent of suite residents. Corridor residents reported too many people on their floor and too many unwanted interactions. Valins and Baum (1973) concluded that corridor designs promoted "excessive social interaction and that such interaction is associated with the experience of crowding" (p. 249).

**FIGURE 17.5**

**The Psychological Effects of Architectural Design**

A corridor dorm and a suite have different psychological effects on students, even when actual space per student is about the same. Valins and Baum reported that students living in corridor dorms complained about being crowded more than students living in suites did.
(Based on Valins & Baum, 1973.)

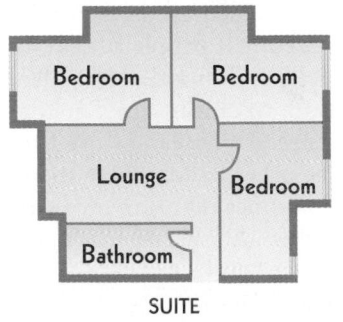

SUITE

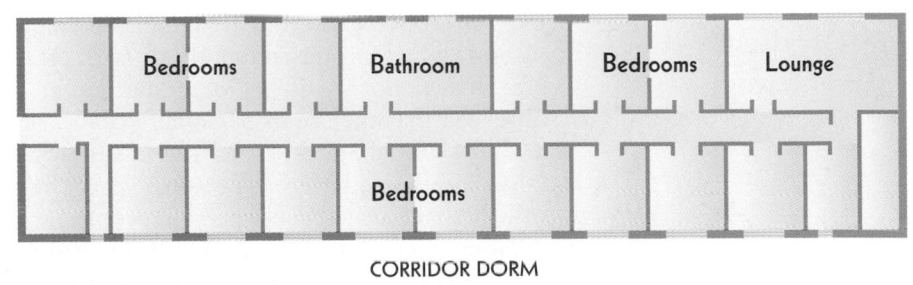

CORRIDOR DORM

If some dormitories produce feelings of crowding, as Valins and Baum have suggested, these feelings should be evident in people's behaviour. In a classic study, Bickman and colleagues (1973) compared the helping behaviour shown by students living in housing of different densities. They used a measure called the *lost-letter technique*, in which unmailed letters were purposely dropped in dormitory corridors. They reasoned that someone finding the letter would assume that a person in the dormitory had dropped it by mistake on the way to the mailbox.

The dependent variable was the number of "lost" letters that were subsequently mailed. The independent variable was the density of housing. The experiment involved high-density dormitories (high-rise, 22-storey towers, each housing more than 500 students), medium-density dorms (4- to 7-storey buildings, each housing about 165 students), and low-density dorms (2- to 4-storey buildings, each housing about 58 students). Letters were left unobtrusively in areas near stairwells and elevators, with no more than one letter per corridor. The letters were addressed, sealed, and stamped but had no return address.

The results showed that helping behaviour was 63 percent in high-density dorms, 87 percent in medium-density dorms, and 100 percent in low-density dorms. When questionnaires were distributed to the students in the various dorms, the answers generally reflected attitudes related to the kind of housing in which the students lived. For example, students in high-density dorms reported feeling less trust, cooperativeness, and responsibility than did students in the lower-density dorms. The researchers concluded that students living in the high-density dormitories behaved in a less socially responsible manner toward other dormitory residents. Baum believes that in situations of high density, people feel stressed, out of control, and crowded. All of this contributes to potential problems in situations of high density—for example, in prisons (Fleming, Baum, & Weiss, 1987).

Although many of the effects of crowding are not consistent across all situations or populations, certain effects seem to be universal. In high-density situations, people feel stressed and sometimes overaroused (Ruback, Pandey, & Begum, 1997). They may feel alone or anonymous, and they may withdraw from the situation. They may become apathetic, may exhibit impaired task performance, and even may become hostile (Malik & Batra, 1998). Maintaining a sense of control and of personal space seems to be a crucial variable (Evans et al., 1998; Morgan & Stewart, 1998).

**PERSONAL SPACE AND CULTURE.** It may be that to help assert their individuality and maintain a sense of personal control, human beings generally try to establish appropriate degrees of personal space. **Personal space** is the area or invisible boundary around an individual that the person considers private. Encroachment on that space causes displeasure and often withdrawal.

The size of your personal space can change, depending on the situation and the people near you. For example, you may walk arm in arm with a family member, but you will avoid physical contact with a stranger. You may stand close to a friend and whisper in his ear, but you will keep a certain distance from an elevator operator or a store clerk.

Anthropologist Edward Hall (1966) suggested that personal space is a mechanism by which people communicate with others. He proposed that people adhere to established norms of personal space that are learned in childhood. Hall also observed that the use of personal space varies from culture to culture. In Canada and the United States, especially in suburban and rural areas, people are used to large homes and generous personal space. In Japan, on the other hand, where there is little space available per person, people are used to small homes that provide little personal space. In general, Western cultures insist on a fair amount of space for people, reserving proximity for intimacy and close friends, while Arab cultures allow much smaller distances between strangers (Rustemli, 1991).

PERSONAL SPACE
The area or invisible boundary around an individual that the person considers private.

To explain the concept of personal space, Hall classified four *spatial zones*, or distances, used in social interactions with other people. The distances are intimate, personal, social, and public. An *intimate distance* (from 0 to 45 centimetres) is reserved for people who have great familiarity with one another. This space is acceptable for comforting someone who is hurt, for lovers, for physicians, and for athletes. The closeness enables a person to hold another person, examine the other's hair and eyes, and hear the other's breath. An acceptable distance for close friends and everyday interactions is *personal distance* (45 centimetres to 1.2 metres). This space is used for most social interactions. At 45 to 60 centimetres, someone might tell a secret to a close friend. At 60 centimetres, people can walk and talk together. At 60 centimetres to 1.2 metres, a person can maintain good contact with a co-worker without seeming too personal or too impersonal. *Social distance* (1.2 to 3.6 metres) is used for business and for interactions with strangers. At 1.2 to 1.8 metres, people are close enough to communicate their ideas effectively but far enough away to remain separated. Physical barriers, such as a desk to separate a clerk, receptionist, or boss from the people with whom the person interacts, may control personal space in the social zone. *Public distance* (3.6 to 7.5 metres or more) minimizes personal contact. This is the distance at which politicians speak at lunch clubs, teachers instruct classes of students, and actors and musicians perform. Public distance is sufficiently great to eliminate personal interaction between individuals and their audiences.

▲ These woman are standing a comfortable personal distance from one another, suggestive of an amicable friendship.

Of course, determining personal space is a tricky endeavour, and researchers are trying to sort out distance estimations (Zakay, Hayduk, & Tsal, 1992) for adults and children (Roques et al., 1997) and for men and women (Idehen, 1997). Figure 17.6 presents generally accepted estimates of the spaces people use when seated and standing.

## Community Psychology

If you live in a community that has faced a challenge before—unemployment, environmental spills, or the call to host the Olympic Games—you know that communities can be mobilized. They can take on a school board or vote mayors in or out of office, and they do so by pooling resources, volunteering, using their

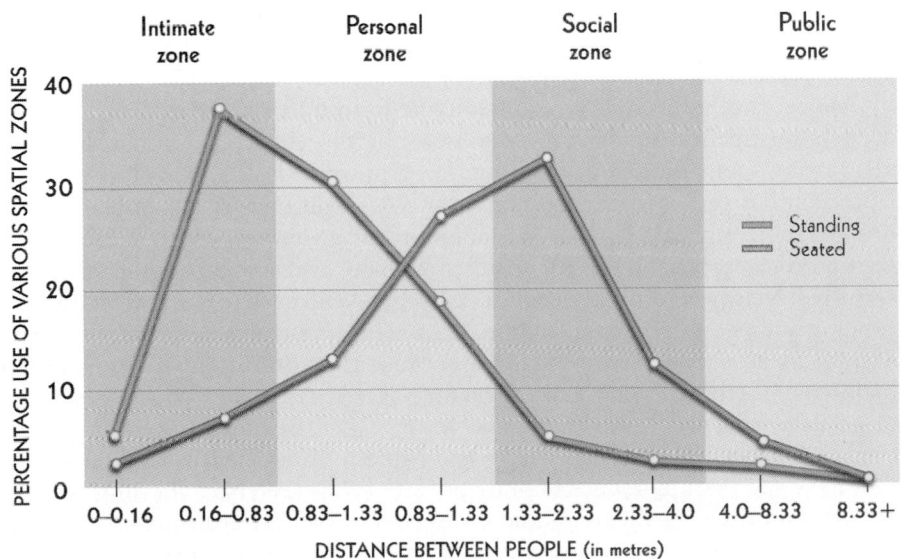

**FIGURE 17.6**

**People's Use of Personal Space When Seated and Standing**
(Based on Altman & Vinsel, 1977.).

When standing, people use primarily the intimate and personal zones. When seated, people use primarily the social and personal zones.

## Be an
# ACTIVE
# LEARNER

**REVIEW**
> How does a stressor affect behaviour? pp. 635–636
> Distinguish between social density and spatial density. p. 637
> What is personal space? p. 638

**THINK CRITICALLY**
> What are the results of the lost-letter experiments? Do you think the same results would happen with students that attend your school? Why or why not?
> How does personal space help people maintain a sense of privacy?
> What are the implications of studying the effects of environmental variables for architectural firms, window designers, and companies that provide heating, ventilation, and air conditioning systems?

**APPLY PSYCHOLOGY**
> Pay attention to your personal space as you leave class. When do you feel encroached upon?

COMMUNITY PSYCHOLOGY
The branch of psychology that seeks to reach out to society to provide services such as community mental health centres and especially to effect social change.

EMPOWERMENT
Helping people in the community enhance their existing skills and develop new skills, knowledge, and motivation so that they can gain control over their own lives.

collective talent, and reaching out. Some communities are more proactive than others and seek to prevent problems before they occur. They toil on school problems and decaying sections of town and they lobby legislators for new funds for community centres. Psychologists today are working at prevention and consider it to be a part of psychology. They are looking not only at individuals but also at whole communities—they seek to influence individuals, families, and the entire social structure (Levine, 1998). They hope to help people develop resilience and a sense of purpose and nurture what is essential for survival and personal growth (Sonn & Fisher, 1998). Access to information, communication within a community, and a sense of social involvement are necessary for the work of these psychologists. *Point/Counterpoint* looks at the effect of the Internet on these kinds of variables.

To a certain extent, this movement in psychology can be traced to the 1960s. In that decade, many psychologists recognized that individual therapy was at best imprecise and at worst inefficient for treating large numbers of people. Researchers and practitioners, as well as politicians, sought a more efficient and effective approach. Community psychology has emerged in response to a widespread desire for a more action-oriented approach to individual and social adjustment. **Community psychology** is a branch of psychology that seeks to reach out to society to provide services such as community mental health centres and especially to effect social change.

The general aims of community psychology are to strengthen existing social support networks and to stimulate the formation of new networks to meet new challenges (Gonzales et al., 1983). A key element is community involvement leading to social change. A church or synagogue group, for example, could mobilize its senior citizens for a foster grandparent program. A community psychologist might help a group develop better fire safety procedures in public housing. The focus of community psychology is often on solving applied behaviour problems. A key element of community psychology is **empowerment**—helping people in the community enhance their existing skills and develop new skills, knowledge, and motivation so that they can gain control over their own lives (Rappaport, 1987). Community psychologists work in schools, churches, planning commissions, and prisons. They plan and set up programs for bringing psychological skills and knowledge into the community. Community psychologists work especially hard at prevention of psychological problems. This often comes in the form of developing neighbourhood organization to build cohesion and resilience to mental health problems (Wandersman & Nation, 1998). Prevention operates at three levels: primary, secondary, and tertiary.

One focus of community psychology is *primary prevention*—reducing the risk of *new* cases of a disorder or counteracting harmful circumstances before they lead to maladjustment. Primary prevention usually targets groups rather than individuals. It may focus on an entire community, on mild-risk groups (such as children from families of low socio-economic status), or on high-risk groups (such as children of schizophrenic parents). Community psychologists may establish drug prevention centres, safe houses for battered women, and suicide hotlines. For example, Geoffrey Nelson and his colleagues (2001) at Wilfred Laurier University reviewed programs aimed at reducing child maltreatment and concluded that most programs are not as effective as they could be because they do not adequately address the major risk factor for child maltreatment: poverty. As such, Canada has a long way to go in promoting family wellness. Many Western European countries such as France, Sweden, and Germany have been able to implement family benefit policies that have successfully reduced family poverty levels (Peters et al., 2001).

In response to growing public awareness of mental health problems, a special kind of primary prevention service agency—the *neighbourhood clinic*—came into

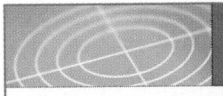

## Has the Internet Left People with Fewer Meaningful Social Contacts?

**POINT:** The Internet is a positive, prosocial way of helping people communicate quickly and efficiently.

**COUNTERPOINT:** Frequent use of the Internet adversely affects social involvement and psychological well-being.

There is no doubt that the Internet is fast and inexpensive and has transformed communication. But is it also changing our lives in harmful ways? Are people cutting themselves off from others as they hunker down over their terminals, communicating with anonymous strangers, or buying anything and everything online? Has the Internet left people with fewer social contacts, seeking entertainment and relationships through a medium that is asocial and anonymous and that promotes a solitary activity?

The Internet is having enormous effects on society. It is accessible to nearly everyone. More than 9.8 billion e-mails are delivered through the Internet every day. This technology gives people greater opportunities to meet, communicate, catch up, get acquainted, develop chat relationships, and share ideas with diverse individuals all over the world at rapid-fire speed. People form new bonds, exchange information, and increase their social contacts. The Internet is a major medium of communication. Sarah Birnie and Peter Horvath (2002) collected data at Acadia University that suggest that rather than serving as a substitute for social contact, the Internet actually supplements the social behaviours of individuals. In fact, the more sociable an individual, the greater their social contacts over the Internet. Although shy people did not use the Internet any more than more social people, they did engage in more intimate socializing on the Internet, perhaps because they felt more comfortable expressing themselves in this more anonymous format (McKenna & Bargh, 2000). Research such as this leads some to think that the Internet is great.

However, some researchers assert that greater use of the Internet is associated with small but reliable increases in loneliness, declines in social involvement, and increases in depression. They assert that using the Internet adversely affects social involvement and psychological well-being. The time people spend on the Internet has displaced other social activities. The new online relationships are mostly superficial or enhance existing friendships at school, work, or house of worship.

The Internet is not all bad or good—for example, people learn computer skills while accessing the Internet, and it provides a quick way to gather information, helping with schoolwork. But are these benefits worth the trade-off? Can accessing the Internet be entertaining and useful without causing disengagement from real life? Can psychologists help design Internet applications that enhance social interactions so as to benefit society? Can the Internet become a more social medium? The research jury is still out.

being. Such clinics help communities cope with problems that may be created by mental illness, unemployment, and lack of education. Some clinics provide free, confidential treatment for such problems as drug addiction, alcoholism, and emotional and psychological disorders. They offer a variety of services, including partial hospitalization programs for people who require hospitalization during the day and outpatient care for people who live at home while receiving therapy. They also offer consultation, education programs, and lectures and literature on such topics as therapy, family planning, and drug rehabilitation.

*Secondary prevention* involves catching problems and identifying new cases in the early stages. Community psychologists offer secondary prevention services in *crisis intervention centres*, which help people deal with short-term stressful situations requiring immediate therapeutic attention. Often the crisis is a specific event; for example, a person may be contemplating suicide, or a woman may have been raped. The focus of crisis intervention is on the immediate circumstances, not on past experiences. Studies show that crisis intervention therapy can be especially effective (Sawicki, 1988), but one problem in evaluating such therapy is that a variety of techniques are used, making controlled comparisons difficult (Slaikeu, 1990).

*Tertiary prevention* focuses on the treatment of full-blown psychological problems. There is considerable overlap between secondary and tertiary prevention, as sometimes issues and problems that are presented as short term or in their early stages may have a long-standing basis. Community psychologists offer help to eliminate or reduce a problem as well as to strengthen existing family or community resources. Sometimes this help is an intervention to protect family members; other times, it consists of counselling, consulting with schools, or calling in other social service agencies. Again, the emphasis is on using existing community resources and empowering individuals to manage their own lives more effectively.

An important aim of community psychology is to serve all members of the community, including people who might not otherwise be able to afford the services of a psychotherapist or counsellor. Community psychologists seek to develop a sense of community in individuals, which has a clear psychological benefit (Brodsky, 1996). Community psychologists are change-oriented. Because they believe that some social conditions and organizational procedures result in maladjusted individuals, they often advocate changes in community institutions and organizations. For example, they seek to improve the court system, develop programs to prevent drug use in schools, help energy conservation groups educate the public, consult with industry about reducing stress on the job, help religious organizations develop volunteer programs to aid the homeless, help hospitals set up preventive-medicine programs, and foster community involvement in educational issues.

## Educational Psychology

Today, all teachers have undergraduate degrees; many have advanced degrees. Teachers now must be trained not only in their content areas but also in sophisticated educational techniques. History teachers need to know history and how to teach it, as well as how to manage classrooms and help individual students meet their special challenges. And this is where educational psychology comes in.

**Educational psychology** is the systematic application of psychological principles to learning and teaching. Psychology has had a long tradition of studying learning principles; psychological researchers have thoroughly explored how people study, learn, and forget. Educators have long focused on instructional techniques and principles of classroom management. *Educational psychologists* bring these two disciplines together. They show how psychological ideas, methods, and theories can be applied to improve learning in individual students and in whole classrooms and to improve the process of teaching itself. In short, they help create better classroom managers (Fox, 1993). A distinction exists between educational psychologists and school psychologists. Although both share many similar concerns, educational psychologists are likely to focus on strategies to improve overall learning and classroom techniques. School psychologists are more likely to focus on interventions to affect individuals, on diagnoses of psychological and learning problems, and on consultations with parents and educators about an individual child's progress or plans.

### PROBLEMS STUDIED BY EDUCATIONAL PSYCHOLOGISTS

Educational psychologists need to know a great deal about students to help promote effective teaching. For example, they seek to discover information about students' backgrounds, interests, abilities, and past learning and to understand how they interact with other students and other teachers and how they go about solving problems. Psychologists usually study these issues in the context of five areas of inquiry in order to put theory into practice. You will recognize these areas from earlier chapters, because educational psychologists apply the lessons of many psychological subdisciplines—from learning, to developmental psychology, to social psychology.

A key focus for educational psychologists is *developmental change*—how and when individuals develop physically, socially, and intellectually. In children these

EDUCATIONAL PSYCHOLOGY
The systematic application of psychological principles to learning and teaching.

processes are rapid, change each year, and dramatically alter the ways a child or adolescent learns and interacts with teachers and other students.

Educational psychologists also study students' backgrounds to learn how *environmental conditions* can affect the learning process. Socioeconomic status is but one of those conditions; parental marital status, use of drugs in the home, and how learning is talked about at home are other important environmental factors.

Classroom learning styles are important to educational psychologists. These psychologists study *behavioural principles of learning* to ensure that the classroom has appropriate order, they study *cognitive processes* to learn how students learn and process new information, and they examine *social interactions* to find out how students are influenced by others and how they can be influenced in positive ways.

▲ Establishing clear classroom rules and pacing a class effectively are important in classroom management.

## PUTTING THEORY INTO PRACTICE: CLASSROOM MANAGEMENT

Studying the principles of psychology is obviously a prerequisite for developing effective classroom techniques. But what are effective classroom techniques? Educational psychologists try to bridge the gap between theory and practice by developing approaches to learning and instruction that optimize student outcomes. For example, educational psychologists have focused on developing individualized educational plans to personalize instruction; they work to develop mastery learning—breaking learning down into a series of discrete steps for students to master one at a time. They also encourage immediate feedback, establish clearly defined objectives, and develop effective classroom management techniques.

Educational psychologists are both theoreticians and practitioners. They try to implement instructional techniques in innovative ways that have measurable outcomes. What if a student acts out in class by verbally abusing another child? Such situations arise throughout the school day, and there are dozens of things an instructor can do. Should a teacher *scold* the child, *ignore* the child, *banish* the child to the school office, *punish* the child for classroom misbehaviour, or *instruct* the child on respect for peers? The answers lie in psychological principles: scolding, ignoring, and banishment are forms of punishment, but the most effective instruction tries to focus on positive behaviours—including how to get along with other people, the value of ideas, and the dignity and power individuals gain from knowledge.

**Be an ACTIVE LEARNER**

REVIEW
> What do community psychologists mean by *empowerment*? p. 640
> What is primary prevention? p. 641
> What are some of the issues studied by educational psychologists? pp. 642–643

THINK CRITICALLY
> How can community psychologists focus on helping groups of people in neighbourhoods and even whole communities to change? How do they do it?
> Why is primary prevention so important to psychologists?
> As a psychologist, what do you think would be the most important part of instruction?
> How do you think teaching should vary according to grade level and subject matter (think Piaget—Chapter 10)?

APPLY PSYCHOLOGY
> What type of curriculum changes, if any, might educational psychologists have made when young children were first exposed to televised educational programming, such as *Sesame Street*?

# Sport Psychology

Imagine lining up a shot—any kind of shot will do. You picture the ball, you think about its final destination, you visualize its trajectory. You shoot. When golfers such as Mike Weir, basketball players such as Vince Carter, or quarterbacks such as Damon Allen prepare to take their shots, they usually imagine them first. In using mental imagery, they are using principles of sport psychology.

**Sport psychology** is the systematic application of psychological principles in sports. Sport psychologists, like any psychologists, recognize that behaviour (in this case, athletic performance) is affected by the individual athlete, the athlete's team, the team leader or coach, and the environment in which these individuals interact. The characteristics of athlete, coach, and environment are each multidimensional; people, their own personal characteristics, how they interact with others, and how

SPORT PSYCHOLOGY

The systematic application of psychological principles to sports.

the environment affects them are all influenced by years of past events, relationships, and successes or failures. Nevertheless, sport psychologists have tried to bring some order to the study of athletic performance. Sport psychologists study the behaviours associated with sports in the traditional ways that psychologists go about things: Some do basic research in sports; others take an educational role, teaching about sport psychology; still others are applied practitioners who help athletes overcome obstacles to achieve their highest potential. Practitioners need to be trained in sports and psychology to work in this area. There exists a whole range of sports behaviours that researchers consider appropriate for study and research, education, and intervention. Among the most important are the topics we will consider here: motivation, activation and arousal, anxiety and performance, and intervention strategies (Cox, Qiu, & Liu, 1993).

## MOTIVATION

If there were simple answers to explain what motivates an athlete—what factors energize, direct, and sustain athletic performance—then the task for sport psychologists, and especially for an athlete's coach, would be dramatically different. But athletic performance is exceedingly complicated. According to one researcher, it takes at least four levels of analysis to understand what motivates a person to perform a sport well (Roberts, 1992):

- *What is the goal?* Is the person seeking competitive abilities or merely mastery of a sport? Is the goal learning to play squash at a national level of competition, or is the goal to have a friendly game in which the athlete knows the rules, feels competent, and has fun playing? Based on such recognition of personal goals, the athlete must then accept goals set by a coach.
- *Is the motivational climate set by friends, parents, and coaches geared toward competition or mastery?* When the climate is geared toward mastery, the athlete's energy level is usually much lower, and so is anxiety.
- *How does the athlete perceive his or her abilities—as high, low, or not relevant?* When people have a strong self-concept of their abilities, they do better in sports. As we saw in Chapter 12, when people have a positive sense of self-efficacy, they do much better at a task.
- *Is the athlete's achievement behaviour adaptive or maladaptive?* Does the athlete set realistic goals and practice schedules and follow training routines, or does the athlete engage in self-defeating behaviours?

To a great extent, this four-step analysis of motivation looks at what energizes and sustains an athlete in sports. But a person who seeks to understand sport psychology must recognize that human beings are not always rational or goal-directed and do not always behave consistently. Their health, love life, family situation, and financial status, to name just a few variables, affect people's behaviour.

Consider how attribution theory might help explain motivations in sports (see p. 462 for a review of attribution theory). If a person attributes his or her failure to a lack of personal ability, this is likely to be detrimental to future motivation and performance. To test this hypothesis, Miserandino (1998) trained members of a boys' high-school basketball team to revise their attributions about their performance so that they were more facilitative and motivational. Half of the participants received feedback about shooting performance and were encouraged to attribute any poor performance to a lack of effort rather than to a lack of ability. The remaining participants received feedback on shooting technique only, with no attributions provided. After a four-week training period, the boys in the attributional group showed more mastery and greater improvement in their shooting. Attributions about the whys of behaviour make a difference.

In the end, enhancing motivation through attribution may be important, but it is only part of a more complex picture. In various sports, high achievers also:

- Set realistic goals
- Announce goals to others
- Chart progress toward goals
- Vary workout regimes
- Take days off so as to avoid burnout and boredom
- Have workout partners
- Try to keep their sport activity fun

The complexity of these situations makes the study of sport psychology resistant to easy explanations, but also more exciting. Researchers have so much to learn, especially about the energizing of behaviour through activation and arousal, our next topic.

## ACTIVATION AND AROUSAL

In our study of motivation in Chapter 9, we saw that, given moderate levels of arousal and moderately difficult tasks, as arousal increased, performance also increased. Arousal generally is viewed as stimulation and excitement—a performance enhancer (for example, a goalie's performance in the Stanley Cup playoffs often can be better than in the regular season). But excessive levels of arousal are associated with poor performance. Yerkes and Dodson characterized such a learning curve as an inverted U (see page 309 for a review of the Yerkes–Dodson law). One need not be a psychologist to recognize that when people are extremely frightened, aroused, or activated, performance suffers. This is certainly true in athletics; dozens of research studies have shown that being activated and aroused increases athletic performance—but only up to a point.

▲ Based on arousal theory, we would guess that Curtis Joseph would perform best when moderately aroused.

The inverted U–shape relationship for arousal and performance is not always orderly, however, especially in sports situations that involve a heavy level of cognitive activity, such as quarterbacking in football or catching in baseball. Researchers know that for every increase in a person's arousal, a corresponding increase (or decrease) in performance is not necessarily evident. Sometimes a small increase in arousal can push some people "over the top" to acute anxiety and poor performance. Young children are less affected by pressure; older children, in contrast, think about options ("My teammate at second base doesn't catch very well, so it makes more sense to throw to first") and are more affected by pressure (French, Spurgeon, & Nevett, 1995). How then is arousal distinct from anxiety?

## ANXIETY AND PERFORMANCE

In any sport, it is never good to prepare excessively either physiologically or psychologically—such overtraining can lead to serious anxiety (Kreider, Fry, & O'Toole, 1998). When an athlete is fearful, tense, and apprehensive and such feelings are associated with arousal, the athlete is suffering from anxiety. Some people, including athletes, feel this way most of the time—trait personality theorists would say that such people have a strong or dominant anxiety trait. A whole range of tests has been developed to measure anxiety in athletes and to discern whether anxiety is related to specific events or is a general trait in a given athlete.

Unlike weekend or casual sports enthusiasts, competitive athletes often reach their peak of anxiety significantly before an athletic event begins, and their highest levels of anxiety may disappear immediately before the event. As they step up to the plate, hoop, skating rink, or scrimmage line, professional athletes often become cool, collected, and in control. Three hours earlier they may have felt overwhelmed by their arousal and fear, but when they have to perform, their anxiety is gone.

If this relationship between anxiety and performance were tidy, psychologists wouldn't fret about precompetitive anxiety. However, like so many other psychological phenomena, anxiety is related to other aspects of an athlete's performance and life. If an athlete's arousal exceeds the level needed for effective performance, anxiety can take over. Similarly, an underaroused athlete also may become anxious and stay anxious throughout an event. So arousal and anxiety are closely related and hard to separate, but separation can be achieved through good intervention strategies. Lisa Rogerson and Dennis Hrycaiko (2002) at the University of Manitoba measured the effectiveness of relaxation and self-talk on the performance of hockey goaltenders during games. Such mental skills training was effective in improving performance and, importantly, in maintaining gains.

## INTERVENTION STRATEGIES

When a person's level of anxiety is sufficiently high that arousal leads to lower performance, interventions can be put in place to help relieve anxiety and arousal. Stress management approaches, described in Chapter 14, have proved to be effective. There is a broad array of such anxiety-reducing techniques.

One widely used technique is *progressive relaxation*, in which athletes are taught to relax slowly and progressively as time passes. Individual muscle relaxation, with progressively deeper muscle-group relaxation, is the goal. Typical steps are suggestions to relax the limbs, to feel heaviness or warmth in the arms and legs, to feel a reduced heart rate, and to sense coolness on the forehead.

*Hypnosis*, the state encouraging uncritical acceptance of suggestions, has been used widely to help athletes achieve deep relaxation, as well as to help them focus their energy and attention. Closely associated with hypnosis is instruction in *meditation* to help an athlete relax and gain control of his or her focus. The technique of meditation is to focus energy and attention on a single thought, idea, sound, or object. (Hypnosis and meditation can help athletes relax and focus, of course, but they will never make a bad athlete into a good one.) Closely associated are the physical and mental techniques involved in yoga. Practitioners claim that yoga is capable of causing profound physiological and psychological changes. Head coach Phil Jackson of the Chicago Bulls made his team go to mandatory yoga sessions a couple of years ago and it seemed to work!

Using *mental imagery* to promote relaxation has been shown to be worthwhile in many sports activities (Overby, 1990), and when mental imagery is combined with other relaxation strategies, the results have proved especially effective (Murphy & Jowdy, 1992). As described earlier, athletes also use mental imagery to "psych up," or practise a sports activity in their thoughts (Murphy, 1990).

*Cognitive interventions* that focus on changing thought patterns about a sport, an event, abilities, or strategies have been especially helpful (Boutcher, 1992). Cognitive strategies often focus on educational issues in the sport in combination with training in relaxation, such as thinking calm thoughts just before a pole vault. Cognitive interventions may teach athletes to think positively, to block out distractions, and to focus on the one part of their body that is crucial in their sport.

*Be an*
**ACTIVE LEARNER**

**REVIEW**
> Identify four levels of analysis needed for an understanding of motivation in sports. pp. 643–644
> Why does high arousal lead to lower performance in sports? p. 645

**THINK CRITICALLY**
> Sport psychologists seek to enhance athletes' performance by improving their physical and emotional condition and their motivation. Does such behaviour management raise any ethical problems for sport psychologists?
> When psychologists say that top sports performance is 90 percent attitude, what do you think they mean?

**APPLY PSYCHOLOGY**
> If you were coaching a team that had made it to the city finals, how would you prepare your team members to do their best under this anxiety-provoking circumstance?
> What does an athlete mean when she says that she is going to focus on each day, one day at a time? Can you devise five specific things that she might do to stay on task?

# Summary and Review

## INDUSTRIAL/ORGANIZATIONAL PSYCHOLOGY

### What is I/O psychology?

> *Industrial/organizational (I/O) psychology* is the study of how individual behaviour is affected by the work environment, co-workers, and organizational practices. It can be divided into four broad areas: human resources psychology, motivation of job performance, job satisfaction, and leadership.   **pp. 612–613**

### What are the goals of job analyses, selection procedures, and training efforts in today's workplace?

> The functional job analysis and the position analysis questionnaire are instruments that have been developed by I/O psychologists for *job analyses*. All such analyses have a similar goal: to ensure that jobs are well defined and doable. Two important tasks of an I/O psychologist are to balance the scope and complexity of jobs and to help employers create jobs that will be motivating.   **pp. 613–614**

> Selection procedures have the basic goal of evaluating job candidates in order to help an employer determine which ones to hire. Application forms, interviews, samples of work, and ability tests are some of the instruments used in selection. Training is the process by which organizations systematically teach employees skills to improve their job performance.   **pp. 614–617**

### What is performance appraisal?

> *Performance appraisal* is the process whereby a supervisor periodically evaluates the job-relevant strengths and weaknesses of subordinates. The problem with performance appraisals is that they are often done inaccurately by people with few evaluative skills and with few diagnostic aids. Multiple performance criteria must enter into an appraisal.   **pp. 618–619**

### How have psychologists tried to help managers motivate workers?

> I/O psychologists help employers find ways to motivate employees to be more productive. *Goal-setting theory* asserts that setting specific, clear, attainable goals for a given task leads to better performance.   **p. 619**

> *Expectancy theories* assert that a worker's effort and desire to work are determined by expectations about the outcome of the work. Vroom suggested that work motivation is determined by expectancy (the belief that hard or extra work will lead to good or improved performance); instrumentality (the belief that good performance will be rewarded); and valence (the value put on rewards that are offered). Lawler and Porter contended that performance is determined by ability, effort, and role perceptions—the

ways people believe they should be doing their jobs.   **p. 620**

### How have psychologists analyzed worker performance and job satisfaction?

> The view that what people bring to a work situation should be balanced by what they receive there compared with others constitutes *equity theory*. Thus, workers' input (what they do) should be balanced by the rewards they receive. If input is not balanced with compensation, people will adjust their work input accordingly.   **p. 621**

> I/O psychologists have identified three basic approaches to motivation management: paternalistic, behavioural, and participatory.   **pp. 622–623**

> There are many sources of job satisfaction, including the work itself, the perceived rewards of the work, the quality of supervision, the support of co-workers, and the work setting. In the end, the overall level of satisfaction depends on the extent to which people feel their expectations for satisfaction are matched by their actual satisfaction.   **pp. 623–625**

### What makes a good leader?

> A leader is a person who influences other people's behaviour toward the attainment of agreed-upon goals. Business leaders can be employee-oriented or task-oriented; the situation or the organization is a key determinant of which type of leader will be more effective. *Transformational leaders*—charismatic leaders who inspire and provide intellectual stimulation—create opportunities to transform an organization, often by empowering employees.   **pp. 625–628**

### KEY TERMS

applied psychology, p. 612; industrial/organizational (I/O) psychology, p. 612; job analyses, p. 613; performance appraisal, p. 618; goal-setting theory, p. 619; expectancy theories, p. 620; equity theory, p. 621; transformational leader, p. 627

## HUMAN FACTORS AND ERGONOMICS

### Describe the field of human factors.

> *Human factors* is the study of the relationship of human beings to machines and to workplaces and other environments. It involves the study of the fit between human anatomy or physiology, the demands of a particular task or piece of equipment, and the environment in which the task occurs. Human factors research can help design work environments that are both efficient and safe. Warnings, labels, and compliance techniques are all helpful in improving safety.   **pp. 628–630**

**What is behaviour-based safety?**

> In behaviour-based safety, effective safety management refers to a wide range of programs that focus on changing the behaviour of workers *and* companies to prevent occupational injuries and illnesses.    **pp. 630–631**

**KEY TERMS**

human factors, p. 629; ergonomics, p. 629

## PSYCHOLOGY AND THE LAW

**What key roles do psychologists play in the legal system?**

> As researchers, psychologists help determine why individuals behave in ways that are unacceptable to society. Psychologists also act as policy or program evaluators, helping governments and other institutions determine whether various policies, agencies, or programs actually work. Psychologists work as advocates for individuals and society, helping to shape social policy in areas such as minority, remedial, and gifted education. Finally, psychologists often serve as expert witnesses, bringing their knowledge to court as consultants.    **pp. 631–633**

**What is the new role of DNA in relationship to the law?**

> DNA analysis can be likened to complex fingerprint analysis—if enough of the identifying features are the same between the DNA of a suspect and some evidence found on an injured person or at the scene of a crime, the DNA profile is determined to be a match. Increasingly forensic psychologists and others are relying on DNA evidence.    **p. 633**

## ENVIRONMENTAL PSYCHOLOGY

**What do environmental psychologists study?**

> *Environmental psychology* is the study of how physical settings and aspects of the environment affect human behaviour, as well as how people can change their environment to meet their psychological needs. *Crowding* is the perception that one's personal space is too limited. Social density is the number of people in a given space; spatial density is the amount of space allocated to a fixed number of people. *Personal space,* as defined by Hall, is the immediate area around an individual that the person considers private. Four spatial zones, or distances, that can be observed in social interactions in Canada are intimate, personal, social, and public.    **pp. 634–639**

**KEY TERMS**

environmental psychology, p. 635; stressor, p. 636; crowding, p. 637; personal space, p. 638

## COMMUNITY PSYCHOLOGY

**What are the goals of community psychology, and what do community psychologists mean by *empowerment*?**

> *Community psychology* seeks to reach out to society by providing psychological services to people who might not otherwise receive them. The general aims of community psychologists are to empower people and to use three levels of prevention strategies to help ward off, treat, or stop psychological problems in the community.    **pp. 639–642**

> *Empowerment* refers to helping people enhance existing skills and develop new skills, knowledge, and motivation so that they can gain control over their own lives.    **p. 641**

**Has the Internet left people with fewer social contacts?**

> The Internet is not all bad or good—people learn computer skills while accessing the Internet, and it helps with schoolwork; but use of the Internet is associated with small but reliable increases in loneliness, declines in social involvement, and increases in depression.    **p. 640**

**KEY TERMS**

community psychology, p. 640; empowerment, p. 640

## EDUCATIONAL PSYCHOLOGY

**What are the goals of and the problems studied by educational psychologists?**

> *Educational psychology* is the systematic application of psychological principles to learning and teaching. To help create effective teaching, educational psychologists seek to understand students' backgrounds, interests, abilities, and past learning; how they interact with other students and other teachers; and how they solve problems.    **pp. 642–643**

**KEY TERM**

educational psychology, p. 642

## SPORT PSYCHOLOGY

**What is sport psychology?**

> *Sport psychology* is the systematic application of psychological principles to sports. Sport psychologists recognize that athletic performance is affected by the athlete, the team leader or coach, and the environment. Sport psychologists study factors such as arousal and performance and have found that Yerkes and Dodson's inverted U-shape relationship between arousal and performance is not always consistent in sports; that is, as arousal increases, performance may or may not increase or decrease smoothly. When anxiety is too high and arousal lowers performance, interventions can help lower arousal and relieve anxiety.    **pp. 643–644**

**Identify four levels of analysis used to understand what motivates a person to perform a sport well.**

> The four levels of analysis ask the following questions: What is the goal? Is the motivational climate set by friends, parents, and coaches geared toward competition or mastery? How does the athlete perceive his or her abilities? And, is the athlete's achievement behaviour

adaptive or maladaptive—does the athlete set realistic goals? **pp. 644–645**

**Identify some intervention strategies that can help athletes improve their performance.**

> One widely used technique to improve sports performance is progressive relaxation, in which athletes are taught to relax individual muscles slowly and progressively. Another technique, hypnosis, has been widely used to help athletes achieve deep relaxation, as well as to help them focus their energy and attention. Closely associated with hypnosis is meditation. Last, mental imagery to promote relaxation and focus is worthwhile in many sports activities. **p. 646**

**KEY TERM**

sport psychology, p. 643

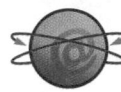 Take advantage of the multimedia resources available with this text! Follow the marginal icons to access the interactive modules on the *HandsOnPsych CD-ROM*; log on to *MyPsychLab* to explore the ebook, study aids, and other online resources; and visit the Companion Website at **www.pearsoned.ca/lefton** for additional exercises and links.

# Statistical Methods

**STATISTICS**
The branch of mathematics that deals with collecting, classifying, and analyzing data.

**DESCRIPTIVE STATISTICS**
A general set of procedures used to summarize, condense, and describe sets of data.

**Research Methods and Statistics**

Scientific progress is in many ways directly linked to researchers' ability to measure and quantify observations; that is, to collect data. **Statistics** is the branch of mathematics that deals with classifying and analyzing data. To rule out coincidence and discover the true causes of behaviour, psychologists control the variables in experiments (as discussed in detail in Chapter 1) and then use statistics to describe, summarize, and present results. These methods and procedures for analyzing data are the topics of this appendix.

## Descriptive Statistics

Researchers use statistics to evaluate and organize data. Specifically, they use **descriptive statistics**—procedures used to summarize, condense, and describe sets of data. Descriptive statistics make it possible for researchers to interpret the results of their experiments. For example, your professors use descriptive statistics to interpret exam results. A statistical description of a 100-point mid-term exam may show that 10 percent of a class scored more than 60 points, 70 percent scored between 40 and 60 points, and 20 percent scored fewer than 40 points. On the basis of this statistical description, the professor might conclude that the test was exceptionally difficult and might arrange the grading so that anyone who earned 61 points or more would receive an A. However, before inferences can be drawn or grades assigned, the data from a research study or the scores on a test must be organized in a meaningful way.

### ORGANIZING DATA: FREQUENCY DISTRIBUTIONS

When psychologists do research, they often produce large amounts of data that must be assessed. Suppose a social psychologist asked parents to monitor the number of hours their children watch television. The parents might report between 0 and 20 hours of TV watching a week. Here is a list of the actual number of hours of TV watching by 100 children in a particular week:

| | | | | | |
|---|---|---|---|---|---|
| 11 | 18 | 5 | 9 | 6 | 20 |
| 9 | 7 | 15 | 3 | 6 | 11 |
| 6 | 1 | 10 | 3 | 4 | 4 |
| 8 | 8 | 9 | 10 | 13 | 12 |
| 16 | 1 | 15 | 9 | 4 | 3 |
| 10 | 5 | 6 | 12 | 8 | 2 |
| 14 | 12 | 6 | 9 | 8 | 12 |
| 10 | 7 | 3 | 14 | 13 | 7 |
| 10 | 17 | 11 | 13 | 16 | 7 |
| 15 | 11 | 9 | 11 | 16 | 8 |
| 14 | 7 | 10 | 10 | 12 | 8 |
| 11 | 1 | 12 | 7 | 6 | 0 |
| 19 | 18 | 9 | 8 | 2 | 5 |
| 9 | 14 | 7 | 10 | 9 | 2 |
| 10 | 4 | 13 | 8 | 5 | 4 |
| 9 | 8 | 5 | 17 | 15 | 17 |
| 5 | 13 | 10 | 11 | | |

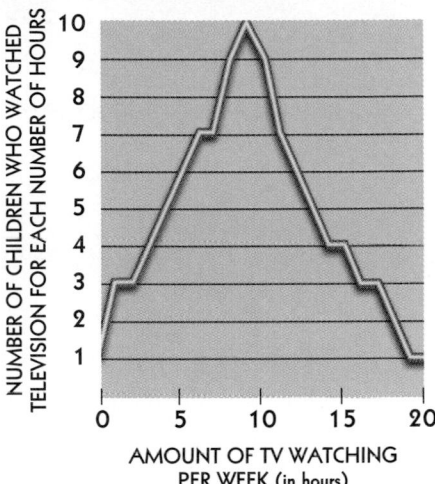

**FIGURE A.1**

**A Frequency Polygon Showing Hours of Television Watched in a Week by 100 Children**

The first step in making these numbers meaningful is to arrange them in a chart or array, organized from the highest to the lowest, showing the number of times each number occurs; this type of organization is known as a **frequency distribution**. As the frequency distribution in Table A.1 (on page 652) shows, 10 children were reported to have watched 9 hours of television in a week—a greater number of children than for any other number of hours of TV watching.

Researchers often construct graphs from the data in frequency distributions. Such graphs, called **frequency polygons**, show the range of possible results or scores (for example, numbers of hours of TV watching) on the horizontal axis, or *abscissa*, and the frequency of each score (for example, the number of children who watched television for each number of hours) on the vertical axis, or *ordinate*. Figure A.1 is a frequency polygon of the data from the frequency distribution in Table A.1. Straight lines connect the data points.

## MEASURES OF CENTRAL TENDENCY

A descriptive statistic that tells which result or score best represents an entire set of scores is a **measure of central tendency**. It is used to summarize and condense data; all the numbers in the distribution are condensed into one number. Also, because almost every group has members who score higher or lower than the rest of the group, researchers often use a measure of central tendency to describe the group *as a whole*.

People often use the word *average* in a casual way to describe a variety of traits or tendencies. A woman asks a clerk to help her find a sweater for her "average-sized" husband. The owner of a new sedan boasts that his car "averages" 40 miles to a gallon of gasoline. A doctor tells her patient that his serum cholesterol level is "average" because it falls halfway between low and high measurements. In each of these cases, the person is using *average* to depict a type of norm, and others understand what the person means, even though not all of these examples are technically "averages." Consider this statement: Men are taller than women are. Because you know that some women are taller than some men are, you assume that the statement means: *On the average,* men are taller than women are. In other words, comparing the heights of all the men and all the women in the world would show that, *on the average,* men are taller.

**FREQUENCY DISTRIBUTION**

A chart or array of scores, usually arranged from the highest to the lowest, showing the number of instances for each score.

**FREQUENCY POLYGON**

Graph of a frequency distribution that shows the number of instances of obtained scores, usually with the data points connected by straight lines.

**MEASURE OF CENTRAL TENDENCY**

A descriptive statistic that tells which result or score best represents an entire set of scores.

| | TABLE A.1 | A Frequency Distribution of the Number of Hours of Television Watched in a Week by 100 Children | |
|---|---|---|---|

| Number of Hours of Television Watched | Individuals Watching Each Number of Hours | Total Number of Individuals Watching |
|:---:|:---:|:---:|
| 0 | I | 1 |
| 1 | III | 3 |
| 2 | III | 3 |
| 3 | IIII | 4 |
| 4 | IIIII | 5 |
| 5 | IIIIII | 6 |
| 6 | IIIIIII | 7 |
| 7 | IIIIIIII | 8 |
| 8 | IIIIIIIII | 9 |
| 9 | IIIIIIIIII | 10 |
| 10 | IIIIIIIII | 9 |
| 11 | IIIIIII | 7 |
| 12 | IIIIII | 6 |
| 13 | IIIII | 5 |
| 14 | IIII | 4 |
| 15 | IIII | 4 |
| 16 | III | 3 |
| 17 | III | 3 |
| 18 | II | 2 |
| 19 | I | 1 |
| 20 | I | 1 |
| | | 100 |

Note that few individuals score very high or very low—most score in the middle range.

Let's look more closely at three measures of central tendency: mean (arithmetic average), mode, and median.

MEAN. How could a researcher investigate the truth of the statement that men are taller than women are? One way would be to measure the heights of thousands of men and women, taking a careful sample from each country, ethnic group, and age group. The researcher could then calculate the average heights of the men and the women in the sample and plot the results on a graph. Table A.2 lists height data from a small sample of men and women. For each group, the measured heights were added together and divided by the number of people in the group. The resulting number is the **mean,** or *arithmetic average,* the measure of central tendency calculated by dividing the sum of scores (the total of all heights) by the total number of scores (in this case, the number of heights). The mean is the most frequently used measure of central tendency.

MODE. Another statistic used to describe the central tendency of a set of data is the mode. The **mode** is the most frequently observed data point. Table A.3 (on page 654) shows the frequencies of all the different heights from Table A.2. It shows, for example, that only one person is 58 inches tall, three are 79 inches tall, and more people are 70 inches tall than are any other single height. The mode of the heights of this group is therefore 70 inches.

MEAN

The measure of central tendency that is calculated by dividing the sum of the scores by the total number of scores; also known as the arithmetic average.

MODE

The measure of central tendency that is the most frequently observed data point.

Calculation of Mean Height for 20 Men and 20 Women

| Men | Height (in inches) | Women | Height (in inches) |
|---|---|---|---|
| Davis | 62 | Leona | 58 |
| Baird | 62 | Golde | 59 |
| Jason | 64 | Marcy | 61 |
| Ross | 67 | Mickey | 64 |
| David | 68 | Sharon | 64 |
| Cary | 68 | Rozzy | 66 |
| Mark | 69 | Bonnie | 66 |
| Evan | 70 | Dianne | 66 |
| Michael | 70 | Cheryl | 66 |
| Davey | 70 | Carol | 67 |
| Steven | 70 | Iris | 67 |
| Morry | 70 | Nancy | 67 |
| Alan | 70 | Theresa | 67 |
| Bernie | 70 | Sylvia | 67 |
| Lester | 70 | Jay | 68 |
| Al | 70 | Linda | 68 |
| Arnold | 73 | Elizabeth | 71 |
| Andrew | 79 | Jesse | 75 |
| Corey | 79 | Gabrielle | 76 |
| Stephen | 79 | Sarah | 77 |
| **Total height** | **1400** | **Total height** | **1340** |

Mean: $\dfrac{\Sigma S}{N} = \dfrac{1400}{20} = 70$ inches

Mean: $\dfrac{\Sigma S}{N} = \dfrac{1340}{20} = 67$ inches

Note. $\Sigma S$ means add up the scores; $N$ means number of scores.

**MEDIAN.** The **median** is the 50 percent point: Half of the observations (or scores) fall above it, and the other half fall below it. Table A.4 presents all the heights of men and women given in Table A.2, arranged from lowest to highest. It shows that half of the heights fall above 68 and half fall below 68. The median of the data set, therefore, is 68. You have probably read news reports that refer to medians, for example: "According to the Statistics Canada, the median family income in Canada rose to $36 000 this year." What this means is that half of Canadian families earned more than this amount and half earned less.

Table A.5 (on page 655) presents a set of data from an experiment on memory. The scores are the numbers of items correctly recalled. There are three groups of participants: a control group, which received no special treatment; one experimental group, which received task-motivating instructions (such as "Think hard" and "Focus your attention"); and a second experimental group, whose members were hypnotized and told under hypnosis that they would have good recall. The results of the study show that the task-motivated group did slightly worse than the control group, with a mean of 10.3 words recalled, compared with the control group's mean of 10.6. But the hypnosis group did better, recalling 15.4 words on average, compared with the control group's average recall of 10.6 words—a difference of 4.8 words. Hypnosis therefore *seemed* to have a positive effect on memory, but we need to do some additional analysis before coming to that conclusion.

MEDIAN

The measure of central tendency that is the data point with 50 percent of all the observations (scores) above it and 50 percent below it.

| TABLE A.3 | The Mode for Men's and Women's Heights |
|---|---|

The mode is 70 inches, the most frequently observed height.

| Height (in inches) | Number of Individuals of Each Height |
|---|---|
| 58 | I |
| 59 | I |
| 60 | |
| 61 | I |
| 62 | II |
| 63 | |
| 64 | III |
| 65 | |
| 66 | IIII |
| 67 | IIIIII |
| 68 | IIII |
| 69 | I |
| 70 | IIIIIIIII  Mode |
| 71 | I |
| 72 | |
| 73 | I |
| 74 | |
| 75 | I |
| 76 | I |
| 77 | I |
| 78 | |
| 79 | III |

| TABLE A.4 | The Median of Men's and Women's Heights |
|---|---|

The median is the height in the middle of the range of heights measured—half of the heights are above the median and half are below.

| Height (in inches) | Height (in inches) |
|---|---|
| 58 | 68 |
| 59 | 68 |
| 61 | 69 |
| 62 | 70 |
| 62 | 70 |
| 64 | 70 |
| 64 | 70 |
| 64 | 70 |
| 66 | 70 |
| 66 | 70 |
| 66 | 70 |
| 66 | 70 |
| 67 | 71 |
| 67 | 73 |
| 67 | 75 |
| 67 | 76 |
| 67 | 77 |
| 67 | 79 |
| 68 | 79 |
| 68 — Median | 79 |

The medians for the control group and the task-motivated group were equal—10.5 words. The difference between the median of the control group and the median of the hypnosis group was 4 words. Hypnosis still seems to have had a positive effect, but the difference between the medians (4 words) is smaller than the difference between the means (4.8 words)—because the median discounts very high and very low scores. For example, if you get a test score of 0 after obtaining five other scores whose average is about 70, the sixth score will drop that *average* substantially; averaging in a sixth score of 60 would not have as large an impact. But with a median, a single extreme score (such as 0 or 120) counts as much as all the other scores. For a sample as small as this one, where a single score can have a big impact, the median is often a better measure of central tendency.

The mean, mode, and median are descriptive statistics that measure central tendency. Each tells researchers something about the average (or typical) person, score, or data item. Sometimes the mean, the mode, and the median are the same; but more often, there is enough variability in a sample (one very tall or very short person in a group of height measurements, for example) that each central tendency measure yields a slightly different result and will be used for different purposes. If you had to guess the height of a woman you had never met, a good guess would be the mean, or average, height for women. If you were a buyer for a clothing store and had to pick one dress size or one shoe size to order, you might be more likely to pick the modal size—the size that occurs more often than any other.

## TABLE A.5 Calculations of Mean and Median Memory Scores for Three Groups (with 10 People in Each Group)

| Person | Scores of Control Group | Scores of Task-Motivated Group | Scores of Hypnosis Group |
|---|---|---|---|
| 1 | 10 | 11 | 16 |
| 2 | 12 | 13 | 14 |
| 3 | 14 | 14 | 16 |
| 4 | 10 | 12 | 12 |
| 5 | 11 | 12 | 10 |
| 6 | 9 | 8 | 9 |
| 7 | 5 | 10 | 15 |
| 8 | 12 | 5 | 12 |
| 9 | 16 | 10 | 18 |
| 10 | 7 | 8 | 32 |
| Total | 106 | 103 | 154 |
| Mean | 10.6 | 10.3 | 15.4 |
| Median | 10.5 | 10.5 | 14.5 |

**Control Group (scores are reordered lowest to highest)**

$$\text{Mean} = \frac{5+7+9+10+10+11+12+12+14+16}{10} = \frac{106}{10} = 10.6$$

Median = 5  7  9  10  $\boxed{10 \quad 11}$  12  12  14  16

$\downarrow$

10.5

The point at which half of the scores fall above and half of the scores fall below is 10.5; that is, 10.5 is the median.

**Task-Motivated Group (scores are reordered lowest to highest)**

$$\text{Mean} = \frac{5+8+8+10+10+11+12+12+13+14}{10} = \frac{103}{10} = 10.3$$

Median = 5  8  8  10  $\boxed{10 \quad 11}$  12  12  13  14

$\downarrow$

10.5

The point at which half of the scores fall above and half of the scores fall below is 10.5; that is, 10.5 is the median.

**Hypnosis Group (scores are reordered lowest to highest)**

$$\text{Mean} = \frac{9+10+12+12+14+15+16+16+18+32}{10} = \frac{154}{10} = 15.4$$

Median = 9  10  12  12  $\boxed{14 \quad 15}$  16  16  18  32

$\downarrow$

14.5

The point at which half of the scores fall above and half of the scores fall below is 14.5; that is, 14.5 is the median.

## MEASURES OF VARIABILITY

A measure of central tendency is a single number that describes a hypothetical "average." In real life, however, people do not always reflect the central tendency because they vary so much. Consequently, knowledge of an average data item or score is more useful when accompanied by knowledge of how all the items or scores in the group are distributed relative to one another. If you know that the mean of a group of numbers is 150, you still do not know how widely dispersed are the numbers that were averaged to calculate that mean. In other words, the mean on the final examination in your psychology class may be 150, and you may have scored 170 (above the mean), but you still do not know how much you can celebrate. Are there few other scores above your score? If there are many others, how much better than you did they do?

Statistics that describe the extent to which scores in a distribution differ from one another are called *measures of variability*. **Variability** is the extent to which scores differ from one another, especially the extent to which they differ from the mean. If all scores obtained are the same, there is no variability; this, however, is unlikely to occur. It is more usual that in any group of people being tested or measured in some way, personal and situational characteristics will cause some to score high and some to score low. If researchers know the extent of the variability, they can estimate the extent to which participants differ from the mean, or "average," person. Two important and useful measures of variability are range and standard deviation.

**RANGE.** The **range** shows the spread of scores in a distribution; it is calculated by subtracting the lowest score from the highest score. If the lowest score on a test is 20 points and the highest is 85, the range is 65 points. The range is unaffected by the mean. In this example, whether the mean is 45, 65, or 74 points, the range remains 65; that is, there is a 65-point spread from the lowest score to the highest.

The range is a relatively crude measure of the extent to which participants vary within a group. In a group of 100 students, for example, the mean score might be 80, and nearly all of the students might have scored within 10 points of that mean. But if the lowest score is 20 and the highest is 85, the range is 65. More precise measures of the spread of scores within a group are available, however. They indicate how scores are distributed as well as the extent of their spread.

**STANDARD DEVIATION.** Consider a reaction-time study that measures how fast people press a button when a light flashes. The following list gives the number of milliseconds (thousandths of a second) it took each of 30 randomly chosen grade 10 students to press the button when the light flashed; clearly, the reaction times vary.

| | | | | | |
|---|---|---|---|---|---|
| 450 | 490 | 500 | 610 | 520 | 470 |
| 480 | 492 | 585 | 462 | 600 | 490 |
| 740 | 700 | 595 | 500 | 493 | 495 |
| 498 | 455 | 510 | 470 | 480 | 540 |
| 710 | 722 | 575 | 490 | 495 | 570 |

If you knew only that the mean reaction time is 540 milliseconds, you might conclude that 540 is the best estimate of how long it takes a grade 10 student to respond to the light. But of course, not everyone reacted in 540 milliseconds; some took more time and some took less. Psychologists say that the data are variable, or that variability exists.

To find out how much variability exists among data, and to quantify it in a meaningful manner, researchers use a statistic called the standard deviation. A **standard deviation** is a descriptive statistic that measures the variability of data from the mean of the sample—that is, the extent to which each score differs from the mean. The calculations for a standard deviation are shown in Table A.6. Here is the general procedure: First, subtract the mean from each score, and then square that difference. Next, add up the squared differences and divide by the number of scores minus 1. (For a small sample, to get a better estimate of the sample's

## TABLE A.6 Computation of the Standard Deviation for a Small Distribution of Scores

| Score | Score − Mean | (Score − Mean)$^2$ |
|-------|--------------|--------------------|
| 10 | 10 − 6 = 4 | 16 |
| 10 | 10 − 6 = 4 | 16 |
| 10 | 10 − 6 = 4 | 16 |
| 5 | 5 − 6 = −1 | 1 |
| 4 | 4 − 6 = −2 | 4 |
| 4 | 4 − 6 = −2 | 4 |
| 4 | 4 − 6 = −2 | 4 |
| 1 | 1 − 6 = −5 | 25 |
| 48 | | 86 |

Standard deviation $= \sqrt{\dfrac{\Sigma(X - \overline{X})^2}{N - 1}}$, where $\Sigma$ means "sum up,"

$X$ is a score, $\overline{X}$ is the mean of the scores, and $N$ is the number of scores.

Sum of scores = 48.

$\overline{X}$ = sum of scores ÷ 8 = 6.

Sum of squared differences from mean = 86.

Average of square differences from mean (dividing by the number of scores − 1) = 86 ÷ 7 = 12.3.

Square root of average square difference from the mean = 3.5.

Standard deviation = 3.5.

---

standard deviation, researchers typically divide by 1 less than the number of scores.) Last, take the square root of the answer. You have now calculated a standard deviation.

A standard deviation gives information about all members of a group, not just an average member. Knowing the standard deviation—that is, the variability associated with a mean— enables a researcher to make more accurate predictions. Table A.7 shows the reaction times for two groups of participants responding to a light. The mean is the same for both groups, but group 1 shows a large degree of variability, whereas group 2 shows little variability. The standard deviation (the estimate of variability) for group 1 participants is substantially higher than that for group 2 participants because the scores differ from the mean much more in the first group than in the second. Since the standard deviation for participants in group 2 is small, a researcher can more confidently predict that any one individual in that group will respond to the light in about 555 milliseconds (the mean response time). However, the researcher cannot make the same prediction for individuals in group 1 with the same confidence, since that group's standard deviation is high.

## TABLE A.7 Reaction Times, Mean Reaction Times, and Standard Deviations for Responses to a Light

Group 1 shows a wider range of scores and thus great variability. Group 2, in contrast, shows a narrow range of scores and little variability.

| Times for Group 1 (in milliseconds) | Times for Group 2 (in milliseconds) |
|-------------------------------------|-------------------------------------|
| 380 | 530 |
| 400 | 535 |
| 410 | 540 |
| 420 | 545 |
| 470 | 550 |
| 480 | 560 |
| 500 | 565 |
| 720 | 570 |
| 840 | 575 |
| 935 | 580 |
| Mean = 555 | Mean = 555 |
| Standard deviation = 197 | Standard deviation = 17 |

# THE NORMAL DISTRIBUTION

**NORMAL DISTRIBUTION**

The approximate distribution of scores expected when a sample is taken from a large population, drawn as a frequency polygon that often takes the form of a bell-shaped curve, known as a normal curve.

The **normal distribution** is the approximate distribution of scores expected when a sample is drawn from a large population; it is drawn as a frequency polygon that takes the form of a bell-shaped curve, known as a *normal curve*. Normal distributions usually have few scores at each extreme and progressively more scores toward the middle. Height, for example, is approximately normally distributed: More people are of average height than are very tall or very short (see Figure A.2). Weights, shoe sizes, IQs, and scores on psychology exams also tend to be normally distributed.

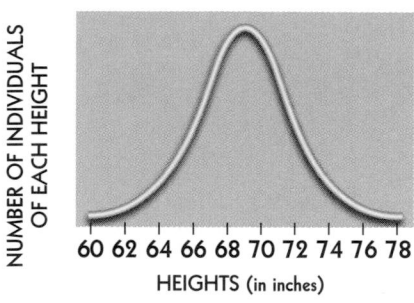

**FIGURE A.2**

**A Normal Curve for Height**

A normal curve for height shows that many more people are of average height than are at the extremes.

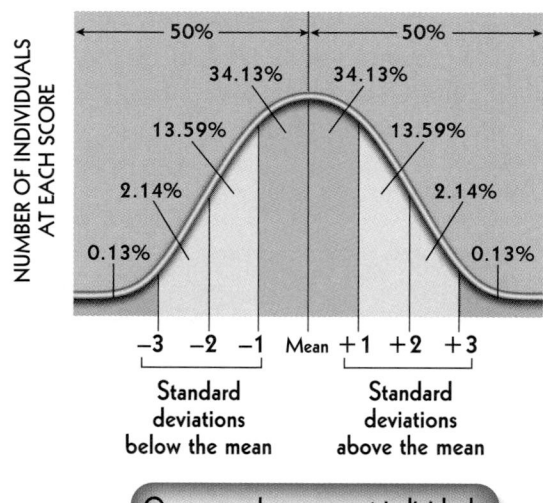

On a normal curve, most individuals score within 6 standard deviations, 3 on either side of the mean.

**FIGURE A.3**

**Percentages of Population for a Normal Curve**

**CHARACTERISTICS OF A NORMAL CURVE.** A normal curve has certain characteristics. The mean, mode, and median are the same; the distribution of scores around that central point is symmetrical. Also, most individuals have a score that occurs within 6 standard deviations—3 above the mean and 3 below it (see Figure A.3).

To understand this phenomenon, look at Figure A.4, which shows a normal curve for test scores. The mean is 50, and the standard deviation is 10 points. Note how each increment of 10 points above or below the mean accounts for fewer and fewer individuals: Scores between 50 and 60 account for 34.13 percent of those tested; scores between 60 and 70 account for 13.59 percent; scores above 70 account for less than 2.5 percent. The sum of these percentages (34.13 + 13.59 + 2.14 + 0.13) represents 50 percent of the scores.

When you know the mean and standard deviation of a set of data, you can estimate where an individual in the sample population stands relative to others. Figure A.5 shows a normal curve representing heights of a sample of men. Dennis is 74 inches tall. His height is 1 standard deviation above the mean, which means that he is taller than 84 percent of the population (0.13 + 2.14 + 13.59 + 34.13 + 34.13 = 84.12 percent). Rob, who is 66 inches tall, is taller than only 16 percent of the population. His height is 1 standard deviation below the mean.

**NORMAL CURVES: A PRACTICAL EXAMPLE.** Your grade on an examination is often determined by how other members of the class do. This is what instructors mean when they say that grades are calculated using a "sliding scale" or a "curve." If the average student in a class answers only 50 percent of the questions correctly, a student who answers 70 percent correctly has done a good job in comparison to the rest of the class. However, if the average student scores 85 percent, then someone who scores only 70 percent has not done so well.

Before they assign grades on a sliding scale, testing services and instructors generally calculate a mean and standard deviation. They then inspect the scores and "slide the scale" to an appropriate level based on those descriptive statistics. Figure A.6 shows scores achieved and grades assigned on a calculus test. The average score is 65 percent; the instructor decides to give students who score 65 percent a C, which she considers an average grade. Those students who do better get an A or a B, depending on how much better than the mean they score; those who do worse get a D or an F, depending on how much below the mean they score.

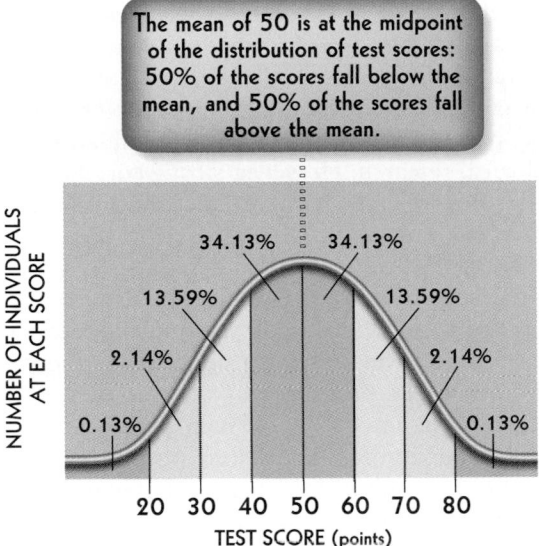

**FIGURE A.4**

**A Normal Curve with a Standard Deviation of 10 Points**

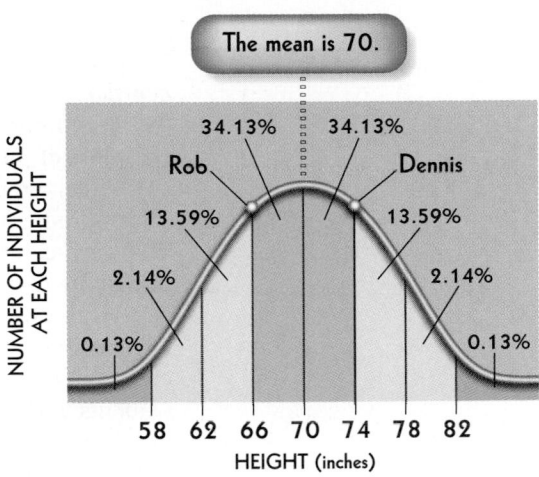

The mean is 70.

**FIGURE A.5**

**A Normal Curve with a Mean of 70 and a Standard Deviation of 4 Inches**

On this normal curve, Dennis's height of 74 inches is 1 standard deviation above the mean height of 70 inches. Rob's height is 66 inches, which is 1 standard deviation below the mean.

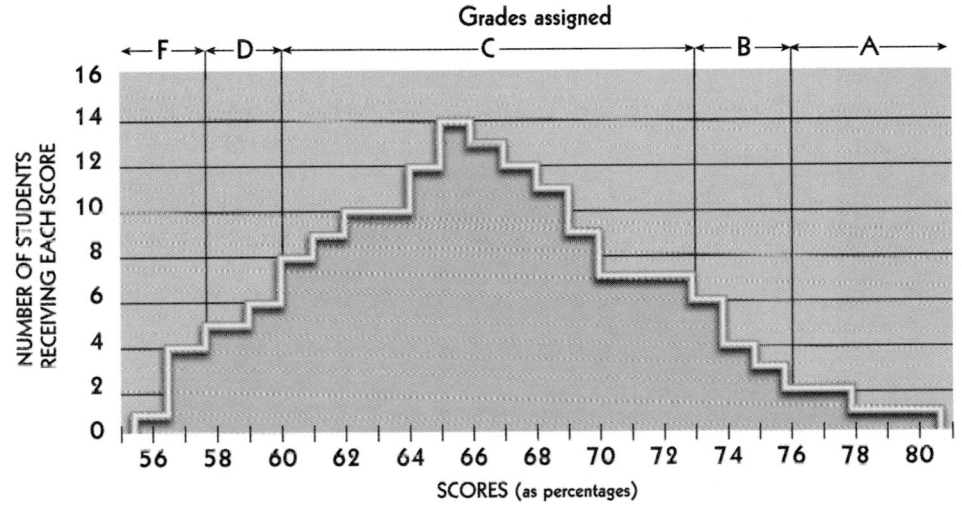

**FIGURE A.6**

**Grading on a Sliding Scale**

To calculate grades on a sliding scale, instructors often draw a graph like this one, showing the number of individuals who received each score. They then figure out the cutoff points for assigning letter grades (A, B, C, D, and F).

## CORRELATION

Sometimes a researcher wants to know about the relationship between two sets of data. For example, an instructor might want to know how strong the relationship was between the scores on test 1 and test 2. In such cases, a correlation will show the strength of this relationship.

A correlation exists when an increase in the value of one variable is regularly accompanied by an increase or a decrease in the value of a second variable. The degree and direction of relationship between two variables is expressed by a numerical value called the **correlation coefficient**. Correlation coefficients range from –1, through 0, to +1. Any correlation coefficient greater or less than 0, regardless of its

CORRELATION COEFFICIENT

A number that expresses the degree and direction of a relationship between two variables, ranging from –1 (a perfect negative correlation) to +1 (a perfect positive correlation).

sign, indicates that the variables are somehow related. When two variables are perfectly correlated, they are said to have a correlation coefficient of 1. Correlation coefficients close to 1 indicate stronger relationships than those close to 0.

When knowing the value of one variable allows a researcher to predict *precisely* the value of the second, the variables are perfectly correlated; a perfect correlation is, of course, a rare occurrence in psychological research. However, strong correlations allow predictions (although not perfect ones). This characteristic of correlation allows researchers to predict the occurrence of one variable if they know the other and know that the correlation between the two is strong. For example, there is a correlation between scores on the SAT and grade-point average during the first year in university or college. The correlation is not perfect (1.00), but it is high enough to allow colleges and universities to use the SAT as a way to select students; they choose students with high SAT scores because those students are more likely to do well.

Most variables are not perfectly correlated, and SAT scores and first-year college or university grade point averages are no exception. Some students receive high scores on the SAT but do poorly in college or university because they party too much, have trouble adapting to the daily routine, become distracted by extracurricular activities, and so forth. Other students get lower SAT scores and still succeed in college or university because they are disciplined students who work hard. The correlation between SAT scores and grades is high but not perfect. Only when the correlation is perfect is the prediction perfect. School admission committees know that they need to look at more than SAT scores in making admission decisions. However, the correlation between scholastic ability tests and grades allows for their use in predicting behaviour.

Before calculating a correlation coefficient, researchers often plot, or graph, their data in a scatter plot. A *scatter plot* is a diagram of data points that shows the relationship between two variables. An individual's score on one variable is measured on the horizontal axis, or x axis; the score on the second variable is measured on the vertical axis, or y axis. Thus, for example, a scatter plot might show 10 people's heights and weights; for each person, there is a height and weight pair. If one person is 6 feet tall and weighs 170 pounds, a dot appears on the graph at the point where 6 feet (on the x axis) and 170 pounds (on the y axis) intersect, as shown in Figure A.7(a). Plotting all 10 points in this way gives a graphic sense of the extent to which these two variables are related. Tall people do tend to weigh more than short people, in general, and when height and weight data are plotted, the graph usually shows that as height increases, so does weight (at least most of the time), indicating a correlation.

FIGURE A.7

**Three Types of Correlations: A Summary**

(a) In a positive correlation, an increase in one variable is associated with an increase in the other variable. (b) In a negative correlation, an increase in one variable is associated with a decrease in the other variable. (c) No correlation exists when changes in one variable are not associated in any systematic way with changes in the other variable.

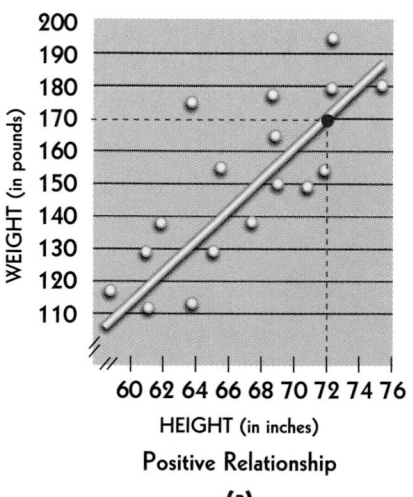

Positive Relationship

(a)

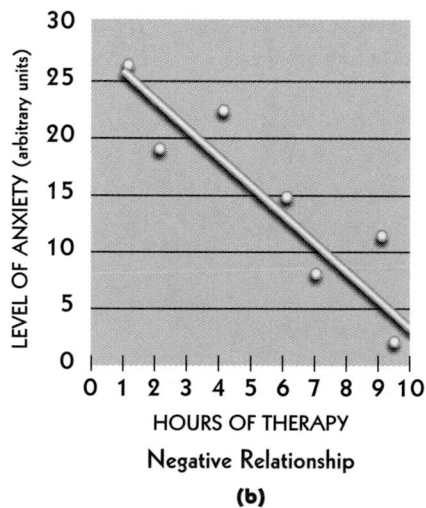

Negative Relationship

(b)

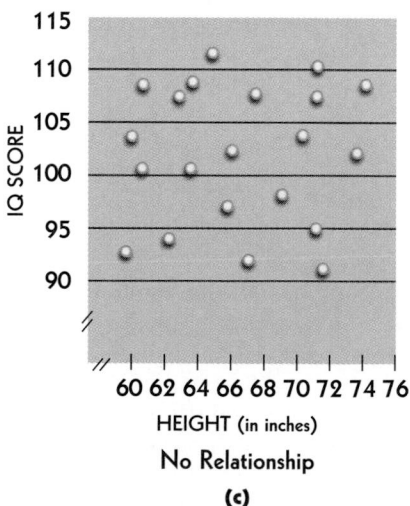

No Relationship

(c)

When one variable shows an increase in value and a second also shows an increase, the two variables are said to be positively related, and the relationship is known as a *positive correlation*. Height and weight show a positive correlation: Generally, as height increases, so does weight—although knowing a person's height does not allow someone to predict his or her weight precisely. The scatter plot in Figure A.7(a) shows a positive direction overall—upward and to the right. These two variables have a correlation coefficient of about 0.65.

On the other hand, if one variable decreases as the other increases, the variables are said to be negatively correlated, and the relationship is known as a *negative correlation*. For example, the relationship between the number of hours of therapy and the extent of anxiety shows a negative correlation—that is, as the number of hours of therapy increases, anxiety decreases; see Figure A.7(b). The scatter plot shows a corresponding movement downward and to the right. These two variables have a negative correlation of about –0.6 or –0.7.

A correlation coefficient of +0.7 is no stronger than one of –0.7. That is, the plus or minus sign changes the *direction,* but not the strength, of a relationship. The strength is shown by the number: The larger the number, the greater the strength of the correlation. A correlation coefficient of –0.8 is stronger than one of +0.7; a correlation coefficient of +0.6 is stronger than one of –0.5.

Some variables show absolutely no correlation; absence of correlation is expressed by a correlation coefficient of 0. Figure A.7(c) plots data for IQ and height. There is no pattern in the scatter plot and thus no correlation between IQ and height; the two variables have a correlation coefficient of 0.

As we saw in Chapter 2, a correlation in no way implies a cause-and-effect relationship. A correlation between two variables simply indicates that if there is an increase in one variable, there will probably be an increase (or decrease) in the other variable. It is only through experimental studies that researchers can make cause-and-effect statements. Many of the studies cited and described in this text are correlational, but far more are experimental. Whenever possible, researchers wish to draw causal inferences. To do so, they use a different type of statistic—inferential statistics.

# Inferential Statistics

Researchers perform experiments so that they can draw causal inferences. Researchers want to be able to tell whether a difference between a control group and an experimental group is due to manipulation of the independent variable, to extraneous variables, or to one or two deviant scores. It turns out that many of the manipulations and controls that researchers devise are necessary if they wish to make sound inferences, the topic we consider next.

Researchers use inferential statistics in making decisions about data—to determine whether their studies have turned out as hypothesized. **Inferential statistics** are procedures used to draw reasonable conclusions (generalizations) about larger populations from small samples of data. There are usually two issues to be explored: First, does the mean of a sample (a small group of people) actually reflect the mean of the larger population? Second, are differences between means (for example, between the mean for a control group and the mean for an experimental group) real and important, or are they merely chance occurrences?

### SIGNIFICANT DIFFERENCES

Psychologists hope to find a **significant difference**—a difference that is statistically unlikely to have occurred because of chance alone and thus is more likely to be due to the experimental conditions. To claim that a difference is significant, a researcher must show that a performance difference between two or more groups is not a

**INFERENTIAL STATISTICS** Procedures used to draw reasonable conclusions (generalizations) about larger populations from small samples of data.

**SIGNIFICANT DIFFERENCE** An experimentally obtained statistical difference that is unlikely to have occurred because of chance alone.

result of chance variations and can be repeated experimentally. Generally, psychologists assume that a difference is statistically significant if the likelihood of its occurring by chance is less than 5 percent—that is, if it would occur by chance fewer than 5 out of 100 times. But many researchers assume a difference is significant only if the likelihood of its occurring by chance is less than 1 percent.

It is difficult to decide whether a difference is significant by looking at the scores. Look back at Table A.5, which shows calculations for a set of memory scores. The results showed that the task-motivated group recalled slightly fewer words, on average, than the control group did. The hypnosis group recalled 4.8 more words, on average, than the control group. Since the hypnosis group did better than the control group, can the researcher conclude that hypnosis is a beneficial memory aid? Did the hypnosis group do significantly better than the control group? Is a 4.8-word difference significant? It is easy to see that if the difference in recall between the two groups had been 10 words, and if the variability within each group had been very small, the difference would be considered significant. Similarly, a 1- or 2-word difference would not be considered significant if the variability within each group was large. In the present case, a 4.8-word difference is not significant; the scores were highly variable, and the study included only a small sample of people. When scores are variable (widely dispersed), both statistical analysts and researchers are unlikely to view a small difference between two groups as significant or important. (See Figure A.8 for an illustration of this point.)

Even if they obtain statistically significant differences, researchers often repeat an experiment and hope that the results will be the same. Repeating an experiment to verify a result is called *replicating* the experiment. If the results of a replicated experiment are the same as the original experiment, a researcher can generally say that the observed difference between the two groups is statistically significant, showing a reliable pattern of difference between control and experimental groups.

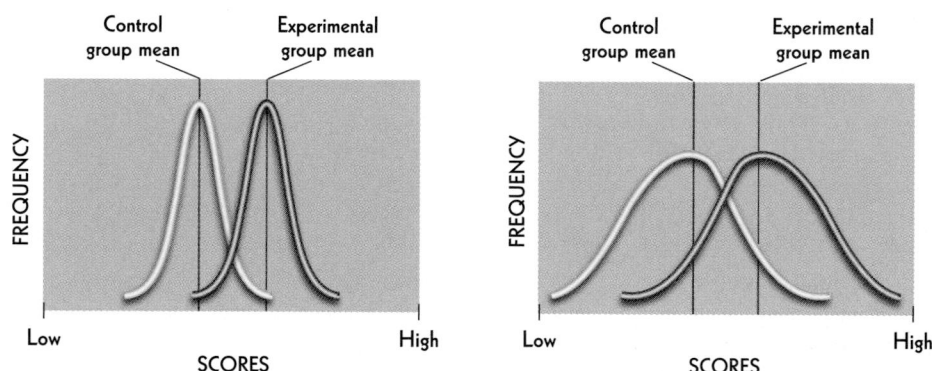

**FIGURE A.8**

**The Possible Outcomes of Experiments Whose Means Are Identical**

In the first graph, the observed scores all cluster around the means—there is little variability. The difference between the means in the first graph is therefore likely to be significant. The means in the second graph (although identical to the ones in the first graph) are unlikely to be deemed significantly different—the scores are too widely distributed. Here, there is too much variability; the means may be affected by extreme scores. Thus, a scientist is less likely to accept these means as different from one another.

# Summary and Review

## DESCRIPTIVE STATISTICS

### What is statistics?

> *Statistics* is the branch of mathematics that deals with classifying and analyzing data. Researchers use statistics to help them understand and interpret the data they gather.   **p. 650**

### How do descriptive statistics help researchers organize data?

> Researchers use *descriptive statistics* to summarize, condense, and describe sets of data. A *frequency distribution* is a way of organizing data to show the number of times each item occurs; the graphic version of a frequency distribution is a *frequency polygon.*   **pp. 650–651**

### How are measures of central tendency used?

> *Measures of central tendency* are descriptive statistics that indicate which single score best represents an entire set of scores. The most frequently used measure of central tendency is the *mean*, or arithmetic average of all the scores. Also used are the *mode*, the most frequently observed score, and the *median*, the data point that has 50 percent of the scores above it and 50 percent below it.   **pp. 652–656**

### What is a measure of variability?

> A measure of *variability* is any statistic that describes the extent to which scores in a distribution differ from one another. One such measure, the *range*, shows the spread of scores in a distribution. Another measure of variability, the *standard deviation*, shows the extent to which individual scores in a distribution vary from the mean.   **pp. 655–657**

### What are the key characteristics of a normal distribution?

> The mean, mode, and median of a *normal distribution*, or normal curve, are generally assumed to be the same, and the scores are distributed symmetrically around that central point.   **pp. 658–659**

## What is correlation, and how is it used?

> A *correlation coefficient* is a number that expresses the degree of relationship between two variables. Correlation coefficients range from +1 to –1. When two variables are perfectly correlated, they are said to have a correlation coefficient of 1. A plus or minus sign in front of the correlation coefficient indicates the direction, not the strength, of a correlation relationship. The strength is shown by the number: The closer the number is to 1, the greater the strength of the correlation.   **pp. 659–661**

## Compare correlational and experimental studies with regard to cause and effect.

> Correlational studies make no statements about cause and effect. They simply show that if there is an increase in one variable, there will probably be an increase or decrease in another variable. This property allows researchers to make predictions based on strong correlations, but only experimental studies allow researchers to make cause-and-effect statements.   **p. 661**

### KEY TERMS

statistics, p. 650; descriptive statistics, p. 650; frequency distribution, p. 651; frequency polygon, p. 651; measure of central tendency, p. 651; mean, p. 652; mode, p. 652; median, p. 653; variability, p. 656; range, p. 656; standard deviation, p. 656; normal distribution, p. 658; correlation coefficient, p. 659

## INFERENTIAL STATISTICS

### What is the role of inferential statistics?

> Researchers use *inferential statistics* to determine whether two or more groups differ from one another and whether the difference is a result of chance. A *significant difference* is one that most likely did not occur by chance and that can be repeated experimentally with similar groups of people. Repeating an experiment to verify a result is called replicating the experiment.   **p. 661–662**

### KEY TERMS

inferential statistics, p. 661; significant difference, p. 661

# Glossary

**Abnormal behaviour** Behaviour characterized as not typical, socially unacceptable, distressing, maladaptive, and/or the result of distorted cognitions.

**Abnormal psychology** The field of psychology concerned with the assessment, treatment, and prevention of maladaptive behaviour.

**Absolute threshold** The statistically determined minimum level of stimulation necessary to excite a perceptual system.

**Accommodation** According to Piaget, the process of modifying previously developed schemes to adapt them to new experiences.

**Accommodation** The change in the shape of the lens of the eye to keep an object in focus on the retina when the object is moved closer to or farther away from the observer.

**Action potential** An electrical current sent down the axon of a neuron, initiated in an all-or-none fashion by a rapid reversal of the electrical balance of the cell membrane. Also known as a spike discharge.

**Actor–observer effect** The tendency to attribute the behaviour of others to dispositional causes but to attribute one's own behaviour to situational causes.

**Adaptation** Occurs when a trait or inherited characteristic has increased in a population.

**Addictive drug** A drug that causes a compulsive physiological need and that, when withheld, produces withdrawal symptoms.

**Adolescence [add-oh-LESS-sense]** The period extending from the onset of puberty to early adulthood.

**Afferent neurons** Neurons that send messages to the spinal cord and brain.

**Ageism** Prejudice against the elderly and the discrimination that follows from it.

**Aggression** Any behaviour designed to harm another person or thing.

**Agnosia** An inability to recognize a sensory stimulus that should be recognizable (because all normal perceptual processes are intact and there is no verbal, memory, or intellectual impairment).

**Agonist [AG-oh-nist]** Chemical that mimics the actions of a neurotransmitter, usually by occupying receptor sites and facilitating neurochemical transfers.

**Agoraphobia [AG-or-uh-FOE-bee-uh]** An anxiety disorder characterized by fear and avoidance of being alone or isolated in open and public places from which escape might be difficult or embarrassing.

**Alcoholic** A problem drinker who also has both a physiological and a psychological need to consume alcohol and to experience its effects.

**Algorithm [AL-go-rith-um]** A simple, precise, and exhaustive problem-solving procedure that follows a set of rules to implement a step-by-step analysis, as in working out a math problem.

**All-or-none** Either at full strength or not at all; a principle by which neurons fire.

**Altruism [AL-true-ism]** Behaviours that benefit other people and for which there is no discernible extrinsic reward, recognition, or appreciation.

**Alzheimer's [ALTZ-hy-merz] disease** A chronic and progressive disorder of the brain that is the most common cause of degenerative dementia.

**Amnesia [am-NEE-zhuh]** Inability to remember information (typically all events within a specific period), usually due to physiological trauma.

**Amplitude** The total energy of a sound wave, which determines the loudness of a sound. Also known as intensity.

**Anal stage** Freud's second stage of personality development, from about age two to about age three, during which children learn to control the immediate gratification they obtain through defecation and to become responsive to the demands of society.

**Androgynous** Having both stereotypically male and stereotypically female characteristics.

**Animistic thinking** The attribution of intentions or animate qualities to some objects or events.

**Anorexia nervosa** An eating disorder characterized by an obstinate and wilful refusal to eat, a distorted body image, and an intense fear of being fat.

**Antagonist** Chemical that opposes the actions of a neurotransmitter, usually by preventing the neurotransmitter from occupying a receptor site.

**Anterograde amnesia** Loss of memory for events and experiences that occurred after the amnesia-causing event.

**Anti-social personality disorder** Personality disorder characterized by egocentricity, behaviour that is irresponsible and that violates the rights of other people, a lack of guilt feelings, an inability to understand other people, and a lack of fear of punishment.

**Anxiety** A generalized feeling of fear and apprehension that may be related to a particular situation or object and is often accompanied by increased physiological arousal.

**Applied psychology** The branch of psychology that uses psychological principles to help solve practical problems of everyday life.

**Appraisal** The evaluation of the significance of a situation or event as it relates to a person's well-being.

**Approach–approach conflict** Conflict that results from having to choose between two equally attractive alternatives or goals.

**Approach–avoidance conflict** Conflict that results from having to choose an alternative or goal that has both attractive and repellent aspects.

**Archetypes [AR-ki-types]** In Jung's theory, the emotionally charged ideas and images that are rich in meaning and symbolism and exist within the collective unconscious.

**Arousal** Activation of the central nervous system, the autonomic nervous system, and the muscles and glands; according to some motivational theorists, organisms seek to maintain optimal levels of arousal by actively varying their exposure to arousing stimuli.

**Assessment** Process of evaluating individual differences among human beings by means of tests, interviews, observations, and recordings of physiological processes.

**Assimilation** According to Piaget, the process by which a person absorbs new ideas and experiences and incorporates them into existing schemes.

**Attachment** The strong emotional tie that a person develops toward significant others.

**Attitudes** Long-lasting patterns of feelings and beliefs about other people, ideas, or objects that are based in a person's past experiences, shape his or her future behaviour, are evaluative in nature, and serve certain functions.

**Attribution**   The process by which a person infers other people's motives and intentions by observing their behaviour.

**Autonomic [au-toe-NOM-ick] nervous system**   The part of the peripheral nervous system that controls the vital and automatic processes of the body, such as heart rate, digestion, blood pressure, and functioning of internal organs.

**Aversive counterconditioning**   A counterconditioning technique in which an aversive or noxious stimulus is paired with a stimulus that elicits an undesired behaviour so that the client will adopt a new, more worthwhile behaviour in response to the familiar stimulus and thus cease the undesired behaviour.

**Avoidance–avoidance conflict**   Conflict that results from having to choose between two equally distasteful alternatives or goals.

**Axon**   A thin, elongated process that leads from the neuron cell body and serves to transmit signals from the cell body through the axon terminal to adjacent neurons, muscles, or glands.

**Babinski reflex**   A reflex in which a newborn projects its toes outward and up when the soles of its feet are touched.

**Backward search**   A heuristic procedure in which a problem solver works backward from the goal or endpoint to the current position, both to analyze the problem and to reduce the steps needed to get from the current position to the goal.

**Behaviour therapy**   A therapy based on the application of learning principles to human behaviour that focuses on changing overt behaviours rather than on understanding subjective feelings, unconscious processes, or motivations. Also known as behaviour modification.

**Behavioural genetics**   Seeks to determine both genetic (nature) and environmental (nurture) contributions to individual variations in human behaviour.

**Behaviourism**   The school of psychological thought that rejects the study of the contents of consciousness and focuses on describing and measuring only that which is observable directly or through assessment instruments.

**Binocular depth cues**   Any visual cues for depth perception that require the use of both eyes.

**Biofeedback**   A technique by which individuals can monitor and learn to control the involuntary activity of some of the body's organs and functions.

**Biological perspective**   The school of psychological thought that examines psychological issues based on how heredity and biological structures affect mental processes and behaviour and that focuses on how physical mechanisms affect emotions, feelings, thoughts, desires, and sensory experiences; also known as the neuroscience perspective.

**Bipolar disorder**   Mood disorder originally known as manic–depressive disorder because it is characterized by behaviour that vacillates between two extremes: mania and depression.

**Body language**   Communication of information through body positions and gestures.

**Bonding**   A special process of emotional attachment that may occur between parents and babies in the minutes and hours immediately after birth.

**Brain**   The part of the central nervous system that is located in the skull and that regulates, monitors, processes, and guides other nervous system activity.

**Brainstorming**   A problem-solving technique that involves considering all possible solutions without making initial evaluative judgments.

**Brightness**   The lightness or darkness of reflected light, determined in large part by the light's intensity.

**Bulimia nervosa**   An eating disorder characterized by repeated episodes of binge eating followed by purging.

**Bystander effect**   The unwillingness of witnesses to an event to help, an effect that increases when there are more observers.

**Case study**   A method of interviewing participants to gain information about their backgrounds, including data on factors such as childhood, family, education, and social and sexual interactions.

**Catatonic [CAT-uh-TONN-ick] type of schizophrenia**   Type of schizophrenia characterized either by displays of excited or violent motor activity or by stupor.

**Categorical speech perception**   The ability to discriminate sounds that belong to the same phonemic class.

**Central nervous system**   One of the two major parts of the nervous system, consisting of the brain and the spinal cord.

**Centration [sent-RAY-shun]**   The tendency to focus on or reason with only the single most salient feature of a task or situation.

**Cerebellum [seh-rah-BELL-um]**   A large structure that is attached to the back surface of the brain stem and that influences balance, coordination, and movement.

**Challenge**   The emotional state that results when circumstances change in a way that requires action or effort.

**Child abuse**   Physical, emotional, or sexual mistreatment of a child.

**Chromosomes**   Microscopic strands of deoxyribonucleic acid (DNA) found in the nucleus (centre) of every body cell.

**Chunks**   Manageable and meaningful units of information that can be easily encoded, stored, and retrieved.

**Circadian [sir-KAY-dee-an] rhythms**   Internally generated patterns of body functions, including hormonal signals, sleep, blood pressure, and temperature regulation, that have an approximate 24-hour cycle and occur even when normal day and night cues are removed.

**Classical conditioning**   A conditioning process in which an originally neutral stimulus, by repeated pairing with a stimulus that normally elicits a response, comes to elicit a similar or identical response. Also known as Pavlovian conditioning.

**Client-centred therapy**   An insight therapy, developed by Carl Rogers, that seeks to help people evaluate the world and themselves from their own perspective by providing them with a nondirective environment and unconditional positive regard. Also known as person-centred therapy.

**Clinical psychologist**   A mental health practitioner who views behaviour and mental processes from a psychological perspective and who uses research-based knowledge to treat persons with serious emotional or behavioural problems or to do research into the causes of behaviour.

**Cognitive dissonance [COG-nuh-tiv DIS-uh-nins]**   The state of discomfort that results when a discrepancy exists between two or more of a person's beliefs or between a person's beliefs and overt behaviour.

**Cognitive psychology**   The study of the overlapping fields of learning, perception, memory, and thought, with a special emphasis on how people attend to, acquire, transform, store, and retrieve knowledge.

**Cognitive theories**   In the study of motivation, an explanation of behaviour that asserts that people actively and regularly determine their own goals and the means of achieving them through thought.

**Collective unconscious**   In Jung's dream theory, a storehouse of primitive ideas and images in the unconscious that is inherited from one's ancestors; these inherited ideas and images, called archetypes, are emotionally charged and rich in meaning and symbolism.

**Colour blindness**   The inability to perceive different hues.

**Community psychology**   The branch of psychology that seeks to reach out to society to provide services such as community mental health centres and especially to effect social change.

**Concept**   A mental category used to classify an event or object according to a common property.

**Concordance rate**   The degree to which a condition or trait is shared by two or more individuals or groups.

**Concrete operational stage** Piaget's third stage of cognitive development (lasting from approximately age 6 or 7 to age 11 or 12), during which the child develops the ability to understand constant factors in the environment, rules, and higher-order symbolism.

**Conditioned response** A response elicited by a conditioned stimulus.

**Conditioned stimulus** A neutral stimulus that, through repeated association with an unconditioned stimulus, begins to elicit a conditioned response.

**Conditioning** A systematic procedure through which associations and responses to specific stimuli are learned.

**Conduction deafness** Deafness resulting from interference with the transmission of sound to the neural mechanism of the inner ear.

**Conflict** The emotional state or condition in which a person has to make difficult decisions about two or more competing motives, behaviours, or impulses.

**Conformity** People's tendency to change attitudes or behaviours to be consistent with other people or with social norms.

**Consciousness (1)** Freud's level of mental life that consists of those experiences that we are aware of at any given time.

**(2)** The general state of being aware of and responsive to events in the environment, including one's own mental processes.

**Conservation** The ability to recognize that perceptual changes (such as the "shape" of a liquid put in a different container) may not indicate that an underlying quality has changed (for example, the liquid still has the same weight, substance, and volume).

**Consolidation** [kon-SOL-ih-DAY-shun] The process of changing a short-term memory to a long-term one.

**Continuous reinforcement** Reinforcement for every occurrence of the targeted behaviour.

**Control group** In an experiment, the comparison group—the group of participants tested on the dependent variable in the same way as the experimental group but for whom the treatment is not given.

**Convergence** The movement of the eyes toward each other in order to keep visual input at corresponding points on the retinas as an object moves closer to the observer.

**Convergent thinking** In problem solving, the process of narrowing down choices and alternatives to arrive at a suitable answer.

**Convolutions** Characteristic folds in the tissues of the cerebral hemispheres and the overlying cortex.

**Coping** Process by which a person takes some action to manage, master, tolerate, or reduce environmental or internal demands that cause or might cause stress and that tax the individual's inner resources.

**Coping strategies** The techniques people use to deal with the stress of changing situations.

**Correlation coefficient** A number that expresses the degree and direction of a relationship between two variables, ranging from 21 (a perfect negative correlation) to 11 (a perfect positive correlation).

**Correlation coefficients** Statistical values that can be calculated between two scores to determine the nature and degree of relatedness between those variables.

**Correlational study** A type of descriptive research design that establishes the degree of relationship between two variables.

**Cortex** The convoluted, or furrowed, exterior covering of the brain's hemispheres, which is about two millimetres thick, consists of six thin layers of nerve cells, and traditionally is divided into a series of lobes, or areas, each with characteristic structures; thought to be involved in both sensory interpretation and complex thought processes.

**Counterconditioning** A process of reconditioning in which a person is taught a new, more adaptive response to a familiar stimulus.

**Creativity** A feature of thought and problem solving that includes the tendency to generate or recognize ideas considered to be high quality, original, novel, and appropriate.

**Critical period** A time in the development of an organism when it is especially sensitive to certain environmental influences; outside of that period the same influences will have far less effect.

**Cross-sectional study** A type of research design that compares individuals of different ages to determine how they differ on a particular important dimension.

**Cross-sectional study** A type of research design that compares individuals of different ages to determine how they differ.

**Crowding** The perception that one's space is too limited.

**CT (computerized tomography) scans** Computer-assisted X-ray images of the brain (or any area of the body) in three dimensions—essentially a computerized series of X-rays that show photographic slices of part of the brain or body.

**Dark adaptation** The increase in sensitivity to light that occurs when the illumination level changes from high to low, causing chemicals in the rods and cones to regenerate and return to their inactive state.

**Debriefing** A procedure to inform participants about the true nature of an experiment after its completion.

**Decay** Loss of information from memory as a result of disuse and the passage of time.

**Deception** Misleading research participants as to the nature or purpose of an experiment or condition in order to study a particular response. Is strictly limited for ethical reasons.

**Decision making** Assessing and choosing among alternatives.

**Declarative memory** Memory for specific information.

**Defence mechanism** An unconscious way of reducing anxiety by distorting perceptions of reality.

**Deindividuation** The process by which individuals in a group lose their self-awareness and concern with evaluation and may engage in anti-normative behaviour.

**Delusions** False beliefs that are inconsistent with reality but are held in spite of evidence that disproves them.

**Demand characteristics** Elements of an experimental situation that might cause a participant to perceive the situation in a certain way or become aware of the purpose of the study and thus bias the participant to behave in a certain way, and in so doing, distort results.

**Dementia** A long-standing impairment of mental functioning and global cognitive abilities in otherwise alert individuals, causing memory loss and related symptoms.

**Dendrites** Thin, bushy, widely branching fibres extending from the neuron cell body that receive signals from neighbouring neurons and carry them back to the cell body.

**Denial** A defence mechanism by which people refuse to accept reality or recognize the true source of their anxiety.

**Dependent variable** The variable in a controlled experiment that is expected to change because of the manipulation of the independent variable.

**Depressive disorders** General category of mood disorders in which people show extreme and persistent sadness, despair, and loss of interest in life's usual activities.

**Descriptive statistics** A general set of procedures used to summarize, condense, and describe sets of data.

**Descriptive studies** A type of research method that allows researchers to measure variables so that they can develop a description of a situation or phenomenon.

**Developmental psychology** The study of the lifelong, age-related processes of change in the physical, cognitive, emotional, and social domains of functioning; such changes are rooted in biological mechanisms that are genetically controlled as well as in social interactions.

**Deviation IQ** A standard IQ test score for which the mean and variability remain constant at all ages.

**Diabetes mellitus [mel-LIGHT-us]** A condition in which too little insulin is produced, causing sugar to be transported insufficiently out of the blood and into body cells.

**Dichromats** People who can distinguish only two of the three basic colours; they have difficulty distinguishing between either red and green or blue and yellow.

**Discrimination** Behaviour targeted at individuals or groups with the aim of holding them apart and treating them differently.

**Disorganized type of schizophrenia** Type of schizophrenia characterized by severely disturbed thought processes, frequent incoherence, disorganized behaviour, and inappropriate affect.

**Displacement** A defence mechanism by which people divert sexual or aggressive feelings for one person onto another person.

**Dissociative amnesia** Dissociative disorder characterized by the sudden and extensive inability to recall important personal information, usually of a traumatic or stressful nature.

**Dissociative disorders** Psychological disorders characterized by a sudden but temporary alteration in consciousness, identity, sensorimotor behaviour, or memory.

**Dissociative identity disorder** Dissociative disorder characterized by the existence within an individual of two or more distinct personalities, each of which is dominant at different times and directs the individual's behaviour at those times; commonly known as multiple personality disorder.

**Divergent thinking** In problem solving, widening the range of possibilities and expanding the options for solutions.

**Double bind** A situation in which an individual is given two different and inconsistent messages.

**Double-blind technique** A research technique in which neither the experimenter nor the participants know who is in the control and experimental groups.

**Dream** A state of consciousness that occurs during sleep and is usually accompanied by vivid visual, tactile, or auditory imagery.

**Dream analysis** A psychoanalytic technique in which a patient's dreams are interpreted and used to provide insight into the individual's unconscious motivations.

**Drive** An internal aroused condition that directs an organism to satisfy physiological needs.

**Drive theory** An explanation of behaviour that assumes that an organism is motivated to act because of a need to attain, re-establish, balance, or maintain some goal that helps with the survival of the organism or the species.

**Drug** Any chemical substance that alters normal biological processes.

**Eclecticism [ek-LECK-ti-sizm]** In psychology, a combination of theories, facts, or techniques; the practice of using whatever clinical and counselling techniques are appropriate for an individual client rather than relying exclusively on the techniques of one school of psychology.

**Educational psychology** The systematic application of psychological principles to learning and teaching.

**Efferent neurons** Neurons that send messages from the brain and spinal cord to other structures in the body.

**Ego** In Freud's theory, the part of personality that seeks to satisfy instinctual needs in accordance with reality.

**Egocentrism [ee-go-SENT-rism]** The inability to perceive a situation or event except in relation to oneself.

**Elaboration likelihood model** A theory suggesting that there are two routes to attitude change: central, which focuses on thoughtful, elaborative considerations, and peripheral, which focuses on less careful, more emotional, and even superficial considerations.

**Elaborative rehearsal** Involves repetition and analysis, in which the stimulus may be associated with (linked to) other information and further processed.

**Electroconvulsive [ee-LECK-tro-con-VUL-siv] therapy (ECT)** A treatment for severe mental illness in which an electric current is briefly applied to the head in order to produce a generalized seizure.

**Electroencephalogram (EEG) [eel-ECK-tro-en-SEFF-uh-low-gram]** Record of electrical brain wave patterns obtained through electrodes placed on the scalp.

**Embryo [EM-bree-o]** The prenatal organism from implantation to the eighth week following conception.

**Emotion** A subjective response (feeling), usually accompanied by a physiological change, which is often interpreted by an individual and then readies the individual for some action that is associated with a change in behaviour.

**Empowerment** Helping people in the community enhance their existing skills and develop new skills, knowledge, and motivation so that they can gain control over their own lives.

**Encoding** The organizing of information so that the nervous system can process it.

**Encoding specificity principle** The notion that the effectiveness of a specific retrieval cue depends on how well it matches up with the originally encoded information.

**Endocrine [END-oh-krin] glands** Ductless glands that secrete hormones directly into the bloodstream, rather than through a specific duct into a target organ.

**Endorphins [en-DOR-finz]** Painkillers produced naturally in the brain and pituitary gland.

**Environmental psychology** The study of how physical settings affect human behaviour and how people change their environment.

**Episodic [ep-ih-SAW-dick] memory** Memory of specific personal events and situations (episodes), tagged with information about time.

**Equity theory** In I/O psychology, the theory that suggests that what people bring to a work situation should be balanced by what they receive compared with other workers; thus, input should be balanced by compensation, or rewards, or workers will adjust their work level and potentially their job satisfaction accordingly.

**Ergonomics** The study of the fit between human anatomy or physiology, the demands of a particular task or piece of equipment, and the environment in which the task occurs.

**Ethics** Rules of proper and acceptable conduct that investigators use to guide psychological research; these rules concern the treatment of animals, the rights of human beings, and the responsibilities of investigators.

**Evolutionary psychology** The psychological perspective that seeks to explain and predict behaviour by analyzing how specific behaviours, over the course of many generations, have led to adaptations that allow the species to survive; it assumes that behaviours that help organisms adapt, be fit, and survive will be passed on to successive generations through a greater chance of reproduction.

**Ex post facto study** A type of research design that contrasts groups of people who differ on some variable of interest to the researcher.

**Expectancy theories (1)** Explanations of behaviour that focus on people's expectations about reaching a goal and their need for achievement as energizing factors.

**(2)** Theories that suggest that a worker's effort and desire to maintain goal-directed behaviour (to work) is determined by expectancies regarding the outcomes of that work.

**Experiment** A procedure in which a researcher systematically manipulates and observes elements of a situation in order to answer a question and, usually, to test hypotheses and make inferences about cause and effect.

**Experimental design** A design in which researchers manipulate an independent variable and measure a dependent variable to determine a cause-and-effect relationship.

**Experimental group**   In an experiment, a group of participants to whom a treatment is given.

**Explicit memory**   Conscious memory that a person is aware of, such as a memory of a word in a list or an event that occurred in the past.

**Extinction [egg-STINK-shun] (1)**   In classical conditioning, the process through which not presenting the unconditioned stimulus gradually reduces the probability of a conditioned response.

**(2)**   In operant conditioning, the process by which the probability of an organism's emitting a conditioned response is reduced when reinforcement no longer follows the response.

**Extrinsic [ecks-TRINZ-ick] motivation**   Motivation supplied by rewards that come from the external environment.

**Factor analysis**   Statistical procedure designed to discover the independent elements (factors) in any set of data.

**Family therapy**   A type of therapy in which two or more people who are committed to one another's well-being are treated at once, in an effort to change the ways they interact.

**Fetus [FEET-us]**   The prenatal organism from the eighth week following conception until birth.

**Fixation**   An excessive attachment to some person or object that was appropriate only at an earlier stage of development.

**Fixed-interval schedule**   A reinforcement schedule in which a reinforcer (reward) is delivered after a specified interval of time, provided that the required response occurs at least once after the interval.

**Fixed-ratio schedule**   A reinforcement schedule in which a reinforcer (reward) is delivered after a specified number of responses has occurred.

**Forebrain**   The largest, most complicated, and most advanced organizationally and functionally of the three divisions of the brain, with many interrelated parts: the thalamus and hypothalamus, the limbic system, the basal ganglia and corpus callosum, and the cortex.

**Formal operational stage**   Piaget's fourth and final stage of cognitive development (beginning at about age 12), during which the individual can think hypothetically, can consider all future possibilities, and is capable of deductive logic.

**Free association**   A psychoanalytic technique in which a person reports to the therapist his or her thoughts and feelings as they occur, regardless of how trivial, illogical, or objectionable their content may appear.

**Frequency**   In sound waves, a measure of the number of times a complete change in air pressure occurs per unit of time; expressed in hertz (Hz), or cycles per second.

**Frequency distribution**   A chart or array of scores, usually arranged from the highest to the lowest, showing the number of instances for each score.

**Frequency polygon**   Graph of a frequency distribution that shows the number of instances of obtained scores, usually with the data points connected by straight lines.

**Frustration**   The emotional state or condition that results when a goal—work, family, or personal—is thwarted or blocked.

**Fulfilment**   In Rogers' theory of personality, an inborn tendency directing people toward actualizing their essential nature and thus attaining their potential.

**Functional fixedness**   The inability to see that an object can have a function other than its stated or usual one.

**Functional MRI (fMRI)**   Imaging technique that registers changes in the metabolism (energy consumption) of cells in various regions of the brain and thus allows observation of activity in the brain as it takes place.

**Functionalism**   The school of psychological thought (an outgrowth of structuralism) that was concerned with how and why the conscious mind works; its main aim was to know how the contents of consciousness functioned and worked together.

**Fundamental attribution error**   The tendency to attribute other people's behaviour to dispositional (internal) causes rather than situational (external) causes.

**Gender identity**   A person's sense of being male or female.

**Gender schema theory**   The theory that children and adolescents use gender as an organizing theme to classify and interpret their perceptions about the world and themselves.

**Generalized anxiety disorder**   An anxiety disorder characterized by persistent anxiety on more days than not for at least six months, sometimes with autonomic hyperactivity, apprehension, problems with motor tension, and difficulty in concentrating.

**Genes**   The fundamental units of hereditary transmission, consisting of DNA.

**Genetic mapping**   Dividing the chromosomes into smaller fragments that can be characterized and ordered (mapped) so that the fragments reflect their respective locations on specific chromosomes.

**Genetics**   The study of heredity, which is the biological transmission of traits and characteristics from parents to offspring.

**Genital [JEN-it-ul] stage**   Freud's last stage of personality development, from the onset of puberty through adulthood, during which the sexual conflicts of childhood resurface (at puberty) and are often resolved (during adolescence).

**Genome**   The total DNA blueprint of heritable traits contained in every cell of the body.

**Genotype**   A person's genetic makeup that is fixed at conception.

**Gestalt [gesh-TALT] psychology**   The school of psychological thought that argued that behaviour cannot be studied in parts but must be viewed as a whole; the focus was on the unity of perception and thinking.

**Goal-setting theory**   A theory that asserts that setting specific, clear, attainable goals for a given task will lead to better performance.

**Grammar**   The linguistic description of how a language functions, especially the rules and patterns used for generating appropriate and comprehensible sentences.

**Grasping reflex**   A reflex in which a newborn vigorously grasps any object touching its palm or fingers or placed in its hand.

**Group**   Two or more individuals who are loosely or cohesively related and who share some common characteristics and goals.

**Group polarization**   Exaggeration of individuals' pre-existing attitudes as a result of group discussion.

**Group therapy**   A psychotherapeutic process in which several people meet as a group with a therapist.

**Groupthink**   The tendency of people in a group to seek agreement with one another when reaching a decision, usually prematurely.

**Halo effect**   The tendency for one particular or outstanding characteristic of an individual (or a group) to influence the evaluation of other characteristics.

**Hawthorne effect**   The finding, based on early research studies at the Hawthorne industrial plant, that people behave differently (usually better) when they know they are being observed.

**Health psychology**   Subfield concerned with the use of psychological ideas and principles to enhance health, prevent illness, diagnose and treat disease, and improve rehabilitation.

**Heritability**   Refers to estimates of the proportion of variation in a trait in a population determined by heredity—with the remainder determined by environment.

**Heuristics [hyoo-RISS-ticks]**   Sets of strategies that act as guidelines, not strict rules and procedures, for discovery-oriented problem solving.

**Higher-order conditioning**   A process by which a neutral stimulus takes on conditioned properties through pairing with a conditioned stimulus.

**Hindbrain**   The most primitive organizationally of the three functional divisions of the brain, consisting of the medulla, the reticular formation, the pons, and the cerebellum.

**Homeostasis**   A tendency to attempt to maintain a constant state of inner stability or balance.

**Hormones**   Chemicals produced by endocrine glands that regulate the activities of specific organs or cells.

**Hue**   The psychological property of light referred to as colour, determined by the wavelengths of reflected light.

**Human factors**   The study of the relationship of human beings to machines and to workplaces and other environments.

**Humanistic psychology**   The school of psychological thought that emphasizes the uniqueness of each human being and the idea that human beings have free will to determine their destiny.

**Humanistic theory**   An explanation of behaviour that emphasizes the entirety of life rather than individual components of behaviour; focuses on human dignity, individual choice, and self-worth.

**Hyperopic [HY-per-OP-ick]**   Having trouble seeing things that are close but able to see objects at a distance. Also known as farsighted.

**Hypnosis**   An altered state of consciousness brought about by procedures that may induce a trance.

**Hypoglycemia [hi-po-gly-SEE-me-uh]**   A condition in which overproduction of insulin results in a very low blood sugar level.

**Hypothalamus**   A relatively small structure of the forebrain, lying just below the thalamus, that acts through its connections with the rest of the forebrain and the midbrain and affects many complex behaviours, such as eating, drinking, and sexual activity.

**Hypothesis**   A tentative statement or idea expressing a causal relationship between two events or variables that are to be evaluated in a research study.

**Id**   In Freud's theory, the source of a person's instinctual energy, which works mainly on the pleasure principle.

**Ideal self**   In Rogers' theory of personality, the self a person would ideally like to be.

**Illusion**   A perception of a physical stimulus that differs from measurable reality and normal expectations about its appearance.

**Imagery**   The creation or recreation of a mental picture of a sensory or perceptual experience.

**Imaginary audience**   A cognitive distortion experienced by adolescents, in which they see themselves as "on stage," with an imaginary audience always watching them.

**Implicit memory**   Memory a person is not aware of possessing; considered an almost unconscious process, implicit memory occurs almost automatically.

**Impression formation**   The process by which a person uses the behaviour and appearance of others to infer their internal states and intentions.

**Independent variable**   The variable in a controlled experiment that the experimenter directly and purposely manipulates to see how the other variables under study will be affected.

**Industrial/organizational (I/O) psychology**   The study of how individual behaviour is affected by the work environment, by co-workers, and by organizational practices.

**Inferential statistics**   Procedures used to draw reasonable conclusions (generalizations) about larger populations from small samples of data.

**Informed consent**   The agreement of participants expressed through a signed document that indicates that they understand the nature of their participation in upcoming research and have been fully informed of the general nature of the research, its goals, and its methods.

**Insight therapy**   Therapy that attempts to discover relationships between unconscious motivations and current abnormal behaviour in order to change that behaviour.

**Insomnia**   A prolonged inability to sleep.

**Insulin**   A hormone produced by the pancreas; facilitates the transport of sugar from the blood into body cells, where it is metabolized.

**Intelligence**   The overall capacity of the individual to act purposefully, to think rationally, and to deal effectively with the environment.

**Interference**   The suppression of one bit of information by another received either earlier or later or the confusion of two pieces of information.

**Interpersonal attraction**   The tendency of one person to evaluate another person (or a symbol or image of another person) in a positive way.

**Interpretation**   In Freud's theory, the technique of providing a context, meaning, or cause of a specific idea, feeling, or set of behaviours; the process of tying a set of behaviours to its unconscious determinant.

**Interview**   A face-to-face meeting in which a series of standardized questions is used to gather detailed information.

**Intimacy**   A state of being or feeling in which each person is willing to self-disclose and to express important feelings and information to the other person; such behaviours are usually reciprocated.

**Intrinsic [in-TRINZ-ick] motivation**   Motivation that leads to behaviours engaged in for no apparent reward except the pleasure and satisfaction of the activity itself.

**Introspection**   A person's description and analysis of what he or she is thinking and feeling; also known as self-examination.

**Job analyses**   Careful descriptions of the various tasks and activities that are required for employees to do their jobs, along with the necessary knowledge, skills, and abilities; such analyses describe what gets done and how it gets done.

**Kinesthesis [kin-iss-THEE-sis]**   The awareness aroused by movements of the muscles, tendons, and joints.

**Language**   A system of symbols, usually words, that convey meaning; in addition, it also has rules for combining symbols to generate an infinite number of messages.

**Latency [LAY-ten-see] stage**   Freud's fourth stage of personality development, from about age seven until puberty, during which sexual urges are inactive.

**Latent content**   The deeper meaning of a dream, usually involving symbolism, hidden content, and repressed or obscured ideas and wishes.

**Latent learning**   Learning that occurs in the absence of any direct reinforcement and that is not necessarily demonstrated in any observable behaviour, though it has the potential to be exhibited.

**Law of Prägnanz [PREG-nants]**   The Gestalt principle that when items or stimuli can be grouped together and seen as a whole, they will be.

**Learned helplessness**   The behaviour of giving up or not responding, exhibited by people or animals exposed to negative consequences or punishment over which they have no control.

**Learning**   A relatively permanent change in an organism that occurs as a result of experiences in the environment.

**Levels-of-processing approach**   A memory theory that suggests that the brain processes and encodes information in different ways, to different extents, and at different levels, depending on how shallow or how deep the degree of analysis.

**Libido [lih-BEE-doe]**   In Freud's theory, the instinctual (and sexual) life force that, working on the pleasure principle and seeking immediate gratification, energizes the id.

**Light**   The portion of the electromagnetic spectrum visible to the eye.

**Limbic system**   An interconnected group of structures (including parts of the cortex, thalamus, and hypothalamus) located deep within the temporal lobe and involved in emotions, memory, motivation, and brain disorders such as epilepsy. Within the limbic system are the hippocampus and the amygdala.

**Linguistics [ling-GWIS-ticks]**  The study of language structure and language change, including speech sounds, meaning, and grammar.

**Logic**  The system or principles of reasoning used to reach valid conclusions or inferences.

**Long-term memory**  The storage mechanism that keeps a relatively permanent record of information.

**Longitudinal study**  A research method that examines a specific group of individuals at different ages to discover changes that occur over time.

**Lucid [LOO-sid] dream**  A dream in which the person is aware of dreaming while it is happening.

**Mainstreaming**  The integration of all children with special needs into regular classroom settings, whenever appropriate, with the support of special education services.

**Maintenance rehearsal**  The repetition of information with little or no interpretation.

**Major depressive disorder**  Depressive disorder characterized by loss of interest in almost all of life's usual activities; a sad, hopeless, or discouraged mood; sleep disturbance; loss of appetite; loss of energy; and feelings of unworthiness and guilt.

**Manifest content**  The overt story line, characters, and setting of a dream—the obvious, clearly discernible events of the dream.

**Mean**  The measure of central tendency that is calculated by dividing the sum of the scores by the total number of scores; also known as the arithmetic average.

**Means–ends analysis**  A heuristic procedure in which the problem solver tries to move closer to a solution by comparing the current situation with the desired goal and determining the most efficient way to get from one to the other.

**Measure of central tendency**  A descriptive statistic that tells which result or score best represents an entire set of scores.

**Median**  The measure of central tendency that is the data point with 50 percent of all the observations (scores) above it and 50 percent below it.

**Meditation**  A state of consciousness induced by a variety of techniques and characterized by concentration, restriction of incoming stimuli, and deep relaxation to produce a sense of detachment.

**Medulla [meh-DUH-lah]**  The most primitive and lowest portion of the hindbrain; controls basic bodily functions such as heartbeat and breathing.

**Memory span**  The limited number of items a person can reproduce from usually one or two chunks.

**Memory**  The ability to remember past events, images, ideas, or previously learned information or skills; the storage system that allows for retention and retrieval of previously learned information.

**Mental retardation**  Below-average intellectual functioning, as measured on an IQ test, accompanied by substantial limitations in functioning that originate before age 18.

**Midbrain**  The second level of the three organizational structures of the brain; it receives afferent signals from other parts of the brain and from the spinal cord, interprets the signals, and either relays the information to a more complex part of the brain or causes the body to act at once; considered important in the regulation of movement.

**Mode**  The measure of central tendency that is the most frequently observed data point.

**Model**  A guideline, perspective, or approach derived from data in one field and used to help describe data in another field.

**Monochromats**  People who are totally colour-blind and cannot discriminate among wavelengths, often because they lack cones in their retinas.

**Monocular [mah-NAHK-you-ler] depth cues**  Depth cues that do not depend on the use of both eyes.

**Morality**  A system of learned attitudes about social practices, institutions, and individual behaviour that allows a person to evaluate situations and behaviour as being right or wrong, good or bad.

**Moro reflex**  A reflex in which a newborn stretches out its arms and legs and cries in response to a loud noise or a sudden, unexpected change in the environment.

**Morpheme [MORE-feem]**  A basic unit of meaning in a language.

**Motivation**  Any condition, although usually an internal one, that can be inferred to initiate, activate, or maintain an organism's goal-directed behaviour.

**Motive**  A specific (usually internal) condition, usually involving some form of arousal, that directs an organism's behaviour toward a goal.

**MRI (magnetic resonance imaging)**  Imaging technique that uses magnetic fields instead of X-rays to produce scans of great clarity and high resolution, distinguishing brain parts as small as one or two millimetres.

**Mutations**  Unexpected changes in the gene replication process that are not always evident in phenotype and create unusual and sometimes harmful characteristics of body or behaviour.

**Myopic [my-OP-ick]**  Able to see things that are close but having trouble seeing objects at a distance. Also known as nearsighted.

**Natural selection**  The principle that those characteristics and behaviours that help organisms adapt, be fit, and survive are the ones that will be passed on to successive generations because flexible, fit individuals have a greater chance of reproduction.

**Naturalistic observation**  A descriptive research method in which researchers study behaviour in its natural context, without observer intervention.

**Nature**  A person's inherited characteristics determined by genetics.

**Need**  A state of physiological imbalance usually accompanied by arousal.

**Need for achievement**  A social need that directs people to strive constantly for excellence and success.

**Negative punishment**  A form of punishment in which a pleasant stimulus is taken away in an effort to decrease an undesirable behaviour.

**Negative reinforcement**  Removal of an aversive stimulus after a particular response to increase the likelihood that the response will recur.

**Nervous system**  The structures and organs that act as the communication system for the body allowing all behaviour and mental processes to take place.

**Neuromodulator**  Chemical substance that functions to increase or decrease the sensitivity of widely distributed neurons to the specific effects of neurotransmitters.

**Neuron [NYER-on]**  The basic unit (a single cell) of the nervous system comprising dendrites, which receive neural signals; a cell body, which generates electrical signals; and an axon, which transmits neural signals. Also known as a nerve cell.

**Neurotransmitter [NYER-oh-TRANS-mitt-er]**  Chemical substance that resides in the axon terminals and within synaptic vesicles and that, when released, moves across the synaptic space and binds to a receptor site on adjacent neurons.

**Non-rapid eye movement (NREM) sleep**  Four distinct stages of sleep during which no rapid eye movements occur.

**Nonverbal communication**  The communication of information by cues or actions that include gestures, tone of voice, vocal inflections, and facial expressions.

**Normal curve**  A bell-shaped graphic representation of data arranged to show what percentage of the population falls under each part of the curve.

**Normal distribution**  The approximate distribution of scores expected when a sample is taken from a large population, drawn as a frequency polygon that often takes the form of a bell-shaped curve, known as a normal curve.

**Norms** The scores and corresponding percentile ranks of a large and representative sample of individuals from the population for which a test was designed.

**Nurture** All non-genetic influences; that is, all prenatal, postnatal, biochemical, and social environmental events.

**Obedience** Compliance with the orders of another person or a group of people.

**Observational learning theory** A theory that suggests that organisms learn new responses by observing the behaviour of a model and then imitating it. Also known as social learning theory.

**Obsessive–compulsive disorder** An anxiety disorder characterized by persistent and uncontrollable thoughts and irrational beliefs (obsessions) that cause performance of intrusive and inappropriate compulsive rituals that interfere with daily life.

**Oedipus [ED-i-pus] complex** Feelings of rivalry with the parent of the same sex and sexual desire for the parent of the other sex, occurring during the phallic stage and ultimately resolved through identification with the parent of the same sex.

**Olfaction [ole-FAK-shun]** The sense of smell.

**Operant [OP-er-ant] conditioning** Conditioning in which the probability that an organism will emit a response is increased or decreased by the subsequent delivery of a reinforcer or punisher. Also known as instrumental conditioning.

**Operational definition** Definition of a variable in terms of the set of methods or procedures used to measure or study that variable.

**Opiate** A drug with pain-relieving and sedative properties that is addictive and produces tolerance.

**Opponent-process theory** Visual theory, proposed by Herring, that colour is coded by stimulation of three types of paired receptors; each pair of receptors is assumed to operate in an antagonistic way so that stimulation by a given wavelength produces excitation (increased firing) in one receptor of the pair and also inhibits the other receptor.

**Optic chiasm [KI-azm]** Point at which half of the optic nerve fibres from each eye cross over and connect to the other side of the brain.

**Oral stage** Freud's first stage of personality development, from birth to about age two, during which the instincts of infants are focused on the mouth as the primary pleasure centre.

**Overjustification effect** The decrease in likelihood that an intrinsically motivated task, after having been extrinsically rewarded, will be performed when the reward is no longer given.

**Paranoid [PAIR-uh-noid] type of schizophrenia** Type of schizophrenia characterized by hallucinations and delusions of persecution or grandeur (or both), and sometimes irrational jealousy.

**Parasympathetic [PAIR-uh-sim-puh-THET-ick] nervous system** The part of the autonomic nervous system that controls the ongoing maintenance processes of the body, such as heart rate, digestion, and blood pressure.

**Partial reinforcement** Reinforcement that is occasional or intermittent.

**Participant** A human individual who takes part in an experiment and whose behaviour is observed for research data collection; previously known as a subject.

**Percentile score** A score indicating what percentage of the test population obtained a lower score.

**Perception** The process whereby an organism selects and interprets sensory input so that it acquires meaning.

**Performance appraisal** The process by which a supervisor periodically evaluates the job-relevant strengths and weaknesses of a subordinate.

**Peripheral [puh-RIF-er-al] nervous system** The part of the nervous system that carries information to and from the central nervous system through a network of spinal and cranial nerves.

**Personal fable** A cognitive distortion experienced by adolescents, in which they believe they are so special and unique that other people cannot understand them and risky behaviours will not harm them.

**Personal space** The area or invisible boundary around an individual that the person considers private.

**Personality** A pattern of relatively permanent traits, dispositions, or characteristics that give some consistency to people's behaviour.

**Personality disorders** Psychological disorders characterized by inflexible and long-standing maladaptive behaviours that typically cause stress and/or social or occupational problems.

**PET (positron emission tomography)** Imaging technique that uses radioactive markers injected into the bloodstream to enable researchers to observe metabolic activity by recording glucose use taking place in the brain; measures local variations in cerebral blood flow, which is correlated with mental activity.

**Phallic [FAL-ick] stage** Freud's third stage of personality development, from about age four through age seven, during which children obtain gratification primarily from the genitals.

**Phenotypes** Observable characteristics.

**Phobic disorders** Anxiety disorders characterized by excessive, unreasonable, and irrational fear of, and consequent attempt to avoid, specific objects or situations.

**Phoneme [FOE-neem]** A basic unit of sound in a language.

**Phonology** The study of the patterns and distribution of speech sounds in a language and the tacit rules for their pronunciation.

**Photoreceptors** The light-sensitive cells in the retina: rods and cones.

**Pitch** The psychological experience that corresponds with the frequency of an auditory stimulus. Also known as tone.

**Pituitary [pit-YOU-ih-tare-ee] gland** The body's master gland located at the base of the brain and closely linked to the hypothalamus; regulates the actions of other endocrine glands; major function is the control of growth hormones.

**Placebo [pluh-SEE-bo]** A treatment that has no effect but is presented as possibly producing certain effects.

**Placebo effect** A therapeutic change that occurs as a result of a person's expectations of change rather than as a result of any specific treatment.

**Placenta [pluh-SENT-uh]** A mass of tissue in the uterus that acts as the life-support system for the fetus by supplying oxygen, food, and antibodies and by eliminating wastes—all by way of the mother's bloodstream.

**Pons** A structure of the hindbrain that provides a link between the medulla and the cerebellum and the rest of the brain; it affects sleep and dreaming.

**Population** The entire group (large or small) of people you might be interested in studying.

**Positive punishment** A form of punishment in which an unpleasant stimulus is added in an effort to decrease an undesirable behaviour.

**Positive reinforcement** Presentation of a rewarding or pleasant stimulus after a particular response, to increase the likelihood that the response will recur.

**Post-traumatic stress disorder (PTSD)** Psychological disorder that may become evident after a person has undergone extreme stress caused by some type of disaster; common symptoms include vivid, intrusive recollections or re-experiences of the traumatic event and occasional lapses of normal consciousness.

**Preconscious** Freud's level of the mind that contains those experiences that are not currently conscious but may become so with varying degrees of difficulty.

**Prejudice** Negative evaluation of an entire group of people, typically based on unfavourable (often incorrect) ideas or stereotypes about the group.

**Preoperational stage** Piaget's second stage of cognitive development (lasting from about age two to age six or seven), during which initial symbolic thought is developed.

**Pressure** The emotional state or condition resulting from the real or imagined expectations of others for certain behaviours or results.

**Prevalence** The percentage of a population displaying a disorder during any specified period.

**Primacy effect** The more accurate recall of items presented first in a series.

**Primary punisher** Any stimulus or event that is naturally painful or aversive to an organism.

**Primary reinforcer** A reinforcer (such as food, water, or the termination of pain) that has survival value for an organism; thus, its value does not have to be learned.

**Proactive [pro-AK-tiv] coping** Taking action in advance of a potentially stressful situation to prevent it, modify it, or prepare for it before it occurs.

**Proactive interference** Decrease in accurate recall of information as a result of the effects of previously learned or presented information. Also known as proactive inhibition.

**Problem solving** The behaviour of individuals when confronted with a situation or task that requires insight or determination of some unknown elements.

**Procedural memory** Memory for skills, including the perceptual, motor, and cognitive skills required to complete complex tasks.

**Projection** A defence mechanism by which people attribute their own undesirable traits to others.

**Projective tests** Devices or instruments used to assess personality, in which examinees are shown a standard set of ambiguous stimuli and asked to respond to the stimuli in their own way.

**Prosocial behaviour** Behaviour that benefits someone else or society but that generally offers no obvious benefit to the person performing it and that may even involve some personal risk or sacrifice.

**Prototype** An abstraction of a pattern, object, or idea stored in memory, against which similar patterns are evaluated to see how closely they resemble each other; it is the best example of a class of items.

**Psychedelic** A consciousness-altering drug that affects moods, thoughts, memory, judgment, and perception and that is usually self-administered for the purpose of producing these results.

**Psychiatrist** A physician (medical doctor) specializing in the treatment of patients with emotional disorders.

**Psychoactive [SYE-koh-AK-tiv] drug** A drug that alters behaviour, thoughts, or emotions by altering biochemical reactions in the nervous system, thereby affecting consciousness.

**Psychoanalysis [SYE-ko-uh-NAL-uh-sis]** A lengthy insight therapy developed by Sigmund Freud that aims at uncovering conflicts and unconscious impulses through special techniques, including free association, dream analysis, and transference.

**Psychoanalyst** A psychiatrist or, occasionally, non-medical practitioner who has studied the technique of psychoanalysis and uses it to treat people with emotional problems.

**Psychoanalytic [SYE-ko-an-uh-LIT-ick] approach** The school of psychological thought developed by Freud, which assumes that psychological maladjustment is a consequence of anxiety resulting from unresolved conflicts and forces of which a person may be unaware; includes the therapeutic technique known as psychoanalysis.

**Psychodynamically [SYE-ko-dye-NAM-ick-lee] based therapies** Therapies based loosely on Freud's psychoanalytic theory, using a part of that approach but rejecting or modifying some of its elements.

**Psycholinguistics** The study of how language is acquired, perceived, understood, and produced.

**Psychological dependence** A compelling desire to use a drug, along with an inability to inhibit that desire.

**Psychologist** A professional who studies behaviour and uses behavioural principles in scientific research or applied settings.

**Psychology** The science of behaviour and mental processes.

**Psychoneuroimmunology [SYE-ko-NEW-ro-IM-you-NOLL-oh-gee]** An interdisciplinary area of study that includes behavioural, neurological, and immune factors and their relationship to the development of disease.

**Psychophysics [SYE-co-FIZ-icks]** The subfield that focuses on the relationship between physical stimuli and people's conscious experience of them.

**Psychostimulant** A drug that in low to moderate doses increases alertness, reduces fatigue, and elevates mood.

**Psychosurgery** Brain surgery used in the past to alleviate symptoms of serious mental disorders.

**Psychotherapy [SYE-ko-THER-uh-pee]** The treatment of emotional or behavioural problems through psychological techniques.

**Psychotic [sye-KOT-ick]** Suffering from a gross impairment in reality testing that interferes with the ability to meet the ordinary demands of life.

**Puberty [PEW-burr-tee]** The period during which the reproductive system matures; it begins with an increase in production of sex hormones and occurs at (and signals) the end of childhood.

**Punishment** The process of presenting an undesirable or noxious stimulus, or removing a desirable stimulus, to decrease the probability that a particular preceding response will recur.

**Questionnaire** A printed form with questions, usually given to a large group of people; used by researchers to gather a substantial amount of data in a short time; also known as a survey.

**Range** A measure of variability that describes the spread between the highest and the lowest scores in a distribution.

**Rape** Forcible sexual assault on an unwilling partner.

**Rapid eye movement (REM) sleep** Stage of sleep characterized by high-frequency, low-voltage brain wave activity, rapid and systematic eye movements, and dreams.

**Rational–emotive therapy** A cognitive behaviour therapy that emphasizes the importance of logical, rational thought processes.

**Rationalization** A defence mechanism by which people reinterpret undesirable feelings or behaviours in terms that make them appear acceptable.

**Raw score** A test score that has not been transformed or converted in any way.

**Reactance** A pattern of feelings and subsequent behaviours aimed at re-establishing a sense of freedom when there is an inconsistency between a person's self-image as being free to choose and the person's realization that someone is trying to force him or her to choose a particular alternative.

**Reaction formation** A defence mechanism by which people behave in a way opposite to what their true but anxiety-provoking feelings would dictate.

**Reasoning** The purposeful process by which people generate logical and coherent ideas, evaluate situations, and reach conclusions.

**Recency effect** The more accurate recall of items presented last in a series.

**Receptive fields** Areas of the retina that, when stimulated, produce a change in the firing of cells in the visual system.

**Reflex** An involuntary, automatic behaviour that occurs in response to a stimulus without prior learning and usually shows little variability from instance to instance.

**Refractory period** The recovery period of a neuron after it fires, during which it cannot fire again; this period allows the neuron to re-establish electrical balance with its surroundings.

**Regression**   A return to a prior stage after a person has progressed through the various stages of development; caused by anxiety.

**Rehearsal**   The process of verbalizing, thinking about, or otherwise acting on or transforming information in order to keep it active in memory.

**Reinforcer**   Any event that increases the probability of a recurrence of the response that preceded it.

**Reliability**   A test's ability to yield the same or similar scores for the same individual through repeated testing.

**Representative sample**   A sample of individuals who match the population with whom they are to be compared on key variables such as socio-economic status and age.

**Repression**   A defence mechanism by which anxiety-provoking thoughts and feelings are forced to the unconscious.

**Residual type of schizophrenia**   A schizophrenic disorder in which the person exhibits inappropriate affect, illogical thinking, and/or eccentric behaviour but seems generally in touch with reality.

**Resilience**   The extent to which people are flexible and respond adaptively to external or internal demands.

**Resistance**   In psychoanalysis, an unwillingness to cooperate by which a patient signals a reluctance to provide the therapist with information or to help the therapist understand or interpret a situation.

**Retinal disparity**   The slight difference between the visual images projected on the two retinas.

**Retrieval**   The process by which stored information is recovered from memory.

**Retroactive [RET-ro-AK-tiv] interference**   Decrease in accurate recall of information as a result of the subsequent presentation of different information. Also known as retroactive inhibition.

**Retrograde [RET-ro-grade] amnesia**   Loss of memory for events and experiences that occurred in a period preceding the amnesia-causing event.

**Rooting reflex**   A reflex in which a newborn turns its head toward a mild stimulus that touches its lips or cheek.

**Saccades [sack-ADZ]**   Rapid voluntary movements of the eyes.

**Sample**   A group of participants who are assumed to be representative of the population about which an inference is being made.

**Saturation**   The depth and richness of a hue determined by the homogeneity of the wavelengths contained in the reflected light; also known as purity.

**Schema [SKEEM-uh]**   A conceptual framework that organizes information and allows a person to make sense of the world.

**Scheme**   In Piaget's view, a specific mental structure; an organized way of interacting with the environment and experiencing it.

**Schizophrenic [SKIT-soh-FREN-ick] disorders**   A group of psychological disorders characterized by a lack of reality testing and by deterioration of social and intellectual functioning and personality, beginning before age 45 and lasting at least six months.

**Scientific method**   In psychology, the techniques used to discover knowledge about human behaviour and mental processes; in experimentation, the scientific method involves stating the problem, developing hypotheses, designing a study, collecting and analyzing data (which often includes manipulating some part of the environment to better understand what conditions can lead to a behaviour or phenomenon), replicating results, and drawing conclusions and reporting results.

**Secondary punisher**   A neutral stimulus with no intrinsic negative effect on an organism that acquires punishment value through repeated pairing with a primary punisher.

**Secondary reinforcer**   A neutral stimulus that has no intrinsic value for an organism initially but that can become rewarding when linked with a primary reinforcer.

**Secondary sex characteristics**   The genetically determined physical features that differentiate the sexes but are not directly involved with reproduction.

**Sedative–hypnotic**   A drug that relaxes and calms people and, in higher doses, induces sleep.

**Self**   In Rogers' theory of personality, the perception an individual has of himself or herself and of his or her relationships to other people and to various aspects of life.

**Self-actualization**   The fundamental human need to strive to fulfil one's potential, thus a state of motivation, according to Maslow; from a humanist's view, a final level of psychological development in which a person attempts to minimize ill health, function fully, have a superior perception of reality, and feel a strong sense of self-acceptance.

**Self-efficacy**   A person's belief that he or she can successfully engage in and execute a specific behaviour.

**Self-fulfilling prophecy**   The creation of a situation that unintentionally allows personal expectancies to influence participants.

**Self-perception theory**   An approach to attitude formation in which people are assumed to infer their attitudes based on observations of their own behaviour.

**Self-serving bias**   People's tendency to evaluate their own positive behaviours as being due to their own internal traits and characteristics, but to blame their failures and shortcomings on external, situational factors.

**Semantic memory**   Memory of ideas, rules, words, and general concepts about the world.

**Semantics [se-MAN-ticks]**   The analysis of the meaning of language, especially of individual words.

**Sensation**   The process in which the sense organ receptor cells are stimulated and relay their initial information to higher brain centres for further processing.

**Sensorimotor stage**   The first of Piaget's four stages of cognitive development (covering roughly the first two years of life), during which the child begins to interact with the environment and the rudiments of memory are established.

**Sensorineural [sen-so-ree-NEW-ruhl] deafness**   Deafness resulting from damage to the cochlea, the auditory nerve, or higher auditory processing centres.

**Sensory memory**   The mechanism that performs initial encoding and brief storage of stimuli. Also known as the sensory register.

**Shape constancy**   The ability to recognize a shape despite changes in the orientation or angle from which it is viewed.

**Shaping**   A gradual training of an organism to give the proper responses through selective reinforcement of behaviours as they approach the desired response.

**Signal detection theory**   The theory that holds that an observer's perception is dependent on the intensity of a stimulus, on the observer's motivation, on the criteria he or she sets up, and on the "noise" present.

**Significant difference**   In an experiment, a difference that is unlikely to have occurred because of chance alone and is most likely due to the systematic manipulation of the independent variable.

**Size constancy**   The ability of the perceptual system to recognize that an object remains constant in size regardless of its distance from the observer or the size of its image on the retina.

**Skinner box**   Named by others for its developer, B. F. Skinner, a box that contains a responding mechanism (usually a lever) capable of delivering a consequence, often a reinforcer, to an organism.

**Sleep**   Non-waking state of consciousness characterized by general unresponsiveness to the environment and general physical immobility.

**Social categorization**   The process of dividing the world into "in" and "out" groups.

**Social cognition**   The thought processes involved in making sense of events, other people, oneself, and the world in general by analyzing and interpreting them.

**Social facilitation**   A change in performance that occurs when people believe they are in the presence of other people.

**Social influence**   The ways in which people alter the attitudes or behaviour of others, either directly or indirectly.

**Social interest**   In Adler's theory, a feeling of oneness with all humanity.

**Social loafing**   A decrease in productivity that occurs when an individual works in a group instead of alone.

**Social need**   An aroused condition that directs people to behave in ways that allow them to feel good about themselves and others and to establish and maintain relationships.

**Social phobia [FOE-bee-uh]**   An anxiety disorder characterized by fear of, and a desire to avoid, situations in which the person might be exposed to scrutiny by others and might behave in an embarrassing or humiliating way.

**Social psychology**   The study of how individuals influence and are influenced by the thoughts, feelings, and behaviours of other people.

**Social support**   The comfort, recognition, approval, and encouragement available from other people, including friends, family members, and co-workers.

**Sociobiology**   A theory based on the premise that even day-to-day behaviours are determined by the process of natural selection—that social behaviours that contribute to the survival of a species are passed on genetically from one generation to the next and account for the mechanisms producing behaviours such as altruism.

**Somatic [so-MAT-ick] nervous system**   The part of the peripheral nervous system that carries information to skeletal muscles and thereby affects bodily movement; it controls voluntary, conscious sensory and motor functions.

**Sound**   The psychological experience that occurs when changes in air pressure take place at the receptive organ for hearing; the resulting tones, or sounds, vary in frequency and amplitude.

**Specific phobia**   An anxiety disorder characterized by irrational and persistent fear of a specific object or situation, along with a compelling desire to avoid it.

**Spinal cord**   The portion of the central nervous system that is contained within the spinal column and transmits signals from the senses to the brain, controls reflexive responses, and conveys signals from the brain to the muscles and glands.

**Split-brain patients**   People whose corpus callosum, which normally connects the two cerebral hemispheres, has been surgically severed.

**Spontaneous recovery**   Recurrence of an extinguished conditioned response following a rest period.

**Sport psychology**   The systematic application of psychological principles to sports.

**Standard deviation**   A descriptive statistic that measures the variability of data from the mean of the sample.

**Standard score**   A score that expresses an individual's position relative to those of others based on the mean score and how scores are distributed around it.

**Standardization**   The process of developing uniform procedures for administering and scoring a test and for establishing norms.

**State-dependent learning**   The tendency to recall information learned in a particular physiological state most accurately when one is again in that physiological state.

**Statistics**   The branch of mathematics that deals with collecting, classifying, and analyzing data.

**Stereotypes**   Fixed, overly simple, often incorrect, and often negative ideas about traits, attitudes, and behaviours attributed to groups of people.

**Stimulus discrimination**   Process by which an organism learns to respond only to a specific reinforced stimulus and not to other irrelevant stimuli.

**Stimulus generalization**   Occurrence of a conditioned response with a stimulus that is similar but not identical to the original conditioned stimulus.

**Storage**   The process of maintaining or keeping information available; it also refers to the locations of memory, which researchers call "memory stores."

**Stress**   A nonspecific response to real or imagined challenges or threats.

**Stress inoculation [in-OK-you-LAY-shun]**   Procedure of teaching people ways to cope with stress and allowing them to practise in realistic situations so they will develop "immunity" to stress.

**Stressor**   A stimulus that affects an organism in physically or psychologically injurious ways and usually elicits feelings such as anxiety, tension, and physiological arousal.

**Structuralism**   The school of psychological thought that considered the organized structure of immediate, conscious experience to be the proper subject matter of psychology.

**Subgoal analysis**   A heuristic procedure in which a task is broken down into smaller, more manageable steps, each of which has a subgoal.

**Sublimation [sub-li-MAY-shun]**   A defence mechanism by which people redirect socially unacceptable impulses toward acceptable goals.

**Subliminal perception**   Perception below the threshold of awareness.

**Substance abuser**   A person who overuses and relies on drugs to deal with stress and anxiety.

**Sucking reflex**   A reflex in which a newborn makes sucking motions when presented with a stimulus to the lips, such as a nipple.

**Superego [sue-pur-EE-go]**   In Freud's theory, the moral aspect of mental functioning, comprising the ego ideal (what a person would ideally like to be) and the conscience and taught by parents and society.

**Superstitious behaviour**   Behaviour learned through coincidental association with reinforcement.

**Survey**   One of the descriptive methods of research; it requires construction of a set of questions to administer to a group of participants.

**Sympathetic nervous system**   The part of the autonomic nervous system that becomes most active in response to emergency situations; it calls up bodily resources as needed for major energy expenditures.

**Symptom substitution**   The appearance of one overt symptom to replace another that has been eliminated by treatment.

**Synapse [SIN-apps]**   The microscopically small space between the axon terminals of one neuron and the receptor sites of another neuron.

**Syntax [SIN-tacks]**   The way that words and groups of words combine to form phrases, clauses, and sentences.

**Systematic desensitization**   A three-stage counterconditioning procedure in which people are taught to relax when presented with stimuli that formerly elicited anxiety.

**Temperament**   Early-emerging and long-lasting individual differences in the intensity and especially the quality of a person's emotional reactions.

**Teratogen [ter-AT-oh-jen]**   A substance that can produce developmental malformations (birth defects) during the prenatal period.

**Thalamus**   A large structure of the forebrain that acts primarily as a routing station to send information to other parts of the brain but probably also performs some interpretive functions; nearly all sensory information proceeds through the thalamus.

**Thanatology**  The study of the psychological and medical aspects of death and dying.

**Theory**  In psychology, a collection of interrelated ideas and facts put forward to describe, explain, and predict behaviour and mental processes.

**Theory of mind**  An understanding of mental states such as feelings, desires, beliefs, and intentions and of the causal role they play in human behaviour.

**Time out**  A punishment procedure in which a person is physically removed from sources of reinforcement in order to decrease the occurrence of undesired behaviours.

**Token economy**  An operant conditioning procedure in which individuals who engage in appropriate behaviour receive tokens that they can exchange for desirable items or activities.

**Tolerance**  Progressive insensitivity to repeated use of a specific drug in the same dosage and at the same frequency of use.

**Trait**  Any readily identifiable stable quality that characterizes how an individual differs from other individuals.

**Transduction**  The process by which a perceptual system analyzes stimuli and converts them into electrical impulses. Also known as coding.

**Transfer-appropriate processing**  Initial processing of information that is similar in modality or type to the processing necessary in the retrieval task.

**Transference**  A psychoanalytic phenomenon in which a therapist becomes the object of a patient's emotional attitudes about an important person in the patient's life, such as a parent.

**Transformational leader**  A charismatic leader who inspires and provides intellectual stimulation to recreate an organization.

**Trichromatic [try-kroe-MAT-ick] theory**  Visual theory, stated by Young and Helmholtz, that all colours can be made by mixing the three basic colours: red, green, and blue; also known as the Young-Helmholtz theory.

**Trichromats**  People who can perceive all three primary colours and thus can distinguish any hue.

**Type A behaviour**  Behaviour pattern characterized by competitiveness, impatience, hostility, and constant efforts to do more in less time.

**Type B behaviour**  Behaviour pattern exhibited by people who are calmer, more patient, and less hurried than Type A individuals.

**Types**  Personality categories in which broad collections of traits are loosely tied together and interrelated.

**Unconditioned response**  An unlearned or involuntary response to an unconditioned stimulus.

**Unconditioned stimulus**  A stimulus that normally produces a measurable involuntary response.

**Unconscious**  Freud's level of mental life that consists of mental activities beyond people's normal awareness.

**Undifferentiated type of schizophrenia**  A schizophrenic disorder that is characterized by a mixture of symptoms and does not meet the diagnostic criteria of any one type.

**Validity**  The ability of a test to measure only what it is supposed to measure and to predict only what it is supposed to predict.

**Variability**  The extent to which scores differ from one another, especially the extent to which they differ from the mean.

**Variable**  A condition or characteristic of a situation or a person that is subject to change (that varies) within or across situations or individuals.

**Variable-interval schedule**  A reinforcement schedule in which a reinforcer (reward) is delivered after predetermined but varying intervals of time, provided that the required response occurs at least once after each interval.

**Variable-ratio schedule**  A reinforcement schedule in which a reinforcer (reward) is delivered after a predetermined but variable number of responses has occurred.

**Vestibular [ves-TIB-you-ler] sense**  The sense of bodily orientation and postural adjustment.

**Visual cortex**  The most important area of the brain's occipital lobe, which receives information from the lateral geniculate nucleus. Also known as striate cortex.

**Vulnerability**  A person's diminished ability to deal with demanding life events.

**Withdrawal symptoms**  Physiological reactions that occur when an addictive drug is no longer administered to an addict.

**Working memory**  The storage mechanism that temporarily holds current or recently attended-to information for immediate or short-term use and that is composed of several subsystems: a component to encode and rehearse auditory information, a visual–spatial "scratch pad," and a central processing mechanism, or executive, that balances and controls information flow.

**Working through**  In psychoanalysis, the repetitive cycle of interpretation, resistance to interpretation, and transference.

**Zygote [ZEYE-goat]**  A fertilized egg.

# References

Blue type indicates a Canadian researcher or a researcher associated with a Canadian university.

Abbott, L. F., Varela, J. A., Sen, K., & Nelson, S. B. (1997). Synaptic depression and cortical gain control. *Science, 275,* 220–224.

Abramowitz, J. S. (1998). Does cognitive-behavioral therapy cure obsessive-compulsive disorder? A meta-analytic evaluation of clinical significance. *Behavior Therapy, 29,* 339–355.

Abrams, M., & Ellis, A. (1994). Stress management and counselling: Rational emotive behaviour therapy in the treatment of stress. *British Journal of Guidance and Counselling, 22,* 39–50.

Abramson, L. Y., Metalsky, G. I., & Alloy, L. B. (1989). Hopelessness depression: A theory-based subtype of depression. *Psychological Review, 96,* 358–372.

Abravanel, E., & DeYong, N. G. (1997). Exploring the roles of peer and adult video models for infant imitations. *Journal of Genetic Psychology, 158*(2), 133–150.

Acocella, J. (1999). *Creating hysteria: Women and multiple personality disorder.* San Francisco: Jossey-Bass.

Ader, R. (1997). The role of conditioning in pharmacotherapy. In A. Harrington (Ed.), *The placebo effect: An interdisciplinary exploration* (pp. 138–165). Cambridge, MA: Harvard University Press.

Ader, R. (2000). True or false: The placebo effect as seen in drug studies is definitive proof that the mind can bring about clinically relevant changes in the body: The placebo effect: If it's all in your head, does that mean you only think you feel better? *Advances in Mind-Body Medicine, 16,* 7–11.

Ader, R. (2001). Psychoneuroimmunology. *Current Directions in Psychological Science, 10,* 94–98.

Ader, R., & Cohen, N. (1975). Behaviorally conditioned immunosuppression. *Psychosomatic Medicine, 37,* 333–340.

Ader, R., & Cohen, N. (1985). CNS-immune system interactions: Conditioning phenomena. *Behavioral and Brain Sciences, 8*(3), 379–426.

Ader, R., & Cohen, N. (1993). Psychoneuroimmunology: Conditioning and stress. *Annual Review of Psychology, 44,* 53–85.

Adler, A. (1927). *Understanding human nature.* New York: Greenberg.

Adler, A. (1964). *Problems of neurosis.* New York: Harper Torchbooks. (Original work published 1929)

Adolphs, R. & Damasio, A. R. (1995). Consciousness and neuroscience, In B. Bromm & J. E. Desmedt (Eds.), *Pain and the brain: From nociception to cognition* (pp. 83–97). New York: Raven.

Adolphs, R., & Damasio, A. R. (2000). Neurobiology of emotion at a systems level. In J. C. Borod (Ed.), *The neuropsychology of emotion: Series in affective science* (pp. 194–213). New York: Oxford University Press.

Adorno, T., Frenkel-Brunswick, E., Levinson, D., & Sanford, R. (1950). *The authoritarian personality.* New York: Harper & Row.

Agnew, H. W., Jr., & Webb, W. B. (1973). The influence of time course variable on REM sleep. *Bulletin of the Psychonomic Society, 2,* 131–133.

Aiello, J. R., & Kolb, K. J. (1995). Electronic performance monitoring and social context: Impact on productivity and stress. *Journal of Applied Psychology, 80,* 339–353.

Aiken, L. R. (1985). *Dying, death, and bereavement.* Boston: Allyn & Bacon.

Aiken, L. R. (1988). *Psychological testing and assessment* (6th ed). Boston: Allyn & Bacon.

Ainsworth, M. D. S. (1979). Infant-mother attachment. *American Psychologist, 34,* 932–937.

Ainsworth, M. S., Blehar, M. C., Waters, E., & Wall, S. (1978). *Patterns of attachment: A psychological study of the strange situation.* Hillsdale, NJ: Lawrence Erlbaum.

Ainsworth, M. S. (1989). Attachments beyond infancy. *American Psychologist, 44*(4), 709–716.

Ajdukovic, M., & Ajdukovic, D. (1998). Impact of displacement on the psychological well-being of refugee children. *International Review of Psychiatry, 10*(3), 186–195.

Aldag, R. J., & Fuller, S. R. (1993). Beyond fiasco: A reappraisal of the groupthink phenomenon and a new model of group decision processes. *Psychological Bulletin, 113,* 533–552.

Al-Issa, I. (1982). Does culture make a difference in psychotherapy? In I. Al-Issa (Ed.), *Culture and psychopathology.* Baltimore: University Park Press.

Allen, K. E., Turner, K. D., & Everett, P. M. (1970). A behavior modification classroom for Head Start children with problem behaviors. *Exceptional Children, 37,* 119–127.

Allgulander, C. (1994). Suicide and mortality patterns in anxiety neurosis and depressive neurosis. *Archives of General Psychiatry, 51,* 708–712.

Allington, R. L. (1981). Sensitivity to orthographic structure in educable mentally retarded children. *Contemporary Educational Psychology, 6,* 135–139.

Allison, T., Ginter, H., McCarthy, G., Nobre, A. C., Puce, A., Luby, M., & Spencer, D. D. (1994). Face recognition in human extrastriate cortex. *Journal of Neurophysiology, 71,* 821–825.

Allport, G. W. (1979). *The nature of prejudice.* Cambridge, MA: Addison-Wesley. (Original work published in 1954.)

Almagor, M., Tellegen, A., & Waller, N. G. (1995). The big seven model: A cross-cultural replication and further exploration of the basic dimensions of natural language trait descriptors. *Journal of Personality and Social Psychology, 69,* 300–307.

Altemeyer, R. (1996). *The authoritarian specter.* Cambridge, MA: Harvard University Press.

Altemeyer, R. (1999). To thine own self be untrue: Self-awareness in authoritarians. *North American Journal of Psychology, 1, 2,* 157–164.

Altman, I., & Vinsel, A. M. (1977). Personal space: An analysis of E. T. Hall's proxemics framework. In I. Altman, A. Rapoport, & J. F. Wohlwill (Eds.), *Human behavior and environment: Vol. 2. Advances in theory and research.* New York: Plenum.

Amaral, D. G. (2000). The functional organization of perception and movement. In E. R. Kandel., J. H. Schwartz, & T. M. Jessell (Eds.), *Principles of neural science.* (337–348). New York: McGraw-Hill.

American Association of University Women Educational Foundation. (1998). *Gender gaps: Where schools still fail our children* (Special Report). Washington, DC: Author.

American Psychiatric Association (2000). *Diagnostic and statistical manual of mental disorders* (4th ed.) (DSM-IV). Washington, DC: (DSM–IV–TR).

American Psychiatric Association. (2001). *The practice of electro-convulsive therapy: Recommendations for treatment, training, and privileging: A task force report of the American Psychiatric Association* (2nd ed.). Washington, DC: APA.

American Psychological Association. (1990). Editor's Note on the Seville Statement on Violence. *American Psychologist, 45*(10), 167.

American Psychological Association (1993). Guidelines for providers of psychological services to ethnic, linguistic, and culturally diverse populations. *American Psychologist, 48,* 45–48.

Ames, E. W. (1990). Spitz revisited: A trip to Romanian "orphanages." *Canadian Psychological Association Developmental Section Newsletter, 9,* 8–11.

Ames, E. W., & Carter, M. (1992). A study of Romanian orphanage children in Canada: Background, sample and procedure. *Canadian Psychology, 33,* 503.

Ames, E. W., & Chisholm, K. (2001). Social and emotional development in children adopted from institutions. In D. B. Bailey, Jr. & J. T. Bruer et al. (Eds.), *Critical thinking about critical periods* (pp. 129–148).

Anderson, A. K., & Phelps, E. A. (2000). Expression without recognition: Contributions of the human amygdala in emotional communication. *Psychological Science, 11,* 106–111.

Anderson, C. A. (1989). Temperature and aggression: Ubiquitous effects of heat on occurrence of human violence. *Psychological Bulletin, 106,* 74–96.

Anderson, C. A., & Anderson, K. B. (1998). Temperature and aggression: Paradox, controversy, and a (fairly) clear picture. In R. G. Geen, E. Donnerstein, et al. (Eds.), *Human aggression: Theories, research, and implications for social policy* (pp. 247–298). San Diego, CA: Academic Press, Inc.

Anderson, C. A., Anderson, K. B., & Deuser, W. E. (1996). Examining an affective aggression framework: Weapon and temperature effects on aggressive thoughts, affect, and attitudes. *Personality and Social Psychology Bulletin, 22*(4), 366–376.

Anderson, C. A. & Bushman, B. J. (2002). The effects of media violence on society. *Science Magazine, 295,* 2377–2379.

Anderson, C. A., & DeNeve, K. M. (1992). Temperature, aggression, and the negative affect escape model. *Psychological Bulletin, 111,* 347–351.

Anderson, C. A., & Dill, K. E. (2000). Video games and aggressive thoughts, feelings, and behavior in the laboratory and in life. *Journal of Personality and Social Psychology, 67,* 772–790.

Anderson, E. N. (1992). A healing place: Ethnographic notes on a treatment centre. *Alcoholism Treatment Quarterly, 9,* 3–4, 1–21.

Anderson, J. R., & Schooler, L. J. (2000). The adaptive nature of memory. In E. Tulving & F. I. Craik (Eds.), *The Oxford handbook of memory* (pp. 557–570). New York: Oxford University Press.

Anderson, J. S., Lampl, I., Gillespie, D. C., & Ferster, D. (2000). The contribution of noise to contrast invariance of orientation tuning in cat visual cortex. *Science, 290,* 1968–1972.

Anderson, N. D., Iidaka, T., Cabeza, R., Kapur, S., McIntosh, A. R., & Craik, F. I. M. (2000). The effects of divided attention on encoding- and retrieval-related brain activity: A PET study of younger and older adults. *Journal of Cognitive Neuroscience 12,* 775–792.

Andreasen, N. C. (1997). Neuroimaging techniques in the investigation of schizophrenia. *Journal of Clinical Psychiatry Monograph Series, 15*(3), 16–19.

Ang, R. P., & Chang, W. C. (1999). Impact of domain-specific locus of control on need for achievement and motivation. *The Journal of Social Psychology, 139,* 527–529.

Annett, M. (1985). *Left, right, hand and brain: The right shift theory.* London: Erlbaum.

Anstey, K. J., Luszcz, M. A., Giles, L. C., & Andrews, G. R. (2001). Demographic, health, cognitive, and sensory variables as predictors of mortality in very old adults. *Psychology and Aging 16,* 3–11.

Appelbaum, P. S., Robbins, P. C., & Monahan, J. (2000). Violence and delusions: Data from the MacArthur Violence Risk Assessment Study. *American Journal of Psychiatry, 157,* 566–572.

Applewhite, S. L. (1995). Curanderismo: Demystifying the health beliefs and practices of elderly Mexican Americans. *Health and Social Work, 20,* 247–253.

Apter, T. (1995). *Secret paths: Women in the new midlife.* New York: Norton.

Archibald, A. B. (2000). Moody girls: Is puberty to blame? *Dissertation Abstracts International: Section B: The Sciences & Engineering, 60*(12-B), 6394.

Ariely, D. (2001). Seeing sets: Representation by statistical properties. *Psychological Science, 12,* 157–162.

Arkowitz, H. (1997). Integrative theories of therapy. In Wachtel, P. L., & Messer, S. B. (Eds.), *Theories of psychotherapy: Origins and evolution* (pp. 227–288). Washington, DC: American Psychological Association.

Armel, K. C., & Ramachandran, V. S. (1999). Acquired synesthesia in retinitis pigmentosa. *Neurocase: Case Studies in Neuropsychology, Neuropsychiatry, and Behavioural Neurology, 5,* 293–296.

Arnedt, J. T., Wilde, G. J. S., Munt, P. W., & MacLean, A. W. (2001). How do prolonged wakefulness and alcohol compare in the decrements they produce on a simulated driving task? *Accident Analysis and Prevention, 33,* 337–344.

Arnett, J. J. (1999). Adolescent storm and stress, reconsidered. *American Psychologist, 54,* 317–326.

Aronson, J., Quinn, D. M., & Spencer, S. J. (1998). Stereotype threat and the academic underperformance of minorities and women. In J. K. Swim, C. Stangor, et al. (Eds.). *Prejudice: The target's perspective* (pp. 83–103). San Diego, CA: Academic Press.

Arseneault, L., Moffitt, T. E., Caspi, A., Taylor, P. J., & Silva, P. A. (2000). Mental disorders and violence in a total birth cohort: Results from the Dunedin Study. *Archives of General Psychiatry, 57,* 979–986.

Arvey, R. D., & Campion, J. E. (1982). The employment interview: A summary and review of recent research. *Personnel Psychology, 35,* 281–322.

Asch, S. E. (1955, November). Opinions and social pressure. *Scientific American,* 31–35.

Ashcraft, M. H. (1989). *Human memory and cognition.* Glenview, IL: Scott, Foresman.

Asthana, H. S., & Mandal, M. K. (1997). Hemiregional variations in facial expression of emotions. *British Journal of Psychology, 88,* 519–525.

Astin, J. A. (1998). Why patients use alternative medicine: Results of a national study. *Journal of the American Medical Association, 279,* 1548–1553.

Astington, J. (1999). What is theoretical about the child's theory of mind? A Vygotskian view of its development. In P. Lloyd, C. Fernhough, et al. (Eds.), *Lev Vygotsky: Critical assessments, future directions, Vol. IV* (pp. 401–418). New York: Routledge.

Astington, J. W. & Gopnick, A. (1988) Knowing you have changed your mind: Children's understanding of representational change. In J.W. Astington & P.L. Harris (Eds.), *Developing theories of mind,* pp. 193–206. Cambridge, England: Cambridge University Press.

Atwood, N. C. (2001). Gender bias in families and its clinical implications for women. *Social Work, 46,* 23–36.

Aube, J., Fichman, L., Saltaris, C., & Koestner, R. (2000). Gender differences in adolescent depressive symptomatology: Towards an integrated social–developmental model. *Journal of Social & Clinical Psychology, 19,* 297–313.

Audia, G., Kristof-Brown, K. G., & Locke, E. A. (1996). Relationship of goals and micro-level work processes to performance on a multi-path manual task. *Journal of Applied Psychology, 81*(5), 483–497.

Averett, S. L., Gennetian, L. A., & Peters, H. E. (2000). Patterns and determinants of paternal child care during a child's first three years of life. *Marriage & Family Review, 29*(2/3), 115–136.

Ayllon, T., & Azrin, N. H. (1965). The measurement and reinforcement behavior of psychotics. *Journal of the Experimental Analysis of Behavior, 8,* 357–383.

Ayllon, T., & Haughton, E. (1964). Modification of symptomatic verbal behavior of mental patients. *Behavior Research and Therapy, 2,* 87–97.

Azrin, N. H., & Holtz, W. C. (1966). Punishment. In W. K. Honig (Ed.), *Operant behavior: Areas of research and application.* New York: Appleton-Century-Crofts.

Bachar, E. (1998). Psychotherapy—an active agent: Assessing the effectiveness of psychotherapy and its curative factors. *Israel Journal of Psychiatry and Related Sciences, 35*(2), 128–135.

Baddeley, A. (1994). The magical number seven: Still magic after all these years? *Psychological Review, 101,* 353–356.

Baddeley, A. (2000). Short-term and working memory. In E. Tulving & F. I. M. Craik (Eds.), *The Oxford handbook of memory* (pp. 77–92). New York: Oxford University Press.

Baddeley, A. D., & Hitch, G. (1974). Working memory. In G. Bower (Ed.), *Recent advances in learning and motivating* (Vol. 8). New York: Academic.

Baddeley, A. D., & Hitch, G. J. (1994). Developments in the concept of working memory. *Neuropsychology, 6,* 485–493.

Bagely, C., & Tremblay, P. (1998). On the prevalence of homosexuality and bisexuality in a random community survey of 750 men aged 18 to 27. *Journal of Homosexuality, 36*(2), 1–18.

Bahrick, H. P. (1984). Semantic memory content in permastore: Fifty years of memory for Spanish learned in school. *Journal of Experimental Psychology: General, 113,* 1–29.

Bahrick, H. P. (2000). Long-term maintenance of knowledge. In E. Tulving and F. I. Craik (Eds.), *The Oxford handbook of memory* (pp. 347–362). New York: Oxford University Press.

Bailey, K. G. (2000). Evolution, kinship, and psychotherapy: Promoting psychological health through human relationships. In P. Gilbert & K. G. Bailey (Eds.), *Genes on the couch: Explorations in evolutionary psychotherapy* (pp. 42–67). New York: Brunner-Routledge.

Baillargeon, R. (1998). Infants' understanding of the physical world. In M. Sabourin, F. Craik, et al. (Eds.), *Advances in psychological science, Vol. II: Biological and cognitive aspects* (pp. 503–529). Hove, England: Psychology Press/Erlbaum, Taylor & Francis.

Baird, J. C., Wagner, M., & Fuld, K. (1990). A simple but powerful theory of the moon illusion. *Journal of Experimental Psychology: Human Perception and Performance, 16*, 675–677.

Baischer, W. (1995). Acupuncture in migraine: Long-term outcome and predicting factors. *Headache, 35*(8), 472–474.

Bak, M., Girvin, J. P., Hambrecht, F. T., Kufta, C. V., Loeb, G. E., & Schmidt, E. M. (1990). Visual sensations produced by intracortical microstimulation of the human occipital cortex. *Medical and Biological Engineering and Computing, 28*, 257–259.

Baker, C. (1993). The stress of settlement where there is no ethnocultural receiving community. In R. R. Masi, & L. L. Mensah (Eds.), *Health and cultures: Programs, services, and care*, Vol. 2. Oakville, ON: Mosaic Press.

Bala, N., Weiler, R., Copple, P., Smith, R., Hornick, J. P., & Paetsch, J. J. (1994). *A police reference manual on youth and violence*. Canadian Research Institute for Law and the Family and Solicitor General Canada.

Balay, J., & Shevrin, H. (1988). The subliminal psychodynamic activation method. *American Psychologist, 3*, 161–174.

Baldwin, E. (1993). The case for animal research in psychology. *Journal of Social Issues, 49*, 121–131.

Ball, K., & Lee, C. (2000). Relationship between psychological stress, coping and disordered eating: A review. *Psychology & Health, 14*, 1007–1035.

Ballen, W. (1997). Freud's views and the contemporary application of hypnosis: Enhancing therapy within a psychoanalytic framework. *Journal of Contemporary Psychotherapy, 27*(3), 201–214.

Balota, D. A., Dolan, P. O., & Duchek, J. M. (2000). Memory changes in healthy older adults. In E. Tulving & F. I. M. Craik (Eds.), *The Oxford handbook of memory* (pp. 395–409). New York: Oxford University Press.

Baltes, P. B. (1987). Theoretical propositions of life-span developmental psychology: On the dynamics between growth and decline. *Developmental Psychology, 23*, 611 626.

Baltes, P. B. (1993). The aging mind: Potential and limits. *Gerontologist, 33*(5), 580–594.

Bamforth, F., Machin, G., & Innes, M. (1996). X-chromosomes inactivation is mostly random in placental tissues of female monozygotic twins and triplets. *American Journal of Medical Genetics, 61*, 209–215.

Band, E. B., & Weisz, J. R. (1988). How to feel better when it feels bad: Children's perspectives on coping with everyday stress. *Developmental Psychology, 24*, 247–253.

Bandura, A. (1969). *Principles of behavior modification*. New York: Holt, Rinehart & Winston.

Bandura, A. (1977a). Self-efficacy: Toward a unifying theory of behavioral change. *Psychological Review, 84*, 191–215.

Bandura, A. (1977b). *Social learning theory*. Englewood Cliffs, NJ: Prentice-Hall.

Bandura, A. (1999). Social cognitive theory of personality. In L. A. Pervin & O. P. John (Eds.), *Handbook of personality: Theory and research* (pp. 154–196). New York: Guilford Press.

Bandura, A. (2000). Exercise of human agency through collective efficacy. *Current Directions in Psychological Science, 9*, 75–78.

Bandura, A. (2001). Social cognitive theory: An agentic perspective. *Annual Review of Psychology, 52*, 1–26.

Bandura, A., Barbaranelli, C., Vittorio Caprara, G., & Pastorelli, C. (2001). Self-efficacy beliefs as shapers of children's aspirations and career trajectories, *Child Development, 72*, 1, 187–206.

Bandura, A., Blanchard, F. B., & Ritter, B. (1969). Relative efficacy of desensitization and modeling approaches for inducing behavioral, affective, and attitudinal changes. *Journal of Personality and Social Psychology, 13*, 173–199.

Bandura, A., & Menlove, F. L. (1968). Factors determining vicarious extinction of avoidance through symbolic modeling. *Journal of Personality and Social Psychology, 8*, 99–108.

Bandura, A., Ross, D., & Ross, S. A. (1963). Imitation of film-mediated aggressive models. *Journal of Abnormal and Social Psychology, 66*, 3–11.

Bandura, A., & Walters, R. (1963). *Social learning and personality development*. New York: Holt, Rinehart & Winston.

Baptista, M. A. S., Siegel, S., MacQueen, G., & Young, L. T. (1998). Predrug cues modulate morphine tolerance, striatal c-Fos, and AP-1 DNA binding. *Neuroreport: An International Journal for the Rapid Communication of Research in Neuroscience, 9*, 3387–3390.

Barbato, G., Barker, C., Bender, C., Giesen, H. A., & Wehr, T. A. (1994). Extended sleep in humans in 14 hour nights (LD 10:14): Relationship between REM density and spontaneous awakening. *Electroencephalography and Clinical Neurophysiology, 90*, 291–297.

Barber, J. (1991). The locksmith model: Accessing hypnotic responsiveness. In S. J. Lynn & J. W. Rhue (Eds.), *Theories of hypnosis: Current models and perspectives* (pp. 241–274). New York: Guilford Press.

Barber, T. X., Spanos, N. P., & Chaves, J. F. (1974). *Hypnosis, imagination, and human potentialities*. New York: Pergamon.

Barbuto, J. E., Jr. (1997). Taking the charisma out of transformational leadership. *Journal of Social Behavior and Personality, 12*(3), 689–697.

Bard, P. (1934). Emotion: The neuro-humoral basis of emotional reactions. In C. Murchison (Ed.), *Handbook of general experimental psychology*. Worcester, MA: Clark University Press.

Bardon, J. I. (1983). Psychology applied to education: A specialty in search of an identity. *American Psychologist, 38*, 185–196.

Baron, R. A. (1993). Interviewers' moods and evaluations of job applicants: The role of applicant qualifications. *Journal of Applied Social Psychology, 23*, 253–271.

Barondes, S. H. (1998). *Mood genes: Hunting for origins of mania and depression*. New York: W. H. Freeman.

Bar-Or, O., Foreyt, J., Bouchard, C., Brownell, K. D., Dietz, W. H., Ravussin, E., Salbe, A. D., Schwenger, S., St. Jeor, S., & Torun, B. (1998). Physical activity, genetic, and nutritional considerations in childhood weight management. *Medicine and Science in Sports and Exercise, 30*(1), 2–10.

Barrett, G. V., & Depinet, R. L. (1991). A reconsideration of testing for competence rather than for intelligence. *American Psychologist, 46*, 1012–1024.

Barron, M., & Kimmel, M. (2000). Sexual violence in three pornographic media: Toward a sociological explanation. *The Journal of Sex Research, 37*, 161–168.

Bartlett, F. C. (1932). *Remembering: A study in experimental and social psychology*. New York: Macmillan.

Bartoshuk, L. M. (2000). Comparing sensory experiences across individuals: Recent psychophysical advances illuminate genetic variation in taste perception. *Chemical Senses, 25*, 447–460.

Bartoshuk, L. M., Duffy, V. B., & Miller, I. J. (1994, December). PTC/PROP taste: Anatomy, psychophysics, and sex effects. Paper presented at the Kirin International Symposium on Bitter Taste. *Physiology and Behavior, 56*(6), 1165–1171.

Bartoshuk, L. M., Duffy, V. B., Reed, D., & Williams, A. (1996). Supertasting, earaches and head injury: Genetics and pathology alter our taste worlds. *Neuroscience and Biobehavioral Reviews, 20*(1), 79–87.

Bass, B. M. (1985). *Leadership and performance beyond expectations*. New York: Free Press.

Bass, B. M. (1990). From transactional to transformational leadership: Learning to share the vision. *Organizational Dynamics, 18*, 19–31.

Bass, B. M. (1997). Does the transactional–transformational leadership paradigm transcend organizational and national boundaries? *American Psychologist, 52*(2), 130 139.

Bass, B. M. (1998). *Transformational leadership: Industrial, military, and educational impact*. Mahwah, NJ: Lawrence Erlbaum Associates, Inc.

Bass, B. M. (2001). Cognitive, social, and emotional intelligence of transformational leaders. In R. E. Riggio & S. E. Murphy (Eds). *Multiple intelligences and leadership. LEA's organization and management series* (pp. 105–118). Mahwah, NJ: Erlbaum.

Bates, E., & Roe, K. (1999). Language development in children with unilateral brain injury. In C. A. Nelson & M. Luciana (Eds.), *Handbook of developmental cognitive neuroscience* (pp. 269–280) Cambridge, MA: The MIT Press.

Bateson, G., Jackson, D. D., Haley, J., & Weakland, J. (1956). Toward a theory of schizophrenia. *Behavioral Science, 1*, 251–264.

Batson, C. D. (1990). How social an animal? *American Psychologist, 45*, 336–346.

Batson, C. D., Batson, J. G., Slingsby, J. K., Harrell, K. L., Peekna, H. M., & Todd, R. M. (1991). Empathic joy and the empathy-altruism hypothesis. *Journal of Personality and Social Psychology, 61*, 413–426.

Bauer, R. M., & Demery, J. A. (2003). Agnosia. In K. M. Heilman & E. Valenstein (Eds), *Clinical neuropsychology* (4th ed.) (pp. 236–295). London: Oxford University Press.

Baum, A. (1987). Crowding. In D. Stokols & I. Altman (Eds.), *Handbook of environmental psychology*. New York: Wiley.

Baum, A., & Posluszny, D. M. (1999). Health psychology: Mapping biobehavioral contributions to health and illness. *Annual Review of Psychology, 50,* 137–164.

Baumeister, R. F., & Tice, D. M. (2001). *The social dimension of sex.* Boston: Allyn and Bacon.

Bavelier, D., Tomann, A., Hutton, C., Mitchell, T., Corina, D., Liu, G., & Neville, H. (2000). Visual attention to the periphery is enhanced in congenitally deaf individuals. *The Journal of Neuroscience, 20* (RC93), 1–6.

Bayley, N. (1969). Consistency and variability in the growth of intelligence from birth to eighteen years. *Journal of Genetic Psychology, 25,* 165–196.

Baynes, K., Eliassen, J. C., Lutsep, H. L., & Gazzaniga, M. S. (1998). Modular organization of cognitive systems masked by interhemispheric integration. *Science, 280,* 902–905.

Bayster, P. G., & Ford, C. M. (2000). The impact of functional issue classification on managerial decision processes: A study in the telecommunications industry. *Journal of Managerial Issues, 12,* 468–483.

Bechara, A., Tranel, D., Damasio, H., Adolphs, R., Rockland, C., & Damasio, A. R. (1995). Double dissociation of conditioning and declarative knowledge relative to the amygdala and hippocampus in humans. *Science, 269,* 1115–1118.

Beck, A. T. (1963). Thinking and depression: 1. Idiosyncratic content in cognitive distortions. *Archives of General Psychiatry, 9,* 324–333.

Beck, A. T. (1967). *Depression: Clinical, experimental, and theoretical aspects.* New York: Hober.

Beck, A. T. (1976). *Cognitive therapy and emotional disorders.* New York: International Universities Press.

Beck, A. T. (1991). Cognitive therapy. *American Psychologist, 46,* 368–375.

Beck, A. T., & Weishaar, M. (1989). Cognitive therapy. In A. Freeman, K. M. Simon, L. E. Beutler, & H. Arkowitz (Eds.), *Comprehensive handbook of cognitive therapy.* New York: Plenum.

Beck, J. (1966). Effects of orientation and of shape similarity on perceptual grouping. *Perception and Psychophysics, 1,* 311–312.

Bee, H. L. (1987). *The journey of adulthood.* New York: Macmillan.

Begg, I. M., Needham, D. R., & Bookbinder, M. (1993). Do backward messages unconsciously affect listeners? No. *Canadian Journal of Experimental Psychology, 47,* 1–14.

Behr, H. (2000). Families and group analysis. In D. Brown & L. Zinkin, (Eds.). *The psyche and the social world: Developments in group-analytic theory.* International Library of Group Analysis (pp. 163–179). London, UK: Jessica Kingsley Publishers, Ltd.

Beitel, A. H., & Parke, R. D. (1998). Paternal involvement in infancy: The role of maternal and paternal attitudes. *Journal of Family Psychology, 12*(2), 268–288.

Bekerian, D. A., & Bowers, J. M. (1983). Eyewitness testimony: Were we misled? *Journal of Experimental Psychology: Learning, Memory, and Cognition, 9,* 139–145.

Belansky, E. S., & Boggiano, A. K. (1994). Predicting helping behaviors: The role of gender and instrumental/expressive self-schemata. *Sex Roles, 30,* 647–662.

Bell, B. E., & Loftus, E. F. (1989). Trivial persuasion in the courtroom: The power of (a few) minor details. *Journal of Personality and Social Psychology, 56,* 669–679.

Bell, S. T., Kuriloff, P. J., & Lottes, I. (1994). Understanding attributions of blame in stranger rape and date rape situations: An examination of gender, race, identification, and students' social perceptions of rape victims. *Journal of Applied Social Psychology, 24*(19), 1719–1734.

Belsky, J. (1999). Modern evolutionary theory and patterns of attachment. In J. Cassidy & P. R. Shaver, *Handbook of Attachment: Theory, Research and Clinical Applications.* New York, NY: Guilford Press.

Bem, D. J. (1972). Self-perception theory. In L. Berkowitz (Ed.), *Advances in experimental social psychology.* New York: Academic.

Bem, D. J. (1996). Exotic becomes erotic: A developmental theory of sexual orientation. *Psychological Review, 103*(2), 320–335.

Bem, D. J. (2000). Exotic becomes erotic: Interpreting the biological corelates of sexual orientation. *Archives of Sexual Behavior, 29,* 531–548.

Bem, D. J., & Honorton, C. (1994). Does psi exist? Replicable evidence for an anomalous process of information transfer. *Psychological Bulletin, 115, 1,* 4–18

Bem, S. L. (1985). Androgyny and gender schema theory: A conceptual and empirical integration. In T. B. Sonderegger (Ed.), *Nebraska symposium on motivation.* Lincoln: University of Nebraska Press.

Bem, S. L. (1993). *The lenses of gender.* New Haven, CT: Yale University Press.

Benbow, C. P., & Arjmand, O. (1990). Predictors of high academic achievement in mathematics and science by mathematically talented students: A longitudinal study. *Journal of Educational Psychology, 82*(3), 430–441.

Bender, S. T. (1999). Attachment style and friendship characteristics in college students. *Dissertation Abstracts International: Section B: The Sciences & Engineering, 60* (5-B), 2407.

Benet-Martinez, V., & Waller, N. G. (1997). Further evidence for the cross-cultural generality of the Big Seven Factor model: Indigenous and imported Spanish personality constructs. *Journal of Personality, 65*(3), 567–598.

Benjamin, L. T., Jr., Durkin, M., Link, M., Vestal, M., & Acord, J. (1992). Wundt's American doctoral students. *American Psychologist, 47,* 123–131.

Bennett, J. B., & Lehman, W. E. K. (1999). The relationship between problem co-workers and quality of work practices: A case study of exposure to sexual harassment, substance abuse, violence, and job stress. *Work and Stress, 13,* 299–311.

Berg, T. R. (1991). The importance of equity perception and job satisfaction in predicting employee intent to stay at television stations. *Group and Organizational Studies, 16,* 268–284.

Berk, L. E. (1994). *Child development* (3rd. ed.). Boston: Allyn & Bacon.

Berkley, K. J. (1997). Sex differences in pain. *Behavioral and Brain Sciences, 20*(3), 371–380.

Berkman, L. F., & Breslow, L. (1983). *Health and ways of living: The Alameda County Study.* New York: Oxford University Press.

Berkowitz, L. (1964). *The effects of observing violence.* San Francisco: Freeman.

Berkowitz, L. (1990). On the formation and regulation of anger and aggression. *American Psychologist, 45,* 494–503.

Berkowitz, L. (1993). Pain and aggression: Some findings and implications. *Motivation and Emotion, 17,* 277–294.

Berkowitz, L. (2000). *Causes and consequences of feelings: Studies in emotion and social interaction.* New York: Cambridge University Press.

Berman, F. E., & Miner, J. B. (1985). Motivation to manage at the top executive level: A test of the hierarchic role-motivation theory. *Personnel Psychology, 38,* 377–391.

Bernstein, D. & Ebbesen, E. (1978). Reinforcement and substitution in humans: A multiple-response analysis. *Journal of the Experimental Analysis of Behavior, 30,* 243–253.

Bernstein, I. L. (1988, September). What does learning have to do with weight loss and cancer? Paper presented at a science and public policy seminar sponsored by the Federation of Behavioral, Psychological, and Cognitive Sciences, Washington, DC.

Bernstein, I. L. (1991). Aversion conditioning in response to cancer and cancer treatment. *Clinical Psychology Review, 11*(2), 185–191.

Bernstein, K. S. (2000). The experience of acupuncture for treatment of substance dependence. *Journal of Nursing Scholarship, 32,* 267–272.

Berry, D. S., & Landry, J. C. (1997). Facial maturity and daily social interaction. *Journal of Personality and Social Psychology, 72*(3), 570–580.

Bersoff, D. M., & Miller, J. G. (1993). Culture, context, and the development of moral accountability judgments. *Developmental Psychology, 29,* 664–676.

Bettencourt, B. A., & Miller, N. (1996). Gender differences in aggression as a function of provocation: A meta-analysis. *Psychological Bulletin, 119,* 422–447.

Betz, N. E. (1992). Counseling uses of career self-efficacy theory. *Career Development Quarterly, 41*(1), 22–26.

Betz, N. E., & Fitzgerald, L. F. (1987). *The career psychology of women.* New York: Academic Press.

Beutler, L. E., Williams, R. E., Wakefield, P. J., & Entwistle, S. R. (1995). Bridging scientist and practitioner perspectives in clinical psychology. *American Psychologist, 50,* 984–994.

Beyer, S. (1998). The accuracy of academic gender stereotypes. *Sex Roles, 41,* 297–306.

Bhatt, R. S. (1997). The interface between perception and cognition: Feature detection, visual pop-out effects, feature integration, and long-term memory in infancy. In C. Rovee-Collier & L. P. Lipsitt (Eds.),

*Advances in infancy research*. Greenwich, CT: Ablex Publishing Corporation.

*Bhinder and the Canadian Human Rights Commision vs. The Canadian National Railway* (1985) 2 S.C.R. 561.

Biaggio, M., Roades, L. A., Staffelbach, D., Cardinali, J., & Duffy, R. (2000). Intracultural and intercultural. Dialogue in psychoanalytic psychotherapy and psychoanalysis. *Journal of Applied Social Psychology, 30,* 1657–1669.

Bickerton, D. (1998). The creation and re-creation of language. In C. B. Crawford & D. L. Krebs (Eds.). *Handbook of evolutionary psychology: Ideas, issues, and applications* (pp. 613–634). Mahwah, NJ: Erlbaum.

Bickman, L., Teger, A., Gabriele, T., McLaughlin, C., Berger, M., & Sunaday, E. (1973). Dormitory density and helping behavior. *Environment and Behavior, 5,* 465–466.

Bird, C. E. (1999). Gender, household labor, and psychological distress: The impact of the amount and division of housework. *Journal of Health and Social Behavior, 40,* 32–45.

Birnie, S. A., & Horvath, P. (2002). Psychological predictors of Internet social communication. *Journal of Computer Mediated Communication, 7,* 4, 1–25.

Bivens, J. A., & Berk, L. E. (1990). A longitudinal study of the development of elementary school children's private speech. *Merrill-Palmer Quarterly, 36,* 443–463.

Black, M. M., Dubowitz, H., & Starr, R. H., Jr. (1999). African American fathers in low income, urban families: Development, behavior, and home environment of their three-year-old children. *Child Development, 70*(4), 967–978.

Blagrove, M. (1996). Problems with the cognitive psychological modeling of dreaming. *The Journal of Mind and Behavior, 17,* 99–134.

Blakemore, C., & Campbell, F. W. (2000). On the existence of neurons in the human visual system selectively sensitive to the orientation and size of retinal images. In S. Yantis, *Visual perception: Essential readings: Key readings in cognition* (pp. 172–189). Philadelphia: Psychology Press/Taylor & Francis.

Blakemore, S., Wolpert, D., & Frith, C. (2000). Why can't you tickle yourself? *Neuroreport, 11,* 11, R11–R16.

Blanc-Garin, J., Fauré, S., & Sabio, P. (1993). Right hemisphere performance and competence in processing mental images in a case of partial interhemispheric disconnection. *Brain and Cognition, 22,* 118–133.

Bland, B. H. (2000). The medial septum: Node of the ascending brainstem hippocampal synchronizing pathways. In R. Numan (Ed.), *The behavioral neuroscience of the septal region* (pp. 115–145). New York: Springer.

Bland, B. H. & Oddie, S. D. (2001). Theta band oscillation and synchrony in the hippocampal formation and associated structures: The case for its role in sensorimotor integration. *Behavioural Brain Research, 127,* 1–2, 119–136.

Blass, T. (1999). The Milgram Paradigm after 35 years: Some things we now know about obedience to authority. In T. Blass (Ed.), *Obedience to authority: Current perspectives on the Milgram paradigm* (pp. 35–59). Mahwah, NJ: Erlbaum.

Blass, T. (2000). The Milgram Paradigm after 35 years: Some things we now know about obedience to authority. In T. Blass (Ed.), *Obedience to Authority: Current Perspectives on the Milgram Paradigm* (pp. 35–59). Mahwah, N.J.: Erlbaum.

Blatt, S. J. (1995). The destructiveness of perfectionism. *American Psychologist, 50,* 1003–1020.

Bleak, J. L., & Frederick, C. M. (1998). Superstitious behavior in sport: Levels of effectiveness and determinants of use in three collegiate sports *Journal of Sport Behavior, 21,* 1–15.

Bleske, A. L., & Buss, D. M. (2000). Can men and women be just friends? *Personal Relationships, 7,* 131–151.

Bloom, F. E. (1981, October). Neuropeptides. *Scientific American,* 148–168.

Blount, S., & Larrick, R. P. (2000). Framing the game: Examining frame choice in bargaining. *Organizational Behavior & Human Decision Processes, 81,* 43–71.

Blum, K., Braverman, E. R., Holder, J. M., Lubar, J. F., Monastra, V. J., Miller, D., Lubar, J. O., Chen, T. H., & Comings, D. E. (2000). Reward deficiency syndrome: A biogenetic model for the diagnosis and treatment of impulsive, addictive, and compulsive behaviors. *Journal of Psychoactive Drugs, 32,* 1–68.

Boachie, A., Goldfield, G. S., & Spettique, W. (2003). Olanzapine use as an adjunctive treatment for hospitalized children with anorexia nervosa: Case reports. *International Journal of Eating Disorders, 33,* 1, 98–103.

Bobo, L., & Kluegel, J. R. (1997). Status, ideology, and dimensions of whites' racial beliefs and attitudes: Progress and stagnation. In S. A. Tuch & J. K. Martin (Eds.), *Racial attitudes in the 1990s: Continuity and change.* Westport, CT: Praeger.

Bodnar, A. G., Ouellette, M., Frolkis, M., Holt, S. E., Chiu, C. P., Morin, G. B., Harley, C. B., Shay, J. W., Lichtsteiner, S., & Wright, W. E. (1998). Extension of life-span by introduction of telomerase into normal human cells. *Science, 279,* 349–352.

Bogren, L., Boren, I., & Thorell, L. (1998). Defense mechanism test and electrodermal activity. *Perceptual & Motor Skills, 87,* 279–290.

Boivin, D. B., Duffy, J. F., Kronauer, R. E., & Czeisler, C. A. (1996). Dose-response relationships for resetting of human circadian clock by light. *Nature, 379,* 540–542.

Bond, C. F., Jr., & Titus, L. J. (1983). Social facilitation: A meta-analysis of 241 studies. *Psychological Bulletin, 94,* 265–292.

Bond, R., & Smith, P. B. (1996). Culture and conformity: A meta-analysis of studies using Asch's (1952b, 1956) line judgement task. *Psychological Bulletin, 119,* 111–137.

Boneva, B., Frieze, I. H., Ferligoj, A., Pauknerová, D., & Orgocka, A. (1998). Achievement, power, and affiliation motives as clues to (e)migration desires: A four-countries comparison. *European Psychologist, 3,* 247–254.

Borg, E., & Counter, S. A. (1989, August). The middle-ear muscles. *Scientific American,* 74–80.

Borkenau, P., & Ostendorf, F. (1998). The Big Five as states: How useful is the five-factor model to describe intraindividual variations over time? *Journal of Research in Personality, 32*(2), 202–221.

Bornstein, R. F. (1989). Exposure and affect: Overview and meta-analysis of research, 1968–1987. *Psychological Bulletin, 106,* 265–289.

Bornstein, R. F. (1992). The dependent personality: Developmental, social, and clinical perspectives. *Psychological Bulletin, 112,* 3–23.

Boronat, C. B., & Logan, G. D. (1997). The role of attention in automatization: Does attention operate at encoding, or retrieval, or both? *Memory and Cognition, 25*(1), 36–46.

Borrie, R. A. (1991). The use of restricted environmental stimulation therapy in treating addictive behaviors. *International Journal of the Addictions, 25,* 995–1015.

Bosma, H., Richard, P., Siegrist, J., & Marmot, M. (1998). Two alternative job stress models and the risk of coronary heart disease. *American Journal of Public Health, 88*(1), 68–74.

Botschner, J. V. (1996). Reconsidering male friendships: A social-development perspective. In C. W. Tolman et al. (Eds.), *Problems of theoretical psychology.* North York, ON: Captus Press.

Bouchard, T. J., Jr., & McGue, M. (1981). Familial studies of intelligence: A review. *Science, 212,* 1055–1058.

Boudreaux, E., Kilpatrick, D. G., Resnick, H. S., Best, C. L., & Saunders, B. E. (1998). Criminal victimization, posttraumatic stress disorder, and comorbid psychopathology among a community sample of women. *Journal of Traumatic Stress, 11,* 665–678.

Boutcher, S. H. (1992). Attention and athletic performance: An integrated approach. In Thelma S. Horn (Ed.), *Advances in sport psychology* (pp. 251–265). Champaign, IL: Human Kinetics.

Bower, G. H. (1981). Mood and memory. *American Psychologist, 36,* 126–148.

Bower, T. G. R. (1966, December). The visual world of infants. *Scientific American,* 80–92.

Bowers, K. S. (1979). Time distortion and hypnotic ability: Underestimating the duration of hypnosis. *Journal of Abnormal Psychology, 88,* 435–439.

Bowers, K. S., Regehr, G., Balthazard, C., & Parker, K. (1990). Intuition in the context of discovery. *Cognitive Psychology, 22,* 72–110.

Bowlby, J. (1977). The making and breaking of affectional bonds: Etiology and psychopathology in the light of attachment theory. *British Journal of Psychiatry, 130,* 201–210.

Bowlby, J. (1988). *A secure base.* New York: Basic Books.

Boyd, B., & Wandersman, A. (1991). Predicting undergraduate condom use with the Fishbein and Ajzen and the Triandis attitude-behavior models: Implications for public health interventions. *Journal of Applied Social Psychology, 21,* 1810–1830.

Boynton, R. M. (1988). Color vision. *Annual Review of Psychology, 39,* 69–101.

Bradley, B. P. (1990). Behavioural addictions: Common features and treatment implications. *British Journal of Addiction, 85*, 1417–1419.

Bradley, C. L., & Marcia, J. E. (1998). Generativity-stagnation: A five-category model. *Journal of Personality, 66*(1), 39–44.

Bradley, J. P., Nicol, A. A. M., Charbonneau, D., & Meyer, J. P. (2002). Personality correlates of leadership development in Canadian forces officer candidates. *Canadian Journal of Behavioural Science, 34*, 2, 92–103.

Branden, N. (1980). *The psychology of romantic love*. Los Angeles: Tarcher.

Brannon, L. (2002). *Gender: Psychological perspectives* (3rd ed.). Boston: Allyn and Bacon.

Brannon, L., & Feist, J. (2000). *Health psychology: An introduction to behavior and health* (4th ed.). Belmont, CA: Wadsworth.

Braun, A. R., Balkin, T. J., Wesensten, N. J., Gwadry, F., Carson, R. E., Varga, M., Baldwin, P., Belenky, G., & Herscovitch, P. (1998). Dissociated pattern of activity in visual cortices and their projections during human rapid eye movement sleep. *Science, 279*, 91–96.

Braun, C. M. J., Denault, C., Cohen, H., & Rouleau, I. (1994). Discrimination of facial identity and facial affect by temporal and frontal lobectomy patients. *Brain & Cognition, 24*, 2, 198–212.

Breger, L. (2000). *Freud: Darkness in the midst of vision*. New York: Wiley.

Brehm, J. W. (1966). *A theory of psychological reactance*. New York: Academic.

Brennan, K. A., Clark, C. L., & Shaver, P. R. (1998). Self-report measurement of adult attachment: An integrative overview. In J. A. Simpson, W. S. Rholes, and others, *Attachment Theory and Close Relationships*. (46–76). New York, NY: Guildford Press.

Brennan, K. A. & Shaver, P. R. (1995). Dimensions of adult attachment, affect regulation, and romantic relationship functioning. *Personality and Social Psychology Bulletin, 21*, 267–283.

Bretschneider, J. G., & McCoy, N. L. (1988). Sexual interest and behavior in healthy 80- to 102-year-olds. *Archives of Sexual Behavior, 17*, 109–129.

Brief, A. P., & Weiss, H. M. (2002). Organizational behavior: Affect in the workplace. *Annual Reviews Psychology, 53*, 279–307.

Broadbent, D. E. (1958). *Perception and communication*. London: Pergamon.

Broberg, A. G., Wessels, H., Lamb, M. E., & Hwang, C. P. (1997). Effects of day care on the development of cognitive abilities in 8-year-olds: A longitudinal study. *Developmental Psychology, 33*(1), 62–69.

Brock, G., McIntire, L., & Macchia, R. J. (2003). Snow on the roof doesn't douse fire below. Presented at the 98th annual meeting of the American Urological Association, 26 April–1 May 2003, Chicago, IL.

Brodsky, A. E. (1996). Resilient single mothers in risky neighborhoods: Negative psychological sense of community. *Journal of Community Psychology, 24*(4), 347–363.

Brody, L. R. (1997). Gender and emotion: Beyond stereotypes. *Journal of Social Issues, 53*(2), 369–392.

Bronfenbrenner, U. (1989, September). Who cares for children? Invited address, UNESCO, Paris.

Bronfenbrenner, U. (1999). Environments in developmental perspective: Theoretical and operational models. In S. L. Friedman & T. D. Wachs (Eds.). *Measuring environment across the life span: Emerging methods and concepts* (pp. 3–28). Washington, DC: American Psychological Association.

Bronson, G. W. (1997). The growth of visual capacity: Evidence from infant scanning patterns. In C. Rovee-Collier & L. P. Lipsitt (Eds.), *Advances in infancy research*. Greenwich, CT: Ablex Publishing Corporation.

Brooks, M. C. (2000). Press start: Exploring the effects of violent video games on boys. In *Dissertation Abstracts International: Section B: The Sciences & Engineering, 60*(12B), 6419.

Broughton, R. (1990). The prototype concept in personality assessment. *Canadian Psychology, 31*, 1, 26–37.

Broughton, R., Boyes, M. C., & Mitchell, J. (1993). DIStance-From-the-PROtotype (DISPRO) personality assessment for children. *Journal of Personality Assessment, 60*, 1, 32–47.

Broughton, R. H. (1987). Distance from the prototype: A multidimensional scaling approach to personality assessment. *Dissertation Abstracts International, 48*, 3-B, 907.

Broughton, R. J. (1991). Field studies of sleep/wake patterns and performance: A laboratory experience. *Canadian Journal of Psychology, 45*, 240–253.

Broughton, R. J., Billings, R., Cartwright, R., Doucette, D. et al. (1994). Homicidal somnambulism: A case report. *Sleep, 17*, 3, 253–264.

Brown, A. S. (1989). *How to increase your memory power*. Glenview, IL: Scott, Foresman.

Brown, G. M. (1994). Light, melatonin and the sleep-wake cycle. *Journal of Psychiatry & Neuroscience, 19*, 345–353.

Brown, K. W., & Moskowitz, D. S. (1998). Dynamic stability of behavior: The rhythms of our interpersonal lives. *Journal of Personality, 66*(1), 105–108.

Brown, N. (1997). Context memory and the selection of frequency estimation strategies. *Journal of Experimental Psychology: Learning, Memory, and Cognition, 23*(4), 898–914.

Brown, R. (1970). The first sentences of child and chimpanzee. In R. Brown (Ed.), *Psycholinguistics: Selected papers*. New York: Free Press.

Brown, R. (1973). *A first language: The early stages*. Cambridge, MA: Harvard University Press.

Brown, R., & Kulik, J. (1977). Flashbulb memories. *Cognition, 5*, 73–99.

Brown, S. C., & Craik, F. I. M. (2000). Encoding and retrieval of information. In E. Tulving & F. I. M. Craik (Eds.), *The Oxford handbook of memory* (pp. 93–107). New York: Oxford University Press.

Browne, B. A. (1998). Gender stereotypes in advertising on children's television in the 1990s: A cross-national analysis. *Journal of Advertising, 27*(1), 83–96.

Bruce, T. J., Spiegel, D. A., & Hegel, M. T. (1999). Cognitive–behaviorial therapy helps prevent relapse and recurrence of panic disorder following alprazolam discontinuation: A long-term follow-up of the Peoria and Dartmouth studies. *Journal of Consulting & Clinical Psychology, 67*, 151–156.

Bruner, J. (1990). *Acts of meaning*. Cambridge, MA: Harvard University Press.

Bruner, J. (1997). Celebrating divergence: Piaget and Vygotsky. *Human Development, 40*, 63–73.

Bryant, R. A., & McConkey, K. M. (1989). Hypnotic blindness: A behavioral and experiential analysis. *Journal of Abnormal Psychology, 98*, 71–77.

Bryden, M. P., Roy, E. A., McManus, I. C, & Bulman-Fleming, M. B. (1997). On the genetics and measurement of human handedness, *Laterality, 2*, 3–4, 317–336.

Buck, R., Losow, J. I., Murphy, M. M., & Costanzo, P. (1992). Social facilitation and inhibition of emotional expression and communication. *Journal of Personality and Social Psychology, 6*, 962–968.

Bukowski, W. M., Sippola, L. K., & Hoza, B. (1999). Same and other: Interdependency between participation in same- and other-sex friendships. *Journal of Youth & Adolescence, 28*, 439–459.

Bukowski, W. M., Sippola, L. K., & Newcomb, A. F. (2000). Variations in patterns of attraction of same- and other-sex peers during early adolescence. *Developmental Psychology, 36*, 2, 147–154.

Burgoon, J. K., Buller, D. B., & Guerrero, L. K. (1995). Interpersonal deception: IX. Effects of social skill and nonverbal communication on deception success and detection accuracy. *Journal of Language & Social Psychology, 14*, 3, 289–311.

Busato, V. V., Prins, F. J., Elshout, J. J., & Hamaker, C. (1999). The relation between learning styles, the Big Five personality traits and achievement motivation in higher education. *Personality and Individual Differences, 26*, 129–140.

Bushman, B. J., & Baumeister, R. F. (1998). Threatened egotism, narcissism, self-esteem, and direct and displaced aggression: Does self-love or self-hate lead to violence? *Journal of Personality & Social Psychology, 75*(1), 219–229.

Bushman, B. J., & Geen, R. G. (1990). Role of cognitive-emotional mediators and individual differences in the effects of media violence on aggression. *Journal of Personality and Social Psychology, 58*, 156–163.

Bushman, B. J., & Phillips, C. M. (2001). If the television program bleeds, memory for the advertisement recedes. *Current Direction in Psychological Science, 10*, 43–47.

Buss, D. M. (1995). Psychological sex differences: Origins through sexual selection. *American Psychologist, 50*, 164–168.

Buss, D. M. (1999). *Evolutionary psychology*. Boston: Allyn and Bacon.

Buss, D. M. (2000a). *The dangerous passion: Why jealousy is as necessary as love and sex*. New York: Free Press.

Buss, D. M. (2000b). The evolution of happiness. *American Psychologist, 55*, 15–23.

Buss, D. M., & Kenrick, D. T. (1998). Evolutionary social psychology. In D. T. Gilbert, S. T. Fiske, & G. Lindzey (Eds.), *The handbook of social psychology* (pp. 982–1019). Boston, MA: The McGraw-Hill Company.

Bussey, K., & Bandura, A. (1999). Social cognitive theory of gender development and differentiation. *Psychological Review, 106,* 676–713.

Butler, S. F., & Strupp, H. H. (1991). Psychodynamic psychotherapy. In M. Hersen, A. E. Kazdin, & A. S. Bellack (Eds.), *The clinical psychology handbook* (2nd ed.). New York; Pergamon.

Cabeza, R., & Nyberg, L. (2000). Imaging cognition II: An empirical review of 275 PET and fMRI studies. *Journal of Cognitive Neuroscience, 12,* 1–47.

Cabeza, R., Rao, S. M., Wagner, A. D., Mayer, A. R., & Schacter, D. L. (2001). Can medial temporal lobe regions distinguish true from false? An event-related functional MRI study of veridical and illusory recognition memory. *Proceedings of the National Academy of Sciences of the United States, 98,* 4805–4810.

Cacioppo, J. T., & Gardner, W. L. (1999). Emotion. *Annual Review of Psychology, 50,* 191–214.

Cacioppo, J. T., Petty, R. E., Feinstein, J. A., & Jarvis, W. B. G. (1996). Dispositional differences in cognitive motivation: The life and times of individuals varying in need for cognition. *Psychological Bulletin, 119,* 197–253.

Caffarella, R. S., & Olson, S. K. (1993). Psychosocial development of women: A critical review of the literature. *Adult Education Quarterly, 43,* 125–151.

Cairns, R. B., & Cairns, B. D. (1994). *Lifelines and risks: Pathways of youth in our time.* Cambridge, England: Cambridge University Press.

Cairns, R. B., & Cairns, B. D. (2000). The natural history and developmental functions of aggression. In A. J. Sameroff, M. Lewis, & S. M. Miller (Eds.), *Handbook of developmental psychopathology* (pp. 403–429). New York: Kluwer/Plenum.

Call, M. J. (1999). Transgenerational attachment, life stress, and the development of disruptive behavior in preschool children. *Dissertation Abstracts International: Section B: The Sciences & Engineering, 60*(4-B), 1884.

Call, V., Sprecher, S., & Schwartz, P. (1995). The incidence and frequency of marital sex in a national sample. *Journal of Marriage and the Family, 57*(3), 639–652.

Calvert, S. L. (1998). *Children's journeys through the information age.* New York: McGraw-Hill.

Calvin, W. H. (1996). *The cerebral code: Thinking a thought in the mosaics of the mind.* Cambridge, MA & London: The MIT Press.

Camara, W. J., & Schneider, D. L. (1994). Integrity tests: Facts and unresolved issues. *American Psychologist, 49,* 112–119.

Cameron, J., & Pierce, W. D. (2002). *Rewards and intrinsic motivation: Resolving the controversy.* Westport, CO: Bergin and Garvey.

Cameron, P., & Cameron, K. (1998). "Definitive" University of Chicago sex survey overestimated prevalence of homosexual identity. *Psychological Reports, 82*(3, Pt.1), 861–862.

Campbell, S. S., & Murphy, P. J. (1998). Extraocular circadian phototransduction in humans, *Science, 279,* 396–399.

Campion, M. A., Palmer, D. K., & Campion, J. F. (1998). Structuring employment interviews to improve reliability, validity, and users' reactions. *Current Directions in Psychological Science, 7*(3), 77–82.

Canadian Centre for Justice Statistics (2002). *Juristat: Crime Statistics in Canada, 2001, 22,* 6 (85-002-XIE; 85-002-XPE) http://www.statcan.ca/Daily/English/020717/d020717b.htm, accessed 7 July 2003.

Canadian Council on Animal Care (1989). *Ethics of animal investigation.* Ottawa.

Canadian Human Rights Commission (1979). *Discrimination in Canada: A survey of knowledge, attitudes and practices concerned with discrimination.*

Canadian Mental Health Association (2002a). *Fact sheet: Bipolar disorder (formerly known as manic depression).*

Canadian Mental Health Association (2002b). *Fact sheet: Schizophrenia.*

Canadian Psychological Association (1998). *Human Relations and Societal Issues: Report of the National Conference on Psychology as a Science.* CPA, http://www.cpa.ca/science/human.htm.

Canadian Psychological Association (2001). *Companion manual to the Canadian code of ethics for psychologists* (3rd ed.). Ottawa: CPA.

Canadian Study of Health and Aging Working Group (1994). Canadian study of health and aging: Study methods and prevalence of dementia. *Canadian Medical Association Journal, 150,* 899–913.

Cannon, W. B. (1927). The James-Lange theory of emotion: A critical examination and an alternative theory. *American Journal of Psychology, 39,* 106–124.

Cannon-Bowers, J. A., & Salas, E. (1998). Team performance and training in complex environments: Recent findings from applied research. *American Psychological Society, 7*(3), 83–87.

Cano, C., Hennessy, K. D., Warren, J. L., & Lubitz, J. (1996). Medicare part A: Utilization and expenditures for psychiatric services: 1995. *Health Care Financing Review, 18,* 177–193.

Caporael, L. R. (2001). Evolutionary psychology: Toward a unifying theory and a hybrid science. *Annual Review of Psychology, 52,* 607–628.

Carlson, N. R. (2001). *Physiology of behaviour* (7th ed.). Boston: Allyn & Bacon.

Carlson-Radvansky, L. A., Covey, E. S., & Lattanzi, K. M. (1999). "What" effects on "Where": Functional influences on spatial relations. *Psychological Science, 10,* 516–521.

Carpendale, J. I. M. (2000). Kohlberg and Piaget on stages and moral reasoning. *Developmental Review, 20,* 181–205.

Carr, M., Borkowski, J. G., & Maxwell, S. E. (1991). Motivational components of underachievement. *Developmental Psychology, 27,* 108–118.

Carstensen, L. L., & Charles, S. T. (1998). Emotion in the second half of life. *Psychological Science, 7,* 144–149.

Carter, B. L., & Tiffany, S. T. (1999). Meta-analysis of cue-reactivity in addiction research. *Addiction, 94,* 327–340.

Carton, J. S., & Nowicki, S. (1994). Antecedents of individual differences in locus of control of reinforcement: A critical review. *Genetic, Social, and General Psychology Monographs, 120*(1), 31–81.

Carton, J. S., Nowicki, S., & Balser, G. M. (1996). An observational study of antecedents of locus of control of reinforcement. *International Journal of Behavioral Development, 19*(1), 161–175.

Casagrande, M., Violani, C., Lucidi, F., & Buttinelli, E. (1996). Variations in sleep mentation as a function of time of night. *International Journal of Neuroscience, 85*(1/2), 19–30.

Casas, J. M., Turner, J. A., Ruiz, de, E., & Christoper, A. (2001). Machismo revisited in a time of crisis: Implications for understanding and counseling Hispanic men. In G. R. Brooks, R. Gary, & G. E. Good (Eds.). *The new handbook of psychotherapy and counseling with men: A comprehensive guide to settings, problems, and treatment approaches, 1 & 2* (pp. 754–779). San Francisco: Jossey-Bass.

Cascio, W. F. (1995). Whither industrial and organizational psychology in a changing world of work? *American Psychologist, 50,* 928–939.

Casey, B. J., Giedd, J. N., & Thomas, K. M. (2000). Structural and functional brain development and its relation to cognitive development. *Biological Psychology, 54,* 241–257.

Caspi, A., & Roberts, B. W. (2001). Target article: Personality development across the life course: The argument for change and continuity. *Psychological Inquiry, 12,* 49–66.

Cassidy, J., & Berlin, L. J. (1994). The insecure/ambivalent pattern of attachment: Theory and research. *Child Development, 65,* 971–991.

Cassidy, T. (2000). Stress, healthiness, and health behaviours: An exploration of the role of life events, daily hassles, cognitive appraisal, and the coping process. *Counselling Psychology Quarterly, 13,* 293–311.

Cattell, R. B. (1949). *Manual for forms A and B: Sixteen personality factors questionnaire.* Champaign, IL: IPAT.

Cavalier, A. R., Ferretti, R. P., & Hodges, A. E. (1997). Self-management within a classroom token economy for students with learning disabilities. *Research in Development Disabilities, 18*(3), 167–178.

Cavanagh, P., & Leclerc, Y. G. (1989). Shape from shadows. *Journal of Experimental Psychology: Human Perception and Performance, 15,* 3–27.

Ceci, S. J. (2000). So near and yet so far: Lingering questions about the use of measures of general intelligence for college admission and employment screening. *Psychology, Public Policy, & Law, 6,* 233–252.

Ceci, S. J., & Bruck, M. (1993). Suggestibility of the child witness: A historical review and synthesis. *Psychological Bulletin, 113,* 403–439.

Ceci, S. J., & Williams, W. M. (1997). Schooling, intelligence, and income. *American Psychologist, 52*(10), 1051–1058.

Celuch, K., & Slama, M. (1995). Getting along and getting ahead as motives for self-presentation: Their impact on advertising effectiveness. *Journal of Applied Social Psychology, 25,* 1700–1713.

Centers for Disease Control and Prevention. (2001). HIV and AIDS—United States, 1981–2000. *Morbidity and Mortality Weekly Report, 50,* 430–433.

Cermak, L. S. (1975). *Improving your memory.* New York: Norton.

Chaleby, K. (2000). Forensic psychiatry and Islamic law. In I. Al-Issa (Ed.), *Al-Junun: Mental illness in the Islamic world* (pp. 71–98). Madison, CT: International Universities Press.

Challis, G. B., & Stam, H. J. (1992). A longitudinal study of the development of anticipatory nausea and vomiting in cancer chemotherapy patients: The role of absorption and autonomic perception. *Health Psychology, 11*(3), 181–189.

Chalmers, D. J. (1996). *Conscious mind: In search of a fundamental theory.* New York: Oxford University Press.

Chambless, D., & Hollon, S. D. (1998). Defining empirically supported therapies. *Journal of Consulting & Clinical Psychology, 66,* 7–18.

Chang, F. I. F., Isaacs, K. R., & Greenough, W. T. (1991). Synapse formation occurs in association with the induction of long-term potentiation in two-year-old rat hippocampus in vitro. *Neurobiology of Aging, 12,* 517–522.

Channouf, A. (2000). Subliminal exposure to facial expressions of emotion and evaluative judgements of advertising messages. *European Review of Applied Psychology, 50,* 19–25.

Charles, G. (1991). Suicide intervention and prevention among northern Native youth. *Journal of Child and Youth Care, 6*(1), 11–17.

Charness N., Clifton, J., & MacDonald L. (1988). Case study of a musical mono-savant. In L. K. Obler & D. A. Fein (Eds), *The exceptional brain: Neuropsychology of talent and special abilities* (pp. 277–293). New York: Guilford Press.

Chase, V. M. (2000). Where to look to find out why: Rational information search in causal hypothesis testing. *Dissertation Abstracts International: Section B: The Sciences & Engineering, 60*(11-B), 5800.

Chassin, L., Collins, R. L., Ritter, J., & Shirley, M. C. (2001). Vulnerability to substance use disorders across the lifespan. In R. E. Ingram, J. M. Price, *Vulnerability to Psychopathology: Risk Across the Lifespan* (165–172). New York: The Guilford Press.

Chassin, L., Pillow, D. R., Curran, P. J., Molina, B. S. G., & Barrera, M., Jr. (1993). Relation of parental alcoholism to early adolescent substance use: A test of three mediating mechanisms. *Journal of Abnormal Psychology, 102,* 3–19.

Chaves, J. F., & Dworkin, S. F. (1997). Hypnotic control of pain: Historical perspectives and future prospects. *International Journal of Clinical and Experimental Hypnosis, 45*(4), 356–376.

Chen, X. (2000). Growing up in a collectivist culture: Socialization and socioemotional development in Chinese children. In A. L. Comunian, U. P. Gielen, *International Perspectives on Human Development* (331–353). Lengerich, Germany: Pabst Science Publishers.

Cheng, Y., Kawachi, I., Coakley, E. H., Schwartz, J., & Colditz, G. (2000). Association between psychosocial work characteristics and health functioning in American women: Prospective study. *British Medical Journal, 320,* 1432–1435.

Cherulnik, P. D., Turns, L. C., & Wilderman, S. K. (1990). Physical appearance and leadership: Exploring the role of appearance-based attribution in leader emergence. *Journal of Applied Social Psychology, 20,* 1530–1539.

Chi, M. T., Hutchinson, J. E., & Robin, A. F. (1989). How inferences about novel domain-related concepts can be constrained by structured knowledge. *Merrill-Palmer Quarterly, 35*(1), 27–62.

Chi, M. T. & Koeske, R. D. (1983). Network representation of a child's dinosaur knowledge. *Developmental Psychology, 19*(1), 29–39.

Chidester, T. R. (1986). Problems in the study of interracial interaction: Pseudo-interracial dyad paradigm. *Journal of Personality and Social Psychology, 50,* 74–79.

Chodorow, N. (1978). *The reproduction of mothering: Psychoanalysis and the sociology of gender.* Berkeley, CA: University of California Press.

Choi, I., Nisbett, R. E., & Norenzayan, A. (1999). Causal attribution across cultures: Variation and universality. *Psychological Bulletin, 125*(1), 47–63.

Chomsky, N. (1957). *Syntactic structures.* The Hague, Netherlands: Mouton.

Chomsky, N. (1999). On the nature, use, and acquisition of language. In W. Ritchie & T. Bhatia (Eds.), *Handbook of child language acquisition.* New York: Academic Press.

Chorpita, B. F., & Barlow, D. H. (1998). The development of anxiety: The role of control in the early environment. *Psychological Bulletin, 124*(1), 3–21.

Christenfeld, N., Gerin, W., Linden, W., & Sanders, M. (1997). Social support effects on cardiovascular reactivity: Is a stranger as effective as a friend? *Psychosomatic Medicine, 59*(4), 388–398.

Cialdini, R. B. (1993). *Influence* (3rd ed.). New York: HarperCollins.

Cialdini, R. B. (2001). Influence: Science and practice. (4th ed.). Boston: Allyn and Bacon.

Cialdini, R. B., Eisenberg, N., Green, B. L., Rhoads, K., & Bator, R. (1998). Undermining the undermining effect of reward on sustained interest. *Journal of Applied Social Psychology, 28*(3), 249–263.

Cialdini, R. B., Trost, M. R., & Newsom, J. T. (1995). Preference for consistency: The development of a valid measure and the discovery of surprising behavioral implications. *Journal of Personality and Social Psychology, 69,* 318–328.

Cialdini, R. B., Wosinska, W., Barrett, D. W., Butner, J. & Gornik-Durose, M. (2001). The differential impact of two social influence principles on individualists and collectivists in Poland and the United States. W. Wosinska & R.B. Cialdini et al. (Eds), *The Practice of Social Influence in Multiple Cultures: Applied Social Research*, Lawrence Erlbaum Assoc., 33–50.

Cicero, T. J. (1994). Effects of paternal exposure to alcohol on offspring development. *Alcohol Health and Research World, 18,* 37–41.

Clark, H. H. (1996). *Using language.* Cambridge, England: Cambridge University Press.

Clarke-Stewart, A., Friedman, S., & Koch, J. B. (1985). *Child development: A topical approach.* New York: Wiley.

Clarkin, J. F., & Hull, J. W. (1991). The brief psychotherapies. In M. Hersen, A. E. Kazdin, & A. S. Bellack (Eds.), *The clinical psychology handbook* (2nd ed.). New York: Pergamon.

Claxon, G. (1975). Why can't we tickle ourselves. *Perceptual and Motor Skills, 41*(1), 335–338.

CNN (2003, April 23). Mel Lastman interview.

Coffey, C. W., Weiner, R. D., Djang, W. T., Figiel, G. S., Soady, S. A. R., Patterson, L. J., Holt, P. D., Spritzer, C. E., & Wilinson, W. E. (1991). Brain anatomic effects of electroconvulsive therapy. *Archives of General Psychiatry, 48,* 1013–1021.

Cohen, S. (1996). Psychological stress, immunity, and upper respiratory infections. *Current Directions in Psychological Science, 5*(3), 86–90.

Cohen, S., Frank, E., Doyle, W. J., Skoner, D. P., Rabin, B. S., & Gwaltney, J. M., Jr. (1998). Types of stressors that increase susceptibility to the common cold in healthy adults. *Health Psychology, 17*(3), 214–223.

Cohen, S., Tyrrell, D. A. J., & Smith, A. P. (1997). Psychological stress in humans and susceptibility to the common cold. In T. W. Miller et al. (Eds.), *Clinical disorders and stressful life events* (pp. 217–235). Madison, CT: International Universities Press, Inc.

Cohn, D. A. (1990). Child-mother attachment of six-year-olds and social competence at school. *Child Development, 61,* 152–162.

Cohn, L. (1991). Sex differences in the course of personality development: A meta-analysis. *Psychological Bulletin, 109,* 252–266.

Cole, A., & Kerns, K. A. (2001). Perceptions of sibling qualities and activities of early adolescents. *Journal of Early Adolescence, 21,* 204–226.

Cole, M. (1999). Culture in development. In B. H. Bornstein & M. E. Lamb (Eds.), *Developmental psychology: An advanced textbook.* Mahwah, NJ: Erlbaum.

Cole, S. W., Kemeny, M. E., Taylor, S. E., Visscher, B. R., & Fahey, J. L. (1996). Accelerated course of human immunodeficiency virus infection in gay men who conceal their homosexual identity. *Psychosomatic Medicine, 58,* 219–231.

Coley, R. L., & Chase-Lansdale, P. L. (1998). Adolescent pregnancy and parenting: Recent evidence and future directions. *American Psychologist, 53,* 152–166.

Collins, N. L., & Miller, L. C. (1994). Self-disclosure and liking: A meta-analytic review. *Psychological Bulletin, 116,* 457–475.

Collins, W. A., & Laursen, B. (2000). Adolescent relationships: The art of fugue. In C. Hendrick & S. S. Hendrick (Eds.), *Close relationships: A sourcebook* (pp. 59–69). Thousand Oaks, CA: Sage.

Collins, W. A., Maccoby, E. E., Steinberg, L., Hetherington, E. M., & Bornstein, M. H. (2000). Contemporary research on parenting: The case for nature and nurture. *American Psychologist, 55,* 218–232.

Colman, H., Nabekura, J., & Lichtman, J. W. (1997). Alterations in synaptic strength preceding axon withdrawal. *Science, 275,* 356–361.

Comer, J. P. (1988, November). Educating poor minority children. *Scientific American*, 42–51.

Comer, J. P., & Woodruff, D. W. (1998). Mental health in schools. *Child & Adolescent Psychiatric Clinics of North America, 7*, 499–513.

Compas, B. E., Haaga, D. A., Keefe, F. J., Leitenberg, H., & Williams, D. A. (1998). Sampling of empirically supported psychological treatment from health psychology: Smoking, chronic pain, cancer, and bulimia nervosa. *Journal of Consulting and Clinical Psychology, 66*, 89–112.

Comuzzie, A. G., & Allison, D. B. (1998). The search for human obesity genes. *Science, 280*, 1374–1377.

Connors, E. (1993). Healing in First Nations: The spirit of the family. In M. Rodway & B. Trute (Eds.), *Ecological perspective in family-centered therapy* (pp. 51–65). Toronto: Edwin Mellen Press.

Constantino, J. M., Grosz, D., Saenger, P., Chandler, D. W., Nandi, R., & Earls, F. J. (1993). Testosterone and aggression in children. *Journal of the American Academy of Child and Adolescent Psychiatry, 32*, 1217–1222.

Conway, M. A., Anderson, S. J., Larsen, S. F., Donnelly, C. M., McDaniel, M. A., McClelland, A. G. R., Rawles, R. E., & Logie, R. H. (1994). The formation of flashbulb memories. *Memory & Cognition, 22*, 326–343.

Conyers, L. M., Enright, M. S., & Strauser, D. R. (1998). Applying self-efficacy theory to counseling college students with disabilities. *Journal of Applied Rehabilitation Counseling, 29*(1), 25–30.

Cooley-Quille, M., Boyd, R. C., Frantz, E., & Walsh, J. (2001). Emotional and behavioral impact of exposure to community violence in inner-city adolescents. *Journal of Clinical Child Psychology, 30*, 199–206.

Coppola, D. M., & O'Connell, R. J. (1988). Behavioral responses of peripubertal female mice towards puberty-accelerating and puberty-delaying chemical signals. *Chemical Senses, 13*, 407–424.

Corbetta, D., & Vereijken, B. (1999). Understanding development and learning of motor coordination in sport: The contribution of dynamic systems theory. *International Journal of Sport Psychology, 30*, 507–530.

Coren, S. (1992). *The left-hander syndrome: The causes and consequences of left handedness.* New York: Vintage Books.

Coren, S. (1996). *Sleep thieves: An eye-opening exploration into the science and mysteries of sleep.* New York: The Free Press.

Coren, S., & Aks, D. J. (1990). Moon illusion in pictures: A multimechanism approach. *Journal of Experimental Psychology: Human Perception and Performance, 16*, 365–380.

Coren, S. & Previc, F. H. (1996). Handedness as a predictor of increased risk of knee, elbow, or shoulder injury, fractures and broken bones. *Laterality, 1*, 2, 139–152.

Corina, D. P. (1999). On the nature of left hemisphere specialization for signed language. *Brain and Language, 69*, 230–240.

Corkin, S. (1984). Lasting consequences of bilateral medial temporal lobectomy: Clinical course and experimental findings in H. M. *Seminar in Neurology, 4*, 249–259.

Cornblatt, B. A., Green, M. F., & Walker, E. F. (1999). Schizophrenia: Etiology and neurocognition. In T. Millon, P. H. Blaney, & R. D. Davis (Eds.), *Oxford textbook of psychopathology* (pp. 277–310). New York: Oxford University Press.

Cosmides, L., & Tooby, J. (1997). Evolutionary psychology: A primer. Retrieved May 13, 2001 from the World Wide Web: http://www.psych.ucsb.edu/research/cep.

Cosmides, L., & Tooby, J. (1999). Toward an evolutionary taxonomy of treatable conditions. *Journal of Abnormal Psychology, 108*, 453–464.

Cosmides, L., & Tooby, J. (2000). Evolutionary psychology and the emotions. In M. Lewis & J. M. Haviland-Jones (Eds.), *Handbook of emotions* (2nd ed., pp. 91–115). New York: Guilford Press.

Costa, P. T., & McCrae, R. R. (1995). Domains and facets: Hierarchical personality assessment using the Revised NEO Personality Inventory. *Journal of Personality Assessment, 64*, 21–50.

Costa, P. T., Jr., & McCrae, R. R. (1998). Trait theories of personality. In D. F. Barone, M. Hersen, et al. (Eds.), *Advanced personality. The Plenum series in social/clinical psychology* (pp. 103–121). New York: Plenum Press.

Costanza, D. P., Fleishman, E. A., & Marshall-Mies, J. (1999). Knowledges. In N. G. Peterson, M. D. Mumford, W. C. Borman, P. R. Jeanneret, & E. A. Fleishman (Eds.), *An occupational information system for the 21st century: The development of O*NET* (pp. 71–90). Washington, DC: American Psychological Association.

Cote, S., & Morgan, L. M. (2002). A longitudinal analysis of the association between emotional regulation, job satisfaction, and intentions to quit. *Journal of Organizational Behaviour, 23*, 8, 947–962.

Courthout, E., Uttl, B., Walsh, V., Hallet, M., & Cowey, A. (2000). Plasticity revealed by transcranial magnetic stimulation of early visual cortex. *Neuroreport: An International Journal for the Rapid Communication of Research in Neuroscience, 11*, 1565–1569.

Courtney, S. M., Petit, L., Maisog, J. M., Ungerleider, L. G., & Haxby J. V. (1998). An area specialized for spatial working memory in human frontal cortex. *Science, 279*, 1347–1351.

Courtney, S. M. & Ungerleider, L. G. (1997). What fMRI has taught us about human vision. *Current Opinion in Neurobiology, 7*, 554–561.

Cowan, N., & Wood, N. L. (1997). Constraints on awareness, attention, processing, and memory: Some recent investigations with ignored speech. *Consciousness & Cognition: An International Journal, 6*, 182–203.

Cox, B. J., & Taylor, S. (1999). Anxiety disorders: Panic and phobias. In T. Millon, P. H. Blaney, & R. D. Davis (Eds.), *Oxford textbook of psychopathology* (pp. 81–113). New York: Oxford University Press.

Cox, R. H., Qiu, Y., & Liu, Z. (1993). Overview of sport psychology. In R. N. Singer, M. Murphey, & L. K. Tennant (Eds.), *Handbook of research on sport psychology* (pp. 3–31). New York: Macmillan.

Coyne, Jerry A. (2000, April 3). Of vice and men—the fairy tales of evolutionary psychology. *New Republic, 222*, 27–34.

Craik, F. I. M. (2001). Effects of dividing attention on encoding and retrieval process. In H. L. Roediger, J. S. Nairne, I. Neath, & A. M. Surprenant (Eds.), *The nature of remembering: Essays in honor of Robert G. Crowder. Science Conference Series* (pp. 55–68). Washington, DC: American Psychological Association.

Craik, F. I. M., & Lockhart, R. S. (1972). Levels of processing: A framework for memory research. *Journal of Verbal Learning and Verbal Behavior, 11*, 671–784.

Craik, F. I. M., Moroz, T. M., Moscovitch, M., Stuss, D. T., Winocur, G., Tulving, E., & Kapur, S. (1999). In search of the self: A positron emission tomography study. *American Psychological Society, 10*(1), 26–34.

Crair, M. C., Gillespie, D. C., & Stryker, M. P. (1998). The role of visual experience in the development of columns in cat visual cortex. *Science, 279*, 565–570.

Crandall, C. S., Preisler, J. J., & Aussprung, J. (1992). Measuring life event stress in the lives of college students: The Undergraduate Stress Questionnaire (USQ). *Journal of Behavioral Medicine, 15*, 627–662.

Crane, J. (1996). Effects of home environment, SES, and maternal test scores on mathematics achievement. *Journal of Educational Research, 89*, 305–314.

Crave, J. (1998). It's a highschool, there must be gangs, right? *Cameron Chronicle: Collingwood's International Newspaper.* http://cses.scbe.on/gangs4.htm, accessed March 1999.

Crawford, C. B., & Anderson, J. L. (1989). Sociobiology. *American Psychologist, 44*, 1449–1459.

Crawford, H. J. (1994). Brain dynamics and hypnosis: Attentional and disattentional processes. *The International Journal of Clinical and Experimental Hypnosis, 42*, 204–232.

Creem, S. H., & Proffitt, D. R. (2001). Grasping objects by their handles: A necessary interaction between cognition and action. *Journal of Experimental Psychology: Human Perception and Performance, 27*, 218–228.

Crespi, T. D. (1988). Effectiveness of time-out: A comparison of psychiatric, correctional and day-treatment programs. *Adolescence, 23*, 805–811.

Crews, F. (1996). The verdict on Freud. *Psychological Science, 7*, 63–68.

Crick, F., & Koch, C. (1998). Contraints on cortical and thalamic projections: The no-strong-loops hypothesis. *Nature, 391*(15), 245–250.

Crick, F., & Mitchison, G. (1983). The function of dream sleep. *Nature, 304*, 111–114.

Crick, N. R., & Rose, A. J. (2000). Toward a gender balanced approach to the study of social emotional development: A look at relational aggression. In P. H. Miller, & E. Kofsky Scholnick (Eds.). *Toward a feminist developmental psychology* (pp. 153–168). Florence, KY: Taylor & Francis/Routledge.

Crittenden, K. S., Fugita, S. S., Bae, H., Lamug, C. B., & Lin, C. (1992). A cross-cultural study of self-report depressive symptoms among college students. *Journal of Cross-Cultural Psychology, 23*, 163–178.

Cronshaw, S. F. (1991). *Industrial psychology in Canada*. Waterloo, ON: North Waterloo Academic Press.

Cross, S. E., & Madson, L. (1997a). Elaboration of models of the self: Reply to Baumeister and Sommer (1997) and Martin and Ruble (1997). *Psychological Bulletin, 122*(1), 51–55.

Cross, S. E., & Madson, L. (1997b). Models of the self: Self-construals and gender. *Psychological Bulletin, 122*(1), 5–37.

Crosson, B. (2000). Systems that support language processes: Verbal working memory. In S. E. Nadeau, L. J. Gonzalez Rothi, & B. Crosson (Eds.), *Aphasia and language: Theory to practice. The science and practice of neuropsychology* (pp. 399–418). New York: Guilford Press.

Crouter, A. C., Bumpas, M. F., Head, M. R., & McHale, S. M. (2001). Implications of overwork and overload for the quality of men's family relationships. *Journal of Marriage and the Family, 63,* 404–416.

Crowl, R. K., & MacGinitie, W. H. (1974). The influence of students' speech characteristics on teachers' evaluations of oral answers. *Journal of Educational Psychology, 66,* 304–308.

Csikszentmihalyi, M. (1996). *Creativity: Flow and the psychology of discovery and invention*. New York: HarperCollins.

Csikszentmihalyi, M. (1997). *Finding flow: The psychology of engagement with everyday life*. New York: Basic Books.

Csikszentmihalyi, M. (2001). The context of creativity. In W. Bennis, G. M. Spreitzer, & T. G. Cummings (Eds.), *The future of leadership: Today's top leadership thinkers speak to tomorrow's leaders* (pp. 116–124). San Francisco: Jossey-Bass.

Culbertson, F. M. (1997). Depression and gender: An international review. *American Psychologist, 52*(1), 25–31.

Cummings, N. A. (1986). The dismantling of our health system: Strategies for the survival of psychological practice. *American Psychologist, 41,* 426–431.

Cummings, N. A., Budman, S. H., & Lawrence, T. J. (1998). Efficient psychotherapy as a viable response to scarce resources and rationing of treatment. *Professional Psychology: Research and Practice, 29*(5), 460–469.

Cunningham, C. L., Dickinson, S. D., Grahame, N. J., Okorn, D. M., & McMullin, C. S. (1999). Genetic differences in cocaine-induced conditioned place preference in mice depend on conditioning trial duration. *Psychopharmacology, 146,* 73–80.

Cunningham, M.R., Roberts, A.R., Barbee, A.P., Druen, P.B., & Wu, C. (1995). "Their ideas of beauty are, on the whole, the same as ours": Consistency and variability in the cross-cultural perception of female physical attractiveness. *Journal of Personality and Social Psychology, 68,* 261–279.

Cutting, A. L., & Dunn, J. (1999). Theory of mind, emotion understanding, language, and family background: individual differences and interrelations. *Child Development, 70*(4), 853–865.

Czeisler, C. A., Johnson, M. P., Duffy, J. F., Brown, E. N., Ronda, J. M., & Kronauer, R. E. (1990). Exposure to bright light and darkness to treat physiologic maladaptation to night work. *New England Journal of Medicine, 322,* 1253–1259.

Damasio, A. R. (1994). *Descartes' error: Emotion, reason, and the human brain*. New York: Putnam.

Damasio, A. R. (2000). A neurobiology for consciousness. In T. Metzinger (Ed.), *Neural correlates of consciousness: Empirical and conceptual questions* (pp. 111–120). Cambridge, MA: The MIT Press.

Damasio, A. R., & Damasio, H. (1992, September). Brain and language. *Scientific American,* 89–95.

Damasio, A. R., & Damasio, H. (2000). Aphasia and the neural basis of language. In M. Mesulam, *Principles of behavioral and cognitive neurology* (2nd ed., pp. 294–315). New York: Oxford University Press.

Damian, M. F. (2001). Congruity effects evoked by subliminally presented primes: Automaticity rather than semantic processing. *Journal of Experimental Psychology: Human Perception and Performance, 27,* 154–165.

Daniel, M. H. (1997). Intelligence testing. *American Psychologist, 52*(10), 1038–1045.

Daniel, M. H. (2000). Interpretation of intelligence test scores. In R. J. Sternberg (Ed.), *Handbook of intelligence* (pp. 477–491). New York: Cambridge University Press.

Danner, R., & Edwards, D. (1992). Life is movement: Exercise for the older adult. *Activities, Adaptation & Aging, 17,* 15–26.

Danziger, K. (1990). *Constructing the subject: Historical origins of psychological research*. New York: Cambridge University Press.

Darley, J. M., & Gross, P. H. (2000). A hypothesis-confirming bias in labeling effects. In C. Stangor (Ed.), *Stereotypes and prejudice: Essential readings, Key Readings in Social Psychology* (pp. 212–225). Philadelphia: Psychology Press/Taylor & Francis.

Dasgupta, N., & Greenwald, A. G. (2001). On the malleability of automatic attitudes: Combating automatic prejudice with images of admired and disliked individuals. *Journal of Personality and Social Psychology, 81,* 800–814.

Davidson, R. J., Jackson, D. C., & Kalin, N. H. (2000). Emotion, plasticity, context, and regulation: Perspectives from affective neuroscience. *Psychological Bulletin, 126,* 890–909.

Davies, M., Stankov, L., & Roberts, R. D. (1998). Emotional intelligence: In search of an elusive construct. *Journal of Personality and Social Psychology, 75*(4), 989–1015.

Davies, M. M. (1997). *Fake, fact, and fantasy: Children's interpretations of television reality*. Mahwah, NJ: Lawrence Erlbaum Associates, Inc.

Dawson, D., Winocur, G., & Moscovitch, M. (1999). The psychosocial environment and cognitive rehabilitation in the elderly. In D.T. Stuss, G. Winocur et al. (Eds.), *Cognitive neurorehabilitation* (pp. 94–108).

DeBono, K. G. (1992). Pleasant scents and persuasion: An information processing approach. *Journal of Applied Social Psychology, 22,* 910–919.

DeCatanzaro, D. (1999). *Motivation and emotion: Evolutionary, physiological, developmental, and social perspectives*. Upper Saddle River, NJ: Prentice Hall.

DeCharms, R. C., Blake, D. T., & Merzenich, M. M. (1998). Optimizing sound features for cortical neurons. *Science, 280,* 1439–1443.

Deci, E. L. (1972). Effects of contingent and non-contingent rewards and controls on intrinsic motivation. *Organizational Behavior and Human Performance, 8,* 217–229.

Deci, E. L. (1975). *Intrinsic motivation*. New York: Plenum.

Deci, E. L., Koestner, R., & Ryan, R. M. (1999). A meta-analytic review of experiments examining the effects of extrinsic rewards on intrinsic motivation. *Psychological Bulletin, 125,* 627–668.

Deco, G., & Schürmann, B. (2000). A neuro-cognitive visual system for object recognition based on testing of interactive attentional top-down hypotheses. *Perception, 29,* 1249–1264.

de Haan, M., & Nelson, C. A. (1997). Recognition of the mother's face by six-month-old infants: A neurobehavioral study. *Child Development, 68*(2), 187–210.

de Jonge, J., Bosma, H., Peter, R., & Siegrist, J. (2000). Job strain, effort-reward imbalance, and employee well-being: A large-scale cross-sectional study. *Social Science & Medicine, 50,* 1317–1327.

DeKeseredy, W., & Kelly, K. (1993). *The incidence and prevalence of woman abuse in Canadian university and college dating relationships: Results from a national survey*. Ottawa: Health Canada, 1993.

De La Casa, L. G., & Lubow, R. E. (2000). Super-latent inhibition with delayed conditioned taste aversion testing. *Animal Learning & Behavior, 28,* 289–399.

Delgado, P. L., Price, D. S., Aghajanian, L. H., Landis, G. K., & Heninger, G. R. (1990). Serotonin function and mechanism of antidepressant action: Reversal of antidepressant-induced remission by rapid depletion of plasma atryptophan. *Archives of General Psychiatry, 47,* 411–418.

DeLongis, A., Folkman, S., & Lazarus, R. S. (1988). The impact of daily stress on health and mood: Psychological and social resources as mediators. *Journal of Personality and Social Psychology, 54,* 486–495.

Dement, W. C., with C. Vaughan. (1999). *The promise of sleep*. New York: Delacorte Press.

Dement, W. C., & Wolpert, E. A. (1958). The relation of eye movements, body motility, and external stimuli to dream content. *Journal of Experimental Psychology, 55,* 543–553.

Denmark, F. I. (1994). Engendering psychology. *American Psychologist, 49,* 329–334.

Dennett, D. C. (1991). *Consciousness explained*. Boston: Little, Brown.

Dennett, D. C. (1996). *Kinds of minds: Toward an understanding of consciousness*. New York: Basic Books.

Denollet, J. (2000). Type D personality: A potential risk factor refined. *Journal of Psychosomatic Research, 49,* 4, 255–266.

DePaulo, B. M. (1992). Nonverbal behavior and self-presentation. *Psychological Bulletin, 111,* 230–243.

DePaulo, B. M., & Friedman, H. S. (1998). Nonverbal communication. In D. T. Gilbert & S. T. Fiske (Eds.). *The handbook of social psychology* (4th ed., pp. 3–40). New York: McGraw-Hill.

DePaulo, B. M., Lindsay, J. J., Malone, B. E., Muhlenbruck, L., Charlton, K., & Cooper, H. (2003). Cues to deception. *Psychological Bulletin, 129,* 1, 74–112.

Deregowski, J. B. (1980). Perception. In H. C. Triandis & J. W. Berry (Eds.), *Handbook of cross-cultural psychology: Vol. 3. Basic processes.* Boston: Allyn & Bacon.

Dershowitz, A. M. (1986). *Reversal of fortune: Inside the von Bulow case.* New York: Random House.

DeSantis, A., & Kayson, W. A. (1997). Defendants' characteristics of attractiveness, race, and sex and sentencing decisions. *Psychological Reports, 81,* 679–683.

Detterman, D. K., & Thompson, L. A. (1997). What is so special about special education? *American Psychologist, 52*(10), 1082–1090.

DeValois, R. L., & Jacobs, G. H. (1968). Primate color vision. *Science, 162,* 533–540.

Devlin, A. S. (1992). Psychiatric ward renovation: Staff perception and patient behavior. *Environment & Behavior, 24,* 1, 66–84.

Devoto, A., Lucidi, F., Violani, C., & Bertini, M. (1999). Effects of different sleep reductions on daytime sleepiness. *Sleep, 22,* 336–343.

de Vries, B., & Walker, L. J. (1986). Moral reasoning and attitudes toward capital punishment. *Developmental Psychology, 22*(4), 509–513.

Diedrich, F. J., Highlands, T. M., Spahr, K. A., Thelan, E., & Smith, L. B. (2001). The role of target distinctiveness in infant perseverative reaching. *Journal of Experimental Child Psychology, 78*(3), 263–290.

Diener, E. (2000). Subjective well-being: The science of happiness and a proposal for a national index. *American Psychologist, 55,* 34–43.

Diener, E., Lusk, R., DeFour, D., & Flax, R. (1980). Deindividuation: Effects of group size, density, number of observers, and group member similarity on self-consciousness and disinhibited behavior. *Journal of Personality and Social Psychology, 39,* 449–459.

Dietvorst, T. F. (1978). Biofeedback assisted relaxation training with patients recovering from myocardial infarction. *Dissertation Abstracts International, 38,* 3389.

Dietz, T. L. (1998). An examination of violence and gender role portrayals in video games: Implications for gender socialization and aggressive behavior. *Sex Roles, 38*(5/6), 425–428.

Dikeos, D. G., Papadimitriou, G. N., Avramopoulos, D., Karadima, G., Daskalopoulou, E. G., Souery, D., Mendlewicz, J., Vassilopoulos, D., & Stefanis, C. N. (1999). Association between the dopamine D3 receptor gene locus (DRD3) and unipolar affective disorder. *Psychiatric Genetics, 9,* 189–195.

DiLalla, D. L., & Gottesman, I. I. (1995). Normal personality characteristics in identical twins discordant for schizophrenia. *Journal of Abnormal Psychology, 104,* 490–499.

DiLalla, L. F., & Jones, S. (2000). Genetic and environmental influences on temperament in preschoolers. In V. J. Molfese, D. L. Molfese, and others, *Temperament and Personality Development Across the Life Span* (33–55). Mahwah, NJ: Lawrence Erlbaum Associates, Inc.

DiLalla, L. F., & Gottesman, I. I. (1991). Biological and genetic contributors to violence: Wisdom's untold tale. *Psychological Bulletin, 109*(1), 125–129.

DiLalla, L. F., Thompson, L. A., Plomin, R., Phillips, K., Fagan, J. F., III, Haith, M. M., Cyphers, L. H., & Fulker, D. W. (1990). Infant predictors of preschool and adult IQ: A study of infant twins and their parents. *Development Psychology, 26,* 759–769.

Dillard, J. P., & Pfau, M. W. (2002). (Eds.), *The persuasion handbook: Developments in theory and practice.* Thousand Oaks, CA: Sage.

DiMatteo, M. R. (1994). Enhancing patient adherence to medical recommendations. *Journal of the American Medical Association, 217,* 79, 83.

DiMatteo, M. R., & DiNicola, D. D. (1982). *Achieving patient compliance: The psychology of the medical practitioner's role.* New York: Pergamon.

D'Imperio, R. L., Dubow, E. F., & Ippolito, M. F. (2000). Resilient and stress-affected adolescents in an urban setting. *Journal of Clinical Child Psychology, 29,* 129–142.

Dimsdale, J. E. (1974). The coping behavior of Nazi concentration camp survivors. *American Journal of Psychiatry, 131,* 792–797.

Dindia, K., & Allen, M. (1992). Sex differences in self-disclosure: A meta-analysis. *Psychological Bulletin, 112,* 106–124.

Dinges, N. G., Atlis, M. M., & Vincent, G. M. (1997). Cross-cultural perspectives on antisocial behavior. In D. M. Stoff, J. Breiling, & J. Wohl (Eds.), *Handbook of antisocial behavior* (pp. 463–473). New York: Wiley.

Dinges, N. G., & Cherry, D. (1995). Symptom expression and the use of mental health services among American ethnic minorities. In J. F.

Aponte, R. Y. Rivers, & J. Wohl (Eds.), *Psychological interventions and cultural diversity* (pp. 40–56). Boston: Allyn and Bacon, Inc.

Dinges, N. G., & Hull, P. V. (1993). Personality, culture, and international studies. In D. Lieberman (Ed.), *Revealing the world: An interdisciplinary reader for international studies.* Dubuque, IA: Kendall-Hunt.

Dion, K., Dion, K., & Pak, A. W. (1992). Personality-based hardiness as a buffer for discrimination-related stress in members of Toronto's Chinese community. *Canadian Journal of Behavioural Science, 24*(4), 517–536.

Dion, K. K., Pak, A. W., & Dion, K. L. (1990). Stereotyping physical attractiveness. *Journal of Cross-Cultural Psychology, 21,* 158–179.

Dion, K. L. (2001). Immigrants' perceptions of housing discrimination in Toronto: The Housing New Canadians Project. *Journal of Social Issues, 57,* 3, 523–539.

DiPlacido, J. (1998). Minority stress among lesbians, gay men, and bisexuals: A consequence of heterosexism, homophobia, and stigmatization. In G. M. Herek (Ed.), *Stigma and sexual orientation: Understanding prejudice against lesbians, gay men, and bisexuals: Vol. 4. Psychological perspectives on lesbian and gay issues* (pp. 138–159). Thousand Oaks, CA: Sage.

Dishion, T. J., McCord, J., & Poulin, F. (1999). When interventions harm. *American Psychologist, 54,* 755–764.

Dixon, M. J., Smilek, D., Cudahy, C., & Merikle, P. (2000). Five plus two equals yellow: Mental arithmetic in people with synaesthesia is not coloured by visual experience. *Nature, 406,* 6794, 365.

Dobash, R. E., & Dobash, R. P. (1998). Cross-border encounters: Challenges and opportunities. In C. M. Renzetti & J. L. Edleson (Series Eds.), *Rethinking violence against women* (Vol. 9, pp. 1–21). Thousand Oaks, CA: Sage.

Dobson, K. S. (1989). A meta-analysis of the efficacy of cognitive therapy for depression. *Journal of Consulting and Clinical Psychology, 57,* 414–419.

Dobson, K. S. (2001). *Handbook of cognitive-behavioral therapies* (2nd ed.). New York: Guilford Press.

Dobson, K. S., & Block, L. (1988). Historical and philosophical bases of the cognitive-behavioral therapies. In K. S. Dobson (Ed.), *Handbook of cognitive-behavioral therapies.* New York: Guilford.

Docherty, N. M., Hall, M. J., & Gordinier, S. W. (1998). Affective reactivity of speech in schizophrenia patients and their nonschizophrenic relatives. *Journal of Abnormal Psychology, 107*(3), 461–467.

Dohrenwend, B. P. (2000). The role of adversity and stress in psychopathology: Some evidence and its implications for theory and research. *Journal of Health and Social Behavior, 41,* 1–19.

Dollard, J., Doob, L. W., Miller, N. E., Mowrer, O. H., & Sears, R. R. (1939). *Frustration and aggression.* New Haven, CT: Yale University Press.

Dollins, A. B., Lynch, H. J., Wurtman, R. J., Deng, M. H., et al. (1993). Effects of illumination on human nocturnal serum melatonin levels and performance. *Physiology and Behavior, 53,* 153–160.

Donnelly, C. M., & McDaniel, M. A. (1993). Use of analogy in learning scientific concepts. *Journal of Experimental Psychology: Learning, Memory, and Cognition, 19,* 975–987.

Donovan, J. M. (1998). Brief couples therapy: Lessons from the history of brief individual treatment. *Psychotherapy: Theory, Research and Practice, 35*(1), 116–129.

Doob, A. N., & McLaughlin, D. S. (1989). Ask and you shall be given: Request size and donations to a good cause. *Journal of Applied Social Psychology, 19,* 1049–1056.

Doty, R. W. A. (1999). Two brains, one person. *Brain Research Bulletin, 50,* 453.

Downey, V. W., & Landry, R. G. (1997). Self-reported sexual behaviours of high school juniors and seniors in North Dakota. *Psychological Reports, 80*(3, Pt. 2), 1357–1358.

Draine, S. C., & Greenwald, A. G. (1998). Replicable unconscious semantic priming. *Journal of Experimental Psychology: General, 127,* 286–303.

Drennen, W. T., & Holden, E. W. (1984). Trait/set interactions in EMG biofeedback. *Psychological Reports, 54,* 843–849.

Dromi, E. (1997). Early lexical development. In M. Barerett (Ed.), *The development of language.* London: UCL.

Drummond, D. C. (2001). Theories of drug craving, ancient and modern. *Addiction, 96,* 33–46.

Dryden, W., & Ellis, A. (1988). Rational-emotive therapy. In K. S. Dobson (Ed.), *Handbook of cognitive-behavioral therapies*. New York: Guilford.

Dryden, W., & Ellis, A. (2001). Rational emotive behavior therapy. In K. S. Dobson (Ed.). *Handbook of cognitive-behavioral therapies* (2nd ed.), (pp. 295–348). New York: Guilford Press.

Dubrovsky, B. (2003). Comment on Ehrlich, Paul and Feldman, Marcus (2003) Genes and culture: What creates our behavioural phenome? *Current Anthropology, 44*, 1, 95–96.

Duckitt, J. (1992). Psychology and prejudice. *American Psychologist, 47*, 1182–1193.

Duffy, R. D., Kalsher, M. J., & Wogalter, M. S. (1993). The effectiveness of an interactive warning in a realistic product-use situation. *Proceedings of the Human Factors and Ergonomics Society, 37th Annual Meeting*, 935–939.

Dumont, M., & Provost, M. A. (1999). Resilience in adolescents: Protective role of social support, coping strategies, self-esteem, and social activities on experience of stress and depression. *Journal of Youth and Adolescence, 28*, 343–363.

Dunant, Y., & Israel, M. (1985, April). The release of acetylcholine. *Scientific American*, 58–83.

Dunbar, K. (1994). Concept discovery in the scientific domain. *Cognitive Science, 17*(3): 397–434.

Duncan, J., Seitz, R. J., Kolodny, J., Bor, D., Herzog, H., Ahmed, A., Newell, F. N., & Emslie, H. (2000). A neural basis for general intelligence. *Science, 289*, 457–460.

Dupont, S., Van de Moortele, P. F., Samson, S., Hasboun, D., Poline, J. B., Adam, C., Lehericy, S., Le Bihan, D., Samson, Y., & Baulac, M. (2000). Episodic memory in left temporal lobe epilepsy: A functional MRI study. *Brain, 123*, 1722–1732.

Durex. (2002). *Global sex survey 2002*. http://www.durex.com/index.html, accessed September 26, 2003.

Dutton, D. G., & Aron, A. P. (1974). Some evidence for heightened sexual attraction under conditions of high anxiety. *Journal of Personality & Social Psychology, 30*, 4, 510–517.

Dwyer, W. O., Leeming, F. C., Cobern, M. K., Porter, B. E., & Jackson, J. M. (1993). Critical review of behavioral interventions to preserve the environment: Research since 1980. *Environment and Behavior, 25*, 275–321.

Eagly, A. H. (1992). Uneven progress: Social psychology and the study of attitudes. *Journal of Personality and Social Psychology, 63*, 693–710.

Eagly, A. H., & Chaiken, S. (1993). *The psychology of attitudes*. Fort Worth, TX: Harcourt Brace Jovanovich.

Eagly, A. H., & Johnson, B. T. (1990). Gender and leadership style: A meta-analysis. *Psychological Bulletin, 108*, 233–256.

Eagly, A. H., Makhijani, M. G., & Klonsky, B. G. (1992). Gender and the evaluation of leaders: A meta-analysis. *Psychological Bulletin, 111*, 1, 3–22.

Eagly, A. H., & Steffen, V. J. (2000). Gender stereotypes stem from the distribution of women and men into social roles. In C. Stangor (Ed.), *Stereotypes and prejudice: Essential reading. Key Readings in Social Psychology* (pp. 142–160). Philadelphia: Psychology Press/Taylor & Francis.

Eaton, M. J., & Dembo, M. H. (1997). Differences in the motivational beliefs of Asian American and non-Asian students. *Journal of Educational Psychology, 89*(3), 433–440.

Edwards, D. C. (1999). *Motivation and emotion: Evolutionary, physiological, cognitive, and social influences*. London: Sage Publications.

Edwards, K. (1998). The face of time: Temporal cues in facial expressions of emotion. *American Psychological Society, 9*(4), 270–276.

Ehrlich, P. & Feldman, M. (2003). Genes and culture: What creates our behavioral phenome? *Current Anthropology, 44*, 1, 87–94.

Ehrlich, P. R. (2000). *Human natures: Genes, cultures, and the human prospect*. Washington, DC: Island Press.

Eich, E. (1995). Searching for mood dependent memory. *Psychological Science, 6*, 67–75.

Eisenberg, N., Shepard, S. A., Faves, R. A., Murphy, B. C., & Guthrie, I. K. (1998). Shyness and children's emotionality, regulation, and coping: Contemporaneous, longitudinal, and across-context relations. *Child Development, 69*(3), 767–790.

Ekman, P. (1992). Facial expressions of emotion: New findings, new questions. *Psychological Science, 3*, 34–38.

Ekman, P. (1993). Facial expression and emotion. *American Psychologist, 48*, 384–392.

Ekman, P. (2003). *Emotions revealed: Recognizing faces and feelings to improve communication and emotional life*. New York: Times Books.

Ekman, P., & Keltner, D. (1997). Universal facial expressions of emotion: An old controversy and new findings. In U. C. Segerstrale, P. Molnar, et al. (Eds.), *Noverbal communication: Where nature meets culture* (pp. 27–46). Mahwah, NJ: Lawrence Erlbaum Associates, Inc.

Ekman, P., O'Sullivan, M., & Frank, M. G. (1999). A few can catch a liar. *Psychological Science, 10*, 3, 253–266.

Eliot, L. (1999). *What's going on in there? How the brain and mind develop in the first five years of life*. New York: Bantam Books.

Elkind, D. (1967). Egocentrism in adolescence. *Child Development, 38*, 4, 1025–1034.

Elkind, D., & Bowen, R. (1979). Imaginary audience behavior in children and adolescents. *Developmental Psychology, 15*(1), 38–44.

Elliot, A., & Devine, P. G. (1994). On the motivational nature of cognitive dissonance: Dissonance as psychological discomfort. *Journal of Personality and Social Psychology, 67*(3), 382–394.

Ellis, A. (1970). *The essence of rational psychotherapy: A comprehensive approach to treatment*. New York: Institute for Rational Living.

Ellis, A. (1988, August). The philosophical basis of rational-emotive therapy (RET). Paper presented at the 96th Annual Convention of the American Psychological Association, Atlanta.

Ellis, A. (1990). How can psychological treatment aim to be briefer and better? The rational-emotive approach to brief therapy. In J. K. Zeig & S. G. Gilligan (Eds.), *Brief therapy myths, methods, and metaphors*, New York: Brunner/Mazel.

Ellis, A. (1999a). Early theories and practices of rational emotive behavior therapy and how they have been augmented and revised during the last three decades. *Journal of Rational Emotive and Cognitive Behavior Therapy, 17*, 69–93.

Ellis, A. (1999b). Reasons why rational emotive behavior therapy is relatively neglected in the professional and scientific literature. *Journal of Rational Emotive and Cognitive Behavior Therapy, 19*, 67–74.

Ellis, A., & Harper, R. A. (1961). *A guide to rational living*. North Hollywood, CA: Wilshire.

Ellis, A., Shaughnessy, M. F., & Mahan, V. (2002). An interview with Albert Ellis about rational emotive therapy. *North American Journal of Psychology, 4*, 3, 355–366.

Ellis, R. J., & Oscar-Berman, M. (1989). Alcoholism, aging, and functional cerebral asymmetries. *Psychological Bulletin, 106*, 128–147.

Engel, A. K., Konig, P., Kreiter, A. K., Schillen, T. B., & Singer, W. (1992). Temporal coding in the visual cortex: New vistas on integration in the nervous system. *Trends in Neurosciences, 15*, 218–226.

Engel, S. A. (1999). Using neuroimaging to measure mental representations: Finding color-opponent neurons in visual cortex. *Psychological Science, 8*, 23–26.

Engen, T., & Engen, E. A. (1997). Relationship between development of odor perception and language. *Enfance, 1*, 125–140.

Epstein, H. T. (2001). An outline of the role of brain in human cognitive development. *Brain & Cognition, 45*(1), 44–51.

Erel, O., Oberman, Y., & Yirmiya, N. (2000). Maternal versus nonmaternal care and seven domains of children's development. *Psychological Bulletin, 126*(5), 727–747.

Ericsson, K. A., & Charness, N. (1994). Expert performance: Its structure and acquisition. *American Psychologist, 49*, 725–747.

Ericsson, K. A., Chase, W. G., & Faloon, S. (1980). Acquisition of a memory skill. *Science, 208*, 1181–1182.

Ericsson, K. A., Krampe, R. T., & Tesch-Römer, C. (1993). The role of deliberate practice in the acquisition of expert performance. *Psychological Review, 100*, 363–406.

Erikson, E. H. (1963). *Childhood and society* (2nd ed.). New York: Norton.

Erikson, E. H. (1968). *Identity: Youth and crisis*. New York: Norton.

Erlenmeyer-Kimling, L., & Jarvik, L. F. (1963). Genetics and intelligence: A review. *Science, 142*, 1477–1479.

Ernst, E. (2000). Prevalence of use of complementary/alternative medicine: A systematic review. *Bulletin of the World Health Organization, 78*, 252–257.

Eron, L. D. (1987). The development of aggressive behavior from the perspective of a developing behaviorism. *American Psychologist, 42*, 435–442.

Ettner, S. L., & Grzywacz, J. G. (2001). Workers' perceptions of how jobs affect health: A social ecological perspective. *Journal of Occupational Health Psychology, 6*, 101–113.

Evans, D. A., Funkenstein, H. H., Albert, M. S., Scherr, P. A., Cook, N. R., Chown, M. J., Hebert, L. E., Hennekens, C. H., & Taylor, J. O. (1989). Prevalence of Alzheimer's disease in a community population of older persons. *Journal of the American Medical Association, 262,* 2551–2556.

Evans, G. W., Hygge, S., & Bullinger, M. (1995). Chronic noise and psychological stress. *Psychological Science, 6,* 333–338.

Evans, G. W., Lepore, S. J., Shejwal, B. R., & Palsane, M. N. (1998). Chronic residential crowding and children's well-being: An ecological perspective. *Child Development, 69*(6), 1514–1523.

Evans, G. W., Rhee, E., Forbes, C., Allen, K. M., & Lepore, S. J. (2000). The meaning and efficacy of social withdrawal as a strategy for coping with chronic residential crowding. *Journal of Environmental Psychology, 4,* 335–342.

Exner, J. E., Jr., Thomas, E. A., & Mason, B. (1985). Children's Rorschachs: Description and prediction. *Journal of Personality Assessment, 49,* 13–14.

Eyer, D. E. (1992). *Mother-infant bonding: A scientific fiction.* New Haven, CT: Yale University Press.

Eysenck, H. J. (1970). *The structure of human personality* (3rd ed.). London: Methuen.

Eysenck, H. J. (1995). *Genius: The natural history of creativity.* Cambridge, England: Cambridge University Press.

Eysenck, H. J. (1998). *A new look at intelligence.* London: Transaction Publishers.

Eysenck, H. J., & Eysenck, S. B. G. (1993). *The Eysenck Personality Questionnaire–Revised.* London: Hodder & Stoughton.

Fabiani, M., Stadler, M. A., & Wessels, P. M. (2000). True but not false memories produce a sensory signature in human lateralized brain potentials. *Journal of Cognitive Neuroscience, 12,* 941–949.

Fagan, J. (1996). A preliminary study of low-income African American fathers' play interactions with their preschool-age children. *Journal of Black Psychology, 22*(1), 7–19.

Fagan, J. (1997). Patterns of mother and father involvement in day care. *Child and Youth Care Forum, 26*(2), 113–126.

Fagan, J., & Silverthorn, A. S. (1998). Research on communication by touch. In E. W. Smith (Ed.), *Touch in psychotherapy: Theory, research, and practice* (pp. 59–73). New York: The Guildford Press.

Fagan, T. K. (1992). Compulsory schooling, child study, clinical psychology, and special education: Origins of school psychology. *American Psychologist, 47,* 2, 236–243.

Fagot, B. I., Rodgers, C. S., & Leinbach, M. D. (2000). Theories of gender socialization. In T. Eckes & H. M. Trautner (Eds.), *The developmental social psychology of gender* (pp. 65–89). Mahwah, NJ: Erlbaum.

Faludi, S. (1999). *Stiffed: The betrayal of the American man.* New York: Morrow.

Fan, X., Chen, M., & Matsumoto, A. R. (1997). Gender differences in mathematics achievement: Findings from the National Educational Longitudinal Study of 1988. *Journal of Experimental Education, 65,* 229–242.

Fancher, R. (1996). *Pioneers of psychology* (3rd ed.). New York: Norton.

Fang, H. (1996). Dopamine receptor studies in human postmortem brain by radioreceptor binding. *International Medical Journal, 3*(4), 265–272.

Fantz, R. L. (1961, May). The origin of form perception. *Scientific American,* 66–72.

Farah, M. J. (1990). *Visual agnosia: Disorders of object recognition and what they tell us about normal vision.* Cambridge, MA: MIT Press.

Farah, M. J., Levinson, K. L., & Klein, K. (1995). Face perception and within-category discrimination in prosopagnosia. *Neuropsychologia, 33*(6), 661–674.

Farah, M. J., O'Reilly, R. C., & Vecera, S. P. (1993). Dissociated overt and covert recognition as an emergent property of a lesioned neural network. *Psychological Review, 100*(4), 571–588.

Farah, M. J., Wilson, K. D., Drain, M., & Tanaka, J. N. (1998). What is special about face perception? *Psychological Review, 105*(3), 482–498.

Fares, I., McCulloch, K. M., & Raju, T. N. (1997). Intrauterine cocaine exposure and risk for sudden infant death syndrome: a meta-analysis. *Journal of Perinatology, 17,* 3, 179–182.

Farmer-Dougan, V. (1998). A disequilibrium analysis of incidental teaching: Determining reinforcement effects. *Behavior Modification, 22,* 78–95.

Farwell, L., & Wohlwend-Lloyd, R. (1998). Narcissistic processes: Optimistic expectations, favorable self-evaluations, and self-enhancing attributions. *Journal of Personality, 66*(1), 65–67.

Fast, J. E., & Frederick, J. A. (1996). Working arrangements and time stress. *Canadian Social Trends, 43,* 14–19.

Federation of Canadian Municipalities (1994). *Youth violence and youth gangs: Responding to community concerns.* Ottawa: Solicitor General and Department of Justice, Government of Canada.

Feeney, D. M. (1987). Human rights and animal welfare. *American Psychologist, 42,* 593–599.

Feingold, A. (1992a). Gender differences in mate selection preferences: A test of the parental investment model. *Psychological Bulletin, 112,* 125–139.

Feingold, A. (1992b). Good-looking people are not what we think. *Psychological Bulletin, 111,* 304–341.

Feldman, L., Holowaty, P., Harvey, B., Rannie, K., Shortt, L., & Jamal, A. (1997). A comparison of the demographic, lifestyle, and sexual behaviour characteristics of virgin and non-virgin adolescents. *The Canadian Journal of Human Sexuality, 6*(3), 197–209.

Fenwick, P., Donaldson, S., Gillies, L., Bushman, J., Fenton, G., Perry, I., Tilsley, C., & Serafinowicz, H. (1977). Metabolic and EEG changes during transcendental meditation. *Biological Psychology, 5,* 101–118.

Fernald, R. D., & White, S. A. (2000). Social control of brains: From behavior to genes. In M. S. Gazzaniga (Ed.), *The new cognitive neurosciences* (pp. 1193–1208). Cambridge, MA: The MIT Press.

Fernandez, E., & Sheffield, J. (1996). Relative contributions of life events versus daily hassles to the frequency and intensity of headaches. *Headache, 36*(10), 595–602.

Fernandez, E., & Turk, D. C. (1992). Sensory and affective components of pain: Separation and synthesis. *Psychological Bulletin, 112,* 205–217.

Ferrie, J. E., Martikainen, P., Shipley, M. J., Marmot, M. G., Stansfeld, S. A., & Smith, G. D. (2001). Employment status and health after privatisation in white collar civil servants: Prospective cohort study. *British Medical Journal, 322,* 647–651.

Festinger, L. (1954). A theory of social comparison processes. *Human Relations, 7,* 117–140.

Festinger, L. (1957). *A theory of cognitive dissonance.* Evanston, IL: Row, Petersen.

Field, T. (1996). Attachment and separation in young children. *Annual Review of Psychology, 47,* 541–561.

Finkel, D., Pedersen, N. L., Berg, S., & Johansson, B. (2000). Quantitative genetic analysis of biobehavioral markers of aging in Swedish studies of adult twins. *Journal of Aging & Health, 12,* 47–68.

Finkel, D., Pedersen, N. L., Plomin, R., & McClearn, G. E. (1998). Longitudinal and cross-sectional twin data on cognitive abilities in adulthood: The Swedish Adoption/Twin Study of Aging. *Developmental Psychology, 34,* 1400–1413.

Fischer, A. R., & Good, G. E. (1998). New directions for the study of gender role attitudes. *Psychology of Women Quarterly, 22,* 371–384.

Fischer, C. T. (1991). Phenomenological-existential psychotherapy. In M. Hersen, A. E. Kazdin, & A. S. Bellack (Eds.), *The clinical psychology handbook* (2nd ed.). New York: Pergamon.

Fischer, J., & Gochros, H. L. (1975). *Planned behavior change: Behavior modification in social work.* New York: Free Press.

Fischer, L., Ames, E. W., Chisholm, K., Savoie, L. (1997). Problems reported by parents of Romanian orphans adopted to British Columbia. *International Journal of Behavioral Development, 20*(1), 67–82.

Fischer, S. E., Lai, S. L., & Monaco, A. P. (2003). Deciphering the genetic basis of speech and language disorders. *Annual Review of Neuroscience, 26,* 57–80.

Fischhoff, B., Downs, J., & de Bruin, W. B. (1998). Adolescent vulnerability: A framework for behavioral interventions. *Applied and Preventive Psychology, 9,* 77–94.

Fish, J. M. (2002). The myth of race. In J. M. Fish (Ed.), *Race and intelligence: Separating science from myth* (pp. 113–141). Mahwah, NJ: Erlbaum.

Fishbain, D. A. (2000). Non-surgical chronic pain treatment outcome: A review. *International Review of Psychiatry, 12,* 170–180.

Fisher, L. A., & Bredemeier, B. J. (2000). Caring about injustice: The moral self-perceptions of professional female bodybuilders. *Journal of Sport & Exercise Psychology, 22*(4), 327–344.

Fishman, D. B., & Franks, C. M. (1997). The conceptual evolution of behavior therapy. In P. L. Wachtel & S. B. Messer (Eds.), *Theories of psychotherapy: Origins and evolution* (pp. 131–180). Washington, DC: American Psychological Association.

Fiske, S. T. (1992). Thinking is for doing: Portraits of social cognition from daguerreotype to laserphoto. *Journal of Personality and Social Psychology, 63,* 877–889.

Fiske, S. T. (1998). Stereotyping, prejudice, and discrimination. In D. T. Gilbert et al. (Eds.), *The handbook of social psychology* (pp. 357–411). New York: McGraw-Hill.

Fiske, S. T. (2000). Stereotyping, prejudice, and discrimination at the seam between the centuries: Evolution, culture, mind, and brain. *European Journal of Social Psychology, 30,* 299–322.

Fiske, S. T. (2001). Effects of power on bias: Power explains and maintains individual, group, and societal disparities. In A. Y. Lee-Chai & J. A. Bargh (Eds.), *The use and abuse of power: Multiple perspectives on the causes of corruption* (pp. 181–193). Philadelphia: Psychology Press/Taylor & Francis.

Fitzgerald, L. F., & Osipow, S. H. (1986). An occupational analysis of counseling psychology. *American Psychologist, 41,* 535–544.

Fivush, R. (2001). Owning experience: Developing subjective perspective in autobiographical narratives. In C. Moore & K. Lemmon (Eds.), *The self in time: Developmental perspectives* (pp. 35–52). Mahwah, NJ: Erlbaum.

Flack, W. F., Laird, J. D., & Cavallaro, L. A. (1999). Separate and combined effects of facial expressions and bodily postures on emotional feelings. *European Journal of Social Psychology, 29,* 2–3, 203–217.

Flaskerud, J. H., & Hu, L. T. (1992). Relationship of ethnicity to psychiatric diagnosis. *Journal of Nervous and Mental Disease, 180,* 296–303.

Flavell, J. H. (1996). Piaget's legacy. *American Psychological Society, 7*(4), 200–203.

Flavell, J. H., & Wellman, H. M. (1977). Metamemory. In R. V. Kail, Jr., & J. W. Hagen (Eds.), *Perspectives on the development of memory and cognition.* Hillsdale, NJ: Erlbaum.

Fleischhacker, W. W., Lemmens P., & van Baclen, B. (2001). A qualitative assessment of the neurological safety of antipsychotic drugs: An analysis of risperidone database. *Pharmacopsychiatry, 34,* 104–110.

Fleischman, D. A., Vaidya, C. J., Lange, K. L., & Gabrieli, J. D. E. (1997). A dissociation between perceptual explicit and implicit memory processes. *Brain & Cognition, 35*(1), 42–57.

Fleming, I., Baum, A., & Weiss, L. (1987). Social density and perceived control as mediators of crowding stress in high-density residential neighborhoods. *Journal of Personality and Social Psychology, 52,* 899–906.

Flint, A. J., & Rifat, S. L. (1998). The treatment of psychotic depression in later life: A comparison of pharmacotherapy and ECT. *International Journal of Geriatric Psychiatry, 13*(1), 23–28.

Flynn, J. R. (1999). Searching for justice: The discovery of IQ gains over time. *American Psychologist, 54*(1), 5–20.

Folkman, S., & Moskowitz, J. T. (2000). Positive affect and the other side of coping. *American Psychologist, 55,* 647–654.

Ford, J. D., Chandler, P., Thacker, B., Greaves, D., Shaw, D., Sennhauser, S., & Schwartz, L. (1998). Family systems therapy after operation Desert Storm with European-theater veterans. *Journal of Marital and Family Therapy, 24*(2), 243–250.

Forest, G., & Godbout, R. (2000). Effects of sleep deprivation on performance and EEG spectral analysis in young adults. *Brain and Cognition, 43,* 195–200.

Forgas, J. P. (1998). Asking nicely? The effects of mood on responding to more or less polite requests. *Personality and Social Psychology Bulletin, 24*(2), 173–185.

Fornai, F., & Orzi, F. (2001). Sexual pheromone or conventional odors increase extracellular lactate without changing glucose utilization in specific brain areas of the rat. *Neuroreport: An International Journal for the Rapid Communication of Research in Neuroscience, 12,* 63–69.

Forsythe, S. M. (1990). Effect of applicant's clothing on interviewer's decision to hire. *Journal of Applied Social Psychology, 20,* 1579–1595.

Fosshage, J. L. (1997). The organizing functions of dream mentation. *Contemporary Psychoanalysis, 33*(3), 429–458.

Foulkes, D. (1985). *Dreaming: A cognitive-psychological analysis.* Hillsdale, NJ: Lawrence Erlbaum.

Foulkes, D. (1990). Dreaming and consciousness. *European Journal of Cognitive Psychology, 2*(1), 39–55.

Foulkes, D. (1996). Dream research. *Sleep, 19*(8), 609–624.

Foulkes, D., & Kerr, N. H. (1994). Point of view in nocturnal dreaming. *Perceptual and Motor Skills, 78*(2), 690.

Foulkes, D., Meier, B., Strauch, I., & Kerr, N. H. (1993). Linguistic phenomena and language selection in the REM dreams of German-English bilinguals. *International Journal of Psychology, 28*(6), 871–891.

Fox, M. (1993). *Psychological perspectives in education.* New York: Cassell Educational.

Frable, D. E. (1989). Sex typing and gender ideology: Two facets of the individual's gender psychology that go together. *Journal of Personality and Social Psychology, 56,* 95–108.

Fraenkel, P., & Pinsof, W. M. (2001). Teaching family therapy-centered integration: Assimilation and beyond. *Journal of Psychotherapy Integration, 11,* 59–85.

Franks, J. J., Bilbrey, C. W., Lein, K. G., & McNamara, T. P. (2000). Transfer-appropriate processing (TAP) and repetition priming. *Memory and Cognition, 28,* 1140–1151.

Frater, E. (2000). Polarized over polygraphs: Polygraph testing in federal government. *National Journal, 32,* 2800–2801.

Frederick, C. M. (2000). Competitiveness: Relations with GPA, locus of control, sex, and athletic status. *Perceptual and Motor Skills, 90,* 413–414.

French, K. E., Spurgeon, J. H., & Nevett, M. E. (1995). Expert-novice differences in cognitive and skill execution components of youth baseball performance. *Research Quarterly for Exercise and Sport, 66,* 194–201.

Freud, S. (1933). *New introductory lectures on psychoanalysis.* New York: Norton.

Freud, S. (1953). The interpretation of dreams. In J. Stachey (Ed.), *The standard edition of the complete psychological works of Sigmund Freud* (Vols. 4 and 5). London: Hogarth. (Original work published 1900.)

Freud, S. (1966). *A general introduction to psychoanalysis* (J. Riviere, Trans.) New York: Washington Square. (Original work published 1920.)

Frey, B. J., & Hinton, G. E. (1999). Variational learning in nonlinear gaussian belief networks. *Neural Computation, 11,* 193–213.

Frezza, M., di Padova, C., Pozzato, G., Terpin, M., Baraona, E., & Lieber, C. S. (1990). High blood alcohol levels in women. *New England Journal of Medicine, 322,* 95–99.

Friedman, M., & Rosenman, R. H. (1974). *Type A behavior and your heart.* Greenwich, CT: Fawcett.

Friedrich, R. W., & Laurent, G. (2001). Dynamic optimization of odor representations by slow temporal patterning of mitral cell activity. *Science, 291,* 889–894.

Fromm, E. (1956). *The art of loving.* New York: Harper & Row.

Fromme, K., Marlatt, G. A., Baer, J. S., & Kivlahan, D. R. (1994). The alcohol skills training program: A group intervention for young adult drinkers. *Journal of Substance Abuse Treatment, 11,* 143–154.

Fulbright, R. K., Shaywitz, S. E., Shaywitz, B. A., Pugh, K. R., Skudlarski, P., Constable, R. T., et al. (1997). Neuroanatomy of reading and dyslexia. *Child & Adolescent Psychiatric Clinics of North America, 6,* 431–445.

Gabriel, M., & Talk, A. C. (2001). A tale of two paradigms: Lessons learned from parallel studies of discriminative instrumental learning and classical eyeblink conditioning. In J. E. Steinmetz, M. A. Gluck, & P. R. Solomon (Eds.), *Model systems and the neurobiology of associative learning: A festschrift in honor of Richard F. Thompson* (pp. 149–185). Mahwah, NJ: Erlbaum.

Gabrieli, J. D. E., Brewer, J. B., Desmond, J. E., & Glover, G. H. (1997). Separate neural bases of two fundamental memory processes in the human medial temporal lobe. *Science, 276,* 264–266.

Gaines, S. O., Jr., & Reed, E. S. (1995). Prejudice: From Allport to DuBois. *American Psychologist, 50,* 96–103.

Gainor, K. A. (2000). Including transgender issues in lesbian, gay, and bisexual psychology: Implications for clinical practice and training. In B. Greene & G. L. Croom (Eds.), *Education, research, and practice in lesbian, gay, bisexual, and transgendered psychology: A resource manual, 5* (pp. 131–160). Thousand Oaks, CA: Sage.

Galambos, N. L., & Tilton-Weaver, L. C. (2000). Adolescents' psychosocial maturity, problem behavior, and subjective age: In search of the adultoid. *Applied Developmental Science, 4*(4), 178–192.

Galin, D. (1974). Implications for psychiatry of left and right cerebral specialization: A neurophysiological context for unconscious processes. *Archives of General Psychiatry, 31,* 572–583.

Gallopin, T., Fort, P., Eggerman, E., Cauli, B., Luppi, P-H., Rossier, J., Audinat, E., Muhlethaler, M., & Serafin, M. (2000). Identification of sleep-promoting neurons in vitro. *Nature, 404,* 992–995.

Gallup, G. G., Jr., Anderson, J. R., & Platek, S. M. (2003). Self-awareness, social intelligence, and schizophrenia. In A. S. David & T. Kircher (Eds.), *The self and schizophrenia: A neuropsychological perspective.* Cambridge: Cambridge University Press.

Gallup, G. G., Jr., & Suarez, S. D. (1985). Alternatives to the use of animals in psychological research. *American Psychologist, 40,* 1104–1111.

Galotti, K. M. (1989). Approaches to studying formal and everyday reasoning. *Psychological Bulletin, 105,* 331–351.

Galotti, K. M., Clinchy, B. M., Ainsworth, K. H., Lavin, B., Annick, F., & Mansfield, A. F. (1999). A new way of assessing ways of knowing: The Attitudes Toward Thinking and Learning Survey (ATTLS). *Sex Roles, 40,* 745–766.

Gannon, P. J., Holloway, R. L., Broadfield, D. C., & Braun, A. R. (1998). Asymmetry of chimpanzee planum temporale: Humanlike pattern of Wernicke's brain language area homolog. *Science, 279,* 220–222.

Gao, F., Levine, S. C., Huttenlocher, J. (2000). What do infants know about continuous quantity? *Journal of Experimental Child Psychology, 77*(1), 20–29.

Garb, H. N., Florio, C. M., & Grove, W. M. (1998). The validity of the Rorschach and the Minnesota Multiphasic Personality Inventory: Results from meta-analyses. *American Psychological Society, 9*(5), 402–404.

Garcia, J., Gustavson, C. R., Kelly, D. J., & Sweeney, M. (1976). Preynlithium aversions: I. Coyotes and wolves. *Behavioral Biology, 16,* 61–72.

Garcia, J., & Koelling, R. A. (1971). The use of ionizing rays as a mammalian olfactory stimulus. In H. Autrum, R. Jung, W. R. Loewenstein, D. M. MacKay, & H. L. Teuber (Eds.), *Handbook of sensory physiology: Vol. 4. Chemical senses* (Pt. 1). New York: Springer-Verlag.

Gardner, H. (1983/1993). *Frames of mind: The theory of multiple intelligences.* New York: Basic Books.

Gardner, H. (1995). Multiple intelligences as a catalyst. *English Journal, 84*(8), 16–18.

Gardner, H. (1998). A reply to Perry D. Kleins multiplying the problems of intelligence by eight. *Canadian Journal of Education, 23,* 96–102.

Gardner, H., & Hatch, T. (1989). Multiple intelligences go to school: Educational implications of the theory of multiple intelligences. *Educational Researcher, 18,* 6.

Gardner, R. A., & Gardner, B. T. (1969). Teaching sign language to a chimp. *Science, 165,* 664–672.

Gardner, W. L., & Avolio, B. J. (1998). The charismatic relationship: A dramaturgical perspective. *Academy of Management Review, 23*(1), 32–58.

Garry, M. & Loftus, E. F. (1994). Pseudomemories without hypnosis. *The International Journal of Clinical and Experimental Hypnosis, 42,* 363–378.

Garwood, A. (1996). The Holocaust and the power of powerlessness: Survivor guilt an unhealed wound. *British Journal of Psychotherapy, 13, 2,* 243–258.

Gatchel, R. J., & Turk, D. C. (1999). Interdisciplinary treatment of chronic pain patients. In R. J. Gatchel & D. C. Turk (Eds.), *Psychosocial factors in pain: Critical perspectives* (pp. 435–444). New York: Guilford Press.

Gates, G. J., & Sonenstein, F. L. (2000). Heterosexual genital sexual activity among adolescent males: 1988 and 1995. *Family Planning Perspectives, 32, 6,* 295–297.

Gavin, J. (2000). Arousing suspicion and violating trust: The lived ideology of safe sex talk. *Culture, Health, and Sexuality, 2,* 117–134.

Gazzaniga, M. S. (1983). Right hemisphere language following brain bisection: A 20-year perspective. *American Psychologist, 38,* 525–537.

Gazzaniga, M. S. (2000). Right hemisphere language following brain bisection: A 20-year perspective. In M. S. Gazzaniga (Ed.), *Cognitive neuroscience* (pp. 411–430). Malden, MA: Blackwell Publishers.

Gazzaniga, M. S., Ivry, R., & Mangun, G. R. (2002). Fundamentals of cognitive neuroscience (2nd ed.). W. W. Norton.

Ge, X., Conger, R. D., Cadoret, R. J., Neiderhiser, J. M., Yates, W., Troughton, E., et al. (1996). The developmental interface between nature and nurture: A mutual influence model of child antisocial behavior and parent behaviors. *Developmental Psychology, 32*(4), 574–589.

Ge, X., Conger, R. D., & Elder, G. H., Jr. (1996). Coming of age too early: Pubertal influences on girls' vulnerability to psychological distress. *Child Development, 67*(6), 3386–3400.

Geary, D. C. (1996). Biology, culture, and cross-national differences in mathematical ability. In R. J. Sternberg, T. Ben-Zeev, et al. (Eds.), *The nature of mathematical thinking. The studies in mathematical thinking and learning series* (pp. 145–171). Mahwah, NJ: Lawrence Erlbaum Associates, Inc.

Geary, D. C. (1998). *Male, female: The evolution of human sex differences.* Washington, DC: American Psychological Association.

Geary, D. C. (2000). Evolution and proximate expression of human paternal investment. *Psychological Bulletin, 126,* 55–77.

Geen, R. G. (1991). Social motivation. *Annual Review of Psychology, 42,* 377–399.

Geen, R. G. (1998). Aggression and antisocial behavior. In D. T. Gilbert, S. T. Fiske, & G. Lindzey (Eds.), *The handbook of social psychology* (4th ed., pp. 317–347). Boston: McGraw-Hill.

Geller, B., & Luby, J. (1997). Child and adolescent bipolar disorder: A review of the past 10 years. *Journal of the American Academy of Child and Adolescent Psychiatry, 36,* 1168–1176.

Geller, B., Zimmerman, B., Williams, M., Bolhofner, K., & Craney, J. L. (2001). Adult psychosocial outcome of prepubertal major depressive disorder. *Journal of the American Academy of Child & Adolescent Psychiatry, 40, 6,* 673–677.

Geller, E. S. (2001a). *The psychology of safety handbook* (2nd ed.). Boca Raton, FL: CRC Press LLC.

Geller, E. S. (2001b). Sustaining participation in a safety improvement process: 10 relevant principles from behavioral science. *American Society of Safety Engineers,* 24–29.

Geller, E. S. (2001c). The future of safety: From conversation to commitment. *Occupational Health & Safety, 1,* 58–63.

George, J. M., & Brief, A. P. (1992). Feeling good—doing good: A conceptual analysis of the mood at work-organizational spontaneity relationship. *Psychological Bulletin, 112,* 310–329.

German, T. P., & Defeyter, M. A. (2001). Immunity to functional fixedness in young children. *Psychonomic Bulletin & Review, 7,* 707–712.

Geschwind, N. (1972, April). Language and the brain. *Scientific American,* 76–83.

Geschwind, N., & Galaburda, A. M. (1985a). Cerebral lateralization: Biological mechanisms, associations, and pathology: I. A hypothesis and a program for research. *Archives of Neurology, 42, 5,* 428–459.

Geschwind, N., & Galaburda, A. M. (1985b). Cerebral lateralization: Biological mechanisms, associations, and pathology: II. A hypothesis and a program for research. *Archives of Neurology, 42, 6,* 521–552.

Geschwind, N., & Galaburda, A. M. (1985c). Cerebral lateralization: Biological mechanisms, associations, and pathology: III. A hypothesis and a program for research. *Archives of Neurology, 42, 7,* 634–654.

Gifford, R. (2002). Making a difference: Some ways environmental psychology has improved the world. In R. B. Brechtel & A. Churchman (Eds.), *Handbook of environmental psychology* (pp. 323–334). New York: John Wiley & Sons.

Gift, T. E., Strauss, J. S., Ritzler, B. A., Kokes, R. F., & Harder, D. W. (1980). How diagnostic concepts of schizophrenia differ. *Journal of Nervous and Mental Disease, 168,* 3–8.

Gillies, R. M., & Ashman, A. F. (1996). Teaching collaborative skills to primary school children in classroom-based work groups. *Learning and Instruction, 6*(3), 187–200.

Gilligan, C. (1982). *In a different voice: Psychological theory and women's development.* Cambridge, MA: Harvard University Press.

Gilligan, C. (1994). In a different voice: Women's conceptions of self and of morality. In B. Puka et al. (Eds.), *Caring voices and women's moral frames: Gilligan's view.* New York: Garland Publishing, Inc.

Gilligan, C. (1997). Remembering Iphigenia: Voice, resonance, and a talking cure. In B. Mark (Ed.), *The handbook of infant, child, and adolescent psychotherapy.* Northvale, NJ: Jason Aronson.

Glaser, R., Rabin, B., Chesney, M., Cohen, S., & Natelson, B. (1999). Stress-induced immunomodulation: Implications for infectious diseases? *Journal of the American Medical Association, 281,* 2268–2270.

Glass, R. M. (2001). Electroconvulsive therapy: Time to bring it out of the shadows. *Journal of the American Medical Association, 285* (10), special issue.

Gleaves, D. H. (1996). The sociocognitive model of dissociative identity disorder: A reexamination of the evidence. *Psychological Bulletin, 120,* 42–59.

Gleicher, F., & Petty, R. E. (1992). Expectations of reassurance influence the nature of fear-stimulated attitude change. *Journal of Experimental Social Psychology, 28*(1), 86–100.

Gleitman, H. (1985). Some trends in the study of cognition. In S. Koch, & D. E. Leary (Eds.), *A century of psychology as science.* New York: McGraw-Hill.

Glenmullen, J. (2001). *Prozac backlash: Overcoming the dangers of Prozac, Zoloft, Paxil, and other antidepressants with safe, effective alternatives.* New York: Touchstone Books/Simon & Schuster, Inc.

Glick, P., Diebold, J., Bailey-Wexner, B., & Zhu, L. (1997). The two faces of Adam: Ambivalent sexism and polarized attitudes toward women. *Personality and Social Psychology Bulletin, 23*(12), 1323–1334.

Glick, P., & Fiske, S. T. (1997). Hostile and benevolent sexism: Measuring ambivalent sexism toward women. *Psychology of Women Quarterly, 21*(1), 119–135.

Goldfried, M. R., & Wolfe, B. E. (1996). Psychotherapy practice and research: Repairing a strained alliance. *American Psychologist, 51*(10), 1007–1016.

Golding, J. (1999). Intimate partner violence as a risk factor for mental disorders: A meta-analysis. *Journal of Family Violence, 14,* 99–101.

Goldin-Meadow, S. (2000). Learning with and without a helping hand. In B. Landau, J. Sabini, J. Jonides, & E. L. Newport (Eds.), *Perception, cognition, and language: Essays in honor of Henry and Lila Gleitman* (pp. 121–137). Cambridge, MA: The MIT Press.

Goldin-Meadow, S., & Mylander, C. (1998). Spontaneous sign systems created by deaf children in two cultures. *Nature, 39,* 279–281.

Goldman, M. S., Brown, S. A., Christiansen, B. A., & Smith, G. T. (1991). Alcoholism and memory: Broadening the scope of alcohol-expectancy research. *Psychological Bulletin, 110,* 137–146.

Goldman-Rakic, P. S. (1998). The prefrontal landscape: Implications of functional architecture for understanding human mentation and the central executive, In A. C. Roberts and T. W. Robbins (Ed.), *The prefrontal cortex: Executive and cognitive functions* (pp. 87–102). Oxford: Oxford University Press.

Goldstein, A. P. (2001). Low-level aggression: New targets for zero tolerance. In J. N. Hughes, A. M. La Greca, & J. C. Conoley (Eds.), *Handbook of psychological services for children and adolescents* (pp. 161–181). New York: Oxford University Press.

Goleman, D. (1995). *Emotional intelligence.* New York: Bantam.

Gonzales, L. R., Hays, R. B., Bond, M. A., & Kelly, J. G. (1983). Community mental health. In M. Hersen, A. E. Kazdin, & A. S. Bellack (Eds.), *The clinical psychology handbook.* New York: Pergamon.

Goodale, M. A. (1996). One visual experience, many visual systems. In T. Inui & J. L. McClelland (Eds.), *Attention and performance: Information integration in perception and communication* (pp. 369–393). Cambridge, MA: MIT Press.

Goodale, M. A., & Humphrey, G. K. (2001). Separate visual systems for action and perception. In E. B. Goldstein (Ed.), *Blackwell handbook of perception* (pp. 311–343). Oxford: Blackwell Publishing.

Goodale, M. A., Milner, A. D., Jakobson, L. S., & Carey, D. P. (1991). A neurological dissociation between perceiving objects and grasping them. *Nature, 349,* 6305, 154–156.

Goodwin, S. A., & Fiske, S. T. (2001). Power and gender: The double-edged sword of ambivalence. In R. K. Unger (Ed.), *Handbook of the psychology of women and gender* (pp. 358–366). New York: Wiley.

Gortmaker, S. L., Kagan, J., Caspi, A., & Silva, P. A. (1997). Daylength during pregnancy and shyness in children: Results from Northern and Southern hemispheres. *Developmental Psychobiology, 31*(2), 107–114.

Gottesman, I. I. (1991). *Schizophrenia genesis: The origins of madness.* New York: Freeman.

Gottman, J. M. (1998). Psychology and the study of marital processes. *Annual Review of Psychology, 49,* 169–187.

Gould, S. J. (1997). Darwinian fundamentalism. *New York Review of Books,* 34–37.

Gould, S. J. (1997, January–February). Interview by Michael Krasny. *Mother Jones,* 60–63.

Goulding, M. M. (1990). Getting the important work done fast: Contract plus redecision. In J. K. Zeig & S. G. Gilligan (Eds.), *Brief therapy myths, methods, and metaphors.* New York: Brunner/Mazel.

Graber, J. A., Britto, P. R., & Brooks-Gunn, J. (1999). What's love got to do with it? Adolescents' and young adults' beliefs about sexual and romantic relationships. In W. Furman, B. B. Brown, & C. Feiring (Eds.),

*Self, social identity, and physical health: Interdisciplinary explorations. Rutgers Series on Self and Social Identity* (pp. 364–395). New York: Cambridge University Press.

Graham, C. J., & Cleveland, E. (1995). Left-handedness as an injury risk factor in adolescents. *Journal of Adolescent Health, 16*(1), 50–52.

Graham, T., & Ickes, W. (1997). When women's intuition isn't greater than men's. In W. Ickes (Ed.), *Empathic accuracy* (pp. 117–143). New York: Guilford Press.

Graig, E. (1993). Stress as a consequence of the urban physical environment. In L. Goldberger & S. Breznitz (Eds.), *Handbook of stress: Theoretical and clinical aspects* (2nd ed., pp. 316–332). New York: Free Press.

Grant, K. J., Henley, A., & Kean, M. (2001). The journey after the journey: Family counselling in the context of immigration and ethnic diversity. *Canadian Journal of Counselling, 35,* 1, 89–100.

Graziano, M. S., Hu, X. T., & Gross, C. G. (1997). Coding the locations of objects in the dark. *Science, 277,* 239–240.

Graziano, M. S. A., & Gross, C. G. (1994). Mapping space with neurons. *Current Directions in Psychological Science, 3,* 164–167.

Greenberg, J. (1990). Employee theft as a reaction to underpayment inequity: The hidden cost of pay cuts. *Journal of Applied Psychology, 75,* 561–568.

Greenberg, R. P., Bornstein, R. F., Greenberg, M. D., Fisher, S., & Seymour, F. (1992). A meta-analysis of antidepressant outcome under "blinder" conditions. *Journal of Consulting and Clinical Psychology, 60,* 664–669.

Greene, K., & Rubin, D. L. (1991). Effects of gender inclusive/exclusive language in religious discourse. *Journal of Language and Social Psychology, 10*(2), 81–98.

Greene, P. E., Bressman, S. B., Ford, B., & Hyland, K. (2000). Parkinsonism, dystonia, and hemiatrophy. *Movement Disorders, 15,* 3, 537–541.

Greenfield, P. M. (1997). You can't take it with you: Why ability assessments don't cross cultures. *American Psychologist, 52*(10), 1115–1124.

Greeno, C. G., & Wing, R. R. (1994). Stress-induced eating. *Psychological Bulletin, 115,* 444–464.

Greeno, J. G. (1989). A perspective on thinking. *American Psychologist, 44,* 134–141.

Greeno, J. G., and the Middle School Mathematics Through Applications Project Group. (1998). The situativity of knowing, learning, and research. *American Psychologist, 53*(1), 5–26.

Greenough, W. T., Black, J. E., Klintsova, A., Bates, K. E., & Weiler, I. J. (1999). Experience and plasticity in brain structure: Possible implications of basic research findings for developmental disorders. In S. H. Broman & J. M. Fletcher (Eds.), *The changing nervous system: Neurobehavioral consequences of early brain disorders* (pp. 51–70). New York: Oxford University Press.

Greenspan, S. I. (1997). *The Growth of the Mind.* MA: Addison-Wesley.

Greenwald, A. G., Banaji, M., Rudman, R., Laurie, A., Farmham, S. D., Nosek, B., & Mellott, D. S. (2002). A unified theory of implicit attitudes, stereotypes, self-esteem, and self-concept. *Psychological Review, 109,* 3–25.

Greenwald, A. G., & Farnham, S. D. (2000). Using the Implicit Association Test to measure self-esteem and self-concept. *Journal of Personality and Social Psychology, 79,* 1022–1038.

Greenwald, A. G., Klinger, M. R., & Schuh, E. S. (1995). Activation by marginally perceptible ("subliminal") stimuli: Dissociation of unconscious from conscious cognition. *Journal of Experimental Psychology: General, 124*(1), 22–42.

Griffin, Z. M., & Bock, K. (2000). What the eyes say about speaking. *Psychological Science, 11,* 274–279.

Gringras, P. (1999). Identical differences. *Lancet, 353,* 9152, 562.

Gross, J. J. (1999). Emotion and emotional regulation. In L. A. Pervin & O. P. John (Eds.), *Handbook of personality: Theory and research* (pp. 525–552). New York: Guilford Press.

Grossberg, S. (1995). The attentive brain. *American Scientist, 83,* 438–449.

Grossenbacher, P. G., & Lovelace, C. T. (2001). Mechanisms of synaesthesia: Cognitive and physiological constraints. *Trends in Cognitive Science, 5,* 36–41.

Grossman, F. K., Pollack, W. S., & Golding, E. (1988). Fathers and children: Predicting the quality and quantity of fathering. *Developmental Psychology, 1,* 91–92.

Grunberg, L., Moore, S., & Greenberg, E. S. (1998). Work stress and problem alcohol behavior: A test of the spillover model. *Journal of Organizational Behavior, 19*(5), 487–502.

Grusec, J. E., Goodnow, J. J., & Kuczynski, L. (2000). New directions in analyses of parenting contributions to children's acquisition of values. *Child Development, 71,* 205–211.

Guerin, P. J., Jr., & Chabot, D. R. (1997). Development of family systems theory. In P. L. Wachtel & S. B. Messer (Eds.), *Theories of psychotherapy: Origins and evolution* (pp. 181–226). Washington, DC: American Psychological Association.

Guilford, J. P. (1967). *The nature of human intelligence.* New York: McGraw-Hill.

Guillemette, J., Hebert, M., Paquet, J., & Dumont, M. (1998). Natural bright light exposure in the summer and winter in subjects with and without complaints of seasonal mood variations. *Biological Psychiatry, 44,* 7, 622–628.

Guimon, J., Goerg, D., Zbinden, E., & Fischer, W. (2001). Combining pharmacotherapy and psychotherapy: A Swiss survey. *European Journal of Psychiatry, 15,* 13–21.

Gulevich, G., Dement, W., & Johnson, L. (1966). Psychiatric and EEG observations on a case of prolonged (264 hours) wakefulness. *Archives of General Psychiatry, 15,* 29–35.

Gulya, M., Rovee-Collier, C., Galluccio, L., & Wilk, A. (1998). Memory processing of a serial list by young infants. *American Psychological Society, 9*(4), 303–307.

Haaga, D. A. F., & Davison, G. C. (1993). An appraisal of rational-emotive therapy. *Journal of Consulting and Clinical Psychology, 61,* 215–220.

Hacking, I. (1997). *Rewriting the soul: Multiple personality and the sciences of memory.* Princeton, NJ: Princeton University Press.

Hackmann, A., Clark, D. M., & McManus, F. (2000). Recurrent images and early memories in social phobia. *Behaviour Research and Therapy, 38,* 601–610.

Haermae, M., Laitinen, J., Partinen, M., & Suvanto, S. (1994). The effect of four-day round trip flights over 10 time zones on the circadian variation of salivary melatonin and cortisol in airline flight attendants. *Ergonomics, 37,* 9, 1479–1489.

Haggarty, J. M., Cernovsky, Z., & Husni, M. (2001). The limited influence of latitude on rates of seasonal affective disorder. *The Journal of Nervous and Mental Disease, 189,* 7, 482–484.

Hajek, P., & Belcher, M. (1991). Dreams of absent-minded transgression: An empirical study of a cognitive withdrawal symptom. *Journal of Abnormal Psychology, 100,* 487–491.

Hales, D. (1999). *Just like a woman: How gender science is redefining what makes us female.* New York: Bantam Books.

Hall, C. C. (1997). Cultural malpractice: The growing obsolescence of psychology with the changing U.S. population. *American Psychologist, 52*(6), 642–651.

Hall, E. T. (1966). *The hidden dimension.* Garden City, NY: Doubleday.

Hall, R. E. (2001). The bell curve: Calculated racism and the stereotype of African American men. *Journal of Black Studies, 32,* 104–119.

Hall, S. M., Havassy, B. E., & Wasserman, D. A. (1991). Effects of commitment to abstinence, positive moods, stress, and coping on relapse to cocaine use. *Journal of Consulting and Clinical Psychology, 59,* 526–532.

Hallman, W. K., & Wandersman, A. H. (1992). Attribution of responsibility and individual and collective coping with environmental threats. *Journal of Social Issues, 48,* 101–118.

Halpern, D. F. (1986). *Sex differences in cognitive abilities.* Hillsdale, NJ: Erlbaum.

Halpern, D. F. (1997). Sex difference in intelligence. *American Psychologist, 52*(10), 1091–1102.

Halpern, D. F., & Coren, S. (1993). Left-handedness and life span: A reply to Harris. *Psychological Bulletin, 114*(2), 235–241.

Hambrick, D. Z., Salthouse, T. A., & Meinz, E. J. (1999). Predictors of crossword puzzle proficiency and moderators of age-cognition relations. *Journal of Experimental Psychology: General, 128,* 131–164.

Hamer, D. H., Hu, S., Magnuson, V. L., Hu, N., & Pattatucci, A. M. L. (1993). A linkage between DNA markers on the X chromosome and male sexual orientation. *Science, 261,* 321–327.

Hamilton, K. E., & Dobson, K. S. (2002a). Cognitive theory of depression: Pretreatment patient predictors of outcome. *Clinical Psychology Review, 22,* 6, 875–894.

Hamilton, K. E., & Dobson, K. S. (2002b). Cognitive-behavioral therapy for depression. In G. G. Hofman & M. C. Thompson (Eds.), *Treating chronic and severe mental disorders: A handbook of empirically supported interventions* (pp. 99–115). New York: Guilford Press.

Haney, C., Banks, W., & Zimbardo, P. (1973). Interpersonal dynamics in a simulated prison. *International Journal of Criminology and Penology, 1,* 69–97.

Hankin, C. S., Spiro, A., III, Miller, D. R., & Kazis, L. (1999). Mental disorders and mental health treatment among U.S. Department of Veterans Affairs outpatients: The Veterans Health Study. *American Journal of Psychiatry, 156,* 1924–1930.

Hannover, B. (2000). Development of the self in gendered contexts. In T. Eckes, H. M. Trautner, and others, *The Developmental Social Psychology of Gender* (177–206). Mahwah, NJ: Lawrence Erlbaum Associates, Inc.

Hardy, P. A. J. (1995). Pain management in old age. *Reviews in Clinical Gerontology, 5*(3), 259–273.

Harkins, S. G., & Szymanski, K. (1988). Social loafing and self-evaluation with an objective standard. *Journal of Experimental Social Psychology, 24,* 354–365.

Harlow, H. F. (1962). The heterosexual affectional system in monkeys. *American Psychologist, 17,* 1–9.

Harlow, H. F., & Zimmerman, R. R. (1958). The development of affectional responses in infant monkeys. *Proceedings of the American Philosophic Society, 102,* 501–509.

Harmatz, M. G., Well, A. D., Overtree, C. E., Kawamura, K. Y., Rosal, M., & Ockene, I. S. (2000). Seasonal variation of depression and other moods: a longitudinal approach. *Journal of Biological Rhythms, 15,* 4, 344–350.

Harmer, C. J., Thilo, K. V., Rothwell, J. C., & Goodwin, G. M. (2001). Transcranial magnetic stimulation of medial–frontal cortex impairs the processing of angry facial expressions. *Nature Neuroscience, 4,* 17–18.

Harper, J. M., Schaalje, B. G., & Sandberg, J. G. (2000). Daily hassles, intimacy, and marital quality in later life marriages. *American Journal of Family Therapy, 28,* 1–17.

Harris, C. R. (1999). The mystery of ticklish laughter. *American Scientist, 87,* 4, 344–351.

Harris, C. R., & Christenfeld, N. (1997). Humor, tickle, and the Darwin-Hecker hypothesis. *Cognition and Emotion, 11*(1), 103–110.

Harris, J. R. (1998). *The nurture assumption: Why children turn out the way they do.* New York: The Free Press.

Harris, K. M., & Morgan, S. P. (1991). Fathers, sons, and daughters: Differential paternal involvement in parenting. *Journal of Marriage and the Family, 53,* 531–544.

Harris, L. J. (1993). Do left-handers die sooner than right-handers? Commentary on Coren and Halpern's (1991) Left-handedness: A marker for decreased survival fitness. *Psychological Bulletin, 114*(2), 203–234.

Harris, M. B., & Knight-Bohnhoff, K. (1996). Gender and aggression: Personal aggressiveness. *Sex Roles, 35*(1/2), 27–42.

Harris, M. M., Gilbreath, B., & Sunday, J. A. (1998). A longitudinal examination of a merit pay system: Relationships among performance ratings, merit increases, and total pay increases. *Journal of Applied Psychology, 83*(5), 825–831.

Hartmann, E. (1995). Making connections in a safe place: Is dreaming psychotherapy? *Dreaming, 5,* 213–228.

Hartmann, E. (1996). Outline for a theory on the nature and functions of dreaming. *Dreaming, 6,* 147–170.

Hartung, C. M., & Widiger, T. A. (1998). Gender differences in the diagnosis of mental disorders: Conclusions and controversies of the DSM-IV. *Psychological Bulletin, 123*(3), 260–278.

Hartup, W. W., & Stevens, N. (1997). Friendships and adaptation in the life course. *Psychological Bulletin, 121*(3), 355–370.

Harvey, E. (1999). Short-term and long-term effects of early parental employment on children of the National Longitudinal Survey of Youth. *Developmental Psychology, 35*(2), 445–459.

Harvey, M. (2000, July). Sleepless in America: A lack of rest reaches epidemic proportions. *American Demographics, 22,* 9–10.

Harvey, M. L., Loomis, R. J., Bell, P. A., & Marino, M. (1998). The influence of museum exhibit design on immersion and psychological flow. *Environment and Behavior, 30*(5), 601–627.

Haskell, T. (1961). Toward a reference group theory of juvenile delinquency. *Social Problems, 8,* 220–230.

Haslam, N. (1997). Evidence that male sexual orientation is a matter of degree. *Journal of Personality and Social Psychology, 73*(4), 862–870.

Hauser, S. T., & Bowlds, M. K. (1990). Stress, coping, and adaptation. In S. S. Feldman & G. R. Elliott (Eds.), *At the threshold*. Cambridge, MA: Harvard University Press.

Haveman, R. B., Wolf, K., Wilson, & Peterson, E. (1997). *Do teens make rational choices? The case of teen nonmarital childbearing*. Discussion Paper 1137-97. Institute for Research on Poverty, University of Wisconsin, Madison.

Hawkins, J. D., Catalano, R. F., & Miller, J. Y. (1992). Risk and protective factors for alcohol and other drug problems in adolescence and early adulthood: Implications for substance abuse prevention. *Psychological Bulletin, 112*, 64–105.

Hayes, J. A., & Mitchell, J. C. (1994). Mental health professionals' skepticism about multiple personality disorder. *Professional Psychology: Research and Practice, 25*, 410–425.

Hayflick, L. (1996). *How and why we age*. New York: Ballantine Books, Inc.

Health Canada (1994). *Suicide in Canada: Update of the report of the task force on suicide in Canada*. Ottawa: Mental Health Division, Health Services Directorate, Health Programs and Services Branch, Health Canada.

Health Canada (1998). *HIV and AIDS in Canada*. Surveillance report to June 30, 1998. Ottawa: Division of HIV/AIDS Surveillance, Bureau of HIV/AIDS, STD, and TB, LCDC, HPB, Health Canada.

Health Canada. (1999). *The statistical report on the health of Canadians*. http://www.hc-sc.gc.ca/hppb/phdd/report/stat/report.html.

Health Canada. (1999). *Survey of attention deficit hyperactivity disorder (ADHD) diagnosis and treatment with methylphenidate among Canadian physicians*. http://www.hc-sc.gc.ca/hpfb-dgpsa/tpd-dpt/adhd_survey_e.html, accessed 10 August 2003.

Health Canada. (2000). *Acting on what we know: Preventing youth suicides in First Nations: Report of the advisory group on suicide prevention*. http://www.hc-sc.gc.ca/fnihb/cp/publications/preventing_youth_suicide.pdf, accessed 6 October 2003.

Health Canada. (2001). *Canadian study on health and aging*. http://www.hc-sc.gc.ca/english/media/releases/1996/96_04bke.htm, accessed 29 September 2003.

Health Canada. (2001). *National clearing house on family violence: Canadian incidence study of reported child abuse and neglect (CIS)*. http://www.hc-sc.gc.ca/pphb-dgpsp/publicat/chirpp-schirpt/20se01/index.html#cis, accessed 7 July 2003.

Health Canada. (2002). HIV and AIDS in Canada: Surveillance report to June 30, 2002. http://www.hc-sc.gc.ca/pphb-dgpsp/publicat/aids-sida/haic-vsac0602/pdf/haic-vsac0602.pdf, accessed 6 July 2003.

Health Canada. (2002). *What is FASD: Fast facts*. http://www.hc-sc.gc.ca/dca-dea/programs-mes/fas-fae_whatis_e.html, accessed 28 September 2003.

Healy, A. F., & McNamara, D. S. (1996). Verbal learning and memory: Does the modal model still work? *Annual Review of Psychology, 47*, 143–172.

Hebb, D. O. (1949). *Organization of behavior*. New York: Wiley.

Hebb, D. O. (1955). Drives and the C. N. S. (conceptual nervous system). *Psychological Review, 62*, 243–254.

Hebb, D. O. (1972). *Textbook of psychology* (3rd ed.). Philadelphia: Saunders.

Hedges, L. V., & Nowell, A. (1995). Sex differences in mental test scores, variability, and numbers of high-scoring individuals. *Science, 269*, 41–45.

Heeger, D. J. (1999). Linking visual perception with human brain activity. *Current Opinion in Neurobiology, 9*, 474–479.

Heilbron, C. L., & Guttman, M. A. J. (2000). Traditional healing methods with First Nations women in group counselling. *Canadian Journal of Counselling, 32*, 1, 3–24.

Heine, S. J., Kitayama, S., & Lehman, D. R. (2001). Cultural differences in self-evaluation: Japanese readily accept negative self-relevant information. *Journal of Cross-Cultural Psychology, 32*, 4, 434–443.

Heine, S. J., Kitayama, S., Lehman, D. R., Takata, T., Ide, E., Leung, C., & Matsumoto, H. (2001). Divergent consequences of success and failure in Japan and North America: An investigation of self-improving motivations and malleable selves. *Journal of Personality and Social Psychology, 81*, 599–615.

Heine, S. J., & Lehman, D. R. (1997a). The cultural construction of self-enhancement: An examination of group-serving biases. *Journal of Personality and Social Psychology, 72*(6), 1268–1283.

Heine, S. J., & Lehman, D. R. (1997b). Culture, dissonance, and self-affirmation. *Personality and Social Psychology Bulletin, 23*(4), 389–400.

Heine, S. J., & Lehman, D. R. (1999). Culture, self-discrepancies, and self-satisfaction. *Personality & Social Psychology Bulletin, 25*, 8, 915–925.

Heinlein, R. (1961). *Stranger in a strange land*. New York: Putnam.

Heise, L., Ellsberg, M., & Gottemoeller, M. (1999). Ending violence against women. *Population Reports,* Series L, No. 11, Baltimore, MD: Johns Hopkins University School of Public Health, Population Information Program.

Hellriegel, D., & Slocum, J. (1992). *Management* (6th ed). Reading, MA: Addison-Wesley.

Helms, J. E. (1992). Why is there no study of cultural equivalence in standardized cognitive ability testing? *American Psychologist, 47*, 1083–1101.

Helweg-Larsen, M., & Collins, B. E. (1997). A social psychological perspective on the role of knowledge about AIDS in AIDS prevention. *American Psychological Society, 6*(2), 23–26.

Hemphill, S. A., & Littlefield, L. (2001). Evaluation of a short-term group therapy program for children with behavior problems and their parents. *Behavior Research & Therapy, 39*(7), 823–841.

Henry, D., Guerra, N., Huesmann, R., Tolan, P., VanAcker, R., & Eron, L. (2000). Normative influences on aggression in urban elementary school classrooms. *American Journal of Community Psychology, 28*, 59–81.

Herbert, T. B., Cohen, S., Marsland, A. L., Bachen, E. A., et al. (1994). Cardiovascular reactivity and the course of immune response to an acute psychological stressor. *Psychosomatic Medicine, 56*, 337–344.

Hermann, D. J., Crawford, M., & Holdsworth, M. (1992). Gender-linked differences in everyday memory performance. *British Journal of Psychology, 83*, 221–231.

Herrnstein, R. J., & Murray, C. (1994). *The bell curve: Intelligence and class structure in American life*. New York: Free Press.

Herz, R. S., & Engen, T. (1996). Odor memory: Review and analysis. *Psychonomic Bulletin & Review, 3*(3), 300–313.

Hespos, S. J., Baillargeon, R. (2001). Reasoning about containment events in very young infants. *Cognition, 78*(3), 207–245.

Hesse, E., & Main, M. (2000). Disorganized infant, child and adult attachment: Collapse in behavioral and attentional strategies. *Journal of the American Psychoanalytic Association, 48*(4), 1097–1127.

Hester, C. (1996). The relationship of personality, gender, and age to Adjective Check List profiles of the ideal romantic partner. *Journal of Psychological Type, 36*, 28–35.

Hewlett, B. S., Lamb, M. E., Shannon, D., Leyendecker, B., & Schoelmerich, A. (1998). Culture and early infancy among central African foragers and farmers. *Developmental Psychology, 34*(4), 653–661.

Higgins, N. C., & Bhatt, G. (2000). Culture moderates the self-serving bias: Etic and emic features of casual attributions in India and in Canada. *Social Behavior and Personality, 29*, 49–61.

Higgins, R. L., & Snyder, C. R. (1990). Self-handicapping from a Heiderian perspective: Taking stock of "bonds." In R. L. Higgins (Ed.), *Self-handicapping: The paradox that isn't. The Plenum Series in social/clinical psychology* (pp. 239–273). New York: Plenum.

Hilgard, E. R. (1965). *Hypnotic susceptibility*. New York: Harcourt, Brace & World.

Hilgard, E. R., Hilgard, J. R., & Barber, J. (1994). *Hypnosis in the relief of pain* (rev. ed.). Stanford: Bruner-Routledge.

Hill, J. O., & Peters, J. C. (1998). Environmental contributions to the obesity epidemic. *Science, 280*, 1371–1374.

Hilsman, R., & Garber, J. (1995). A test of the cognitive diathesis-stress model of depression in children: Academic stressors, attributional style, perceived competence, and control. *Journal of Personality and Social Psychology, 69*, 370–380.

Hindmarch, I. (2001). Expanding the horizons of depression: Beyond the monoamine hypothesis. *Human Psychopharmacology: Clinical and Experimental, 16*, 203–218.

Hines, D. (1997). Arguments for prescription privileges for psychologists. *American Psychologist, 52*(3), 270–271.

Hinsz, V. B., Matz, D. C., & Patience, R. A. (2001). Does women's hair signal reproductive potential? *Journal of Experimental Social Psychology, 37*, 166–172.

Hinton, G., Plaut, D. C., & Shallice, T. (1993, April). Simulating brain damage. *Scientific American*, 76–83.

Hinton, P. R. (2000). *Stereotypes, cognition, and culture*. Philadelphia: Psychology Press/Taylor and Francis.

Hiramoto, R. N., Rogers, C. F., Demissie, S., Hseuh, C., Hiramoto, N. S., Lorden, J. F., & Ghanta, V. K. (1997). Psychoneuroendocrine immunology: Site of recognition, learning, and memory in the immune system and the brain. *International Journal of Neuroscience, 92,* 259–286.

Hirsch, H. V. B., & Spinelli, D. N. (1971). Modification of the distribution of receptive field orientation in cats by selective exposure during development. *Experimental Brain Research, 13,* 509–527.

Hirschfeld, R. M. A., Keller, M. B., Panico, S., Arons, B. S., Barlow, D., Davidoff, F., Endicott, J., Froom, J., Goldstein, M., Gorman, J. M., Guthrie, D., Marek, R. G., Maurer, T. A., Meyer, R., Phillips, K., Ross, J., Schwenk, T. L., Sharfstein, S. S., Thase, M. E., & Wyatt, R. J. (1997). The National Depressive and Manic Depressive Association consensus statement on the undertreatment of depression. *Journal of the American Medical Association, 277*(4), 333–340.

Hiscock, M., & Kinsbourne, M. (1987). Specialization of the cerebral hemispheres. *Learning Disabilities, 20,* 130–143.

Hobfoll, S. E., & Shirom, A. (2001). Conservation of resources theory: Application to stress and management in the workplace. In R. T. Golembiewski (Ed.), *Handbook of organizational behavior* (2nd ed., pp. 57–80). New York: Marcel Dekker.

Hobson, J. A. (1989). *Sleep*. New York: Freeman.

Hobson, J. A. (1994). *The chemistry of conscious states: How the brain changes its mind*. Boston: Little, Brown.

Hobson, J. A. (1999). *Consciousness*. New York: Freeman.

Hobson, J. A., & McCarley, R. W. (1977). The brain as a dream state generator: An activation-synthesis of the dream process. *American Journal of Psychiatry, 134,* 1335–1348.

Hochschild, A. (1997). *The time bind*. New York: Metropolitan Books.

Hodges, E. V. E., Boivin, M., Vitaro, F., & Bukowski, W. M. (1999). The power of friendship: Protection against an escalating cycle of peer victimization. *Developmental Psychology, 35,* 1, 94–101.

Hodges, J. R. (2000). Memory in the dementias. In E. Tulving & F. I. M. Craik (Eds.), *The Oxford handbook of memory* (pp. 441–459). New York: Oxford University Press.

Hoffart, A. (1996). In vivo cognitive therapy of panic attacks. *Journal of Cognitive Psychotherapy, 10*(4), 281–289.

Hoffman, P. D., Fruzzetti, A. E., & Swenson, C. R. (1999). Dialectical behavior therapy—Family skills training. *Family Process, 38,* 399–414.

Hoffmann, A. A., & Hercus, M. J. (2000). Environmental stress as an evolutionary force. *BioScience, 50,* 217–226.

Hofstede, G. (1983). National cultures revisited. *Behavior Science Research, 18,* 285–305.

Hogan, R., Curphy, G. J., & Hogan, J. (1994). What we know about leadership: Effectiveness and personality. *American Psychologist, 49,* 493–504.

Hogan, R., Hogan, J., & Roberts, B. W. (1996). Personality measurement and employment decisions. *American Psychologist, 51*(5), 469–477.

Holden, C. (2000, April 7). Global survey examines impact of depression. *Science, 288,* 39–40.

Holden, R. R., & Scholtz, D. (2002). The Holden Psychological Screening Inventory in the prediction of Canadian Forces basic training outcome. *Canadian Journal of Behavioural Science, 34,* 2, 104–110.

Holder, M. D., Yirmiya, R., Garcia, J., & Raizer, J. (1989). Conditioned taste aversions are not readily disrupted by external excitation. *Behavioral Neuroscience, 103,* 605–611.

Holland, J. C. (1999). Use of alternative medicine—a marker for distress? *New England Journal of Medicine, 340,* 1758–1759.

Holland, M. K. (1975). *Using psychology: Principles of behavior and your life*. Boston: Little, Brown.

Hollis, K. L. (1997). Contemporary research on Pavlovian conditioning: A "new" functional analysis. *American Psychologist, 52*(9), 956–965.

Holloway, F. A. (1977). State-dependent retrieval based on time of day. In B. Ho, D. Chute, & D. Richards (Eds.), *Drug discrimination and state-dependent learning*. New York: Academic.

Holmes, D. S. (1984). Mediation and somatic arousal reduction. *American Psychologist, 39,* 1–10.

Holmes, T. H., & Rahe, R. H. (1967). The Social Readjustment Rating Scale. *Journal of Psychosomatic Research, 11,* 213–218.

Hong, Y., Morris, M., Chiu, C., & Benet-Martinez, V. (2000). Multicultural minds: A dynamic constructivist approach to culture and cognition. *American Psychologist, 55,* 709–720.

Honts, C. R. (1994). Psychophysiological detection of deception. *Current Directions in Psychological Science, 3,* 77–82.

Hood, B. M., Willen, J. D., & Driver, J. (1998). Adult's eyes trigger shifts of visual attention in human infants. *American Psychological Society, 9*(2), 131–134.

Hooley, J. M., & Candela, S. F. (1999). Interpersonal functioning in schizophrenia. In T. Millon, P. H. Blaney, & R. D. Davis (Eds.), *Oxford textbook of psychopathology* (pp. 311–338). New York: Oxford University Press.

Hoosain, Z., & Roopnarine, J. L. (1994). African-American fathers' involvement with infants: Relationship to their functioning style, support, education, and income. *Infant Behavior and Development, 17,* 175–184.

Horn, J. L. (2002). Selections of evidence, misleading assumptions, and oversimplifications: The political message of The Bell Curve. In J. M. Fish (Ed.), *Race and intelligence: Separating science from myth* (pp. 297–325). Mahwah, NJ: Lawrence Erlbaum Associates.

Horne, J. (1988). *Why we sleep*. New York: Oxford University Press.

Horney, K. (1937). *The neurotic personality of our time*. New York: Norton.

Hornstein, G. A. (1992). The return of the repressed. *American Psychologist, 47,* 254–263.

Horwitz, A. V., Widom, C. S., McLaughlin, J., & White, H. R. (2001). The impact of childhood abuse and neglect on adult mental health: A prospective study. *Journal of Health and Social Behavior, 42,* 184–201.

Hout, M. (2002). Test scores, education, and poverty. In J. M. Fish (Ed.), *Race and intelligence: Separating science from myth* (pp. 329–354). Mahwah, NJ: Erlbaum.

Howe, D. (1999). The main change agent in psychotherapy is the relationship between therapist and client. In C. Feltham (Ed.), *Controversies in psychotherapy and counseling* (pp. 95–103). London: Sage.

Howe, M. J. A., & Smith, J. (1988). Calendar calculating in "idiots savants": How do they do it? *British Journal of Psychology, 79,* 371–386.

Howes, C., Hamilton, C. E., & Philipsen, L. C. (1998). Stability and continuity of child-caregiver and child-peer relationships. *Child Development, 69*(2), 418–426.

Howes, C., & Tonyan, H. (1999). Peer relations. In L. Balter & C. S. Tamis-LeMonda (Eds.), *Child psychology: A handbook of contemporary issues* (pp. 143–157). Philadelphia: Psychology Press/Taylor & Francis.

Hoyt, I. P., Nadon, R., Register, P. A., Chorny, J., Fleeson, W., Grigorian, E. M., & Otto, L. (1989). Daydreaming, absorption, and hypnotizability. *The International Journal of Clinical and Experimental Hypnosis, 37,* 332–342.

Hubel, D. H., & Wiesel, T. N. (1962). Receptive fields, binocular interaction, and functional architecture in the cat's visual cortex. *Journal of Physiology, 160,* 106–164.

Hubel, D. H., & Wiesel, T. N. (2000). Receptive fields and functional architecture of monkey straite cortex. In S. Yantis (Eds.), *Visual perception: Essential readings, key readings in cognition* (pp. 147–167). Philadelphia: Psychology Press/Taylor & Francis.

Hudak, M. A. (1993). Gender schema theory revisited: Men's stereotypes of American women. *Sex Roles, 28,* 279–293.

Hudspeth, A. J. (1983, January). The hair cells of the inner ear. *Scientific American,* 54–73.

Huffman, L. C., Bryan, Y. E., del Carmen, R., Pedersen, F. A., Doussard-Roosevelt, J. A., & Porgess, S. W. (1998). Infant temperament and cardiac vagal tone: Assessments at twelve weeks of age. *Child Development, 69*(3), 624–635.

Hultsch, D. F., Hertzog, C., Small, B. J., & Dixon, R. A. (1999). Use it or lose it: Engaged lifestyle as a buffer of cognitive decline in aging? *Psychology and Aging, 14,* 245–263.

Humphreys, K. (1996). Clinical psychologists as psychotherapists: History, future, and alternatives. *American Psychologist, 51,* 190–197.

Hunsley, J., Lee, C. M., & Wood, J. M. (2003). Controversial and questionable assessment techniques. In S. O. Lilienfeld, S. J. Lynn et al. (Eds.), *Science and pseudoscience in clinical psychology* (pp. 39–76). New York: Guilford Press.

Hunt, M. (1974). *Sexual behavior in the 1970s*. New York: Dell.

Hurvich, L., & Jameson, D. (1974). Opponent processes as a model of neural organization. *American Psychologist, 30,* 88–102.

Huttenlocher, J. (1998). Language input and language growth. *Preventive Medicine, 27*(2), 195–199.

Huttenlocher, J.; Newcombe, N; & Vasilyeva, M. (1999). Spatial scaling in young children. *Psychological Science, 10*(5), 393–398.

Hyde, J. S. (1996). Gender and cognition: A commentary on current research. *Learning & Individual Differences, 8,* 33–38.

Hyde, J. S., Fennema, E., & Lamon, S. J. (1990). Gender differences in mathematics performance: A meta-analysis. *Psychological Bulletin, 107,* 139–155.

Hyde, J. S., & Linn, M. C. (1988). Gender differences in verbal ability: A meta-analysis. *Psychological Bulletin, 104,* 53–69.

Ida, Y., & Bryden, M. P. (1996). A comparison of hand preference in Japan and Canada. *Canadian Journal of Experimental Psychology, 50,* 2, 234–239.

Idehen, E. E. (1997). The influence of gender and space sharing history on the conceptions of privacy by undergraduates. *Ife Psychologia: An International Journal, 5*(1), 59–75.

Ilgen, D. R. (1999). Teams embedded in organizations: Some implications. *American Psychologist, 54*(2), 129–139.

Ingbar, D. H., & Gee, J. B. L. (1985). Pathophysiology and treatment of sleep apnea. *Annual Review of Medicine, 36,* 369–395.

Ingledew, D. K., Hardy, L., & Cooper, C. L. (1997). Do resources bolster coping and does coping buffer stress? An organizational study with longitudinal aspect and control for negative affectivity. *Journal of Occupational Health Psychology, 2,* 118–133.

Ingram, R. E., Scott, W., & Siegle, G. (1999). Depression: Social and cognitive aspects. In T. Millon, P. H. Blaney, & R. D. Davis (Eds.), *Oxford textbook of psychopathology* (pp. 203–226). New York: Oxford University Press.

Inhelder, B., & Piaget, J. (1958). *The growth of logical thinking from childhood to adolescence.* New York: Basic Books.

Inhoff, A. W., Starr, M., & Shindler, K. L. (2000). Is the processing of words during eye fixations in reading strictly serial? *Perception & Psychophysics, 62,* 1474–1484.

Innes, J. M., & Young, R. F. (1975). The effect of presence of an audience, evaluation apprehension, and objective self-awareness on learning. *Journal of Experimental Social Psychology, 11,* 35–42.

Inzlicht, M., & Ben-Zeev, T. (2000). A threatening intellectual environment: Why females are susceptible to experiencing problem-solving deficits in the presence of males. *Psychological Science, 11,* 365–371.

Ionescu, M. D. (2000). Sex differences in memory estimates for pictures and words. *Psychological Reports, 87,* 315–322.

Isabella, R. A., Belsky, J., & von Eye, A. (1989). Origins of infant- mother attachment: An examination of interactional synchrony during the infant's first year. *Developmental Psychology, 25,* 12–21.

Ito, T. A., Larsen, J. T., Smith, N. K., & Cacioppo, J. T. (1998). Negative information weighs more heavily on the brain: The negativity bias in evaluative categorizations. *Journal of Personality and Social Psychology, 75*(4), 887–900.

Ittelson, W. H., & O'Hanlon, T. (1976). Behavioural science and the rationalization of architectural design. *World Hospital, 12,* 1, 59–62.

Izard, C. E. (1990). Facial expressions and the regulation of emotions. *Journal of Personality and Social Psychology, 58*(3), 487–498.

Izard, C. E. (1997). Emotions and facial expressions: A perspective from differential emotions theory. In J. A. Russell, J. M. Fernandez-Dols, et al. (Eds.), *The psychology of facial expression. Studies in emotion and social interaction, 2nd series* (pp. 57–77). New York: Cambridge University Press.

Izard, C. E., & Saxton, P. M. (1988). Emotions. In R. C. Atkinson, R. J. Herrnstein, G. Lindzey, & R. D. Luce (Eds.), *Stevens handbook of experimental psychology: Vol. 1. Perception and motivation.* New York: Wiley.

Izquierdo, I., & Medina, J. H. (1997). The biochemistry of memory formation and its regulation by hormones and neuromodulators. *Psychobiology, 25*(1), 1–9.

Jaccard, J., Helbig, D. W., Wan, C. K., Gutman, M. A., & Kritz-Silverstein, D. C. (1990). Individual differences in attitude-behavior consistency: The prediction of contraceptive behavior. *Journal of Applied Social Psychology, 20,* 575–617.

Jackson, D. N., & Tremblay, P. F. (2002). The six factor personality questionnaire. In R. deBoele & U. Groningen (Eds.), *Big five assessment* (pp. 354–372). Ashland, OH: Hogrefe & Huber Publishers.

Jackson, J. M., & Latané, B. (1981). All alone in front of all those people: Stage fright as a function of number and type of co-performers and audience. *Journal of Personality and Social Psychology, 40,* 73–85.

Jackson, L. M., & Esses, V. M. (2000). Effects of perceived economic competition on people's willingness to help empower immigrants. *Group Processes & Intergroup Relations, 3,* 4, 419–435.

Jackson, S. E., & Schuler, R. S. (1990). Human resource planning: Challenges for industrial/organizational psychologists. *American Psychologist, 45,* 223–239.

Jackson, S. E., & Schuler, R. S. (1995). Understanding human resource management in the context of organizations and their environments. *Annual Review of Psychology, 46,* 237–264.

Jackson, S. R. (2000). Perception, awareness, and action: Insights from blindsight. In Y. Rossetti & A. Revonsuo (Eds.), *Beyond dissociation: Interaction between dissociated implicit and explicit processing: Advances in consciousness research* (pp. 73–98). Amsterdam: John Benjamins Publishing Company.

Jacob, S., & McClintock, M. K. (2000). Psychological state and mood effects of steroidal chemosignals in women and men. *Hormones & Behavior, 37,* 57–78.

Jacobs, B., Schall, M., & Scheibel, A. B. (1993). A quantitative dendritic analysis of Wernicke's area. II. Gender, hemispheric, and environmental factors. *Journal of Comprehensive Neurology, 237,* 97–111.

Jacobs, L., Berscheid, E., & Walster, E. (1971). Self-esteem and attraction. *Journal of Personality and Social Psychology, 17,* 84–91.

Jacobs, R. A. (1997). Nature, nurture, and the development of functional specializations: A computational approach. *Psychonomic Bulletin and Review, 4*(3), 299–309.

Jacobs, R. A., & Kosslyn, S. M. (1994). Encoding shape and spatial relations: The role of receptive field size in coordinating complementary representations. *Cognitive Science, 18,* 361–386.

Jacobson, N. S., Christensen, A., Prince, S. E., Cordova, J., & Eldridge, K. (2000). Integrative behavioral couple therapy: An acceptance-based, promising new treatment for couple discord. *Journal of Consulting & Clinical Psychology, 68,* 351–355.

Jaffee, S., & Hyde, J. S. (2000). Gender differences in moral orientation: A meta-analysis. *Psychological Bulletin, 126,* 703–726.

James, W. (1884). What is an emotion? *Mind, 9,* 188–205.

James, W. (1890). *Principles of psychology.* New York: Dover.

James, W. (1896). *The will to believe.* London: Longman, Green.

Jamison, K. R. (1993). *Touched with fire: Manic-depressive illness and the artistic temperament.* New York: Simon & Schuster.

Jamison, K. R. (1996). Mood disorders, creativity, and the artistic temperament. In J. J. Schildkraut & A. Otero. *Depression and the spiritual in modern art: Homage to Miró* (pp. 15–32). Oxford, UK: Wiley.

Jan, J. E., Espezel, H., & Appleton, R. E. (1994). The treatment of sleep disorders with melatonin. *Developmental Medicine and Child Neurology, 36,* 97–107.

Janik, V. M. (2000). Whistle matching in wild bottlenose dolphins. *Science, 289,* 1355–1357.

Janis, I. L. (1983). The role of social support in adherence to stressful decisions. *American Psychologist, 38,* 142–160.

Jansen, A. S. P., Nguyen, X. V., Karpitskiy, V., Mettenleiter, T. C., & Loewy, A. D. (1995). Central command neurons of the sympathetic nervous system: Basis of the fight-or-flight response. *Science, 270,* 644–646.

Janssen, T., & Carton, J. S. (1999). The effects of locus of control and task difficulty on procrastination. *Journal of Genetic Psychology, 160,* 436–442.

Jarrett, M. E., & Lethbridge, D. J. (1994). Looking forward, looking back: Women's experience with waning fertility during midlife. *Qualitative Health Research, 4,* 370–384.

Jaynes, J. (1976). *The origin of consciousness in the breakdown of the bicameral mind.* Boston: Houghton Mifflin.

Jazwinski, S. M. (1996). Longevity, genes, and aging. *Science, 273,* 54–59.

Jenkins, G. D., Jr., Mitra, A., Gupta, N., & Shaw, J. D. (1998). Are financial incentives related to performance? A meta-analytic review of empirical research. *Journal of Applied Psychology, 83*(5), 777–787.

Jenkins, H. M., & Harrison, R. H. (1960). Effect of discrimination training on auditory generalization. *Journal of Experimental Psychology, 59,* 244–253.

Jensen, A. R. (1969). How much can we boost IQ and scholastic achievement? *Harvard Educational Review, 39,* 1–123.

Jensen, A. R. (1970). Can we and should we study race differences? In J. Hellmuth (Ed.), *Disadvantaged child* (Vol. 3). New York: Brunner/Mazel.

Jensen, A. R. (1987). Psychometric g as a focus on concerted research effort. *Intelligence, 11*, 193–198.

Jerome, L., & Segal, A. (2001). Benefit of long-term stimulants on driving in adults with ADHD. *Journal of Nervous & Mental Disease, 189*(1), 63–64.

Job, R. F. S., & Barnes, B. W. (1995). Stress and consumption: Inescapable shock, neophobia, and quinine finickiness in rats. *Behavioral Neuroscience, 109*, 106–116.

John, E. R., Chesler, P., Bartlett, F., & Victor, I. (1968). Observational learning in cats. *Science, 159*, 1489–1491.

Johnsen, K., Espnes, G. A., & Gillard, S. (1998). The associations between Type A/B behavioural dimension and Type 2/4 personality patterns. *Personality and Individual Differences, 25*(5), 937–945.

Johnson, B. T., & Eagly, A. H. (1989). Effects of involvement on persuasion: A meta-analysis. *Psychological Bulletin, 106*, 290–314.

Johnson, D. L. (1997). Weight loss for women: Studies of smokers and nonsmokers using hypnosis and multi-component treatments with and without overt aversion. *Psychological Reports, 80*(3, Pt. 1), 931–933.

Johnson, E. K., & Jusczyk, P. W. (2001). Word segmentation by 8-month olds: When speech cues count more than statistics. *Journal of Memory and Language, 44*, 548–567.

Johnson, J. G., Cohen, P., Smailes, E. M., Kasen, S., & Brook, J. S. (2002). Television viewing and aggressive behavior during adolescence and adulthood. *SCIENCE Magazine, 295*, 2468–2471.

Johnson, J. S., Shenkman, K. D., Newport, E. L., & Medin, D. L. (1996). Indeterminacy in the grammar of adult language learners. *Journal of Memory and Language, 35*, 335–352.

Johnson, L. C., Slye, E. S., & Dement, W. (1965). Electroencephalographic and autonomic activity during and after prolonged sleep deprivation. *Psychosomatic Medicine, 27*, 415–423.

Johnson, S., & Lebow, J. (2000). The "coming of age" of couple therapy: A decade review. *Journal of Marital & Family Therapy, 26*, 23–38.

Johnson, S. H. (1998). Cerebral organization of motor imagery: Contralateral control of grip selection in mentally represented prehension. *American Psychological Society, 9*(3), 219–222.

Johnson, T. F. (1995). Aging well in contemporary society. *American Behavioral Scientist, 39*(2), 120–130.

Jonah, N. (1996). *Risk, vulnerability, resiliency—Health system implications IV: Selected applications of the concepts of risk and resiliency. A guide to the literature on the effectiveness of prevention of mental health problems for those at risk.* Ottawa: Health Canada

Jonas, E., Schulz-Hardt, S., Frey, D., & Thelen, N. (2001). Confirmation bias in sequential information search after preliminary decisions: An expansion of dissonance theoretical research on selective exposure to information. *Journal of Personality and Social Psychology, 80*, 557–571.

Joncas, S., Zadra, A., Paquet, J., & Montplaisir, J. (2002). The value of sleep deprivation as a diagnostic tool in adult sleepwalkers. *Neurology, 58*, 936–940.

Jones, C. J., & Meredith, W. (2000). Developmental paths of psychological health from early adolescence to later adulthood. *Psychology and Aging, 15*, 351–360.

Jones, J. M., Bennet, S., Olmsted, M. P., Lawson, M. L., & Rodin, G. (2001). Disordered eating attitudes and behaviours in teenaged girls: A school based study. *Canadian Medical Association Journal, 165*, 5, 547–552.

Jonides, J., Schumacher, E. H., Smith, E. E., & Lauber, E. J. (1997). Verbal working memory load affects regional brain activation as measured by PET. *Journal of Cognitive Neuroscience, 9*(4), 462–475.

Jouvet, M. (1999). *The paradox of sleep: The story of dreaming* (L. Garey, Trans.). Cambridge, MA: The MIT Press.

Judge, T. A., Locke, E. A., Durham, C. C., & Kluger, A. N. (1998). Dispositional effects on job and life satisfaction: The role of core evaluations. *Journal of Applied Psychology, 83*(1), 17–34.

Julien, R. M. (1995). *A primer of drug action: A concise, nontechnical guide to the actions, uses, and side effects of psychoactive drugs (7th ed.).* New York: W. H. Freeman & Co.

Jussim, L., Nelson, T. E., Manis, M., & Soffin, S. (1995). Prejudice, stereotypes, and labeling effects: Sources of bias in person perception. *Journal of Personality and Social Psychology, 68*, 228–246.

Kagan, B. L., Leskin, G., Haas, B., Wilkins, J., & Foy, D. (1999). Elevated lipid levels in Vietnam veterans with chronic posttraumatic stress disorders. *Biological Psychiatry, 45*(3), 374–377.

Kagan, J. (1997). Temperament and the reactions to unfamiliarity. *Child Development, 68*(1), 139–143.

Kagan, J., Reznick, J. S., & Snidman, N. (1987). The physiology and psychology of behavioural inhibition in children. *Child Development, 58*, 1459–1473.

Kahana, B., Deimling, G., & Bowman, K. (2000, October 15). Post traumatic stress reactions among elderly long-term cancer survivors. *The Gerontologist*, p. 354.

Kail, R., & Hall, L. K. (2001). Distinguishing short-term memory from working memory. *Memory and Cognition, 29*, 1–9.

Kaitz, M., Lapidot, P., Bronner, R., & Eidelman, A. I. (1992). Parturient women can recognize their infants by touch. *Developmental Psychology, 28*, 35–39.

Kalick, S. M., Zebrowitz, L. A., Langlois, J. H., & Johnson, R. M. (1998). Does human facial attractiveness honestly advertise health? Longitudinal data on an evolutionary question. *Psychological Science, 9*(1), 8–13.

Kandel, E., & Abel, T. (1995). Neuropeptides, adenyl cyclase, and memory storage. *Science, 268*, 825–826.

Kandel, E. R. (2001). The molecular biology of memory storage: A dialogue between genes and synapses. *Science, 294*, 5544, 1030–1038.

Kanner, A. D., Coyne, J. C., Schaefer, C., & Lazarus, R. S. (1981). Comparison of two modes of stress measurement: Daily hassles and uplifts versus major life events. *Journal of Behavioral Medicine, 4*, 1–39.

Kaplan, D. W., Feinstein, R. A., Fisher, M. M., Klein, J. D., Olmedo, L. F., Rome, E. S., & Yancy, W. S. (2001). Condom use by adolescents. *Pediatrics, 107*, 1463–1469.

Karabenick, S. A., & Collins, E. J. (1997). Relation of perceived instructional goals and incentives to college students' use of learning strategies. *Journal of Experimental Education, 65*(4), 331–341.

Karasek, R. A. (1979). Job demands, job decision latitude, and mental strain: Implications for job redesign. *Administrative Science Quarterly, 24*, 285–308.

Karau, S. J., & Williams, K. D. (2000). Understanding individual motivation in groups: The collective effort model. In M. E. Turner (Ed.), *Groups at work: Theory and research. Applied social research* (pp. 113–141). Mahwah, NJ: Erlbaum.

Katsuki, Y. (1961). Neutral mechanisms of auditory sensation in cats. In W. A. Rosenblith (Ed.), *Sensory communication*. Cambridge, MA: MIT Press.

Katz, J., & Beach, S. R. H. (2000). Looking for love? Self-verification and self-enhancement effects on initial romantic attraction. *Society for Personality and Social Psychology, 26*, 1526–1539.

Kaufman, A. S. (1983). Some questions and answers about the Kaufman Assessment Battery for Children (K-ABC). *Journal of Psychoeducational Assessment, 1*, 205–218.

Kaye, K., Elkind, L., Goldberg, D., & Tytun, A. (1989). Birth outcomes for infants of drug abusing mothers. *New York State Journal of Medicine, 89*(5), 256–261.

Kazdin, A. E. (2000). *Psychotherapy for children and adolescents: Directions for research and practice.* New York: Oxford University Press.

Kazdin, A. E. (2001). Bridging the enormous gaps of theory with therapy research and practice. *Journal of Clinical Child Psychology, 30*, 59–66.

Keane, T. M. (1998). Psychological effects of military combat. In B. P. Dohrenwend et al. (Eds.), *Adversity, stress, and psychopathology* (pp. 52–65). New York: Oxford University Press.

Keefe, F. J., & France, C. R. (1999). Pain: Biopsychosocial mechanisms and management. *Current Directions in Psychological Science, 8*, 137–140.

Keefe, K., & Berndt, T. J. (1996). Relations of friendship quality to self-esteem in early adolescence. *Journal of Early Adolescence, 16*(1), 110–129.

Keenan, J. P., Nelson, A., O'Connor, M., Pascual-Leone, A. (2001). Self-recognition and the right hemisphere. *Nature, 409*, 6818, 305.

Keenan, J. P., Wheeler, M., Gallup, G. G., Jr., & Pascual-Leone, A. (2000). Self-recognition and the right prefrontal cortex. *Trends in Cognitive Science, 4*, 338–344.

Kelley, H. H. (1972). Attribution in social interaction. In E. E. Jones et al. (Eds.), *Attribution: Perceiving the causes of behavior*. Morristown, NJ: General Learning Press.

Kelley, H. H. (1973). Process of causal attribution. *American Psychologist, 28*, 107–128.

Kelly, A. E., & McKillop, K. J. (1996). Consequences of revealing personal secrets. *Psychological Bulletin, 120*(3), 450–465.

Kelly, T. A., & Strupp, H. H. (1992). Patient and therapist values in psychotherapy: Perceived changes, assimilation, similarity, and outcome. *Journal of Consulting and Clinical Psychology, 60,* 34–40.

Keltner, D., & Ekman, P. (2000). Facial expressions and emotion. In M. Lewis & J. M. Haviland-Jones (Eds.), *Handbook of emotions* (2nd ed., pp. 236–249). New York: Guilford Press.

Kemppainen, J. K., Levine, R. E., Mistal, M., & Schmidgall, D. (2001). HAART adherence in culturally diverse patients with HIV/AIDS: A study of male patients from a Veterans Administration hospital in Northern California. *AIDS Patient Care and STD's, 15,* 117–127.

Kendall, P. C., Krain, A., & Treadwell, K. R. H. (1999). Generalized anxiety disorder. In R. T. Ammerman, M. Hersen, et al. (Eds.), *Handbook of prescriptive treatments for children and adolescents* (2nd ed.) (pp. 155–171). Boston: Allyn & Bacon, Inc.

Kendler, K. S., Neale, M., Kessler, R., Heath, A., & Eaves, L. (1992). A population-based twin study of major depression in women. *Archives of General Psychiatry, 49,* 257–266.

Kendler, K. S., Neale, M., Kessler, R., Heath, A., & Eaves, L. (1993). A twin study of recent life events and difficulties. *Archives of General Psychiatry, 50,* 789–796.

Kendler, K. S., Neale, M. C., Heath, A. C., Phil, D., et al. (1994). A twin-family study of alcoholism in women. *American Journal of Psychiatry, 151,* 707–715.

Kennedy, M. B. (2000, October 27). Signal-processing machines at the postsynaptic density. *Science, 290,* 750–754.

Kenrick, D. T. (2001). Evolutionary psychology, cognitive science and dynamical systems: Building an integrative paradigm. *Current Directions in Psychological Science, 10,* 1, 13–17.

Kerns, K. A. (1998). Individual differences in friendship quality: Links to child-mother attachment. In W. M. Bukowski et al. (Eds.), *The company they keep: Friendship in childhood and adolescence.* New York: Cambridge University Press.

Kerr, N., & Bruun, S. E. (1983). Dispensability of member effort and group motivation losses: Free-rider effects. *Journal of Personality and Social Psychology, 44,* 78–94.

Kessler, R. C. (2000). Psychiatric epidemiology: Selected recent advances and future directions. *Bulletin of the World Health Organization, 78,* 464–474.

Kessler, R. C., Berglund, P., Demler, O., Jin, R., Koretz, D., Merikangas, K. R., Rush, A. J., Walters, E. E., & Wang, P. S. (2003). The epidemiology of major depressive disorder: Results from the National Comorbidity Survey Replication (NCS-R). *JAMA: Journal of the American Medical Association, 289,* 23, 3095–3105.

Kessler, R. C., McGonagle, K. A., Zhao, S., Nelson, C. B., Hughes, M., Eshleman, S., Wittchen, H-U., & Kendler, K. S. (1994). Lifetime and 12-month prevalence of *DSM-III-R* psychiatric disorders in the United States. *Archives of General Psychiatry, 51,* 8–19.

Ketelaar, T., & Ellis, B. J. (2000). Are evolutionary explanations unfalsifiable? Evolutionary psychology and the Lakatosian philosophy of science. *Psychological Inquiry, 11,* 1–21.

Kettl, P. A., & Bixler, E. O. (1993). Alcohol and suicide in Alaskan Natives. *American Indian and Alaskan Mental Health Research, 5*(2), 34–45.

Kety, S. S., Wender, P. H., Jacobsen, B., Ingraham, L. J., Jansson, L., Faber, B., & Kinney, D. K. (1994). Mental illness in the biological and adoptive relatives of schizophrenic adoptees: Replication of the Copenhagen study in the rest of Denmark. *Archives of General Psychiatry, 51,* 442–455.

Kidd, S. A. (2003a). Street youth: Coping and interventions. *Child & Adolescent Social Work Journal, 20,* 4, 235–261.

Kidd, S. A. (2003b). The need for improved operational definition of suicide attempts: Illustrations from the case of street youth. *Death Studies, 27,* 5, 449–455.

Kidd, S. A., & Kral, M. J. (2002). Suicide and prostitution among street youth. *Adolescence, 37,* 146, 411–430.

Kiecolt-Glaser, J. K., Page, G. G., Marucha, P. T., MacCallum, R. C., & Glaser, R. (1998). Psychological influences on surgical recovery: Perspectives from psychoneuroimmunology. *American Psychologist, 53*(11), 1209–1218.

Kier, C., & Lewis, C. (1997). Infant-mother attachment in separated and married families. *Journal of Divorce and Remarriage, 26*(3/4), 185–194.

Kihlstrom, J. F., Barnhardt, T. M., & Tataryn, D. J. (1992). The psychological unconscious. *American Psychologist, 47,* 788–791.

Kilbourne, B. K. (1989). A cross-cultural investigation of the foot-in-the-door compliance induction procedure. *Journal of Cross-Cultural Psychology, 20,* 3–38.

Kilgard, M. P., & Merzenich, M. M. (1998). Cortical map reorganization enabled by nucleus basalis activity. *Science, 279,* 1714–1718.

Kilpatrick, D. G., Acierno, R., Saunders, B., Resnick, H. S., Best, C. L., & Schnurr, P. P. (2000). Risk factors for adolescent substance abuse and dependence data from a national sample. *Journal of Consulting and Clinical Psychology, 68,* 19–30.

Kim, C., & Kwok, Y. S. (1998). Navajo use of native healers. *Archives of Internal Medicine, 158,* 2245–2249.

Kim, H., & Markus, H. R. (1999). Deviance or uniqueness, harmony or conformity? A cultural analysis. *Journal of Personality and Social Psychology, 77,* 785–800.

Kim, J. J., & Fanselow, M. S. (1992). Modality-specific retrograde amnesia of fear. *Science, 256,* 675–677.

Kim, S. R. (1997). Relationships between young children's day care experience and their attachment relationships with parents and socioemotional behavior problems. *Korean Journal of Child Studies, 18*(2), 5–18.

Kimura, D. (2000). *Sex and cognition.* Cambridge, MA: MIT Press.

Kimura, D. (2002, Special Issue: The Hidden Mind). Sex differences in the brain. *Scientific American, 12,* 32–37.

Kindlon, D., Thompson, M., & Baker, T. (1999). *Raising Cain: Protecting the emotional life of boys.* New York: Ballantine Books.

Kinnunen, T., & Zamansky, H. S. (1996). Hypnotic amnesia and learning: A dissociation interpretation. *American Journal of Clinical Hypnosis, 38*(4), 247–253.

Kirsch, I., & Lynn, S. J. (1998b). Dissociation theories of hypnosis. *Psychological Bulletin, 123*(1), 100–115.

Kirsch, I., & Sapirstein, G. (1999). Listening to Prozac but hearing placebo: A meta-analysis of antidepressant medications. In I. Kirsch (Ed.), *How expectancies shape experience* (pp. 303–320). Washington, DC: American Psychological Association.

Kirsch, I., Silva, C. E., Comey, G., & Reed, S. (1995). A spectral analysis of cognitive and personality variables in hypnosis: Empirical disconfirmation of the two-factor model of hypnotic responding. *Journal of Personality and Social Psychology, 69,* 167–175.

Kirshnit, C. E., Richards, M. H., & Ham, M. (1988, August). Athletic participation and body-image during early adolescence. Paper presented at the 96th Annual Convention of the American Psychological Association, Atlanta.

Kitayama, S., & Burnstein, E. (1994). Social influence, persuasion, and group decision making. In S. Shavitt & T. C. Brock (Eds.), *Persuasion: Psychological insights and perspectives* (pp. 175–194). Boston: Allyn & Bacon.

Klammer, J., Skarlicki, D. P., & Barclay, L. (2002). Speaking up in the Canadian military: The roles of voice, being heard, and generation in predicting civic virtue. *Canadian Journal of Behavioural Science, 34,* 2, 122–130.

Klar, A. J. S. (1996). A single locus, RGHT, specifies preference for hand utilization in humans. *Cold Spring Harbor Symposium for Quantitative Biology, 61,* 59–65.

Klar, Y., & Giladi, E. E. (1997). No one in my group can be below the group's average: A robust positivity bias in favor of anonymous peers. *Journal of Personality and Social Psychology, 73*(5), 885–901.

Klaus, M. H., & Kennell, J. H. (1983). *Bonding: The beginnings of parent-infant attachment* (Rev. ed.). New York: New American Library.

Klein, P. D. (1997). Multiplying the problems of intelligence by eight: A critique of Gardner's theory. *Canadian Journal of Education, 22,* 377–394.

Kliegl, R., Philipp, D., Luckner, M., & Krampe, R. (2001). Face memory skill acquisition. In N. Charness, D. C. Parks, & B. A. Sable (Eds.), *Communication, technology, and aging: Opportunities and challenges for the future* (pp. 169–186). New York: Springer.

Kline, D. W., Kline, T. J., Fozard, J. L., Kosnik, W. et al. (1992). Vision, aging, and driving: The problems of older drivers. *Journal of Gerontology, 47,* 1, P27–P34.

Kling, K. C., Hyde, J. S., Showers, C. J., & Buswell B. N. (1999). Gender differences in self-esteem: a meta-analysis. *Psychological Bulletin, 125,* 4, 470–500.

Klinke, R., Kral, A., Heid, S., Tillein, J., & Hartmann, R. (1999). Recruitment of the auditory cortex in congenitally deaf cats by long-term cochlear electrostimulation. *Science, 285,* 1729–1733.

Klonoff, E. A., Landrine, H., & Campbell, R. (2000). Sexist discrimination may account for well-known gender differences in psychiatric symptoms. *Psychology of Women Quarterly, 24*, 93–99.

Klonoff-Cohen, H., & Lam-Kruglick, P. (2002). Maternal and paternal recreation drug use and sudeen infant death syndrome. *Journal of the American Academy of Child & Adolescent Psychiatry, 41*, 2, 147.

Klusman, L. E. (1998). Military health care providers' views on prescribing privileges for psychologists. *Professional Psychology: Research and Practice, 29*(3), 223–229.

Knapp, S., & VandeCreek, L. (2000). Recovered memories of childhood abuse: Is there an underlying professional consensus? *Professional Psychology: Research and Practice, 31*, 365–371.

Knee, C. R. (1998). Implicit theories of relationships: Assessment and prediction of romantic relationship initiation, coping, and longevity. *Journal of Personality and Social Psychology, 74*(2), 360–368.

Knight, K. H., Elfenbein, M. H., & Martin, M. B. (1997). Relationship of connected and separate knowing to the learning styles of Kolb, formal reasoning, and intelligence. *Sex Roles, 37*, 401–414.

Knoblich, G., & Ohlsson, S. (1999). Constraint relaxation and chunk decomposition in insight problem solving. *Journal of Experimental Psychology: Learning, Memory, & Cognition, 25*, 1534–1555.

Kohan, A., & O'Connor, B. P. (2002). Police officer job satisfaction in relation to mood, well-being, and alcohol consumption. *Journal of Psychology, 136*, 3, 307–318.

Kohlberg, L. (1969). The cognitive-developmental approach to socialization. In D. A. Goslin (Ed.), *Handbook of socialization theory and research*. Chicago: Rand McNally.

Kohn, A. (1993). *Punished by rewards: The trouble with gold stars, incentive plans, A's, praise, and other bribes*. Boston: Houghton Mifflin.

Kolb, B. (1999). The twentieth century belongs to neuropsychology. *Brain Research Bulletin, 50*, 409–410.

Kolb, B., & Wishaw, I. Q. (1996). *Fundamentals of human neuropsychology*. New York: W. H. Freemen.

Koob, G. F. (2000). Neurobiology of addiction: Toward the development of new therapies. In S. D. Glick & I. M. Maisonneuve (Eds.), *New medications for drug abuse. Annals of the New York Academy of Sciences* (pp. 170–185). New York: New York Academy of Sciences.

Koob, G. F., Wall, T. L., & Bloom, F. E. (1989). Nucleus accumbens as a substrate for the aversive stimulus effects of opiate withdrawal. *Psychopharmacology, 98*, 530–534.

Koolstra, C. M., van der Voort, T. H., & van der Kamp, L. J. (1997). Television's impact on children's reading comprehension and decoding skills: A 3-year panel study. *Reading Research Quarterly, 32*(2), 128–152.

Kopp, C. B., & Kaler, S. R. (1989). Risk in infancy: Origins and implications. *American Psychologist, 44*, 224–230.

Kopta, S. M., Howard, K. I., Lowry, J. L., & Beutler, L. E. (1994). Patterns of symptomatic recovery in psychotherapy. *Journal of Consulting and Clinical Psychology, 62*, 1009–1016.

Kopyov, O. V., Jacques, D., Lieberman, A., Duma, C. M., & Rogers, R. L. (1996). Clinical study of fetal mesencephalic intracerebral transplants for the treatment of Parkinson's disease. *Cell Transplantation, 5*(2), 327–337.

Koriat, A., Goldsmith, M., & Pansky, A. (2000). Toward a psychology of memory accuracy. *Annual Review of Psychology, 51*, 481–537.

Koski, L., & Petrides, M. (2001). Time-related changes in task performance after lesions restricted to the frontal cortex. *Neuropsychologia, 39*, 268–281.

Koss, M. P. (2000). Blame, shame, and community justice reponses to violence against women. *American Psychologist, 55*, 1332–1343.

Koss, M. P., Gidycz, C. A., & Wisniewski, N. (1987). The scope of rape: Incidence and prevalence of sexual aggression and victimization in a national sample of higher education students. *Journal of Consulting and Clinical Psychology, 55*, 162–170.

Kosslyn, S. M. (1975). Information representation in visual images. *Cognitive Psychology, 7*, 341–370.

Kosslyn, S. M. (1987). Seeing and imagining in the cerebral hemispheres: A computational approach. *Psychological Review, 94*, 148–175.

Koulack, D. (1991). *To catch a dream*. Albany: State University of New York Press.

Kozyk, J. C., Touyz, S. W., & Beumont, P. J. (1998). Is there a relationship between bulimia nervosa and hazardous alcohol use? *International Journal of Eating Disorders, 24*(1), 95–99.

Kral, M. J., Burkhardt, K. J., & Kidd, S. (2002). The new research agenda for cultural psychology. *Canadian Psychology, 43*, 3, 154–162.

Krantz, D. S., & McCeney, M. K. (2002). Effects of psychological and social factors on organic disease: A critical assessment of research on coronary heart disease. *Annual Review of Psychology, 53*(1), 341–369.

Kranzler, H. R., & Anton, R. F. (1994). Implications of recent neuropsychopharmacologic research for understanding the etiology and development of alcoholism. *Journal of Consulting and Clinical Psychology, 62*, 1116–1126.

Kranzler, J. H. (1997). Educational and policy issues related to the use and interpretation of intelligence tests in the schools. *School Psychology Review, 26*, 150–162.

Kreider, R. B., Fry, A. C., & O'Toole, M. L. (1998). Overtraining in sport. *International Journal of Sport Psychology, 27*(3), 269–285.

Kreiman, G., Koch, C., & Fried, I. (2000). Imagery neurons in the human brain. *Nature, 408*, 357–361.

Krell, R., & Sherman, M. I. (1997). *Medical and psychological effects of concentration camps on Holocaust survivors*. New Brunswick, NJ: Transaction.

Kremen, A. M., & Block, J. (1998). The roots of ego-control in young adulthood: Links with parenting in early childhood. *Journal of Personality and Social Psychology, 75*, 1062–1075.

Kring, A. M., & Gordon, A. H. (1998). Sex differences in emotion: Expression, experience, and physiology. *Journal of Personality and Social Psychology, 74*, 686–703.

Krisel, W. (2001). Letter to the editor. *Archives of Sexual Behavior, 30*, 457.

Krosnick, J. A., Jussim, L. J., & Lynn, A. R. (1992). Subliminal conditioning of attitudes. *Personality and Social Psychology Bulletin, 18*(2), 152–162.

Kruley, P., Sciama, S. C., & Glenberg, A. M. (1994). On-line processing of textual illustrations in the visuospatial sketchpad: Evidence from dual-task studies. *Memory and Cognition, 22*, 261–272.

Kuczaj, S. A. (1998). Is an evolutionary theory of language play possible? *Cahiers de Psychologie Cognitive, 17*, 135–154.

Kudoh, N., Tajima, H., Hatayama, T., Maruyama, K., Shoji, Y., Hayashi, T., & Nakanishi, M. (1991). Effects of room environment on human cognitive activities. *Tohoku Psychologica Folia, 50*, 45–54.

Kugihara, N. (1999). Gender and social loafing in Japan. *Journal of Social Psychology, 139*, 516–526.

Kuhl, P. K., Andruski, J. E., Chistovich, I. A., Chistovich, L. A., Kozhevnikova, E. V., Ryskina, V. L., Stolyarova, E. I., Sundberg, U., & Lacerda, F. (1997). Cross-language analysis of phonetic units in language addressed to infants. *Science, 277*, 684–686.

Kuiper, N. A., & Martin, R. A. (1998). Laughter and stress in daily life: Relation to positive and negative affect. *Motivation and Emotion, 22*(2), 133–153.

Kuncel, N. R., Hezlett, S. A., & Ones, D. S. (2001). A comprehensive meta-analysis of the predictive validity of the graduate record examinations: Implications for graduate student selection and performance. *Psychological Bulletin, 127*, 162–181.

Kupperbusch, C., Matsumoto, D., Kooken, K., Loewinger, S., Uchida, H., Wilson-Cohn, C., & Yrizarry, N. (1999). Cultural influences on nonverbal expressions of emotion. In P. Philippot & R. S. Feldman (Eds.), *The social context of nonverbal behavior: Studies in emotion and social interaction* (pp. 17–44). New York; Paris, France: Cambridge University Press: Editions de la Maison des Sciences de l'Homme.

Kurzban, R., Tooby, J., & Cosmides, L. (2001). Can race be erased? Coalitional computation and social categorization. *Proceedings of the National Academy of Science USA, 98*, 15387–15392.

Kush, R. R., & Fleming, L. M. (2000). An innovative approach to short-term cognitive therapy in the combined treatment of anxiety and depression. *Group Dynamics: Theory, Research, and Practice, 4*, 176–183.

Kutchins, H., & Kirk, S. A. (1997). *Making us crazy. DSM: The psychiatric bible and the creation of mental disorders*. New York: The Free Press.

Lachter, J., Durgin, F., & Washington, T. (2000). Disappearing percepts: Evidence for retention failure in metacontrast masking. *Visual Cognition, 7*, 269–279.

LaDue, R. (1994). Coyote returns: Twenty sweats does not an Indian expert make. *Women's Therapy, 15*, 1, 93–111.

LaFerla, J. J., Anderson, D. L., & Schalch, D. S. (1978). Psychoendocrine response to sexual arousal in human males. *Psychosomatic Medicine, 40*, 166–172.

Lafferty, P., Beutler, L. E., & Crago, M. (1989). Differences between more and less effective psychotherapists: A study of select therapist variables. *Journal of Consulting and Clinical Psychology, 57,* 76–80.

Laible, D. J., & Thompson, R. A. (2000). Mother-child discourse, attachment security, shared positive affect, and early conscience development. *Child Development, 71(5),* 1424–1440.

Laird, J. (2000). Culture and narrative as central metaphors for clinical practice with families. In D. H. Demo, K. R. Allen, & M. A. Fine (Eds.). *Handbook of family diversity* (pp. 338–358). New York: Oxford University Press.

Lakkis, J., Ricciardelli, L. A., & Williams, R. J. (1999). Role of sexual orientation and gender-related traits in disordered eating. *Sex Roles, 41,* 1–16.

Lakoff, R. T. (2000). *The language war.* Los Angeles: University of California Press.

Lam, R. W., & Levitan, R. D. (2000). Pathophysiology of seasonal affect disorder: A review. *Journal of Psychiatry & Neuroscience, 35, 5,* 469–480.

Lam, R. W., Tam, E. M., Yatham, L. N., Shiah, I., & Zis, A. P. (2001). Seasonal depression: The dual vulnerability hypothesis revisited. *Journal of Affective Disorders, 63,* 1–3, 123–132.

Lambert, A. J. (1995). Stereotypes and social judgment: The consequences of group variability. *Journal of Personality and Social Psychology, 68,* 388–403.

Lamerson, C. D. (2002). Psychology in the Canadian Forces. *Canadian Journal of Behavioural Science, 34,* 2, 71–74.

Landrine, H., Klonoff, E. A., & Brown-Collins, A. (1992). Cultural diversity and methodology in feminist psychology. *Psychology of Women Quarterly, 16,* 145–163.

Landy, S., & Tam, K. K. (1998). *Yes, parenting does make a difference to the development of children in Canada.* Growing Up in Canada: National Longitudinal Survey of Children and Youth. Ottawa: Human Resources Development Canada and Statistics Canada.

Laner, M. R., Benin, M. H., & Ventrone, N. A. (2001). Bystander attitudes toward victims of violence: Who's worth helping? *Deviant Behavior, 22,* 23–42.

Lang, P. J. (1994). The varieties of emotional experience: A meditation on James-Lange theory. *Psychological Review, 101,* 211–221.

Langdon, D., & Warrington, E. K. (2001). The role of the left hemisphere in verbal and spatial reasoning tasks. *Cortex, 36,* 691–702.

Lange, C. G. (1922). *The emotions* (English translation). Baltimore: Williams & Wilkins. (Original work published 1885.)

Langer, E. J., & Rodin, J. (1976). The effects of choice and enhanced personal responsibility for the aged: A field experiment in an institutional setting. *Journal of Personality and Social Psychology, 34,* 191–198.

Langer, L. L. (1991). *Holocaust testimonies: The ruins of memory.* New Haven, CT: Yale University Press.

Langlois, J. H., Ritter, J. M., Roggman, L. A., & Vaughn, L. S. (1991). Facial diversity and infant preferences for attractive faces. *Developmental Psychology, 27,* 79–84.

Langlois, J. H., Roggman, L. A., & Rieser-Danner, L. A. (1990). Infants' differential social responses to attractive and unattractive faces. *Developmental Psychology, 26,* 153–159.

Langman, B., & Cockburn, A. (1975). Sirhan's gun. *Harper's, 250,* 16–27.

Langlois, J. H., Roggman, L. A., & Musselman, L. (1994). What is average and what is not average about attractive faces? *Psychological Science, 5(4),* 214–220.

Lapp, J., & Attridge, M. (2000). Worksite interventions reduce stress among high school teachers and staff. *International Journal of Stress Management, 7,* 229–232.

Lapsley, D. K. (1993). Toward an integrated theory of adolescent ego development: The "new look" at adolescent egocentrism. *American Journal of Orthopsychiatry, 63(4),* 562–571.

La Roche, M. J. (1999). Culture, transference, and countertransference among Latinos. *Psychotherapy: Theory, Research, Practice, and Training, 36,* 389–397.

Larrick, R. P., Morgan, J. N., & Nisbett, R. E. (1990). Teaching the use of cost-benefit reasoning in everyday life. *Psychological Science, 1,* 362–370.

Larson, R., & Ham, M. (1993). Stress and "storm and stress" in early adolescence: The relationship of negative events with dysphoric affect. *Developmental Psychology, 29,* 130–140.

Larson, R., & Pleck, J. (1999). Hidden feelings: Emotionality in boys and men. In D. Bernstein (Ed.), *Nebraska Symposium on Motivation, 1999: Gender and motivation* (pp. 25–74). Lincoln: University of Nebraska Press.

Larson, R. W. (2000). Toward a psychology of positive youth development. *American Psychologist, 55,* 170–183.

Latané, B., & Darley, J. M. (1970). *The unresponsive bystander: Why doesn't he help?* New York: Meredith.

Latané, B., Williams, K., & Harkins, S. (1979). Many hands make light work: The causes and consequences of social loafing. *Journal of Personality and Social Psychology, 37,* 822–832.

Latham, G. P., Daghighi, S., & Locke, E. A. (1997). Implications of goal-setting theory for faculty motivation. In J. L. Bess et al. (Eds.), *Teaching well and liking it: Motivating faculty to teach effectively* (pp. 125–142). Baltimore, MD: Johns Hopkins University Press.

Laumann, E. O., Gagnon, J. H., Michael, R. T., & Michaels, S. (1994). *The social organization of sexuality: Sexual practices in the United States.* Chicago: The University of Chicago Press.

Laumann, E. O., & Mahay, J. (2002). The social organization of women's sexuality. In G. M. Wingood & R. J. DiClemente (Eds.), *Handbook of women's sexual and reproductive health: Issues in women health* (pp. 43–70). New York: Kluwer Academic/Plenum Publishers.

Laumann, E. O., Paik, A., & Rosen, R. C. (1999). Sexual dysfunction in the United States: Prevalence and predictors. *Journal of the American Medical Association, 281,* 537–544.

Laurent, G. (1999). A systems perspective on early olfactory coding. *Science, 286,* 723–728.

Lavie, P. (1996). *The enchanted world of sleep.* New Haven, CT and London: Yale University Press.

Lavie, P. (2001). Sleep-wake as a biological rhythm. *Annual Review of Psychology, 52,* 277–303.

Lawler, E. E., & Porter, L. W. (1967). Antecedent attitudes of effective managerial performance. *Organizational Behavior and Human Performance, 2,* 122–142.

Lawler, J. J., & Elliot, R. (1996). Artificial intelligence in HRM: An experimental study of an expert system. *Journal of Management, 22(1),* 85–111.

Lawrence, E., Eldridge, K., Christensen, A., & Jacobson, N. S. (1999). Intergrative couple therapy: The dyadic relationship of acceptance and change. In J. M. Donovan (Ed.), *Short-term couple therapy, The Guilford Family Therapy Series* (pp. 226–261). New York: Guilford Press.

Laws, D. R. (2001). Olfactory aversion: Notes on procedure, with speculation on its mechanism of effect. *Sexual Abuse: A Journal of Research and Treatment, 13,* 4, 275–287.

Lazarus, A. A., & Fay, A. (1990). Brief psychotherapy: Tautology or oxymoron? In J. K. Zeig & S. G. Gilligan (Eds.), *Brief therapy myths, methods, and metaphors.* New York: Brunner/Mazel.

Lazarus, R. S. (1991). *Emotion and adaptation.* New York: Oxford University Press.

Lazarus, R. S. (1993). From psychological stress to the emotions: A history of changing outlooks. *Annual Review of Psychology, 44,* 1–21.

Leahey, T. H. (1992). The mythical revolutions of American psychology. *American Psychologist, 47,* 308–318.

Lebow, J. L., & Gurman, A. S. (1995). Research assessing couple and family therapy. *Annual Review of Psychology, 46,* 27–57.

LeDoux, J. (1996). *The emotional brain: The mysterious underpinnings of emotional life.* New York: Simon and Schuster.

LeDoux, J. E. (1995). Emotion: Clues from the brain. *Annual Review of Psychology, 46,* 209–235.

LeDoux, J. E., & Phelps, E. A. (2000). Emotional networks in the brain. In M. Lewis & J. M. Haviland-Jones (Eds.), *Handbook of emotions* (2nd ed., pp. 157–172). New York: Guilford Press.

Lee, C., Ashford, S. J., & Bobko, P. (1990). Interactive effects of "Type A" behavior and perceived control on worker performance, job satisfaction, and somatic complaints. *Academy of Management Journal, 33,* 870–881.

Lee, M., Lei, A., & Sue, S. (2001). The current state of mental health research on Asian Americans. *Journal of Human Behavior in the Social Environment, 3,* 159–178.

Lee, T. M. C. (1996). Phototherapy for SAD: A meta-analytic review. *Dissertation Abstracts International: Section B: The Sciences & Engineering, 57,* 3-B, 1745.

Lefcourt, H. M. (1992). Durability and impact of the locus of control construct. *Psychological Bulletin, 112,* 411–414.

Lefcourt, H. M., & Davidson-Katz, K. (1991). Locus of control and health. In C. R. Snyder & D. R. Forsyth (Eds.), *Handbook of social and clinical psychology* (pp. 246–266). New York: Pergamon.

Lefcourt, H. M., & Thomas, S. (1998). Humor and stress revisited. In W. Ruch et al. (Eds.), *The sense of humor: Explorations of a personality characteristic. Humor research: 3* (pp. 179–202). Berlin: Walter De Gruyter.

Leibowitz, H. W. (1971). Sensory, learned, and cognitive mechanisms of size perception. *Annals of the New York Academy of Sciences, 1988,* 47–62.

Leikin, R., & Zaslavsky, O. (1997). Facilitating student interactions in mathematics in a cooperative learning setting. *Journal for Research in Mathematics Education, 28*(3), 331–354.

Lenneberg, E. H. (1967). *Biological foundations of language.* New York: Wiley.

Leon, M. (1992). The neurobiology of filial learning. *Annual Review of Psychology, 43,* 377–399.

Leonard, B. E. (2001). The immune system, depression, and the action of antidepressants. *Progress in Neuro-Psychopharmacology and Biological Psychiatry, 25,* 767–780.

Lesch, K. P., Bengel, D., Heils, A., Sabol, S. Z., Greenberg, B. D., Petri, S., Benjamin, J., Müller, C. R., Hamer, D. H., & Murphy, D. L. (1996). Association of anxiety-related traits with a polymorphism in the serotonin transporter gene regulatory region. *Science, 274,* 1527–1531.

Lester, B. M & Dreher, M. (1989). Effects of marijuana use during pregnancy on newborn cry. *Child Development, 60*(4), 765–771.

LeVay, S. (1991). A difference in hypothalamic structure between heterosexual and homosexual men. *Science, 253,* 1034–1037.

LeVay, S., & Hamer, D. H. (1994, May). Evidence for a biological influence in male homosexuality. *Scientific American,* 44–49.

Levi, L. (1990). Occupational stress. *American Psychologist, 46,* 1142–1145.

Levin, D. (2000). Race as a visual feature: Using visual search and perceptual discrimination tasks to understand face categories and the cross-race recognition deficit. *Journal of Experimental Psychology: General, 129,* 559–574.

Levin, D. J. (1990). *Alcoholism.* New York: Hemisphere.

Levine, E. L., Ash, R. A., Hall, H., & Sistrunk, F. (1983). Evaluation of job analysis methods by experienced job analysts. *Academy of Management Journal, 26,* 339–348.

Levine, M. (1998). Prevention and community. *American Journal of Community Psychology, 26*(2), 189–206.

Levine, R. L., & Stadtman, E. R. (1992). Oxidation of proteins during aging. *Generations, 16,* 39–42.

Levine, R. V., Martinez, T. S., Brase, G., & Sorenson, K. (1994). Helping in 36 U.S. cities. *Journal of Personality and Social Psychology, 67,* 69–82.

Levinson, D. J. (1978). *The seasons of a man's life.* New York: Knopf.

Levinson, D. J. (1980). Toward a conception of the adult life course. In N. J. Smelser & E. H. Erikson (Eds.), *Themes of work and love in adulthood.* Cambridge, MA: Harvard University Press.

Levinson, D. J. (1996). *The seasons of a woman's life.* New York: Alfred A. Knopf.

Levitt, A. J., Boyle, M. H., Joffe, R. T., & Baumal, Z. (2000). Estimated prevalence of the seasonal subtype of major depression in a Canadian community sample. *Canadian Journal of Psychiatry, 45,* 7, 650–654.

Levy, G. D. (1999). Gender-typed and non-gender-typed category awareness in toddlers. *Sex Roles, 41,* 851–873.

Lewin, K. K. (1970). *Brief psychotherapy.* St. Louis, MO: Warren H. Green.

Lewinsohn, P. M. (1974). Classical and theoretical aspects of depression. In I. S. Calhoun, H. E. Adams, & K. M. Mitchell (Eds.), *Innovative treatment methods in psychopathology.* New York: Wiley Interscience.

Lewinsohn, P. M., Rohde, P., Klein, D. N., & Seeley, J. R. (1999). Natural course of adolescent major depressive disorder: I. Continuity into young adulthood. *Journal of the American Academy of Child and Adolescent Psychiatry, 38*(1), 56–63.

Lewinsohn, P. M., Rohde, P., Klein, D. N., Seeley, J. R., & Fischer, S. A. (1993). Age-cohort changes in the lifetime occurrence of depression and other mental disorders. *Journal of Abnormal Psychology, 102*(1), 110–120.

Lewinsohn, P. M., & Talkington, J. (1979). Studies on the measurement of unpleasant events and relations with depression. *Applied Psychological Measurement, 3,* 83–101.

Lewis, M. (1995). Self-conscious emotions. *American Scientist, 83,* 68–78.

Lewis, M., & Feiring, C. (1989). Infant, mother, and mother-infant interaction behavior and subsequent attachment. *Child Development, 60,* 831–837.

Ley, P. (1997). Compliance among patients. In A. Baum, S. Newman, J. Weinman, R. West, & C. McManus (Eds.), *Cambridge handbook of psychology, health, and medicine* (pp. 281–284). Cambridge, UK: Cambridge University Press.

Li, H. Z., & Browne, A. J. (2000). Defining mental illness and accessing mental health services: Perspectives of Asian Canadians. *Canadian Journal of Community Mental Health, 19,* 1, 143–159.

Lidz, T. (1973). *The origin and treatment of schizophrenic disorders.* New York: Basic Books.

Lilienfield, S. O., Lynn, S. J., Kirsch, I., Chaves, J. F., Sarbin, T. R., Ganaway, G. K., & Powell, R. A. (1999). Dissociative identity disorders and the sociocognitive model: Recalling the lessons of the past. *Psychological Bulletin, 125,* 507–523.

Lilla, I., Szikriszt, E., Ortutay, J., Berecz, M., Gyoergy, F., & Attila, N. (1998). Psychological factors contributing to the development of coronary artery disease—a study of rigidity and the A-type behaviour pattern. *Psychiatria Hungarica, 13*(2), 169–180.

Lillo-Martin, D. (1997). The modular effects of sign language acquisition. In Marschark, M., Siple, P., et al. (Eds.), *Relations of language and thought* (pp. 62–109). New York: Oxford University Press.

Lilly, J. C. (1956). Mental effects of reduction of ordinary levels of physical stimuli on intact, healthy persons. *Psychiatric Research Reports. No. 5.* 1–9.

Lin, K. M. (2001). Biological differences in depression and anxiety across races and ethnic groups. *Journal of Clinical Psychiatry, 62* (Suppl. 13), 13–19.

Lin, Y., McKeachie, W. J., & Kim, Y. C. (2001). College student intrinsic and/or extrinsic motivation and learning. *Learning & Individual Differences, 13,* 3, 251–258.

Linberg, M. A., Beggs, A. L., Chezik, D. D., & Ray, D. (1982). Flavor-toxicosis associations: Tests of three hypotheses of long delay learning. *Physiology and Behavior, 29,* 439–442.

Lindfors, O., Hannula, J., Aalber, V., Kaarento, K., Kaipainen, M., & Pylkkaenen, K. (1995). Assessment of the effectiveness of psychotherapy. *Psychiatria Fennica, 26,* 150–164.

Link, B. G., Monahan, J., Stueve, A., & Cullen, F. T. (1999). Real in their consequences: A sociological approach to understanding the association between psychotic symptoms and violence. *American Sociological Review, 64,* 316 332.

Link, B. G., Phelan, J. C., Bresnahan, M., Stueve, A., & Pescosolido, B. A. (1999). Public conceptions of mental illness: Labels, causes, dangerousness, and social distance. *American Journal of Public Health, 89,* 1328–1333.

Linn, M. C., & Petersen, A. C. (1985). Emergence and characterization of sex differences in spatial ability: A meta-analysis. *Child Development, 56,* 1479–1498.

Lisanby, S. H., Maddox, J. H., Prudic, J., Devanand, D. P., & Sackeim, H. A. (2000). The effects of electroconvulsive therapy on memory of autobiographical and public events. *Archives of General Psychiatry, 57,* 581–590.

Livingstone, M. S. & Tsao, D. Y. (1999). Receptive fields of disparity-selective neurons in macaque striate cortex. *Nature Reviews Neuroscience, 2,* 825–832.

Locher, P., Unger, R., Sociedade, P., & Wahl, J. (1993). At first glance: Accessibility of the physical attractiveness stereotype. *Sex Roles, 28,* 729–743.

Locke, E. A. (1996). Motivation through conscious goal setting. *Allied and Preventive Psychology, 5*(2), 117–124.

Locke, E. A., & Latham, G. P. (1990a). Work motivation: The high performance cycle. In U. Kleinbeck, H. Quast, H. Thierry, & H. Hacker (Eds.), *Work motivation.* Hillsdale, NJ: Erlbaum.

Lockman, P., & Summers, R. (1999). Perceptions of poison: Ages four and seven. *Journal of Toxicology: Clinical Toxicology, 37,* 596.

Loeber, R., & Stouthamer-Loeber, M. (1998). Development of juvenile aggression and violence: Some common misconceptions and controversies. *American Psychologist, 53*(2), 242–259.

Loehlin, J. C. (1992). *Genes and environment in personality development.* Newbury Park, CA: Sage.

Loftus, E. F. (1979). The malleability of human memory. *American Scientist, 67,* 310–320.

LoLordo, V. M., & Taylor, T. L. (2001). Effects of uncontrollable aversive events: Some unsolved puzzles. In R. R. Mowrer & S. B. Klein (Eds.), *Handbook of contemporary learning theories* (pp. 119–154). Mahwah, NJ: Erlbaum.

Long, B. C. (1998). Coping with workplace stress: A multiple-group comparison of female managers and clerical workers. *Journal of Counseling Psychology, 45,* 65–78.

Longworth, C., Honey, G., & Sharma, T. (1999). Functional magnetic resonance imaging in neuropsychiatry. *British Medical Journal, 319,* 1551–1554.

Lore, R. K., & Schultz, L. A. (1993). Control of human aggression. *American Psychologist, 48,* 16–25.

Lorenz, K. (1964). Ritualized fighting. In J. D. Carthy & F. J. Ebling (Eds.), *The natural history of aggression.* New York: Academic Press.

Losa, E. G. (1999). Self-conditioned suppression in parenteral opiate drug addicts. *Psiquis: Revista de Psiquiatria, Psicologia Medica y Psicosomatica, 20,* 47–50.

Louie, K., & Wilson, M. A. (2001). Temporally structured replay of awake hippocampal ensemble activity during rapid eye movement sleep. *Neuron, 29,* 145–156.

Low, B. (2000). *Why sex matters.* Princeton, NJ: Princeton University Press.

Lowe, M. R., Gleaves, D. H., & Murphy-Eberenz, K. P. (1998). The relation of dieting and bingeing in bulimia nervosa. *Journal of Abnormal Psychology, 107*(2), 263–271.

Lowell, E. L. (1952). The effect of need for achievement on learning and speed of performance. *Journal of Psychology, 33,* 31–40.

Lubart, T. I. (1999). Creativity across cultures. In R. J. Sternberg (Ed.), *Handbook of creativity* (pp. 339–350). Cambridge, MA: Cambridge University Press.

Luger, G. F., Bower, T. G. R., & Wishart, J. G. (1983). A model of the development of the early infant object concept. *Perception, 12,* 21–34.

Lundin, R. W. (1961). *Personality: An experimental approach.* New York: Macmillan.

Luria, A. R. (1968). *The mind of the mnemonist.* New York: Basic Books.

Lush, J. L. (1937). *Animal breeding plans.* Ames, IA: Collegiate Press.

Lykken, D. T., McGue, M., Tellegen, A., & Bouchard, T. J., Jr. (1992). Emergenesis. *American Psychologist, 47,* 1565–1577.

Lymburner, J. A., & Roesch, R. (1999). The insanity defense: Five years of research (1993-1997). *International Journal of Law and Psychiatry, 22,* 213–240.

Lynn, M., & Mynier, K. (1993). Effect of server posture on restaurant tipping. *Journal of Applied Social Psychology, 23,* 678–685.

Lynn, R., & Martin, T. (1997). Gender differences in extraversion, neuroticism, and psychoticism in 37 nations. *Journal of Social Psychology, 137,* 369–373.

Lynn, S. J. (1992). A non-state view of hypnotic involuntariness. *Contemporary Hypnosis, 9*(1), 21–27.

Lynn, S. J., Lock, T. G., Myers, B., & Payne, D. G. (1997). Recalling the unrecallable: Should hypnosis be used to recover memories in psychotherapy? *American Psychological Society, 6*(3), 79–83.

Lyubomirsky, S., & Tucker, K. L. (1998). Implications of individual differences in subjective happiness for perceiving, interpreting, and thinking about life events. *Motivation and Emotion, 22*(2), 155–186.

Maas, J. B. (1998). *Power sleep.* New York: Villard.

Macaluso, E., Frith, C. D., & Driver, J. (2000). Modulation of human visual cortex by crossmodal spatial attention. *Science, 289,* 1206–1208.

Maccoby, E. E. (1998). *The two sexes: Growing up apart, coming together.* Cambridge, MA: Harvard University Press.

Maccoby, E. E. (2000). Perspectives on gender development. *International Journal of Behavioral Development, 24,* 398–406.

Machado, L., & Rafal, R. D. (2000). Strategic control over saccadic eye movements: Studies of the fixation offset effect. *Perception & Psychophysics, 62,* 1236–1242.

Machin, G. (1996). Some causes of genotypic and phenotypic discordance in monozygotic twin pairs. *American Journal of Medical Genetics, 61,* 216–228.

MacKay, N. J., & Covell, D. (1997). The impact of women in advertisements on attitudes toward women. *Sex Roles, 36*(9/10), 573–576.

MacLeod, C. M. (1991). Half a century of research on the Stroop effect: An integrative review. *Psychological Bulletin, 109,* 163–203.

MacWhinney, B. (1998). Models of the emergence of language. *Annual Review of Psychology, 49,* 199–227.

Maddux, J. E., & Meier, L. J. (1995). Self-efficacy and depression. In J. E. Maddux (Ed.), *Self-efficacy, adaptation, and adjustment: Theory, research, and application* (pp. 143–169). New York: Plenum.

Madigan, M. F., Jr., Dale, J. A., & Cross, J. D. (1997). No respite during sleep: Heart-rate hyperreactivity to rapid eye movement sleep in angry men classified as Type A. *Perceptual and Motor Skills, 85* (3, Pt. 2), 1451–1454.

Maguire, E. A., Burgess, N., Donnett, J. G., Frackowiak, R. S. J., Frith, C. D., & O'Keefe, J. (1998). Knowing where and getting there: A human navigation network. *Science, 280,* 921–924.

Mahoney, M. J. (1977). Reflections on the cognitive-learning trend in psychotherapy. *American Psychologist, 32,* 5–13.

Mahrer, A. R., & Nadler, W. P. (1986). Good moments in psychotherapy: A preliminary review, a list, and some promising research avenues. *Journal of Consulting and Clinical Psychology, 54,* 10–15.

Maier, N. R. F., & Klee, J. B. (1941). Studies of abnormal behavior in the rat: 17. Guidance versus trial and error and their relation to convulsive tendencies. *Journal of Experimental Psychology, 29,* 380–389.

Maier, S. F., Peterson, C., & Schwartz, B. (2000). From helplessness to hope: The seminal career of Martin Seligman. In J. E. Gillham (Ed.), *The science of optimism and hope: Research essays in honor of Martin E. P. Seligman. Laws of Life Symposia Series* (pp. 11–37). Philadelphia: Templeton Foundation Press.

Main, M., & Solomon, J. (1990). Procedures for identifying infants as disorganized/disoriented during the Ainsworth Strange Situation. In M. T. Greenberg, D. Cicchetti, et al. (Eds.). *Attachment in the preschool years: Theory, research, and intervention. The John D. and Catherine T. MacArthur Foundation series on mental health and development.* Chicago: University of Chicago Press.

Mainemer, H., Gilman, L. C., & Ames, E. W. (1998). Parenting stress in families adopting children from Romanian orphanages. *Journal of Family Issues, 19,* 2, 164–180.

Malamuth, N. M. (1996). The confluence model of sexual aggression: Feminist and evolutionary perspectives. In D. M. Buss & N. M. Malamuth (Eds.), *Sex, power, conflict: Evolutionary and feminist perspectives* (pp. 269–295). New York: Oxford University Press.

Malik, A., & Batra, P. (1998). Effect of crowding on a complex task. *Journal of Personality and Clinical Studies, 13*(1/2), 87–91.

Malinowski, J. C. (2001). Mental rotation and real-world wayfinding. *Perceptual and Motor Skills, 92,* 19–30.

Malle, B. F., Knobe, J., O'Laughlin, M. J., Pearce, G. E., & Nelson, S. E. (2000). Conceptual structure and social functions of behavior explanations beyond person–situation attributions. *Journal of Personality and Social Psychology, 79,* 309–326.

Malone, J. L. (2000). Working with Aboriginal women: Applying feminist therapy in a multicultural counselling context. *Canadian Journal of Counselling, 34,* 1, 33–42.

Mangan, B. (1993). Dennett, consciousness, and the sorrows of functionalism. *Consciousness and Cognition, 2,* 1–17.

Mann, J. J., Malone, D. M., Diehl, D. J., P., J., Cooper, T. B., & Mintun, M. A. (1996). Demonstration in vivo of reduced serotonin reponsivity in the brain of untreated depressed patients. *American Journal of Psychiatry, 153*(2), 174–182.

Mannuzza, S., Schneier, F. R., Chapman, T. F., Liebowitz, M. R., Klein, D. F., & Fyer, A. J. (1995). Generalized social phobia: Reliability and validity. *Archives of General Psychiatry, 52,* 230–237.

Maquet, P., Smith, C., & Stickgold, R. (2003). *Sleep and brain plasticity.* New York: Oxford University Press.

March, J. S., Leonard, H. L., & Swedo, S. E. (1995). Obsessive-compulsive disorder. In J. S. March (Ed.), *Anxiety disorders in children and adolescents* (pp. 251–275). New York: Guilford.

Marcia, J. E. (2002). Identity and psychosocial development in adulthood. *Identity, 2,* 1, 7–28.

Marcovitch, S., Goldberg, S., Handley-Derry, M., & MacGragor, D. (1994). *Recovery from early institutional care: Predictors of attachment and development for internationally adopted Romanian orphans.* Final report to Health Canada, Mental Health Division.

Marcus, G. F., Vijayan, S., Bandi, R., & Vishton, P. M. (1999). Rule learning by seven-month-old infants. *Science, 283,* 77–79.

Marini, Z., & Case, R. (1994). The development of abstract reasoning about the physical and social world. *Child Development, 65,* 1, 147–159.

Maris, R., & Silverman, M. M. (1995). *Suicide prevention: Toward the year 2000.* New York: Guilford.

Markowitsch, H. J. (2000). Neuroanatomy of memory. In E. Tulving & F. I. M. Craik (Eds.), *The Oxford handbook of memory* (pp. 465–484). New York: Oxford University Press.

Markowitsch, H. J., & Tulving, E. (1994). Cognitive processes and cerebral cortical fundi: Findings from positron-emission tomography studies. *Proceedings of the National Academy of Sciences of the United States of America, 91,* 10507–10511.

Marks, I. M. et al. (1986). *Behavioral psychotherapy: Pocketbook of clinical management.* Bristol, England: John Wright.

Marks, L. E. (2000). Synesthesia. In E. Cardena, S. J. Lynn, & S. Krippner (Eds.), *Varieties of anomalous experience: Examining the scientific evidence* (pp. 121–149). Washington, DC: American Psychological Association.

Marks, W. B., Dobell, W. H., & MacNichol, J. R. (1964). The visual pigments of single primate cones. *Science, 142,* 1181–1183.

Marlatt, G. A., Larimer, M. E., Baer, J. S., & Quigley, L. A. (1993). Harm reduction for alcohol problems: Moving beyond the controlled drinking. *Behavior Therapy, 24,* 461–504.

Marschark, M., Yuille, J. C., Richman, C. L., & Hunt, R. R. (1987). The role of imagery in memory: On shared and distinctive information. *Psychological Bulletin, 102,* 28–41.

Martenyi, F., Dossenbach, M., Mraz, K., & Metcalfe, S. (2001). Gender differences in the efficacy of fluoxetime and maprotiline in depressed patients. A double-blind trial of antidepressants with serotonergic reuptake inhibition profile. *European-Neuropsychopharmacology, 11,* 227–232.

Martin, R., & Haroldson, S. (1977). Effect of vicarious punishment on stuttering frequency. *Journal of Speech and Hearing Research, 20,* 21–26.

Martin, C. L. (2000). Cognitive theories of gender development. In T. Eckes, H. M. Trautner, and others, *The Developmental Social Psychology of Gender* (91–121). Mahwah, NJ: Lawrence Erlbaum Associates, Inc.

Martino, G., & Marks, L. E. (2001). Synesthesia: Strong and weak. *Current Directions in Psychological Science, 10,* 61–65.

Marucha, P. T., Kiecolt-Glaser, J. K., & Favagehi, M. (1998). Mucosal wound healing is impaired by examination stress. *Psychosomatic Medicine, 60,* 362–365.

Masia, C. L., & Chase, P. N. (1997). Vicarious learning revisited: A contemporary behavior analytic interpretation. *Journal of Behavior Therapy and Experimental Psychiatry, 28*(1), 41–51.

Masotto, C., & Racagni, G. (1995). Biological aspects of schizophrenia. *Rivista di Psichiatria, 30*(4), 34–46.

Masters, W. H., Johnson, V. E., & Kolodny, R. C. (1994). *Heterosexuality.* New York: HarperCollins.

Maté, G. (2003). Who really should take a time-out. *Globe and Mail,* 1 March, F9.

Mather, K. (1949). *Biometrical genetics: A study of continuous variation.* London: Methuen.

Mathews, F. (1990). *An exploratory typology of youth gangs in Metropolitan Toronto.* Toronto: Central Toronto Youth Services.

Mathews, F. (1993). *Youth gangs on youth gangs.* Ottawa: Minister of Supply and Services.

Matsui, T., & Onglatco, M. L. U. (1990). Relationships between employee quality circle involvement and need fulfillment in work as moderated by work type: A compensatory or a spillover model? In U. Kleinbeck, H. Quast, H. Thierry, & H. Hacker (Eds.), *Work motivation.* Hillsdale, NJ: Erlbaum.

Matsumoto, D. (1994). *People: Psychology from a cultural perspective.* Pacific Grove, CA: Brooks/Cole.

Matsumoto, D. (2000). Culture and self: An empirical assessment of Markus and Kitayama's theory of independent and interdependent self-construal. *Asian Journal of Social Psychology, 2,* 289–310.

Matsumoto, D., & Kudoh, T. (1993). American-Japanese cultural differences in attributions of personality based on smiles. *Journal of Nonverbal Behavior, 17,* 231–243.

Matthews, K., Owens, J., Kuller, L., Sutton-Tyrell, K., & Jansen-McWilliams, L. (1998). Are hostility and anxiety associated with carotid atherosclerosis in healthy postmenopausal women? *Psychosomatic Medicine, 60,* 633–638.

Max, D. T. (2001, May 6). To sleep no more. *New York Times.* Retrieved May 10, 2001 from the World Wide Web: www.nytimes.com/2001/05/06/magazine/06INSOMNIA.html.

Mayer, J. D., Salovey, P., & Caruso, D. (2000). Models of emotional intelligence. In R. J. Sternberg (Ed.). *Handbook of intelligence* (pp. 396–420). New York: Cambridge University Press.

Mazure, C. M., Bruce, M., Maciejewski, P. K., & Jacobs, S. C. (2000). Adverse life events and cognitive-personality characteristics in the prediction of major depression and antidepressant response. *American Journal of Psychiatry, 157,* 896–903.

McBride, A. B. (1990). Mental health effects of women's multiple roles. *American Psychologist, 45,* 381–384.

McBurney, D. H., Gaulin, S. J. C., Devineni, T., & Adams, C. (1997). Superior spatial memory of women: Stronger evidence for the gathering hypothesis. *Evolution & Human Behavior, 18,* 165–174.

McCall, V. W., Reboussin, B. A., Cohen, W., & Lawton, P. (2001). Electroconvulsive therapy is associated with superior symptomatic and functional change in depressed patients after psychiatric hospitalization. *Journal of Affective Disorders, 63,* 17–25.

McCann, I. L., & Pearlman, L. A. (1990). *Psychological trauma and the adult survivor: Theory, therapy and transformation.* New York: Brunner/Mazel.

McCartney, K., Harris, M. J., Bernieri, F. (1990). Growing up and growing apart: A developmental meta-analysis of twin studies. *Psychological Bulletin, 107,* 226–237.

McCaul, K. D., Gladue, B. A., & Joppa, M. (1992). Winning, losing, mood, and testosterone. *Hormones and Behavior, 26,* 486–504.

McCaul, K. D., Jacobson, K., & Martinson, B. (1998). The effects of a state-wide media campaign on mammography screening. *Journal of Applied Social Psychology, 28*(6), 504–515.

McCauley, C. (1989). The nature of social influence in groupthink: Compliance and internalization. *Journal of Personality and Social Psychology, 57,* 250–260.

McClearn, G. E., Johansson, B., Berg, S., Pedersen, N. L., Ahern, F., Petrill, S. A., & Plomin, R. (1997). Substantial genetic influence on cognitive abilities in twins 80 or more years old. *Science, 276,* 1560–1563.

McClelland, D. C. (1958). Methods of measuring human motivation. In J. W. Atkinson (Ed.), *Motives in fantasy, action, and society.* Princeton, NJ: Van Nostrand.

McClelland, D. C. (1961). *The achieving society.* Princeton, NJ: Van Nostrand.

McClelland, D. C. (1998). Identifying competencies with behavioral-event interviews. *Psychological Science, 9,* 331–339.

McClintock, M. K. (1971). Menstrual synchrony and suppression. *Nature, 229,* 244–245.

McClintock, M. K. (1996). Menstrual synchrony and suppression. *Foundations of Animal Behavior: Classic Papers with Commentaries,* 438–439. Chicago: University of Chicago Press.

McConkey, K. M., & Kinoshita, S. (1988). The influence of hypnosis on memory after one day and one week. *Journal of Abnormal Psychology, 97,* 48–53.

McCormick, E. J., Jeanneret, P. R., & Mecham, R. C. (1972). A study of job characteristics and job dimensions as based on the Position Analysis Questionnaire (PAQ) [Monograph]. *Journal of Applied Psychology, 56,* 347–368.

McCormick, L., Nielsen, T., Ptito, M., & Hassainia, F. (1997). REM sleep dream mentation in right hemispherectomized patients. *Neuropsychologia, 35*(5), 695–701.

McCormick, R. (1998). The facilitation of healing for the First Nations people of British Columbia. *Canadian Journal of Native Education, 21,* 2, 251–322.

McCormick, R. (2000). Aboriginal traditions in the treatment of substance abuse: Let the good spirits guide you. *Canadian Journal of Counselling, 34,* 1, 25–32.

McCracken, L. M. (1997). "Attention" to pain in persons with chronic pain: A behavioral approach. *Behavior Therapy, 28,* 271–284.

McCrady, B. S. (1994). Alcoholics anonymous and behavior therapy: Can habits be treated as diseases? Can diseases be treated as habits? *Journal of Consulting and Clinical Psychology, 62,* 1159–1166.

McCrae, R. R., & Costa, P. T. (1999). A Five Factor theory of personality. In L. A. Pervin & O. P. John (Eds.). *Handbook of personality theory and research* (pp. 139–153). New York: Guilford Press.

McCrae, R. R., & Costa, P. T., Jr. (1997). Personality trait structure as a human universal. *American Psychologist, 52,* 509–516.

McCrae, R. R., Costa, P. T., Jr., Del Pilar, G. H., Rolland, J. P., & Parker, W. D. (1998). Cross-cultural assessment of the five-factor model: The revised NEO personality inventory. *Journal of Cross-Cultural Psychology, 29*(1), 171–188.

McCrae, R. R., Costa, P. T., Jr., Hrebickova, M., Ostendorf, F., Angleitner, A., Avia, M. D., Sanz, J., Sanchez-Bernardos, M. L., Kusdil, M. E., Woodfield, R., Saunders, P. R., & Smith, P. B. (2000). Nature over nurture: Temperament, personality, and life span development. *Journal of Personality and Social Psychology, 78,* 173–186.

McCubbin, M., & Cohen, D. (1999). Empirical, ethical, and political perspectives on the use of methylphenidate. *Ethical Human Sciences and Services, 1,* 81–101.

McDermott, D. (2001). Parenting and ethnicity. In Marvin J. Fine, S. W. Lee, *Handbook of Diversity in Parent Education: The Changing Faces of Parenting and Parent Education* (73–96). San Diego, CA: Academic Press, Inc.

McEwen, B. S. (1999). Lifelong effects of hormones on brain development: Relationship to health and disease. In L.A. Schmidt & J. Schulkin, (Eds), *Extreme Fear, Shyness, and Social Phobia: Origins, Biological Mechanisms, and Clinical Outcomes,* pp. 173–192. Oxford University Press, Series in Affective Science.

McGaugh, J. L. (2002). The amygdala regulates memory consolidation. In L. R. Squire & D. L. Schacter (Eds.), *Neuropsychology of memory* (3rd ed) (pp. 437–449). New York: Guilford Press.

McGill, M. E., & Slocum, J. W., Jr. (1998). A little leadership, please? *Organizational Dynamics, 26*(3), 39–49.

McGinty, D., & Szymusiak, R. (1988). Neuronal unit activity patterns in behaving animals: Brainstem and limbic system. *Annual Review of Psychology, 39,* 135–168.

McGlone, J., & Wands, K. (1991). Self-report of memory function in patients with temporal lobe epilepsy and temporal lobectomy. *Cortex, 27,* 1, 19–28.

McGue, M., & Bouchard, T. J. (2000). Genetic and environmental influences on human behavioral differences. *Annual Review of Neuroscience, 21,* 1–24.

McGuffin, P., Rijsdijk, F., Andrew, M., Sham, P., Katz, R., & Cardno, A. (2003). The heritability of bipolar affective disorder and the genetic relationship to unipolar depression. *Archives of General Psychiatry, 60,* 497–502.

McGuffin, P., Riley, B., & Plomin, R. (2001, February 16). Toward behavioral genomics. *Science, 291,* 1232–1249.

McGuire, S., & Clifford, J. (2000). Genetic and environmental contributions to loneliness in children. *Psychological Science, 11,* 487–491.

McHale, S., Updegraff, K. A., Helms-Erikson, H., & Crouter, A. C. (2001). Sibling influences on gender development in middle childhood and early adolescence: A longitudinal study. *Developmental Psychology, 37,* 115–125.

McKeachie, W. J. (2003). William James's talks to teachers (1899) and McKeachie's teaching tips (1999). *Teaching of Psychology, 30,* 1, 40–43.

McKelvey, M. W., & McKenry, P. C. (2000). The psychosocial well-being of black and white mothers following marital dissolution. *Psychology of Women Quarterly, 24,* 4–14.

McKelvie, S. J. (1984). Relationship between set and functional fixedness: A replication. *Perceptual and Motor Skills, 58*(3), 996–998.

McKenna, K. Y. A., & Bargh, J. A. (2000). Plan 9 from cyberspace: The implications of the Internet for personality. *Personality and Social Psychology Review, 4,* 1, 57–75.

McKenzie, B. E., Tootell, H. E., & Day, R. H. (1980). Development of visual size constancy during the 1st year of human infancy. *Developmental Psychology, 16,* 163–174.

McKenzie, D. (1997). *Canadian profile: Alcohol, tobacco, and other drugs.* Ottawa: Canadian Centre on Substance Abuse.

McLaughlin, L. A., & Braun, K. L. (1998). Asian and Pacific islander cultural values: Considerations for health care decision making. *Health and Social Work, 23,* 116–126.

McLoyd, V. C. (1998). Socioeconomic disadvantage and child development. *American Psychologist, 53*(2), 185–204.

McLynn, F. (1997). *Carl Gustav Jung: A biography.* New York: St. Martin's Press.

McMahon, T. J., & Luthar, S. S. (2000). Women in treatment: Within gender differences in the clinical presentation of opioid-dependent women. *Journal of Nervous and Mental Disease, 88,* 679–687.

McManus, I. C., Porac, C., Bryden, M. P., & Boucher, R. (1999). Eye-dominance, writing hand, and throwing hand. *Laterality, 4,* 2, 173–192.

McNally, R. J. (1994). Cognitive bias in panic disorder. *Current Directions in Psychological Science, 3,* 129–132.

McNally, R. J., Hornig, C. D., Otto, M. W., & Pollack, M. H. (1997). Selective encoding of threat in panic disorder: Application of a dual priming paradigm. *Behaviour Research and Therapy, 35*(6), 543–549.

McNeil, J. E., & Warrington, E. K. (1993). Prosopagnosia: A face-specific disorder. *The Quarterly Journal of Experimental Psychology, 46A*(1), 1–10.

McNeill, D. (1970). Explaining linguistic universals. In J. Morton (Ed.), *Biological and social factors in psycholinguistics.* London: Logos.

Meadows, S. (1998). Children learning to think: Learning from others? Vygotskian theory and educational psychology. *Educational and Child Psychology, 15*(2), 6–13.

Mecklinger, A. (2000). Interfacing mind and brain: A neurocognitive model of recognition memory. *Psychophysiology, 37,* 565–582.

Mehlhorn, G., Holborn, M., & Schliebs, R. (2000). Induction of cytokines in glial cells surrounding cortical beta-amyloid plaques in transgenic Tg2576 mice with Alzheimer pathology. *International Journal of Developmental Neuroscience, 18,* 423–431.

Meichenbaum, D. (1974). *Cognitive behavior modification.* Morristown, NJ: General Learning.

Meichenbaum, D. (1993). Changing conceptions of cognitive behavior modification: Retrospect and prospect. *Journal of Consulting and Clinical Psychology, 61,* 202-204.

Meichenbaum, D., & Cameron, R. (1973). Training schizophrenics to talk to themselves: A means of developing attentional controls. *Behavior Therapy, 4,* 515–534.

Meichenbaum, D., & Cameron, R. (1983). Stress inoculation training: Toward a general paradigm for training coping skills. In D. Meichenbaum & M. E. Jaremko (Eds.), *Stress reduction and prevention* (pp. 115–154). New York: Plenum.

Meinz, E. J., & Salthouse, T. A. (1997). The effects of age and experience on memory for visually presented music. *Journals of Gerontology Series B—Psychological Sciences and Social Sciences, 53B*(1), P60–P69.

Melfi, C. A., Croghan, T. W., Hanna, M. P., & Robinson, R. L. (2000). Racial variation in antidepressant treatment in a Medicaid population. *Journal of Clinical Psychiatry, 61,* 16–21.

Melton, G. B., Petrila, J., Poythress, N. G., & Slobogin, C. (1987). *Psychological evaluations for the courts.* New York: Guilford.

Meltzoff, A. N. (1988). Imitation of televised models by infants. *Child Development, 59,* 1221–1229.

Meltzoff, A. N. (1996). The human infant as imitative generalist: A 20–year progress report on infant imitation with implications for comparative psychology. In C. M. Heyes et al. (Eds.), *Social learning in animals: The roots of culture.* San Diego, CA: Academic Press.

Meltzoff, A. N., & Moore, M. K. (2001). "Discovery procedures" for people and things—The role of representation and identity. In F. Lacerda, C. von Hofsten, & M. Heimann (Eds.), *Emerging cognitive abilities in early infancy* (pp. 213–230). Mahwah, NJ: Erlbaum.

Melville, J. (1977). *Phobias and obsessions,* Putnam Pub Group.

Melzack, R. (1990, February). The tragedy of needless pain. *Scientific American,* 27–33.

Melzack, R. (1999). From the gate to the neuromatrix. *Pain* (Suppl. 6), S121–S126.

Melzack, R. & Wall, P. D. (1965). Pain mechanisms: A new theory. *Science, 150,* 971–979.

Merikle, P. M. (2000). Subliminal perception. In A. E. Kazdin (Ed.), *Encyclopedia of Psychology,* Vol. 7 (pp 497-499). New York: Oxford University Press.

Merrill, S. S., & Verbrugge, L. M. (1999). Health and disease in midlife. In S. L. Willis & J. D. Reid (Eds.), *Life in the middle: Psychological and social development in middle age* (pp. 77–103). San Diego, CA: Academic Press.

Merton, R. K. (1949). Merton's typology of prejudice and discrimination. In R. M. MacIver (Ed.), *Discrimination and national welfare.* New York: Harper & Row.

Merzenich, M. M., Jenkins, W. M., Johnston, P., Schreiner, C., Miller, S. L., & Tallal, P. (1996). Temporal processing deficits of language-learning impaired children ameliorated by training. *Science, 271,* 77–81.

Mesquita, B. (2001). Emotions in collectivist and individualist contexts. *Journal of Personality and Social Psychology, 80,* 68–74.

Messer, S. B., & Wachtel, P. L. (1997). The contemporary psychotherapeutic landscape: Issues and prospects. In P. L. Wachtel & S. B. Messer, (Eds.), *Theories of psychotherapy: Origins and evolution* (pp. 1–27). Washington, DC: American Psychological Association.

Metcalfe, J., Funnell, M., & Gazzaniga, M. S. (1995). Right-hemisphere memory superiority: Studies of a split-brain patient. *Psychological Science, 6,* 157–164.

Meyer, R. G., & Salmon, P. (1988). *Abnormal psychology* (2nd ed.). Boston: Allyn & Bacon.

Meyers-Levy, J., & Maheswaran, D. (1991). Exploring differences in males' and females' processing strategies. *Journal of Consumer Research, 18,* 63–70.

Micallef, J., & Blin, O. (2001). Neurobiology and clinical pharmacology of obsessive–compulsive disorder. *Clinical-Neuropharmacology, 24,* 191–207.

Michael, R. T., Wadsworth, J., Feinleib, H., Johnson, A. M., Laumann, E. O., & Wellings, K. (1998). Private sexual behavior, public opinion, and public health policy related to sexually transmitted diseases: A U.S.-British comparison. *American Journal of Public Health, 88(5),* 749–754.

Michalos, A. C., & Zumbo, B. D. (2001). Ethnicity, modern prejudice and the quality of life. *Social Indicators Research, 53,* 189–222.

Miczek, K. A., Mirsky, A. F., Carey, G., Debold, J., & Raine, A. (2001). An overview of biological influences on violent behavior. In D. P. Barash (Ed.), *Understanding violence* (pp. 31–46). Boston: Allyn and Bacon.

Middaugh, S. J. (1990). On clinical efficacy: Why biofeedback does—and does not—work. *Biofeedback and Self-Regulation, 15,* 191–208.

Middleton, B., Arendt, J., & Stone, B. M. (1997). Complex effects of melatonin on human circadian rhythms in constant dim light. *Journal of Biological Rhythms, 12(5),* 467–477.

Miklowitz, D. J. (1994). Family risk indicators in schizophrenia. *Schizophrenia Bulletin, 20,* 137–150.

Miles, D. R., & Carey, G. (1997). Genetic and environmental architecture of human aggression. *Journal of Personality and Social Psychology, 72,* 207–217.

Milgram, S. (1963). Behavioral study of obedience. *Journal of Abnormal and Social Psychology, 67,* 371–378.

Milgram, S. (1965). Liberating effects of group pressure. *Journal of Personality and Social Psychology, 1,* 127–134.

Millar, M. G., & Millar, K. (1990). Attitude change as a function of attitude type and argument type. *Journal of Personality and Social Psychology, 39,* 217–228.

Miller, G. A. (1956). The magical number seven plus or minus two: Some limits on our capacity for processing information. *Psychological Review, 63,* 81–97.

Miller, G. A. (1965). Some preliminaries to psycholinguistics. *American Psychologist, 20,* 15–20.

Miller, J. (2000). Measurement error in subliminal perception experiments: Simulation analyses of two regression methods. *Journal of Experimental Psychology: Human Perception & Performance, 26,* 1461–1477.

Miller, J. G., & Bersoff, D. M. (1999). Development in the context of everyday family relationships: Culture, interpersonal morality, and adaptation. In M. Killen & D. Hart (Eds.). *Morality in everyday life* (pp. 259–282).

Miller, L. C. (1990). Intimacy and liking: Mutual influence and the role of unique relationships. *Journal of Personality and Social Psychology, 59,* 50–60.

Miller, M. E., & Bowers, K. S. (1993). Hypnotic analgesia: Dissociated experience or dissociated control? *Journal of Abnormal Psychology, 102,* 29–38.

Miller, N. E. (1944). Experimental studies of conflict. In J. M. Hunt (Ed.), *Personality and behavioral disorders* (Vol. 1). New York: Ronald Press.

Miller, N. E. (1959). Liberalization of basic S-R concepts: Extensions to conflict behavior, motivation, and social learning. In S. Koch (Ed.), *Psychology: A study of a science* (Vol. 2). New York: McGraw-Hill.

Miller, N. E. (1969). Learning of visceral and glandular responses. *Science, 163,* 434–445.

Miller, P. F., Light, K. C., Bragdon, E. E., Ballenger, M. N., Herbst, M. C., Maixner, W., Hinderliter, A. L., Atkinson, S. S., Koch, G. G., & Sheps, D. S. (1993). Beta-endorphin response to exercise and mental stress in patients with ischemic heart disease. *Journal of Psychosomatic Research, 37,* 455–465.

Miller, P. H., & Aloise, P. A. (1989). Young children's understanding of the psychological causes of behavior: A review. *Child Development, 60,* 257–285.

Miller, P. J. O., & Bain, D. E. (2000). Whining-pod variation in the sound production of a pod of killer whales, *Orcinus orca. Animal Behavior, 60,* 617–628.

Miller, R. P., Cosgrove, J. M., & Doke, L. (1990). Motivating adolescents to reduce their fines in a token economy. *Adolescence, 25,* 97–104.

Milner, B. (1966). Amnesia following operation on the temporal lobes. In C. W. M. Whitty & O. L. Zangwill (Eds.), *Amnesia.* London: Butterworth.

Milner, B., Corkin, S., & Teuber, H. L. (1968). Further analysis of hippocampal amnesic syndrome: 14–year follow-up study of H. M. *Neuropsychologia, 6,* 215–234.

Milner, P. M. (1991). Brain stimulation reward: A review. *Canadian Journal of Psychology, 45,* 1–36.

Milton, J., & Wiseman, R. (1999). Does psi exist? Lack of replication of an anomalous process of information transfer. *Psychological Bulletin, 125,* 4, 387–391

Mindell, J. A. (1999). Empirically supported treatments in pediatric psychology: Bedtime refusal and night wakings in young children. *Journal of Pediatric Psychology. Vol 24(6),* 465–481.

Mineka. (1992). Evolutionary memories, emotional processing, and the emotional disorders. *The Psychology of Learning and Motivation, 28,* 161–206.

Mischel, W. (1999). Personality coherence and dispositions in a cognitive-affective personality system (CAPS) approach. In D. Cervone & Y. Shoda (Eds.), *The coherence of personality: Social– cognitive bases of consistency, variability, and organization* (pp. 37–66). New York: Guilford Press.

Mischel, W., & Shoda, Y. (1998). Reconciling processing dynamics and personality dispositions. *Annual Review of Psychology, 49,* 229–258.

Mischel, W., & Shoda, Y. (1999). Integrating dispositions and processing dynamics within a unified theory of personality: The cognitive–affective personality system. In L. A. Pervin & O. P. John (Eds.), *Handbook of personality: Theory and research* (pp. 197–218). New York: Guilford Press.

Miscrandino, M. (1998). Attributional retraining as a method of improving athletic performance. *Journal of Sport Behavior, 21(3),* 286–297.

Mishima, K., Okawa, M., Hishikawa, Y., Hozumi, S., Hori, H., & Takahashi, K. (1994). Morning bright light therapy for sleep and behavior disorders in elderly patients with dementia. *Acta Psychiatrica Scandinavica, 89,* 1–7.

Mishler, E. G., & Waxler, N. E. (1968). Family interaction processes and schizophrenia: A review of current theories. In E. G. Mishler & N. E. Waxler (Eds.), *Family processes and schizophrenia.* New York: Science House.

Mitchell, K. J., Johnson, M. K., Raye, C. L., & D'Esposito, M. (2000). FMRI evidence of age-related hippocampal dysfunction in feature binding in working memory. *Cognitive Brain Research, 10(1–2),* 197–206.

Mitler, M. M., Miller, J. C., Lipsitz, J. J., & Walsh, J. K. (1997). The sleep of long-haul truck drivers. *New England Journal of Medicine, 337(11),* 755–761.

Mohr, D., Likosky, W., Bertagnolli, A., Goodkin, D., Van Der Wende, J., Dwyer, P., & Dick, L. (2000). Telephone administered cognitive–behavioral therapy for the treatment of depressive symptoms in multiple sclerosis. *Journal of Consulting and Clinical Psychology, 68,* 356–361.

Mokdad, A. H., Serdula, M. K., Dietz, W. H., Bowman, B. A., Marks, J. S., & Kaplan, J. P. (2000). The continuing epidemic of obesity in the United States. *Journal of the American Medical Association, 284,* 1650–1651.

Molnar, B. E., Buka, S. L., & Kessler, R. C. (2001). Child sexual abuse and subsequent psychopathology: Results from the National Comorbidity Survey. *American Journal of Public Health, 91,* 753–760.

Monahan, J. L., Murphy, S. T., & Zajonc, R. B. (2000). Subliminal mere exposure: Specific, general, and diffuse effects. *Psychological Science, 11,* 462–466.

Moncrieff, J. (1997). Lithium: Evidence reconsidered. *British Journal of Psychiatry, 171,* 113–119.

Monnier, J., Stone, B. K., Hobfoll, S. E., & Johnson, R. J. (1998). How antisocial and prosocial coping influence the support process among men and women in the U.S. Postal Service. *Sex Roles, 39,* 1–19.

Monteith, M. J., Zuwerink, J. R., & Devine, P. G. (1994). Prejudice and prejudice reduction: Classic challenges, contemporary approaches. In P. G. Devine (Ed.), *Social cognition: Impact on social psychology.* San Diego, CA: Academic Press, Inc.

Monteleone, P., Luisi, M., Colurcio, B., Casarosa, E., Monteleone, P., Ioime, R., Genazzani, A. R., & Maj, M. (2001). Plasma levels of neuroactive steroids are increased in untreated women with anorexia nervosa or bulimia nervosa. *Psychosomatic Medicine, 63,* 62–68.

Montepare, J. M., & Zebrowitz-McArthur, L. (1988). Impressions of people created by age-related qualities of their gaits. *Journal of Personality and Social Psychology, 55,* 547–556.

Montgomery, D., Miville, M. L., Winterowd, C., Jeffries, B., & Baysden, M. F. (2000). American Indian college students: An exploration into resiliency factors revealed through personal stories. *Cultural Diversity and Ethnic Minority Psychology, 6,* 387–398.

Montgomery, G. H., & Bovbjerg, D. H. (1997). The development of anticipatory nausea in patients receiving adjuvant chemotherapy for breast cancer. *Psychology & Behavior, 61,* 737–741.

Montgomery, G. H., Tomoyasu, N., Bovbjerg, D. H., Andrykowski, M. A., Currie, V. E., Jacobsen, P. B., & Redd, W. H. (1998). Patients' pretreatment expectations of chemotherapy-related nausea are an independent predictor of anticipatory nausea. *Annals of Behavioral Medicine, 20,* 104–108.

Montgomery-St. Laurent, T., Fullenkamp, A. M., & Fischer, R. B. (1988). A role for the hamster's flank gland in heterosexual communication. *Physiology and Behavior, 44,* 759–762.

Moore, T. E. (1995). Subliminal self-help auditory tapes: An empirical test of perceptual consequences. *Canadian Journal of Behavioural Science, 27*(1), 9–20.

Moorhead, G., Ference, R., & Neck, C. P. (1991). Group decision fiascoes continue: Space shuttle challenger and a revised groupthink framework. *Human Relations, 44*(6), 539–550.

Morgan, C. A., III, Kingham, P., Nicolaou, A., & Southwick, S. M. (1998). Anniversary reactions in Gulf War veterans: A naturalistic inquiry 2 years after the Gulf War. *Journal of Traumatic Stress, 11*(1), 165–171.

Morgan, D. G., & Stewart, N. J. (1998). High versus low density special care units: Impact on the behaviour of elderly residents with dementia. *Canadian Journal on Aging, 17*(2), 143–165.

Morgan, W. P. (1992). Hypnosis and sport psychology. In J. Rhue, S. J. Lynn, & I. Kirsch (Eds.), *Handbook of clinical hypnosis.* Washington, DC: American Psychological Association.

Morin, C. M., Stone, J., McDonald, K., & Jones, S. (1994). Psychological management of insomnia: A clinical replication series with 100 patients. *Behavior Therapy, 25,* 291–309.

Morren, M. (1998). Hostility as a risk factor for coronary heart disease. *Psycholoog, 33*(3), 101–108.

Morris, C. D., Bransford, J. D., & Franks, J. J. (1977). Levels of processing versus transfer appropriate processing. *Journal of Verbal Learning and Verbal Behavior, 16*(5), 519–533.

Morris, M. W., & Peng, K. (1994). Culture and cause: American and Chinese attributions for social and physical events. *Journal of Personality and Social Psychology, 67,* 949–971.

Moscovitch, M., & Winocur, G. (1995). Frontal lobes, memory, and aging. In J. Grafman, K. J. Holyoak et al. (Eds.), *Structure and functions of the human prefrontal cortex. Annals of the New York Academy of Sciences, Vol. 769* (pp. 119–150).

Moser, E. I., Krobert, K. A., Moser, M. B., & Morris, R. G. (1998). Impaired spatial learning after saturation of long-term potentiation. *Science, 281,* 2038–2042.

Moskowitz, B. A. (1978, November). The acquisition of language. *Scientific American,* 92–108.

Most, S. B., Simons, D. J., Scholl, B. J., Jimenez, R., Clifford, E., & Chabris, C. F. (2001). How not to be seen: The contribution of similarity and selective ignoring to sustained inattentional blindness. *Psychological Science, 12,* 9–17.

Mottron, L., Belleville, S., Stip, E., & Morasse, K. (1998). Atypical memory performance in an autistic savant, *Memory, 6,* 6, 593–607.

MRC, NSERC, & SSHRC (1998). *Tri-council policy statement: Ethical conduct for research involving humans.* Ottawa: MRC, NSERC, SSHRC.

Mueser, K. T., Bellack, A. S., Morrison, R. L., & Wade, J. H. (1990). Gender, social competence, and symptomatology in schizophrenia: A longitudinal analysis. *Journal of Abnormal Psychology, 99,* 138–147.

Mullen, B., Anthony, T., Salas, E., & Driskell, J. E. (1994). Group cohesiveness and quality of decision making: An integration of tests of the groupthink hypothesis. *Small Group Research, 25,* 189–204.

Mullen, B., & Copper, C. (1994). The relation between group cohesiveness and performance: An integration. *Psychological Bulletin, 115,* 210–227.

Mumford, M. D., Feldman, J. M., Hein, M. B., & Nagao, D. J. (2001). Tradeoffs between ideas and structure: Individuals versus group performance in creative problem solving. *Journal of Creative Behavior, 35*(1), 1–23.

Murachver, T., Pipe, M. E., Gordon, R., & Owens, J. L. (1996). Do, show, and tell: Children's event memories acquired through direct experience, observation, and stories. *Child Development, 67*(6), 3029–3044.

Murphy, G. E., Wetzel, R. D., Robins, E., & McEvoy, L. (1992). Multiple risk factors predict suicide in alcoholism. *Archives of General Psychiatry, 49,* 459–463.

Murphy, S. M. (1990). Models of imagery in sport psychology: A review. *Journal of Mental Imagery, 14,* 153–172.

Murphy, S. M., & Jowdy, D. P. (1992). Imagery and mental practice. In Thelma S. Horn (Ed.), *Advances in sport psychology* (pp. 221–250). Champaign, IL: Human Kinetics.

Murphy, S. T. (1998). The impact of factual versus fictional media portrayals on cultural stereotypes. *The Annals of the American Academy of Political and Social Sciences, 560,* 165–178.

Murray, H. A. (1938). *Explorations in personality.* New York: Oxford University Press.

Murray, J. B. (1995). Evidence for acupuncture's analgesic effectiveness and proposals for the physiological mechanisms involved. *Journal of Psychology, 129*(4), 443–461.

Murray, J. G. (1994). Dimensions of multiple personality disorder. *Journal of Genetic Psychology, 155,* 233–246.

Myers, D. G. (2000). The funds, friends, and faith of happy people. *American Psychologist, 55,* 56–67.

Myers, I. B. (1962). *Myers-Briggs type indicator manual.* Princeton, NJ: Educational Testing Service.

Myerson, J., Rank, M. R., Raines, F. Q., & Schnitzler, M. A. (1998). Race and general cognitive ability: The myth of diminishing returns to education. *American Psychological Society, 9*(2), 139–142.

Nace, E. P. (1987). *The treatment of alcoholism.* New York: Brunner/ Mazel.

Nadel, L., & Bohbot, V. (2001). Consolidation of memory. *Hippocampus, 11,* 56–60.

Nair, E. (2000). Health and aging: A perspective from the Far East. *Journal of Adult Development, 7,* 121–126.

Narrow, W. E., Regier, D. A., & Rae, D. S. (1993). Use of services by persons with mental and addictive disorders: Findings from the National Institute of Mental Health Epidemiologic Catchment Area Program. *Archives of General Psychiatry, 50,* 95–107.

Nash, M. (1987). What, if anything, is regressed about hypnotic age regression? A review of the empirical literature. *Psychological Bulletin, 102,* 42–52.

Nash, R. A. (1996). The serotonin connection. *Journal of Orthomolecular Medicine, 11*(1), 35–44.

Nass, C., Moon, Y., Fogg, B. J., & Reeves, B. (1995). Can computer personalities be human personalities? *International Journal of Human Computer Studies, 43*(2), 223–239.

Nathan, B. R., & Tippins, N. (1990). The consequences of halo "error" in performance ratings: A field study of the moderating effect of halo on test validation results. *Journal of Applied Psychology, 75,* 290–296.

Nathan, P. E. (1988). The addictive personality is the behavior of the addict. *Journal of Consulting and Clinical Psychology, 56,* 183–188.

Nathan, P. E., & Langenbucher, J. W. (1999). Psychopathology: Description and classification. *Annual Review of Psychology, 50,* 79–108.

Nathan, P. E., & Skinstad, A. H. (1987). Outcomes of treatment for alcohol problems: Current methods, problems, and results. *Journal of Consulting and Clinical Psychology, 55,* 332–340.

Nathans, J. (1989, February). The genes for color vision. *Scientific American*, 42–49.

National Advisory Council on Aging (1997). How many people have hearing impairment? *Aging Vignettes, Number 88*. National Advisory Council on Aging.

National Crime Prevention Centre. (1999, December 9–10). National Forum on Youth Gangs. http://www.sgc.gc.ca/Publications/Policing/199912_e.pdf, accessed 2 July 2003.

Nauta, W. J. H., & Feirtag, M. (1986). *Fundamental neuroanatomy*. New York: Freeman.

Navon, D. (1990). How critical is the accuracy of an eyewitness's memory? Another look at the issue of lineup diagnosticity. *Journal of Applied Psychology, 75*, 506–510.

Neisser, U. (1967). *Cognitive psychology*. Englewood Cliffs, NJ: Prentice-Hall.

Neisser, U., & Libby, L. K. (2000). Remembering life events. In E. Tulving & F. I. M. Craik (Eds.), *The Oxford handbook of memory* (pp. 315–332). New York: Oxford University Press.

Nelson, D. L., McKinney, V. M., & Gee, N. R. (1998). Interpreting the influence of implicitly activated memories on recall and recognition. *Psychological Review, 105*(2), 299–324.

Nelson, G., Laurendeau, M.-C., & Chamberland, C. (2001). A review of programs to promote family wellness and prevent the maltreatment of children. *Canadian Journal of Behavioural Science, 33*, 1, 1–13.

Nelson, T. D. (2002). *Psychology of prejudice*. Boston: Allyn & Bacon.

Nestle, M., Wing, R., Birch, L., DiSogra, L., Drewnowski, A., Middleton, S., Sigman-Grant, M., Sobal, J., Winston, M., & Economos, C. (1998). Behavioral and social influences on food choices. *Nutrition Reviews, 56*, S50–71.

Neugarten, B. (1968). Adult personality: Toward a psychology of the life cycle. In B. Neugarten (Ed.), *Middle age and aging* (pp. 137–147). Chicago: University of Chicago Press.

Neumann, R., & Strack, F. (2000). Experiential and nonexperiental routes of motor influence on affect and evaluation. In H. Bless & J. P. Forgas (Eds.), *The message within: The role of subjective experience in social cognition and behavior* (pp. 52–68). Philadelphia: Psychology Press/Taylor & Francis.

Neumark-Sztainer, D., Story, M., Hannan, P. J., Beuhring, T., & Resnick, M. D. (2000). Disordered eating among adolescents: Associations with sexual/physical abuse and other familial/psychosocial factors. *International Journal of Eating Disorders, 28*, 249–258.

Neville, H. J., & Bavelier, D. (2000). Specificity and plasticity in neurocognitive development in humans. In M. S. Gazzaniga (Ed.), *The new cognitive neurosciences* (pp. 83–98). Cambridge, MA: The MIT Press.

Newcomb, A. F., Bukowski, W. M., & Bagwell, C. L. (1999). Knowing the sounds: Friendship as a developmental context. In W. A. Collins, B. Laursen, and others, *Relationships as Developmental Contexts. The Minnesota Symposia on Child Psychology*. (63–84). Mahwah, NJ: Lawrence Erlbaum Associates, Inc.

Newcomb, M. D., & Bentler, P. M. (1989). Substance use and abuse among children and teenagers. *American Psychologist, 44*, 242–248.

Newcombe, N. S., & Huttenlocher, J. (2000). *Making Space: the Development of Spatial Representation and Reasoning*. Cambridge, MA: The MIT Press.

Newman, L. S., Duff, K. J., & Baumeister, R. F. (1997). A new look at defensive projection: Thought suppression, accessibility, and biased person perception. *Journal of Personality and Social Psychology, 72*(5), 980–1001.

Ng, V. W. K., Eslinger, P. J., Williams, S., Brammer, M., Bullmore, E. T., Andrew, C. M., Suckling, J., Morris, R. G., & Benton, A. L. (2000). Hemispheric preference in visuospatial processing: A complementary approach with fMRI and lesion studies. *Human Brain Mapping, 10*, 80–86.

Niaura, R., & Goldstein, M. G. (1995). Cardiovascular disease, Part II: Coronary artery disease and sudden death and hypertension. In Stoudemire, A. (Ed). *Psychological factors affecting medical conditions*. (pp. 39–56). Washington, DC, US: American Psychiatric Association.

NICHD Early Child Care Research Network (1997). The effects of infant child care on infant-mother attachment security: Results of the NICHD study of early child care. *Child Development, 68*(5), 860–879.

Nichoff, D. (1999). *The biology of violence: How understanding the brain, behavior, and environment can break the vicious circle of aggression*. New York: The Free Press.

Nilsson, K. M. (1990). The effect of subject expectations of "hypnosis" upon vividness of visual imagery. *The International Journal of Clinical and Experimental Hypnosis, 38*, 17–24.

Nisbett, R. E. (1972). Hunger, obesity, and the ventromedial hypothalamus. *Psychological Review, 79*, 433–453.

Nolen-Hoeksema, S. (2000). The role of rumination in depressive disorders and mixed anxiety/depressive symptoms. *Journal of Abnormal Psychology, 109*, 504–511.

Nolen-Hoeksema, S., Larson, J., & Grayson, C. (1999). Explaining the gender difference in depressive symptoms. *Journal of Personality and Social Psychology, 77*, 1061–1072.

Norman, D. A. (1990). *Design of everyday things*. New York: Doubleday.

Norman, R. A., Tataranni, P. A., Pratley, R., Thompson, D. B., Hanson, R. L., Prochazka, M., Baier, L., Ehm, M. G., Sakul, H., Foroud, T., Garvey, W. T., Burns, D., Knowler, W. C., Bennett, P. H., Bogardus, C., & Ravussin, E. (1998). Autosomal genomic scan for loci linked to obesity and energy metabolism in Pima Indians. *American Journal of Human Genetics, 62*(3), 659–668.

North, A. C., Linley, A., & Hargreaves, D. J. (2000). Social loafing in a co-operative classroom task. *Educational Psychology, 20*, 389–392.

Northouse, P. G. (2001). *Leadership theory and practice* (2nd ed.). Thousand Oaks, CA: Sage.

Nyberg, L., & Cabeza, R. (2000). Brain imaging of memory. In E. Tulving and F. I. Craik (Eds.), *The Oxford handbook of memory* (pp. 501–519). New York: Oxford University Press.

Nyberg, L., Cabeza, R., & Tulving, E. (1996). PET studies of encoding and retrieval: The HERA model. *Psychonomic Bulletin and Review, 3*(2), 135–148.

Nyhuus, K. (1998). *Chasing ghosts: Asian organized crime investigation in Canada*. R.C.M.P.

Oberbauer, A. M., Rundstadler, J. A., Murray, A. D., & Havel, P. J. (2001). Obesity and elevated plasma leptin concentration in oMTIA-o growth hormone transgenic mice. *Obesity Research, 9*, 51–58.

O'Brien, C. P., Childress, A. R., Ehrman, R., & Robbins, S. J. (1998). Conditioning factors in drug use: Can they explain compulsion? *Journal of Psychopharmacology, 12*(1), 15–22.

O'Connor, F. L. (1998). The role of serotonin and dopamine in schizophrenia. *Journal of the American Psychiatric Nurses Association, 4*(4), S30–S34.

O'Connor, T., & Plomin, R. (2000). Developmental behavioral genetics. In A. J. Sameroff, M. Lewis, & S. M. Miller (Eds.), *Handbook of developmental psychopathology* (pp. 217–235). New York: Kluwer Academic/Plenum Publishers.

O'Connor, T. G., Rutter, M., Beckett, C., Keaveney, L., & Kreppner, J. M. (2000). English & Romanian Adoptees Study Team. The effects of global severe privation on cognitive competence: Extension and longitudinal follow-up. *Child Development, 71*, 2, 376–390.

Oddone-Paolucci, E., Genuis, M. L., & Violato, C. (2001). A meta-analysis of the published research on the effects of child sexual abuse. *Journal of Psychology, 135*, 17–36.

Okuda-Ashitaka, E., Minami, T., Tachibana, S., Yosihara, Y., Nishiuchi, Y., Kimura, T., & Ito, S. (1998). Nocistatin, a peptide that blocks nociceptin action in pain transmission. *Nature, 392*, 286–289.

Olausson, B., & Sagvik, J. (2000). Pain threshold changes following acupuncture, measured with cutaneous argon laser and electrical tooth pulp stimulation, a comparative study. *Progress in Neuro-Psychopharmacology & Biological Psychiatry, 24*, 385–395.

Olds, J. (1955). Physiological mechanisms of reward. *Nebraska Symposium on Motivation, 3*, 73–139.

Olds, J. (1969). The central nervous system and the reinforcement of behavior. *American Psychologist, 24*, 114–132.

Olds, J., & Milner, P. (1954). Positive reinforcement produced by electrical stimulation of septal area and other regions of rat brain. *Journal of Comparative and Physiological Psychology, 47*, 419–427.

Olfson, M., Marcus, S. C., Druss, B., Elinson, L., Tanielian, T., & Pincus, H. A. (2002). National trends in the outpatient treatment of depression. *Journal of the American Medical Association, 287*, 203–209.

Olivardia, R., Pope, H. G., Jr., Mangweth, B., & Hudson, J. L. (1995). Eating disorders in college men. *American Journal of Psychiatry, 152*, 1279–1283.

Oliver, J. M., & Novak, B. B. (1993). Depression, Seligman's "modernity" hypothesis, and birth cohort effects in university students. *Journal of Social Behavior and Personality, 8*, 99–110.

Oliver, W. (2000). Preventing domestic in the African American community: The rationale for popular culture interventions. *Violence Against Women, 6,* 533–549.

Olness, K. (1993). Hypnosis: The power of attention. In D. Goleman & J. Gurin (Eds.), *Mind/body medicine: How to use your mind for better health* (pp. 277–290). Yonkers, NY: Consumer Reports Books.

O'Mara, S. M., Commins, S., & Anderson, M. (2000). Synaptic plasticity in the hippocampal area CA1-subiculum projection: Implications for theories of memory. *Hippocampus, 10,* 447–456.

*Ontario Human Rights Commision and O'Malley (Vincent) vs. Simpson-Sears* (1985) 2 S.C.R. 536.

Ornstein, R. (1997). *The right mind: Making sense of the hemisphere.* New York: Harcourt Brace and Company.

Ornstein, R. E. (1976). A science of consciousness. In P. R. Lee, R. E. Ornstein, D. Galin, A. Deikman, & C. T. Tart (Eds.), *Symposium on consciousness* (San Francisco, 1974). New York: Viking.

Ornstein, R. E. (1977). *The psychology of consciousness* (2nd ed.). New York: Harcourt Brace Jovanovich.

Orth-Gomér, K. (1998). Psychosocial risk factor profile in women with coronary heart disease. In K. Orth-Gomér, M. Chesney, & N. K. Wenger (Eds.), *Women, stress, and heart disease* (pp. 25–38). Mahwah, NJ: Erlbaum.

Osborne, J. W. (1997). Race and academic disidentification. *Journal of Educational Psychology, 89*(4), 728–735.

Ostrea, E. M., Jr., Ostrea, A. R., & Simpson, P. M. (1997). Mortality within the first 2 years in infanys exposed to cocaine, opiate, or cannabinoid during gestation. *Pediatrics, 100,* 1, 79–83.

Otto, L. B. (2000). Youth perspectives on parental career influence. *Journal of Career Development, 27*(2), 111–118.

Ouimette, P. C. (1997). Psychopathology and sexual aggression in nonincarcerated men. *Violence and Victims, 12,* 390–395.

Overby, L. Y. (1990). A comparison of novice and experienced dancers' imagery ability. *Journal of Mental Imagery, 14,* 173–184.

Owens, L., Shute, R., & Slee, P. (2000). Guess what I just heard: Indirect aggression amongst teenage girls. *Aggressive Behavior, 26,* 67–83.

Pagano, R. W., Rose, R. M., Stivers, R. M., & Warrenburg, S. (1976). Sleep during transcendental meditation. *Science, 191,* 308–310.

Paikoff, R. L., Parfenoff, S. H., Williams, S. A., & McCormick, A. (1997). Parenting, parent-child relationships, and sexual possibility situations among urban African American preadolescents: Preliminary findings and implications for HIV prevention. *Journal of Family Psychology, 11,* 11–22.

Paivio, A. (1971). *Imagery and verbal processes.* New York: Holt, Rinehart & Winston.

Palatnik, A., Frolov, K., Fux, M., & Benjamin, J. (2001). Double-blind, controlled, crossover trial of inositol versus fluvoxamine for the treatment of panic disorder. *Journal of Clinical Psychopharmacology, 21,* 335–339.

Palmer, G. (2000). Resilience in child refugees: An historical study. *Australian Journal of Early Childhood, 25*(3), 39+.

Pan, C., Morrison, R. S., Ness, J., Fugh-Berman, A., & Leipzig, R. M. (2000). Complementary and alternative medicine in the management of pain, dyspnea, and nausea and vomiting near the end of life: A systematic review. *Journal of Pain & Symptom Management, 20,* 374–387.

Panksepp, J. (2000). Emotions as natural kinds within the mammalian brain. In M. Lewis & J. M. Haviland-Jones (Eds.), *Handbook of emotions* (2nd ed., pp. 137–156). New York: Guilford Press.

Pantin, H. M., & Carver, C. S. (1982). Induced competence and the bystander effect. *Journal of Applied Social Psychology, 12,* 100–111.

Papini, M. R., & Bitterman, M. E. (1990). The role of contingency in classical conditioning. *Psychological Review, 97,* 396–403.

Papp, P. (2000). Gender differences in depression: His or her depression. In P. Papp (Ed.), *Couples on the fault line: New directions for therapists* (pp. 130–551). New York: Guilford Press.

Paradis, C. M., Hatch, M., & Friedman, S. (1994). Anxiety disorders in African Americans: An update. *Journal of the National Medical Association, 86,* 609–612.

Park, H. S., Bauer, S. C., & Sullivan, L. M. (1998). Gender differences among top-performing elementary school students in mathematical ability. *Journal of Research and Development in Education, 31*(3), 133–141.

Parke, R. D. (1995). Fathers and families. In M. H. Bornstein (Ed.), *Handbook of parenting. Vol. III: Status and social conditions of parenting.* Mahwah, NJ: Lawrence Erlbaum Associates.

Parker, D. E. (1980, November). The vestibular apparatus. *Scientific American,* 118–135.

Parkin, A. J. (2001). The structure and mechanisms of memory. In B. Rapp (Ed.), *The handbook of cognitive neuropsychology: What deficits reveal about the human mind* (pp. 399–422). Philadelphia: Psychology Press/Taylor & Francis.

Parks, C. A., Hesselbrock, M. N., Hesselbrock, V. M., & Segal, B. (2001). Gender and reported health problems in treated alcohol-dependent Alaska natives. *Journal of Studies on Alcohol, 62,* 286–293.

Parvizi, J., & Damasio, A. (2001). Consciousness and the brainstem. *Cognition, 79,* 135–159.

Patrick, C. J. (1994). Emotion and psychopathy: Startling new insights. *Psychophysiology, 31,* 319–330.

Paulus, P. B. (1998). Developing consensus about groupthink after all these years, *Organizational Behavior & Human Decision Processes, 73*(2-3), 362–374.

Paunonen, S. V. (2003). Big five factors of personality and replicated predictions of behavior. *Journal of Personality & Social Psychology, 84,* 2, 411–422.

Pavlov, I. P. (1927). *Conditioned reflexes.* London: Oxford University Press.

Payne, D. G., Neuschatz, J. S., Lampinen, J. M., & Lynn, S. J. (1997). Compelling memory illusions: The characteristics of false memories. *American Psychological Society, 6*(3), 56–60.

Payne, J. W., Bettman, J. R., & Johnson, E. J. (1992). Behavioral decision research: A constructive processing perspective. *Annual Review of Psychology, 43,* 87–132.

Pearlmann, S. F. (1993). Late mid-life astonishment: Disruptions to identity and self-esteem. *Women and Therapy, 14,* 1–12.

Pedersen, D. M., & Wheeler, J. (1983). The Müller-Lyer illusion among Navajos. *Journal of Social Psychology, 121,* 3–6.

Peltonen, L., & McKusick, V. (2001, February 16). Dissecting human disease in the postgenomic era. *Science, 291,* 1224–1229.

Pendergrast, M. (1997). Memo to Pope: Ask the real questions, please. *American Psychologist, 52,* 989–990.

Penfield, W., & Boldrey, E. (1937). Somatic motor and sensory representation in the cerebral cortex of man as studied by electrical stimulation. *Brain, 60,* 4, 389–443.

Penfield, W., & Rasmussen, T. (1950). *The cerebral cortex of man: A clinical study of localization of function.* New York: Macmillan.

Peng, K., & Nisbett, R. (1999). Culture, dialectics, and reasoning about contradiction. *American Psychologist, 54,* 741–754.

Penn, D. L., Corrigan, P. W., Bentall, R. P., Racenstein, J. M., & Newman, L. (1997). Social cognition in schizophrenia. *Psychological Bulletin, 121*(1), 114–132.

Pennebaker, J. W. (1997). *Opening up: The healing power of expressing emotions* (rev. ed.). New York: Guilford Press.

Pennebaker, J. W., & Graybeal, A. (2001). Patterns of natural language use: Disclosure, personality, and social integration. *Current Directions in Psychological Science, 10,* 90–93.

Pennebaker, J. W., & King, L. A. (1999). Linguistic styles, language use, and an individual difference. *Journal of Personality and Social Psychology, 77,* 1296–1312.

Pepperberg, I. (1994). Numerical competence in an African gray parrot (Psittacus erithacus). *Journal of Comparative Psychology, 108*(1), 36–44.

Pepperberg, I., Brese, K.J., & Harris, B. J. (1991). Solitary play during acquisition of English vocalizations by an African Grey Parrot (Psittacus erithacus): Possible parallels with children's monologue speech. *Applied Psycholinguistics, 12*(2), 151–178.

Perkins, D. N., & Grotzer, T. A. (1997). Teaching intelligence. *American Psychologist, 52*(10), 1125–1133.

Perloff, R. M. (2001). *Persuading people to have safer sex: Applications of social science to the AIDS crisis.* Mahwah, NJ: Erlbaum.

Perner, J., & Ruffman, T. (1995). Episodic memory and autonoetic consciousness: Developmental evidence and a theory of childhood amnesia. *Journal of Experimental Child Psychology, 59*(3), 516–548.

Perrett, D. I., Lee, K. J., Penton-Voak, I., Rowland, D., Yoshikawa, S., Burt, D. M., Henzi, S. P., Castles, D. L., & Akamatsu, S. (1998). Effects of sexual dimorphism on facial attractiveness. *Nature, 394,* 884–887.

Perry, B. D. (1994). Neurobiological sequelae of childhood trauma: Post traumatic stress disorders in children. In M. Murburg (Ed.), *Catecholamines in PTSD* (pp. 253–276). Washington, DC: American Psychiatric Press, Washington.

Perry, B. D. (1999). The memories of states: How the brain stores and retrieves traumatic experience. In J. Goodwin & R. Attias (Eds.), *Splintered reflections: Images of the body in trauma* (pp. 9–38). New York: Basic Books.

Perry, B. D. (2002). Childhood experience and the expression of genetic potential: What childhood neglect tells us about nature and nurture. *Brain & Mind, 3,* 1, 79–100.

Persky, H. (1978). Plasma testosterone level and sexual behavior of couples. *Archives of Sexual Behavior, 7,* 157–173.

Peselow, E. D., Sanfilipo, M. P., & Fieve, R. R. (1995). Relationship between hypomania and personality disorders before and after successful treatment. *American Journal of Psychiatry, 152,* 232–238.

Pesut, D. J. (1990). Creative thinking as a self-regulatory metacognitive process: A model for education, training and further research. *Journal of Creative Behavior, 24,* 105–110.

Peters, R. DeV., Peters, J. E., Laurendeau, M.-C., Chamberland, C., & Peirson, L. (2001). Social policies for promoting the well-being of Canadian children and families. In I. Prilleltensky, G. Nelson, & L. Peirson (Eds.), *Promoting family wellness and preventing child maltreatment.* Toronto: University of Toronto Press.

Petersen, R. C., Stevens, J. C., Ganguli, M., Tangalos, E. G., Cummings, J. L., & DeKosky, S. T. (2001). Practice parameter: Early detection of dementia: Mild cognitive impairment (an evidence-based review). *Neurology, 56,* 9, 1133–1142.

Peterson, C. (2000). Optimistic explanatory style and health. In J. E. Gillham (Ed.), *The science of optimism and hope: Research essays in honor of Martin E. P. Seligman. Laws of Life Symposia Series* (pp. 145–161). Philadelphia: Templeton Foundation Press.

Peterson, C., & Seligman, M. E. P. (1984). Causal explanations as a risk factor for depression: Theory and evidence. *Psychological Review, 91,* 347–374.

Peterson, L. R., & Peterson, M. J. (1959). Short-term retention of individual verbal items. *Journal of Experimental Psychology, 58,* 193–198.

Peterson, S. (2002). Grade eight students' talk about classroom writing. *Gender and Education, 14,* 4, 351–356.

Petrill, S. A., Plomin, R., Berg, S., Johansoon, B., Pedersen, N. L., Ahern, F., & McClearn, G. E. (1998). The genetic and environmental relationship between general and specific cognitive abilities in twins age 80 and older. *Psychological Science, 9*(3), 183–189.

Petrinovich, L. (1997). Evolved behavioral mechanisms. In M. E. Bouton & M. S. Fanselow (Eds.), *Learning, motivation, and cognition: The functional behavioralism of Robert C. Bolles* (pp. 13–30). Washington, DC: American Psychological Association.

Pettigrew, T. F. (1997). The affective component of prejudice: Empirical support for the new view. In S. A. Tuch & J. K. Martin (Eds.), *Racial attitudes in the 1990s: Continuity and change* (pp. 76–90). New York: Praeger.

Pettigrew, T. F., Jackson, J. S., Brika, J. B., Lemaine, G., Meertens, R. W., Wagner, U., & Zick, A. (1998). Outgroup prejudice in Western Europe. In W. Stroebe, M. Hewstone, et al. (Eds.), *European Review of Social Psychology, Vol. 8.* (pp. 241–273). Chichester, England: John Wiley & Sons, Inc.

Petty, R. E., & Cacioppo, J. T. (1985). The elaboration likelihood model of persuasion. In L. Berkowitz (Ed.), *Advances in experimental social psychology* (Vol. 19). New York: Academic.

Petty, R. E., Cacioppo, J. T., Strathman, A. J., & Priester, J. R. (1994). To think or not to think: Exploring two routes to persuasion. In S. Shavitt & T. C. Brock (Eds.), *Persuasion: Psychological insights and perspectives* (pp. 113–148). Boston: Allyn & Bacon.

Petty, R. E., Schumann, D. W., Richman, S. A., & Strathman, A. J. (1993). Positive mood and persuasion: Different roles for affect under high- and low-elaboration conditions. *Journal of Personality and Social Psychology, 64,* 5–20.

Petty, R. E., Wegener, D. T., & White, P. H. (1998). Flexible correction processes in social judgment: Implications for persuasion. *Social Cognition, 16*(1), 93–113.

Petty, R. E., & Wegener, D. T. (1999). The elaboration likelihood model: Current status and controversies. In S. Chaiken & Y. Trope (Ed.), *Dual process theories in social psychology* (pp. 37–72). New York: Guilford Press.

Pfister, H. P., & Muir, J. L. (1992). Prenatal exposure to predictable and unpredictable novelty stress and oxytocin treatment affects offspring development and behavior in rats. *International Journal of Neuroscience, 62,* 227–241.

Phares, V., & Compas, B. E. (1993). Fathers and developmental psychopathology. *Current Directions in Psychological Science, 2,* 162–165.

Phillips, D., Liu, G., Kwok, K., Jarvinen, J.N., Zhang, W. & Abramson, I. (2002). "The Hound of the Baskervilles effect: Natural experiment on the influence of psychological stress on timing of death": Reply. *BMJ (British Medical Journal), 324*(7345), 1098–1099.

Phillipps, M. (1999). Problems with the polygraph. *Science, 286,* 413.

Phillips, M., Brooks-Gunn, J., Duncan, G. J., Klebanov, P., & Crane, J. (1998). Family background, parenting practices, and the Black–White test score gap. In C. Jencks, M. Phillips (Eds.), *The Black–White test score gap* (pp. 103–145). Washington, DC: Brookings Institution.

Phillips, N. A., & McGlone, J. (1995). Grouped data do not tell the whole story: Individual analysis of cognitive change after temporal lobectomy. *Journal of Clinical & Experimental Neuropsychology, 17,* 5, 713–724.

Philpot, C. L. (2001). Family therapy for men. In G. R. Brooks (Ed.), *The new handbook of psychotherapy and counseling with men: A comprehensive guide to settings, problems, and treatment approaches, 1 & 2* (pp. 622–636). San Francisco: Jossey-Bass.

Piaget, J. (1932). *The moral judgment of the child.* London: Routledge & Kegan Paul.

Pillard, R. C., & Bailey, M. J. (1998). Human sexual orientation has a heritable component. *Human Biology, 70,* 347–365.

Pinel, J. P. J. (2003). *Biopsychology* (5th ed.). Boston: Pearson.

Pinker, S. (1994). *The language instinct: How the mind creates language.* New York: Morrow.

Pinker, S. (1997). *How the mind works.* New York: Norton.

Pinker, S. (1999). *Words and rules.* New York: Basic Books.

Pinker, S. (2002). *The blank slate: The denial of human nature in modern intellectual life.* London: Penguin.

Pipher, M. (1994). *Reviving Ophelia: Saving the selves of adolescent girls.* New York: Ballantine Books.

Pirenne, M. H. (1967). *Vision and the eye* (2nd ed.). London: Chapman and Hall.

Place, U. T. (2000). Consciousness and the zombie within: A functional analysis of the blindsight evidence. In Y. Rossetti & A. Revonsuo (Eds.), *Beyond dissociation: Interaction between dissociated implicit and explicit processing. Advances in consciousness research* (pp. 295–329). Amsterdam: John Benjamins Publishing Company.

Plant, E. A., Hyde, J. S., Keltner, D., & Devine, P. G. (2000). The gender stereotyping of emotions. *Psychology of Women Quarterly, 24,* 81–92.

Plath, S. (1971). *The bell jar.* New York: HarperCollins Publishers.

Plomin, R., & Caspi, A. (1999). Behavior genetics and personality. In L. A. Pervin & O. P. John (Eds.), *Handbook of personality: Theory and research* (pp. 251–276). New York: Guilford Press.

Plomin, R., & Crabbe, J. (2000). DNA. *Psychological Bulletin, 126,* 806–828.

Plomin, R., & DeFries, J. C. (1999). The genetics of cognitive abilities and disabilities. In S. J. Ceci & W. M. Williams (Eds.), *The nature-nurture debate: The essential readings. Essential readings in developmental psychology* (pp. 177–195). Malden, MA: Blackwell Publishers.

Plomin, R., DeFries, J. C., Craig, I. C., & McGuffin, P. (Eds.). (2002). *Behavioral genetics in a postgenomic era.* Washington, DC: APA Books.

Plomin, R., Fulker, D. W., Corley, R., & DeFries, J. C. (1997). Nature, nurture, and cognitive development from 1 to 16 years: A parent-offspring adoption study. *Psychological Science, 8*(6), 442–447.

Plotkin, W. B. (1980). The role of attributions of responsibility in the facilitation of unusual experiential states during alpha training: An analysis of the biofeedback placebo effect. *Journal of Abnormal Psychology, 89,* 67–78.

Plous, S. (1996). Attitudes toward the use of animals in psychological research and education. *American Psychologist, 51*(11), 1167–1180.

Pollack, W. (1998). *Real boys: Rescuing our sons from the myths of boyhood.* New York: Random House.

Polonsky, A., Blake, R., Braun, J., & Heeger, D. J. (2000). Neuronal activity in human primary visual cortex correlates with perception during binocular rivalry. *Nature Neuroscience, 3,* 1153–1159.

Pope, K. S. (2000). Pseudoscience, cross-examination, and scientific evidence in the recovered memory controversy. *Psychology, Public Policy, and Law, 4,* 1160–1181.

Porter, B. E., Leeming, F. C., & Dwyer, W. O. (1995). Solid waste recovery: A review of behavioral programs to increase recycling. *Environment and Behavior, 27*, 122–152.

Porter, L. S., & Stone, A. A. (1995). Are there really gender differences in coping? A reconsideration of previous data and results from a daily study. *Journal of Social and Clinical Psychology, 14*, 2, 184–202.

Posner, M. I., DiGirolamo, G. J., & Fernandez-Duque, D. (1997). Brain mechanisms of cognitive skills. *Conscious Cognition, 6*(2/3), 267–290.

Posner, M. I., & Mitchell, R. F. (1967). Chronometric analysis of classification. *Psychological Review, 74*, 392–409.

Posner, M. I., & Pavese, A. (1998). Anatomy of word and sentence meaning. *Proceedings of the National Academy of Sciences, 95*(3), 899–905.

Post, R. M., Frye, M. A., Dnicoff, K. D., Leverich, G. S., Kimbrell, T. A., & Dunn, R. T. (1998). Beyond lithium in the treatment of bipolar illness. *Neuropsychopharmacology, 19*(3), 206–219.

Powers, P. C., & Geen, R. G. (1972). Effects of the behavior and the perceived arousal of a model on instrumental aggression. *Journal of Personality and Social Psychology, 23*, 175–184.

Powers, S. I., Hauser, S. T., & Kilner, L. A. (1989). Adolescent mental health. *American Psychologist, 44*, 200–208.

Pozzi, M. E. (2000). Ritalin for whom? Understanding the need for Ritalin in psychodynamic counseling with families of under 5s. *Journal of Child Psychotherapy, 26*(1), 25–43.

Prados, J., Chamizo, V. D., & Mackintosh, N. J. (1999). Latent inhibition and perceptual learning in a swimming-pool navigation task. *Journal of Experimental Psychology: Animal Behavior Processes, 25*(1), 37–44.

Pratkanis, A. R. (2001). Propaganda and deliberative persuasion: The implications of Americanized mass media for established and emerging democracies. In W. Wosinska, R. B. Cialdini, D. W. Barrett, & J. Reykowski (Eds.), *The practice of social influence in multiple cultures. Applied social research* (pp. 259–285). Mahwah, NJ: Erlbaum.

Pratkanis, A. R., Eskenazi, J., & Greenwald, A. G. (1994). What you expect is what you believe (but not necessarily what you get): A test of the effectiveness of subliminal self-help audiotapes. *Basic and Applied Social Psychology, 15*, 251–276.

Pratkanis, A. R., & Turner, M. E. (1999). Groupthink and preparedness for the Loma Prieta earthquake: A social identity maintenance analysis of causes and preventions. In R. Wageman (Ed.), *Research on managing groups and teams: Groups in context* (pp. 115–136). Stamford, CT: JAI Press.

Premack, D. (1962). Reversibility of the reinforcement relation. *Science, 136*, 255–257.

Premack, D. (1965). Reinforcement theory. In D. Levine (Ed.), *Nebraska Symposium on Motivation* (Vol. 13, pp. 123–180). Lincoln: University of Nebraska Press.

Premack, D. (1971). Language in chimpanzees? *Science, 172*, 808–822.

Price, T. S., Eley, T. C., Dale, P. S., Stevenson, J., Saudino, K., & Plomin, R. (2000). Genetic and environmental covariation between verbal and nonverbal cognitive development in infancy. *Child Development, 71*(4), 948–959.

Prinz, R. J., Smith, E. P., Dumas, J. E., Laughlin, J. E., White, D. W., & Barron, R. (2001). Recruitment and retention of participants in prevention trials involving family-based interventions. *American Journal of Preventive Medicine, 20* (Suppl 1), 31–37.

Prinz, R. N., Vitiello, M. V., Raskind, M. A., & Thorphy, M. J. (1990). Geriatrics: Sleep disorders and aging. *New England Journal of Medicine, 323*, 520–526.

Prokopcakova, A. (1998). Drug experimenting and pubertal maturation in girls. *Studia Psychologica, 40*, 287–290.

Proshansky, H. M., & O'Hanlon, T. (1977). Environmental psychology: Origins and development. In D. Stokols (Ed.), *Perspectives on environment and behavior: Theory, research, and application*. New York: Plenum.

Prudic, J., Olfson, M., & Sackeim, H. A. (2001). Electro-convulsive therapy practices in the community. *Psychological Medicine, 31*, 929–934.

Prudic, J., Peyser, S., & Sackeim, H. A. (2000). Subjective memory complaints: A review of patient self-assessment of memory after electroconvulsive therapy. *Journal of ECT, 16*, 121–132.

Puffer, S. M. (1987). Prosocial behavior, noncompliant behavior, and work performance among commission salespeople. *Journal of Applied Psychology, 72*, 615–621.

Putnam, F. W., & Carlson, E. B. (1998). Trauma, memory, and dissociation. *Progress in Psychiatry, 54*, 27–55.

Putnam, W. H. (1979). Hypnosis and distortions in eyewitness memory. International *Journal of Clinical and Experimental Hypnosis, 27*, 437–448.

Quigley, B., Gaes, G. G., & Tedeschi, J. T. (1989). Does asking make a difference? Effects of initiator, possible gain, and risk on attributed altruism. *Journal of Social Psychology, 129*, 259–267.

Rachlin, H. (1995). Things that are private and things that are mental. In J. T. Todd & E. K. Morris (Eds.), *Modern perspectives on B. F. Skinner and contemporary behaviorism* (pp. 179–183). Westport, CT: Greenwood.

Rahe, R. H. (1989). Recent life change stress and psychological depression. In T. W. Miller (Ed.), *Stressful life events*. Madison, WI: International Universities Press.

Rahola, J. G. (2001). Antidepressants: Pharmacological profile and clinical consequences. *International Journal of Psychiatry in Clinical Practice, 5* (Suppl. 1), S19–S28.

Raine, A., Lenczk, T., Bihrle, S., LaCasse, L., & Colletti, P. (2000). Reduced prefrontal gray matter volume and reduced autonomic activity in antisocial personality disorder. *Archives of General Psychiatry, 57*, 119–127, 128–129.

Rainville, P., Hofbauer, R. K., Paus, T., Duncan, G. H., Bushnell, M. C., & Price, D. D. (1999). Cerebral mechanisms of hypnotic induction and suggestion. *Journal of Cognitive Neuroscience, 11*, 110–125.

Rajaram, S., Srinivas, K., & Roediger, H. L., III. (1998). A transfer-appropriate processing account of context effects in word-fragment completion. *Journal of Experimental Psychology: Learning, Memory and Cognition, 24*, 993–1004.

Ramachandran, V. S. (2000). Memory and the brain: New lessons from old syndromes. In D. L. Schacter & E. Scarry (Eds.), *Memory, brain, and belief* (pp. 87–114). Cambridge, MA: Harvard University Press.

Ramey, C. T., & Campbell, F. A. (1984). Preventive education for high-risk children: Cognitive consequences of the Carolina Abecedarian Project. *American Journal of Mental Deficiency, 88*, 515–523.

Ramey, C. T., & Campbell, F. A. (1992). Poverty, early childhood education, and academic competence: The Abecedarian experiment. In A. Huston (Ed.), *Children in poverty* (pp. 190–221). New York: Cambridge University Press.

Ramey, C. T., Campbell, F. A., Burchinal, M., Skinner, M. L., Gardner, D. M., & Ramsey, S. L. (2000). Persistent effects of early intervention on high-risk children and their mothers. *Applied Developmental Science, 4*, 2–14.

Ramey, C. T., Ramey, S. L., & Lanzi, R. G. (2001). Intelligence and experience. In R. J. Sternberg & E. L. Grigorenko (Eds.), *Environmental effects on cognitive abilities* (pp. 83–115). Mahwah, NJ: Erlbaum.

Ramey, S. L. (1999). Head Start and preschool education. *American Psychologist, 54*(5), 344–346.

Ramey, S. L., & Sackett, G. P. (2000). The early caregiving environment: Expanding views on nonparental care and cumulative life experiences. In A. J. Sameroff, M. Lewis, & S. M. Miller (Eds.), *Handbook of developmental psychopathology* (2nd ed., pp. 365–380). New York: Kluwer/Plenum.

Rapcsak, S. Z., Polster, M. R., Comer, J. F., & Rubens, A. B. (1994). False recognition and misidentification of faces following right hemisphere damage. *Cortex, 30*(4), 565–583.

Rappaport, J., (1987). Terms of empowerment/exemplars of prevention: Toward a theory for community psychology. *American Journal of Community Psychology, 2*, 121–148.

Rasmussen, L. E. L., & Krishnamurthy, V. (2000). How chemical signals integrate Asian elephant society: The known and the unknown. *Zoo Biology, 19*, 405–423.

Raven, B. H. (1998). Groupthink, Bay of Pigs, and Watergate reconsidered. *Organizational Behavior and Human Decision Processes, 73*, 352–361.

Ravussin, E., Lillioja, S., Knowler, W. C., Christin, L., Freymond, D., Abbott, W. G. H., Boyce, V., Howard, B. V., & Bogardus, C. (1988). Reduced rate of energy expenditure as a risk factor for body-weight gain. *New England Journal of Medicine, 318*, 467–472.

Rayner, K. (1998). Eye movements in reading and information processing: 20 years of research. *Psychological Bulletin, 124*(3), 372–422.

Rayner, K., Reichle, E. D., & Pollatsek, A. (2000). Eye movement control in reading: Updating the E-Z reader model to account for initial fixation locations and refixations. In A. Kennedy, R. Radach, D. Heller, & J. Pynte (Eds.), *Reading as a perceptual process* (pp. 701–719). Amsterdam: North-Holland/Elsevier Science Publishers.

Raz, S., & Raz, N. (1990). Structural brain abnormalities in the major psychoses: A quantitative review of the evidence from computerized imaging. *Psychological Bulletin, 208,* 93–108.

Rechtschaffen, A. (1998). Current perspectives on the function of sleep. *Perspectives in Biology and Medicine, 41,* 359–370.

Ree, M. J., Earles, J. A., & Teachout, M. S. (1994). Predicting job performance: Not much more than g. *Journal of Applied Psychology, 79,* 518–524.

Reed, C. F. (1984). Terrestrial passage theory of the moon illusion. *Journal of Experimental Psychology: General, 113,* 489–516.

Reeder, H. M. (2000). I like you...as a friend: The role of attraction in cross-sex friendship. *Journal of Social and Personal Relationship, 17,* 329–348.

Reichle, E. D., Carpenter, P. A., & Just, M. A. (2000). The neural bases of strategy and skill in sentence-picture verification. *Cognitive Psychology, 40,* 261–295.

Reisenzein, R. (1983). The Schachter theory of emotion: Two decades later. *Psychological Bulletin, 94,* 239–264.

Reiss, D., Neiderhiser, J. M., Hetherington, E. M., & Plomin, R. (2000). *The relationship code.* Cambridge, MA: Harvard University Press.

Reiss, D., & Price, R. H. (1996). National research agenda for prevention research: The National Institute of Mental Health Report. *American Psychologist, 51*(11), 1109–1115.

Renault, B., Signoret, J. L., Debruille, B., Breton, F., & Bolgert, F. (1989). Brain potentials reveal covert facial recognition in proposopagnosia. *Neuropsychologica, 27,* 905–912.

Rescorla, R. A. (1977). Pavlovian 2nd-order conditioning: Some implications for instrumental behavior. In H. Davis & H. Herwit (Eds.), *Pavlovian-operant interactions.* Hillsdale, NJ: Erlbaum.

Rescorla, R. A. (1978). Some implications of a cognitive perspective on Pavlovian conditioning. In S. H. Hulse, H. Fowler, & W. Honig (Eds.), *Cognitive process in animal behavior.* Hillsdale, NJ: Erlbaum.

Rescorla, R. A. (1988). Pavlovian conditioning: It's not what you think it is. *American Psychologist, 43,* 151–160.

Rescorla, R. A. (2001a). Experimental extinction. In R. R. Mowrer & S. B. Klein (Eds.), *Handbook of contemporary learning theories* (pp. 119–154). Mahwah, NJ: Erlbaum.

Rescorla, R. A. (2001b). Retraining of extinguished Pavlovian stimuli. *Journal of Experimental Psychology: Animal Behavior Processes, 27,* 115–124.

Resnick, M. D., Bearman, P. S., Blum, R. W., Bauman, K. E., Harris, K. M., Jones, J., Tabor, J., Beuhring, T., Sieving, R. E., Shew, M., Ireland, M., Bearinger, L. H., & Udry, R. (1997). Protecting adolescents from harm: Findings from the National Longitudinal Study on Adolescent Health. *Journal of the American Medical Association, 278*(10), 823–831.

Restak, R. M. (1994). *The modular brain: How new discoveries in neuroscience are answering age-old questions about memory, free will, consciousness, and personal identity.* New York: Macmillan.

Restle, F. (1970). Moon illusion explained on the basis of relative size. *Science, 167,* 1092–1096.

Rhode, D. L. (1997). *Speaking of sex: The denial of gender inequality.* Cambridge, MA: Harvard University Press.

Rhodes, N., & Wood, W. (1992). Self-esteem and intelligence affect influenceability: The mediating role of message reception. *Psychological Bulletin, 111,* 156–171.

Rice, G., Anderson, C., Risch, N., & Ebers, G. (1999). Male homosexuality: Absence of linkage to microsatellite markers at Xq28. *Science, 284,* 665–667.

Richardson, J. T. E., & Zucco, G. M. (1989). Cognition and olfaction: A review. *Psychological Bulletin, 105,* 352–360.

Richardson, K. (2000). *The making of intelligence.* New York: Columbia University Press.

Riegel, B., & Bennett, J. A. (2000). Cardiovascular disease in elders: Is it inevitable? *Journal of Adult Development, 7,* 101–112.

Rieger, E., Touyz, S. W., Swain, T., & Beumont, P. J. V. (2001). Cross-cultural research on anorexia nervosa: Assumptions regarding the role of body weight. *International Journal of Eating Disorders, 29,* 205–215.

Riehle, A., Grun, S., Diesmann, M., & Aertsen, A. (1997). Spike synchronization and rate modulation differentially involved in motor cortical function. *Science, 278,* 1950–1953.

Ring, K., Wallston, K., & Corey, M. (1970). Mode of debriefing as a factor affecting subjective reaction to a Milgram-type obedience experiment: An ethical inquiry. *Representative Research in Social Psychology, 1,* 67–88.

Rips, L. J. (1990). Reasoning. *Annual Review of Psychology, 41,* 321–353.

Roberts, G. C. (1992). *Motivation in sport and exercise: Conceptual constraints and convergence* (pp. 3–29). Champaign, IL: Human Kinetics.

Roberts, R. E., Roberts, C. R., & Chen, I. G. (2000). Fatalism and risk of adolescent depression. *Psychiatry: Interpersonal and Biological Processes, 63,* 239–252.

Robinson, J. L., Kagan, J., Reznick, J. S., & Corley, R. P. (1992). The heritability of inhibited and uninhibited behaviour: A twin study. *Developmental Psychology, 28,* 1030–1037.

Robinson, T. E., & Berridge, K. C. (2000). The psychology and neurobiology of addiction: An incentive-sensitization view. *Addiction, 95,* 91–117.

Robinson, T. N., Wilde, M. L., Navracruz, L. C., Haydel, K. F., & Varady, A. (2001). Effects of reducing children's television and video game use on aggressive behavior: A randomized controlled trial. *Archives of Pediatrics and Adolescent Medicine, 155,* 17–23.

Rochat, F., Maggioni, O., & Modigliani, A. (1999). The dynamics of obeying and opposing authority: A mathematical model. In T. Blass (Ed.), *Obedience to authority: Current perspectives on the Milgram paradigm* (pp. 161–192). Mahwah, NJ: Erlbaum.

Rock, I., & Palmer, S. (1990). The legacy of Gestalt psychology. *Scientific American, 263*(6), 84–90.

Rodin, J., & Langer, E. J. (1977). Long-term effects of a control-relevant intervention with the institutionalized aged. *Journal of Personality and Social Psychology, 35,* 897–902.

Rodriguez, E., George, N., Lachaux, J. P., Martinerie, J., Renault, B., & Varela, F. J. (1999). Perception's shadow: Long-distance synchronization of human activity. *Nature, 397,* 430–433.

Roediger, H. L., & McDermott, K. B. (1995). Creating false memories: Remembering words not presented in lists. *Journal of Experimental Psychology: Learning, Memory, and Cognition, 21,* 803–814.

Roeser, R. W., Eccles, J. S., & Sameroff, A. J. (2000). School as a context of early adolescents' academic and social-emotional development: A summary of research findings. *Elementary School Journal, 100,* 443–471.

Roethlisberger, F. J., & Dickson, W. J. (1939). *Management and the worker.* Cambridge, MA: Harvard University Press.

Rogers, C. R. (1951). *Client-centered therapy.* Boston: Houghton Mifflin.

Rogers, C. R. (1957). The necessary and sufficient conditions of therapeutic personality change. *Journal of Consulting Psychology, 21,* 95–103.

Rogers, C. R. (1980). *A way of being.* Boston: Houghton Mifflin.

Rogers, M., & Smith, K. H. (1993). Public perceptions of subliminal advertising: Why practitioners shouldn't ignore this issue. *Journal of Advertising Research, 33*(2), 10–18.

Rogerson, L. J., & Hrycaiko, D. W. (2002). Enhancing competitive performance of ice hockey goaltenders using centering and self-talk. *Journal of Applied Sport Psychology, 14,* 1, 14–26.

Rogoff, B., & Morelli, G. (1989). Perspectives on children's development from cultural psychology. *American Psychologist, 44,* 343–348.

Rohland, B. M. (2001). Self-report of improvement following hospitalization for electroconvulsive therapy: Relationship to functional status and service use. *Administration and Policy in Mental Health, 28,* 193–203.

Rohner, R. P. (1998). Father love and child development: History and current evidence. *Psychological Science, 7*(5), 157–161.

Romano, S. T., & Bordieri, J. E. (1989). Physical attractiveness stereotypes and students' perceptions of college professors. *Psychological Reports, 64,* 1099–1102.

Romans, S. E. (2001). Gender issues in psychiatry. *Hong Kong Journal of Psychiatry, 10,* 4, 7–11.

Romero, A. J. (2000). Assessing and treating Latinos: Overview of research. In I. Cuellar & F. A. Paniagua (Eds.), *Handbook of multicultural mental health* (pp. 209–223). San Diego, CA: Academic Press.

Roques, P., Lambin, M., Jeunier, B., & Strayer, F. F. (1997). Multivariate analysis of personal space in a primary school classroom. *Enfance, 4,* 451–468.

Rosch, E. (1973). Natural categories. *Cognitive Psychology, 4,* 328–350.

Rosch, E. (1978). Principles of categorization. In E. Rosch & B. B. Lloyd (Eds.), *Cognition and categorization* (pp. 27–48). Hillsdale, NJ: Erlbaum.

Rose, S. A., & Feldman, J. F. (1995). Prediction of IQ and specific cognitive abilities at 11 years from infancy measures. *Developmental Psychology, 31,* 685–696.

Rose, S. D. (1999). Group therapy: A cognitive–behavorial interactive approach. In J. R. Price, D. R. Hescheles, & A. R. Price (Eds.), *A guide to starting psychotherapy groups* (pp. 99–113). San Diego, CA: Academic Press.

Rosebush, P. A. (1998). Psychological intervention with military personnel in Rwanda. *Military Medicine, 163*(8), 559–563.

Rosenberg, H. (1993). Prediction of controlled drinking by alcoholics and problem drinkers. *Psychological Bulletin, 113,* 129–139.

Rosenbluth, R., Grossman, E. S., & Kaitz, M. (2000). Performance of early-blind and sighted children on olfactory tasks. *Perception, 29,* 101–110.

Rosenthal, R. (2002). Experimenter and clinician effects in scientific inquiry and clinical practice. *Prevention & Treatment, 5,* Article 38, posted 18 October.

Rosenthal, R., & Jacobson, L. (1966). Teachers' expectancies: Determinates of pupils' I.Q. gains. *Psychological Reports, 19,* 115–118.

Ross, C. A. (1999). Dissociative disorders. In T. Millon, P. H. Blaney, & R. D. Davis (Eds.), *Oxford textbook of psychopathology* (pp. 466–481). New York: Oxford University Press.

Ross, H. S., & Lollis, S. P. (1987). Communication within infant social games. *Developmental Psychology, 2,* 241–248.

Ross, L., Bierbrauer, G., & Hoffman, S. (1976). The role of attribution processes in conformity and dissent. *American Psychologist, 31,* 148–157.

Ross, S. M., & Offermann, L. R. (1997). Transformational leaders: Measurement of personality attributes and work group performance. *Personality and Social Psychology Bulletin, 23*(10), 1078–1086.

Rossini, P. M., & Pauri, F. (2000). Neuromagnetic integrated methods tracking human brain mechanisms of sensorimotor areas "plastic" reorganisation. *Brain Research Reviews, 33,* 131–154.

Rotter, J. B. (1990). Internal versus external control of reinforcement. *American Psychologist, 45,* 489–493.

Rout, U. (1999). Gender differences in stress, satisfaction, and mental well-being among general practitioners in England. *Psychology, Health, and Medicine, 4,* 345–354.

Rowe, D. C., Jacobson, K. C., Van den Oord, E. J. C. G. (1999). Genetic and environmental influences on vocabulary IQ: parental education level as moderator. *Child Development, 70*(5), 1151–1162.

Rowland, D. L., Greenleaf, W. J., Dorfman, L. J., & Davidson, J. M. (1993). Aging and sexual function in men. *Archives of Sexual Behavior, 22,* 545–558.

Rozin, P. (1999). Food is fundamental, fun, frightening, and far-reaching. *Social Research, 66,* 9–30.

Ruback, R. B., Pandey, J., & Begum, H. A. (1997). Urban stressors in South Asia: Impact on male and female pedestrians in Delhi and Dhaka. *Journal of Cross-Cultural Psychology, 28*(1), 23–43.

Rubenzahl, S. A., & Corcoran, K. J. (1998). The prevalence and characteristics of male perpetrators of acquaintance rape: New research methodology reveals new findings. *Violence Against Women, 4,* 713–725.

Rudy, D., & Grusec, J. F. (2001). Correlates of authoritarian parenting in individualist and collectivist cultures and implications for understanding the transmission of values. *Journal of Cross-Cultural Psychology, 32,* 202–212.

Ruggieri, V., Milizia, M., Sabatini, N., & Tosi, M. T. (1983). Body perception in relation to muscular tone at rest and tactile sensitivity. *Perceptual and Motor Skills, 56*(3), 799–806.

Rumbaugh, D. M., Gill, T. V., & Von Glaserfeld, E. D. (1973). Reading and sentence completion by a chimpanzee (Pan troglodytes). *Science, 182,* 731–733.

Rumelhart, D. E. (1997). The architecture of mind: A connectionist approach. In J. Haugeland (Ed.), *Philosophy, psychology, artificial intelligence* (pp. 205–232). Cambridge, MA: The MIT Press.

Rumiati, R. I., & Humphreys, G. W. (1997). Visual object agnosia without alexia or propagnosia: Arguments for separate knowledge stores. *Visual Cognition, 4*(2), 207–217.

Rushton, P. (1988). Race differences in behaviour: A review and evolutionary analysis. *Personality and Individual Differences, 9*(6), 1009–1024.

Russell, J. A. (1994). Is there universal recognition of emotion from facial expression? A review of the cross-cultural studies. *Psychological Bulletin, 115,* 102–141.

Rustemli, A. (1991). Crowding effects of density and interpersonal distance. *The Journal of Social Psychology, 132,* 51–58.

Rutter, M., Pickles, A., Murray, R., & Eaves, L. (2001). Testing hypotheses on specific, environmental causal effects on behavior. *Psychological Bulletin, 127,* 291–324.

Rybak, I. A., Gusakova, V. I., Golovan, A. V., Podladchikova, L. N., & Shevtsova, N. A. (1998). A model of attention-guided visual perception and recognition. *Vision Research, 38,* 2387–2400.

Rycroft, P. J. (2001). An evaluation of short-term group therapy for battered women. *Dissertation Abstracts International: Section B: The Sciences & Engineering, 61*(7-B). Univ. Microfilms International.

Sabini, J., Siepmann, M., & Stein, J. (2001). The really fundamental attribution error in social psychological research. *Psychological Inquiry, 12*(1), 1–15.

Sackeim, H. A. (2001). Functional brain circuits in major depression and remission. *Archives of General Psychiatry, 58,* 649–650.

Sackett, P. R. (1994). Within-group norming and other forms of score adjustment in preemployment testing. *American Psychologist, 49,* 11, 929–954.

Sackett, P. R. (2001). High-stakes testing in employment, credentialing, and higher education: Prospects in a post-affirmative-action world. *American Psychologist, 56,* 4, 302–318.

Sackett, P. R. (2003). The status of validity generalization research: Key issues in drawing inferences from cumulative research findings. In K. R. Murphy (Ed.), *Validity generalization: A critical review. Applied Psychology Series* (pp. 91–114). Mahwah, NJ: Lawrence Erlbaum Associates.

Sacks, O. (1985). *The man who mistook his wife for a hat and other clinical tales.* New York: Summit Books.

Sagrestano, L. M., McCormick, S. H., Paikoff, R. L., & Holmbeck, G. N. (1999). Pubertal development and parent–child conflicts in low-income, urban, African American adolescents. *Journal of Research on Adolescence, 9,* 85–107.

Sakata, S., Shinohara, J., Hori, T., & Sugimoto, S. (1995). Enhancement of randomness by flotation rest (restricted environmental stimulation technique). *Perceptual and Motor Skills, 80*(3, Pt. 1), 999–1010.

Sakitt, B., & Long, G. M. (1979). Cones determine subjective offset of a stimulus but rods determine total persistence. *Vision Research, 19,* 1439–1443.

Salminen, S., & Glad, T. (1992). The role of gender in helping behavior. *The Journal of Social Psychology, 132,* 131–133.

Salt, R. E. (1991). Affectionate touch between fathers and preadolescent sons. *Journal of Marriage and the Family, 53,* 545–554.

Salthouse, T. A. (1999). Theories of cognition. In V. L. Bengtson, K. W. Schaie, et al. (Eds.), *Handbook of theories of aging* (pp. 196–208). New York: Springer Publishing Co.

Salthouse, T. A. (2000). Pressing issues in cognitive aging. In D. C. Park & N. Schwarz (Eds.), *Cognitive aging: A primer* (pp. 43–54). Philadelphia: Psychology Press/Taylor & Francis.

Salzberg, H. C., & DePiano, F. A. (1980). Hypnotizability and task motivating suggestions: A further look at how they affect performance. *International Journal of Clinical and Experimental Hypnosis, 28,* 261–271.

Samoriski, G. M., & Gross, R. A. (2000). Functional compartmentalization of opioid desensitization in primary sensory neurons. *Journal of Pharmacology & Experimental Therapeutics, 294,* 500–509.

Sande, G. N., Goethals, G. R., & Radloff, C. E. (1988). Perceiving one's own traits and others: The multifaceted self. *Journal of Personality and Social Psychology, 54,* 13–20.

Sanders, G. S., & Simmons, W. L. (1983). Use of hypnosis to enhance eyewitness accuracy: Does it work? *Journal of Applied Psychology, 68,* 70–77.

Sanders, M. S., & McCormick, E. J. (1993). *Human factors in engineering and design* (7th ed.). New York: McGraw-Hill.

Sankis, L. M., Corbitt, E. M., & Widiger, T. A. (1999). Gender bias in the English language. *Journal of Personality and Social Psychology, 77,* 1289–1295.

Santos, M. D., Leve, C., & Pratkanis, A. R. (1994). Hey buddy, can you spare seventeen cents? Mindful persuasion and the pique technique. *Journal of Applied Social Psychology, 224,* 755–764.

Sapp, M. (1996). Potential negative sequelae of hypnosis. *Australian Journal of Clinical Hypnotherapy and Hypnosis, 17*(2), 73–78.

Sass, L. A. (2001). Schizophrenia, modernism, and the "creative imagination": On creativity and psychopathology. *Creativity Research Journal, 13*(1), 55–74.

Sattler, J. M. (1992). *Assessment of children: Revised and updated* (3rd ed.). San Diego: Jerome M. Sattler.

Saumier, D., Arguin, M., & Lassonde, M. (2001). Prosopagnosia: A case study involving problems in processing configural information. *Brain and Cognition, 46,* 1–2, 255–259.

Sawicki, S. (1988). Effective crisis intervention. *Adolescence, 23,* 83–88.

Scarr, S. (1998). American child care today. *American Psychologist, 53*(2), 95–108.

Schacter, D. L. (1996). *Searching for memory: The brain, the mind, and the past.* New York: Basic Books.

Schacter, D. L. (1997). False recognition and the brain. *American Psychological Society, 6*(3), 65–70.

Schacter, D. L. (2001). *The seven sins of memory: How the mind forgets and remembers.* Boston: Houghton Mifflin.

Schachter, S., & Singer, J. E. (1962). Cognitive, social, and physiological determinants of emotional state. *Psychological Review, 69,* 379–399.

Schafe, G. E., & Bernstein, I. L. (1996). Taste aversion learning. In E. D. Capaldi (Ed.), *Why we eat what we eat: The psychology of eating* (pp. 31–51). Washington: American Psychological Association.

Schafe, G. E., Sollars, S. I., & Bernstein, I. L. (1995). The CS-US interval and taste aversion learning: A brief look. *Behavioral Neuroscience, 109*(4), 799–802.

Schaie, K. W. (1993). The Seattle longitudinal studies of adult intelligence. *Current Directions in Psychological Science, 2,* 171–175.

Schaie, K. W. (2000). The impact of longitudinal studies on understanding development from young adulthood to old age. *International Journal of Behavioral Development, 24,* 257–266.

Schaller, M. (1991). Social categorization and the formation of group stereotypes: Further evidence for biased information processing in the perception of group-behavior correlations. *European Journal of Social Psychology, 21*(1), 25–35.

Schaeffer, J., & Plaat, A. (1997). Kasparov versus Deep Blue: The rematch, *Journal of the International Computer Chess Association. 20*(2), pp. 95–101.

Schaeffer, J. (1997). *One jump ahead: Challenging human supremacy in checkers.* New York, Springer-Verlag.

Schatzman, M. (1992). Freud: Who seduced whom? *New Scientist,* 34–37.

Scheibel, A. B., Conrad, T., Perdue, S., Tomiyasu, U., & Wechsler, A. (1990). A quantitative study of dendrite complexity in selected areas of the human cerebral cortex. *Brain Cognition, 12,* 85–101.

Scher, A., & Mayseless, O. (2000). Mothers of anxious/ambivalent infants: Maternal characteristics and child-care context. *Child Development, 71*(6), 1629–1639.

Scher, M. (2001). Male therapist, male client: Reflections on critical dynamics. In G. R. Brooks & G. E. Good (Eds.), *The new handbook of psychotherapy and counseling with men: A comprehensive guide to settings, problems, and treatment approaches, 1 & 3* (pp. 719–733). New York: Jossey-Bass.

Scherer, K. R. (1997). The role of culture in emotion-antecedent appraisal. *Journal of Personality and Social Psychology, 73,* 902–922.

Scherer, K. R., Wallbott, H. G., & Summerfield, A. B. (1986). *Experiencing emotion: A cross-cultural study.* Cambridge, UK: Cambridge University Press.

Schiff, M., Duyme, M., Dumaret, A., & Tomkiewicz, S. (1982). How much could we boost scholastic achievement and IQ scores? A direct answer from a French adoption study. *Cognition, 12,* 165–196.

Schiller, P. H. (1998). The neural control of visually guided eye movements. In J. E. Richards (Ed.), *Cognitive neuroscience of attention: A development perspective* (pp. 3–50). Mahwah, NJ: Erlbaum.

Schinka, J. A., Dye, D. A., & Curtiss, G. (1997). Correspondence between five-factor and RIASEC models of personality. *Journal of Personality Assessment, 68*(2), 355–368.

Schlaug, G., Jöncke, L., Huang, Y., Staiger, J. F., & Steinmetz, H. (1995). Increased corpus callosum size in musicians. *Neuropsychologia, 33*(8), 1047–1055.

Schmidt, D. F., & Boland, S. M. (1986). Structure of perceptions of older adults: Evidence for multiple stereotypes. *Psychology and Aging, 1,* 255–260.

Schmidt, F. L., & Hunter, J. E. (1998). The validity and utility of selection methods in personnel psychology: Practical and theoretical implications of 85 years of research findings. *Psychological Bulletin, 124*(2), 262–274.

Schmidt, F. L., Onex, D. S., & Hunter, J. E. (1992). Personnel selection. *Annual Review of Psychology, 43,* 627–670.

Schmidt, L. A., Fox, N. A., Rubin, K. H., Hu, S., & Hamer, D. H. (2002). Molecular genetics of shyness and aggression in preschoolers. *Personality & Individual Differences, 33,* 2, 227–238.

Schmit, M. J., & Ryan, A. M. (1993). The big five in personnel selection: Factor structure in applicant and nonapplicant populations. *Journal of Applied Psychology, 78,* 966–974.

Schmitz, J. M., Averill, P., Stotts, A. L., Moeller, F. G., Rhoades, H. M., & Grabowski, J. (2001). Fluoxetine treatment of cocaine-dependent patients with major depressive disorder. *Drug & Alcohol Dependence, 63,* 207–214.

Schmitz, S. (1999). Gender differences in acquisition of environmental knowledge related to wayfinding ability, spatial anxiety, and self-estimated environmental competencies. *Sex Roles, 41,* 71–94.

Schneiderman, N., Antoni, M. H., Saab, P. G., & Ironson, G. (2001). Health psychology: Psychosocial and biobehavioral aspects of chronic disease management. *Annual Review of Psychology, 52,* 555–580.

Schnur, E., Brooks-Gunn, J., & Shipman, V. C. (1992). Who attends programs serving poor children? The case of Head Start attendees and nonattendees. *Journal of Applied Developmental Psychology, 13,* 405–421.

Schnyder, U., Moergeli, H., Klaghofer, R., & Buddeberg, C. (2001). Incidence and prediction of posttraumatic stress disorder symptoms in severely injured accident victims. *American Journal of Psychiatry, 158,* 594–599.

Scholl, B. J. (2000). Attenuated change blindness for exogenously attended items in a flicker paradigm. *Visual Cognition, 7,* 377–396.

Schooler, C., Neumann, E., Caplan, L. J., & Roberts, B. R. (1997). A time course analysis of Stroop interference and facilitation: Comparing normal individuals and individuals with schizophrenia. *Journal of Experimental Psychology: General, 126*(1), 19–36.

Schooler, J. W., & Fich, F. (2000). Memory for emotional events. In E. Tulving and F. I. Craik (Eds.), *The Oxford handbook of memory* (pp. 379–392). New York: Oxford University Press.

Schramke, C. J., & Bauer, R. M. (1997). State-dependent learning in older and younger adults. *Psychology and Aging, 12*(2), 255–262.

Schredl, M., Dombrowe, C., Bozzer, A., & Morlock, M. (1999). Do subliminal stimuli affect dream content? Methodological issues and empirical data. *Sleep & Hypnosis, 1,* 181–185.

Schulberg, H. C., & Rush, A. J. (1994). Clinical practice guidelines for managing major depression in primary care practice: Implications for psychologists. *American Psychologist, 49,* 34–41.

Schultz, A., Williams, D., Israel, B., Becker, A., Parker, E., James, S. A., & Jackson, J. (2000). Unfair treatment, neighborhood effects, and mental health in the Detroit metropolitan area. *The Journal of Health and Social Behavior, 41,* 314–333.

Schultz, G., & Melzack, R. (1999). A case of referred pain evoked by remote light touch after partial nerve injury. *Pain, 81,* 199–202.

Schurr, K. T., Ruble, V., Palomba, C., Pickerill, B., & Moore, D. (1997). Relationships between the MBTI and selected aspects of Tinto's model for college attrition. *Journal of Psychological Type, 40,* 31–42.

Schusterman, R. J. & Gisiner, R. C. (1996). Pinnipeds, porpoises, and parsimony: Animal language research viewed from a bottom-up perspective. In R. W. Mitchell, N. S. Nicholas, & H. L. Miles (Eds.), *Anthropomorphism, anecdotes, and animals* (pp. 370–382). New York: State University of New York Press.

Schwartz, B., & Robbins, S. J. (1995). *Psychology of learning and behavior.* New York: Norton.

Schwartzman, A. E., Gold, D., Andres, D., Arbuckle, T. Y., & Chaikelson, J. (1987). Stability of intelligence: A 40-year follow-up. *Canadian Journal of Psychology, 41,* 244–256.

Schwarz-Stevens, K. S., & Cunningham, C. L. (1993). Pavlovian conditioning of heart rate and body temperature with morphine: Effects of CS duration. *Behavioral Neuroscience, 107,* 1039–1048.

Schweiger, U., Deuschle, M., Körner, A., Lammers, C. H., Schmider, J., Gotthardt, U., Holsboer, F., & Heuser, I. (1994). Low lumbar bone mineral density in patients with major depression. *American Journal of Psychiatry, 151,* 1691–1693.

Sclafani, A. (1997). Learned controls of ingestive behavior. *Appetite, 29,* 153–158.

Scott, K., Brady, R., Cravchik, A., Morozov, P., Rzhetsky, A., Zuker, C., & Axel, R. (2001). A chemosensory gene family encoding candidate gustatory and olfactory receptors in *Drosophila. Cell, 104,* 661–673.

Sears, G., & Rowe, P. M. (2003). A personality-based similar-to-me effect in the employment interview: Conscientiousness, affect- versus competence-mediated interpretations, and the role of job relevance. *Canadian Journal of Behavioural Science, 35,* 1, 13–24.

Segal, N. L., & MacDonald, K. B. (1998). Behavioral genetics and evolutionary psychology: Unified perspective on personality research. *Human Biology, 70,* 159–174.

Seidenberg, M. S. (1997). Language acquisition and use: Learning and applying probabilistic constraints. *Science, 275,* 1599–1603.

Selekman, M. D. (1993). Solution-oriented brief therapy with difficult adolescents. In S. Friedman (Ed.), *The new language of change: Constructive collaboration in psychotherapy* (pp. 138–157). New York: Guilford Press.

Seligman, M. E. P. (1976). *Learned helplessness and depression in animals and humans.* Morristown, NJ: General Learning.

Seligman, M. E. P. (1988, August). *Learned helplessness.* G. Stanley Hall lecture at the American Psychological Association Convention, Atlanta.

Seligman, M. E. P. (1991). *Learned optimism.* New York: Knopf.

Seligman, M. E. P. (1995). The effectiveness of psychotherapy. *American Psychologist, 50,* 965–974.

Seligman, M. E. P., & Csikszentmihalyi, M. (2000). Positive psychology. *American Psychologist, 55,* 5–14.

Sell, R. L., Wells, J. A., & Wypij, D. (1995). The prevalence of homosexual behavior and attraction in the United States, the United Kingdom and France: Results of national population-based samples. *Archives of Sexual Behavior, 24,* 235–248.

Selye, H. (1956). *The stress of life.* New York: McGraw-Hill.

Selye, H. (1976). *Stress in health and disease.* London: Butterworth.

Sen, M. G., Yonas, A., & Knill, D. C. (2001). Development of infants' sensitivity to surface contour information for spatial layout. *Perception, 30,* 167–176.

Severiens, S., & Ten-Dam, G. (1997). Gender and gender identity differences in learning styles. *Educational Psychology, 17*(1/2), 79–93.

Shallice, T., Fletcher, P., Frith, C. D., Grasby, P., Frackowiak, R. S. J., & Dolan, R. J. (1994). Brain regions associated with acquisition and retrieval of verbal episodic memory. *Nature, 368,* 633–635.

Shalowitz, M. U., Berry, C. A., Rasinski, K. A., & Dannhausen-Brun, C. A. (1998). A new measurement of contemporary life stress: Development, validation, and reliability of the CRISYS (Crisis in Family Systems). *Health Services Research, 33,* 1381–1382.

Shamir, B. (1992). Attribution of influence and charisma to the leader: The romance of leadership revisited. *Journal of Applied Social Psychology, 22,* 386–407.

Shammi, P. & Stuss, D. T. (1999). Humour appreciation: A role of the right frontal lobe. *Brain, 122,* 657–666.

Shanab, M. E., & Yahya, K. A. (1978). A cross-cultural study of obedience. *Bulletin of the Psychonomic Society, 11,* 267–269.

Sharit, J., & Czajia, S. J. (1999). Performance of a computer-based troubleshooting task in the banking industry: Examining the effects of age, task experience, and cognitive abilities. *International Journal of Cognitive Ergonomics, 3*(1), 1–22.

Shatz, C. J. (1992, September). The developing brain. *Scientific American,* 61–67.

Shatz, S. M. (2000). The relationship of locus of control and social support to adult nursing home residents. *Dissertation Abstracts International: Section B: The Sciences & Engineering, 61*(3-B), 1655.

Shaywitz, B. A., Shaywitz, S. E., Pugh, K. R., Constable, R. T., Skudlarski, P., Fulbright, R. K., Bronen, R. A., Fletcher, J. M., Shankweiler, D. P., Katz, L., & Gore, J. C. (1995). Sex differences in the functional organization of the brain for language. *Nature, 373,* 607–609.

Shaywitz, S. E., Shaywitz, B. A., Pugh, K. R., Fullbright, R. K., & Constable, R. T. (1998). Functional disruption in the organization of the brain for reading in dyslexia. *Proceedings of the National Academy of Sciences, 95*(5), 2636–2641.

Shedler, J., & Block, J. (1990). Adolescent drug use and psychological health. *American Psychologist, 45,* 612–630.

Sheehan, P. W., & Tilden, J. (1983). Effects of suggestibility and hypnosis on accurate and distorted retrieval from memory. *Journal of Experimental Psychology: Learning, Memory and Cognition, 9*(2), 283–293.

Sheehy, G. (1995). *New passages: Mapping your life across time.* New York: Random House.

Sheehy, G. (1998). *Understanding men's passages: Discovering the new map of men's lives.* New York: Random House.

Sheeran, P., Abraham, C., & Orbell, S. (1999). Psychosocial correlates of heterosexual condom use: A meta-analysis. *Psychological Bulletin, 125*(1), 90–132.

Shelton, C. M. (2000). *Achieving moral health: An exercise plan for your conscience.* New York: Crossroad.

Shen, B., & McNaughton, B. L. (1996). Modeling the spontaneous reactivation of experience-specific hippocampal cell assemblies during sleep. *Hippocampus, 6*(6), 685–692.

Shepard, S., & Metzler, D. (1988). Mental rotation: Effects of dimensionality of objects and type of task. Journal of Experimental Psychology: *Human Perception and Performance, 14,* 3–11.

Shepperd, J. A. (1993). Productivity loss in performance groups: A motivation analysis. *Psychological Bulletin, 113,* 67–81.

Sher, L. (1998). The role of the immune system and infection in the effects of psychological factors on the cardiovascular system. *Canadian Journal of Psychiatry, 43*(9), 954–955.

Shergill, S. S., Brammer, M. J., Williams, S. C. R., Murray, R. M., & McGuire, P. K. (2000). Mapping auditory hallucinations in schizophrenia using functional magnetic resonance imaging. *Archives of General Psychiatry, 57,* 1033–1038.

Sheridan, M. S. (1985). Things that go beep in the night: Home monitoring for apnea. *Health and Social Work, 10,* 63–70.

Sherin, J. E., Shiromani, P. J., McCarley, R. W., & Saper, C. B. (1996). Activation of ventrolateral preoptic neurons during sleep. *Science, 271,* 216–219.

Sherrington, R., Rogaev, E. I., Liang, Y., Rogaeva, E. A., Levesque, G., Ikeda, M., Chi, H., Lin, C., Li, G., Holman, K., Tsuda, T., Mar, L., Foncin, J. F., Bruni, A. C., Montesi, M. P., Sorbi, S., Rainero, I., Pinessi, L., Nee, L., Chumakov, I., Pollen, D., Brookes, A., Sanseau, P., Polinsky, R. J., Wasco, W., Da Silva, H. A. R., Haines, J. L., Pericak-Vance, M. A., Tanzi, R. E., Roses, A. D., Fraser, P. E., Rommens, J. M., & St. George-Hyslop, P. H. (1995). Cloning of a gene bearing missense mutations in early-onset familial Alzheimer's disease. *Nature, 375,* 754–760.

Shimamura, A. P., & Squire, L. R. (1986). Memory and metamemory: A study of the feeling-of-knowing phenomenon in amnesic patients. *Journal of Experimental Psychology: Learning, Memory, and Cognition, 12,* 452–460.

Shiner, R. L. (1998). How shall we speak of children's personalities in middle childhood? A preliminary taxonomy. *Psychological Bulletin, 124*(3), 308–332.

Shobe, K. K., & Kihlstrom, J. F. (1997). Is traumatic memory special? *Current Directions in Psychological Science, 6*(3), 70–74.

Shonkoff, J. P. (2000). *From neurons to neighborhoods: The science of early childhood development.* Briefing presented at the National Research Council and Institute of Medicine, Washington, DC.

Shostrom, E. L. (1974). *Manual for the Personal Orientation Inventory.* San Diego, CA: Educational and Industrial Testing Service.

Shum, M. S. (1998). The role of temporal landmarks in autobiographical memory processes. *Psychological Bulletin, 124*(3), 423–442.

Shute, V. J., Pellegrino, J. W., Hubert, L., & Reynolds. R. W. (1983). The relationship between androgen levels and human spatial abilities. *Bulletin of the Psychonomic Society, 21,* 465–468.

Siegel, E. F. (1979). Control of phantom limb pain by hypnosis. *American Journal of Clinical Hypnosis, 21,* 285–286.

Siegel, J. M. (1990). Stressful life events and use of physician services among the elderly: The moderating role of pet ownership. *Journal of Personality and Social Psychology, 58,* 1081–1086.

Siegel, S. (1984). Pavlovian conditioning and heroin overdose: Reports by overdose victims. *Bulletin of the Psychonomic Society, 22*(5), 428–430.

Siegel, S. (1999). Drug anticipation and drug addiction: The 1998 H. David Archibald lecture. *Addiction, 94,* 1113–1124.

Siegel, S., & Allan, L. G. (1996). The widespread influence of the Rescorla-Wagner model. *Psychonomic Bulletin and Review, 3*(3), 314–321.

Siegel, S., Baptista, M. A. S., Kim. J. A., McDonald, R. V., & Weise-Kelly, L. (2000). Pavlovian psychopharmacology: The associative basis of tolerance. *Experimental & Clinical Psychopharmacology, 8,* 276–293.

Siegel, S., & MacCrae, J. (1984). Environmental specificity of tolerance. *Trends in Neurosciences, 7*(5), 140–143.

Siegman, A. W. & Boyle, S. (1993). Voices of fear and anxiety and depression: The effects of speech rate and loudness on fear and anxiety and sadness and depression. *Journal of Abnormal Psychology, 102,* 3, 430–437.

Sigelman, L. (1997). Blacks, whites, and the changing of the guard in black political leadership. In S. A. Tuch & J. K. Martin (Eds.), *Racial attitudes in the 1990s: Continuity and change.* Westport, CT: Praeger.

Sigman, M. (1995). Nutrition and child development: More food for thought. *Current Directions in Psychological Science, 4,* 52–55.

Silverman, I., Choi, J., Mackewn, A., Fisher, M., Moro, J., & Olshansky, E. (2000). Evolved mechanisms underlying wayfinding: Further studies on the hunter-gatherer theory of spatial sex differences. *Evolution & Human Behavior, 21,* 201–213.

Silverman, J. G., Raj, A., Mucci, L. A., & Hathaway, J. E. (2001). Dating violence against adolescent girls and associated substance use, unhealthy weight control, sexual risk behavior, pregnancy, and suicidality. *Journal of the American Medical Association, 286,* 572–579.

Silverman, L. H. (1983). The subliminal psychodynamic activation method: Overview and comprehensive listing of studies. In J. Masling (Ed.), *Empirical studies of psychoanalytic theories* (Vol. 1, pp. 69–100). Hillsdale, NJ: Erlbaum.

Silverstein, L. B., & Auerbach, C. F. (1999). Deconstructing the essential father. *American Psychologist, 54*(6), 397–407.

Simons, A. D., Gordon, J. S., Monroe, S. M., & Thase, M. (1995). Toward an integration of psychologic, social, and biologic factors in depression. *Journal of Consulting and Clinical Psychology, 63,* 369–377.

Simons, D. J., & Chabris, C. F. (1999). Gorillas in our midst: Sustained inattentional blindness for dynamic events. *Perception, 28,* 1059–1074.

Simons, D. J., Franconeri, S. L., & Reimer, R. L. (2000). Change blindness in the absence of a visual disruption. *Perception, 29,* 1143–1154.

Simonton, D. K. (1988). Age and outstanding achievement: What do we know after a century of research? *Psychological Bulletin, 104,* 251–267.

Simpson, J. R., Oenguer, D., Akbudak, E., Conturo, T. E., Ollinger, J. M., Snyder, A. Z., Gusnard, D. A., & Raichle, M. E. (2000). The emotional modulation of cognitive processing: An fMRI study. *Journal of Cognitive Neuroscience, 12* (Suppl. 2), 157–170.

Singer, L. M., Brodzinsky, D. M., Ramsay, D., Steir, M., & Waters, E. (1985). Mother infant attachment in adoptive families. *Child Development, 56,* 1543–1551.

Singer, W. (1995). Development and plasticity of cortical processing architectures. *Science, 270,* 758–763.

Singh, S., & Darroch, J. (2000). Adolescent pregnancy and childbearing: levels and trends in developed countries. *Family Planning Perspectives, 32,* 14–23.

Sinha, B. K., Willson, L. R., & Watson, D. C. (2000). Stress and coping among students in India and Canada. *Canadian Journal of Behavioural Science, 32,* 218–225.

Siple, P. (1997). Universals, generalizability, and the acquisition of signed language. In M. Marschark, P. Siple, D. Lillo-Martin, R. Campbell, & V. S. Everhart, *Relations of language and thought: The view from sign language and deaf children* (pp. 24–61). New York: Oxford University Press.

Skarlicki, D. P., & Latham, G. P. (1995). Organizational citizenship behaviour and performance in a university setting. *Canadian Journal of Administrative Sciences, 12,* 175–181.

Skinner, B. F. (1938). *The behavior of organisms.* New York: Appleton-Century-Crofts.

Skinner, B. F. (1948). Superstition in the pigeon. *Journal of Experimental Psychology, 38,* 168–172.

Skinner, B. F. (1987). *Upon further reflection.* Englewood Cliffs, NJ: Prentice-Hall.

Skinner, B. F. (1988, June). Skinner joins aversives debate. *American Psychological Association APA Monitor, 22.*

Skoog, G., & Skoog, I. (1999). A 40–year follow-up of patients with obsessive-compulsive disorder. *Archives of General Psychiatry, 56,* 121–132.

Slaikeu, K. A. (1990). *Crisis intervention* (2nd ed.). Boston: Allyn & Bacon.

Smart, R., & Peterson, C. (1994). Stability versus transition in women's career development: A test of Levinson's theory. *Journal of Vocational Behavior, 45,* 241–260.

Smellie, P. (1999). Feeding stereotypes. *The Quill, 87*(2), 25–27.

Smith, E. E. (1997). Working memory: A view from neuroimaging. *Cognitive Psychology, 33*(1), 5–42.

Smith, E. E., Jonides, J., Koeppe, R. A., & Awh, E. (1995). Spatial versus object working memory: PET investigations. *Journal of Cognitive Neuroscience, 7*(3), 337–356.

Smith, K. H., & Rogers, M. (1994). Effectiveness of subliminal messages in television commercials: Two experiments. *Journal of Applied Psychology, 79,* 866–874.

Smith, L. B. & Thelen, E. (1993). *A dynamic systems approach to development: Applications.* MIT Press/Bradford Books Series in Cognitive Psychology.

Smith, M. (1996). Aboriginal street gangs in Winnipeg. *Alberta Sweetgrass.* Edmonton.

Smith, M. C. (1983). Hypnotic memory enhancement of witnesses: Does it work? *Psychological Bulletin, 94,* 387–407.

Smith, M. L., Glass, G. V., & Miller, T. I. (1980). *The benefits of psychotherapy.* Baltimore: Johns Hopkins University Press.

Smith, M. W., Mendoza, R. P., & Lin, K. M. (1999). Gender and ethnic differences in the pharmacogenetics of psychotropics. In M. Herrera & W. B. Lawson (Eds.), *Cross-cultural psychiatry* (pp. 323–341). New York: Wiley.

Smith, S. L., Wilson, B. J., Kunkel, D., Linz, D., Potter, J., Colvin, C. M., & Donnerstein, E. (1998). *National television violence study. Volume III.* London: Sage Publications.

Sneed, C. D., McCrae, R. R., & Funder, D. C. (1998). Lay conceptions of the five-factor model and its indicators. *Personality & Social Psychology Bulletin, 24*(2), 115–126.

Snider, V. E., Frankenberger, W., Aspenson, M. R. (2000). The relationship between learning disabilities and Attention Deficit Hyperactivity Disorder: A national survey. *Developmental Disabilities Bulletin, 28*(1), 18–38.

Soares, J. C., & Mann, J. (1997). The functional neuroanatomy of mood disorders. *Journal of Psychiatric Research, 31*(4), 393–432.

Sobell, L. C., Cunningham, J. A., & Sobell, M. B. (1996). Recovery from alcohol problems with and without treatment: Prevalence in two population surveys. *American Journal of Public Health, 86,* 966–972.

Sobell, M. B., & Sobell, L. C. (1982). Controlled drinking: A concept coming of age. In K. R. Blanstein & J. Polivy (Eds.), *Self-control and self-modification of emotional behavior.* New York: Plenum.

Soderstrom, M., Dolbier, C., Leiferman, J., & Steinhardt, M. (2000). The relationship of hardiness, coping strategies, and perceived stress to symptoms of illness. *Journal of Behavioral Medicine, 23,* 311–328.

Sokolov, R. (1999). Culture and obesity. *Social Research, 66,* 31–38.

Solomon, P. R., Flynn, D., Mirak, J., Brett, M., Coslov, N., & Groccia, M. E. (1998). Five-year retention of the classically conditioned eyeblink response in young adult, middle-aged, and older humans. *Psychology and Aging, 13*(2), 186–192.

Solowij, N. (1998). *Cannabis and cognitive functioning.* Cambridge, England: Cambridge University Press.

Solso, R. L. (1979). *Cognitive psychology.* New York: Harcourt, Brace Jovanovich.

Sommerich, C. M., Joines, S. M. B., & Psihogios, J. P. (2001). Effects of computer monitor viewing angle and related factors on strain, performance, and preference outcomes. *Human Factors, 43,* 39–55.

Sonn, C. C., & Fisher, A. T. (1998). Sense of community: Community resilient responses to oppression and change. *Journal of Community Psychology, 26*(5), 457–472.

Sonnenborg, F. A., Anderson, O. K., & Arendt-Nielsen, L. (2000). Modular organization of excitatory and inhibitory reflex receptive fields elicited by electrical stimulation of the foot sole in man. *Clinical Neurophysiology, 11,* 2160–2169.

Sosik, J. J., Kahai, S. S., & Avolio, B. J. (1998). Transformational leadership and dimensions of creativity: Motivating idea generation in computer-mediated groups. *Creativity Research Journal, 11*(2), 111–121.

Spangler, W. D. (1992). Validity of questionnaire and TAT measures of need for achievement: Two meta-analyses. *Psychological Bulletin, 112,* 140–154.

Spanos, N. P. (1991). A sociocognitive approach to hypnosis. In S. J. Lynn & J. W. Rhue (Eds.), *Theories of hypnosis: Current models and perspectives* (pp. 324–361). New York: Guilford Press.

Spanos, N. P. (1994). Multiple identity enactments and multiple personality disorder: A sociocognitive perspective. *Psychological Bulletin, 116,* 143–165.

Spear, L. P. (2000). Neurobehavioral changes in adolescence. *Current Directions in Psychological Science, 9,* 111–114.

Spears, R., & Haslam, S. A. (1997). Stereotyping and the burden of cognitive load. In R. Spears (Ed.), *The social psychology of stereotyping and group life.* Oxford, England: Blackwell Publishers, Inc.

Speck, O., Ernst, T., Braun, J., Koch, C., Miller, E., & Chang, L. (2000). Gender differences in the functional organization of the brain for working memory. *Neuroreport: An International Journal for the Rapid Communication of Research in Neuroscience, 11,* 2581–2585.

Spelke, E. S., Breinlinger, K., Macomber, J., & Jacobson, K. (1992). Origins of knowledge. *Psychological Review, 99*(4), 605–632.

Spelke, E. S., & von Hofsten, C. (2001). Predicted reaching for occluded objects by 6-month-old infants. *Journal of Cognition & Development, 2,* 3, 261–281.

Sperling, G. (1960). The information available in brief visual presentations. *Psychological Monographs, 15,* 201–293.

Sperry, R. W. (1985). Consciousness, personal identity, and the divided brain. In D. F. Benson & E. Zaidel (Eds.), *The dual brain: Hemispheric specialization in humans* (pp. 11–26). New York: Guilford.

Sporer, S. L. (1993). Eyewitness identification accuracy, confidence, and decision times in simultaneous and sequential lineups. *Journal of Applied Psychology, 78,* 22–33.

Springer, P. J. (2000). The relationship between learned helplessness and work performance in registered nurses. *Dissertation Abstracts International: Section B: The Sciences & Engineering, 60*(12-B), 6407.

Springer, S. P., & Deutsch, G. (1998). *Left brain, right brain: Perspectives from cognitive neuroscience* (5th ed.). New York: Freeman.

Sprock, J., & Yoder, C. Y. (1997). Women and depression: An update on the report of the APA Task Force. *Sex Roles, 36*(5/6), 269–303.

Squire, L. R., & Kandel, E. R. (1999). *Memory: From mind to molecules.* New York: Freeman.

Stagner, R. (1988). *A history of psychological theories.* New York: Macmillan.

Stajkovic, A. D., & Luthans, F. (1998). Self-efficacy and work-related performance: A meta-analysis. *Psychological Bulletin, 124*(2), 240–261.

Stake, J. E. (1997). Integrating expressiveness and instrumentality in real-life settings: A new perspective on the benefits of androgyny. *Sex Roles, 37*(7/8), 541–564.

Stalker, C. A., Levene, J. E., & Coady, N. F. (1999). Solution focused brief therapy—one model fits all? *Families in Society, 80,* 468–477.

Starzomski, A., & Nussbaum, D. (2000). The self and the psychology of domestic homicide–suicide. *International Journal of Offender Therapy and Comparative Criminology, 44,* 468–479.

Stassen, H. H., Ragaz, M., & Reich, T. (1997). Age-of-onset or age-cohort changes in the lifetime occurrence of depression? *Psychiatric Genetics, 7,* 27–34.

Staszewski, J. J. (1987). The psychological reality of retrieval structures: An investigation of expert knowledge (doctoral dissertation, Cornell University, 1987). *Dissertation Abstracts International, 48,* 2168B.

Staszewski, J. J. (1988). Skilled memory and expert mental calculation. In M. T. H. Chi, R. Glaser, & M. J. Farr (Eds.), *The nature of expertise.* Hillsdale, NJ: Erlbaum.

Statistics Canada (2001, 25 January). *The daily: Television viewing.* http://www.statcan.ca/english/freepub/82-221-XIE/00601/high/drink/htm, accessed 3 October 2003.

Statistics Canada (2001, June). *Self esteem in health indicators.* Catalogue no. 82-221-XIE. http://www.statcan.ca/english/freepub/82-221-XIE/00601/high/esteem.htm, accessed 2 July 2003.

Statistics Canada (2002). *Table 052-0001—Projected population, by age group and sex, Canada, provinces and territories, July 1, 2000–2026, annual (persons).* http://cansim2.statcan.ca/cgiwin/cnsmcgi.exe?Lang=E&RootDir=CII/&ResultTemplate=CII/CII_pick&Array_Pick=1&ArrayId=0520001, accessed 29 September 2003.

Statistics Canada (2003). *Canadian community health survey: Mental health and well being: 2002.* http://www.statcan.ca/Daily/English/030903/d030903a.htm, accessed 6 October 2003.

Statistics Canada (2003, 18 June). *Causes of death.* Catalogue Number 84-208-XIE.

Statistics Canada (2003). 2001 Canadian census data. Obtained at http://www.statcan.ca/english/Pgdb/demo10a.htm, accessed September 23, 2003.

St. Clair, D. M., St. Clair, J. B., Swainson, C. P., Bamforth, F., & Machin, G. A. (1998). Twin zygosity testing for medical purposes. *American Journal of Medical Genetics, 77,* 412–414.

Steele, C. M. (1997). A threat in the air: How stereotypes shape intellectual identity and performance. *American Psychologist, 52*(6), 613–629.

Steele, C. M. (1999). The psychology of self-affirmation: Sustaining the integrity of the self. In R. F. Baumeister (Ed.), *The self in social psychology, Key Readings in Social Psychology* (pp. 372–390). Philadelphia: Psychology Press/Taylor & Francis.

Steele, C. M., & Aronson, J. (2000). Stereotype threat and the intellectual test performance of African Americans. In C. Stangor (Ed.), *Stereotypes and prejudice: Essential readings, Key Readings in Social Psychology* (pp. 369–389). Philadelphia: Psychology Press/ Taylor & Francis.

Steele, C. M., & Josephs, R. A. (1990). Alcohol myopia. *American Psychologist, 45,* 921–933.

Stein, A. D., Karel, T., & Zuidema, R. (1999). Carrots and sticks: Impact of an incentive/disincentive employee flexible credit benefit plan on health status and medical costs. *American Journal of Health Promotion, 13,* 260–267.

Stein, B. E., Wallace, M. T., Stanford, T. R., & Jiang, W. (2002). Cortex governs multisensory integration in the midbrain. *The Neuroscientist, 8,* 306–314.

Stein, M., Jang, K., & Livesley, W. J. (2002). Heritability of social anxiety-related concerns and personality characteristics: A twin study. *The Journal of Nervous and Mental Disease, 190,* 4, 219–224.

Stein, M. B. (1998). Neurobiological perspectives on social phobia: From affiliation to zoology. *Biological Psychiatry, 44,* 1277–1285.

Stein, M. B., Walker, J. R., & Forde, D. R. (2000). Gender differences in susceptibility to posttraumatic stress disorder. *Behaviour Research and Therapy, 38,* 619–628.

Steinberg, M. (1995). *Handbook for the assessment of dissociation: A clinical guide.* Washington, DC: American Psychiatric Press.

Steiner, I. D. (1982). Heuristic models of groupthink. In M. Brandstatter, J. H. Davis, & G. Stocker-Kreichgauer (Eds.), *Group decision making.* New York: Academic.

Sternberg, R. J. (1985). *Beyond IQ.* Cambridge, England: Cambridge University Press.

Sternberg, R. J. (1997a). The concept of intelligence and its role in lifelong learning and success. *American Psychologist, 52*(10), 1030–1037.

Sternberg, R. J. (1998). A balance theory of wisdom. *Review of General Psychology, 2*(4), 347–365.

Sternberg, R. J. (2000a). Identifying and developing creative giftedness. *Roeper Review, 23,* 60–64.

Sternberg, R. J. (2000b). Implicit theories of intelligence as exemplar stories of success: Why intelligence test validity is in the eye of the beholder. *Psychology, Public Policy, & Law, 6,* 159–167.

Sternberg, R. J. (2001a). Successful intelligence: A unified view of giftedness. In C. F. M. van Lieshout & P. G. Heymans (Eds.), *Developing talent across the life span* (pp. 43–65). Philadelphia: Psychology Press/Taylor & Francis.

Sternberg, R. J. (2001b). What is the common thread of creativity?: Its dialectical relation to intelligence and wisdom. *American Psychologist, 56,* 360–362.

Sternberg, R. J., Castegon, J. L., Prieto, M. D., Hautamaki, J., & Grigorenko, E. L. (2001). Confirmatory factor analysis of the Sternberg Triarchic Abilities Test in three international samples: An empirical test of the triarchic theory of intelligence. *European Journal of Psychological Assessment, 17*(1), 1–16.

Sternberg, R. J., & Grigorenko, E. L. (2000a). Practical intelligence and its development. In R. Bar-On, & J. D. A. Parker (Eds.), *The handbook of emotional intelligence: Theory, development, assessment, and application at home, school, and in the workplace* (pp. 215–243). San Francisco: Jossey-Bass.

Sternberg, R. J., & Grigorenko, E. L. (2000b). Theme-park psychology: A case study regarding human intelligence and its implications for education. *Educational Psychology Review, 12*(2), 247–268.

Sternberg, R. J., Grigorenko, E. L., & Bundy, D. A. (2001). The predictive value of IQ. *Merrill-Palmer Quarterly, 47,* 1–41.

Sternberg, R. J., & Lubart, T. I. (1993). Creative giftedness: A multivariate investment approach. *Gifted Child Quarterly, 37*(1), 7–15.

Sternberg, R. J., & Lubart, T. I. (1996). Investing in creativity. *American Psychologist, 51*(7), 677–688.

Sternberg, R. J., & Lubart, T. I. (1999). The concept of creativity: Prospects and paradigms. In R. J. Sternberg (Ed.), *Handbook of creativity* (pp. 3–15). New York: Cambridge University Press.

Sternberg, R. J., & Williams, W. M. (1997). Does the Graduate Record Examination predict meaningful success in the graduate training of psychologists? *American Psychologist, 52*(6), 630–641.

Sterrett, E. A. (1998). Use of a job club to increase self-efficacy: A case study of return to work. *Journal of Employment Counseling, 35*(2), 69–78.

Stewart, S., Stinnett, H., & Rosenfeld, L. B. (2001). Sex differences in desired characteristics of short-term and long-term relationship partners. *Journal of Social and Personal Relationships, 17*, 843–853.

Stickgold, R., James, L., & Hobson, J. A. (2000). Visual discrimination learning requires sleep after training. *Nature Neuroscience, 3*, 1237–1238.

Stilwell, B. M., Galvin, M. R., Kopta, S. M. (2000). *Right vs Wrong: Raising a Child With a Conscience.* Bloomington, IN: Indiana University Press.

Stitzer, M. L. (1988). Drug abuse in methadone patients reduced when rewards/punishments clear. *Alcohol, Drug Abuse, and Mental Health, 14*, 1.

Stokols, D. (1995). The paradox of environmental psychology. *American Psychologist, 50*, 821–837.

Stoléru, S., Grégoire, M. C., Gérard, D., Decety, J., Lafarge, E., Cinotti, L., Lavenne, F., LeBars, D., Vernet-Maury, E., Rada, H., Collet, C., Mazoyer, B., Forest, M. G., Magnin, F., Spira, A., & Comar, D. (1999). Neuroanatomical correlates of visually evoked sexual arousal in human males. *Archives of Sexual Behavior, 28*(1), 1–19.

Stone, J., Perry, Z. W., & Darley, J. M. (1997). "White men can't jump": Evidence for the perceptual confirmation of racial stereotypes following a basketball game. *Basic and Applied Social Psychology, 19*(3), 291–306.

Stone, J., Wiegand, A. W., Cooper, J., & Aronson, E. (1997). When exemplification fails: Hypocrisy and the motive for self-integrity. *Journal of Personality and Social Psychology, 72*(1), 54–65.

Stone, R. (2000). Stress: The invisible hand in Eastern Europe's death rates. *Science, 288*, 1732–1733.

Stoolmiller, M. (1999). Implications of the restricted range of family environments for estimates of heritability and nonshared environment in behavior-genetic adoption studies. *Psychological Bulletin, 125*, 392–409.

Stowell, J. R., Kiecolt-Glaser, J. K., & Glaser, R. (2001). Perceived stress and cellular immunity: When coping counts. *Journal of Behavioral Medicine, 24*, 323–339.

Streissguth, A. P., Barr, H. M., & Martin, D. C. (1983). Maternal alcohol use and neonatal habituation assessed with the Brazelton Scale. *Child Development, 54*, 1109–1118.

Streissguth, A. P., Barr, H. M., Sampson, P. D., Darby, B. L., & Martin, D. C. (1989). IQ at age 4 in relation to maternal alcohol use and smoking during pregnancy. *Developmental Psychology, 25*, 3–11.

Striegel-Moore, R. H., & Cachelin, F. M. (1999). Body image concerns and disordered eating in adolescent girls: Risk and protective factors. In N. G. Johnson, M. C. Roberts, & J. Worell (Eds.), *Beyond appearance: A new look at adolescent girls* (pp. 85–108). Washington, DC: American Psychological Association.

Stringer, P. (1998). One night Vygotsky had a dream: "Children learning to think..." and implications for educational psychologists. *Educational and Child Psychology, 15*(2), 14–20.

Stroganova, T. A., Tsetlin, M. M., Malykh, S. B., Malakhovskaya, E. V. (2000). Biological principles of individual differences of children of the second half-year of life: Communication II. The nature of individual differences in temperamental features. *Human Physiology, 26*(3), 281–289.

Stroop, J. R. (1935). Studies of interference in serial verbal reactions. *Journal of Experimental Psychology, 18*, 643–662.

Stuart, E. W., Shimp, T. A., & Engle, R. W. (1987). Classical conditioning of consumer attitudes: Four experiments in an advertising context. *Journal of Consumer Research, 14*, 334–349.

Sturges, J. S. (1994). Family dynamics. In J. L. Ronch, W. V. Ornum, & N. C. Stilwell (Eds.), *The counseling sourcebook: A practical reference on contemporary issues* (pp. 358–372). New York: Crossroad.

Sturges, J. W., & Rogers, R. R. (1996). Preventive health psychology from a developmental perspective: An extension of protection motivation theory. *Health Psychology, 15*, 158–166.

Stuss, D. T. (1991). Self, awareness and the frontal lobes: A neuropsychological perspective. In J. Strauss & G. R. Goethals (Eds.), *The self: Interdisciplinary approaches* (pp. 255–278). New York: Springer-Verlag.

Sue, D. (2001). Asian American masculinity and therapy: The concept of masculinity in Asian American males. In G. R. Brooks & G. E. Good (Eds.), *The new handbook of psychotherapy and counseling with men: A comprehensive guide to settings, problems, and treatment approaches, 1 & 2* (pp. 780–795). San Francisco: Jossey-Bass.

Suedfeld, P. (1990). Restricted environmental stimulation and smoking cessation: A 15-year progress report. *International Journal of the Addictions, 25*, 861–888.

Suedfeld, P. (1998). What can abnormal environments tell us about normal people? Polar stations as natural psychology laboratories. *Journal of Environmental Psychology, 18*, 95–102.

Suedfeld, P. (2000). Reverberations of the Holocaust fifty years later: Psychology's contributions to understanding persecution and genocide. *Canadian Psychology, 41*, 1–9.

Suedfeld, P. (2003). Canadian space psychology: The future may be almost here. *Canadian Psychology, 44*, 2, 85–91.

Suedfeld, P. (2003). Specific and general attributional patterns of Holocaust survivors. *Canadian Journal of Behavioural Science, 35*, 2, 133–141.

Suedfeld, P., & Bruno, T. (1990). Flotation REST and imagery in the improvement of athletic performance. *Journal of Sport and Exercise Psychology, 12*(1), 82–85.

Suedfeld, P., Collier, D. E., & Hartnett, B. D. (1993). Enhancing perceptual-motor accuracy through flotation REST. *Sport Psychologist, 7*(2), 151–159.

Suedfeld, P., & Coren, S. (1989). Perceptual isolation, sensory deprivation, and rest: Moving introductory psychology texts out of the 1950s. *Canadian Psychology, 30*(1), 17–29.

Suedfeld, P., Fell, C., & Krell, R. (1998). Structural aspects of survivors' thinking about the Holocaust. *Journal of Traumatic Stress, 11*, 323–336.

Suedfeld, P., Krell, R., Wiebe, R. E., & Steel, G. D. (1997). Coping strategies in the narratives of Holocaust survivors. *Anxiety, Stress & Coping, 10*, 2, 153–179.

Suedfeld, P., & Schwartz, G. (1981). *Restricted environmental stimulation therapy (REST) as a treatment for autistic children.* Annual meeting of the American Psychological Association, Los Angeles, California.

Suedfeld, P. & Soriano, E. (1998). Separating the qualitative to quantitative dimension from the data versus analyses distinction: Another way to study Holocaust survivors. *The Reference Librarian, 61/62*, 315–338.

Suedfeld, P., Steel, G., Wallbaum, A., Bluck, S., Lively, N., & Capozzi, L. (1994). Explaining the effects of stimulus restriction: Testing the dynamic hemispheric asymmetry hypothesis. *Journal of Environmental Psychology, 14*, 87–100.

Suedfeld, P., & Steel, G. D. (2000). The environmental psychology of capsule habitats. *Annual Review of Psychology, 51*, 227–253.

Sugihara, Y., & Katsurada, E. (2000). Gender-role personality traits in Japanese culture. *Psychology of Women Quarterly, 24*, 309–318.

Suh, E., Diener, E., Oishi, S., & Triandis, H. C. (1998). The shifting basis of life satisfaction judgments across cultures: Emotions versus norms. *Journal of Personality and Social Psychology, 74*, 482–493.

Suinn, R. M. (2001). The terrible twos—anger and anxiety: Hazardous to your health. *American Psychologist, 56*, 27–36.

Sullivan, M. J. L., Bishop, S. R., & Pivik, J. (1995). The pain catastrophizing scale: Development and validation. *Psychological Assessment, 7*, 524–532.

Sullivan, P. F., Bulik, C. M., Fear, J. L., & Pickering, A. (1998). Outcome of anorexia nervosa: A case-control study. *American Journal of Psychiatry, 155*(7), 939–946.

Summers, T. P., & Hendrix, W. H. (1991). Modeling the role of pay equity perceptions: A field study. *Journal of Occupational Psychology, 64*, 145–157.

Sun, L-C., & Roopnarine, J. L. (1996). Mother-infant, father-infant interaction and involvement in childcare and household labor among Taiwanese families. *Infant Behavior and Development, 19*(1), 121–129.

Sutker, P. B. & Allain, A. N. (1988). Issues in personality conceptualizations of addictive behaviors. *Journal of Consulting and Clinical Psychology, 56*, 172–182.

Suzuki, K. (1998). The role of binocular viewing in a spacing illusion arising in a darkened surround. *Perception, 27*, 355–361.

Suzuki, L. A., & Valencia, R. (1997). Race-ethnicity and measured intelligence: Educational implications. *American Psychologist, 52*(10), 1103–1114.

Swaab, D. F., & Hofman, M. A. (1995). Sexual differentiation of the human hypothalamus in relation to gender and sexual orientation. *Trends in Neuroscience, 18*, 264–270.

Swim, J., Borgida, E., Maruyama, G., & Myers, D. G. (1989). Joan McKay versus John McKay: Do gender stereotypes bias evaluations? *Psychological Bulletin, 105*, 409–429.

Szasz, T. (1984). *The therapeutic state: Psychiatry in the mirror of current events* (p. 502). Buffalo, NY: Prometheus.

Szasz, T. (1987). *Insanity: The idea and its consequences*. New York: Wiley.

Szeszko, P. R., Robinson, D., Alvir, J. M. J., Bilder, R. M., Lencz, T., Ashtan, M., Wu, H., & Bogerts, B. (1999). Orbital frontal and amygdala column reductions in obsessive–compulsive disorder. *Archives of General Psychiatry, 56*, 913–919.

Szymanski, K., & Harkins, S. G. (1993). The effect of experimenter evaluation on self-evaluation within the social loafing paradigm. *Journal of Experimental Social Psychology, 29*, 268–286.

Takahashi, J. S. (1999). Narcolepsy genes wake up the sleep field. *Science, 285*, 2076–2077.

Takaku, S. (2000). Culture and status as influences on account giving: A comparison between the United States and Japan. *Journal of Applied Social Psychology, 30*(2), 371–388.

Takeichi, M., & Sato, T. (2000). Studies on the psychosomatic functioning of ill-health according to Eastern and Western medicine: 4. The verification of possible links between ill-health, lifestyle illness and stress-related disease. *American Journal of Chinese Medicine, 28*, 9–24.

Takeuchi, J. (2000). Treatment of a biracial child with schizophreniform disorder: Cultural formulation. *Cultural Diversity and Ethnic Minority Psychology, 6*, 93–101.

Takkouche, B. (2001). A cohort study of stress and the common cold. *Journal of the American Medical Association, 285*, 3070.

Talwar, S. K., Xu, S., Hawley, E. S., Weiss, S. A., Moxon, K. A., & Chapin, J. K. (2002). Rat navigation guided by remote control. *Nature, 417*, 37–38.

Tannen, D. (2001). But what do you mean? Men and women in conversation. In J. M. Henslin (Ed.), *Down to earth sociology: Introductory readings* (11th ed.) (pp. 168–173). New York: Free Press.

Tardif, T., & Wellman, H. M. (2000). Acquisition of mental state language in Mandarin and Cantonese speaking children. *Developmental Psychology, 36*(1), 25–43.

Tarter, R. E., & Vanyukov, M. (1994). Alcoholism: A development disorder. *Journal of Consulting and Clinical Psychology, 62*(6), 1096–1107.

Tasman, A., Riba, M. B., & Silk, K. R. (2000). *The doctor–patient relationship in pharmacotherapy: Improving treatment effectiveness*. New York: Guilford Press.

Tataranni, P. A., Young, J. B., Bogardus, C., & Ravussin, E. (1997). A low sympathoadrenal activity is associated with body weight gain and development of central adiposity in Pima Indian men. *Obesity Research, 5*(4), 341–347.

Tate, D. F., Wing, R. R., & Winett, R. A. (2001). Using Internet-based technology to deliver a behavioral weight loss program. *Journal of the American Medical Association, 285*, 1172–1177.

Taubman-Ben-Ari, O. (2000). The effects of reminders of death on reckless driving: A terror management perspective. *Current Directions in Psychological Science, 9*, 196–199.

Taylor, S. E., Kemeny, M. E., Reed, G. M., Bower, J. E., & Gruenwald, T. L. (2000). Psychological resources, positive illusions, and health. *American Psychologist, 55*, 99–109.

Taylor, S. E., Klein, L. C., Lewis, B. P., Gruenwald, T. L., Gurung, R. A. R., & Updegraff, J. A. (2000). Biobehavioral responses to stress in females: Tend-and-befriend, not fight-or-flight. *Psychological Review, 107*, 411–429.

Taylor, S. E., Repetti, R. L., & Seeman, T. (1997). Health psychology: What is an unhealthy environment and how does it get under the skin? In J. T. Spence, J. M. Darley, & D. J. Foss (Eds.), *Annual Review of Psychology, Vol. 48*. Palo Alto, CA: Annual Reviews, Inc.

Taylor, W. R., He, S., Levick, W. R., & Vaney, D. I. (2000). Dendritic computation of direction selectivity by retinal ganglion cells. *Science, 289*, 2347–2350.

Tchernichovski, O., Mitra, P. P., Lints, T., & Nottebohm, F. (2001). Dynamics of the vocal imitation process: How a zebra finch learns its song. *Science, 291*, 2564–2569.

Teevan, R. C., & McGhee, P. E. (1972). Childhood development of fear of failure motivation. *Journal of Personality and Social Psychology, 21*, 345–348.

Tempo, P. M., & Saito, A. (1996). Techniques of working with Japanese-American families. In G. Yeo, D. Gallagher-Thompson, et al. (Eds.), *Ethnicity and the dementias* (pp. 109–112). Washington, DC: Taylor & Francis.

Tenenbaum, J. B., de Silva, V., & Langford, J. C. (2000). A global geometric framework for nonlinear dimensionality reduction. *Science, 290*, 2319–2323.

Tennen, H., Affleck, G., Armeli, S., & Carney, M. A. (2000). A daily process approach to coping: Linking theory, research, and practice. *American Psychologist, 55*, 626–636.

Tennov, D. (1981). *Love and limerance*. Briarcliffe Manor, NY: Stein & Day.

Tepper, B. J. (1998). 6-n-propylthiouracil: A genetic marker for taste, with implication for food preference and dietary habits. *American Journal of Human Genetics, 63*, 1271–1276.

Terrace, H. S. (1985). In the beginning was the "name." *American Psychologist, 40*, 1011–1028.

Tesser, A. (2001). On the plasticity of self-defense. *Current Directions in Psychological Science, 10*, 66–69.

Tesser, A., & Beach, S. R. H. (1998). Life events, relationship quality, and depression: An investigation of judgment discontinuity in vivo. *Journal of Personality and Social Psychology, 74*(1), 36–52.

Teuchmann, K., Totterdell, P., & Parker, S. K. (1999). Rushed, unhappy, and drained: An experience sampling study of relations between time pressure, perceived control, mood, and emotional exhaustion in a group of accountants. *Journal of Occupational Health Psychology, 4*, 37–54.

Thach, W. T. (1998). A role for the cerebellum in learning movement coordination. *Neurobiology of Learning & Memory, 70*, 177–188.

Thelen, E. (1994). Three-month-old infants can learn task-specific patterns of interlimb coordination. *Psychological Science, 5*, 280–285.

Thelan, E., & Corbetta, D. (2002). Microdevelopment and dynamic systems: Applications to infant motor development. In N. Granott & J. Parziale (Eds.), *Microdevelopment: Transition processes in development and learning* (pp. 59–79). Cambridge Studies in Cognitive Perceptual Development. New York: Cambridge University Press.

Thomas, A., & Chess, S. (1977). *Temperament and development*. New York: Brunner/Mazel.

Thomas, E. K. (2000). Domestic violence in African-American communities: A comparative analysis of two racial/ethnic minority cultures and implications for mental health service provision for women of color. *Psychology: A Journal of Human Behavior, 37*, 32–43.

Thompson, R. A. (2001). Sensitive periods in attachment? Bailey, D. B. Jr. (Ed); Bruer, J. T. (Ed); et al. *Critical Thinking about Critical Periods* (pp. 83–106). Paul H. Brookes Publishing Co, Baltimore MD.

Thompson, R. A., & Nelson, C. (2001). Developmental science and the media: Early brain development. *American Psychologist, 56*(1), 5–15.

Thompson, T. L., & Zerbinos, E. (1997). Television cartoons: Do children notice it's a boy's world? *Sex Roles, 37*(5/6), 415–432.

Thomson, R., Murachver, T., & Green, J. (2001). Where is the gender in gendered relationships? *Psychological Science, 12*, 171–175.

Tice, D. M., & Baumeister, R. F. (1985). Masculinity inhibits helping in emergencies: Personality does predict the bystander effect. *Journal of Personality and Social Psychology, 49*, 420–428.

Tiedemann, J. (2000). Parents' gender stereotypes and teachers' beliefs as predictors of children's concept of their mathematical ability in elementary school. *Journal of Educational Psychology, 92*(1), 144–151.

Tiggemann, M., & Williamson, S. (2000). The effect of exercise on body satisfaction and self-esteem as a function of gender and age. *Sex Roles, 43*, 119–127.

Timberlake, W., & Farmer-Dougan, V. A. (1991). Reinforcement in applied settings: Figuring out ahead of time what will work. *Psychological Bulletin, 110*, 379–391.

Tjaden, P. G., & Thoennes, N. (2000). *Full report of the prevalence, incidence, and consequences of violence against women: Findings from* the *Violence Against Women Survey*. Washington, DC: National Institute of Justice.

Tjosvold, D. (1987). Participation: A close look at its dynamics. *Journal of Management, 13,* 739–750.

Tkachuk, G. A., & Martin, G. L. (1999). Exercise therapy for patients with psychiatric disorders: Research and clinical implications. *Professional Psychology: Research & Practice, 30,* 275–282.

Toch, H. (2001). Altruistic activity as correctional treatment. *International Journal of Offender Therapy and Comparative Criminology, 44,* 270–278.

Tomasello, M. (2000). *Culture and cognitive development: Psychological science* (pp. 37–40). Malden, MA: Blackwell Publishers.

Tooby, J., & Cosmides, L. (1997, June 26). On Stephen Jay Gould's "*Darwinian Fundamentalism*" and "*Evolution: The Pleasures of Pluralism*" [Letter to the editor]. *The New York Review of Books.*

Tovee, M. J., & Cohen-Tovee, E. M. (1993). The neural substrates of face processing models: A review. *Cognitive Neuropsychology, 10(6),* 505–528.

Trachtenberg, J. T., Trepel, C., & Stryker, M. P. (2000). Rapid extragranular plasticity in the absence of thalamocortical plasticity in the developing primary visual cortex. *Science, 287,* 2029–2032.

Tracy, R. J., & Barker, C. H. (1994). A comparison of visual versus auditory imagery in predicting word recall. *Imagination, Cognition and Personality, 13,* 147–161.

Trappey, C. (1996). A meta-analysis of consumer choice and subliminal advertising. *Psychology and Marketing, 13(5),* 517–530.

Triandis, H. C., & Gelfand, M. J. (1998). Converging measurement of horizontal and vertical individualism and collectivism. *Journal of Personality and Social Psychology, 74,* 118–128.

Trierweiler, S. J., Neighbors, H. W., Munday, C., Thompson, E. E., Binion, V. J., & Gomez, J. P. (2000). Clinician attributions associated with the diagnosis of schizophrenia in African American and non–African American patients. *Journal of Consulting and Clinical Psychology, 68,* 171–175.

Trimble, J. E. (2000). Social psychological perspectives on changing self-identification among American Indians and Alaska Natives. In R. H. Dana (Ed.), *Handbook of cross-cultural and multicultural personality assessment. Personality and Clinical Psychology Series* (pp. 197–222). Mahwah, NJ: Erlbaum.

Trites, D., Galbraith, F. D., Sturdavent, M., & Leckwart, J. F. (1970). Influence of nursing-unit design on the activities and subjective feelings of nursing personnel. *Environment and Behavior, 2,* 203–234.

Tritt, K., Loew, T. H., Meyer, M., Werner, B., & Peseschkian, N. (2000). Positive psychotherapy: Effectiveness of an interdisciplinary approach. *European Journal of Psychiatry, 13,* 231–242.

Troisi, A., & McGuire, M. T. (2000). Psychotherapy in the context of Darwinian psychiatry. In P. Gilbert & K. G. Bailey (Eds.), *Genes on the couch: Explorations in evolutionary psychotherapy* (pp. 3–27). Philadelphia: Brunner-Routledge.

Tronick, E. Z., Morelli, G. A., & Ivey, P. K. (1992). The Efe forager infant and toddler's pattern of social relationships: Multiple and simultaneous. *Developmental Psychology, 28,* 568–577.

Trull, T. J., & Geary, D. C. (1997). Comparison of the Big-Five Factor structure across samples of Chinese and American adults. *Journal of Personality Assessment, 69(2),* 324–341.

Tuckman, A. (1996). Isn't it about time psychologists were granted prescription privileges? *Psychotherapy in Private Practice, 15(2),* 1–14.

Tulving, E. (1972). Episodic and semantic memory. In E. Tulving & W. Donaldson (Eds.), *Organization of memory*. New York: Academic Press.

Tulving, E. (1993). What is episodic memory? *Current Directions in Psychological Science, 2,* 67–70.

Tulving, E., Kapur, S., Craik, F. I. M., Moscovitch, M., & Houle, S. (1994). Hemispheric encoding/retrieval asymmetry in episodic memory: Positron emission tomography findings. *Proceedings of the National Academy of Sciences USA, 91,* 2016–2020.

Turkheimer, E. (2000). Three laws of behavior genetics and what they mean. *Current Directions in Psychological Science, 9,* 160–164.

Turkington, C. (1996). *12 steps to a better memory.* New York: Macmillan.

Tversky, A., & Kahneman, D. (1973). Availability: A heuristic for judging frequency and probability. *Cognitive Psychology, 4,* 207–232.

Tziner, A., & Murphy, K. R. (1999). Additional eveidence of attitudinal influences in performance appraisal. *Journal of Business and Psychology, 13(3),* 407–419.

Uba, L. (1994). *Asian Americans: Personality patterns, identity, and mental health.* New York: Guilford.

Ullian, E. M., Sapperstein, S. K., Christopherson, K. S., & Barres, B. A. (2001, January 26). Control of synapse number by glia. *Science, 291,* 657–661.

Ullman, S. E., Karabatsos, G., & Koss, M. P. (1999). Alcohol and sexual aggression in a national sample of college men. *Psychology of Women Quarterly, 23,* 673–689.

Underwood, G. (1994). Subliminal perception on TV. *Nature, 370,* 103.

Ungerleider, L. G., & Mishkin, M. (1982). Two cortical visual systems. In D. J. Ingle, M. A. Goodale, & R. J. W. Mansfield (Eds.), *Analysis of visual behavior* (pp. 549–586). Cambridge, MA: MIT Press.

Ursano, R. J., Fullerton, C. S., Kao, T., & Bhartiya, V.R. (1995). Longitudinal assessment of posttraumatic stress disorder and depression after exposure to traumatic death. *Journal of Nervous and Mental Disease, 183,* 36–42.

Vahava, O., Morell, R., Lynch, E. D., Weiss, S., Kagan, M. E., Ahituv, N., et al. (1998). Mutation in transcription factor POU4F3 associated with inherited progressive hearing loss in humans. *Science, 279,* 1950–1954.

Vaillant, G. E., & Milofsky, E. S. (1982). The etiology of alcoholism: A prospective view. *American Psychologist, 37,* 494–503.

Valenstein, E. S. (1986). *Great and desperate cures: The rise and decline of psychosurgery and other radical treatments for mental illness.* New York: Basic Books.

Valenstein, E. S. (1998). *Blaming the brain: The truth about drugs and mental health.* New York: The Free Press.

Valins, S., & Baum, A. (1973). Residential group size, social interaction, and crowding. *Environment and Behavior, 5,* 421–435.

Vallerand, R. J., & Bissonnette, R. (1992). Intrinsic, extrinsic, and amotivational styles as predictors of behavior: A prospective study. *Journal of Personality, 60, 3,* 599–620.

Van Fleet, D. D., & Atwater, L. (1997). Gender-neutral names: Don't be so sure! *Sex Roles, 37(1/2),* 111–123.

Van Horn, D. H. A., & Frank, A. F. (1998). Substance-use situations and abstinence predictions in substance abusers with and without personality disorders. *American Journal of Drug & Alcohol Abuse. Vol 24(3),* 395–404.

Van Laar, C. (2001). Declining optimism in ethnic minority students: The role of attributions and self-esteem. In F. Salili & C. Chiu (Eds.), *Student motivation: The culture and context of learning. Plenum Series on Human Exceptionality* (pp. 79–104). New York: Kluwer/Plenum.

Vartanian, L. R. (2000). Revisiting the imaginary audience and personal fable constructs of adolescent egocentrism: A conceptual review. *Adolescence, 35,* 639–661.

Vartanian, L. R., & Powlishta, K. K. (1996). A longitudinal examination of the social-cognitive foundations of adolescent egocentrism. *Journal of Early Adolescence, 16(2),* 157–178.

Veniegas, R. C., & Peplau, L. A. (1997). Power and the quality of same-sex friendships. *Psychology of Women Quarterly, 21(2),* 279–297.

Venter, J. C., Adams, M. D., Myers, G. W., Li, P. W., Mural, R. J., Sutton, G. W., et al. (2001, February 16). The sequence of the human genome. *Science, 291,* 1304–1351.

Vianna, M. R. M., Izquierdo, L. A., Barros, D. M., de Souza, M. M., Rodrigues, C., Sant'Anna, M. K., Medina, J. H., & Izauierdo, I. (2001). Pharmacological differences between memory consolidation of habituation to an open field and inhibitory avoidance learning. *Brazilian Journal of Medical & Biological Research, 34,* 233–240.

Videbech, P. (2000). PET measurements of brain glucose metabolism and blood flow in major depressive disorder: A critical review. *Acta Psychiatrica Scandinavica, 101,* 11–20.

Villani, S. (2001). Impact of media on children and adolescents: A 10-year review of the research. *Journal of the American Academy of Child and Adolescent Psychiatry, 40,* 392–401.

Villeneuve, C. (2001). *Emphasizing the interpersonal in psychotherapy: Families and groups in the era of cost containment.* Philadelphia: Brunner-Routledge.

Visser, M. (1999). Food and culture: Interconnections. *Social Research, 66,* 117–132.

Vitiello, M. V. (1989). Unraveling sleep disorders of the aged. Paper presented at the annual meeting of the Association of Professional Sleep Societies, Washington, DC.

Vogel, G. W. (1991). Sleep-onset mentation. In S. J. Ellman & J. S. Antrobus (Eds.), *The mind in sleep: Psychology and psychophysiology* (2nd ed., pp. 125–142). New York: Wiley.

Von Senden, M. (1932). *Raum- und Gestaltauffassung bei operierten: Blindgeborernin vor und nach der Operation.* Leipzig, Germany: Barth.

Vroom, V. H. (1964). *Work and motivation.* New York: Wiley.

Vroom, V. H. (1974). A new look at managerial decision making. *Organizational Dynamics, 5,* 66–80.

Vroom, V. H. (1997). Can leaders learn to lead? In R. P. Vecchio et al. (Eds.), *Leadership: Understanding the dynamics of power and influence in organizations* (pp. 278–291). Notre Dame, IN: University of Notre Dame Press.

Vroom, V. H., & Jago, A. G. (1995). Situation effects and levels of analysis in the study of leader participation. *Leadership Quarterly, 6*(2), 169–181.

Vroom, V. H., & Yetton, P. W. (1973). *Leadership and decision-making.* Pittsburgh: University of Pittsburgh Press.

Vroon, P. (1997). *Smell: The secret seducer.* New York: Farrar, Straus & Giroux.

Vygotsky, L. S. (1962). *Thought and language* (E. Hanfmann & G. Vakar, Eds. and Trans.). Cambridge, MA: MIT Press. (Original work published in 1934.)

Vygotsky, L. S. (1978). *Mind in society: The development of higher mental processes.* Cambridge, MA: Harvard University Press. (Original works published 1930, 1933, and 1935.)

Wacholtz, E. (1996). Can we learn from the clinically significant face processing deficits prosopagnosia and Capgras delusion? *Neuropsychology Review, 6*(4), 203–257.

Wadsworth, J., McEwan, J., Johnson, A. M., Wellings, K., et al. (1995). Sexual health for women: Some findings of a large national survey discussed. *Sexual and Marital Therapy, 10*(2), 169–188.

Wakefield, J. C. (1999). Evolutionary versus prototype analyses of the concept of disorder. *Journal of Abnormal Psychology, 108,* 374–399.

Waldie, K., & Mosley, J. L. (2000). Hemispheric specialization for reading. *Brain & Language, 75*(1), 108–122.

Waldron, I. (1997). Changing gender roles and gender differences in health behavior. In D. S. Gochman (Ed.), *Handbook of health behavior research I: Personal and social determinants* (pp. 303–328). New York: Plenum.

Walker, E., Hoppes, E., Mednick, S., Emory, E., & Schulsinger, F. (1983). Environmental factors related to schizophrenia in psychophysiologically labile high-risk males. *Journal of Abnormal Psychology, 90,* 313–320.

Walker, L. J., Hennig, K. H., & Krettenauer, T. (2000). Parent and peer contexts for children's moral reasoning development. *Child Development, 71*(4), 1033–1048.

Walker, L. J., & Pitts, R. C. (1998). Naturalistic conceptions of moral maturity. *Developmental Psychology, 34*(3), 403–419.

Walker, L. S., Garber, J., Smith, C. A., Van Slyke, D. A., & Claar, R. L. (2001). The relation of daily stressors to somatic and emotional symptoms in children with and without recurrent abdominal pain. *Journal of Consulting and Clinical Psychology, 69,* 85–91.

Walker, S., Richardson, D. S., & Green, L. R. (2000). Aggression among older adults: The relationship of interaction networks and gender role to direct and indirect responses. *Aggressive Behavior, 26,* 145–154.

Walker-Andrews, A. S. (1986). Intermodal perception of expressive behaviors: Relation of eye and voice? *Developmental Psychology, 22,* 373–377.

Walker-Andrews, A. S. (1997). Infants' perception of expressive behavior: Differentiation of multimodal information. *Psychological Bulletin, 121*(3), 437–456.

Wall, P. (2000). *Pain: The science of suffering.* New York: Columbia University Press.

Wallbaum, A. B., Rzewnicki, R., & Steele, H. (1991). Progressive muscle relaxation and restricted environmental stimulation therapy for chronic tension headache: A pilot study. *International Journal of Psychosomatics, 38,* Special Issue, 33–39.

Walsh, B. T., & Devlin, M. J. (1998). Eating disorders: Progress and problems. *Science, 280,* 1387–1390.

Walsh, K. W. (1999). *Neuropsychology: A clinical approach* (4th ed.). Churchill: Livingstone.

Walton, G. E., & Bower, T. G. R. (1993). Newborns form "prototypes" in less than 1 minute. *Psychological Science, 4,* 203–205.

Wamala, S. P., Mittleman, M. A., Horsten, M., Schenck-Gustafsson, K., & Orth-Gómer, K. (2000). Job stress and the occupational gradient in coronary heart disease risk in women: The Stockholm Female Coronary Risk Study. *Social Science & Medicine, 51,* 481–489.

Wampold, B. E., Mondin, G. W., Moody, M., Stich, F., Benson, K., & Ahn, H. (1997). A meta-analysis of outcome studies comparing bona fide psychotherapies: Empirically, "all must have prizes." *Psychological Bulletin, 122*(3), 203–215.

Wandersman, A., & Nation, M. (1998). Urban neighborhoods and mental health: Psychological contributions to understanding toxicity, resilience, and interventions. *American Psychologist, 53*(6), 647–656.

Wandersman, A. H., & Hallman, W. K. (1993). Are people acting irrationally? *American Psychologist, 48,* 681–686.

Wang, A., Gao, L., Shinfuku, N., Zhang, H., Zhao, C., & Shen, Y. (2000). Longitudinal study of earthquake-related PTSD in a randomly selected community sample in North China. *American Journal of Psychiatry, 157,* 1260–1266.

Warren, S. L., Schmitz, S., & Emde, R. N. (1999). Behavioral genetic analyses of self-reported anxiety at 7 years of age. *Journal of the American Academy of Child & Adolescent Psychiatry, 38*(11), 1403–1408.

Washton, A. M. (1989). *Cocaine addiction.* New York: Norton.

Waters, E., Weinfield, N. S., & Hamilton, C. E. (2000). The stability of attachment security from infancy to adolescence and early adulthood: General discussion. *Child Development, 71*(3), 703–706.

Watson, J. B. (1924). *Behaviorism.* Chicago: University of Chicago Press.

Webb, W. B., & Agnew, H. W., Jr. (1975). The effects on subsequent sleep of an acute restriction of sleep length. *Psychophysiology, 12,* 367–370.

Weber-Fox, C. M., & Neville, H. J. (1999). Functional neural subsystems are differentially affected by delays in second language immersion: ERP and behavioral evidence in bilinguals. In D. Birdsong and others, *Second Language Acquisition and the Critical Period Hypothesis. Second Language Acquisition Research* (23–38). Mahwah, NJ: Lawrence Erlbaum Associates, Inc.

Webster, R. (1995). Why Freud was wrong: Sin, science, and psychoanalysis. New York: Basic Books.

Weidner, G. (2000). Why do men get more heart disease than women? An international perspective. *Journal of American College Health, 48,* 291–294.

Weine, S. M., Kuc, G., Dzudza, E., Razzano, L., & Pavkovic, I. (2001). PTSD among Bosnian refugees: A survey of providers' knowledge, attitudes and service patterns (posttraumatic stress disorder). *Community Mental Health Journal, 37,* 261–272.

Weingartner, H. (1977). Human state-dependent learning. In B. T. Ho, D. Richards, & D. L. Chute (Eds.), *Drug discrimination and state-dependent learning.* New York: Academic.

Weingartner, H., Adefris, W., Eich, J. E., & Murphy, D. L. (1976). Encoding-imagery specificity in alcohol state-dependent learning. *Journal of Experimental Psychology, 2,* 83–87.

Weinstein, N. D., Rothman, A. J., & Sutton, S. R. (1998). Stage theories of health behavior: Conceptual and methodological issues. *Health Psychology, 17,* 290–299.

Weisberg, R. B., Brown, T. A., Wineze, J. P., & Barlow, D. H. (2001). Casual attributions and male sexual arousal: The impact of attributions for a bogus erectile difficulty on sexual arousal, cognitions, and affect. *Journal of Abnormal Psychology, 110,* 324–334.

Weise-Kelly, L., & Siegel, S. (2001). Self-administration cues as signals: Drug self-administration and tolerance. *Journal of Experimental Psychology: Animal Behavior Processes, 27,* 125–136.

Weisfeld, G. E. (1993). The adaptive value of humor and laughter. *Ethology and Sociobiology, 14*(2), 141–169.

Wellman, H. M., Phillips, A. T., & Rodriguez, T. (2000). Young children's understanding of perception, desire, and emotion. *Child Development, 71*(4), 895–912.

Wells, G. L. (1993). What do we know about eyewitness identification? *American Psychologist, 48,* 553–571.

Wells, G. L., Luus, C. A. E., & Windschitl, P. D. (1994). Maximizing the utility of eyewitness identification evidence. *Current Directions in Psychological Science, 3,* 194–197.

Werker, J. F., & Tees, R. C. (1999). Influences on infant speech processing: Toward a new synthesis. *Annual Review of Psychology, 50,* 509–535.

Werker, J. F., & Tees, R. C. (2002). Cross-language speech perception: Evidence for perceptual reorganization during the first year of life. *Infant Behavior & Development, 25,* 1, 121–133.

Werker, J. F., & Vouloumanos, A. (1999). Speech and language processing in infancy: A neurocognitive approach. In C. A. Nelson & M. Luciana (Eds.), *Handbook of developmental cognitive neuroscience* (pp. 269–280). Cambridge, MA: The MIT Press.

Werler, M. M., Mitchell, A. A., & Shapiro, M. B. (1989). The relation of aspirin use during the first trimester of pregnancy to congenital cardiac defects. *New England Journal of Medicine, 321,* 1639–1642.

Werner, N. E., & Crick, N. R. (1999). Relational aggression and social psychological adjustment in a college sample. *Journal of Abnormal Psychology, 108,* 615–623.

West, M. A. (1980). Meditation and the EEG. *Psychological Medicine, 10,* 369–375.

West, M. A. (1982). Meditation and self-awareness: Physiological and phenomenological approaches. In G. Underwood (Ed.), *Aspects of consciousness: Vol. 3. Awareness and self-awareness.* London: Academic.

Westen, D. (1998). The scientific legacy of Sigmund Freud: Toward a psychodynamically informed psychological science. *Psychological Bulletin, 124,* 333–371.

Westgaard, R. H. (2000). Work related musculoskeletal complaints: Some ergonomics challenges upon the start of a new century. *Applied Ergonomics, 6,* 569–580.

Wheeler, M. A. (2000). Episodic memory and autonoetic awareness. In E. Tulving & F. I. M. Craik (Eds.), *The Oxford handbook of memory* (pp. 597–608). New York: Oxford University Press.

Wheeler, S. C., Jarvis, W. B. G., & Petty, R. E. (2001). Think unto others: The self-destructive impact of negative racial stereotypes. *Journal of Experimental Social Psychology, 37,* 273–180.

Whicker, K. M., Bol, L., & Nunnery, J. A. (1997). Cooperative learning in the secondary mathematics classroom. *Journal of Educational Research, 91*(1), 42–48.

White, N. M., & Milner, P. M. (1992). The psychobiology of reinforcers. *Annual Review of Psychology, 43,* 443–471.

WHO International Consortium in Psychiatric Epidemiology. (2000). Cross-national comparisons of the prevalences and correlates of mental disorders. *Bulletin of the World Health Organization, 78,* 413–426.

Whorf, B. L. (1956). *Language, thought, and reality: Selected writings of Benjamin Lee Whorf* (J. B. Carroll, Ed.). New York: Wiley.

Widiger, T. A., Frances, A. J., Pincus, H. A., Davis, W. W., & First, M. B. (1991). Toward an empirical classification for the DSM-IV. *Journal of Abnormal Psychology, 100,* 280–288.

Widiger, T. A., & Sankis, L. M. (2000). Adult psychopathology: Issues and controversies. *Annual Review of Psychology, 51,* 377–404.

Wiley, J. (1998). Expertise as mental set: The effects of domain knowledge in creative problem solving. *Memory & Cognition, 26,* 716–730.

Williams, C. (2001). *You snooze, you lose? Sleep patterns in Canada.* Statistics Canada, Catalogue no. 11-008.

Williams, J. (2000). *Unbending gender: Why family and work conflict and what to do about it.* New York: Oxford University Press.

Williams, K., Harkins, S., & Latané, B. (1981). Identifiability as a deterrent to social loafing: Two cheering experiments. *Journal of Personality and Social Psychology, 40,* 303–311.

Williams, K. J., Suls, J., Alliger, G. M., Learner, S. M., & Wan, C. K. (1991). Multiple role juggling and daily mood states in working mothers: An experience sampling study. *Journal of Applied Psychology, 76,* 664–674.

Williams, M. L., Elwood, W. N., & Bowen, A. M. (2000). Escape from risk: A qualitative exploration of relapse to unprotected anal sex among men who have sex with men. *Journal of Psychology and Human Sexuality, 11,* 25–49.

Williams, T. M. (1985). Implications of a natural experiment in the developed world for research on television in the developing world. *Journal of Cross-Cultural Psychology, 16,* 3, 263–287.

Williams, T. M., Zabrack, M. L., & Joy, L. A. (1982). The portrayal of aggression on North American television. *Journal of Applied Social Psychology, 12,* 5, 360–380.

Williams, S. L., Kinney, P. J., & Falbo, J. (1989). Generalization of therapeutic changes in agoraphobia: The role of perceived self-efficacy. *Journal of Consulting and Clinical Psychology, 57,* 436–442.

Williams, W. M., & Ceci, S. J. (1997). Are Americans becoming more or less alike? Trends in race, class, and ability differences in intelligence. *American Psychologist, 52*(11), 1226–1235.

Williamson, R. C. (1991). *Minority languages and bilingualism: Case studies in maintenance and shift.* Norwood, NJ: Ablex.

Willis, S. L., & Schaie, K. W. (1999). Intellectual functioning in midlife. In S. L. Willis & J. D. Reid, *Life in the middle: Psychological and social development in middle age* (pp. 233–247). San Diego, CA: Academic Press.

Willoughby, J. C., & Glidden, L. M. (1995). Fathers helping out: Shared child care and marital satisfaction of parents of children with disabilities. *American Journal on Mental Retardation, 99,* 399–406.

Wilson, D. A. (2000). Comparison of odor receptive field plasticity in the rat olfactory bulb and anterior piriform cortex. *Journal of Neurophysiology, 84,* 3036–3042.

Wilson, E. O. (1975). *Sociobiology: A new synthesis.* Cambridge, MA: Harvard University Press.

Wilson, E. O. (1998). *Consilience: The unity of knowledge.* New York: Alfred A. Knopf.

Wilson, F. A. W., & Goldman-Rakie, P. S. (1994). Viewing preferences of rhesus monkeys related to memory for complex pictures, colours and faces. *Behavioral Brain Research, 60,* 79–89.

Wilson, G. T., Loeb, K. L., Walsh, B. T., Labouvie, E., Petkova, E., Liu, X., & Waternaux, C. (1999). Psychological treatments of bulimia nervosa predictors and processes of change. *Journal of Consulting and Clinical Psychology, 67,* 451–459.

Wilson, M., & Daly, M. (1998). Lethal and nonlethal violence against wives and the evolutionary psychology of male sexual proprietariness. In R. E. Dobash & R. P. Dobash (Eds.), *Rethinking violence against women. Sage Series on Violence Against Women, Vol. 9* (pp. 199–230). UK: Sage.

Wilson, M. E. (1992). Factors determining the onset of puberty. In A. A. Gerall, H. Moltz, A. A. Gerall, H. Moltz, & I. L. Ward (Eds.), *Sexual differentiation: Handbook of behavioral neurobiology* (pp. 275–312). New York: Plenum.

Wing, R. R., & Jeffery, R. W. (1999). Benefits of recruiting participants with friends and increasing social support for weight loss and maintenance. *Journal of Consulting & Clinical Psychology, 67,* 132–138.

Winner, E. (1997). Exceptionally high intelligence and schooling. *American Psychologist, 52*(10), 1070–1081.

Winner, E. (2000). Giftedness: Current theory and research. *Psychological Science, 9,* 153–156.

Winocur, G., McDonald, R. M., & Moscovitch, M. (2001). Anterograde and retrograde amnesia in rats with large hippocampal lesions. *Hippocampus, 11,* 27–42.

Winsler, A., Carlton, M. P., & Barry, M. J. (2000). Age-related changes in preschool children's systematic use of private speech in a natural setting. *Journal of Child Language, 27*(3), 665–687.

Winsler, A., Diaz, R. M., Atencio, D. J., McCarthy, E. M., & Adams Chabay, L. (2000). Verbal self-regulation over time in preschool children at risk for attention and behavior problems. *Journal of Child Psychology & Psychiatry & Allied Disciplines, 41,* 7, 875–886.

Wise, R. A. (1996). Neurobiology of addiction. *Current Opinion in Neurobiology, 6,* 243–251.

Wittrock, M. C. (2000). Knowledge acquisition and education. *Journal of Mind & Behavior, 21,* 205–212.

Witztum, E., & Buchbinder, J. T. (2001). Strategic culture sensitive therapy with religious Jews. *International Review of Psychiatry, 13,* 117–124.

Wodak, R., & Benke, G. (1997). Gender as a sociolinguistic variable: New perspectives on variation studies. In F. Coulmas (Ed.), *The handbook of sociolinguistics.* Oxford, England: Blackwell.

Wolpe, J. (1958). *Psychotherapy by reciprocal inhibition.* Stanford, CA: Stanford University Press.

Wong, R. O. L., Chernjavsky, A., Smith, S. J., & Shatz, C. J. (1995). Early functional neural networks in the developing retina. *Nature, 374,* 716–718.

Woods, S. C., Schwartz, M. W., Baskin, D. G., & Seeley, R. J. (2000). Food intake and the regulation of body weight. *Annual Review of Psychology, 51,* 255–278.

Woodward, S. A., Lenzenweger, M. F., Kagan, J., Snidman, N., & Arcus, D. (2000). Taxonic structure of infant reactivity: Evidence from a taxometric perspective. *Psychological Science, 11*(4), 296–301.

Woodward, W. R. (1982). The "discovery" of social behaviorism and social learning theory, 1870–1980. *American Psychologist, 37,* 396–410.

Wordsdell, A. S., Iwata, B. A., Hanley, G. P., Thompson, R. H., & Kahng, S. (2000). Effects of continuous and intermittent reinforcement for problem behavior during functional communication training. *Journal of Applied Behavior Analysis, 33,* 2, 167–179.

Wright, J. C., Huston, A. C., Vandewater, E. A., Bickham, D. S., Scantlin, R. M., Kotler, J. A., Caplovitz, A. G., Lee, J. H., Hofferth, S., & Finkelstein, J. (2001). American children's use of electronic media in

1997: A national survey. *Journal of Applied Developmental Psychology, 22,* 31–47.

Wynn, K. (2002). Do infants have numerical expectations or just perceptual preferences? Comment. *Developmental Science, 5,* 2, 207–209.

Wynn, K., Bloom, P., & Chiang, W-C. (2002). Enumeration of collective entities by 5-month-old infants. *Cognition, 83,* 3, B55–B62.

Wynn-Dancy, L. M., & Gillam, R. B. (1997). Accessing long-term memory: Metacognitive strategies and strategic action in adolescents. *Topics in Language Disorders, 18*(1), 32–44.

Wyszecki, G., & Stiles, W. S. (1967). *Color science: Concepts and methods, quantitative data, and formulas.* New York: Wiley.

Yancey, S. W., & Phelps, E. A. (2001). Functional neuroimaging and episodic memory: A perspective. *Journal of Clinical & Experimental Neuropsychology, 23,* 32–48.

Yarmey, A. D. (2001). Earwitness descriptions and speaker identification. *Forensic Linguistics, 8,* 113–122.

Yehuda, R., Schmeidler, J., Wainberg, M., Binder-Brynes, K., & Duvdevani, T. (1998). Vulnerability to posttraumatic stress disorder in adult offspring of Holocaust survivors. *American Journal of Psychiatry, 155*(9), 1163–1171.

Yoder, K. A., Whitbeck, L. B., & Hoyt, D. R. (2003). Gang involvement and membership among homeless youth and runaway youth. *Youth & Society, 34,* 4, 441–467.

Yohannes, A. M., Connolly, M. J., & Baldwin, R. C. (2001). A feasibility study of antidepressant drug therapy in depressed elderly patients with chronic obstructive pulmonary disease. *International Journal of Geriatric Psychiatry, 16,* 451–454.

York, J. L., & Welte, J. W. (1994). Gender comparisons of alcohol consumption in alcoholic and nonalcoholic populations. *Journal of Studies on Alcohol, 55,* 743–750.

Young, S. J., Longstaffe, S., & Tenenbein, M. (1999). Inhalant abuse and the abuse of other drugs. *American Journal of Drug & Alcohol Abuse, 25*(2), 371–375.

Young, T. J., & French, L. A. (1993). Suicide and social status among Native Americans. *Psychological Reports, 73,* 461–462.

Youngstedt, S. D., O'Connor, P. J., & Dishman, R. K. (1997). The effects of acute exercise on sleep: A quantitative synthesis. *Sleep, 20*(3), 203–214.

Youniss, J., McLellan, J. A., & Yates, M. (1999). Religion, community service, and identity in American youth. *Journal of Adolescence, 22,* 243–255.

Zajonc, R. B. (1965). Social facilitation. *Science, 149,* 269–274.

Zakay, D., Hayduk, L. A., & Tsal, Y. (1992). Personal space and distance misperception: Implications of a novel observation. *Bulletin of the Psychonomic Society, 30,* 33–35.

Zangwill, O. L., & Blakemore, C. (1972). Dyslexia: Reversal of eye movements during reading. *Neuropsychologia, 10,* 371–373.

Zanna, M. P. (1994). On the nature of prejudice. *Canadian Psychology, 35,* 1, 11–23.

Zarcone, J. R., Crosland, K., Fisher, W. W., Worsdell, A. S., & Herman, K. (1999). A brief method for conduction a negative-reinforcement assessment. *Research in Developmental Disabilities, 20,* 107–124.

Zeki, S. (1993) *A vision of the brain.* Oxford: Blackwell Scientific Publications.

Zemore, S. E., Fiske, S., & Hyun-Jeong, K. (2000). Gender stereotypes and the dynamics of social interaction. In T. Eckes & H. S. Hanns (Eds.), *The Developmental Social Psychology of Gender* (pp. 207–241). Mahwah, NJ: Erlbaum.

Zhang, F., Shogo, E., Cleary, L. J., Eskin, A., & Byrne, J. H. (1997). Role of transforming growth factor in long-term synaptic facilitation in Aplysia. *Science, 275,* 1318–1320.

Zhou, Z. (2001). American and Chinese children's knowledge of basic relational concepts. *School Psychology International, 22,* 5–21.

Ziel, H. K. (1999). Complementary alternative medicine: Boon or boondoggle? *Skeptic, 7,* 86–89.

Zigler, E. F., & Hodapp, R. M. (1991). Behavioral functioning in individuals with mental retardation. *Annual Review of Psychology, 42,* 29–50.

Zillmann, D. (1994). Cognition excitation interdependencies in the escalation of anger and angry aggression. In M. Potegal & J. F. Knutson (Eds.), *The dynamics of aggression: Biological and social processes in dyads and groups* (pp. 45–71). Hillsdale, NJ: Erlbaum.

Zimbardo, P. G., Maslach, C., & Haney, C. (2000). *Reflections on the Stanford prison experiment: Genesis, transformations, consequences.* Mahwah, NJ: Erlbaum.

Zimmerman, L. (2000). *The SE switch: Evolution and our self-esteem.* Orlando, FL: Rivercross.

Zola, S. M., & Squire, L. R. (2000). The medial temporal lobe and the hippocampus. In E. Tulving and F. I. Craik (Eds.), *The Oxford handbook of memory* (pp. 485–500). New York: Oxford University Press.

Zoucha, R., & Husted, G. L. (2000). Culturally congruent care to individual patients by health care professional: The differences between transculturalism and multiculturalism are explored. *Issues in Mental Health Nursing, 21,* 324–340.

Zuber, J. A., Crott, H. W., & Werner, J. (1992). Choice shift and group polarization: An analysis of the status of arguments and social decision schemes. *Journal of Personality and Social Psychology, 62,* 50–61.

Zuckerman, M. (1990). Some dubious premises in research and theory on racial differences. *American Psychologist, 45,* 1297–1303.

Zuckerman, M. (1999). *Vulnerability to psychopathology: A biosocial model.* Washington, DC: American Psychological Association.

# Name Index

Abbott, L.F., 55
Abel, T., 221
Abraham, C., 522
Abramowitz, J.S., 544, 596
Abrams, M., 597
Abramson, L.Y., 551
Abravanel, E., 350
Acocella, J., 554
Ader, R., 178, 512, 513
Adler, A., 414, 421, 422, 423, 424, 426, 433, 435, 446
Adolphs, R., 132, 255
Adorno, T., 469
Agnew, H.W.Jr., 136, 141
Aiello, J.R., 475
Aiken, L.R., 408, 443
Ainsworth, M.D.S., 366, 367
Ajdukovic, D., 504
Ajdukovic, M., 504
Aks, D.J., 108
Al-Issa, I., 25
Aldag, R.J., 478
Allain, A.N., 153
Allan, L.G., 172, 178, 179
Allen, K.E., 193
Allen, M., 489
Allgulander, C., 540
Allington, R.L., 299
Allison, D.B., 317
Allison, T., 98
Alloy, L.B., 551
Allport, G.W., 413, 414, 428, 429, 447, 468
Almagor, M., 432
Aloise, P.A., 351
Altemeyer, R., 469
Alzheimer, A., 407
Amaral, D.G., 61
American Association of University Women Educational Foundation, 296
American Association on Mental Retardation, 298
American Psychiatric Association, 607
American Psychological Association, 479, 539
Ames, E.W., 368
Anderson, A.K., 328
Anderson, C.A., 439, 483, 636
Anderson, D.L., 80
Anderson, E.N., 581
Anderson, J.L., 485
Anderson, J.R., 212, 234
Anderson, J.S., 97, 98
Anderson, K.B., 636
Anderson, M., 69, 197
Anderson, O.K., 98
Andreasen, N.C., 69
Ang, R.P., 324
angwill, O.L., 99
Annett, M., 72
Anstey, K.J., 403
Anton, R.F., 155
Appelbaum, P.S., 563
Appleton, R.E., 142
Applewhite, S.L., 524
Apter, T., 402
Arboleda-Florez, J., 533
Archibald, A.B., 382
Arendt, J., 142
Arendt-Nielson, L., 98
Arguin, M., 96
Ariely, D., 243
Arjmand, O., 79

Arkowitz, H., 577
Armel, K.C., 104
Arnedt, J.T., 138
Arnett, J.J., 382
Aron, A.P., 330
Aronson, J., 285, 465
Arseneault, L., 563
Arvey, R.D., 616
Asch, S.E., 471
Ashcraft, M.H., 242
Ashford, S.J., 616
Ashman, A.F., 198
Aspenson, M.R., 371
Aspinwall, L., 519
Astin, J.A., 525
Astington, J., 339, 360
Atlis, M.M., 259
Attridge, M., 527
Atwater, L., 374
Atwood, N.C., 582
Aube, J., 390
Audia, G., 622
Auerbach, C.F., 373
Aussprung, J., 500, 501
Averett, S.L., 373
Avolio, B.J., 628
Ayllon, T., 591, 592
Azrin, N.H., 188, 592

Bachar, E., 576
Baddeley, A.D., 214, 215, 216
Bagely, C., 321, 322
Bagwell, C.L., 374
Bahrick, H.P., 224, 226
Bailey, K.G., 602
Bailey, M.J., 323
Baillargeon, R., 354, 358
Bain, D.E., 269
Baird, J.C., 109
Baischer, W., 122
Bak, M., 95
Baker, C., 506
Bala, N., 387
Balay, J., 88
Baldwin, R.C., 605
Ball, K., 395
Ballen, W., 149
Balota, D.A., 220
Balser, G.M., 437
Baltes, P.B., 340, 403
Bamforth, F., 47
Band, E.B., 508
Bandura, A., 10, 200, 201, 202, 325, 414, 436, 438, 439, 440, 441, 447, 594
Banks, W., 454
Baptista, M.A.S., 179
Bar-Or, O., 317
Barbato, G., 136
Barber, J., 150
Barbuto, J.E.Jr., 628
Barclay, L., 620
Bard, P., 326, 327, 331, 334, 337
Bardon, J.I., 36
Bargh, J.A., 641
Barker, C.H., 227
Barker, T., 392
Barlow, D.H., 540
Barnes, B.W., 515
Barnett, L., 241
Barnhardt, T.M., 88
Baron, R.A., 614
Barondes, S.H., 549, 552

Barr, H.M., 346
Barrett, G.V., 290
Barron, M., 439
Barry, M.J., 359
Bartlett, F., 230, 233, 236
Bartoshuk, L.M., 117
Bass, B.M., 627, 628
Bates, E., 264
Bateson, G., 560
Batra, P., 638
Batson, C.D., 485, 487
Bauer, R.M., 96, 224
Bauer, S.C., 386
Baum, A., 514, 520, 521, 524, 637, 638
Baumeister, R.F., 396, 421, 482, 487
Bavelier, D., 111, 346
Bayley, N., 295
Baynes, K., 260, 266
Bayster, P.G., 252
Beach, S.R.H., 489, 503, 508
Bechara, A., 65
Beck, A.T., 10, 550, 597, 598, 599
Beck, J., 111
Bee, H.L., 403
Begg, I.M., 88, 89
Begum, H.A., 638
Behr, H., 601
Beitel, A.H., 373
Bekerian, D.A., 233
Belansky, E.S., 487
Belcher, M., 145
Bell, B.E., 233
Bell, S.T., 464
Belleville, S., 274
Belsky, J., 366, 369
Bem, D.J., 124, 323, 459, 460
Bem, S.L., 78, 390, 392
Ben-Zeev, T.L., 198
Bender, S.T., 395
Benet-Martinez, V., 432
Benin, M.H., 487
Benjamin, L.T.Jr., 6
Benke, G., 258
Bennett, J.A., 408
Bennett, J.B., 507
Bentler, P.M., 151
Berg, T.R., 621
Berk, L.E., 348, 359
Berkley, K.J., 119
Berkman, L.F., 520
Berkowitz, L., 121, 481
Berlin, L.J., 366
Berman, F.E., 616
Bernardo, P., 564
Berndt, T.J., 393
Bernieri, F., 43
Bernstein, I.L., 176, 177
Bernstein, K.S., 122
Berridge, K.C., 57
Berry, D.S., 455
Berscheid, E., 489
Bersoff, D.M., 364, 464
Bettencourt, B.A., 484
Bettman, J.R., 251
Betz, N.E., 437, 440
Beumont, P.J., 395
Beutler, L.E., 34, 578
Beyer, S., 439
Bhatt, G., 465
Bhatt, R.S., 350
Biaggio, M., 582
Bickerton, D., 264

NAME INDEX

Coffey, C.W., 607
Cohen, D., 371
Cohen, N., 178, 512, 513
Cohen, S., 513, 520, 607
Cohen-Tovee, E.M., 96
Cohn, D.A., 367
Cohn, L., 389
Cole, A., 391, 392
Cole, M., 366
Cole, S.W., 507
Coley, R.L., 396
College of Psychologists of Ontario, 31
Collier, D.E., 91
Collins, B.E., 522
Collins, E.J., 200
Collins, N.L., 489
Collins, W.A., 374, 383, 384
Colman, H., 75
Comer, J.P., 188
Commins, S., 197
Compas, B.E., 150, 526
Comuzzie, A.G., 317
Conger, R.D., 384
Connolly, M.J., 605
Connors, E., 581
Constantino, J.M., 480
Conway, M.A., 225
Conyers, L.M., 438
Cooley-Quille, M., 505
Cooper, C.L., 518
Copper, C., 475
Coppola, D.M., 118
Corbetta, D., 98, 354
Corbitt, E.M., 258
Corcoran, K.J., 568
Coren, S., 72, 91, 108, 133, 134, 138
Corey, M., 475
Corkin, S., 207, 236
Cornblatt, B.A., 558, 559
Cosgrove, J.M., 592
Cosmides, L., 46, 132, 133, 254, 294, 307, 327, 331, 470, 536
Costa, P.T., 430, 442, 444
Costanza, D.P., 617
Cote, S., 624
Counter, S.A., 113
Courtney, S.M., 212
Covell, D., 482
Covey, E.S., 98
Cowan, N., 90
Cox, B.J., 540, 542
Cox, R.H., 644
Coyne, J.A., 46
Crabbe, J., 42
Crago, M., 578
Craik, F.I.M., 197, 209, 210, 212, 215, 233, 243
Crair, M.C., 75
Crandall, C.S., 500, 501
Crane, J., 295
Crave, J., 387
Crawford, C.B., 485
Crawford, H.J., 148
Crawford, M., 226
Creem, S.H., 97
Crespi, T.D., 593
Crews, F., 422
Crick, F., 68, 98, 139
Crick, N.R., 484
Crittenden, K.S., 538
Cronshaw, S.F., 632
Cross, J.D., 511
Cross, S.E., 489
Crosson, B., 256
Crott, H.W., 477
Crouter, A.C., 508
Crowl, R.K., 284
Csikszentmihalyi, M., 248, 434, 435, 551
Culbertson, F.M., 546
Cummings, N.A., 582, 583
Cunningham, C.L., 171
Cunningham, J.A., 600
Cunningham, M.R., 488

Curphy, G.J., 628
Curtiss, G., 432
Cutting, A.L., 360
Czajia, S.J., 403
Czeisler, C.A., 134

da Vinci, L., 107
Daghighi, S., 622
Dale, J.A., 511
Dalton, J., 103
Daly, M., 480
Damasio, A.R., 61, 65, 132, 255, 257, 266, 271
Damian, M.F., 88
Daniel, M.H., 280, 285
Danner, R., 408
Danziger, K., 6
Darkness Visible, 545
Darley, J.M., 29, 284, 469, 486, 487
Darroch, J., 320
Dasgupta, N., 465
Davidson, R.J., 328
Davidson-Katz, K., 437
Davison, G.C., 597
Dawson, D., 403
Day, R.H., 105
De Bruin, W.B., 385
De Haan, M., 350
De Jonge, J., 507
De La Casa, L.G., 176
De Vries, B., 364
DeBono, K.G., 458
DeCatanzaro, D., 307
DeCharms, R.C., 113
Deci, E.L., 311, 312, 313, 623
Deco, G., 98
Defeyter, M.A., 246
DeFries, J.C., 292
Deimling, G., 504
DeKeseredy, W., 568
Delgado, P.L.C., 56
DeLongis, A., 503
Dembo, M.H., 324
Dement, W., 135, 137
Dement, W.C., 138, 139, 140, 141, 144
Demery, J.A., 96
DeNeve, K.M., 636
Denmark, F.I., 26
Dennett, D.C., 132
Denollet, J., 495
DePaulo, B.M., 335, 461, 462
DePiano, F.A., 150
Depinet, R.L., 290
Dershowitz, A.M., 233
DeSantis, A., 488
Design of Everyday Things, 629
Detterman, D.K., 297
Deuser, W.E., 636
Deutsch, G., 74
DeValois, R.L., 103
Devine, P.G., 469
Devlin, A.S., 635
Devlin, M.J., 394
Devoto, A., 138
DeYong, N.G., 350
Diagnostic and Statistical Manual of Mental Disorders, 536, 537, 538, 539, 540, 541, 548, 553, 556, 561, 568, 569, 602
Dickson, W.J., 611
Diedrich, F.J., 354
Diener, D., 333
Diener, E., 435, 478
Dietvorst, T.F., 148
Dietz, T.L., 484
DiGirolamo, G.J., 257
Dikeos, D.G., 549
DiLalla, D.L., 558
DiLalla, L.F., 295, 370, 479, 480
Dill, K.E., 483
Dillard, J.P., 455
DiMatteo, M.R., 524, 525
D'Imperio, R.I., 515
Dimsdale, J.E., 504

Dindia, K., 489
Dinges, N.G., 259
DiNicola, D.D., 525
Dion, K., 468, 488, 506
DiPlacido, J., 506
Dishion, T.J., 382
Dishman, R.K., 135, 139
Dixon, M.J., 104
Dobash, R.E., 480
Dobash, R.P., 480
Dobell, W.H., 101, 103
Dobson, K.S., 596, 598, 599
Docherty, N.M., 560
Dodson, J.D., 309, 336, 645, 648
Dohrenwend, B.P., 503
Doke, L., 592
Dolan, P.O., 220
Dollard, J., 481
Dollins, A.B., 142
Donnelly, C.M., 252
Donovan, J.M., 583
Doob, A.N., 457
Doty, R.W.A., 74
Downey, V.W., 320
Downs, J., 385
Draine, S.C., 88
Drcher, M., 347
Drennen, W.T., 148
Driver, J., 97, 350
Dromi, E., 261
Drummond, D.C., 179
Dryden, W., 596
Dubow, E.F., 515
Dubowitz, H., 373
Dubrovsky, B., 46
Duchek, J.M., 220
Duckitt, J., 468
Duff, K.J., 421
Duffy, R.D., 631
Duffy, V.B., 117
Dumont, M., 515
Dunant, Y., 55
Dunbar, K., 252
Duncan, J., 275
Dunn, J., 360
Dupont, S., 70
Durex, 320
Durgin, F., 91
Dutton, D.G., 330
Dworkin, S.F., 149
Dwyer, W.O., 635
Dye, D.A., 432

Eagly, A.H., 452, 453, 456, 467, 626
Earles, J.A., 614
Early Child Care Research Network, 367
Eaton, M.J., 324
Ebbesen, E., 195
Ebbinghaus, H., 222, 230, 236
Eccles, J.S., 382
Edwards, D., 408
Edwards, D.C., 306
Edwards, K., 329
Ehrlich, P., 46
Eich, E., 225
Eisenberg, N., 370
Ekman, P., 326, 329, 332, 335, 461
Elder, G.H.Jr., 384
Elfenbein, M.H., 198
Eliot, L., 260
Elkind, D., 386
Elkind, L., 347
Elliot, R., 255
Ellis, A., 10, 583, 596, 597, 598
Ellis, B.J., 46
Ellis, R.J., 155
Ellsberg, M., 567
Elwood, W.N., 527
Emde, R.N., 370
Engel, A.K., 68
Engel, S.A., 103
Engen, E.A., 118
Engen, T., 118

McGuffin, P., 42, 44
McGuire, M.T., 602
McGuire, S., 49
McHale, S., 391
McIntire, L., 398
McKeachie, W.J., 199
McKelvey, M.W., 508
McKelvie, S.J., 247
McKenna, K.Y.A., 641
McKenry, P.C., 508
McKenzie, B.E., 105
McKenzie, D., 153
McKillop, K.J., 489
McKinney, V.M., 219
McKusick, V., 49
McLaughlin, D.S., 457
McLaughlin, L.A., 524
McLoyd, V.C., 292
McLynn, F., 145
McMahon, T.J., 582
McManus, F., 542
McManus, I.C., 72, 74
McNally, R.J., 542
McNamara, D.S., 213
McNaughton, B.L., 236
McNeil, J.E., 96
McNeill, D., 263
Meadows, S., 359, 360
Mecham, R.C., 614
Mecklinger, A., 98
Medical Research Council, 27, 28
Medina, J.H., 225
Mehlhorn, G., 28
Meichenbaum, D., 519, 598
Meier, L.J., 551
Meinz, E.J., 403
Melfi, C.A., 580
Melton, G.B., 633
Meltzoff, A.N., 350, 354, 483
Melville, J., 544
Melzack, R., 66, 121, 122, 126
Mendoza, R.P., 580
Menlove, F.L., 202
Meredith, W., 397, 405
Merikle, P., 88, 104
Merrill, S.S., 398
Merton, R.K., 468
Merzenich, M.M., 75, 98, 113
Mesquita, B., 332
Messer, S.B., 583
Metalsky, G.I., 551
Metcalfe, J., 73
Metzler, D., 228
Meyer, R.G., 565
Meyers-Levy, J., 198
Micallef, J., 544
Michael, R.T., 320
Michalos, A., 506
Miczek, K.A., 480
Middaugh, S.J., 148
Middleton, B., 142
Miklowitz, D.J., 560
Miles, D.R., 480
Milgram, S., 473, 474, 475, 484, 492
Millar, K., 455
Millar, M.G., 455
Miller, G.A., 10, 215, 243, 265, 266
Miller, I.J., 117
Miller, J., 88, 89
Miller, J.G., 364, 464
Miller, J.Y., 155
Miller, L.C., 489
Miller, M.E., 56, 149
Miller, N., 484, 497
Miller, N.E., 147
Miller, P.H., 351
Miller, P.J.O., 269
Miller, R.P., 592
Miller, T.I., 576
Milner, B., 207, 219, 236
Milner, P.M., 65, 185
Milofsky, E.S., 155
Milton, J., 124

Mineka, 177
Miner, J.B., 616
Mischel, W., 436, 440, 441, 442, 447
Miserandino, M., 644
Mishima, K., 142
Mishkin, M., 66
Mishler, E.G., 560
Mitchell, A.A., 347
Mitchell, J., 431
Mitchell, J.C., 554
Mitchell, R.F., 243
Mitchell, T., 69
Mitchison, G., 139
Mitler, M.M., 138
Modigliani, A., 473
Mohr, D., 596
Mokdad, A.H., 318
Molnar, B.E., 567
Monaco, A.P., 11
Monahan, J.L., 88, 563
Moncrieff, J., 604
Monnier, J., 507
Monteith, M.J., 469
Monteleone, P., 394
Montepare, J.M., 462
Montgomery, D., 516
Montgomery, G.H., 177
Montgomery St-Laurent, T., 118
Moore, M.K., 354
Moore, S., 498
Moore, T.E., 88, 89
Moorhead, G., 478
Morelli, G., 353, 366
Morgan, C.A.III, 503
Morgan, D.G., 638
Morgan, J.N., 200
Morgan, L., 624
Morgan, W.P., 149
Morin, C.M., 141
Morren, M., 511
Morris, C.D., 211
Morris, M.W., 463
Moscovitch, M., 197, 403
Moser, E.I., 75
Moskowitz, B.A., 262
Moskowitz, D.S., 428, 440
Moskowitz, J.T., 517, 518
Mosley, L., 73
Most, S.B., 91
Mottron, L., 274
Mueser, K.T., 561
Muir, J.L., 345
Mullen, B., 475, 477
Mumford, M.D., 248
Murachver, T., 202, 258
Murphy, G.E., 565
Murphy, K.R., 619
Murphy, P.J., 134
Murphy, S.M., 646
Murphy, S.T., 88, 483
Murphy-Eberenz, K.P., 395
Murray, C., 294, 295
Murray, H.A., 321
Murray, J.B., 122
Murray, J.G., 554
Musselman, L., 488
Myers, D.G., 329, 333, 435
Myers, I.B., 444
Myerson, J., 294
Mylander, C., 264
Mynier, K., 462

Nabekura, J., 75
Nace, E.P., 154
Nadel, L., 196
Nair, E., 405
Narrow, W.E., 574
Nash, M., 148
Nash, R.A., 122
Nathan, B.R., 284
Nathan, P.E., 153, 155, 538, 555, 561, 562, 563
Nathans, J., 103

Nation, M., 640
National Advisory Council on Aging, 115
National Crime Prevention Centre, 387
National Institutes of Health, 371
Natural Science and Engineering Research Council, 27, 28
Nauta, W.J.H., 51, 53
Neale, M., 549
Neck, C.P., 478
Needham, D.R., 88, 89
Neisser, U., 10, 218, 243
Nelson, C., 346
Nelson, C.A., 350
Nelson, D.L., 219
Nelson, G., 640
Nelson, T.D., 467
Nestle, M., 316
Neugarten, B., 382
Neumann, R., 326
Neumark-Sztainer, D., 389
Nevett, M.E., 645
Neville, H.J., 346
Newcomb, A.F., 374, 389
Newcomb, M.D., 151
Newcombe, N.S., 355
Newman, L.S., 421
Newport, E.L., 346
Newsom, J.T., 459
Ng, V.W.K., 69
Niaura, R., 512
Niehoff, D., 480
Nilsson, K.M., 149
Nisbett, R.E., 200, 253, 311, 313, 314, 465
Nolen-Hoeksema, S., 546, 547
Norenzayan, A., 465
Norman, D., 629
Norman, R.A., 317
North, A.C., 477
Northouse, P.G., 626
Novak, B.B., 546
Nowell, A., 297, 386
Nowicki, S., 437
Nunnery, J.A., 200
Nussbaum, D., 480
Nyberg, L., 69, 212, 219
Nyhuus, K., 388

O' Mara, S.M., 197
Oberbauer, A.M., 317
Oberman, Y., 367
O'Brien, C.P., 179
O'Connell, R.J., 118
O'Connor, B., 623
O'Connor, F.L., 558
O'Connor, P.J., 135, 139
O'Connor, T., 49
Oddie, S.D., 68
Oddone-Paolucci, E., 567
Offermann, L.R., 628
O'Hanlon, T., 635
Ohlsson, S., 245
Okuda-Ashitaka, E., 122
Olausson, B., 122
Olds, J., 65, 185
Olfson, M., 603, 607
Olivardia, R., 395
Oliver, J.M., 546
Oliver, W., 580
Olness, K., 150
Olson, C., 564
Olson, S.K., 402
Ones, D.S., 291
Onex, D.S., 614
Onglatco, M.L.U., 623
Orbell, S., 522
O'Reilly, R.C., 96
Ornstein, R., 71, 72, 74, 131, 132
Ornstein, R.E., 131
Orth-Gómer, K., 511, 516
Orzi, F., 118
Osborne, J.W., 465
Oscar-Berman, M., 155
Osipow, S.H., 35

Vereijken, B., 98
Vianna, M.R.M., 196
Videbech, P., 545, 559
Villani, S., 439, 483
Villeneuve, C., 601
Vincent, G.M., 259
Violato, C., 567
Visser, M., 315, 316
Vitiello, M.V., 141
Von Eye, A., 366
Von Glaserfeld, E.D., 268
Von Helmholtz, H., 101
Von Hofsten, C., 354
Von Senden, M., 97
Vouloumanos, A., 264
Vroom, V.H., 620, 627, 647
Vroon, P., 117
Vygotsky, L.S., 275, 276, 280, 301, 342,
    353, 359, 360, 361, 378, 384

Wacholtz, E., 96
Wachtel, P.L., 583
Wadsworth, J., 320
Wagner, M., 109
Wakefield, J.C., 536
Walbott, H.G., 332
Waldie, K., 73
Waldron, I., 523
Walk, 351
Walker, E.F., 558, 559, 560
Walker, J.R., 505
Walker, L.J., 362, 364
Walker, L.S., 508
Walker, S., 484
Walker-Andrews, A., 350
Wall, P., 121, 122
Wall, P.D., 121
Wall, S., 366
Wall, T.L., 122
Wallbaum, A.B., 91
Waller, N.G., 432
Wallston, K., 475
Walsh, B.T., 394
Walsh, K.W., 73
Walster, E., 489
Walters, R., 201
Walton, G.E., 350
Wamala, S.P., 507
Wampold, B.E., 576
Wandersman, A.H., 455, 496, 640
Wands, K., 76
Wang, A., 504
Warren, S.L., 370
Warrington, E.K., 96, 260
Washington, T., 91
Washton, A.M., 158
Wasserman, D.A., 158
Waters, E., 366, 375
Watson, D.C., 517
Watson, J.B., 8, 9, 12, 37, 42, 130, 170,
    180
Waxler, N.E., 560
Webb, W.B., 136, 141
Weber, E., 87
Weber-Fox, C.M., 346
Webster, R., 419, 421
Wechsler, D., 273, 275, 285, 286, 287, 297,
    299, 301, 302
Wegener, D.T., 456
Weidner, G., 512
Weine, S.M., 504
Weinfield, N.S., 375

Weingartner, H., 223
Weinstein, N.D., 522
Weisberg, R.B., 464
Weise-Kelly, L., 152
Weisfeld, G.E., 120
Weishaar, M., 597
Weiss, H.M., 624
Weiss, L., 638
Weisz, J.R., 508
Wellman, H.M., 131, 360, 374
Wells, G.L., 233
Wells, J.A., 321
Welte, J.W., 153
Werker, J.F., 261, 264
Werler, M.M., 347
Werner, J., 477
Werner, N.E., 484
Wertheimer, M., 7, 110
Wessels, P.M., 235
West, M.A., 149
Westen, D., 422
Westgaard, R.H., 629
Wheeler, M.A., 218
Wheeler, S.C., 468
Whicker, K.M., 200
Whitbeck, L.B., 566
White, D., 76
White, N.M., 185
White, S.A., 46
WHO International Consortium in
    Psychiatric Epidemiology, 546
Whorf, B.L., 259
Widiger, T.A., 258, 537, 538
Wiesel, T.N., 97, 98, 113
Wilderman, S.K., 488
Wiley, J., 247
Wiliams, C., 138
Willen, J.D., 350
Williams, C.D., 193, 592
Williams, J., 508, 582
Williams, K., 476
Williams, K.D., 477
Williams, K.J., 402
Williams, M.L., 527
Williams, R.J., 318
Williams, S.L., 542
Williams, T., 33
Williams, T.M., 439
Williams, W.M., 277, 291, 292, 294
Williamson, R.C., 259
Williamson, S., 408
Willis, S.L., 403
Willson, L.R., 517
Wilson, D.A., 117
Wilson, E.O., 242, 485
Wilson, F.A.W., 350
Wilson, G.T., 596
Wilson, M., 480
Wilson, M.A., 146
Wilson, M.E., 383
Windschitl, P.D., 233
Wing, R.R., 317
Winner, E., 297
Winocur, G., 197, 403
Winsler, A., 195, 359
Wise, R.A., 65
Wiseman, R., 124
Wishart, J.G., 105
Wishaw, I., 65
Wisniewski, N., 567
Witmer, L., 36
Witzum, E., 580

Wodak, R., 258
Wogalter, M.S., 631
Wohlwend-Lloyd, R., 464
Wolfe, B.E., 576, 578
Wolpe, J., 593
Wolpert, E.A., 144
Wong, R.O.L., 351
Wood, J.M., 444
Wood, N.L., 90
Wood, W., 456
Woodruf, D.W., 188
Woods, S.C., 314, 315, 317, 318
Woodward, S.A., 370
Woodward, W.R., 201
Worsdell, A.S., 192
Wright, J.C., 484
Wundt, W., 6, 7, 9, 37, 130
Wurtman, R.J., 142
Wynn, K., 354
Wynn-Dancy, L.M., 200
Wypij, D., 321
Wyszecki, G., 103

Yahya, K.A., 474
Yancey, S.W., 260
Yarmey, A.D., 233
Yates, M., 388
Yehuda, R., 504
Yerkes, R.M., 309, 336, 645, 648
Yetton, P.W., 627
Yirmiya, N., 367
Yoder, C.Y., 546
Yoder, K.A., 566
Yohannes, A.M., 605
Yonas, A., 106
York, J.L., 153
Young, R.F., 476
Young, S.J., 371
Young, T., 101
Young, T.J., 565
Youngstedt, S.D., 135, 139
Youniss, J., 388

Zabrack, M.L., 439
Zajonc, R.B., 88, 475
Zakay, D., 639
Zamansky, H.S., 149
Zanna, M., 467
Zarcone, J.R., 192
Zaslavsky, O., 200
Zebrowitz-McArthur, L., 462
Zeki, S., 66
Zemore, S.E., 467
Zhang, F., 75
Zhou, Z., 260
Ziel, H.K., 525
Zigler, E.F., 296, 300
Zillmann, D., 482
Zimbardo, P.G., 454
Zimmerman, L., 45
Zimmerman, R.R., 365
Zola, S.M., 219
Zoucha, R., 580
Zuber, J.A., 477
Zucco, G.M., 259
Zuckerman, M., 291, 514, 542, 545, 549,
    551, 552, 558, 564
Zuidema, R., 526
Zumbo, B., 506
Zuwerink, J.R., 469

# Subject Index

Abecedarian Project, 296
ablation, 68
abnormal behaviour
    *see also* mental disorders
    atypical nature of, 532
    and culture, 539
    defined, 532–533
    diagnosis of, 536–539
    *Diagnostic and Statistical Manual of Mental Disorders (DSM–IV–TR)*, 536–539
    diathesis-stress model, 551
    distorted cognitions, 533
    distress, 532
    legal model, 564
    maladaptive nature of, 532
    maladjustment, 533
    mental status examination, 547
    perspectives on. *See* abnormal psychology
    physical examination, 547
    prevalence, 537
    psychiatric history, 547
abnormal psychology
    behavioural model, 535
    biopsychosocial approach, 536
    cognitive model, 535
    defined, 534
    eclectic approach, 536
    evolutionary model, 536
    humanistic model, 534–535
    medical-biological model, 534
    modelling, 533–534
    psychodynamic model, 534
    sociocultural model, 535
Aboriginal communities
    spiritual and community healing, 581
    and suicide, 565–566
absentmindedness, 232–233
absolute thresholds, 87
accommodation, 107
accuracy, 13
acetylcholine, 56
achievement
    motivation, 322–324
    need for achievement, 321
    self-efficacy and, 325
    Thematic Apperception Test (TAT), 324
acquaintance rape, 567–568
acrophobia, 542
action potentials, 54–55
activation, 645
actor-observer effect, 464
acupuncture, 122
adaptation, 45, 353
addictive drug, 151
Adler's individual psychology, 421–424
adolescence
    adolescent egocentrism, 386
    androgyny, 392
    beginning of, 347

cognitive development, 384–386
cultural context, 383
defined, 382
emotional development, 386–389
friendships, 393–396
gender identity, 389–390
gender schema theory, 390
genital stage, 419
imaginary audience, 386
and life-and-death decisions, 385
life structures, 401
menarche, 383
multiple contexts, 382–383
parental influence, 389
peer groups, 389
personal fable, 386
physical development, 383–384
puberty, 382, 383–384
secondary sex characteristics, 383
self-image, 388
sexual behaviour, 396
sibling influences, 391–392
social development, 386–389
storm and stress, 382
suicide, 565–566
youth gangs, 387–388
adolescent egocentrism, 386
adoption studies, 48
adrenal cortex, 80
adrenal glands, 80
adrenal medulla, 80
adult stage theories
    early adulthood, 401
    ego integrity *vs.* despair, 400
    Erikson's stage theory, 400
    gender differences, 402
    generativity *vs.* stagnation, 400
    identity *vs.* role confusion, 400
    intimacy *vs.* isolation, 400
    late adulthood, 402
    Levinson's life structures, 400–402
    middle adulthood, 401
    midlife crisis, 401
adulthood
    adult stage theories, 399–402
    aging theories, 399
    careers and, 397
    cognitive changes, 402–403
    identity, 399–402
    late adulthood. *See* late adulthood
    life-span perspective, 397
    life structures, 401–402
    menopause, 398
    personality development, 403–404
    sensation in, 398
    sexual changes, 398
    social development, 399–402
advertising, classical conditioning in, 170
affective responses, 440
afferent neurons, 51
age bias, 26

age regression, 148
ageism, 405–406
aggression
    as acquired drive, 479–481
    biological perspective, 480
    cognitive perspective, 481–482
    cultural context, 484
    defined, 479
    environmental influences, 480
    excitation transfer theory, 482
    frustration-aggression hypothesis, 481
    gender differences, 484
    and hormones, 480
    imitation of, 592
    nativists, 479
    psychoanalytic theory, 419–420
    psychological aggression, 484
    sexual aggression, 482
    social cognitive neuroscience, 480
    *thanatos*, 479
aging theories, 399
agnosias, 66, 96
agonists, 57
agoraphobia, 541–542
agreeableness-antagonism, 430
AIDS prevention, 521–522
alcohol
    adolescent use of, 382
    alcohol-related problems, 154–155
    consumption statistics, 153
    effects of, 153–154
    medical problem of, 155
    problem drinkers, 154–155
    social problem of, 155
    treatment programs, 155
    warning signs of alcoholism, 156
alcoholics, 154–155
Alcoholics Anonymous, 155, 600
algorithm, 245
all-or-none, 55
allocation of attention, 90
Allport's personal disposition theory, 428–429
altered state of consciousness
    described, 131
    drugs and. *See* substance use and abuse
    hypnosis, 148–150
alternative-form method, 283
alternative medicine, 525
altruism, 485–486
Alzheimer's disease
    and acetylcholine, 56
    causes and treatment, 408
    defined, 407
    described, 220, 407
    irreversible dementias, 407
    neurotransplantation techniques, 75
American Sign Language, 259
amnesia, 236
amphetamines, 157–158
amplitude, 112

behavioural genetics
  *see also* genetics
  defined, 46
  described, 46–48
  genetic mapping, 48–49
  heritability, 47–48
behavioural medicine psychologists, 35
behavioural model of abnormality, 535
behavioural regulation theorists, 195
behavioural self-regulation, 195
behaviourism
  defined, 8
  described, 8–9
  developmental theories, 341
belief in small numbers, 252
beliefs, 440
bell curve, 294–295
bias
  age, 26
  class bias, 26
  confirmation bias, 211, 253
  cultural bias, 26, 289–291
  described, 16
  disabilities, 26
  ethnic bias, 26
  gender bias, 26
  group diversity, within *vs.* between, 27
  IQ tests, 289–291
  rater bias, 615
  in research, 25–27
  self-fulfilling prophecy, 289
  self-serving bias, 465
Big Five, 430–432
biofeedback, 147–148
biological perspective
  *see also* evolutionary psychology
  aggression, 480
  aging, 399
  amnesia, 236
  and chimpanzee studies, 267–268
  defined, 10
  described, 10–11
  dreams, 146–147
  encoding, 211–212
  Eysenck's factor theory, 430
  language, 263–264
  language acquisition, 265–266
  major depressive disorder, 549, 551
  memory storage, 219–221
  schizophrenic disorders, 558
  sexual orientation, 323
  temperament, 370
biologically based therapy
  described, 574
  drug therapy, 603–606
  electroconvulsive therapy (ECT), 607
  psychosurgery, 606–607
biopsychosocial approach to abnormal
  behaviour, 536
bipolar affective disorder, 44
bipolar disorder, 551–552
birth defects, 346
birth order hypotheses, 424
bisexual orientation, 321
blindsight, 255
body language, 462
bona fide occupational qualifications
  (BFOQs), 632
bonding, 365–366
borderline personality disorder, 562

bottom-up processing, 86
the brain
  *see also* brain and behaviour connections
  aging brain, and Alzheimer's
    disease, 220
  amygdala, 65, 327, 328
  basal ganglia, 65
  cerebellum, 63
  cerebral hemispheres, 61
  corpus callosum, 61, 66, 73
  cortex, 65
  critical periods, 346
  cross-section of, 62
  electrical stimulation, and
    reinforcement, 185
  five key operating principles, 61
  forebrain, 64–67
  function of, 60
  gender differences, 74
  hemispheric specialization, 71–74
  hindbrain, 62–63
  hippocampus, 65
  hypothalamus, 64
  information processing, 208–209
  limbic system, 64–65
  main divisions, 61–62
  malleability, 75
  medulla, 63
  memory. *See* memory
  midbrain, 63–64
  monitoring techniques. *See* brain-
    monitoring techniques
  organization of, 61–67
  plasticity, 75
  pons, 63
  prefrontal lobotomy, 607
  reticular formation, 63
  split brain, 71–74
  striate cortex, 93
  structure of, and language
    acquisition, 266
  substantia nigra, 64
  superior colliculus, 64
  temporal lobectomies, effect of, 76
  thalamus, 64
  visual cortex, 93
brain and behaviour connections
  aging brain, and Alzheimer's
    disease, 220
  art, creativity, and intelligence, 298
  conditioning in addicts, 179
  critical periods, 346
  described, 33
  eating disorders, 394–395
  forensic psychology, 633–634
  identical twins, 47
  language, 260
  melatonin, 142
  mental disorders, brain imaging of, 559
  personality traits, genetics of, 431
  prosopagnosia, 96
  Prozac, 605
  psychoneuroimmunology, 513
  social phobia, 452
  temporal lobectomies, effect of, 76
brain dominance, 71
brain-monitoring techniques
  CT (computerized tomography)
    scans, 69

electroencephalogram (EEG), 68–69,
  135
  function of, 70–71
  functional MRI (fMRI), 69–70
  MRI (magnetic resonance imaging), 69
  PET (positron emission tomography), 69
  single unit recording, 68
  transcranial magnetic stimulation
    (TMS), 71
brainstorming, 248–249
brief therapy, 582–583
brightness, 100
British Society for the Study of Psychic
  Phenomena, 124
Broca's area, 66
bulimia nervosa, 394, 395
bystander apathy, 486
bystander effect, 486–487

Canada
  adopted Romanian orphans, 368–369
  aging population, 404
  Canadian psychologists, work of, 34
  the North, 34
Canadian Charter of Rights and
  Freedoms, 364, 632
Canadian Psychological Association, 5, 30,
  170
Canadian Society for Brain, Behaviour, and
  Cognitive Science, 30
Cannon-Bard theory, 326, 327
cardinal trait, 413, 429
career in psychology, 31–34
case studies, 24, 104, 539
castration anxiety, 418
catastrophes, 503–505
catatonic type of schizophrenia, 557
categorical speech perception, 261
Cattell's trait theory, 429
causation, *vs.* correlation, 20–21, 44
central nervous system
  the brain. *See* the brain
  defined, 60
  described, 51, 60
  spinal cord, 60–61
central tendency, 618
central traits, 429
centration, 355
cerebellum, 63
cerebral hemispheres, 61
challenge, 498
change, 341
child abuse, 567
child development
  *see also* developmental psychology
  anal stage, 418
  cognitive development, 351–361
  critical periods, 346
  emotional development, 365–372
  latency stage, 419
  moral reasoning, 362–364
  oral stage, 418
  phallic stage, 418–419
  physical development, 344–351
  social development, 372–376
childhood, 347
children
  gender schema theory, 390
  language acquisition, 260
    *see also* language acquisition

commitment, 490
common fate principle, 111
communication, and smell, 118–119
communications, 455
community interventions, and health, 527
community psychologists, 36, 577
community psychology, 639–642
companionate love, 490
comparative study, 466
competencies, 440
completers, 564
computers. *See* artificial intelligence
concentrative meditation, 149–150
concept, 243
concept formation, 243–244
conception, 344
concordance rate, 558
concrete operational stage, 356–357
conditioned response, 168
conditioned stimulus, 168
conditioned taste aversion, 177
conditioning, 167
    *see also* learning
conduction deafness, 115
cones, 93–95, 101
confirmation bias, 211, 253
conflict
    approach-approach conflict, 497
    approach-avoidance conflict, 497
    avoidance-avoidance conflict, 497
    defined, 497
conformity
    Asch's classic conformity
      experiment, 471
    and attribution, 472
    background authority, 473
    defined, 470
    expediency, 472
    groups and, 471, 472
    and independence, 472
    information, amount of, 472
    Milgram's obedience
      experiment, 473–475
    obedience, 473–474
    position within a group, 472
    public nature of behaviour, 472
    relative competence of group, 472
    social conformity approach, 472
congruence, 588
congruent partner, 433
conscience, 416
conscientiousness-undirectedness, 430
consciousness
    altered state of consciousness, 131
    biofeedback, 147–148
    control of, 147–151
    defined, 131
    described, 130–131, 415
    dreams, 141–147
    drugs. *See* substance use and abuse
    dualism, 130
    evolutionary perspective, 132–133
    hypnosis, 148–150
    levels of, 131
    materialism, 130
    meditation, 149–151
    metacognition, 131
    and philosophy, 133
    preconscious, 415
    sleep. *See* sleep

study of, 130
theories of, 131–133
unconscious, 415
consensus, 463
consequentiality, 225
conservation, 356–357
consistency, 458, 463
    *see also* cognitive consistency
consolidation, 221
consolidation process, 196–197
construct validity, 284
content validity, 284
continuous reinforcement, 190
continuous view, 341
control groups, 17–18
conventional morality, 363
convergence, 93, 108
convergence zones, 255, 266
convergent thinking, 248
conviction, 453
convolutions, 65
cooperative learning, 199–200
coping
    *see also* coping strategies
    defined, 514
    effective coping, 519
    influencing factors, 514–516
    personal resources, 515
    resilience, 514, 515–516
    rumination, 546
    sense of control, 515
    social support, 516
coping strategies
    defined, 516
    described, 516–517
    emotion-focused coping, 517
    proactive coping, 518–519
    problem-focused coping, 517–518
    stress inoculation, 519
core sleep, 134
corporal punishment, 188
corpus callosum, 61, 66, 73
correlation, 20–21, 44, 659–660
correlation coefficients, 20–21, 44, 659–660
correlational study, 44
cortex
    behaviour, role in, 65
    Broca's area, 66
    central fissure`, 66
    convolutions, 65
    defined, 65
    division of, 66
    frontal lobe, 66
    lateral fissure, 66
    neocortex, 65
    occipital lobe, 66
    parietal lobe, 66
    phantom limb phenomenon, 66
    somatosensory cortex, 66
    temporal lobe, 66
    Wernicke's area, 66
counselling psychologists, 35
counterconditioning
    aversive counterconditioning, 594
    defined, 593
    described, 593
    modelling, 594–595
    systematic desensitization, 593–594
crack, 158
creative power, 423

creativity, 248–249, 298
crisis intervention centres, 641
critical periods, 346
critical thinking, 21–23, 249, 536
cross-sectional research design, 342–343
cross-sectional study, 356
crowding
    architectural design, effects of, 637–638
    and culture, 638–639
    defined, 637
    personal space, 637–639
    social density, 637
    spatial density, 637
CT (computerized tomography) scans, 69
cultural bias in IQ tests, 289–291
cultural differences. *See* culture
cultural diversity, 25
culturally patterned dialogue, 359
culture
    and abnormal behaviour, 539
    achievement motivation, 324
    and adolescence, 383
    and aggression, 484
    and behaviour, 45
    collectivist cultures, 333
    described, 26
    and eating disorders, 394
    and emotion, 332–333
    emotion, perception of, 329
    and facial expressions, 329
    health care and, 523
    and hunger, 315–316
    individualist cultures, 333
    and intelligence, 291
    and language, 258–259
    and late adulthood, 404
    and love, 490
    and personal space, 638–639
    and personality, 440–442
    and reasoning, 253
    and self-serving bias, 466
    and shyness, 370
    and therapy, 579–581

dark adaptation, 94
data collection methods
    case studies, 24
    interviews, 24
    naturalistic observation, 24
    questionnaire, 23–24
    summary of approaches, 25
    surveys, 23–24
date rape, 567–568
day care, 367–369
deafness, 114–115
death, 408
debriefing, 29, 474–475
decay, 231
deception, 474–475
deception in research, 29–30
decision making
    analogies, 252
    availability heuristic, 251, 252
    barriers, 252–253
    belief in small numbers, 252
    confirmation bias, 253
    defined, 250
    educated guess, 250–251
    gambler's fallacy, 252
    overconfidence, 253

insomnia, 141
instinct, 307
instrumental conditioning. *See* operant conditioning
instrumentality, 620
insulin, 80, 315
intelligence
    Abecedarian Project, 296
    analytic dimension, 278
    associative abilities, 275
    bell curve, 294–295
    cognitive abilities, 275
    creative dimension, 278
    cultural dimensions of, 291
    emotional intelligence, 278–280
    evolutionary perspective, 293–294
    exceptional individuals. *See* exceptional individuals
    Flynn effect, 293
    and gender differences, 296–297
    and genetics, 294–295
    heritability, 292–293
    practical dimension, 278
    and race, 294–295
    theories of, 275–278
    working definition, 274
intelligence quotient (IQ), 282–283
intelligence test development
    deviation IQ, 283
    intelligence quotient (IQ), 282–283
    measurement, 281
    normal curve, 281–282
    norms, 281
    percentile score, 282
    process, 281–283
    raw score, 282
    reliability, 283
    representative sample, 281
    scores, 282
    standard error of measurement, 283
    standard score, 282
    standardization, 281
    validity, 284–285
intelligence tests
    critique of validity of, 284–285
    cultural adaptation, measurement of, 291
    cultural bias and, 289–291
    development of. *See* intelligence test development
    experiment expectancy effect, 289
    halo effect, 284
    history of, 280
    Kaufman Assessment Battery for Children (K-ABC), 287–288
    learned information, 284
    location of, 284
    stability of test scores, 295
    Stanford-Binet Intelligence Scale, 285–286
    stereotype threat, 285
    test-wise individuals, 284–285
    Wechsler intelligence scales, 286–287
    Woodcock-Johnston III, 288
intelligence theories
    factor theories, 275
    Gardner's multiple intelligences, 276–277, 279
    Jensen's two-level theory, 275
    Sternberg's triarchic theory, 277–278

two-factor theory of intelligence, 275
    Vygotsky's theory, 276
    Wechsler's theory, 275
intensity, 112
interaural intensity difference, 114
interaural time difference, 114
interference
    in attention, 232–233
    defined, 231
    in memory, 231–232
    proactive interference (inhibition), 232
    retroactive interference (inhibition), 232
internal attribution, 462
internal locus of control, 437
Internet, and social involvement, 641
interneurons, 52
interpersonal attraction
    defined, 487
    physical attractiveness, 488
    proximity, 487–488
    shared attraction, 489
    similar attitudes, 489
interpretation, 584
interval schedules, 190–191
interviews, 24
intimacy, 489, 490
intimacy *vs.* isolation, 400
intimate partner violence, 567
intimate relationships, 489–490
intrinsic motivation, 311–312, 619
intrinsically motivated behaviours, 194
introspection, 7
introverts, 430
investment theory of creativity, 249
IQ tests. *See* intelligence tests
irrational behaviours, 596, 597, 598
irreversible dementias, 407

James, William, 7, 18, 25, 130
James-Lange theory, 326
Jensen's two-level theory of intelligence, 275
jet lag, 134
job analyses, 613–614
job interviews, and "similar-to-me" effect, 615
job performance
    behavioural approaches, 623
    culture and, 619
    equity theory, 621–622
    expectancy theories, 620–621
    goal-setting theory, 619–620
    individualism, 619
    intrinsically motivated behaviour, 619
    masculinity, 619
    and motivation, 619–623
    motivation management, 622–623
    motivation and need, 619–620
    participatory approach, 623
    paternalistic approach, 622–623
    power distance, 619
    self-efficacy, 622
    uncertainty avoidance, 619
job satisfaction, 623–625
Jungian therapy, 145
Jung's analytical psychology, 425, 444

Kanzi, 268
Kaufman Assessment Battery for Children (K-ABC), 287–288
kinesthesis, 123–124

Koffka, Kurt, 7, 110
Kohlberg's theory of moral development, 362–364
Köhler, Wolfgang, 110
Korsakoff's syndrome, 236

Lana, 268
language
    biological basis, 263–264
    and the brain, 260
    categorical speech perception, 261
    and culture, 258–259
    defined, 257
    evolutionary basis of, 263–264
    gender differences in usage, 258
    and gender stereotypes, 258
    grammar, 263
    linguistic structures, 260
    linguistics, 259–260
    morphemes, 261
    morphology, 261
    phoneme, 261
    phonology, 260, 261
    pragmatics, 257
    productive vocabulary, 260
    psycholinguistics, 259
    receptive vocabulary, 260
    semantics, 260, 261–262
    as social tool, 257–258
    structure, 261–263
    syntax, 260, 262–263
    and thought, 258–259
language acquisition
    biological theories, 265–266
    brain structure, 266
    chimpanzee studies, 267–268
    convergence zones, 266
    dolphins, 269
    lateralization, 266
    learning readiness, 266
    learning theories, 264–265
    naturalistic observation study, 265
    social interaction theories, 269
    whales, 269
language acquisition device (LAD), 265
late adulthood
    ageism, 405–406
    Alzheimer's disease. *See* Alzheimer's disease
    cultural context, 404
    death, 408
    dementias, 406–407
    health, 406–408
    irreversible dementias, 407
    multiple infarct dementia, 407
    myths, 405–406
    realities of, 405–406
    reversible dementias, 407
    senility, 406
    statistics, 404
    stereotypes, 405–406
    terminal drop, 408
    treatment of older people, 404
latency stage, 419
latent content, 145
latent learning, 199
lateralization, 266
the law, and psychology, 631–634
law of closure, 111
law of continuity, 111

law of Prägnanz, 110
law of proximity, 111
law of similarity, 111
Lazarus, Richard, 10
Lazarus approach, 331
leadership
    behaviours, 626
    effective leadership, 628
    leadership effectiveness theories, 627
    situational leadership theory, 627
    trait theories of, 626
    transformational leadership, 627–628
    Vroom's leadership model, 627
learned helplessness, 188–189, 550–551
learned information, 284
learning
    behavioural analysis, 426
    biological perspective, 195–197
    and chemotherapy, 177
    classical conditioning. See classical
        conditioning
    cognitive learning, 197–202
    consolidation process, 196–197
    cooperative learning, 199–200
    defined, 166
    gender differences, 198
    group learning, 200
    language acquisition. See language
        acquisition
    to learn, 199–200
    major depressive disorder, 549–550
    and nervous system, 196–197
    observational learning theory, 200–202
    operant conditioning. See operant
        conditioning
    state-dependent learning, 223–225
    types of, 195, 201
left-handedness, 72
legal defences
    brain scan defences, 71
    homicidal somnambulism, 143
    Twinkie defence, 76–77
legal model of abnormal behaviour, 564
legal psychology, 631
leniency, 618
leptin, 315, 318
levels-of-processing approach, 210–211
Levinson's life structures, 400–402
libido, 419
lie detectors, and emotion, 335
life-and-death decisions, and
    adolescence, 385
life stages in human development, 344
life structures, 400–402
lifestyle factors, 399
limbic system, 64–65, 326
linguistic structures, 260
linguistics, 259–260
lithium carbonate, 604
Locke, John, 6
locus of control, 436–437, 515
logic, 250
long-term memory
    declarative memory, 217
    defined, 216
    described, 216
    episodic memory, 218
    explicit memory, 218–219
    implicit memory, 218–219
    long-term potentiation, 221

    procedural memory, 217
    research on, 224
    semantic memory, 218
long-term potentiation, 221
longitudinal research design, 342–343
longitudinal study, 391, 428
love
    as behaviour, 490
    classifications of, 490
    companionate love, 490
    consummate love, 490
    cultural variations, 490
    definitions of, 489–490
    passionate love, 490
    varieties of love, 490
low socio-economic groups, 505
lowballing technique, 457
LSD (lysergic acid diethylamide), 159
lucid dream, 144

mainstreaming, 300
maintenance rehearsal, 215–217
major depressive disorder
    age and, 546
    biological theories, 549
    biopsychosocial model, 551
    causes, 548–551
    clinical evaluation, 547
    cognitive theories, 549–550
    defined, 545
    delusions, 545
    diathesis-stress model, 551
    duration of, 546
    vs. dysthymic disorder, 547
    learned helplessness, 550–551
    learning theories, 549–550
    onset of, 546
    prevalence, 546
    reality testing, 546
    rumination, 546
    symptoms, 545–546
    vulnerability, 551
maladjustment, 533
mandala, 145, 425
manic-depressive disorder. See bipolar
    disorder
manifest content, 145
marijuana, 159–160
Maslow, Abraham, 10, 432–433
Maslow's hierarchy of needs, 313
mate selection, 395–396
materialism, 130
maternal employment, 367–369
MDMA
    (methylenedioxymethamphetamine), 158
mean, 652
means-ends analysis, 246
measures of central tendency, 651–654
measures of retention, 221–222
measures of variability, 655–657
mechanistic needs, 307
median, 653–654
medical-biological model of
    abnormality, 534
meditation, 149–151, 646
medium tasters, 117
medulla, 63
Meichenbaum's theory, 598–599
melatonin, 142
memory

autobiographical memory, 218
chunks, 215
declarative memory, 217
defined, 208
elaborative rehearsal, 215
encoding, 209, 212
encoding specificity principle, 211, 223
episodic memory, 218
explicit memory, 218–219
extraordinary memory, 226–227
failure of. See forgetting
flashbulb memory, 225
forgetting. See forgetting
and gender, 226
implicit memory, 218–219
information processing, 208–209
long-term memory, 216–219
maintenance rehearsal, 215–217
pictorial memory, 222
procedural memory, 217
recovered memories, 235–237
rehearsal, 215, 216
retention, measures of, 221–222
retrieval, 209, 221–229
semantic memory, 218
sensory memory, 213–214
short-term memory, 214–216
short-term working memory, 214–216
storage, 209, 212–221
three-process approach, 209
working memory, 216
memory enhancement, 233
memory span, 215
memory stores, 213
memory trace, 231
menarche, 383
menopause, 398
mental age, 280
mental disorders
    see also abnormal behaviour
    anxiety disorders, 540–544
    child abuse and, 567
    diagnoses associated with
        violence, 563–566
    dissociative disorders, 552–554
    domestic violence, 567
    and intimate partner violence, 567
    mood disorders, 544–552
    personality disorders, 561–563
    rape and, 567–568
    schizophrenia, 553–561
    social construction of, 533
    suicide, 564–566
    unacceptability of, 532
    and violence, 563–568
mental imagery, 646
mental processes, 5
mental retardation
    defined, 298
    education and, 300
    employment, 300
    levels of retardation, 299
    mainstreaming, 300
    mild retardation, 299
    moderate retardation, 299
    profound retardation, 299
    severe retardation, 299
mental set, 247–248
mental shortcuts, 461
mere exposure effect, 455

metacognition, 131, 200, 210
method of constant stimuli, 87
method of limits, 87
method of successive
  approximations, 181–182
midbrain, 63–64
mild retardation, 299
Milgram's obedience experiment, 473–475
Miller, George, 10
mindful meditation, 149
Minnesota Multiphasic Personality
  Inventory - 2nd Edition, 445
minor tranquilizers, 156
Mischel's cognitive-affective personality
  system, 440
mob violence, 478–479
mode, 652
modelling, 457, 533–534, 594–595
moderate retardation, 299
monochromats, 103
monocular depth cues, 106–107
monozygotic twins, 47, 48
mood disorders
  depressive disorders, 544–551
  described, 544
moon illusion, 108
moral reasoning
  conventional morality, 363
  gender differences, 364
  Kohlberg's theory of moral
    development, 362–364
  morality, 362
  Piaget's theory of moral
    development, 362
  postconventional morality, 363–364
  preconventional morality, 363
morality, 362
Moro reflex, 349
morphemes, 261
morphology, 261
motivated forgetting, 234–237
motivation
  achievement, 321–325
  behavioural approaches, 623
  defined, 306
  drive, 307
  emotion, interconnection with, 325
  extrinsic motivation, 311–312
  extrinsically motivated behaviour, 194
  hunger, 314–318
  intrinsic motivation, 311–312, 619
  intrinsically motivated behaviours, 194
  and job performance, 619–623
  need, 307
  participatory approach, 623
  paternalistic approach, 622–623
  sexual behaviour, 318–323
  sport psychology, 644–645
  study of, 306
motivation theories
  arousal theory, 308–309
  cognitive theories, 310–312
  drive theory, 307–308
  evolutionary theories, 306–307
  expectancy theories, 310–311
  extrinsic motivation, 311–312
  humanistic theory, 312–313
  intrinsic motivation, 311–312
  prejudice and, 468
motive, 310

motor neurons, 52
MRI (magnetic resonance imaging), 69
Müller-Lyer illusion, 108
multiculturalism, 580
multiple baseline case study procedure, 186
multiple infarct dementia, 407
multiple intelligences theory, 276–277, 279
multiple personality disorder, 553–554
mutations, 50
myelin sheath, 52
myelinated axons, 52
Myers-Briggs Type Indicator, 444
myopic, 93

narcissism, 429
narcissistic personality disorder, 562
narcolepsy, 140
nativists, 479
natural selection, 45, 294
naturalistic observation, 24, 265
nature, 42–43, 340
nearsighted, 93
need for achievement, 321
  see also achievement
needs
  see also motivation
  defined, 307
  and job performance, 619–620
  Maslow's hierarchy of needs, 313
  social need, 310
negative instance, 244
negative punishment, 185
negative reinforcement, 183
neighbourhood clinic, 641
Neisser, Ulric, 10
neonatal development, 344
nerve cell. See neurons
nerves, 51
nervous system
  autonomic nervous system, 58–60
  central nervous system, 51, 60–61
  communication in, 51–57
  consolidation process, 196–197
  defined, 51
  described, 51
  and learning, 196–197
  neurons, 51–55
  neurotransmitters, 55, 56–57
  organization of, 58–61
  parasympathetic nervous system, 59–60
  peripheral nervous system, 51, 58–60
  smooth functioning of, 51
  somatic nervous system, 58
  sympathetic nervous system, 59
neural networks, 255–257
neuroanatomy, 68
neuroleptics, 604–605
neuromatrix theory, 121–122
neuromodulators, 57
neurons
  action potentials, 54–55
  afferent neurons, 51
  all-or-none proposition, 55
  axon, 52
  axon terminals, 52
  communication of, 53
  defined, 51
  dendrites, 52
  described, 51
  efferent neurons, 51

electrochemical processes, 53
excitatory PSPs, 55
glial cells, 52
inhibitory PSPs, 55
interneurons, 52
motor neurons, 52
myelin sheath, 52
nerve pathways, 51
neuron impulse, 54
neurotransmitters. See neurotransmitters
parts of, 52–53
postsynaptic potential (PSP), 55
refractory period, 55
sensory neurons, 52
suprachiasmic nucleus (SC), 140
synapses, 53
types of, 52
neuropeptides, 56
neuropsychologists, 36
neuroscience perspective. See biological
  perspective
neuroticism, 430
neuroticism-stability, 430
neurotransmitters
  acetylcholine, 56
  and behaviour, 56–57
  defined, 55
  described, 55
  dopamine, 56
  drug addiction and, 57
  gamma-aminobutyric acid (GABA), 56
  key neurotransmitters, 56
  neuromodulators, 57
  norepinephrine, 56
  number of, 56
  postsynaptic potential (PSP), 55
  psychopharmacology, 57
  research, 56–57
  reuptake, 55
  serotonin, 56
newborns and infants
  attachment, 366–367
  Babinski reflex, 349
  cephalocaudal trend, 347
  Fantz's viewing box, 349–350
  grasping reflex, 349
  growth, 347–348
  learned responses, 349
  Moro reflex, 349
  oral stage, 418
  perception, 349–350
  primary reflexes, 349
  proximodistal trend, 348
  reflexes, 349
  rooting reflex, 349
  sucking reflex, 349
  visual cliff method, 351
night terrors, 141
Nim, 268
nine-dot problem, 248
noise, 636
non-rapid eye movement (NREM)
  sleep, 135–137
non-tasters, 117
nonverbal communication
  body language, 462
  defined, 461
  eye contact, 462
  facial expressions, 461
norepinephrine, 56

normal curve, 281–282, 658
normal distribution, 281, 658
norms, 281
the North, 34
note taking, 200
novel response, 248
nurture, 42–43, 340

obedience, 473–474
obesity
    evolutionary explanations, 316–317
    physiological explanations, 316–317
    prevalence, 316
    psychological explanations, 317–318
object permanence, 354
objectivity, 12–13
observational learning theory
    attitude formation, 454
    described, 201
    key variables, 202
    laboratory studies, 202
    learner's characteristics, 202
    prejudice, 468
    situation, 202
    type and power of model, 202
obsessive-compulsive disorders, 543–544
Occupational Safety and Health Act
    (OSHA), 631
Oedipus complex, 418–419
olfaction, 117–119
olfactory aversion, 186
olfactory epithelium, 117
openness to experience, 430
operant conditioning
    attitude formation, 454
    and behaviour therapy, 591–593
    behavioural analysis, 426
    behavioural self-regulation, 195
    B.F. Skinner, 179–180
    in daily life, 194–195
    defined, 180
    described, 180
    E.L. Thorndike, 179–180
    extinction, 192–194, 592
    extrinsically motivated behaviour, 194
    frequency of consequences, 190–192
    intrinsically motivated behaviours, 194
    key variables in, 189–195
    pioneers of, 179–180
    process of, 181
    punishment, 185–189, 592–593
    reinforcement, 182–185
    schedules of reinforcement, 190–192
    shaping, 181–182
    Skinner box, 181
    spontaneous recovery, 193–194
    stimulus discrimination, 192
    stimulus generalization, 192
    strength of consequences, 189
    time consuming nature of, 182
    time out, 593
    timing of consequences, 189
    token economies, 591–592
operational definitions, 18
operational diagnosis, 583
opiates, 156–157
opponent-process theory, 102–103
optic chiasm, 95
optional sleep, 134
oral stage, 418

organization, 199
original response, 248
ossicles, 113
outgroup, 475
overconfidence, 253
overjustification effect, 312
overt actions, 5

pain
    acupuncture, 122
    and anxiety, 123
    chronic pain, 526
    endorphins, 122
    and hypnosis, 123, 149
    lack of ability to feel pain, 121
    management, 122–123, 526
    neuromatrix theory, 121–122
    perception of, 121
    periodic pain, 526
    physical sources, 123
    progressive pain, 526
    psychological sources, 123
    receptors for, 121
    study of, 121
paired associate tasks, 222
pancreas, 80
panic attacks, 542
paradoxical sleep, 136
parallel distributed processing (PDP), 256
paranoid personality disorder, 562
paranoid type of schizophrenia, 556–557
parasympathetic nervous system, 59–60
parental influence, 389
Parkinson's disease
    basal ganglia, 65
    and dementia, 407
    dopamine and, 56
    neurotransplantation techniques, 75
Parks, Kenneth, 143
partial reinforcement, 190
participants, 17, 22, 27–29
passionate love, 490
pathological use, 152
Pavlov, Ivan, 167–168
Pavlovian conditioning. See classical
    conditioning
peer groups, 389
peer relations, 393–396
penis envy, 419
percentile score, 282
perception
    see also sensation
    bottom-up processing, 86
    categorical speech perception, 261
    common process, 87
    constancy, perception of, 98
    defined, 86
    depth perception, 106–108
    electrochemical basis of, 95–99
    extrasensory perception (ESP), 124
    face perception, 96
    Fantz's viewing box, 349–350
    illusions, 108–109
    inattentional blindness, 91–92
    infant perception, 349–350
    law of Prägnanz, 110
    of loudness, 113
    pain, 121
    perceptual constancies, 103–105

restricted environmental
    stimulation, 90–91
selective attention, 89–90
sensation, reliance on, 86
signal detection theory, 87–88
subliminal perception, 88–89
top-down processing, 86
visual perception, 103–111
perceptual constancies, 103–105
perceptual disorders, 556
perceptual span, 100
perceptual systems
    absolute thresholds, 87
    described, 86
    difference threshold, 87
    psychophysics, 87–88
performance appraisal, 618–619
performance improvement, and
    psychology, 32
periodic pain, 526
peripheral feedback hypothesis, 326
peripheral nervous system
    autonomic nervous system, 58–60
    defined, 58
    described, 51, 58
    parasympathetic nervous system, 59–60
    somatic nervous system, 58
    sympathetic nervous system, 59
person-centred therapy. See client-centred
    therapy
personal disposition theory, 428–429
personal fable, 386
personal goals and values, 440
Personal Orientation Inventory (POI), 445
personal space
    architectural design, effects of, 637–638
    and culture, 638–639
    defined, 638
    intimate distance, 639
    personal distance, 639
    public distance, 639
    social density, 637
    social distance, 639
    spatial density, 637
    spatial zones, 639
personality
    cultural context, 440–442
    defined, 414
    described, 414
    happiness, 435
    influences on, 414
    psychosexual stages of
        development, 416–419
    traits, 428
        see also traits
    types, 428
personality assessment
    assessment, defined, 442
    described, 444
    goals of, 442
    Myers-Briggs Type Indicator, 444
    personality inventories, 443–445
    projective tests, 442–443
    Rorschach Inkblot Test, 443
    Thematic Apperception Test (TAT), 443
personality development, 403–404
personality disorders
    anti-social personality disorder, 562
    borderline personality disorder, 562
    characteristics of, 561

classes, 561
defined, 561
dependent personality disorder, 562–563
described, 561
histrionic personality disorder, 562
narcissistic personality disorder, 562
paranoid personality disorder, 562
personality inventories
Eysenck Personality Questionnaire, 444
humanistic theories, 445
Minnesota Multiphasic Personality
Inventory - 2nd Edition, 445
Personal Orientation Inventory
(POI), 445
Revised NEO-Personality Inventory, 444
Sixteen Personality Factor Test, 444
and trait theories, 444
personality theories
Adler's individual psychology, 421–424
Allport's personal disposition
theory, 428–429
archetypes, 425
birth order hypotheses, 424
Cattell's trait theory, 429
cognitive-affective personality
system, 440
cognitive approaches, 435–440
collective unconscious, 425
Eysenck's factor theory, 429–430
Five Factor Model, 430–432
humanistic approaches, 432–435
Jung's analytical psychology, 425
locus of control, 436–437
positive psychology, 434–435
and prejudice, 469
psychodynamic theories, 414–425
purpose of, 414
self-actualization, 432–433
self-efficacy, 438–440
self theory, 433–434
Skinner's behavioural analysis, 426–427
social interest, 423
trait and type theories, 427–432
persuasion
ask-and-you-shall-be-given
technique, 457
audience, 456
central route, 456
cognitive approaches, 456–458
communications, 455
communicator, 455
door-in-the-face technique, 457
elaboration likelihood model, 456–458
face-to-face communication, 456
foot-in-the-door technique, 457
incentives technique, 457
lowballing technique, 457
medium of communication, 455–456
mere exposure effect, 455
modelling, 457
openness to, 456
peripheral route, 458
techniques, 457
persuasive argument explanation, 477
PET (positron emission tomography), 69
phallic stage, 418–419
phantom limb phenomenon, 66
phenotypes, 50
pheromones, 118–119, 320
phobias, 175, 329

phobic disorders
acrophobia, 542
agoraphobia, 541–542
claustrophobia, 542
defined, 541
described, 541
hematophobia, 542
panic attacks, 542
social phobia, 452, 542
specific phobia, 542–543
phoneme, 261
phonetic sensitivity, 261
phonology, 260, 261
photoreceptors, 93
phrenologists, 67
physical attractiveness, 488
physical development
adolescence, 383–384
growth spurts, 383
neonatal development, 344
newborns and infants, 347–351
prenatal development, 344–347
secondary sex characteristics, 383
sexual changes in adulthood, 398
physiological approach
aging, 399
Cannon-Bard theory, 327
cognitive appraisal, 502
emotion, 326–327
facial feedback hypothesis, 326
general adaptation syndrome, 498–499
Hassles Scale, 503
Holmes-Rahe scale, 499–501
hunger, 314–315
James-Lange theory, 326
obesity, 316–317
peripheral feedback hypothesis, 326
Social Readjustment Rating
Scale, 499–500
stress, 498–503
physiological needs, 307–308
physiological psychologists, 36
physiological reactions, 5
Piaget's theory of cognitive development
adaptation, 353
animistic thinking, 355
assimilation, 353
centration, 355
concrete operational stage, 356–357
conservation, 356–357
egocentrism, 355
formal operational stage, 357–358
key concepts, 353–354
object permanence, 354
in perspective, 358
preoperational stage, 355
schemes, 353
sensorimotor stage, 354–355
stages of cognitive
development, 353–358
Piaget's theory of moral development, 362
pictorial memory, 222
pinna, 113
pitch, 112
placebo, 20
placebo effects, 575
placenta, 344
plasticity, 75

pleasure principle, 416
pleasures centres, 65
Plomin, Robert, 11
polarization of cell membrane, 53
pollution, 636
polydrug users, 153
polygraph device, 335
pons, 63
Ponzo illusion, 108
population, 18
position analysis questionnaire, 614
positive instance, 244
positive psychology, 434–435
positive punishment, 185
positive reinforcement, 182
positive well-being, 435
post-traumatic stress disorder (PTSD), 503
postconventional morality, 363–364
postsynaptic potential (PSP), 55
pragmatics, 257
precognition, 124
preconscious, 415
preconventional morality, 363
predictive validity, 284
predispositions. See biological perspective
prefrontal lobotomy, 607
pregnancy. See prenatal development
prejudice
ageism, 405–406
authoritarian personality, 469
causes of, 468–469
cautious bigots, 468
cognitive approach, 469
defined, 467
described, 467
discrimination, 467
elimination of, 470
evolutionary perspective, 469
legislation against, 470
motivational theory, 468
personality theories, 469
racism and reactivity, 506
reducing, 470
reverse discrimination, 468–474
sexism, 467
social categorization, 469
social learning theory, 468
tokenism, 468
Premack principle, 183
prenatal development
birth defects, 346
blastocyst, 344
conception, 344
critical periods, 346
differentiation process, 344
drug use during, 347
embryo, 344
fetal alcohol syndrome (FAS), 347
fetus, 344
harmful environmental effects, 345–347
major developments, 345
placenta, 344
teratogens, 346–347
umbilical cord, 344
preoperational stage, 355
pressure, 497–498
prevalence, 537
prevention, vs. treatment, 578
primacy effects, 227
primary aging, 399

psychostimulants, 157–158
psychosurgery, 606–607
psychotherapy
    behaviour therapy, 577,
        589–595
    brief therapy, 582–583
    cognitive therapy, 577,
        595–599
    culture and, 579–581
    defined, 574
    eclectic approach, 577
    effectiveness of, 576
    and gender, 582
    goals of, 579
    group therapy, 599–602
    humanistic therapy, 577,
        586–599
    insight therapy, 583
    operational diagnosis, 583
    placebo effects, 575
    psychoanalysis, 583–586
    psychodynamically based
        therapies, 577, 583–586
    research on, 576
    signs of good progress, 576
    therapists, choice
        of, 577–578
    types of, 576–579
psychotherapy integration, 577
psychotic, 555
psychoticism, 430
psychotropic drugs, 603–606
puberty, 382, 383–384
punisher, 180
punishment
    in behaviour
        therapy, 592–593
    corporal punishment, 188
    defined, 185
    and learned
        helplessness, 188–189
    limitations of, 188–189
    nature of punishers, 186–187
    negative punishment, 185
    olfactory aversion, 186
    plus reinforcement, 187
    positive punishment, 185
    primary punisher, 186
    secondary
        punishers, 186–187
    strength of
        consequences, 189
    timing of consequences, 189
purity, 101

quasi-experimental design, 506
questionnaire, 23–24

racism and reactivity, 506
random assignment, 17
range, 656
rapid eye movement (REM)
    sleep, 135–137
rater bias, 615
ratio schedules, 190, 191–192
rational-emotive
    therapy, 596–597
rationalization, 420
raw score, 282
reactance, 460

reaction formation, 421
reality principle, 416
reality testing, 546
reasoning
    and culture, 253
    defined, 250
    evolutionary
        perspective, 253–254
    logic, 250
recall, 222
recency effects, 227
receptive fields, 97–98
receptive vocabulary, 260
recessive genes, 49–50
recognition, 222
reconstruction, 222
recovered memories, 235–237
referential naming, 268
reflex, 167, 349
refractory period, 55
regressions, 420
rehearsal, 215, 216
reinforcement
    avoidance conditioning, 183
    behavioural analysis, 426
    electrical brain
        stimulation, 185
    escape conditioning, 183
    negative reinforcement, 183
    plus punishment, 187
    positive reinforcement, 182
    schedules of reinforcement.
        See schedules of
        reinforcement
    strength of
        consequences, 189
    superstitious behaviours, 184
    timing of consequences, 189
reinforcement schedules. See
    schedules of reinforcement
reinforcers
    defined, 190
    nature of, 183–184
    Premack principle, 183
    primary reinforcer, 184
    probable behaviours, 183
    reward as, 180
    secondary reinforcer, 184
    specific situations, 184
relationship therapy, 602
relationships
    attraction, 487–489
    ending of, 490
    equity theory, 489
    friendships, 489
    intimate
        relationships, 489–490
    love, 489–490
    physical attractiveness, 488
    proximity, 487–488
    shared attraction, 489
    similar attitudes, 489
relearning, 222, 230
reliability
    alternative-form method, 283
    defined, 283
    in performance
        appraisals, 619
    split-half method, 283
    test-retest, 283

repeated measures design, 615
replication of results, 16
representative sample, 281, 322
representativeness, 461
repression, 234–237, 420
research
    see also research methods
    bias, avoidance of, 25–27
    conclusions, 22
    confounded results, 18
    control groups, 17–18
    correlation
        coefficients, 20–21, 44
    critical thinking, 21–23
    debriefing, 29
    deception, 29–30
    ethics. See ethics
    evaluation, 21–23
    expectancy effects, 19–20
    extraneous variables, 18
    guidelines, 27–29
    hypothesis, 17
    methodology, 22
    operational definitions, 18
    participants, 17, 22
    pitfalls to avoid, 19–20
    purpose, 22
    repeatability, 22
    sample size, 18–19
    significant differences, 19
    variables, 16–17
research methods
    case studies, 539
    comparative study, 466
    correlational study, 44
    cross-sectional research
        design, 342–343
    cross-sectional study, 356
    data collection
        methods, 23–24
    descriptive research, 44
    descriptive studies, 146
    in developmental
        psychology, 342–343
    double-blind technique, 20,
        575
    ex post facto study, 224
    experiment, 16
    experimental design, 289
    experimental groups, 17–18
    experimental research
        study, 14–15
    longitudinal research
        design, 342–343
    longitudinal study, 391, 428
    multiple baseline case study
        procedure, 186
    naturalistic observation, 265
    quasi-experimental
        design, 506
    random assignment, 17
    repeated measures
        design, 615
    representative sample, 322
    surveys, 322
research (specific studies)
    correlation vs. causation, 44
    culture, and abnormal
        behaviour, 539
    dreams, and mazes, 146

experiment expectancy
    effect, 289
job interviews, and "similar-
    to-me" effect, 615
language acquisition, 265
long-term memory, 224
on neurotransmitters, 56–57
olfactory aversion, and
    deviant sexual
    behaviour, 186
personality traits, stability
    of, 428
preoperational stage,
    cognitive limitations
    during, 356
racism and reactivity, 506
self-perceptions, and
    culture, 466
sex surveys, 322
sibling influences, 391–392
synesthesia, 104
residual type of
    schizophrenia, 557
resilience, 514, 515–516
resistance, 585
resistance to extinction, 193, 499
restricted environmental
    stimulation, 90–91
restricted environmental
    stimulation therapy (REST), 91
retention, measures of, 221–222
reticular formation, 63
retinal disparity, 108
retrieval
    cues, 223
    defined, 221
    extraordinary
        memory, 226–227
    facilitation of, 227–229
    failure of, 223–225
    flashbulb memory, 225
    imagery, 227–228
    measures of
        retention, 221–222
    pictorial memory, 222
    primacy effects, 227
    recall, 222
    recency effects, 227
    recognition, 222
    reconstruction, 222
    relearning, 222
    state-dependent
        learning, 223–225
    success of, 223–225
retroactive interference
    (inhibition), 232
retrograde amnesia, 236
reuptake, 604
reverse discrimination, 468–474
reversible dementias, 407
Revised NEO-Personality
    Inventory, 444
Ritalin, 371
rods, 93–95
Rogerian therapists. See client-
    centred therapy
Rogers, Carl, 10
Roger's self theory, 433–434
rooting reflex, 349
Rorschach Inkblot Test, 443

Rotter's locus of control, 436–437
rumination, 546
runner's high, 56

saccades, 99
sadism, 429
safer-sex campaign, 527
sample, 18
sample size, 18–19
Sarah, 268
saturation, 101
saving method, 230
scaffolding, 360
Schachter-Singer approach, 330–331
schedules of reinforcement
    continuous reinforcement, 190
    described, 190
    fixed-interval schedule, 190
    fixed-ratio schedule, 191
    interval schedules, 190–191
    partial reinforcement, 190
    ratio schedules, 190, 191–192
    use of, 192
    variable-interval schedule, 191
    variable-ratio schedule, 191–192
scheduling, 199
schema, 231, 436
schemes, 353
schizophrenic disorders
    anti-psychotic drugs, 604–605
    biological factors, 558
    catatonic type of schizophrenia, 557
    causes, 557–561
    characteristics of, 555–556
    concordance rate, 558
    defined, 554–555
    delusions, 555
    disorganized type of schizophrenia, 557
    dopamine theory of schizophrenia, 558
    double bind, 560
    emotional disorders, 556
    environmental factors, 560–561
    hallucinations, 556
    inappropriate affect, 556
    nature and nurture, 561
    negative symptoms, 555
    paranoid type of
        schizophrenia, 556–557
    perceptual disorders, 556
    positive symptoms, 555
    psychotic, 555
    residual type of schizophrenia, 557
    thought disorders, 555
    treatment of, 57
    types of schizophrenia, 556–557
    undifferentiated type of
        schizophrenia, 557
    vulnerability, 561
school psychologists, 36, 642
schools of psychological thought
    behaviourism, 8–9
    biological perspective, 10–11
    broadening of, 8–12
    cognitive psychology, 10
    described, 6
    early traditions, 6–8
    eclecticism, 12
    evolutionary psychology, 11–12
    functionalism, 7
    Gestalt psychology, 7–8

    humanistic psychology, 9–10
    psychoanalytic approach, 8
    structuralism, 6–7
science of psychology
    accuracy, 13
    hypothesis, 13–15
    objectivity, 12–13
    scientific endeavour, principles of, 12–13
    scientific method, 13–16
    skepticism, 13
    theory, 15
scientific method
    conclusions, 16
    data collection and analysis, 15–16
        see also data collection methods
    defined, 13
    hypotheses, development of, 13–15
    problem, statement of, 13
    replication of results, 16
    reporting results, 16
    study, design of, 15
seasonal affective disorder (SAD), 548
secondary aging, 399
secondary prevention, 641
secondary punishers, 186–187
secondary reinforcer, 184
secondary sex characteristics, 383
secondary traits, 429
sedative-hypnotic
    alcohol, 153–155
    barbiturates, 156
    defined, 153
    minor tranquilizers, 156
    tranquilizers, 156
selection procedures, 614–616
selective attention, 89–90
selective serotonin reuptake inhibitors
    (SSRIs), 604
self, 433
self-actualization, 10, 312, 425, 432–433, 434
self-concept, 433–434
self-efficacy, 325, 622
self-examination, 7
self-fulfilling prophecy, 19–20, 289, 533
self-instruction, 598–599
self-perception theory, 459
self-serving bias, 465
self theory
    congruent partner, 433
    empathy, 433
    fulfilment, 433
    fully functioning person, 434
    ideal self, 433–434
    psychological stagnation, 434
    self-actualization, 434
    self-concept, 433–434
    unconditional positive regard, 433
Selye's general adaptation
    syndrome, 498–499
semantic memory, 218
semantic networks, 222
semantics, 260, 261–262
sensation
    see also perception
    in adulthood, 398
    bottom-up processing, 86
    defined, 86
    perception, reliance on, 86
    top-down processing, 86

sensorimotor stage, 354–355
sensorineural deafness, 115
sensory adaptation, 117
sensory memory, 213–214
sensory neurons, 52
sensory register, 213–214
sensory systems
    hearing, 111–115
    kinesthesis, 123–124
    olfaction, 117–119
    skin senses, 119–123
    smell, 117–119
    synesthesia, 104
    taste, 115–117
    touch, 119
    vestibular sense, 123–124
    visual system. See visual system
separation anxiety, 366
serial position curve, 227
serial recall tasks, 222
serotonin, 56
severe retardation, 299
sex drive, 419–420
sex hormones, 319
sex surveys, 322
sexism, 467
sexist discrimination, 506
sexual assault, 567–568
sexual behaviour
    adolescence, 396
    influences on, 319
    initiation of sex drive, 319–320
    sex hormones, 319
    sexual orientation, 321–649, 323
    study of sexuality, 320–321
    thought, role of, 320
sexual changes in adulthood, 398
sexual orientation, 321–649, 323, 506–507
sexuality. See sexual behaviour
shadow, 425
sham rage, 326
shape constancy, 106
shaping, 181–182
sharing, 373–374
short-term memory, 214–216
short-term working memory, 214–216
shyness, 370
sibling influences, 391–392
sick role, 524
sickness, psychology of. See illness
signal detection theory, 87–88
significant differences, 19, 661–662
"similar-to-me" effect, 615
situational leadership theory, 627
Sixteen Personality Factor Test, 444
size constancy, 105
skepticism, 13
skin senses
    described, 119
    pain, 120–123
    touch, 119
Skinner, B.F., 9, 179–180
Skinner box, 181
Skinner's behavioural analysis, 426–427
sleep
    amount required, 135
    changes in sleep patterns, 136
    circadian rhythms, 133–134
    circadian theory of, 139
    core sleep, 134

variable-interval schedule, 191
variable-ratio schedule, 191–192
variables
    defined, 16
    dependent variable, 17
    extraneous, 18
    independent variable, 16–17
ventrolateral preoptic area (VLPO), 140
vestibular sense, 123–124
violence
    *see also* aggression
    child abuse, 567
    effect of observation of, 439
    intimate partner violence, 567
    and mental disorders, 563–568
    mob violence, 478–479
    rape, 567–568
    as risk factor for mental
        disorders, 567–568
    spouse abuse, 567
    television violence, 482–483
visual acuity, 94
visual cliff method, 351
visual cortex, 93
visual perception
    constancies, 103–105
    depth perception, 106–108
    form, 103–105
    Gestalt laws of organization, 109–111
    illusions, 108–109
    law of Prägnanz, 110
    shape constancy, 106
    size constancy, 105

visual system
    colour vision, 100–103, 104
    duplicity theory of vision, 93–94
    electrochemical basis of
        perception, 95–99
    electrochemical changes in, 98
    evolutionary psychology, 99
    eye, structure of, 92–95
    eye movements, 99–100
    feature detectors, 97
    hypercomplex cells, 97
    hyperopic, 93
    lateral geniculate nucleus, 93
    myopic, 93
    object form and colour, 98
    parallel processing, 98
    receptive fields, 97–98
    saccades, 99
    serial processing, 98
    spatial location, 98
Vroom's leadership model, 627
vulnerability, 551, 561
Vygotsky's sociocultural theory, 359–360
Vygotsky's theory of intelligence, 276

Washoe, 267
Watson, John B., 8–9, 42, 130
wear-and-tear theory, 399
Wechsler Adult Intelligence Scale
    (WAIS), 286
Wechsler-Bellevue Intelligence Scale, 286
Wechsler Intelligence Scale for Children
    (WISC), 286

Wechsler intelligence scales, 286–287
Wechsler Preschool and Primary Scale of
    Intelligence (WPPSI), 287
Wechsler's theory of intelligence, 275
weight stability, 314
Wernicke's area, 66
Wertheimer, Max, 7, 110
whales, 269
wise old man, 425
withdrawal symptoms, 152
women
    *see also* gender differences
    discrimination in workplace, 402
    life stages of, 402
    menopause, 398
    and post-traumatic stress disorder
        (PTSD), 505
    self-efficacy, 440
    and sexism, 467
        *see also* gender stereotypes
Woodcock-Johnston III, 288
working memory, 216
working through, 585
workplace wellness programs, 526–527
Wundt, Wilhelm, 6, 130

Yerkes-Dodson principle, 309
Young-Helmholtz theory, 101
youth gangs, 387–388

Zen meditation techniques, 151
zone of proximal development, 359–360

# Credits

## Chapter Opening Art

**Chapter 1:** Jacob Lawrence, *The Library*, 1960. Tempera on fibre-board, 24 × 29⅞ in. Copyright Smithsonian American Art Museum, Washington DC/Art Resource, NY. Smithsonian American Art Museum, Washington DC, U.S.A.

**Chapter 2:** Santiago Hernandez, *Reflector*, 1966. Alkyd on panel. Collection of Kenneth L. Freed.

**Chapter 3:** Alexander Calder, *Untitled*, 1947. Gouache and ink on paper, 57.6 × 83.8 cm. © Copyright 2002, Estate of Alexander Calder/Artists Rights Society, New York. Copyright Art Resource, NY. Private Collection.

**Chapter 4:** Andy Warhol, *Marilyn Monroe's Lips*, 1962. Synthetic polymer paint and silkscreen ink on canvas, two panels, each 82 × 80 in. © 2002, The Andy Warhol Foundation for the Visual Arts/Artists Rights Society, New York/Art Resource, NY.

**Chapter 5:** Lyonel Feininger, *Architecture II, The Man of Potin*, 1921. © Copyright Artists Rights Society, New York/VG Bild-Kunst, Bonn. Copyright Nimatallah/Art Resource, NY. Fundacion Coleccion Thyssen-Bornemisza, Madrid, Spain.

**Chapter 6:** Jonathan Green, *Colored Clothes*, 1988. Oil on Canvas, 23.5 × 23.5 in. Collection of Carroll Greene, Jr. Photograph by Tim Stamm.

**Chapter 7:** Stuart Davis, *Abstraction*, 1937. Watercolour and gouache on paper, 17⅞ × 23⅛ in. Copyright Smithsonian American Art Museum, Washington, DC/Art Resource, NY. Smithsonian American Art Museum, Washington, DC, U.S.A. © Estate of Stuart Davis/Licensed by VAGA, New York, NY.

**Chapter 8:** Lee Krasner, *Composition*, 1943. © Copyright 2002, The Pollock-Krasner Foundation/Artists Rights Society, New York. Copyright Smithsonian American Art Museum, Washington, DC/Art Resource, NY. Smithsonian American Art Museum, Washington, DC, U.S.A.

**Chapter 9:** Ruby Pearl, *Solitude*, 1998. Courtesy of Gateway Arts, Brookline, Massachusetts, Private Collection.

**Chapter 10:** Maud Lewis, 1903–1970, *Children Skiing*, no date. Oil on pulpboard, 26.0 × 35.8, Collection of Art Gallery of Nova Scotia, Gift of Peter Moore, 1994, 1994.279.

**Chapter 11:** Christopher Pratt, *Summer of the Karmann Ghia*, 1998, original singed lithograph.

**Chapter 12:** Margarett Sargent, *Beyond Good and Evil* (self-portrait), ca. 1930. Oil on canvas, 40 × 23 in. Gift of Honor Moore, Davis Museum and Cultural Center, Wellesley College, Wellesley, Massachusetts. Photograph by Steve Briggs.

**Chapter 13:** Pegi Nicol McLeod 1904–49, *Young Girl at Window*, n.d., oil on canvas, 80.7 × 68.5 cm, McMichael Canadian Art Collection, Purchase 1985, 1985.40.

**Chapter 14:** George Tooker, *Government Bureau*, 1956. Egg tempera on wood, 19⅝ × 29⅝ in. The Metropolitan Museum of Art, George A. Hearn Fund, 1956. (56.78) Photograph © 1984 The Metropolitan Museum of Art.

**Chapter 15:** Stanton MacDonald-Wright, *The Prophecy—Sleep Suite 2*, 1955. AM 1977-610. Copyright CNAC/ MNAM/Dist. Réunion des Musées Nationaux/Art Resource, NY. Musée National d'Art Moderne, Centre Georges Pompidou, Paris, France.

**Chapter 16:** Claude Fourel, *Fish*, 2000. Courtesy of Gateway Arts, Brookline, Massachusetts, Private Collection.

**Chapter 17:** Joseph Stella, *The Voice of the City of New York Interpreted: The Bridge*, 1920–1922. Oil on and tempera on canvas, 88½ × 54 in. Collection of The Newark Museum, 37.288e. Copyright The Newark Museum/Art Resource, NY.

## Figures and Tables

**Chapter 3:** Figure 3.4, p. 93: From Dowling, J. E., & Boycott, B. B. (1966). Proceedings of the Royal Society (London), B166, 80–111, Figure 7. Reprinted by permission. Figure 3.5, p. 94: From Pirenne, M. H. (1967). Vision and the eye, 32. London: Chapman and Hall, Ltd. Reprinted by permission. Figure 3.13, p. 101: Reprinted from Vision Research, 4, MacNichol, Edward F. Jr., Retinal mechanisms of color vision, 119–133, Copyright 1964, with kind permission from Elsevier Science Ltd., The Boulevard, Langford Lane, Kidlington 0X5 1GB, UK. Figure 3.14, p. 102, Baron/Eerhard/Ozier, Psychology, 3/C/e, Pearson Education Canada, Figure 3.8, p. 102. Figure 3.20, p. 110, (bottom right): From Beck, Jacob (1966). Effects of orientation and of shape similarity on perceptual grouping. Perception and Psychophysics, 1, 300–302. Reprinted by permission of Psychonomic Society, Inc.

**Chapter 4:** Figure 4.1, p. 135: From Some must watch while some must sleep by Dement, William C., Copyright © 1972 by William C. Dement. Used by permission of the Stanford Alumni Association and William C. Dement. Figure 4.2, p. 137: Reprinted with permission from Roffwarg, Howard P., Muzio, Joseph N., & Dement, William C. (1966). Ontogenetic development of human sleep-dream cycle. Science, 152, 604–619. Copyright 1966 American Association for the Advancement of Science. Figure 4.3, p. 153: From Ray, Oakley, & Ksir, Charles (1993). Drugs, society, and human behavior, ed. 6, 1993, 192, 194. St. Louis, MO: Mosby-Year Book, Inc. Reprinted by permission.

**Chapter 6:** Figure 6.9, p. 228: (top): From Kosslyn, Stephen. M. (1975). Information representation in visual images. Cognitive Psychology, 7, 341–370. Reprinted by permission of Academic Press, Inc. Figure 6.10, p. 228 (bottom): Reprinted with permission from Shepard, R. N., & Metzler, J. (1971). Mental rotation of three-dimensional objects. Science, 171, 701–703. Copyright 1971 by American Association for the Advancement of Science.

**Chapter 8:** Table 8.1, p. 276: Adapted from Gardner, H., & Hatch, T. (1989). Multiple intelligences go to school: Educational implications of the theory of multiple intelligences. Educational Researcher, 18(8), 6. Reprinted by permission of the authors with adaptation based on personal communication from H. Gardner (1996).

**Chapter 9:** Figure 9.6, p. 329: Copyright David Matsumoto and Paul Ekman.

**Chapter 10:** Figure 10.2, p. 348: From Berk, Laura (1993). Infants, children, and adolescents, 166. Copyright © 1993 by Allyn and Bacon. Reprinted by permission; Figure 10.3, p. 348: From Frankenberg, W. K., & Dobbs, J. B. (1967). The Denver Developmental Screening Tests. Journal of Pediatrics, 71, 191. Reprinted by permission of Mosby-Yearbook, Inc. Figure 10.5, p. 352: From Clarke-Stewart, A., Friedman, S., & Koch, J. (1985). Child development: A topical approach, 191. Copyright © 1985. Reprinted by permission of John Wiley & Sons, Inc. Figure 10.6, p. 357: © Susan Avishai 1995. Reprinted by permission.

**Chapter 11:** Figure 11.2, p. 405: Adapted from Statistics Canada, "Canadian Population by Sex and Age Group," www.statcan.ca/english/Pgdb/demo10a.htm, Accessed June 19, 2003. Figure 11.3, p. 407: http://www.hc-sc.gc.ca/english/media/releases/1996/96_04bke.htm, Health Canada, 1996. Reproduced with the permission of the Minister of Public Works and Government Services Canada, 2004.

**Chapter 12:** Table 12.5, p. 445: From Cattell, R.B. (1979), Personality and learning theory, 1, 61–73. New York: Springer Publishing Company, Inc. Copyright © 1979. Adapted by permission.

**Chapter 13:** Figure 13.7, p. 474: From Milgram, S. (1963). Behavioral study of obedience. Journal of Abnormal and Social Psychology, 67, 371–378. Copyright © 1963 by Alexandra Milgram. Adapted by permission.

Chapter 14: Figure 14.2, p. 499: Figure from Selye, Hans (1976). The stress of life, Revised Edition. Copyright 1976. Reproduced with permission of The McGraw-Hill Companies; Table 14.1, p. 500: Reprinted from Journal of Psychosomatic Research, II, Holmes, T. H., & Rahe, R. H., Social readjustment rating scale, 213–218, Copyright 1967, with permission from Elsevier Science. Table 14.2, p. 501: From Crandall, C.S., Preisler, J.J., & Aussprung, J. (1992). Measuring life event stress in the lives of college students: The Undergraduate Stress Questionnaire (USQ). Journal of Behavioral Medicine, 15, 627–662. Reprinted by pemission of Kluwer Academic/Plenum Publishers. Table 14.3, p. 503: From Kanner, A. D., Coyne, J. C., Schaefer, C., & Lazarus, R. S. (1981). Comparison of two modes of stress measurement: Daily hassles and uplifts versus major life events. Journal of Behavioral Medicine, 4, 1–39. Reprinted by permission of Kluwer Academic/Plenum Publishers. Figure 14.8, p. 521: *HIV and AIDS in Canada*, Health Canada, 2002. Reproduced with the permission of the Minister of Public Works and Government Services Canada, 2004.

Chapter 15: Table 15.6, p. 565: From Meyer, Robert. G., & Salmon, Paul. (1988). Abnormal psychology, 2nd ed., 333 and the work of Edwin Shneidman and Norman Farberow. Copyright © 1988 by Allyn and Bacon. Reprinted by permission.

Chapter 16: Table 16.1, p. 576: From Mahrer, A. R., & Nadler, W. P. (1986). Good moments in psychotherapy: A preliminary review, a list, and some promising research avenues. Journal of Consulting and Clinical Psychology, 54, 10–15. Copyright © 1986 by the American Psychological Association. Adapted with permission; Figure 16.3, p. 591: Reprinted from Behavior Research and Therapy, 2, Ayllon, T., & Haughton, T., Modification of symptomatic verbal behavior of mental patients, 87–97, Copyright 1964, with permission from Elsevier Science Ltd., Pergamon Imprint, The Boulevard, Langford Lane, Kidlington 0X5 1GB, UK; Figure 16.4, p. 592: From Ayllon, T., & Azrin, N. H. (1965). The measurement and reinforcement of behavior of psychotics. Journal of the Experimental Analysis of Behavior, 8, 357–383. Copyright 1965 by the Society for the Experimental Analysis of Behavior, Inc. Reprinted by permission; Table 16.4, p. 598: From Ellis, Albert, & Harper, Robert A. A guide to rational living. © 1989, 1961. Reprinted by permission.

Chapter 17: Figure 17.4, p. 624: Reprinted fom Locke, E. A., & Schweiger, D. M. (1979). Participation in decision-making: One more look. In B. M. Staw (ed.), Research in organizational behavior, 1. Copyright © 1979, with permission from Elsevier Science. Figure 17.5, p. 637: From Baum, Andrew & Valins, Stuart (1977). Suite-style dorm and traditional corridor dorm figure. Architecture and social behavior: Psychological studies of social density. Mahwah, NJ: Lawrence Erlbaum Assoc., Inc. Reprinted by permission. Figure 17.6, p. 639: From Altman, I., & Vinsel, A. M. (1977). Personal space: An analysis of E. T. Hall's proxemics framework. In I. Altman, A. Rapoport, & J. F. Wohlwill (eds.), Human behavior and environment: Vol. 2. Advances in theory and research. New York: Kluwer Academic/Plenum Publishers. Reprinted by permission.

## Photos

Chapter 1: p. 8, Freud Museum, London; p. 9 (top), National Library of Medicine; (bottom), Corbis/Bettmann; p. 13, Brian Smith; p. 15, Jonathan Nourok/PhotoEdit; p. 17, Lilo Hess/TimePix; p. 24, Will Hart; p. 26, Canapress/Regina Leader-Post/Pat Pettit; p. 28, A. Ramey/PhotoEdit; p. 34, Canapress/Paul Chiasson.

Chapter 2: p. 47, Copyright © Michael Newman/PhotoEdit; p. 49, CNRI/SPL/Science Source/Photo Researchers; p. 53, Andrew Leonard/Science Source/Photo Researchers; p. 54, Omikron/ Science Source/Photo Researchers; p. 57, Canadian Press EDMS; p. 58, Kent Miles/Getty Images; p. 61, CP Photo/Jonathan Hayward; p. 68, Robert Holmgren/Peter Arnold Inc.; p. 69, Wellcome Department of Cognitive Neurology/SPL/Science Source/Photo Researchers; p. 70, Professor K. Ugurbil/Peter Arnold, Inc.

Chapter 3: p. 90 (top) John Maier, Jr./The Image Works; (bottom) Patrick Molnar/ Getty Images; p. 91, Benjamin Ailes; p. 94, Ralph C. Eagle, Jr., MD/Science Source/Photo Researchers; p. 96, Alain Morvan/Gamma Liaison; p. 99, Arthur Tilley/Getty Images; p. 106, Mike Yamashita/Woodfin Camp & Associates; p. 108 (left), CORBIS; (right), Bettmann/CORBIS; p. 109 (top), Ron Pretzer/ Luxe; (bottom),

M.C. Escher's *Relativity* © 1998 Cordon Art B.V.-Baarn-Holland. All rights reserved; p. 116, Omikron/ Science Source/Photo Researchers; p. 120, © Masterfile/www.masterfile.com; p. 124, Michael Justice/The Image Works.

Chapter 4: p. 133, © Reuters NewMedia Inc./CORBIS; p. 134, HMS/Index Stock Imagery; p. 136 (top) Will and Deni McIntyre/Science Source/Photo Researchers; (bottom) Ted Spagna/Science Source/Photo Researchers; p. 138, UPI/CORBIS; p. 142, Bonnie Kamin; p. 145, The Granger Collection, New York; p. 147, Will & Deni McIntyre/Photo Researchers; p. 148, Brian Phillips/The Image Works; p. 149, Robert Sorbo; p. 153, A. Lichtenstein/The Image Works; p. 158, James Prince/Science Source/Photo Researchers.

Chapter 5: p. 167, Blair Seitz/Science Source/Photo Researchers; p. 170, Archives of the History of American Psychology/The University of Akron; p. 177, Stan Wayman/Science Source/Photo Researchers; p. 181, AP/ Wide World Photos; p. 182, Tony Freeman/PhotoEdit; p. 187 (top left), Brian Smith; (top right), Omikron/Science Source/Photo Researchers; (bottom left), First Light/Jan Milne; (bottom right), Jim Pickerell; p. 194, Michael Newman/ PhotoEdit; p. 198, Will Faller; p. 200, Paul Conklin/PhotoEdit; p. 202, Offshoot Special Collections.

Chapter 6: p. 208, Hulton/Archive/Getty Images; p. 213, Keith Kent/Science Photo Library/Photo Researchers; p. 215, Brian Smith; p. 218, Will Hart; p. 219, Jeff Greenberg/PhotoEdit; p. 220, David Young-Wolff/PhotoEdit; p. 223, Bettmann/CORBIS; p. 225, AP/Wide World Photos; p. 226, Robert E. Daemmrich/Getty Images; p. 230, Archives of the History of American Psychology/The University of Akron; p. 232, Bob Daemmrich/The Image Works; p. 290, Michael Newman/PhotoEdit; p. 234, Marley Soltes/Seattle Times.

Chapter 7: p. 244 (left), Stephen J. Krasemann/The National Audubon Society Collection/Photo Researchers; (right), Tim Davis/The National Audubon Society Collection/Photo Researchers; p. 246, AP/Wide World Photos; p. 252, CP Photo/Paul Chiasson; p. 255, Jonathan Schaeffer/University of Alberta; p. 258, Dana White/PhotoEdit; p. 259, Kal Muller/Woodfin Camp & Associates; p. 260, D. Greco/The Image Works; p. 263, The Image Works/John Eastcott; p. 267, Susan Kuklin/Science Source/Photo Researchers.

Chapter 8: p. 274, AP Photo/Jessica Griffin; p. 276, Bill Aron/PhotoEdit; p. 280, Archives of the History of American Psychology/The University of Akron; p. 291, Alan Oddie/PhotoEdit; p. 293, Robert Azzi/Woodfin Camp & Associates; p. 296, Bob Daemmrich/The Image Works; p. 299, Bob Daemmrich/The Image Works.

Chapter 9: p. 311, Ed Lallo/Getty Images; p. 315, Richard Howard; p. 316, Catherine Karnow/Woodfin Camp & Associates; p. 317 (top), Donna Day/Getty Images; (bottom), Jose Galvez/PhotoEdit; p. 318, Index Stock Imagery, Inc/William Thompson; pp. 323 and 324, Lew Merrim/Photo Researchers; p. 325, CP Photo/Jonathan Hayward; p. 326, AP/Wide World Photos; p. 329, Copyright David Matsumoto and Paul Ekman; p. 332, © Stock Image/SuperStock; p. 333, © 2003 Masterfile Corporation; p. 335, Dreamworks/Shooting Star.

Chapter 10: p. 341, AP/Wide World Photos; p. 345 (top and middle), Petit Format-Nestle/Science Source/Photo Researchers; (bottom), J. Stevenson/SPL/Science Source/ Photo Researchers; p. 347, Jean Shifrin/Associated Press/The Atlanta Journal and Constitution; p. 349, (top), Charles Gupton/Stock, Boston; (bottom), Spencer Grant/Stock, Boston; p. 350 (top), Courtesy of Dr. David Linton; (bottom), from Meltzoff, A.N., and Moore, M.K. "Imitation of facial and manual gestures by human neonates," Science, 198, 75, copyright 1977 by American Association for the Advancement of Science; p. 351, courtesy of J. Campos, B. Bertenthal, and R. Kermoran; p. 352 (top left), SuperStock; (top right), Laura Dwight/Peter Arnold, Inc.; (middle left), James A. Sugar/Black Star; (middle right), Laura Dwight/ Peter Arnold, Inc.; (bottom left), Andy Cox/Getty Images; (bottom right), Richard Hutchings/Photo Researchers; p. 355, © Jose Luis Pelaez, Inc./CORBIS; p. 359, Robert Brenner/PhotoEdit; p. 362, David Young-Wolff/ PhotoEdit; p. 365, Martin Rogers/Stock, Boston; p. 366, Robert Harbison; p. 370, Ken Cavanagh/Photo Researchers; p. 373, David Lassman/Syracuse Newspapers/The Image Works; p. 374, Robert Harbison.

Chapter 11: p. 382, Strauss/Curtis/Off Shoot Stock Special Collections; p. 383, David Young-Wolff/PhotoEdit; p. 384, Bob Daemmrich/Stock, Boston; p. 386, David Young-Wolff/Getty Images; p. 387, © Dick

Hemingway; p. 394, AP/Wide World Photos; p. 396, Color Day Production/Getty Images; p. 398, Will Faller; p. 400, Michael Newman/PhotoEdit; pp. 405 and 408, David Young-Wolff/PhotoEdit.

Chapter 12: p. 413, Everett Collection; p. 418, Tom Prettyman/PhotoEdit; p. 421, Mary Evans Picture Library; p. 425 (top), National Library of Medicine; (bottom), Alison Wright/Stock Boston; p. 429, Archives of the History of American Psychology/The University of Akron; p. 430 (top), Photofest; (bottom), Novastock/PhotoEdit; p. 433, (top) Corbis/Bettmann; (bottom), Roger Ressmeyer/Corbis; p. 435, Phil Banko/Getty Images; p. 439, Mary Kate Denny/PhotoEdit; p. 441, Alon Reininger/Contact/Woodfin Camp & Associates; p. 443, Lew Merrim/Monkmeyer.

Chapter 13: p. 453, CP Photo/London Free Press/Morris Lamont; p. 454, Philip G. Zimbardo; p. 455, MADD Canada; p. 458, Canapress/Rene Johnston; p. 462, Charles Gupton/Getty Images; p. 466, First Light/Mark Stephenson; p. 467, Alon Reininger/Contact Press Images/PictureQuest; p. 471, William Vandevert/Scientific American; p. 473, Courtesy of the Milgram Estate; p. 479 (top), Andrew Lichtenstein/The Image Works; (bottom), Tony Bock, Toronto Star; p. 483, Michael Newman/PhotoEdit; p. 484, PhotoDisc, Inc.; p. 488, D. Perrett, I. Penton-Voak, M. Burk/University of St. Andrews/SPL/Science Source/Photo Researchers.

Chapter 14: p. 499, Courtesy of Hans Selye; p. 500, Tony Stone Images/Kaluzny/Thatcher; p. 504, AP/Wide World Photos; p. 505, Canapress/Paul Chiasson; p. 507, © Owen Franken/CORBIS/Magmaphoto.com; p. 508, Jon Bradley/Getty Images; p. 515, Peter Scholey/Getty Images; p. 517, David Young-Wolff/PhotoEdit; p. 518, David Madison/Getty Images; p. 520, Bob Daemmrich/Stock, Boston; p. 522, Michael Newman/PhotoEdit; p. 527, Rick Strange/Index Stock Imagery.

Chapter 15: p. 532, Calgary Herald/Peter Brosseau; p. 534, National Library of Medicine; p. Bettmann/CORBIS; p. 542, Will Hart; p. 544, Brian Smith; p. 545, Will Hart; p. 548, Colin McConnell/Toronto Star; p. 557, Everett Collection; p. 559, NIH/Science Source/Photo Researchers; p. 562, Chris Craymer/Getty Images Inc.; p. 564, AP/Wide World Photos; p. 566, Canapress/Brandon Sun/Bruce Bumstead; p. 567, Bill Aron/PhotoEdit.

Chapter 16: p. 575, Photofest; p. 580, Frank Siteman/Stock Boston; p. 581, Dauphin Friendship Centre Aboriginal Festival; p. 582, Will Hart; p. 584, AP/Wide World Photos; p. 587, Michael Rougier/TimePix; p. 593, PH Merrill Publishing; p. 594, Lori Adamski Peek/Getty Images; p. 600, Will Hart; p. 604, Louisa Preston; p. 607, Will and Deni McIntyre/Science Source/Photo Researchers.

Chapter 17: p. 613, Frank LaBua/Prentice Hall Inc.; p. 614, Michael Newman/PhotoEdit; p. 615, Will Hart; p. 617, Kerbs/Monkmeyer; p. 623, Charles Gupton/Getty Images; p. 626, Andrew MacNaughton (1999); p. 628, Dale Brazao/Toronto Star; p. 629, From Anthony D. Andre and Leon D. Segal, "Design Functions," Ergonomics in Design, April 1993, p. 5, copyright 1993 by the Human Factors and Ergonomics Society, reprinted by permission, all rights reserved; p. 631, Paul McCusker; p. 632, Tony Stone Images/David Young-Wolff; p. 635, Gary Wagner/Stock Boston; p. 637, Rod Rolle/Getty Images; p. 639, Brian Smith; p. 643, Will Faller; p. 645, Canapress/AP Photo/Chris Gardner.